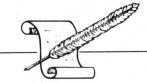

HISTORIC
DOCUMENTS
OF
1974

Cumulative Index 1972-74

Congressional Quarterly, Inc.

Ref
1974

Historic Documents of 1974

Major Contributor: Diantha Johnson Allenby

Other Contributors: Buel W. Patch, Elizabeth Wehr
Cumulative Index: Mary Neumann
Cover Design: Howard Chapman
Production Manager: Donald R. Buck

Library of Congress Catalog Card Number 72-97888
International Standard Book Number: 0-87187-069-X

Copyright 1975 by Congressional Quarterly Inc.
1414 22nd Street, N.W., Washington, D.C. 20037

Printed in the United States of America

FOREWORD

Publication of *Historic Documents of 1974* carries through a third year the project launched by Congressional Quarterly Service and Editorial Research Reports with *Historic Documents 1972*. The purpose of this continuing series of volumes is to give students, scholars, librarians, journalists and citizens convenient access to documents of basic importance in the broad range of public affairs.

To place the documents in perspective, each entry is preceded by a brief introduction containing background materials, in some cases a short summary of the document itself and, where necessary, relevant subsequent developments. We believe this editorial input will prove increasingly useful in future years when the events and questions now covered are less fresh in one's memories and the documents may be hard to find or unobtainable.

The year 1974 was dominated by the climax of the Watergate drama. Richard Nixon became the first President in American history to resign from office. Gerald Ford and Nelson Rockefeller attained the two highest offices in the land without ever facing a national electorate. As the year ended, the trial of the Watergate cover-up conspirators drew to a close with a verdict reached on New Year's Day 1975—bringing to a conclusion, one hoped, a sorry chapter in American history.

The nation's economy struggled with double-digit inflation and by year's end had slumped into a deep recession. Inflation at home was dwarfed by inflation rates abroad as the entire world economy was afflicted by a shortage of oil and energy. And in the third world, millions struggled with a more elemental shortage—food.

These developments added substantially to the usual outpouring of presidential statements, court decisions, commission reports, special studies and speeches of national or international importance. We have selected for inclusion in this book as many as possible of the documents that in our judgment will be of more than transitory interest. Where space limitations prevented reproduction of the full texts, the excerpts used were chosen to set forth the essentials and, at the same time, preserve the flavor of the materials.

Robert A. Diamond
Book Service Editor

Washington, D.C.
January 1975

How to Use This Book

The documents are arranged in chronological order. If you know the approximate date of the report, speech, statement, court decision or other document you are looking for, glance through the titles for that month in the Summary of the Table of Contents below. For more detailed information on an entry in which you are interested, see the comprehensive Table of Contents that follows.

If the Table of Contents does not lead you directly to the document you want, make a double check by turning to the subject Index at the end of the book. There you may find references not only to the particular document you seek but also to other entries on the same or a related subject. The Index in this volume is the third of a projected **five-year cumulative index** of Historic Documents.

The introduction to each document is printed in italic type. The document itself, printed in roman type, follows the spelling, capitalization and punctuation of the original or official copy. Where the full text is not given, omissions of material are indicated by the customary series of dots.

Summary Table of Contents

JANUARY

FEBRUARY

MARCH

APRIL

MAY

JUNE

JULY

AUGUST

SEPTEMBER

OCTOBER

NOVEMBER

DECEMBER

TABLE OF CONTENTS
January

February

March

Ellsberg Break-In Indictments

Nixon on Campaign Reform

End of Arab Oil Embargo

Sirica Decision on Grand Jury Report on Nixon

April

May

Supreme Court on Wiretapping

*Excerpts from the Supreme Court ruling on abuses of
the federal wiretapping statute by former Attorney
General John N. Mitchell and his Justice Department
subordinates* 391

June

July

Budget Reform Legislation

Senate Watergate Report

Supreme Court on Nixon's Tapes

Court on Cross-District Busing

Impeachment Articles

Sentencing of the "Plumbers"

August

Self-Incriminating Nixon Tapes

September

Ford's Vietnam Amnesty Plan

U.N. General Assembly Opening

Kennedy's Rejection of 1976 Presidential Race

Reversal of Calley Conviction

Summit on the U.S. Economy

October

U.S.-Polish Relations

Ford's Testimony on Nixon Pardon

Agreement on Soviet Jewish Emigration

November

Report on "Project Independence"

Arafat's U.N. Speech

U.N. World Food Conference

Ford's Asian Summits

December

Ford's Recession-Fighting Plan

U.S.-French Relations: Ford and Giscard D'Estaing

Swearing-In of Vice President Rockefeller

End of Watergate Coverup Trial

January

MILK FUND AND ITT STATEMENTS
January 8, 1974

President Nixon released two separate background papers Jan. 8 defending his role in two controversial administration decisions made in 1971, one related to raising federal milk price supports and the other to settling an antitrust case against International Telephone and Telegraph Corporation. In both papers, Nixon termed "utterly false" charges that the two decisions had been taken in response to promises of political contributions. Nixon said in one paper that political and economic considerations, not a $427,500 contribution from dairy industry groups to the Nixon 1972 re-election campaign, guided the administration's decision to reverse an earlier decision by the secretary of agriculture and approve higher milk price supports in March 1971. In the paper on ITT, the President said a promise from an ITT subsidiary to help defray the costs of the 1972 Republican national convention had nothing to do with the President's attempt to block a 1971 Justice Department appeal of an antitrust case against ITT. The uncommon dual defense of presidential decisions was, according to the White House, another facet of "Operation Candor" by which President Nixon apparently hoped to recapture his plummeting personal credibility which had been severely damaged by the widening Watergate scandal. ("Operation candor," see Historic Documents 1973, pp. 947-949.)

The paper on raising milk subsidies met head-on accusations initially made by consumer activist Ralph Nader that the increase had been tied to the dairymen's contribution pledge to Nixon's campaign. Citing improper political motivations for the increase, Nader and three consumer groups had sued in U.S. District Court in January 1972 for a rollback in the milk price supports. That case was still pending when Nixon released his

3

statement. *The paper on Nixon's role in the ITT matter challenged the contention first made by columnist Jack Anderson in February 1972 that Nixon had ordered the Justice Department to drop an antitrust suit against the large conglomerate in response to an ITT subsidiary's offer to underwrite the cost of the Republican convention in San Diego, California. Anderson's publication of a secret inter-office memorandum, purportedly written by ITT Washington lobbyist Dita Beard to the head of ITT's Washington office and linking settlement of the ITT antitrust case with the contribution pledge, fueled the controversy even after the Republican convention site was switched in May 1972 to Miami Beach.* (See Historic Documents 1972, p. 395-406).

The Milk Fund

The milk fund paper acknowledged for the first time that Nixon personally had made the decision on March 23, 1971, to reverse the decision made two weeks before by then Secretary of Agriculture Clifford M. Hardin and thereby to increase the federal government support of milk prices. Hardin had said previously that he reversed his first position on his own initiative. The paper also revealed that the President had been informed of the dairymen's intended $2-million contribution to his 1972 campaign prior to making the price support decision. According to the paper, the President was informed in a 1970 memo of the campaign pledge from the Associated Milk Producers Inc., the largest dairy cooperative. But at no time, the statement added, did Nixon discuss the contributions with the dairy industry. The White House also noted that the dairy contributions fell far short of the expected total, made up less than one per cent of total contributions to Nixon and represented only a fraction of dairy gifts to congressional candidates.

The White House defended the milk support decision on the ground that its economic consequences had been "beneficial to the entire country." Specifically, the document said, the decision had kept increases in the price of milk to the consumer low and had not cost the federal government any additional money. The statement also detailed the President's Nov. 17, 1973, contention that "Congress put a gun to our head" on the milk support issue. (See Historic Documents 1973, p. 947-949, 963-964). *After former Agriculture Secretary Hardin's initial decision on March 8, 1971, that price supports would not go up, the White House noted that 29 senators and more than 100 representatives began a push to boost price supports. Vetoing such a bill, the statement argued, would be "politically disastrous in some of the Midwestern states." The White House also made it clear that it was seriously concerned by the financial influence of the dairy groups in the 1972 congressional campaigns. This concern and the possibility of alienating the farm vote influenced the President's decision to approve the increase.*

ITT Antitrust Suit

In the paper on the ITT antitrust suit, the White House branded charges that Nixon had ordered the case dropped in return for a convention con-

tribution pledge from Sheraton Hotel Corporation, an ITT subsidiary, "totally without foundation." The document claimed that Nixon did not know about any financial commitment from Sheraton at the time of his order. Rather, the White House said, the President "had concluded that the ITT litigation was inconsistent with his own views of antitrust policy" because it was an attack on "bigness" more than an attempt to ensure corporate competition. When it appeared that former U.S. Solicitor General Erwin N. Griswold might resign in protest, the statement added, Nixon was dissuaded from pursuing his order to drop the appeal.

The Justice Department suit had sought to divest ITT of three companies it had acquired. The lower court decision on the first divestiture case went against the department, but the department expressed confidence that it could win on appeal. According to the White House paper's version of events leading to the settlement, the President ordered then Deputy Attorney General Richard G. Kleindienst not to file the appeal on April 19, 1971. On April 21, 1971, according to this account, former Attorney General John N. Mitchell advised the President against ordering that the appeal be dropped, warning that Griswold was prepared to resign if there were no appeal. The statement added that Mitchell "feared legislative repercussions if the matter were dropped entirely." At that point, the White House said, Nixon withdrew his April 19 order and authorized the Justice Department to proceed with the case as it wished. ITT and the department reached a settlement out of court in July 1971.

Nixon Conversation With Kleindienst

Nixon's admission that he spoke with Kleindienst concerning the ITT appeal corroborated reports that Kleindienst's October 1973 testimony to Watergate prosecutors contradicted his earlier account of the ITT appeal decision. Kleindienst had maintained in testimony before the Senate Judiciary Committee in early 1972 at the time of his confirmation hearings to become attorney general that no one in the White House had pressured him to dispose of the ITT case in any particular way. But the New York Times reported Oct. 30 that during discussions with Watergate prosecutors, Kleindienst had amended that testimony. According to sources close to the prosecution team quoted in the Times account, Kleindienst had acknowledged that President Nixon had ordered him to drop the suit and contended that his threat to resign forced the President to withdraw the order. In a statement Oct. 30, 1973, in response to the Times story, the White House also admitted for the first time that Nixon had talked with Kleindienst about the suit, but denied that there had been an attempt to obstruct the case for political or other reasons. On March 16, 1974, Kleindienst pleaded guilty in U.S. District Court in Washington, D.C. to a misdemeanor charge based on his failure to tell members of the Senate Judiciary Committee of his conversations with Nixon concerning the ITT appeal. Kleindienst thus became the first former attorney general in history to be convicted of a criminal offense commited while in office. (See p. 407-410.)

Excerpts from the text of President Nixon's Jan. 8 statements on presidential involvement in 1971 decisions to increase the level of federal milk price supports and to drop Justice Department antitrust action against ITT:

Milk Support Price Decision

Summary—The Milk Price Decision

The Charge

It has been publicly alleged that President Nixon in 1971, in exchange for a promise of political contributions from the dairy industry ordered an increase in the level of Federal support prices for milk. That charge has been frequently denied and is totally false.

The Facts

On March 12, 1971, the Secretary of Agriculture announced that the price of milk for the 1971-72 marketing year would be supported by the Federal Government at approximately 80 per cent of parity. His announcement was made in the face of strong pressure from the dairy industry for a support level between 85 and 90 percent of parity; the industry, along with its supporters in the Congress, argued that the 80 percent level would lead to underproduction and would not represent a fair return on farm investments.

Subsequent to Secretary Hardin's announcement, there was a concerted effort in the Congress to pass legislation forcing the President to raise price supports to a minimum of 85 percent of parity. In the House of Representatives, 125 Members introduced or consponsored legislation for higher support prices. In the Senate, 29 Members introduced such legislation. Support for mandatory legislation came from both sides of the aisle, but was predominantly Democratic.

On March 23, 1971, following a meeting with representatives of the dairy industry who argued the merits of their case, and then a meeting with key advisers who agreed that the Congress would likely force his hand, the President decided that the milk support level should be raised to 85 percent of parity for the coming year. His decision was announced by Secretary Hardin on March 25.

It is fallacious to suggest that the President's decision was influenced by a promise of political contributions from the dairy industry. The President had been informed of the dairy industry's intentions to raise funds for the 1972 campaign, but he at no time discussed the contributions with the dairy industry and the subject was not mentioned in his meetings of March 23, 1971. It is also worth noting that the ultimate contributions by the dairy industry to the President's reelection effort (1) were far less than the industry leaders had hoped to raise; (2) were far less than the dairy industry gave to other candidates for the House and Senate, including many prominent Democrats; and (3) represented less than one percent of the total contributions to President Nixon's reelection campaign.

How the Decision Was Made: The President's action took several factors into account:

—intensive Congressional pressure;

—the economic merits of the case itself, as presented by the industry leaders in the meeting with the President; and as weighed by the President's advisers;

—traditional political considerations relating to the needs of the farm States.

The Results: The economic consequences of the decision have been beneficial to the entire country.

—The price of milk to the consumer did not skyrocket, as some feared. Rather, the price of milk to the consumer in the year in question rose at the lowest rate of recent years. It also rose at a rate significantly below the general rate of inflation.

—The cost to the Government of the milk price support program did not go up as a result of the President's decision. It went down.

—Government inventories of surplus dairy products did not expand. In fact, they went down. No massive surplus was created.

—The level of dairy production was ample to meet the needs of consumers but was not excessive, and thus did not burden the Government with special expenditures....

I. The Decisions of March 1971

The decision announced each year by the Secretary of Agriculture of the price at which the Government will support milk prices has a significant impact on the Nation's dairy farmers. In 1970, Secretary Hardin had announced that for the marketing year running from April 1, 1970, through March 31, 1971, the Government would support manufacturing milk at $4.66 per 100 pounds, or at 85 percent of parity. This figure represented an increase of 38 cents and an increase of 2 percent of the parity rate over the year before (1969-1970).

As the 1971-72 marketing season approached, the question within the Government was whether to continue supporting the milk price at $4.66 per 100 pounds or to raise the price. Because a grain shortage and other factors had increased the costs of production for dairy farmers, a continuation of the $4.66 price meant that the parity rate would actually fall to approximately 80 percent. To the farmers, a drop in parity rate would result in a possible loss of income which in turn could deter production. The farmers therefore advocated an increase in the price support to $5.21 per 100 pounds, or 90 percent of parity; at the very least, they argued, the Government should raise the price to $4.92 per 100 pounds and thereby maintain the current parity rate of 85 percent. At the Department of Agriculture, it was feared that such price increases might encourage excess production on the farms, raise the prices of dairy products for consumers, and ultimately force the Government to purchase the surplus products.

The dairy industry, which had become highly organized in the 1960's, moved to exert maximum, direct pressure on the Secretary of Agriculture in early 1971: In a few weeks, over 13,000 letters from milk producers were received by the Department of Agriculture.

At the same time, the dairy industry worked to achieve its objectives indirectly through Members of the Congress who agreed with industry views. The upper Midwestern affiliate of the Associated Milk Producers, Inc. (AMPI) estimated that its members alone sent some 50,000 letters to Congressmen on the subject of milk supports. Between February 23 and March 12, 1971, some 25 Senators and 65 Congressmen wrote the Secretary of Agriculture to urge that the $4.66 support price be increased. Some 20 Senators and 53 Representatives indicated that they wanted to see the price raised to a full 90 percent of parity ($5.21 per cwt.). Four Senators and eight Representatives adopted a more restrained position, asking that the price be raised to at least 85 percent of parity ($4.92).

Some of the letters openly referred to the fact that spokesmen for the dairy cooperatives—AMPI, Dairymen, Inc., or their affiliates— had written or called upon the Congressmen to ask for support. A number of letters were apparently drafted by lobbying groups.

Many of the Members also took to the floor of the House and Senate to express their concern....

After March 7, when the Associated Press reported that Secretary Hardin might raise the support level to 85 percent of parity, Senators Hubert Humphrey (D., Minn.), Vance Hartke (D., Ind.), Walter Mondale (D., Minn.), and Fred Harris (D., Okla.), as well as Congressmen Ed Jones (D., Tenn.), Robert McClory (R., Ill.), and Vernon Thomson (R., Wis.), all made floor speeches in favor of a 90 percent level....

While their colleagues were marshaling support in open floor speeches, senior Democratic leaders in the Congress were expressing their concerns privately to representatives of the Administration. On February 10, the Chairman of the House Ways and Means Committee, Wilbur Mills (D., Ark.), arranged a meeting in the office of Speaker Carl Albert (D., Okla.) to discuss the dairy issue. Represesatives of the dairy industry had apparently asked for the meeting to plead their case. In attendance were Harold Nelson and David Parr from AMPI; Congressmen Mills, Albert and John Byrnes (R., Wis.); William Galbraith, head of Congressional liaison for the Department of Agriculture; and Clark MacGregor, then Counsel to the President for Congressional Relations.

The Congressional leaders continued to make their views known in several private conversations thereafter. According to Mr. MacGregor's records, Congressman Mills urged him on at least six occasions in late February and early March to urge the President to raise the support price. Congressman Mills and Speaker Albert also telephoned the Director of the Office of Management and Budget, George Shultz, with the same request. Mr. Shultz sent a memorandum to John Ehrlichman at the White House indicating the substance of the Mills request for a rise in the support level.

Nevertheless, on March 12, Secretary Hardin announced that the price support for the coming year would be approximately 80 percent of parity—not 90 percent as the dairy industry wanted. The Secretary's announcement acknowledged that some dairymen believed that the support price should be increased. But, he said, higher support prices might lead to excessive supplies and large surpluses. Mr. Hardin believed his action was "in the long-term best interests of the dairy producers."

Immediately following the Agriculture Department announcement of March 12, 1971, a campaign was initiated on Capitol Hill by both Democrats and Republicans for mandatory legislation to increase the parity level to 85 or 90 percent. *Thirty separate bills* were introduced in the House of Representatives between March 16 and March 25 with this specific goal in mind. *One hundred and twenty-five Members of the House of Representatives* introduced or cosponsored legislation to support the price of manufacturing milk at a level of not more than 90 percent nor less than 85 percent. In other words, 85 percent would be an absolute floor for price supports. Of these Representatives, 29 were Republicans and 96 were Democrats. Two Congressmen, one from each side of the aisle, also introduced legislation for a mandatory level of 90 percent of parity.

In the Senate, 28 Senators, led by Democratic Senator Gaylord Nelson of Wisconsin, introduced legislation on March 16, 1971, that would have required support levels at a minimum of 85 percent of parity. Of the Nelson bill sponsors, one was a Republican (Senator Cook of Kentucky) and 27 were Democrats (Senators Allen, Bayh, Burdick, Bentsen, Cranston, Eastland, Eagleton, Fulbright, Gravel, Hart, Harris, Hollings, Hartke, Hughes, Inouye, Long, Mondale, McGee, McGovern, Muskie, Moss, Nelson, Proxmire, Sparkman, Stevenson, Symington, Tunney). Three days later, Senator Hubert Humphrey sponsored his own bill seeking higher parity.

Phase-out of Subsidies

Philosophically, the Nixon Administration had hoped to gradually move away from Federal policies which provide massive subsidies to agriculture. These subsidies had initially been instituted during the Depression years....During the ensuing decades, when these support policies might have been phased out, they instead became political footballs, tossed about in the Congress, aided and abetted by well-organized farm lobby groups.

The dairy support question proved to be no exception. On March 28, 1971, for instance, the *Minneapolis Tribune* quoted an aide of Senator Gaylord Nelson to the effect that representatives of AMPI, who were operating out of a three-room hotel suite in Washington, played a major role in the preparation of the Senator's bill. According to this acount, AMPI also provided some of the research material which the Senator used for a public statement.

With 29 Senators and more than 100 Congressmen actively spearheading the effort to achieve an increased parity rate for the dairy industry, it thus became increasingly clear that mandatory legislation would be enacted and, further, that a Presidential veto of such legislation could well be overridden. Moreover, if the President were to try to force his will in this matter (i.e., to push parity down to 80 percent), it could be politically disastrous in some of the Midwestern States and, in the light of known Congressional intentions, would be both foolish and futile....

With the pressures from Capitol Hill mounting rapidly, President Nixon during the afternoon of March 23 met with seven of his senior advisers to explore the situation with regard to milk price supports. This was the President's second meeting of the day concerning dairy matters. As will be discussed below, the President and other Administration officials met that morning with dairy representatives in response to a long-standing appointment. Meeting with the President that afternoon were John Connally, then Secretary of the Treasury; Clifford Hardin, then Secretary of Agriculture; Under Secretary of Agriculture J. Phil Campbell; George Schultz, then Director of the Office of Management and Budget; John D. Ehrlichman, then Assistant to the President for Domestic Affairs; John Whitaker, then Deputy Assistant to the President for Domestic Affairs; and Donald Rice, then Associate Director of the Office of Management and Budget. The discussion was frank and wide-ranging. It included an appraisal of the support which the milk price legislation had on Capitol Hill and the fact that the legislation had the support of two of the most powerful legislators in the country—Speaker of the House of Representatives Carl Albert and the Chairman of the House Ways and Means Committee, Wilbur Mills.

The political power of the dairy industry lobby was also brought to the President's attention in the March 23 meeting. Secretary Connally said that their votes would be important in several Midwestern States and he noted that the industry had political funds which would be distributed among House and Senate candidates in the coming election year—although neither the Secretary nor anyone else discussed possible contributions to the President's campaign. Mr. Connally argued that the milk industry's case also had merit on strictly economic grounds, and rising costs for dairy producers were mentioned.

The President himself concluded that the final decision came down to the fact that the Congress was going to pass the higher support legislation, and he could not veto it without alienating the farmers—an essential part of his political constituency. It was also believed that by raising the support level in 1971, similar action in 1972 could be precluded—thus holding the price line for 2 years.

The fundamental themes running through this March 23 meeting were two: (1) the unique and very heavy pressures being placed upon the President by the Democratic majority leadership in the Congress and (2) the political advantages and disadvantages of making a decision regarding a vital political constituency.

After the President announced his decision there was discussion of the great power of the House Democratic leadership (which was then pressing for the milk price support increase) and how that power might be enlisted in support of certain of the President's key domestic legislation if the Administration acknowledged the key role these leaders played in securing the reversal of Secretary Hardin's March 12 decision. The meeting concluded with a discussion of the manner in which the decision would be announced and implemented.

Two days later, on March 25, Secretary Hardin officially announced the decision to raise the support level to approximately 85 percent of parity for the 1971-72 marketing season....

The response on Capitol Hill demonstrates the political realities that the President faced....

On April 1, Democratic Senator George McGovern of South Dakota, who had actively sought a rise in price support, noted that he had joined other senators in hoping supports would be set at 85 percent. "This reversal," said Senator McGovern, "can be considered a victory for those in Congress who spoke out vigorously on behalf of the dairy farmers."

On April 5, Senator Nelson,... went on to say that "the [Administration's] decision obviously was the result of S. 1277, which was cosponsored by 27 Senators, and a companion measure in the House which likewise had substantial support.... The Secretary of Agriculture responded to the outpouring of Congressional and farmer concern over the initial decision on price supports by adjusting the support level upward...."

This Congressional pressure was "the gun to our head" that President Nixon referred to in his November 17, 1973, press conference.

It is also worth noting that in 1972, a year after the struggle over a legislatively mandated support level for milk, the Congress enacted legislation which requires that milk be supported at a level no lower than 85 percent in future years.

II. The Dairy Industry Contributions and Lobbying Activities

The lobbying and contribution activities of the dairy industry...[not] unexpectedly...undertook to cover every available base. But there was no arrangement or understanding between the industry and the President as has been so widely and falsely alleged.

The very nature of the Governmental process—with decisions frequently being made within the executive branch on the administration of critical dairy programs and with dairy legislation constantly under review in the Congress—encouraged the dairy farmers to organize and become a potent political force in recent years. There are now three major dairy cooperatives in the United States: AMPI, Mid-America Dairies (Mid Am) and Dairymen, Inc. (DI). Together these cooperatives have over 66,000 members and account for about 25 percent of all the milk produced in the United States.

These dairy organizations not only represent in Washington the interests of their members, they also exert influence through the ballot box and through political contributions. Their activity is not unlike the fundraising and contributing activities of a number of special interest groups such as the Committee on Political Education (COPE) of the AFL-CIO.

The record shows the following lobbying and contribution activities by the dairy industry representatives between 1969 and 1971:

1969-1970

President Nixon had no direct contact with any of the members of these dairy organizations until 1970 when AMPI officials invited him to address their annual convention in Chicago in September. The President was unable to accept the invitation, and Secretary Hardin spoke in his place.

Although he could not attend the convention, the President—as he frequently does—placed a courtesy phone call on September 4, 1970, to the general manager of AMPI, Mr. Harold Nelson. He also spoke with Secretary Hardin, who was with Mr. Nelson. During that conversation, the President invited the dairy leaders to meet with him in Washington and to arrange a meeting with a larger delegation of dairy leaders at a later date....

The meeting...according to the President's diary, lasted...9 minutes....

Mr. Parr has stated in a sworn deposition that it was essentially a social visit. He and Mr. Nelson invited the President to address the next AMPI convention in 1971 and also expressed a hope that he would meet with other dairy industry leaders. Mr. Parr also remembers that the men spoke about the economic plight of the dairy farmer.

Contributions from Dairymen

Although money was not discussed in the meeting between AMPI representatives and the President in September of 1970, it is evident that raising and making political contributions to both Democrats and Republicans were important, continuous, and conspicuous activities of the dairymen during 1970, 1971, and 1972.

During the late 1960's each of the three major dairy cooperatives established a trust fund in order to raise and distribute money to political candidates....

In August of 1969, an attorney for AMPI delivered to Mr. Herbert Kalmbach the sum of $100,000. Mr. Kalmbach deposited the funds in a trustee account he maintained at the Security Pacific National Bank in Newport Beach, Calif. The account contained political contributions remaining from the 1968 election campaign. The President had no knowledge of this contribution.

Reports on file with the Clerk of the House of Representatives showed that contributions to Congressional candidates in 1969 and 1970 by [certain dairy cooperatives] totaled over $500,000. The bulk of the money was earmarked for Democratic candidates. Representatives of the dairy co-ops have indicated in an Associated Press account of December 17, 1973, that Republican candidates received approximately $135,000, or less than 30 percent of the funds.

Some members of the White House Staff knew that the dairymen were giving financial support to Republican and Democratic candidates in Senate elections in 1970. One member of the staff, Charles W. Colson, asserted in a memorandum to the President that AMPI had pledged $2 million to the 1972 campaign. (Whether any such pledge was actually made is unknown, but the total amount given to the President's 1972 campaign was $427,000. As noted below, AMPI's campaign contributions to other candidates during this period were even more generous). That memorandum was attached to a Presidential briefing paper for the courtesy meeting between the President and the AMPI representatives in September of 1970. It was suggested in the memorandum that the President acknowledge AMPI's support. No suggestion was made that any commitment whatsoever be made to do any substantive act. There was also no mention of the asserted pledge during the meeting.

Another reference to fundraising was in a letter addressed to the President on December 16, 1970, from Patrick J. Hillings, a former Congressman who had suceeded Mr. Nixon in his Congressional seat after the latter had been elected to the Senate....

The fact is that the action taken by the President on import quotas was less favorable to the dairy industry than the steps recommended by the Tariff Commission. The Commission, a body of impartial experts, had recommended on economic grounds and pursuant to statutory requirements that imports be closed off entirely for three dairy products (ice cream, certain chocolate products, and animal feeds containing milk derivatives) and that much lower import quotas be set for a fourth item, low-fat cheese. Rather than closing off imports—an action that would have been more favorable to the dairy industry—the President instead reduced the import quotas on each item, permitting all four goods to continue their competition with American dairy products.

1971

The President next met with dairy representatives at 10:30 a.m. on March 23, 1971, in the Cabinet Room of the White House....

Contrary to allegations which have since been made, the meeting had been scheduled more than 3 weeks *before* the March 12 announcement on price supports by Secretary Hardin. As noted above, the meeting stemmed from an invitation first extended on September 4, 1970, when the President spoke by telephone to Harold Nelson of AMPI. In January of 1971, Secretary Hardin recommended to the White House that the meeting be placed on the President's schedule. Thereafter, in February, the White House arranged the March meeting....

[T]he meeting was taken up with the dairy leaders pleading their case for higher supports and with other Administration officials expressing concerns about overproduction and higher retail prices. There was no mention whatsoever of campaign contributions. Nor were any conclusions regarding dairy supports reached at the meeting, as the President pressed the attendees as to whether or not they could control overproduction. Much was said by the dairy representatives of the higher costs of their doing business.

Prior to this meeting, a staff memorandum was prepared as a briefing paper for the President. That paper briefly noted that the dairy lobby—like organized labor—had decided to spend political money and that Pat Hillings and Murray Chotiner were involved. There was no suggestion that the President should give special treatment to the dairymen. In fact, that same paper discussed in much more detail the pressure which was coming from the Congress for higher supports; that the Congress was acting at Speaker Albert's instigation; that the Democratic leadership wanted to embarass the President; and that a bill for higher supports would probably be passed, thus presenting the President with a very tough veto situation.

There were no other discussions between the President and the dairy industry representatives prior to the President's decision on the afternoon of March 23, 1971.

There are a number of mistaken notions with regard to these lobbying efforts of the dairy industry. One is that they had a substantial influence upon the President's decisions. That is untrue. Another is that the dairy contributions represented a substantial portion of the total funding of the President's reelection effort. The truth is that the contributions from the dairymen, amounting to some $427,000, constituted less than one percent of the total.

It should be further noted that from the perspective of the dairymen, their contributions to President Nixon's campaign organizations were not the major focus of their efforts. According to the Congressional Quarterly of March 17, 1973, reports publicly filed by the political arms of the cooperatives show the following total contributions by the political arms of the dairy cooperatives to all political candidates from April 7, 1972, through December 31, 1972....

The Congressional Quarterly account reports that of the $1.5 million contributed by the dairy cooperatives to political campaigns after April 7, 1972, $95,000 went to support the candidacy of President Nixon. Thus, after April 7, 1972, President Nixon's campaign received less than one-fifteenth of the available funds distributed by the dairy trusts. The rest—more than $1.4 million—flowed into the campaigns of Senate and Congressional candidates and to primary contestants in the Democratic Presidential race.

A great number of the Congressional and Senatorial candidates to whom dairy funds were given were also leaders in the effort to legislate a mandatory increase in milk supports in March of 1971....

III. Consequences of President's Decision

Although the President's decision of March 23 was based largely on political realities, unrelated to campaign contributions, it also proved to be sound economics. Here, in brief, were the economic results:

Milk Production: ...Supplies had become sufficiently low by the late 1960s that Secretary Hardin's decision to raise the milk support level in 1970 was based in large part upon his desire to increase production.... The additional increase in the support price to $4.93 as a result of the March 25 announcement provided still further assurances against the resumption of a downward trend in production....

Cost of Milk to the Consumer: The average retail price per half gallon of milk has been rising steadily since 1965...but...the 1971-72 increase was the smallest of all the years...and was considerably less than the rate of general inflation. These reductions in the rate of milk inflation in 1971 and 1972 are directly related to the President's decision of March 23 because the announcement of March 25 encouraged the production of milk to a level higher than it otherwise would have been. Thus, because supplies increased, market price increases have been less than they otherwise would have been.

Cost of the Milk Support Program to the Government: Net expenditures for the dairy price support program and related costs (butter, cheese, dried milk, and similar products) were...during the fiscal year in question—1972—...considerably lower than the year before. It dropped again the following year.

Government Inventories of Dairy Products: ...The aim is thus to achieve a balance in the Commodity Credit Corporation (CCC) stockpiles. As of January 1971, there was some concern that the stocks might fall too low if production of milk were reduced. As it turned out, the butter, processed cheese, and nonfat dry milk stocks in the CCC dipped between a high of 257.9 million pounds to a low of 62.7 million pounds during 1971, even with increased production of milk, but it is a virtual certainty they would have been even lower if the decision had not been made to raise the parity level to 85 percent....

On the basis of all four of the indices above...it would appear that the March 25 reversal of the milk support decision in fact proved to have substantial benefits for all segments of the Nation's economy.

IV. Conclusions

The information contained in this discussion can be summarized as follows:

—Immediately after the Agriculture Department first announced on March 12 that milk would be supported at approximately 80 percent of parity, pressures developed on Capitol Hill for mandatory legislation to increase the parity level to 85-90 percent. Several of the President's advisers believed that the legislation would be enacted and that a Presidential veto of such legislation would be politically disastrous for Mr. Nixon in several States.

—Except for the fear that a rise in supports would create problems of overproduction, several advisers believed the dairymen's case to be meritorious due to the rising costs of fuel, feed, and labor for those producing dairy products. In fact, the corn blight of 1970 considerably reduced many supplies of feed grain for the 1971 marketing year.

—With the Congress putting "a gun to our head" and with his senior advisers supporting him, the President decided that the parity level should be increased to 85 percent.

—Economically, the President's decision to raise the support level proved to be sound and beneficial for the Nation.

—While the President had been advised that the dairymen had decided to make contributions towards the reelection effort of 1972, this did not influence the President's decision to raise the level of supports.

The ITT Antitrust Decision

In the thousands of pages of testimony and analysis regarding the ITT case since 1971, the only major charge that has been publicly made against President Nixon is that in return for a promise of a political contribution from a subsidiary of ITT, the President directed the Justice Department to settle antitrust suits against the corporation.

That charge is totally without foundation:

—The President originally acted in the case because he wanted to avoid a Supreme Court ruling that would permit antitrust suits to be brought against large American companies simply on the basis of their size. He did not direct the settlement or participate in the settlement negotiations directly or indirectly. The only action taken by the President was a telephoned instruction on April 19, 1971, to drop a pending appeal in one of the ITT cases. He rescinded that instruction 2 days later.

—The actual settlement of the ITT case, while avoiding a Supreme Court ruling, caused the corporation to undertake the largest single divestiture in corporate history. The company was forced to divest itself of subsidiaries with some $1 billion in annual sales, and its acquisitions were restricted for a period of 10 years.

—The President was unaware of any commitment by ITT to make a contribution toward expenses of the Republican National Convention at the time he took action on the antitrust case. In fact, the President's antitrust actions took place entirely in April of 1971—several weeks before the ITT pledge was even made.

I. President's Interest in Antitrust Policy

Mr. Nixon made it clear during his 1968 campaign for the President that he stood for an antitrust policy which would balance the goals of free competition in the marketplace against the avoidance of unnecessary government interference with free enterprise. One of Mr. Nixon's major antitrust concerns in that campaign was the Government's treatment of conglomerate mergers.... Mr. Nixon expressed his dissatisfaction with existing conglomerate policies:

"The Department of Justice has recently proposed guidelines for 'conglomerates' but the guidelines have not provided any substantial criteria on which businessmen can safely depend. Moreover, there is the problem of unsettled case law on the question. My administration will make a real effort, and a successful one, I believe, to clarify this entire 'conglomerate' situation...."

To help resolve the issues involved, Mr. Nixon during his campaign appointed a Task Force on Productivity and Competition, headed by Professor George Stigler of the University of Chicago and including several eminent academicians. The task force presented its report to the newly inaugurated President on February 18, 1969. The group recognized public fears that conglomerates posed a "threat of sheer bigness" but said these fears were "nebulous" and should not be converted into an aggressive antitrust policy on the basis of knowledge then available. "We strongly recommend," stated the report, "that the Department (of Justice) decline to undertake a program of action against conglomerate enterprises...."

A similar view was set forth by many outside the Government. In an article in Fortune in September of 1969, Robert Bork, then a professor of antitrust law at the Yale Law School...noted that unless conglomerates mergers were involved in horizontal price-fixing within an industry, there was no economic foundation for believing that they were anti-competitive....

A second major concern of the President and his advisers was their fear that the ability of U.S. companies to compete in the world market might be threatened by antitrust actions against conglomerates. The United States faced a shrinking balance of trade surplus and the President and many of his advisers felt that U.S. multinational companies could play an important role in improving the balance.

The President feared that antitrust action against those companies which was based upon something other than a clear restraint of trade would render them less able to compete with the government sheltered and sponsored industrial giants of Europe and Asia....

Peter Peterson, Director of the President's Council on International Economic Policy, wrote:

> ...the Japanese government sees itself as a partner with business in facilitating economic growth.... The situation is far different from that in the United States—where...major efforts of the government are devoted not to growth and stimulation, but to restraint and regulation of business and labor...."

This view, along with a great deal of other data on foreign trade, was communicated to the President by Mr. Peterson on April 8, 1971—only a few days before the President intervened in the ITT matter.

The President and his advisers (but not Attorney General Mitchell, who had disqualified himself on matters related to ITT) were thus seriously concerned about two aspects of antitrust policy which would eventually bear on the ITT matter: 1) the policy of attacking bigness *per se* and whether such policy had any economic justification, and 2) the need to prevent misguided antitrust attacks upon U.S. companies in competition with large foreign industrial entities.

II. Background on the ITT Litigation

The Justice Department in 1969 initiated civil litigation against the International Telephone and Telephone Co., a major "conglomerate," for alleged violations of the antitrust laws. The allegations involved acquisitions by ITT of the Grinnell Corporation, the Hartford Fire Insurance Company, and the Canteen Corporation. These were only the latest and among the largest of a series of acquisitions made by ITT in the years since

1963, a period in which favorable tax laws, among other things, made acquisitions popular.

Under Assistant Attorney General McLaren, the Antitrust Division of the Justice Department was concerned with the implementation of an antitrust policy which attacked the general merger trend not only because the effect of the corporate growth "may be substantially to lessen competition," conduct clearly proscribed by the antitrust laws, but also because of the economic concentration itself.

Other experts, including many of the President's advisers, did not see the role of antitrust law in such all-encompassing terms. They believed that to use the law of antitrust to achieve political and economic aims beyond prevention of restraint of trade was unsound. If there were dangers such as Mr. McLaren and his colleagues feared from conglomerates, President Nixon and his advisers, along with other experts, preferred solving them through legislation.

Executives of ITT were also concerned about the Justice Department action, and talked with various administration officials to learn their views. The chief executive officer of ITT, Harold Geneen, was sufficiently concerned that he attempted to talk to the President personally about these issues in the summer of 1969. The President's advisers thought that such a meeting was not appropriate, and the meeting was not held.

Other White House officials, however, did talk to various representatives of ITT about antitrust policy. Those discussions invariably focused on the legal and economic issues of whether antitrust suits should be pursued simply because companies are large or rather because they are actually restraining trade in a tangible way. Papers relating to those conversations have been voluntarily turned over to the Special Prosecutor.

III. Making The ITT Cases Consistent With Administration Policy On Antitrust

During the latter part of 1970, there was a question among White House advisers about whether the antitrust actions against the ITT were consistent with the notion of keeping hands off companies unless they had committed some clear restraint of trade rather than simply becoming large in size, and generally whether the ITT suits were consistent with administration policy on antitrust.

While these discussions were taking place, the Justice Department lawsuits against ITT were continuing. The Justice Department's actions against ITT to enjoin the acquisitions of the Grinnell Corporation and Hartford Fire Insurance Company were presented to the United States District Court for the District of Connecticut on September 17, 1969. The court (Chief Judge Timbers, presiding) issued a Memorandum of Decision on October 21, 1969, denying the Government's motion for a preliminary injunction to enjoin the proposed acquisitions by ITT, but directing that "hold separate" orders be entered to preserve the status quo, pending a trial and a decision on the merits.

Subsequently, a trial of the Grinnell case on the merits was held on September 15, 1970, and concluded on October 30, 1970. The court again refused to find that ITT had violated the antitrust laws.

As a result of this litigation and pending a determination to appeal the adverse judgment to the Supreme Court of the United States, Assistant Attorney General McLaren discussed a compromise settlement with ITT during 1970. He indicated he would recommend that ITT be allowed to keep the Grinnell Corporation, but divest itself of the Canteen Corporation and not proceed with its pending acquisition of the Hartford Fire Insurance Company.

By the spring of 1971, the President, based on the information and advice he had received, had concluded that the ITT litigation was inconsistent with his own views on antitrust policy. The Department of Justice and some of the President's advisers continued to maintain, however, that the cases were not an attack on bigness and were based on clear anticompetitive effects of the acquisitions.

On April 19, 1971, in a meeting with John Ehrlichman and George Shultz, then Director of the Office of Management and Budget, the President was told by Mr. Ehrlichman that the Justice Department had filed an appeal with the Supreme Court in the Grinnell case which Mr. Ehrlichman described as an "attack on a conglomerate." Mr. Ehrlichman further told the President that he believed that prosecution of the case was contrary to the President's antitrust policy and that, as a result, he had tried to persuade the Justice Department not fo file a jurisdictional statement (due the following day) so as to terminate the appeal. He indicated, however, that he had been unsuccessful with the Justice Department.

The President expressed irritation with the failure of the head of the Antitrust Division, Mr. McLaren, to follow his policy. He then placed a telephone call to Deputy Attorney General Kleindienst and ordered that the appeal not be filed. The meeting continued [and]...Mr. Shultz expressed the view that conglomerates had been unfairly criticized.

The Justice Department, on April 20, 1971, requested and was granted a delay in filing the appeal which was due that day. On the following day, April 21, 1971, Mr. John N. Mitchell, the Attorney General, advised the President that in his judgment it was inadvisable for the President to order no appeal to the Supreme Court in the Grinnell case. The Attorney General reasoned that, as a personal matter, Mr. Erwin N. Griswold, Solicitor General of the United States, had prepared his brief for appeal and would resign were the appeal not to proceed. The Attorney General further feared legislative repercussions if the matter were dropped entirely. Based upon the Attorney General's recommendations, the President reversed his decision of April 19, 1971, and authorized the Department of Justice to proceed with the case in accordance with his own determinations. He said that he did not care about ITT as such, but that he wanted the Attorney General to see that his antitrust policy was carried out.

At the end of the same month, April 1971, the President approved a proposal for creating a central clearinghouse for information about

Government antitrust policy within the White House, to ensure that the President's views on the subject could be made known to all the operating agencies.

On April 29, 1971, a meeting of ITT representatives, Department of Justice and Department of Treasury officials was held at the Department of Justice wherein ITT made a presentation concerning the financial ramifications of the proposed divestiture actions. Following the meeting, the Department of Justice requested that the Treasury Department and an outside consultant specializing in financial analysis evaluate the ITT claims. These evaluations were made in addition to the Justice Department's own analysis of competitive effect.

Based on the completed assessment, Assistant Attorney General McLaren, on June 17, 1971, sent a memorandum to the Deputy Attorney General outlining a proposed settlement. This proposal was subsequently communicated to ITT representatives and after further negotiations a final settlement, extremely similar to Mr. McLaren's June 17 proposal, was agreed upon in principle on July 31, 1971, and final consent judgments were entered by the United States District Courts on September 24, 1971. On the first trading day after the settlement was announced the common stock of ITT fell 11 percent, from 62 to 55 on investor reaction to the terms of the settlement....

After the consent judgments were made public, several authorities offered their opinions as to the reasonableness of the settlements as opposed to pursuing the appeal to the United States Supreme Court. Former Solicitor General Erwin N. Griswold...found the settlement "extremely favorable" to the Justice Department....

Archibald Cox [said]:

"It was proper for the President to have an interest in such a major case.... 'There was nothing improper in voicing his own opinion.' He added that he thought the Government received a fair settlement in the case."

Mr. McLaren described it as a "tough" settlement which would have immediate deterrent effect in the antitrust area and was therefore preferable to waiting 3 or 4 years for a Supreme Court ruling.

IV. Selection of San Diego for Republican National Convention

The separate and unrelated process of decisionmaking regarding the Republican National Convention began in 1971, when the site selection committee started to examine prospective sites.

In the 1971 selection process, six cities were seriously considered for the 1972 convention....

On June 29, 1971, the San Diego City Council adopted a resolution authorizing the mayor of the city of San Diego to submit a bid on the Republican National Convention to be held in San Diego, and to offer financial support of $1,500,000. Of this amount, $600,000 was to be used for city services, such as police and fire protection, extra public works responsibilities and other service requirements connected with a convention.

The remaining $900,000 to be used for facilities, rents, and other convention requirements was conditioned upon contributions in cash and services by other State and local governmental agencies, individuals, corporations and organizations.

A large part of the cash portion of the bid was committed by the Sheraton Hotel Corporation, a subsidiary of ITT, about June 1, 1971, and subsequently confirmed on July 21, 1971. A new Sheraton hotel was under construction in San Diego and Sheraton apparently felt that television publicity for the hotel and the chain would be a worthwhile business investment. The exact provisions of the donation were and are unclear. Apparently ITT-Sheraton offered $200,000 with some requirement of matching by other San Diego businessmen as to one-half of the commitment. In any event, a payment of $100,000 to the San Diego Convention and Visitor's Bureau was returned when the convention site was changed.

The White House Staff report to Chief of Staff H. R. Haldeman on possible convention sites made no mention of ITT. Rather, it recommended San Diego because of California's Republican Governor, San Diego's Republican Congressman, its proximity to the Western White House, its outstanding climate, its relatively large bid in money and services, the importance of California in the electoral tally, the attractive outdoors atmosphere of the town, and the excellent security which could be offered.

The President, himself, informed Senator Robert Dole, Chairman of the Republican National Committee, that whatever Senator Dole and the site selection committee decided was agreeable to him. Subsequently, the President approved the selection of San Diego by the site selection committee....

WHITE HOUSE TAPE ERASURES
January 15, 1974

A panel of six tape experts reported to Federal District Chief Judge John J. Sirica Jan. 15 that at least five, or as many as nine, "separate and contiguous" erasures were the cause of a mysterious 18-minute buzzing noise that wiped out a White House tape recording of a June 20, 1972, conversation between President Nixon and former White House Chief of Staff H. R. Haldeman. Dealing another blow to the President's already weakened credibility, the tape experts rejected the White House contention that the gap had been caused accidentally by President Nixon's personal secretary as she was transcribing the conversations. The conversation had dealt with the break-in at the Democratic National Headquarters in the Watergate complex three days before, according to Haldeman's personal notes placed into evidence at hearings on the 18-minute gap before Sirica in November. Those notes also indicated that during the June 20 meeting, President Nixon directed Haldeman to launch a public relations counter-offensive to offset the burglary. The tape recording of the June 20 meeting had been subpoenaed by former Special Watergate Prosecutor Archibald Cox to determine whether or not Nixon knew of or participated in the Watergate cover-up.

After nearly two months of analyzing the tape, the experts concluded that the gap had been caused by manually stopping and starting a Uher 5000 tape recorder similar to the one used by Nixon's secretary Rose Mary Woods, and not by "any single, continuous operation" as the White House had suggested. Rose Mary Woods had testified before Sirica Nov. 26 that she caused a 4-5 minute gap by pressing the wrong button when she answered a telephone call and by keeping her foot on the recorder's foot pedal during the conversation. The tape specialists found that "whether the foot pedal was used or not, the recording controls must have been operated by hand in the making of each segment" of the five to nine erasures.

Questioned by Assistant Special Prosecutor Richard Ben-Veniste as to whether the erasures had been deliberate, one panel member said in court Jan. 15 that the variations on the tape were "thoroughly consistent" with a deliberately erased tape. Another member of the panel agreed with Ben-Veniste that if the erasures had been an accident, "it would have to be an accident that was repeated at least five times." President Nixon's lawyer James D. St. Clair asked whether defects in the Uher recorder used by Miss Woods may have caused the markings on the tape that indicated separate erasures. One expert denied that defects could have made the markings.

St. Clair Jan. 15 indicated that the White House would consult its "own" experts, although the six-man panel had been selected jointly Nov. 21, 1973, by the White House and the special Watergate prosecutor's office. Deputy White House Press Secretary Gerald L. Warren Jan. 16 denied that President Nixon himself had deliberately or accidentally erased the 18-minute segment, basing his comments on "many discussions about this matter with the President."

But public, congressional and other official reactions to the findings were markedly more concerned. Public opinion polls showed widespread disbelief of the White House's accidental erasure theory. In Congress, many Republicans and Democrats agreed that the report on the tape had further undermined Nixon's credibility and underscored the necessity of an impeachment inquiry. Sen. Henry M. Jackson (D Wash.) said, "the burden has shifted for the President and his White House aides to explain what went on." Special Watergate Prosecutor Leon Jaworski requested the FBI to investigate the erasure and to report directly to him.

Since former presidential aide Alexander P. Butterfield disclosed the existence of tape recordings of White House conversations July 16, 1973, (See Historic Documents 1973, p. 697-701), *the White House tapes had triggered a controversial struggle over obtaining the tapes for evidence in the investigations of various Watergate cases. Cox had subpoenaed nine taped conversations despite White House arguments that executive privilege and the need to safeguard the confidentiality of administration conversations precluded release of the tapes. (See* Historic Documents 1973, p. 737-751.) *Two courts ordered President Nixon to relinquish the recordings or reach a compromise acceptable to Cox (see* Historic Documents 1973, p. 839-857). *Nixon had ordered that Cox be fired over his refusal to accept a resultant White House compromise, an order that led to the resignations of the Attorney General and the Deputy Attorney General. (*Historic Documents 1973, 859-880.) *Abruptly, the White House reversed its position Oct. 23, 1973, and released the nine subpoenaed tapes. And on Nov. 21, 1973, Nixon lawyers reported to the court that an 18-minute gap existed in the June 20, 1972, conversation.*

The six tape experts and a seventh expert hired solely by the White House confirmed June 4 the original findings on the cause of the 18-minute gap after more extensive experimentation. The tape panel's final 287-page report to Judge Sirica restated their belief that at least five manual erasures, not a foot pedal nor a malfunction of the Uher recorder, caused the gap. The White House expert, Michael H.L. Hecker of the Stanford Research Institute, said that the theories that defects in the recorder caused the gap have been disproved when scrutinized theoretically or experimentally." However, he held out the possibility that "an acceptable hypothesis can be advanced by other scientists." Sirica forwarded a copy of the report to the Watergate Special Prosecutor for an investigation into "the possibility of unlawful destruction of evidence" on the subpoenaed White House tape recordings.

Text of advisory panel's report to Judge John J. Sirica, submitted Jan. 15, 1974, on gaps in the White House tape recording of June 20, 1972:

In response to your request we have made a comprehensive technical study of the White House tape of June 20, 1972, with special attention to a section of buzzing sounds that lasts approximately 18.5 minutes. Paragraphs that follow summarize our findings and indicate the kinds of tests and evidence on which we base the findings.

Magnetic signatures that we have measured directly on the tape show that the buzzing sounds were put on the tape in the process of erasing and re-recording at least five,and perhaps as many as nine, separate and contiguous segments. Hand operation of keyboard controls on the Uher 5000 recorder was involved in starting and again in stopping the recording of each segment.

The magnetic signatures observed on the tape show conclusively that the 18.5-minute section could not have been produced by any single, continuous operation. Further, whether the foot pedal was used or not, the recording controls must have been operated by hand in the making of each segment.

'Were Done Directly'

The erasing and recording operations that produced the buzzing section were done directly on the tape we received for study. We have found that this tape is 1,814.5 feet long, which lies within a normal range for tapes sold as 1,800 feet in length. We have examined the entire tape for physical splices and have found none. Other tests that we have made thus far are consistent with the assumption that the tape is an original and not a re-recording.

A Uher 5000 recorder, almost surely the one designated as Government exhibit #60, was used in producing the 18.5-minute section. Support for this conclusion includes recorder operating characteristics that we measured and found to correspond to signal characteristics observed on the evidence tape.

The buzzing sounds themselves originated in noise picked up from the electrical power line to which the recorder was connected. Measurements of the frequency spectrum of the buzz showed that it is made up of a 60 cycles per second fundamental tone, plus a large number of harmonic tones at multiples of 60.

Especially strong are the third harmonic at 180 and the fifth harmonic at 300 cycles per second. As many as 40 harmonics are present in the buzz and create its "raucous" quality.

Variations in the Buzz

Variations in the strength of the buzz, which during most of the 18.5-minute section is either "loud" or "soft," probably arose from several causes including variations in the noise on the power line, erratic functioning of the recorder, and changes in the position of the operator's hand while running the recorder. The variations do not appear to be caused by normal machine operations.

Can speech sounds be detected under the buzzing? We think so. At three locations in the 18.5-minute section, we have observed a fragment of speech-like sound lasting less than one second.

Each of the fragments lies exactly at a place on the tape that was missed by the erase head during the series of operations in which the several segments of erasure and buzz were put on the tape. Further, the frequency spectra of the sounds in these fragments bear a reasonable resemblance to the spectra of speech sounds.

Can the speech be recovered? We think not. We know of no technique that could recover intelligible speech from the buzz section. Even the fragments that we have observed are so heavily obscured that we cannot tell what was said.

The attached diagram [omitted] illustrates the sequence of sound events in the 18.5-minute section. Also illustrated is a sequence of Uher operations "erase-record on" and "erase-record off" that are consistent with signatures that we measured on the evidence tape. The five segments that can be identified unequivocally are labeled "1" through "5." In addition, the diagram shows four segments of uncertain ending.

In developing the technical evidence on which we have based the findings reported here, we have used laboratory facilities, measuring instruments and techniques of several kinds, including digital computers located in three different laboratories, specialized instruments for measuring frequency spectra and wave forms, techniques for "developing" magnetic marks that can be seen and measured directly on the tape, techniques for measuring the performance characteristics of recorders and voice-operated switches, and statistical methods for analyzing experimental results.

In summary we have reached complete agreement on the following conclusions:

1. The erasing and recording operations that produced the buzz section were done directly on the evidence tape.

2. The Uher 5000 recorder designated Government exhibit #60 probably produced the entire buzz section.

3. The erasures and buzz recordings were done in at least five, and perhaps as many as nine, separate and contiguous segments.

4. Erasure and recording of each segment required hand operation of keyboard controls of the Uher 5000 machine.

5. Erased portions of the tape probably contained speech originally.

6. Recovery of the speech is not possible by any method known to us.

7. The evidence tape, in so far as we have determined, is an original and not a copy.

Respectfully submitted,

RICHARD H. BOLT

FRANKLIN S. COOPER

JAMES L. FLANAGAN

JOHN G. (JAY) McKNIGHT

THOMAS G. STOCKHAM JR.

MARK R. WEISS

EGYPTIAN-ISRAELI DISENGAGEMENT

January 18, 1974

Egypt and Israel signed two agreements Jan. 18 to separate their forces along the Suez Canal, action termed a first step toward settlement of the October 1973 war and the establishment of a permanent peace in the Middle East. (See Historic Documents 1973, p. 881-896, 897-909, 931-937.) *Following intensive efforts Jan. 11-17 by U.S. Secretary of State Henry A. Kissinger to bring the two sides closer together, announcement of the disengagement was made Jan. 17 simultaneously in Cairo, Jerusalem and Washington. Several hours later, U.S. officials in Jerusalem disclosed the existence of the second agreement to define military limits within the disengagement zones following the troop pullback. The agreements provided for Israel's maintenance of troops at points key to the defense of the Sinai Peninsula and Egypt's renewed access to its Third Army, trapped by surrounding Israeli forces since the second week of the October war.*

The first agreement called for a pullback of Egyptian and Israeli troops along the Suez Canal and the establishment of disengagement zones. Israel was to abandon its bridgehead on the west bank of the Suez and pull back its forces on the east bank to designated zones 5 to 7½ miles wide, 14-20 miles from the canal. But Israel also retained positions at the Mitla and Gidi Passes, thereby controlling the major routes into the Sinai. This fact was judged particularly significant in light of Egypt's claim to absolute sovereignty over the entire Sinai Penisula. Egypt likewise was to retain troops on the east bank in a 5 to 7½ mile zone. The opposing troops were to be divided by United Nations Emergency Force (U.N.E.F.) troops holding a buffer zone.

Egyptian and Israeli chiefs of staff signed the disengagement accord Jan. 18 at Kilometer 101 on the Suez-Cairo road. Major General Mohammed Abdel el-Gamasy signed for Egypt and Lt. General David Elazer for Israel. Technical details of the disengagement were completed Jan. 24 by these officials, troop movement began Jan. 25 and the agreed disengagement was completed March 6.

Copies of the second agreement, defining the limitations on troops and arms within the disengagement zones, were signed the same day in Aswan, Egypt, by President Anwar Sadat and in Jerusalem by Israeli Premier Golda Meir. Secretary Kissinger attended both ceremonies. Details of this second accord were kept secret, although high Israeli officials reported that it called for Egypt's ground-to-air missiles to be withdrawn to seven miles west of the canal where they would continue to protect Egyptian forces but where they would not pose a threat to Israel's first line of defense. In addition, Egypt was to reduce its forces from 70,000 men and 700 tanks on the east bank of the Suez Canal to 7,000 troops and 30 tanks. Israel would complete a comparable reduction of forces.

Kissinger's Diplomacy

The disengagement agreement was the outcome of a week of negotiations mediated by Kissinger through a series of discussions with Egyptian officials in Aswan and with Israelis in Jerusalem. Kissinger had embarked on the diplomatic effort after largely unsuccessful Geneva peace talks on a Middle East settlement broke off Jan. 9. The importance of United Nations actions in halting sporadic Egyptian-Israeli fighting since the October cease-fire was emphasized by an invitation from Egypt and Israel for the commander of the United Nations Emergency Force (U.N.E.F.) to attend the signing ceremony at Kilometer 101. Although the Soviets had joined the United States in cosponsoring the U.N. resolution that brought about the October cease-fire and in cosponsoring the peace talks in Geneva their role went unnoticed in the announcements and the signings.

The arms limitation agreement reportedly emerged from a U.S. proposal offered by Kissinger. A State Department official Jan. 21 cited "eight or nine" assurances that Kissinger had established with the Egyptians and the Israelis during mediation efforts on this accord. Among the points the official cited were (1) that the United States had informed Israel of its understanding that Egypt would reopen the Suez Canal to international shipping, including Israeli cargo ships, following the troop pullback, (2) that Egypt would formally announce the end of its blockade of the Bab-el Mandeb strait at the entrance to the Red Sea, although Egypt had actually lifted the blockade following a secret agreement with the United States and Israel in November 1973, (3) that Israel would continue to have U.S. support, including military support, although no formal treaty would be signed, and (4) that the U.N.E.F. buffer zone would operate until disbanded by the U.N. Security Council, unlike the situation in 1967 when Egypt uni-laterally ordered the troops withdrawn.

Reaction to the agreements emphasized their preliminary nature. Presi-dent Nixon called them "the first significant step toward a permanent peace in the Middle East." But he stressed "the difficulties that lie ahead" in resolving other aspects of the Arab-Israeli dispute in order to establish a permanent peace in the area. He said Americans could "be proud of the role that our government has played, and particularly the role that has been played by Secretary Kissinger and his colleagues."

President Sadat hailed the accords as a "turning point" in the troubled history of the Middle East, but said the stalled Middle East peace talks on a permanent peace would not reopen until a disengagement agreement between Israel and Syria could be reached. On Jan. 23, at the conclusion of a six day tour of eight Arab states to gain support for the troop disengage-ment agreement with Israel, a mission he called a "complete success," Sadat said he noted a shift in American policy in the Middle East, away from "total and unconditional support" of Israel toward "a balance of power" in the area. (Israeli-Syrian disengagement, 435-439.)

Israeli defense minister Moshe Dayan called the pacts "good and satisfactory," attributing the successful outcome of negotiations to Egypt's sincere desire for peace. The Palestinian Liberation Organization, representing various guerrilla groups, split in its reaction to the accords. Although Yasir Arafat, leader of the Al Fatah, a major commando group, conveyed his support to Sadat Jan. 21, other high-ranking members regard-ed the agreements as "surrender to the American plan," and vowed to con-tinue the war against Israel "until all occupied Palestinian soil is liberated."

Text of the accord signed Jan. 18 by Israel and Egypt on the separation of their forces on the Suez front. The arms and troop limitation agreement was not released:

[A]

Egypt and Israel will scrupulously observe the cease-fire on the land, sea and air called for by the U.N. Security Council and will refrain from the time of the signing of this document from all military or paramilitary ac-tions against each other.

[B]

The military forces of Egypt and Israel will be separated in accordance with the following principles:

1. All Egyptian forces on the east side of the canal will be deployed west of the line designated as line A on the attached map. All Israeli forces in-cluding those west of the Suez Canal on the Bitter Lakes will be deployed east of the line designated as line B on the attached map.

2. The area between the Egyptian and Israeli lines will be a zone of disengagement in which the United Nations Emergency Force will be stationed. The U.N.E.F. will continue to consist of units from countries that are not permanent members of the Security Council.

3. The area between the Egyptian line and the Suez Canal will be limited in armament and forces.

4. The area between the Israeli line, line B on the attached map, and the lines designated as line C on the attached map, which runs along the western base of the mountains where the Gidi and Mitla passes are located, will be limited in armament and forces.

5. The limitations referred to in paragraphs 3 and 4 will be inspected by U.N.E.F. Existing procedures of the U.N.E.F., including the attaching of Egyptian and Israeli liaison officers to U.N.E.F., will be continued.

[C]

The detailed implementation of the disengagement of forces will be worked out by military representatives of Egypt and Israel, who will agree on the stages of this process. These representatives will meet no later than 48 hours after the signature of this agreement at Kilometer 101 under the aegis of the United Nations for this purpose. They will complete this task within five days. Disengagement will begin within 48 hours after the completion of the work of the military representatives, and in no event later than seven days after the signature of this agreement. The process of disengagement will be completed not later than 40 days after it begins.

[D]

This agreement is not regarded by Egypt and Israel as a final peace agreement. It constitutes a first step toward a final, just and durable peace according to the provisions of Security Council Resolution 338 and within the framework of the Geneva Conference.

For Egypt:

MOHAMMED ABDEL GHANY AL-GAMASY
Major General

For Israel:

DAVID ELAZAR
Lieut. Gen., Chief of Staff of Israel Defense Forces

SENTENCING OF EGIL KROGH
January 24, 1974

"However national security is defined, I now see that none" of the reasons for the burglary of the office of Daniel Ellsberg's psychiatrist "could justify the invasion of the rights of the individuals" involved. With these words, Egil Krogh Jr., the former co-director of the secret White House investigative unit called the "plumbers," sought to explain his rejection of the national security rationale that had led to his directing the break-in at the office of Dr. Lewis Fielding, Ellsberg's psychiatrist. The occasion was Kroth's sentencing in U.S. District Court in Washington, D.C. Jan. 24, 1974, following his plea of guilty to the charges of violating the civil rights of Fielding. Krogh, who had been named undersecretary of transportation at age 33 and had been considered among the brightest young men in the Nixon White House, thus became the first major former White House aide to be sentenced to prison for Watergate-related activities. He was ordered to serve six months of a two-to-six year prison sentence with an additional 18 months of unsupervised probation for his part in the Fielding break-in which eventually led to the dismissal of the Pentagon Papers Case. (See Historic Documents 1973, p. 537-548; Historic Documents 1972, p. 491-497.) Although Krogh accepted sole responsibility for engineering the burglary and did not implicate President Nixon, he nonetheless attributed his actions to "the intensity of the national security concern expressed by the President" which "fired up and overshadowed every aspect of the unit's work."

In a 12-page statement released by his lawyers after sentencing, Krogh explained that as a result of "an urgent assignment" from President Nixon after the unauthorized publication in 1971 of a secret Defense Department

33

study on Vietnam, a document that came to be known as the Pentagon Papers, he had sought to compile detailed information on Daniel Ellsberg who released a copy of the papers to the New York Times. *The material, Krogh said, was to be used to prevent further disclosures, to urge Ellsberg to reveal his true intentions and to discredit Ellsberg as an antiwar spokesman. One result of Krogh's efforts was the burglary of the office of Lewis Fielding, a psychiatrist Ellsberg had consulted. That burglary was "dictated by the national security interest as I then understood it, said Krogh.*

When initially indicted for the break-in, Krogh had pleaded "not guilty" to burglary charges filed in a California court and to perjury charges in the U.S. District Court in Washington, D.C., pitching his pleas to the necessity of maintaining national security. But U.S. District Judge Gerhard A. Gesell struck down Krogh's legal defense, saying, "We would have no society" if persons could burglarize and lie to a grand jury when guided by some vague notion of national security. Gesell's remarks, said Krogh, "spurred my reappraisal" of previous events. On Nov. 30, 1973, Krogh switched his plea to guilty of one charge of violating Fielding's civil rights. In his statement he repented, saying, "rights of the individual cannot be sacrificed to the mere assertion of national security."

Krogh's assessment of the White House use of the term "national security" renewed the public debate on two questions: the tone of the Nixon administration and the ultimate responsibility for the actions of White House subordinates. During an interview Jan. 27, 1974, with CBS newsman Mike Wallace, Krogh addressed himself to both questions. In the White House, he said, "there was an attitude perhaps, that was created by some discussions among staff people that demonstrators and others...were out to destroy his [Nixon's] policies, a feeling of us versus them." He acknowledged that the White House at times considered political enemies as enemies of the state. Asked who set the tone of the White House atmosphere, Krogh replied: "The climate is set by the top man." In his statement after sentencing, Krogh appeared to be claiming that without the White House paranoia of "us versus them" and without excessive concerns allegedly for national security, he never would have acted as he did.

"National Security" Barred Asking "Is This Right?"

Krogh's explanation in his statement of the acquiescence by White House aides to undertake what later came to be considered improper, if not illegal activity, seemed to rest with the use of the term "national security." Said Krogh: "The invocation of national security stopped me from asking the question, 'is this the right thing to do.'" Discrediting Ellsberg, Krogh said, "which today strikes me as repulsive and an inconceivable national security goal, at the time would have appeared a means of blocking the possibility that he would become such a popular figure that others possessed of classified information would be encouraged to emulate him. More broadly, it would serve to diminish any influence he might have in mobilizing op-

position to the course of ending the Vietnam war that had been set by the President. And that course was the very definition of national security. Freedom of the President to pursue his planned course was the ultimate national security objective."

In rejecting the values he said had seemed "natural" when he worked at the Nixon White House, Krogh dramatized accusations that the Nixon Administration operated in isolation and added another voice to the chorus questioning President Nixon's leadership of his subordinates. In ending his statement, Krogh made an incisive pitch to potential young government employees: "I hope they will recognize that the banner of national security can turn perceived patriotism into actual disservice. When contemplating a course of action, I hope they will never fail to ask 'Is this right?' "

> *Text of the statement by Egil Krogh Jr., released by his lawyer Jan 24 following Krogh's sentencing in U.S. District Court for his role in the break-in at the office of Daniel Ellsberg's psychiatrist:*

In describing the offense to which I have pleaded guilty, and the nature of my role in it, I am hampered by the fact that my present evaluation is totally antagonistic to the understanding I had at the time. I feel unable to set forth what happened without continuing on to discuss how my present contrary appraisal developed.

And the process of reappraisal has been so extensive and so agonizing that my present evaluation is very firmly fixed, which makes recounting my feelings at the time of the offense all the more difficult. I have been aided by a review of the files in the Executive Office Building on Dec. 13 and 14, 1973.

This case involves the work of the special investigation unit established within the White House to deal with the problem of unauthorized disclosure of classified information.

My role began on July 15 or 16, 1971, in San Clemente. At that time, John Ehrlichman informed me that the President wanted me to perform an urgent assignment in response to the unauthorized disclosure of the Pentagon Papers. The entire resources of the Executive Branch were to be brought to bear on this task, and I was to make certain that the relevant departments and agencies treated the matter as one of highest priority.

Because Dr. Daniel Ellsberg had been identified as responsible for the leak of the Pentagon papers, he was to be a vital part of the inquiry. Specifically, his motivations, his possible collaborators, and his potential for further disclosures were to be determined to the greatest extent possible.

"Zeal Comparable to...Investigating Alger Hiss"

In that connection, Mr. Ehrlichman instructed me that the President had directed that I read his book, "Six Crises," and particularly the chapter on Alger Hiss, in preparation for this assignment. The message that I drew from this chapter was the President's concern that we proceed with respect to the Pentagon Papers and Dr. Ellsberg with a zeal comparable to that he exercised as a congressman in investigating Alger Hiss.

Mr. Ehrlichman instructed me that David Young of Dr. Kissinger's staff would be working with me on this assignment and that we should form a small unit for the purpose. Mr. Young was to devote full time to the unit. My participation was to be part time, for I was to continue my ongoing responsibilities, particularly solidification of the Vietnam drug program and creation of a Cabinet committee to fight international narcotics traffic.

As it happened, these latter assignments occupied most of my time in August. Finally, Mr. Ehrlichman instructed me that the activities of the unit were to be impressed with the highest classification and kept secret even within the White House staff. To handle our assignment Mr. Young and I received some of the most sensitive security clearances.

Mr. Young and I arranged for space in the Executive Office Building, and elaborate special security systems were installed. Mr. E. Howard Hunt was assigned to the unit on the basis of his extensive prior experience with the Central Intelligence Agency. Mr. G. Gordon Liddy, with whom I had worked on matters of narcotics law enforcement and gun control while he was at the Treasury Department, came to the unit because of his prior experience with the Federal Bureau of Investigation.

A damage assessment prepared by the C.I.A. prior to establishment of the unit reported grounds to suspect that a full set of the Pentagon papers had reached the Soviet Embassy. I was early informed that similar intelligence had been furnished by the F.B.I. Yet *The New York Times* had received only a partial set. This development reinforced suspicion that Dr. Ellsberg or one of his collaborators, if any, may have had some sort of foreign involvement.

Nixon Directs Expansion of Unit

On July 24, I was summoned to the President's office with Mr. Ehrlichman. This meeting followed by one day the appearance in *The New York Times* of the fallback [negotiating] position of the United States in the SALT talks at Helsinki.

The President appeared deeply troubled by this unauthorized disclosure and directed me to expand the work by the unit to cover it. He described the matter of unauthorized disclosures as intolerable, directed the extensive administration of polygraph tests, and made clear that the protection of national security information must outweigh any individual reluctance to be polygraphed.

He discussed the creation of a new security classification which would condition access to national security information upon advance agreement to submit to polygraphing. He was deeply concerned that any future disclosure of such information could only undermine the SALT and Vietnam peace negotiations. His intense determination was evident. He instructed that further leaks *would not be allowed* and made me feel personally responsible for carrying out this instruction.

The work of the unit went forward with regard to the SALT leak, the Pentagon papers, Dr. Ellsberg, and some other unauthorized disclosures. Polygraphing was immediately begun (although on a far more limited scale than originally envisioned). Dr. Ellsberg's extensive knowledge of classified national security information in addition to the Pentagon papers was ascertained. The intensity of the national security concern expressed by the President fired up and overshadowed every aspect of the unit's work.

It was in this context that the Fielding incident, the break-in into the office of Dr. Ellsberg's psychiatrist, took place. Doubtless, this explains why John Dean has reported that I told him that instructions for the break-in had come directly from the Oval Office. In fact, the July 24 meeting was the only direct contact I had with the President on the work of the unit.

I have just listened to the tape of that meeting, and Dr. Ellsberg's name did not appear to be mentioned. I had been led to believe by the White House statement of May 22, 1973, that the President had given me instructions regarding Dr. Ellsberg in the July 24, 1971 meeting. It must be that those instructions were relayed to me by Mr. Ehrlichman. In any event, I received no specific instruction or authority whatsoever regarding the break-in from the President, directly or indirectly.

As I stated in the affidavit I filed before Judge Byrne, Mr. Ehrlichman gave the unit authority to engage in covert activity to obtain information on Dr. Ellsberg. The precise nature of that authorization and the extent to which it specifically covered the break-in are matters that will be the subject of testimony in the prosecution pending in California and that may be involved in a prosecution in the District of Columbia. So are the origination of the idea of a break-in and the manner of its formulation.

I have expressed the desire, to which the special prosecutor has acceded to defer any testimony until after sentencing. I would simply say that I considered that a break-in was within the authority of the unit and that I did not act to foreclose one from occurring despite the opportunity to do so. Indeed, I was under the clear impression that such operations were by no means extraordinary by the C.I.A. abroad and, until 1966, by the F.B.I. in this country—an impression confirmed by former officers of both agencies on the unit's staff.

Aims of Fielding Burglary

The break-in [of Dr. Fielding's office] came about because the unit felt it could leave no stone unturned in the investigation of Dr. Ellsberg. The aims of the operation were many:

(A) To ascertain if Dr. Ellsberg acted alone or with collaborators;

(B) To ascertain if Dr. Ellsberg in fact had any involvement with the Soviets or other foreign power;

(C) To ascertain if Dr. Ellsberg had any characteristics that would cause him to make further disclosures;

(D) To ascertain if prosecution of Dr. Ellsberg would induce him to make further disclosures that he otherwise would not.

The potential uses of the above information were also multiple. Primary, of course, was preventing further disclosures by Dr. Ellsberg and putting an end to whatever machinery for disclosure might have been developed. It was also thought, particularly by E. Howard Hunt, that the sought information could be useful in causing Dr. Ellsberg himself to declare his true intentions. Finally, there is the point that has been most stressed in the current investigative process—the potential use of the information in discrediting Dr. Ellsberg as an antiwar spokesman.

My best recollection is that I focused on the prevention of further leaks by Dr. Ellsberg and the termination of any machinery he may have established for such disclosures. That was the use most central to the assignment of the unit as I understood it. But my precise focus is fundamentally not important to my guilt or innocence, because at the time of the operation I did not consider it necessary to assign relative weightings to the potential uses of the sought information. All of them were dictated by the national security interest as I then understood it.

Break-in Damage Was Disturbing

To my knowledge, the break-in netted nothing. When I saw the photographs that had been taken of the damage done, I immediately felt that a mistake had been made. The visibility of physical damage was somehow disturbing beyond the theoretical impression of covert activity. I recommended to Mr. Ehrlichman that no further actions of that sort be undertaken. He concurred and stated that he considered the operation to have been in excess of his authorization.

My participation in the work of the unit progressively diminished, and for all intents and purposes ended in November, 1971. I was recalled to the unit for a few days in December, 1971, in connection with the India-Pakistan conflict leak. In that period, I was asked to authorize a wire tap in connection with a highly sensitive aspect of that leak. I declined and was thereupon removed from the unit the same day. I learned in reviewing the unit's files on Dec. 17, 1973, that the tap was effected after my removal along with another one in the same investigation. These are the only instances of wiretapping by the unit of which I am aware, and I first learned of them on Dec. 13.

In August, 1972, I was deposed at the Department of Justice in connection with the grand jury investigation of the Watergate break-in. I had been repeatedly instructed by Mr. Ehrlichman that the President considered the work of the unit a matter of the highest national security and that I was under no circumstances to discuss it.

I was specifically advised by John Dean that the Fielding incident was not relevant to and would not be touched upon in the deposition. The Assistant United States Attorney who conducted the deposition himself advised me that he was not interested in pursuing national security matters.

In the course of the deposition, I was asked questions relating to travel by Messrs. Hunt and Liddy. I answered the questions by interpreting them as excluding national security and thus the travel of Liddy and Hunt to California for the Fielding incident. This interpretation was highly strained, reflecting a desperate effort on my part to avoid any possible disclosure of the work of the unit in accordance with the instructions of the President that had been relayed to me by Mr. Ehrlichman.

Subsequently, in April, 1973, when Judge Byrne requested persons having knowledge of the Fielding incident to file affidavits with him, I determined that a disclosure of my role was imperative. Because I was still operating under the instructions of the President that the work of the unit was not to be revealed under any circumstances, I sought the advice of Attorney General-designate Elliot Richardson and requested Mr. Ehrlichman to seek the President's permission for me to explain my involvement in the incident.

Mr. Ehrlichman informed me on May 2 that the President had authorized me to make a statement, and I submitted an affidavit setting forth details of my role in the Fielding incident on May 4. In describing the travel to California by Messrs. Liddy and Hunt, that affidavit was inconsistent, and intentionally so, with the answers I had given in my deposition (except for the strained interpretation I have described).

I was indicted for false declarations on the basis of those answers in October this year. In moving to dismiss the indictment, my counsel argued with my approval, that...[official immunity] extended to criminal prosecutions, and that the authority and discretion possessed by an official in my position embraced false statements to protect classified national security information from unauthorized disclosure.

The court rejected that argument as fundamentally incompatible with the very existence of our society. That ruling, and the questions asked by the judge in the course of the argument, spurred my reappraisal of my whole conception of the Fielding incident.

"Key is...'national security' "

While I early concluded that the operation had been a mistake, it is only recently that I have come to regard it as unlawful. I see now that the key is the effect that the term "national security" had on my judgment. The very words served to block critical analysis. It seemed at least presumptuous if not unpatriotic to inquire into just what the significance of national security was.

When the issue was the proper response to a demonstration, for example, it was natural for me to question whether the proposed course was not excessive. The relative rankings of the rights of demonstrators and the protection of law and order could be debated, and the range of possible accommodations explored without the subjects of patriotism and loyalty even rising to the level of consciousness. But to suggest that national security was being improperly invoked was to invite a confrontation with patriotism and loyalty and so appeared to be beyond the scope and in contravention of the faithful performance of the duties of my office.

Freedom of President "Ultimate...Objective"

Yet what is national security? I mentioned that all of the potential uses of the information sought in the Fielding incident were consistent with my then concept of national security. The discrediting of Dr. Ellsberg, which today strikes me as repulsive and an inconceivable national security goal, at the time would have appeared a means of blocking the possibility that he would become such a popular figure that others possessed of classified information would be encouraged to emulate him. More broadly, it would serve to diminish any influence he might have in mobilizing opposition to the course of ending the Vietnam war that had been set by the President. And that course was the very definition of national security. Freedom of the President to pursue his planned course was the ultimate national security objective.

The fact that I do not recall this use as my personal motivating force provides scant comfort. I can recollect that I would have accepted the rationalization I have just described. The invocation of national security stopped me from asking the question, "is this the right thing to do."

My experience in the months since my resignation from government, during which I have been under intense investigation and multiple indictments has also affected my view. I have throughout this most difficult period been free, first because I had not yet been indicted and later on recognizance. And I perceive this freedom as the very essence of our society and our system.

This freedom for me is not a privilege but a right protected by our Constitution. It is one of a host of rights that I as an American citizen am fortunate to share with Dr. Ellsberg and Dr. Fielding. These rights of the individual cannot be sacrificed to the mere assertion of national security.

National security is obviously a fundamental goal and a proper concern of any country. It is also a concept that is subject to a wide range of definitions, a factor that makes all the more essential a painstaking approach to the definition of national security in any given instance.

But however national security is defined, I now see that none of the potential uses of the sought information could justify the invasion of the rights of the individuals that the break-in necessitated. The understanding I have come to is that these rights are the definition of our nation. To invade them unlawfully in the name of national security is to work a destructive force upon the nation, not to take a protective measure....

I see now that the sincerity of my motivation was not a justification but indeed a contributing cause of the incident. I hope that the young men and women who are fortunate enough to have an opportunity to serve in government can benefit from this experience and learn that sincerity can often be as blinding as it is worthy. I hope they will recognize that the banner of national security can turn perceived patriotism into actual disservice. When contemplating a course of action, I hope they will never fail to ask, "Is this right?"

STATE OF THE UNION MESSAGE —AND REBUTTAL

January 30, February 1, 1974

President Nixon pledged to forestall a recession, check inflation and break the back of the energy crisis in his State of the Union message delivered in person to a joint session of Congress Jan. 30. In the nationally televised address, Nixon emphasized the past accomplishments of his administration amd vowed to continue his efforts to bring a lasting peace to the world. At the same time, he proposed "new initiatives which are ripe for action in 1974," including proposals for welfare reform, mass transit and national health insurance. By far the most dramatic section of the speech, a postscript on his on-going Watergate troubles, came after Nixon had closed his notes and after his escort of congressional leaders had risen to usher him out of the chamber. In a carefully worded statement of his Watergate position, he pledged to cooperate with the House Judiciary Committee's impeachment inquiry with "only one limitation," that he would not do anything that "impairs the ability of Presidents of the future to make the great decisions" essential to the nation and the world.

Two days later, on Feb. 1, Senate Majority Leader Mike Mansfield (D Mont.) replied to President Nixon's message and underlined the contrast in public visibility of the White House and Congress as well as differences in style between the leadership of the two branches of government. In his nationally televised speech, and during the question-and-answer period with reporters that followed, Mansfield rebutted Nixon's contention that the Watergate investigations should come to a swift end, saying that "the crimes of Watergate" must be taken through the judicial system "for however long may be necessary." There were few similarities between Nixon's and Mansfield's statements. While Nixon refused to release his message to the press before he delivered it, Mansfield made the text of his reply available to newsmen nearly eight hours in advance. Nixon left the House chamber immediately after his speech, with White House spokesmen indicating that he intended to hold a press conference at some later date; Mansfield held a conference with the members of the press immediately following his address. (Nixon news conference, Feb. 25, see p. 145-154.)

Fight Against Impeachment

Nixon's fourth state of the union message to be delivered in person (he sent written messages to Congress in 1973), (see Historic Documents 1973, p. 209-225; 303-329), *was interpreted by many onlookers primarily as a warning to Congress that Nixon was prepared for a vigorous fight against impeachment. At one point, he expressed hope that a legacy of peace would be the hallmark of "the eight years of my Presidency." Later, he asked Congress for cooperation on new programs "in these final three years of my Administration." Reaffirming previous statements that he would not resign* (see Historic Documents 1973, p. 913), *he said, "I want you to know that I have no intention whatever of ever walking away from the job that the people elected me to do for the people of the United States." These references to his determination to remain in office drew standing ovations from Nixon's congressional supporters and from many of the family members and friends seated in the surrounding galleries. But, in contrast, Nixon's references to White House-imposed limitations on the impeachment inquiry brought hisses and boos from congressional Democrats. To Nixon's statements that "I believe the time has come to bring that [Watergate] investigation and the other investigations of the matter to an end. One year of Watergate is enough," Senate Watergate Committee Chairman Sam J. Ervin, Jr. (D N.C.) retorted, "If the President would not have spent time withholding information from our investigation, we could have ended it months ago,"*

Before beginning his address, Nixon submitted a longer, more specific 22,000-word message to Congress, giving details of the legislative actions he would ask. These proposals underscored his belief that taxes should not be increased and that increases in federal spending should be held to a minimum. On energy, he stressed the need for emergency legislation that "would permit additional restrictions on energy consumption and would postpone temporarily Clean Air Act requirements," a windfall profits excise tax, unemployment insurance for people adversely affected by the energy crunch and mandatory reporting by major energy industries. Nixon called on Congress with "special urgency" to complete action on trade reform, asking the Senate to delete provisions in a House-passed bill forbidding the President to grant trade credits or preferred tariff status to Soviet goods unless the Soviet government eased its restrictions on emigration by Soviet Jews.

On the economy, Nixon pledged: "There will be no recession in the United States of America." He said he would "continue to watch the wage-price situation closely and to pursue a policy of gradual, selective decontrol except in particularly troublesome areas," actions he said would "cushion the economic slowdown we expect during 1974 without providing additional stimulus for inflation." Nixon also urged Congress to take action on his tax reform legislation which would establish a minimum taxable income among other revisions.

Saying that he would recommend a "substantial increase" in the fiscal 1975 Defense Department budget, Nixon said the increases "are necessary to improve the readiness of our armed forces, to build up levels of essential equipment and supplies and to preserve present force levels in the face of rising costs." In the areas of crime and personal privacy, Nixon asked Congress to pass legislation that would stiffen criminal penalties on the one hand and limit the collection of personal data on the other. To continue the fight against crime, Nixon asked Congress to reform the Federal Criminal Code and to restore the death penalty for several "especially heinous" crimes including hijacking, kidnapping and bombing. To ensure the right of privacy to all Americans, Nixon said he had ordered an "extensive Cabinet-level review...of both government and industry practices as they relate to the right of privacy." Appropriate legislation to ensure the balance between legitimate needs for information and privacy would be forthcoming, he said.

Excerpts from the text of President Nixon's nationally televised State of the Union Message to Congress Jan. 30, excerpts from his more detailed written message and excerpts from Senate Majority Leader Mike Mansfield's Feb. 1 speech presenting a congressional view of the state of the union:

THE STATE OF THE UNION

The President's Address Delivered Before a Joint Session of the Congress.
January 30, 1974

Mr. Speaker, Mr. President, my colleagues in the Congress, our distinguished guests, my fellow Americans:

We meet here tonight at a time of great challenge and great opportunities for America. We meet at a time when we face great problems at home and abroad that will test the strength of our fiber as a Nation. But we also meet at a time when that fiber has been tested and it has proved strong.

America is a great and good land, and we are a great and good land because we are a strong, free, creative people and because America is the single greatest force for peace anywhere in the world. Today, as always in our history, we can base our confidence in what the American people will achieve in the future on the record of what the American people have achieved in the past.

Tonight, for the first time in 12 years, a President of the United States can report to the Congress on the state of a Union at peace with every nation of the world. Because of this, in the 22,000-word message on the state of the Union that I have just handed to the Speaker of the House and the President of the Senate, I have been able to deal primarily with the problems of peace—with what we can do here at home in America for the American people—rather than with the problems of war....

Record of Nixon's Presidency

It was 5 years ago on the steps of this Capitol that I took the oath of office as your President. In those 5 years, because of the initiatives undertaken by this Administration, the world has changed. America has changed. As a result,...America is safer today, more prosperous today, with greater opportunity for more of its people than ever before in our history.

Five years ago America was at war in Southeast Asia. We were locked in confrontation with the Soviet Union. We were in hostile isolation from a quarter of the world's people who lived in Mainland China.

Five years ago our cities were burning and besieged.

Five years ago our college campuses were a battleground.

Five years ago crime was increasing at a rate that struck fear across the nation.

Five years ago the spiraling rise in drug addiction was threatening human and social tragedy of massive proportion, and there was no program to deal with it.

Five years ago—as young Americans had done for a generation before that—America's youth still lived under the shadow of the military draft.

Five years ago there was no national program to preserve our environment. Day by day our air was getting dirtier, our water was getting more foul.

And 5 years ago American agriculture was practically a depressed industry with 100,000 farm families abandoning the farm every year.

As we look at America today we find ourselves challenged by new problems. But we also find a record of progress to confound the professional criers of doom and prophets of despair. We met the challenges we faced 5 years ago, and we will be equally confident of meeting those that we face today.

Let us see for a moment how we have met them. After more than 10 years of military involvement, all of our troops have returned from Southeast Asia and they have returned with honor. And we can be proud of the fact that our courageous prisoners of war, for whom a dinner was held in Washington tonight, that they came home with their heads high, on their feet and not on their knees.

In our relations with the Soviet Union, we have turned away from a policy of confrontation to one of negotiation. For the first time since World War II, the world's two strongest powers are working together toward peace in the world. With the People's Republic of China after a generation of hostile isolation, we have begun a period of peaceful exchange and expanding trade.

Peace has returned to our cities, to our campuses. The 17-year rise in crime has stopped. We can confidently say today that we are finally beginning to win the war against crime. Right here in this Nation's Capital—which a few years ago was threatening to become the crime capital of the world—the rate in crime has been cut in half. A massive campaign against drug abuse has been organized. And the rate of new heroin addiction, the most vicious threat of all, is decreasing rather than increasing.

For the first time in a generation no young Americans are being drafted into the Armed Services of the United States. And for the first time ever we have organized a massive national effort to protect the environment. Our air is getting cleaner. Our water is getting purer, and our agriculture, which was depressed, is prospering. Farm income is up 70 percent, farm production is setting alltime records, and the billions of dollars the taxpayers were paying in subsidies has been cut to nearly zero.

Overall, Americans are living more abundantly than ever before today. More than 2½ million new jobs were created in the past year alone. That is the biggest percentage increase in nearly 20 years. People are earning more. What they earn buys more, more than ever before in history. In the past 5 years the average American's real spendable income—that is what you really can buy with your income, even after allowing for taxes and inflation—has increased by 16 percent.

Despite this record of achievement, as we turn to the year ahead we hear once again the familiar voice of the perennial prophets of gloom telling us now that because the need to fight inflation, because of the energy shortage, America may be headed for a recession.

"There Will Be No Recession"

Let me speak to that issue head on. There will be no recession in the United States of America. Primarily due to our energy crisis, our economy is passing through a difficult period. But I pledge to you tonight that the full powers of this Government will be used to keep America's economy producing and to protect the jobs of America's workers.

We are engaged in a long and hard fight against inflation. There have been, and there will be in the future, ups and downs in that fight. But if this Congress cooperates in our efforts to hold down the cost of government, we shall win our fight to hold down the cost of living for the American people....

Looking at the year 1974 which lies before us, there are 10 key areas in which landmark accomplishments are possible this year in America. If we make these our national agenda, this is what we will achieve in 1974:

We will break the back of the energy crisis; we will lay the foundation for our future capacity to meet America's energy needs from America's own resources.

And we will take another giant stride toward lasting peace in the world—not only by continuing our policy of negotiation rather than confrontation where the great powers are concerned but also by helping toward the achievement of a just and lasting settlement in the Middle East.

We will check the rise in prices, without administering the harsh medicine of recession, and we will move the economy into a steady period of growth at a sustainable level.

We will establish a new system that makes high-quality health care available to every American in a dignified manner and at a price he can afford.

We will make our States and localities more responsive to the needs of their own citizens.

We will make a crucial breakthrough toward better transportation in our towns and in our cities across America.

We will reform our system of Federal aid to education, to provide it when it is needed, where it is needed, so that it will do the most for those who need it the most.

We will make an historic beginning on the task of defining and protecting the right of personal privacy for every American.

And we will start on a new road toward reform of a welfare system that bleeds the taxpayer, corrodes the community, and demeans those it is intended to assist.

And together with the other nations of the world, we will establish the economic framework within which Americans will share more fully in an expanding worldwide trade and prosperity in the years ahead, with more open access to both markets and supplies.

First Priority: Energy

In all of the 186 State of the Union messages delivered from this place in our history, this is the first in which the one priority, the first priority, is energy. Let me begin by reporting a new development which I know will be welcome news to every American. As you know we have committed ourselves to an active role in helping to achieve a just and durable peace in the Middle East, on the basis of full implementation of Security Council Resolutions 242 and 338. The first step in the process is the disengagement of Egyptian and Israeli forces which is now taking place.

Because of this hopeful development I can announce tonight that I have been assured, through my personal contacts with friendly leaders in the Middle Eastern area, that an urgent meeting will be called in the immediate future to discuss the lifting of the oil embargo.

This is an encouraging sign. However, it should be clearly understood by our friends in the Middle East that the United States will not be coerced on this issue.

Regardless of the outcome of this meeting, the cooperation of the American people in our energy conservation program has already gone a long way towards achieving a goal to which I am deeply dedicated. Let us do everything we can to avoid gasoline rationing in the United States of America.

Last week I sent to the Congress a comprehensive special message setting forth our energy situation, recommending the legislative measures which are necessary to a program for meeting our needs. If the embargo is lifted, this will ease the crisis, but it will not mean an end to the energy shortage in America. Voluntary conservation will continue to be necessary. And let me take this occasion to pay tribute once again to the splendid spirit of cooperation the American people have shown which has made possible our success in meeting this emergency up to this time.

Nixon's Energy Program

The new legislation I have requested will also remain necessary. Therefore, I urge again that the energy measures that I have proposed be made the first priority of this session of the Congress. These measures will require the oil companies and other energy producers to provide the public with the necessary information on their supplies. They will prevent the injustice of windfall profits for a few as a result of the sacrifices of the millions of Americans. And they will give us the organization, the incentives, the authorities needed to deal with the short-term emergency and to move toward meeting our long-term needs....

As we move toward the celebration 2 years from now of the 200th anniversary of this Nation's independence, let us press vigorously on toward the goal I announced last November for Project Independence. Let this be our national goal. At the end of this decade in the year 1980, the United States will not be dependent on any other country for the energy we need to provide our jobs, to heat our homes, and to keep our transportation moving.

To indicate the size of the Government commitment, to spur energy research and development, we plan to spend $10 billion in Federal funds over the next 5 years. That is an enormous amount. But during the same 5 years, private enterprise will be investing as much as $200 billion—and in 10 years, $500 billion—to develop the new resources, the new technology, the new capacity America will require for its energy needs in the 1980's. That is just a measure of the magnitude of the project we are undertaking.

But America performs best when called to its biggest tasks. It can truly be said that only in America could a task so tremendous be achieved so quickly, and achieved not by regimentation, but through the effort and ingenuity of a free people, working in a free system.

Turning now to the rest of the agenda for 1974, the time is at hand this year to bring comprehensive high quality health care within the reach of every American. I shall propose a sweeping new program that will assure comprehensive health insurance protection to millions of Americans who cannot now obtain it or afford it, with vastly improved protection against catastrophic illnesses. This will be a plan that maintains the high standards of quality in America's health care. And it will not require additional taxes.

Now I recognize that other plans have been put forward that would cost $80 billion or even $100 billion and that would put our whole health care system under the heavy hand of the Federal Government. This is the wrong approach. This has been tried abroad, and it has failed. It is not the way we do things here in America. This kind of plan would threaten the quality of care provided by our whole health care system. The right way is one that builds on the strengths of the present system and one that does not destroy those strengths, one based on partnership, not paternalism. Most important of all, let us keep this as the guiding principle of our health programs. Government has a great role to play, but we must always make sure that our doctors will be working for their patients and not for the Federal Government.

Revenue Sharing Enacted

Many of you will recall that in my State of the Union address 3 years ago I commented that "Most Americans today are simply fed up with government at all levels," and I recommended a sweeping set of proposals to revitalize State and local governments, to make them more responsive to the people they serve. I can report to you today that as a result of revenue sharing passed by the Congress, and other measures, we have made progress toward that goal. After 40 years of moving power from the States and the communities to Washington, D.C., we have begun moving power back from Washington to the States and communities and, most important, to the people of America.

In this session of the Congress, I believe we are near the breakthrough point on efforts which I have suggested, proposals to let people themselves make their own decisions for their own communities, and in particular on those to provide broad new flexibility in Federal aid for community development, for economic development, for education. And I look forward to working with the Congress, with members of both parties in resolving whatever remaining differences we have in this legislation so that we can make available nearly $5½ billion to our States and localities to use not for what a Federal bureaucrat may want, but for what their own people in those communities want. The decision should be theirs.

I think all of us recognize that the energy crisis has given new urgency for the need to improve public transportation, not only in our cities but in rural areas as well. The program I have proposed this year will give communities not only more money but also more freedom to balance their own transportation needs. It will mark the strongest Federal commitment ever to the improvement of mass transit as an essential element of the improvement of life in our towns and cities.

One goal on which all Americans agree is that our children should have the very best education this great Nation can provide.

In a special message last week, I recommended a number of important new measures that can make 1974 a year of truly significant advances for our schools and for the children they serve. If the Congress will act on these proposals, more flexible funding will enable each Federal dollar to meet better the particular need of each particular school district. Advance funding will give school authorities a chance to make each year's plans knowing ahead of time what Federal funds they are going to receive. Special targeting will give special help to the truly disadvantaged among our people. College students faced with rising costs for their education will be able to draw on an expanded program of loans and grants. These advances are a needed investment in America's most precious resource, our next generation. And I urge the Congress to act on this legislation in 1974.

One measure of a truly free society is the vigor with which it protects the liberties of its individual citizens. As technology has advanced in America, it has increasingly encroached on one of those liberties—what I term the right of personal privacy. Modern information systems, data banks, credit records, mailing list abuses, electronic snooping, the collection of personal data for one purpose that may be used for another—all these have left millions of Americans deeply concerned by the privacy they cherish.

And the time has come, therefore, for a major initiative to define the nature and extent of the basic rights of privacy and to erect new safeguards to ensure that those rights are respected.

I shall launch such an effort this year at the highest levels of the Administration, and I look forward again to working with this Congress in establishing a new set of standards that respect the legitimate needs of society, but that also recognize personal privacy as a cardinal principle of American liberty.

Welfare Reform

Many of those in this Chamber tonight will recall that it was 3 years ago that I termed the Nation's welfare system "a monstrous, consuming outrage—an outrage against the community, against the taxpayer, and particularly against the children that it is supposed to help."

That system is still an outrage. By improving its administration, we have been able to reduce some of the abuses. As a result, last year, for the first time in 18 years, there has been a halt in the growth of the welfare case load. But as a system, our welfare program still needs reform as urgently today as it did when I first proposed in 1969 that we completely replace it with a different system.

In these final 3 years of my Administration, I urge the Congress to join me in mounting a major effort to replace the discredited present welfare system with one that works, one that is fair to those who need help or cannot help themselves, fair to the community, and fair to the taxpayer. And let us have as our goal that there will be no Government program which makes it more profitable to go on welfare than to go to work....

America's own prosperity in the years ahead depends on our sharing fully and equitably in an expanding world prosperity. Historic negotiations will take place this year that will enable us to ensure fair treatment in international markets for American workers, American farmers, American investors, and American consumers.

It is vital that the authorities contained in the trade bill I submitted to the Congress be enacted so that the United States can negotiate flexibly and vigorously on behalf of American interests. These negotiations can usher in a new era of international trade that not only increases the prosperity of all nations but also strengthens the peace among all nations.

In the past 5 years, we have made more progress toward a lasting structure of peace in the world than in any comparable time in the Nation's history. We could not have made that progress if we had not maintained the military strength of America. Thomas Jefferson once observed that the price of liberty is eternal vigilance. By the same token, and for the same reason, in today's world, the price of peace is a strong defense as far as the United States is concerned.

Reduction of Defense Budget

In the past 5 years, we have steadily reduced the burden of national defense as a share of the budget, bringing it down from 44 percent in 1969 to 29 percent in the current year. We have cut our military manpower over the past 5 years by more than a third, from 3½ million to 2.2 million.

In the coming year however, increased expenditures will be needed. They will be needed to assure the continued readiness of our military forces, to preserve the present force levels in the face of rising costs, and to give us the military strength we must have if our security is to be maintained and if initiatives for peace are to succeed.

The question is not whether we can afford to maintain the necessary strength of our defense, the question is whether we can afford not to maintain it, and the answer to that question is no. We must never allow America to become the second strongest nation in the world.

I do not say this with any sense of belligerence, because I recognize the fact that is recognized around the world. America's military strength has always been maintained to keep the peace, never to break it....

In this year 1974 we will be negotiating with the Soviet Union to place further limits on strategic nuclear arms. Together with our allies, we will be negotiating with the nations of the Warsaw Pact on mutual and balanced reduction of forces in Europe. And we will continue our efforts to promote peaceful economic development in Latin America, in Africa, in Asia. We will press for full compliance with the peace accords that brought an end to American fighting in Indochina, including particularly a provision that promised the fullest possible accounting for those Americans who are missing in action.

And having in mind the energy crisis to which I have referred to earlier, we will be working with other nations of the world toward agreement on means by which oil supplies can be assured at reasonable prices on a stable basis in a fair way to the consuming and producing nations alike.

All of these are steps toward a future in which the world's peace and prosperity, and ours as well as a result, are made more secure.

Throughout the 5 years that I have served as your President, I have had one overriding aim, and that was to establish a new structure of peace in the world that can free future generations of the scourge of war. I can understand that others may have different priorities. This has been and this will remain my first priority and the chief legacy I hope to leave from the 8 years of my Presidency.

This does not mean that we shall not have other priorities, because as we strengthen the peace we must also continue each year a steady strengthening of our society here at home. Our conscience requires it, our interests require it, and we must insist upon it.

As we create more jobs, as we build a better health care system, as we improve our education, as we develop new sources of energy, as we provide more abundantly for the elderly and the poor, as we strengthen the system of private enterprise that produces our prosperity, as we do all of this and even more, we solidify those essential bonds that hold us together as a nation....

We cannot afford to neglect progress at home while pursuing peace abroad. But neither can we afford to neglect peace abroad while pursuing progress at home. With a stable peace, all is possible, but without peace, nothing is possible.

In the written message that I have just delivered to the Speaker and to the President of the Senate, I commented that one of the continuing challenges facing us in the legislative process is that of the timing and pacing of our initiatives, selecting each year among many worthy projects those that are ripe for action at that time.

Rare Opportunity for Peace

What is true in terms of our domestic initiatives is true also in the world. This period we now are in in the world—and I say this as one who has seen so much of the world, not only in these past 5 years, but going back over many years—we are in a period which presents a juncture of historic forces unique in this century. They provide an opportunity we may never have again to create a structure of peace solid enough to last a lifetime and more, not just peace in our time, but peace in our children's time as well. It is on the way we respond to this opportunity, more than anything else, that history will judge whether we in America have met our responsibility. And I am confident we will meet that great historic responsibility which is ours today.

It was 27 years ago that John F. Kennedy and I sat in this Chamber, as freshmen Congressmen, hearing our first State of the Union address delivered by Harry Truman. I know from my talks with him as members of the Labor Committee, on which we both served, that neither of us then even dreamed that either one or both might eventually be standing in this place that I now stand in now and that he once stood in before me. It may well be that one of the freshmen Members of the 93rd Congress, one of you out there, will deliver his own State of the Union message 27 years from now, in the year 2001.

Well, whichever one it is, I want you to be able to look back with pride and to say that your first years here were great years and recall that you were here in this 93rd Congress when America ended its longest war and began its longest peace.

Mr. Speaker, and Mr. President and my distinguished colleagues and our guests:

I would like to add a personal word with regard to an issue that has been of great concern to all Americans over the past year. I refer, of course, to the investigations of the so-called Watergate affair.

As you know, I have provided to the Special Prosecutor voluntarily a great deal of material. I believe that I have provided all the material that he needs to conclude his investigations and to proceed to prosecute the guilty and to clear the innocent.

I believe the time has come to bring that investigation and the other investigations of this matter to an end. One year of Watergate is enough.

And the time has come, my colleagues, for not only the executive, the President, but the Members of Congress, for all of us to join together in devoting our full energies to these great issues that I have discussed tonight which involve the welfare of all of the American people in so many different ways as well as the peace of the world.

I recognize that the House Judiciary Committee has a special responsibility in this area, and I want to indicate on this occasion that I will cooperate with the Judiciary Committee in its investigation. I will cooperate so that it can conclude its investigation, make its decision, and I will cooperate in any way that I consider consistent with my responsibilities to the Office of the Presidency of the United States.

There is only one limitation. I will follow the precedent that has been followed by and defended by every President from George Washington to Lyndon B. Johnson of never doing anything that weakens the Office of the President of the United States or impairs the ability of the Presidents of the future to make the great decisions that are so essential to this Nation and to the world.

Another point I should like to make very briefly. Like every Member of the House and Senate assembled here tonight, I was elected to the office that I hold. And like every Member of the House and Senate, when I was elected to that office, I knew that I was elected for the purpose of doing a job and doing it as well as I possibly can. And I want you to know that I have no intention whatever of ever walking away from the job that the people elected me to do for the people of the United States.

Now, needless to say, it would be understatement if I were not to admit that the year 1973 was not a very easy year for me personally or for my family. And as I have already indicated, the year 1974 presents very great and serious problems as very great and serious opportunities are also presented.

But my colleagues this I believe: With the help of God, who has blessed this land so richly, with the cooperation of the Congress, and with the support of the American people, we can and we will make the year 1974 a year of unprecedented progress toward our goal of building a structure of lasting peace in the world and a new prosperity without war in the United States of America.

The President's Message to the Congress. January 30, 1974

To the Congress of the United States:

...I have started with certain basic premises:

—The basic tax burden on the American taxpayer should not be increased.

—Our new initiatives, therefore, should be scaled to what can prudently be spent given the level of revenues that would be generated by the existing tax structure at full utilization of our resources.

—Increases in Federal Spending should be kept to a minimum, but the budget should be flexible enough to be used, if necessary, to maintain jobs and prosperity.

—It is essential that we break the old habit of regarding any Federal program, once established, as permanent; we must learn to scrap old programs that are no longer effective or needed in favor of new ones that are. This is the only way we can afford to do what must be done.

Within these guidelines, there are a number of major new initiatives which are ripe for action in 1974—several of which can be milestones on our march to a life of greater freedom, greater opportunity and greater prosperity for all.

In particular, 1974 can be the year in which:

—First, we not only break the back of the energy crisis, but also, through Project Independence, lay the foundation for our future capacity to meet America's energy needs from America's own resources—at reasonable prices and with adequate environmental protection.

—Second, we take another giant stride toward lasting peace in the world—not only by continuing our policy of negotiation rather than confrontation where the great powers are concerned, but also by helping toward the achievement of a just and lasting settlement in the Middle East.

—Third, we will check the rise in prices, without administering the harsh medicine of recession, and move the economy into a period of steady growth at a sustainable level.

—Fourth, we establish a new system of comprehensive health insurance that makes high quality health care available to every American in a dignified manner and at a price he or she can afford.

—Fifth, we continue to build a new era of achievement and responsiveness in State and local government, by cutting the strings of too tight Federal control that have bound the hands of State and local officials in community and economic development programs.

—Sixth, we make a crucial breakthrough toward better transportation by strengthening the ability of local communities to deal with their transportation problems.

—Seventh, we reform our system of Federal aid to education to provide it when it is needed, where it is needed, and so that it will do the most for those who need it most.

—Eighth, we make an historic beginning on the task of defining and protecting the right of personal privacy.

—Ninth, we start on a new road toward reform of a welfare system that bleeds the taxpayer, corrodes the community and demeans those it is meant to assist.

—And tenth, together with the other nations of the world, we establish the economic framework within which Americans will share more fully in an expanding world trade and prosperity in the years ahead, with more open access to both markets and supplies.

Meeting our Energy Needs

At the start of this Congressional session, the number one legislative concern must be the energy crisis.

The cooperative efforts of the American people, together with measures already taken by the Administration, have significantly reduced the immediate impact of the energy crisis....The immediate energy crisis began with the oil embargo imposed in the Middle East last fall. But the embargo only hastened a shortage that was already anticipated....

Irrespective of the possibility of restoring the flow of Middle East oil, we must act now to ensure that we are never again dependent on foreign sources of supply for our energy needs. We must continue to slow the rise in our rate of consumption, and we must sharply increase our domestic production....As we seek to act domestically to increase fuel supplies, we will act internationally in an effort to obtain oil at reasonable prices. Unreasonable increases in the cost of so vital a commodity as oil poses a threat to the entire structure of international economic relations. Not only U.S. jobs, prices and incomes are at stake, but the general pattern of international cooperation is at stake as well....Those measures which I request be given the highest priority are the following:

—A special energy act which would permit additional restrictions on energy consumption and would postpone temporarily certain Clean Air Act requirements for power plants and automotive emissions;

—A windfall profits tax which would prevent private profiteering at the expense of public sacrifice;

—Unemployment insurance for people in areas impacted by serious economic dislocation; and

—Mandatory reporting by major energy companies on their inventories, their production and their reserves.

I am also asking that the Congress quickly establish the Federal Energy Administration and the Energy Research and Development Administration to provide the appropriate organizational structure for administering the national energy policy, as we work toward the establishment of a Department of Energy and Natural Resources.

International Trade Barriers

...There are still many unnecessary barriers to trade which need to be lowered or removed....This is why I call upon the Congress with special urgency to complete action on my proposed Trade Reform Act, in order to provide the authority we will need to negotiate effectively for reductions in barriers to trade, to improve the trading system, and to manage trade problems at home more effectively.

As the Senate considers this legislation, I would draw its attention particularly to provisions added in the House which would seriously impede our efforts to achieve more harmonious international relationships. These provisions would effectively prevent both the extension of non-discriminatory tariff treatment and of credits to certain Communist countries unless they followed a policy which allowed unrestricted emigration. I am convinced that such a prohibition would only make more difficult the kind of cooperative effort between the United States and other governments which is necessary if we are to work together for peace in the Middle East and throughout the world....

The Domestic Economy

Despite our general prosperity, inflation remains a most serious economic problem, not only in the United States but also for the rest of the world....Because domestic prices cannot be isolated from international prices, worldwide inflationary pressures have helped to drive up prices here at home.

Inflation has been a continuous problem for nearly a decade, and it got worse in 1973. The result has been that people have come to expect continuing price increases—and to behave accordingly in their own economic life. Their behavior, in turn, adds further to inflationary pressures, contributing to a vicious inflationary spiral which is difficult to break.

Some people have said that the best way to wring these inflationary expectations out of our economy is by taking the economy into a recession. I disagree. It is true that a lower level of economic activity would reduce demand and...lower the pressure for higher prices. [But]...the cost of such a policy in terms of increased unemployment would simply be unacceptable.

By the same token, I also reject the notion that we should totally ignore inflation and concentrate solely on stimulating higher levels of employment. This policy would also involve too high a cost since it would unleash a further acceleration of the inflation rate.

In developing my economic policy for 1974, I have chosen what I believe is a sound middle road: to cushion the economic slowdown we expect during 1974 without providing additional stimulus for inflation. We expect this policy to reduce the rate of inflation by the end of the year. Should there appear to be a serious threat of a severe slowdown, then we will act promptly and vigorously to support the economy....Accordingly, I will continue to watch the wage-price situation closely and to pursue a policy of gradual, selective decontrol except in particularly troublesome areas.

At the same time, those Federal programs that will help reduce inflation by increasing the supply of scarce resources will be strengthened. One key area where we can look forward to expanded supplies is that of food. With a new national farm policy that encourages rather than discourages output, we achieved a record harvest in 1973 and another record harvest now appears likely in 1974. Increased agricultural output is the only sure way to bring food prices down—and increased output is what our new policies are producing....

Another most pressing economic problem—and a major contributor to inflation—is the energy crisis....Unfortunately, our growing dependence on imports made our entire economy more vulnerable to outside forces. That vulnerability has been tested in recent months....

To a large extent, our flexible, adaptable economy will solve the longer run energy problem through the normal workings of the marketplace. As energy prices reach somewhat higher levels than the bargain rates of the past, conservation will be encouraged while domestic energy production will be expanded....It is essential, therefore, that we seek a more reasonable price for oil in the world market.

It is also imperative that we review our current and prospective supplies of other basic commodities. I have therefore directed that a comprehensive report and policy analysis be made...so that governmental actions can properly anticipate and help avoid other damaging shortages.

Even with the inflation and energy problems, 1973 was a year of many important economic gains for American people.

First, employment in 1973 increased...3.3 percent...the largest since 1955....

Second, the purchasing power of the American people reached new highs last year....

Perspective on 1974

We have known for some time that a slowdown in economic growth is inevitable in 1974. It has been clear that our economy has simply been growing at an unsustainable rate....Unfortunately, the very mild slowdown which we anticipated for 1974 now threatens to be somewhat more pronounced because of the oil embargo, the resulting shortages, and the oil price increase.

We expect, therefore, that during the early part of this year output will rise little if at all, unemployment will rise somewhat and inflation will be high. Our objective, however, is to turn this situation around so that later in the year output will be rising more rapidly, while unemployment will stop rising and will then decline, and the rate of inflation will slow.

Role of the Federal Budget

The budget that I will recommend to the Congress next week will help us achieve our goals for this period. It will support the economy, resisting a major slowdown, but it will not provide the degree of stimulation that could accelerate inflation. If future events suggest that a change in fiscal policy is desirable, I will promptly recommend the appropriate changes. In particular, I will not hesitate to use the stimulus of fiscal policy if it becomes necessary to preserve jobs in the face of an unexpected slackening in economic activity...

The Federal budget remains an essential tool in the fight against inflation....

I have noted with satisfaction that most Members of the Congress have also recognized the need for budgetary discipline, and that work is going forward to establish a more systematic budgeting procedure.... I urge the Congress to enact a workable budget reform in this legislative session....

Tax Reform

Last April, the Secretary of the Treasury presented to the Congress a set of Administration proposals for major and fundamental tax reform. Included in these proposals were the establishment of a minimum taxable income so that no one could avoid paying a fair share of the tax burden, the establishment of new rules for taxing income from foreign sources, and also a limitation on artificial accounting losses to eliminate so-called "tax shelters." I urge the Congress to consider the Administration's tax reform proposals early in the year.

I have also been concerned about the excessive burdens imposed on our low income elderly families by State and local property taxes. To deal with this problem, I have proposed a refundable tax credit for those low income elderly persons whose property taxes exceed five percent of their income. The proposal would also provide equivalent relief for the low income elderly individual who pays rent. I again urge the Congress to enact this very important proposal....

Economic Security

One of the most significant legislative achievements of 1973 was the enactment of the Comprehensive Employment and Training Act (CETA). A form of manpower revenue sharing, this bill transfers from the Federal Government to States and localities significant control over the design and operation of programs to improve the employability of the unemployed and the underemployed....

Other proposals related to economic security that I made to the Congress last year, and on which I again urge action, include:

—The establishment of minimum vesting, funding and fiduciary standards for private pension programs, so that workers could have greater assurance of receiving the pensions they expect and deserve when they retire....

—Extension to State and local governments of the law forbidding employment discrimination against older workers.

—Improvement of the Federal-State unemployment insurance program in several ways: by increasing the State limits that keep some unemployed workers from receiving a reasonable proportion of their normal wage, by extending coverage to farmworkers, and by prohibiting payment of benefits to strikers while assuring benefits to non-participants unemployed as a result of a strike....

Income Security

...I plan to make a major new effort to replace the current maze of welfare programs with a system that works....

In the development of my proposal, I will be guided by five principles:

(1) All Americans who are able to work should find it more rewarding to work than to go on welfare. Americans would strongly prefer to have good jobs rather than a Federal handout. While we should provide cash assistance to those in need, we must always encourage complete self-support for those who are capable of it.

(2) Cash assistance is what low-income people need most from the Federal Government. The people themselves, not the Federal Government, know their own needs best.

(3) We need to focus Federal help on those who need it most. People in need should receive equal treatment from the Federal Government regardless of their place of residence.

(4) The new system should be as simple as possible to administer with rules that are clear and understandable. It should be based on objective criteria rather than the personal judgment of administering officials. And it should be efficient.

(5) This new approach should not require an increased tax burden for any of us. Too much of the income of all of us now goes to support Government. We help no one—certainly not those in poverty—by weakening our free enterprise system by even higher taxation.

Starting from these basic principles, I believe we can develop a new system which would ensure that those who can help themselves do help themselves, and which would allow those who cannot help themselves to live with dignity and self-respect.

Improving our People's Health

...As one of my major new initiatives for 1974, I shall soon submit to the Congress a comprehensive health insurance proposal which would:

—Make available health insurance protection to millions of Americans who currently cannot obtain or afford the private health coverage they need.

—Provide all Americans with vastly improved protection against catastrophic illness.

—Place a new emphasis on preventive health care.

—Provide State and Federal subsidies for low-income families, and for those whose special health risks would otherwise make them uninsurable or insurable only at exorbitant expense.

My comprehensive health insurance proposal will build upon the strengths of the existing health system, rather than destroying it. It will maintain the high quality of medical care without requiring higher taxes. It will be based on partnership, not paternalism. And most importantly, it will require doctors to work for their patients, not for the Federal Government....

Improving Education

...In special messages to the Congress on education in the past, I set forth five major proposals to improve American education. They were:

—A new program of student assistance to help to ensure—for the first time in the Nation's history—that no qualified person is barred from attending college by lack of money.

—A National Institute of Education to be the focal point for educational research and development aimed at increasing our knowledge of how to help students learn.

—A National Foundation for Higher Education, to encourage innovation in learning beyond high school.

—An Emergency School Aid program to assist desegregating school districts.

—A thorough reform of the programs for Federal support of elementary and secondary education, consolidating the myriad separate categorical grant programs in order to transfer educational decisions back to the State and local levels where they belong.

The first four of these basic proposals have been enacted, in whole or in part, and a great deal has already been accomplished through them. As for the fifth, reform of Federal funding for elementary and secondary education, I believe that 1974 should be the year of its enactment.

College Student Assistance

...Since the present student assistance programs are targeted to help the neediest, and because the costs of higher education have risen dramatically, many middle income students are now finding it increasingly difficult to make ends meet. I therefore also recommend that the limit on total borrowing be increased so that professional and other graduate students will be able to find adequate student loans....

Assisting School Desegregation

...By the 1975-1976 school year, the bulk of the problems incident to "de jure" segregation should have passed. However, to provide assistance to those other school districts which may still be required to take special desegregation measures as the result of court rulings, I have budgeted an additional $75 million for fiscal year 1975. In addition, the Federal Government will continue to provide civil rights education advisory activities to local districts to assist them in meeting any remaining problems.

Busing

... I shall continue to support the passage of legislation which makes busing only a last resort—tightly circumscribed even then. I will also continue to work with the Congress to revise my proposals in light of unfolding events in this area....

59

Non-Public Schools

...I continue to support legislation which permits tax credits for parents who pay to send their children to non-public schools....

Protection Against Crime and Invasions of Privacy

Over the past five years I have had no higher domestic priority than rolling back the tide of crime and violence which rose in the 1960s. I am therefore especially pleased with the progress we are making on this front....Key elements of our strategy to do so—most of which will require the assistance of the Congress—include:

—Comprehensive reform of the Federal Criminal Code...

—Restoration of the death penalty under the Federal Criminal Code for several especially heinous specific crimes which result in the death of innocent victims. Examples of such crimes are hijacking, kidnapping, or bombing.

—Increased Federal assistance to State and local law enforcement agencies....

—Increasing the resources available to the U.S. Attorneys' offices throughout the Nation—offices which have, in the last three years, increased the number of criminal convictions by 28 percent....

Protecting the Right of Privacy

One of the basic rights we cherish most in America is the right of privacy. With the advance of technology, that right has been increasingly threatened....

Privacy, of course, is not absolute; it may conflict, for example, with the need to pursue justice. But where conflicts occur, an intelligent balance must be struck....

I have therefore ordered an extensive Cabinet-level review—which will be undertaken this year—both of government and industry practices as they relate to the right of privacy, of the conflicts that arise and the balances that must be struck between legitimate needs for information and the right of privacy, and of those measures—including appropriate legislation—that can be taken to ensure that these balances are properly struck....

Improving Transportation

The energy crisis has made urgent what once seemed only necessary: the building of a transportation system that permits all Americans to travel efficiently and at reasonable cost....It is my hope that 1974 will be the year when we make major advances by enacting two critical transportation bills.

One of these proposals, which I will send to the Congress in the near future, would give our communities not only more money but also more freedom to balance their own transportation needs—and it will mark the largest Federal commitment ever to the improvement of public transportation. This bill would increase Federal assistance for metropolitan areas by nearly 50 percent over the level of fiscal year 1974. More than two-thirds of those funds would be allocated by formula to State and local governments and those governments could better determine their own transportation priorities, choosing between construction of highways or public transit systems, or the purchase of buses or rail cars. Additional transit aid would also be made available to rural communities for the first time.

Under this bill resources would also be available for the first time to augment the operating funds for public transportation systems in both urban and rural areas. By permitting Federal resources to be used for operating purposes, this proposal should make it unnecessary to establish a new categorical grant program for transit operating subsidies, as is now contemplated in bills before the Congress.

As a second major transportation initiative this year, I shall propose that we modernize the regulatory system governing railroad operations. This legislation would make it easier for railroads to consolidate service on a sustainable basis. It would make changes in the system of rate regulation to allow rail carriers to compete more effectively with one another and with alternative modes of freight transportation. Discriminatory State and local taxation of interstate carriers would be barred. It would also provide $2 billion in Federal loan guarantee authority to finance improvements in rights-of-way, terminal and rail plant facilities, and rolling stock, where necessary, which would be a major step in our effort to improve the Nation's railroad system....

Campaign Reform

For several years it has been clear that reforms were needed in the way we elect public officials. The intense public focus placed on the campaign abuses of 1972 has now generated sufficient support for this issue that we now have an opportunity to make a genuine breakthrough....

I have now decided to submit a comprehensive set of Administration proposals on campaign reform for consideration by the Congress during this session. While I do not believe mine will be the only workable proposals, I do hope they will lead to meaningful debate and reform in this critical area....

Strengthening Our Free World Partnerships

As our relationships with old adversaries are changing, so are our relationships with old friends. Western Europe and Japan have put behind them the post-war struggle to rebuild their economies, re-order their societies and reestablish their political force. Their success in these endeavors is something we helped to foster and in which we can take pride. But now times have changed and our past role in their success cannot be the sole basis for a continuing relationship. We must instead adjust our relationships to recognize their new economic capacities and their international political objectives....

61

Maintaining a Strong Defense

This year, I will recommend a substantial increase in the 1975 budget for the Department of Defense. These increases are necessary to improve the readiness of our armed forces, to build up levels of essential equipment and supplies to preserve present force levels in the face of rising costs.

Conclusion

Throughout these five years, I have had one overriding aim: to establish a structure of peace in the world that can free future generations from the scourge of war. Others may have different priorities; this has been and will remain my first priority, the chief legacy that I hope to leave from the eight years of my Presidency.

As we strengthen the peace, we must also continue each year a steady strengthening of our society here at home....

As we create more jobs, as we build a better health care system, and improve education; as we develop new sources of energy, as we provide more abundantly for the elderly and the poor, as we strengthen the system of private enterprise that produces our prosperity—as we do all this and more, we solidify those essential bonds that hold us together as a Nation. Even more importantly, we advance what in the final analysis government in America is all about: more freedom more security, a better life, for each one of the 211 million individual persons who are America....

RICHARD NIXON

The White House,
January 30, 1974

Excerpts from the text of Senate Majority Leader Mike Mansfield's speech on a congressional view of the State of the Union, nationally televised Feb. 1:

Wednesday evening President Nixon addressed a joint session of Congress, through the medium of radio and television, he also spoke directly to the nation. His State of the Union Address was welcomed by the Congress. It will receive full and cooperative consideration. Whatever the legal difficulties which confront the Administration, the regular business of the nation must come first. The President put it first. Insofar as the Congress is concerned, it will be first....

Twelve months ago the 93rd Congress convened after a sweeping victory for a Republican President in the 1972 election. From that same election, however, there also came an increase in the Democratic Majority in the Senate and a continuing Democratic Majority in the House of Representatives....

The Congressional Majority accepted the President's electoral mandate. At the same time we concluded that there was also a mandate to the Legislative Branch. Therefore, we moved promptly to reinforce the nation's system of checks and balances against an accumulation of power in the Executive Branch. This accumulation did not begin in the present Administration. It had been going on, administration after administration, Democratic and Republican, for decades. Nevertheless, there were, at the outset of the 93rd Congress the following evidences of an ominous shift to one-branch government:

(1) Excessive Executive curtailment of public information in the name of national security;
(2) Arbitrary Executive impoundment of appropriated funds;
(3) Unwarranted Executive attacks on the national press;
(4) Executive pre-emption of sole authority over the Federal budget;
(5) Multiplying expressions of Executive contempt for Congress and, by extention, for the people who elect the Congress;
(6) Executive usurpation of sole control over changes in the basic organizational structure of the government; and,
(7) Illegal invasions of personal privacy by Executive agents.

To the Congress, these were flashpoints of a danger to freedom and we were determined to act on them. In my judgment, we did what we set out to do. The erosion of the system of checks and balances was halted. A greater Congressional impact began to be registered on all of the basic decisions of the Federal government....

The bitter and tragic experience of Viet Nam led us, moreover, to act against a repetition elsewhere. Now, any military intrusion into another nation—and hopefully, we have seen the last—is conditioned on the expressed consent of Congress as prescribed in the War Powers Act. Hereafter, what this nation may find necessary to do abroad in a military sense is a question that must be openly considered. It must be decided not alone by the President. It must be decided by the President together with the men and women in the Congress who answer directly to the people. That is a basic Constitutional concept. That is an essential concept for the continued existence of freedom in this nation.

The past year also witnessed major contributions from the Congress over a range of domestic questions. New farm legislation was passed calling for the removal of all limitations on the production of food. Hopefully, this legislation will undo some of the damage done by subsidized sales of grains abroad at bargain-basement prices.

Last year, we sold millions of tons of grain to the Soviet Union. This year, the Soviet Union is offering to sell some of it back to us—at almost three times the price. Who pays for this sort of flim-flam? The people of the nation pay for it in the skyrocketing costs of all foodstuffs.

In the last session, Congress acted twice on its own initiative to try to keep Social Security benefits in line with rising prices. The way was also cleared for building the Alaska pipeline. New emphasis was given to urban mass transportation. Measures were adopted to encourage emergency medical services and health maintainence systems throughout the nation. Legislation of significance to veterans became law after a Presidential veto....

At this point, I wish to speak with the utmost candor on the Congress and Watergate and the related questions of impeachment and resignation. I raise these matters reluctantly. Nevertheless, they must be raised because they have been widely discussed by the public and, on Wednesday, reference was made to them by the President. The question of a Presidential resignation, as in the case of a Vice-Presidential resignation, is not one for the Congress. The President has stated his intentions bluntly in that regard. Insofar as the Congress is concerned, that closes the matter of resignation.

Impeachment is a responsibility of the Congress. The question is now before the House of Representatives where it belongs at this time under the Constitution. It is being handled properly and deliberately. On the basis of available information, I would anticipate that it will be dealt with fully in this session.

What has been done by the Senate Watergate Committee is also within the Constitutional responsibility of the Congress. That work, too, I would anticipate, will be completed during this session in legislative recommendations....As for the crimes of Watergate—and there were crimes—they cannot be put to rest by Congress. Nor can any words of the President's or from me mitigate them. The disposition of crimes is a function of the Justice Department and the Courts. Insofar as I can see, Mr. Leon Jaworski, the special prosecutor, is doing his job and so, too, are the courts. There the matter must rest for however long may be necessary. Whether it is months or years, there are no judicial shortcuts....

To excise Watergate and what it implies before it becomes fatal to liberty is a fundamental responsibility of this government....

The people of this nation, in their overwhelming number, do not want government by the whim or the will of the most powerful and influential. That is the nub of the problem. It is incumbent on us to foreclose an excessive intrusion of great wealth, whether corporate, labor, personal or whatever, into the electoral process. That is a solemn and urgent obligation...

In my judgment, we shall not come finally to grips with the problem except as we are prepared to pay for the public business of elections with public funds....

Today, the petroleum situation threatens the jobs, the business and even the basic maintenance of the homes of millions of Americans. We have become aware, suddenly, of an abject dependency on decisions made by governments five thousand miles away and by a handful of executives in petroleum companies scattered around the world....Under the stress of the energy shortage and other economic difficulties, there is the danger of a crumbling of international cooperation, notably, as it involves our relations with Western Europe and Japan. That, indeed, would be the final straw. The consequences of devil-take-the-hindmost economic policies among free nations would be disastrous to all concerned and might well initiate the general erosion of world peace....

As for the energy crisis at home, the immediate responsibility of government is to make certain that the shortage does not devastate the economy and that the price of past neglect is borne equitably by all Americans. If that means rationing, then let us not hesitate to use this device. Surely a price roll back will also be considered by the Congress. Surely the tax benefits accorded the major oil concerns on investments outside the United States by this Government, as well as excessive oil profits, will be scrutinized by the Congress....

The energy crisis has shocked this nation. In so doing, it has also shown us in a sudden flash the precarious manner in which our national economic life has come to be organized....

To say that we have been extravagant with our resources is to put it mildly. We spend nearly $3 billion a year on air-conditioning and less than $150 million on air pollution control. We throw away 60 billion beverage containers a year, yet spend only $5 million to research recycling techniques. Pollution is building dead seas off the coast of New York, New Jersey, the Great Lakes states and elsewhere. Yet, during the recent recess the President chose to impound $3 billion that had been appropriated for the treatment of waste.

It would be my hope that the concern of the Government will not stop with the energy shortage. The need is to take a careful look not only at the flashing of this single danger but at the whole integrated switchboard of our national existence....In short, we need to think ahead and begin to make the hard political choices between what is more important to the nation and what is less, between what is enduring and what is transitory....

It seems to me that it would be helpful in this connection to bring together on a regular basis representatives of the Executive Branch and the Legislative Branch with those of industry, labor and other areas of our national life. The fusion of ideas and interests from these sources should help us to establish useful economic yardsticks....There is a great deal that is right in this nation. There is a strong, decent, industrious and compassionate people. There is a bountiful land. There is intelligence, inventiveness and vitality. If, working together, today, we will put these attributes to use for the benefit of all, there need be no fear for the nation's tomorrow. That is the responsibility of this government. It is the responsibility of the President, the elected members of Congress, the appointed officials of government and the civil service. Nor is it a responsibility confined to the now. We owe this nation more than a decent present. We owe this nation leadership in the reach for a decent future. In 1974 this Congress—your Congress—will do its part fully in meeting that responsibility....

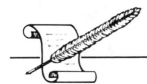
February

ANNUAL ECONOMIC REPORT
February 1, 1974

Accepting inflation, economic stagnation and rising unemployment as inevitable for the first part of 1974, President Nixon and the Council of Economic Advisers Feb. 1 outlined policies the Nixon administration planned to use to guide the economy into recovery later in 1974. In his annual economic message to Congress, Nixon emphasized that continuing inflation and the effect of the energy shortage would continue to shape the economic picture. In a separate report to Congress, accompanying the President's message, the Council of Economic Advisers called for fiscal and monetary policies to encourage a moderate economic upturn in the latter part of the year. Unlike President Nixon's pledge in the state of the union message (see p. 41-65), the council's outlook did not rule out a brief recession during 1974.

Whereas Nixon—already beleaguered with political problems—had promised to avoid a recession, the council's report conceded that there would be "a fairly low rate of increase of production, which might in fact for a while be negative." But that prospect "does not appear to presage a very long or severe slowdown," the council maintained. "How soon a revival will come, and how strong it will be," they said, will "depend on events and policies of 1974." By cautiously charting the economic prospects of the upcoming year, the council avoided repetition of the optimistic predictions of the previous year which had failed to materialize. (See Historic Documents 1973, p. 185-191.)

If the economy could be steered onto a course of moderate expansion, the council predicted, the gross national product (GNP) could be expected to *grow by 8 per cent during 1974, reaching $1,390-billion by the end of the year. Of that 8 per cent growth, however, inflation would account for 7 per cent, leaving real economic growth at only 1 per cent for the year. With that level of activity, the council estimated that unemployment during 1974 would average "a little above 5½ per cent." Between 1972 and 1973, by contrast, the gross national product grew by 11.5 per cent—the largest annual increase in 22 years—with nearly 8 per cent of that figure attributable to inflation. For 1973, unemployment averaged 4.9 per cent.*

Throughout their report, the council members—Chairman Herbert Stein, William J. Fellner and Gary L. Seevers—stressed the economic uncertainties posed by the energy crisis. Inflation, the slowdown of output and the reduction of demand, they said, "are intensified by the higher prices and reduced imports of oil."

In contrast to the administration's past optimism about containing inflation, the council's 1974 report conceded that "a high rate of price and wage increases, although possibly not as high as in 1973, seems inevitable in the first part of 1974." The report predicted that large increases during late 1973 in wholesale prices—including crude oil and food prices—would show up in rising retail prices during 1974. "The rate of wage increases had been drifting up during 1973," the report continued, "and since the cost of living was also continuing to rise rapidly, this trend of wages was unlikely to be reversed soon." But while the pace of inflation was predetermined for early 1974, according to the report, the council found that "beyond the early months, the course of inflation is as yet undetermined." They concluded that "as we go through the year, the course of prices will be less and less a reverberation of what happened in 1973 and increasingly the outcome of events and policies in 1974."

To contain inflation and revitalize the economy, the council found the most appropriate goal to be "a moderate expansion, one which will bring a halt to the rise in unemployment and yet resist an upsurge of inflation outside the food and fuel sectors and get the benefit of a much lower rate of further price increase in these two sectors." If accomplished, that path "would leave real output approximately flat, and perhaps declining for an interval, in the first half of the year but would bring a rise by somewhat more than the normal trend rate in the second half," the report said. After rapid acceleration in the first half of the year, it added, inflation would "subside to rates significantly below those experienced in 1973."

Economic Advisers' Policy Recommendations

The report prescribed federal policies that would aim "to keep the dip in the early part of the year from going too far and to assist the revival later in the year, but to avoid stimulating too rapid a surge." The report's policy recommendations included: (1) fiscal measures to restrain the early decline, but avoid overstimulation of the recovery, and back-up measures to be held ready to provide additional stimulus if needed; (2) continued growth of the money supply at rates allowed during the last half of 1973; (3) steps to encourage a revival of housing construction; (4) effective management of the energy shortage; (5) continuation of the ongoing process of freeing prices from government controls; and (6) cooperation with other nations in order to assure a reliable flow of oil and to head off a round of competitive currency depreciations, trade restrictions and deflationary policies that could plunge the world into general recession.

Excerpts from Chapter 1 of the Annual Report of the Council of Economic Advisers, submitted to Congress Feb. 1. The chapter deals with the economic outlook and proposed goals for 1974:

The Annual Report
of the Council of Economic Advisers

CHAPTER 1

Economic Problems and Policies

For eight years economic policy and the news about the economy have been dominated by inflation. The story has been a frustrating one. Over the period from the end of 1965 to the end of 1973 consumer prices rose by 45 percent, or an average rate of 4.8 percent a year.... But in the last of the 8 years the rate of inflation was higher than in any of the others. During the 8 years the inflation came in various forms—sometimes led by wages, sometimes by prices, by foods, by oil; sometimes it was domestic and sometimes imported....

There is by now a great deal of inflation built into our system. For one thing, both workers and employers are now used to high increases in money wages which reflect the expectation of rapid inflation, and only gradually can these be moderated. Inflation is similarly built into the level of interest rates. The public is highly sensitive to inflation and reacts in an inflationary way to any news which confirms its expectation of inflation.... Whoever undertakes now to fight inflation must be prepared to stay the long course.... Experience extending over almost a decade teaches us that if we do not fight inflation effectively it will accelerate.

The American people have prospered over the past 8 years. Our real incomes have risen. Our real consumption expenditures have risen, and our real assets have risen, in total and per capita. These are facts of great importance. But they do not relieve us of the need to bring inflation under control, and to accept the cost of doing so for the sake of avoiding the greater costs of an accelerating inflation.

We have specific problems, too, aside from the general inflation problem.... [T]he American people...want to maintain an adequate defense, to clean up the environment, to provide more generously for the disadvantaged, to improve standards of health, and also to continue to raise the quality of their lives in all the ways that involve more private consumption.... Beneath the tide of inflation the basic economic problem of increasing production goes on and requires attention, even in a country as rich as ours.

The problems of specific price increases must be distinguished from the general inflation problem. Increases in some individual product or service prices beyond the average are essential, if we are to maintain supplies and allocate shortages. The attempt to suppress the increase of particular prices, while it may be necessary in emergencies, is in general not an effective way to combat inflation and is harmful to production.

Where We Stand at the Outset of 1974

We enter 1974 in a condition of high inflation and in the early stage of a slowdown, one result of which will be to reduce the rate of inflation, although not immediately. All the features of this situation—the high rate of inflation, the slowdown of output, and the slowdown of demand—are intensified by the higher prices and reduced imports of oil. Moreover, the oil situation makes the period ahead even more than usually difficult to predict....

The rapid price and wage increases that were being experienced at the end of 1973 will undoubtedly be carried on and passed through in the early part of 1974. In the fourth quarter of last year, wholesale industrial prices other than for energy products rose at an annual rate in excess of 11 percent. Much of this rise will appear in retail prices in early 1974. Similarly, large increases that have already occurred in crude oil prices have not yet been fully reflected in retail prices. Wholesale food prices were also rising as the year ended, and the outlook was that tight supplies would boost retail prices in the first months of 1974. The rate of wage increases had been drifting up during 1973, and since the cost of living was also continuing to rise rapidly, this trend of wages was unlikely to be reversed soon.

Thus, a high rate of price and wage increases, although possibly not as high a rate as in 1973, seems inevitable in the first part of 1974. But beyond the early months, the course of inflation is as yet undetermined. Prices of oil and related products will not go on rising at the rate of late 1973 and early 1974, but will presumably reach some new high level from which they will be no more likely to rise than to fall. There is also a prospect of larger world food supplies. In general, as we go through the year the course of prices will be less and less a reverberation of what happened in 1973 and increasingly the outcome of events and policies in 1974.

The year 1974 also began with demand rising less rapidly than during most of 1973 and production possibly not rising at all. In the fourth quarter of 1973, total expenditures for the purchase of output rose at an annual rate of about 9½ percent, compared to about 12 percent in the year ending in the third quarter. Real output rose at the rate of about 1 percent after an increase of about 5½ percent in the preceding year. There seems little doubt that this sluggishness will continue in the early part of 1974 and that total output may decline. Automobile production is being cut back sharply, partly because of the effect of high prices and shortages of gasoline on the demand for large cars. The recent weakness of housing starts and permits indicates declining residential construction during the first part of the year. The high prices for oil being paid to foreign suppliers will hold down expenditures for U.S. output. There will be some cases, although one cannot be sure how many, in which production is held back by shortages of energy or energy-related materials.

Just as a high inflation rate seems predetermined for the early part of the year, so does a fairly low rate of increase of production, which might in fact for a while be negative. But the situation at the beginning of the year does not appear to presage a very long or severe slowdown. There are a number of factors tending to support the expansion of the economy, including substantial planned increases of business fixed investment. How soon a revival will come, and how strong it will be, also depend on events and policies of 1974.

General Economic Implications
of the Energy Problem

The nature of the problems with which policy has to contend in 1974 depends substantially on the energy situation—on the volume of oil imports, on their prices, and on the policies adopted in the United States. Total imports of oil expected in 1974, before measures were taken by some exporting countries beginning in October 1973 to curtail shipments and raise prices, were about 40 percent of expected petroleum consumption in 1974. This was about 20 percent of expected energy consumption in 1974, since petroleum would have supplied about 50 percent of total energy use. The countries participating in the embargo of the United States had been expected to supply, directly and indirectly, about 16 percent of our petroleum use and 8 percent of our energy use. This would have been the extent of the initial supply reduction if the embargo had been fully effective.

This curtailment of supply does, of course, lead to adaptations. Prices of oil imported into the United States are free from price control, as are prices of oil produced by certain small (stripper) wells and of "new" oil produced by other wells in excess of their base period production. These prices can be passed on in prices of refined products. Thus, a shortage of oil in the United States raises the prices of oil in these categories and increases the supply, both of imported oil and of domestic oil, offsetting some of the initial effects of the curtailment. Also the higher prices reduce the quantity consumers and businesses want to buy. Therefore, the whole initial curtailment does not appear as a gap between desired quantities and available quantities.... Although prices of petroleum products in the United States rose very rapidly after October 1973, and this apparently served to cut down the desired consumption, they had not risen enough by the end of January to eliminate shortages. The impact of the remaining shortages is being distributed through the economy by allocations and other controls, by voluntary conservation measures, and to some extent by a first-come-first served process.

The Secretary of State has recently expressed the hope that the embargo on the export of oil to the United States from some Arab countries would soon be lifted. The effect of such action on the U.S. economy would depend upon the price and production policies of the oil-exporting countries. The higher their production levels, and the lower the world price, the smaller will be the current economic problems for the United States and for other importing countries....

This combination of limited oil imports and higher prices will have four kinds of economic effects in the United States and in other oil-importing countries.

1. Limitation on capacity to produce. Beyond some point, inadequacy in the supply of energy can make it impossible to produce certain products, or high energy prices can make it impossible to produce certain products at costs at which they can be sold. However, it does not appear that this point will be exceeded or that our capacity to produce will be significantly curtailed by the energy situation.... Maintenance of capacity to produce in the presence of import curtailment will depend on limiting consumption use of petroleum products, especially the use of heating oil for homes and gasoline for personal transportation.... Concentration of the available supply in the uses most essential for production and employment will be brought about in part by higher prices....

2. Restraint on the demand for output. The reduced availability and higher price of gasoline will curtail the demand for large automobiles, for the services of motels, and for other tourist services. The shortage of heating oil and gasoline will cut the demand for new houses. How serious these effects are will depend in part on the amount of the cut in oil supplies or on the rise in the price. One should note that the effect of a price rise can be as great as the effect of a shortage in diverting expenditures from oil-related products....

3. The real income loss due to costlier energy. ...The initial loss of capacity to produce caused by the curtailment of energy supplies will in time be offset by shifts of production in directions that use less energy. The initial loss of demand for output associated with energy will in time be compensated for by a shift of consumers' demands to other products, and possibly by an increase in demand for American products by the oil-exporting countries. In addition...we shall have to pay more of our own products or assets to foreigners in exchange for their oil,...we shall have to devote more of our own resources to producing energy domestically, and...we shall have to accept methods of production or forms of consumption we would not have chosen if more oil had been available at a lower price.

How much these costs will amount to is exceedingly difficult to estimate. A clue to their magnitude is given by the fact that the increased cost of U.S. oil imports due to the oil price rises of October and December 1973 would be less than 1 percent of the gross national product (GNP) in 1974, with a volume of imports that would have occurred at the pre-October prices. This is probably an outside estimate of the costs in 1974 (aside from the transitional costs already noted) because there would be adaptations of various kinds. The amount is large and justifies a strenuous effort to reduce it, by getting the foreign price down and by developing cheaper sources at home. Whether the cost will continue to rise, relative to GNP, will depend on the costs of producing additional amounts of energy from new sources.

4. Balance of payments and other international consequences. All of the other oil-importing countries of the world will suffer the effects of the cut in supplies and the increase in prices of oil. In fact, most of these countries will be more seriously affected than the United States, because their imports of oil are larger relative to their total supply of energy and to their total GNP.... In any case there will be a marked slowdown, and possibly an absolute decline, in demand and output in most of the countries of the world with which we do business, except for the oil-exporting countries.

This outcome will influence the United States in a number of ways. It should help to retard the increases in prices of industrial raw materials, just as the worldwide boom contributed to their rise.... Oil prices will be lower here than elsewhere, at least for a time, because of the price control on a large part of our oil supply; and this situation will tend to stimulate exports of products with a large oil component, such as petrochemicals. On the other hand, the reduction of income and activity abroad and the depreciation of foreign currencies will tend to cut our exports. This factor will probably be the dominant one, although its net effect is likely to be small except for one reservation to be noted.

At present prices of oil, the oil import bills of the industrialized countries will be so large that many if not all of them will have current account deficits—that is, their foreign expenditures for goods and services will exceed their foreign earnings. This will be true even after allowing for the added purchases that the oil-exporting countries may make from the industrialized countries. The oil-exporting countries will have large current account surpluses, which in one form or another will be invested in financial or real assets in the industrialized countries.

This combination of transactions does not require any decline in the level of economic activity in the industrialized world—aside from the transitional difficulties already noted—or slowdown in the rate of growth. In fact, there may be a stimulus to the rate of growth, as the higher oil prices extract funds from consumption and return them to investment via the investment of the oil-exporting countries. However, there could be severe repercussions if the financial aspects of these transactions are not well managed.

Several possibilities can be envisaged which could lead to cumulative recession. One possibility is that some of the industrialized countries might lose large amounts of monetary reserves, or incur large liquid liabilities to the oil-exporting countries which would impel the industrialized countries to try to build up their reserves. Or industrialized countries having current account deficits might feel it important to correct those deficits, even though their overall balances of payments are not in deficit. Some countries will have overall deficits and might try to correct that situation. In any event, the single-country response is likely to be to try to export more and import less, either by squeezing down the economy at home or by checking imports and spurring exports. That is, the single-country response could well either create recession at home or export recession. If many countries are following this policy at once, the compound result could be a large and unnecessary decline in the world economy.

Goals for 1974

The goals for 1974 must be realistically connected with the conditions existing at the beginning of the year. As we have already explained, we believe that the conditions existing at the beginning of the year make it extremely likely that inflation will continue at a high rate through the early part of 1974. A slow rate of economic expansion is also likely during this period, and possibly a decline, with rising unemployment. After some period, probably after the first half of the year, the course of the economy will be influenced more by policies still to be adopted. The idea of a "goal" is more relevant to this later period than to the months immediately at hand. For this later period, three possible paths for the economy can be distinguished.

1. Total spending can accelerate strongly, bringing production quickly back to a full-employment level. This path would create new price pressures which would replace the diminishing pressures expected in energy and food and contribute to an acceleration of wage increases.

2. The contraction can continue, with unemployment rising throughout the year. Anti-inflationary pressure would be strengthened along this path.

3. The economy can begin a moderate expansion, one which will bring a halt to the rise in unemployment and yet resist an upsurge of inflation outside the food and fuel sectors and get the benefit of a much lower rate of further price increase in these two sectors. There would be an expectation that a significant reduction of price increases in food and fuel would be followed in time by a reduction elsewhere if the economic environment is not overheated. This would be accompanied by a gradual decline of the unemployment rate.

The third possible path is most consistent with attaining as well as maintaining the goals of the Employment Act. The first is a prescription for undiminished and probably accelerating inflation. The second exacts too high a price in unemployment.

Of course, no one knows with certainty or precision the relations among output, unemployment, and prices along any of these paths. They only reflect general emphases which can be utilized as guides to policy. Moreover, even if the desired path could be precisely described, no one could precisely describe the policy that would achieve it. All of these usual uncertainties are heightened this year by the difficulty of foreseeing the effects of the radical change in the energy situation. This unusual degree of uncertainty makes it more important than ever that we be prepared with means for adapting policy if events seem to be moving outside a reasonable range of the roughly defined target path.

What is implied by the path that at present seems to us the best of the feasible ones for the economy, given the inescapable effects of the energy shortage, is an increase of about 8 percent in the nominal value of GNP from calendar 1973 to 1974, to about $1,390 billion. Of this rise, about 1 percent would be an increase in real output and about 7 percent an increase of prices (as measured by the GNP deflator). Changes from calendar 1973 to 1974 are, of course, significantly influenced by what has already happened in 1973; and hence changes so expressed do not describe an expected path for 1974, though they are implied in any expected path. As for the expected path during 1974, this would leave real output approximately flat, and perhaps declining for an interval, in the first half of the year but would bring a rise by somewhat more than the normal trend rate in the second half. Inflation would be rapid in the early part of the year, mainly as a consequence of energy and food prices, and then subside to rates significantly below those experienced in 1973. Unemployment for the year would average a little above 5½ percent.

We would emphasize two aspects of this path. First, it is at the same time our view of a feasible target and a prediction of what will be achieved if the planned policy is carried through. Second, that the path is feasible and that it will be achieved by the planned policy are both uncertain to a significant degree. This means that the target or the policy may have to be changed as new information emerges, although changes involve costs and should not be made unless the case for them is clear.

A description of the implications of this path for the main sectors of the economy appears at the end of this chapter.

Policies for Achieving the 1974 Goals

The general contour of the economy described for 1974 is consistent with the private forces now apparently at work. In the early months of the year, consumers will make the move to spending a larger part of their income on an imported product—namely oil—because of the higher price. This will tend to reduce their spending for the purchase of other goods and services and will offset the rise of other categories of demand, such as business investment and government spending. But the adjustment to spending more money on imported oil will be completed early in the year; this drag on the expansion of the economy will then be removed and the expansive forces will become more effective. (Expenditures for foreign oil will not decline, but they will not be rising significantly.) As the year progresses, housing construction will rise in response to greater availability of credit and greater certainty about the distribution of fuel oil and gasoline; and production of new automobiles will increase as the manufacturers improve their ability to turn out small cars. Meanwhile, the period of maximum increase of energy prices and food prices should have passed.

The main functions of policy will be to keep the dip in the early part of the year from going too far and to assist the revival later in the year, but to avoid stimulating too rapid a surge.

1. *Fiscal policy.* The budget proposed by the President will tend to restrain the decline of the economy during 1974 but would inject no fiscal stimulus to push the economy above its average rate of expansion. If the economy were operating at about the same rate of utilization of the labor force in 1974 as in 1973, the size of the budget surplus would change very little between the 2 years. Thus one can say approximately that if the economy were moving along its normal growth path the budget would not be tending to divert the economy from that path in either direction.

However, if the economy operates, as expected, at a lower rate of activity relative to its potential in calendar 1974 than in calendar 1973, the budget will swing significantly toward deficit. This change will result chiefly from the lower level of receipts accruing to the Federal Government at lower levels of economic activity, and partly from higher unemployment compensation payments. As a consequence, private incomes after taxes rise relative to output, thus sustaining demand and moderating the slowdown....

In calendar year 1972, unlike 1973, Federal receipts were swollen by exceptionally large net overwithholding of personal income tax estimated to amount to about $9 billion. An estimate of the economic effect of the budget in 1972 and 1973 depends heavily on the impact attributed to this overwithholding. If the amount overwithheld was less like a personal tax than like personal saving accruing in the form of a government obligation, fiscal policy moved in a restrictive direction from 1972 to 1973. Thus, if the amount overwithheld is subtracted from recorded receipts, there was a swing of about $14 billion from deficit to surplus between the 2 years on the assumption of a constant rate of economic activity at full employment. Over $3 billion of that swing would have been due to the higher rate of inflation in 1973, but the remaining $10 billion would represent an independent fiscal policy force restraining even the normal rate of growth. Such restraint was appropriate, given the inflationary condition of the time. Since we had in 1973 both a reduction of unemployment and an increase in the rate of inflation, the actual swing from deficit to surplus was larger—about $17 billion, or about $26 billion if overwithholding is excluded from actual 1972 receipts.

If the overwithheld amount is treated like any other tax receipt, little shift in the full-employment budget position appears between 1972 and 1973. However, exclusion of the overwithholding from receipts seems to us to come closer to representing the economic effect of the budget, and the full-employment estimates in Table 1 are calculated in that way. On this basis it appears that whereas the direction of fiscal policy was significantly restrictive from 1972 to 1973 it is fairly neutral from 1973 to 1974, offering support if the economy declines but otherwise not exerting any upward or downward push.

The foregoing observations relate to the balance of Federal receipts and expenditures in the national income and product accounts. These accounts are more useful for analysis of overall economic impact than the unified budget accounts stressed in the Budget Message, primarily because they exclude certain expenditures which do not enter directly into the stream of U.S. income or expenditure. The references to the behavior of the surplus or deficit at a constant rate of economic activity are to calculations of the surplus as it would be at the actual or forecast rate of inflation if the economy were operating at 4 percent unemployment and at an annual growth rate of 4 percent (rather than the 4.3 percent used in Council Reports of the past 4 years). The level of these surpluses depends on the unemployment rate chosen, but the year-to-year changes in the surplus are not sensitive to the unemployment rate chosen if the chosen rate is approximately stable from year to year. Reference to a higher unemployment rate would reduce the levels of the surpluses but not have much effect on the year-to-year changes.

It is also useful to try to take the effect of changing inflation rates out of the change in the surplus because such a procedure gives a clearer picture of the budget changes that are autonomous, that is, not responses to economic fluctuations. An increase in the inflation rate will affect both receipts and expenditures, but it will affect receipts much more promptly and hence increase the surplus. This increase in the surplus tends to restrain the expansion and thus the increase of the inflation rate. But it is also a symptom of not having prevented a rise of the inflation rate and so is evidence of anti-inflationary policy only in a rather negative sense. Unfortunately, the effect of the change in the inflation rate can be measured only very approximately....

In view of the uncertainties facing us, it is extremely important to be prepared with fiscal measures to support or restrain the economy if it is clearly running outside the general track described here for 1974. The Administration is now in the process of preparing for support action. A decision to take such measures would have to be made with great caution, however, in view of the additional supply bottlenecks that might be caused by the energy shortage.

Greater protection for those unemployed because of the prospective conditions, and greater assurance against an even more serious slowdown, would have been provided if Congress had enacted the proposal submitted by the Administration last year to improve the unemployment compensation system. The President has again strongly urged the Congress to act promptly on these proposals; he will also submit additional unemployment insurance amendments to extend the duration of benefits and expand coverage in labor market areas that have large increases in unemployment.

2. *Monetary policy.* Because of the lag which we believe exists between changes in money and changes in economic activity, the influence of monetary policy on the economy during 1974 will largely result from the monetary expansion during the second half of 1973 and the first half of 1974. The monetary expansion in the second half of 1973 can be described

by an increase in the narrowly defined money stock (M₁) of somewhat under 5 percent and an increase in the broadly defined money stock (M₂) of
about 8 percent at annual rates. Continued growth in M₂ at approximately
this rate would be consistent with our expectations concerning the increase
in money GNP during 1974. At present we expect money GNP to increase
by about 8 percent during the year. For more than a decade the propor-
tionate increase of money GNP tended to be the same as that of M₂, though
in some years the deviations from this proportionality were substantial,
and half-yearly deviations were often quite large. Hence, the foregoing conclusion seems reasonable, barring the emergence of further evidence as yet
unforeseen.

The prospect for trends in interest rates is particularly difficult to
appraise at present. Inflationary expectations tend to raise money rates,
while the temporary slowdown of business activity is apt to have the contrary influence for a while, even though business fixed investment is likely
to rise at a rate well above that of GNP. Among the interest-reducing influences, the prospective capital inflows resulting directly or indirectly
from current account surpluses of the oil-exporting countries also need to
be taken into account. All this relates to interest rates in general. Terms on
which mortgage credit is available will be influenced by the success that
depository institutions have in attracting new savings funds in competition
with market alternatives, and by the subsidization policies of the Administration with respect to this category of borrowers.

As will be explained in Chapter 2, by steepening inflationary expectations an overgenerous increase in the money supply would steepen rather
than moderate trends in money rates of interest.

3. *Housing policy.* The economic path described for 1974 implies a bot-
toming out of housing starts in the first quarter of 1974 at a level only
slightly below the fourth quarter of 1973 followed by a rise beginning in the
spring. The Administration took a number of steps in September 1973 to
cushion the decline then under way. In January a two-pronged action was
taken to revive the mortgage market. The Department of Housing and
Urban Development was authorized to purchase mortgages on up to 200,-
000 housing units at 7¾ percent, substantially below the prevailing market
interest rate. In addition, the maximum interest rates on FHA-VA
mortgages were lowered to 8¼ percent from 8½ percent, thereby setting
the pattern for reduced mortgage rates.

4. *Managing the energy shortage in the United States.* If the economy
is to follow the general path we have outlined it will be essential that output not be seriously hampered by the shortage of energy. This stipulation
means, first, that the total supply of fuels made available for industrial
production, including transportation related to it, must be adequate to sustain the aggregate level of economic activity projected for the year. Second,
the supply must be distributed among users...[to avoid] bottlenecks.

How easily these two conditions can be met will depend upon the volume
of oil imports. We believe that the volume of imports will be sufficient to

permit their fulfillment, but it would be imprudent to assume that they can be met without care in the distribution of energy among various uses.

The rise in prices of petroleum products which has been occurring helps to bring about the desired distribution. As the prices rise, the less valuable uses—which tend to be those which generate the least output and employment—are foregone. At a higher price, a factory which uses oil for space heating will cut down the temperature before it cuts down the use of oil in the production process. A higher price will cause a consumer to cut down the use of his car for pleasure driving, rather than for getting to work. It is commonly said that the use of energy will be reduced relatively little by a price increase. That may or may not be correct. But even if the cut in energy use is "relatively little" compared to a price increase, the price increases that have occurred or are in prospect are sufficiently large to have a substantial effect on the total use of energy and its distribution.

The oil price increases that have taken place under the controls program have been justified as a necessary means of increasing supply and maintaining orderly markets. Imported oil, "new" oil, and oil from small wells are exempt from control. Other oil is controlled and sells at prices considerably below those of uncontrolled oil, but the control price has been raised on two occasions to keep the price spread from becoming too large. Although necessitated by supply considerations, these price increases have played a useful role in the allocation of supply. To make sure that the price increases do not yield excessive profits that are not justified by their contribution to increasing supply, the Administration has proposed an Emergency Windfall Profits Tax. This tax would take a large proportion, up to 85 percent, of the additional revenue earned by producers of crude oil as a result of higher prices.

Other methods are being used to distribute supplies of oil in ways that will meet production requirements. The Federal Energy Office (FEO) has encouraged refineries to limit the production of gasoline in order to increase the production of other products more essential to industrial output. This enforces a cut in automobile driving, although it does not solve the question of who gets the available gasoline. The FEO has taken steps to prepare for coupon rationing of gasoline, although it is believed that a combination of increased supplies, higher prices, and conservation measures, largely voluntary, will make such rationing unnecessary.

The Emergency Petroleum Allocation Act of 1973 requires the establishment of a system of mandatory allocation of oil products, and the FEO has now set up such a system. It specifies limits to the amounts of petroleum products that refineries or distributors can deliver to described classes of customers (but stops short of individual consumers). The limits are generally described in percentages of current requirements or base-period use. The limits differ by class of user, in accord with FEO's estimate of the essentiality of the use to the productive process and to society. Such a system necessarily involves elaborate paperwork and a large degree of arbitrariness. Confidence that the economy will not be seriously hampered rests upon the expectation that increased supply and higher prices will narrowly limit the shortages to be distributed by the allocation system.

A third method, which seems to have been highly effective, has been voluntary conservation. This has been especially useful in stretching out the supplies of gasoline and home heating oil, but it has also helped to bring about a reduction in the nonproductive use of energy in industry.

The measures taken in recent months to deal with the energy shortage are too numerous to recount here. What further steps may be needed cannot now be foreseen. It must be emphasized, however, that satisfactory progress through 1974 will depend upon a flexible use of prices, allocations, and voluntary measures to channel energy efficiently into industry.

5. Wage and price controls. When Phase IV controls were instituted in August, the President announced that it would be our policy to work our way and feel our way out of controls. There would be no pre-set terminal date and we should avoid a disorderly transition, but the determination would be to end the system of comprehensive controls. This policy has been followed in the last 5 months. A number of industries have been decontrolled since Phase IV began and the pace of decontrol has been accelerating.

Experience under Phase IV has shown the wisdom of pressing on with the removal of controls. The controls have not recently been very effective in restraining inflation, and the general uncertainty cast over the economic process by the actual or potential operations of a detailed control system endangers the healthy economic expansion we seek. The last point is very important. Too many business decisions for too long a period ahead are being influenced by puzzlement over the kinds of controls businesses will be subjected to. We badly need business investment and economic growth in the years ahead, and continuation of general controls tends to interfere with that aim.

Just how fast the process of decontrol should properly go, and what residue of controls will endure, if any, cannot now be precisely told. But achievement of the desired reduction of inflation during the year does not, in our opinion, depend upon any significant influence from the controls.

6. *International cooperation.* The ability of the United States to get through the economic uncertainties of 1974 successfully would be enhanced by reasonable stability in the rest of the world, especially in the industrialized countries that are the chief suppliers and customers of the United States. There are two main things the United States can do to further that stability.

First, the United States can take the lead in an international effort to bring about a reliable international flow of oil at reasonable prices. Powerful moves by the United States and other industrialized countries to develop energy sources as potential alternatives to the oil now controlled by a few nations will be helpful in normalizing the flow of oil. The President has called the first of a series of international meetings on this subject to take place February 11.

Second, the United States can participate in a common effort to assure that the effects of high oil prices on the balance of payments do not lead the industrialized countries into a round of competitive deflation, depreciation, or trade restriction. This effort should include consideration of possible ways to supplement the now existing means of providing temporary support to countries finding themselves in a critical financial condition as a result of greatly enlarged oil import costs.

Goals Beyond 1974

Concern with the stabilization problems of 1974 should not divert attention from those other problems whose consequences will come chiefly after 1974 but which need to be dealt with now and continuously. Most of these problems arise from the need to increase our ability to produce—in total as well as in particular directions. This emphasis on ability to produce is essentially an emphasis on efficiency, on managing our resources so that we get as much out of them as we can. It is neutral about what should be produced and even about how much should be produced, only stressing the ability to produce more of what is wanted, if it is wanted.

We think emphasis on ability to produce is important at this time, because in the years ahead the desire of the American people for more output is likely to be especially strong, and unusual obstacles may hinder fulfillment of this demand. The need to devote more resources to obtaining energy will be a drag on output. The country is almost certainly ending the period of large transfers of the labor force out of agriculture into other pursuits. By 1980, we will probably come to the end of a period in which the labor force grew much more rapidly than the population and thus helped to raise output per capita. Environmental considerations may tend to slow down the growth of output, at least as output is usually measured.

For these reasons, emphasis on the capacity to produce—on efficiency and productivity—is especially important now. Of course, even in the field vaguely labeled "economic" the Nation always deals with a multiplicity of goals. For example, the distribution of the national income among persons will always be a subject of concern. We hope that the information presented in Chapter 5 will be illuminating in this connection. The Nation has other goals about the uses of the national output. One sees evidence, for example, of a great interest in devoting more of the national output to improvement of health, and in achieving that aim more efficiently. The President will be submitting suggestions to this end. It seems most useful for us to concentrate here on the problem of production.

Many aspects of Government policy affecting capacity to produce are discussed in more detail in later chapters of this report. We present here only a brief survey of the field.

DEVELOPMENT OF LOW-COST ENERGY FOR THE FUTURE

Throughout the 1960s the United States employed quantitative restrictions on petroleum imports to limit dependence on foreign sources of supply. However, the availability of imported petroleum at a price below the domestic price led to a weakening of the import restrictions and in 1973 to abandonment of the quota system altogether. As a result, imports have provided a rapidly expanding share of the domestic market.

The energy crisis that occurred in late 1973 as a result of the embargo by some of the oil-exporting countries alerted the Nation to the risk of depending on imports for a commodity that is vital to our economic well-being, and the supply of which is largely controlled by a few countries. Reductions in oil shipments to the United States and a sharp rise in the price of imported oil have caused substantial economic disruption. Had these events occurred later, when the United States was projected to be even more dependent on imported petroleum, the loss of jobs and the effect on incomes might have been far greater.

Oil imports may become more readily available, and the price may decline. However, the possibility of a subsequent sharp price rise or supply curtailment makes it risky for the United States to remain heavily dependent on imports to supply domestic needs.

The Nation has the capability to become self-sufficient in energy production. This capability will, however, require substantial capital investment and large expenditure on research and development. The private sector will be willing to make the needed investment only if there is a reasonable assurance that returns will be adequate to justify the commitment of resources to long-term investments.

In response to this situation, the President has announced Project Independence, a program to develop the capability for self-sufficiency in energy production by 1980. The choice of policies to implement Project Independence should be made largely on economic grounds. Because energy can be expected to cost more in the 1980s than it did in 1972, important changes in production methods, in the composition of output, and in consumption will occur. These changes will develop most rapidly, and with the least cost to society, if relative prices are allowed to allocate resources and to influence production decisions. There are many uncertainties regarding which of the new energy technologies will prove to be economic. By relying on the market mechanism to guide production decisions, we can avoid becoming locked into production methods and energy sources that prove to be uneconomic.

A major component of Project Independence is a program of Government-funded research and development to accelerate the development of technologies that will ensure an adequate supply of low-cost energy for the future. Although the private sector will continue to undertake most of the energy research and development, there is a need for a more active Government role. In part this is because the returns from expenditure on research and development will be heavily influenced by Federal policies regarding environmental control, leasing of mineral rights, and import restrictions. In addition, the development of new energy technologies to some extent involves expanding our knowledge of fundamental processes. In such cases, although the research and development provides a large gain to the economy as a whole, there may be little opportunity for any one firm to derive a large enough part of this gain to warrant undertaking the research. Moreover, private research and development is usually oriented toward projects with a relatively quick payoff, whereas much of the needed expenditure must be devoted to the development of energy sources that may not be competitive for some time.

SAVING AND PRIVATE INVESTMENT

To keep output per worker rising rapidly, when the labor force is also rising rapidly, requires a high rate of investment in productive facilities. Our total investment requirements in the years ahead will be greatly increased by the need to invest in energy development and environmental improvements.

These energy and environmental investments do not raise productivity as conventionally measured, though the former may prevent a decline in productivity if energy shortages would otherwise continue, and the latter may also prevent an ultimate decline in productivity. Both types of investment thus represent part of the increased resource costs imposed on energy-using or environment-using industries, in one case by adverse supply developments and in the other by social choice. Environmental benefits enhance economic well-being, and increased reliance on domestic sources of energy adds to security of production. Still, one can probably say, the American people expect rapidly rising output of the ordinary, marketable kind; and this expectation will require rapidly rising total investment to accommodate rising energy and environmental investment along with increasing investments of other kinds.

Part of total investment is provided through the Federal budget, in the form of direct expenditures for capital purposes, loans to private businesses and individuals, or grants and loans to States and localities. The budget for fiscal 1975 includes $19 billion for such outlays, excluding defense and excluding expenditures for education, training, health, and research and development. The largest single item is expenditures for transportation, primarily highways, followed by expenditures for public works.

These direct investments in the Federal budget make a useful contribution to economic growth, if they are wisely selected and well managed. Such direct investments have numerous advocates in the Federal budget-making process. But attention needs to be called to another way in which the Federal budget could contribute to investment and growth, although it has few advocates: running a budget surplus, or at least avoiding a budget deficit except under appropriate conditions.

If the Federal Government runs a deficit and borrows under conditions of strong private investment demand, its borrowing absorbs funds which would otherwise have been invested in private projects. Unless all of that deficit is used to finance direct Government investment, which is unlikely, the deficit depresses total investment. On the other hand, if the Government runs a surplus in these circumstances, it will repay some of its debt and make more funds available for private investment, unless the surplus is generated by taxes all of which come out of private saving, an unlikely condition. When there is a great deal of slack in the economy, a budget deficit will help to support the level of economic activity needed to supply both the incentive to invest and the savings for investment. However, when productive resources are fully utilized, the smaller the Federal deficit is, or the larger the Federal surplus, the higher private investment is likely to be. This fact partly explains the principle adopted by the Administration that expenditures should not exceed, and at times may properly be less than, the receipts that would be collected at full employment.

Government policy affects incentives for private investment, in total and in particular sectors, in a number of ways, including policies relating to taxes, international trade, and international financial policy, as well as credit guarantees, subsidies, and so on. All of these involve well-known conflicts of objectives and difficulties of measuring costs and benefits. We may now be running into a problem which is new, at least in magnitude, and potentially very serious: the uncertainty created for private investment, and all private long-term commitments, by Government economic controls that are unprecedented in scope and unpredictable in operation. Taken together, the price and wage controls, the controls connected with the energy shortage, and the environmental regulations add up to a massive entry of Government into the affairs of almost every business in the country. The management of these controls involves a great many close or arbitrary decisions, to be made in many instances by a very few people. They could go either way, and the private businessman who must invest in the light of these controls cannot tell which way they will go.

These uncertainties could become a major obstacle to new private investment, even though we do not now see good evidence of its having already happened. Concern on this score is not a conclusive argument for avoiding controls. And it does argue for as much stability as can be achieved in the management of the controls that are inescapable.

THE FINANCIAL SYSTEM

In his 1970 Economic Report the President said:

Because our expanding and dynamic economy must have strong and innovative financial institutions if our national savings are to be utilized effectively, I shall appoint a commission to study our financial structure and make recommendations to me for needed changes.

After studying the findings of this commission (the Hunt Commission), the President, on August 3, 1973, sent to Congress a series of recommendations. In them a more efficient financial system is envisioned, in which financial institutions can operate with greater freedom and less imposed specialization. By fostering more competition among financial institutions, the proposed measures would improve the efficiency of our financial system in channeling funds from savers to borrowers. Savings would earn the highest rate of return the competitive market structure could allow, and the savings would be put to the most productive use. Under such a system, interest rates would play a greater role in determining the volume and the distribution of funds. Social projects deserving priorities, such as low- and moderate-income housing, would be taken care of with subsidies instead of regulations.

Among the recommendations, interest rate ceilings on deposits would be phased out over a period of 5½ years. Federally chartered thrift institutions would be authorized to offer third party payment plans, including negotiable orders of withdrawal (NOW's) and credit cards to individuals and corporations; but they would also be given expanded lending powers in making consumer and real estate loans and in acquiring high-grade private debt securities. National banks would likewise be able to offer NOW accounts and make real estate loans with fewer restrictions. Interest ceilings on Government-backed mortgages would be removed, and a mortgage interest tax credit of up to 3½ percent to financial institutions and up to 1½ percent to individuals supplying mortgage funds would be made available.

The President's recommendations, if enacted by Congress, would strengthen the financial markets in general and mortgage markets in particular. The expanded lending and borrowing powers would increase the flow of funds into financial institutions. Further, the mortgage tax credit would reduce the dependence of the mortgage market on thrift institutions by encouraging other types of financial institutions, as well as individuals, to invest in mortgages. The resulting mortgage market would be less vulnerable to a credit squeeze than it has been, and the burden of monetary restraint would be more evenly distributed throughout the economy.

On another financial matter, the time may be at hand when a move in the direction of greater uniformity of reserve requirements among depository institutions is warranted. Varying reserve arrangements among State and federally supervised banks have resulted in removing an increasing proportion of the money supply from the direct influence of Federal Reserve requirements and have made short-term shifts of deposits among member and nonmember institutions a source of uncertainty in the implementation of monetary policy. Care must be taken that any change in the reserve structure of the Nation's banks should not work to the disadvantage of smaller institutions or change the balance among supervisory authorities; but within these constraints it now appears desirable that deposits which form the money supply should be subject to direct influence by the Federal Reserve, regardless of the source of supervision of the institutions that hold them....

TRANSPORTATION REFORM

Last year the Congress passed and on January 2, 1974, the President signed the Regional Rail Reorganization Act, which is a pragmatic attempt to deal with the pervasive insolvency of railroads in the heavily industrialized Midwest and Northeast. Several of the eight principal bankrupt railroads had threatened liquidation, and such a bill was needed because the risk of even a very short period of suspended service was too great to be tolerated. If the services of the Northeast's railroads are so vital to the rest of the economy, one must ask why so many of them were in such a weakened financial condition. Factors more general and basic than those that normally cause bankruptcy are responsible.

Poor management and unrealistically rigid labor contracts are popular explanations of the railroads' inability to adapt to changing technology and a changing economy. These proximate causes largely reflect, however, a more fundamental cause—inefficient and intransigent governmental regulation.

Governmental regulation of the railroads can be traced to two sources. The public wanted the Government to protect them from the industry in a time of near monopoly and the members of the industry wanted the Government to protect them from each other. This "protection" has been expensive for both the railroads and the public. The elaboration of regulations intended to provide this protection has created a complex set of specifications for the behavior of firms that has tended to ossify with time. As a result railroad companies have increasingly given up control of fundamental management decisions to the Interstate Commerce Commission (ICC) in return for the policing of industry competition by the agency. Moreover, railroad management's attention began to focus more on the rules that delimited its discretion than upon the underlying economic realities in the markets in which they operated. As these realities changed, railroad management found itself increasingly inept at adjusting—the result being an increasing incidence of bankruptcy.

The Transportation Improvement Act

The Transportation Improvement Act of 1974, proposed by the Administration, is an important first step toward solving some of the more general problems of the railroad industry. It is also an imperative step toward a long-term solution of the problem of the bankrupt railroad; because the viability of the rail system that will emerge from the wreck of the Penn Central will depend in an important way upon successful regulatory reform. Among the more important reforms facilitated by the bill would be liberalization and rationalization of procedures for the "abandonment" of unprofitable lines. In 1971 the railroads were required by the ICC to maintain service on 21,000 miles, about 10 percent of the total, of lightly traveled track for which revenues were less than operating costs.

To cover these losses, railroads must charge higher rates on profitable routes. This subsidization distorts resource use and interferes with the efficiency of the entire transportation system, and hence the entire economy, as well as increasing the financial problems of the rail industry. Requiring railroads to continue to operate short and uneconomic branch lines diverts traffic that could be carried more efficiently by truck; and conversely the higher rates on longer hauls result in a diversion to trucks of freight that could be moved more efficiently by rail. Since trucks use considerably more fuel (and emit more pollutants) than trains per ton-mile of freight carried, the magnitude of this inefficiency grows directly with the increasing relative scarcity of energy supplies.

The proposed act will also facilitate the substitution of truck transportation for rail services on abandoned lines, by...authorizing truck service between any point on the abandoned line and connecting rail service points.

Need for Further Reform

Although enactment of this bill will add to the efficiency of the rail industry, several basic problems remain on the agenda for transportation reform in the coming year. The longer-term viability of the Nation's railroads will require substantial investments in improved technology, and in improvement and diversification of types of freight service, as well as investments to rehabilitate deteriorating physical facilities.

It is vital, however, that a comprehensive evaluation of the regulatory and institutional structure of both the railroads and the entire surface transportation industry be completed *before* such investments are made. Many aspects of modern railroad operation are not determined by either technological or profitability considerations. They are adaptations to obsolete regulatory policies and labor practices. Investment in conventional railroad technology as it exists today may inhibit productivity and actually reinforce the resistance to the institutional reforms that will be required for the development of a more rational and efficient surface transportation system in the future.

Changes in corporate structure may also be desirable. Costs of transferring freight from one railroad to another significantly reduce the savings that rails enjoy relative to trucks on long-haul shipments. This would imply that end-to-end mergers of railroads might be important mechanisms for reducing the real cost of rail transportation. Yet formidable administrative barriers must be surmounted by companies attempting end-to-end mergers under current regulatory practices.

The Administration's concern with the efficiency of the surface transportation system is not limited to stopping the spreading insolvency that infects the railroad industry. It will be difficult to exploit fully the opportunities for increasing productivity in the railroad industry unless major changes take place concurrently in the trucking industry.

The regulation of trucks in interstate common carriage that began in the midst of the Great Depression has also evolved into a web of regulatory constraints. Restrictions on entry into market areas, limitations on the type of goods carried, and mandated "gateways"—creating required routes which may be so circular as to be bizarre—have resulted in an industry burdened with regulatory inefficiency. Partially loaded trucks, often required to return empty even when alternative cargoes are available, are common. Such inefficiency is a result of regulatory policy. There are no technological reasons why the motor freight industry could not operate as an essentially competitive sector of the economy.

A comprehensive analysis of the trucking industry is now under way and will provide a basis for the design of a comprehensive set of regulatory reform proposals to be completed by the fall of 1974.

EFFICIENT INTERNATIONAL EXCHANGE

Economic growth is significantly enhanced by an openness to foreign economies which permits a relatively free international exchange of goods and capital based on economic incentive. International trade makes goods available that might otherwise be lacking, or only available at much higher costs. It can also make available to domestic producers ideas about new products, new product designs, or new methods of production. For producers it can be an added incentive to adopt more efficient methods of production.

We have been reminded in recent months that in some circumstances there can be a danger, both political and economic, in excessive dependence on foreign supplies. The United States must guard itself against this danger, by unilateral or multilateral action. However, if this objective is realistically defined it will be found not to limit greatly the scope for beneficial expansion of international trade.

Despite a fairly extensive removal of trade barriers in the past 25 years, substantial barriers to international trade and investment remain in effect. The inefficient location of productive facilities because of these barriers constitutes a loss of economic welfare to the country as a whole. Efforts to negotiate a reduction of the remaining trade barriers are therefore important toward improving the efficiency of the U.S. economy. The trade legislation now before Congress would give the President authority to negotiate a substantial reduction of such barriers.

Negotiations in the trade area also have to deal with the economic interdependence that results from trade. Abrupt economic shifts emanating from abroad can from time to time create a temporary economic dislocation at home which needs to be moderated or offset by government measures. Since such measures will have further repercussions abroad, governments need to agree on some basic rules and procedures that they can follow when their interests conflict. Multilateral negotiations are designed to improve some of the current rules and procedures, as well as to reduce existing trade barriers.

An international monetary system is a prerequisite for the efficient exchange of goods and capital. Without such a system, international exchange is confined to barter. To function efficiently, the international monetary system has to provide sufficient quantities of commonly accepted means of payment and a procedure for adjusting the relationship between one currency and another. It also has to provide a set of rules on such questions as the conversion of one currency into another, restrictions on the conversion of currencies, transfers of liquid funds from one country to another, as well as a set of procedures for resolving differences in national approaches to such problems. The current negotiations to reform the international monetary system are designed to improve the existing rules and procedures.

SUPPLEMENT

Prospects for 1974

Earlier in this chapter we noted that 1974 would be a year of little output growth and considerable inflation but that in both respects the second half of the year should be better than the first. The energy crisis has clouded near-term prospects much more than usual. There is great uncertainty, not only about the overall GNP change and its distribution between price and real volume but also about the components of demand. It seems fairly likely that this year's 8 percent increase in nominal GNP should reflect slower rates of increase, compared to last year, in consumption, gross private domestic investment, and net exports, and a faster rate in combined government purchases. The specific changes are much less certain, but the Council presents the following projections of individual demand components underlying this year's overall total.

Business Fixed Investment

The Council expects nonresidential fixed investment to show a rise of about 12 percent from 1973 to 1974. It is likely to be the major source of strength in demand this year. Despite the small rise in production in the final quarter of 1973, the condition of shortages that prevailed in many industries earlier in 1973 continued through the end of the year. Capacity utilization was still very high, especially in the basic materials industries. Delivery times were still long. Aside from the automobile industry, inventories were rather low relative to output and sales. All of these were indicative of tight supply conditions that constituted a strong simulus for business to invest in new plant and equipment in the coming year.

This is not to say that the character of investment demand will be the same as in 1972 or 1973. The slowdown of the rise in aggregate demand during 1973 and the leveling in profits are likely to bring a smaller rise in new investment initiatives than in the preceding 2 years. Even so, the large volume of new investment under way assures a sizable increase in real expenditures in 1974. Unfilled order backlogs in capital goods industries at the end of December were some 35 percent greater than they had been a year earlier.

In early 1974 the Commerce Department released a survey which showed that businessmen were planning a rise of 12 percent in capital expenditures in the coming year. The rise was particularly large for manufacturing—17 percent—and planned increases within manufacturing were above average (21 percent) for materials-producing industries. The Commerce Department survey is broadly consistent with a McGraw-Hill survey, which was run about 2 months earlier, projecting an overall rise of 14 percent from 1973 to 1974.

Neither of these surveys sheds any light on the effect of the energy crisis on investment plans; and because of variations in sample coverage and for other reasons, the difference in results between the two surveys is not considered significant. The Council believes that on balance the energy crisis may result in some reduction in business purchases of cars and trucks, but aside from this the negative and positive effects of the energy crisis on investment will be roughly offsetting. Some industries directly affected by the crisis have already cut back investment (airlines, for example), while some firms in other industries may be holding back on commitments until

91

they understand the implications that the current crisis holds for future fuel supplies. On the other hand, the crisis is stimulating capital outlays to support the search for new energy sources in this country, and conversions to other types of fuel will entail new capital expenditures.

Inventory Investment

Inventory investment is likely to be a little higher this year than in 1973—perhaps by $2 billion. In the final quarter of 1973 there was a very large increase in inventory accumulation, a good part of which represented a rise of retail stocks of new cars. Even so, total nonfarm stocks relative to total output measured in real terms at the end of 1973 were low, gauged by post-World War II experience. The first half of this year should see a working off of unwanted automobile stocks at the same time that other industries continue to accumulate inventories in an effort to restore more normal relationships between stocks and output.

Residential Construction

Housing starts in the final quarter of 1973 appeared to be reflecting the effects of the stringency in mortgage markets last summer, and possibly temporary effects arising out of the energy crisis. Very late in the year there were reports that builders were uncertain about the impact of reduced fuel supplies on new construction, while potential buyers of homes in outlying areas were hesitant because of uncertainty about the availability of gasoline for extended commuting. But this, and the extent to which homeowners were making new expenditures for better insulation of their homes, cannot be considered hard information. While there is no assurance about improved energy supplies, the coming months should at least dispel the present uncertainty and permit those builders and those consumers who can buy and rent new homes to make decisions.

A more fundamental factor concerns financial conditions. Net inflows into savings and loan associations have risen since late summer, and thrift institutions now have more funds available for mortgage lending. On the basis of past experience this improvement in the availability of mortgage funds should be reflected in a turnaround in starts this spring. Recent actions taken by the Federal Government should also help spur the recovery. The reduction in FHA and VA mortgage rates in January should help make these programs more attractive to home purchasers, and increased purchases of mortgages by GNMA should increase the supply of mortgage funds for these programs.

The underlying demand for housing—as measured by the need to provide shelter for new households and for the replacement of houses removed from the housing stock—remains strong. However, the inventory of unsold homes at the start of the year is likely to act temporarily as a brake on new starts and dampen the increase after this spring. For all of 1974 the Council foresees starts of approximately 1-2/3 million private units, which would represent a decline of almost 20 percent from the 1973 total. Outlays are expected to decline by 15 percent.

Government Purchases

Federal purchases of goods and services, after rising very little from 1972 to 1973, are expected to increase about 10 percent in the coming year, with increases in both defense and nondefense outlays. State and local purchases, further supported by the revenue sharing program, are expected to rise by 12 percent, which is close to the increase of the preceding year.

Net Exports

Prior to the energy crisis it was expected that net exports would show a further improvement from 1973 to 1974. The effect of the devaluation of the dollar and the continued strength of foreign demand were expected to stimulate exports. The slower growth of output in the United States was expected to slow the growth in imports. Thus, a further moderate improvement over the high rate of net exports that prevailed in the second half of 1973 appeared to be a reasonable prospect.

The oil crisis has drastically modified this outlook. For the time being at least, foreign countries are expecting much slower real growth than they anticipated previously. While exports will be greater than in 1973, they will not rise as much as they would have without the crisis. The main factor affecting imports is the huge increase in prices of imported oil. Cutbacks in the physical volume of crude oil and refined products will be much more than offset by the rise in price. The full effect of the price rise should be felt by the second quarter. In nominal terms the net exports are expected to fall close to zero for 1974 as a whole.

Consumer Spending

Consumer expenditures are likely to increase about as much as GNP in 1974. Spending should be rather sluggish in the first half but should show a marked improvement in the second.

Consumers had already shown a pronounced reaction to the energy crisis in late 1973, when they reduced their purchases of domestically produced cars from an annual rate of 10 million units in the third quarter to about 8 million units in the fourth. The decrease was much more than had been anticipated by forecasters prior to the energy crisis, and the fact that large car purchases were weak, while long delivery times were required for small car purchases, pointed up the special influence of the crisis on auto demand. It is not clear whether the cutback by consumers had run its course by early January, when dealer sales of domestic cars were running at a seasonally adjusted annual rate of about 7-1/3 million units. As small car supplies improve through the year consumers should come into the market in increasing numbers, although the pickup in car purchases is not likely to be appreciable until this summer. Another reason for the improvement in consumer spending from the first to the second half of 1974 is that the major downward adjustment of demand resulting from reduced gasoline supplies and higher prices is likely to be completed in the first half of this year.

Prior to the energy crisis some slowdown in the growth of consumer spending had been expected in the first half of 1974 because of the earlier shift in fiscal and monetary policy and the independent effect of the housing decline. Offsetting these influences is the stimulation from sharp increases in Federal transfer payments. These include the 7 percent social security increase scheduled for this April and the further 4 percent increase in July; the rise in payments due to the federalization of adult welfare programs; increased payments for food stamps and increased retirement benefits for Federal workers and veterans. All told, Federal transfer payments to persons as measured in the national accounts are scheduled to rise by $14 billion (annual rate) from the second half of 1973 to the first half of 1974. As an offset, the increase in the taxable wage base this January from $10,800 to $13,200 will reduce personal income by $2 billion, as calculated in the national income accounts. In fact, this rise will be felt by those consumers whose wages exceed $10,800 only in the second half of the calendar year, as employers make deductions from employees' earnings for a longer period than under the old taxable base. Although the net fiscal stimulus will have run its course by midyear, the pickup elsewhere in the economy in the second half should serve to increase consumer incomes and spending....

NIXON'S 1975 BUDGET

February 4, 1974

Charting an uncertain course between inflation and recession, President Nixon Feb. 4 sent Congress a $304.4-billion fiscal 1975 budget stressing fiscal flexibility in a slumping, energy-short economy. Outlining plans for "moderate restraint" through an expected $9.4-billion deficit, the President carefully reserved the option of shifting the budget toward greater stimulus "to support the economy if that should be necessary." In sharp contrast to Nixon's fiscal 1974 budget message (see Historic Documents 1973, p. 169-183), his fiscal 1975 proposals in both wording and substance were conciliatory to Congress and conventional in direction. Few innovations were offered, and the administration's 1973 proposals to dismantle federal social programs on a wholesale basis were not renewed. Beset by Watergate and economic discontent, the administration in effect accepted continuation of most trends and instead concentrated its efforts on guiding the economy away from recession.

Like the fiscal 1975 budget itself, the congressional reaction to the President's proposals could be characterized as restrained and in most cases predictable. Conservatives complained about the expected rise in spending even as inflation persisted and liberals complained that spending would not rise enough to offset the effects of inflation. House Appropriations Committee Chairman George Mahon (D Texas), whose committee would take an active part in the eventual shape of the fiscal 1975 budget, expressed special concern about the budget's prediction that the national debt would rise by $16.3-billion during fiscal 1974 and another $19.8-billion during fiscal 1975. Less restrained in their reactions were a number of liberals who found the President's proposals for spending on *domestic programs inadequate. "This 1975 budget is essentially a 'standpat' budget," Sen. Hubert H. Humphrey (D Minn.) complained Feb. 7. "It moves us no closer to the goals we have set for ourselves." Humphrey argued that the budget's apparent increases in domestic spending initiatives in fact did no more than offset the impact of inflation on the persons the programs were designed to help. In some cases, he added, the increases failed to match rising living costs.*

Outlays, Revenues, Deficit

Even without bold program initiatives, built-in spending increases in Nixon's 1975 budget dictated a projected $29.8-billion increase in federal outlays above expected fiscal 1974 levels, putting the anticipated spending total above $300-billion for the first time. The new federal efforts the President did propose—notably national health insurance and stepped-up energy research—called for relatively little spending increases in fiscal 1975. The largest increase in the budget was a $6.3-billion additional request for defense spending. But the bulk of the over-all fiscal 1975 increases were outlays mandated to meet federal obligations for Social Security benefits to retired persons, veterans, the poor and the unemployed, health benefits, interest on the federal debt and similar commitments not subject to immediate control. The only cutbacks targeted in the budget were aimed at halting construction of hospitals under the Hill-Burton grant program, phasing out special education aid for federally impacted areas and ending the antipoverty activities of the Office of Economic Opportunity, which the Nixon administration had attempted to dismantle in 1973. (See Historic Documents 1973, p. 453-464.)

According to the budget, federal revenues were expected to increase by $25-billion during fiscal 1975. In making this projection, the administration counted heavily on continued economic expansion and previously enacted payroll tax changes for the bulk of the increase. Of that $25-billion increment, the administration attributed only a net increase of $1.3-billion to tax changes through proposed legislation. The budget estimated fiscal 1975 revenue from the President's proposed windfall profits tax on crude oil at $3-billion, but nearly $2-billion of that would be offset by the administration's own limited tax-reform proposals and by proposed liberalized deductions for pension plan contributions.

In calculating a $9.4-billion fiscal 1975 deficit, the budget followed the unified budget concept used since fiscal 1969 by combining federal funds and trust fund transactions. While the unified budget figures gave a more comprehensive look at the budget's fiscal impact, it obscured a projected $17.9-billion federal funds deficit that would be offset by a $8.4-billion trust fund surplus. A substantial part of the federal funds deficit was due to transactions with trust funds, primarily federal fund payments to social insurance trust funds and interest on the federal debt held by the trust funds.

Nixon's message renewed familiar themes—greater state and local government responsibility, reliance on individual private initiatives, restraint of the federal government's role. Underscoring the continuation of previous budgetary trends, Nixon noted the growth of spending on income security and health programs, the shrinking share of outlays devoted to defense, and a shift "away from support for direct federal operations and toward benefit payments to individuals and grants to state and local governments." Reversing one trend, however, the fiscal 1975 budget projected an increase of 22,200 civilian employees in the federal government, reflecting expanded work forces for most major domestic agencies. The budget documents also estimated that civilian pay and benefit costs would reach $34.2-billion and military pay and benefit costs $22.6-billion. The budget carried Nixon's recommendation for a 7.5 per cent pay raise during 1974 for high-level federal officials, including members of Congress.

'Avoid A Recession'

The administration took a strong stand against a severe economic downturn. Frederic V. Malek, the assistant director of the Office of Management and Budget told reporters Feb. 2 that "we are prepared to do whatever is necessary to avoid a recession. The President is very firm about that. If it means busting the budget, then he will bust the budget rather than keep people out of jobs." In his budget message, Nixon accepted "some slowdown in the growth of demand" as necessary economic adjustment from 1973's inflationary boom, but he vowed that "this slowdown should not be permitted to go too far." To keep that from happening, Nixon said the administration "will be prepared to use a range of measures...tailored to the special conditions of the energy shortage." But no specifics were given on what recession-countering actions the administration was preparing. In his message, Nixon only suggested that Congress enact his 1973 proposals to raise standards and extend coverage under the unemployment insurance system.

Briefing reporters on the budget Feb. 2, Treasury Secretary George P. Shultz refused to describe the economic conditions that the administration would define as recession. Offering "my own list" of stimulative measures that could be used to counter too steep a downturn, Shultz contended that tax cuts—a proposal gaining support in Congress—"should be at the end of the line" because of the need to maintain federal revenue. "But if we must, we must," he conceded.

In addition to fiscal 1975 budget authority, the President asked Congress for $10.4-billion in supplemental fiscal 1974 appropriations—mostly for defense and pay raises—and hinted that an additional $3.4-billion would be sought for 1974 if Congress approved proposed programs. If Congress granted all of Nixon's additional requests for fiscal 1974 appropriations, total budget authority for the ongoing fiscal year would increase to $202.6-billion from the $188.3-billion given congressional approval during 1973.

Congressional Reaction

Many Democrats criticized the administration's approach to inflation and to the effect of rising costs on limited individual budgets. In Feb. 6 remarks, Rep. John Brademas (D Ind.) asserted that "although at first glance the budget indicates that the President has not proposed the savage slashes...that he suggested last year, his proposals are not cause for optimism." While Congress could be "thankful that the President has not proposed deep slashes" in programs for the elderly, Brademas went on, administration economic policies permitting rapid inflation "make standing still a step to the rear." Making similar complaints, Sen. Frank Church (D Idaho) found the budget "characterized by retrenchment or standpatism at a time when inflationary pressures are driving up the operating costs of services programs for the elderly." Sen. Alan Cranston (D Calif.) said the President's proposals for veterans programs "show he is not aware of the harsh realities of life in today's overheated economy for returning veterans...."

Nixon's budget came under harsh attack from at least one House Republican conservative. Rep. Jack F. Kemp (R N.Y.), generally an administration supporter, termed the fiscal 1975 proposals "the worst conceived of any on record—at least of any Republican president on record." The budget, Kemp complained, "embodies the worst of Keynesian economic principles—planned deficits, the use of the government's spending power to compensate for declines in other segments of the economy—all at the taxpayer's expense."

Text of President Nixon's Feb. 4 budget message to the Congress:

BUDGET MESSAGE OF THE PRESIDENT

To the Congress of the United States:

The Federal budget must be both a consistent statement of our national objectives and a responsible plan for achieving them. The budget that I propose for fiscal year 1975 meets these standards. It places special emphasis on:

—the proper fiscal balance to keep the economy on the track to sustained high employment and more stable prices;

—a strong defense force in support of our efforts to build an enduring structure of peace in the world;

—a comprehensive energy program to deal with current shortages and to reestablish our ability to be self-sufficient in energy;

—the New Federalism philosophy of strengthening the role of State and local governments, and of the individual citizen;

—basic reforms of major domestic programs; and

—efficient management of the Federal Government in the years ahead, through a more intensive focus on the tangible results that programs achieve.

In the face of economic uncertainty, my budget recommendations provide for a fiscal policy that would support high employment while restraining inflation. It would maintain the flexibility to take further action, if needed, to offset the effects of energy shortages. My budget recommendations hold the rise of Federal spending to the minimum increases necessary.

The budget recommends total outlays of $304.4 billion in 1975, $29.8 billion more than in 1974, and anticipates receipts of $295 billion, a $25 billion increase over 1974. About 90% of the increase in outlays between 1974 and 1975 represents mandatory spending increases that are unavoidable under current law.

Under conditions of full employment—conventionally defined as a 4% unemployment rate—Federal receipts would be substantially higher and outlays somewhat lower than these figures. Thus, on a *full employment basis* the budget shows a surplus of $4 billion in 1974 increasing to $8 billion in 1975.

The budget proposes increases for defense activities so that we can increase our defense preparedness and preserve present force levels in the face of rising costs. These proposals reflect minimum prudent levels of defense spending consistent with maintaining adequate armed forces to assure our national security.

The budget includes my program, Project Independence, to reestablish our capability for self-sufficiency in energy. I plan Federal funding of $10 billion for the accelerated energy research and development component of this program over the next 5 years. Other measures already underway or proposed will help reduce low-priority energy use and minimize economic dislocations due to shortages. Our vigorous diplomatic efforts to restore an acceptable pattern of world trade in petroleum will complement these measures.

The budget carries forward the New Federalism philosophy. This philosophy stresses the need to recognize the different roles appropriate to each level of government, and to the private sector—thereby strengthening individual choice and self-reliance in America. The New Federalism calls for Federal support in meeting national problems and holds that State and local authorities are best able to make decisions on local and statewide needs in accordance with local conditions and community aspirations. Federal aid in the areas of law enforcement, manpower, and rural development incorporate the principles of the New Federalism. I now propose to apply this philosophy in major reforms of Federal assistance for health, education, community development, and transportation.

Our welfare system is inefficient and inequitable. I urge the Congress to work with my Administration in developing a new system that is simple, fair, and compassionate.

I am once again proposing a comprehensive plan for national health insurance that would make adequate insurance against the costs of health care available to *all* Americans. This far-reaching reform is long overdue. I urge early congressional action on it. The budget proposes measures to prepare for this program.

Federal taxes impose a large burden on the Nation. Each Federal program, therefore, must be managed as efficiently as possible, and each must be subject to continuous scrutiny as to how well it meets today's highest priority needs. This budget supports the major management initiatives I have undertaken to ensure that Federal programs produce results that truly satisfy the needs of the American people—and do so at the lowest possible cost to the taxpayer.

The end of American combat involvement in the Vietnam war and the reduction of cold war tensions in recent years have contributed to a significant shift in the composition of the Federal budget. Defense outlays remained virtually constant from 1968 to 1974, despite substantial cost increases and the pay raises which have accompanied the transition to an all-volunteer armed force. These added costs were offset by large savings resulting from reductions in men and materiel. Defense costs have been a decreasing share of our national budget, falling from 44% of Federal spending in 1969 to an estimated 29% in 1975.

Conversely, Federal nondefense spending has increased from 56% of Federal spending in 1969 to 71% in this budget. In the process, the form that Federal spending takes has shifted dramatically away from support for direct Federal operations and toward benefit payments to individuals and grants to State and local governments.

When I took office as President in 1969, defense outlays were nearly one-fifth more than combined outlays for aid to individuals under human resource programs and for aid to State and local governments. While our defenses are being maintained and strengthened, this budget proposes spending nearly *twice* as much money for aid to individuals and to State and local governments as for defense. This dramatic shift in Federal spending both reflects and supports the New Federalism.

The Budget and The Economy

During the past year, our economy operated at close to full capacity. In fact, the Nation's capacity for producing basic materials was used at a higher rate than in any previous year since World War II. New jobs were created for about 2¾ million people. Unemployment fell from a 5.4% average rate in the second half of calendar year 1972 to a 4.7% rate in the second half of 1973. At the same time, adverse weather and other conditions cut into the world's food supplies, including ours, while the policies of exporting countries cut supplies of oil and raised its price sharply.

These developments created a severe inflation during calendar year 1973, particularly in prices of food and energy. Our budget policy has been a key element in the effort to control that inflation. Strict limitation of expenditures in 1973 applied fiscal restraint to an economy that was expanding at an unsustainable rate. The budget totals recommended here continue a policy of fiscal responsibility as part of a continuing anti-inflation program.

There is now evidence that the economy is slowing down. In part this is due to the energy shortage, which limits our ability to produce some products and reduces demand for others. Our energy-use policies are designed to minimize the adverse impact of the energy shortage on the economy, but some effect is inescapable.

Some slowdown in the growth of demand is appropriate to help check inflation. This is especially true in view of supply limitations. But this slowdown should not be permitted to go too far. Therefore, I propose a budget which will continue a posture of moderate restraint rather than greatly intensifying that restraint. Also, my Administration is developing and will be prepared to use a range of measures to support the economy if that should be necessary—measures tailored to the special conditions of the energy shortage. Along these lines, the Congress should enact the proposals I made last year to improve our regular unemployment insurance system by establishing higher minimum benefit standards and extending coverage to farm workers.

Under conditions of full employment the budget outlays I propose would be less than the receipts from present and proposed taxes by about $4 billion in 1974 and $8 billion in 1975. A 4% rate of unemployment is used as a measure of full employment in calculating these surpluses. These surpluses, following a small full-employment deficit in 1973, and rising somewhat from 1974 to 1975, are consistent with our objective of moderate restraint.

In large part, the estimated increase in the full-employment surplus is the result of the high inflation rate experienced in calendar year 1973 and expected to continue for the first half of 1974. In the short run, inflation increases receipts more than it increases outlays. Thus, it increases for a time the surplus that would be achieved at high employment. This means that the budget has the effect of restraining inflation. The rising full-employment surpluses estimated here are largely the product of an inflation that is proceeding too rapidly. To use the size of these surpluses as an invitation or an excuse for more spending would only make the inflation rate worse.

A 4% unemployment rate is used in calculating full-employment receipts and outlays as a conventional standard which approximately removes the effects on the budget estimates of year-to-year changes in the level of economic activity. To serve this purpose the unemployment rate used for the calculations must be reasonably stable from year to year. However, this does not mean that the feasible and proper target for unemployment is always represented by the same figure. In fact, as a result of changes in the composition of the labor force, a 4% overall unemployment rate today would mean much tighter conditions in labor markets than would have been true ten or twenty years ago.

The estimates of receipts in this budget include the windfall profits tax on oil producers which I have proposed. This tax would recapture the excess profits that these producers would otherwise realize due to rising oil prices.

I continue to urge action on the tax reform and simplification proposals that were discussed with Congress last year. These proposals would not appreciably affect the *overall* tax burden on the economy; they would simply distribute it more equitably.

Our ability to carry out sound fiscal policy and to provide the resources needed to meet emerging problems is limited by decisions made in the past. The portion of the budget subject to discretionary control has shrunk in recent years primarily because of the relative decline in controllable defense spending, the growth in mandatory grants to State and local governments, and the growth in human resource programs (which largely take the form of benefit payments, set by law, to individuals and families). In 1975, over $223 billion in outlays, or nearly three-quarters of the budget, will be *virtually uncontrollable* in the short run due to existing law and prior-year commitments. This represents a substantial decline in the controllability of the budget since 1967, when only 59% of outlays were uncontrollable.

Just as each budget is heavily influenced by commitments embodied in those that have preceded it, so each, in turn, strongly influences those that follow. Therefore, the future impact of current decisions must be taken into account by projecting future available resources and the known claims against these resources. This is why the 1975 budget presents detailed projections of its 1976 spending implications; this is also the reason that all five budgets submitted by my Administration have contained 5-year projections of full employment outlays and receipts.

The costs of existing programs and of the new programs I have proposed will rise over time in response to growth in the number of eligible beneficiaries for programs such as social security and other entitlement programs, and in response to price increases. The rise in outlays for existing and currently proposed programs, however, will be less rapid than the rise in tax receipts. Thus, by 1979, receipts are projected to reach about $428 billion on a full-employment basis, while outlays for existing and proposed programs will be $391 billion. This leaves a budget margin—a margin which can be used for tax reduction, new initiatives, or retirement of public debt—of about $37 billion for 1979. This compares with a margin of $10 billion projected for 1976. The 1979 margin is a relatively small one—less than 9% of the projected 1979 receipts—to cover the exigencies of the next 5 years. But it is indicative of longer-term fiscal health if proper fiscal discipline is exercised.

TOWARD A LASTING WORLD PEACE

The overriding goal of American foreign policy is to build a lasting world peace, a peace resting on the solid foundation of mutual respect among all nations.

We have made great progress toward this objective during the past few years. During this Administration we have:

—ended American combat involvement in the war in Vietnam;

—ended the draft;

—established more cooperative relations with the Soviet Union;

—developed promising new relationships with the People's Republic of China;

—concluded an initial strategic arms limitation treaty with the Soviet Union; and

—provided diplomatic leadership toward a Middle East peace settlement.

Building sound foundations for a durable peace requires patient and skillful diplomacy. To be effective, statesmanship must be backed by credible military strength. The 1975 budget provides for the defense forces essential to protect our national security and to maintain the credibility and effectiveness of our diplomatic efforts to preserve world peace.

Increases in spending for military functions are necessary for both 1974 and 1975. Outlays of $85.8 billion are proposed for 1975, compared to $79.5 billion for 1974. These figures include the outlay impacts of proposed supplemental appropriations. These increases are required to improve the readiness of our armed forces, to build up levels of essential equipment and supplies, and to meet today's higher costs of maintaining force levels. They would also provide for a vigorous research and development effort that would enable us to produce new weapon systems if they are needed to maintain the strategic balance.

Because of the urgency I attach to a strong defense effort, I am recommending supplemental appropriations for 1974. An increase of $2.8 billion in budget authority is proposed to improve combat readiness and modernize forces, to augment munitions stock levels in accordance with lessons learned in the Middle East war, and to meet higher fuel costs.

The increases proposed for defense should be viewed in the context of the substantial—but prudent—reduction in our defense forces that has taken place since I took office. This reduction has resulted primarily from our success in bringing about a general easing of world tensions, in achieving mutual arms limitations, and in improving weapons systems and military efficiency. We have 36% fewer men under arms today than we had in 1968. In constant dollar terms, we will spend substantially less for defense in 1975 than we did in 1964, before the Vietnam buildup began.

The dollar costs of defense manpower are much higher with an all-volunteer armed force than they were under the draft. The Nation is now paying the full real costs of its defense in dollar terms; we no longer "tax" the young by commanding their services at less than their market value. I hope that we will never again need a draft.

Strengthening international economic cooperation is essential to our quest for peace. Expansion of peaceful trade relationships helps bind together the peoples of the world. We have already made considerable progress toward international monetary reform, progress which has helped bring about dramatic improvement in our balance of payments. The Trade Reform Act, now before the Congress, would authorize U.S. participation in a new round of international discussions to reduce trade barriers. Failure to enact this measure in a responsible form could result in a wave of trade protectionism that would undermine the economic well-being of all nations. I urge the Congress to approve it.

This budget provides for the continuation of our foreign assistance programs to strengthen the economies of developing nations, to provide humanitarian assistance and disaster relief, and to help friendly nations provide for their own defense.

MEETING THE NATION'S NEEDS FOR ENERGY AND BASIC RESOURCES

Until recent years, this country was largely self-sufficient in energy production. The rapidly growing demands of our households and industries for more and more energy, however, have now outstripped available low-cost domestic supplies. During the past few years we have become dangerously dependent on imported petroleum, which until recently was low in price. Development of relatively high-cost domestic sources has lagged.

Three years ago, in the first energy message delivered to the Congress by any President, I warned that the long era of abundant low-cost supplies of energy was drawing to a close. I proposed an expanded program to produce greater supplies of clean energy. Last April, in my second energy message, I warned that if existing trends continued unchecked, the Nation would face a serious energy problem; I proposed legislative action to meet this challenge. Since then, I have repeated my previous warnings and proposed urgent measures to restore our capability for energy self-sufficiency. The interruption of oil exports by Arab countries following the Middle East war last October has aggravated the energy problem and underscored sharply the need for this country to regain its ability to be self-sufficient in energy. I have taken all responsible actions I can within my existing authority to meet this challenge.

The 1975 budget reflects a comprehensive national energy policy to deal with current shortages and provides funds to initiate the Federal portion of Project Independence, an accelerated private and governmental effort to reestablish our capability for self-sufficiency in energy by 1980. I anticipate that the research and development component of this program will require about $10 billion in Government funds during its first 5 years; greater amounts may be needed thereafter. These funds will complement an even larger research and development investment in the private sector, which I will continue to encourage.

Higher prices will be necessary to stimulate development of adequate supplies of fuel through the mechanism of the free market. To assure that this will not result in excess profits for oil producers, I have proposed an emergency windfall profits tax on these producers.

Other elements of my comprehensive national energy policy include:

—reorganization of Federal administrative machinery to deal more effectively with short- and long-term energy needs;

—stringent energy conservation measures and mandatory allocation of petroleum products as long as shortages persist;

—mandatory reporting of oil production, inventories, reserves, and costs;

—modernization of regulations for railroads in order to permit energy savings and other economies;

—policies to accelerate development of domestic oil and gas reserves, including removal of ceilings on wellhead prices for new natural gas, production from the Elk Hills, Calif., Naval Petroleum Reserve, and development by private industry of western oil shale and of off-shore oil and gas deposits;

—measures to permit increased use of our vast coal reserves, including environmental safeguards for surface mining, conversion of oil-fired electric powerplants to coal, improvement of mining techniques, and accelerated efforts to develop technology for coal gasification, coal liquefaction, advanced combustion systems, and pollution control;

—development of fast breeder nuclear reactors, which will greatly increase the amount of energy recoverable from our nuclear fuel resources;

—more timely approval of sites for energy facilities and accelerated construction of nuclear powerplants; and

—increased research on advanced energy sources, including fusion power, and geothermal and solar energy.

The budget provides for $1.5 billion in outlays for direct energy research and development programs in 1975, compared to $942 million in 1974. An additional $128 million in outlays is provided in 1975 for complementary basic research and for environmental and health effects research. I will submit additional details on this accelerated effort to the Congress shortly.

The Federal Government alone cannot overcome the energy crisis. Project Independence will require a maximum effort by private industry as well. The measures proposed in this budget provide the essential governmental leadership to get this joint public and private program underway. In addition, every American household and every American business must economize on energy usage if we are to share temporary shortages equitably, as we must, and reestablish our energy independence in the long run.

The energy crisis has brought to the fore the need for a realistic balancing of the demands of economic growth and the demands of environmental protection. Shortages of "clean" fuels will mean that some temporary variances from air quality plans will be necessary to meet high priority energy needs. The progress we have made in pollution control in recent years, however, along with reductions in energy consumption, should insure that overall air quality will continue to improve.

The adverse impact of energy shortages on the economy could be aggravated by shortages of other raw materials. A comprehensive study on supplies of metal ores and other basic resources and our needs for them is now underway. This study will help insure that our policies properly anticipate potential problems.

We must also do everything we can to avoid a shortage of agricultural commodities such as we experienced last year. For many years this country enjoyed abundant agricultural production. This abundance not only met domestic needs, but aided greatly in alleviating hunger and malnutrition abroad. In 1972, however, adverse conditions throughout much of the world created widespread agricultural shortages. Food costs began to spiral, both here and abroad.

My Administration made a number of important program changes in 1973 to bring more farm land into production and to increase farm output. These steps, combined with favorable weather conditions, made 1973 a record crop year; farm income reached an all-time high level. Agricultural income now depends more upon the private market, and less upon the Government, than has been the case for over 3 decades. In 1973, direct Government payments to farmers experienced their largest dollar decline in history.

HELPING PEOPLE
THROUGH STATE AND LOCAL GOVERNMENTS

Ours is a *federal* system of government. Our Constitution, now nearly two centuries old, provides for a logical division of responsibilities among:

—a strong national government, concerned with essential national needs;

—State and local governments close to, and responsive to, the needs of individuals and local communities; and

—private citizens endowed with civil liberties that are secure from governmental encroachment.

During the first century and a half of our national experience, State and local governments were able to meet community and State needs from their own revenue sources. They were financially independent of the Federal Government. During the past 40 years, however, the needs of State and local governments have outstripped their resources. The Federal Government has therefore come to play a larger and larger role in financing their day-to-day operations. In the 4 years between 1969 and 1973, Federal grants to States and localities doubled. In 1973 this financial aid, disbursed through literally hundreds of separate programs, provided more than 20% of total State and local revenues.

Unfortunately, these Federal programs have all too often been accompanied by regulations and restrictions which have stifled innovation and initiative on the part of State and local officials, severely limiting the ability of those officials most familiar with problems at the local level to respond to local needs.

In response to this problem I have applied a philosophy of government that has come to be known as the New Federalism. It calls for each level of government to focus its attention on the functions most appropriate to that level. By strengthening the resources and responsibilities of State and local governments, it permits their policies and programs to reflect local needs more sensitively.

Broader sharing of Federal revenues with State and local governments is helping to make this philosophy a reality. Under the General Revenue

Sharing program, now in its second year, State and local governments receive over $6 billion a year for use in meeting State and local needs as they see them.

This Administration has also sought to substitute broad-based formula grants for narrow categorical grant programs, giving State and local governments significant discretion as to how funds are used and insuring that Federal aid is more equitably distributed among recipients. These principles now apply to several major areas of Federal assistance.

The *Law Enforcement Assistance* program has demonstrated the feasibility of broad-based formula grants. Aid under this program is being increased from $28 million in 1969 to $747 million in 1975 and is helping to make the streets of America safer.

The *Comprehensive Employment and Training Act* which I signed in December extends these same grant principles to manpower programs. Under this Act, the Federal Government will no longer specify the types, methods, and proportions of various manpower services to be provided. Instead, State and local governments will be able to use the funds allocated to them to provide the mix of services which they decide best meets the needs of their areas. The budget provides for $2 billion in outlays for this program in 1975.

New authorities under the *Rural Development Act* are being implemented this year in a manner which is supportive of State and local development plans and priorities.

I urge congressional action to achieve similar reform in additional areas this year:

The principles embodied in the *Education Grants Consolidation and Reform* I proposed last year deserve priority attention. State and local education agencies should have greater freedom to direct Federal assistance toward meeting what they view as high priority local needs. I will continue to work with the Congress, therefore, on legislation to consolidate and improve education grant programs.

The *Better Communities Act* would replace several ineffective grant and loan programs with a more streamlined approach to the problems of urban areas. This act would allow localities to decide for themselves how to allocate community development funds. The budget proposes funding for this program of $2.3 billion in 1975.

The *Unified Transportation Assistance Program* I am proposing this year would provide $2.3 billion in highway and mass transit funds, and permit States and localities to allocate these grant funds flexibly, in accordance with local conditions and priorities. Since transportation is a major consumer of energy and is strongly affected by the energy crisis, high priority must be given to enabling States and localities to make decisions on transportation systems based on their assessment of economy, energy conservation, environmental impact, and safety considerations.

I am proposing legislation for a new *Economic Adjustment Assistance* program. This legislation would permit States and communities to respond flexibly to problems of economic change and unemployment.

Another central feature of the New Federalism is strengthening the ability of State and local governments to perform effectively. The *Responsive Governments Act* would broaden Federal assistance available for improving State and local planning, decisionmaking, and management capabilities.

I urge the earliest possible enactment of all these measures.

In parallel with these legislative initiatives, my Administration is continuing its efforts to consolidate and streamline categorical grant programs, to simplify complex and burdensome procedures, and to remove unnecessary, inflexible program restrictions.

As part of this same effort, Federal programs are being decentralized along uniform regional lines, and the Federal Regional Councils are being strengthened to facilitate coordination of Federal with State and local activities at the operating level.

The budget accelerates our programs for aiding State and local governments in improving water quality. The Environmental Protection Agency has allotted $4 billion to the States for 1975 to make grants for municipal sewage treatment plants, a $1 billion increase over the allotment for 1974. Priorities for grants within these allotments will be determined by the States. A total of $6.9 billion was made available for this program in 1973 and 1974, more than twice the amount made available in the preceding 2 years.

STRENGTHENING THE ROLE OF THE INDIVIDUAL

Abraham Lincoln believed that:

> "The legitimate object of Government is to do for a community of people whatever they need to have done, but cannot do at all, or cannot do so well, for themselves, in their separate and individual capacities. *In all that the people can individually do as well for themselves, government ought not to interfere.*"

I share this belief. This philosophy underlies the efforts of my Administration to strengthen the role of the individual in American society. It is a cornerstone of the New Federalism.

I believe that government policy should seek to maintain an economic environment in which all who are able to work can find employment and adequate earnings. For those unable to support themselves, government should help to provide the means necessary to meet personal and family needs, while preserving individual dignity and self-respect.

My Administration has consistently endeavored to strengthen the role of the individual in American society and to ensure that all Americans enjoy equality of opportunity in education, in employment, in business, and in housing. We have consistently worked to improve assistance for the retired, the disabled, and the unemployed.

Reflecting these concerns, Federal human resource programs have grown dramatically. Between 1969 and 1975, outlays for these programs will have increased by 139%, while outlays for all other programs will have risen only 26%.

The national health insurance plan I am proposing represents another major step toward improving the lives of individual Americans. My proposal calls for basic reform in the financing of medical care. It would bring comprehensive insurance protection against medical expenses within reach of all Americans, including millions of people who cannot now obtain adequate insurance coverage. Costs of coverage for low-income families would be federally supported, with payments scaled according to family income.

It will take several years for this reform to become fully operational. In the interim, the 1975 budget provides $26.3 billion for existing health programs. Under this budget, the momentum of cancer, heart, and other research initiatives would be sustained, and total funding for biomedical research would exceed $2 billion in 1975, almost double the 1969 level. To support continued reform of our medical care system, the budget proposes a total of $125 million in 1974 and 1975 to demonstrate health maintenance organization concepts throughout the Nation. I am also proposing a Health Resources Planning Act to enhance State and regional capabilities and responsibilities for planning and regulating health services.

The rapid growth of human resource programs in recent years has brought about many improvements in the well-being of the American people. Higher social security benefits and extension of the Medicare program, for example, have increased the economic security of the elderly and the disabled. Cash benefits under social security programs will rise from $26.2 billion in 1969 to $62.9 billion in 1975. They now reach 29 million beneficiaries. Five social security benefit increases have been enacted since 1969. Taken together, these increases total nearly 70%, far exceeding the increases in the cost of living, and in average wages, over this period. I continue to urge enactment of legislation to reform private pension plans, legislation which would further strengthen the economic security of millions of Americans in their retirement years.

The Supplemental Security Income program began operation on January 1, 1974, replacing the various State public assistance programs for the aged, the blind, and the disabled with a more uniform and equitable national system. This broad reform provides higher benefits for these disadvantaged groups. In addition, Federal assumption of responsibility for these programs will provide substantial fiscal relief to State and local governments.

Also during the past month, food stamp benefits have been increased by over 20%, and the program has been extended to those parts of the country where it was not available before. Outlays for food stamps will be $3.9 billion in 1975, 78% higher than the 1973 level.

I propose further measures to improve the income security of Americans, including:

—reform of pensions for veterans and their dependents, with provisions for automatic cost-of-living adjustments in benefits, and better matching of pensions to family need;

—an increase in education benefits for veterans to help meet cost increases since these benefits were last raised;

—automatic cost-of-living increases for the aged, blind, and disabled beneficiaries of the Supplemental Security Income program;

—transfer of food stamps and related nutrition programs to the Department of Health, Education, and Welfare, to improve coordination of income maintenance programs; and

—continued priority efforts to develop a practical program of direct cash assistance for housing.

One of the major unfinished pieces of business of my Administration is the replacement of the current welfare system with a new system that *works*. Figures collected over the past year are grim testimony to the fact that our current welfare system is a mess; these figures show that fully 40% of the payments made are incorrect. I intend to make new proposals to solve this continuing problem.

As we begin this effort, I hope that the debate can focus on the substance of the issues, not on superficial labels. I believe that the majority of the American people agree on the principles that should guide Federal income assistance:

—the system should provide strong work incentives for those able to help themselves;

—income assistance should be provided in cash, rather than in kind, so that families can make their own spending decisions;

—the system should be as simple as possible, replacing the chaotic rules and overlapping programs that we have now;

—the levels of support provided should reflect the compassionate spirit of the American people toward those who cannot provide for themselves; and

—Federal aid should be provided on an equitable basis nationwide. I believe that the Administration and the Congress, working together, can *and must* find a solution that accords with these principles.

IMPROVING MANAGEMENT IN THE FEDERAL GOVERNMENT

The recommendations contained in this budget are part of a broad effort by my Administration, working with the Congress and with State and local officials, to improve public services at all levels. The New Federalism is a crucial element of this broad endeavor. A second, complementary element consists of improving the efficiency and effectiveness of Federal programs in carrying out Federal responsibilities.

Concern for meeting problems must extend beyond the well-intended commitment of public funds. What really matters are the tangible results produced through the effective use of these funds—results measured in terms of better lives for all Americans.

Since I assumed office as President, I have encouraged extensive efforts to streamline and revitalize the organization and management of the Federal Government. These efforts are helping to ensure that the taxpayers get their money's worth from the Government.

To enable the Federal Government to meet emerging challenges more effectively, several new organizations have been created during my Administration, and existing ones have been improved. Among these new offices are Action, the Environmental Protection Agency, the Council on Environmental Quality, the National Oceanic and Atmospheric Administration, the Domestic Council, the Office of Management and Budget, the Drug Enforcement Administration, the Consumer Product Safety Commission, the Council on International Economic Policy, and the Federal Energy Office.

In 1971 I proposed creation of four new departments, including a department to be responsible for energy and natural resources. I continue to urge congressional approval of this proposal as revised in legislation submitted last year. In addition, I ask the Congress to join me in renewing consideration of other departmental reorganization legislation that will permit more effective management of the Government.

During the past 25 years, Presidents have been able to make many improvements in Government organization under Presidential Reorganization Plan Authority. This legislation has now expired. I urge the Congress to restore this authority as soon as possible in order to facilitate continued modernization of our governmental structure.

Good organization is only a first step toward improving governmental performance. Government can be effective only if the public service can develop and retain capable leadership. In response to this need, this Administration has placed high priority on the identification and development of the most able career managers. We intend to intensify this effort.

Increasing the effectiveness of individual programs is another essential step in improving overall governmental performance. During the past year I have launched an intensive effort to strengthen the management of major Federal activities. The emphasis in this management initiative is not on producing a great display of activity, nor on merely rearranging work processes; the emphasis is on producing significant *results*. To help keep a constant focus on program results, I have asked each major department and agency to work with me in developing a set of specific objectives to be achieved during fiscal year 1974. As we approach 1975, we will identify further objectives. Currently, we are working toward more than 200 such objectives, ranging from international monetary reform to improvement of opportunities for minorities and women.

These objectives will not simply be identified and then filed away and forgotten. Specific results are to be achieved by specific deadlines. These commitments will be reviewed continually and will guide day-to-day operations until the objectives are met.

Congressional procedures, too, are in need of reform—particularly those that deal with the budget. In my last three budget messages I encouraged the Congress to reform its procedures for considering the budget. I noted that the Congress faced a fundamental problem because it lacks a system for relating each individual spending decision—whether or not it is part of the appropriation process—to overall budget totals. The need for a more systematic congressional process was once again illustrated during the session just concluded. Congressional actions, taken together, increased spending totals over my proposals by $3.8 billion in 1974 and by $8.2 billion in 1975.

The Congress is currently moving toward a new budgetary system. I commend this action and urge that the final procedures worked out by the Congress recognize the necessary and proper role of the President and his responsibility for efficient administration of the executive branch. I am particularly concerned about provisions which would subject some of the most routine financial actions of the executive branch to veto by either house of the Congress.

CONCLUSION

The proposals set forth in this budget are constructive and forward-looking. They meet the Federal Government's responsibility to provide vigorous national leadership toward the solution of major national problems. They do so within the bounds of fiscal prudence.

But the Federal Government cannot do everything. It should not be expected to. Nor can money alone solve all our problems. Recognizing these limitations, my Administration has made an intensive effort to identify and *do well* those things which the Federal Government should do. By the same token, this budget, like my previous ones, stresses the revitalization of individual initiative and of State and local capabilities. It represents an important further step in my efforts to restore a proper balance of individual and governmental power in America.

FEBRUARY 4, 1974   RICHARD NIXON

WORLD ECONOMIC REPORT

February 7, 1974

The Nixon administration issued a warning Feb. 7 on the dangers of individual countries attempting to better their economic condition—at the expense of other nations—in the face of food and petroleum shortages. In a message accompanying the second Annual Report of the Council on International Economic Policy, President Nixon stressed the necessity of interdependence among nations in coping with food shortages and the oil crisis. "It is particularly important," he said, "that we move forward in a multinational attempt to reduce trade barriers so that individual nations are not tempted to 'go it alone' in seeking solutions." The Council of International Economic Policy echoed Nixon's expressed desires for cooperation in trade to reduce the impact of shortages: "A number of observers believed that current international economic negotiations have been obviated by more pressing food and petroleum problems, but in fact the need for cooperative approaches has increased. No country can take major unilateral actions without risking retaliation and turmoil in world economic relations." The administration's warnings on the outcome of unilateral economic expediency took on special significance in light of French and British agreements with Saudi Arabia to safeguard imported oil supplies. Later, on March 4, Common Market countries approached Arab states with a proposal for special cooperation, unilateral action seemed aimed at ensuring continuing oil supplies. (See p. 185.)

The international economic report stated that monopolistic price fixing and contrived shortages, such as those apparent in the oil situation, were unlikely to recur. This prediction was based on the belief that other nations and groups controlling vital resources were not in a position to risk unemployment, substantial reduction of accumulated assets, curtailment

*of economic growth and changes in consumer demands that could per-
manently alter the market for the resource. Instead, the report emphasized
that the goal of ensuring adequate raw material supplies—including food
and oil—could best be attained by international economic cooperation.*

*On the impact of the oil price increases and shortages, the administration
admitted that there would be a "significant short-term impact on both the
domestic economy of all nations and on international economic
relationships." However, because of the "unprecedented" nature of the oil
situation, the long-term outlook remained "uncertain." Among the
ramifications of the oil crisis for domestic economies, the administration
cited reduced consumer purchasing power, reduction of demand for
petroleum-based products, deferral of some business investment and consumer purchases, somewhat higher unemployment, a continuing high rate
of inflation, and reduction of economic growth. But because the oil-derived
revenue of oil producing nations was expected to rise at a greater rate than
their demand for foreign goods and services, large surpluses of funds were
predicted. If these revenues were invested or deposited in industrialized
nations—as appeared likely—they would tend to drive down interest rates
and thereby stimulate new investments worldwide.*

*In encouraging greater cooperation in trade, the administration looked to
Congress to cooperate in expanding U.S. trading in a more open and
equitable world economic system. It criticized Congress's attempt to tie
reduced tariff priviledges for the Soviet Union to that country's emigration
policies. The report stated that the goal of detente would be aided by "the
elimination of U.S. provisions that discriminate against communist
countries."*

*Excerpts from the International Economic Report of the
President, submitted to Congress Feb. 7:*

I. Progress Toward Achieving the Nation's
International Economic Goals

US INTERNATIONAL ECONOMIC POLICIES

1973 was a year in which significant progress was made toward the
Nation's most critical international economic goals, but it also was a year
when man's ability to cooperate was tested by newly emerging problems....

At the same time, we have seen the appearance of serious and unprecedented problems that will test the effectiveness and resilience of existing economic relationships among nations. New resource stringen-
cies—some real, some artificial—are having serious and complex effects
which no nation alone can resolve. The Arab petroleum producers' selective
embargo and enormous increases in petroleum prices have forced all oil-
importing nations to reevaluate their domestic and international economic

policies. Large price increases in basic commodities were transmitted to all nations and as a consequence world inflation has reached levels well above any that have occurred for decades. To meet these and other challenges—which pose problems as severe for the poor nations as for the rich—the United States has called for broad international cooperation in devising innovative solutions....

US Policies and the Changing World Economy

The progress achieved under the institutions and modes of cooperation established in the immediate post-World War II period has brought fundamental changes in the economic relationships among nations.... Although the United States remains preeminent, other countries have narrowed the economic gap. As we expected—and encouraged—significant economic progress has occurred in Western Europe, and Japan has emerged as a major center of economic power. Many less developed countries have made impressive economic strides after centuries of near stagnation. And more recently, we have seen an easing of East-West tensions coupled with a dramatic increase in commerce between countries in both areas.

These changes are natural and needed elements of world economic progress. But the progress achieved has also created new problems. The flow of goods, services, and capital among nations has reached a magnitude such that few nations, if any, can effectively isolate themselves from economic events elsewhere. Each nation's prosperity is increasingly dependent on that of other nations, with a growing share of each country's output being exported. The growing dependence on imported goods is also having far-reaching repercussions, especially when those goods are critical raw materials in short supply....

Reconciling Domestic and International Policy Goals

Governments must direct the bulk of their efforts at maximizing the social and economic well-being of their own citizens—creating new jobs, upgrading workers whose jobs have become obsolete, securing needed natural resources, and maintaining stable prices. But in meeting these responsibilities, governments sometimes take actions which adversely affect the economies of other countries. To minimize these destructive frictions, and to contribute to efforts to construct a lasting world peace, each country's need for freedom to deal with its domestic problems must be balanced with the need to achieve international economic cooperation.... A number of observers believe that current international economic negotiations have been obviated by more pressing food and petroleum problems, but in fact the need for cooperative approaches has increased. No country can take major unilateral actions without risking retaliation and turmoil in world economic relations....

Creating a Freer and More Equitable World Trading System

The rapid expansion of international commerce and the resulting growth in prosperity during the past quarter of a century reflect in part the ability of nations to abide by common rules and to reduce barriers inhibiting foreign trade. The principles governing trade relations between countries accounting for the bulk of world trade are contained in the General Agreement on Tariffs and Trade (GATT), which went into effect in 1948.... Further progress will require that all nations reach agreements:

- Reducing, harmonizing or eliminating tariffs on a broad scale.

- Reducing nontariff barriers (NTBs). In some cases, these trade-distorting measures have reduced or nullified the benefits of tariff cuts. They are particularly hard to deal with because many are difficult to identify and quantify. National policies and protective measures distorting agricultural trade and production, such as the Common Agricultural Policy of the European Community (EC), have proven particularly intractable at the negotiating table. Other NTBs range from import quotas to safety standards.

- Improving the guidelines of the international trading system and expanding their scope to include new problem areas and to provide greater flexibility. Some trade barriers have remained largely outside the rules, such as export restraints, product standards and government procurement practices. Other rules are too rigid in not permitting countries to utilize trade policy effectively for the correction of international payments imbalances or for the easing of inflationary pressures.

- Introducing an improved international "safeguard" system relating to measures taken to avoid disruption of national markets through sudden increases in competition from imports.

- Strengthening enforcement of international codes. Improved incentives and penalties are needed to ensure that the GATT codes of conduct are adhered to by all.

- Taking account of the special needs of less developed countries (LDCs).

- Providing for equitable access to supplies at reasonable prices....

Trade Legislation

...The Trade Reform Act of 1973 passed by the House of Representatives (HR 10710) on 11 December 1973 is in most respects consistent with the purposes for which the original Administration proposals were designed. In brief, it:

- provides the US negotiators the authorities needed to achieve more open access to markets and supplies, with a strong and proper emphasis on both equity and reciprocity;

- eases access to escape clause relief and adjustment assistance for American industries, workers and individual firms suffering injury or threat of injury from growing import competition;

- broadens the range of actions the United States can take in responding to unfair international trade practices;

• introduces several new authorities that can be used to manage domestic and international economic policies more effectively;

• allows the United States to fulfill its international pledge to establish a plan of generalized tariff preferences for the less developed countries of the world.

There are a few areas, however, where it is of very great importance that substantial improvements be made in the bill adopted by the House. The first of these concerns the conditions attached to the President's authority for expanding normal commercial relationships with nonmarket economy countries, including the USSR. It is important that there be a meaningful and constructive dialogue with the Senate, during its consideration of the trade bill, concerning the ways the vital interests of this country are served by a policy of detente and the important role of peaceful economic contacts.

The elimination of US provisions that discriminate against communist countries not only makes economic sense but is also important to the continued development of normal peaceful relationships with these countries. The denial of credits and nondiscriminatory tariff treatment, although aimed primarily at the USSR's emigration policies, would also hinder the US trade that has been developed with several other communist countries and deprive us of the jobs and income that this trade is already creating. Export-Import Bank credits help US exporters meet foreign competition for sales to communist countries that otherwise would be made by other developed countries which provide similar financing. Non-discriminatory tariff treatment will allow communist countries to increase their dollar earnings and therefore to make more purchases here.

Failure to accord the communist countries the same commercial treatment we give virtually all other trading nations would seriously undermine our efforts to involve these countries more fully in the world community. Furthermore, Soviet agreement to settle its outstanding Lend-Lease obligations is dependent on US ceasing to discriminate against imports from the USSR. Greater interchange and cooperation in our economic relations promise similar expansion of relations in other areas of importance. Such developments are very much in our interest because they give the communist countries a vested interest in the continued peace and prosperity of the world.

A second area of concern is the adoption by the House of a very restrictive approach to certain countervailing duty provisions. This approach could force actions contrary to US interests before international negotiations could be undertaken to alter other countries' subsidy practices.

EC and GATT Article XXIV:6

The United States warmly welcomed the enlargement of the EC [European Community] to include the United Kingdom, Denmark, and Ireland.

We took this position with the full knowledge that the enlargement of the Community would disadvantage some US exports....

While adoption of the Common External Tariff will result in the reduction of duties on some products exported to the new member states, the EC has not yet offered the United States adequate compensating tariff reductions to offset their proposed withdrawals of concessions and duty increases. We are continuing to explore with the EC various possible ways of reaching an equitable settlement....

Two New Problems: Food and Petroleum

The world economy faced two severe shocks in 1973—in agricultural products and in petroleum. Since both of these commodities are basic to the well-being and economic strength of every country, shortages and dramatic price increases have had serious political ramifications. And there is an important link between petroleum and food: oil provides the fuel for tractors and for the transport of foodstuffs; it is also a basic input to fertilizer products.

Today's agricultural problems stem from adverse natural conditions and the worldwide economic boom.... In contrast, the petroleum crisis was wrought by man. By joint action in the OPEC, the major oil exporters have substantially raised prices unilaterally, and have thus been able to reap large monopoly profits. In many cases these revenues far exceed the amount of money the producers can effectively spend in the short run, leading to the enormous accumulation of foreign exchange. Although higher prices alone had already begun to force consuming nations to reevaluate their energy policies, the October oil production cutback imposed by the Arab governments for political reasons has had much deeper repercussions. The realization that a few countries, by altering their crude oil production levels can have such a severe impact on the world economy has led to serious reappraisals of most countries' energy policies. The further drastic price increase announced in December has accelerated these reappraisals....

Ensuring Adequate Raw Material Supplies

...As the industrial nations have increasingly competed for raw material supplies, the producing nations have found that they can utilize their resources to achieve economic and sometimes political gains. Some producers have sought higher prices for their products, some have demanded increased or full domestic ownership of production facilities, and some have pressed for having the raw product processed further at home rather than abroad.

Restriction of commodity supply has, however, many repercussions. It is an oversimplification to view the producing nations as being in a position to determine market conditions. In many cases they will not be able to take advantage of the unusual short-run circumstances that permitted the oil producers' actions in 1973. In these nations, crude oil production cutbacks do not significantly increase unemployment. Further, given their high reserve asset levels, the oil-producing countries could easily accept a reduction in sales volume—especially at the new higher prices. Countries controlling other resources, however, cannot count on such an advantageous combination of circumstances: demand for any given resource can, at any time, be increasing much more slowly, or even dropping in the course of a world economic slowdown, putting the producing countries in a poor bargaining position and even leading to severe competition among producers for markets. Many countries do not have enough foreign reserve assets to permit them to curtail production and still maintain economic growth. Furthermore, many extractive industries employ significant numbers of workers, and a production cutback could have serious domestic political consequences.

In the longer run, major restrictions imposed by producer nations on the supply of any commodity—or large price increases—will tend to prove counter-productive for the producers. Consumers will undoubtedly find it in their best interest, for both economic and national security reasons, to further exploit their own domestic sources of raw materials, develop synthetics or find substitute products....

SOME IMPLICATIONS OF THE ENERGY CRISIS FOR THE UNITED STATES AND THE WORLD ECONOMY

... In 1973 oil producers took advantage of tight supply and heavy competition for resources through two major actions. First, in a move directly related to the Arab-Israeli war, the Arab oil nations embargoed oil to the United States and the Netherlands, and reduced supply to other customers, highlighting the significance of the Arab countries in the world supply picture. Second, the Organization of Petroleum Exporting Countries (OPEC) took advantage of their monopoly position and crude oil prices nearly quadrupled during the past year.

Unless cooperative actions can be taken to moderate the price increases and to adjust to the dislocations caused by them, both oil consumer and producer nations may find themselves in a worsening economic position....

Short-term Constraints on Expanding Oil Supply

There is little that major industrial nations can do immediately to reduce their dependence on imported oil. In the United States, domestic non-oil energy sources such as coal, nuclear power, and natural gas will in time significantly increase their current level of production. Alaskan production and new discoveries in off-shore areas will not increase domestic crude oil production substantially in the next year or two, but output is increasing in traditional production areas, particularly from stripper wells.

While imports supply about one-third of our oil needs, Western Europe and Japan rely on imports for virtually 100% of their supply....

At present, the Middle East has proved oil reserves capable of meeting the growing import needs of the United States, Europe, and Japan.... The Middle Eastern countries, however, may not expand production sufficiently to meet the short-run needs of the importing nations. Kuwait, over a year before the October 1973 Middle East war, had decided to limit production to 3 million barrels per day. Some Arab states argued that their oil assets were increasing in value more rapidly in the ground than they would as currency in the bank. Another factor which may prevent Middle East production from increasing to meet the world's oil needs is the use of oil as a political tool.

US Steps To Increase and Diversify Domestic Energy Sources

There is no reason why the United States cannot become independent in energy. As President Nixon has declared, the technical and financial effort required will be comparable to that expended on the Apollo program which put a man on the moon. Nevertheless, it is already clear what steps will be necessary.

1. Construction in the next several years of the long-delayed Alaska pipeline, which offers the means of tapping our large Alaskan reserves and compensating for production declines.

2. Decontrol of prices on new suppliers of natural gas, to encourage the exploration which by 1980 should result in greatly expanded domestic production.

3. A program to accelerate leasing of lands on the outer continental shelf for exploration and development of oil and gas reserves.

4. A crash program of research and development in economical techniques of coal gasification and liquefaction and development of shale oil designed to make the vast reserves of these energy resources available as fast as possible.

5. The passage of a national powerplant siting bill to provide simplified procedures for the siting and approving of electric energy facilities. The speeding up of the licensing and construction of nuclear powerplants in order to reduce the time required to bring them on-line from ten to six years.

6. An expedited program of research and development to speed the realization of the fast breeder reactor and other nuclear plants.

7. Stepped-up Federal energy research and development programs for non-depletable power sources (for the 1990s) such as geothermal, solar, and fusion.

8. A massive conservation effort designed to reduce in the short term unnecessary consumption of energy for electrical utilities, transportation, home heating, industrial and commercial usage, etc.

Expanding and Diversifying Our Foreign Energy Sources

Although it will remain the goal of the United States to achieve the capability for national self-sufficiency in energy by 1980, self-sufficiency does not mean autarky or isolation.... In other words, in addition to developing domestic resources, we must diversify our international sources of energy to the greatest extent possible so that no one country or likely combination of countries will be able to influence our policies by manipulating the supply or price of our energy. Nor is this the only reason for the United States to maintain an outward-looking energy posture. US companies can provide important international services in exploration, development, and marketing of new sources of energy. It is also in our interest to see new foreign sources of energy developed in order to have adequate supplies of energy available for international economic growth.

The Rise of Oil Prices: Implications for the World Economy

Export prices have now been divorced from factors such as costs and return to capital and are largely determined by the producer governments. Beginning in February 1971 with the Tehran Pact, effective control over oil prices has rested increasingly with producer countries working through the Organization of Petroleum Exporting Countries (OPEC). Posted prices rose approximately 70% between October 1970 and October 1973. In October 1973, the Persian Gulf producers announced unilaterally that posted prices would rise another 70% immediately. Libya joined them in announcing larger price increases. Nigeria, Venezuela, and Canada—the three largest suppliers to the United States—also declared substantial increases in their export prices—in some cases beyond those imposed for oil from the Persian Gulf. Then in December, the Shah of Iran announced on behalf of the Persian Gulf members of OPEC that the posted prices announced in October would be doubled beginning 1 January 1974....

Price and Balance of Payments Impacts

The drastic increases in oil prices will have a significant short-term impact on both the domestic economies of all nations and on international economic relationships. However, because a price change of this magnitude for a basic industrial product has no modern precedent, the extent of the impact is uncertain.

Impact on Domestic Economies

...The higher oil prices will accentuate [a worldwide economic] slowdown by reducing consumer purchasing power, slowing demand for petroleum-based products, and causing deferral of some business investment as well as consumer purchases. The result will be a reduction in economic growth, somewhat higher unemployment than expected and, of course, a continuing high rate of inflation with increased oil costs adding to other price pressures.

The reduction of growth, however, should be only temporary. The duration of the expected slowdown will depend largely on the ability of each economy to adjust to the new price structure.... Further, all nations must cooperate to avoid a competitive trade war, which could lead to a serious recession: some nations might be tempted to try to stimulate employment during this difficult period by providing export incentives or imposing import barriers, and such "exporting of unemployment" could provoke retaliation by other countries.

Impact on the World Economy

The price increases will also affect balance-of-payments accounts and international financial markets. The consuming countries' oil import bill will

increase dramatically this year if current crude oil prices are maintained....
Exporting countries' revenues will increase in 1974 to nearly $100 billion or
three-and-a-half times the 1973 level....

Most producers will be able to spend only a small part of their increased
revenues on foreign goods and services.... In all, oil producing countries will
probably have extremely large surpluses to invest or deposit abroad....
While the international financial markets will be able to absorb these investment funds, their magnitude will probably depress interest rates.
Lower interest rates, should, in turn, stimulate new investments in productive facilities....

MEETING OF OIL-CONSUMING NATIONS

February 13, 1974

Four months after the start of the Arab states' embargo on oil shipments to the West, the major oil consuming nations took initial steps to ease the energy crisis through cooperative action. The North Atlantic nations and Japan wound up a three-day conference in Washington, Feb. 13, by agreeing to form an energy action group and setting forth guidelines for it to follow. Only France registered important exceptions to this procedure. To join in unified action, the French seemed to fear, would jeopardize the "favored-nation" status which so far had kept that country well supplied with oil.

In an effort to head off a stampede to unilateral, competitive oil deals, the United States had taken the lead in organizing the February conference. On Jan. 9, France had concluded the first phase of a formal oil agreement with Saudi Arabia, and Britain also was reported to be negotiating with the Arabs. French opposition to joint U.S.-European action was voiced by Foreign Minister Michel Joubert, who attended the Washington talks, but who accused the United States of exploiting the energy crisis to its own advantage.

The fragile U.S.-European initiative of February faltered when, on March 4, the European Economic Community (EEC) independently offered a major assistance program to 20 Arab nations (see p. 185). The stage had been set for U.S.-E.E.C. rivalry on energy policy at a December 1973 E.E.C. conference in Copenhagen which endorsed the principle of cooperative action by its nine member nations. During the same months, the United States also was proposing to act jointly with Europe and Japan on energy *problems. In a Dec. 12 speech Secretary of State Henry A. Kissinger warned that insufficiency of supply was a more serious problem than the existing boycott. Without stabilized prices and new sources of supply, he predicted, there would be "disaster for everyone." By that he apparently meant a world-wide depression equally devastating to both oil producers and oil consumers. Kissinger's views appeared again when the Washington conference instructed its action group to set up a meeting of "consumer and producer countries...at the earliest possible opportunity."*

A multilateral energy meeting did take place on April 9, but it was at a special session of the General Assembly at the United Nations, and was called by Algeria, not by the Energy Coordination Group (ECG) established by the February conference. (See p. 255). In the intervening months, the oil embargo had been lifted (on March 18) and pressures on oil supplies had eased. (See p. 221). The ECG met—without French participation—in February, April and June to discuss government surveillance of international companies, multilateral reduction of energy consumption and plans to pool emergency supplies of consumer countries.

The prospect of unified action by major oil-consuming nations had triggered angry Arab comments. A Feb. 10 broadcast on Libyan radio called the Washington conference "an aggressive act against the oil-producing states, particularly the Arab states." Algerian President Houari Boumediene, speaking at the U.N. special session in April, said that "the idea behind the Washington Conference is more in the nature of preliminary confrontation than the reflection of a desire for international cooperation." Boumediene had been more blunt in February when he charged that the talks were "directed toward creation of an imperialist protectorate over energy resources."

> *Excerpts from the text of the Feb. 13, 1974, communique of the Washington Energy Conference. Italicized material represents sections rejected by France.*

International Monetary Fund
Text of Feb. 13 Communique of
Energy Conference

Summary Statement

1. Foreign Ministers of Belgium, Canada, Denmark, France, the Federal Republic of Germany, Ireland, Italy, Japan, Luxembourg, The Netherlands, Norway, the United Kingdom, the United States met in Washington from Feb. 11 to 13, 1974. The European Community was represented as such by the president of the council and the president of the commission. Finance ministers, ministers with responsibility for energy affairs, economic affairs and science and technology affairs also took part in the meeting. The secretary general of the OECD [Organization for Economic Cooperation and Development] also participated in the meeting.

The ministers examined the international energy situation and its implications and charted a course of action to meet this challenge which requires constructive and comprehensive solutions. To this end they agreed on specific steps to provide for effective international cooperation. The ministers affirmed that solutions to the world's energy problem should be sought in consultation with producer countries and other consumers.

Analysis of Situation

2. They noted that during the past three decades progress in improving productivity and standards of living was greatly facilitated by the ready availability of increasing supplies of energy at fairly stable prices. They recognized that the problem of meeting growing demand existed before the current situation and that the needs of the world economy for increased energy supplies require positive long-term solutions.

3. They concluded that the current energy situation results from an intensification of these underlying factors and from political developments.

4. They reviewed the problems created by the large rise in oil prices and agreed with the serious concern expressed by the International Monetary Fund's Committee of Twenty at its recent Rome meeting over the abrupt and significant changes in prospect for the world balance of payments structure.

5. They agreed that present petroleum prices presented the structure of world trade and finance with an unprecedented situation. They recognized that none of the consuming countries could hope to insulate itself from these developments, or expect to deal with the payments impact of oil prices by the adoption of monetary or trade measures alone. In their view, the present situation, if continued, could lead to a serious deterioration in income and employment, intensify inflationary pressures, and endanger the welfare of nations. They believed that financial measures by themselves will not be able to deal with the strains of the current situation.

6. They expressed their particular concern about the consequences of the situation for the developing countries and recognized the need for efforts by the entire international community to resolve this problem. At current oil prices the additional energy costs for developing countries will cause a serious setback to the prospect for economic development of these countries.

General Conclusions

7. They affirmed, that, in the pursuit of national policies, whether in the trade, monetary or energy fields, efforts should be made to harmonize the interests of each country on the one hand and the maintenance of the world economic system on the other. Concerted international cooperation between all the countries concerned including oil producing countries could

help to accelerate an improvement in the supply and demand situation, ameliorate the adverse economic consequences of the existing situation and lay the groundwork for a more equitable and stable international energy relationship.

8. They felt that these considerations taken as a whole made it essential that there should be a substantial increase of international cooperation in all fields. Each participant in the conference stated its firm intention to do its utmost to contribute to such an aim, in close cooperation both with the other consumer countries and with the producer countries.

9. *They concurred in the need for a comprehensive action program to deal with all facets of the world energy situation by cooperative measures. In so doing they will build on the work of the OECD. They recognized that they may wish to invite, as appropriate, other countries to join with them in these efforts. Such an action program of international cooperation would include, as appropriate, the sharing of means and efforts, while concerting national policies, in such areas as:*

• *The conservation of energy and restraint of demand.*

• *A system of allocating oil supplies in times of emergency and severe shortages.*

• *The acceleration of development of additional energy sources so as to diversify energy supplies.*

• *The acceleration of energy research and development programs through international cooperative efforts.*

10. With respect to monetary and economic questions, they decided to intensify their cooperation and to give impetus to the work being undertaken in the IMF, the World Bank and the OECD on the economic and monetary consequences of the current energy situations, in particular to deal with balance of payments disequilibria. They agreed that:

• *In dealing with the balance of payments impact of oil prices they stressed the importance of avoiding competitive depreciation and the escalation of restrictions on trade and payments or disruptive actions in external borrowing.*

• *While financial cooperation can only partially alleviate the problems which have recently arisen for the international economic system, they will intensify work on short-term financial measures and possible longer-year longer-term financial measures and possible longer-term mechanisms to reinforce existing official and market credit facilities.*

• *They will pursue domestic economic policies which will reduce as much as possible the difficulties resulting from the current energy cost levels.*

• They will make strenuous efforts to maintain and enlarge the flow of development aid bilaterally and through multilateral institutions, on the basis of international solidarity embracing all countries with appropriate resources.

11. Further, they have agreed to accelerate wherever practicable their own national programs of new energy sources and technology which will help the overall worldwide supply and demand situation.

12. They agreed to examine in detail the role of international oil companies.

13. They stressed the continued importance of maintaining and improving the natural environment as part of developing energy sources and agreed to make this an important goal of their activity.

14. They further agreed that there was need to develop a cooperative multilateral relationship with producing countries, and consuming countries that takes into account the long-term interests of all. They are ready to exchange technical information with these countries on the problem of stabilizing energy supplies with regard to quantity and prices.

15. They welcomed the initiatives in the U.N. to deal with the larger issues of energy and primary products at a worldwide level and in particular for a special session of the U.N. General Assembly.

Coordinating Group

16. *They agreed to establish a coordinating group headed by senior officials to direct and to coordinate the development of the actions referred to above. The coordinating group shall decide how best to organize its work. It should:*

● *Monitor and give focus to the tasks that might be addressed in existing organizations.*

● *Establish such ad hoc working groups as may be necessary to undertake tasks for which there are presently no suitable bodies.*

● *Direct preparations of a conference of consumer and producer countries which will be held at the earliest possible opportunity and which, if necessary, will be preceded by a fourth meeting of consumer countries.*

17. *They agreed that the preparations for such meetings should involve consultations with developing countries and other consumer and producer countries.*

EXPULSION OF SOLZHENITSYN
February 13, 1974

The Soviet government sent Nobel Prize author Alexander Solzhenitsyn into exile Feb. 13 and stripped him of his Soviet citizenship in an unusual effort to rid the country of one of its most outspoken social and political critics. Solzhenitsyn, who had waged an ever-increasing attack on Soviet repression of dissidents, thus became the most prominent Soviet citizen deported since Joseph Stalin expelled Leon Trotsky in 1929. The expulsion capped months of increasing confrontation between the internationally acclaimed author and Soviet officials, exacerbated by the December 1973 publication in Paris of The Gulag Archipelago, 1918-1956, *an account of the campaign of terror and mass killing during Stalin's regime.*

Relief mingled with outrage as news of the banishment spread around the world. Asylum was offered to the outcast by foreign government officials, including Secretary of State Henry A. Kissinger, who said Solzhenitsyn would be welcome to reside in the United States, although the author's plight must not be allowed to impede efforts toward detente. In the Soviet Union, dissidents expressed concern over the loss of a noted leader and voiced fears that the author's exile foreshadowed their own undoing.

For Solzhenitsyn, the final drama began the evening of Feb. 12 when seven Soviet police officers forced him from his wife's Moscow apartment where he lived periodically under a law that prevented him from staying in Moscow for more than three consecutive days. In rapid succession, the 55-year-old author and historian was, according to later accounts, taken to a Moscow prison, stripped of his clothing and belongings and charged with

129

treason, a crime punishable under Soviet law by ten years of hard labor or by death. But the day after his arrest, Solzhenitsyn learned that he had been declared a "non-person" and would be expelled from the country. Hours later, he was flown to Frankfurt, West Germany.

TASS, the Soviet press agency, issued a statement declaring that Solzhenitsyn had been deprived of his citizenship by a decree of the Presidium of the Supreme Soviet for "performing systematically actions that are incompatible with being a citizen of the U.S.S.R." The statement added that the author's family would be allowed to join him in exile and take with them his extensive library "when they deem it necessary," action which seemed intended to cool Western reactions to the expulsion.

With the deportation, Solzhenitsyn came full circle in a writing career that had initially won praise from the Kremlin. Former Soviet party chief Nikita Khrushchev, in his own attempt to discredit Stalin, had lauded Solzhenitsyn's first officially published novel, One Day in the Life of Ivan Denisovich, *an account of prison camp life based on Solzhenitsyn's 11 years in Stalinist camps. The author's later novels, however, met with official hostility and were banned, although they became best-sellers in the West. After Solzhenitsyn had become a leading member of the Soviet dissidents' "democratic movement," and had been awarded in 1970 the Nobel Prize for Literature, the difficulty of muting his criticism of Soviet domestic policies markedly increased. His international acclaim sheltered him from a three-year purge that left many other members of the dissident movement in asylums and prisons.*

Final Showdown With Soviet Authorities

With the publication of Gulag *in December 1973, the lines for a showdown were drawn. An official campaign was launched to denounce Solzhenitsyn and thereby defuse his attacks on Stalin's terrorist tactics. Solzhenitsyn met it head-on with even more pointed remarks. He announced that if he were arrested, he would have published abroad five sequels to* Gulag, *accounts purportedly detailing repressive tactics under Khrushchev and his successor, Leonid I. Brezhnev. Tension mounted in early February when Solzhenitsyn and his wife twice defied summonses to appear before authorities and it seemed that Soviet officials would have to take strong action to discipline and silence the outspoken author. Soviet sources said Feb. 13 that his refusal to comply with the summonses prompted official actions to "expedite" the banishment.*

In the past, trial and imprisonment on charges of anti-Soviet agitation had been the more common fate of dissidents. But such a trial of Solzhenitsyn following on recently voiced Western support for Russian dissidents (see Historic Documents 1973, p. 791-800), and coming at a time of ongoing negotiations between the Soviet Union and several Western nations in various fields, could have caused repercussions. Another Soviet tactic was revocation of citizenship while a critic was temporarily abroad, but it was for that very reason that Solzhenitsyn had declined to go abroad to receive the Nobel Prize. The chosen tactic, banishment, was a special solution, apparently without legal basis in the Soviet Union and therefore requiring a special Supreme Soviet decree.

Text of an essay by Alexander Solzhenitsyn, "Live Not By Lies," dated Feb. 12, 1974, the day Soviet police broke into Solzhenitsyn's wife's Moscow apartment and arrested him, and published Feb. 18, in the New York Times.

Live Not By Lies

At one time we dared not even to whisper. Now we write and read *samizdat*, and sometimes when we gather in the smoking room at the Science Institute we complain frankly to one another: What kind of tricks are they playing on us, and where are they dragging us? Gratuitous boasting of cosmic achievements while there is poverty and destruction at home. Propping up remote, uncivilized regimes. Fanning up civil war. And we recklessly fostered Mao Tse-tung at our expense—and it will be we who are sent to war against him, and will have to go. Is there any way out? And they put on trial anybody they want, and they put sane people in asylums—always they, and we are powerless.

Things have almost reached rock bottom. A universal spiritual death has already touched us all, and physical death will soon flare up and consume us both and our children—but as before we still smile in a cowardly way and mumble without tongues tied: But what can we do to stop it? We haven't the strength.

We have been so hopelessly dehumanized that for today's modest ration of food we are willing to abandon all our principles, our souls, and all the efforts of our predecessors and all the opportunities for our descendants—but just don't disturb our fragile existence. We lack staunchness, pride and enthusiasm. We don't even fear universal nuclear death, and we don't fear a third world war. We have already taken refuge in the crevices. We just fear acts of civil courage.

Fear to Step Alone

We fear only to lag behind the herd and to take a step alone—and suddenly find ourselves without white bread, without heating gas and without a Moscow registration.

We have been indoctrinated in political courses, and in just the same way was fostered the idea to live comfortably, and all will be well for the rest of our lives: You can't escape your environment and social conditions. Everyday life defines consciousness. What does it have to do with us? We can't do anything about it.

But we can—everything. But we lie to ourselves for assurance. And it is not they who are to blame for everything—we ourselves, only we. One can object; but actually you can think anything you like. Gags have been stuffed into our mouths. Nobody wants to listen to us, and nobody asks us. How can we force them to listen? It is impossible to change their minds.

It would be natural to vote them out of office—but there are no elections in our country. In the West people know about strikes and protest demonstrations—but we are too oppressed, and it is a horrible prospect for us: How can one suddenly renounce a job and take to the streets? Yet the other fatal paths probed during the past century by our bitter Russian history are, nevertheless, not for us, and truly we don't need them.

"Infamous Methods Breed Infamous Results"

Now that the axes have done their work, when everything which was sown has sprouted anew, we can see that the young and presumptuous people who thought they would make our country just and happy through terror, bloody rebellion and civil war were themselves misled. No thanks, fathers of education! Now we know that infamous methods breed infamous results. Let our hands be clean!

The circle—is it closed? And is there really no way out? And is there only one thing left for us to do, to wait without taking action? Maybe something will happen by itself? It will never happen as long as we daily acknowledge, extoll, and strengthen—and do not sever ourselves from—the most perceptible of its aspects: Lies.

When violence intrudes into peaceful life, its face glows with self-confidence, as if it were carrying a banner and shouting: "I am violence. Run away, make way for me—I will crush you. But violence quickly grows old. And it has lost confidence in itself, and in order to maintain a respectable face it summons falsehood as its ally—since violence can conceal itself with nothing except lies, and the lies can be maintained only by violence. And violence lays its ponderous paw not every day and not on every shoulder: It demands from us only obedience to lies and daily participation in lies—all loyalty lies in that.

Key: Non-participation in Lies

And the simplest and most accessible key to our self-neglected liberation lies right here: Personal nonparticipation in lies. Though lies conceal everything, though lies embrace everything we will be obstinate in this smallest of matters: Let them embrace everything, but not with any help from me.

This opens a breach in the imaginary encirclement caused by our inaction. It is the easiest thing to do for us, but the most devastating for the lies. Because when people renounce lies it simply cuts short their existence. Like an infection, they can exist only in a living organism.

We do not exhort ourselves. We have not sufficiently matured to march into the squares and shout the truth out loud or to express aloud what we think. It's not necessary.

It's dangerous. But let us refuse to say that which we do not think!

Well-Rooted Cowardice

This is our path, the easiest and most accessible one, which takes into account our inherent cowardice, already well-rooted. And it is much easier—it's dangerous even to say this—than the sort of civil disobedience which Gandhi advocated.

Our path is not to give conscious support to lies about anything whatsoever! And once we realize where lie the perimeters of falsehood—each sees them in his own way.

Our path is to walk away from this gangrenous boundary. If we did not paste together the dead bones and scales of ideology, if we did not sew together rotting rags, we would be astonished how quickly the lies would be rendered helpless and subside.

That which should be naked would then really appear naked before the whole world.

So in our timidity, let each of us make a choice: Whether consciously to remain a servant of falsehood—of course, it is not out of inclination, but to feed one's family, that one raises his children in the spirit of lies—or to shrug off the lies and become an honest man worthy of respect both by one's children and contemporaries.

Path to Liberation

And from that day onward he:

• Will not henceforth write, sign or print in any way a single phrase which in his opinion distorts the truth.

• Will utter such a phrase neither in private conversation nor in the presence of many people, neither on his own behalf nor at the prompting of someone else, neither in the role of agitator, teacher, educator, nor in a theatrical role.

• Will not depict, foster or broadcast a single idea which he can see is false or a distortion of the truth, whether it be in painting, sculpture, photography, technical science or music.

• Will not cite out of context, either orally or written, a single quotation so as to please someone, to feather his own nest, to achieve success in his work, if he does not share completely the idea which is quoted, or if it does not accurately reflect the matter at issue.

• Will not allow himself to be compelled to attend demonstrations or meetings if they are contrary to his desire or will, will neither take into hand nor raise into the air a poster or slogan which he does not completely accept.

• Will not raise his hand to vote for a proposal with which he does not sincerely sympathize, will vote neither openly nor secretly for a person whom he considers unworthy or of doubtful abilities.

133

• Will not allow himself to be dragged to a meeting where there can be expected a forced or distorted discussion of a question.

• Will immediately walk out of a meeting, session, lecture, performance or film showing if he hears a speaker tell lies, or purvey ideological nonsense or shameless propaganda.

• Will not subscribe to or buy a newspaper or magazine in which information is distorted and primary facts are concealed.

Of course, we have not listed all of the possible and necessary deviations from falsehood. But a person who purifies himself will easily distinguish other instances with his purified outlook.

No, it will not be the same for everybody at first. Some, at first, will lose their jobs. For young people who want to live with the truth, this will, in the beginning, complicate their young lives very much, because the required recitations are stuffed with lies, and it is necessary to make a choice.

Daily Challenge

But there are no loopholes for anybody who wants to be honest: On any given day, any one of us will be confronted with at least one of the above-mentioned choices even in the most secure of the technical sciences. Either truth or falsehood: Toward spiritual independence, or toward spiritual servitude.

And he who is not sufficiently courageous even to defend his soul—don't let him be proud of his "progressive" views, and don't let him boast that he is an academician or a people's artist, a merited figure, or a general—let him say to himself: I am in the herd, and a coward. It's all the same to me as long as I'm fed and warm.

Even this path, which is the most modest of all paths of resistance, will not be easy for us. But it is much easier than self-immolation or a hunger strike: The flames will not envelop your body, your eyeballs will not burst from the heat, and brown bread and clean water will always be available to your family.

Czechoslovakian Example

A great people of Europe, the Czechoslovaks, whom we betrayed and deceived: Haven't they shown us how a vulnerable breast can stand up even against tanks if there is a worthy heart within it?

You say it will not be easy? But it will be the easiest of all possible resources. It will not be an easy choice for a body, but it is the only one for a soul. No, it is not an easy path. But there are already people, even dozens of them, who over the years have maintained all these points and live by the truth.

So you will not be the first to take this path, but will join those who have already taken it. This path will be easier and shorter for all of us if we take it by mutual efforts and in close rank. If there are thousands of us, they will not be able to do anything with us. If there are tens of thousands of us, then we would not even recognize our country.

If we are too frightened, then we should stop complaining that someone is suffocating us. We ourselves are doing it. Let us then bow down even more, let us wait, and our brothers the biologists will help to bring nearer the day when they are able to read our thoughts.

And if we get cold feet, even taking this step, then we are worthless and hopeless, and the scorn of Pushkin should be directed to us:

"Why should cattle have the gifts of freedom?

"Their heritage from generation to generation is the belled yoke and the lash."

IMPEACHABLE OFFENSES: TWO VIEWS

February 21, 28, 1974

*By a historic 410-4 roll-call vote Feb. 6, 1974, the House of Represen-
tatives approved a resolution authorizing the "Committee on the
Judiciary...to investigate fully...whether sufficient grounds exist for the
House...to exercise its constitutional power to impeach Richard M. Nixon,
President of the United States of America." The dramatic action marked
the first time since 1867 and only the second time in American history that
the House had formally authorized an investigation of grounds for impeachment of a president. Initiation of the inquiry immediately raised
questions over what presidential actions constituted impeachable offenses
within the meaning of the constitutional language covering such offenses:
"Treason, Bribery, or other high Crimes and Misdemeanors." Two contrasting views presented in late February clearly marked the lines of partisan dissent. On Feb. 21, the bipartisan impeachment inquiry staff of the
Judiciary Committee presented to the committee its view that an impeachable offense did not require criminal conduct on the part of the
President. Democrats on the committee largely agreed; Republicans were
less certain. A week later, on Feb. 28, President Nixon's legal team, headed
by Chief Counsel James D. St. Clair, published an analysis concluding that
impeachment required an indictable offense, a position supported by many
Republicans on the House Judiciary Committee.*

*The committee staff found that "To limit impeachable conduct to
criminal offenses would be incompatible with the evidence concerning the
constitutional meaning of the phrase...and would frustrate the purpose
that the framers intended for impeachment." Committee Democrats
generally agreed; committee Republicans, however, generally favored an*

137

interpretation requiring criminal offenses as a necessary basis for impeachment.

The impeachment inquiry staff's report, designed to illuminate the historical meaning of "high crimes and misdemeanors," was prepared by the staff and was endorsed both by Special Counsel John M. Doar, who had been selected by Democrats on the committee, and by Special Minority Counsel Albert E. Jenner Jr., who had been chosen by Republicans. But the report, as ranking Republican Edward Hutchinson (Mich.) pointed out, was a report to the committee, not a report of the committee.

Judiciary committee members, however, split roughly along party lines in their reactions to the report. "It has been my view all along that grounds for impeachment need not arise out of criminal conduct," said Chairman Peter W. Rodino (D N.J.), signaling his agreement with the staff report. But Hutchinson disagreed: "There should be criminality involved." Describing the report as a "useful document," Robert McClory (R Ill.) took a middle position between Rodino and Hutchinson, saying that he felt not every crime was an impeachable offense—using manslaughter as an example—and that some impeachable offenses might not be defined as crimes. The memorandum from the staff, he pointed out, was not the unanimous view—or even the consensus of the staff—but merely contained the points on which the staff could agree.

Apparent in the report's findings was the conclusion that the constitution provided no rigid formula for grounds for impeachment. "The framers did not write a fixed standard. Instead they adopted from English history a standard sufficiently general and flexible to meet future circumstances and events, the nature and character of which they could not foresee." But to determine the meaning that "high crimes and misdemeanors" should properly have in the 1974 inquiry, the report took a long look at the English precedents for the use of impeachment: "Two points emerge from the 400 years of English parliamentary experience with the phrase," the staff found. "First, the particular allegations of misconduct alleged damage to the state," they said. "Second, the phrase...was confined to parliamentary impeachments," they found, and then "particular allegations of misconduct under that heading were not necessarily limited to...crimes."

Committee Staff: Abuse of Duties

Moving then to scrutinize the intention of the men who wrote those words into the Constitution, the staff report examined the debates at the Constitutional Convention and later at the state conventions called to ratify the new Constitution. This evidence, concluded the report, indicated that the framers intended impeachment to "reach offenses against government, and especially abuses of constitutional duties." Looking at the 13 American impeachments, 10 of which had been of federal judges, the report found that each of those impeachments had "involved charges of misconduct incompatible with the official position of the officeholder." According to the report: "This conduct falls into three broad categories: ex-

ceeding the constitutional bounds of the powers of office...behaving in a manner grossly incompatible with the proper function and purpose of the office; and employing the power of the office for improper purpose or for personal gain."

In practice, the staff found, the House in impeachment cases "has placed little emphasis on criminal conduct. Less than one-third of the eighty-three articles [of impeachment] the House has adopted have explicitly charged the violation of a criminal statute." A pattern of conduct, rather than specific individual acts, often has been the primary charge against an impeachable official. To restrict impeachable offenses to crimes would be to define the function of presidential impeachment too narrowly, the staff concluded. The criminal law applies to all citizens, they asserted, but impeachment of a president is the remedy for his abuse of powers that only he possesses.

St. Clair: Only Indictable Offenses

The President's Chief Counsel, St. Clair, took the view that only a criminal offense is sufficient for impeachment. (Nixon's views, see p. 145, 189.) "The evidence is conclusive on all points; a President may only be impeached for indictable crimes. That is the lesson of history, logic, and experience," concluded "An Analysis of The Constitutional Standard for Presidential Impeachment," by the President's lawyers, headed by St. Clair. Released the afternoon of Feb. 28, the analysis clearly took issue with the report made public a week before by the House Judiciary Committee's impeachment staff. The men who wrote the Constitution reacted against the English practice of political impeachments which demonstrated parliamentary supremacy, St. Clair's analysis stated. They rejected that use of impeachment in order to preserve an independent executive, it said. The language they adopted to define causes for impeachment—"treason, bribery, or other high crimes and misdemeanors"—meant, according to the analysis, "such criminal conduct as justified the removal of an office holder from that office." Furthermore, the analysis stated, "in light of English and American history and usage from the time of Blackstone onwards, there is no evidence to attribute anything but a criminal meaning to the unitary phrase, 'other high crimes and misdemeanors.' "

Continuing to narrow the definition of "high crimes and misdemeanors," St. Clair interpreted the phrase as requiring not only "a criminal offense, but one of a very serious nature committed in one's governmental capacity." The most notable lesson to be learned from the impeachment of Andrew Johnson, St. Clair wrote, "is that impeachment of a President should be resorted to only for cases of the gravest kind—the commission of a crime in the Constitution or a criminal offense against the laws of the United States."

> *Excerpts from the Feb. 21 memorandum prepared by the impeachment inquiry staff of the House Judiciary Committee on the constitutional grounds for presidential impeachment, followed by excerpts from a contrasting*

analysis of that subject by James D. St. Clair and other White House lawyers, released Feb. 28:

Excerpts from impeachment staff report entitled "Constitutional Grounds for Presidential Impeachment."

The Historical Origins of the Impeachment Process

"The Constitution provides that the President '...shall be removed from Office on Impeachment for, and Conviction of, Treason, Bribery, or other high Crimes and Misdemeanors.' The framers could have written simply 'or other crimes'.... They did not do that.... They adopted instead a unique phrase used for centuries in English parliamentary impeachments....

"Two points emerge from the 400 years of English parliamentary experience with the phrase.... First, the particular allegations of misconduct, alleged damage to the state in such forms as misapplication of funds, abuse of official power, neglect of duty, encroachment on Parliament's prerogatives, corruption, and betrayal of trust. Second, the phrase...was confined to parliamentary impeachments; it had no roots in the ordinary criminal law, and the particular allegations of misconduct under that heading were not necessarily limited to common law or statutory derelictions or crimes.

"The Intention of the Framers. The debates on impeachment at the Constitutional Convention... focus principally on its applicability to the President.... Impeachment was to be one of the central elements of executive responsibility....

"The framers intended impeachment to be a constitutional safeguard of the public trust, the powers of government conferred upon the President...and the division of powers....

"The American Impeachment Cases. ...Does Article III, section 1 of the Constitution, which states that judges 'shall hold their Offices during good Behavior,' limit the relevance of the ten impeachments of judges with respect to presidential impeachment standards as has been argued...? It does not....

"Each of the thirteen American impeachments involved charges of misconduct incompatible with the official position of the officeholder. This conduct falls into three broad categories: (1) exceeding the constitutional bounds of the powers of the office in derogation of the powers of another branch of government; (2) behaving in a manner grossly incompatible with the proper function and purpose of the office; and (3) employing the power of the office for an improper purpose or for personal gain....

"In drawing up articles of impeachment, the House has placed little emphasis on criminal conduct. Less than one-third of the eighty-three articles the House has adopted have explicitly charged the violation of a criminal statute or used the word 'criminal' or 'crime' to describe the conduct alleged....

140

"Much more common in the articles are allegations that the officer has violated his duties or his oath or seriously undermined public confidence in his ability to perform his official functions....

"All have involved charges of conduct incompatible with continued performance of the office; some have explicitly rested upon a 'course of conduct'.... Some of the individual articles seem to have alleged conduct that, taken alone, would not have been considered serious....

The Criminality Issue

"The central issue...is whether requiring an indictable offense as an essential element of impeachable conduct is consistent with the purposes and intent of the framers.

"Impeachment and the criminal law serve fundamentally different purposes. Impeachment is the first step in a remedial process.... The purpose...is not personal punishment; its function is primarily to maintain constitutional government....

"The general applicability of the criminal law also makes it inappropriate as the standard.... In an impeachment proceeding a President is called to account for abusing powers which only a President possesses.

"Impeachable conduct...may include the serious failure to discharge the affirmative duties imposed on the President by the Constitution. Unlike a criminal case, the cause for removal...may be based on his entire course of conduct in office....It may be a course of conduct more than individual acts that has a tendency to subvert constitutional government.

"To confine impeachable conduct to indictable offenses may well be to set a standard so restrictive as not to reach conduct that might adversely affect the system of government. Some of the most grievous offenses against our constitutional form of government may not entail violations of the criminal law....

"To limit impeachable conduct to criminal offenses would be incompatible with the evidence...and would frustrate the purpose that the framers intended....

Conclusion

"In the English practice and in several of the American impeachments, the criminality issue was not raised at all. The emphasis has been on the significant effects of the conduct....Impeachment was evolved...to cope with both the inadequacy of criminal standards and the impotence of courts to deal with the conduct of great public figures. It would be anomalous if the framers, having barred criminal sanctions from the impeachment remedy...intended to restrict the grounds for impeachment to conduct that was criminal.

"The longing for precise criteria is understandable.... However, where the issue is presidential compliance with the constitutional requirements and limitations on the presidency, the crucial factor is not the intrinsic quality of behavior but the significance of its effects upon our constitutional system or the functioning of our government.

Excerpts from St. Clair's study, "An Analysis of the Constitutional Standard for Presidential Impeachment":

English Background of Constitutional Impeachment Provisions

"The Framers felt that the English system permitted men...to make arbitrary decisions, and one of their primary purposes in creating a Constitution was to replace this arbitrariness with a system based on the rule of law.... They felt impeachment was a necessary check on a President who might commit a crime, but they did not want to see the vague standards of the English system that made impeachment a weapon to achieve parliamentary supremacy....

"To argue that the President may be impeached for something less than a criminal offense, with all the safeguards that definition implies, would be a monumental step backwards into all those old English practices that our Constitution sought to eliminate. American impeachment was not designed to force a President into surrendering executive authority...but to check overtly criminal actions as they are defined by law....

"The terminology 'high crimes and misdemeanors' should create no confusion or ambiguity.... It was a unitary phrase meaning crimes against the state, as opposed to those against individuals.... It is as ridiculous to say that 'misdemeanor' must mean something beyond 'crime' as it is to suggest that in the phrase 'bread and butter issues' butter issues must be different from bread issues....

The Constitutional Convention

"It is evident from the actual debate and from the events leading up to it that Morris' remark that 'An election of every four years will prevent maladministration,' expressed the will of the Convention. Thus, the impeachment provision adopted was designed to deal exclusively with indictable criminal conduct.... The Convention rejected all non-criminal definitions of impeachable offenses.... To distort the clear meaning of the phrase 'treason, bribery or other high crimes and misdemeanors' by including non-indictable conduct would thus most certainly violate the Framers' intent."

Legal Meaning of Impeachment Provision

"Just as statutes are to be construed to uphold the intent of the drafters...so should we uphold the intent of the drafters of the Constitution that impeachable offenses be limited to criminal violations. Also as penal statutes have been strictly construed in favor of the accused, so should we construe the impeachment provisions of the Constitution....

American Impeachment Precedents

"Some of the proponents of presidential impeachment place great emphasis on the cases involving federal judges to support the proposition that impeachment will lie for conduct which does not of itself constitute an indictable offense. This view is apparently most appealing to those broad constructionists who, favoring a severely weakened Chief Executive, argue that certain non-criminal 'political' offenses may justify impeachment....

"The Framers...distinguished between the President and judges concerning the standard to be employed for impeachment. Otherwise the 'good behavior' clause is a nullity....

"The precedent...asserted by the House in 1804 that a judge may be impeached for breach of good behavior was reasserted again with full force over one hundred years later in 1912....

"The fact that the House...felt it necessrary to make a distinction in the impeachment standards between the Judiciary and the Executive reinforces the obvious—that the words 'treason, bribery, and other high crimes and misdemeanors' are limited solely to indictable crimes and cannot extend to misbehavior....

"The acquittal of President Johnson over a century ago strongly indicates that the Senate has refused to adopt a broad view of 'other high crimes and misdemeanors'...Impeachment of a President should be resorted to only for cases of the gravest kind—the commission of a crime named in the Constitution or a criminal offense against the laws of the United States. If there is any doubt as to the gravity of an offense or as to a President's conduct or motives, the doubt should be resolved in his favor. This is the necessary price for having an independent executive....

Conclusion: Proper Standard for Presidential Impeachment

"Any analysis that broadly construes the power to impeach and convict can be reached only...by placing a subjective gloss on the history of impeachment that results in permitting Congress to do whatever it deems most politic. The intent of the Framers, who witnessed episode after episode of outrageous abuse of the impeachment power by the self-righteous English Parliament, was to restrict the *political* reach of the impeachment power.

"Those who seek to broaden the impeachment power invite the use of power 'as a means of crushing political adversaries or ejecting them from office,'.. The acceptance of such an invitation would be destructive to our system of government and to the fundamental principle of separation of powers.... The Framers never intended that the impeachment clause serve to dominate or destroy the executive branch of the government...."

NIXON ON IMPEACHMENT
February 25, 1974

As the House Judiciary Committee began its investigation into his possible impeachment, President Nixon told reporters at a nationally televised news conference Feb. 25 that he did not believe he would be impeached and that he would not resign to save Republicans from losses at the polls in November. "I want my party to succeed," Nixon said, "but more important, I want the presidency to survive. And it is vitally important in this nation that the presidency of the United States not be hostage to what happens to the popularity of a president at one time or another." Nixon's reiterated contention that he would not resign and his opinion that he would not be impeached came after numerous predictions that the House Judiciary Committee would report a bill of impeachment to the full House and that Republican pressure, exerted in the face of election year worries, would lead Nixon to resign if impeachment appeared likely or did, in fact, occur. Thus, the news conference was interpreted as an attempt to salvage Nixon's severely tarnished image and thereby bring public pressure opposing impeachment to bear on Congress. (Subsequent efforts, see p. 189, 287.)

Responding to reporters' questions for the first time since Oct. 26, 1973, (see Historic Documents 1973, p. 897-909), *Nixon parried questions that concentrated heavily on Watergate-related issues. On impeachment, he said he accepted the opinion of his White House counsel and some constitutional lawyers that "a criminal offense on the part of the President is the requirement for impeachment," rather than some other criteria such as dereliction of duty. Asked if it would not be in his best interest and that of the country to have the question of his involvement in Watergate resolved by impeachment, Nixon said: "Well, a full impeachment trial in the Senate under our Constitution comes only when the House determines that there is an impeachable offense. It is my belief that the House, after it conducts its inquiry, will not reach that determination. I do not expect to be impeached." Nixon also reiterated his position that he would cooperate with the House Judiciary Committee's staff investigation of impeachment so long as his cooperation did not interfere with his concept of executive privilege.*

In the course of the 30-minute question-and-answer session, Nixon also revealed that he had refused a request to testify before a Watergate grand jury and that his counter-offer, to respond to questions in writing or to meet with the Watergate special prosecutor, had been turned down. On the subject of his controversial tax payments, Nixon said he would withdraw the federal income tax deduction he claimed for donating his vice presidential papers if it were determined that the deduction was improper. (See p. 235.) At another point, Nixon spoke of the effect of the Soviet expulsion of Alexander Solzhenitsyn (see p. 129) on Soviet-American detente. He said that although the Soviets "don't like our system or approve of it and I don't like their system or approve of it," both powers should nonetheless continue to work toward avoiding confrontations.

Nixon had opened the news conference with a statement on the energy situation. Saying he believed the crisis in that area to have passed, he said that nonetheless a serious problem remained. He faulted Congress' handling of the energy issue, saying he would veto the pending Emergency Energy Bill if Congress passed it in its current form. His reasons, he said, were that the congressional measures would not solve the problem of gasoline shortages, but rather, through a proposed gasoline price rollback, would increase the likelihood of gasoline rationing. On Feb. 27, Congress cleared the energy bill; Nixon vetoed it March 6.

Excerpts from the text of President Nixon's Feb. 25 news conference, as made available by the White House:

THE PRESIDENT: Won't you be seated, please.

Ladies and Gentlemen, before going to your questions, I have a brief report on the energy situation, the progress we have made to date and also the problems that we have in the future.

You will recall that last October when we saw the energy crisis developing as a result of the embargo and other matters, that there were dire predictions that we would have problems with home heating oil and even fuel to run our factories.

As a result of the cooperation of the American people—and they deserve most of the credit—and also the management on the part of Mr. Simon and his organization, we have now passed through that crisis. The home fuel oil, as far as it is concerned, as we know, has been furnished, no one has suffered as a result. As far as our plants are concerned, all have had the fuel that is required to keep the plants going.

The major problem that remains is...getting gas..... I have seen this problem as I have driven around in the Miami area and also in the Washington area. The gas lines, the fact, too, that in the Eastern States generally, we do have a problem of shortage of gasoline, which has been, of course, very difficult for many people going to work, going to school or what have you....

As far as the entire situation is concerned, I am able to report tonight that as a result of the cooperation of the American people, as a result, too, of our own energy conservation program within the Government, that I now believe confidently that there is much better than an even chance that there will be no need for gas rationing in the United States.

As far as that is concerned, however, I should point out that while the crisis has passed, the problem still remains and it is a very serious one.

Having reported somewhat positively up to this point, let me point out some of the negative situations that we confront.

One has to do with Congress. The Congress, of course, is working hard on this problem, but I regret to say that the bill presently before the Congress is one that if it reaches my desk in its present form, I will have to veto it.

I will have to veto it because what it does is simply to manage the shortage rather than to deal with the real problem and what should be our real goal, and that is to get rid of the shortage.

For example, there is a provision in the bill, the present bill, that provides for a rollback of prices. Now this, of course, would be immediately popular, but it would mean if we did have such a rollback that we would not only have more and longer gas lines, but a rollback of prices would lead to shortages which would require, without question, rationing all over the country.

That would mean 17,000 to 20,000 more Federal bureaucrats to run the system at a cost of $1½ billion a year. And this we should avoid. This we can avoid....

Executive Privilege

THE PRESIDENT: Miss Thomas, I think you are No. 1 tonight.

Q: Mr. President, to heal the divisions in this country, would you be willing to waive Executive privilege to give the Judiciary Committee what it says it needs to end any question of your involvement in Watergate?

A: Miss Thomas, as you know, the matter of the Judiciary Committee's investigation is now being discussed by White House Counsel, Mr. St. Clair, and Mr. Doar. As I indicated in my State of the Union Address, I am prepared to cooperate with the committee in any way consistent with my constitutional responsibility to defend the office of the Presidency against any action which would weaken that office and the ability of future Presidents to carry out the great responsibilities that any President will have.

Mr. Doar is conducting those negotiations with Mr. St. Clair, and whatever is eventually arranged, which will bring a prompt resolution of this matter, I will cooperate in.

Inflation

Q: Mr. President, John Dunlop, the price controller, has said, "I don't think we know how to restrain inflation." How confident are you that in the latter half of the year we can restrain inflation?

A: Mr. Cormier, the problem of inflation is still a very nagging one. The last figures, as you know, the 1 percent increase in one month of the Consumer Price Index, was a very troublesome one.

Looking to the future, we are keenly aware of this problem, and we are preparing to deal with it.

First, we believe that it is vitally important to get at the source of the problem. One is in the field of energy. The way to get at the source of the problem in the field of energy is to increase supplies. I have already directed my comments to that point.

The other is in the field of food, and in the field of food we have the same objective—to increase supplies. Secretary Butz indicates to me and to other members of the Cabinet and the Cost of Living Council that he expects that our supplies through the balance of this year of food will go up and that that will have a restraining influence as far as food costs are concerned.

With regard to inflation, I should point out, too, that almost two-thirds of the price increase, the increase in prices last year, which was at a very high rate, was due to energy and also to the problem of food.

By getting at these two problems and by continuing our Cost of Living Council activities in the areas Secretary Shultz has testified to, I believe that we will bring inflation under control as the year goes on, but I would not underestimate the problem.

We are going to continue to fight it. It is going to have to take responsibility on the part of the Congress to keep the budget within the limits that we have laid out. It is also going to take an effort on the part of our farmers, an effort on the part of the Administration in the field of energy and the rest, so that we can get the supplies up because the answer to higher prices is not simply controls.

Controls have been tried and controls have been found wanting. The answer to higher prices is to get up the supplies that will bring the prices down.

Cooperation With Committee

Q: Mr. President, to follow up Miss Thomas' question, you say you will cooperate with the Judiciary Committee, but you can't say yet precisely to what extent. Can you tell us if you anticipate you will be able to cooperate at least to the extent you cooperated with Mr. Jaworski in terms of turning over to the Judiciary Committee roughly the same tapes and documents that Mr. Jaworski has?

A: Well, this is a matter, Mr. Jarriel, that has been discussed by Mr. St. Clair with Mr. Doar and the decision will be made based on what arrangements are developed between the two for the confidentiality of those particular items where they must remain confidential, and also based on whether or not turning over to the committee will, in any way, jeopardize the rights of defendants or impair the ability of the prosecution to carry on its proper functions in the cases that may develop. It is a matter that we are talking about and it is a matter where we will be cooperative within those guidelines.

Impeachable Offense

Q: Mr. President, may I follow on to my colleague's question and also to Miss Thomas' question. Within the past week or ten days, the House Judiciary Committee and the Justice Department have issued differing interpretations of what by Constitution definition is an impeachable offense for a President.

Now, as we all know, you are an experienced student of the Constitution, and I think people would be interested to know what you consider to be an impeachable offense for a President, particularly on the dividing line, whether it requires the House to determine that they believe that the President may have committed a crime or whether dereliction of duty, not upholding the Constitution, is enough in itself to constitute an impeachable offense?

A: Well, Mr. Rather, you don't have to be a constitutional lawyer to know that the Constitution is very precise in defining what is an impeachable offense. And in this respect it is the opinion of White House counsel and a number of other consititutional lawyers, who are perhaps more up to date on this than I am at this time, that a criminal offense on the part of the President is the requirement for impeachmetnt.

This is a matter which will be presented, however, to the committee by Mr. St. Clair in a brief which he presently is preparing.

Gas Prices, Supply

Q: Mr. President, I would like to follow up on your discussion of the energy situation. When you said that the crisis is ended, that the problem is still with us, I think for most people the problem is waiting for a long time in line for gasoline and another part of it is the price of gasoline going up as it has been.

What can you tell the American people about when lines for gasoline may become shorter under your program and what do you see in terms of the future of the price of gasoline?

A: I believe that the lines for gasoline will become shorter in the spring and summer months....

As far as the price of gasoline is concerned, I would be less than candid if I were not to say that the price of gasoline is not going to go down until more supplies of gasoline come into the country and also until other fuels come on stream which will reduce the pressure which is upward on the price of gasoline.

Obviously too, when the embargo is lifted, that is, and will have some effect on the price of gasoline....

Request for Testimony

Q: Mr. President, has the Special Prosecutor requested your testimony in any form; and if asked, will you testify?

A: Well, I believe it is a matter of record that the Special Prosecutor transmitted a request that I testify before the Grand Jury and on constitutional grounds, I respectfully declined to do so.

I did offer, of course, to respond to any interrogatories that the Special Prosecutor might want to submit or to meet with him personally and answer questions. And he indicated that he did not want to proceed in that way.

Impeachment Trial

Q: Mr. President, under the—however the impeachable offense is defined under the system, the impeachment proceeding is the courtroom of the President—you have said many times that these matters belong in the courts. So, won't it be in your best interest and in the best interest of the country to have this matter finally resolved in a proper judicial form, a full impeachment trial in the Senate?

A: Well, a full impeachment trial in the Senate under our Constitution comes only when the House determines that there is an impeachable offense. It is my belief that the House, after it conducts its inquiry, will not reach that determination. I do not expect to be impeached....

The Economy

Q: Mr. President, you have told the American people that there will be no recession this year. If the unemployment rate should go above 5½ percent of the labor force, what do you plan to do about this as an anti-recession move and would that include the tax cut?

A: ...We are going through what I would say is a down turn in the economy at this point, but not a recession. And for the balance of the year, the prospects are good. They are good because we are going to be dealing with the energy crisis—what was a crisis—as a problem. That will be helpful.

We expect to have an increase insofar as food is concerned, and as far as other elements of the economy are concerned, there are very great areas of strength. The last half of the year we expect to be on an upward curve rather than the down curve....

We will not stand by and allow this country—because of the energy crisis, and because of some of the problems we have had on the inflation front—stand by and allow a recession to occur. That is why I have been so positive in saying there will be no recession....

Veterans Administrator

Q: Mr President, sir,...I don't think you are fully informed about some of the things that are happening in the Government in a domestic way. I am sure it is not your fault, but maybe the people you appointed to office aren't giving you the right information.

For example, I have discovered the Veterans Administration has absolutely no means of telling precisely what is the national problem regarding the payments of checks to boys going to school under the G.I. bill and many a young man in this country is being disillusioned totally by his Government these days because of the hardships being put upon him.

A: Well, this is a question which you very properly bring to the attention of the Nation. It is a question that has already been brought to my attention, I am sure, by a number of people...and the question...is very simply this. Mr. Don Johnson of the Veterans Administration, as you know, acted expeditiously when we had a case in California. We have another one in Illinois at the present time.

There are great numbers of veterans. We have an adequate program to deal with it, and I can assure you that when any matter is brought to my attention, or to his, we will deal with it as quickly as we can because our Vietnam veterans and all veterans deserve whatever the law provides for them and I will see that they get it.

Q: He is the very man I am talking about who is not giving you the correct information. He stood up here at the White House the other day and gave us false information. He has no real system for getting the statistics on this problem.

A: Well, if he isn't listening to this program I will report to him just what you said. (Laughter)

He may have heard even though he wasn't listening to the President. (Laughter)

Advice to Candidates

Q: Mr. President, this is a political question.

A: The others weren't political? [Laughter]

Q: Jerry Ford's old House seat was won by a Democrat who campaigned mainly on the theme that you should be removed or impeached or that you should resign. What advice could you give Republican candidates this year to counter that argument?

A: First, I want Republican candidates to win where they are deserving candidates, and second, I recall the year 1948 when we confidently expected to gain in the House and when Mr. Fulbright, as you may recall, called for President Truman's resignation in the spring because the economy was in a slump, and President Truman had other problems, and we proceeded to campaign against Mr. Truman. He was the issue. We took a bad licking in the Congress in 1948.

What my advice to the candidates very simply would be is this: It is that nine months before an election, no one can predict what can happen in this country. What will affect the election in this year, 1974, is what always affects elections—peace and prosperity.

On the peace front, we are doing well, and I think we will continue to do well. With regard to the prosperity issue, the bread and butter issue, as I have already indicated, I think that this economy is going to be moving up.

I think, therefore, it will be a good year for those candidates who stand for the Administration.

Income Taxes

Q: Mr. President, as you prepare to sign your income tax returns for this year, do you intend to pay State or local income taxes, and have you had any second thoughts about your claimed deduction for the gift of the Vice Presidential papers?

A: With regard to any State taxes or concern, I will pay any that the law requires. As I understand, in California a ruling has been made, apparently, that even though I have a residence in California that there is not a requirement that I pay California taxes.

I would be glad to pay those taxes and, of course, deduct that from my Federal income tax liability as others can do if they desire to do so.

With regard to the gift of papers that I made to the Government, there is no question about my intent. All of my Vice Presidential papers were delivered to the Archives in March, four months before the deadline. The paper work on it apparently was not concluded until after that time.

This raises a legal question as to whether or not the deduction, therefore, is proper. That is why I voluntarily asked the Senate control committee of the House and Senate to look into the matter and to advise me as to whether or not the deduction was a proper one. If it was not a proper one, I, of course, will be glad to pay the tax. [Tax report, see p. 235-245.]

Solzhenitsyn's Expulsion

Mr. Healy.

Q: Mr. President, what is your personal reaction to the expulsion by the Soviet Union of Alexander Solzhenitsyn and will it in any way affect our policy of detente?

A: I am, of course, an admirer of a man who has won a Nobel prize for literature and one who has also shown, as he has shown, such great courage.

Second, as far as our relations with the Soviets are concerned, if I thought that breaking relations with the Soviets or turning off our policy of negotiation and turning back to confrontation would help him or help thousands of others like him in the Soviet Union, we might do that.

On the other hand, I look back to the years of confrontation, and I find that men like him, as a matter of fact, rather than being sent to Paris, would have been sent to Siberia or probably worse.

As far as our relations with the Soviets are concerned, we shall continue. We shall continue to negotiate, recognizing that they don't like our system or approve of it, and I don't like their system or approve of it....

No Resignation

Q: Mr. President, you have said on many occasions that you would not resign from the office to which you were elected, but what if within the next few months it became evident that your party was going to suffer a disastrous defeat in this year's election, would you then reconsider your resolve on this?

A: No. I want my party to succeed but more important, I want the Presidency to survive, and it is vitally important in this Nation that the Presidency of the United States not be hostage to what happens to the popularity of a President at one time or another. The stability of this office, the ability of the President to continue to govern, the ability, for example of this President to continue the great initiatives which have led to a more peaceful world than we have had for a generation, and to move on the domestic front in the many areas that I have described, all of these things, these goals, are yet before us.

We have a lot of work left to do, more than three years left to do, and I am going to stay here until I get it done.

Q: Mr. President, you have made a very strong defense on the confidentiality of Presidential documents and other matters, and you have launched a program to protect the privacy of citizens of the United States.

In light of this, would you explain how you happened to issue an Executive Order last year, once modified, to allow the Agriculture Department to examine key points of individual income tax returns of America's three million farmers and a Justice Department advisory opinion saying that this Executive Order should serve as a model for all the Federal Government departments?

A: Well, as a matter of fact, in the privacy message, which, as you know, I issued on Saturday, I did not raise this question specifically, but certainly I want that question, along with others, considered, because in this whole area of privacy, it isn't just a question of those who run credit bureaus and banks and others with their huge computers, but the Federal Government itself, in its activities, can very much impinge on the privacy of individuals.

This is a matter that I think should be considered by the commission that I have appointed which is chaired, as you know, by the Vice President.

Kalmbach Plea

Q: Thank you, Mr. President.

Your personal lawyer, Herb Kalmbach, entered a plea of guilty today to a criminal charge of accepting $100,000 in exchange for an Ambassadorial post. In your capacity as President you approve of Ambassadors and send the nominations to the Senate, were you consulted in any manner on this engagement, and this contribution, by Mr. Kalmbach, or anyone else in the White House, and have you done any research on this in the White House to determine who is responsible for it?

A: The answer to the first question is no; the answer to the second question is yes, and I would go further and say that Ambassadorships have not been for sale, to my knowledge; Ambassadorships cannot be purchased, and I would not approve an Ambassadorship unless the man or woman was qualified clearly apart from any contributions....

Fair Share of Taxes

Q: Mr. President, thank you very much. To follow on an earlier question about taxes, April 21, 1969, was a significant day for you in taxes and for the country, too. That is the notary date on the deed that allowed you to give your papers to the Government and pay just token taxes for two years. On that same date, you had a tax reform message in which you said, and I quote, "special preferences in the law permit far too many Americans to pay less than their fair share of taxes. Too many others bear too much of the tax burden."

Now, Mr. President, do you think you paid your fair share of taxes?

A: Well, I would point out that those who made deductions such as I made in this particular instance, included John Kenneth Galbraith, Jerome Weisner, Vice President Humphrey, President Johnson, a number of others. I did not write that law. When it was brought to my attention, rather vigorously by President Johnson when I saw him shortly after my election, he thought that it would be wise for me to give my papers to the Government and take the proper deduction.

I did that. Under the circumstances, as you know now, that deduction is no longer allowed. As far as I am concerned, I think that was probably a proper decision....

▼▼▼

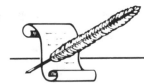
March

WATERGATE COVER-UP INDICTMENT

March 1, 1974

Seven former White House aides and officials of President Nixon's 1972 re-election campaign committee were indicted by a federal grand jury March 1 on charges of conspiring to impede the investigation of the June 1972 break-in at the Democratic National Committee's headquarters at the Watergate complex in Washington, D.C. Three of Nixon's closest aides during his first term—Attorney General John M. Mitchell and former presidential assistants H. R. Haldeman and John D. Ehrlichman— were charged with conspiracy and obstruction of justice. Mitchell and Haldeman were also charged with giving false testimony to the Senate committee that investigated Watergate, and Mitchell and Ehrlichman were charged with lying to FBI agents and the grand jury. Other aides indicted on various counts of conspiracy, obstruction of justice and false declarations were Charles W. Colson, former special counsel to the President; Robert C. Mardian, former assistant attorney general and political consultant to Nixon's re-election committee; Kenneth W. Parkinson, attorney for the re-election committee; and Gordon C. Strachan, former assistant to Haldeman. Colson pleaded guilty June 3 to one count of violating the civil rights of a person in connection with his part in the break-in at the office of Daniel Ellsberg's psychiatrist. (See p. 205.) In exchange for his future cooperation, the government agreed to drop all other charges pending against him. (See p. 443.) Colson, along with all of the other men indicted March 1, had pleaded not guilty at the arraignment March 9. The long-awaited indictment capped a highly publicized 20-month investigation of the Watergate burglary and cover-up. (See Historic Documents, 1973, p. 413-425, 499-512, 549-556, 563-574, 659-679, 697-701, 737-751, 839-857, 859-880, 897-909, 947-964.)

At the same time, the grand jury gave U.S. District Judge John J. Sirica a sealed report dealing with the jury's conclusions on President Nixon's involvement in the cover-up of the Watergate crime. The secret report was accompanied by a briefcase containing documents to support the findings. After silently reading in court a covering letter to the report, Sirica said he would hold the materials in his custody until he decided whether or not to forward them to the House Judiciary Committee for its presidential impeachment probe. On March 18, Sirica ruled to turn over the information to the committee. (See p. 225-232.) While most politicians avoided any comment on the March 1 indictment of former Nixon administration officials, several key officials in both parties predicted that pressure would be increased to impeach President Nixon.

Conspiracy Alleged

In returning the indictment, the grand jury charged all seven men with conspiring to impede the investigation into the Watergate burglary. "It was part of the conspiracy," the indictment stated, "that the conspirators would corruptly influence, obstruct, and impede...the due administration of justice...for the purpose of concealing the identities of the persons who were responsible for, participated in, and had knowledge of (a) the activities which were the subject of the investigation and trial and (b) other illegal and improper activities." The conspirators also worked, the indictment stated, to obstruct justice, to lie to government agencies and to defraud the government of its right to have the officials of the Central Intelligence Agency (CIA), the FBI and the Justice Department "transact their official business honestly and impartially, free from corruption, fraud, improper and undue influence, dishonesty, unlawful impairment and obstruction.

"Among the means by which the conspirators would carry out the aforesaid conspiracy," the indictment continued, were the following: "The conspirators would direct G. Gordon Liddy to seek the assistance of Richard G. Kleindienst, then attorney general...in obtaining the release from the District of Columbia jail of one or more of the persons who had been arrested on June 17, 1972, in the offices of the Democratic National Committee...; would at various times remove, conceal, alter and destroy...documents, papers, records and objects...; would plan, solicit, assist and facilitate the giving of false, deceptive, evasive and misleading statements and testimony...; would give false, misleading, evasive and deceptive statements and testimony...; would covertly raise, acquire, transmit, distribute and pay cash funds to and for the benefits of the defendants [in the original case]..; would make and cause to be made offers of leniency, executive clemency and other benefits to E. Howard Hunt, Jr., G. Gordon Liddy, James W. McCord Jr. and Jeb. S. Magruder..; would attempt to obtain CIA financial assistance for persons who were subjects of the investigation...and...would obtain information from the FBI and the Department of Justice concerning the progress of the investigation." Forty-

five overt acts were listed in support of the conspiracy charge, for which the maximum penalty was five years in prison and a $5,000 fine.

Obstruction of Justice

Mitchell, Haldeman, Ehrlichman, Strachan, Parkinson and Colson were also charged with one count of obstruction of justice for their success in impeding the investigation and the due administration of justice. This obstruction was accomplished, the indictment stated, by providing cash and other benefits to the seven original Watergate defendants—Bernard L. Barker, Virgilio R. Gonzales, Eugenio R. Martinez, McCord, Frank L. Sturgis and Hunt—"for the purpose of concealing...the identities of the persons who were responsible for, participated in and had knowledge of the activities which were the subject of the investigation and trial." The maximum penalty for this charge is five years in prison and a $5,000 fine.

Mitchell's Involvement

In addition to his indictment for conspiracy and obstruction of justice in the Watergate investigation, Mitchell was indicted on four different counts of lying—twice before the grand jury, once before the Senate Watergate committee and once to FBI agents. When Mitchell on July 5, 1972, told FBI agents that he knew nothing of the Watergate burglary other than what he had read in the newspapers, he was knowingly making "false, fictitious and fraudulent statements," said the indictment.

Ehrlichman's Role

In addition to charges of conspiracy and obstruction of justice, Ehrlichman was charged with two counts of lying to the grand jury and one count of lying to FBI agents. The indictment said that when Ehrlichman told FBI agents late in July 1973 that he had no information relating to the Watergate burglary other than what he had read in the newspapers, he was knowingly making "false, fictitious, and fraudulent statements." When Ehrlichman in May 1973 told the grand jury that he had not approved the raising of money for the defense of the original Watergate defendants and their families, and that he had not said this money-raising and its purpose should be kept secret, he knew those statements, too, were false, said the indictment.

Haldeman: Perjury

In addition to charges of conspiracy and obstruction of justice, Haldeman was also charged with three counts of perjury, all relating to his testimony before the Senate Watergate committee. According to the indictment, when on July 30, 1973, he told the Senate committee that no one in the summer of 1972 was aware that the funds raised and provided to Watergate defendants were a response to blackmail or were "hush money," Haldeman knew that these statements were false. When on July 30-31, 1973, Haldeman told the committee that Nixon had told Dean on March 21, 1973, it would be wrong to pay the blackmail money Hunt was demanding, he knew that those statements also were false, the indictment said.

159

In addition to the charges of conspiracy and obstruction of justice, Strachan was also charged on one count of lying to the grand jury. Strachan told the grand jury on April 11, 1973, that on his own iniative he had taken $350,000 in cash in November 1972 from the safe where it had been kept and on his own initiative had returned it to Frederick LaRue rather than to the campaign committee treasurer. The indictment said he knew he was lying when he gave this testimony. Strachan's trial, however, was severed from those of the other defendants Sept. 30 because of complications concerning his indictment and his contention that he had provided prosecutors with information under a promise of immunity.

One of the grand jury's charges, that Haldeman had lied to the Senate Watergate committee, called into direct question the accuracy of a public statement by the President. At his Aug. 22, 1973, press conference, a month after Haldeman's testimony on the subject, Nixon answered a question about the March 21 meeting with Dean. Nixon recalled Dean's mentioning a figure of $1-million for the original Watergate defendants. Nixon said he asked Dean: "how do you get around clemency because they're not going to stay in jail simply because their families are being taken care of?" Then Nixon added: "And so that was why I concluded, as Mr. Haldeman recalls, perhaps, and did testify very effectively, when I said, 'John, it's wrong, it won't work, we can't give clemency and we've got to get this story out.' " Haldeman was indicted for knowingly making a false statement when he quoted Nixon as having said "it's wrong."

Text of the indictment returned March 1 by the Watergate grand jury. The italicized *material was underscored in the original document:*

Introduction

1. On or about June 17, 1972, Bernard L. Barker, Virgilio R. Gonzalez, Eugenio R. Martinez, James W. McCord Jr. and Frank L. Sturgis were arrested in the offices of the Democratic National Committee, located in the Watergate office building, Washington, D.C., while attempting to photograph documents and repair a surreptitious electronic listening device which had previously been placed in those offices unlawfully.

2. At all times material herein, the United States attorney's office for the District of Columbia and the Federal Bureau of Investigation were parts of the Department of Justice, a department and agency of the United States, and the Central Intelligence Agency was an agency of the United States.

3. Beginning on or about June 17, 1972, and continuing up to and including the date of filing of this indictment, the Federal Bureau of Investigation and the United States attorney's office for the District of Columbia were conducting an investigation, in conjunction with a grand jury of the United States District Court for the District of Columbia which had been duly impaneled and sworn on or about June 5, 1972, to determine whether violations of 18 U.S.C. 371, 2511 and 22 D.C. Code 1801 (b), and of other statutes of the United States and the District of Columbia, had been committed in the District of Columbia and elsewhere, and to identify the

individual or individuals who had committed, caused the commission of, and conspired to commit such violations.

4. On or about Sept. 15, 1972, in connection with the said investigation, the grand jury returned an indictment in Criminal Case No. 1827-72 in the United States District Court for the District of Columbia charging Bernard L. Barker, Virgilio R. Gonzalez, E. Howard Hunt Jr., G. Gordon Liddy, Eugenio R. Martinez, James W. McCord Jr. and Frank L. Sturgis with conspiracy, burglary and unlawful endeavor to intercept wire communications.

5. From in or about January, 1969, to on or about March 1, 1972, John N. Mitchell, the defendant, was attorney general of the United States. From on or about April 9, 1972, to on or about June 30, 1972, he was campaign director of the Committee to Re-Elect the President.

6. At all times material herein up to on or about April 30, 1973, Harry R. Haldeman, the defendant, was assistant to the President of the United States.

7. At all times material herein up to on or about April 30, 1973, John D. Ehrlichman, the defendant, was assistant for domestic affairs to the President of the United States.

8. At all times material herein up to on or about March 10, 1973, Charles W. Colson, the defendant, was special counsel to the President of the United States.

9. At all times material herein, Robert C. Mardian, the defendant, was an official of the Committee to Re-Elect the President.

10. From on or about June 21, 1972, and all times material herein, Kenneth W. Parkinson, the defendant, was an attorney representing the Committee to Re-Elect the President.

11. At all times material herein up to in or about November, 1972, Gordon Strachan, the defendant, was a staff assistant to Harry R. Haldeman at the White House. Thereafter he became general counsel to the United States Information Agency.

Count One

12. From on or about June 17, 1972, up to and including the date of the filing of this indictment, in the District of Columbia and elsewhere, John N. Mitchell, Harry R. Haldeman, John D. Ehrlichman, Charles W. Colson, Robert C. Mardian, Kenneth W. Parkinson and Gordon Strachan, the defendants, and other persons to the grand jury known and unknown, unlawfully, willfully and knowingly did combine, conspire, confederate and agree together and with each other, to commit offenses against the United States, to wit, to obstruct justice in violation of Title 18, United States Code, Section 1503, to make false statements to a government agency in violation of Title 18, United States Code, Section 1001, to make false declarations in violation of Title 18, United States Code, Section 1623, and to defraud the United States and agencies and departments thereof, to wit, tne Central Intelligence Agency (C.I.A.), the Federal Bureau of Investigation (F.B.I.) and the Department of Justice, of the government's right to

161

have the officials of these departments and agencies transact their official business honestly and impartially, free from corruption, fraud, improper and undue influence, dishonesty, unlawful impairment and obstruction, all in violation of Title 18, United States Code, Section 371.

13. It was a part of the conspiracy that the conspirators would corruptly influence, obstruct and impede, and corruptly endeavor to influence, obstruct and impede, the due administration of justice in connection with the investigation referred to in Paragraph 3 above and in connection with the trial of Criminal Case No. 1827-72 in the United States District Court for the District of Columbia, for the purpose of concealing and causing to be concealed the identities of the persons who were responsible for, participated in, and had knowledge of (a) the activities which were the subject of the investigation and trial, and (b) other illegal and improper activities.

14. It was further a part of the conspiracy that the conspirators would knowingly make and cause to be made false statements to the F.B.I. and false material statements and declarations under oath in proceedings before and ancillary to the grand jury and a court of the United States, for the purposes stated in paragraph thirteen (13) above.

15. It was further a part of the conspiracy that the conspirators would, by deceit, craft, trickery and dishonest means, defraud the United States by interfering with and obstructing lawful governmental functions of the C.I.A., in that the conspirators would induce the C.I.A. to provide financial assistance to persons who were subjects of the investigation referred to in paragraph three (3) above, for the purposes stated in paragraph thirteen (13) above.

16. It was further a part of the conspiracy that the conspirators would, by deceit, craft, trickery and dishonest means, defraud the United States by interfering with and obstructing the lawful governmental functions of the F.B.I. and the Department of Justice, in that the conspirators would obtain and attempt to obtain from the F.B.I. and the Department of Justice information concerning the investigation referred to in paragraph three (3) above, for the purposes stated in paragraph thirteen (13) above.

17. Among the means by which the conspirators would carry out the aforesaid conspiracy were the following:

(a) The conspirators would direct G. Gordon Liddy to seek the assistance of Richard G. Kleindienst, then attorney general of the United States, in obtaining the release from the District of Columbia jail of one or more of the persons who had been arrested on June 17, 1972 in the offices of the Democratic National Committee in the Watergate office building in Washington, D.C., and G. Gordon Liddy would seek such assistance from Richard G. Kleindienst.

(b) The conspirators would at various times remove, conceal, alter and destroy, attempt to remove, conceal, alter and destroy, and cause to be removed, concealed, altered and destroyed, documents, papers, records and objects.

(c) The conspirators would plan, solicit, assist and facilitate the giving of false, deceptive, evasive and misleading statements and testimony.

(d) The conspirators would give false, misleading, evasive and deceptive statements and testimony.

(e) The conspirators would covertly raise, acquire, transmit, distribute and pay cash funds to and for the benefit of the defendants in Criminal Case No. 1827-72 in the United States District Court for the District of Columbia, both prior to and subsequent to the return of the indictment on Sept. 15, 1972.

(f) The conspirators would make and cause to be made offers of leniency, executive clemency and other benefits to E. Howard Hunt Jr., G. Gordon Liddy, James W. McCord Jr., and Jeb S. Magruder.

(g) The conspirators would attempt to obtain C.I.A. financial assistance for persons who were subjects of the investigation referred to in paragraph three (3) above.

(h) The conspirators would obtain information from the F.B.I. and the Department of Justice concerning the progress of the investigation referred to in paragraph three (3) above.

18. In furtherance of the conspiracy, and to the effect the objects thereof, the following overt acts, among others, were committed in the District of Columbia and elsewhere:

Overt Acts

1. On or about June 17, 1972, John N. Mitchell met with Robert C. Mardian in or about Beverly Hills, Calif., and requested Mardian to tell G. Gordon Liddy to seek the assistance of Richard G. Kleindienst, then attorney general of the United States, in obtaining the release of one or more of the persons arrested in connection with the Watergate break-in.

2. On or about June 18, 1972, in the District of Columbia, Gordon Strachan destroyed documents on the instructions of Harry R. Haldeman.

3. On or about June 19, 1972, John D. Ehrlichman met with John W. Dean 3rd at the White House in the District of Columbia, at which time Ehrlichman directed Dean to tell G. Gordon Liddy that E. Howard Hunt Jr. should leave the United States.

4. On or about June 19, 1972, Charles W. Colson and John D. Ehrlichman met with John W. Dean 3rd at the White House in the District of Columbia, at which time Ehrlichman directed Dean to take possession of the contents of E. Howard Hunt Jr.'s safe in the Executive Office Building.

5. On or about June 19, 1972, Robert C. Mardian and John N. Mitchell met with Jeb S. Magruder at Mitchell's apartment in the District of Columbia, at which time Mitchell suggested that Magruder destroy documents from Magruder's files.

6. On or about June 20, 1972, G. Gordon Liddy met with Fred C. LaRue and Robert C. Mardian at LaRue's apartment in the District of Columbia, at which time Liddy told LaRue and Mardian that certain "commitments" had been made to and for the benefit of Liddy and other persons involved in the Watergate break-in.

7. On or about June 24, 1972, John N. Mitchell and Robert C. Mardian met with John W. Dean 3rd at 1701 Pennsylvania Avenue in the District of

Columbia, at which time Mitchell and Mardian suggested to Dean that the C.I.A. be requested to provide covert funds for the assistance of the persons involved in the Watergate break-in.

8. On or about June 26, 1972, John D. Ehrlichman met with John W. Dean 3rd at the White House in the District of Columbia, at which time Ehrlichman approved a suggestion that Dean ask Gen. Vernon A. Walters, deputy director of the C.I.A., whether the C.I.A. could use covert funds to pay bail and salaries of the persons involved in the Watergate break-in.

9. On or about June 28, 1972, John D. Ehrlichman had a conversation with John W. Dean 3rd in the White House in the District of Columbia, during which Ehrlichman approved the use of Herbert W. Kalmbach to raise cash funds to make covert payments to and for the benefit of persons involved in the Watergate break-in.

10. On or about July 6, 1972, Kenneth W. Parkinson had a conversation with William O. Bittman in or about the District of Columbia, during which Parkinson told Bittman that "Rivers is O.K. to talk to," ["Rivers" was a code name used by Anthony Ulasewicz.]

11. On or about July 7, 1972, Anthony Ulasewicz delivered approximately $25,000 in cash to William O. Bittman at 815 Connecticut Avenue, Northwest, in the District of Columbia.

12. In or about mid-July, 1972, John N. Mitchell and Kenneth W. Parkinson met with John W. Dean 3rd at 1701 Pennsylvania Avenue in the District of Columbia, at which time Mitchell advised Dean to obtain F.B.I. reports of the investigation into the Watergate break-in for Parkinson and others.

13. On or about July 17, 1972, Anthony Ulasewicz delivered approximately $40,000 in cash to Dorothy Hunt at Washington National Airport.

14. On or about July 17, 1972, Anthony Ulasewicz delivered approximately $8,000 in cash to G. Gordon Liddy at Washington National Airport.

15. On or about July 21, 1972, Robert C. Mardian met with John W. Dean 3rd at the White House in the District of Columbia, at which time Mardian examined F.B.I. reports of the investigation concerning the Watergate break-in.

16. On or about July 26, 1972, John D. Ehrlichman met with Herbert W. Kalmbach at the White House in the District of Columbia, at which time Ehrlichman told Kalmbach that Kalmbach had to raise funds with which to make payments to and for the benefit of the persons involved in the Watergate break-in, and that it was necessary to keep such fund-raising and payments secret.

17. In or about late July or August, 1972, Anthony Ulasewicz made a delivery of approximately $43,000 in cash at Washington National Airport.

18. In or about late July or early August, 1972. Anthony Ulasewicz made a delivery of approximately $18,000 in cash at Washington National Airport.

19. On or about Aug. 29, 1972, Charles W. Colson had a conversation with John W. Dean 3rd, during which Dean advised Colson not to send memorandums to the authorities investigating the Watergate break-in.

20. On or about Sept. 19, 1972, Anthony Ulasewicz delivered approximately $53,000 in cash to Dorothy Hunt at Washington National Airport.

21. On or about Oct. 13, 1972, in the District of Columbia, Fred C. LaRue arranged for the delivery of...$20,000...to William O. Bittman.

22. On or about Nov. 13, 1972, in the District of Columbia, E. Howard Hunt Jr. had a telephone conversation with Charles W. Colson, during which Hunt discussed with Colson the need to make additional payments to and for the benefits of the defendants in criminal case No. 1827-72 in the United States District Court for the District of Columbia.

23. In or about mid-November, 1972, Charles W. Colson met with John W. Dean 3rd at the White House in the District of Columbia, at which time Colson gave Dean a tape recording of a telephone conversation between Colson and E. Howard Hunt Jr.

24. On or about Nov. 15, 1972, John W. Dean 3rd met with John D. Ehrlichman and Harry R. Haldeman at Camp David, Md., at which time Dean played for Ehrlichman and Haldeman a tape recording of a telephone conversation between Charles W. Colson and E. Howard Hunt Jr.

25. On or about Nov. 15, 1972, John W. Dean 3rd met with John N. Mitchell in New York City...[and] played for Mitchell a tape recording of the telephone conversation between Charles W. Colson and E. Howard Hunt Jr.

26. On or about Dec. 1, 1972, Kenneth W. Parkinson met with John W. Dean 3rd at the White House in the District of Columbia, at which time Parkinson gave Dean a list of anticipated expenses of the defendants during the trial of criminal case No. 1827-72 in the United States District Court for the District of Columbia.

27. In or about early December, 1972, Harry R. Haldeman had a telephone conversation with John W. Dean 3rd, during which Haldeman approved the use of a portion of a cash fund of approximately $350,000, then being held under Haldeman's control, to make additional payments to and for the benefit of the defendants in criminal case No. 1827-72 in the United States District Court for the District of Columbia.

28. In or about early December, 1972, Gordon Strachan met with Fred C. LaRue at LaRue's apartment in the District of Columbia, at which time Strachan delivered approximately $50,000 in cash to LaRue.

29. In or about early December, 1972, in the District of Columbia, Fred C. LaRue arranged for the delivery of approximately $40,000 in cash to William O. Bittman.

30. On or about Jan. 3, 1973, Charles W. Colson met with John W. Dean 3rd at the White House in the District of Columbia, at which time Colson, Ehrlichman and Dean discussed the need to make assurances to E. Howard Hunt Jr. concerning the length of time E. Howard Hunt Jr. would have to spend in jail if he were convicted in criminal case No. 1827-72 in the United States District Court for the District of Columbia.

31. In or about early January, 1973, Harry R. Haldeman had a conversation with John W. Dean 3rd, during which Haldeman approved the use of

the balance of the cash fund referred to in overt act No. 27 to make additional payments to and for the benefit of the defendants in criminal case No. 1827-72 in United States District Court for the District of Columbia.

32. In or about early January, 1973, Gordon Strachan met with Fred C. LaRue at LaRue's apartment in the District of Columbia, at which time Strachan delivered approximately $300,000 in cash to LaRue.

33. In or about early January, 1973, John N. Mitchell had a telephone conversation with John W. Dean 3rd, during which Mitchell asked Dean to have John C. Caulfield give an assurance of executive clemency to James W. McCord Jr.

34. In or about mid-January, 1973, the District of Columbia, Fred C. LaRue arranged for the delivery of approximately $20,000 in cash to a representative of G. Gordon Liddy.

35. On or about Feb. 11, 1973, in Rancho LaCosta, Calif., John D. Ehrlichman and Harry R. Haldeman met with John W. Dean 3rd and discussed the need to raise money with which to make additional payments to and for the benefit of the defendants in criminal case No. 1827-72 in the United States District Court for the District of Columbia.

36. In or about late February, 1973, in the District of Columbia, Fred C. LaRue arranged for the delivery of approximately $25,000 in cash to William O. Bittman.

37. In or about late February, 1973, in the District of Columbia, Fred C. LaRue arranged for the delivery of...$35,000 in cash to...Bittman.

38. On or about March 16, 1973, E. Howard Hunt Jr. met with Paul O'Brien at 815 Connecticut Avenue, Northwest, in the District of Columbia, at which time Hunt told O'Brien that Hunt wanted...$120,000.

39. On or about March 19, 1973, John D. Ehrlichman had a conversation with John W. Dean 3rd at the White House in the District of Columbia, during which Ehrlichman told Dean to inform John N. Mitchell about the fact that E. Howard Hunt Jr. had asked for approximately $120,000.

40. On or about March 21, 1973, from approximately 11:15 a.m. to approximately noon, Harry R. Haldeman and John W. Dean 3rd attended a meeting at the White House in the District of Columbia, at which time there was a discussion about the fact that E. Howard Hunt Jr. had asked for approximately $120,000.

41. On or about March 21, 1973, at approximately 12:30 p.m., Harry R. Haldeman had a telephone conversation with John N. Mitchell.

42. On or about the early afternoon of March 21, 1973, John N. Mitchell had a conversation with Fred C. LaRue during which Mitchell authorized LaRue to make a payment of approximately $75,000 and for the benefit of E. Howard Hunt Jr.

43. On or about the evening of March 21, 1973, in the District of Columbia, Fred C. LaRue arranged for the delivery of approximately $75,000 in cash to William O. Bittman.

44. On or about March 22, 1973, John D. Ehrlichman, Harry R. Haldeman and John W. Dean 3rd met with John N. Mitchell at the White

House in the District of Columbia, at which time Mitchell assured Ehrlichman that E. Howard Hunt Jr. was not a "problem" any longer.

45. On or about March 22, 1973, John D. Ehrlichman had a conversation with Egil Krogh at the White House in the District of Columbia, at which time Ehrlichman assured Krogh that Ehrlichman did not believe that E. Howard Hunt Jr. would reveal certain matters.

(Title 18, United States Code, Section 371.)

Count Two

The grand jury further charges:

1. From on or about June 17, 1972, up to and including the date of the filing of this indictment, in the District of Columbia and elsewhere, John N. Mitchell, Harry R. Haldeman, John D. Ehrlichman, Charles W. Colson, Kenneth W. Parkinson and Gordon Strachan, the defendants, unlawfully, willfully and knowingly did corruptly influence, obstruct and impede, and did corruptly endeavor to influence, obstruct and impede the due administration of justice in connection with an investigation being conducted by the Federal Bureau of Investigation and the United States attorney's office for the District of Columbia, and in connection with the trial of criminal case No. 1827-72 in the United States District Court for the District of Columbia, by making cash payments and offers of other benefits to and for the benefit of the defendants in Criminal Case No. 1827-72 in the United States District Court for the District of Columbia, and to others, both prior to and subsequent to the return of the indictment on Sept. 15, 1972, for the purpose of concealing and causing to be concealed the identities of the persons who were responsible for, participated in, and had knowledge of the activities which were the subject of the investigation and trial, and by other means.

(Title 18, United States Code, Section 1503 and the number 2.)

Count Three

The grand jury further charges:

On or about July 5, 1972, in the District of Columbia, John N. Mitchell, the defendant, did knowingly and willfully make false, fictitious and fraudulent statements and representations to agents of the Federal Bureau of Investigation, Department of Justice, which department was then conducting an investigation into a matter within its jurisdiction, namely, whether violations of 18 U.S.C. 371, 2511, and 22 D.C. Code 1801 (b), and of other statutes of the United States and the District of Columbia had been committed in the District of Columbia and elsewhere in connection with the break-in at the Democratic National Committee headquarters at the Watergate office building on June 17, 1972, and to identify the individual or individuals who had committed, caused the commission of, and conspired to commit such violations, in that he stated that he had no knowledge of the break-in at the Democratic National Committee headquarters other than what he had read in newspaper accounts of that indicent.

(Title 18, United States Code, Section 1001.)

Count Four

The grand jury further charges:

1. On or about Sept. 14, 1972, in the District of Columbia, John N. Mitchell, the defendant, having duly taken an oath that he would testify truthfully, while testifying in a proceeding before the June, 1972, grand jury, a grand jury of the United States duly impaneled and sworn in the United States District Court for the District of Columbia, did knowingly make false material declarations as hereinafter set forth.

2. At the time and place alleged, the June 1972, grand jury of the United States District Court for the District of Columbia was conducting an investigation in conjunction with the United States Attorney's Office of the District of Columbia and the Federal Bureau of Investigation to determine whether violations if Title 18, United States Code, Sections 371, 2511 and 22D.C. Code No. 1801 (b), and of other statutes of the United States and of the District of Columbia, had been committed in the District of Columbia, and elsewhere and to identify the individual or individuals who had committed, caused the commission of, and conspired to commit such violations.

3. It was material to the said investigation that the said grand jury ascertain the identity and motives of the individual or individuals who were responsible for, participated in, and had knowledge of unlawful entries into, and electronic surveillance of the offices of the Democratic National Committee, located in the Watergate office building in Washington, D.C., and related activities.

4. At the time and place alleged, John N. Mitchell, the defendant, appearing as a witness under oath at the proceeding before the said grand jury, did knowingly declare with respect to the material matters alleged in Paragraph 3 as follows:

Q. Was there any program, to your knowledge, at the committee, or any effort made to organize a covert or clandestine operation, basically, you know, illegal in nature, to get information or to gather intelligence about the activities of any of the Democratic candidates for public office or any activities of the Democratic Party?

A. *Certainly not, because if there had been, I would have shut it off as being entirely nonproductive at that particular time of the campaign.*

Q. Did you have any knowledge, direct or indirect, of Mr. Liddy's activities with respect to any intelligence-gathering effort with respect to the activities of the Democratic candidates or its party?

A. *None whatsoever, because I didn't know there was anything going on of that nature, if there was. So I wouldn't anticipate having heard anything about his activities in connection with it.*

5. The underscored portions of the declarations quoted in Paragraph 4, [in italics above] made by John N. Mitchell, the defendant, were material to the said investigation and, as he then and there well knew, were false.

(Title 18, United States Code, Section 1623.)

Count Five

The grand jury further charges:

1. On or about April 20, 1973, in the District of Columbia, John N. Mitchell, the defendant, having duly taken an oath and sworn that he would testify truthfully, and while testifying in a proceeding before the June, 1972, grand jury, a grand jury of the United States duly impaneled and sworn in the United States District Court for the District of Columbia, did knowingly make false material declarations as hereinafter set forth.

2. At the time and place alleged, the June, 1972, grand jury of the United States District Court for the District of Columbia was conducting an investigation in conjunction with the United States attorney's office for the District of Columbia and the Federal Bureau of Investigation to determine whether violations of Title 18, United States Code, Sections 371, 2511 and 22 D.C. Code 1801 (b), and of other statutes of the United States and of the District of Columbia had been committed in the District of Columbia and elsewhere, and to identify the individual or individuals who had committed, caused the commission of, and conspired to commit such violations.

3. It was material to the said investigation that the said grand jury ascertain the identity and motives of the individual or individuals who were responsible for, participated in, and had knowledge of efforts to conceal, and to cause to be concealed, information relating to unlawful entries into, and electronic surveillance of, the offices of the Democratic National Committee located in the Watergate office building in Washington, D.C., and related activities.

4. At the time and place alleged, John N. Mitchell, the defendant, appearing as a witness under oath at a proceeding before the said grand jury, did knowingly declare with respect to the material matters alleged in Paragraph 3 as follows:

Q. Did Mr. LaRue tell you that Mr. Liddy had confessed to him?

A. *No, I don't recall that, no.*

Q. Did Mr. Mardian tell you that he'd confessed to him?

A. *No.*

Q. Do you deny that?

A. Pardon me?

Q. Do you deny that?

A. *I have no recollection of that.*

Q. So Mr. Mardian did not report to you that Mr. Liddy had confessed to him?

A. *Not to my recollection, Mr. Glanzer.*

Q. That would be something that you would remember, if it happened, wouldn't you?

A. Yes, I would.

Q. I didn't ask you that, I asked you were you told by either Mr. Mardian or Mr. LaRue or anybody else, at the committee, prior to June 28th, 1972, that Mr. Liddy had told them that he was involved in the Watergate break-in?

A. *I have no such recollection.*

The underscored portions [set in italics above] of the declarations quoted in Paragraph 4, made by John N. Mitchell, the defendant, were material to the said investigation and, as he then and there well knew, were false.

(Title 18, United States Code, Section 1623.)

Count Six

The grand jury further charges:

1. On or about July 10 and July 11, 1973, in the District of Columbia, John N. Mitchell, the defendant, having duly taken an oath before a competent tribunal, to wit, the Select Committee on Presidential Campaign Activities, a duly created and authorized committee of the United States Senate conducting official hearings and inquiring into a matter in which a law of the United States authorizes an oath to be administered that he would testify truly, did willfully, knowingly and contrary to such oath state material matters hereinafter set forth which he did not believe to be true.

2. At the time and place alleged, the said committee was conducting an investigation and study, pursuant to the provisions of Senate Resolution 60 adopted by the United States Senate on Feb. 7, 1973, of the extent, if any, to which illegal, improper or unethical activities were engaged in by any persons, acting either individually or in combination with others, in the Presidential election of 1972, or in any related campaign or canvass conducted by or in behalf of any person seeking nomination or election as the candidate of any political party for the office of President of the United States in such election, for the purpose of determining whether in its judgment any occurrences which might be revealed by the investigation and study indicated the necessity or desirability of the enactment of new legislation to safeguard the electoral process by which the President of the United States is chosen.

3. It was material to the said investigation and study that the said committee ascertain the identity and motives of the individual or individuals who were responsible for, participated in, and had knowledge of efforts to conceal, and to cause to be concealed information relating to (A) unlawful entries into, and electronic surveillance of, the offices of the Democratic National Committee located in the Watergate office building in Washington, D.C., and (B) related activities, through such means as the destruction of documents and other evidence of said facts.

4. At the times and place alleged, John N. Mitchell, the defendant, appearing as a witness under oath before the said committee, did willfully and knowingly state with respect to the material matters alleged in Paragraph 3 as follows:

July 10, 1973:

MR. DASH. Was there a meeting in your apartment on the evening that you arrived in Washington on June 19, attended by Mr. LaRue, Mr. Mardian, Mr. Dean, Mr. Magruder—

MR. MITCHELL. Magruder and myself, that is correct.

MR. DASH. Do you recall the purpose of that meeting, the discussion that took place there?

MR. MITCHELL. I recall that we had been traveling all day and, of course, we had very little information about what the current status was of the entry of the Democratic National Committee, and we met at the apartment to discuss it. They were, of course, clamoring for a response from the committee because of Mr. McCord's involvement, etc., etc., and we had quite a general discussion of the subject matter.

MR. DASH. Do you recall any discussion of the so-called either Gemstone files or wire-tapping files that you had in your possession?

MR. MITCHELL. *No, I had not heard of the Gemstone files as of that meeting and, as of that date, I had not heard that anybody there at that particular meeting knew of the wire tapping aspects of that or had any connection with it.*

July 11, 1973:

SENATOR WEICKER. Now, on June 19, Mr. Magruder has testified and Mr. LaRue has stated that Mr. Mitchell, that you instructed Magruder to destroy the Gemstone files, to in fact, have a bonfire with them.

SENATOR WEICKER. Did you suggest that any documents be destroyed, not necessarily Gemstone?

MR. MITCHELL. To the best of my recollection.

SENATOR WEICKER. At the June 19 meeting at your apartment?

Did you suggest that any documents be destroyed, not necessarily Gemstone or not necessarily documents that relate to electronic surveillance?

MR. MITCHELL. *To the best of my recollection, when I was there there was no such discussion of the destruction of documents. That was not the type of a meeting we were having.*

5. The underscored portions [set in italics above] of the declarations quoted in Paragraph 4, made by John N. Mitchell, the defendant, were material to the said investigation and study and, as he then and there well knew, were false.

(Title 18, United States Code, Section 1621.)

Count Seven

The Grand Jury further charges:

1. On or about July 30, 1973, in the District of Columbia Harry R. Haldeman, the defendant, having duly taken an oath before a competent tribunal, to wit, the Select Committee on Presidential Campaign Activities, a duly created and authorized committee of the United States Senate conducting official hearings and inquiring into a matter in which a law of the United States authorizes an oath to be administered, that he would testify truly, did willfully, knowingly and contrary to such oath state material matters hereinafter set forth which he did not believe to be true.

2. At the time and place alleged, the said committee was conducting an investigation and study, pursuant to the provisions of Senate Resolution

60 adopted by the United States Senate on Feb. 7, 1973, of the extent, if any, to which illegal, improper or unethical activities were engaged in by any persons, acting either individually or in combination with others, in the Presidential election of 1972, or in any related campaign or canvass conducted by or in behalf of any person seeking nomination or election as the candidate of any political party for the office of President of the United States in such election, for the purpose of determining whether in its judgment any occurrences which might be revealed by the investigation and study indicated the necessity or desirability of enactment of new legislation to safeguard the electoral process by which the President of the United States is chosen.

3. It was material to the said investigation and study that the said committee ascertain the identity and motives of the individual or individuals who were responsible for, participated in and had knowledge of efforts to conceal, and to cause to be concealed, information relating to (A) unlawful entries into, and electronic surveillance of, the offices of the Democratic National Committee located in the Watergate office building in Washington, D.C. and (B) related activities, through such means as the payment and promise of payment of money and other things of value to participants in these activities and to their families.

4. At the time and place alleged, Harry R. Haldeman, the defendant, appearing as a witness under oath before said committee, did willfully and knowingly state with respect to the material matters alleged in Paragraph 3 as follows:

I was told several times, starting in the summer of 1972, by John Dean and possibly also by John Mitchell that there was a need by the committee for funds to help take care of the legal fees and family support of the Watergate defendants. The committee apparently felt obliged to do this.

Since all information regarding the defense funds was given to me by John Dean, the counsel to the President, and possibly by John Mitchell, and since the arrangements for Kalmbach's collecting funds and for transferring the $350,000 cash fund were made by John Dean, and since John Dean never stated at the time that the funds would be used for any other than legal legal [sic] and proper purposes, I had no reason to question the propriety or legality of the process of delivering the $350,000 to the committee via LaRue or of having Kalmbach raise the funds.

I have no personal knowledge of what was done with the funds raised by Kalmbach or with the $350,000 that was delivered by Strachan to LaRue.

It would appear that, at the White House at least, John Dean was the only one who knew that the funds were for "hush money," if, in fact, that is what they were for. The rest of us relied on Dean and all thought that what was being done was legal and proper.

No one, to my knowledge, was aware that these funds involved either blackmail or "hush money" until this suggestion was raised in March of 1973.

5. The underscored [set in italics above] portion of the statements quoted in Paragraph 4, made by Harry R. Haldeman, the defendant, was

material to the said investigation and study and, as he then and there well knew, was false.

(Title 18, United States Code, Section 1621.)

Count Eight

The grand jury further charges:

1. On or about July 30 and July 31, 1973, in the District of Columbia, Harry R. Haldeman, the defendant, having duly taken an oath before a competent tribunal, to wit, the Select Committee on Presidential Campaign Activities, a duly created and authorized committee of the United States Senate conducting official hearings and inquiring into a matter in which a law of the United States authorizes an oath be administered, that he would testify truly, did willfully, knowingly and contrary to such oath state material matters hereinafter set forth which he did not believe to be true.

2. At the times and place alleged, the said committee was conducting an investigation and study, pursuant to the provisions of the Senate Resolution 60 adopted by the United States Senate on Feb. 7, 1973, of the extent, if any, to which illegal, improper or unethical activities were engaged in by any persons, acting either individually or in combination with others, in the Presidential election of 1972, or in any related campaign or canvass conducted by or in behalf of any person seeking nomination or election as the candidate of any political party for the office of President of the United States in such election, for the purpose of determining whether in its judgment any occurrences which might be revealed by the investigation and study indicated the necessity or desirability of the enactment of new legislation to safeguard the electoral process by which the President of the United States is chosen.

3. It was material to the said investigation and study that the said committee ascertain the identity and motives of the individual or individuals who were responsible for, participated in, and had knowledge of efforts to conceal, and to cause to be concealed, information relating to (A) unlawful entries into, and electronic surveillance of, the offices of the Democratic National Committee located in the Watergate office building in Washington, D.C., and (B) related activities, through such means as the payment and promise of payment of money and other things of value to participants in these activities and to their families.

4. At the times and place alleged, Harry R. Haldeman, the defendant, appearing as a witness under oath before said committee, did willfully and knowingly state with respect to the material matters alleged in Paragraph 3 as follows:

July 30, 1973:

I was present for the final 40 minutes of the President's meeting with John Dean on the morning of March 21. While I was not present for the first hour of the meeting, I did listen to the tape of the entire meeting.

Following is the substance of that meeting to the best of my recollection.

173

He [Dean] also reported on a current Hunt blackmail threat. He said Hunt was demanding $120,000 or else he would tell about the seamy things he had done for Ehrlichman. The President pursued this in considerable detail, obviously trying to smoke out what was really going on. He led Dean on regarding the process and what he would recommend doing. He asked such things as—"Well, this is the thing you would recommend? We ought to do this? Is that right?" And he asked where the money would come from. How it would be delivered. And so on. He asked how much money would be involved over the years and Dean said "probably a million dollars—but the problem is that it is hard to raise." The President said, "There is no problem in raising a million dollars, we can do that, *but it would be wrong.*"

July 31, 1973:

SENATOR BAKER...What I want to point out to you is that one statement in your addendum seems to me to be of extraordinary importance and I want to test the accuracy of your notetaking from those tapes, and I am referring to the last, next to the last, no the third from the last sentence on page 2. "The President said there is no problem in raising a million dollars. We can do that but it would be wrong."

Now, if the period were to follow "we can do that," it would be a most damning statement. If, in fact, the tapes clearly show he said "but it would be wrong," it is an entirely different context. Now, how sure are you, Mr. Haldeman, that those tapes, in fact, say that?

MR. HALDEMAN. *I am absolutely positive that the tapes—*

SENATOR BAKER. Did you hear it with your own voice?

MR. HALDEMAN. *With my own ears, yes.*

SENATOR BAKER. I mean with your own ears. Was there any distortion in the quality of the tape in that respect?

MR. HALDEMAN. No I do not believe so.

SENATOR ERVIN. Then the tape said that the President said that there was no problem raising a million dollars.

MR. HALDEMAN. Well, I should put that the way it really came, Mr. Chairman, which was that Dean said when the President said how much money are you talking about here and Dean said over a period of years probably a million dollars, but it would be very hard—it is very hard to raise that money. And the President said it is not hard to raise it. We can raise a million dollars. *And then got into the question of, in the one case before I came into the meeting making a statement that it would be wrong* and in exploration of this getting into the—trying to find out what Dean was talking about in terms of a million dollars.

SENATOR ERVIN. Can you point—are you familiar with the testimony Dean gave about his conversations on the 13th and the 21st of March with the President?

MR. HALDEMAN. I am generally familiar with it, yes sir.

SENATOR ERVIN. Well, this tape corroborates virtually everything he said except that he said that the President could be—that the President said there would be no difficulty about raising the money and you say the only difference in the tape is that the President also added that but that would be wrong.

MR. HALDEMAN. And there was considerable other discussion about what you do, what Dean would recommend, what should be done, how—what this process is and this sort of thing. It was a very—there was considerable exploration in the area.

5. The underscored [set in italics above] portions of the statements quoted in Paragraph 4, made by Harry R. Haldeman, the defendant, were material to the said investigation and study and, as he then and there well knew, were false.

(Title 18, United States Code, Section 1621.)

Count Nine

The grand jury further charges:

1. On or about August 1, 1973, in the District of Columbia, Harry R. Haldeman, the defendant, having duly taken oath before a competent tribunal, to wit, the Select Committee on Presidential Campaign Activities, a duly created and authorized committee of the United States Senate conducting official hearings and inquiring into a matter in which a law of the United States authorizes an oath to be administered, that he would testify truly, did willfully, knowingly and contrary to such oath state material matters hereinafter set forth which he did not believe to be true.

2. At the time and place alleged, the said committee was conducting an investigation and study, pursuant to the provisions of Senate Resolution 60 adopted by the United States Senate on Feb. 7, 1973, of the extent, if any, to which illegal, improper or unethical activities were engaged in by any persons, acting either individually or in combination with others, in the Presidential election of 1972, or in any related campaign or canvass conducted by or in behalf of any person seeking nomination or election as the candidate of any political party for the office of President of the United States in such election, for the purpose of determining whether in its judgment any occurrences which might be revealed by the investigation and study indicated the necessity or desirability of the enactment of new legislation to safeguard the electoral process by which the President of the United States is chosen.

3. It was material to the said investigation and study that the said committee ascertain the identity and motives of the individual or individuals who were responsible for, participated in, and had knowledge of efforts to conceal, and to cause to be concealed, information relating to (A) unlawful entries into, and electronic surveillance of, the offices of the Democratic National Committee located in the Watergate office building in Washington, D.C., and (B) related activities, through such means as the commission of perjury and subornation of perjury.

4. At the time and place alleged, Harry R. Haldeman, the defendant, appearing as a witness under oath before the said committee, did willfully and knowingly state with respect to the material matters alleged in Paragraph 3 as follows:

SENATOR GURNEY. Let's turn to the March 21 meeting....Do you recall any discussion by Dean about Magruder's false testimony before the grand jury?

MR. HALDEMAN. There was a reference to his feeling that Magruder had known about the Watergate planning and break-in ahead of it, in other words, that he was aware of what had gone on at Watergate. *I don't believe there was any reference to Magruder committing perjury.*

5. The underscored [set in italics above] portion of the statements quoted in Paragraph 4, made by Harry R. Haldeman, the defendant, was material to the said investigation and study and, as he then and there well knew, were false.

(Title 18, United States Code, section 1621.)

Count Ten

The grand jury further charges:

On or about July 21, 1973, in the District of Columbia, John D. Ehrlichman, the defendant, did knowingly and willfully make false, fictitious and fraudulent statements and representation to agents of the Federal Bureau of Investigation, Department of Justice, which department was then conducting an investigation into a matter within its jurisdiction, namely, whether violations of 18 U.S.C 371, 2511, and 22 D.C. Code 801(B), and of other statutes of the United States and the District of Columbia, had been committed in the District of Columbia and elsewhere in connection with the break-in at the Democratic National Committee headquarters at the Watergate office building on June 17, 1972, to identify the individual or individuals who had committed, caused the commission of, and conspired to commit such violations, in that he stated that he had neither received nor was he in the possession of any information relative to the break-in at the Democratic National Committee headquarters on June 17, 1972, other than what he had read in the way of newspaper accounts of that incident.

(Title 18, United States Code, Section 1001.)

Count Eleven

The grand jury further charges:

1. On or about May 3, and May 9, 1973, in the District of Columbia, John D. Ehrlichman, the defendant, having duly taken an oath that he would testify truthfully, and while testifying in a proceeding before the June, 1972, grand jury, a grand jury of the United States, duly impaneled and sworn in the United States District Court for the District of Columbia, did knowingly make false material declarations as hereinafter set forth.

2. At the times and place alleged, the June, 1972, grand jury of the United States District Court for the District of Columbia was conducting an investigation in conjunction with the United States attorney's office for the District of Columbia and the Federal Bureau of Investigation to determine whether violations of Title 18, United States Code, Sections 371, 2511, and 22 D.C. Code 1801 (B) and of other statutes of the United States and of

the District of Columbia and elsewhere, and to identify the individual or individuals who had committed, caused the commission of, and conspired to commit such violations.

3. It was material to the said investigation that the said grand jury ascertain the identity and motives of the individual or individuals who were responsible for, participated in, and had knowledge of efforts to conceal, and to cause to be concealed, information relating to unlawful entries into, and electronic surveillance of, the offices of the Democratic National Committee located in the Watergate office building in Washington, D.C., and related activities.

4. At the time and place alleged, John D. Ehrlichman, the defendant, appearing as a witness under oath at a proceeding before the said grand jury, did knowingly declare with respect to the material matters alleged in Paragraph 3 as follows:

May 3, 1973:

Q. Mr. Ehrlichman, going back to that first week following the Watergate arrest, did you have any conversations besides those on Monday with Mr. Dean?

A. Yes, I did.

Q. Will you relate those to the ladies and gentlemen of the grand jury?

A. Well, I don't recall the content specifically of most of them. I know that I saw Mr. Dean because my log shows that he was in my office. I think it was four times that week, once in a large meeting—excuse me, more than four times.

He was in alone twice on Monday, and in the large meeting that I have described. He was in twice alone on other occasions, and then he was in a meeting that I had with Patrick Gray—well, that was the following week. It was a span of seven days, within the span of seven days.

Q. All right, Now at any of those meetings with Mr Dean, was the subject matter brought up of a person by the name of Gordon Liddy?

A. *I can't say specifically one way or the other.*

Q. So you neither confirm or deny that anything with respect to Mr. Liddy was brought up at any of those meetings, is that correct, sir?

A. I don't recall whether Mr. Liddy was being mentioned in the press and would have been the subject of an inquiry by somebody from the outside. If he would have, then it is entirely probable that his name came up.

Q. All right. Let's assume for a moment that Mr. Liddy's name did not in that first week arise in the press. Can you think of any other context in which his name came up excluding any possible press problem with respect to the name of Liddy?

A. *I have no present recollection of that having happened.*

Q. So you can neither confirm or deny whether or not the name of Gordon Liddy came up in the course of any conversation you had with Mr. Dean during that week or for that matter with anyone else?

A. That's right, unless I had some specific event to focus on. Just to take those meetings in the abstract, I can't say that I have any recollection of them having happened in any of those.

Q. All right. Let's take the example or did anyone advise you, directly or indirectly, that Mr. Liddy was implicated or involved in the Watergate affair?

A. Well, they did at some time, *and I don't know whether it was during that week or not.*

Q. To the best of your recollection, when was that done, sir?

A. *I'm sorry but I just don't remember.*

Q. Well, who was it that advised you of that?

A. I think it was Mr. Dean, but I don't remember when he did it.

Q. Would it have been within a month of the investigation? Within three months of the investigation?

A. *I'm sorry but I just don't know.*

Q. You can't even say then whether it was within a week, a month, or three months? Is that correct, sir?

A. Well, I think it was fairly early on, but to say it was within a week or two weeks or something, I just don't know.

Q. Now Mr. Dean advised you that Mr. Liddy was implicated. Did you advise the United States attorney or the attorney general, or any other law enforcement agency immediately or at any time after?

A. *No. I don't think it was private information at the time I heard it.*

Q. Well, did you inquire to find out whether or not it was private information?

A. *To the best of my recollection, when I first heard it it was not in the nature of exclusively known to Dean, or anything of that kind.*

Q. Well, was it in the newspapers that he was involved?

A. *I'm sorry. I just don't remember. It probably was, but I just don't recall.*

Q. You mean the first time you found out from Mr. Dean that Liddy was involved, Mr. Ehrlichman, it was in the same newspaper or the newspapers that you yourself could have read?

A. No, no. I am telling you that I cannot remember the relationship of time, but my impression is that he was not giving me special information that was not available to other people.

A lot of Mr. Dean's information came out of the Justice Department apparently, and I think the impression I had was whatever he was giving us by way of information was known to a number of other people. That's what I meant by special information.

May 9, 1973

Q. When did you first become aware that Mr. Liddy was involved?

A. I don't know.

Q. You don't know?

A. No, sir.

Q. Did you ever become aware of it?

A. Well, obviously I did, but I don't know when that was.

Q. Was it in June?

A. *I say I don't know.*

Q. Who told you?

A. *I don't know.*

Q. How did you learn it?

A. *I don't recall.*

The underscored portions [set in italics above] of the declarations quoted in Paragraph 4, made by John D. Ehrlichman, the defendant, were material to the said investigation and, as he then and there well knew, were false.

(Title 18, United States Code, Section 1625.)

Count Twelve

The grand jury further charges:

1. On or about May 3, and May 9, 1973, in the District of Columbia, John D. Ehrlichman, the defendant, having duly taken an oath that he would testify truthfully, and while testifying in a proceeding before the June, 1972, grand jury of the United States, duly impaneled and sworn in the United States District Court for the District of Columbia, did knowingly make false material declarations as hereafter set forth.

2. At the time and place alleged, the June, 1972, grand jury of the United States District Court for the District of Columbia was conducting an investigation in conjunction with the United States attorney's office for the District of Columbia and the Federal Bureau of Investigation to determine whether violations of Title 18, United States Code, Sections 371, 2511 and 22 D.C. Code 1801(B), and other statutes of the United States and of the District of Columbia had been committed in the District of Columbia and elsewhere, and to identify the individual or individuals who had committed, caused the commission of, and conspired to commit such violations.

3. It was material to the said investigation that the said grand jury ascertain the identity and motives of the individual or individuals who were responsible for, participated in, and had knowledge of efforts to conceal, and to cause to be concealed, information relating to unlawful entries into and electronic surveillance of, the offices of Democratic National Committee located in the Watergate Office building in Washington, D.C., and related activities.

4. At the times and place alleged, John D. Ehrlichman, the defendant, appearing as a witness under oath at a proceeding before the said grand jury, did knowingly declare with respect to the material matters alleged in paragraph 3 as follows:

May 3, 1973:

Q. Now with respect to that, what further information did you receive that really related to this fundraising for the defendants and the defense counsel and their families?

A. I had a call from Mr. Kalmbach within four or five days to verify whether or not I had in fact talked to John Dean. I said that I had.

Q. This was a telephone call, sir?

A. I think it was. It may have been during a visit. I'm not sure. I used to see Mr. Kalmbach periodically about all kinds of things.

It may have been during a visit, but I think it was just a phone call.

He said substantially that John Dean had called me and said that I had no objection, and I said, "Herb, if you don't have any objection to doing it, I don't have any objection to your doing it, obviously."

He said, "No, I don't mind," and he went ahead.

Q. So far as you recall the only conversation that you recall is Mr. Kalmbach saying to you, "John Dean has asked me to do this," and you stated that you had no objection. He said that he was checking with you to determine whether you and any objection or not?

A. He was checking on Dean.

Q. On Dean?

A. Yes.

Q. And you said to him, "If you don't have any objection then I don't have any objection.

A. *Right.*

Q. Was there any discussion between the two of you as to the purpose for which this money was to be raised?

A. I don't think so.

Q. Did you in any way approve the purpose for which this money was being given?

A. *No, I don't think so, I don't recall doing so.*

Q. Based on your testimony for the background of this, there would have been no basis for your approval or for you to affirm that?

A. That's right. That's why I say I don't believe that I did.

Q. And your best recollection is that you did not?

A. That's right.

Q. Do you have any recollection of Mr. Kalmbach inquiring of you whether or not this was appropriate, sir?

A. Are you questioning me with respect to that?

Q. Yes.

A. *No, I don't.*

Q. He did not, to the best of your recollection?

A. *I don't have any recollection of his doing so.*

Q. You have expressed, say back six or seven months ago, to Mr. Kalmbach that the raising of the money should be kept as a secret matter, and it would be either political dynamite, or comparable words, if it ever got out, when Mr. Kalmbach came to see you?

A. *No, I don't recall ever saying that.*

5. The underscored portions of the declarations [set in italics above] quoted in Paragraph 4, made by John D. Ehrlichman, the defendant, were material to the said investigation and, as he then and there well knew, were false.

(Title 18, United States Code, Section 1623.)

Count Thirteen

The grand jury further charges:

1. On or about April 11, 1973, in the District of Columbia, Gordon

Strachan, the defendant, having duly taken an oath that he would testify truthfully, and while testifying in a proceeding before the June 1972, grand jury, a grand jury of the United States, duly impaneled and sworn in the United States District Court for the District of Columbia, did knowingly make false material declarations as hereafter set forth.

2. At the time and place alleged, the June, 1972, grand jury of the United States District Court for the District of Columbia was conducting an investigation in conjunction with the United States attorney's office for the District of Columbia and the Federal Bureau of Investigation to determine whether violations of Title 18, United States Code, Sections 371, 2511 and 22 D.C. Code 1801 (B), and of other statutes of the United States and of the District of Columbia had been committed in the District of Columbia and elsewhere, and to identify the individual or individuals who had committed, caused the commission of, and conspired to commit such violations.

3. It was material to the said investigation that the said grand jury ascertain the identity and motives of the individual or individuals who were responsible or participated in, and had knowledge of efforts to conceal, and to cause to be concealed, information relating to unlawful entries into, and electronic surveillance of the offices of the Democratic National Committee located in the Watergate office building in Washington, D.C., and related activities.

4. At the time and place alleged, Gordon Strachan, the defendant, appearing as a witness under oath at a proceeding before the said grand jury, did knowingly declare with respect to the material matters alleged in Paragraph 3 as follows:

Q. Did you, yourself, ever receive any money from the Committee for the Re-Election of the President, or from the Finance Committee to Re-elect the President?

A. Yes, sir, I did.

Q. Can you tell the ladies and gentlemen of the grand jury about that?

A. Yes, sir. On April 6, 1972, I received $350,000 in cash.

Q. From whom?

A. From Hugh Sloan.

Q. What was done with the money after you received it from Mr. Sloan on April 6th?

A. I put it in the safe.

Q. Was the money ever used?

A. Pardon?

Q. Was the money ever used?

A. No, the money was not used.

Q. To your knowledge, was it ever taken out of the safe?

A. No.

Q. To your knowledge, is it still there?

A. No, it is not.

Q. Where is it?

A. *I returned it to the committee, at Mr. Haldeman's direction, at the end of November.*

181

Q. November of '72?

A. Yes, '72, or early December.

Q. To whom did you return it?

A. To Fred LaRue.

Q. Where did that transfer take place?

A. I gave it to Mr. LaRue in his apartment.

Q. That was either late November or early December?

A. That's correct.

Q. Well, let me ask you this: Why would it have been given to Mr. LaRue at his apartment as opposed to being given to the committee?

A. Well, Mr. LaRue is a member of the committee and he just asked me to bring it by on my way home from work.

Q. After Mr. Haldeman told you to return the money, what did you do? Did you contact someone to arrange for delivery?

A. Yes, I contacted Mr. LaRue.

Q. That was at Mr. Haldeman's suggestion or direction?

A. No.

Q. Why is it that you would have called Mr. LaRue?

A. I don't think Stans was in the country at that time. He was not available.

Q. What position did Mr. LaRue occupy that would have made you call him?

A. He was the senior campaign official.

Q. That's the only reason you called him?

A. *That's correct.*

Q. No one suggested you call him?

A. *No.*

Q. Was anyone present in Mr. LaRue's apartment at the hotel when you delivered the money to him?

A. No.

Q. Did you ever tell anyone to whom you had given the money? Did you report back to either Mr. Haldeman or anyone else that you had delivered the money?

A. I don't think so. I could have mentioned that I had done it. When I received an order, I did it.

Q. Did you get a receipt for the money?

A. No, I did not.

Q. Did you ask for it?

A. No, I did not.

JUROR. Why?

THE WITNESS. I did not give a receipt when I received the money, so I didn't ask for one when I gave it back.

JUROR. Did someone count the money when it came in and when it went out, so they knew there were no deductions made from that $350,000?

THE WITNESS. Yes, I counted the money when I received it, and I counted it when I gave it back.

JUROR. You solely counted it; no one else was with you?

THE WITNESS. I counted it when I received it alone, and I counted it in front of Mr. LaRue when I gave it back.

JUROR. You had that money in the White House for seven months and did nothing with it?

THE WITNESS. That's correct.

Q. So who told you to give it to Mr. LaRue?

A. *I decided to give it to Mr. LaRue.*

Q. On your own initiative?

A. *That's correct.*

Q. Who do you report to?

A. Mr. Haldeman.

Q. Did you report back to Mr. Haldeman that you gave it to Mr LaRue?

A. No, I did not.

Q. You just kept this all to yourself?

A. He was a senior official at the campaign, I gave it back to him. He said he would account for it, and that was it.

Q. Who told you to go to Mr. LaRue and give him the money.

A. *I decided that myself.*

Q. Do you have a memo in your file relating to this incident?

A. No, I do not.

Q. Did you discuss this incident with anybody afterwards?

A. Yes, I told Mr. Haldeman afterwards that I had given the money to Mr. LaRue.

Q. What did he say to you?

A. Fine. He was a senior campaign official.

Q. What time of day was it that you gave it to Mr. LaRue?

A. In the evening, after work.

Q. Does the finance committee or the Committee to Re-Elect the President conduct its business in Mr. LaRue's apartment?

A. No. It was a matter of courtesy. He's a senior official. He asked me to drop it by after work.

THE FOREMAN. Do you have any idea why Mr. LaRue asked you to return this money to his apartment, where actually you could just walk across 17th Street?

THE WITNESS. No, I do not.

THE FOREMAN. And you could have had the protection of the Secret Service guards with all that money, if you were afraid someone might snatch it from you.

THE WITNESS. I wouldn't ask for the Secret Service guards protection.

JUROR. Why not?

THE WITNESS. They protect only the President and his family.

THE FOREMAN. Or the White House guards, whoever. I mean, I find it somewhat dangerous for a person to be carrying this amount of money in Washington, in the evening, and you accompanied by your brother, when it would have been much easier and handier just to walk across 17th Street.

THE WITNESS. I agree, and I was nervous doing it, but I did it.

THE FOREMAN. I'm still puzzled. You get the money from the treasurer or whatever Mr. Sloan's position was in the committee—shall we say on an official basis, between the disburser and you as the receiver, and the money sits in the safe for seven months; then Mr. Haldeman decides it has to go back to the committee. You call Mr. LaRue—you don't call Mr. Sloan and say "Hugh, seven months ago you gave me this $350,000 and we haven't used any of it; I'd like to give it back to you since I got it from you," but you call Mr. LaRue.

THE WITNESS. Mr. Sloan was no longer with the committee at the time.

THE FOREMAN. Well, whoever took Mr. Sloan's place.

THE WITNESS. Mr. Barret took Mr. Sloan's place.

THE FOREMAN. Why didn't you call him.

THE WITNESS. *I honestly don't know.*

Q. When you got to Mr. LaRue's apartment was he expecting you?

A. Yes. I said I would be by.

Q. And no one was present when you were there?

A. No, sir.

Q. Was the money counted?

A. Yes sir, I counted it.

JUROR. It must have taken a long time to count that money.

THE WITNESS. It did. It took about 45 minutes. It takes a long time to count it.

Q. How did you carry this money?

A. In a briefcase.

Q. Did you take the briefcase back, or did you leave it?

A. No, I left the briefcase.

Q. Whose briefcase was it?

A. Gee, I think it was mine. I'm honestly not sure.

Q. Did you ever get the briefcase back?

A. I don't think so.

Q. Have you spoken to Mr. LaRue since that day?

A. No—well, I ran into him at a party two weeks ago.

Q. Did you have a discussion?

A. No, just talked to him.

5. The underscored portions [set in italics above] of the declarations quoted in Paragraph 4, made by Gordon Strachan, the defendant were material to the said investigation and, as he then and there well knew, were false.

(Title 18, United States Code, Section 1623.)

EEC OFFER TO ARAB STATES

March 4, 1974

On March 4, less than a month after endorsing joint action with the United States, Canada and Japan to work to guarantee continued production and equitable distribution of energy supplies to combat current energy shortages, the nine Common Market countries of the European Economic Community (EEC) approached twenty Arab countries with an independent offer to explore long-term economic, technical and cultural cooperation. The proposal called for Arab representatives to confer with the EEC's President of the Council of Ministers, Walter Scheel, also foreign minister of West Germany, about possible cooperative efforts; establishment of working groups to discuss possible areas of cooperation; and eventually a ministerial meeting between leaders of the Arab and European states, if such a meeting appeared worthwhile. The foreign ministers of the Arab League, meeting in Tunis, Tunisia, March 25-28, agreed to establish a nine-member delegation to negotiate with the EEC on economic and technological cooperation.

Even though oil and political issues were not mentioned specifically as areas of cooperation in the March offer, the EEC's proposal appeared to deal a setback to U.S.-backed attempts at unified action by all oil-consuming nations, rather than competitive unilateral actions, in assuring continued oil supplies. According to the New York Times, the EEC move was viewed also as a victory for France which had preferred action through existing European organizations. France, which had already signed agreements for continued oil supplies with several Arab states, had opposed establishment of a coordinating council to plan for a meeting between oil-producing and oil-consumer countries, a proposal that had come forward at the U.S.-initiated meeting of oil-consuming nations in Washington, D.C., Feb. 11-13, 1974. (See p. 123-127.) The council was to include officials from not only Western Europe, but also the United States, Canada and Japan.

Because European nations obtained three-fourths of their oil supplies from Arab producers, the EEC offer was seen as a unilateral move to better the European position among Arab oil producers. The EEC's previous declaration on the Middle East, issued in November 1973 during the Arab-Israeli war, the most tense period of oil shortages, also had been widely interpreted as an attempt by the Common Market countries to gain greater political favor with the Arab states. Faced in November with the likelihood that Arab oil supplies would be cut off unless European states neutralized their support of Israel, the EEC declaration had urged a return of Egyptian and Israeli forces to lines held before Israeli troops isolated the Egyptian III Corps on the west bank of the Suez Canal. (See Historic Documents, 1973, p. 931-937.)

U.S. Reaction

U.S. anger at the EEC offer to the Arab states apparently was not dispelled by assurances from Scheel that any new actions would run parallel to and not interfere with follow-up actions to the Washington energy conference. On March 11, Secretary of State Henry A. Kissinger bluntly told a group of congressmen's wives that "the biggest problem American foreign policy confronts is...how to bring our friends to a realization that there are greater common interests than simple self-assertiveness." Kissinger subsequently apologized for his comments for which he apparently had not expected press coverage. But in the same week President Nixon postponed a U.S.-EEC meeting in Bonn which would have dealt with a draft declaration on relations between the U.S. and EEC. Nixon also warned the nine that they must work with the U.S. "on the economic and political front," or else America "will go separately." "Going separately" might involve significant troop reductions in Europe, Nixon said. Unidentified officials in the Nixon administration were reported to have said that the U.S. government was reevaluating its policy towards France in view of what it considered the French policy of trying to isolate the U.S. from Europe. Kissinger was said to believe that the EEC offer to the Arabs had been inspired by the French.

Background of EEC Offer

Groundwork for the EEC's offer had been laid at the December 1973 summit conference of the nine countries in Copenhagen. Out of that meeting came recommendations for agreement with oil-producing nationals to trade European economic and industrial assistance for stable energy supplies. Though not officially invited to Copenhagen, the foreign ministers of

Algeria, Tunisia, the Sudan and the Union of Arab Emirates had appeared at the talks to emphasize that any solution to the energy crisis would have to include producing as well as consuming countries. To end the current Arab-imposed embargo on shipments of oil to the West, the Arabs said they would require strong support of their demands for the return of Arab territories held by Israel since the June 1967 war.

Following is an unofficial translation of the text of a proposal issued by the European Economic Community to Arab states, March 4:

[1]

The nine Governments of the member states of the European Community confirm the importance they attach to the talks that took place in Copenhagen, on Dec. 14 and 15 with the Foreign Ministers of Algeria, Sudan and Tunisia as well as the Ministers of State of the Arab Emirates, who, speaking in the name of all the Arab countries, expressed the wish that the countries of the Community should develop their relations with the Arab world and engage with it in long-term cooperation in all fields, notably the economic, technical and cultural.

[2]

The nine wish, on their part, to continue the dialogue thus begun and develop from it mutually beneficial cooperation including in relations, existing or developing, with the Community.

[3]

In the first analysis, the nine believe that this cooperation should be realized by concrete actions, in numerous fields like industry, agriculture, energy and raw materials, transportation, science and technology, financial cooperation and training of cadres, for example.

[4]

The first objective of the Arab and European governments would be, in the opinion of the latter, to organize among themselves as soon as possible contacts which would permit them to express their initial views on the character to be developed and on the efforts to be made to undertake it. The nine propose, as a first step, and at as soon a date as possible, a meeting between their own President, the Foreign Minister of the Federal Republic of Germany [and EEC president] and the representative or representatives that the Arab governments wish to designate. The Foreign Minister of the Federal Republic of Germany will undertake these meetings in his double capacity, presiding over the political cooperation of the nine and over the European Economic Council.

[5]

In light of the results of the foregoing the nine are prepared to undertake afterward, at the European and Arab expert level, for example at a working group level, a study of the ways and means of cooperation between them, to arrive at concrete recommendations, as soon as possible.

[6]

If the results of their work justify it, in the opinion of the two parties, a conference of the foreign ministers of the Community and of the Arab countries can be organized to take the necessary decisions.

NIXON ON WATERGATE
AND RESIGNATION
March 6-19, 1974

President Nixon spoke out on Watergate before newsmen and two enthusiastic public audiences March 6-19 following the March 1 indictment of seven former White House and campaign aides on charges of covering up the Watergate scandal (see p. 157). During a nationally televised news conference from the White House March 6, Nixon made his strongest denial to date that he had authorized either clemency or the payment of "hush money" for the defendants in the 1972 Watergate break-in. But he acknowledged that he had discussed these matters in some detail before rejecting them. In Chicago March 16 before the city's Executives' Club, the President emphasized his determination not to yield to the House Judiciary Committee's demands for more White House documents and recordings of taped conversations. In Houston March 19, speaking before the National Association of Broadcasters, he repeated assertions that he would not resign nor do anything to weaken the office of the presidency.

Nixon used the nationally televised White House news conference March 6 as his forum for rebutting implications that had arisen the week before. One of the seven former White House aides or Nixon re-election committee officials indicted March 1 in the Watergate coverup was H. R. Haldeman, the President's former chief of staff. And one charge against Haldeman was that he had lied to the Senate Watergate investigating committee in saying that Nixon had told John W. Dean III, former presidential counsel, that "there is no problem in raising $1-million...but it would be wrong." The conversation between Dean and Nixon occurred March 21, 1973, and was recorded on a White House tape. The tape was one of 19 turned over to Watergate Special Prosecutor Leon Jaworski. Its contents had not been

189

made public. They were important to Nixon's credibility, because the President had corroborated Haldeman's version. Nixon acknowledged at the news conference that the transcript of the tape could be interpreted differently by different people, "but I know what I meant, and I also know what I did."

In recounting the March 21 meeting with Dean, Nixon told reporters that he had learned for the first time at the meeting that money had been paid to the Watergate defendants for their silence, not just for their legal expenses. The President said he informed Dean, in these exact words: "It is wrong; that is for sure."

Nixon went on to say that he meant "the whole transaction was wrong, the transaction for the purpose of keeping this whole matter covered up.... I never at any time authorized clemency for any of the defendants. I never at any time authorized the payment of money to any of the defendants."

Nixon expressed willingness to meet at some time with leaders of the House Judiciary Committee, which was conducting the impeachment investigation, and answer questions under oath. A prior step, responding in writing to the committee's questions, had been offered by Nixon's lawyer, James D. St. Clair. In court the day of the news conference, St. Clair had offered the committee all the records that had been given earlier to the special prosecutor.

In response to a later question, however, the President balked at a suggestion that giving the committee all the tapes and documents it sought would speed up settlement of the case. On the contrary, Nixon replied, it would delay a conclusion for as long as a year. Completion of the investigation could take months, he said, "if all that is really involved...is to cart everything that is in the White House down to a committee, and to have them paw through it on a fishing expedition." But Nixon later repeated what he had said earlier—he wanted to remove the cloud over the White House. To do so, he said, he had cooperated with the special prosecutor and with the Judiciary Committee.

Chicago Speech

In a question-and-answer session before the Executives Club of Chicago March 15, President Nixon was asked: "Do you not think that the entire incident (Watergate) has begun to affect the quality of life in this country, particularly the great deal of uncertainties that people have about it, and also has begun to affect the concept of ethics, particularly in our young people? And for these reasons alone, would it not be better if you resigned at this time and allowed yourself the public forum as a private citizen to answer all accusations on all parts?"

This was Nixon's answer, as transcribed by Congressional Quarterly *from a tape recording:*

"Let me respond...first, by saying that of course Watergate has had a disturbing effect not only on young people but on other people. It was a wrong and very stupid action, to begin with. I have said that. I believe it now. Second, as far as Watergate is concerned, it has been carried on, it has been, I believe, over-publicized, and a lot of charges have been made that frankly have proved to be false...."

In Chicago, Nixon again remarked on his March 21, 1973, meeting with former White House counsel John Dean. Nixon said he "learned for the first time on March 21 of 1973 that the blackmail attempt was being made in the White House—not on March 13," and "learned for the first time at that time that payments had been made to the defendants." But he said he wanted to correct "what may have been a misapprehension when I spoke to the press on March the 6th in Washington." He said: "It was alleged that the payments that had been made to defendants were made for the purpose of keeping them still. However, Mr. Ehrlichman, Mr. Haldeman, Mr. Mitchell have all denied that that was the case, and they certainly should be allowed the right in court to establish their innocence or guilt without our concluding that that was the case."

Later, responding to the question "Why doesn't the President resign?" Nixon said: "Because if the President resigned when he was not guilty of charges, then every president in the future could be forced out of office by simply leveling the charges and getting the media to carry them, and getting a few congressmen and senators who were on the other side to exploit them."

Houston Appearance

President Nixon said March 19 that Sen. James L. Buckley's (Cons-R N.Y.) statement earlier in the day calling on him to voluntarily resign had not caused him to reassess his position on resignation. During the question-and-answer session before the National Association of Broadcasters in Houston, Texas, Nixon said: "...While it might be an act of courage to run away from a job that you were elected to do, it also takes courage to stand and fight for what you believe is right, and that is what I intend to do."

Nixon repeated his determination to protect the principle of presidential confidentiality in the face of demands by the House Judiciary Committee's special impeachment study staff that he turn over more Watergate-related tapes and documents. "It is difficult to find a proper way to meet the demands of the Congress," he said. "I am trying to do so and trying to be as forthcoming as possible. But I also have another responsibility. I must think not of myself, but I must think also of future presidents of this country, and I am not going to do anything and I am not going to give up to any demand that I believe would weaken the presidency of the United States. I will not participate in the destruction of the office of the president of the United States while I am in this office."

Nixon argued that to give the committee staff free access to presidential documents and tapes would reduce the candor of future presidential advisers, since they would be afraid that their private conversations might eventually become public knowledge. If this became the case, Nixon said, a president "isn't going to get the variety of views he needs to make the right kind of decision."

Excerpts from President Nixon's remarks March 6 to newsmen at a nationally televised news conference, March 16 to the Executives' Club of Chicago and March 19 to the National Association of Broadcasters meeting in Houston, Texas:

THE PRESIDENT'S NEWS CONFERENCE OF MARCH 6, 1974

QUESTIONS

MATERIALS FOR HOUSE JUDICIARY COMMITTEE

Q. Mr. President, your lawyer announced today that you will turn over to the House Judiciary Committee all of the materials that you made available to the Special Prosecutor. I am wondering, sir, what about other materials that the committee might want to see that the Prosecutor didn't see?

THE PRESIDENT. ...Mr. St. Clair [White House Counsel]...has made, I think, a very forthcoming offer. He has indicated that we will respond to any written interrogatories under oath that the committee may have on matters that they do not think are covered adequately by the materials that have been submitted to Mr. Jaworski. And, in addition, he has indicated that in the event that that is not satisfactory, in order to bring the matter to a complete and, we hope, early conclusion, that the President will be glad to meet with members of the committee, perhaps the Chairman and the ranking minority member of the committee, at the White House to answer any further questions under oath that they may have....

CONVERSATIONS AT MARCH 21ST MEETING

Q. Mr. President, Mr. Haldeman, your former top aide in the White House, has been charged with perjury because he testified that you said it would be wrong to pay hush money to silence the Watergate defendants, and last August you said that was accurate. Can you, and will you, provide proof that you did indeed say it would be wrong?

THE PRESIDENT: Miss Thomas, it would be improper, as, of course, you know, for me to comment on the substance of any charges or indictment that have been made against any of the defendants in this matter. However, it is proper for me to comment on what I said and what I did on the 21st of March, which is the date in question.

On that occasion, Mr. Dean asked to see me, and when he came into the office, soon after his arrival he said that he wanted to tell me some things that he had not told me about the Watergate matter. And for the first time, on March 21, he told me that payments had been made to defendants for the purpose of keeping them quiet, not simply for their defense.

If it had been simply for their defense, that would have been proper, I understand. But if it was for the purpose of keeping them quiet—you describe it as "hush money"—that...would have been an obstruction of justice.

I examined him at great length. We examined all of the options at great length during our discussion, and we considered them on a tentative basis—every option as to what the defendants would do, as to who in the White House might be involved, and other information that up to that time had not been disclosed to me by Mr. Dean.

Then we came to what I considered to be the bottom line. I pointed out that raising the money, paying the money, was something that could be done, but I pointed out that that was linked to clemency, that no individual is simply going to stay in jail because people are taking care of his family or his counsel...and that unless a promise of clemency was made, that the objective of so-called "hush money" would not be achieved.

I am paraphrasing what was a relatively long conversation.

I then said that to pay clemency was wrong. In fact, I think I can quote it directly. I said, "It is wrong; that is for sure." Mr. Haldeman was present when I said that. Mr. Dean was present. Both agreed with my conclusion.

Now, when individuals read the entire transcript of the 21st meeting or hear the entire tape where we discussed all of these options, they may reach different interpretations, but I know what I meant, and I also know what I did.

I meant that the whole transaction was wrong, the transaction for the purpose of keeping this whole matter covered up. That was why I directed that Mr. Haldeman, Mr. Ehrlichman, Mr. Dean, and Mr. Mitchell, who was then in New York, meet in Washington that evening, if possible—it turned out that they could not meet until the next day—so that we could find out what would be the best way to get the whole story out.

I also know what I did with regard to clemency and with regard to the payment of the money to any of the defendants. And after we had met on the 22nd, I sent Mr. Dean to Camp David to write a full report of everything that he knew.

That report was not forthcoming, and, consequently, on the 30th of August (March), a week later, I directed Mr. Ehrlichman to conduct an independent investigation, which he did conduct, and presented to me on the 14th of April.

And also on the 30th, on that same day—Mr. Ziegler announced this to the press corps, after I had issued the direction—I directed that all members of the White House Staff who were called by the grand jury should appear before the grand jury and testify fully with regard to any knowledge whatever they had with regard to their involvement, if they were involved, or anybody else's involvement.

In other words, the policy was one of full disclosure, and that was the decision that was made at the conclusion of the meeting....

CLEMENCY

Q. Without regard to past events or hush money or anything like that, would you now consider granting clemency to any former assistants who might ultimately be convicted?

THE PRESIDENT. The matter of clemency, Mr. Theis, is something that can only be granted and only be considered on an individual basis, depending upon the circumstances involved. I can only say that under no circumstances has any defendant or potential defendant been offered clemency. That would be improper, and I will not engage in that activity....

Q. Mr. President, to follow up on an earlier answer, as I understand it, you said that you are not ruling out the possibility that you might grant clemency to a former aide. Is that correct, you are really not ruling that out, and if so, why?

THE PRESIDENT. No,...I am simply saying that I am not ruling out granting clemency to any individual depending upon a personal tragedy or something of that sort.

What I am saying, that I am not going to grant clemency because they happen to be involved in Watergate— that I am ruling out....

MATERIALS FOR IMPEACHMENT INVESTIGATION

Q. Mr. President,....you spoke of an expeditious conclusion of the impeachment hearings in the House. Would it not serve the purpose of a speedy conclusion of these hearings for you to give the committee whatever materials, tapes, and documents they consider pertinent to their investigation?

THE PRESIDENT. It would not lead to a speedy conclusion; it would delay it in my opinion. Because if all that is really involved in this instance is to cart everything that is in the White House down to a committee and to have them paw through it on a fishing expedition, it will take them a matter of months, so that they can complete their investigation and, we trust, their decision by the first of May, which I understand is Mr. Rodino's object, but it would take them months and perhaps even as long as a year....

IMPEACHABLE OFFENSES

Q. Mr. President, your attorneys have taken what is seen as the narrow view on impeachment, saying that impeachment should be limited to very serious crimes committed in one's official capacity. My question is, would you consider the crimes returned in the indictments last week, those of perjury, obstruction of justice, and conspiracy, to be impeachable crimes if they did apply to you?

THE PRESIDENT. Well, I have also quit beating my wife. *[Laughter]*

Of course, the crime of perjury is a serious crime, and, of course, the crime of obstruction of justice is a serious crime and would be an impeachable offense, and I do not expect that the House committee will find that the President in guilty of any of these crimes to which you have referred.

When you refer to a narrow view of what is an impeachable crime, I would say that might leave in the minds of some of our viewers and listeners, a connotation which would be inaccurate. It is the constitutional view. The Constitution is very precise. Even Senator Ervin agrees that that view is the right one, and if Senator Ervin agrees, it must be the right one....

MARCH 21, 1973, MEETING

Q. Mr. President, you said earlier, if my notes are correct, that on March 21, Mr. Dean told you for the first time that payments were made to defendants to keep them quiet and that you considered a number of options. Did you not consider the option of blowing the whistle, of turning that information over to the authorities immediately, and on reflection now do you think you should have?

THE PRESIDENT. As a matter of fact, among the options we considered was getting out a full report, a report that he would write. Among the options we considered the next day—and we started to consider it that day—was to have everybody testify before the Ervin committee and waive executive privilege, which was a course of action which Attorney General Mitchell recommended.

Yes, the option of a full disclosure at that time by everybody concerned was one that was considered. The difficulty that I had was that for months these matters had not been brought to my attention. I had not been informed of the payments to the defendants. I had not been informed with regard to the alleged coverup. I had not been informed about the possible involvement of some White House aides.

I felt it was my responsibility to conduct my own investigation with all the assistance I could get from those who could provide information before moving to what would be a proper way of getting this story out to the country....

Q. Mr. President, I have a followup on that question right there, on the March 21st meeting. You have referred to your own personal desire to have complete disclosure, and you have also mentioned here this evening that anybody who heard the tape of that March 21st meeting, or different people hearing that tape, or reading the transcript, might get different impressions. Have you ever considered the option of making that tape and transcript public so that the American people can read it, and hear it, and make their own judgment on what happened at that meeting?

THE PRESIDENT. Yes, I have. We have a problem there, however, in that that tape, as well as others, as was, I think, probably implied at least in the hearing today, affects the rights of the defendants and also the possibilities of the prosecution, and under the circumstances, of course, we must be, to a certain extent, guided by that.

I think eventually the entire tape will be made available....

PAYMENTS TO DEFENDANTS

Q. Mr. President, just to follow up an earlier question about Watergate and the indictments, I was wondering if you figured out, sir, why the payment of $75,000 in alleged hush money occurred the same day you said you disapproved of the practice? I am talking about the March 21st conversation.

THE PRESIDENT. I have no information as to when a payment was made, to what you have referred. All I have information on is as to my own actions and my own directions, and my actions and directions were clear and very precise. I did not authorize payments, and I did not have knowledge of payments to which you have referred.

MR. CORMIER. Thank you Mr. President....

The Executives' Club of Chicago

The President's Remarks in a Question-and-Answer Session at a Luncheon Meeting of the Club, March 15, 1974

COOPERATION WITH SPECIAL PROSECUTOR AND HOUSE JUDICIARY COMMITTEE

Q. Mr. President, you said on many occasions that you are willing to cooperate with the Special Prosecutor and Congress in this Watergate situation, but going beyond a certain point might tend to weaken the future constitutional relationship between the Presidency and Congress. Now I agree, but I think there is a great deal of confusion among the public and maybe not enough of a point made. And I wonder if you would care to make a few additional comments on that point.

THE PRESIDENT. ...Now first, being reasonable it seems to me would be that the committee should first examine what it has, because Mr. Jaworski, the Special Prosecutor, said that he had what he considered to be the full story of Watergate, and we want the full story out.

It has been before the Special Prosecutor, and it is now before the committee.

Second, with regard to additional requests, there are those who I think very logically would raise the question: Well, why not just give the members of the Judiciary Committee the right to come in and have all of the tapes of every Presidential conversation, a fishing license or complete right to go in and go through all of the Presidential files in order to find out whether or not there is a possibility that some action had been taken which might be and might result in an impeachable offense.

The reason why we cannot go that far, the reason why we have gone probably as far as we have and even in going that far have weakened the office of the Presidency is very simply this: It isn't a question that the President has something to hide; it is the fact that every President, Democrat and Republican from the founding of this Republic, has recognized the necessity of protecting the confidentiality of Presidential conversations with his associates, with those who come to see him, be they Congressmen or Senators or people from various parts of the country to give advice. And if that confidentiality principle is completely destroyed, future Presidents will not have the benefit of the kind of advice that an executive needs to make the right decision. He will be surrounded by a group of eunuchs insofar as their advice is concerned, always fearful that sometime in the future if they happen to have given an opinion which turned out to be wrong that then they would be held responsible for it—wrong, I am not referring to being illegal, but wrong in terms of whether or not it worked....

WATERGATE AND THE QUESTION OF RESIGNATION

Q. Mr. President, forgetting all other considerations of whether the Watergate situation was or is as publicized or not because it is still in the process of being litigated, do you not think that the entire incident has begun to affect the quality of life in this country, particularly in the great deal of uncertainties that people have about it, and also begun to influence the concepts of ethics, particularly of our young people, and for those reasons alone would it not be better that you resign at this time and allow yourself the public forum as a private citizen to answer all accusations on all parts?

THE PRESIDENT. Now ladies and gentlemen, that is a perfectly proper question, and it has been raised not only by the gentleman who has asked it but by several respected publications in this area as well as in other parts of the country, and some Members of Congress as well.

Let me respond to it first by saying that of course Watergate has had a disturbing effect not only on young people but on other people. It was a wrong and very stupid action to begin with. I have said that and I believe it now.

Second, as far as Watergate is concerned, it has been carried on, it has been I believe overpublicized, and a lot of charges have been made that frankly have proved to be false.

I am sure that many people in this audience have read, at one time or other, either in your news magazines, possibly in a newspaper, certainly heard on telvision and radio such charges as this: That the President helped to plan the Watergate thing before and had knowledge of it; that the President was informed of the cover-up on September 15th of 1973; that the President was informed that payments were being made on March 13 and that a blackmail attempt was being made on the White House on March 13 rather than on March 21 when I said was the first time those matters were brought to my attention; that the President had authorized the issuance of clemency or a promise of clemency to some of the defendants and that the President had ordered the burglarizing—again, a very stupid act apart from the fact of its being wrong and illegal—of Dr. Ellsberg's psychiatrist's office in California.

Now, all of those charges have been made. Many of the Americans, perhaps a majority, believe them. They are all totally false, and the investigations will prove it, whatever the Congress does, the tapes, et cetera, when they all come out, will establish that they are false.

The President learned for the first time on March 21st of 1973 that a blackmail attempt was being made on the White House, not on March 13. The President learned for the first time at that time that payments had been made to the defendants, and let me point out that payments had been made but—correcting what may have been a misapprehension when I spoke to the press on March 6 in Washington—it was alleged that the payments that had been made to defendants were made for the purpose of keeping them still.

However, Mr. Ehrlichman, Mr. Haldeman, Mr. Mitchell have all denied that that was the case, and they certainly should be allowed the right in court to establish their innocence or guilt without our concluding that that was the case.

But be that as it may, Watergate has hung over the country, and it continues to hang over the country. It will continue to as the Judiciary Committee continues its investigation not only of voluminous documents that we have already presented to the Special Prosecutor, not only of all the material they have from the Ervin committee that has conducted months of hearings—and they have access to that—but in addition, scores of tapes and thousands of documents more, which would mean that not just one year but two years or three years we are going to have this hanging over the country.

That is why I want a prompt and just conclusion and will cooperate, as I indicated in answer to the first question, with the committee consistent with my responsibility to defend the office of the Presidency to get that prompt and just conclusion.

Now, under these circumstances, because the impression has been created, as you have very well indicated, doubts, mistrust of the President—I recognize that—why doesn't the President resign? Because if the President resigned when he was not guilty of charges, then every President in the future could be forced out of office by simply leveling some charges and getting the media to carry them and getting a few Congressmen and Senators who were on the other side to exploit them.

Why doesn't the President resign because his popularity is low? I already have referred to that question. Because if the time comes in this country when a President makes decisions based on where he stands in the polls rather than what is right or what is wrong, we will have a very weak President.

The Nation and the world need a strong President. Now, personally, I will say finally, from a personal standpoint, resignation is an easy copout. Resignation, of course, might satisfy some of my good friendly partisans who would rather not have the problem of Watergate bothering them. But on the other hand, apart from the personal standpoint, resignation of this President on charges of which he is not guilty, resignation simply because he happened to be low in the polls, would forever change our form of government. It will lead to weak and instable Presidencies in the future and I will not be a party to the destruction of the Presidency of the United States....

DEFINITION OF "IMPEACHABLE OFFENSE"

Q. Mr. President, there is a debate over the definition of an "impeachable offense." Should this question be determined by Congress or the judiciary?

THE PRESIDENT. I think it is determined by the Constitution. And I think the Constitution very clearly, as Mr. St. Clair, our very able counsel, pointed out in his brief to the Judiciary Committee, the Constitution in this case defines an impeachable offense, as I indicated earlier, as being treason, bribery, or other high crimes and misdemeanors.

Now, this President is not guilty of any of those crimes, and as far as the Congress is concerned, it would seem to me that—particularly members of the Judiciary Committee, all schooled in the law—would want to follow the Constitution rather than to broaden that definition to include something that the Constitution-framers did not have in mind....

PRESIDENTIAL TESTIMONY

Q. Mr. President, intense two-way loyalty has been a hallmark of your public life and your Administration. If it can be shown to you conclusively that your in-person testimony on behalf of your former colleagues is vital to their defense, would you not consider stepping forward and taking the witness stand?

THE PRESIDENT. I believe that for the President of the United States to appear in a court of law, any court of law, for the purpose of testifying, would be setting a precedent that would be most unfortunate. I believe that any information that I have has been made available, which could affect the guilt or innocence of the individuals involved, and I think the appearance of the President of the United States in any one of these cases would be a precedent which we would regret later....

NATIONAL ASSOCIATION OF BROADCASTERS

The President's Remarks in a Question-and-Answer Session at the Association's Annual Convention in Houston, Texas. March 19, 1974

QUESTIONS

SENATOR BUCKLEY AND THE QUESTION OF RESIGNATION

Q. ...You said repeatedly that you will not resign, and yet today, Senator James Buckley called for you to perform an extraordinary act of statesmanship and courage, voluntary resignation as he put it, the only way by which the Watergate crisis can be resolved.

Would you comment on the import of this statement coming from a conservative United States Senator, and whether it might cause you to reassess your position?

THE PRESIDENT. Well first, it does not cause me to reassess my position, although I, of course, do respect the point of view expressed by the Senator and by others, perhaps some sitting here, who share that view....

[I]t perhaps would be an act of courage to resign. I should also point out, however, that while it might be an act of courage to run away from a job that you were elected to do, it also takes courage to stand and fight for what you believe is right, and that is what I intend to do....

The Constitution provides a method by which a President can be removed from office, impeachment—impeachment for treason, and other high crimes and misdemeanors. Now, if a President is not guilty of those crimes, if only charges have been made which he knows are false, and if simply because as a result of those false charges and as a result of his falling in the polls he decides to resign, it would mean that every future President would be presiding over a very unstable Government in the United States of America.

The United States and the free world, the whole world, needs a strong American President, not an American President who every time the polls go down, says, "Well, maybe I'd better resign."...

RELATIONS WITH THE PRESS

Q. Mr. President, Carl Connerton, KWBA Radio at Baytown. In the early portion of 1960, you made a statement at what you called your last press conference, stating that the press wouldn't have Nixon to kick around anymore. Here it is mid-1970, do you feel that the press is kicking Nixon around again?

THE PRESIDENT. ...[T]here is always—as my friend, now retired, of the *Washington Star*, Jack Horner, senior White House correspondent for many years, said, "There is always an adversary relationship between the President and the press"—that is healthy, that is good.

I think the press has a right to criticize the President, and I think the President has the right of self-defense. I would suggest, also, that we should follow this rule: The President should treat the press just as fairly as the press treats him.

PAYMENTS TO WATERGATE DEFENDANTS

Q. ...Mr. President, I wonder if you would explain the difference between a statement you made last August regarding payments to the Watergate defendants and what you said at your press conference this month.

You will recall that in August, you said you were told that the funds were being raised for attorneys' fees and this month that Mr. Dean had told you the money was to be used for keeping defendants quiet, not simply for their defense. Could you explain the difference between those statements?

THE PRESIDENT. Well, as I stated in Chicago, my statement on March 6 was incorrect insofar as it said that I learned that payments had been made prior to the time that the demand for blackmail by Mr. Hunt—alleged demand for blackmail, I should say, since it has not yet been tried—that payments had been made for the purpose of keeping defendants still.

I should have said they were alleged to have been made, because as a matter of fact, those who were alleged to have made payments to defendants for their defense fees and for their support, Mr. Ehrlichman, Mr. Haldeman, Mr. Mitchell, all have denied that that was the case. They have said it was only for the support of the defendants and only for their attorney's fees, which would be completely proper.

Under the circumstances, therefore, it would not be appropriate for me to say anything further on this point, because these men have a right, now, in a court of law, to establish their innocence or to have established the guilt, if they are guilty, of whether or not the payments were made for one purpose or the other....

WATERGATE

Q. Mr. President .... You made the statement that to drag out Watergate is to drag down this country. Do you feel that this country would be better off tonight and in the immediate years ahead if the Watergate break-in had gone undetected and that the actions of that group of people had never been reported to the American people?

THE PRESIDENT. Certainly not. The action was wrong; the action was stupid. It should never have happened. It should not have been covered up, and I have done the very best that I can over the past year to see that it is uncovered.

I have cooperated completely with not only the grand jury but also with other investigative agencies and have waived executive privilege perhaps further than I should in terms of the office of the Presidency in order to cooperate.

When something happens like this, to say "Cover it up, forget it," when it is wrong, this of course is completely against our American system of values, and I would very, very seriously deplore it.

I would also suggest, not by way of defense, but I was often criticized after the 1960 campaign that I always ran my own campaigns. In the year 1972, I am afraid I was too busy with the trip to China, the decision on May 8 with regard to the bombing and mining in the Haiphong area, the trip to the Soviet Union, the negotiations in Vietnam which brought that war to a conclusion, that I frankly paid too little attention to the campaign.

Now, I don't intend to be in another campaign, needless to say, but I also want to say that if I had any advice for candidates in the future, "Run your own campaign, regardless of what the press says"....

COOPERATION WITH SPECIAL PROSECUTOR
AND HOUSE JUDICIARY COMMITTEE

Q. Thank you, Mr. President. Dan Rather, with CBS News, Mr. President, Mr. President—[Applause]

THE PRESIDENT. Are you running for something? *[Laughter]*

Q. No sir, Mr. President; are you? *[Laughter]*

Mr. President, I believe earlier that you said that you had cooperated completely with the grand jury investigation. It was my impression—and I could be wrong about this—but that the record shows that that is not quite the fact, that number one, that the grand jury asked that you come down and tell your side of some stories they had heard, and that you declined to do that, and number two, that the Special Watergate Prosecutor, Mr. Jaworski, indicated in a letter to the Senate that he did not get all of the evidence that he thought he needed, and I would be interested in hearing you reconcile what I believe is on the record of these previous statements.

My basic question is this: That in recent days you have, in effect, attempted to define the limits of the House Judiciary Committee investigation, what evidence that they have access to. Now since the Constitution, and I think without qualification, clearly assigns to the House of Representatives impeachment investigations, how can the House meet its constitutional responsibilities while you, the person under investigation, are allowed to limit their access to potential evidence?

THE PRESIDENT. Which one of the questions do you want me to answer? *[Laughter]*

First, with regard to the first part of the question, Mr. Rather, what I was referring to with regard to cooperation was that Mr. Jaworski, at the time he handed down the indictments, said that he had the full story on Watergate. You reported that on CBS, I think, as did other reporters, quite properly.

Now as far as appearing before the grand jury was concerned, I respectfully declined to do so, and incidentally, I would advise no President of the United States to appear before any grand jury. That would be not in the interest of the Presidency of the United States.

Now, if you would repeat your second question so that we can keep our train of thought.

MR. RATHER. Well, the second question had to do with the House impeachment investigation. I pointed out that you have sought to limit, to define the limits of that investigation, what evidence they have access to and what evidence they should not have access to.

Now, given the constitutional assignment to the House of Representatives of an impeachment investigation without qualification, how can the House committee do its job as long as you, the person under investigation, is allowed to limit their access to potential evidence?

THE PRESIDENT. Well, Mr. Rather, referring to the House of Representatives, just like the President, it is bound by the Constitution. The Constitution says specifically that a President shall be impeached for treason, bribery, or other high crimes or misdemeanors.

It is the Constitution that defines what the House should have access to and the limits of its investigation, and I am suggesting that the House follow the Constitution. If they do, I will....

PRINCIPLE OF CONFIDENTIALITY

Q. Mr. President, Tom Brokaw of NBC News. Following on my colleague, Mr. Rather's question, you referred here tonight as you have in the past, about what you call the precedents of past Presidents in withholding White House material from the House Judiciary Committee. But other Presidents protecting confidentiality of their conversations were not the subject of impeachment investigations, Mr. President, and in fact many of them wrote that the House Judiciary Committee, at least Congress, had the right to demand White House materials in the course of impeachment investigations. And history shows that Andrew Johnson gave up everything that the Congress asked him for when he was the subject of an impeachment investigation.

So, Mr. President, my question is this: Aren't your statements to that matter historically inaccurate or at least misleading?

THE PRESIDENT. Mr. Brokaw, it is true, as you say, that the only other President who was exposed to an impeachment investigation was Andrew Johnson, and in so far as that particular part of your question is concerned, you are correct.

However, in so far as the principle of confidentiality is concerned, that principle still stands, and it affects an impeachment investigation, as well as any other investigation. Because in the future if all that a Congress under the control of an opposition party had to do in order to get a President out of office was to make an unreasonable demand to go through all of the files of the Presidency, a demand which a President would have to refuse, then it would mean that no President would be strong enough to stay in office to resist that kind of demand and that kind of pressure. It would lead to instability. And it would destroy, as I have indicated before, the principle of confidentiality.

With regard to the problem, I simply want to say this: It is difficult to find a proper way to meet the demands of the Congress. I am trying to do so and trying to be as forthcoming as possible. But I also have another responsibility. I must think not of myself but I must think also of future Presidents of this country, and I am not going to do anything, and I am not going to give up to any demand that I believe would weaken the Presidency of the United States. I will not participate in the destruction of the office of the President of the United States while I am in this office....

▼▼▼

ELLSBERG BREAK-IN INDICTMENTS
March 7, 1974

Three former White House officials and three Cuban-Americans were indicted by a federal grand jury in Washington, D.C., March 7 on charges of conspiring to violate the civil rights of Dr. Lewis J. Fielding, Daniel Ellsberg's psychiatrist, by burglarizing his office in September 1971. Indicted were John D. Ehrlichman, former assistant to the President for domestic affairs; Charles W. Colson, former special counsel to the President; G. Gordon Liddy, former staff assistant to the President; Bernard L. Barker and Eugenio Martinez, convicted for the June 1972 Watergate break-in; and Felipe de Diego. Ehrlichman also was charged with lying to FBI agents and to the grand jury about his knowledge of the Fielding burglary. Liddy also was indicted on a separate count of contempt of Congress for his refusal to testify before the House Armed Services Special Subcommittee on Intelligence. Named as co-conspirators were Egil Krogh Jr., who was already serving a six-month prison term for his role in the Fielding burglary; E. Howard Hunt Jr., who was granted immunity by U.S. District Judge John J. Sirica March 28, 1973, for his part in it, and David R. Young, another member of the White House "plumbers," who was granted immunity May 16, 1973. (Krogh Sentencing, see p. 33-40.)

The indictments, the second set handed up against former Nixon administration officials in less than a week, (see p. 157-184), followed by ten months the disclosure that White House agents of a secret unit known as the "plumbers" had burglarized Fielding's Beverly Hills, Calif., office in an attempt to gain information on Daniel Ellsberg. That revelation and the government's inability to produce records of what information had been obtained from that search forced the abrupt dismissal May 11, 1973, of all charges against Ellsberg and Anthony J. Russo Jr. The pair had been accused of espionage and theft for allegedly stealing a secret Pentagon study on the history of the Vietnam war from the files of the Rand Corporation in Santa Monica, Calif., where they both worked, and forwarding copies of part of the study to the New York Times and other newspapers. (See Historic Documents 1973, p. 537-548; Historic Documents 1972, p. 491-498.) The disclosure of the White House connection in the dismissal of the Pentagon Papers trial widened the so-called "Watergate" investigation to include not only a probe of the burglary and wiretapping of the Democratic National Committee headquarters, but also other areas of questionable Nixon administration conduct. Nixon's alleged role in and knowledge of the Fielding break-in and the withholding of information about it also became a factor in the impeachment investigation. (See p. 655-660 and p. 713-763.)

32-Month-Long Conspiracy

According to the first indictment, part of the conspiracy which began about July 1, 1971, and continued until the time of the indictment, was a plan "that the conspirators would, without legal process, probable cause, search warrant or other lawful authority, covertly and unlawfully enter the offices of Dr....Fielding...with intent to search for confidential information concerning Daniel Ellsberg, thereby injuring, oppressing, threatening, and intimidating Dr....Fielding in the free exercise and enjoyment of the right and privilege secured him by the Fourth Amendment to the Constitution of the United States to be secure in his person, house, papers and effects against unreasonable searches and seizures, and that they would thereafter conceal such activities, so as to prevent Dr....Fielding from securing redress for the violation of such right and privilege." The break-in occurred Sept. 3, 1971.

Listing 19 overt acts in support of the conspiracy charge, the grand jury cast Ehrlichman, Colson, Krogh and Young in the roles of those who had conceived and authorized the burglary, which actually was carried out by Baker, de Diego and Martinez under the supervision of Liddy and Hunt. In addition to the charge of conspiracy, Ehrlichman was charged with four counts of lying, once to FBI agents and three times to the grand jury. According to the indictment, Ehrlichman May 1, 1973, "did knowingly and willfully make false, fictitious and fraudulent statements" when he told FBI agents that "it had been over a year since he had seen anything on the 'Pentagon Papers' investigation, and that he had not seen any material covering the White House investigation of the...case for more than a year." Ehrlichman May 14, 1973, told the grand jury that he did not know until after the Fielding burglary that the burglars were looking for a psychological profile of Ellsberg. When he made those statements, "he then and there well knew (that they) were false," the indictment claimed. Thirdly, Ehrlichman May 14, 1973, told the grand jury that he was not aware of the fact, before the Labor Day 1971 break-in, that an effort was directed toward obtaining information from Ellsberg or his psychiatrist. When he denied that knowledge, he knew his statements were false, according to the indictment. And according to the fourth, Ehrlichman May 14, 1973, told the grand jury that he knew of no files related to the Pentagon Papers investigation or other plumbers operations in the possession of anyone except Krogh. When he made those statements, said the indictment, he knew they were false. The maximum penalty for lying to FBI agents is a $10,000 fine and five years in prison. The maximum penalty for lying to a grand jury is the same.

The indictments followed by two months the guilty plea and sentencing of the former codirector of the secret "plumbers" unit, Egil Krogh, who had been sentenced to six months in prison Jan. 24 for approving the Fielding burglary. (See p. 33-40.) Krogh said at his sentencing that he believed he had become overzealous and exceeded his authority when he directed the Fielding break-in. But he said the atmosphere within the Nixon White House had made the action seem appropriate at the time. The defendants named in the March 7 indictments, however, denied their actions had been improper and defended them on the basis of legitimate national security concerns. In late May, it appeared that the case might be dismissed over President Nixon's refusal to release evidence subpoenaed by Ehrlichman for his defense. On June 3, in a surprise move, Colson pleaded guilty to one charge of obstructing justice by disseminating damaging material on Ellsberg. In return, the government agreed to drop all other charges pending against Colson. As part of the agreement, Colson consented to give sworn testimony and release documents in his possession for the prosecution of relevant cases.

Effect on Impeachment Probe

The indictment of figures in the Fielding break-in case held special significance for the presidential impeachment probe and Colson's access to information and his knowledge of prior White House actions threatened to damage the President's case if Colson's testimony differed with previous presidential statements. In one lengthy statement on Watergate, released by the White House May 22, 1973, Nixon had described the White House concern for national security following the publication of the Pentagon Papers study. As a result of the leak, Nixon said, he had approved the creation of the "plumbers" unit "whose purpose was to stop security leaks and to investigate other sensitive matters." He said he told the unit's director, Krogh, "that as a matter of first priority, the unit should find out all it could about Mr. Ellsberg's associates and his motives." Nixon added that "because of the emphasis I put on the crucial importance of protecting national security, I can understand how highly motivated individuals could have felt justified in engaging in specific activities that I would have disapproved had they been brought to my attention." (See Historic Documents 1973, p. 563-574.)

At his Aug. 22, 1973, news conference at San Clemente, Calif., Nixon responded to a question on why he waited a month to disclose to the Pentagon Papers trial judge that the burglary of Fielding's office had occurred. Nixon had previously acknowledged that he learned of the break-in March 17; he directed that information on the burglary be forwarded to the trial judge April 25. Nixon replied to the questions, saying "since no evidence was developed" against Ellsberg from the burglary, "there was no requirement that it be presented to the jury that was hearing the case." At the same news conference, Nixon also responded to a question on the propriety of his meeting with the trial judge in that case to discuss the judge's appointment to the directorship of the FBI. Confronting charges that the action had been a subtle attempt to influence the outcome of the trial, Nixon said Ehrlichman had told the judge, William Matthew Byrne Jr., that "under no circumstances will we talk to you...if he [Byrne] felt that it would in any way compromise his handling of the Ellsberg case." Byrne made the decision that he would talk to Ehrlichman and later to Nixon, Nixon said. (See Historic Documents 1973, p. 737-751.)

The trial of the indicted men: Ehrlichman, Liddy and the Cuban-Americans, began in Washington, D.C., June 26. (For outcome, see p. 411-417 and p. 661-669.)

> *Text of the indictments handed up by a federal grand jury in Washington, D.C., March 7, against John D. Ehrlichman, Charles W. Colson, G. Gordon Liddy, Bernard L. Barker, Eugenio Martinez and Felipe de Diego:*

Count One

The grand jury charges:

1. At all times material herein up to on or about April 30, 1973, John D. Ehrlichman, the defendant, was acting in the capacity of an officer and employe of the United States government, as assistant for domestic affairs to the President of the United States.

2. At all times material herein up to on or about March 10, 1973, Charles W. Colson, the defendant, was acting in the capacity of an officer and employe of the United States government, as special counsel to the President of the United States.

3. From on or about July 20, 1971, up to on or about Dec. 19, 1971, G. Gordon Liddy, the defendant, was acting in the capacity of an officer and employe of the United States government, as staff assistant to the President of the United States.

4. From on or about July 1, 1971, up to and including the date of the filing of this indictment, in the District of Columbia and elsewhere, John D. Ehrlichman, Charles W. Colson, G. Gordon Liddy, Bernard L. Barker, Felipe de Diego, and Eugenio R. Martinez, the defendants, and Egil Krogh Jr., David R. Young, E. Howard Hunt Jr., named herein as co-conspirators but not as defendants, unlawfully, willfully and knowingly did combine, conspire, confederate and agree together and with each other to injure,

oppress, threaten, and intimidate Dr. Lewis J. Fielding, a citizen of the United States, in the free exercise and enjoyment of rights and privileges secured to him by the Constitution and laws of the United States, in violation of Title 18, United States Code, Section 241 (A).

5. It was part of the conspiracy that the conspirators would, without legal process, probable cause, search warrant, or other lawful authority, covertly and unlawfully enter the offices of Dr. Lewis J. Fielding at 450 North Bedford Drive, Beverly Hills, Calif., with intent to search for confidential information concerning Daniel Ellsberg, thereby injuring, oppressing, threatening, and intimidating Dr. Lewis J. Fielding in the free exercise and enjoyment of the right and privilege secured to him by the Fourth Amendment to the Constitution of the United States to be secure in his person, house, papers and effects against unreasonable searches and seizures, and that they would thereafter conceal such activities, so as to prevent Dr. Lewis J. Fielding from securing redress for the violation of such right and privileges.

6. Among the means by which the conspirators would carry out the aforesaid conspiracy were the following: (a) On or about Sept. 1, 1971, the conspirators would travel and cause others to travel to the State of California; (b) On or about Sept. 3, 1971, the conspirators would, without legal process, probable cause, search warrant or other lawful authority, covertly and unlawfully enter and cause to be entered the offices of Dr. Lewis J. Fielding located in Beverly Hills, Calif., (c) On or about Sept. 3, 1971, the conspirators would unlawfully and unreasonably search and cause to be searched the said offices of Dr. Lewis J. Fielding; and (d) On or about Sept. 3, 1971, the conspirators would conduct such unlawful and unreasonable search in a manner designed to conceal the involvement of officials and employes of the United States government.

7. In furtherance of the conspiracy, and in order to effectuate the objects thereof, the following overt acts, among others, were committed in the District of Columbia and elsewhere:

Overt Acts

1. On or about July 27, 1971, Egil Krogh Jr. and David R. Young sent a memorandum to John D. Ehrlichman, which discussed a request for the preparation of a psychiatric study on Daniel Ellsberg.

2. On or about July 28, 1971, E. Howard Hunt Jr. sent a memorandum to Charles W. Colson entitled "Neutralization of Ellsberg" which discussed a proposal to "obtain Ellsberg's files from his psychiatric analyst."

3. On or about July 30, 1971, Egil Krogh Jr. and David R. Young sent a memorandum to John D. Ehrlichman which informed Ehrlichman that the Central Intelligence Agency had been "instructed to do a thorough psychological study on Daniel Ellsberg."

4. On or about Aug. 3, 1971, Egil Krogh Jr. and David R. Young sent a memorandum to Charles W. Colson which referred to the memorandum described in overt act No. 2 and which stated that "we will look into" the suggestions made by E. Howard Hunt Jr.

5. On or about Aug. 11, 1971, John D. Ehrlichman approved a covert operation proposed by Egil Krogh Jr. and David R. Young to examine all the medical files still held by Ellsberg's psychoanalyst if he were given an "assurance it is not traceable."

6. On or about Aug. 23, 1971, John D. Ehrlichman and David R. Young had a conversation in which Ehrlichman and Young discussed financing for "special project H1," a planned entry into the offices of Dr. Lewis J. Fielding to obtain confidential information concerning Daniel Ellsberg.

7. In late Aug. 1971, Charles W. Colson had a telephone conversation with Egil Krogh Jr. in which Colson and Krogh discussed providing money for E. Howard Hunt Jr. and G. Gordon Liddy.

8. During the week of Aug. 22, 1971, Charles W. Colson and David R. Young had a conversation in which Colson and Young discussed providing money for E. Howard Hunt Jr. and G. Gordon Liddy and preparing a plan to disseminate information regarding Daniel Ellsberg.

9. On or about Aug. 26, 1971, David R. Young sent a memorandum to John D. Ehrlichman which referred to "Hunt/Liddy Project No. 12 and stated that Charles W. Colson would get "the information out" on Ellsberg.

10. On or about Aug. 27, 1971, John D. Ehrlichman sent a memorandum to Charles W. Colson entitled "Hunt/Liddy Special Project No. 1" which requested Colson to prepare a "game plan" for the use of materials to be derived from the "proposed undertaking by Hunt and Liddy."

11. On or about Aug. 30, 1971, G. Gordon Liddy had a meeting with Egil Krogh Jr., David R. Young and E. Howard Hunt Jr. in which there was a discussion of the means by which there would be a nontraceable entry into the office of Dr. Lewis J. Fielding.

12. On or about Aug. 30, 1971, John D. Ehrlichman had a telephone conversation with Egil Krogh Jr. and David R. Young in which Krogh and Young assured Ehrlichman that the planned entry into the office of Dr. Lewis J. Fielding would not be traceable.

13. On or about Aug. 31, 1971, Charles W. Colson had a telephone conversation in which he arranged to obtain $5,000 in cash.

14. On or about Sept. 1, 1971, Charles W. Colson arranged for the transfer of $5,000 from the Trust for Agricultural Political Education in order to repay the $5,000 cash described in overt act No. 13.

15. On or about Sept. 1, 1971, Charles W. Colson caused the delivery of $5,000 in cash to Egil Krogh Jr.

16. On or about Sept. 1, 1971, Egil Krogh Jr. delivered $5,000 in cash to G. Gordon Liddy.

17. On or about Sept. 1, 1971, G. Gordon Liddy and E. Howard Hunt Jr. traveled from Washington, D.C., via Chicago, Ill., to Los Angeles, Calif., for the purpose of meeting with Bernard L. Barker, Felipe de Diego and Eugenio R. Martinez.

18. On or about Sept. 3, 1971, Bernard L. Barker, Felipe de Diego and Eugenio R. Martinez searched the offices of Dr. Lewis J. Fielding

located in Beverly Hills, Calif., for the purpose of obtaining confidential information concerning Daniel Ellsberg.

19. On or about March 27, 1973, John D. Ehrlichman caused the removal of certain memoranda related to the entry into the offices of Dr. Lewis J. Fielding from files maintained at the White House in which such memoranda would be kept in the ordinary course of business.

(Title 18, United States Code, Section 241.)

Count Two

The grand jury further charges:

On or about May 1, 1973, in the District of Columbia, John D. Ehrlichman, the defendant, did knowingly and willfully make false, fictitious and fraudulent statements to agents of the Federal Bureau of Investigation, Department of Justice, which department was then conducting an investigation into a matter within its jurisdiction pursuant to an order of the United States District Court for the Central District of California to investigate whether, as a result of an entry conducted by White House employes into the offices of Dr. Lewis J. Fielding located in Beverly Hills, Calif., there had been obtained information which might taint the prosecution in the criminal case of United States of America v. Russo (No. 93 73-CD-WMB), the trial of which was then pending before said court, in that he stated that it had been over a year since he had seen anything on the "Pentagon papers" investigation, and that he had not seen any material covering the White House investigation of the "Pentagon papers" case for more than a year.

(Title 18, United States Code, Section 1001.)

Count Three

The grand jury further charges:

1. On or about May 14, 1973, in the District of Columbia, John D. Ehrlichman, the defendant, having duly taken an oath that he would testify truthfully in a proceeding before the June, 1972, grand jury, a grand jury of the United States duly empaneled and sworn in the United States District Court for the District of Columbia, did make false material declarations as hereinafter set forth.

2. At the time and place alleged, the said grand jury was conducting an investigation in conjunction with the United States attorney's office for the District of Columbia, and the Federal Bureau of Investigation to determine whether violations of 18 U.S.C. Secs. 371, 1001, 1503, 1621, 1623, 2511, and 22 D.C. Code 1801 (b), and of other statutes of the United States and of the District of Columbia, had been committed in the District of Columbia and elsewhere, and to identify the individual or individuals who had committed, caused the commission of and conspired to commit such violations.

3. It was material to said investigation that the grand jury ascertain, among other things, the identity and motives of the individual or individuals who were responsible for, participated in, and had knowledge of

an entry into the offices of Dr. Lewis J. Fielding, located in Beverly Hills, Calif., and related activities.

4. At the time and place alleged, John D. Ehrlichman, the defendant, appearing as a witness under oath before the said grand jury, did knowingly declare with respect to the aforesaid material matters alleged in Paragraph 3 as follows:

Q. Very well, sir. Now there came a time when this operation became concerned with Dr. Ellsberg himself, is that not correct? A. Yes.

Q. And then there was an attempt or a decision made to find out as much about Dr. Ellsberg as could be done, is that correct.? A. Yes.

Q. And even part of that investigation was going to center on his psychological profile, his mental attitudes, his habits, and possible motivations. Is that correct?

A. *Well, I learned about that after the fact,* but that is my understanding of the decision that was made.

Q. When you say you learned about it after the fact, what do you mean by that, sir?

A. *Well, I learned after the break-in that they were looking for information for what they call a psychological profile. I was not aware of that before the fact.*

Q. So before the fact you were not aware that there was an attempt by Mr. Krogh, or persons working under his supervision or authority, to—there was no attempt made by these people to ascertain information that would be helpful in drawing out the psychological profile if I understood what you just said. Is that right?

A. I didn't know if they made an attempt or not. I was just saying that I didn't learn of it until after I learned of the break-in.

Q. Just so that the grand jury and we are clear on this, prior to receiving information about the break-in, you had no information, direct or indirect, that a psychological profile of Dr. Ellsberg was being drawn up?

A. *I can't recall hearing of a psychological profile until after I had heard of the break-in.*

5. The (italicized) portions of the material declarations quoted in Paragraph 4, made by John D. Ehrlichman, the defendant, were material to the said investigation and, as he then and there well knew, were false. (Title 18, United States Code, Section 1623).

Count Four

The grand jury further charges:

1. On or about May 14, 1973, in the District of Columbia, John D. Ehrlichman, the defendant, having duly taken an oath that he would testify truthfully in a proceeding before the June, 1972, grand jury, a grand jury of the United States duly empaneled and sworn in the United States District Court for the District of Columbia, did make false material declarations as hereinafter set forth.

2. At the time and place alleged, the said grand jury was conducting an investigation in conjunction with the United States attorney's office for

the District of Columbia and the Federal Bureau of Investigation to determine whether violations of 18 U.S.C. Secs. 371, 1001, 1503, 1621, 1623, 2511, and 22 D.C. Code 1801 (b), and of other statutes of the United States and of the District of Columbia, had been committed in the District of Columbia and elsewhere, and to identify the individual or individuals who had committed, caused the commission of, and conspired to commit such violations.

3. It was material to said investigation that the grand jury ascertain, among other things, the identity and motives of the individual or individuals who were responsible for, participated in, and had knowledge of an entry into the offices of Dr. Lewis J. Fielding, located in Beverly Hills, Calif., and related activities.

4. At the time and place alleged, John D. Ehrlichman, the defendant, appearing as a witness under oath before the said grand jury, did knowingly declare with respect to the aforesaid material matters alleged in Paragraph 3 as follows:

Q. Now were you aware before this break-in, which took place on or about Sept. 3, 1971, that an effort was going to be directed towards obtaining information from Dr. Ellsberg or Dr. Ellsberg's psychiatrist?

A. *Ahead of the fact? No.*

5. The (italicized) portions of the material declarations quoted in Paragraph 4, made by John D. Ehrlichman, the defendant, were material to the said investigation and, as he then and there well knew, were false.

(Title 18, United States Code, Section 1623.)

Count Five

The grand jury further charges:

1. On or about May 14, 1973, in the District of Columbia, John D. Ehrlichman, the defendant, having duly taken an oath that he would testify truthfully in a proceeding before the June, 1972, grand jury, a grand jury of the United States duly empaneled and sworn in the United States District Court for the District of Columbia, did make false material declarations as hereinafter set forth.

2. At the time and place alleged, the said grand jury was conducting an investigation in conjunction with the United States attorney's office for the District of Columbia and the Federal Bureau of Investigation to determine whether violations of 18 U.S.C. Secs. 371, 1001, 1503, 1621, 1623, 2511, and 22 D.C. Code 1801 (b), and of other statutes of the United States and the District of Columbia, had been committed in the District of Columbia and elsewhere, and to identify the individual or individuals who had committed, caused the commission of and conspired to commit such violations.

3. It was material to said investigation that the grand jury ascertain, among other things, the identity and motives of the individual or individuals who were responsible for, participated in, and had knowledge of an entry into the offices of Dr. Lewis J. Fielding, located in Beverly Hills, Calif., and related activities.

4. At the time and place alleged, John D. Ehrlichman, the defendant, appearing as a witness under oath before the said grand jury, did knowingly declare with respect to the aforesaid material matters alleged in Paragraph 3 as follows:

Q. You indicate here that you did maintain a newspaper clipping file on the Pentagon papers case. A. Right.

Q. But you say there were other papers in addition? A. I think there were some others. There was a small file and it just went out. I didn't have occasion to look at it before it went, but it went.

Q. You mentioned a moment ago, in response to Mr. Silbert's question, that there were some files. Did you have a file relating to . . .

A. No. I don't believe I kept a file.

Q. Who had a file? A. I think Mr. Krogh had a file.

Q. Anybody else have a file? A. *I don't know.*

Q. So as far as you know, prior to the break-in, whenever that was, I think it was sometime in September, Sept. 3, the only person that had a file that you knew of was Mr. Krogh?

A. *I believe that's right.* I, of course, had a great many other things going on. He would, from time to time, post me on the whole Pentagon papers matter.

This was not just Ellsberg. At that time there were all kinds of things going on. There were lawsuits involving the New York Times. There was a lot of activity going on.

He would inform me from time to time of things that would happen. But I kept no paper as I recall. I would move paper out if any came in on this, and usually sign it over to Krogh.

Q. And subsequent to the break-in, did you learn that there were any files anywhere in existence? A. I think there were a number of files both before and after.

Q. In whose hands? A. Well, I assume Krogh. I think that he would be the one that I would always look to for paper work on this with the exception of—I do recall running across this very bulky clipping file that we had in our office, and why we had it I don't know.

But at sometime or another we accumulated a tremendous amount of newspaper clipping on this case. That was the whole Pentagon papers case.

Q. Any other files in the custody of anybody else involved in this operation? A. *Not that I know of. I would assume that Krogh had them all.*

Q. Did you ever learn that anybody had any files before or after Sept. 3?

A. *No, I don't believe so.*

5. The (italicized) portions of the material declarations quoted in Paragraph 4, made by John D. Ehrlichman, the defendant, were material to the said investigation and, as he then and there well knew, were false.

(Title 18, United States Code, Section 1623.)

NIXON ON CAMPAIGN REFORM
March 8, 1974

President Nixon came out in favor of a federal libel law March 8 to give greater protection to political candidates and public officials from attacks by the media and political opponents. The proposal was one of several campaign reform measures set forth in a message to Congress and in a radio address to the nation. The President also recommended more detailed financial disclosures by candidates, severe curbs on cash transactions, tighter controls against "dirty tricks," and a shortening of presidential campaigns. But Nixon indicated that he would veto legislation providing for public campaign financing or campaign spending ceilings.

The Nixon campaign reform package differed from other pending campaign reform bills in three major ways. One was its rejection of public financing of elections. Said Nixon: "One thing we don't need in this country is to add politicians to the federal dole." Public financing, he said, is "a raid on the public treasury." A second point of variance was the overall campaign spending ceiling. Whereas other proposals placed formulated limits on the amount of money spent in federal elections, the Nixon plan did not. Thirdly, Nixon's $15,000 proposed limit on contributions to presidential primary and general election campaigns and $3,000 limit for congressional primaries and general elections far exceeded the limits of other major bills under consideration.

Although Nixon's campaign reform package addressed many of the problems that had arisen from his own presidential re-election campaign, the recommendation for a federal libel law introduced a new issue into the debate over campaign practices that until then had focused almost exclusively on campaign finance.

In calling for the libel law, Nixon said he had asked the Justice Department "to explore the possibility of legislation to reaffirm certain private rights of public figures so that people interested in running for public office can have greater reassurance of recourse against slanderous attacks on them and their families." Complaining that "landmark Supreme Court decisions have severely restricted a public figure's ability to gain redress against grievances," the President said he was trying to achieve balance in his proposal. "These reforms are not intended to restrict vigorous debate, but to enhance it, to help give it dignity and integrity, and to improve the prospects for good and decent people who today flinch from political participation because of their fear of slanderous attacks." (Supreme Court ruling on "right to reply," see p. 523.) The United States, however, had not had a federal libel law since the Alien and Sedition Acts of 1798. In 1964, the Supreme Court ruled in The New York Times v. Sullivan *that public officials, public figures and newsworthy persons had to present strict proof of "actual malice" or "reckless disregard of whether it was false" in order to maintain a libel suit.*

Procedures for Contributions

To regulate financial disclosures, Nixon proposed a requirement that the source and recipient of every political contribution be identified, except contributions from national party organizations. The effect would be to curb the power of large, special interest donors who pool their funds. By this method, many individual contributions that added up to large contributions to candidates had remained anonymous. Individual donors would be limited to one contribution of no more than $3,000 in any House or Senate race and $15,000 in any presidential race. However, the ceilings would apply only to each election, so that a contributor would be able to give money in primaries, runoffs and general elections. If enacted, the program would also ban foreign contributions above $50; loans; donations of appreciated property; and "in kind" contributions such as supplies, campaign workers and use of airplanes unless accounted for in the contribution ceiling.

To restrict the flow of large sums of cash, the Nixon plan would require that all payments of campaign expenditures above $50 be paid by check and from a candidate's campaign account, to be held in a single bank. The provisions for one bank and one political fund-raising committee were aimed at ending the proliferation of committees used to evade campaign finance laws.

Nixon also called for legislation to make so-called campaign "dirty tricks," covered in general statutes, into federal crimes. These would include "disruptive and willfully misleading activities" such as rigging public opinion polls, "coercive activities" such as using demonstrators to "impede entry at a campaign rally," and fraudulent election day practices such as ballot box stuffing. Presidential campaigns would be shortened under the proposals by prohibiting any presidential primaries before May 1 and by legislating that nominating conventions be held in September of an election year. Nixon also asked for repeal of the federal "equal time" provisions of the 1934 Communications Act, action aimed at relieving stations and networks of obligations to grant equal air time to minor party candidates and thereby stimulating television and radio coverage of political debates.

Immediate Opposition

Massachusetts Democrat Sen. Edward M. Kennedy and the citizen's lobby Common Cause immediately attacked the Nixon proposals as an attempt to blunt public financing of political campaigns, a movement both had helped to lead. In a statement, Kennedy called the reform package "a thinly veiled attempt by the President to obstruct or even kill the most effective response Congress has yet made to Watergate." Common Cause asserted that Nixon's 1972 re-election campaign "constitutes the greatest case ever made for controlling campaign finance abuses through public financing of elections."

Excerpts from President Nixon's radio address to the nation March 8 on campaign reform:

Campaign Reform

...Ten months ago I spoke out on the need for campaign reform. I asked the Congress to create a commission to fashion the remedies that we need. The Congress has failed to act on that proposal. Consequently, today I am sending to the Congress a comprehensive set of proposals to get the job done.

These proposals present reform that will work, not reform that will sugar-coat our problems with the appearance of change or rob our people of their basic freedoms. These proposals address four major areas: campaign finances, campaign practices, campaign duration, and encouragement of candidate participation.

Of all of these, campaign financing is the central concern with which we must deal as we move to improve our electoral process. It provides the best example of our need to deal with the causes of campaign abuses rather than simply with the symptoms of those abuses.

Each year elections become more expensive. In 9 months of 1972 alone, it has been estimated that the Presidential campaign cost $100 million, spent by the two candidates and their committees.

Many millions more were spent on Congressional races. Many of these costs cannot be avoided because Americans put a premium on knowing what their candidates stand for, seeing them in their hometowns, meeting them face to face.

The answer to this is not artificial limits on campaign expenditures by candidates. These limits would not only raise constitutional questions, they would also be unrealistic and, in many situations, unfair.

In a free society we should never put a ceiling on the open and vigorous communication of ideas, specifically when that communication helps to inform the voter's choice. Instead, we should deal with the growing influx of money into politics by establishing broad and rigorously enforced financial disclosure requirements.

With expanded disclosure, our voters would then have the necessary information to assess the philosophy, the personal associations, the political and economic allegiances of the candidates.

To this end, I have proposed that each candidate have only one political committee as his or her authorized campaign organization, and that committee would have to designate one depository for all campaign funds.

Now this measure would insure full accountability for campaign finance and eliminate the unhealthy proliferation of political committees which are used to conceal campaign donations.

I have also proposed that each individual donor be specifically tied to his campaign contribution. By linking donations to the original donor, the influence of special interest groups...would be sharply reduced.

Proposed Limits on Contributions

Beyond requiring greater public disclosure of campaign contributions, I also ask for limits on the size of donations to Federal election campaigns. No contribution above $3,000 could be made by an individual donor to a House or Senate election campaign. For Presidential elections, a ceiling limit of $15,000 would apply and the need for small contributions would rise accordingly. We would also put an end to contributions from organizations which are hidden in the form of services, such as the donated use of private aircraft, the loan of campaign workers whose salaries are paid by third parties, and other types of non-monetary contributions.

We should stop the large flow of cash in campaigns by requiring that all donations over $50 be made by check or other negotiable instrument. We should ban all political loans in order to end the practice of disguising donations as loans, and, finally, I have proposed that all campaign contributions from foreign accounts and foreign citizens be flatly prohibited....

Unlike arbitrary limitations on campaign expenditures, [these requirements] would fulfill the right of the American citizen to learn about all candidates and the views which they seek to communicate.

I am also taking this opportunity to share with you my reasons for opposing a raid on the public treasury to pay for political campaigns. This is popularly called public financing.

In reality it is compulsory financing by the American taxpayer of political campaigns. It is unhealthy, it reduces our freedoms, and it would ...[undermine] the very foundation of our democratic process.

Underwriting political campaigns from the United States Treasury would not only divert tax dollars from pressing national needs, but would also require taxpayers to sponsor political candidates and parties with which they might totally disagree....

In effect, that process would be taxation without representation. It would, in other words, violate the very precept for which our Nation declared its independence and fought a war for that independence. You work too hard for your money to have it spent on candidates or in campaigns that you don't know about or don't care about or even oppose.

Thomas Jefferson, who so eloquently committed to words the spirit of the Revolution, said, at another time, "To compel a man to furnish contributions of money for the propagation of opinions which he disbelieves and abhors is sinful and tyrannical."

The courts have already struck down this type of financing when labor unions have tried to make campaign contributions from compulsory dues, and I see no reason now to place this same type of burden on the back of the American taxpayer. One thing we don't need in this country is to add politicians to the Federal dole.

Public financing could give incumbents unfair advantages over relatively unknown but capable challengers, and at this time in our history, this Nation, all of our legislative bodies, particularly the Congress of the United States, needs new blood, new leadership.

Moreover, it would close off the one avenue that hundreds of thousands of citizens choose to participate in, the electoral process.

Our goal should be to disclose donations, not to foreclose them. We need to open up the election process, not put it in the closed hands of Washington bureaucrats.

I have also proposed reform in the area of campaign practices. We must firmly move to prohibit the organized and intentional disruption of a candidate's campaign by his opponent as well as to prevent the use of tactics which impede or deny entry at a campaign rally.

I recall in the campaign of 1968 the violent demonstrations that took place where Senator Humphrey and I were concerned, demonstrations which had the effect finally in some cases of denying us the right to speak.

Once and for all, we should move to end such anti-democratic practices as stuffing ballot boxes, the rigging of voting machines, other practices which affect the electoral process in the most pernicious manner.

Plan to Shorten Campaigns

The third general area of reform in which I have submitted proposals to the Congress deals with the length of campaigns. Campaigns should be true tests of a candidate's appeal to the voters, rather than endurance contests.

To shorten Presidential campaigns, I have recommended moving primary elections later into the election year, and I have urged both national parties to schedule their 1976 nominating conventions in September instead of in July or August.

Now that would still provide for a national campaign of approximately 2 months. When you consider, for example, that in Great Britain a campaign is scheduled for no longer than 3 weeks, it would seem that a 2-month campaign in the United States would be adequate for the purpose of having each candidate get his views across to the people.

Finally, we must take steps to encourage more good people to run for public office. While closely observing constitutional requirements, I believe that we can reaffirm a public figure's private rights so that people interested in running for public office can have greater assurance of recourse against slanderous attacks on them or their families. Good and decent men and women should not have to flinch from political participation because of their fear of such attacks.

We have here, incidentally, a constitutional problem, which must eventually probably be decided by the courts, but unfortunately, some libel lawyers have interpreted recent Supreme Court decisions, particularly the decision in *Sullivan v. The New York Times*, as being virtually a license to lie where a political candidate, a member of his family, or one of his supporters or friends is involved.

Protection Against Slander

This is wrong. It is necessary that a change be made so that a candidate who runs for public office knows that he has recourse in case of such an attack which is totally untrue and would otherwise give him a right to sue for libel.

Other measures which would encourage a wider choice for the voters by reducing the cost of campaigning, include the repeal of the equal time provision of the Communications Act, allowing for more free broadcast coverage of candidates.

I have also urged the Congress to examine its own benefits of incumbency which have mounted over the years, so competent challengers have a more even chance in House and Senate campaigns.

I am aware of the great interests and expertise that the Congress possesses in the election process, and I am grateful for the counsel, the recommendations which have been contributed to me by several Members of Congress in preparing my remarks on this occasion and the legislation that will be presented. It is fully my intention to work closely with the Congress, with leaders of both parties, to achieve progress in improving the conduct of our campaigns....

If our campaigns, like the communications of ideas in every arena of public life, are to remain free and spirited, they will frequently be caustic and hard-hitting. That is the case in all free countries. Some excesses and abuses will inevitably occur, but if we are guided by a sense of realism, we can go far to improve the process.

More than anything else, it is my desire to open up the election process, eliminate the abuses which cross boundaries of fair play, and to let the American people know as much as possible about their candidates....

The reforms I have put forward today may not provide the panacea that some seek for all the abuses, but they do provide the basis for the workable progress that we do all seek....

END OF ARAB OIL EMBARGO
March 18, 1974

In a decision which strained Arab unity, seven members of the Organization of Petroleum Exporting Countries (OPEC) announced on March 18, in Vienna, that they would lift the oil embargo in force against the United States since October 1973. The decision to resume oil shipments had been reached a week earlier when Arab oil ministers met in Tripoli, but because Libya bitterly opposed the move, the ministers made their formal announcement in Vienna instead of in the Libyan capital. Joining the dissent were Syria which, with Libya, refused to approve the decision, and Algeria which made its approval provisional until a scheduled June 1 oil meeting. Iraq boycotted both the Tripoli and Vienna talks.

The dissidents charged that the United States had not gone far enough in furthering Arab interests. But in the view of the majority this country had demonstrated its good will by using its influence to get Israel to carry out a military disengagement with Egypt (see p. 29) and to agree to contacts with Syria to negotiate a similar pullback (see p. 435-439).

OPEC members had stopped shipping oil to the United States and the Netherlands in reprisal for U.S. and Dutch support of Israel during the Arab-Israel war which began Oct. 6. Later OPEC extended the embargo to Denmark and, in a gesture toward third-world solidarity, to South Africa, Portugal and Rhodesia. Coupled with the ban on shipping was a sharp cutback in crude-oil production which slashed supplies by 25 per cent in November, taking five million barrels of Arab oil a day off the world market. The cutback led to a huge increase in oil prices which, by March 1974, were 300 per cent above the prices of the previous spring. The ensuing

*scramble for oil severely strained U.S.-European relations, particularly
when the European Economic Community (Common Market) approached
the Arabs in March with a long-term assistance offer. (See p. 185.)*

U.S. Reaction

*Termination of the embargo was met with official silence in Washington,
in part because the move had been expected, but also because the OPEC
statement announcing the end of the embargo said nothing about restoring
the disruptive production cutbacks. The White House made no comment
and reportedly instructed government agencies to remain silent on the
Arab move. Saudi Arabia, which reportedly had pressed unsuccessfully for
lowered oil prices, pledged on March 18 to increase crude-oil production—though not to pre-war levels—and to resume shipments to the United
States. The Netherlands and Denmark would still be embargoed, according
to the Saudi Petroleum Minister Sheik Ahmed Saki al-Yamani, because
the two countries had "not made clear their position on asking for a full
[Israeli] withdrawal from occupied territories."*

*Though pleased with the "clear change of policy" by the major industrial
countries, the Arabs found that their "oil weapon" had cut also against the
less prosperous, non-aligned nations, which were severely hurt by the
spiraling oil prices. Pressured by mounting criticism of Arab policies from
third-world nations, Algeria sought a special U.N. General Assembly session on raw materials which met April 10 in New York. (See p. 255.)*

> *Text of Arab statement, March 18, 1974, on end of oil
> embargo:*

The Arab oil ministers held a series of meetings during the period of
March 13 and 18 at Tripoli and Vienna, during which they heard the report
presented by Sheik Ahmed Zaki al-Yamani, Minister of Petroleum and
Mineral Resources of the Kingdom of Saudi Arabia and by Belaid
Abdesalam, Minister of Energy and Industry of the Algerian Popular
Democratic Republic, concerning the results of the second part of their trip,
which included Spain, Italy, West Germany and Japan.

The ministers studied the political analysis presented by the two said
ministers, which was based on their talks with the officials of the respective countries they visited.

The ministers re-evaluated the results of the Arab oil measures in the
light of its main objective, namely to draw the attention of the world to the
Arab cause in order to create the suitable political climate for the implementation of Security Council Resolution 242, which calls for the complete withdrawal from the Arab-occupied territories, and for the restoration of the legitimate rights of the Palestinian people.

The ministers took cognizance of the fact that the said measures made
world public opinion aware of the importance of the Arab world for the
welfare of world economy, and consequently it became receptive to the
legitimate rights of the Arab nations, which led to the gradual isolation of

Israel and paved the way for the assumption of political stances which openly condemn Israel's expansionist policy.

European Policy Shift

Indicative of such stances were the clear change of policy of the European Community represented by its joint declaration of Nov. 6, 1973, the positions assumed by Belgium, Italy, West Germany and Japan which were even more just and clear and also the signs which began to appear in various American circles calling (in various degrees) for the need of an even-handed policy vis-a-vis the Middle East and the Arab world.

It appeared to the ministers that the American official policy as evidenced lately by the recent political events assumed a new dimension vis-a-vis the Arab-Israeli conflict.

Such a dimension, if maintained, will lead America to assume a position which is more compatible with the principle of what is right and just toward the Arab-occupied territories and the legitimate rights of the Palestinian people.

The Arab oil ministers are aware of the fact that oil is a weapon which can be utilized in a positive manner in order to lead to results, the effectiveness of which may surpass those if the oil weapon was used in a negative manner.

Therefore, they came out with resolutions in which the oil weapon was used in a positive manner, the purpose of which was to encourage the countries which showed readiness and willingness to work for a just remedy to the cause which would lead to the complete termination of the Israeli occupation and to the restoration of the legitimate rights of the Palestinian people.

Israeli Responsibility

Israel alone will bear the dangerous responsibility if the forthcoming events lead to the undertaking of more severe oil measures, in addition to the other various resources which the Arab world can master in order to join the battle of destiny.

Israel alone is to be blamed for the effects suffered by the countries which came under the embargo or which suffered as a result of the reduction of the oil production, and it remains responsible today for the maintaining of the production of Arab oil, at the level which is below the needs of the market.

In light of the principles, facts and objectives mentioned previously, the Arab oil ministers decided at the conclusion of their meetings the following:

FIRST: To treat Italy and the Republic of West Germany as friendly countries and to meet their petroleum needs.

SECOND: To lift the embargo on oil supplies to the United States, it being understood that this decision as much as all the other decisions shall be subject to the review on the occasion of the meeting to be held by the Arab oil ministers June 1, 1974, in Cairo.

The ministers emphasized their support for all the Arab countries in their just struggle and to the Syrian Arab Republic at the present time during which it endeavors to reach the means which would eventually lead to the full liberation of its territory and to the complete liberation of all the Arab-occupied territories, first of which comes Jerusalem.

The Syrian Arab Republic did not give its assent to the decision to lift the embargo. On its part Libya did not give its assent to lifting the embargo nor to any increase in production.

SIRICA DECISION ON
GRAND JURY REPORT ON NIXON
March 18, 1974

U.S. District Judge John J. Sirica decided March 18 that he would turn over to the House Judiciary Committee a secret grand jury report and a briefcase full of supporting evidence bearing on President Nixon's alleged involvement in the Watergate scandal. The decision followed conflicting arguments voiced at a hearing before Sirica March 6 by the President's Watergate defense lawyer James D. St. Clair; John J. Wilson, lawyer for two Watergate defendants; the House Judiciary Committee's majority counsel John M. Doar; the committee's minority counsel, Albert E. Jenner Jr.; and Philip A. Lacovara, special counsel to the special Watergate prosecution force. The U.S. Court of Appeals upheld Sirica's decision March 21.

The federal grand jury empaneled June 5, 1972, had given the briefcase and sealed report to Sirica March 1 along with the indictment of seven former White House and Nixon re-election committee officials. (Indictments, see p. 157-184.) Following delivery, the materials became the stakes of a struggle over whether the Judiciary Committee should receive the report and evidence as recommended by the grand jury. Despite the grand jury request and the Judiciary Committee's attempts to obtain the documents, Sirica had delayed a decision, concerned that his action might prejudice the trial of the seven men indicted on charges of conspiring to cover up the Watergate case and White House involvement in it. Although it became known later that the report named Nixon as an unindicted co-conspirator, the White House had officially adopted a position of neutrality c 1 the disposition of the material. Objections to its release had come from the lawyers for three of the seven men indicted March 1.

"We deal in a matter of the most critical moment to the nation, an impeachment investigation involving the President of the United States," said Sirica in his decision. "It would be difficult to conceive of a more compelling need than that of this country for an unswervingly fair inquiry based on all the pertinent information." Sirica declared there was no doubt why the grand jury had requested that the report and briefcase be forwarded to the Judiciary Committee. During its investigation into the Watergate break-in and cover-up, the jury had heard evidence material to the impeachment inquiry underway in the House committee. The report was "a simple and straightforward compilation of information gathered by the grand jury" and "draws no accusatory conclusions.... It renders no moral or social judgments."

Referral: "Obligatory"

After a lengthy examination of the history and precedents, Sirica concluded that "the court...would be unjustified in holding that the grand jury was without authority to pass the report on to the impeachment probe." Rather, he wrote, "delivery to the committee is eminently proper, and indeed, obligatory." Sirica said, in reference to the President, that since "the report's subject is referred to in his public capacity, and on balance with the public interest, any prejudice to his legal rights caused by disclosure to the committee would be minimal.... The President would not be left without a forum in which to adjudicate any charges against him that might employ report materials." Furthermore, said Sirica, "the President of the United States has not objected to its release."

Avoid News Leaks

Although he delayed the effective date of his order for two days to allow for an appeal, Sirica expressed doubt that the coverup defendants were in a proper legal position to appeal the ruling. Mention of them in the report was incidental, he pointed out; they could respond to any such references at their trial, and none of the references went beyond the charges against them in the indictment. With regard to Nixon's request that White House lawyer James D. St. Clair be allowed to review the contents of the report if it were to be turned over to the committee, Sirica left that decision to House Judiciary Committee Chairman Peter W. Rodino, Jr. (D N.J.). In closing, Sirica added his request to that of the grand jury, that the committee consider and use the report "with due regard for avoiding any unnecessary interference with the court's ability to conduct fair trials of persons under indictment." Sirica's ruling resolved the differences over what should be done with the sealed report and accompanying evidence that had surfaced in his courtroom March 6.

Confounding reports that the March 6 court hearing had been requested by the White House to enable it to object formally to Sirica's turning over the report to the committee, St. Clair told Sirica that the White House made no recommendation on the disposition of the report. "Whatever you decide to do with it is quite appropriate from our point of view," he said. However, St. Clair expressed concern at the "serious breach of grand jury secrecy" that had produced front-page stories over the weekend of March 1. The stories said that the sealed envelope contained a report that the grand jury had found Nixon was implicated in the Watergate coverup. St. Clair labeled those stories a "gross distortion of the facts" concerning the contents of the envelope. Later in the day, Sirica stated that St. Clair had been allowed to read the summary report contained in that envelope before the hearing.

Objections To Release

If the White House did not object to transmittal of the report by Sirica, defense counsel Wilson did. Wilson, the 73-year-old attorney for former presidential assistants H. R. Haldeman and John D. Ehrlichman, challenged the grand jury's power to make the report and Sirica's power to release it. Special grand juries, authorized by a 1970 administration-supported law, could issue such reports concerning the misbehavior of public officials, said Wilson—but a regular grand jury, such as this one, could not. "A regular grand jury," he asserted, "has no power to do other than indict or ignore." Warning that he would appeal any decision to release the report, even to the House Judiciary Committee, Wilson argued the danger of prejudicial publicity, which he said would make it difficult or impossible to find an unbiased jury to try the Watergate coverup case. "Whether our clients are the targets of the report or are mentioned...this extra-judicial act prejudices their case, and should be expunged as illegal and improper," he said.

The Committee's Case

"Has there been any discussion by the committee of the advisability, the feasibility of delaying [its inquiry] until after the coverup trial?" asked Sirica of majority committee council Doar. "I feel strongly, as Mr. Wilson does...concerning this problem of pre-trial publicity.... What harm would be done by waiting for this trial, which will begin Sept. 9?" he asked. Both Doar and St. Clair opposed the suggestion of delay.

Jenner, counsel for the Republicans on the Judiciary Committee, similarly argued for release of the materials. "This is the presidency" at issue, Jenner stated. "The people of this country are very anxious that...the House Judiciary Committee proceed with all deliberate speed" to resolve the matter of impeachment. "Your Honor has the briefcase.... You are a citizen. The House...respects you as an officer of a coordinate branch of the government, but however you came into possession of these documents, it is your responsibility to aid and assist the House...in discharging its predominant responsibility."

On behalf of the grand jury and the government, Philip A. Lacovara, counsel for the special prosecutor, argued that the grand jury had the *authority to make the sealed report. He asked that Sirica grant the grand jury's request to pass on the materials to the House Judiciary Committee. "This is an unprecedented situation....We believe it would be unthinkable for any court to hold that this grand jury must remain mute" on matters relevant to the impeachment inquiry, he continued. The contents of the envelope were not "an accusatory presentment," said Lacovara. Rule 6(e), he said, did not prevent their being passed on to the committee. "Neither Congress nor the [Supreme] Court [in approving this rule] would have cut off access of a grand jury involving matters of the highest national importance" by tieing the hands of a judge or jury and preventing the transfer of such information to the House, whose need for it must be considered of "supervening importance," he argued.*

Wilson nevertheless appealed Sirica's March 18 decision to the U.S. Court of Appeals, which March 21 upheld Sirica's ruling. Wilson, rather than carrying his case to the Supreme Court, conceded defeat in the legal battle to bar disclosure of the materials. On March 25 the report and brief-case were delivered to the House Judiciary Committee.

Excerpts from U.S. District Court Judge John J. Sirica's decision March 18 to turn over a sealed grand jury report and briefcase of evidence to the House Judiciary Committee:

IN THE UNITED STATES DISTRICT COURT FOR THE DISTRICT OF COLUMBIA

IN RE REPORT AND RECOMMENDATION OF JUNE 5, 1972 GRAND JURY CONCERNING TRANSMISSION OF EVIDENCE TO THE HOUSE OF REPRESENTATIVES

Misc. No. 74-21

OPINION

On March 1, 1974, in open court, the June 5, 1972, Grand Jury lodged with the Court a sealed Report...accompanied by a two-page document entitled *Report and Recommendation* which is in effect a letter of transmittal describing in general terms the Grand Jury's purpose in preparing and forwarding the Report and the subject matter of its contents. The transmittal memorandum further strongly recommends that accompanying materials be submitted to the Committee on the Judiciary of the House of Representatives for its consideration. The Grand Jury states it has heard evidence that it regards as having a material bearing on matters within the primary jurisdiction of the Committee in its current inquiry, and notes further its belief that it ought now to defer to the House of Representatives for a decision on what action, if any, might be warranted in the circumstances.

After having had an opportunity to familiarize itself with the contents of the Report, the Court invited all counsel who might conceivably have an interest in the matter, without regard to standing, to state their positions concerning disposition. The President's position, through counsel, is that he has no recommendation to make, suggesting that the matter is entirely within the Court's discretion. He has requested that should the Report be released his counsel have an opportunity to review and copy the materials. The House Judiciary Committee through its Chairman has made a formal request for delivery of the Report materials. The Special Prosecutor has urged on behalf of the Grand Jury that its Report is authorized under law and that the recommendation to forward the Report to the House be honored. Finally, attorneys for seven persons named in an indictment returned by the same June, 1972 Grand Jury on March 1, 1974, just prior to delivery of the Grand Jury Report, have generally objected to any disclosure of that Report, and in one instance recommended that the Report be expunged or returned to the Jury.

Having carefully examined the contents of the Grand Jury Report, the Court is satisfied that there can be no question regarding their materiality to the House Judiciary Committee's investigation. Beyond materiality, of course, it is the Committee's responsibility to determine the significance of the evidence, and the Court offers no opinion as to relevance. The questions that must be decided, however, are twofold: (1) whether the Grand Jury has power to make reports and recommendations, (2) whether the Court has power to disclose such reports, and if so, to what extent.

I.

...[T]he instant Report is not the first delivered up by a grand jury, and that, indeed grand juries have historically published reports on a wide variety of subjects....

On this historical basis, with reliance as well upon principles of sound public policy, a number of federal courts have upheld and defined the general scope of grand jury reportorial prerogatives....

The Report here at issue suffers from none of the objectionable qualities noted...[earlier]. It draws no accusatory conclusions. It deprives no one of an official forum in which to respond. It is not a substitute for indictments where indictments might properly issue. It contains no recommendations, advice or statements that infringe on the prerogatives of other branches of government. Indeed, its only recommendation is to the Court, and rather than injuring separation of powers principles, the Jury sustains them by lending its aid to the House in the exercise of that body's constitutional jurisdiction. It renders no moral or social judgments. The Report is a simple and straightforward compilation of information gathered by the Grand Jury, and no more.

Having considered the cases and historical precedents, and noting the absence of a contrary rule in this Circuit, it seems to the Court that it would be unjustified in holding that the Grand Jury was without authority to hand up this Report. The Grand Jury has obviously taken care to assure that its Report contains no objectionable features, and has throughout acted in the interests of fairness. The Grand Jury having thus respected its own limitations and the rights of others, the Court ought to respect the Jury's exercise of its prerogatives.

II.

Beyond the question of issuing a report is the question of disclosure. It is here that grand jury authority ends and judicial authority becomes exclusive....

We begin here with the fact that the Grand Jury has recommended disclosure; not public dissemination, but delivery to the House Judiciary Committee with a request that the Report be used with due regard for the constitutional rights of persons under indictment. Where, as here, a report is clearly within the bound of propriety, the Court believes that it should presumptively favor disclosure to those for whom the matter is a proper concern and whose need is not disputed. Compliance with the established standards here is manifest and adds its weight in favor of at least limited divulgence, overbalancing objections, and leading the Court to the conclusion that delivery to the Committee is eminently proper, and indeed, obligatory. The Report's subject is referred to in his public capacity, and, on balance with the public interest, any prejudice to his legal rights caused by disclosure to the Committee would be minimal. As noted earlier, the Report is not an indictment, and the President would not be left without a forum in which to adjudicate any charges against him that might employ Report materials. The President does not object to release.

The only significant objection to disclosure, is the contention that release of the Report beyond the Court is absolutely prohibited by Rule 6(e), Federal Rules of Criminal Procedure....Counsel objecting to release draw particular attention to the statement "[persons may disclose matters occurring before the grand jury] only when so directed by the court preliminarily to or in connection with a judicial proceeding...."

In their "Notes" accompanying Rule 6(e) the Advisory Committee on Rules, responsible for drafting Federal Rules, explains the intent of that paragraph as follows:

> 1. This rule continues the traditional practice of secrecy on the part of members of the grand jury, *except when the court permits a disclosure,*...

Here, for all purposes relevant to this decision, the Grand Jury has ended its work. There is no need to protect against flight on anyone's part, to prevent tampering with or restraints on witnesses or jurors, to protect grand jury deliberations, to safeguard unaccused or innocent persons with secrecy. The person on whom the Report focuses, the President of the United States, has not objected to its release to the Committee. Other persons are involved only indirectly. Those persons who are not under indictment have already been the subject of considerable public testimony and will no doubt be involved in further testimony, quite apart from this Report. Those persons who are under indictment have the opportunity at trial for response to any incidental references to them. And although it has not been emphasized in this opinion, it should not be forgotten that we deal in a matter of the most critical moment to the Nation, an impeachment investigation involving the President of the United States. It would be difficult to conceive of a more compelling need than that of this country for an unswervingly fair inquiry based on all the pertinent information.

These considerations might well justify even a public disclosure of the Report, but are certainly ample basis for disclosure to a body that in this setting acts simply as another grand jury. The Committee has taken elaborate precautions to insure against unnecessary and inappropriate disclosure of these materials. Nonetheless, counsel for the indicted defendants, some having lived for a considerable time in Washington, D.C., are not persuaded that disclosure to the Committee can have any result but prejudicial publicity for their clients. The Court, however, cannot justify non-disclosure on the basis of speculation that leaks will occur, added to the further speculation that resultant publicity would prejudice the rights of defendants in *United States v. Mitchell, et al.* We have no basis on which to assume that the Committee's use of the Report will be injudicious or that it will disregard the plea contained therein that defendants' rights to fair trials be respected.

Finally, it seems incredible that grand jury matters should lawfully be available to disbarment committees and police disciplinary investigations and yet be unavailable to the House of Representatives in a proceeding of so great import as an impeachment investigation. Certainly Rule 6(e) cannot be said to mandate such a result. If indeed that Rule merely codifies existing practice, there is convincing precedent to demonstrate that common law practice permits the disclosure here contemplated. In 1811, the presentment of a county grand jury in the Mississippi Territory specifying charges against federal territorial Judge Harry Toulmin, was forwarded to the House of Representatives for consideration in a possible impeachment action. Following a committee investigation, the House found the evidence inadequate to merit impeachment and dismissed the matter. Though such grand jury participation appears not to have occurred frequently, the precedent is persuasive....Principles of grand jury secrecy do not bar this disclosure.

III.

Consistent with the above, therefore, the Court orders that the Grand Jury *Report and Recommendation*, together with accompanying materials be delivered to the Committee on the Judiciary, House of Representatives. The only individuals who object to such order are defendants in the *United States v. Mitchell, et al.* case currently pending in this court. Their standing is dubious at best given the already stated facts that (1) their mention in the Report is incidental, (2) their trials will provide ample opportunity for response to such references, none of which go beyond allegations in the indictment, and (3) considerations of possible adverse publicity are both premature and speculative. Their ability to seek whatever appellate review of the Court's decision might be had, is therefore questionable. Nevertheless, because of the irreversible nature of disclosure, the Court will stay its order for two days from the date thereof to allow defendants an opportunity to pursue their remedies, if any, should they desire to do so.

The President's request to have counsel review the Report's contents has not received comment form the Committee counsel due to their feeling that such comment would be inappropriate. It is the Court's view that this request is more properly the Committee's concern, and it therefore defers to the Chairman for a response to the President's counsel.

Having ruled that the Recommendation of the Grand Jury and request of the House Judiciary Committee should be honored, the Court relinquishes its own control of the matter, but takes advantage of this occasion to respectfully request, with the Grand Jury, that the committee receive, consider and utilize the Report with due reguard for avoiding any unnecessary interference with the Court's ability to conduct fair trials of persons under indictment.

Signed: John J. Sirica
Chief Judge

March 18, 1974

▼▼▼

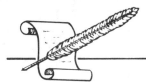
April

REPORT ON NIXON'S TAXES

April 3, 1974

Six months after it was disclosed that he had paid only nominal sums in federal income taxes during his first term as President, Richard M. Nixon April 3 received a bill for nearly half a million dollars in taxes he allegedly should have paid for those years. In December 1973, Nixon had asked the congressional Joint Committee on Internal Revenue Taxation to review his tax returns for 1969 through 1972. Those returns had been the subject of much speculation and questioning after disclosure of his small tax payments and of the circumstances surrounding his major tax deduction over those years, his gift of vice presidential papers to the National Archives. The President had said that he would abide by the findings of the joint committee. When released April 3, the joint committee's report found that the President owed $476,531 in taxes and interest. An Internal Revenue Service (IRS) report that the President had received April 2, which was not made public, contained similar findings. Five hours after receiving the committee report, Nixon announced that he would not contest the findings but would pay the IRS bill of more than $467,000. The White House later said that this payment would "almost wipe out" the President's personal savings and probably would force him to obtain a loan in order to pay the entire amount.

The political impact·of the tax matter—a crucial question for a President already the subject of a House impeachment inquiry—was initially unclear. Rep. Wilbur D. Mills (D Ark.), vice chairman of the Joint Committee on Internal Revenue Taxation, repeated an earlier assertion that the staff report would put pressure on Nixon to resign. Mills had predicted March 17 that Nixon would be out of office by November, 1974, because of

Republican pressure and public disapproval of his income tax payments. The chairman of the House Republican Conference, Rep. John B. Anderson (R Ill.), said Nixon's decision to pay was "more seemly than going into tax court and litigating." But, he said, "It would be almost fatuous to deny that this is a minus in the whole equation as far as the President is concerned." Indeed, few Members of Congress mustered an argument to back up the claim that Nixon would benefit from a finding that he had not paid the taxes he should have paid during his first term. Even before the disclosure of the tax findings, key Republicans had continued to make clear their distance from the problems surrounding the President. At a meeting of Republican leaders from the Midwest on March 30, Vice President Ford directed stinging criticism at the Committee for the Re-election of the President: "The political lesson of Watergate is this. Never again must America allow an arrogant, elite guard of political adolescents like CREEP to bypass the regular party organization and dictate the terms of a national election."

In announcing that Nixon would pay the amount set by the IRS, the White House noted that the still-secret IRS report "rebuts any suggestion of fraud on the part of the President," and the Joint Committee staff's report "offers no facts which would support any such charge." The White House said Nixon had decided to pay the taxes even though he was convinced his lawyers "can make a very strong case" against the major adverse findings. The White House said he would settle without quarrel because of his Dec. 8, 1973, pledge to abide by the findings of the Joint Committee. "In view of the fact that the staff report indicates that the proper amount to be paid must be determined by the Internal Revenue Service, he [Nixon] has today instructed payment of the $432,787.13 set forth by the Internal Revenue Service, plus interest," the White House said. (White House statement, below.)

The White House reported June 20, 1974, that the President had paid the delinquent taxes assessed for 1970, 1971 and 1972, but had yet to pay the taxes for 1969, a year for which the statute of limitations had expired. But the White House reaffirmed Nixon's intention to pay the 1969 tax debt. The same day, following a session of the House Judiciary Committee which was looking into the Nixon tax debt as part of the impeachment inquiry, members of the committee confirmed reports that the Internal Revenue Service had levied a five per cent penalty against Nixon for negligence in the preparation of his tax returns.

The decision by Nixon to pay the taxes dealt a heavy blow to his financial status. In Nixon's December financial disclsure, the White House cited an audit performed by the accounting firm of Coopers & Lybrand, which showed that as of May 31, 1973, Nixon and his wife had cash holdings of about $433,000. A White House official said Nixon probably would use part of his savings to pay the $467,000 the IRS said he owed. He probably would "get a loan to pay the rest of it," the official said. No family "likes to wipe *out its entire savings," he added.* The Wall Street Journal *noted April 4 that Nixon legally would have three years after paying the taxes in which he could contest the IRS rulings in the courts and seek a refund.*

Report Findings

The Joint Committee's staff found that Nixon owed $171,055 in additional taxes for 1969 and the following amounts, including interest, for the other years: $110,048 for 1970, $100,214 for 1971 and $95,114 for 1972. A major part of the 210-page staff report and its 783-page documentary appendix dealt with charitable deductions taken by Nixon for the gift of his vice presidential papers from 1969 through 1972. The $482,018 total taken in deductions for the papers "should not, in the staff's view, be allowed because the gift was made after July 25, 1969, the date when the provisions of the Tax Reform Act of 1969, disallowing such deductions, became effective," the report stated. In the introduction to the report, the staff declared its belief that it should not consider "whether there was, or was not, fraud or negligence" in the preparation of Nixon's returns, because to do so might prejudge impeachment proceedings. However, the section of the report dealing with the papers cited inconsistencies in some of the accounts of Nixon's intent to donate the papers and when they were legally turned over.

"[T]he staff believes that for purposes of the tax deduction there needs to be some expression that the delivery of these papers represented a gift of a specific portion of the papers," according to the report. "The staff has no evidence that any such expression, either oral or written, was made on or before July 25, 1969; and no one at the National Archives or the General Services Administration has indicated any awareness that any portion of the papers delivered on March 26-27, 1969, was to be given to the United States as of that date. They believed, rather, that the papers were delivered for storage purposes and that there would be future gifts from among the papers that had been delivered, but not that a gift had been made as of that date."

Nixon's tax lawyers conceded that the deed transferring the papers was not signed until April 1970, about nine months after the law allowing such deductions was changed. They contended, however, that the deed replaced an earlier document which they said had been destroyed and that, for this reason, the 1970 deed was back-dated. The committee staff rejected this explanation and noted that the deed was not signed by Nixon, but by Edward Morgan, then a presidential counselor. The staff said there was "no evidence that he was authorized to sign for the President."

Nixon's Property

The staff claimed that, because of erroneous estimates involved in Nixon's sale of a large parcel of his San Clemente, Calif., estate to his friends, Charles G. Rebozo and Robert Abplanalp in 1970, a capital gain of $117,836 should have been declared. Nixon's tax accountant had held that the Presi-

dent did not receive any gain on the sale, even though independent auditors who reviewed Nixon's finances at his request found that he should have declared a capital gain of $117,370. The committee staff's finding was based on its commission of a Santa Ana, Calif., engineering firm and a local real estate appraiser to determine independently the fair market value of the property sold and the property retained.

Concluding that Nixon's principal residence was not San Clemente, as his tax accountants had held, the committee staff found that Nixon was not allowed to defer recognition of his capital gain on the 1969 sale of his New York City cooperative apartment. Nixon had argued that he did not move to declare a capital gain because he had reinvested the proceeds of the New York sale in the San Clemente property, which he declared was his principal residence. The staff held that Nixon should have declared a $151,848 capital gain. The committee staff declared also that the President should have reported $11,617 in capital gains from the 1972 sale of a Florida lot. Nixon reported a gain on 60 per cent of the sale, but his daughter, Tricia Nixon Cox, reported the rest. The staff held that the entire amount should have been reported by the President.

Business Expenses

The staff recommended disallowance of four categories of business expenses that the President had claimed as deductions: business use of his San Clemente residence, business use of his Key Biscayne, Fla., residence, depreciation expenses of a cabinet table he bought for use in the White House and business expenses that the staff found could not be adequately substantiated. The President had claimed a total of $85,399 in deductions. The staff suggested the government should reimburse Nixon for his furniture expenditures and pay him $4,816.84 for the cabinet table. While accepting the argument that all of Nixon's use of government aircraft was connected with his duties as President, the staff held that the personal use of such aircraft by Nixon's family and friends should be classified as taxable income totaling $27,015.19.

The staff combed through government-financed improvements to Nixon's Key Biscayne and San Clemente residences and found "those undertaken primarily for the President's personal benefit" to have cost $92,298, which the staff concluded should be declared as taxable income. At San Clemente, these improvements included an exhaust fan, den windows, heating system, gazebo, boundary surveys, sewer, handrails, paving, cabana, stair rail to a beach, railroad crossing and warning signals, landscape construction and maintenance. Key Biscayne improvements included a shuffleboard court, fence and hedge system, landscape construction and maintenance.

Aftermath of Tax Report

In the aftermath of the Joint Committee on Internal Revenue Taxation staff's report, the House Judiciary Committee, the Watergate special prosecutor and the franchise tax board of the state of California followed up on investigation of President Nixon's tax payments. On April 8, it was disclosed that Nixon's handling of his income taxes was being investigated by the House Judiciary Committee. The charge that Nixon had attempted to defraud the government by means of his faulty tax deductions was incorporated in an article of impeachment rejected by the committee July 30. (See p. 655-662.)

The IRS said on April 4 that it would not seek to impose any penalty on Nixon for civil fraud in connection with his tax returns for 1969-1972. The agency also said it was closing its audit of the case. But Attorney General William B. Saxbe disclosed April 9 that the IRS had referred to the Watergate special prosecutor the question of whether there was fraud in the preparation of Nixon's tax returns. On April 10 the New York Times *reported that IRS Commissioner Donald C. Alexander had asked that the Watergate special prosecutor initiate a grand jury investigation into a possible criminal conspiracy stemming from Nixon's claim of a $576,000 tax deduction for his vice presidential papers.*

On April 12, California's franchise tax board ruled that President and Mrs. Nixon owed $4,302 for 1969 and 1970 on the share of their income originating in that state. Martin Huff, executive officer of the board, said the assessment resulted from an inquiry requested by the Joint Committee on Internal Revenue of the California Legislature. Arthur Blech, Nixon's accountant who prepared the contested tax returns, said previously that he had been ordered by White House aides to take some of the deductions that were declared improper by the congressional investigators.

> *Text of the introduction and summary of recommendations of the April 3 report by the staff of the Joint Committee on Internal Revenue Taxation on President Nixon's income taxes for 1969-1972; followed by text of the statement issued by the White House April 3 on the President's decision to settle his back taxes:*

The staff report:

Introduction

On December 8, 1973, President Nixon made public his tax returns and asked the Joint Committee on Internal Revenue Taxation to examine whether two transactions, a gift of his papers claimed as a deduction in 1969 and the sale of 23 acres of land at San Clemente, were correctly reported on his tax returns. The full text of the letter dated December 8, 1973, which President Nixon wrote to Chairman Wilbur D. Mills is as follows:

"Dear Mr. Chairman: Recently there have been many questions in the press about my personal finances during my tenure as President.

"In order to answer these questions and to dispel public doubts, I am today making public a full accounting of my financial transactions since I assumed this office. This accounting includes copies of the income tax returns that Mrs. Nixon and I have filed for the years 1969-72; a full, certified audit of our finances; a full, certified report on the real and personal property we own; an analysis of our financial transactions, including taxes, from January 1, 1969 through May 31, 1973, and other pertinent documents.

"While these disclosures are the most exhaustive ever made by an American President, to the best of my knowledge, I recognize that two tax-related items may continue to be a subject of continuing public questioning. Both items are highly complex and, in the present environment, cannot easily be resolved to the public's satisfaction even with full disclosure of information.

"The first transaction is the gift of certain pre-Presidential papers and other memorabilia which my wife and I claimed as a tax deduction of $576,-000 on our 1969 return and have carried forward, in part, in each subsequent year. The second item in question is the transfer by us, through the Title Insurance and Trust Co., to the B&C Investment Co. of the beneficial interest in 23 acres of land in San Clemente, California in 1970. I have been consistently advised by counsel that this transaction was correctly reported to the Internal Revenue Service. The IRS has also reviewed these items and has advised me that they were correctly reported.

"In order to resolve these issues to the full satisfaction of the American people, I hereby request the Joint Committee on Internal Revenue Taxation to examine both of these transactions and to inform me whether, in its judgment, the items have been correctly reported to the Internal Revenue Service. In the event that the committee determines that the items were incorrectly reported, I will pay whatever tax may be due. I also want to assure you that the committee will have full access to all relevant documents pertaining to these matters and will have the full cooperation of my office.

"I recognize that this request may pose an unusual challenge for the committee, but I believe your assistance on this matter would be a significant public service.

"With warmest regards,
"Sincerely,

s/RICHARD NIXON."

On December 12, 1973, the Joint Committee on Internal Revenue Taxation met in executive session and decided to conduct a thorough examination of the President's income tax returns for the years 1969 through 1972 and to submit a report to the President and to the Congress on its findings.

The committee decided not to confine its examination to the two items mentioned by President Nixon in his letter quoted above, but rather to examine all tax items for the years 1969 through 1972. (President Nixon's tax returns for these years are reproduced...in the Appendix [omitted]). The committee believed that the broader examination was necessary in part because various items on a tax return are often so interrelated that distortions result if a comprehensive review is not made. Probably more important, however, is that so many questions have been raised about the tax returns of the President for these years that the committee believed the general public can only be satisfied by a thorough examination of the President's taxes. From the standpoint of the tax system alone, this confidence of the general public is essential since ours is basically a voluntary assessment system which has maintained its high level of effectiveness only because the general public has confidence in the basic fairness of the collection system.

At its meeting, the committee instructed its staff to conduct a thorough examination of the President's tax matters for the years 1969-1972 and to prepare a report to the committee on its findings. This is that report.

The staff first would like to thank the Internal Revenue Service for its fine cooperation in the examination of these returns. In every respect, the staff found the Internal Revenue Service cooperative and helpful. About the same time President Nixon asked the Joint Committee to examine his returns, the Internal Revenue Service began an examination of the President's return for 1970 and reopened the years 1971 and 1972 (the general statute of limitations having expired on the 1969 return). The staff has exchanged information with the Internal Revenue Service in numerous cases, and the two also have conducted many joint interviews. However, the conclusions reached in this report are those of the staff alone and in no way are intended as indicative of any reexaminations made by the Internal Revenue Service.

Generally, it is the responsibility of the taxpayer to substantiate his deductions or to show why other items should not be included in his return. However, in this case, because of the office held by the taxpayer, it has not been possible to call upon him for the usual substantiation. The unique position of the Presidency has also raised other questions in these returns which the staff comments on at the appropriate points in this report. Although the staff has not been able to contact the taxpayer in this case, he has been represented by counsel, Kenneth W. Gemmill and H. Chapman Rose. The counsel have been helpful in the staff examination of the President's returns, and they have supplied most of the information requested.

In its examination of the President's tax returns, the staff conducted approximately 30 interviews with persons involved in different aspects of the President's tax matters. In a number of cases, this represents more than one interview with the same person. In addition, the staff has made contact with numerous other possible sources of information, has on two occasions sent staff members to California to consider various tax issues, and on another occasion has sent staff personnel to New York to carry out the examination. This is in addition to information the staff received through numerous investigations made by the Internal Revenue Service personnel. Finally, the staff has employed experts to help it appraise the value of the San Clemente property—an engineering firm and an appraisal firm, both in California. The staff believes that it has conducted an extensive examination.

As is true in any examination of a tax return, however, it is not possible to give assurance that all items of income have been included. The staff report contains recommendations on two categories of income which it believes should have been included but were not; namely, improvements made by the Government to the San Clemente and Key Biscayne properties which the staff believes primarily represent personal economic benefits to the President, and economic benefits obtained by family and friends from the use of Government aircraft for personal purposes.

The staff did not examine the President's income tax returns for years prior to 1969. In the course of its examination of the returns for 1969-72, however, the staff found that because of interrelationships of prior years' returns it was necessary to consider a limited number of items relating to prior years' returns, since they affect returns for the years in question. In addition, the staff has limited its recommendations to income tax matters, although in this examination it found instances where the employment taxes were not paid and gift tax returns not filed.

The staff has made no attempt in this report to draw any conclusions whether there was, or was not, fraud or negligence involved in any aspect of the returns, either on the part of the President or his personal representatives. The staff believes that it would be inappropriate to consider such matters in view of the fact that the House Judiciary Committee presently has before it an impeachment investigation relating to the President and that members of the Joint Committee on Internal Revenue Taxation, along with members of the House and Senate, may subsequently be called upon to pass judgment on any charges which may be brought as a result of that investigation. The staff believes that neither the House nor the Senate members of the Joint Committee would want to have pre-judged any issue which might be brought in any such proceedings.

The staff in preparing this report recognizes that an examination by a committee staff, possibly with the publication of the recommendations does not retain for the taxpayer his usual rights of review which are available to him under the appellate procedure in the Internal Revenue Service and through the courts. For this reason, the staff has attempted to examine matters with great care before making a recommendation which will result in greater tax payments. At the same time, however, the staff has attempted to follow the standards which it believes, under the law, are required to be applicable to taxpayers generally, and the staff has not withheld recommendations because of the office of the taxpayer involved. The staff, in any case, believes it should be emphasized that this is a report only. It is not a demand for payment of taxes. Any tax payment is a matter for consideration by the taxpayer and the Internal Revenue Service.

Summary of Recommendations

The report which follows is divided into ten separate parts. Each of these deals with one or more major questions with respect to the tax returns of the President. In most cases the report indicates first the scope of the examination and then presents an analysis of points of law which may be involved. This is followed by a summary of staff recommendations, and finally the staff presents an analysis of these recommendations.

The staff recommendations would make the following increases in the President's taxes for the years involved:

Year	Proposed Deficiency	Interest	Deficiency plus interest
1969	$171,055	—	$171,055
1970	93,410	$16,638	110,048
1971	89,667	10,547	100,214
1972	89,890	5,224	95,114
Total	$444,022	$32,409	$476,431

Should the President decide to reimburse the Government for the General Services Administration improvements which the staff believes were primarily personal in nature, he would pay $106,262. In addition, if he should decide to reimburse the Government for the amount determined by the staff to represent the cost for the personal trips of his family and friends, this would amount to $27,015. On the other hand, if the President were to receive reimbursement for the expense which he paid for the table located in the cabinet room in the White House for which the staff believes the Government should have paid, the amount he should receive would be $4,816.84. If the President were to make the reimbursements referred to above, he would be allowed to take deductions in the year of the payments, since the amounts were treated as taxable income in the years under examination in which they occurred.

The major causes of the deficiencies resulting from the staff examination are set forth below.

(1) The charitable deductions ($482,018) taken for a gift of papers from 1969-1972 should not, in the staff's view, be allowed because the gift was made after July 25, 1969, the date when the provisions of the Tax Reform Act of 1969 disallowing such deductions became effective. The staff believes that in view of the restrictions and retained rights contained in the deed of the gift of papers, that the deed is necessary for the gift. The deed (dated March 27, 1969) which purportedly was signed on April 21, 1969, was not signed (at least by all parties) until April 10, 1970 and was not delivered until after that date. It should also be noted that this deed was signed by Edward Morgan (rather than the President), and the staff found no evidence that he was authorized to sign for the President. In addition, the deed stated that its delivery conveyed title to the papers to the United States and since the deed was not delivered until after April 10, 1970, it is clear that title could not have been conveyed by way of the deed until after July 25, 1969. Furthermore, because the gift is so restricted, in the opinion of the staff, it is a gift of a future interest in tangible personal property, which is not deductible currently under law, even if the gift was valid in all other respects, that is, it had been made and the deed delivered prior to July 25, 1969. President Nixon's 1968 gift of papers contains the same

restrictions as the second gift so that in the staff's opinion it, too, is a non-deductible gift of a future interest. As a result, the staff believes that the amount of the 1968 gift in excess of what was deducted in 1968 is not available to be carried over into 1969.

(2) In 1970, no capital gain was reported on the sale of the President's excess San Clemente acreage. The staff believes that there was an erroneous allocation of basis between the property retained and the property sold and that a capital gain of $117,836 should have been reported.

(3) The staff believes that the President is not allowed to defer recognition of his capital gain on the sale of his New York City cooperative apartment because it does not view the San Clemente residence in which he reinvested the proceeds of the sale (with one year) as his principal residence. Also, the staff believes this gain is larger than the $142,912 reported on the 1969 tax return, because the President's cost basis should be reduced by the depreciation and amortization allowable on the New York apartment resulting from its use in a trade or business by Mr. Nixon. The staff determined that the amount of depreciation and amortization allowable is $8,936. The staff measures the total capital gain at $151,848, which in its view should be reported as income in 1969.

(4) The staff believes that depreciation on the San Clemente house and on certain furniture purchased by the President, business expense deductions taken on the San Clemente property, as well as certain expenditures from the White House "guest fund" are not proper business expenses and are not allowable deductions. These deductions totalled $85,399 during the years under examination. In the case of the purchase of part of the furniture, however, the staff believes the Government should reimburse President Nixon for his expenditure.

(5) In the case of capital gain on the sale of the Cape Florida Development lots in 1972, 60 percent was reported by President Nixon and 40 percent was reported by his daughter Patricia. The staff believes the entire amount should be reported as income to the President. Thus, in the view of the staff, he should report $11,617 (this is the amount allocated to his daughter from the installment payment in 1972) as a capital gain in 1972 and the remainder of the gain 1973. On this basis, Mrs. Cox should also file an amended return and not include any of this gain for 1972 (or in 1973). Also, on this basis President Nixon could deduct as interest part of the payment he made in 1973 to Patricia on the money she loaned him. She, of course, should report the interest as income in 1973.

(6) The staff believes President Nixon should declare as income the value of flights in Government planes taken by his family and friends when there was no business purpose for the furnishing of the transportation. The staff was given no information about family and friends on flights where the President was a passenger. However, for other flights the first-class fare costs of his family and friends are estimated to be $27,015 for the years 1969 through 1972. From April 1971 through March 1972 and again after November 7, 1972, President Nixon paid for most of such travel expense himself.

(7) The staff believes that President Nixon should declare as income $92,298 in improvements made to his Key Biscayne and San Clemente estates. The only improvements taken into account for this purpose, the staff believes, were those undertaken primarily for the President's personal benefit.

(8) The staff believes the President should be allowed an additional $1,007 in sales tax deductions.

(9) The staff believes that $148 of gasoline tax deductions should not be allowed for 1969 through 1971. However, the staff has determined that an additional $10 in gasoline tax deductions is allowable for 1972.

(10) Several other income items should be reported on President Nixon's tax returns, although these are entirely offset by deductions and hence do not increase taxable income.

Each adjustment in tax by year is shown in Table 1.

White House statement, April 3:

We have learned of the decision by the Joint Committee on Internal Revenue Taxation to release a staff analysis of the President's taxes before the Committee itself has had opportunity to evaluate the staff views, and before the President's tax counsel could advise the Committee of their views on the many legal matters in dispute in that report.

Yesterday the President received a statement from the Internal Revenue Service indicating its view, also, that he should pay an additional tax.

The President's tax counsel have advised him that the positions they have sought to present to the Committee, as outlined in their brief, are valid and compelling. His intent to give the papers was clear. Their delivery was accomplished in March, 1969, four months before the July deadline. His intent as to the amount of the gift was stated to his counsel. Because of these facts the President's tax counsel strongly affirm that those various issues could be sharply and properly contested in court proceedings such as are open to an ordinary taxpayer to review the decisions of the Internal Revenue Service.

The President believes that his tax counsel can make a very strong case against the major conclusions set forth in the Committee's staff report. However, at the time the President voluntarily requested the Committee to conduct its examination of his tax returns, he stated that he would abide by the Committee's judgment. In view of the fact that the staff report indicates that the proper amount to be paid must be determined by the Internal Revenue Service, he has today instructed payment of the $432,787.13 set forth by the Internal Revenue Service, plus interest.

It should be noted that the report by the Internal Revenue Service rebuts any suggestion of fraud on the part of the President. The Committee's staff report offers no facts which would support any such charge.

Any errors which may have been made in the preparation of the President's returns were made by those to whom he delegated the responsibility for preparing his returns and were made without his knowledge and without his approval.

▼▼▼

HEARST KIDNAPPING
April 3, 1974

One of the most widely reported kidnapping cases in decades began the evening of Feb. 5, 1974, when Patricia Hearst, granddaughter of the late newspaper magnate, William Randolph Hearst, was forcibly taken from a Berkeley, Calif., apartment she occupied with her fiance, Steven Weed. Weed was beaten semi-conscious during the abduction. The kidnappers identified themselves two days later, on a tape recording sent to a Berkeley radio station, as members of a radical terrorist group called the Symbionese Liberation Army (SLA).

At the time of the kidnapping, two acknowledged SLA members were in jail awaiting trial on charges of murdering the superintendent of Oakland, Calif., schools the previous November. Little was known about the group beyond the source of its name which, apparently, was taken from a 1959 novel dealing with an armed commando group in a ghetto uprising. The book, The Spook Who Sat by the Door, *used the word "symbiology," a biological or psychological term for separate organisms living together. A stated purpose of the SLA was to unite downtrodden minorities.*

For a few months after the February kidnapping, a series of tape recordings and letters was received by California radio stations, newspapers and Miss Hearst's parents dealing with the status of Patricia, conditions for her release, and her apparent conversion to SLA ideology. A Feb. 12 letter instructed Patricia's father, San Francisco Examiner *president and publisher Randolph A. Hearst, to set up a four-week food distribution program for "all people [in California] with welfare cards, Social Security pension cards, food stamps, disabled veteran cards, medical cards, parole or probation* *papers and jail or bail release slips." In a tape recording accompanying the letter, Patricia said she was well and wanted her parents to meet SLA demands. The estimated cost of a food program of the scale and quality demanded by the SLA was $400-million, a figure which Hearst said far exceeded his resources. Instead, he devised a $2-million food giveaway plan. The first distribution, Feb. 21 in East Oakland, was disorganized and provoked fights and looting. A second distribution a week later, at 10 San Francisco Bay area centers, was carried out smoothly.*

Patricia's Conversion to SLA

Meanwhile, the SLA, in a tape-recorded message received Feb. 21, characterized Hearst's program as "throwing a few crumbs to the people" and demanded an additional $4-million worth of food. On a tape received March 9, after a 17-day silence, Miss Hearst also condemned the food program and again urged her father to meet SLA demands. "I know you have enough money," she said. An April 2 SLA message indicated that Patricia would be released, but the next day she declared by tape recording that she had "chosen to stay and fight" with the SLA for the "freedom of oppressed people."

The authenticity of Patricia Hearst's decision to remain with the SLA was the subject of much public debate. Her father, who had just placed in escrow an additional $4-million to be used for food giveaways if his daughter was released, was skeptical. "I don't believe she [would] change her philosophy that quickly," he said. Friends who described Patricia as a sunny, apolitical person questioned her newly acquired militancy. However, Miss Hearst was photographed holding a sawed-off carbine during a San Francisco bank robbery on April 15 which was attributed to the SLA. Although the Federal Bureau of Investigation (FBI) suggested she might have been acting under stress, a bank guard who witnessed the robbery asserted that she "absolutely was a participant."

Miss Hearst confirmed that she took part in the robbery of her own free will in a tape recording received April 24. She called "ridiculous" public speculation that she had been brainwashed by the SLA. In another tape received June 7, in which she used her adopted revolutionary name, "Tania," she reaffirmed her determination to continue the terrorist fight with the SLA. Six members of the group had died the previous month in a shootout and fire that erupted after police surrounded an SLA hideout in Los Angeles. Patricia was not present during the shootout but in the tape she said she had "died in the house...but out of the ashes I was reborn." She added: "I know what I have to do," an apparent reference to revolutionary action. Following the June 7 tape, Patricia dropped from sight and was presumed to be with other surviving SLA members, thought to number only two at most.

An FBI warrant for Patricia Hearst's arrest was issued May 19, and on June 6 a San Francisco federal grand jury indicted her for participation in

the April bank robbery. In early July, FBI Director Clarence W. Kelley said
that investigators did not know where the group was. Throughout the case
there had been speculation that Patricia's commitment to radical politics
preceded her kidnapping and that she had conspired in her abduction. Her
family and friends dismissed such theories as improbable.

Transcripts of two tape-recorded messages of Patricia
Hearst received Feb. 12, 1974, and April 3, 1974:

The Feb. 12 message:

Mom, Dad, I'm okay. I had a few scrapes and stuff, but they washed
them up and they're okay and I caught a cold, but they're giving me pills for
it and stuff, I'm not being starved or beaten or unnecessarily frightened.

I've heard some press reports and so I know that Steve and the neighbors
are okay and that no one was really hurt, and I also know that the SLA
members here are very upset about press distortions of what's been
happening. They have nothing to do with the August 7th movement; they
have not been shooting down helicopters or shooting down innocent people
in the streets.

I'm kept blindfolded usually so that I can't identify anyone. My hands are
often tied, but generally they're not. I'm not gagged or anything, I'm comfortable, and I think you can tell that I'm not really terrified or anything,
and I'm okay.

I was very upset to hear about the police rushing in on that house in
Oakland, and I was just really glad that I wasn't there, and I would
appreciate if everyone would just calm down and not try to find me and not
try to make identifications because they're not only endangering me but
they're endangering themselves.

I'm with a combat unit that's armed with automatic weapons and there's
also a medical team here and there's no way that I will be released until
they let me go, so it wouldn't do any good for somebody to come in here and
try to get me out by force. These people aren't just a bunch of nuts, they've
been really honest with me, but they're perfectly willing to die for what
they're doing, and I want to get out of here, but the only way I'm going to is
if we do it their way.

"Do What They Say"

I just hope that you'll do what they say, Daddy, and do it quickly. I have
been starting and stopping this tape myself so that I can collect my
thoughts, that's why there are so many stops in it. I'm not being forced to
say anything. I think it's important that you take their requests very
seriously about not arresting any other SLA members and about following
their good-faith requests to the letter, and I just want to get out of here and
see everyone again and to be back with Steve.

The SLA is very interested in seeing how you're taking this Dad to make
sure that you're really serious and listening to what they're saying. And
they think you've been taking this whole thing a lot more seriously than the

police or the FBI and other federal people have been taking it, and it seems to be getting to the point where they're not worried about you as much as they're worried about other people, or at least I am.

It's really up to you to make sure that the people don't jeopardize my life by charging in and doing stupid things, and I hope that you'll make sure that they don't do anything else like that Oakland house business.

The SLA people have really been honest with me and I feel pretty sure that I'm going to get out of here if everything goes the way they want it to, and I think you should feel that way, too, and try not to worry so much. I know it's hard. I heard that Mom is really upset and that everybody was at home, and I hope that this puts you a little bit at ease so that you know that I really am all right. I just hope that I can get back to everybody real soon.

SLA: Soldiers Fighting and Aiding People

The SLA has ideological ties with the IRA, the people's struggle in the Philippines and the Socialist people in Puerto Rico and their struggle for independence and they consider themselves to be soldiers who are fighting and aiding these people.

I am a prisoner of war and so are the two men in San Quentin. [Two SLA members in San Quentin Prison awaiting trial on charges of murdering Oakland School Superintendent Marcus Foster in November, 1973]

I'm being treated in accordance with the Geneva Convention and one of the conditions being that I am not being tried for crimes which I'm not responsible for.

I'm here because I'm a member of a ruling class family and I think you can begin to see the analogy. The men in San Quentin are being held and they're going to be tried simply because they are members of the SLA and not because they've done anything.

Witnesses to the shooting of Foster saw black men and two white men have been arrested for that.

You're being told this so you'll understand why I was kidnapped. And so that you'll understand that whatever happens to the two prisoners is going to happen to me. You have to understand that I am held being innocent the same way that the two men in San Quentin are innocent and they are simply members of the group and have not actually done anything themselves to warrant their arrest.

SLA: "Declared War Against the Government"

They apparently were part of an intelligence unit and never executed anyone themselves. The SLA has declared war against the government and it's important that you understand that they know what they are doing and you understand what their actions mean and that you realize that this is not considered by them to be just a simple kidnapping and that you don't treat it that way and say I don't know why she was taken. I'm telling you now why this happened so that you'll know so that you'll have something to use, the knowledge to try to get me out of here. If you can get that food thing organized before the 19th then that's okay and it will just speed up my release.

Today is Friday the eighth and in Kuwait they, the commandos, negotiated the release of their hostages and they left the country. Bye.

Transcript received with a tape-recorded message of Patricia Hearst, April 3:

I would like to begin this statement by informing the public that I wrote what I am about to say. It's what I feel. I have never been forced to say anything on any tape. Nor have I been brainwashed, drugged, tortured, hypnotized or in any way confused. As George Jackson wrote, "It's me, the way I want it, the way I see it."

Mom, Dad, I would like to comment on your efforts to supposedly secure my safety. The PIN [People in Need, the Hearst food program] giveaway was a sham. You attempted to deceive the people, the SLA and me with statements about your concern for myself and the people. You were playing games—stalling for time—which the FBI was using in their attempts to assassinate me and the SLA elements which guarded me.

You continued to report that you did everything in your power to pave the way for negotiations for my release—I hate to believe that you could have been so unimaginative as to not even have considered getting Little and Remiro released on bail. [Two SLA members in San Quentin Prison awaiting trial on charges of murdering Oakland school superintendent Marcus Foster in November 1973.] While it was repeatedly stated that my conditions would at all times correspond with those of the captured soldiers, when your own lawyer went to inspect the "hole" at San Quentin, he approved the deplorable conditions there—another move which potentially jeopardized my safety.

My mother's acceptance of the appointment to a second term as a U.C. [University of California] regent, as you well know, would have caused my immediate execution had the SLA been less 'together' about their political goals. Your actions have taught me a great lesson, and, in a strange kind of way I'm grateful to you.

"I Have Changed, Grown"

Steven, [Weed, Miss Hearst's fiance] I know that you're beginning to realize that there is no such thing as neutrality in time of war. There can be no compromise as your experiences with the FBI must have shown you. You have been harassed by the FBI because of your supposed connections with so-called radicals, and some people have gone so far as to suggest that I arranged my arrest. We both know what really came down that Monday night—but you don't know what's happened since then. I have changed—grown. I've become conscious and can never go back to the life we led before. What I'm saying may seem cold to you and to my old friends, but love doesn't mean the same thing to me anymore.

My love has expanded as a result of my experiences to embrace all people. It's grown into an unselfish love for my comrades here, in prison and on the streets. A love that comes from the knowledge that "no one is free until we are all free." While I wish that you could be a comrade, I don't expect it—all I expect is that you try to understand the changes I've gone through.

"I Have Chosen to Stay and Fight"

I have been given the choice of (1) being released in a safe area, or (2) joining the forces of the Symbionese Liberation Army and fighting for my freedom and the freedom of all oppressed people. I have chosen to stay and fight.

One thing which I learned is that the corporate ruling class will do anything in their power in order to maintain their position of control over the masses, even if this means the sacrifice of one of their own. It should be obvious that people who don't even care about their own children couldn't possibly care about anyone else's children. The things which are precious to these people are their money and power—and they will never willingly surrender either. People should not have to humiliate themselves by standing in lines in order to be fed, nor should they have to live in fear for their lives and the lives of their children....

"Dad...You Are A Liar"

Dad, you said that you were concerned with my life, and you also said that you were concerned with the life and interests of all oppressed people in this country, but you are a liar in both areas and as a member of the ruling class. I know for sure that yours and Mom's interests are never the interests of the people. Dad, you said you would see about getting more job opportunities for the people, but why haven't you warned the people what is to happen to them—that actually the few jobs they still have will be taken away.

You, a corporate liar, of course will say that you don't know what I am talking about, but I ask you then to prove it, tell the poor and oppressed people of this nation what the corporate state is about to do, warn black and poor people that they are about to be murdered down to the last man, woman and child. If you're so interested in the people why don't you tell them what the energy crisis really is. Tell them how it's nothing more than a manufactured strategy, a way of hiding industry's real intentions. Tell the people that the energy crisis is no more than a means to get public approval for a massive program to build nuclear power plants all over this nation.

Tell the people that the entire corporate state is, with the aid of this massive power supply, about to totally automate that entire industrial state, to the point that in the next five years all that will be needed will be a small class of button pushers; tell the people, Dad, that all of the lower class and at least half of the middle class will be unemployed in the next three years, and that the removal of expendable excess, the removal of un-

252

needed people has already started. I want you to tell the people the truth. Tell them how the law and order programs are just a means to remove so-called violent (meaning aware) individuals from the community in order to facilitate the controlled removal of unneeded labor force from this country, in the same way that Hitler controlled the removal of the Jews from Germany.

"You Would Also Kill Me If Necessary"

I should have known that if you and the rest of the corporate state were willing to do this to millions of people to maintain power and to serve your needs you would also kill me if necessary to serve these same needs. How long will it take before white people in this country understand that what happens to a black child must sooner or later happen to a white child. How long will it take before we all understand that we must fight for our freedom.

I have been given the name of Tania after a comrade who fought alongside Che [Guevara] in Bolivia for the people of Bolivia. I embrace the name with the determination to continue fighting with her spirit. There is no victory in the half-assed attempts at revolution. I know Tania dedicated her life to the people. Fighting with local dedication and an intense desire to learn which I will continue in the oppressed American people's revolution. All colors of string in the web of humanity yearn for freedom....

It is in the spirit of Tania that I say, "PATRIA O MUERTE. VENCEREMOS."

BOUMEDIENE'S SPEECH TO SPECIAL
U.N. SESSION ON RAW MATERIALS
April 10, 1974

*Speaking at a special U.N. session on raw materials and world
development, Algerian President Houari Boumediene on April 10 urged the
underdeveloped "third world" nations to take control of any of their natural
resources held by foreign interests. Only national control of raw materials
could guarantee economic growth and political self-determination to the
underdeveloped nations, Boumediene said. The Algerian president's
speech, which also advocated a policy whereby producing nations would fix
the prices of raw materials, gained impact by coming as it did in the wake
of the Arab oil embargo. (See p. 221.) Boumediene spelled out the implications of steps taken by the Arab nations when he declared that the
"OPEC [Organization of Petroleum Exporting Countries] action is really
the first illustration...[of] the great possibilities of a union of the raw
materials-producing countries."*

*Boumediene's proposals gave additional impetus to the concept of third-
world action affirmed at a conference of nonaligned nations in Algiers in
September 1973. There, 76 member nations of Asia, Africa and Latin
America had approved a resolution calling on developing nations to form
separate "producer associations" for each of the major raw material
products they sell to the world. Without mentioning the use of natural
resources as a political weapon, the resolution was clearly intended to
counter the power of multinational companies and to "reinforce...the
negotiating power" of underdeveloped countries.*

*The third-world unity demonstrated at Algiers in September suffered a
setback when Arab oil-production cutbacks and price increases resulted in*

quadrupled oil bills—and huge debts—for poor nations. Algeria had sought to convene the April U.N. session to deflect mounting criticism of Arab policy by underdeveloped nations whose requests for oil price rollbacks had been refused by the Arabs. Since March 1972, 20 black African nations had severed diplomatic ties with Israel in the name of third-world solidarity. In a reciprocal move the Arabs had extended the oil embargo to Rhodesia, Portugal and South Africa. But the spiraling oil prices and the alleged failure of the Arabs to hand over a promised $200-million development grant to the African Development Bank caused black African nations to question the wisdom of siding with the Arabs in the Middle East dispute. This discontent was reported at a March 19 meeting of the non-aligned nations' coordinating bureau in Algiers, called to prepare for the U.N. session.

In his U.N. speech Boumediene minimized the damage done by rising oil prices to underdeveloped countries, but he also urged continued foreign assistance to poor nations and he said that an $80-billion debt owed by underdeveloped countries should be canceled or renegotiated. Boumediene charged that the third-world nations—such as Vietnam, Chile and the Middle East countries—had become battlegrounds on which the industrialized nations fought out their conflicts. Frequently citing his own country's recent history of nationalization and social reorganization, Boumediene called on the nonaligned nations to work together for self-determination.

American Reaction to Speech

Official American reaction to Boumediene's speech came in an address to the U.N. General Assembly by Secretary of State Henry A. Kissinger on April 15. Kissinger pledged a major effort by the United States to help developing countries, but he warned commodity producers against jointly raising prices in imitation of the Arab oil embargo. Such action, he warned, would produce "global inflation followed by global recession from which no nation could escape."

The participation in the U.N. meeting of four heads of state from Africa in addition to Boumediene, with high-ranking ministers from Western Europe, China and the Soviet Union, was viewed in a New York Times report as reflecting both concern for the economic situation and recognition of the emerging influence of the underdeveloped countries.

> *Excerpts from address by Algerian President Houari Boumediene at special U.N. General Assembly session on raw materials, April 10, 1974:*

Mr. Chairman.

The extraordinary session in which we are assembled today is the direct result of the worsening tensions at work in international relations....

Our Assembly bears witness to the fact that these concerns, made more acute and thrown into sharper relief by recent events, are widely shared throughout the world.

Before taking up the precise issues on which we are meeting here, it would be well in order to set our work in its true context, to recall the basic conclusions agreed upon by the Heads of State of the Non-aligned Countries [in September 1973]....The raison d'etre of non-alignment is the defense of just causes against any and all forms of political hegemony and economic domination. Its aim is above all the emancipation of all peoples in a context of international cooperation based on the equality of States, the respect of sovereignty and the establishment of a just peace throughout the world....

[T]he increase in the number of independent States, far from leading to a just participation of all in the responsibilities of international life, has led on the contrary to an ever greater concentration of decision-making power in the hands of a restricted circle of powers.... It follows that imperialist objectives seem to take precedence over the requisites of true democratization....

In this particular context it is the aim of the Non-Aligned Countries in order to insure the conditions for true world-wide security, to achieve general and complete disarmament through a world-wide conference—disarmament which implies not only the prohibition of nuclear testing and destruction of nuclear stockpiles but also the dismantling of military bases and the withdrawal of foreign troops from all the regions of the world....

PRIORITY OF PRIORITIES

While Man inaugurated the present decade by conquering space, demonstrating by this prestigious achievement that his scientific and technological capacity is on a par with the most difficult problems posed by nature, his failure in the face of the dramatic problems of deprivation and poverty that beset the world remains total.

Posed a quarter of a century ago by the community of nations as one of the major world priorities, the problem of development has today become the priority of priorities which we must all face, and without further delay, if we wish to avert the tragic possibility that this problem might one day become a source of uncontrollable conflagration.

Any real political determination to launch a frontal attack on the problem of development should in the first place recognize the allocation of world resources as a central issue.... [An] appropriate stand [must] be taken regarding the recognition of human priorities. This should in the end lead to a profound reorganization of economic relations between rich and poor countries, tending toward a distribution of the benefits of growth and progress—a distribution which, in order to be equitable, must be in accord with the needs, priorities and legitimate interests of the parties concerned.

It must be recognized first of all that in the world in which we live all the strings of the world economy are in the hands of a minority composed of the highly developed countries. By virtue of its dominant position, this minority proceeds at will in determining the allocation of world resources in accordance with an order of priorities of its own....

Under multifarious historical guises the colonialist and neo-colonialist phenomenon has at all times revolved about the issue of the appropriation of world resources by the stronger to the detriment of the weaker.

In fact, the colonial and imperialist powers accepted the principle of the right of peoples to self-determination only when they had already succeeded in setting up the institutions and the machinery that would perpetuate the system of pillage established in the colonial era.

PRICE FIXING AND THE THIRD WORLD

Owing to the fact that the developed countries have virtual control of the raw materials markets and what practically amounts to a monopoly on manufactured products and capital equipment, while at the same time they hold monopolies on capital and services, they have been able to proceed at will in fixing the prices of both the raw materials that they take from the developing countries and the goods and services that they furnish these countries.

Consequently they are in a position to drain the resources of the Third World through a multiplicity of channels, to their own advantage....

THE DIALECTIC OF STRUGGLE AND SELF-RELIANCE

Placing development action within a dialectic of struggle, on the international level, and counting first and foremost on oneself and one's own resources, on the domestic level, are emerging more and more clearly as the two chief components of the only course open to the developing countries....

[N]o action could have fit more neatly into the logic of the basic concerns of the developing countries than what was undertaken by the oil-exporting countries.

The OPEC action is really the first illustration, and at the same time the most concrete and the most spectacular illustration, of the importance of raw material prices for our countries, the vital need for the producing countries to control the levers of price control, and lastly, the great possibilities of a union of raw-materials-producing countries. In this light this action should be viewed by the developing countries not as a problem—in other words, not from the standpoint advanced by those who wish to divide the Third World—but as an example and a source of hope.

The fact is that, following the decisions taken by the oil-producing countries, the action that should be placed on the Third World agenda is to extend what has been achieved by the oil-producing countries in order to include all the basic raw materials produced by the developing countries.

Moreover (and it is this that is also feared in certain industrialized countries in the guise of the display of emotion over oil) this very extension has in fact already begun, since in Africa, in Asia and in Latin America, with respect to raw materials and commodities such as copper, iron ore, bauxite, rubber, coffee, cocoa, peanuts and other items there are already visible, unmistakable signs of a new strength developing in producers' organizations

Yet the promising prospects that are thus opening up before the developing countries in the area of effective recovery of their natural resources must not cause us to lose sight of the extremely serious obstacles that will not fail to stand in our way....

Above and beyond the arguments that industrialized countries put forward regarding the fair price of petroleum and the fears that they display over its alleged effects on their economies, what most offends them and elicits a violent reaction from them is, first and foremost, the fact that for the first time in history developing countries have been able to take the liberty of fixing the prices of their raw materials themselves.

In the eyes of the most highly developed countries this precedent entails the imminent danger of rapidly spreading to all raw materials and commodities, and it is this precedent that some of them are absolutely bent on neutralizing by pressing for the formation of a coalition of industrialized countries against the oil-producing countries. The twofold aim of this coalition is to check the action of the OPEC countries and to exert the dissuasive force of the industrialized nations on other developing countries that are producers of raw materials....

THE RISING PRICES OF PRODUCTS

Unquestionably, the situation prevailing in certain countries, already alarming in every respect, can only grow worse owing to the effects of more or less concomitant rises in the prices of the products imported by them.

The price of wheat doubled from July 1972 to July 1973, and nearly doubled again during the second half of 1973. The price of sugar has quadrupled in less than three years.

The prices of the fertilizers most commonly used in the developing countries almost doubled between June 1972 and September 1973, and these excessive increases were brought about solely by the industrialized countries....

True, oil, which for decades had been sold at a very low price, recently underwent a readjustment and is now valued at a new level. This readjustment elicited violent reactions on the part of the industrialized countries, which mobilized all their machinery of propaganda and deception in an attempt to distort the basic facts of the problem.

The fact is, however, that the fundamental difference that explains the greatly dissimilar reactions caused by rises in fertilizer and wheat prices on the one hand, and the price of oil, on the other, resides in the fact that the proceeds of the increase went to developed countries in the first instance and to developing countries in the second....

Is there any need to mention, furthermore, that for the 25 countries classified by the UN in the category of the least developed nations, the impact of the rising cost of food products is 70% greater on their balance of payment than the effect of the increased price of oil?...

The poorer countries also pay the price of machinery, manufactured foods and other products and services with which they are provided by the industrialized countries. Over the last five years the price of steel has been multiplied by 3, the price of cement by 4, that of wood by 2.5 and that of tractors by 2, to mention only the few products that play a strategic part in development....

There are also the transfers of capital effected by foreign companies out of developing countries in which they possess means of production or engage in export trade....

Lastly there is indebtedness, which for the developing countries amounts to approximately 80 billion dollars owed to the industrialized countries. The service on this debt, which for the current year will be in the vicinity of 9 billion dollars, is one of the factors that compel the developing countries to borrow continually and thus chronically aggravate their balance-of-payments positions still further.

FIVE STRATEGIES FOR INITIATING DEVELOPMENT

If we want to give...[development] a real chance of success, we consider it necessary to base it on the following guidelines:

1) The developing countries must take over their natural resources, which implies, essentially, nationalizing the exploitation of these resources and controlling the machinery governing the determination of their prices;

2) A coherent and integrated process of development must be launched, which includes, in particular, the development of all agricultural potential and the achievement of in-depth industrialization essentially based, wherever possible, on the local processing of the natural resources, mineral or agricultural, of each country concerned;

3) The aid of the international community, based fundamentally on the financial, technological and commercial contributions of the rich and developed countries to those whose development is to be promoted, must be mobilized....

4) It will be necessary to eliminate, or at the least lighten the burdens and attenuate the circumstances which presently weigh on the developing countries and very often ultimately cancel the results of the efforts and sacrifices which these countries devote to their development;

5) A special program must be worked out and put into effect to procure more concentrated aid for those peoples who are recognized by the United Nations community as being the most deprived.

NATIONALIZATION IS AN ACT OF DEVELOPMENT

By enabling us to keep within our own countries all the financial flows generated by the development of our natural resources, by giving us the opportunity to have these resources bear fruit at home, thus promoting our development, and by reintegrating our mines and our plantations into our own economies, nationalization immediately provides us with new resources which can be mobilized for development. It thus constitutes one of the means which make it possible or easier for us to embark upon the process of economic take-off....

RECOVERY OF REVENUE IS A MAJOR OBJECTIVE

Further, the experience that many of us have by now acquired alerts us to the danger that the effects of nationalization may well be reduced or even completely obliterated if we are cheated of our revenue, the recovery of which is the principal objective of nationalization through price manipulation. Thus we see that the power to fix prices and the control of the related mechanisms are corollaries to the goal of recovering natural resources and indispensable extensions of nationalization.

While nationalization can be accomplished by action on the national level, control over prices cannot be achieved without a strategy based on the solidarity of the producing countries, united by their common interest.

Thus, in order to recover the revenue which is our due, we must create, product by product, common fronts among exporting countries, which will enable us collectively to defend our rights and to fix the prices of our products at appropriate levels, in accordance with our interests and the requirements of harmonious development of the world economy....

Development, nevertheless, is not merely a matter of seeking ways to maximize export revenues from the sale of raw materials. In truth, this maximization should be no more than a means of sustaining and speeding up development, which actually consists in mobilizing all agricultural potential and in industrialization, especially in local processing of raw materials to the fullest possible extent.

AGRICULTURE: OUR PRIMARY CONCERN

...Whatever choices we make in economic policy and whatever options other development factors may present, the full realization of our agricultural potential must in any event remain a very important element of our development policy and be aimed, as much as possible, at self-sufficiency as regards our food needs.

With regard to industrialization, the philosophy which has prevailed until now among those concerned with international development has been based on the postulate that, since the productivity of the factors of production is low in developing countries, they should postpone until later, if not forever, their entry into the industrial age....

In lieu of industrialization, our peoples should then content themselves with a series of superficial transformations such as the assembly, clothing or packaging industries which are no more than a new form of exploitation of their labor and which further deprive their economies of real possibilities for creating and promoting jobs—possibilities which exist only in genuine industrialization.

Consequently, our nations would be condemned to seeing their human resources continually bled and exploited, not only in their own countries but even in the developed countries, where their emigrant workers today make up the bulk of the sub-proletariat and where their technical and scientific personnel are attracted and enticed by the opportunities for promotion and progress of which they are deprived by the chronic immobility in their own countries....

The obstacles to development are not inevitably determined by geography or sociology but are the consequence of underdevelopment. Experience has shown that these obstacles gradually vanish under the impact of investment. It is from the very logic of the vicious circle of chronic immobility that the dialectic of development springs: instead of waiting for the obstacles to disappear or diminish before embarking upon development, it is essential to start with development action, which amounts to removing obstacles through development itself....

This industrial revolution is a necessary and urgent goal toward which every country of the Third World must strive. This task cannot be delegated. In other words, if each country is to be the true master of its own destiny, it must take on the responsibility of its own development itself: this implies, first and foremost, mobilizing all its human and material resources....

It is...clear, however, that all of the efforts of the countries of the Third World, however considerable and worthwhile, would not suffice in the face of the immense requirements of development with the support and assistance which the international community and more particularly, the developed countries must furnish them....

The first reason for this necessity is equity and world peace; the second is that the development of the countries of the Third World will trigger a continuing increase in demand which will result in considerable expansion of markets available to the developed countries.

This implies paying the developing countries fair prices for their raw materials and also the protection of the purchasing power of those prices against inflation and all the uncertainties and insecurity inherent in the functioning of the international monetary system....

The impact of the price of oil in overall cost makeup has always been ridiculously small; it remains so today; thus, if we wish to throttle inflation, it is necessary to attack the most significant items of expenditure....

AN END TO RUINOUS EXPENDITURES AND WASTE

In particular, it is necessary to eliminate the phenomena of overconsumption and gadgetization and, more generally, the waste, which runs rampant throughout the developed countries....

The way in which the international monetary system functions at present compromises the expansion of world commerce and, in particular, thwarts all attempts of the countries of the Third World to conquer underdevelopment....

The reform of the international monetary system must be based upon the necessity of giving Third World countries the right to participate, on a democratic basis, in its conception and operation.

In this regard, one could not accept as valid solutions the ideas which have been propagated around the world for some time which seek to lend credence to the idea that the control of inflation and the stability of the international monetary system require non-revalorization of the price of raw materials....

FOREIGN AID

As for financial aid for development, the criteria for its definition and utilization call for a thoroughgoing re-examination.

Foreign aid makes sense and has constructive significance only if it is based upon a recognition of the priorities of the developing countries as well as on an evaluation of the resource requirements of these countries after what is due them has been fully restored to them.

If a repetition of the failures of the decade of development is to be avoided, this aid must be significantly greater that it has been in the past....

MORE NON-REIMBURSABLE ASSISTANCE

Additionally, in order not to weigh too heavily on the balance of payments of the poorer countries, foreign aid should include a larger share of non-reimbursable assistance. In this regard, it would be highly desirable to examine the problem of the present indebtedness of the developing countries. In this examination one should consider the cancellation of the debt in a great number of cases and, in other cases, refinancing on better terms as regards maturity dates, deferrals and rates of interest.... Development aid should not be accompanied by any condition establishing a link between its existence and the maintenance of extremely low prices for raw materials. This link, which is acknowledged by many industrialized countries today, is nothing but the recognition by them that foreign aid was merely a sort of restitution of the poorer countries of a minimal portion of the value of their resources.

Finally...it is the developed countries that hold the major part of world wealth and it is therefore from them that the major part of foreign aid should come.

263

NEEDS OF POOR VS. NEEDS OF RICH

Between the needs of the poorer countries, *viz.* nutrition, schools, hospitals, and the means for the struggle against underdevelopment on the one hand, and, on the other, the needs of the rich countries, i.e., not only the unlimited growth of their wealth, but also the continuation of ruinous expenditures for political and prestige purposes, the question arises as to which of these needs are to be sacrificed for the others. The raw materials problem, therefore, is indeed posed in terms of opposition between priorities of the developed countries and those of the developing countries and, in connection with that opposition, in terms of the distribution of world resources for the satisfaction of those priorities....

The countries of the Third World recognize today the conditions which could permit them to enter upon the path of development and progress; moreover, they cannot be ignorant of the dark future which would be their destiny if they let slip away the opportunities that they now have for joining the battles and making the efforts and the sacrifices necessary for their well-being.

For the developed countries...must accept the conditions of the economic emancipation of the peoples of the Third World and agree to the transformations which this emancipation entails for the economic order presently established in the world.

If the debates and decisions of this Assembly could give us the hope of attaining such a result, then the development of the peoples of the Third World and the victories to be won against poverty, disease, illiteracy and insecurity will not be the revenge of the poorer countries over the wealthier countries, but a victory for all mankind.

▼▼▼

KENT STATE PARENTS: RIGHT TO SUE

April 17, 1974

Four years after Allison Krause, Jeffrey Glenn Miller, William K. Schroeder and Sandra Lee Scheuer were killed by gunfire as National Guardsmen tried to quell an anti-war demonstration at Kent State University, their parents won from the Supreme Court the right to be heard in their suit against the officials who sent the National Guard to the Ohio campus in May 1970. The decision came April 17, three weeks after eight men who were in 1970 members of the Ohio National Guard were indicted by a federal grand jury in connection with the student deaths. Only a "narrow threshold question" was decided by the court—but it was a crucial one. Were the then-governor James Rhodes, the president of the university, the commander of the national guard, and the other officials whom the parents sought to sue absolutely protected from such suits by the Eleventh Amendment or the doctrine of executive immunity? Had the court answered "yes," the parents' suit would have been finally foreclosed. But the answer was unanimously "no," allowing the parents at least the right to be heard initially by the federal district court which had originally dismissed their case.

The parents charged that the officials had deprived their children of their civil rights—and their lives—by "intentionally, recklessly, willfully and wantonly" sending the National Guard to the campus. The court, in its opinion written by Chief Justice Warren E. Burger, made clear that it intimated no view on that claim. When a federal court first reviews such a complaint, Burger wrote, it must consider "not whether a plaintiff will ultimately prevail, but whether...(he) is entitled to offer evidence to support the claims." The federal district court had cited the Eleventh Amendment in dismissing the parents' suit, an amendment that states that federal judicial power does not extend to a suit by citizens against a state. However, wrote Burger, since the 1907 decision—Ex parte Young—"it has been settled that the Eleventh Amendment provides no shield for a state official confronted by a claim that he had deprived another of a federal right under the color of state law." Just such a claim was raised by the parents in this case, the court held, and so the Eleventh Amendment did not apply.

Only A Qualified Immunity

An absolute executive immunity had been cited by the appeals court, sixth circuit, as part of the reason for upholding the dismissal of the case. But the Supreme Court found that executive immunity—although a necessary protection for officials required to make difficult decisions in their jobs—was only a qualified protection. "It can hardly be argued at this late date," wrote Burger, referring to a key provision of the Civil Rights Act of 1871 which had been interpreted to allow such suits, "that under no circumstances can the officers of state government be subject to liability."

In dismissing the parents' cases, the two lower courts "erroneously accepted as a fact the good faith of the governor and took judicial notice that 'mob rule existed at Kent State University.' There was no opportunity afforded...[the parents] to contest the facts assumed in that conclusion.... Further proceedings are required. The complaining parties are entitled to be heard more fully."

Justice William O. Douglas did not take part in the decision.

> *Excerpts from the text of the Supreme Court's ruling April 17, 1974:*

NOS. 72-914 AND 72-1318

Sarah Scheuer, Administra- trix, Etc., Petitioner, 72-914 *v.* James Rhodes et al. Arthur Krause, Administra- tor of the Estate of Allison Krause, et al Petitioners, 72-1318 *v.* James Rhodes et al.	On Writs of Certiorari to the United States Court of Appeals for the Sixth Circuit.

[April 17, 1974]

...MR. CHIEF JUSTICE BURGER delivered the opinion of the Court.

We granted certiorari in these cases to resolve whether the District Court correctly dismissed civil damage actions...on the ground that these actions were, as a matter of law, against the State of Ohio, and hence barred by the Eleventh Amendment to the Constitution and, alternatively, that the actions were against state officials who were immune from liability for the acts alleged in the complaints. These cases arise out of the same period of alleged civil disorder on the campus of Kent State University in Ohio during May 1970....

In these cases the personal representatives of the estates of three students who died in that episode seek damages against the Governor, the Adjutant-General and his Assistant, various named and unnamed officers and enlisted members of the Ohio National Guard and the President of Kent State University....

The District Court dismissed the complaints for lack of jurisdiction over the subject matter on the theory that these actions, although in form against the named individuals, were, in substance and effect, against the State of Ohio and thus barred by the Eleventh Amendment. The Court of Appeals affirmed the action of the District Court, agreeing that the suit was in legal effect one against the State of Ohio and, alternatively, that the common law doctrine of executive immunity barred action against the state officials who are respondents here.... We are confronted with the narrow threshold question whether the District Court properly dismissed the complaint. We hold that dismissal was inappropriate at this stage of the litigation and accordingly reverse the judgment and remand for further proceedings. We intimate no view on the merits of the allegations since there is no evidence before us at this stage.

I

The complaints in these cases are not identical but their thrust is essentially the same. In essence the defendants are alleged to have "intentionally, recklessly, willfully and wantonly" caused an unnecessary deployment of the Ohio National Guard on the Kent State campus and, in the same manner, ordered the Guard members to perform allegedly illegal actions which resulted in the death of plaintiffs' decedents. Both complaints allege that the action was taken "under color of state law" and that it deprived the decedents of their lives and rights without due process of law. Fairly read, the complaints allege that each of the named defendants, in undertaking such actions, acted either outside the scope of his respective office or, if within the scope, acted in an arbitrary manner, grossly abusing the lawful powers of office....

The issue is not whether a plaintiff will ultimately prevail but whether the claimant is entitled to offer evidence to support the claims. Indeed it may appear on the face of the pleadings that a recovery is very remote and unlikely but that is not the test. Moreover, it is well-established that, in passing on a motion to dismiss, whether on the ground of lack of jurisdiction over the subject matter or for failure to state a cause of action, the allegations of the complaint should be construed favorably to the pleader....

II

The Eleventh Amendment to the Constitution of the United States provides: "The judicial power of the United States shall not be construed to extend to any suit in law and equity, commenced or prosecuted against one of the United States by citizens of another State...." It is well-established that the Amendment bars suits not only against the State when it is the named party but when it is the party in fact....

However...it has been settled that the Eleventh Amendment provides no shield for a state official confronted by a claim that he had deprived another of a federal right under the color of state law. *Ex parte Young* teaches that when a state officer acts under a state law in a manner violative of the Federal Constitution, he

> "comes into conflict with the superior authority of that Constitution and he is in that case stripped of his official or representative character and is subjected *in his person* to the consequences of his individual conduct. The State has no power to impart to him any immunity from responsibility to the supreme authority of the United States." (Emphasis supplied.)....

Analyzing the complaint in light of these precedents, we see that petitioners allege facts that demonstrate they are seeking to impose individual and personal liability on the *named defendants* for what they claim—but have not yet established by proof—was a deprivation of federal rights by these defendants under the color of state law. Whatever the plaintiffs may or may not be able to establish as to the merits of their allegations, their claims, as stated in the complaints, given the favorable reading required by the Federal Rules of Civil Procedure, are not barred by the Eleventh Amendment. Consequently, the District Court erred in dismissing the complaint for lack of jurisdiction.

III

The Court of Appeals relied upon the existence of an absolute "executive immunity" as an alternative ground for sustaining the dismissal of the complaint by the District Court.... While the...doctrine that the "King could do not wrong" did not protect all government officers from personal liability, the common law soon recognized the necessity of permitting officials to perform their official functions free from the threat of suits for personal liability. This official immunity apparently rested, in its genesis, on two mutually dependent rationales: (1) the injustice, particularly in the absence of bad faith, of subjecting to liability an officer who is required, by the legal obligations of his position, to exercise discretion; (2) the danger that the threat of such liability would deter his willingness to execute his office with the decisiveness and the judgment required by the public good.

In this country, the development of the law of immunity for public officials has been the product of constitutional provision as well as legislative and judicial processes. The Federal Constitution grants absolute immunity to Members of both Houses of the Congress with respect to any speech, debate, vote, report or action done in session....

Although the development of the general concept of immunity, and the mutations which the underlying rationale has undergone in its application to various positions are not matters of immediate concern here, it is important to note, even at the outset, that one policy consideration seems to pervade the analysis: the public interest requires decisions and action to enforce laws for the protection of the public. Mr. Justice Jackson expressed this general proposition succinctly, stating "it is not a tort for the government to govern...." Public officials, whether Governors, Mayors or police, legislators or judges who fail to make decisions when they are needed or who do not act to implement decisions when they are made do not fully and faithfully perform the duties of their offices. Implicit in the idea that officials have some immunity—absolute or qualified—for their acts, is a recognition that they may err. The concept of immunity assumes this and goes on to assume that it is better to risk some error and possible injury from such error than not to decide or act at all.

For present purposes we need determine only whether there is an absolute immunity.... If the immunity is qualified, not absolute, the scope of that immunity will necessarily be related to facts as yet not established either by affidavits, admissions or a trial record. Final resolution of this question must take into account the functions and responsibilities of these particular defendants in their capacities as officers of the state government, as well as the purposes of [the law]. In neither of these inquiries do we write on a clean slate. It can hardly be argued, at this late date, that under no circumstances can the officers of state government be subject to liability under this statute....

When a court evaluates police conduct relating to an arrest its guideline is "good faith and probable cause." In the case of higher officers of the executive branch, however, the inquiry is far more complex since the range of decisions and choices—whether the formulation of policy, of legislation, of budgets, or of day-to-day decisions—is virtually infinite. In common with police officers, however, officials with a broad range of duties and authority must often act swiftly and firmly at the risk that action deferred will be futile or constitute virtual abdication of office. Like legislators and judges, these officers are entitled to rely on traditional sources for the factual information on which they decide and act. When a condition of civil disorder in fact exists, there is obvious need for prompt action and decisions must be made in reliance on factual information supplied by others. While both federal and state laws plainly contemplate the use of force when the necessity arises, the decision to invoke military power has traditionally been viewed with suspicion and skepticism since it often involves the temporary suspension of some of our most cherished gifts—government by elected civilian leaders, freedom of expression, of assembly and association. Decisions in such situations are more likely than not to arise in an atmosphere of confusion, ambiguity, and swiftly moving events and when, by the very existence of some degree of civil disorder, there is often no consensus as to the appropriate remedy. In short, since the options which a chief executive and his principal subordinates must consider are far broader and far more subtle than those made by officials with less responsibility, the range of discretion must be comparably broad....

These considerations suggest that, in varying scope, a qualified immunity is available to officers of the executive branch of Government, the variation dependent upon the scope of discretion and responsibilities of the office and all the circumstances as they reasonably appeared at the time of the action on which liability is sought to be based. It is the existence of reasonable grounds for the belief formed at the time and in light of all the circumstances, coupled with good faith belief, that afford basis for qualified immunity of executive officers for acts performed in the course of official conduct....

IV

This case, in its present posture, presents no occasion for a definitive exploration of the scope of immunity available to state executive officials nor, because of the absence of a factual record, does it permit a determination as to the applicability of the foregoing principles to the respondents here. The District Court acted before an answer was filed and without any evidence other than the copies of the proclamations issued by Respondent Rhodes and brief affidavits of the Adjutant General and his assistant.... There was no opportunity afforded petitioners to contest the facts assumed in that conclusion. There was no evidence before the Court from which such a finding of good faith could be properly made and, in the circumstances of these cases, such a dispositive conclusion could not be judicially noticed. We can readily grant that a declaration of emergency by the chief executive of a State is entitled to great weight but it is not conclusive....

The documents properly before the District Court at this early pleading stage specifically placed in issue whether the Governor and his subordinate officers were acting within the scope of their duties under the Constitution and laws of Ohio; whether they acted within the range of discretion permitted the holders of such office under Ohio law and whether they acted in good faith both in proclaiming an emergency and as to the actions taken to cope with the emergency so declared. Similarly, the complaint places directly in issue whether the lesser officers and enlisted personnel of the Guard acted in good faith obedience to the orders of their superiors. Further proceedings, either by way of summary judgment or by trial on the merits, are required. The complaining parties are entitled to be heard more fully than is possible on a motion to dismiss a complaint.

We intimate no evaluation whatever as to the merits of the petitioners' claims or as to whether it will be possible to support them by proof. We hold only that, on the allegations of their respective complaints, they were entitled to have them judicially resolved.

The judgement of the Court of Appeals is reversed and remanded for further proceedings consistent with this opinion.

CHINA'S REPORT ON LIN PIAO PLOT
April 20, 1974

On April 20 the government of the People's Republic of China released its first detailed account of an alleged plot for a coup d'etat by its late defense minister, Lin Piao. Once the designated successor to Chairman Mao Tse-tung, Lin reportedly died in a plane crash in Mongolia in 1971 following an aborted attempt to assassinate Mao and overthrow the Chinese government. Official denunciations of Lin—the April 20 attack was the latest in a series dating back to the 10th Chinese Communist Party Congress in August 1973 (see Historic Documents, 1973, p. 767-778)—*apparently evidenced a prolonged political struggle whose full extent was unclear to veteran China-watchers.*

Since the 1973 Party Congress, a new Cultural Revolution-type campaign had been building in China. Newspapers, radio broadcasts and wall posters assailed Lin and the Chinese philosopher Confucius. Both figures were accused of attempting to restore the old regimes of their day. The public declamations on revolutionary ideology were interpreted as a cloak for a power struggle within the party leadership, possibly a reassertion of power by the aging Mao.

The April 20 report on Lin came from the New China News Agency, which quoted from an article published in Hung Chi (Red Flag), *the Chinese Communist Party's theoretical journal. According to that article, Lin planned to seize power Sept. 8, 1971. "To prepare public opinion," the publication said, Lin's followers had three million pamphlets printed and distributed in southern Fukien province from January to September 1971. Gaining control of the mass media was reportedly the first stage of a plot,* known as "Outline of Project 571," devised by Lin at the second plenary session of the 9th Party Congress in 1970. The article also accused Lin of having disobeyed orders as a general during the 1945-49 civil war.

Lin was first officially denounced by name at the August 1973 congress where he was posthumously expelled from the party. The following February, a Communist Party newspaper officially acknowledged that "a serious class struggle and a thoroughgoing revolution in the realm of ideology in China" was going on under the direction of Mao. As the drive intensified, western literary, artistic and political figures, including Italian filmmaker Michaelangelo Antonioni, American scholar Owen Lattimore, and the composers Respighi, Beethoven and Schubert, came under attack. In February, Antonioni's 1972 documentary China was called "degrading to the working people of the vast third world." Lattimore, a China specialist, was branded a "reactionary historian" for having described Confucious as an enlightened philosopher. The "foreign" music of Beethoven and Schubert was said to deserve criticism and Respighi's Pines of Rome was said to express "decadent sentiments." (The Respighi piece had been conducted in Peking by the American orchestra leader Eugene Ormandy in September 1973.) Chinese figures also were criticized, particularly those associated with the recent opera production of suspicious ideology, Three Trips to Tao Feng. But the prime targets for attack were Lin and Confucius.

Growth of Anti-Lin Campaign

According to reports, activists were forming "study groups" and "mass criticism groups," thereby mobilizing wide support for the ideological campaign. By late March individual party officials were being attacked by name in wall posters. The first hint that the drive was more than a paper phenomenon appeared in a Communist Party newspaper editorial of April 10 which stressed the need to "promote production." This suggested to western observers that the campaign had disrupted industrial centers.

Further evidence of internal disturbances—though not on the scale of those during the 1966-69 Cultural Revolution—coincided with the official announcement of Lin's alleged plot. On April 17 the Reuters news agency reported the public executions of 30 persons in Canton; that city, with the surrounding Kwang-tung province, had reportedly been Lin's power base for many years. Though not unheard of in China, public executions were rare and generally were interpreted as a sign of high social tension. The last time they were known to have occurred was during the crackdown on youthful extremists during the final stages of the Cultural Revolution. The Reuters report was based on accounts of travelers who had seen posters in Canton listing names and ages of the victims and accusing them of opposition to the ideological campaign.

By August, the campaign appeared to have subsided without any clear resolution. Wall posters denouncing local party officials had been replaced *by notices stressing the need for "production." Weak links in production were acknowledged in the Chinese press and evidence of coal shortages was reported in the West. Reasons for the pause in the campaign against Lin and Confucius were not clear. Observers suggested that the Peking leadership either wished to protect the economy from further damage by social disruption, or wished to present a unified front as the 25th anniversary of Communist rule in China (Oct. 1, 1974) drew near.*

> *Excerpts from the article on* Lin Piao in the Period of the War of Liberation of the Northeast, *published in* Hung-chi (Red Flag), *April 1, 1974. The article was the first official report of the details of Lin Piao's alleged plot:*

In August 1970 the great leader Chairman Mao and the Party Central Committee smashed the conspiracy of the Lin Piao anti-Party clique for a counter-revolutionary coup d'etat at the Second Plenary Session of the 9th Party Central Committee. In early 1971, at an important moment of the extremely sharp struggle between the two lines, the Hsinhua Bookstore of Fukien Province published a booklet entitled "Lin Piao in the Period of the War of Liberation of the Northeast." The release of this reactionary booklet caused a big stir for a while. From January to September there were successively three editions and seven impressions of more than three million copies. Either sold or presented as gifts, they were distributed to many provinces and cities throughout the country. It was also incorporated into a senior middle school textbook, and it was even prepared to translate into foreign languages. In this booklet the author audaciously extols Lin Piao as "commander," "an extraordinary genius," "a wise leader who is consistently correct," thus energetically preparing public opinion for Lin Piao's counter-revolutionary armed coup d'etat.

This is an unusual counter-revolutionary political incident. To thoroughly expose and criticize this big poisonous weed which created public opinion for the renegade and traitor Lin Piao to usurp Party leadership and seize political power, to find out its origin, and to eliminate its pernicious influence in the course of the struggle to criticize Lin Piao and Confucius—this will help us further settle accounts with the crimes of Lin Piao and his diehard clique in plotting to restore the old order.... Judging by both the timing of its release and its content, it was closely coordinated with the conspiracy of the Lin Piao anti-Party clique in staging a counter-revolutionary armed coup d'etat.

In March 1971, Lin Piao and his diehard clique, hiding in a dark corner, formulated a plan for a counter-revolutionary armed coup d'etat entitled "Outline of 'Project 571'." One of the tasks called for by the plan was to "grasp the public opinion tools and launch a political offensive." Published in January, this booklet was an important "public opinion tool" for them to "launch a political offensive...." In July, the author of this booklet...sent people to the publishing organ and several times a day inquired about the progress, demanding that it be printed, bound and distributed fast and setting the deadline for the "completion of the printing before September."

Comrades should note that these words should not be ignored, for they spoke for the counter-revolutionary conspiracy of Lin Piao and company. Right on September 8, Lin Piao launched his counter-revolutionary armed coup d'etat, vainly attempting to murder the great leader Chairman Mao and to set up a separate Central Committee. After this conspiracy fell through, on September 13 Lin Piao and his several diehard associates privately took a plane to defect to Soviet revisionism in betrayal of the Party and country and died in a crash at Undur Khan in Mongolia. This was a breath-taking time table. It irrefutably proves that the release of this booklet was an organized, planned and directed conspiratorial activity....

Theory of Genius

This reactionary booklet fanatically lauded Lin Piao....

To praise Lin Piao as an "extraordinary genius" and as "a man who is different from others" was to uphold the counter-revolutionary theoretical program of the "theory of genius." At the Second Plenary Session of the 9th Party Central Committee, Chairman Mao severely criticized the idealist "theory of genius" advocated by Lin Piao and company. However, Lin Piao and his diehard clique audaciously resisted Chairman Mao's criticism and continued to preach this reactionary view, declaring that "it is necessary to recognize the genius, learn from the genius, publicize the genius, and protect the genius." Who was the genius? The reactionary booklet, mincing no words, answered that the genius was Lin Piao. And not merely a "genius," but an "extraordinary genius," that is, the so-called "supergenius." In propagating the reactionary idealist "theory of genius" in such a fanatical manner, Lin Piao and his diehard clique peddled the "theory of Heavenly mandate" advocated by Confucius and Mencius in a vain attempt to prove that they were the "noblest" and supermen whose brains were different from those of others and who were "bestowed by Heaven"....

Chairman Mao points out: "The use of novels to carry out anti-Party activities is a big invention. In order to overthrow a political power, it is always necessary first to create the public opinion, to do work in the ideological sphere. This is true for the revolutionary classes and for the counter-revolutionary classes." Some use novels to oppose the Party, others use operas to oppose the Party, and still others use memoirs to oppose the Party. Although the forms are different, the goal is the same.... If we fail to pay attention to the class struggle in the ideological sphere and instead take it lightly, we will suffer greatly....

Lin's Military Orders

As everyone knows, in 1948 the nationwide political and military situation was very favorable to us and the time for the strategic battle of decision had already become ripe.... With the wisdom and courage characteristic of a proletarian revolutionary, the great leader Chairman Mao promptly organized the three big campaigns...and resolutely decided to fight a strategic battle of decision with the Kuomintang reactionary army by starting with the Northeast theater.... Lin Piao time and again opposed Chairman Mao's strategic decisions....

In the course of the Liaohsi-Shenyang campaign, Lin Piao had consistently taken the Right opportunist stand and over-estimated the strength of the enemy while under-estimating the strength of the people. He failed to see that the time for the strategic battle of decision had come. He was blind to the possibility of basically toppling the Kuomintang reactionaries within a short period of time.... A host of facts show that throughout the entire Liaohsi-Shenyang campaign, the struggle between two kinds of military thinking and two military lines was extremely acute. The victory of the Liaohsi-Shenyang campaign was a result of the triumph of Chairman Mao's correct proletarian military line over Lin Piao's Right opportunist line, was a result of the implementation of Chairman Mao's correct line by the broad masses of commanders and fighters of our army, and was a great victory for Chairman Mao's strategic thinking. No forgery can obliterate the historical fact that the great leader Chairman Mao was the leader and organizer of the victorious war of liberation of the Northeast....

In order to create for Lin Piao the myth of so-called "talented military strategist," a whole section of this reactionary booklet was devoted to lauding Lin Piao's so-called "tactical principles" such as "one-point and two-directions".... Actually, Lin Piao's "tactical principles" were nothing but sinister stuff cooked up by him to counter Chairman Mao's ten major military principles....

But through the pen of the author of this booklet, the truth was twisted in such a way that "all the enemy-occupied big cities in the Northeast" were captured under Lin Piao's "tactical guidance." Such a performance of distorting the true facts was really despicable....

In view of the massive distribution of this booklet and the spread of its pernicious influence throughout the country, the time has now come to thoroughly settle accounts with the plot of releasing this booklet. Chairman Mao points out: "Where there are mistakes, these should be criticized; where there are poisonous weeds, a struggle should be waged against them." In the course of the struggle to criticize Lin Piao and Confucius, to penetratingly uncover and criticize this big poisonous weed will enable us to receive a profound education in class struggle and the line struggle by negative example.

NIXON FOREIGN AID MESSAGE

April 24, 1974

President Nixon sent to Congress April 24 a $5.18-billion foreign aid request for fiscal 1975 which included $250-million in assistance to Egypt as part of a $907.5-million request for aid to the Middle East. Indochina reconstruction assistance totaling $939.8-million was also requested. The President called the aid package "the minimum which the United States can prudently afford to invest if we are to maintain the present degree of international equilibrium and advance our efforts to construct a durable peace with prosperity." But the President could expect an uphill fight on Capitol Hill where the ranks of foreign aid opponents had been growing. Although Congress appropriated $5.8-billion for foreign aid in fiscal 1974—the largest amount since the Korean War—the final amount was still more than $1-billion less than requested. In addition, the fiscal 1974 total had been boosted by $2.2-billion in emergency security assistance for Israel.

In his message to Congress making the request, Nixon asserted that "we have an opportunity to achieve a significant breakthrough for world peace" in the Middle East. He called his aid proposal for the region "a vital complement" to U.S. attempts to negotiate a peace settlement. The $250-million in security supporting assistance proposed for Egypt was reported to include $20-million for clearing operations in the Suez Canal, $80-million in farm and industrial goods purchases and $150-million for reconstruction of war-damaged cities. Also included in the Middle East aid proposal were $350-million for Israel ($300-million in military credit sales and $50-million in security supporting assistance) and $207.5-million for Jordan ($100-million in military grants assistance, $77.5-million in security supporting assistance and $30-million in military credit sales).

In addition, the President proposed a $100-million "special requirement fund" which he said could be used for peacekeeping forces, refugee aid and development projects. There was some speculation that this might include aid to Syria, although an Israeli-Syrian troop disengagement pact had not then been reached. (See p. 435.) State Department spokesman John King was reported as saying that prospects of aid to Syria could not be excluded and White House Deputy Press Secretary Gerald L. Warren said such aid was conceivable.

Indochina Assistance

Assistance in the reconstruction of Indochina was termed "no less critical" than U.S. aid to the Middle East. Calling his $939.8-million aid proposal for South Vietnam, Cambodia and Laos "actually austere," Nixon told Congress that U.S. efforts in assisting these countries to become self-sufficient was "nearing success." Included in the Indochina package were proposals for a reported $750-million for South Vietnam, $110-million for Cambodia, $55.2-million for Laos and the balance for regional programs and support costs. The President also requested $1.45-billion for military assistance to South Vietnam in his fiscal 1975 defense budget. Funds for military assistance to Cambodia and Laos were included in the regular foreign aid bill.

Funding Request

President Nixon proposed a funding level of $1.143-billion for development assistance. Included in this over-all total were requests for $873.3-million for functional aid categories and $153.9-million for international organizations. Other assistance requests included $25-million for the Overseas Private Investment Corporation and $42.5-million for international narcotics control, as well as the $939.8-million for Indochina and $100-million for the Middle East special requirements fund. The bulk of the Middle East aid requests were included in the overall military assistance categories.

The President requested a total of $985-million in military grant assistance and $555-million for foreign military sales credits to finance an $872.5-million program. In addition, a total of $385.5-million was proposed for security supporting assistance. The foreign aid message also called for $1,005.6-million for international financial institutions. Although this did not include the $1.5-billion contribution to the International Development Association proposed by the administration but rejected by the House on Jan. 23, 1974, Nixon urged the House to reconsider its action. The Senate Foreign Relations Committee approved the contribution April 23, 1974.

Secretary of State Henry A. Kissinger tried to sell President Nixon's $5.18-billion fiscal 1975 foreign aid program to the House Foreign Affairs Committee June 4-5. At the hearings, committee members made it clear that they liked the salesman, but were doubtful about the product. Kissinger said the aid programs were "key elements" in maintaining *improved relations in the Mideast and Indochina. Nearly half of the aid would go to those two areas. Kissinger also disclosed that $100-million in the proposed program, labeled a "special requirements fund," might be given to Syria for rebuilding in war-damaged areas, particularly the provincial capital of Quneitra. He stressed to the committee that no commitments had been made to Syria about the $100-million during the lengthy negotiations leading to the Israeli-Syrian military disengagement pact signed May 31. He said he had told the Syrians he would ask Congress for the $100-million if an accord were signed and implemented.*

The administration's program in the Mideast was "designed to further the momentum that the peace process has now acquired," Kissinger testified. The proposed $907.5-million for the area would provide Israel with assistance needed for maintaining its security, would be a tangible recognition of "our new and fruitful relations with various Arab countries," and would foster peaceful development in the area, he said. The President's proposal provided for $350-million for Israel for military equipment, $207.5-million for Jordan for military and economic aid, and $250-million to Egypt for economic assistance, plus the $100-million special requirements fund. Kissinger pledged to "consult closely" with Congress on the use of the fund.

Commenting on administration requests for aid to Indochina, Kissinger said the United States had a "moral obligation to persevere" in that area and that renewed warfare would put pressure on developing relationships with other world powers with interests there.

Kissinger's message on the necessity of the foreign aid program to U.S. interests was reinforced June 5 by Defense Secretary James R. Schlesinger, who defended the military assistance program as "essential to the success of our hopes for a greater measure of Middle East peace." In testimony before the House Foreign Affairs Committee, Schlesinger justified major military grant and sales programs to the Mideast as a tool for preserving "an incomplete and fragile peace" and as recognition of the nation's "vital need" to have access to oil reserves in the area. "Denial or curtailment of this access would represent a threat to the security and economic well-being of the United States and other free-world nations," he said. On Indochina, Schlesinger said that the conflict in Southeast Asia had "demonstrated the problems that can result from the direct involvement of American forces" and added that the military assistance program could help to avoid such involvement in the future.

Congressional Reaction

Committee Chairman Thomas E. Morgan (D Pa.) told reporters after a closed session with Kissinger that members of the committee had made clear to him their "severe reservations" about the aid program. Those reservations included sentiment that the overall levels of money requested were too high—particularly for Indochina; questions about con-

tinuing aid to India, which exploded its first nuclear device May 18; questions about continued aid to oil-rich countries; and doubts about the U.S. role in reopening the Suez Canal. The committee questioned Kissinger repeatedly about secret commitments he might have made to Egypt or Syria in negotiating the ceasefire. Kissinger said there had been "no commitments, expressed or implied."

The concern surfaced again in questioning of Schlesinger, who said he had no knowledge of any assurances to Israel on continuing aid. H. R. Gross (R Iowa) said, "I'd like to know how far these commitments go. I am waiting to see all the commitments that have been made in the Middle East." Peter H. B. Frelinghuysen (R N.J.) gave an indication of the tough selling job the President faced with his program when he said that "if experience is any guide, some severe slashing will be made" in the request. Another indication came from Sen. Barry Goldwater (R Ariz.), who criticized the possible aid to Syria as inappropriate "to a country we have never attacked, never been particularly friendly to, and whose aid we have never particularly sought." He said it was time for a "long thoughtful discussion" of the U.S. aid program, which he said had been largely a failure from its beginning.

Text of President Nixon's foreign aid message to Congress April 24, 1974:

FOREIGN ASSISTANCE PROGRAMS

The President's Message to the Congress Proposing Legislation To Authorize Funding for Fiscal Year 1975. April 24, 1974

To the Congress of the United States:

For more than twenty five years, America has generously provided foreign assistance to other nations, helping them to develop their economies, to meet the humanitarian needs of their people and to provide for their own defense.

During this era foreign aid has become an indispensable element of our foreign policy. Without it, America would risk isolating herself from responsible involvement in an international community upon which the survival of our own economic, social and political institutions rests. With the continuation of a healthy foreign aid program, this Nation can continue to lead world progress toward building a lasting structure of peace.

Now that we have ended the longest war in our history and no American troops are serving in combat for the first time in more than a decade, there is a temptation to turn inward, abandoning our aid programs and the critical needs facing many of our friends in the process.

We must not succumb to that temptation. If we lay down the burden now, we will foreclose the peaceful development of many of the nations of the world and leave them at the mercy of powerful forces, both economic and political. Moreover, we will deny ourselves one of the most useful tools we have for helping to shape peaceful relationships in the most turbulent areas of the world.

Many of the nations which were once dependent upon our direct assistance for their survival are now managing their own economic and defense needs without our aid. Those nations which still need our aid will not need it indefinitely. We expect those nations we help to help themselves. We have made it clear that we do not intend to be the world's policeman, that our aid is not a substitute for their self-reliance, and that we do not intend to do for others what they should be expected to do for themselves.

But as long as there are governments which seek to change the frontiers and institutions of other nations by force, the possibility of international conflict will continue to exist. And as long as millions of people lack food, housing, and jobs; starvation, social unrest and economic turmoil will threaten our common future.

Our long-range goal is to create an international environment in which tolerance and negotiation can replace aggression and subversion as preferred methods of settling international disputes. While this goal is not as distant as it once was, present circumstances do not now permit reduction in foreign assistance. We must not only maintain our efforts, but also make special efforts in two critical areas of the world—the Middle East and Indochina.

In the Middle East, we have an opportunity to achieve a significant breakthrough for world peace. Increased foreign aid will be a vital complement to our diplomacy in maintaining the momentum toward a negotiated settlement which will serve the interests of both Israel and the Arab nations.

In Indochina our assistance is no less critical. South Vietnam, Cambodia, and Laos are trying to make the difficult transition from war to peace. Their ability to meet their defense needs while laying the foundations for self-sustaining social and economic progress requires continued and substantial amounts of American aid.

To meet these continuing and special needs, I am proposing to the Congress a total foreign aid budget of $5.18 billion for fiscal year 1975. In my judgment, these amounts represent the minimum which the United States can prudently afford to invest if we are to maintain the present degree of international equilibrium and advance our efforts to construct a durable peace with prosperity.

Toward Peace in the Middle East

The hope for a lasting solution to the Arab-Israeli dispute is stronger today than at any time in the previous quarter century. American diplomatic initiatives have helped create the conditions necessary for an end to conflict and violence. While our diplomatic efforts must and will continue, there is already much that can be done to supplement and consolidate what has been achieved so far. I am therefore requesting a Special Assistance program for the Middle East, and have asked the Congress to provide the following:

—For Israel: $50 million in security supporting assistance and $300 million in military credit sales. Israel's continued ability to defend herself reduces the prospect of new conflict in the Middle East, and we must continue to assist her in maintaining that ability.

—For Egypt: $250 million in supporting assistance. These funds would be used for the tasks which come with peace: clearing the Suez Canal, repairing the damage in adjacent areas, and restoring Egyptian trade.

—For Jordan: $100 million in military assistance grants, $77.5 million in security supporting assistance, and $30 million in military credit sales. Jordan has been a moderating force in the Arab world and these funds will enable her to maintain a position of moderation and independence which will be crucial to a permanent settlement in the area.

—For a Special Requirements Fund: $100 million. This fund will be used for new needs that may arise as the outlines of a peaceful settlement take shape, including provision for peacekeeping forces, refugee aid or settlement, and development projects.

All of this aid will contribute to the confidence these nations must have in the United States and in their own security if they are to have the base from which to negotiate a lasting settlement. It will strengthen moderate forces in an area where only moderation can form the basis for a settlement acceptable to all.

Toward Reconstruction of Indochina

Another area of acute and continuing concern to this Government is Southeast Asia. Our aid in Indochina is no less crucial than our aid in the Middle East in achieving a peaceful outcome which protects our interests and reflects our past involvement in these two areas. I am asking the Congress to authorize the appropriation of $939.8 million to assist South Vietnam, Cambodia and Laos in their efforts to shift their economies from war to peace and to accelerate the reconstitution of their societies.

We have already invested heavily in these countries. Progress has been significant, and we are nearing success in our efforts to assist them in becoming self-sufficient. Although our total request is higher than last year, the budget I am proposing is actually austere. We must recognize that a modest increase in economic assistance now will permit the development of viable, self-supporting economies with lower requirements for assistance within a few years.

The South Vietnamese face an unusually difficult task in reconstructing their economy and caring for their war-torn population even as the effort to end hostilities goes forward. Progress in reconstruction, economic development and humanitarian programs, which offer the hope of a better life for the people there, should make it clear that a peaceful settlement of political disputes is in the interest of all.

This year and next the South Vietnamese face several related challenges which make increased U.S. economic assistance essential:

—They must resettle more than a million refugees and displaced persons.

—They must provide the investments needed to create productive jobs for several hundred thousand who have lost jobs with the withdrawal of U.S. forces.

—They must meet the much higher costs of such essential imports as fertilizer and other critical resources caused by worldwide inflation.

—They must provide for the orphans, the disabled, and for widows who can never recover their wartime losses.

—They must continue to support the military forces needed to preserve movement toward peace so long as hostile forces continue to be deployed within South Vietnam and supported from outside.

The South Vietnamese have made laudable efforts to solve their own problems. They have increased their taxes—a 40 percent increase in real terms in 1973. They have expanded their exports, which were virtually eliminated by the war—doubling exports in 1972 and again in 1973. They have sharply reduced the consumption of imported goods, including a notable reduction in petroleum. But after more than a decade of war, they cannot reconstruct their economy and their society alone. Increased U.S. assistance is needed now to support the increasing efforts of the Vietnamese to achieve peace and self-sufficiency as soon as possible.

In Laos, a peaceful political solution to the conflict is in motion and the people there can finally look forward to a secure and stable environment. The problems of resettling refugees and establishing a viable economy, however, will provide a major test of the Laotian government's ability to work in the interests of all. Our continued assistance is essential to permit this underdeveloped, land-locked country to reconstruct its economy after so many years of war.

Continued U.S. assistance is also essential to alleviate the hardships facing the Cambodian people, many of them refugees with little opportunity to support themselves until hostilities subside.

The investment I am now seeking—an investment to sustain the peace, to overcome the human suffering resulting from the war, and to give the people of Indochina a chance to stand on their own feet—is small in comparison with what we have committed over the years in Indochina. But the potential return on this investment is large in enhancing the prospect of peace both in Indochina and around the world.

Development Assistance

U.S. assistance programs—both bilateral and multilateral—have made a very substantial contribution to the economic growth of the developing nations over the past decade.

In spite of encouraging progress, it is estimated that 40 percent of the total population in all the developing countries still remain trapped in conditions of poverty beyond the reach of the market economy. These people continue to exist below minimal levels of nutrition, literacy, and health.

It is clear that in the modern world, peace and poverty cannot easily endure side by side. In the long term, we must have peace without privation, or we may not have a durable peace at all. All that we have worked, and fought, and sacrificed to achieve will be in jeopardy as long as hunger, illiteracy, disease, and poverty are the permanent condition of 40 percent of the populace in developing nations of the world. But the progress which we have been able to help bring about thus far demonstrates that this need not be a permanent condition. Our developmental assistance continues to be needed to maintain and expand this record of progress.

To provide this needed assistance I am asking the Congress to authorize for fiscal year 1975 the appropriation of $255.3 million for functional development assistance programs in addition to the $618 million already authorized by last year's Foreign Assistance Act.

These additional funds will permit the Agency for International Development to assist developing nations in increasing food production. The widespread hardship caused by recent pressures on world food supplies calls for greater efforts by all to raise agricultural productivity. Population growth combined with recent crop failures in many parts of the world have led to the lowest grain stock levels in many years as well as high prices. In some cases, famine is threatening entire populations, and the world shortage of food makes it difficult to provide the assistance needed to avert tragedy. But food aid alone does not provide a solution. Developing nations must increase their own agricultural productivity, and almost 60 percent of AID's development assistance programs will be aimed at achieving this goal.

We will continue to reorient our development assistance programs, as jointly endorsed by the Congress and the Administration, to concentrate more directly on acute human problems in poor countries. AID will thus focus on providing family planning and basic health services, strengthening education and other human resource programs, increasing food production, and improving nutrition.

A strong bilateral U.S. foreign aid program can be fully effective, however, only if it is complemented by continued, active multilateral assistance efforts. Pending before the Congress is legislation to authorize United States contributions of $1.5 billion to the International Development Association (IDA). Appropriations for those contributions will be spread over a number of years beginning in 1976.

The International Development Association has a 14-year history of excellence in providing development loans to the poorest nations. We have negotiated a reduction in the United States' share of the total contributions to IDA from 40 percent to 33 percent, thereby shifting additional responsibility for international lending to other nations. It is inconceivable that the United States should abandon such a successful international activity, and I urge the House of Representatives to reconsider its recent vote denying the IDA authorization. Such a step would constitute a false economy in violation of the very principles toward which we would hope to move in providing foreign development assistance.

Also pending is legislation to authorize contributions of $362 million for the ordinary capital and $50 million for the special resources of the Asian Development Bank (ADB). The performance of the IDA is being matched today by the newer Asian Development Bank. The African Development Fund of the African Development Bank has excellent prospects of playing an increasingly critical role in a continent whose need has been most recently highlighted by severe drought.

It is imperative that these authorizations as well as those for our bilateral programs be enacted. It is equally imperative that appropriations be enacted in the full amount necessary to fulfill our responsibilities in these institutions and in the Inter-American Development Bank, for which authorizing legislation has been enacted.

The United States is currently engaged in negotiations relating to international monetary and trade reform. It should be recognized that less developed nations will play an important role in the success of these important initiatives. These nations will look to the United States to continue our leadership in the development assistance field as well as in trade and monetary reform.

Security Assistance

The security of our allies and of nations friendly to us is an essential consideration in the foreign and national security policies of the United States. Not all are capable of providing for their security, and our assistance enables those countries to assume primary responsibility for their own defense. It gives them the confidence to negotiate with potential adversaries from a position of strength and to resist subversion and intimidation. The effectiveness and wisdom of these policies is being proven today in the Middle East and Southeast Asia.

There can be no real peace in the world so long as some governments believe that they can successfully obtain by force or threat of force what they cannot obtain by peaceful competition or negotiation. Our security assistance programs reduce the likelihood that such calculations will be made and thereby increase the incentives to resolve international disputes by peaceful means.

Just as security assistance can ease the impact of large and unexpected defense burdens on the economies of friendly nations, it can also strengthen their economies and thereby allow a greater use of military sales credits as opposed to grants. We need a flexible military credit sales program to encourage and facilitate the self-reliance of friendly states and to help gradually reduce the cost to the United States of providing security assistance.

I am asking the Congress to authorize the appropriations for fiscal year 1975 of $985 million for grant military assistance, $555 million for foreign military sales credits to finance an $872.5 million program, and $385.5 million for security supporting assistance.

Conclusion

The United States has only recently emerged from more than a decade of direct involvement in a long, bitter, and costly war. It is not remarkable that we should see a strong sentiment in the land for giving up the difficult duties of world leadership. But temporary sentiment must not obscure the long-range interest of our Nation.

The percentage of America's gross national product dedicated to foreign assistance is small. It is less, indeed, than that of some other nations. But it is a wise investment, undertaken with bipartisan support in the interest of our own Nation, in the interests of our historical role as a generous and courageous defender of freedom and human rights, and in the interests of world peace.

With our assistance, other nations have reached a point where they can share this burden. But we have not yet reached the point where we can safely lay it down.

The amounts I am requesting for fiscal year 1975 are the minimum essential to support the responsible and constructive American role of international leadership and cooperation, a role which it is in our national interest to continue and strengthen.

RICHARD NIXON

The White House,
   April 24, 1974.

NIXON ON WHITE HOUSE TRANSCRIPTS

April 29, 1974

Asserting he had "nothing to hide," President Nixon announced in a nationally televised address April 29 that he would turn over the next day to the House Judiciary Committee White House-edited transcripts of 49 tape-recorded discussions he had held with his advisers concerning the Watergate scandal. Disregarding his own rule that private presidential conversations were protected from disclosure by the doctrine of executive privilege, Nixon also said that the 1,308 pages of transcripts would be made available to the public.

Release of the transcripts constituted President Nixon's response to a House Judiciary Committee subpoena April 11, 1974, for the original tape recordings of 42 conversations. The committee had requested and then subpoenaed the tapes for use in its investigation into the possible impeachment of President Nixon. Another subpoena, issued March 15, by Special Watergate Prosecutor Leon Jaworski, had sought 64 tape recordings of presidential discussions—including 20 which were transcribed and released by the White House—for use in the trial of former White House aides indicted March 1, 1974, for conspiring to cover up the Watergate case. (See p. 157.) In order that the Judiciary Committee might be assured of the relevance and accuracy of the White House transcripts, the President said the chairman and ranking Republican of the committee could listen to the original recordings at the White House and compare them with the transcripts.

"I realize these transcripts will provide grist for many sensational stories in the press," Nixon said in his April 29 telecast. But, he added, "the basic question at issue today is whether the President personally acted improper-

287

*ly in the Watergate matter." This was "the question that will be answered
by these transcripts that I have ordered published tomorrow." Nixon conceded that "parts will seem to be contradictory with one another, and parts
will be in conflict with some of the testimony given in the Senate
Watergate hearings." But "although the words may be ambiguous—though
the discussions may have explored many alternatives—the record of my actions is totally clear now, and I still believe it was totally correct then."*

Republicans Support Nixon Action

*Among Republicans, the President found some outspoken support for his
submission of edited transcripts instead of the original recordings subpoenaed by the House Judiciary Committee. "I have no patience with people who whine and say, 'But the President didn't do it the way we
wanted,'" said Sen. Barry Goldwater (R Ariz.). "I believe the President has
gone as far as he possibly could on the question of materials sought by the
House Judiciary Committee." Rep. Charles E. Wiggins (R Calif.), an influential member of the Judiciary Committee, said April 30: "I view the
submission of the President to be a good-faith effort on his part to comply
with the legitimate demands of our committee for evidence."*

*Most members of the Judiciary Committee, however, voiced dissatisfac-
tion with the President's action. Chairman Peter W. Rodino Jr. (D N.J.)
said May 1: "The procedure suggested by the President for Mr. Hutchinson
and me to come to the White House to review the subpoenaed tape recordings to determine the relevance and accuracy of the partial transcripts is
not compliance with our subpoena." Members of the committee objected
also to the medium—a televised speech—that Nixon chose for his response
to their subpoena. Rep. James R. Mann (D S.C.) chided the President for
"mounting his electronic throne" instead of simply informing the committee whether the materials it sought did or did not exist.*

House Judiciary Committee's Response

*The committee vigorously debated what response it should make to the
White House. A move to cite the President in contempt of Congress for
refusing to turn over the original tapes failed May 1 when the committee
instead voted, 20-18, simply to inform Nixon that he had "failed to comply"
with the committee's subpoena. Those who had pushed for a more strongly
worded response pointed out that without possession of the tapes
themselves, the committee had no way to determine whether the tapes had
been tampered with before the transcripts were made. (Tapes Experts'
Report, see p. 23-27.) Reaction to the President's decision to release
transcripts was limited initially to the Judiciary Committee's criticism of
the President for not complying in full with its subpoena. Later reactions,
based on readings of the transcripts, focused on the content of what Nixon
had released. Senate Republican Leader Hugh Scott (R Pa.) May 7
described the contents of the transcripts as "disgusting" and "immoral." On*

May 9, House Minority Leader John J. Rhodes (R Ariz.) urged Nixon to consider resigning the presidency. The same day, the Chicago Tribune, *a longtime Nixon supporter, urged the House to act quickly on a bill of impeachment. And on May 10, Sen. Richard S. Schweiker of Pennsylvania became the third Republican senator to ask Nixon to resign. The first two had been Edward W. Brooke (R Mass.) and James L. Buckley (Cons-R N.Y.).*

Crumbling of Support for Nixon

In part, the crumbling of support for the President resulted from a feeling that the transcripts indicated his involvement in "high crimes and misdemeanors" which would justify his impeachment. (Debate on Impeachable Offenses, see p. 137.) *But more damaging than the factual substance of the transcribed conversations was their tone. Laced with embarrassing characterizations, and with gaps marked "expletive deleted," "characterization deleted" or "unintelligible," the transcripts were seen as providing a most unflattering portrait of Nixon the man. As the* Chicago Tribune *editorialized: "We saw the public man in his first administration and we were impressed. Now in about 300,000 words we have seen the private man and we are appalled." By mid-July, the controversy over the transcripts had been compounded by a report from the House Judiciary Committee to the effect that some of the transcripts made public by the White House omitted entire sections of dialogue pertaining to Watergate or contained language markedly different from that found by the committee's staff. The staff discovered the discrepancies when, using superior electronic equipment, it examined the tapes of six conversations the committee had received from the Watergate grand jury.* (See Transcripts, p. 301.)

In the courts, the second front in the battle over release of the original tape recordings, President Nixon's decision to claim executive privilege and release transcripts, but not the actual recordings, eventually brought a decision from the Supreme Court requiring Nixon to surrender the tapes subpoenaed by Jaworski. White House lawyers had sought in the U.S. District Court May 2 to quash the special Watergate prosecutor's subpoena for tapes and documents relating to 64 conversations held following the break-in at the Watergate June 17, 1972. (See Historic Documents 1973, p. 413-425; 563-574; 659-679; 737-751.) *First a decision by U.S. District Court Judge John J. Sirica on May 20 and then by the Supreme Court July 24 ordered Nixon to comply with the special prosecutor's subpoena and release the tapes.* (Supreme Court Ruling, see p. 621-638.)

Text of President Nixon's televised speech April 29 announcing his decision to turn over to the House Judiciary Committee White House-edited transcripts of presidential conversations:

The President's Address to the Nation Announcing His Answer to the Subpoena from the House Judiciary Committee. April 29, 1974

Good Evening:

I have asked for this time tonight in order to announce my answer to the House Judiciary Committee's subpoena for additional Watergate tapes, and to tell you something about the actions I shall be taking, about what I hope they will mean to you and about the very difficult choices that were presented to me.

These actions will at last, once and for all, show that what I knew and what I did with regard to the Watergate break-in and coverup were just as I have described them to you from the very beginning.

I have spent many hours during the past few weeks thinking about what I would say to the American people if I were to reach the decision I shall announce tonight. And so, my words have not been lightly chosen; I can assure you they are deeply felt.

It was almost 2 years ago, in June 1972, that five men broke into the Democratic National Committee headquarters in Washington. It turned out that they were connected with my reelection committee, and the Watergate break-in became a major issue in the campaign.

Watergate Investigated "Thoroughly"

The full resources of the FBI and the Justice Department were used to investigate the incident thoroughly. I instructed my staff and campaign aides to cooperate fully with the investigation. The FBI conducted nearly 1,500 interviews. For 9 months—until March 1973— I was assured by those charged with conducting and monitoring the investigations that no one in the White House was involved.

Nevertheless, for more than a year, there have been allegations and insinuations that I knew about the planning of the Watergate break-in and that I was involved in an extensive plot to cover it up. The House Judiciary Committee is now investigating these charges.

On March 6, I ordered all materials that I had previously furnished to the Special Prosecutor turned over to the committee. These included tape recordings of 19 Presidential conversations and more than 700 documents from private White House files.

On April 11, the Judiciary Committee issued a subpoena for 42 additional tapes of conversations which it contended were necessary for its investigation. I agreed to respond to that subpoena by tomorrow.

In these folders that you see here on my left are more than 1,200 pages of transcripts of private conversations I participated in between September 15, 1972, and April 27 of 1973, with my principal aides and associates with regard to Watergate. They include all the relevant portions of all of the subpoenaed conversations that were recorded, that is, all portions that relate to the question of what I knew about Watergate or the coverup and what I did about it.

They also include transcripts of other conversations which were not subpoenaed, but which have a significant bearing on the question of Presidential actions with regard to Watergate. These will be delivered to the committee tomorrow.

In these transcripts. portions not relevant to my knowledge or actions with regard to Watergate are not included, but everything that is relevant is included—the rough as well as the smooth, the strategy sessions, the exploration of alternatives, the weighing of human and political costs.

As far as what the President personally knew and did with regard to Watergate and the coverup is concerned, these materials—together with those already made available—will tell it all.

I shall invite Chairman Rodino and the committee's ranking minority member, Congressman Hutchinson of Michigan, to come to the White House and listen to the actual, full tapes of these conversations, so that they can determine for themselves beyond question that the transcripts are accurate and that everything on the tapes relevant to my knowledge and my actions on Watergate is included. If there should be any disagreement over whether omitted material is relevant, I shall meet with them personally in an effort to settle the matter. I believe this arrangement is fair, and I think it is appropriate.

For many days now I have spent many hours of my own time personally reviewing these materials, and personally deciding questions of relevancy. I believe it is appropriate that the committee's review should also be made by its own senior elected officials, and not by staff employees.

The task of Chairman Rodino and Congressman Hutchinson will be made simpler than was mine by the fact that the work of preparing the transcripts has been completed. All they will need to do is to satisfy themselves of their authenticity and their completeness.

Confidentiality Heightened Mystery

Ever since the existence of the White House taping system was first made known last summer, I have tried vigorously to guard the privacy of the tapes. I have been well aware that my effort to protect the confidentiality of Presidential conversations has heightened the sense of mystery about Watergate and, in fact, has caused increased suspicions of the President. Many people assume that the tapes must incriminate. the President, or that otherwise, he would not insist on their privacy.

But the problem I confronted was this: Unless a President can protect the privacy of the advice he gets, he cannot get the advice he needs.

This principle is recognized in the constitutional doctrine of executive privilege, which has been defended and maintained by every President since Washington and which has been recognized by the courts whenever tested as inherent in the Presidency. I consider it to be my constitutional responsibility to defend this principle.

Three factors have now combined to persuade me that a major unprecedented exception to that principle is now necessary.

First, in the present circumstances, the House of Representatives must be able to reach an informed judgment about the President's role in Watergate.

Second, I am making a major exception to the principle of confidentiality because I believe such action is now necessary in order to restore the principle itself, by clearing the air of the central question that has brought such pressures upon it—and also to provide the evidence which will allow this matter to be brought to a prompt conclusion.

Third, in the context of the current impeachment climate, I believe all the American people, as well as their Representatives in Congress, are entitled to have not only the facts but also the evidence that demonstrates those facts.

"President Has Nothing to Hide"

I want there to be no question remaining about the fact that the President has nothing to hide in this matter.

The impeachment of a President is a remedy of last resort; it is the most solemn act of our entire constitutional process. Now, regardless of whether or not it succeeded, the action of the House in voting a formal accusation requiring trial by the Senate would put the Nation through a wrenching ordeal it has endured only once in its lifetime, a century ago, and never since America has become a world power with global responsibilities.

The impact of such an ordeal would be felt throughout the world, and it would have its effect on the lives of all Americans for many years to come.

Because this is an issue that profoundly affects all the American people, in addition to turning over these transcripts to the House Judiciary Committee, I have directed that they should all be made public—all of these that you see here.

To complete the record, I shall also release to the public transcripts of all those portions of the tapes already turned over to the Special Prosecutor and to the committee that relate to Presidential actions or knowledge of the Watergate affair.

During the past year, the wildest accusations have been given banner headlines and ready credence, as well. Rumor, gossip, innuendo, accounts from unnamed sources of what a prospective witness might testify to have filled the morning newspapers and then are repeated on the evening newscasts day after day.

Time and again, a familiar pattern repeated itself. A charge would be reported the first day as what it was—just an allegation. But it would then be referred back to the next day and thereafter as if it were true.

The distinction between fact and speculation grew blurred. Eventually, all seeped into the public consciousness as a vague general impression of massive wrongdoing, implicating everybody, gaining credibility by its endless repetition.

The basic question at issue today is whether the President personally acted improperly in the Watergate matter. Month after month of rumor, insinuation, and charges by just one Watergate witness—John Dean—suggested that the President did act improperly.

This sparked demands for an impeachment inquiry. This is the question that must be answered. And this is the question that will be answered by these transcripts that I have ordered published tomorrow.

These transcripts cover hour upon hour of discussions that I held with Mr. Haldeman, John Ehrlichman, John Dean, John Mitchell, former Attorney General Kleindienst, Assistant Attorney General Petersen, and others with regard to Watergate.

They were discussions in which I was probing to find out what had happened, who was responsible, what were the various degrees of responsibility, what were the legal culpabilities, what were the political ramifications, and what actions were necessary and appropriate on the part of the President.

I realize that these transcripts will provide grist for many sensational stories in the press. Parts will seem to be contradictory with one another, and parts will be in conflict with some of the testimony given in the Senate Watergate committee hearings.

I have been reluctant to release these tapes not just because they will embarrass me and those with whom I have talked—which they will—and not just because they will become the subject of speculation and even ridicule—which they will—and not just because certain parts of them will be seized upon by political and journalistic opponents—which they will.

I have been reluctant because in these and in all the other conversations in this office, people have spoken their minds freely, never dreaming that specific sentences or even parts of sentences would be picked out as the subjects of national attention and controversy.

Confidentiality Essential to Presidency

I have been reluctant because the principle of confidentiality is absolutely essential to the conduct of the Presidency. In reading raw transcripts of these conversations, I believe it will be more readily apparent why that principle is essential and must be maintained in the future. These conversations are unusual in their subject matter, but the same kind of uninhibited discussion—and it is that—the same brutal candor, is necessary in discussing how to bring warring factions to the peace table or how to move necessary legislation through Congress.

Names are named in these transcripts. Therefore, it is important to remember that much that appears in them is no more than hearsay or speculation, exchanged as I was trying to find out what really happened, while my principal aides were reporting to me on rumors and reports that they had heard, while we discussed the various, often conflicting stories that different persons were telling.

As the transcripts will demonstrate, my concerns during this period covered a wide range. The first and obvious was to find out just exactly what had happened and who was involved.

A second concern was for the people who had been, or might become, involved in Watergate. Some were close advisers, valued friends, others whom I had trusted. And I was also concerned about the human impact on others, especially some of the young people and their families who had come to Washington to work in my Administration, whose lives might be suddenly ruined by something they had done in an excess of loyalty or in the mistaken belief that it would serve the interests of the President.

And then I was quite frankly concerned about the political implications. This represented potentially a devastating blow to the Administration and to its programs, one which I knew would be exploited for all it was worth by hostile elements in the Congress as well as in the media. I wanted to do what was right, but I wanted to do it in a way that would cause the least unnecessary damage in a highly charged political atmosphere to the Administration.

And fourth, as a lawyer, I felt very strongly that I had to conduct myself in a way that would not prejudice the rights of potential defendants.

And fifth, I was striving to sort out a complex tangle, not only of facts but also questions of legal and moral responsibility. I wanted, above all, to be fair. I wanted to draw distinctions, where those were appropriate, between persons who were active and willing participants on the one hand, and on the other, those who might have gotten inadvertantly caught up in the web and be technically indictable but morally innocent.

Despite the confusions and contradictions, what does come through clearly is this:

John Dean charged in sworn Senate testimony that I was "fully aware of the coverup" at the time of our first meeting on September 15, 1972. These transcripts show clearly that I first learned of it when Mr. Dean himself told me about it in this office on March 21—some 6 months later.

Incidentally, these transcripts—covering hours upon hours of conversations—should place in somewhat better perspective the controversy over the 18½ minute gap in the tape of the conversation I had with Mr. Haldeman back in June of 1972.

Now, how it was caused is still a mystery to me and I think to many of the experts, as well. But I am absolutely certain, however, of one thing: that it was not caused intentionally by my secretary, Rose Mary Woods, or any of my White House assistants. And certainly if the theory were true that during those 18½ minutes Mr. Haldeman and I cooked up some sort of a Watergate coverup scheme, as so many have been quick to surmise, it hardly seems likely that in all of our subsequent conversations—many of them are here—which neither of us ever expected would see the light of day, there is nothing remotely indicating such a scheme; indeed, quite the contrary.

Record of My Actions Is Totally Clear

From the beginning, I have said that in many places on the tapes there were ambiguities—statements and comments that different people with different perspectives might interpret in drastically different ways—but although the words may be ambiguous, though the discussions may have explored many alternatives, the record of my actions is totally clear now, and I still believe it was totally correct then.

A prime example is one of the most controversial discussions, that with Mr. Dean on March 21—the one in which he first told me of the coverup, with Mr. Haldeman joining us midway through the conversation.

His revelations to me on March 21 were a sharp surprise, even though the report he gave to me was far from complete, especially since he did not reveal at that time the extent of his own criminal involvement.

I was particularly concerned by his report that one of the Watergate defendants, Howard Hunt, was threatening blackmail unless he and his lawyer were immediately given $120,000 for legal fees and family support, and that he was attempting to blackmail the White House, not by threatening exposure on the Watergate matter, but by threatening to reveal activities that would expose extremely sensitive, highly secret national security matters that he had worked on before Watergate.

I probed, questioned, tried to learn all Mr. Dean knew about who was involved, what was involved. I asked more than 150 questions of Mr. Dean in the course of that conversation.

He said to me, and I quote from the transcripts directly: "I can just tell from our conversation that these are things that you have no knowledge of."

It was only considerably later that I learned how much there was that he did not tell me then—for example, that he himself had authorized promises of clemency, that he had personally handled money for the Watergate defendants, and that he had suborned perjury of a witness.

I knew that I needed more facts. I knew that I needed the judgments of more people. I knew the facts about the Watergate coverup would have to be made public, but I had to find out more about what they were before I could decide how they could best be made public.

Blackmail Threat: National Security Problem

I returned several times to the immediate problem posed by Mr. Hunt's blackmail threat, which to me was not a Watergate problem, but one which I regarded, rightly or wrongly, as a potential national security problem of very serious proportions. I considered long and hard whether it might in fact be better to let the payment go forward, at least temporarily, in the hope that this national security matter would not be exposed in the course of uncovering the Watergate coverup.

I believed then, and I believe today, that I had a responsibility as President to consider every option, including this one, where production of sensitive national security matters was at issue—protection of such matters. In the course of considering it and of "just thinking out loud," as I put it at one point, I several times suggested that meeting Hunt's demands might be necessary.

But then I also traced through where that would lead. The money could be raised. But money demands would lead inescapably to clemency demands, and clemency could not be granted. I said, and I quote directly from the tape: "It is wrong, that's for sure." I pointed out, and I quote again from the tape: "But in the end we are going to be bled to death. And in the end it is all going to come out anyway. Then you get the worst of both worlds. We are going to lose, and the people are going to—"

And Mr. Haldeman interrupts me and says: "And look like dopes!"

And I responded, "And in effect look like a coverup. So that we cannot do."

Now I recognize that this tape of March 21 is one which different meanings could be read in by different people. But by the end of the meeting, as the tape shows, my decision was to convene a new grand jury and to send everyone before the grand jury with instructions to testify.

Whatever the potential for misinterpretation there may be as a result of the different options that were discussed at different times during the meeting, my conclusion at the end of the meeting was clear. And my actions and reactions as demonstrated on the tapes that follow that date show clearly that I did not intend the further payment to Hunt or anyone else to be made. These are some of the actions that I took in the weeks that followed in my effort to find the truth, to carry out my responsibilities to enforce the law.

As the tape of our meeting on March 22, the next day, indicates, I directed Mr. Dean to go to Camp David with instructions to put together a written report. I learned 5 days later, on March 26, that he was unable to complete it. And so on March 27 I assigned John Ehrlichman to try to find out what had happened, who was at fault, and in what ways and to what degree.

One of the transcripts I am making public is a call that Mr. Ehrlichman made to the Attorney General on March 28, in which he asked the Attorney General to report to me, the President, directly, any information he might find indicating possible involvement of John Mitchell or by anyone in the White House. I had Mr. Haldeman separately pursue other, independent lines of inquiry.

Throughout, I was trying to reach determinations on matters of both substance and procedure on what the facts were and what was the best way to move the case forward. I concluded that I wanted everyone to go before the grand jury and testify freely and fully. The decision, as you will recall, was publicly announced on March 30, 1973. I waived executive privilege in order to permit everybody to testify. I specifically waived executive privilege with regard to conversations with the President, and I waived the attorney-client privilege with John Dean in order to permit him to testify fully and, I hope, truthfully.

"Everybody Is to Tell the Truth"

Finally, on April 14—3 weeks after I learned of the coverup from Mr. Dean—Mr. Ehrlichman reported to me on the results of his investigation. As he acknowledged, much of what he had gathered was hearsay, but he had gathered enough to make it clear that the next step was to make his findings completely available to the Attorney General, which I instructed him to do.

And the next day, Sunday, April 15, Attorney General Kleindienst asked to see me, and he reported new information which had come to his attention on this matter. And although he was in no way whatever involved in Watergate, because of his close personal ties, not only to John Mitchell but to other potential people who might be involved, he quite properly removed himself from the case.

We agreed that Assistant Attorney General Henry Petersen, the head of the Criminal Division, a Democrat and career prosecutor, should be placed in complete charge of the investigation.

Later that day I met with Mr. Petersen. I continued to meet with him, to talk with him, to consult with him, to offer him the full cooperation of the White House, as you will see from these transcripts, even to the point of retaining John Dean on the White House staff for an extra 2 weeks after he admitted his criminal involvement because Mr. Petersen thought that would make it easier for the prosecutor to get his cooperation in breaking the case if it should become necessary to grant Mr. Dean's demand for immunity.

On April 15, when I heard that one of the obstacles to breaking the case was Gordon Liddy's refusal to talk, I telephoned Mr. Petersen and directed that he should make clear not only to Mr. Liddy but to everyone that—and now I quote directly from the tape of that telephone call—"As far as the President is concerned, everybody in this case is to talk and to tell the truth." I told him if necessary I would personally meet with Mr. Liddy's lawyer to assure him that I wanted Liddy to talk and to tell the truth.

From the time Mr. Petersen took charge, the case was solidly within the criminal justice system, pursued personally by the Nation's top professional prosecutor with the active, personal assistance of the President of the United States.

I made clear there was to be no coverup.

Let me quote just a few lines from the transcripts—you can read them to verify them—so that you can hear for yourself the orders I was giving in this period.

Speaking to Haldeman and Ehrlichman, I said: "... It is ridiculous to talk about clemency. They all knew that."

Speaking to Ehrlichman, I said: "We all have to do the right thing...We just cannot have this kind of a business..."

Speaking to Haldeman and Ehrlichman, I said: "The boil had to be pricked...We have to prick the boil and take the heat. Now that's what we are doing here."

Speaking to Henry Petersen, I said: "I want you to be sure to understand that you know we are going to get to the bottom of this thing."

Speaking to John Dean, I said: "Tell the truth. That is the thing I have told everybody around here."

And then speaking to Haldeman: "And you tell Magruder, now Jeb, this evidence is coming in, you ought to go to the grand jury. Purge yourself if you're perjured and tell this whole story.

"I Am Confident in the American People"

I am confident that the American people will see these transcripts for what they are, fragmentary records from a time more than a year ago that now seems very distant, the records of a President and of a man suddenly being confronted and having to cope with information which, if true, would have the most far-reaching consequences not only for his personal reputation but, more important, for his hopes, his plans, his goals for the people who had elected him as their leader.

If read with an open and a fair mind and read together with the record of the actions I took, these transcripts will show that what I have stated from the beginning to be the truth has been the truth: that I personally had no knowledge of the break-in before it occurred, that I had no knowledge of the coverup until I was informed of it by John Dean on March 21, that I never offered clemency for the defendants, and that after March 21 my actions were directed toward finding the facts and seeing that justice was done fairly and according to the law.

The facts are there. The conversations are there. The record of actions is there.

To anyone who reads his way through this mass of materials I have provided, it will be totally abundantly clear that as far as the President's role with regard to Watergate is concerned, the entire story is there.

As you will see, now that you also will have this mass of evidence I have provided, I have tried to cooperate with the House Judiciary Committee. And I repeat tonight the offer that I have made previously: to answer written interrogatories under oath and if there are then issues still unresolved to meet personally with the Chairman of the committee and with Congressman Hutchinson to answer their questions under oath.

As the committee conducts its inquiry, I also consider it only essential and fair that my counsel, Mr. St. Clair, should be present to cross-examine witnesses and introduce evidence in an effort to establish the truth.

I am confident that for the overwhelming majority of those who study the evidence that I shall release tomorrow—those who are willing to look at it fully, fairly, and objectively—the evidence will be persuasive and, I hope, conclusive.

We live in a time of very great challenge and great opportunity for America.

We live at a time when peace may become possible in the Middle East for the first time in a generation.

We are at last in the process of fulfilling the hope of mankind for a limitation on nuclear arms—a process that will continue when I meet with Soviet leaders in Moscow in a few weeks.

We are well on the way toward building a peace that can last, not just for this but for other generations as well.

And here at home, there is vital work to be done in moving to control inflation, to develop our energy resources, to strengthen our economy so that Americans can enjoy what they have not had since 1956: full prosperity without war and without inflation.

Every day absorbed by Watergate is a day lost from the work that must be done—by your President and by your Congress—work that must be done in dealing with the great problems that affect your prosperity, affect your security, that could affect your lives.

"Get Watergate Behind Us"

The materials I make public tomorrow will provide all the additional evidence needed to get Watergate behind us and to get it behind us now.

Never before in the history of the Presidency have records that are so private been made so public.

In giving you these records—blemishes and all—I am placing my trust in the basic fairness of the American people.

I know in my own heart that through the long, painful, and difficult process revealed in these transcripts, I was trying in that period to discover what was right and to do what was right.

I hope and I trust that when you have seen the evidence in its entirety, you will see the truth of that statement.

As for myself, I intend to go forward, to the best of my ability with the work that you elected me to do. I shall do so in a spirit perhaps best summed up a century ago by another President when he was being subjected to unmerciful attack. Abraham Lincoln said:

"I do the very best I know how—the very best I can; and I mean to keep doing so until the end. If the end brings me out all right, what is said against me won't amount to anything. If the end brings me out wrong, ten angels swearing I was right would make no difference."

Thank you and good evening.

COMPARISON OF WHITE HOUSE, HOUSE JUDICIARY TRANSCRIPTS

April 30, 1974 — July 9, 1974

It was, beyond question, one of the most remarkable documents ever to come out of the White House. The volume of Watergate-related tape transcripts made public by President Nixon April 30 contained the "brutal candor" that he had promised in his televised speech April 29 (see p. 287), even though the White House had excised the coarsest language and the rawest characterizations of persons. But the 1,308-page book did little to resolve the major question remaining from the inquiries into the June 17, 1972, break-in at the Democratic National Committee offices and the subsequent coverup: What did the President know and when did he learn it? If anything, Nixon's disclosure of the transcripts increased pressure on him to resign or be impeached. Reading the transcripts was like peering into the soul of the Nixon presidency, and many of those who took the trouble—including some Nixon supporters—did not like what they saw.

Senate Minority Leader Hugh Scott (R Pa.) said after reading 800 pages that the transcripts revealed "a shabby, disgusting, immoral performance" by all of those involved in the recorded conversations. "I am enormously disturbed that there was not enough showing of moral indignation," said Scott, who had said in January that the White House had shown him transcripts proving John W. Dean III, Nixon's former counsel, had lied in accusing the President of complicity in the coverup. The transcripts cost Nixon the support of The Chicago Tribune, conservative voice of the American heartland where Nixon counted much of his constituency. No one reading the transcripts, the Tribune wrote in a May 9 editorial, could "continue to think Mr. Nixon has upheld the standards and high dignity of the presidency. "He is humorless to the point of being inhumane," the editorial said. "He is devious. He is vacillating. He is profane. He is willing to be led. He displays dismaying gaps in his knowledge...his loyalty is minimal."

As the House Judiciary Committee began hearings May 9 on whether or not Nixon should be impeached, Rep. John B. Anderson of Illinois, chairman of the House Republican Conference, said that the President should resign. Another Republican official, House Minority Leader John J. Rhodes of Arizona, said that Nixon should consider stepping down. To counter Scott and others who found in the transcripts indications that the Nixon presidency was amoral or immoral, the Rev. John McLaughlin, a Jesuit priest and deputy assistant to the President, said that such a suggestion was "erroneous, unjust and contains an element of hypocrisy."

Contents of Transcripts

It was in response to the House Judiciary Committee's subpoena of the tapes of 42 recorded conversations that the President submitted the transcripts and made them public at the same time. The committee May 1 voted to send Nixon a letter saying that the transcripts "failed to comply with the committee's subpoena of April 11, 1974." (See p. 288.) The transcripts actually covered 46 conversations, four more than the committee subpoenaed. The White House presumably offered the four extra transcripts so that excerpts from them could be used in a 50-page White House summary that prefaced the transcript volume. All four extra transcripts were mentioned in the summary, which argued that the tapes, taken in their entirety, proved Nixon's innocence in the coverup. "In all of the thousands of words spoken, even though they often are unclear and ambiguous, not once does it appear that the President of the United States was engaged in a criminal plot to obstruct justice," the brief stated.

The transcripts covered only a portion of the tapes sought by the Senate Watergate committee and the special prosecutor, Leon Jaworski, who also sought White House tapes of recorded conversations dealing with dairy industry campaign contributions, settlement of antitrust charges against International Telephone and Telegraph Corporation, and other matters. But Nixon made it clear that no further tapes or other materials related to Watergate would be released. His lawyer, James D. St. Clair, said May 7 that the President believed that all relevant material on Watergate had been turned over to the authorities and that "the full story is out." But the Supreme Court differed in its opinion July 24 and other, crucial tapes were released later in the year. (See p. 621-638 and 673-682.) In all, the transcripts covered 1,254 pages, not counting the summary or contents pages.

Gaps and Silences

Nixon said in his April 29 speech that the transcripts would contain ambiguities and contradictions that could be subject to different interpretations. But reporters found other problems with the transcripts for which the White House had no ready answer. For example, The New York

Times *reported May 7 that there were indications of unaccountable silences or gaps in transcripts of an April 14, 1973, conversation of Nixon, Haldeman and Ehrlichman and a March 22, 1973, meeting of Nixon, Dean, Haldeman, Ehrlichman and John N. Mitchell, former manager of the Nixon re-election campaign. The* Times *article noted that the March 22 meeting was reported as lasting from 1:57 to 3:34 p.m. But the transcript ended immediately after Ehrlichman mentioned that "it is 3:16."*

In a similar development, The Washington Post *reported May 14 that "as the result of an apparent accident, the edited White House transcripts contain two different versions of a portion of the same conversation" on April 16, 1973, between Nixon and Assistant Attorney General Petersen. The article said that the apparent mistake, acknowledged by the White House, "demonstrates the problems in making an accurate transcript." The conversation, duplicated on three consecutive pages with variations in some words and phrases, dealt with the preparation of a public statement Nixon made the following day about the Watergate scandal. Special Prosecutor Leon Jaworski and the House Judiciary Committee had contended throughout the tapes controversy that only the actual tapes would constitute acceptable evidence in their investigations.*

House Judiciary Committee Transcripts

On July 9, following weeks of controversy over the accuracy of the White House transcripts, the House Judiciary Committee released its version of eight conversations. The committee's 218-page book contained transcripts of conversations that took place Sept. 15, 1972, and Feb. 28, March 13, March 21 (a.m.), March 21 (p.m.), March 22, April 16 (a.m.) and April 16 (p.m.), 1973. According to the House Judiciary Committee version of the transcripts, President Nixon was more deeply implicated in the Watergate coverup than the White House had admitted to date. During a March 22, 1973, meeting, the transcript of which was never before released, Nixon told John W. Dean III and John N. Mitchell: "I don't give a shit what happens. I want you all to stonewall it, let them plead the Fifth Amendment, coverup or anything else, if it'll save it—save the plan. That's the whole point." Nixon evidently was referring to the then pending hearings before the Senate Watergate committee. The President said he would prefer that Watergate information be released "the other way" if it seemed clear it would be made public by leaks anyway. He apparently was talking about a suggestion that the committee accept a written report from Dean. (See p. 385.)

"(W)ith the number of jackass people that they've got that they can call, they're going to—the story they can get out through leaks, charges, and so forth, and innuendos, will be a hell of a lot worse than the story they're going to get out by just letting it out there," Nixon declared. Nixon's statements were contained in the end part of the March 22 meeting that the White House had not released to the committee, the special prosecutor or

the public. According to The Los Angeles Times, *committee lawyers were able to copy the statements from a tape when a Secret Service agent at the White House supervising the copying inadvertently let the recorder run past the previously transcribed part of the conversation. White House officials, however, denied that report.*

White House Response to Committee Action

White House reaction to the committee transcripts was swift. Press Secretary Ronald L. Ziegler accused the committee of dribbling out its impeachment evidence piecemeal in a "hypoed public relations campaign" designed to prejudice the public against Nixon. He contended that the transcripts in their entirety and actions subsequently taken by Nixon showed he was innocent of coverup allegations. Ziegler said July 10 that Nixon's statements about aides taking the Fifth Amendment and about a "coverup" were "of dubious relevancy."

Nixon on Coverup

The President had said repeatedly that he first learned of the ongoing White House coverup from Dean, his former counsel, on March 21, 1973, and that he immediately began an intensive effort to end it. But portions of the March 22 conversation made public for the first time by the Judiciary Committee left the impression that Nixon was actually aware of—and participating in—the coverup long before March 21. At crucial points in the dialogue, the committee transcript reinforced that impression while the White House version played it down.

March 13, 1973, Conversation

Both versions, for example, had the President asking Dean on March 13 if it was too late to "go the hang-out road"—that is, tell everything and hope for the best. The committee had the President answering himself immediately: "Yes, it is." But according to the White House, Dean said, "Yes, I think it is." (See p. 336.) The White House found most of the President's next remark inaudible, but the committee deciphered it as: "The hang-out road's going to have to be rejected. I, some, I understand it was rejected." Earlier in the March 13 conversation, Dean told the President that H.R. Haldeman's aide, Gordon Strachan, knew about the Watergate break-in in advance. In the committee version, Nixon asked if Strachan would lie to the grand jury, and Dean answered: "He'll go in and stonewall it and say, 'I don't know anything about what you are talking about.' He has already done it twice, as you know, in interviews." The White House version omitted Nixon's question. It interpreted Dean's remark as more tentative: "He can go in and stonewall, and say, 'I don't know anything about what you are talking about.' He has already done it twice you know, in interviews."

In both versions, the President commented: "I suppose we can't call that justice, can we?" But he gave no instructions to stop Strachan. At one point in the March 13 discussion, the committee transcript had Dean telling the President: "A lot of people around here had knowledge that something was going on over there [at the re-election committee]." That remark did not appear in the White House version.

The wiretap at the Democratic National Committee's Watergate headquarters had revealed nothing before the break-in ended it, Dean told Nixon as the discussion continued. "They were just getting started," he explained. According to the committee transcript, Nixon responded: "Yeah. Yeah. But, uh, Bob [presumably Haldeman] one time said something about the fact we got some information about this or that or the other, but, I, I think it was about the convention, what...they were planning...." The White House version varied slightly: "Yeah. Bob one time said something to me about something...this or that or something, but I think it was something about the convention, I think it was about the convention problems they were planning something." When Dean offered the opinion that Mitchell did not know about the re-election committee's intelligence-gathering operation, the White House version of Nixon's response was: "I don't think that Mitchell knew about this sort of thing." In the committee version, it came out: Dean: I don't think he knew it was there. President: You kidding? Dean: I don't— President: You don't think Mitchell knew about this thing?

March 21, 1973, Conversation

The committee's version of the crucial March 21 conversation, when Nixon contended he first learned the full scope of the coverup, suggested that even then the President was unwilling to let the truth come out. When Dean warned that he, Haldeman, Ehrlichman and Mitchell might be indicted, the White House transcript recorded Nixon's response as: "If it really comes down to that, we would have to (unintelligible) some of the men." In the committee transcript, the response was: "Well if it really comes down to that, we cannot, maybe— We'd have to shed it in order to contain it again." Then Dean told the President that he could "just tell from our conversation that...these are things that you have no knowledge of." The White House interpreted Nixon's answer as, "You certainly can!" But the committee transcript had the President saying instead: "The absurdity of the whole damned thing, bugging and so on."

When the March 21 discussion turned to the strategy for handling the Watergate grand jury, Dean warned of the risk of perjury by White House officials. In the committee version, Nixon interjected: "That's right. Just be damned sure you say I don't...remember; I can't recall, I can't give any honest, an answer to that that I can recall. But that's it." In the White House transcript, the same line read: "But you can say I don't remember. You can say I can't recall. I can't give any answer to that that I can recall."

But that's it." In the White House transcript, the same line read: "But you can say I don't remember. You can say I can't recall. I can't give any answer to that that I can recall."

At another meeting in the late afternoon of March 21, Nixon, Dean, Haldeman and Ehrlichman continued to weigh the merits of "stonewalling it," telling all or releasing selected facts in a report prepared by Dean. According to the White House, Nixon outlined the report option this way: "I asked for a written report, which I do not have, which is very general, understand. I am thinking now in far more general terms, having in mind the facts, that where specifics are concerned, make it very general, your investigating of the case." The committee's version of that statement read: "I ask for a, a written report, which I think, uh, that—which is very general, understand. Understand, [laughs] I don't want to get all that God damned specific. I'm thinking now in far more general terms, having in mind the fact that the problem with a specific report is that, uh, this proves this one and that one...and you just prove something that you didn't do at all."

Later the same day, Ehrlichman commented that on the Watergate break-in, White House Press Secretary Ronald L. Ziegler could tell the press that no one at the White House "had notice of it, knowledge of it, participated in the planning or aided or abetted it any way." He added: "And it happens to be true...as for that transaction." According to the committee transcript, Nixon laughed and said: "Sure. As for that transaction."

During the March 22 conversation, the White House transcript had the President saying that a "flexible" stand on executive privilege could be used "in order to get off the coverup line." In the committee version, the same remark came out: "in order to get on with the coverup plan."

Payments to Defendants

Both versions of the transcripts included discussions about cash payments from the White House to the original Watergate break-in defendants—allegedly to buy their silence. In the committee's edition, the President came across as more unequivocally in favor of the payments and aware of their implications. Most of the payment discussions took place on March 21, 1973, the day Dean explained to Nixon that funds for the defendants' legal fees had been distributed under the false cover of a legal defense committee organized for the defendants of Cuban descent. According to the White House transcript, Nixon told Dean: "I would certainly keep that cover for whatever it is worth." In the committee version, Nixon said: "Well, whether it's maybe too late to do anything about it, but I would certainly keep that [laughs], that cover for whatever it's worth."

In a discussion of a possible public explanation for the payments, the committee transcribers quoted Nixon as saying: "As far as what happened up to this time, our cover there is just going to be the Cuban Committee did this for them up through the election." In the White House transcript, the remark was less precise and ended with a question mark: "far as what has *happened up to this time, are covered on their situation, because the Cuban Committee did this for them during the election?" At another point in the committee edition, the President interrupted Dean's description of the perils of laundering money to say, "Well, the main point, now, is the people who will need the money [unintelligible]. Well of course, you've got the surplus from the campaign. That we have to account for. But if there's any other money hanging around—" In the White House version, the President said only: "Well, of course you have a surplus from the campaign. Is there any other money hanging around?"*

Dean had told Nixon earlier on March 21 that it would take about $1-million to keep the defendants quiet. The President's comment on that came out differently in the two versions. According to the White House, he said: "Well, it sounds like a lot of money, a million dollars. Let me say that I think we could get that. I know money is hard to raise." In the committee transcript, the remark read: "But let's now come back to the money, a million dollars, and so forth and so on. Let me say that I think you could get that in cash, and I know money is hard, but there are ways. That could be [unintelligible]."

Payments to Howard Hunt

The question of whether the President authorized a $75,000 payment received by Watergate defendant E. Howard Hunt Jr. the evening of March 21 was considered crucial to the impeachment inquiry. Nixon had denied approving the payment and had contended that he never heard about Hunt's demands for money until March 21. The possibility that the President was aware of the Hunt payments before then was raised by a remark included in the committee transcript but not the White House version. In a Feb. 28, 1973, conversation with Dean, Nixon commented on the expected grand jury appearance of Herbert W. Kalmbach, his personal attorney, who raised money for the defendants. Kalmbach had revealed nothing incriminating up to that point, Nixon said, but added: "Oh well, it, it'll be hard for him, he—'cause it'll, it'll get out about Hunt." Both versions then continued with Nixon saying: "I suppose the big thing is the financing transaction they'll go after. How did the money get to the Bank of Mexico, and so forth and so on."

"Your major guy to keep under control is Hunt," Nixon told Dean March 21, according to the committee transcript. In the White House version, the line ended with a question mark. The committee transcript had Nixon adding that Hunt knew "about a lot of other things," but in the White House version, the President instead asked Dean: "Does he know a lot?" Dean advised against continuing the payments to the defendants indefinitely. In the committee transcript, Nixon cut in with: "But at the moment, don't you agree that you'd better get the Hunt thing? I mean, that's worth it, at the moment." According to the White House edition, that

comment trailed off with: "that's where that—" instead of "that's worth it, at the moment."

Nixon said later, according to the committee version, that Hunt's "price is pretty high, but, at least, uh, we should, we should buy the time on that...." In the White House version it came out: "at least we can buy the time...." Told that providing Hunt's immediate $120,000 demand was imperative, Nixon asked Dean March 21, in the White House version: "Would you agree that that's the prime thing that you damn well better get that done?" In the committee transcript, "the prime thing" became "a buy time thing." The committee version filled in the deleted expletive in Nixon's next comment: "Well for Christ's sakes get it in a, in a way that, uh—who's, who's going to talk to him?..."

Comparisons of the transcripts released April 30, 1974, by the White House and July 9 by the House Judiciary Committee follow. White House transcripts of five presidential conversations have been excerpted and are contrasted—only where a significant difference exists—with excerpts from the House Judiciary Committee's transcripts of those same conversations. Conversations between President Nixon and his aides on Sept. 15, 1972; Feb. 28, March 13, March 21, and March 22, 1973 are included. Where minor word differences exist between the two versions, not affecting the substance of the conversation, only the White House version has been provided. Portions of the transcripts printed in standard, or Roman type, represent the White House text. Italicized portions are excerpts from the House Judiciary Committee transcripts and immediately follow the White House text from which they differ. Triple asterisks (* * *) mark the beginning and the end of extensive comparative sections. In those cases, double asterisks (* *) divide the White House version from the House Judiciary Committee version that follows.

September 15, 1972

Meeting: The President, Haldeman and Dean, Oval Office (5:27 —6:17 p.m.):

Following is the text of a recorded conversation among President Nixon, presidential counsel John W. Dean III, and White House chief of staff H. R. Haldeman on Sept. 15, 1972.

On the same day, a federal grand jury indicted G. Gordon Liddy, E. Howard Hunt Jr. and five other men in connection with the break-in at the Watergate offices of the Democratic National Committee.

Dean testified before the Senate Watergate committee in June 1973 that this was the first conversation he had with Nixon about Watergate, that the President congratulated him about doing "a good job," and that he left the meeting "with the impression that the President was well aware of what had been going on regarding the success of keeping the White House out of the Watergate scandal...."

The transcript, among those supplied to the House Judiciary Committee April 30, 1974, was edited by the White House to delete expletives, personal characterizations and irrelevancies. The participants are identified by initials—P for President, D for Dean and H for Haldeman.

This opens just as Dean comes in the door.

P. Hi, how are you? You had quite a day today didn't you. You got Watergate on the way didn't you?

D. We tried.

H. How did it all end up?

D. Ah, I think we can say well at this point. The press is playing it just as we expect.

H. Whitewash?

D. No, not yet—the story right now—

P. It is a big story.

H. Five indicted plus the WH former guy and all that.

D. Plus two White House fellows.

H. That is good that takes the edge off whitewash, really, that was the thing (Nixon campaign manager John N.) Mitchell kept saying, that to people in the country Liddy and Hunt (G. Gordon Liddy and E. Howard Hunt Jr., Watergate conspirators) were big men. Maybe that is good.

P. How did MacGregor (Clark MacGregor, who succeeded Mitchell as campaign manager) handle himself?

D. I think very well he had a good statement which said that the Grand Jury had met and that it was now time to realize that some apologies may be due.

H. Fat chance.

D. Get the damn (inaudible)

H. We can't do that.

P. Just remember, all the trouble we're taking, we'll have a chance to get back one day. How are you doing on your other investigations?

H. What has happened on the bug? *...on the what?*

D. The second bug there was a bug found in the telephone of one of the men at the DNC (Democratic National Committee).

P. You don't think it was left over from the other time?

D. Absolutely not, the Bureau has checked and re-checked the whole place after that night. The man had specifically checked and re-checked the telephone and it was not there.

P. What the hell do you think was involved?

D. I think DNC was planted.

P. You think they did it?

D. Uh huh

P. (Expletive deleted) do they really want to believe that we planted that?

H. Did they get anything on the finger prints?

D. No, nothing at all either on the telephone or on the bug. The FBI has unleashed a full investigation over at the DNC starting with (Democratic chairman Lawrence F.) O'Brien right now.

H. Laughter. Using the same crew—

D. The same crew—the Washington Field Office.

P. What kind of questions are they asking him?

D. Anything they can think of because O'Brien is charging them with failing to find all the bugs.

H. Good, that will make them mad.

* * *

D. So (acting FBI director L. Patrick) Gray is pissed and his people are pissed off. So maybe they will move in because their reputation is on the line. I think that is a good development.

* *

D. *So, so, Gray is pissed now and his people are kind of pissed off. So they're moving in because their reputation's on the line. That's, uh, do you think that's a good development?*

* * *

P. I think that is a good development because it makes it look so (adjective deleted) funny. Am I wrong?

D. No, no sir. It looks silly. If we can find that the DNC planted that, the whole story will reverse....

Bigger Investigation Than Of JFK Slaying

D. The resources that have been put against this whole investigation to date are really incredible. It is truly a larger investigation than was conducted against the after inquiry of the JFK assassination.

P. Oh.... Yes (Expletive deleted). (Sen. Barry) Goldwater (R Ariz.) put it in context when he said "(expletive deleted) everybody bugs everybody else. You know that."

D. That was priceless.

P. It happens to be totally true. We were bugged in '68 on the plane and in '62 even running for Governor—(expletive deleted) thing you ever saw.

D. It is a shame that evidence to the fact that that happened in '68 was never around....

H. I have some stuff too—on the bombing incident and too in the bombing halt stay.

P. The difficulty with using it, of course, is it reflects on (former President Lyndon B.) Johnson. If it weren't for that, I would use it. Is there any way we could use it without using his name—saying that the DNC did it? No—the FBI did the bugging.

D. That is the problem—would it reflect on Johnson or (former Vice President Hubert H.) Humphrey?

H. Johnson. Humphrey didn't do it.

P. Oh, hell no.

H. He was bugging Humphrey, too.

P. (Expletive deleted)....

[Someone asked the President if he wanted Mitchell's call—he said, "Yeah...."]

P. Well are you still alive?

I was just sitting here with John Dean and he tells me you were going to be sued or something. Good. Good. Yeah. Good. Sure. Well I tell you just don't let this keep you or your colleagues from concentrating on the big game. This thing is just one of those side issues and a month later everybody looks back and wonders what all the shooting was about. OK, John. Good night. Get a good night's sleep. And don't bug anybody without asking me? OK? Yeah. Thank you.

D. Three months ago I would have had trouble predicting there would be a day when this would be forgotten, but I think I can say that 54 days from now nothing is going to come crashing down to our surprise.

P. That what?

D. Nothing is going to come crashing down to our surprise.

'Way You Have Handled All This...Skillful'

P. Oh well, this is a can of worms as you know a lot of this stuff that went on. And the people who worked this way are awfully embarrassed. But the way you have handled all this seems to me has been very skillful putting your fingers in the leaks that have sprung here and sprung there. The Grand Jury is dismissed now?

D. That is correct. They have completed and they have let them go so there will be no continued investigation prompted by the Grand Jury's inquiry, the GAO (General Accounting Office) report referred over to Justice is on a shelf right now because they have hundreds of violations—they have violations of (Sen. George) McGovern (D S.D.), of (Sen.) Humphrey (D Minn.), violations of (Sen.

Henry M.) Jackson (D Wash.), and several hundred Congressional violations. They don't want to start prosecuting one any more than they prosecute the other.

P. They definitely will not prosecute us unless they prosecute the others.

D. Well, we are talking about technical violations referred over also.

P. What about watching the McGovern contributors and all that sort of thing?

D. We have (inaudible) eye out on that. His I understand is not in full compliance.

P. He asked?

D. No....

H. He may be getting $900,000 from somebody. He may have two or three angels.

P. I don't think he is getting a hell of a lot of small money. I don't believe (expletive deleted) Have you had the P.O. checked yet?

H. That is John's area. I don't know.

P. Well, let's have it checked.

Only Problems Are Human Problems

D. Well as I see it, the only problems we may have are the human problems and I will keep a close watch on that....

P. You mean on this case?

D. On this case. There is some bitterness between the Finance Committee and the Political Committee—they feel they are taking all the heat and all the people upstairs are bad people—not being recognized.

*   *   *

P. We are all in it together. This is a war. We take a few shots and it will be over. We will give them a few shots and it will be over. Don't worry. I wouldn't want to be on the other side right now. Would you?

*   *

P. *They're all in it together.*

D. *That's right.*

P. *They should just, uh, just behave and, and, recognize this, this is, again, this is war. We're getting a few shots. It'll be over. Don't worry. [Unintelligble] I wouldn't want to be on the other side right now. Would you? I wouldn't want to be in Edward Bennet Williams', Williams' position after this election.*

D. *No. No.*

P. *None of these bastards—*

D. *He, uh, he's done some rather unethical things that have come to light already, which in—again, Richey has brought to our attention.*

P. *Yeah.*

D. *He went down—*

H. *Keep a log on all that.*

D. *Oh, we are, on these. Yeah.*

P. *Yeah.*

H. *Because afterwards that is a guy,*

P. *We're going after him.*

H. *that is a guy we've got to ruin.*

D. *He had, he had an ex parte—*

P. *You want to remember, too, he's an attorney for the Washington Post.*

D. *I'm well aware of that.*

P. *I think we are going to fix the son-of-a-bitch. Believe me. We are going to. We've got to, because he's a bad man.*

D. *Absolutely.*

P. *He misbehaved very badly in the Hoffa matter. Our—some pretty bad conduct, there, too, but go ahead.*

* * *

D. Along that line, one of the things I've tried to do, I have begun to keep notes on a lot of people who are emerging as less than our friends because this will be over some day and we shouldn't forget the way some of them have treated us.

* *

D. *Well, that's, uh, along that line, uh, one of the things I've tried to do, is just keep notes on a lot of the people who are emerging as,*

P. *That's right.*

D. *as less than our friends.*

P. *Great.*

D. *Because this is going to be over some day and they're—We shouldn't forget the way some of them have treated us.*

* * *

Nixon Orders Enemies' List

P. I want the most comprehensive notes on all those who tried to do us in. They didn't have to do it. If we had a very close election and they were playing the other side I would understand this. No—they were doing this quite deliberately and they are asking for it and they are going to get it. We have not used the power in this first four years as you know. We have never used it. We have not used the Bureau and we have not used the Justice Department but things are going to change now. And they are either going to do it right or go.

D. What an exciting prospect.

P. Thanks. It has to be done. We have been (adjective deleted) fools for us to come into this election campaign and not do anything with regard to the Democratic Senators who are running, et cetera. And who the hell are they after? They are after us. It is absolutely ridiculous. It is not going to be that way any more.

H. Really, it is ironic that we have gone to extremes. You and your damn regulations. Everybody worries about not picking up a hotel bill.

D. I think you can be proud of the White House staff. It really has had no problems of that sort. And I love this GAO audit that is going on now. I think they have some suspicion that even a cursory investigation is going to discover something here. I don't think they can find a thing. I learned today, incidentally, and have not confirmed it, that the GAO auditor who is down here is here at the Speaker of the House's request.

P. That surprises me.

H. Well, (expletive deleted) the Speaker of the House. Maybe we better put a little heat on him.

P. I think so too.

H. Because he has a lot worse problems than he is going to find down here.

D. That's right.

H. That is the kind of thing that, you know, we really ought to do is call the Speaker and say, "I regret to say your calling the GAO down here because of what it is going to cause us to do to you."

P. Why don't you see if (former presidential counselor Bryce N.) Harlow will tell him that.

H. Because he wouldn't do it—he would just be pleasant and call him Mr. Speaker....

'Trying to Cut Our Losses'

P. You really can't sit and worry about it all the time. The worst may happen but it may not. So you just try to button it up as well as you can and hope for the best, and remember basically the damn business is unfortunately trying to cut our losses.

D. Certainly that is right and certainly it has had no effect on you. That's the good thing.

H. No, it has been kept away from the White House and of course completely from the President.... The only tie to the White House is the (former presidential special counsel Charles W.) Colson effort they keep trying to pull in.

D. And, of course, the two White House people of lower level—indicted—one consultant and one member of the Domestic Staff. That is not very much of a tie.

H. That's right. Or (convicted mass murderer Charles M.) Manson. (expletive deleted). If they had been killers. Isn't that true?

H. It is certainly true.

P. These (characterization deleted) they have had no way. They ought to move the trial away from—

D. There has been extensive clipping on the part of the counsel in this case. They may never get a fair trial. They may never get a jury that will convict them. The *Post*, you know, that they have a real large team assigned to cover this case. Believe me, the Maury Stans story about his libel suit that he had so much coverage in the *Evening News* they put way back on page 8 of the *Post* and did not even cover it in total....

* *

H. *The Post is—*

P. *The Post has asked—it's going to have its problems.*

H. *[Unintelligible]*

D. *The networks, the networks are good with Maury coming back three days in a row and—*

P. *That's right. Right. The main thing is the Post is going to have damnable, damnable problems out of this one. They have a television station*

D. *That's right, they do.*

P. *and they're going to have to get it renewed.*

H. *They've got a radio station, too.*

P. *Does that come up too? The point is, when does it come up?*

D. *I don't know. But the practice of non-licensees filing on top of licensees has certainly gotten more,*

P. *That's right.*

D. *more active in the, in the area.*

P. *And it's going to be God damn active here.*

D. *[Laughs]*

P. *Well, the game has to be played awfully rough. I don't know— Now, you, you'll follow through with—who will over there? Who —Timmons, or with Ford, or—How's it going to operate?...*

February 28, 1973

Meeting: The President, Dean in the Oval Office (9:12—10-23 a.m.):

The President and Dean discuss the planned hearings by the Senate Watergate committee.

D. ...I would suspect if we are going to get any insight to what that Committee is going to do, it is going to be through [GOP Sen. Edward] Gurney. I don't know about [GOP Sen. Lowell] Weicker...

P. Weicker, I think the line to Weicker is through [Pat] Gray. Gray has to shape up here and handle himself well too. Do you think he will?

D. I do. I think Pat has had it tough. He goes up this morning as you know. He is ready. He is very comfortable in all of the decisions he has made, and I think he will be good.

P. But he is close to Weicker—that is what I meant.

D. Yes, he is.

P. And so, Gray...

D. He has a lead in there—yes.

P. One amusing thing about the Gray thing, and I knew this would come. They say Gray is a political crony and a personal crony of the President's. Did you know that I have never seen him socially?

D. Is that correct? No, I didn't.

P. I think he has been to a couple White House events, but I have never seen him separately.

D. The Press has got him meeting you at a social function. And, back in 1947, (inaudible) is something I have read.

P. Maybe at a [Adm. Arthur] Radford party or something like that. That's all. I don't know. But Gray is somebody that I know only— He was Radford's assistant, used to attend [National Security Council] meetings. He has never been a social friend. Edgar Hoover, on the other hand, I have seen socially at least a hundred times. He and I were very close friends.

D. This is curious the way the press—

P. (expletive deleted)—Hoover was my crony. He was closer to me than Johnson, actually although Johnson used him more. But as for Pat Gray, (expletive deleted) I never saw him.

D. While it might have been a lot of blue chips to the late Director, I think we could have been a lot better off during this whole Watergate thing if he had been alive. Because he knew how to handle that Bureau—knew how to keep them in bounds.

P. Well, Hoover performed. He would have fought. That was the point. He would have defied a few people. He would have scared them to death. He has a file on everybody....

The President and Dean go on to discuss the motives of the Democratic members of the Senate Watergate Committee.

P. I frankly say that I would rather they would be partisan—rather than for them to have a façade of fairness and all the rest. [Sam] Ervin always talks about his being a great Constitutional lawyer. (expletive deleted) He's got [Howard] Baker totally toppled over to him. Ervin works harder than most of our Southern gentlemen. They are great politicians. They are just more clever than the minority...

D. I am convinced that he has shown that he is merely a puppet for Kennedy in this whole thing. The fine hand of the Kennedys' is behind this whole hearing...

P. Uh, huh.

D. He has kept this quiet and constant pressure on this thing. I think this fellow Sam Dash, who has been selected Counsel, is a Kennedy choice. I think this is also something we will be able to quietly and slowly document. Leak this to the press, and the parts and cast become much more apparent.

P. Yes, I guess the Kennedy crowd is just laying in the bushes waiting to make their move. I had forgotten, by the way, we talk about Johnson using the FBI. Did your friends tell you what Bobby did?

D. I haven't heard but I wouldn't be—

P. Johnson believed that Bobby bugged him.

D. That wouldn't surprise me.

P. Bobby was a ruthless (characterization omitted.) But the FBI does blatantly tell you that—or [former FBI assistant director William] Sullivan told you about the New Jersey thing. He did use a bug up there for intelligence work. (inaudible)...

The President and Dean turn to the subject of news leaks, and then to a discussion of White House strategy with respect to the investigation of the Watergate break-in.

...**D.** I have got to say one thing. There has never been a leak out of my office. There never will be a leak out of my office. I wouldn't begin to know how to leak and I don't want to learn how you leak...

* * *

P. This happens all the time. Well, you can follow these characters to their Gethsemane. I feel for those poor guys in jail, particularly for Hunt with his wife dead.

D. Well there is every indication they are hanging in tough right now.

P. What the hell do they expect though? Do they expect clemency in a reasonable time? What would you advise on that?

D. I think it is one of those things we will have to watch very closely. For example,—

P. You couldn't do it, say, in six months.

D. No, you couldn't. This thing may become so political as a result of these hearings that it is a vendetta. This judge [John Sirica] may go off the deep end in sentencing, and make it so absurd that its clearly injustice that they have been heavily—

P. Is there any kind of appeal left?

D. Right. Liddy and [former CRP security chief James] McCord, who sat through the trial, will both be on appeal and there is no telling how long that will last. It is one of these things we will just have to watch.

P. My view though is to say nothing about them on the ground that the matter is still in the courts and on appeal. Second, my view is to say nothing about the hearings at this point, except that I trust they will be conducted the proper way and I will not comment on the hearings while they are in process. Of course if they break through—if they get muckraking— It is best not to cultivate that thing here at the White House. If it is done at the White House

317

again they are going to drop the (adjective deleted) thing. Now there, of course, you say but you leave it all to them. We'll see as time goes on. Maybe we will have to change our policy. But the President should not become involved in any part of this case. Do you agree with that?

D. I agree totally, sir. Absolutely. That doesn't mean that quietly we are not going to be working around the office. You can rest assured that we are not going to be sitting quietly.

P. I don't know what we can do. The people who are most disturbed about this (unintelligible) are the (adjective deleted) Republicans. A lot of these Congressmen, financial contributors, et cetera, are highly moral. The Democrats are just sort of saying, "(expletive deleted) fun and games!"

D. Well, hopefully we can give them [political prankster Donald] Segretti.

P. (Expletive deleted) He was such a dumb figure, I don't see how our boys could have gone for him. But nevertheless, they did. It was really juvenile! But, nevertheless, what the hell did he do? What in the (characterization deleted) did he do? Shouldn't we be trying to get intelligence? Weren't they trying to get intelligence from us?...

* *

P. *This happens all the time. Well, you can, uh, follow these characters to the, to their Gethsemane. I, I feel for those poor guys in jail, I mean, I don't know—particularly for Hunt. Hunt with his wife, uh, dead. It's a tough thing.*

D. *Well,*

P. *We have to do [unintelligible]*

D. *every indication*

P. *You will have to do—*

D. *that they're, they're hanging in tough right now.*

P. *What the hell do they expect, though? Do they expect that they will get clemency within a reasonable time?*

D. *I think they do. [Unintelligible] going to do.*

P. *What would you say? What would you advise on that?*

D. *Uh, I think it's one of those things we'll have to watch very closely. For example—*

P. *You couldn't do it, you couldn't do it, say in six months?*

D. *No.*

P. *No.*

D. *No, you couldn't. This thing may become so political as a result of these*

P. *Yeah.*

D. *hearings that it is, it, it, is more—*

P. *A vendetta?*

D. *Yeah, it's a vendetta. This judge may, may go off the deep end in sentencing, and make it so absurd that, uh, it's clearly in injustice.*

P. Yeah.

D. That they have been heavily—

P. Are they going to feel—Uh, is there any kind of appeals left?

D. Right. Liddy, Liddy and McCord, who sat through the trial, will both be on appeal.

P. Uh huh.

D. And, uh, there is no telling how long that will last. I think this is one of the, one of these things we'll just have to watch.

P. My view is: say nothing about the event on the ground that the matter is still in the courts and on appeal.

D. That's right.

P. That's my position. Second, my view is to say nothing about the hearings at this point, except that "I trust that they will be conducted in the proper way," and, "I will not comment on the hearings while they are in process." [Unintelligible.] And then I, of course if they break through—if they get a lot luckier—But you see, it's best not to cultivate—and I get Ziegler to do the same—it's best not to elevate that thing here to the White House. Cause I don't want the White House gabbing around about the God damned thing. Now there, of course, you'd say, "But you leave it all to them."

[High frequency tone for four seconds.]

P. our policy. But the President should not become [unintelligible] on this case. Do you agree to that?

D. I agree totally, sir. Absolutely. Now, that doesn't mean that quietly we're not going to be working around the [unintelligible]. But, uh, you can rest assured that, uh, we're not going to be sitting quietly.

P. I don't know what we can do. The people that are most disturbed about this [unintelligible] now are the God damned Republicans. A lot of these Congressmen, financial contributors, and so forth are highly moral. The Democrats are just sort of saying, "Oh, Christ, fun and games. Fun and games."

D. Well, hopefully we can—

P. Take that Segretti thing: Ha, Jesus Christ. He was sort of a clownish figure, I don't see how our boys [laughs], could have gone for him. But nevertheless, they did. It was, it was really—shall we say, juvenile, the way that was handled. But nevertheless, what the hell did he do? What in the name of God did he do? Should, shouldn't we get, be trying to get intelligence? Weren't they trying to get intelligence from us?...

* * *

P. ...[A]ll this business is a battle and they are going to wage the battle. A lot of them have enormous frustrations about those elections, state of their party, etc. And their party has its problems. We think we have had problems, look at some of theirs. [Democratic

319

chairman Robert] Strauss has had people and all the actors, and they haven't done that well you know.

D. Well, I was—we have come a long road on this thing now. I had thought it was an impossible task to hold together until after the election until things started falling out, but we have made it this far and I am convinced we are going to make it the whole road and put this thing in the funny pages of the history books rather than anything serious because actually—

P. It will be somewhat serious but the main thing, of course, is also the isolation of the President.

D. Absolutely! Totally true!

P. Because that, fortunately, is totally true.

D. I know that sir!

P. (expletive deleted) Of course, I am not dumb and I will never forget when I heard about this (adjective deleted) forced entry and bugging. I thought, what in the hell is this? What is the matter with these people? Are they crazy? I thought they were nuts! A prank! But it wasn't! It wasn't very funny. I think that our Democratic friends know that, too. They know what the hell it was. They don't think we'd be involved in such.

D. I think they do too.

P. Maybe they don't. They don't think I would be involved in such stuff. They think I have people capable of it. And they are correct, in that [former adviser Charles] Colson would do anything...now I will not talk to you again until you have something to report to me.

D. Alright, sir.

P. But I think it is very important that you have these talks with our good friend [Attorney General Richard] Kleindienst.

D. That will be done.

P. Tell him we have to get these things worked out. We have to work together on this thing. I would build him up. He is the man who can make the difference. Also point out to him what we have. (expletive deleted) Colson's got (characterization deleted), but I really, really,—this stuff here—let's forget this. But let's remember this was not done by the White House. This was done by the Committee to Re-elect, and Mitchell was the Chairman, correct?

D. That's correct!

P. And Kleindienst owes Mitchell everything. Mitchell wanted him for Attorney General. Wanted him for Deputy, and here he is. Now, (expletive deleted). Baker's got to realize this, and that if he allows this thing to get out of hand he is going to potentially ruin John Mitchell. He won't. Mitchell won't allow himself to be ruined. He will put on his big stone face. But I hope he does and he will. There is no question what they are after. What the Committee is after is somebody at the White House. They would like to get Haldeman or Colson, Ehrlichman.

D. Or possibly Dean. You know, I am a small fish....

March 13, 1973

Meeting: The President, Haldeman and Dean, Oval Office (12:42-2 p.m.):

Following is the text of a recorded conversation between President Nixon and his counsel, John W. Dean III, on March 13, 1973. White House Chief of Staff H. R. Haldeman participates briefly in the beginning of the conversation. In his testimony to the Senate Watergate committee, Dean said that in his conversation he and Nixon discussed the money demands of the Watergate burglars and that the President said it would be 'no problem' to raise $1-million. There is no reference to these subjects in the White House transcript of the March 13 conversation. This discussion is contained in the March 21, 1973, transcript. (March 21, text, p. 340.)

H. Say, did you raise the question with the President on (former presidential special counsel Charles W.) Colson as a consultant?

D. No, I didn't.... The thought was as a consultant, without doing any consulting, he wants it for continued protection on—

H. Solely for the purpose of executive privilege protection, I take it....

P. What happens to (White House appointments secretary Dwight L.) Chapin?

D. Well, Chapin doesn't have quite the same problem in appearing as Colson will.

H. Yeah—you have the same problems of Chapin appearing as Colson.

P. Well, can't—that would be such an obvious fraud to have both of them as consultants, that that won't work. I think he is right. You would have to leave Chapin.

H. Well, you can't make Chapin a consultant, because we have already said he is not.

D. Yeah.

H. Because we wanted the separation. The question is, are you then, as of now, the way they have interpreted executive privilege, is that you are not going to let Chapin testify.

P. Anybody.

H. Because it applies to executive privilege by the former people in relation to matters while they were here.... Colson is concerned with what he is doing from now on, and he would apply the consulting tactic if he were called with regard to actions taken now...that relate to the Watergate action.

D. The problem is, I think, he will be out stirring up counter-news attacks and things of this nature.

P. (expletive deleted) Is he supposed to do that and be consulting with the President on it?

D. No, no. But he is consulting. It is a wide open consultantship. It doesn't mean he would be consulting with you.

H. Yeah. Your idea was just to put this in the drawer, in case.

D. Put it in the drawer, and then decide it.

H. It would be a consultant without pay.

D. I wouldn't even tell Chuck this. Just tell Chuck there is something in the drawer.

H. There is no reason to tell Chuck is there? Why....

P. I would tell Chuck. Tell him he is not to say anything, frankly.

H. The point would be to date it back on Saturday, so it is that day....

* * *

P. Before we get into that I was wondering about that jackassery about some kid who (unintelligible)—which of course is perfectly proper course of action if it works. I would expect we were heavily infiltrated that way too.

* *

P. *Before going into that, uh, I was wondering on that...[unintelligible] jackassery about some kid who was infiltrating peace groups, which of course is perfectly proper. Christ, I hope they were. I would hope, I would expect we were heavily infiltrated that way, too....*

* * *

D. The only problem there Mr. President is that....

P. Did he get paid?

D. He was paid.

P. By check?

D. He was paid by personal check of another person over there who, in turn, was taking it out of expense money. The ultimate source of the money—and this is ticklish—is that it is pre-April 7th money, and there could be some potential embarrassment for Ken Reitz (Kenneth C. Reitz, Nixon's 1972 youth director) along the way.

P. Oh!

D. So he is. But I think it is a confined situation. Obviously it is something that will come up in the Ervin Committee, but it is not another new Liddy-Hunt (Watergate conspirators G. Gordon Liddy and E. Howard Hunt Jr.) operation.

P. It is just a (adjective deleted) thing.

D. Oh, it is.

P. What happened to the kid? Did he just decide to be a hero?

D. That's right. He probably chatted about it around school, and the word got out, and he got confronted with it and he knew he had chatted about it, so there he was. It's absurd, it really is. He didn't do anything illegal.

P. Illegal? Of course not! Apparently you haven't been able to do anything on my project of getting on the offensive?

D. But I have, sir, to the contrary!

P. Based on Sullivan, have you kicked a few butts around?

D. I have all of the information that we have collected. There is some there, and I have turned it over to Baroody (presidential special assistant William J. Baroody Jr.). Baroody is having a speech drafted for (Sen.) Barry Goldwater (R Ariz.). And there is enough material there to make a rather sensational speech just by: Why in the hell isn't somebody looking into what happened to President Nixon during his campaign? Look at these events! How do you explain these? Where are the answers to these questions? But, there is nothing but threads. I pulled all the information.

P. Also, the Senator should then present it to the Ervin Committee and demand that that be included. He is a Senator, a Senator....

D. What I am working on there for Barry is a letter to Senator Ervin that this has come to my attention, and why shouldn't this be a part of the inquiry? And he can spring out 1964 and quickly to '72. We've got a pretty good speech there, if we can get out our materials.

P. Good!...

'Need Any IRS Stuff?'

P. Do you need any IRS (Internal Revenue Service) stuff?

D. There is no need at this hour for anything from IRS, and we have a couple of sources over there that I can go to. I don't have to go around with (IRS commissioner) Johnnie (M.) Walters or anybody, but we can get right in and get what we need. [**P.** *Talk to Elliot Gompers.*] I have been preparing the answers for the briefing book and I just raised this with Ron; in my estimation, for what it is worth, that probably this week will draw more Watergate questions than any other week we are likely to see, given the Gray (Acting FBI Director L. Patrick Gray III) hearings, the new revelations—they are not new, but they are now substantiated—about (Nixon personal attorney Herbert W.) Kalmbach and Chapin that have been in the press.

P. To the effect of what phase?

D. That Chapin directed Kalmbach to pay (Donald H.) Segretti, the alleged saboteur, somewhere between $35 and $40,000. There is an awful lot of that hot in the press now. There is also the question of Dean appearing, not appearing—Dean's role. There are more stories in the *Post* this morning that are absolutely inaccurate about my turning information over to the Re-Election Committee for some woman over there. Mrs. (Judy) Hoback signed an affidavit and gave it to (Sen.) Birch Bayh (D Ind.), and said that "I was brought into (former Nixon campaign deputy manager Robert C.) Bob Mardian's office within 48 hours after a private interview I had with the jury and confronted with it." How did they know that? It came from internal sources over there. That's how they knew it!

P. From what?

D. Internal sources—this girl had told others that she was doing this, and they just told. They just quickly sent it to the top that she was out on her own....

Dean assists the President in preparing for possible questions at a news conference.

P. Well, now, with regard to the question, etc., it would be my opinion not to dodge it just because there are going to be questions.

D. Well you are probably going to get more questions this week. And the tough questions. And some of them don't have easy answers. For example, did Haldeman know that there was a Don Segretti out there? That question is likely.

P. Did he? I don't know.

D. Yes, he had knowledge that there was somebody in the field doing prankster-type activities.

* * *

P. Well, I don't know anything about that. What about my taking, basically, just trying to fight this thing one at a time. I am only going to have to fight it later, and it is not going to get any better. I think the thing to say is, "this is the matter being considered by the Committee and I am not going to comment on it." I don't want to get into the business of taking each charge that comes up in the Committee and commenting on it: "It is being considered by the Committee. It is being investigated and I am not going to comment on it."

* *

P. *Uh huh.... So I don't know that. [Unintelligible].... Yes, but what about, what about my taking, uh, basically just trying to have to fight this thing at one time. I can fight it later, but it's not going to get any better. I don't think that the way to get into this, did he know or not, I think the thing to say "This is a matter being considered by a committee and I'm not going to comment upon it while it's being—I don't want to get into the business of taking each charge that comes up in the Committee and commenting on it. It is being considered by, and it's being investigated. I'm not going to comment on it."*

* * *

D. That is exactly the way I have drafted these. I have checked them generally.

P. I will just cut them off, I think, John, if I start breaking down, you see like I have done the Court thing on the Watergate stuff, I am not going to comment on it. I know all of these questions. I am not going to comment on it. That is a matter for the Committee to determine. Then, I will repeat the fact that as far as the Watergate matter is concerned, I am not going to comment on it, on anything else. Let the Committee find out. What would you say? You don't agree with that?

D. Well, the bottom line, on a draft that (unintelligible). But if you have nothing to hide, Mr. President, here at the White House, why aren't you willing to spread on the record everything you know about it? Why doesn't the Dean Report be made public? Why doesn't everything come out? Why does (White House press secretary Ronald L.) Ziegler stand up there and bob and weave, and no comment? That's the bottom line.

P. Alright. What do you say to that?

D. Well....

P. We are furnishing information. We will....

D. We have cooperated with the FBI in the investigation of the Watergate. We will cooperate with the investigation of, the proper investigation by the Senate.

P. We will make statements.

D. And indeed we have nothing to hide.

P. All this information, we have nothing to hide. We have to handle it. You see, I can't be in the position of basically hunkering down because you have a lot of tough questions on Watergate, and not go out and talk on their issues because it is not going to get better. It is going to get worse.

D. I would agree. I think its cycled somewhat. I think after the Gray thing takes one course or the other, there will be a dead period of news on Watergate until the Ervin Hearings start again. This has obviously sparked the news again.

P. Well, let me just run over the questions again. If it is asked, what about Mr. Haldeman, Mr. Segretti, etc., etc. that is a matter being considered by the Senate Committee and I am not going to comment on it.

D. That is correct. That is specifically in their resolution.

P. I am not going to comment on something being investigated by the Committee. As I have already indicated, I am just not going to comment. Do you approve such tactics? Another question—?

D. Did Mr. Chapin's departure have something to do with his involvement with Mr. Segretti?

P. (inaudible) *[No. The answer's "No." And, uh, "But what about, uh, what about Mr. Dean?"]* What about Mr. Dean? My position is the same. We have cooperated with the Justice Department, the FBI—completely tried to furnish information under our control in this matter. We will cooperate with the Committee under the rules I have laid down in my statement on Executive Privilege....

D. Well, then you will get a barrage of questions probably, on will you supply—will Mr. Haldeman and Mr. (presidential assistant John D.) Ehrlichman and Mr. Dean go up to the Committee and testify?

P. No, absolutely not.

D. Mr. Colson?

P. No. Absolutely not. It isn't a question of not—Ziegler or somebody had said that we in our executive privilege statement it was interpreted as meaning that we would not furnish information and all that. We said we will furnish information, but we are not going to be called to testify. *[...but we are not going to publicly testify.]* That is the position. Dean and all the rest will grant you information. Won't you?

D. Yes, indeed I will!

P. My feeling, John, is that I better hit it now rather than just let it build up where we are afraid of these questions and everybody, etc., and let Ziegler go out there and bob and weave around. I know the easy thing is to bug out, but it is not....

D. You're right. I was afraid. For the sake of debate, but I was having reservations. It is a bullet biter and you just have to do it. These questions are just not going to go away. Now the other thing that we talked about in the past, and I still have the same problem, is to have a "here it all is" approach. If we do that....

'Let it All Hang Out'

P. And let it all hang out.

D. And let it all hang out. Let's with a Segretti—etc.

P. We have passed that point.

D. Plus the fact, they are not going to believe the truth! That is the incredible thing!

P. They won't believe the truth, and they have committed seven people!

D. That's right! They will continually try to say that there is (unintelligible).

P. They hope one will say one day, "Haldeman did it," and one day, one will say I did it. When we get to that question—they might question his political savvy, but not mine! Not on a matter like that!

D. I have a thing on Sullivan (William C. Sullivan, assistant to former FBI director J. Edgar Hoover) I would like to ask you. Sullivan, as I told you, had been talking with me and I said Bill I would like for my own use to have a list of some of the horribles that you are aware of. He hasn't responded back to me, but he sent me a note yesterday saying John I am willing at any time to testify to what I know if you want me to. What he has, as we already know, he has something that has a certain degree of a dynamite situation already—the '68 Presidency, surveillance of Goldwater....

D. Now the other thing, if we were going to use a package like this: Let's say in the Gray hearings—where everything is cast that we are the political people and they are not—that Hoover was above reproach, which is just not accurate, total (expletive omitted). The person who would destroy Hoover's image is going to be this man Bill Sullivan. Also it is going to tarnish quite severely....

P. Some of the FBI.

D. ...some of the FBI. And a former President. He is going to lay it out, and just all hell is going to break loose once he does it. It is going to change the atmosphere of the Gray hearings and it is going to change the atmosphere of the whole Watergate hearings. Now the risk....

P. How will it change?

D. Because it will put them in context of where government institutes were used in the past for the most flagrant political purposes.

P. How can that help us?

D. How does it help us?

P. I am being the devil's advocate.... Why is Sullivan willing to do this?....

Plan to Set Up A Domestic Intelligence System

D. ...What Bill Sullivan's desire in life is, is to set up a domestic national security intelligence system, a White House program. He says we are deficient. He says we have never been efficient, because Hoover lost his guts several years ago. If you recall he and Tom Huston (White House aide Tom Charles Huston) worked on it. Tom Huston had your instructions to go out and do it and the whole thing just crumbled.

P. (inaudible)

D. That's all Sullivan really wants. Even if we could put him out studying it for a couple of years, if you could put him out in the CIA or someplace where he felt—put him there....

P. We will do it....

P. Could we go after the Bureau? I don't know whether we could or not.

D. Not quite after the Bureau. What they are doing is taking the testimony of somebody who is going after the Bureau.

P. I know that. I am just thinking. They will look down the road and see what the result of what they are doing is, won't they? I would think so. Would they go after Johnson? Let's look at the future. How bad would it hurt the country, John, to have the FBI so terribly damaged?

D. Do you mind if I take this back and kick it around with (presidential special counsel Richard A.) Dick Moore? These other questions. I think it would be damaging to the FBI, but maybe it is time to shake the FBI and rebuild it. I am not so sure the FBI is everything it is cracked up to be. I am convinced the FBI isn't everything the public thinks it is.

P. No.

D. I know quite well it isn't.

P. If we can get (District of Columbia police chief) Jerry (V.) Wilson in there—*[rather than a political appointee]* What is your feeling at the moment about Gray? Can he hang in there? Should he?

D. They have an executive session this afternoon to invite me to testify.

P. Sure.

D. There is no question, they are going to invite me to testify. I would say, based on how I handle: (1) the formal letter that comes out of the Committee asking for information, and I programmed that if they do get specific as to what in the hell they do want to know, that I've got to lay it out in a letter sent down here so I can be responsive, fully responsive.

P. Respond to the letter in full! *[Respond to the letter.]*

D. I feel I can respond to the letter in full. I feel I have nothing to hide, as far this issue Gray raised.

P. Would you respond under oath?

D. I think I would be willing to, yes, give it under oath.

P. That is what I would say: that is, what I would prepare in the press thing. He will respond under oath in a letter. He will not appear in a formal session. They might then say, "would he be willing to be questioned under oath?"

D. That is not what the question is. Yes, I would be willing to be questioned under oath, but we are not going up.

P. No, no! Here?

D. No. I think that would be a hell of a bad precedent.

P. Just so we don't cross that bridge. I agree, but you would respond in writing. That's it. OK.

D. After that, if we have been responsive, their argument for holding up Gray's confirmation based on me should be gone. Sure, it can raise more questions than answers, but it should work. The effect of the letter we have taken the central points that they want answers to, given them the responses, given them something in Eastland's hand. And he can say, "alright, it is time to vote." And Eastland says he has the votes to get Gray through. Now, what happens on the Senate Floor is something else, because (Sen. Robert C.) Byrd (D W.Va.) is posing very perceptive, and controlling that Southern bloc.

P. Uh, uh! October! Byrd is running for leader of the whole Senate....

P. My feeling is that they [the Senate] would like to have an excuse not to [confirm L. Patrick Gray III as FBI Director.]....

'Gray...Should Not Head FBI'

P. ...Gray, in my opinion, should not be the head of the FBI. After going through the hell of the hearings, he will not be a good Director, as far as we are concerned.

D. I think that is true. I think he will be a very suspect Director. Not that I don't think Pat won't do what we want—I do look at him a little differently than Dick in that regard. Like he is still keeping in close touch with me. He is calling me. He has given me his hot line. We talk at night, how do you want me to handle this, et cetera? So he still stays in touch, and he is still being involved, but he can't do it because he is going to be under such surveillance by his own people—every move he is making—that it would be a difficult thing for Pat. Not that Pat wouldn't want to play ball, but he may not be able to.

P. I agree. That's what I meant....

D. ...What would be nice for all is to get Gray voted out of the Committee, with a positive vote, enough to get him out of the Committee, and then lock him in limbo there.

P. What is Moore's judgment about Sullivan? What does he think?

D. He said it speaks dynamite. And we both feel that it is the way it would be done, that would be the secret.... We would have to decide, should the White House not be involved or should we be involved? If we are going to play with it, we are probably going to say that we are involved and structure it in a way that there is nothing improper with our involvement.

P. The difficulty with the White House being involved is that if we are involved in this (expletive depleted) that is why it ought to be that he just....

D. I suppose the answer is to say to him, "you have intimated a few things to me, the proper place to take that information is to the Senate Judiciary Committee or to the Attorney General, possibly." And then have him take it to the Committee. Or is that too close to the President still?

P. Well, he works for the Attorney General, doesn't he?

D. If he takes it to (Attorney General Richard G.) Kleindienst, Kleindienst is going to say, "Bill just don't do it because you are going to take DeLoach's name down with it, and DeLoach is a friend of ours."

P. (Expletive deleted)

D. Something I have always thought.

P. Nobody is a friend of ours. Let's face it! Don't worry about that sort of thing.

D. Something I can kick around with Dick Moore. But first of all, it will have to be thought through every inch of the way. Either late yesterday afternoon—it wasn't when I talked with Bob—he was quite excited about it. Ehrlichman said, gave a very good, "uh huh." I said I am not going to rush anything on this. We have a little bomb here that we might want to drop at one time down the road. Maybe the forum to do it in is something totally out of context between the Gray hearings and the Watergate hearings. Maybe we need to go to the *U.S. News*, sir. Who knows what it would be, but we ought to consider every option, now that we've got it.

* * *

P. Rather than going to a hearing, do "Meet the Press," and that
will force the hearing to call him. That is quite the way to do it.
Have him give an interview to *U.S. News* "Wires in the Sky" or
something. A respected reporter—why not give it to Molenhoff
(Clark R. Mollenhoff of the *Des Moines Register and Tribune*)?....

* *

P. *Rather than doing it in a hearing, doing it in the press. Then that
will force the hearing to call him. That's another way you can do
on this. Have him be selected to...give an interview. I would do it
in United States News. Do it in [unintelligible] wire service guy
or something. A respected damn reporter. Why not go to a jackass
like Mollenhoff? No, he's too close to use....*

* * *

P. ...What happened to this Texas guy that gets his money back?
Was he—

D. All hell broke loose for him that week. This was Allan

P. No, no. Allan—

D. Allan, not Duncan nor (unintelligible). All hell broke loose for
Allan for this reason: He—the money apparently originally came
out of a subsidiary of one of Allan's corporations down in Mexico.
It went to a lawyer in Mexico who put it down as a fee billed to the
subsidiary, and then the lawyer sent it back into the States, and it
came back up here. But the weakness of it is that the Mexican lawyer: (1) didn't have a legitimate fee, (2) it could be corporate contribution. So Allan had personally put a note up with the corporation to cover it. Allan, meanwhile, is having problems with his wife,
and a divorce is pending. And tax problems—

P. (inaudible) Watergate—

D. I don't know why that went in the letter. It wasn't used for the
Watergate. That is the interesting thing.

P. It wasn't?

D. No it was not. What happened is that these Mexican checks came
in. They were given to Gordon Liddy, and said, "why don't you get
these cashed?" Gordy Liddy, in turn, put them down to this fellow
(Watergate conspirator Bernard) Barker in Florida, who said he
could cash these Mexican checks, and put them with your Barker's
bank account back in here. They could have been just as easily
cashed at the Riggs Bank. There was nothing wrong with the checks.
Why all that rigamorole? It is just like a lot of other things that
happened over there. God knows what it was all done. It was totally
unnecessary, and it was money that was not directly involved in
the Watergate. It wasn't a wash operation to get money back to
Liddy and the like.

P. Who is going to be the first *[worst]* witness up there?

D. Sloan (Hugh W. Sloan Jr., treasurer of the Nixon re-election finance committee).

P. Unfortunate.

D. No doubt about it—

P. He's scared?

'He's Scared, He's Weak'

D. He's scared, he's weak. He has a compulsion to cleanse his soul by confession. We are giving him a lot of stroking. Funny thing is this fellow goes down to the Court House here before Sirica (Judge John J. Sirica of the U.S. District Court for the District of Columbia), testifies as honestly as he can testify, and Sirica looks around and called him a liar. He just said—Sloan just can't win! So Kalmbach has been dealing with Sloan. Sloan is like a child. Kalmbach has done a lot of that. The person who will have a greater problem as a result of Sloan's testimony is Kalmbach and Stans. So they are working closely with him to make sure that he settles down.

P. Kalmbach will be a good witness, knowing what Kalmbach has been through.

D. Kalmbach has borne up very well. In fact, I decided he may be—

P. Kalmbach is somewhat embarrassed, as he is, they say lawyer for the President. Well, hell I don't need a lawyer. He and (Frank) DeMarco (Jr.), his other partner, handle our pay *[handle that property]* out there.

D. He is sensitive on that point. He saw a transcript of a briefing where Ron was saying, "well he is really not, right nomenclature, 'personal attorney.' " Herb said, "well, gee whiz, I don't know whether Ron knows what all I do." And I said, "well, don't worry about it."

P. What I meant is—I don't care about it, but I mean—it is just the fact that it is played that way, that he is in talking to me all the time. I don't ask him anything. I don't talk to him about anything. I don't know, I see Herb once a year when we see and sign the income tax returns.

D. That's right!

P. Now, true, he handles our San Clemente property and all the rest, but he isn't a lawyer in the sense that most people have a lawyer.

D. No, no. Although when you had an estate claim, he has some dovetailing on it.

P. Anyway we don't want to back off of him.

D. No, he is solid.

P. He will—how does he tell his story? He has a pretty hard row to hoe—he and Stans have.

D. He will be good. Herb is the kind of guy who will check, not once nor twice, on his story—not three times—but probably fifty to a hundred times. He will go over it. He will know it. There won't be a whole in it. Probably he will do his own Q & A. He will have people cross-examine him from ten ways. He will be ready as (former Nixon campaign director) John Mitchell will be ready as Maury Stans will be ready.

P. Mitchell is now studying, is he?

D. He is studying. Sloan will be the worst witness. I think (former Nixon re-election campaign official Jeb Stuart) Magruder will be a good witness. This fellow, Bart Porter (Herbert L. Porter, former official of the Nixon re-election committee), will be a good witness. They have already been through Grand Jury. They have been through trial. They did well. And then, of course, people around here.

P. None will be witnesses.

D. They won't be witnesses?

P. Hell, no. They will make statements. That will be the line which I think we have to get across to Ziegler in all his briefings where he is constantly saying we will provide information. That is not the question. It is how it is to be furnished. We will not furnish it in a formal session. That would be a break down of the privilege. Period. Do you agree with that?

D. I agree. I agree. I have always thought that's the bottom line, and I think that is the good thing that is happening in the Gray hearings right now. If they send a letter down with specific questions, I send back written interrogatories sworn. He knows, the lawyer, that you can handle written interrogatories, where cross examination is another ball game.

P. That's right!

D. You can make a person look like they're inaccurate even if they are trying to tell the truth.

P. Well now, really, you can't mean that! All the facemaking and all that. Written interrogatories you can handle?

D. Can be artfully, accurately answered and give the full information....

P. ...I noticed in the news summary (White House aide Patrick J.) Buchanan was viewing with alarm the grave crisis in the confidency of the Presidency, etc.

D. Well the best way—

P. How much?

D. Pardon?

P. How much of a crisis? It will be—I am thinking in terms of the point is, everything is a crisis, (expletive deleted) it is a terrible lousy thing—it will remain a crisis among the upper intellectual types, the soft heads, our own, too—Republicans—and the Democrats and the rest. Average people won't think it is much of a crisis unless it affects them. (unintelligible)

D. I think it will pass. I think after the Ervin hearings, they are going to find so much—there will be some new revelations. I don't think that the thing will get out of hand. I have no reason to believe it will.

P. Oh, yes—there would be new revelations.

D. They would be quick (inaudible). They would want to find out who knew—

P. Is there a higher up?

D. Is there a higher up?

P. Let's face it, I think they are really after Haldeman.

D. Haldeman and Mitchell.

P. *[Mitchell—I mean.]* Colson is not a big enough name for them. He really isn't. He is, you know, he is on on the government side, *[he is a thorn in their side]* but Colson's name doesn't bother them so much. They are after Haldeman and after Mitchell. Don't you think so?

*   *   *

D. Sure. They are going to take a look and try to drag them, but they're going to be able to drag them into the election—

*   *

D. *That's right. Or I bet they'd take Ehrlichman if they could drag him in but they've been unable to drag him in in any way.*

*   *   *

P. In any event, Haldeman's problem is Chapin isn't it?

D. Bob's problem is circumstantial.

P. Why is that? Let's look at the circumstantial. I don't know, Bob didn't know any of those people like the Hunts and all that bunch. Colson did, but Bob didn't. OK? *[But Bob did know Chapin.]*

D. That's right.

P. Now where the hell, or how much Chapin knew I will be (expletive deleted) if I know.

D. Chapin didn't know anything about the Watergate.

P. Don't you think so?

'Strachan...He Knew'

D. Absolutely not.

P. Strachan?

D. Yes.

P. He knew?

D. Yes.

P. About the Watergate?

D. Yes.

P. Well, then *[Bob knew;]* he probably told Bob. He may not have.

D. He was judicious in what he relayed, but Strachan is as tough as nails. He can go in and stonewall, and say, "I don't know anything about what you are talking about." He has already done it twice you know, in interviews.

P. I guess he should, shouldn't he? I suppose we can't call that justice, can we?

D. Well, it is a personal loyalty to him. He doesn't want it any other
way. He didn't have to be told. He didn't have to be asked. It just
is something that he found was the way he wanted to handle the
situation.

P. But he knew? He knew about Watergate? Strachan did?

D. Yes.

P. I will be damned! Well that is the problem in Bob's case. Not
Chapin then, but Strachan. Strachan worked for him, didn't he?

D. Yes. They would have one hell of a time proving that Strachan
had knowledge of it, though.

P. Who knew better? Magruder?

D. Magruder and Liddy.

P. Oh, I see. The other weak link for Bob is Magruder. He hired him
et cetera.

D. That applies to Mitchell, too.

P. Mitchell—Magruder. Where do you see Colson coming into it? Do
you think he knew quite a bit and yet, he could know quite a great
deal about a lot of other things and not know a lot about this. I
don't know.

D. Well I have never—

Colson Was Very Close to Hunt

P. He sure as hell knows Hunt. That we know. Was very close to him.

D. Chuck has told me that he had no knowledge, specific knowledge,
of the Watergate before it occurred. There have been tidbits that I
have raised with Chuck. I have not played any games with him. I
said, "Chuck, I have indications—"

P. What indications? The lawyer has to know everything.

D. That's right. I said, "Chuck, people have said that you were involved in this, involved in that, involved in all of this. He said,
"that is not true, etc." I think that Chuck had knowledge that
something was going on over there, [a lot of people around here
had knowledge that something was going on over there,] but he
didn't have any knowledge of the details of the specifics of the
whole thing.

P. There must have been an indication of the fact that we had poor
pickings. Because naturally anybody, either Chuck or Bob, were
always reporting to me about what was going on. If they ever got
any information they would certainly have told me that we got
some information, but they never had a thing to report. What was
the matter? Did they never get anything out of the damn thing?

D. I don't think they ever got anything, sir.

P. A dry hole?

D. That's right.

P. (Expletive deleted)

D. Well, they were just really getting started.

P. Yeah. Bob one time said something to me about something, this or that or something, but I think it was something about the Convention. I think it was about the convention problems they were planning something. I assume that must have been MacGregor—not MacGregor, but Segretti.

* * *

D. No, Segretti wasn't involved in the intelligence gathering piece of it at all.

* *

D. *No.*

P. *Bob must have known about Segretti.*

D. *Well, I—Segretti really wasn't involved in the intelligence gathering to speak of at all.*

* * *

P. Oh, he wasn't? Who the hell was gathering intelligence?

D. That was Liddy and his outfit.

P. Apart from Watergate?

* * *

D. That's right. Well you see Watergate was part of intelligence gathering, and this was their first thing. What happened is—

* *

P. *Well, that's a perfectly legitimate thing. I guess that's what it was.*

D. *What happened is they—*

* * *

P That was such a stupid thing!

D. It was incredible—that's right. That was Hunt.

* * *

P. To think of Mitchell and Bob would have allowed—would have allowed—this kind of operation to be in the campaign committee!

D. I don't think he knew it was there.

P. I don't think that Mitchell knew about this sort of thing.

D. Oh, no, no! Don't misunderstand me. I don't think that he knew the people. I think he knew that Liddy was out intelligence gathering. I don't think he knew that Liddy would use a fellow like (Watergate conspirator James W.) McCord, (expletive deleted), who worked for the Committee. I can't believe that.

* *

P. *[Unintelligible] to think that Mitchell and Bob would allow, would have allowed this kind of operation to be in the Committee.*

D. *I don't think he knew it was there.*

P. *You kidding?*

D. *I don't—*

P. *You don't think Mitchell knew about this thing?*

D. *Oh, no, no, no. Don't mis—I don't think he knew that people—I think he knew that Liddy was out intelligence-gathering.*

P. *Well?*

D. *I don't think he knew that Liddy would use a fellow like McCord, for God's sake, who worked for the Committee. I can't believe that. Uh, you know, that—...*

* * *

P. Hunt?

D. I don't think Mitchell knew about Hunt either.

P. Well Mitchell thought, well, gee, and I hired this fellow and I told him to gather intelligence. Maybe Magruder says the same thing.

D. Magruder says—as he did in the trial—well, of course, my name has been dragged in as the guy who sent Liddy over there, which is an interesting thing. Well what happened they said is that Magruder asked—he wanted to hire my deputy over there as Deputy Counsel and I said, "No way. I can't give him up."

P. Was Liddy your deputy?

D. No, Liddy never worked for me. He wanted this fellow Fred (F.) Fielding who works for me. Look, he said, Magruder said to me, "will you find me a lawyer?" I said, "I will be happy to look around." I checked around the White House, (Egil) Krogh (Jr.) said, "Liddy might be the man to do it—he would be a hell of a writer. He has written some wonderful legal opinions over here for me, and I think he is a good lawyer." So I relayed that to Magruder.

P. How the hell does Liddy stand up so well?

'A Strange Man'

D. He's a strange man, Mr. President.

P. Strange or strong?

D. Strange and strong. His loyalty is—I think it is just beyond the pale. Nothing—

P. He hates the other side too, doesn't he?

D. Oh, absolutely! He really is.

* * *

P. Is it too late to go the hang-out road?

* *

P. *Uh, is it too late to, to, frankly, go the hang-out road? Yes, it is.*

D. Yes, I think it is. The hang-out road—

* * *

P. The hang-out road (inaudible).

* *

P. *The hang-out road's going to have to be rejected. I, some, I understand it was rejected.*

* * *

D. It was kicked around Bob and I and—
P. Ehrlichman always felt it should be hang-out.
D. Well, I think I convinced him why he would not want to hang-out either. There is a certain domino situation here. If some things start going, a lot of other things are going to start going, and there can be a lot of problems if everything starts falling. So there are dangers, Mr. President. I would be less than candid if I didn't tell you there are. There is a reason for not everyone going up and testifying.
P. I see. Oh no, no, no! I didn't mean to have everyone go up and testify.
D. Well I mean they're just starting to hang-out and say here's our story—
P. I mean put the story out PR people, here is the story, the true story about Watergate.
D. They would never believe it.
P. *That's the point.*
D. The two things they are working on are Watergate—
P. Who is "they?"
D. The press, (inaudible), the intellectuals,—
P. The Packwoods?
D. Right—They would never buy it as far as one White House involvement in Watergate which I think there is just none for that incident which occurred at the Democratic National Headquarters. People here we just did not know that was going to be done. I think there are some people who saw the fruits of it, but that is another story. I am talking about the criminal conspiracy to go in there. The other thing is that the Segretti thing. You hang that out, and they wouldn't believe that. They wouldn't believe that Chapin acted on his own to put his old friend Segretti to be a (political prankster) Dick Tuck on somebody else's campaign. They would have to paint it into something more sinister, more involved, part of a general plan.

* * *

P. Shows you what a master Dick Tuck is. Segretti's hasn't been a bit similar.

* *

P. *[Expletive deleted], it's not sinister. None of it is.... Segretti's stuff isn't, been a bit sinister.*

* * *

D. They are quite humorous as a matter of fact.

P. As a matter of fact, it is just a bunch of (characterization deleted). We don't object to such damn things anyway. On, and on and on. No, I tell you this is the last gasp of our hardest opponents. They've just got to have something to squeal about it.

D. It is the only thing they have to squeal—

P. (Unintelligible) They are going to lie around and squeal. They are having a hard time now. They got the hell kicked out of them in the election. There is not a *[they're going to]* Watergate around in this town, not so much our opponents, even the media, but the basic thing is the establishment. The establishment is dying, and so they've got to show that the despite the successes we have had in foreign policy and in the election, they've got to show that it is just wrong just because of this. They are trying to use this as the whole thing.

D. Well, that is why I keep coming back to this fellow Sullivan. It could change the picture.

P. How could it change though? Saying here is another—

D. Saying here is another and it happens to be Democrats. You know, I know I just—

'If...Get Kennedy Into It'...

P. If he would get (Sen. Edward M.) Kennedy (D Mass.) into it, too, I would be a little more pleased.

D. Let me tell you something that lurks at the bottom of this whole thing. If, in going after Segretti, they go after Kalmbach's bank records, you will recall sometime back—perhaps you did not know about this—I apologize. That right after Chappaquidick somebody was put up there to start observing and within six hours he was there for every second of Chappaquidick for a year, and for almost two years he worked for (Treasury aide John J.) Jack Caulfield.

P. Oh, I have heard of Caulfield.

D. He worked for Caulfield when Caulfield worked for John, and when I came over here I inherited Caulfield and this guy was still on this same thing. If they get to those bank records between the start of July of 1969 through June of 1971, they say what are these about? Who is this fellow up in New York that you paid? There comes Chappaquidick with vengeance. This guy is a twenty year detective on the New York City Police Department.

P. In other words we—

D. He is ready to disprove and how that—

P. (unintelligible)

D. If they get to it—that is going to come out and this whole thing can turn around on that. If Kennedy knew the bear trap he was walking into—

P. How do we know—why don't we get it out anyway?

D. Well, we have sort of saved it.

P. Does he have any records? Are they any good?

D. He is probably the most knowledgeable man in the country. I think he ran up against walls and they closed the records down. There are things he can't get, but he can ask all of the questions and get many of the answers as a 20 year detective, but we don't want to surface him right now. But if he is ever surfaced, this is what they will get.

Kalmbach Funds

P. How will Kalmbach explain that he hired this guy to do the job on Chappaquidick? Out of what type of funds?

D. He had money left over from the pre-convention—

P. Are they going to investigate those funds too?

D. They are funds that are quite legal. There is nothing illegal about those funds. Regardless of what may happen, what may occur, they may stumble into this in going back to, say 1971, in Kalmbach's bank records. They have already asked for a lot of his bank records in connection with Segretti, as to how he paid Segretti.

P. Are they going to go back as far as Chappaquidick?

D. Well this fellow worked in 1971 on this. He was up there. He has talked to everybody in that town. He is the one who has caused a lot of embarrassment for Kennedy already by saying he went up there as a newspaperman, by saying: "Why aren't you checking this? Why aren't you looking there?" Calling the press people's attention to things. Gosh, the guy did a masterful job. I have never had the full report."

P. Coming back to the Sullivan thing, you will now talk to Moore and then what?

D. I will see if we have something that is viable. And if it's—

P. You plan to talk with him again.

D. Yes he asked me last night to give him a day or so to get all his recollections together, and that was yesterday. So I thought I would call him this evening and say, "Bill, I would just like to know—"

P. You see, right after you talk to him it will become known. So maybe the best thing to say is that he is to turn this over and be maligned. But anyway, the Committee is going to say the White House turned over information on the FBI. I don't know how the (expletive deleted) we get it down there?

D. I think I can kick it around with Dick Moore. He and I do very well just bounding these things back and forth and coming up with something. We would never be embarrassed about it.

P. To give it to a newsman, it would be a hell of a break for a newspaper, a hell of a story! The *Star* just ran a whole story on a real bomb on the FBI. Then the Committee member, the man you would use, for example, in this case would be to tell Gurney, and to say, "look! We are on to something very hot here. I can't tell you any more. Go after it, you'll get your other end this fall." Then he goes. It seems to me that's a very effective way to get it out.

D. Uh huh. It seems to me that I don't think Sullivan would give up the White House. Sullivan—if I have one liability in Sullivan here, it is his knowledge of the earlier (unintelligible) that occurred here.

P. That we did?

D. That we did.

P. Well, why don't you just tell him—he could say, "I did no political work at all. My work in the Nixon Administration was solely in the national security." And that is thoroughly true!

D. That is true.

P. Well, good luck.

D. Thank you, sir.

P. It is never dull is it?

D. Never.

March 21, 1973

Following is the text of the most controversial of the transcripts President Nixon furnished to the House Judiciary Committee April 30, 1974. The transcript, as edited by the White House, is of a recorded conversation in the Oval Office March 21, 1973, among Nixon, presidential counsel John W. Dean III and White House chief of staff H. R. Haldeman.

The three men discussed the possibility that the Watergate burglars might demand up to $1 million for their silence. In his Senate Watergate committee testimony, Dean contended that this conversation took place March 13, before a payment had been made to an attorney for one of the burglars, E. Howard Hunt Jr.

Participants in the conversation are identified by initials—P for the President, D for Dean and H for Haldeman.

...**D.** The reason that I thought we ought to talk this morning is because in our conversations, I have the impression that you don't know everything I know and it makes it very difficult for you to make judgments that only you can make on some of these things and I thought that—

P. In other words, I have to know why you feel that we shouldn't unravel something?

D. Let me give you my over-all first.

P. In other words, your judgment as to where it stands, and where we will go.

'A Cancer...That Is Growing'

D. I think that there is no doubt about the seriousness of the problem we've got. We have a cancer within, close to the Presidency, that is growing. It is growing daily. It's compounded, growing geometrically now, because it compounds itself. That will be clear if I, you know, explain some of the details of why it is. Basically, it is because (1) we are being blackmailed; (2) people are going to start perjuring themselves very quickly that have not had to perjure themselves to protect other people in the line. And there is no assurance—

P. That that won't bust?

D. That that won't bust. So let me give you the sort of basic facts, talking first about the Watergate; and then about (political saboteur Donald H.) Segretti; and then about some of the peripheral items that have come up. First of all on the Watergate: how did it all start, where did it start? O.K.! It started with an instruction to me from Bob Haldeman to see if we couldn't set up a perfectly legitimate campaign intelligence operation over at the Re-Election Committee. Not being in this business, I turned to somebody who had been in this business, (Treasury aide John J.) Jack Caulfield. I don't remember whether you remember Jack or not. He was your original bodyguard before they had the candidate protection, an old city policeman.

P. Yes, I know him.

D. Jack worked for John and then was transferred to my office. I said Jack came up with a plan that, you know—a normal infiltration, buying information from secretaries and all that sort of thing. He did, he put together a plan. It was kicked around. I went to Ehrlichman with it. I went to Mitchell with it, and the consensus was that Caulfield was not the man to do this. In retrospect, that might have been a bad call because he is an incredibly cautious person and wouldn't have put the situation where it is today. After rejecting that, they said we still need something so I was told to look around for someone who could go over to 1701 (1701 Pennsylvania Ave., NW, Nixon re-election committee headquarters) and do this. That is when I came up with Gordon Liddy. They needed a lawyer. Gordon had an intelligence background from his FBI service. I was aware of the fact that he had done some extremely sensitive things for the White House while he had been at the White House and he had apparently done them well. Going out into Ellsberg's (Daniel Ellsberg released the Pentagon Papers) doctor's office—

P. Oh, yeah.

D. And things like this. He worked with leaks. He tracked these things down. So the report that I got from (White House aide Egil) Krogh was that he was a hell of a good man and not only that a good lawyer and could set up a proper operation. So we talked to Liddy. He was interested in doing it. I took Liddy over to meet (campaign director John N.) Mitchell. Mitchell thought highly of him because Mitchell was partly involved in his coming to the White House to work for Krogh. Liddy had been at Treasury before that. Then Liddy was told to put together his plan, you know, how he would run an intelligence operation. This was after he was hired over there at the Committee. (Nixon campaign aide Jeb Stuart) Magruder called me in January and said I would like to have you come over and see Liddy's plan.

P. January of '72?

D. January of '72.

D. "You come over to Mitchell's office and sit in a meeting where Liddy is going to lay his plan out." I said I don't really know if I am the man, but if you want me there I will be happy to. So I came over and Liddy laid out a million dollar plan that was the most incredible thing I have ever laid my eyes on: all in codes, and involved black bag operations, kidnapping, providing prostitutes to weaken the opposition, bugging, mugging teams. It was just an incredible thing.

"Did Mitchell Go Along?"

P. Tell me this: Did Mitchell go along—?

D. No, no, not at all. Mitchell just sat there puffing and laughing. I could tell from—after Liddy left the office I said that is the most incredible thing I have ever seen. He said I agree. And so Liddy was told to go back to the drawing board and come up with something realistic. So there was a second meeting. They asked me to come over to that. I came into the tail end of the meeting. I wasn't there for the first part. I don't know how long the meeting lasted. At this point, they were discussing again bugging, kidnapping and the like. At this point I said right in front of everybody, very clearly, I said, "These are not the sort of things (1) that are ever to be discussed in the office of the Attorney General of the United States —that was where he still was—and I am personally incensed." And I am trying to get Mitchell off the hook. He is a nice person and doesn't like to have to say no when he is talking with people he is going to have to work with.

P. That's right.

D. So I let it be known. I said "You all pack that stuff up and get it the hell out of here. You just can't talk this way in this office and you should re-examine your whole thinking."

P. Who all was present?

D. It was Magruder, Mitchell, Liddy and myself. I came back right after the meeting and told Bob, "Bob, we have a growing disaster on our hands if they are thinking this way," and I said, "The White House has got to stay out of this and I, frankly, am not going to be involved in it." He said, "I agree John." I thought at that point that the thing was turned off. That is the last I heard of it and I thought it was turned off because it was an absurd proposal.

P. Yeah.

D. Liddy—I did have dealings with him afterwards and we never talked about it. Now that would be hard to believe for some people, but we never did. That is the fact of the matter.

P. Well, you were talking with him about other things.

D. We had so many other things.

P. He had some legal problems too. But you were his adviser, and I understand you had conversations about the campaign laws, etc. Haldeman told me that you were handling all of that for us. Go ahead.

D. Now. So Liddy went back after that and was over at 1701, the Committee, and this is where I come into having put the pieces together after the fact as to what I can put together about what happened. Liddy sat over there and tried to come up with another plan that he could sell. (1) They were talking to him, telling him that he was putting too much money in it. I don't think they were discounting the illegal points. Jeb is not a lawyer. He did not know whether this is the way the game was played and what it was all about. They came up, apparently, with another plan, but they couldn't get it approved by anybody over there. So Liddy and Hunt apparently came in to see (White House counsel Charles W.) Chuck Colson, and Chuck Colson picked up the telephone and called Magruder and said, "You all either fish or cut bait. This is absurd to have these guys over there and not using them. If you are not going to use them, I may use them." Things of this nature.

P. When was this?

D. This was apparently in February of '72.

P. Did Colson know what they were talking about?

D. I can only assume, because of his close relationship with Hunt, that he had a damn good idea what they were talking about, a damn good idea. He would probably deny it today and probably get away with denying it. But I still—unless Hunt (Watergate conspirator E. Howard Hunt Jr.) blows on him—

P. But then Hunt isn't enough. It takes two doesn't it?

D. Probably. Probably. But Liddy was there also and if Liddy were to blow—

'Criminal Liability in the White House'

P. Then you have a problem—I was saying as to the criminal liability in the White House.

D. I will go back over that, and take out any of the soft spots.

P. Colson, you think was the person who pushed?

D. I think he helped to get the thing off the dime. Now something else occurred though—

P. Did Colson—had he talked to anybody here?

D. No I think this was—

P. Did he talk with Haldeman?

D. No, I don't think so. But here is the next thing that comes in the chain. I think Bob was assuming, that they had something that was proper over there, some intelligence gathering operation that Liddy was operating. And through (Haldeman assistant Gordon D.) Strachan, who was his tickler, he started pushing them to get some information and they—Magruder—took that as a signal to probably go to Mitchell and to say, "They are pushing us like crazy for this from the White House." And so Mitchell probably puffed on his pipe and said, "Go ahead," and never really reflected on what it was all about. So they had some plan that obviously had, I gather, different targets they were going to go after. They were going to infiltrate, and bug, and do all this sort of thing to a lot of these targets. This is knowledge I have after the fact. Apparently after they had initially broken in and bugged the DNC (Democratic National Committee) they were getting information. The information was coming over here to Strachan and some of it was given to Haldeman, there is no doubt about it.

P. Did he know where it was coming from?

D. I don't really know if he would.

P. Not necessarily?

D. Not necessarily. Strachan knew it. There is no doubt about it, and whether Strachan—I have never come to press these people on these points because it hurts them to give up that next inch, so I had to piece things together. Strachan was aware of receiving information, reporting to Bob. At one point Bob even gave instructions to change their capabilities from (Sen. Edmund S.) Muskie to (Sen. George) McGovern, and passed this back through Strachan to Magruder and apparently to Liddy. And Liddy was starting to make arrangements to go in and bug the McGovern operation.

P. They had never bugged Muskie, though, did they?

D. No, they hadn't, but they had infiltrated it by a secretary.

P. By a secretary?

D. By a secretary and a chauffeur. There is nothing illegal about that. So the information was coming over here and then I, finally, after—. The next point in time that I became aware of anything was on June 17th when I got the word that there had been this break-in at the DNC and somebody from our Committee had been caught in the DNC. And I said, "Oh, (expletive deleted)." You know, eventually putting the pieces together—

P. You knew what it was.

D. I knew who it was. So I called Liddy on Monday morning and said, "First, Gordon, I want to know whether anybody in the White House was involved in this." And he said, "No, they weren't." I said, "Well I want to know how in (adjective deleted) name this happened." He said, "Well, I was pushed without mercy by Magruder to get in there and to get more information. That the information was not satisfactory. That Magruder said, 'The White House is not happy with what we are getting.' "

P. The White House?

D. The White House. Yeah!

P. Who do you think was pushing him?

D. Well, I think it was probably Strachan thinking that Bob wanted things, because I have seen that happen on other occasions where things have said to have been of very prime importance when they really weren't.

P. Why at that point in time I wonder? I am just trying to think. We had just finished the Moscow trip. The Democrats had just nominated McGovern. I mean, (expletive deleted), what in the hell were these people doing? I can see their doing it earlier. I can see the pressures, but I don't see why all the pressure was on them.

Reason: Information About Convention

D. I don't know, other than the fact that they might have been looking for information about the conventions.

P. That's right.

D. Because, I understand that after the fact that there was a plan to bug (Democratic chairman Lawrence) Larry O'Brien's suite down in Florida. So Liddy told me that this is what had happened and this is why it had happened.

P. Where did he learn that there were plans to bug Larry O'Brien's suite?

D. From Magruder, long after the fact.

P. Magruder is (unintelligible).

D. Yeah. Magruder is totally knowledgeable on the whole thing.

P. Yeah.

D. Alright now, we have gone through the trial. I don't know if Mitchell has perjured himself in the Grand Jury or not.

P. Who?

D. Mitchell. I don't know how much knowledge he actually had. I know that Magruder has perjured himself in the Grand Jury. I know that Porter has perjured himself in the Grand Jury.

P. Who is (Herbert L.) Porter? (unintelligible)

D. He is one of Magruder's deputies. They set up this scenario which they ran by me. They said, "How about this?" I said, "I don't know. If this is what you are going to hang on, fine."

P. What did they say in the Grand Jury?

D. They said, as they said before the trial in the Grand Jury, that Liddy had come over as Counsel and we knew he had these capacities to do legitimate intelligence. We had no idea what he was doing. He was given an authorization of $250,000 to collect information, because our surrogates were out on the road. They had no protection, and we had information that there were going to be demonstrations against them, and that we had to have a plan as to what liabilities they were going to be confronted with and Liddy was charged with doing this. We had no knowledge that he was going to bug the DNC.

P. The point is, that is not true?

D. That's right.

P. Magruder did know it was going to take place?

D. Magruder gave the instructions to be back in the DNC.

P. He did?

D. Yes.

P. You know that?

D. Yes.

P. I see. O.K.

'No One Over Here Knew That'

D. I honestly believe that no one over here knew that. I know that as God is my maker, I had no knowledge that they were going to do this.

P. Bob didn't either, or wouldn't have known that either. You are not the issue involved. Had Bob known, he would be.

D. Bob—I don't believe specifically knew that they were going in there.

P. I don't think so.

D. I don't think he did. I think he knew that there was a capacity to do this but he was not given the specific direction.

P. Did Strachan know?

D. I think Strachan did know.

P. (unintelligible) Going back into the DNC—Hunt, etc.—this is not understandable!

D. So—those people are in trouble as a result of the Grand Jury and the trial. Mitchell, of course, was never called during the trial. Now—

P. Mitchell has given a sworn statement, hasn't he?

D. Yes, Sir.

P. To the Jury?

D. To the Grand Jury.—

P. You mean the Goldberg arrangement?

D. We had an arrangement whereby he went down with several of them, because of the heat of this thing and the implications on the election, we made an arrangement where they could quietly go into the Department of Justice and have one of the assistant U.S. Attorneys take their testimony and then read it before the Grand Jury.

P. I thought Mitchell went.

D. That's right, Mitchell was actually called before the Grand Jury. The Grand Jury would not settle for less, because the jurors wanted him.

P. And he went?

D. And he went.

P. Good!

Dean: I Worked on Containment

D. I don't know what he said. I have never seen a transcript of the Grand Jury. Now what has happened post June 17? I was under pretty clear instructions not to investigate this, but this could have been disastrous on the electorate if all hell had broken loose. I worked on a theory of containment—

P. Sure.

D. To try to hold it right where it was.

P. Right.

D. There is no doubt that I was totally aware of what the Bureau was doing at all times. I was totally aware of what the Grand Jury was doing. I knew what witnesses were going to be called. I knew what they were asked, and I had to.

P. Why did (Assistant Attorney General Henry E.) Petersen play the game so straight with us?

D. Because Petersen is a soldier. He kept me informed. He told me when we had problems, where we had problems and the like. He believes in you and he believes in this Administration. This Administration has made him. I don't think he has done anything improper, but he did make sure that the investigation was narrowed down to the very, very fine criminal thing which was a break for us. There is no doubt about it.

P. Do you honestly feel that he did an adequate job?

D. They ran that investigation out to the fullest extent they could follow a lead and that was it.

P. But the way is, where I suppose he could be criticized for not doing an adequate job. Why didn't he call Haldeman? Why didn't he get a statement from Colson? Oh, they did get Colson!

D. That's right. But as based on their FBI interviews, there was no reason to follow up. There were no leads there. Colson said, "I have no knowledge of this" to the FBI. Strachan said, "I have no knowledge." They didn't ask Strachan any questions about Watergate. They asked him about Segretti. They said, "what is your connection with Liddy?" Strachan just said, "Well, I met him over there." They never really pressed him. Strachan appeared, as a result of some coaching, to be the dumbest paper pusher in the bowels of the White House.

P. I understand.

D. Alright. Now post June 17th: These guys immediately—It is very interesting. (Dean sort of chuckled) Liddy, for example, on the Friday before—I guess it was on the 15th, no, the 16th of June—had been in Henry Petersen's office with another member of my staff on campaign compliance problems. After the incident, he ran (Attorney General Richard G.) Kleindienst down at Burning Tree Country Club and told him "you've got to get my men out of jail." Kleindienst said, "You get the hell out of here, kid. Whatever you have to say, just say to somebody else. Don't bother me." But this has never come up. Liddy said if they all got counsel instantly and said we will ride this thing out. Alright, then they started making demands. "We have to have attorneys fees. We don't have any money ourselves, and you are asking us to take this through the election." Alright, so arrangements were made through Mitchell, initiating it. And I was present in discussions where these guys had to be taken care of. Their attorneys fees had to be done. (Nixon personal attorney Herbert W.) Kalmbach was brought in. Kalmbach raised some cash.

P. They put that under the cover of a Cuban Committee, I suppose?

D. Well, they had a Cuban Committee and they had—some of it was given to Hunt's lawyer, who in turn passed it out. You know, when Hunt's wife was flying to Chicago with $10,000 she was actually, I understand after the fact, now, was going to pass that money to one of the Cubans—to meet him in Chicago and pass it to somebody there.

'Keep That Cover'

P. (Unintelligible) but I would certain keep that cover for whatever it is worth.

D. That's the most troublesome post-thing because (1) Bob is involved in that; (2) John is involved in that; (3) I am involved in that; (4) Mitchell is involved in that. And that is an obstruction of justice.

P. In other words, the bad it does. You were taking care of witnesses. How did Bob get in it?

D. Well, they ran out of money over there, Bob had $350,000 in a safe over here that was really set aside for polling purposes. And there was no other source of money, so they came over and said you all have got to give us some money. I had to go to Bob and say, "Bob, they need some money over there." He said "What for." So

I had to tell him what it was for because he wasn't just about to send money over there willy-nilly. And John was involved in those discussions. And then we decided there was no price too high to pay to let this thing blow up in front of the election.

P. I think we should be able to handle that issue pretty well. May be some lawsuits.

D. I think we can too. Here is what is happening right now. What sort of brings matters to the (unintelligible). One, this is going to be a continual blackmail operation by Hunt and Liddy and the Cubans. No doubt about it. And McCord (Watergate conspirator James W. McCord Jr.), who is another one involved. McCord has asked for nothing. McCord did ask to meet with somebody, with Jack Caulfield who is his old friend who had gotten him hired over there. And when Caulfield had him hired, he was a perfectly legitimate security man. And he wanted to talk about commutation, and things like that. And as you know Colson has talked indirectly to Hunt about commutation. All of these things are bad, in that they are problems, they are promises, they are commitments. They are the very sort of things that the Senate is going to be looking most for. I don't think they can find them, frankly.

P. Pretty hard.

D. Pretty hard. Damn hard. It's all cash.

P. Pretty hard I mean as far as the witnesses are concerned.

"The Blackmail Is Continuing"

D. Alright, now, the blackmail is continuing. Hunt called one of the lawyers from the Re-Election Committee on last Friday to leave it with him over the weekend. The guy came in to see me to give a message directly to me. From Hunt to me.

P. Is Hunt out on bail?

D. Pardon?

P. Is Hunt on bail?

D. Hunt is on bail. Correct. Hunt now is demanding another $72,000 for his own personal expenses; another $50,000 to pay attorneys fees; $120,000. Some (1) he wanted it as of the close of business yesterday. He said, "I am going to be sentenced on Friday, and I've got to get my financial affairs in order." I told this fellow O'Brien (Paul L. O'Brien, an attorney for the Nixon re-election committee). "If you want money, you came to the wrong man, fellow. I am not involved in the money. I don't know a thing about it. I can't help you. You better scramble about elsewhere." O'Brien is a ball player. He carried tremendous water for us.

P. He isn't Hunt's lawyer?

D. No he is our lawyer at the Re-Election Committee.

P. I see.

D. So he is safe. There is no problem there. So it raises the whole question. Hunt has now made a direct threat against Ehrlichman. As a result of this, this is his blackmail. He says, "I will bring John Ehrlichman down to his knees and put him in jail. I have done enough seamy things for he and Krogh, they'll never survive it."

P. Was he talking about Ellsberg?

D. Ellsberg, and apparently some other things. I don't know the full extent of it.

P. I don't know about anything else.

D. I don't know either, and I hate to learn some of these things. So that is that situation. Now, where are all the soft points? How many people know about this? Well, let me go one step further in this whole thing. The Cubans that were used in the Watergate were also the same Cubans that Hunt and Liddy used for this California Ellsberg thing, for the break in out there. So they are aware of that. How high their knowledge is, is something else. Hunt and Liddy, of course, are totally aware of it, of the fact that it is right out of the White House.

P. I don't know what the hell we did that for!

D. I don't know either.

P. What in the (expletive deleted) caused this? (unintelligible)

Cubans' Lawyer Knew Of Other Schemes

D. Mr. President, there have been a couple of things around here that I have gotten wind of. At one time there was a desire to do a second story job on the Brookings Institute where they had the Pentagon papers. Now I flew to California because I was told that John had instructed it and he said, "I really hadn't, it is a misimpression, but for (expletive deleted), turn it off." So I did. I came back and turned it off. The risk is minimal and the pain is fantastic. It is something with a (unintelligible) risk and no gain. It is just not worth it. But—who knows about all this now? You've got the Cubans' lawyer, a man by the name of (Henry R.) Rothblatt, who is a no good, publicity seeking (characterization deleted), to be very frank with you. He has had to be pruned down and tuned off. He was canned by his own people because they didn't trust him. He didn't want them to plead guilty. He wants to represent them before the Senate. So F. Lee Bailey, who was a partner of one of the men representing McCord, got in and cooled Rothblatt down. So that means that F. Lee Bailey has knowledge. Hunt's lawyer, a man by the name of (William O.) Bittmann, who is an excellent criminal lawyer from the Democratic era of Bobby Kennedy, he's got knowledge.

P. He's got some knowledge?

D. Well, all the direct knowledge that Hunt and Liddy have, as well as all the hearsay they have. You have these two lawyers over at the Re-election Committee who did an investigation to find out the facts. Slowly, they got the whole picture. They are solid.

P. But they know?

D. But they know. You've got, then an awful lot of the principals involved who know. Some people's wives know. Mrs. Hunt was the savviest woman in the world. She had the whole picture together.

P. Did she?

D. Yes. Apparently, she was the pillar of strength in that family before the death.

P. Great sadness. As a matter of fact, there was a discussion with somebody about Hunt's problem on account of his wife and I said, of course commutation could be considered on the basis of his wife's death, and that is the only conversation I ever had in that light.

D. Right.

The "Soft Spots"

D. So that is it. That is the extent of the knowledge. So where are the soft spots on this? Well, first of all, there is the problem of the continued blackmail which will not only go on now, but it will go on while these people are in prison, and it will compound the obstruction of justice situation. It will cost money. It is dangerous. People around here are not pros at this sort of thing. This is the sort of thing Mafia people can do: washing money, getting clean money, and things like that. We just don't know about those things, because we are not criminals and not used to dealing in that business.

P. That's right.

D. It is a tough thing to know how to do.

P. Maybe it takes a gang to do that.

D. That's right. There is a real problem as to whether we could even do it. Plus there is a real problem in raising money. Mitchell has been working on raising some money. He is one of the ones with the most to lose. But there is no denying the fact that the White House, in Ehrlichman, Haldeman and Dean are involved in some of the early money decisions.

P. How much money do you need?

D. I would say these people are going to cost a million dollars over the next two years.

P. We could get that. On the money, if you need the money you could get that. You could get a million dollars. You could get it in cash. I know where it could be gotten. It is not easy, but it could be done. But the question is who the hell would handle it? Any ideas on that?

D. That's right. Well, I think that is something that Mitchell ought to be charged with.

P. I would think so too.

D. And get some pros to help him.

P. Let me say there shouldn't be a lot of people running around getting money—*[We should set up a little—]*

D. Well he's got one person doing it who I am sure is—

P. Who is that?

D. He has Fred LaRue (Frederick C. LaRue, a Nixon campaign aide)
doing it. Now Fred started out going out trying to solicit money
from all kinds of people.

P. No!

D. I had learned about it, and I said, "(expletive deleted) It is just
awful! Don't do it!" People are going to ask what the money is for.
He has apparently talked to Tom Pappas (Thomas A. Pappas, a
Nixon fund raiser).

P. I know.

D. And Pappas has agreed to come up with a sizeable amount, I
gather.

P. What do you think? You don't need a million right away, but you
need a million? Is that right?

D. That is right.

Nixon: You Need Cash?

P. You need it in cash don't you? I am just thinking out loud here
for a moment. Would you put that through the Cuban Committee:

D. No.

P. It is going to be checks, cash money, etc. How if that ever comes
out, are you going to handle it? Is the Cuban Committee an obstruction of justice, if they want to help?

D. Well they have priests in it.

P. Would that give a little bit of a cover?

D. That would give some for the Cubans and possibly Hunt. Then
you've got Liddy. McCord is not accepting any money. So he is not
a bought man right now.

P. OK. Go ahead.

D. Let me continue a little bit right here now. When I say this is a
growing cancer, I say it for reasons like this. Bud Krogh, in his testimony before the Grand jury, was forced to perjure himself. He is
haunted by it. Bud said, "I have not had a pleasant day on my
job." He said, "I told my wife all about this. The curtain may ring
down one of these days, and I may have to face the music, which
I am perfectly willing to do."

P. What did he perjure himself on, John?

D. Did he know the Cubans. He did.

P. He said he didn't?

D. That is right. They didn't press him hard.

P. He might be able to. I am just trying to think. Perjury is an awful
hard rap to prove. If he could just say that I—well, go ahead.

D. Well, so that is one perjury. Mitchell and Magruder are potential

perjurers. There is always the possibility of any one of these individuals blowing. Hunt, Liddy. Liddy is in jail right now, serving his
time and having a good time right now. I think Liddy in his own
bizarre way is the strongest of all of them. So there is that possibility.

* * *

P. Your major guy to keep under control is Hunt?
D. That is right.
P. I think. Does he know a lot?

* *

P. *Well, your, your major guy to keep under control is Hunt.*
D. *That is right.*
P. *I think. Because he knows.*

* * *

D. He knows so much [*P. About a lot of other things.*] He could
sink Chuck Colson. Apparently he is quite distressed with Colson.
He thinks Colson has abandoned him. Colson was to meet with
him when he was out there after, you know, he had left the White
House. He met with him through his lawyer. Hunt raised the question he wanted money. Colson's lawyer told him Colson wasn't do-
ing anything with money. Hunt took offense with that immediately,
and felt Colson had abandoned him.
P. Just looking at the immediate problem, don't you think you have
to handle Hunt's financial situation damn soon?
D. I think that is—I talked with Mitchell about that last night and—
P. It seems to me we have to keep the cap on the bottle that much,
or we don't have any options.
D. That's right.
P. Either that or it all blows right now?
D. That's the question.
P. We have Hunt, Krogh. We'll go ahead with the other ones.
D. Now we've got Kalmbach.
P. *Yeah, that's a tough one.*
D. Kalmbach received, at the close of the '68 campaign in January of
1969, he got a million $700,000 to be custodian for. That came down
from New York, and was placed in safe deposit boxes here. Some
other people were on the boxes. And ultimately, the money was
taken out to California. Alright, there is knowledge of the fact that
he did start with a million seven. Several people know this. Now
since 1969, he has spent a good deal of this money and accounting
for it is going to be very difficult for Herb. For example, he has spent
close to $500,000 on private polling. That opens up a whole new
thing. It is not illegal, but more of the same thing.
P. Everybody does polling.

D. That's right. There is nothing criminal about it. It's private polling.

P. People have done private polling all through the years. There is nothing improper.

D. That's right. He sent $400,000, as he has described to me, somewhere in the South for another candidate. I assume this was 400,000 that went to (Alabama Gov. George C.) Wallace.

* * *

P. Wallace?

* *

P. *Wallace. [Nixon offers the name before Dean.]*

* * *

D. Right. He has maintained a man who I only know by the name of "Tony," who is the fellow who did the Chappaquiddick study.

P. I know about that.

D. And other odd jobs like that. Nothing illegal, but closer. I don't know of anything that Herb has done that is illegal, other than the fact that he doesn't want to blow the whistle on a lot of people, and may find himself in a perjury situation.

P. *Well, if he, uh, he could—because he will be asked about that money!*

D. Well, what will happen when they call him up there—and he has no immunity? They will say, "How did you pay Mr. Segretti?" He will say, "Well, I had cash on hand." "How much cash did you have on hand?" Where does it go from there? Where did you get the cash? A full series of questions. His bank records indicate he had cash on hand, because some of these were set up in trustee accounts.

P. How would you handle him, John, for example? Would you just have him put the whole thing out? *I don't think so. I mean I* don't mind the $500,000 and the $400,000.

D. No—that doesn't bother me either. As I say, Herb's problems are politically embarrassing, but not criminal.

* * *

P. Well he just handled matters between campaigns. These were surveys etc., etc. There is no need to account for that. There is no law that requires his accounting for that.

* *

P. *Well, they're embarrassing, sure—he, he just handled matters that were between campaigns, before anything was done. There were surveys, etc. There is no need to account for that. No law requires him to account for that.*

* * *

D. Ah, now

P. Sources of money. There is no illegality in having a surplus in cash after a campaign.

D. No, the money—it has always been argued by Stans that it came in the pre-convention primary for the 1968 race, and it was just set aside. That all can be explained.

* * *

P. How about the other probabilities?

* *

P. How do your other vulnerabilities go together?

* * *

D. We have a runaway Grand Jury up in the Southern District. They are after Mitchell and (campaign finance director Maurice H.) Stans on some sort of bribe of influence peddling [*P. On Vesco.*] with (financier Robert L.) Vesco. They are also going to try to drag Ehrlichman into that. Apparently Ehrlichman had some meetings with Vesco, also. Don Nixon Jr. (Donald A. Nixon, the President's nephew) came in to see John a couple of times about the problem.

* * *

P. Not about Vesco, but about Don Jr.? Ehrlichman never did anything for Vesco?

* *

P. Not about the complaint.
D. That, there's, uh—the fact of the matter is—
P. [Unintelligible] about a job.
D. That's right. And, and, and, uh, I—
P. We're, is it—Ehrlichman's totally to blame on that.
D. Yeah, well, I think the White House—
P. [Unintelligible]

* * *

D. No one at the White House has done anything for Vesco.
P. ...Matter of—not for the prosecutor.
P. Well Ehrlichman doesn't have to appear there?
D. Before that Grand Jury? Yes he could very well.

* * *

P. He couldn't use Executive Privilege?

* *

P. Uh, we couldn't presume immunity there?

* * *

D. Not really. Criminal charge, that is a little different. That would be dynamite to try to defend that.
P. Use the Flanigan analogy?
D. Right! That's pretty much the over-all picture. And probably the most troublesome thing is the Segretti thing. Let's get down to that. Bob has indicated to me that he has told you a lot of it, that he, indeed did authorize it. He did not authorize anything like

ultimately evolved. He was aware of it. He was aware that (Nixon appointments secretary Dwight L.) Chapin and Strachan were looking for somebody. Again, this is one that has potential that Dwight Chapin should have a felony in this. He has to disprove a negative. The negative is that he didn't control and direct Segretti.

P. Wouldn't the felony be perjury again?

D. No, the felony in this instance would be a potential use of one of the civil rights statutes, where anybody who interferes with the campaign of a candidate for national office.

P. Why isn't it under civil rights statutes for these clowns demonstrating against us?

D. I have argued for that very purpose.

P. Really?

D. Yes, I have.

P. We were closer—nuts interfering with the campaign.

D. That is exactly right.

P. I have been sick about that because it is so bad the way it has been put out on the PR side. It has ended up on the PR side very confused.

D. What really bothers me is this growing situation. As I say, it is growing because of the continued need to provide support for the Watergate people who are going to hold us up for everything we've got, and the need for some people to perjure themselves as they go down the road here. If this thing ever blows, then we are in a cover-up situation. I think it would be extremely damaging to you and the—

P. Sure. The whole concept of Administration justice. Which we cannot have!

D. That is what really troubles me. For example, what happens if it starts breaking, and they do find a criminal case against a Haldeman, a Dean, a Mitchell, an Ehrlichman? That is—

* * *

P. If it really comes down to that, we would have to (unintelligible) some of the men.

* *

P. *Well, if it really comes down to that, we cannot, maybe—We'd have to shed it in order to contain it again.*

* * *

Dean: We'll Carve It Away From You

D. That's right. I am coming down to what I really think, is that Bob and John and John Mitchell and I can sit down and spend a day, or however long, to figure out one, how this can be carved away from you, so that it does not damage you or the Presidency. It just can't! You are not involved in it and it is something you shouldn't—

P. That is true!

D. I know, sir. I can just tell from our conversation that these are things that you have no knowledge of.

P. You certainly can! *[The absurdity of the whole damned thing...]* Buggings, etc.! Let me say I am keenly aware of the fact Colson, et al., were doing their best to get information as we went along. But they all knew very well they were supposed to comply with the law. There was no question about that! You feel that really the trigger man was really Colson on this then?

D. No. He was one of us. He was just in the chain. He helped push the thing.

P. All I know about is the time of ITT, he was trying to get something going there because ITT was giving us a bad time.

D. I know he used Hunt.

P. I knew about that. I didn't know about it, *[I did know about it,]* but I knew there was something going on. But I didn't know it was a Hunt.

D. What really troubles me is one, will this thing not break some day and the whole thing—domino situation—everything starts crumbling, fingers will be pointing. Bob will be accused of things he has never heard of and deny and try to disprove it. It will get real nasty and just be a real bad situation. And the person who will be hurt by it most will be you and the Presidency, and I just don't think—*[Nixon agrees with Dean, interrupting with "yeah" throughout.]*

P. First, because I am an executive I am supposed to check these things.

D. That's right.

P. Let's come back to this problem. What are your feelings yourself, John? You know what they are all saying. What are your feelings about the chances? *[Options]*

D. I am not confident that we can ride through this. I think there are soft spots.

P. You used to be— *[comfortable]*

D. I am not comfortable for this reason. I have noticed of recent— since the publicity has increased on this thing again, with the Gray hearings, that everybody is now starting to watch after their behind. Everyone is getting their own counsel. More counsel are getting involved. How do I protect my ass. *[You know: "How do I protect my own ass?"]*

P. They are scared.

D. That is bad. We were able to hold it for a long time. *[P. Yeah, I know]* Another thing is that my facility to deal with the multitude of people I have been dealing with has been hampered because of Gray's blowing me up into the front page.

P. Your cover is broken?

D. That's right and its—

Nixon: Is Complete Disclosure Best?

P. So what you really come to is what we do. Let's suppose that you and Haldeman and Ehrlichman and Mitchell say we can't hold this? What then are you going to say? What are you going to put out after it. Complete disclosure, isn't that the best way to do it?

D. Well, one way to do it is—

P. That would be my view.

D. One way to do it is for you to tell the Attorney General that you finally know. Really, this is the first time you are getting all the pieces together.

P. Ask for another Grand Jury?

D. Ask for another Grand Jury. The way it should be done though, is a way—for example, I think that we could avoid criminal liability for countless people and the ones that did get it could be minimal.

P. How?

D. Well, I think by just thinking it all through first as to how. You know, some people could be granted immunity.

P. Like Magruder?

'Some People Are Going...to Jail'

D. Yeah. To come forward. But some people are going to have to go to jail. That is the long and short of it, also.

P. Who? Let's talk about—

D. Alright. I think I could. For one.

P. You go to jail?

D. That's right.

P. Oh, hell no! I can't see how you can.

D. Well, because—

P. I can't see how. Let me say I can't see how a legal case could be made against you, John.

D. It would be tough but, you know, I can see people pointing fingers. You know, to get it out of their own, put me in an impossible position. Just really give me a (unintelligible). *[disproving too many negatives.]*

P. Oh, no! Let me say I got the impression here—But just looking at it from a cold legal standpoint: you are a lawyer, you were a counsel—doing what you did as counsel. You were not—What would you go to jail for?

D. The obstruction of justice.

P. The obstruction of justice?

D. That is the only one that bothers me.

P. Well, I don't know. I think that one. I feel it could be cut off at the pass, maybe, the obstruction of justice.

D. You know one of the—that's why—

P. Sometimes it is well to give them something, and then they don't want the bigger push? *[bigger fish.]*

D. That's right. I think that, I think that with proper coordination with the Department of Justice, Henry Petersen is the only man I know bright enough and knowledgeable enough in the criminal laws and process that could really tell us how this could be put together so that it did the maximum to carve it away with a minimum of damage to individuals involved.

P. Petersen doesn't know does he? *[doesn't know the whole story?]*

D. That's right. No. I know he doesn't know. I know he doesn't now. I am talking about somebody who I have over the years grown to have enough faith in—you constantly. *[I am talking about somebody who I have over the years grown to have faith in.]* It would have to put him in a very difficult situation as the Head of the Criminal Division of the United States Department of Justice, and the oath of office—

P. No. Talking about your obstruction of justice, though, I don't see it.

D. Well, I have been a conduit for information on taking care of people out there who are guilty of crimes.

P. Oh, you mean like the blackmailers?

D. The blackmailers. Right.

Nixon: Could You Contain the Blackmailers With Money?

P. Well, I wonder if that part of it can't be—I wonder if that doesn't —let me put it frankly: I wonder if that doesn't have to be continued? Let me put it this way: let us suppose that you get the million bucks, and you get the proper way to handle it. You could hold that side?

D. Uh, huh.

P. It would seem to me that would be worthwhile.

D. Well, that's one problem.

P. I know you have a problem here. You have the problem with Hunt and his clemency.

D. That's right. And you are going to have a clemency problem with the others. They are all going to expect to be out and that may put you in a position that is just untenable at some point. You know, the Watergate Hearings just over, Hunt now demanding clemency or he is going to blow. And politically, it's impossible for you to do it. You know, after everybody—

P. That's right!

D. I am not sure that you will ever be able to deliver on the clemency. It may be just too hot.

P. You can't do it politically until after the '74 elections, that's for sure. Your point is that even then you couldn't do it.

D. That's right. It may further involve you in a way you should not be involved in this.

P. No—it is wrong that's for sure.

D. Well—there have been some bad judgments made. There have been some necessary adjustments made.

P. Before the election?

D. Before the election and in the wake the necessary ones, you know, before the election. You know, with me there was no way, *[to me, there was no way]* but the burden of this second Administration *[P. We're all in on it.]* is something that is not going to go away.

P. No, it isn't.

D. It is not going to go away, Sir!

P. It is not going to go away.

D. Exactly.

P. The idea, well, that people are going to get tired of it and all that sort of thing.

D. Anything will spark it back into life. It's got to be,—It's got to be—

P. It is too much to the partisan interest to others to spark it back into life.

D. And it seems to me the only way—

P. Well, also so let's leave you out of it. I don't think on the obstruction of justice thing—I take that out. I don't know why I think you may be over that cliff. *[I don't think on the obstruction of justice thing—I think that one we can handle. I don't know why I feel that way, but I—]*

D. Well, it is possible.

P. Who else do you think has—

D. Potential criminal liability?

P. Yeah.

D. I think Ehrlichman does. I think that uh—

P. Why? *[Why Ehrlichman? What'd he do?]*

D. Because of this conspiracy to burglarize the Ellsberg doctors' office.

P. That is, provided Hunt's breaks?

D. Well, the funny—let me say something interesting about that. Within the files—

P. Oh, I thought of it. The picture! *[Oh, I saw that. The picture.]*

D. Yes, sir. That is not all that buried. And while I think we've got it buried, there is no telling when it is going to pop up. Now the Cubans could start this whole thing. When the Ervin Committee starts running down why this mysterious telephone was here in the White House listed in the name of a secretary, some of these secretaries have a little idea about this, and they can be broken down just so fast. That is another thing I mentioned in the cycle—in the circle. Liddy's secretary, for example, is knowledgeable. Magruder's secretary is knowledgeable.

P. Sure. So Ehrlichman on the—

D. What I am coming in today with is: I don't have a plan on how to solve it right now, but I think it is at the juncture that we should begin to think in terms of how to cut the losses; how to minimize the further growth of this thing, rather than further compound it by, you know, ultimately paying these guys forever. I think we've got to look—

P. But at the moment, don't you agree it is better to get the Hunt thing that's where that—*[better get the Hunt thing? I mean, that's worth it, at the moment.]*

D. That is worth buying time on.

P. That is buying time, I agree.

D. The Grand Jury is going to reconvene next week after Sirica sentences. But that is why I think that John and Bob have met with me. They have never met with Mitchell on this. We have never had a real down and out with everybody that has the most to lose and it is the most danger for you to have them have criminal liabilities. I think Bob has a potential criminal liability, frankly. In other words, a lot of these people could be indicted.

P. Yeah.

D. They might never be convicted but just the thought of spending nights.

P. Suppose they are?

D. I think that would be devastating.

P. Suppose the worst—that Bob is indicted and Ehrlichman is indicted. And I must say, we just better then try to tough it through. You get the point.

D. That's right.

P. If they, for example, say let's cut our losses and you say we are going to go down the road to see if we can cut our losses and no more blackmail and all the rest. And then the thing blows cutting Bob and the rest to pieces. You would never recover from that, John.

D. That's right.

'Better to Fight It Out'

P. It is better to fight it out. Then you see that's the other thing. It's better to fight it out and not let people testify, and so forth. And now, on the other hand, we realize that we have these witnesses— that we have these weaknesses—in terms of blackmail.

D. There are two routes. One is to figure out how to cut the losses and minimize the human impact and get you up and out and away from it in any way. In a way it would never come back to haunt you. That is one general alternative. The other is to go down the road, just hunker down, fight it at every corner, every turn, don't let people testify—cover it up is what we really are talking about. Just keep it buried, and just hope that we can do it, hope that we make good decisions at the right time, keep our heads cool, we make the right moves.

P. And just take the heat?

D. And just take the heat.

P. Now with the second line of attack. You can discuss this (unintelligible) the way you want to. Still consider my scheme of having you brief the Cabinet, just in very general terms and the leaders in very general terms and maybe some very general statement with regard to my investigation. Answer questions, basically on the basis of what they told you, not what you know. Haldeman is not involved. Ehrlichman is not involved.

D. If we go that route, Sir, I can give a show we can sell them just like we were selling Wheaties in our position. There's no—

P. The problem that you have are these mine fields down the road. I think the most difficult problem are the guys who are going to jail. I think you are right about that.

D. I agree.

Nixon: We Can't Give Them Clemency

P. Now. And also the fact that we are not going to be able to give them clemency.

D. That's right. How long will they take? How long will they sit there? I don't know. We don't know what they will be sentenced to. There's always a chance—

P. Thirty years, isn't it?

D. It could be. You know, they haven't announced yet, but it—

P. Top is 30 years, isn't it?

D. It is even higher than that. It is about 50 years. It all—

P. So ridiculous!

D. And what is so incredible is, he is (unintelligible).

P. People break and enter, etc., and get two years. No weapons! No results! What the hell are they talking about?

D. The individuals who are charged with shooting (Sen.) John Stennis are on the street. They were given, you know, one was put out on his personal recognizance rather than bond. They've got these fellows all stuck with $100,000 bonds. It's the same Judge, (John J.) Sirica, let one guy who is charged with shooting a United States Senator out on the street.

P. Sirica?

D. Yes—it is phenomenal.

P. What is the matter with him? I thought he was a hard liner.

D. He is. He is just a peculiar animal, and he set the bond for one of the others somewhere around 50 to 60,000. But still, that guy is in. Didn't make bond, but still 60 thousand dollars as opposed to $100,000 for these guys is phenomenal.

P. When could you have this meeting with these fellows as I think time is of the essence. Could you do it this afternoon?

D. Well, Mitchell isn't here. It might be worth it to have him come down. I think that Bob and John did not want to talk to John Mitchell about this, and I don't believe they have had any conversation with him about it.

P. Well, I will get Haldeman in here now.

D. Bob and I have talked about it, just as we are talking about it this morning. I told him I thought that you should have the facts and he agrees. Of course, we have some tough problems down the road if we—(inaudible). *[P. Let me say, though that Hunt [unintelligible] hard line, and that a convicted felon is going to go out and squeal [unintelligible] as we about this [unintelligible] decision [unintelligible] turns on that.]* Let me say (unintelligible) How do we handle all (unintelligible) who knew all about this in advance? Let me have some of your thoughts on that.

D. Well we can always, you know, on the other side charge them with blackmailing us. This is absurd stuff they are saying, and

*   *   *

P. See, the way you put it out here, letting it all hang out, it may never get there.

     *   *

P. *That's right. You see, even the way you put it out here, of course if it all came out, it may never, it may not—never, never get there.*

*   *   *

Haldeman Entrance

(Haldeman enters the room)

P. I was talking to John about this whole situation and he said if we can get away from the bits and pieces that have broken out. *and I think, we, uh, so that we can get away from the bits and pieces that have broken out.* He is right in recommending that there be a meeting at the very first possible time. I realize Ehrlichman is still out in California but, what is today? Is tomorrow Thursday?

H. (unintelligible)

D. That's right.

P. He does get back. Could we do it Thursday? This meeting—you can't do it today, can you?

D. I don't think so. I was suggesting a meeting with Mitchell.

P. Mitchell, Ehrlichman, yourself and Bob, that is all. Now, Mitchell has to be there because he is seriously involved and we are trying to keep him with us. We have to see how we handle it from here on. We are in the process of having to determine which way to go, and John has thought it through as well as he can. I don't want Moore (Richard A. Moore, special presidential counsel) there on this occasion. You haven't told Moore all of this, have you?

D. Moore's got, by being with me, has more bits and pieces I have had
to give him.

P. Right.

D. Because he is making judgments—

P. The point is when you get down to the PR, once you decide it,
what to do, we can let him know so forth and so on. But it is the
kind of thing that I think what really has to happen is for you to
sit down with those three and for you to tell them exactly what you
told me.

D. Uh, huh.

P. It may take him about 35 or 40 minutes. In other words he knows,
John knows, about everything and also what all the potential
criminal liabilities are, whether it is—like that thing—what, about
obstruction?

D. Obstruction of justice. Right.

P. So forth and so on. I think that's best. Then we have to see what
the line is. Whether the line is one of continuing to run a kind of
stone wall, *[a total stone wall,]* and take the heat from that,
having in mind the fact that there are vulnerable points there; the
vulnerable points being, the first vulnerable points would be obvious. That would be one of the defendents, either Hunt, because
he is most vulnerable in my opinion, might blow the whistle and
his price is pretty high, but at least we can buy the time *[but at
least we should buy the time]* on that as I pointed out to John.
Apparently, who is dealing with Hunt at the moment now? Colson's—

*   *   *

D. Well, Mitchell's lawyer and Colson's lawyer both.

*   *

D. *Well, uh, Mitchell's lawyer and, uh.*

P. *Colson's lawyer [unintelligible]*

D. *Colson's lawyer, both.*

*   *   *

P. Who is familiar with him? At least he has to know before he is
sentenced.

H. Who is Colson's lawyer? Is he in his law firm?

D. David Shapiro. Right. The other day he came up and—

H. Colson has told him everything, hasn't he?

D. Yep, I gather he has. The other thing that bothered me about that
is that he is a chatterer. He came up to Fred (F.) Fielding, of my
office, at Colson's going away party. I didn't go over there. It was
the Blair House the other night. He said to Fred, he said, "well,
Chuck has had some mighty serious words with his friend Howard
and has had some mighty serious messages back." Now, how does
he know what Fielding knows? Because Fielding knows virtually
nothing.

P. Well,—

H. That is where your dangers lie, in all these stupid human errors developing.

Nixon: Secretaries May Crack

P. Sure. The point is Bob, let's face it, the secretaries, the assistants know all of this. The principals may be as hard as a rock, but you never know when they, or some of their people may crack. But, we'll see, we'll see. Here we have the Hunt problem that ought to be handled now. Incidentally, I do not feel that Colson should sit in this meeting. Do you agree?

D. No. I would agree.

P. Ok. How then—who does sit on Colson? Because somebody has to, don't they?

D. Chuck—

P. Talks too much.

D. I like Chuck, but I don't want Chuck to know anything that I am doing, frankly.

P. Alright.

H. I think that is right. I think you want to be careful not to give Chuck any more knowledge than he's already got.

D. I wouldn't want Chuck to even know of the meeting, frankly.

P. Ok. Fortunately, with Chuck it is very—I talk to him about many, many political things, but I have never talked with him about this sort of thing. *['cause he's, uh, he's very harmful, I mean I don't think—he must be damn sure I don't know anything. And I don't.]* Very probably, I think he must be damn sure that I didn't know anything. And I don't. In fact, I am surprised by what you told me today. From what you said, I gathered the impression, and of course your analysis does not for sure indicate that Chuck knew that it was a bugging operation [for certain.]

D. That's correct. I don't have—Chuck denies having knowledge.

P. Yet on the other side of that is that Hunt had conversations with Chuck. It may be that Hunt told Chuck that it was bugging, and so forth and so on.

D. Uh, uh, uh, uh. They were very close. They talk too much about too many things. They were intimate on this sort of—

Colson Loves To Talk

H. That's the problem. Chuck loves (unintelligible). Chuck loves what he does and he loves to talk about it.

P. He also is a name dropper. Chuck may have gone around and talked to Hunt and said, well I was talking to the President, and the President feels we ought to get information about this,...etc.

D. Well, Liddy is the same way.

P. Well, I have talked about this and that and the other thing. I have never talked to anybody, but I have talked to Chuck and John and the rest and I am sure that Chuck might have even talked to him along these lines.

H. Other than—Well, anything could have happened. I was going.

D. I would doubt that seriously.

H. I don't think he would. Chuck is a name dropper in one sense, but not in that sense. I think he very carefully keeps away from that, except when he is very intentionally bringing the President in for the President's purposes.

Colson Was The Trigger Man

P. He had the impression though apparently he, as it turns out, he was the trigger man. Or he may well have been the trigger man where he just called up and said now look here Jeb go out and get that information. And Liddy and Hunt went out and got it at that time. This was February. It must have been after—

D. This was the call to Magruder from Colson saying, "fish or cut bait." Hunt and Liddy were in his office.

H. In Colson's office?

D. In Colson's office. And he called Magruder and said, "Let's fish or cut bait in this operation. Let's get it going."

H. Oh, really?

D. Yeah. This is Magruder telling me that.

H. Of course. That—now wait, Magruder testified—

D. Chuck also told me that Hunt and Liddy were in his office when he made the call.

H. Oh, ok.

D. So it was corroborated by the principal.

H. Hunt and Liddy haven't told you that, though?

D. No.

H. You haven't talked to Hunt and Liddy?

D. I talked to Liddy once right after the incident.

P. The point is this, that it is now time, though, that Mitchell has got to sit down, and know where the hell all this thing stands, too. You see, John is concerned, as you know, about the Ehrlichman situation. It worries him a great deal because, and this is why the Hunt problem is so serious, because it had nothing to do with the campaign. It has to do with the Ellsberg case. I don't know what the hell the—(unintelligible)

H. But what I was going to say—

P. What is the answer on this? How you keep it out, I don't know. You can't keep it out if Hunt talks. You see the point is irrelevant. It has gotten to this point—

P. And in effect, look like a cover-up. So that we can't do. Now the other line, however, if you take that line, that we are not going to continue to cut our losses, that means then we have to look square in the eye as to what the hell those losses are, and see which people can—so we can avoid criminal liability. Right?

D. Right.

* * *

P. And that means keeping it off you. Herb has started this Justice thing. We've got to keep it off Herb. You have to keep it, naturally, off of Bob, off Chapin, if possible, Strachan, right?

* *

P. *And that means, we got to, we've got to keep it off of you, uh, which I [unintelligible] obstruction of justice thing. We've got to keep it off Ehrlichman. We've got to keep it, naturally, off of Bob, off Chapin, if possible, and Strachan. Right?*

* * *

D. Uh, huh

P. And Mitchell. Right?

D. Uh, huh

H. And Magruder, if you can.

P. John Dean's point is that if Magruder goes down, he will pull everybody with him.

H. That's my view. Yep, I think Jeb, I don't think he wants to. And I think he even would try not to, but I don't think he is able not to.

D. I don't think he is strong enough.

'Jackasses Who Are in Jail'

P. Another way to do it then Bob, and John realizes this, is continue to try to cut our losses. Now we have to take a look at that course of action. First it is going to require approximately a million dollars to take care of the jackasses who are in jail. That can be arranged. That could be arranged. But you realize that after we are gone, and assuming we can expend this money, then they are going to crack and it would be an unseemly story. Frankly, all the people aren't going to care that much.

D. That's right.

P. People won't care, but people are going to be talking about it, there is no question. And the second thing is, we are not going to be able to deliver on any of a clemency thing. You know Colson has gone around on this clemency thing with Hunt and the rest?

D. Hunt is now talking about being out by Christmas.

H. This year?

D. This year. He was told by O'Brien, who is my conveyor of doom back and forth, that hell, he would be lucky if he were out a year

from now, or after Ervin's hearings were over. He said how in the
Lord's name could you be commuted that quickly? He said, "Well,,
that is my commitment from Colson."

H. By Christmas of this year?

D. Yeah.

H. See that, really, that is verbal evil. *[that is very believable.]* Colson is—That is your fatal flaw in Chuck. He is an operator in expediency, and he will pay at the time and where he is to accomplish
whatever he is there to do. And that, and that's—I would believe
that he has made that commitment if Hunt says he has. I would
believe he is capable of saying that.

P. The only thing we could do with him would be to parole him like
the (unintelligible) situation. *[parole him for a period of time because of his family situation.]* But you couldn't buy clemency.
[couldn't provide clemency.]

Kleindienst Can Pull Off Paroles

D. Kleindienst has now got control of the Parole Board, and he said
to tell me we could pull paroles off now where we couldn't before.
So—

H. Kleindienst always tells you that, but I never believe it. *[Klein-
dienst always tells you that, and then never delivers.]*

P. Paroles—let the (unintelligible) worry about that. Parole, in
appearance, etc., is something I think in Hunt's case, you could do
Hunt, but you couldn't do the others. You understand.

D. Well, so much depends on how Sirica sentences. He can sentence
in a way that makes parole even impossible.

P. He can?

D. Sure. He can do all kind of permanent sentences.

P. (unintelligible)

D. Yeah. He can be a (characterization deleted) as far as the whole
thing.

H. Can't you appeal an unjust sentence as well as an unjust? *[an unjust conviction?]*

D. You have 60 days to ask the Judge to review it. There is no Appellate review of sentences.

H. There isn't?

P. The judge can review it.

H. Only the sentencing judge can review his own sentence?

P. Coming back, though, to this. So you got that hanging over. Now?
If—you see, if you let it hang there, you fight with them at all or
they part— The point is, your feeling is that we just can't continue
to pay the blackmail of these guys?

D. I think that is our great jeopardy.

P. Now, let me tell you. We could get the money. There is no problem in that. We can't provide the clemency. Money could be provided. Mitchell could provide the way to deliver it. That could be done. See what I mean?

H. Mitchell says he can't, doesn't he?

D. Mitchell says—there has been an interesting phenomena all the way along. There have been a lot of people having to pull oars and not everybody pulls them all the same time, the same way, because they develop self-interests.

H. What John is saying, everybody smiles at Dean and says well you better get something done about it.

D. That's right.

H. Mitchell is leaving Dean hanging out on him. None of us, well, maybe we are doing the same thing to you.

D. That's right.

H. But let me say this. I don't see how there is any way that you can have the White House or anybody presently in the White House involved in trying to gin out this money.

D. We are already deeply enough in that. That is the problem, Bob.

P. I thought you said—

H. We need more money.

*   *   *

D. Well, in fact when—

*   *

P. *I thought you said you could handle the money?*

D. *Well, in fact when—*

*   *   *

P. Kalmbach?

D. Well, Kalmbach

H. He's not the one.

D. No, but when they ran out of that money, as you know it came out of *[as you know they came after]* the 350,000 that was over here.

P. And they knew that? *[And they used that, right?]*

D. And I had to explain what it was for before I could get the money.

LaRue Has Money Back

H. In the first place, that was put back to LaRue.

D. That's right.

H. It was put back where it belonged. It wasn't all returned in a lump sum. It was put back in pieces.

D. That's right.

P. Then LaRue used it for this other purpose?

D. That's right.

P. *Well, I think they can get that.*

H. And the balance was all returned to LaRue, but we don't have any receipt for that. We have no way of proving it.

D. And I think that was because of self-interest over there. Mitchell—

H. Mitchell told LaRue not to take it at all.

D. That's right.

H. That is what you told me.

D. That's right. And then don't give them a receipt.

P. Then what happened? LaRue took it, and then what?

D. It was sent back to him because we just couldn't continue piecemeal giving. Every time I asked for it I had to tell Bob I needed some, or something like that, and he had to get Gordon Strachan to go up to his safe and take it out and take it over to LaRue. And it was just a forever operation.

P. Why did they take it all? *[Why didn't they take it all to him?]*

D. I just sent it along to them.

H. We had been trying to get a way to get that money back out of here anyway. And what this was supposed to be was loans. This was immediate cash needs that was going to be replenished. Mitchell was arguing that you can't take the $350,000 back until it is all replenished. Isn't that right?

D. That is right.

H. They hadn't replenished, so we just gave it all back anyway.

P. I had a feeling we could handle this one.

D. Well, first of all, I would have a hell of a time proving it. That is one thing.

P. I just have a feeling on it. Well, it sounds like a lot of money, a million dollars. Let me say that I think we could get that. I know money is hard to raise. But the point is, what we do on that—Let's look at the hard problem—

D. That has been, thus far, the most difficult problem. That is why these fellows have been on and off the reservation all the way along.

P. So the hard place is this. Your feeling at the present time is the hell with the million dollars. I would just say to these fellows I am sorry it is all off and let them talk. Alright?

D. Well,—

P. That's the way to do it isn't it, if you want to do it clean?

'What Do You Need Tomorrow?'

H. That's the way. We can live with it, because the problem with the blackmailing, that is the thing we kept raising with you when you said there was a money problem. When you said we need $20,000, or $100,000, or something. We said yeah, that is what you need today. But what do you need tomorrow or next year or five years from now?

P. How long?

D. That was just to get us through November 7th, though.

H. That's what we had to have to get through November 7th. There is no question.

D. These fellows could have sold out to the Democrats for one-half a million.

P. These fellows though, as far as what has happened up to this time, are covered on their situation, because the Cuban Committee did this for them during the election?

D. Well, yeah. We can put that together. That isn't of course quite the way it happened, but—

P. I know, but that's the way it is going to have to happen.

D. It's going to have to happen.

P. Finally, though, so you let it happen. So then they go, and so what happens? Do they go out and start blowing the whistle on everybody else? Isn't that what it really gets down to?

D. Uh, huh.

P. So that would be the clean way—Right!

D. Ah—

P. Is that—you would go so far as to recommend that?

D. No, I wouldn't. I don't think necessarily that is the cleanest way. One of the things that I think we all need to discuss is, is there some way that we can get our story before a Grand Jury, so that they can really have investigated the White House on this. I must say that I have not really thought through that alternative. We have been so busy on the other containment situation.

P. John Ehrlichman, of course, has raised the point of another Grand Jury. I just don't know how you could do it. On what basis. I would call for it, but I—

D. That would be out of the question.

Nixon Wants Another Grand Jury

P. I hate to leave with differences in view of all this stripped land. I could understand this, but I think I want another Grand Jury proceeding and we will have the White House appear before them. Is that right John?

D. Uh huh.

P. That is the point, see. Of course! That would make the difference. I want everybody in the White House called. And that gives you a reason not to have to go before the Ervin and Baker Committee. It puts it in an executive session, in a sense.

H. Right.

D. That's right.

H. And there would be some rules of evidence, aren't there?

D. There are rules of evidence.

P. Rules of evidence and you have lawyers.

H. You are in a hell of a lot better position than you are up there.

D. No, you can't have a lawyer before the Grand Jury.

P. Oh, no. That's right.

H. But you do have rules of evidence. You can refuse to talk.

D. You can take the 5th Amendment.

P. That's right.

H. You can say you have forgotten too can't you?

D. Sure but you are chancing a very high risk for perjury situation.

P. But you can say I don't remember. *Just be damned sure you say I don't remember;* You can say I can't recall. I can't give you answer to that that I can recall.

H. You have the same perjury thing on the Hill don't you?

D. That's right.

P. Oh hell, yes.

H. And the Ervin Committee is a hell of a lot worse to deal with.

D. That's right.

P. The Grand Jury thing has its in view of this thing. Suppose we have a Grand Jury thing. What would that do to the Ervin Committee? Would it go right ahead?

D. Probably. Probably.

P. If we do that on a Grand Jury, we would then have a much better cause in terms of saying, "Look, this is a Grand Jury, in which the prosecutor—How about a special prosecutor? We could use Peterson, or use another one. You see he is probably suspect. Would you call in another prosecutor?

Dean: I Want Petersen On Our Side

D. I would like to have Petersen on our side, if I did this thing. *[I would like to have Petersen on our side, advising us [laughs] frankly.]*

P. Well, Petersen is honest. There isn't anybody about to question him is there?

D. No, but he will get a barrage when these Watergate hearings start.

P. But he can go up and say that he has been told to go further with the Grand Jury and go in to this and that and the other thing. Call everybody in the White House, and I want them to come and I want them to go to the Grand Jury.

D. This may happen without even our calling for it when these—

P. Vesco?

D. No. Well, that is one possibility. But also when these people go back before the Grand Jury here, they are going to pull all these criminal defendants back before the Grand Jury and immunize them.

P. Who will do this? *[And immunize them: Why? Who? Are you going to—On what?]*

D. The U.S. Attorney's Office will.

P. To do what?

D. To let them talk about anything further they want to talk about.

P. But what do they gain out of it?

D. Nothing.

P. To hell with it!

D. They're going to stonewall it, as it now stands. Excepting Hunt. That's why his threat. *[That's the leverage in his threat.]*

H. It's Hunt opportunity.

'Come Up With $120,000'

P. That's why for your immediate things you have no choice but to come up with the $120,000, or whatever it is. Right?

D. That's right.

P. Would you agree that that's the prime thing *[the buy time thing]* that you damn well better get that done? *[But fast.]*

D. Obviously he ought to be given some signal anyway.

P. (Expletive deleted), get it. In a way that—who is going to talk to him? Colson? He is the one who is supposed to know him?

D. Well, Colson doesn't have any money though. That is the thing. That's been one of the real problems. They haven't been able to raise a million dollars in cash. (Unintelligible) has been just a very difficult problem as we discussed before. Mitchell has talked to Pappas, and John asked me to call him last night after our discussion and after you had met with John to see where that was. And I said, "Have you talked to Pappas?" He was at home, and Martha picked up the phone so it was all in code. I said, "Have you talked to the Greek?" And he said, "Yes, I have." I said, "Is the Greek bearing gifts?" He said, "Well, I'll call you tomorrow on that."

P. Well look, what it is you need on that? When—I am not familiar with the money situation.

D. It sounds easy to do and everyone is out there doing it and that is where our breakdown has come every time.

P. Well, if you had it, how would you get it to somebody?

D. Well, I got it to LaRue by just leaving it in mail boxes and things like that. *Well, I gather LaRue just leaves it in mail boxes and things like that, and tells Hunt to go pick it up.* And someone phones Hunt to come and pick it up. As I say, we are a bunch of amateurs in that business.

H. That is the thing that we thought Mitchell ought to be able to know how to find somebody who would know how to do all that sort of thing, because none of us know how to.

D. That's right. You have to wash the money. You can get a $100,000 out of a bank, and it all comes in serialized bills.

P. I understand.

D. And that means you have to go to Vegas with it or a bookmaker in New York City. I have learned all these things after the fact. I will be in great shape for the next time around.

H. (Expletive deleted)

P. Well, of course you have a surplus from the campaign. Is there any other money hanging around? *[But if there's any other money hanging around—]*

H. Well, what about the money we moved back out of here?

D. Apparently, there is some there. That might be what they can use. I don't know how much is left.

P. Kalmbach must have some.

D. Kalmbach doesn't have a cent.

P. He doesn't?

D. *See the new law—*

H. That $350,000 that we moved out was all that we saved. Because they were afraid to because of this. That is the trouble. We are so (adjective deleted) square that we get caught at everything.

P. Could I suggest this though: let me go back around—

H. Be careful—

P. The Grand Jury thing has a feel. Right? It says we are cooperating well with the Grand Jury.

D. Once we start down any route that involves the criminal justice system, we've got to have full appreciation that there is really no control over that. While we did an amazing job of keeping us in on the track *[keeping the thing on the track]* before while the FBI was out there, and that was the only way they found out where they were going—*[and that was only because...I had a [unintelligible] of where they were going.]*

P. But you've got to (unintelligible). Let's take it to a Grand Jury. *[Right. But you haven't got that now because everybody else is going to have a lawyer. Let's take the new Grand Jury.]* A new Grand Jury would call Magruder again, wouldn't it?

D. Based on what information? For example, what happens if Dean goes in and gives a story. You know, that here is the way it all came about. It was supposed to be a legitimate operation and it obviously got off the track. I heard—before, but told Haldeman that we shouldn't be involved in it. Then Magruder can be called in and questioned again about all those meetings and the like. And it again he'll begin to change his story as to what he told the Grand Jury the last time, that way, he is in a perjury situation.

H. Except that is the best leverage you've got with Jeb. He has to keep his story straight or he is in real trouble, unless they get smart and give him immunity. If they immunize Jeb, then you have an interesting problem.

D. We have control over who gets immunized. I think they wouldn't do that without our—

P. But you see the Grand Jury proceeding achieves this thing. If we go down that road—(unintelligible) *[I'm just thinking of how how the President looks.]* We would be cooperating. We would be cooperating through a Grand Jury. Everybody would be behind us.

That is the proper way to do this. It should be done in the Grand Jury, not up there under the kleig lights of the Committee. Nobody questions a Grand Jury. And then we would insist on Executive Privilege before the Committee, flat out say, "No we won't do that. It is a matter before the Grand Jury, and so on, and that's that."

H. Then you go the next step. Would we then—The Grand Jury is in executive session?

D. Yes, they are secret sessions.

H. Alright, then would we agree to release our Grand Jury transcripts?

D. We don't have the authority to do that. That is up to the Court and the Court, thus far, has not released the ones from the last Grand Jury.

P. They usually are not.

D. It would be highly unusual for a Grand Jury to come out. What usually happens is—

H. But a lot of the stuff from the Grand Jury came out.

P. Leaks.

D. It came out of the U.S. Attorney's office, more than the Grand Jury. We don't know. Some of the Grand Jurors may have blabbered, but they were—

P. Bob, it's not so bad. It's bad, but it's not the worst place.

H. I was going the other way there. I was going to say that it might be to our interest to get it out.

Leaks Could Be Controlled

P. Well, we could easily do that. Leak out certain stuff. We could pretty much control that. We've got so much more control. Now, the other possibility is not to go to the Grand Jury. We have three things. (1) You just say the hell with it, we can't raise the money, sorry Hunt you can say what you want, and so on. He blows the whistle. Right?

D. Right.

P. If that happens, that raises some possibilities about some criminal liabilities, because he is likely to say a hell of a lot of things and will certainly get Magruder in on it.

D. It will get Magruder. It will start the whole FBI investigation going again.

P. Yeah. It would get Magruder, and it could possibly get Colson.

D. That's right. Could get—

P. Get Mitchell. Maybe. No.

H. Hunt can't get Mitchell.

D. I don't think Hunt can get Mitchell. Hunt's got a lot of hearsay.

P. Ehrlichman? *[He could on the other thing—except Ehrlichman [unintelligible]]*

D. Krogh could go down in smoke.

P. On the other hand—Krogh says it is a national security matter. Is that what he says?

D. Yeah, but that won't sell ultimately in a criminal situation. It may be mitigating on sentences but it won't, in the main matter.

P. Seems we're going around the track. You have no choice on Hunt but to try to keep—

D. Right now, we have no choice.

P. But my point is, do you ever have any choice on Hunt? That is the point. No matter what we do here now, John, whatever he wants if he doesn't get it—immunity. *[No matter what we do here now, John,...Hunt eventually, if he isn't going to get commuted and so forth,]* etc., he is going to blow the whistle.

D. What I have been trying to conceive of is how we could lay out everything we know in a way that we have told the Grand Jury or somebody else, so that if a Hunt blows, so what's new? It's already been told to a Grand Jury and they found no criminal liability and they investigated it in full. We're sorry fellows—And we don't, it doesn't—

*   *   *

P. (Unintelligible) for another year.

D. That's right.

P. And Hunt would get off by telling them the Ellsberg thing.

D. No Hunt would go to jail for that too—he should understand that.

P. That's a point too. I don't think I would throw that out. I don't think we need to go into everything. (adjective deleted) thing Hunt has done.

D. No.

P. Some of the things in the national security area. Yes.

H. Whoever said that anyway. We laid the groundwork for that.

*   *

D. *We don't, it doesn't—*

P. *Including Ehrlichman's use of Hunt on the other deal?*

D. *That's right.*

P. *You'd throw that out?*

D. *Uh, well, Hunt will go to jail for that too—he's got to understand that.*

*   *   *

P. But here is the point, John. Let's go the other angle, is to decide if you open up the Grand Jury: first, it won't be any good, it won't be believed. And then you will have two things going: the Grand Jury and the other things, committee, etc. The Grand Jury appeals to me from the standpoint, the President makes the move. All these charges being bandied about, etc., the best thing to do is that I have asked the Grand Jury to look into any further charges. All charges have been raised. That is the place to do it, and not before a Committee of the Congress. Right?

D. Yeah.

Third Opinion: Endure It

P. Then, however, we may say, (expletive deleted), we can't risk that, or she'll break loose there. That leaves you to your third thing.

D. Hunker down and fight it.

P. Hunker down and fight it and what happens? Your view is that it is not really a viable option.

D. It is a high risk. It is a very high risk.

P. Your view is that what will happen on it, that it's going to come out. That something is going to break loose, and—

D. Something is going to break and—

P. It will look like the President

D. is covering up—

P. Has covered up a huge (unintelligible) *[uh, uh, this—Right?]*

D. That's correct.

H. But you can't (inaudible) *[contain the charge.]*

P. You have now moved away from the hunker down—

D. Well, I have moved to the point that we certainly have to take a harder look at the other alternative, which we haven't before.

P. The other alternative is—

D. Yes, the other choices.

'Middle Ground of Grand Jury'

P. As a matter of fact, your middle ground of Grand Jury. I suppose there is a middle ground of a public statement without a transcript. *[but without a grand jury.]*

D. What we need also, Sir

H. But John's view is if we make the public statement that we talked about this morning, the thing we talked about last night—each of us in our hotel, *[If each of us...make moves,]* he says that will immediately lead to a Grand Jury.

P. Fine—alright, fine.

H. As soon as we make that statement, they will have to call a Grand Jury.

P. They may even make a public statement *[Then maybe we make a public statement]* before the Grand Jury, in order to—

H. So it looks like we are trying to do it over.

D. Here are public statements, and we want full Grand Jury investigations by the U.S. Attorney's office.

P. If we said that the reason we had delayed this is until after the sentencing— You see that the point is that the reason time is of the essence, we can't play around on this. If they are going to sentence on Friday, we are going to have to move on the (expletive deleted) thing pretty fast. See what I mean?

D. That's right.

P. So we really have a time problem.

D. The other thing is that the Attorney General could call Sirica, and say that, "The government has some major developments that it is considering. Would you hold sentencing for two weeks?" If we set ourselves on a course of action.

P. Yep, yep.

D. See, the sentencing may be in the, wrong perspective right now. I don't know for certain, but I just think there are some things that I am not at liberty to discuss with you, but I want to ask that the Court withhold two weeks sentencing.

H. So then the story is out: "Sirica delays sentencing Watergate"—

D. I think that could be handled in a way between Sirica and Kleindienst that it would not get out. Kleindienst apparently does have good rapport with Sirica. He has never talked since this case developed, but—

H. or P. *Why not?*

P. That's helpful. So Kleindienst should say that he is working on something and would like to have a week. I wouldn't take two weeks. I would take a week.

D. I will tell you the person that I feel we could use his counsel on this, because he understands the criminal process better than anybody over here does.

P. Petersen?

Petersen Is Crucial

D. Yes, Petersen. It is awkward for Petersen. He is the head of the criminal division. But to discuss some of things with him, we may well want to remove him from the head of the Criminal Division and say, "That related to this case, you will have no relation." Give him some special assignment over here where he could sit down and say, "Yes, this is an obstruction, but it couldn't be proved," so on and so forth. We almost need him out of there to take his counsel. I don't think he would want that, but he is the most knowledgeable.

P. How could we get him out?

D. I think an appeal directly to Henry—

P. Why couldn't the President call him in as Special Counsel to the White House for the purpose of conducting an investigation. Rather than a Dean in office, having him the Special Counsel to represent us before the Grand Jury.

D. I have thought of that. That is one possibility.

H. On the basis that Dean has now become a principal, rather than a Counsel.

D. I could recommend that to you.

H. Petersen is planning to leave, anyway.

D. Is he?

P. You could recommend it and he could come over and I would say, "Now Petersen, we want you to get to the bottom of the damn thing. Call another Grand Jury or anything else." Correct? Well, now you gotta know whether Kleindienst can get Sirica to hold off. Right? Second, you have to get Mitchell down here. And you and Ehrlichman and Mitchell by tomorrow.

H. Why don't we do that tonight?

P. I don't think you can get Mitchell that soon, can you?

H. John?

P. It would be helpful if you could.

D. It would be better if he could come down this afternoon.

P. It would be very helpful to get going. Actually, I am perfectly willing to meet with the group. I don't know whether I should.

H. Do you think you want to?

P. Or maybe have Dean report to me at the end. See what conclusions you have reached. I think I need to stay away from the Mitchell subject *[Mitchell side of it]* at this point, do you agree?

D. Uh, huh.

D. Unless we see, you know, some sort of a reluctant dragon there.

H. You might meet with the rest of us, but I am not sure you would want to meet with John in this group at this time. *[OK, let me see if I can get it done.]*

Need For New Plan After Election

P. Alright. Fine. And my point is that I think it is good, frankly, to consider these various options. And then, once you decide on the right plan, you say, "John," you say, "No doubts about the right plan before the election. You handled it just right. You contained it. And now after the election we have to have another plan. Because we can't for four years have this thing eating away." *[we can't have this thing—you're going to be eaten away.]* We can't do it.

H. We should change that a little bit. John's point is exactly right. The erosion here now is going to you, and that is the thing that we have to turn off at whatever cost. We have to turn it off at the lowest cost we can, but at whatever cost it takes.

D. That's what we have to do.

P. Well, the erosion is inevitably going to come here, apart from anything and all the people saying well the Watergate isn't a major issue. It isn't. But it will be. It's bound to. (Unintelligible) *[...Although Ron Ziegler]* has to go out. Delaying is the greater danger to the White House area. We don't, I say that the White House can't do it. Right?

D. Yes, Sir.

March 22, 1973

*Following is the text of the end portion of the House Judiciary Com-
mittee's transcript of the conversation of this day. This material does not
appear in the White House transcript of the conversation. "P" is the
President, "M" is John Mitchell and "D" is John Dean.*

M. *Believe me, it's a lot of work.*

P. *Oh, great. I may [unintelligible]. Well, let me tell you, you've done
a hell of a job here.*

P. *I didn't mean for you. I thought we had a boy here. No, you, uh,
John, uh, carried a very, very heavy load. Uh, both Johns as a matter of fact, but, uh, I was going to say, uh, uh, John Dean is, uh,
[unintelligible] got—put the fires out, almost got the damn thing
nailed down till past the election and so forth. We all know what it
is. Embarrassing God damn thing the way it went, and so forth.
But, in my view, uh, some of it will come out; we will survive it.
That's the way it is. That's the way you've got to look at it.*

D. *We were within a few miles months ago, but, uh, we're—*

P. *The point is, get the God damn thing over with.*

D. *That's right.*

P. *That's the thing to do. That's the other thing that I like about this.
I'd like to get— But you really would draw the line on— But, I
know, we can't make a complete cave and have the people go up
there and testify. You would agree on that?*

M. *I agree.*

P. *You agree on that, John?*

D. *If we're in the posture of everything short of giving them public session [unintelligible] and the whole deal. You're not hiding anything.*

P. *Yeah. Particularly if, particularly if we have the Dean statement.*

D. *And they've been given out.*

P. *And your view about the Dean statement is to give that to the
Committee and not make it public, however.*

D. *That's correct. I think that's—*

P. *And say it's, uh—*

M. *Give it to the Committee for the purpose—*

P. *—the purpose of their investigation.*

M. *[Unintelligible] to limit the number of witnesses*

P. *Yeah.*

M. *which are called up there, instead of a buck-shot operation.*

P. *And say here, and also say, "This may help you in your investigation."*

M. *Right.*

P. *"This is everything we know, Mr. Senator." That's what I was
preparing to say. "This is everything we know; I know nothing more.
This is the whole purpose, and that's that. If you need any further
information, my, our counsel will furnish it, uh, that is not in here."*

It'd be tempting to—"but this is all we know. Now, in addition to that, you are welcome to have, have people, but you've got to have—" I think that the best way to have it is in executive session, but incidentally, you say executive session for those out of Government as well as in?

M. *That's right.*

P. *Chapin and Colson should be called in.*

D. *[Unintelligible]*

P. *I would think so.*

M. *Sure. Because you have the same problem.*

P. *You see we ask—but your point—we ask for, uh, the privilege, and at least, you know, we, we, our statement said it applies to former as well as present [unintelligible]*

D. *Now, our statement—you leave a lot of flexibility that you normally—for one thing, taking the chance appearing, and uh, however, informal relationships will always be worked out [unintelligible]*

P. *Informal relations.*

D. *That's right.*

M. *You have the same basis—*

P. *Well, it might. When I say that, that, that—the written interrogatory thing is not as clear [unintelligible] maybe Ervin is making it that way, but I think that's based on what may be, uh, we said that the—I don't think I said we would only write, in, in the press conference, written interrogatories.*

D. *That's right. I don't think—*

P. *I didn't say that at all.*

D. *Ervin just jumped to that conclusion as a result of my letter to, uh—*

P. *I think that's what it was.*

D. *I think that's what's happened.*

P. *Not that your letter was wrong—it was right. But, uh, the whole written interrogatory, we didn't discuss other possibilities.*

M. *With respect to your ex-employes, you have the same problem of getting into areas of privileged communications. You certainly can make a good case for keeping them in executive session.*

P. *That's right.*

M. *[Unintelligible]*

P. *And, and in this sense the precedent for working—you can do it in cases in the future, which [unintelligible] executive session, and then the privilege can be raised without having, uh, on a legal basis, without having the guilt by the Fifth Amendment, not like pleading the Fifth Amendment—*

M. *Right.*

P. *the implication always being raised.*

M. *[Unintelligible] and self-protection in that view?*

P. *What? Yeah.*

D. *[Unintelligible] Fifth Amendment.*

P. That's right. That's what we're going to do here.

M. Those—boy, this thing has to be turned around. Got to get you off the lid.

P. Right.

D. All right.

P. All right, fine, Chuck.

M. Good to see you.

P. How long were you in Florida? Just, uh—

M. I was down there overnight. I was four hours on the witness stand testifying for the Government in these, uh, racket cases involving wiretapping. The God damn fool Judge down there let them go all over the lot and ask me any questions that they wanted to. Just ridiculous. You know, this had, all has to do with the discretionary act of signing a piece of paper that I'm authorized by the statute. There were 27 hood lawyers that questioned me.

P. You know, uh, the, uh, you, you can say when I [unintelligible] I was going to say that the, uh— [Picks up phone] Can you get me Prime Minister Trudeau in Canada, please. [Hangs up] I was going to say that Dean has really been, uh, something on this.

M. That he has, Mr. President, no question about it. He's a very—

P. Son-of-a-bitching tough thing.

M. You've got a very solid guy that's handled some tough things. And I also want to say these lawyers that you have think very highly of him. I know that John spends his time with certain ones—

P. Dean? Discipline is very high.

M. Parkinson, O'Brien.

P. Yes, Dean says it's great. Well, you know I feel for all the people, you know, I mean everybody that's involved. Hell, is all we're doing is their best to [unintelligible] and so forth. [Unintelligible]. That's that's why I can't let you go, go down. John? It's all right. Come in.

D. Uh—

P. Did you find out anything?

D. I was, I went over to Ziegler's office. They have an office over there. Paul O'Brien'll be down here in a little while to see you. I'm going over to Ziegler's office and finish this up now.

M. Are you coming back?

D. Yes, I'll come back over here then.

P. Yeah. Well, when you come back—he can, uh, is that office open for John now?

D. Yes.

Nixon: Stonewall It, Plead the 5th, Save the Plan

P. Then he can go over there as soon [unintelligible] this. But, uh, the, uh, the one thing I don't want to do is to—Now let me make this clear. I, I, I thought it was, uh, very, uh, very cruel thing as it turned out—although at the time I had to tell [unintelligible]—what happened to Adams. I don't want it to happen with Watergate—the Watergate matter. I think he made a, made a mistake, but he shouldn't have been sacked, he shouldn't have been—And, uh, for that reason, I am perfectly willing to—I don't give a shit what happens. I want you all to stonewall it, let them plead the Fifth Amendment, cover-up or anything else, if it'll save it—save the plan. That's the whole point. On the other hand, uh, uh, I would prefer, as I said to you, that you do it the other way. And I would particularly prefer to do it that other way if it's going to come out that way anyway. And that my view, that, uh, with the number of jackass people that they've got that they can call, they're going to—The story they get out through leaks, charges and so forth, and innuendos, will be a hell of a lot worse than the story they're going to get out by just letting it out there.

M. Well—

P. I don't know. But that's, uh, you know, up to this point, the whole theory has been containment, as you know, John.

M. Yeah.

P. And now, now we're shifting. As far as I'm concerned, actually from a personal standpoint, if you weren't making a personal sacrifice—it's unfair—Haldeman and Dean. That's what Eisenhower—that's all he cared about. He only cared about—Christ, "Be sure he was clean." Both in the fund thing and the Adams thing. But I don't look at it that way. And I just—that's the thing I am really concerned with. We're going to protect our people, if we can.

M. Well, the important thing is to get you up above it for this first operation. And then to see where the chips fall and, uh, and, uh, get through this Grand Jury thing up here. Uh, then the Committee is another question. [Telephone rings] What we ought to have is a reading as to what is [telephone rings] coming out of this Committee and we, if we handle the cards as it progresses. [Telephone rings]

P. Yeah. But anyway, we'll go on. And, uh, I think in order—it'll probably turn out just as well, getting them in the position of, even though it hurts for a little while.

M. Yeah.

P. You know what I mean. People say, "Well, the President's [unintelligible]," and so forth. Nothing is lasting. You know people get so disturbed about [unintelligible]. Now, when we do move [unintelligible] we can move, in a, in a, in a, in the proper way.

M. If you can do it in a controlled way it would help and good, but, but, but the other thing you have to remember is that this stuff is going to come out of that Committee, whether—

P. That's right.

M. And it's going to come out no matter what.

P. As if, as if I, and then it looks like I tried to keep it from coming out.

M. That's why it's important that that statement go up to the Committee.

P. *[Picks up phone.] Hello. I don't want to talk. Sure. [Hangs up.] Christ. Sure, we'll—*

M. *It's like these Gray, Gray hearings. They had it five days running that the files were turned over to John Dean, just five days running—the same story.*

P. *Same story.*

M. *Right.*

P. *The files should have been turned over.*

M. *Just should have, should have demanded them. You should have demanded all of them.*

P. *(Unintelligible) what the hell was he doing as counsel to the President without getting them? He was—I told him to conduct an investigation, and he did.*

M. *I know.*

P. *Well, it's like everything else.*

M. *Anything else for us to—*

P. *Get on that other thing. If Baker can—Baker is not proving much of a need up to this point. He's smart enough.*

M. *Howard is smart enough, but, uh, we've got to carry him. Uh, I think he has and I've been puzzling over a way to have a liaison with him and, and, uh—*

Baker Thinks We're Tapping His Phone

P. *He won't talk on the phone with anybody, according to Kleindienst. He thinks his phone is tapped.*

M. *He does?*

P. *Who's tapping his phone?*

M. *I don't know.*

P. *Who would he think would tap his phone? I guess maybe that we would.*

M. *I don't doubt that.*

P. *He must think that Ervin—*

M. *Maybe.*

P. *Or, or a newspaper.*

M. *Newspaper, or, or the Democratic party, or somebody. There's got to be somebody to liaison with Kleindienst to get in a position where—It's all right from foreknowledge through Kleindienst.*

P. *You really wonder if you take Wally Johnson and, uh—He's a pretty good boy, isn't he?*

M. *Yeah. [Unintelligible]*

P. *You might, you might throw that out to Dean. Dean says he doesn't want to be in such a, such a public position. He talked to the Attorney General [unintelligible] Wally Johnson. And he said that—*

M. *Well, he will be in the Department.*

P. *Yeah.*

M. *Talking to the Department.*

P. *(Unintelligible) Mansfield's down there—*

M. *Everything else under control?*

P. *Yeah, we're all doing fine. I think, though, that as long as, uh, everyone and so forth, is a, uh—(unintelligible) still (unintelligible)*

M. *All of Washington—the public interest in this thing, you know.*

P. *Isn't Nash, (unintelligible) Earl Nash worries the shit out of us here in regard, regarding (unintelligible)*

M. *Just in time.*

P. *But the point is that, uh, I don't—There's no need for him to testify. I have nothing but intuition, but hell, I don't know. I, but—Again you really have to protect the Presidency, too. That's the point.*

M. *Well this does no violence to the Presidency at all, this concept—*

P. *This whole scenario.*

M. *Yeah.*

P. *No, it, uh, uh, d—, that's what I mean. The purpose of this scenario is to clean the Presidency. (Unintelligible) what they say "All right. Here's the report, we're going to cooperate with the Committee," and so forth and so on. The main thing is to answer (unintelligible) and that should be a God damned satisfactory answer, John.*

M. *It should be.*

P. *Shouldn't it.*

M. *It answers all of their complaints they've had to date.*

P. *That's right. They get cross-examination.*

M. *Right. They get everything but the public spectacle.*

P. *Public spectacle. And the reason we don't have that is because you have to argue.*

M. *They have to argue and—*

P. *On a legal and you don't want them to be, uh, used as a, uh, uh, for unfairly, to, to have somebody charged.*

M. *It's our fault that you have somebody charged with not answering the Committee's questions (unintelligible) to John, make sure you put it in, make sure that you put it again in the argument, the clean record, and that's the reason why you have an executive session. Because the record that comes out of it is clean. But, uh, in areas of dispute—*

P. *I'd rather think, though, that all of their yakking about this, uh, we often said, John—we've got problems.*

M. *[Unintelligible]*

P. *Might cost them [unintelligible]. Think of their problems. They, those bastards are really—they're just really something. Where is their leadership?*

M. *They don't have any leadership, and they're leaping on every new issue....*

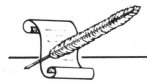

May

SUPREME COURT ON WIRETAPPING
May 13, 1974

"The Attorney General, or any Assistant Attorney General specially designated by the Attorney General, may authorize an application to a federal judge...for...an order authorizing or approving the interception of wire or oral communications," stated Title III of the Omnibus Crime Control and Safe Streets Act of 1968. Passed over the vigorous opposition of President Lyndon B. Johnson and his attorney general, Ramsey Clark, this language authorized official law enforcement use of wiretaps and electronic surveillance under the supervision of the federal courts. Even as Johnson signed the massive bill, he asked Congress to repeal this section. Clark refused to make use of the new powers. But not so his successor.

John N. Mitchell, attorney general during President Nixon's first term, seized with enthusiasm this new law enforcement tool. In October 1970, he called it "a key factor" in the administration's effort to crack down on organized crime. "It has amply demonstrated its effectiveness" and "has won an appropriate place in the American legal structure." Reported use of wiretaps mushroomed. Whereas 33 wiretaps were authorized by the Nixon administration in 1969, 206 were reported in 1972.

But Mitchell was careless about observing the letter of this 1968 law—and often, when he or a specially designated assistant attorney general were unavailable, the application for the wiretap would be signed by some other assistant. This fact came to light after persons who were the subjects of such surveillance were indicted and challenged use of this evidence against them. Several of these defendants argued that disregard of the precise statutory procedure for obtaining court approval of the wiretap meant that—as the 1968 law provided—the wiretap was unlawful and its products must be suppressed.

On May 13, 1974, a unanimous Supreme Court agreed with the defendants in a move predicted to require the reversal of convictions, the dropping, or the complete rebuilding, of 60 federal cases involving 626 persons—most of whom were charged with some involvement in organized crime. "Congress did not intend the power to authorize wiretap applications to be exercised by any individuals other than the Attorney General or an Assistant Attorney General specially designated by him," wrote Justice Byron R. White, himself once deputy attorney general. "Evidence secured by wire interceptions pursuant to a court order issued in response to an application which was, in fact, not authorized by one of the statutorily designated officials must be suppressed," White continued.

Authorization Violation

In the case at hand, the surveillance of suspected drug dealer Dominic Nicholas Giordano was approved on the basis of an application signed by Mitchell's executive assistant, Sol Lindenbaum, not Assistant Attorney General Will Wilson, as it appeared to be. "Plainly enough," White wrote, "the executive assistant is neither the Attorney General nor a specially designated Assistant Attorney General." The attorney general could delegate other duties, but not this one: Congress set up a "critical precondition" for any court-approved wiretap—"the mature judgment of a particular responsible Department of Justice official." The court also rejected the administration's argument that even if the approval procedure had not been proper, the evidence obtained by the wiretaps should not be suppressed. Citing the language of Title III, White stated "that the provision for pre-application approval [by specific persons] was intended to play a central role in the statutory scheme and that suppression must follow when it is shown that this statutory requirement has been ignored."

The court was divided, 5-4, over whether the same ruling applied to information obtained from surveillance approved as an extension of the original wiretap. The five-man majority felt that that information should also be suppressed. Not so the dissenters, all four Nixon nominees. Justice Lewis F. Powell Jr., Chief Justice Warren E. Burger and Justices Harry A. Blackmun and William H. Rehnquist found the extensions sufficiently justified by independent evidence other than that obtained by the original surveillance and felt that it should not be suppressed. (U.S. v. Giordano)

In a related case involving two cases of surveillance in which the official authorizing the application for the wiretap was misidentified, the court again unanimously invalidated one instance—in which Mitchell's executive assistant had actually approved the application although Wilson's signature had appeared on it. However, the court again split 5-4 over the validity of a wiretap application purportedly approved by Wilson but actually approved by Mitchell. With White's vote, the four Nixon nominees became a majority upholding the validity of this surveillance, since Mitchell did have the authority to grant such approval. (U.S. v. Chavez)

In dissent, Justices William O. Douglas, William J. Brennan Jr., Potter Stewart and Thurgood Marshall argued that to erroneously assign responsibility for the decision by misidentifying the person approving the application was a serious flaw, invalidating the application and the wiretap: "It is clear that this personal responsibility and political accountability, relied on by Congress to check the reckless use of electronic surveillance is rendered a mere chimera when the official actually authorizing a wiretap application is not identified until years after the tap has occurred.... In eviscerating Congress' intent to fix responsibility in the application...the court destroys a significant deterrent to reckless or needless electronic surveillance."

Allowing this sort of application to stand in spite of the misidentification, the court preserved 99 more government cases, involving 807 defendants, in which Mitchell's actual approval had been concealed by this sort of faulty identification. Despite the number of cases involved, Douglas wrote, these wiretaps and this evidence should be ruled invalid. Numbers do not "vitiate our duty to enforce the congressional scheme as written," he said. "The failure of a prosecution in a particular case pales in comparison with the duty of this court to nourish and enhance respect for the evenhanded application of the law."

Excerpts from Supreme Court opinions on federal wiretapping procedures in the cases of U.S. v. Giordano and U.S. v. Chavez, May 13, 1974:

No. 72-1057

United States, Petitioner, v. Dominic Nicholas Giordano et al.	On Writ of Certiorari to the United States Court of Appeals for the Fourth Circuit.

[May 13, 1974]

MR. JUSTICE WHITE delivered the opinion of the Court.

Title III of the Omnibus Crime Control and Safe Streets Act of 1968...prescribes the procedure for securing judicial authority to intercept wire communications in the investigation of specified serious offenses. The Court must here determine whether the Government sufficiently complied with the required application procedures in this case and whether, if not, evidence obtained as a result of such surveillance, under a court order based on the applications, is admissible at the criminal trial of those whose conversations were overheard. In particular, we must decide whether the provision...conferring power on the "Attorney General, or any Assistant Attorney General specially designated by the Attorney General" to "authorize an application to a Federal judge...for...an order authorizing or approving the interception of wire or oral communications" by federal investigative agencies seeking evidence of certain designated offenses permits the Attorney General's Executive Assistant to validly authorize a wiretap application to be made. We conclude that Congress did not intend the power to authorize wiretap applications to be exercised by any individuals other than the Attorney General or an Assistant Attorney General specially designated by him and that primary or derivative evidence secured by wire interceptions pursuant to a court order issued in response to an application which was, in fact, not authorized by one of the statutorily designated officials must be suppressed....

I

In the course of an initial investigation of suspected narcotics dealings on the part of respondent Giordano, it developed that Giordano himself sold narcotics to an undercover agent on October 5, 1970, and also told an informant to call a specified number when interested in transacting narcotics business. Based on this and other information, Francis Brocato, an Assistant United States Attorney, on October 16, 1970, submitted an application to the Chief Judge of the District of Maryland for an order permitting interception of the communications of Giordano, and of others as yet unknown, to or from Giordano's telephone. The application recited that Assistant Attorney General Will Wilson had been specially designated by the Attorney General to authorize the application. Attached to the application was a letter from Will Wilson to Brocato which stated that Wilson had reviewed Brocato's request for authorization and had made the necessary probable cause determinations and which then purported to authorize Brocato to proceed with the application to the court. Also attached were various affidavits of law enforcement officers stating the reasons and justification for the proposed interception. Upon reviewing the application, the Chief Judge issued an order on the same day authorizing the interception "pursuant to application authorized by the Assistant Attorney General...Will Wilson, who has been specially designated in this proceeding by the Attorney General...to exercise the powers conferred on him...." On November 6, the same judge extended the intercept authority based on an application similar in form to the original, but also including information obtained from the interception already authorized and carried out and extending the authority to conversations of additional named individuals calling from or to Giordano's telephone. The interception was terminated on November 18 when Giordano and the other respondents were arrested and charged with violations of the narcotics laws.

Suppression hearings followed pretrial notification by the Government...that it intended to use in evidence the results of the court-authorized interceptions of communications on Giordano's telephone. It developed at the hearings that the applications for interception authority presented to the District Court had inaccurately described the official who had authorized the applications and that neither the initial application for the October 16 order nor the application for the November 6 extension order had been approved and authorized by Assistant Attorney General Will Wilson, as the applications had indicated. An affidavit of the Executive Assistant to the Attorney General divulged that he, the Executive Assistant, had reviewed the request for authorization to apply for the initial order, had concluded from his "knowledge of the Attorney General's actions on previous cases that he would approve the request if submitted to him[,]" and, because the Attorney General was then on a trip away from Washington, D.C., and pursuant to authorization by the Attorney General for him to do so in such circumstances, had approved the request and caused the Attorney General's initials to be placed on a memorandum to Wilson instructing him to authorize Brocato to proceed. The affidavit also stated that the Attorney General himself had approved the November 6 request for extension and had initialed the memorandum to Wilson designating him to authorize Brocato to make application for an extension order. It was also revealed that although the applications recited that they had been authorized by Will Wilson, he had not himself reviewed Brocato's applications, and that his action was at best only formal authorization to Brocato. Furthermore, it became apparent that Wilson did not himself sign either of the letters bearing his name and accompanying the applications to the District Court. Instead, it appeared that someone in Wilson's office had affixed his signature after the signing of the letters had been authorized by a Deputy Assistant Attorney General in the Criminal Division who had, in turn, acted after the approval of the request for authorization had occurred in and had been received from the Office of the Attorney General.

The District Court sustained the motions to suppress on the ground that the officer in the Justice Department approving each application had been misidentified in the applications and intercept orders.... On the Government's pretrial appeal...the Court of Appeals affirmed on the different ground that the authorization of the October 16 wiretap application by the Attorney General's Executive Assistant violated...the statute and struck at "the very heart" of Title III, thereby requiring suppression of the wiretap and derivative evidence....

II

The United States contends that the authorization of intercept applications by the Attorney General's Executive Assistant was not inconsistent with the statute and that even if it were, there being no constitutional violation, the wiretap and derivative evidence should not have been ordered suppressed. We disagree with both contentions.

Turning first to whether the statute permits the authorization of wiretap applications by the Attorney General's Executive Assistant, we begin with the language...which provides that "the Attorney General, or any Assistant Attorney General specially designated by the Attorney General, may authorize" an application for intercept authority. Plainly enough, the Executive Assistant is neither the Attorney General nor a specially designated Assistant Attorney General; but the United States argues that...functions of the Department of Justice, with some exceptions, [are vested] in the Attorney General, and that Congress characteristically assigns newly created duties to the Attorney General rather than to the Department of Justice, thus making essential the provision for delegation....

As a general proposition, the argument is unexceptionable. But...the power of the Attorney General in this respect is specifically limited to delegating his authority to "any Assistant Attorney General specially designated by the Attorney General." ...Congress does not always contemplate that the duties assigned to the Attorney General may be freely delegated.... [P]recise language forbidding delegation was not employed in the legislation before us; but we think...[the law,] fairly read, was intended to limit the power to authorize wiretap applications to the Attorney General himself and to any Assistant Attorney General he might designate. This interpretation of the statute is also strongly supported by its purpose and legislative history....

Congress legislated in considerable detail in providing for applications and orders authorizing wiretapping and evinced the clear intent to make doubly sure that the statutory authority be used with restraint and only where the circumstances warrant the surreptitious interception of wire and oral communications. These procedures were not to be routinely employed as the initial step in criminal investigation. Rather, the applicant must state and the court must find that normal investigative procedures have been tried and failed to reasonably appear to be unlikely to succeed if tried or to be too dangerous. The Act plainly calls for prior, informed judgment of enforcement officers desiring court approval for intercept authority, and investigative personnel may not themselves ask a judge for authority to wiretap or eavesdrop. The mature judgment of a particular, responsible Department of Justice official is interposed as a critical precondition to any judicial order.

The legislative history of the Act supports this view.... [I]t is apparent that Congress desired to centralize and limit this authority where it was feasible to do so, a desire easily implemented in the federal establishment by confining the authority to approve wiretap applications to the Attorney General or a designated Assistant Attorney General. To us, it appears wholly at odds with the scheme and history of the Act...to permit the Attorney General to delegate his authority at will, whether it be to his Executive Assistant or to any officer in the Department other than an Assistant Attorney General.

III

We also reject the Government's contention that even if the approval by the Attorney General's Executive Assistant of the October 16 application did not comply with the statutory requirements, the evidence obtained from the interceptions should not have been suppressed. The issue does not turn on the judicially fashioned exclusionary rule aimed at deterring violations of Fourth Amendment rights, but upon the provisions of Title III....

Section 2515 provides that no part of the contents of any wire or oral communication, and no evidence derived therefrom, may be received at certain proceedings, including trials, "if the disclosure of that information would be in violation of this chapter." What disclosures are forbidden, and are subject to...suppression of evidence on the following grounds:

"(i) the communication was unlawfully intercepted;

"(ii) the order of authorization or approval under which it was intercepted is insufficient on its face; or

"(iii) the interception was not made in conformity with the order of authorization or approval."

The Court of Appeals held that the communications the Government desired to offer in evidence had been "unlawfully intercepted" within the meaning of paragraph (i), because the October application had been approved by the Executive Assistant to the Attorney General rather than by the Attorney General himself or a designated Assistant Attorney General. We have already determined that delegation to the Executive Assistant was indeed contrary to the statute; but the Government contends that approval by the wrong official is a statutory violation only and that paragraph (i) must be construed to reach constitutional, but not statutory, violations. The argument is a straightforward one.... On the one hand, the unlawful interceptions referred to in paragraph (i) must include some constitutional violations.... On the other hand (ii) and (iii) plainly reach some purely statutory defaults without constitutional overtones, and these omissions cannot be deemed unlawful interceptions under paragraph (i), else there would have been no necessity for paragraphs (ii) and (iii)....

We have already determined that Congress intended not only to limit resort to wiretapping to certain crimes and situations where probable cause is present but also to condition the use of intercept procedures upon the judgment of a senior official in the Department of Justice that the situation is one of those warranting their use. It is reasonable to believe that such a precondition would inevitably foreclose resort to wiretapping in various situations where investigative personnel would otherwise seek intercept authority from the court and the court would very likely authorize its use. We are confident that the provision for pre-application approval was intended to play a central role in the statutory scheme and that suppression must follow when it is shown that this statutory requirement has been ignored....

IV

Even though suppression of the wire communications intercepted under the October 16, 1970 order is required, the Government nevertheless contends that communications intercepted under the November 6 extension order are admissible because they are not "evidence derived" from the contents of communications intercepted under the October 16 order.... This position is untenable.

Under §2518, extension orders do not stand on the same footing as original authorizations but are provided for separately.... Under subsection (1)(e), applications for extensions must reveal previous applications and orders, and under (1)(f) must contain "a statement setting forth the results thus far obtained from the interception, or a reasonable explanation of the failure to obtain such results." Based on the application, the court is required to make the same findings that are required in connection with the original order; that is, it must be found not only that there is probable cause in the traditional sense and that normal investigative procedures are unlikely to succeed but also that there is probable cause for believing that particular communications concerning the offense will be obtained through the interception and for believing that the facilities or place from which the wire or oral communications are to be intercepted are used or will be used in connection with the commission of such offense or are under lease to the suspect or commonly used by him.

In its November 6 application, the Government sought authority to intercept the conversations of not only Giordano, who alone was expressly named in the initial application and order, but of nine other named persons who were alleged to be involved with Giordano in narcotics violations. Based on the attached affidavit, it was alleged that there was probable cause to believe that communications concerning the offense involved would be intercepted, particularly those between Giordano and the other named individuals, as well as those with others as yet unnamed, and that the telephone listed in the name of Giordano and whose monitoring was sought to be continued "has been used, and is being used and will be used, in connection with the commission of the offenses described.".…

It is apparent from the foregoing that the communications intercepted pursuant to the extension order were evidence derived from the communications invalidly intercepted pursuant to the initial order. In the first place, the application sought and the order granted authority to intercept the communications of various named individuals not mentioned in the initial order. It is plain from the affidavit submitted that information about most of these persons was obtained through the initial illegal interceptions. It is equally plain that the telephone monitoring and accompanying surveillance were coordinated operations, necessarily intertwined. As the Government asserted, the surveillance and conventional investigative techniques "would be completely ineffective except as an adjunct to electronic interception." That the extension order and the interceptions under it were not in fact the product of the earlier electronic surveillance is incredible.…

It is urged in dissent that the information obtained from the illegal October 16 interception order may be ignored and that the remaining evidence submitted in the extension application was sufficient to support the extension order. But whether or not the application, without the facts obtained from monitoring Giordano's telephone, would independently support original wiretap authority, the Act itself forbids extensions of prior authorizations without consideration of the results meanwhile obtained.

Obviously, those results were presented, considered and relied on in this case. Moreover, as previously noted, the Government itself had stated that the wire interception was an indispensable factor in its investigation and that ordinary surveillance alone would have been insufficient. In our view, the results of the conversations overheard under the initial order were essential, both in fact and in law, to any extension of the intercept authority. Accordingly, communications intercepted under the extension order are derivative evidence and must be suppressed. The judgment of the Court of Appeals is

Affirmed

MR. JUSTICE POWELL, with whom the CHIEF JUSTICE, MR. JUSTICE BLACKMUN, and MR. JUSTICE REHNQUIST join, concurring in part and dissenting in part.

...For the reasons stated below, however, I dissent from the Court's conclusion, stated in Part IV of its opinion, that evidence obtained under the two "pen register" extension orders and under the November 6 extension of the interception order must also be suppressed....

The Government contends that, putting aside all evidence derived from the invalid original wiretap order, the independent and untainted evidence submitted to the District Court constituted probable cause for issuance of both pen register extension orders and the wiretap extension order, and in the latter case also satisfied the additional requirements.... Preoccupied with the larger issues in the case, the District Court summarily dismissed this contention insofar as it related to the pen register extension orders....

...The question is not whether the application for that order relied in part on communications intercepted under the invalid original order but whether, putting aside that tainted evidence, the independent and lawful information stated in the supporting affidavit suffices to show both probable cause and satisfaction of the various additional requirements of Title III....

In light of the substantiality and detail of the untainted allegations offered in support of the application for the wiretap extension order, I find no basis for the majority's rather summary conclusion that the communications intercepted under that extension order were derivatively tainted by the improper authorization of the application for the original wiretap order. Because neither the District Court nor the Court of Appeals has considered this question, I would remand the case with instructions that the issue be settled in accord with the principles set forth in this opinion.

No. 72-1319

United States, Petitioner,   On Writ of Certiorari
                 v.   to the United States
Umberto Jose Chavez et al.   Court of Appeals for
                                               the Ninth Circuit.

[May 13, 1974]

MR. JUSTICE WHITE delivered the opinion of the Court.

This case...concerns the validity of procedures followed by the Justice Department in obtaining judicial approval to intercept wire communications under Title III of the Omnibus Crime Control and Safe Streets Act of 1968,...and the propriety of suppressing evidence gathered from court-authorized wiretaps where the statutory application procedures have not been fully satisfied.... Title III limits who, among federal officials, may approve submission of a wiretap application to the appropriate District Court, to the Attorney General or an Assistant Attorney General he specially designates,...and delineates the information each application must contain, upon what findings an interception order may be granted, and what the order shall specify....

I

Respondents were all indicted for conspiracy to import and distribute heroin.... In addition, respondent Umberto Chavez was separately charged...with using and causing others to use a telephone between California and Mexico, and performing other acts, in order to facilitate unlawful narcotics activity, and respondent James Fernandez was charged...with traveling between California and Mexico and performing other acts, for the same purpose. Upon notification that the Government intended to introduce evidence obtained from wiretaps of Chavez' and Fernandez' phones at trial, respondents filed motions to suppress, challenging the legality of the Justice Department's application procedures leading to the issuance by the District Court of the two orders permitting the wire interceptions. Affidavits filed in opposition by the former Attorney General and his Executive Assistant represented that the application submitted for the February 18, 1971 order authorizing interception of wire communications to and from the Chavez phone had been personally approved by the Attorney General, whereas the application for the February 25, 1971 order to intercept communications to and from the Fernandez phone had been approved by his Executive Assistant at a time when the Attorney General was unavailable, and pursuant to an understanding that the Executive Assistant, applying the Attorney General's standards as he understood them could act for the Attorney General in such circumstances....

The District Court held that the evidence secured through both wiretaps had to be suppressed for failure of either of the individuals who actually authorized the applications to be "identified to Chief Judge Carter,

Congress or the public" in the application or orders, as mandated.... Moreover, evidence obtained under the February 25 wiretap order on the Fernandez phone was separately suppressed, because the Government admitted that "neither the Attorney General nor a specially designated Assistant Attorney General ever authorized the application....

The Court of Appeals affirmed in all respects. With respect to the Chavez tap, the Court of Appeals assumed, as had the District Court, that the Attorney General had personally approved the request for authority to apply for the interception order, as his affidavit stated. Nonetheless, the misidentification of Assistant Attorney General Wilson as the authorizing official was deemed to be a "misrepresentation" and an "apparently deliberate deception of the courts by the highest law officers in the land,"...which required suppression of evidence gathered from the tap for failure to comply with [the U.S. Code]. Congress was held to have "intended to eliminate any possibility that the authorization of wiretap applications would be institutional decisions[,]" and the Court of Appeals was fearful that if the misidentification which occurred in this case were approved, "there would be nothing to prevent future Attorneys General from remaining silent if a particular wiretap proved embarrassing"....

We agree with those other courts of appeals that misidentifying the Assistant Attorney General as the official authorizing the wiretap application to be made does not require suppression of wiretap evidence when the Attorney General himself has actually given the approval; hence, we reverse that portion of the judgment suppressing the Chavez wiretap evidence, and remand for further proceedings to permit the District Court to address other challenges to the Chavez wiretap evidence which respondents had made but the District Court did not find it necessary to consider....

II

The application and order for the Chavez wiretap did not correctly identify the individual authorizing the application.... Of this there is no doubt. But it does not follow that because of this deficiency in reporting, evidence obtained pursuant to the order was not used at the trial of respondents. There is no claim of any constitutional infirmity arising from this defect, nor would there be any merit to such a claim, and we must look to the statutory scheme to determine if Congress has provided that suppression is required for this particular procedural error....

...Failure to correctly report the identity of the person authorizing the application...when in fact the Attorney General has given the required preliminary approval to submit the application, does not represent a...failure to follow Title III's precautions against the unwarranted use of wiretapping or electronic surveillance and does not warrant the suppression of evidence gathered pursuant to a court order resting upon the application....

Respondents suggest that the misidentification of Assistant Attorney General Wilson as the authorizing official was calculated to mislead the

District Court in considering the wire interception applications, and certainly had the effect of misleading him, since the interception order also misidentified the authorizing official in reliance on the statements made in the application. We do not perceive any purpose to be served by deliberate misrepresentation by the Government in these circumstances. To the contrary, we think it cannot be seriously contended that had the Attorney General been identified as the person authorizing the application, rather than his subordinate, Assistant Attorney General Wilson, the district judge would have had any greater hesitation in issuing the interception order.... [W]e cannot say that misidentification was in any sense the omission of a requirement that must be satisfied if wiretapping or electronic surveillance is to be lawful under Title III.

Neither the District Court nor the Court of Appeals made clear which of the grounds...was relied upon to suppress the Chavez wiretap evidence. Respondents rely on each of the first two grounds, *i.e.*, that the communications were "unlawfully intercepted" and that the Chavez interception order is "insufficient on its face." Support for the latter claim is drawn from the District Court decision in *United States* v. *Focarile*...which concluded that an order incorrectly identifying who authorized the application is equivalent to an order failing to identify anyone at all as the authorizing official. We find neither of these contentions persuasive.

Here, the interception order clearly identified "on its face" Assistant Attorney General Wilson as the person who authorized the application to be made.... That this has subsequently been shown to be incorrect does not detract from the facial sufficiency of the order. Moreover...the Attorney General authorized the application, as he also had the power to do.... In no realistic sense, therefore, can it be said that the order failed to identify an authorizing official who possessed statutory power to approve the making of the application.

The claim that communications to and from the Chavez phone were "unlawfully intercepted" is more plausible, but does not persuade us, given the purposes to be served by the identification requirements and their place in the statutory scheme of regulation.... [W]e did not go so far as to suggest that every failure to comply fully with any requirement provided in Title III would render the interception of wire or oral communications "unlawful" ....

In the present case, the misidentification of the officer authorizing the wiretap application did not affect the fulfillment of any of the reviewing or approval functions required by Congress.... Requiring identification of the authorizing official in the application facilitates the court's ability to conclude that the application has been properly approved...; requiring identification in the court's order also serves to "fix responsibility" for the source of preliminary approval. This information contained in the application and order further aids the judge in making reports.... An annual report of the authorizing officials...must also be filed...and is to contain the same information with respect to each application made as is required of the issuing or denying judge.... Finally, a summary of the information...is to be filed with Congress in April of each year.... The purpose of these reports is "to form the basis for a public evaluation" of the operation of Title III and to "assure the community that the system of court-order electronic surveillance...is properly administered...." While adherence to the identification reporting requirements...thus can simplify the assurance that those who Title III makes responsible for determining when and how wiretapping and electronic surveillance should be conducted have fulfilled their roles in each case, they do not establish a substantive role to be played in the regulatory system.

Nor is there any legislative history concerning these sections, to suggest that they were meant, by themselves, to occupy a central, or even functional, role in guarding against unwarranted use of wiretapping or electronic surveillance....

When it is clearly established, therefore, that authorization of submission of a wiretap or electronic surveillance application has been given by the Attorney General himself, but the application, and, as a result, the interception order, incorrectly state that approval has instead been given by a specially designated Assistant Attorney General, the misidentification, by itself, will not render interceptions conducted under the order "unlawful" within the meaning of § 2518 (10)(a)(i) or the disclosure of the contents of intercepted communications, or derivative evidence, otherwise "in violation of" Title III.... Hence, the suppression of the Chavez wiretap evidence on the basis of the misidentification of Assistant Attorney General Wilson as the authorizing official was in error. Though we deem this result to be the correct one under the suppression provisions of Title III, we also deem it appropriate to suggest that strict adherence by the Government to the provisions of Title III would nonetheless be more in keeping with the responsibilities Congress has imposed upon it when authority to engage in wiretapping or electronic surveillance is sought.

The judgment of the Court of Appeals is affirmed in part, reversed in part, and remanded for further proceedings consistent with this opinion.

It is so ordered.

MR. JUSTICE DOUGLAS, with whom MR. JUSTICE BRENNAN, MR. JUSTICE STEWART, and MR. JUSTICE MARSHALL concur, concurring in part and dissenting in part....

...I join the opinion of the Court in *Giordano*...and I therefore concur in the Court's suppression of the evidence seized in that wiretap. In *Chavez*, however, the Court finds that suppression is not warranted for the violations...which the Court admits occurred in the Chavez wiretap itself. I dissent from this conclusion, hereinafter referred to as the holding of *Chavez*....

I

Chavez...represents a class of cases where the Justice Department violated the "identification requirement...which requires that each application made to the District Court for a wiretap order "shall include...the identity of...the officer authorizing the application." Because the District Courts in this class of cases were supplied with misinformation as to the identity of the person who authorized the applications made to them, the orders they entered approving the use of electronic surveillance violated § 2518 (4)(d) of Title III, which provides that *such orders "shall specify...the identity of...the person authorizing the application"*....

By creating the identification provisions, which required the authorizing official to be made known at the time of an application, [Congress] established a mechanism by which a person's responsibility was to be acknowledged immediately, not a device by which the identity of the person authorizing the application would remain hidden until it was discovered that an instance of electronic surveillance had been productive and not offensive to public sensibilities.

Immediate acknowledgment of responsibility for authorizing electronic surveillance is not an idle gesture. It lessens or eliminates the ability of officials to later disavow their responsibility for surveillance. By adding the identification provisions...Congress took a step toward stripping from responsible officials the ability to choose after the fact whether to accept or deny that responsibility by coming forward and filing an affidavit. "Fixing" of responsibility in the application and order can have no other meaning; it simply does not comprehend a situation where responsibility is concealed or unsettled....

But it is clear that this personal responsibility and political accountability, relied on by Congress to check the reckless use of electronic surveillance, is rendered a mere chimera when the official actually authorizing a wiretap application is not identified until years after the tap has occurred, when he might already be out of office, when the usefulness of the tap is already established, when it is clear that the surveillance was not abusive, and then only through voluntary admissions or the sifting of potentially contradictory affidavits. Responsibility is hardly "focused," and the "lines of responsibility" are gossamer at best. This is why Congress added the demand that responsibility be immediately *fixed*. The procedures which the Court sanctions in *Chavez* stretch the unequivocally expressed desire of Congress to *fix responsibility* in the application and order well beyond the breaking point.

In eviscerating Congress' intent to fix responsibility in the application and order, the Court destroys a significant deterrent to reckless or needless electronic surveillance. It allows the official authorizing a wiretap to remain out of the harsh light of public scrutiny at the crucial beginning of the wiretap process, only to emerge later when he chooses to identify himself. Knowledge that personal responsibility would be immediately focused and immutably fixed, whatever the outcome of surveillance, be it profitable or profligate, successful or embarrassing, forces an official to be circumspect in initially authorizing an electronic invasion of privacy. This is why Title III requires more than a judicial determination of probable cause; it also requires an accountable political official to exercise political judgment, and it requires that the political official be immediately identified and his responsibility fixed when an application is filed. The identification procedures, by fixing responsibility, obviously serve to "limit the use of intercept procedures to those situations clearly calling for the employment of this extraordinary investigative device," thereby requiring suppression even under the test the Court adopts in *Chavez*....

I accordingly dissent in part in *Chavez*.

▼▼▼

KLEINDIENST PLEADS GUILTY
May 16, 1974

Richard G. Kleindienst, former Attorney General under President Richard M. Nixon, pleaded guilty May 16 in a District of Columbia federal district court to a misdemeanor charge based on his failure to testify fully and accurately at his confirmation hearings before the Senate Judiciary Committee in the spring of 1972. The minor criminal charge related to Kleindienst's failure to tell the committee that President Nixon had personally ordered him in 1971 to drop an appeal in a government antitrust case against the International Telephone and Telegraph Corporation (I.T.T.). At the time he received the President's order, which he did not act on, Kleindienst was supervising the Justice Department's antitrust cases against I.T.T. as deputy attorney general. During his Senate testimony a year later, he was acting attorney general. Kleindienst was the first cabinet-level officer to be convicted in a matter related to the Watergate scandal. He was also the first former attorney general to be convicted for an act committed while in office.

The I.T.T. affair arose out of press allegations that a July 1971 out-of-court settlement of the antitrust suit against Grinnell, an I.T.T. subsidiary, had been made as a result of a pledge by I.T.T. officials to contribute as much as $400,000 to help finance the 1972 Republican convention then scheduled for San Diego, California. The settlement had been considered favorable to I.T.T. In April 1971, while the case was still pending, then presidential aide John D. Ehrlichman, according to Kleindienst, told him to drop any plans to appeal a key item in the suit. When Kleindienst refused to comply, the President himself in a telephone call directed him to abandon the appeal.

In a May 16 statement on his guilty plea, Kleindienst confirmed the Ehrlichman and Nixon calls and said he had considered resigning in protest after receiving them but "realized that if I did so the case might not be appealed, which would be tantamount to compliance with the order." Instead, Kleindienst said, he decided to offer his resignation at a later time. He conveyed his intentions to the President, who subsequently retracted the order. Kleindienst said he had concealed the incident from the Senate committee because he thought Nixon's order "ill conceived, quickly retracted...privileged and...not the focus of the committee's inquiry." But he had been "wrong," he said, "in not having been more candid."

Kleindienst's faulty testimony was given during Senate committee confirmation hearings in March and April 1972, reopened at his request after press reports had raised questions about his role in the I.T.T. case. Kleindienst's nomination as attorney general had been unanimously approved by the committee in February 1972. But doubts about his original testimony followed reports late in February about a confidential memo, credited to an I.T.T. lobbyist, which dealt with the putative $400,000 pledge (see Historic Documents, 1972, p. 395). During the March and April sessions, Kleindienst consistently denied to the Judiciary Committee that he had been pressured to come to terms with the corporation."I was not," he stated, "interfered with by anybody at the White House."

Senate approval of Kleindienst's nomination was given June 8, 1972, but the Judiciary Committee, judging its I.T.T. investigation inconclusive, referred the hearing record to the Justice Department to determine whether any witness had committed perjury. In June 1973, the Justice Department turned the investigation over to the Watergate special prosecutor, then Archibald Cox.

White House Admits Role in ITT Case

The possibility that Kleindienst gave false or misleading information during his confirmation hearing was raised publicly once again in August 1973. The Senate Watergate investigating committee made public at that time a White House memorandum which hinted at direct involvement of the President in the I.T.T. settlement, contrary to Kleindienst's account. Dated March 1972, the memorandum had been written by Charles W. Colson, then special counsel to the President. In October 1973, according to press reports, Kleindienst acknowledged to the special prosecutor's office that Nixon had tried to intercede on behalf of I.T.T. In response to those reports, the White House stated briefly, for the first time, that Nixon had discussed the suit with Kleindienst. A presidential white paper issued the following January defended the President's action and said it was not a quid pro quo for actual or promised campaign contributions from I.T.T. (White paper, see p. 3-21.)

The Plea Bargain

Kleindienst's guilty plea followed months of bargaining with Special Watergate Prosecutor Leon Jaworski. In the end, Kleindienst was charged with a relatively minor offense in return for cooperating with the prosecution's I.T.T. investigation. In a letter to Kleindienst's attorney confirming the plea-bargaining arrangement, Jaworski said he would drop further charges arising from Kleindienst's testimony on the I.T.T. case before the Senate committee and the Watergate grand juries. The letter, which was made public, said that if new evidence was developed, Kleindienst could still be prosecuted.

The incomplete testimony before the Senate committee had exposed Kleindienst to felony charges for perjury. As a lawyer, he would have been subject to automatic disbarment if convicted of a felony charge. Jaworski's decision not to bring perjury charges provoked public debate over the merits of plea-bargaining in cases as important as the Watergate coverup and associated abuses. The decision was reportedly a factor in the resignation of three members of the special prosecutor's staff who contended that Kleindienst should have been charged with a felony. However, Jaworski's letter to Kleindienst's attorney noted that the special prosecutor's investigation had "failed to disclose any criminal conduct...in the manner in which he [Kleindienst] handled the I.T.T. antitrust cases. In one of the cases he successfully opposed a direct presidential order to abandon an appeal and leave the government without relief." Another mitigating factor in Kleindienst's case was reported to be his substantial efforts while in office to block the Watergate coverup.

On June 7, Kleindienst received the minimum sentence under law, a $100 fine and one month in jail, both suspended. Chief U.S. District Court Judge George L. Hart Jr., who sentenced Kleindienst, placed him on one-month unsupervised probation. In announcing the sentence, Hart described Kleindienst's crime as a "technical violation" of the law. It was "not the type of violation that reflects a mind bent on deception.... Rather, it reflects a heart that is too loyal," the judge said.

> *Statement by Richard G. Kleindienst after he pleaded guilty to a misdemeanor charge in federal district court, May 16, 1974:*

I have entered a plea of guilty before Chief Judge George L. Hart Jr., of the United States District Court for the District of Columbia, to a misdemeanor (Title 2, United States Code, Section 192), namely that I refused to answer certain questions asked of me during my confirmation hearings in 1972 before the Committee on the Judiciary of the United States Senate. I wish to make the following statement:

On April 19, 1971, while I was Deputy Attorney General, I received a call from John Ehrlichman [assistant to the President for domestic affairs], who said that the President ordered me to drop the appeal in U.S. *v.* I.T.T. (Grinnell), which had to be filed the next day in order to keep the case alive.

After I refused Mr. Ehrlichman's instruction, the President called me and directed me to drop the appeal. When the President hung up, I considered immediately resigning but realized that if I did so the case might not be appealed, which would be tantamount to compliance with the order.

Reply to 'Insinuation'

Instead, I decided to get the extension of time and then offer my resignation, which I did by asking John Mitchell [Attorney General] to convey my plans to the President. Shortly thereafter the President retracted his order and the case was in fact appealed to the Supreme Court. Subsequently this case was won by the Government when it and two others involving I.T.T. were settled.

After I had been nominated for Attorney General one year later, charges were made that the I.T.T. cases had been settled because I.T.T. had made a contribution relating to the Republican National Convention.

So far as I was aware, these charges were false and I therefore asked that my confirmation hearings be reopened in order to dispel any insinuation of impropriety on the part of the Department of Justice or myself.

As the special prosecutor has indicated, I did not fully answer questions by the Senate Committee on the Judiciary which would have elicited the circumstances surrounding the extension of time in the Grinnell appeal. I was less than candid because I viewed the President's order as ill conceived, quickly retracted, in my opinion privileged and in any event not the focus of the committee's inquiry, which dealt with the reasons why the three I.T.T. cases were settled during the summer of 1971.

Kleindienst Admits Error in Lack of Candor

I was wrong in not having been more candid with the committee and I sincerely regret it. It is my earnest prayer that in due time history will record that in I.T.T. the Department of Justice fulfilled its charge fairly and fully to enforce the laws of the United States without fear, interference or favor. So far as I know, this is the truth.

In making my guilty plea to the misdemeanor which I have described, I do so out of respect for the criminal justice system of the United States and the indisputable fact that the system must have equal application to all. This same respect for the criminal justice system required that I voluntarily and fully cooperate with the Watergate special prosecution force, and I am morally certain that I have done so.

COURT REJECTION OF "NATIONAL SECURITY" DEFENSE

May 24, 1974

U.S. District Court Judge Gerhard A. Gesell ruled May 24 that former White House aides could not use "national security" as a legal justification for their role in the break-in at the office of Dr. Lewis J. Fielding, a Los Angeles psychiatrist consulted by Pentagon Papers defendant Daniel Ellsberg. Former White House aides John D. Ehrlichman and Charles W. Colson had been indicted March 7 along with convicted Watergate break-in conspirators G. Gordon Liddy, Bernard L. Barker, Eugenio Martinez and Felipe De Diego on charges of conspiring to violate the civil rights of Fielding by the September 1971 burglary of his office. Together the men had been charged with planning and carrying out the burglary in search of psychiatric records on Ellsberg. (See Historic Documents 1973, p. 537-548.)

Ehrlichman and Colson based their defense of the conspiracy charges on the necessity to protect national security under authority of the President. But Judge Gesell struck down that defense, grounding his opinion on the 4th Amendment of the Constitution. "The 4th Amendment protects the privacy of citizens against unreasonable and unrestrained intrusion by government officials and their agents. It is not theoretical. It lies at the heart of our free society." Gesell conceded that an invasion without a warrant of a home or of an office had been approved by the Supreme Court "under carefully delineated emergency circumstances." But he denied that these exceptional circumstances were met by the facts of the Fielding break-in. "On the contrary," he said, the burglary "had been meticulously planned over a period of more than a month. The search of Dr. Fielding's office was therefore clearly illegal under the unambiguous mandate of the 4th Amendment."

Gesell flatly rejected the defendents' contention that the President had the right to suspend 4th Amendment guarantees by virtue of his special responsibilities for foreign affairs and national security. He said that recent Supreme Court decisions allowing warrantless wiretapping for gathering of intelligence had no applicability to the defendants' case.

Rejecting the defendants' position that they had been following a presidential order, Gesell said that an April 29 letter received by the Court from President Nixon "did not, in fact, give any specific directive permitting national security break-ins, let alone this intrusion." Gesell quoted from the letter describing a meeting in 1971 between the President, Ehrlichman and Egil Krogh Jr., a former White House aide who had directed the group which had carried out the Fielding break-in. According to Nixon: "it was my intent...that the fullest authority of the President under the Constitution and the law should be used if necessary to bring a halt to these disclosures [such as Ellsberg's alleged leaking of the Pentagon Papers to the press].... I did not have prior knowledge of the break-in...nor was I informed of it until March 17, 1973." Gesell therefore dismissed the contention that the defendants had been operating on a direct order from the President.

Gesell also rejected "the contention that the President could delegate his alleged power to suspend constitutional rights to non-law enforcement officers in the vague, informal, inexact terms noted" in Nixon's letter. The defendants had declared that even lacking a direct presidential order, they had properly followed through on general authority. "Whatever accommodation is required between the guarantees of the 4th Amendment and the conduct of foreign affairs," said Gesell, "it cannot justify a casual, ill-defined assignment to White House aides and part-time employees granting them an uncontrolled discretion to select, enter and search the homes and offices of innocent American citizens without a warrant."

Following are excerpts from the text of an opinion by U.S. District Court Judge Gerhard A. Gesell May 24 on the national security aspects of the break-in case involving the former psychiatrist of Daniel Ellsberg:

Five defendants stand indicted for conspiring to injure a Los Angeles psychiatrist in the enjoyment of his Fourth Amendment rights by entering his offices without a warrant for the purpose of obtaining the doctor's medical records relating to one of his patients, a Daniel Ellsberg, then under Federal indictment for revealing top secret documents.

They now claim that broad pre-trial discovery into the alleged national security aspects of this case is essential to the presentation of their defense, in that it will establish (1) that the break-in was legal under the Fourth Amendment because the President authorized it for reasons of national security, and (2) that even in the absence of such authorization the national security information available to the defendants at that time, led them to the good-faith, reasonable belief that the break-in was legal and justified in the national interest.

The court has carefully considered these assertions, which have been fully briefed and argued over a two-day period, and finds them to be unpersuasive as a matter of law.

In approaching these issues, it is well to recall the origins of the Fourth Amendment and the crucial role that it has played in the development of our constitutional democracy. That amendment provides:

"The right of the people to be secure in their persons, houses, papers, and effects, against unreasonable searches and seizures, shall not be violated, and no warrants shall issue, but upon probable cause, supported by oath or affirmation, and particularly describing the place to be searched, and the persons or things to be seized."

"Heart of Free Society"

The Fourth Amendment protects the privacy of citizens against unreasonable and unrestrained intrusion by government officials and their agents. It is not theoretical. It lies at the heart of our free society. As the Supreme Court recently remarked, "No right is held more sacred."....

Indeed, the American Revolution was sparked in part by the complaints of the colonists against the issuance of writs of assistance, pursuant to which the King's revenue officers conducted unrestricted, indiscriminate searches of persons and homes to uncover contraband.... The Fourth Amendment was framed against this background and every state in the Union, by its own constitution, has since reinforced the protections and the security which that amendment was designed to achieve.

Thus the security of one's privacy against arbitrary intrusion by governmental authorities has proven essential to our concept of ordered liberty. When officials have attempted to justify law enforcement methods that ignore the structures of this amendment on grounds of necessity, such excuses have proven fruitless, for the Constitution brands such conduct as lawless, irrespective of the end to be served.

Steady Court Position

Throughout the years the Supreme Court of the United States, regardless of changes in its composition or contemporary issues, has steadfastly applied the amendment to protect a citizen against the warrantless invasion of his home or office, except under carefully delineated emergency circumstances....

No right so fundamental should now, after the long struggle against governmental trespass, be diluted to accommodate conduct of the very type the amendment was designed to outlaw.

The break-in charges in this indictment involve a search by agents of the executive branch of the Federal Government. It is undisputed that no warrant was obtained and no magistrate gave his approval.

Moreover, none of the traditional exceptions to the warrant requirement are claimed and none existed; however desirable the break-in may have appeared to its instigators, there is no indication that it had to be carried out quickly, before a warrant could have been obtained.

On the contrary, it had been meticulously planned over a period of more than a month. The search of Dr. Fielding's office was therefore clearly illegal under the unambiguous mandate of the Fourth Amendment....

Defendants contend that even though the Fourth Amendment would ordinarily prohibit break-ins of this nature, the President has the authority, by reason of his special responsibilities over foreign relations and national defense, to suspend its requirements, and that he did so in this case. Neither assertion is accurate.

Many of the landmark Fourth Amendment cases in this country and in England concerned citizens accused of disloyal or treasonous conduct, for history teaches that such suspicions foster attitudes within a government that generate conduct inimical to individual rights....

Strict Limits Enforced

The judicial response to such executive overreaching has been consistent and emphatic: the Government must comply with the strict constitutional and statutory limitations on trespassory searches and arrests even when known foreign agents are involved....

To hold otherwise, except under the most exigent circumstances, would be to abandon the Fourth Amendment to the whim of the executive in total disregard of the amendment's history and purpose.

Defendants contend that, over the last few years, the courts have begun to carve out an exception to this traditional rule for purely intelligence-gathering searches deemed necessary for the conduct of foreign affairs.

However, the cases cited are carefully limited to the issue of wiretapping, a relatively nonintrusive search....and the Supreme Court has reserved judgment in this unsettled area....

The court cannot find that this recent, controversial judicial response to the special problem of national security wiretaps indicates an intention to obviate the entire Fourth Amendment whenever the President determines that an American citizen, personally innocent of wrongdoing, has in his possession information that may touch upon foreign policy concerns....

Blank Check Opposed

Such a doctrine, even in the context of purely information gathering searches, would give the executive a blank check to disregard the very heart and core of the Fourth Amendment and the vital privacy interests that it protects. Warrantless criminal investigatory search—which this break-in may also have been—would, in addition, undermine vital Fifth and Sixth Amendment rights.

The facts presented pretrial lead the court to conclude as a matter of law that the President not only lacked the authority to authorize the break-in but also that he did not in fact give any specific directive permitting national security break-ins, let alone this particular intrusion.

The President has repeatedly and publicly denied prior knowledge or authorization of the Fielding break-in, and the available transcripts of the confidential tape recordings support that claim.

No defendant has presented any evidence to the contrary, and neither Ehrlichman nor Colson, the two defendants who had the greatest access to the President, contend that such specific authorization was given to anyone. The special prosecutor has uncovered nothing to the contrary.

Although there is no recording of the crucial San Clemente meeting between the President, Ehrlichman and Krogh, their similar accounts of that conversation reflect intense Presidential concern with the need to plug the national security leaks and a belief that Dr. Ellsberg might be involved, but no specific reference either to Dr. Fielding or to trespassory searches. The President described that meeting in the following terms:

> "I consider the problem of such disclosures most critical to the national security of the United States and it was my intent, which I believe I conveyed, that the fullest authority of the President under the Constitution and the law should be used if necessary to bring a halt to these disclosures. I considered the successful prosecution of anyone responsible for such unauthorized disclosures a necessary part of bringing to an end this dangerous practice of making such unauthorized disclosures. I did not have prior knowledge of the break-in of Dr. Fielding's office, nor was I informed of it until March 17, 1973."

Such comments simply cannot be interpreted to direct a break-in in violation of the Fourth Amendment.

Defendants adopt the fall-back position that even if the President did not specifically authorize the Fielding break-in, he properly delegated to one or more of the defendants or unindicted co-conspirators the authority to approve national security break-ins.

Of course, since the President had no such authority in the first place, he could not have delegated it to others. Beyond this, however, the court rejects the contention that the President could delegate his alleged power to suspend constitutional rights to nonlaw enforcement officers in the vague, informal, inexact terms noted above.

Even in the wiretap cases the courts have stressed the fact that the President had specifically delegated the authority over "national security" wiretaps to his chief legal officer, the Attorney General, who approved each such tap....

Whatever accommodation is required between the guarantees of the Fourth Amendment and the conduct of foreign affairs, it cannot justify a casual, ill-defined assignment to White House aides and part-time employees granting them an uncontrolled discretion to select, enter and search the homes and offices of innocent American citizens without a warrant....

Defendants contend that, even if the break-in was illegal, they lacked the specific intent necessary to violate Section 241 because they reasonably believed that they had been authorized to enter and search Dr. Fielding's office. As explained above, however, such authorization was not only factually absent but also legally insufficient, and it is well established that a mistake of law is no defense in a conspiracy case to the knowing performance of acts which, like the unauthorized entry and search at issue here, are malum in se [bad in itself]....

As the Supreme Court said in Screws v. United States,...(1945), "The fact that the defendants may not have been thinking in constitutional terms is not material [to a charge under Section 242, a related specific intent statute], where their aim was not to enforce local law but to deprive a citizen of a right and that right was protected by the Constitution."

No Basis for Protection

Here, defendants are alleged to have intended to search Dr. Fielding's office without a warrant, and their mistaken belief that such conduct did not offend the Constitution would not protect them from prosecution under Section 241.... The cases cited by the defendants are not to the contrary. United States v. Guest,...(1966), requires only that the acts which violate Federal rights must have been the primary purpose of the conspiracy rather than an incidental side effect. And United States v. Murdock,...(1933), merely reflects the rule that mistake of law often is a defense to malum prohibition [an act prohibited as wrongful] crimes requiring specific intent, such as those created by the Federal tax laws....

Mistake of law may also excuse an act if it resulted from good faith reliance upon a court order or decision,...or upon the legal advice of an executive officer charged with interpreting or enforcing the law in question....

This principle, however, cannot be stretched to encompass a mistake based upon the assurances of an alleged co-conspirator with regard to the criminality of acts that are malum in se [evil in itself]....

Defendants nonetheless are entitled to present factual material that negatives the claim that they conspired to break in. This will, of course, permit them to explain contracts and activities which may imply collaboration as to the break-in but which they contend was collaboration in pursuit of different, more legitimate efforts to tighten security and prevent leaks within the Government establishment.

Questions of Intent

This material, of course, will necessarily also reflect upon the underlying questions of intent and apparently will require the presentation of some evidence bearing on the defendant's knowledge and authority in national security areas. Discovery to this end—within strict limits—should be permitted by specific, particularized documentary discovery adequate to corroborate their factual contentions as to the legitimate reasons for their association.

To the extent that the special prosecutor has not already produced all material relevant to these limited issues within the possession of his office, the Department of Justice and the F.B.I., defendants may demand such production....

Defendants may pursue such material in the possession of other Government agencies or private parties by means of tightly framed subpoenas duces tecum [for documents and records]....

These subpoenas must be confined to documents the defendants wrote, received, or read, and a strict rule of relevance and materiality will be applied. Cumulative material will be rejected.... All documents subpoenaed shall be produced in court....if evidence relevant and material to the defense is suppressed despite a sufficiently specific demand from one of the defendants, the Court will use the full range of its sanctions, including dismissal, if necessary to insure that defendants received a fair trial....

Defendants' motions for dismissal because of the danger of exposing national security information is denied.

▼▼▼

BURNS ON INFLATION
May 26, 1974

Arthur F. Burns, chairman of the Board of Governors of the Federal Reserve System, warned in a May 26 speech at Jacksonville, Illinois, that "debilitating" inflation threatened the social and political future of the United States. The rapidly rising rate of inflation, Burns said, was more the result of "awesome" federal spending levels than of skyrocketing food and fuel costs. He called for restraint in spending by individuals and government and asserted that the Federal Reserve would continue to oppose "swift growth in money and credit." Burns' gloomy analysis contrasted sharply with relatively optimistic administration statements on the economy.

In a nationwide radio address May 25, President Nixon had declared that the recent economic "storms are abating," and that "the worst is behind us." And the President's Council of Economic Advisers, in an unusual midyear report to Congress, predicted May 28 that inflation would drop to a level "in the neighborhood of 7 per cent by the final quarter of 1974." Burns' pessimistic statements brought a sharp rebuke from White House Press Secretary Ronald L. Ziegler who declared, "the President is right and Burns is wrong on economic prospects." But Burns' views found some support within the administration. In a May 27 interview, Treasury Secretary William E. Simon also urged fiscal restraint and called the nation's inflation rate "totally unacceptable."

As measured by the May Consumer Price Index of the Bureau of Labor Statistics, inflation had expanded at an annual rate of 12 per cent in the previous three months. That rate was the highest in many years, exceeded only by a 13 per cent rate of inflation in the first quarter of 1951, during the

*Korean War. On May 17 government officials announced that the
economy's performance had been worse than anticipated during the first
quarter of 1974. The "real" Gross National Product—that is, the nation's
output of goods and services adjusted to reflect inflation—had dropped at
an annual rate of 6.3 per cent. Although corporate profits were up 10 per
cent, the increase was credited largely to greatly increased oil company
earnings and the impact of inflation on business inventories. The oil
crisis—brought on in part by the Arab oil embargo following the Arab-
Israeli war—and the subsequent effects of the crisis on auto production,
housing construction and other major sectors of the American economy,
had been blamed for the economic slowdown. The Council of Economic
Advisers based its 7 per cent prediction on a belief that increases in food
and energy prices would level off.*

*No slowdown in inflation occurred in the months immediately following
the Burns speech. By late June, according to the Consumer Price Index, inflation was rising at an adjusted annual rate of 13.2 per cent, reflecting
significant increases in the prices of food, cars, clothing, fuel, appliances
and services. When compared with the previous 12 months, wholesale
prices were 16.4 per cent higher than the index level in May 1973. Unabated
inflation prompted a special address on the economy by President Nixon in
late July. In August, shortly after Gerald R. Ford became President he
promised to chair a "domestic summit conference" on the nation's "number one problem." (See p. 861-880.)*

> *Excerpts from speech by Arthur F. Burns at Commence-
> ment exercises of Illinois College, Jacksonville, Illinois,
> May 26, 1974:*

...Inflation is not a new problem for the United States, nor is it confined
to our country. Inflationary forces are now rampant in every major industrial nation of the world. Inflation is raging also in the less developed
countries, and apparently in socialist countries as well as those that practice free enterprise.

The gravity of our current inflationary problem can hardly be
overestimated. Except for a brief period at the end of World War II, prices
in the United States have of late been rising faster than in any other
peacetime period of our history. If past experience is any guide, the future
of our country is in jeopardy. No country that I know of has been able to
maintain widespread economic prosperity once inflation got out of hand.
And the unhappy consequences are by no means solely of an economic
character. If long continued, inflation at anything like the present rate
would threaten the very foundations of our society....

A large part of the recent upsurge in prices has been due to special factors. In most years, economic trends of individual nations tend to diverge.
But during 1973 a business-cycle boom occurred simultaneously in the
United States and in every other major industrial country. With production rising rapidly across the world, prices of labor, materials, and finished
products were bid up everywhere.

To make matters worse, disappointing crop harvests in a number of countries in 1972 forced a sharp run-up in the prices of food last year. The manipulation of petroleum supplies and prices by oil-exporting countries gave another dramatic push to the general price level last autumn and early this year. The influence of these factors is still being felt in consumer markets.

Recently, our price level has also reacted strongly to the removal of wage and price controls—a painful, but essential adjustment in the return to free markets.

These special factors, however, do not account for all of our inflation. For many years, our economy and that of other nations has had a serious underlying bias toward inflation which has simply been magnified by the special influences that I have mentioned.

Rising Aspirations

Ironically, the roots of that bias lie chiefly in the rising aspirations of people everywhere. We are a nation in a hurry for more and more of what we consider the good things of life. I do not question that yearning. Properly directed, it can be a powerful force for human betterment. Difficulties arise, however, when people in general seek to reach their goals by means of short cuts; and that is what has happened.

Of late, individuals have come to depend less and less on their own initiative, and more on government, to achieve their economic objectives. The public nowadays expects the government to maintain prosperous economic conditions, to limit such declines in employment as may occasionally occur, to ease the burden of job loss or illness or retirement, to sustain the incomes of farmers, homebuilders, and so on. These are laudable objectives, and we and other nations have moved a considerable distance toward their realization. Unfortunately, in the process of doing so, governmental budgets have gotten out of control, wages and prices have become less responsive to the discipline of market forces, and inflation has emerged as the most dangerous economic ailment of our time.

The awesome imbalance of the Federal budget is probably the contributory factor to inflation that you have heard the most about. In the past five years, the total Federal expenditures have increased about 50 per cent. In that time span, the cumulative budget deficit of the Federal government, including government-sponsored enterprises, has totaled more than $100 billion. In financing this deficit, and also in meeting huge demands for credit by businesses and consumers, tremendous pressures have been placed on our credit mechanisms and the supply of money has grown at a rate inconsistent with price stability.

The Effects of Inflation

...The prices of virtually everything...have been rising and are still going up. For the typical American worker, the increase in weekly earnings during the past year, while sizeable in dollars, has been wiped out by inflation. In fact, the real weekly take-home pay of the average worker is now below what it was a year ago. Moreover, the real value of accumulated savings deposits has also declined, and the pressure of rising prices on family budgets has led to a worrisome increase in delinquency rates on home mortgages and consumer loans.

Many consumers have responded to these developments by postponing or cancelling plans for buying homes, autos, and other big-ticket items. Sales of new autos began to decline in the spring of 1973, and so too did sales of furniture and appliances, mobile homes, and newly built dwellings. The weakness in consumer markets, largely engendered by inflation, slowed our economic growth rate last year some months before the effects of the oil shortage began to be felt.

Actually, the sales of some of our nation's leading business firms have been on the wane for a year or more. Their costs, meanwhile, have continued to soar with increasing wage rates and sharply rising prices of materials.

The effect on business profits was ignored for a time because accountants typically reckon the value of inventories—and also the value of machinery and equipment used up in production—at original cost, rather than at current inflated prices. These accounting practices create an illusory element in profits—an element that is not available for distribution to stockholders in view of the need to replace inventories, plant, and equipment at appreciably higher prices. Worse still, the illusory part of profits is subject to income tax, thus aggravating the deterioration in profits. This result is especially unfortunate because of the shortage of industrial capacity that now exists in key sectors of our economy—particularly in the basic materials area.

By early this year, a confrontation with economic reality could no longer be put off. Major business corporations found that the volume of investable funds generated internally was not increasing fast enough to finance the rising costs of new plants and equipment, or of the materials and supplies needed to rebuild inventories. Businesses began to scramble for borrowed funds at commercial banks and in the public markets for money and capital. Our financial markets have therefore come under severe strain. Interest rates have risen sharply; savings flows have been diverted from mortgage lending institutions; security dealers have experienced losses; prices of common stocks have declined; the liquidity of some enterprises has been called into question; and tensions of a financial nature have spilled over into international markets.

Social and Political Impact

Concerned as we all are about the economic consequences of inflation, there is even greater reason for concern about the impact on our social and political institutions. We must not risk the social stresses that persistent inflation breeds. Because of its capricious effects on the income and wealth of a nation's families and businesses, inflation inevitably causes disillusionment and discontent. It robs millions of citizens who in their desire to be self-reliant have set aside funds for the education of their children or their own retirement, and it hits many of the poor and elderly especially hard.

In recent weeks, governments have fallen in several major countries, in part because the citizens of those countries had lost confidence in the ability of their leaders to cope with the problem of inflation. Among our own people, the distortions and injustices wrought by inflation have contributed materially to distrust of government officials and of government policies, and even to some loss of confidence in our free enterprise system. Discontent bred by inflation can provoke profoundly disturbing social and political change, as the history of other nations teaches. I do not believe I exaggerate in saying that the ultimate consequence of inflation could well be a significant decline of economic and political freedom for the American people.

There are those who believe that the struggle to curb inflation will not succeed and who conclude that it would be better to adjust to inflation rather than to fight it. On this view, contractual payments of all sorts—wages, salaries, social security benefits, interest on bank loans and deposits and so on—should be written with escalator clauses so as to minimize the distortions and injustices that inflation normally causes.

This is a well-meaning proposal, but it is neither sound nor practical. For one thing, there are hundreds of billions of dollars of outstanding contracts—on mortgages, public and private bonds, insurance policies, and the like—that as a practical matter could not be renegotiated. Even with regard to new undertakings, the obstacles to achieving satisfactory escalator arrangements in our free and complex economy, where people differ so much in financial sophistication, seem insuperable. More important still, by making it easier for many people to live with inflation, escalator arrangements would gravely weaken the discipline that is needed to conduct business and government affairs prudently and efficiently. Universal escalation, I am therefore convinced, is an illusory and dangerous quest. The responsible course is to fight inflation with all the energy we can muster and with all the weapons at our command.

Monetary Policy

One essential ingredient in this struggle is continued resistance to swift growth in money and credit. The Federal Reserve System, I assure you, is firmly committed to this task. We intend to encourage sufficient growth in supplies of money and credit to finance orderly economic expansion. But we are not going to be a willing party to the accommodation of rampant inflation.

As this year's experience has again indicated, a serious effort to moderate the growth of money and credit during a period of burgeoning credit demand results in higher interest rates—particularly on short-term loans. Troublesome though this rise in interest rates may be, it must for a time be tolerated. For, if monetary policy sought to prevent a rise in interest rates when credit demands were booming, money and credit would expand explosively, with devastating effects on the price level. Any such policy would in the end be futile, even as far as interest rates are concerned, because these rates would soon reflect the rise in the price level and therefore go up all the more. We must not let that happen.

But I cannot emphasize too strongly that monetary policy alone cannot solve our stubborn inflationary problem. We must work simultaneously at lessening the powerful underlying bias toward inflation that stems from excessive total demands on our limited resources. This means, among other things, that the Federal budget has to be handled more responsibly than it has been in the past.

Incredible though it may seem, the Congress has been operating over the years without any semblance of a rational budget plan. The committees that consider spending operate independently of the committees that consider taxes, and appropriations themselves are treated in more than a dozen different bills annually. All of this means that the Federal budget never really gets considered as a whole—a fact which helps explain why it is so often in deficit.

Fortunately, after many years of advocacy by concerned citizens and legislators, this glaring deficiency in the Congressional budget process is about to be remedied. Bills that would integrate spending and taxing decisions have passed both the House and the Senate. This is a most encouraging development, and we may confidently expect final action soon by the Congress on this landmark legislation.

Procedural changes, however, will mean little unless the political will exists to exploit the changes fully. And this can happen only if the American people understand better the nature of the inflation we have been experiencing and demand appropriate action by their elected representatives....

Individual Initiative

In the great "town hall" tradition of America, much can be accomplished if people organize themselves—in their offices, trade unions, factories, social clubs, and churches—to probe beneath the superficial explanations of inflation that are the gossip of everyday life. Productivity councils in local communities and enterprises, established for the purpose of improving efficiency and cutting costs, can be directly helpful in restraining inflation.

While I am on the subject of what individuals can do to be helpful, let me note the need for rediscovery of the art of careful budgeting of family expenditures. In some of our businesses, price competition has atrophied as a mode of economic behavior, in part because many of our families no longer exercise much discipline in their spending. We have become a nation of impulse shoppers, of gadget buyers. We give less thought than we should to choosing among the thousands of commodities and services available in our markets. And many of us no longer practice comparative price shopping—not even for big-ticket items. Careful spending habits are not only in the best interest of every family; they could contribute powerfully to a new emphasis on price competition in consumer markets.

I do not expect that the path back to reasonable price stability can be traveled quickly. Indeed, our government will need to take numerous steps to reduce the inflationary bias of our economy besides those I have emphasized. The forces of competition in labor and product markets need to be strengthened—perhaps by establishing wage and price review boards to minimize abuses of economic power, certainly through more vigorous enforcement of the anti-trust laws, besides elimination of barriers to entry in skilled occupations, reduction of barriers to imports from abroad, and modification of minimum wage laws to improve job opportunities for teenagers. Impediments to increased production that still remain in farming, construction work, and other industries need to be removed. And greater incentives should be provided for enlarging our capacity to produce industrial materials, energy, and other products in short supply.

But if inflation cannot be ended quickly, neither can it be eliminated without cost. Some industries will inevitably operate for a time at lower rates of production than they would prefer. Government cannot—and should not—try to compensate fully for all such occurrences. Such a policy would involve negating with one hand what was being attempted with the other.

But government does have a proper ameliorative role to play in areas, such as housing, where the incidence of credit restraint has been disproportionately heavy. The special burden that has fallen on homebuilding should be lightened, as is the intent of the housing aids which the Administration recently announced. And my personal judgment is that it would be advisable, too, for government to be prepared, if need be, to expand the roster of public-service jobs. This particular means of easing especially troublesome situations of unemployment will not add permanently to governments costs. And in any event, it would conflict much less with basic anti-inflation objectives than would the conventional alternative of general monetary or fiscal stimulus. A cut in personal income taxes, for instance, would serve to perpetuate budget deficits. Not only that, it might prove of little aid to the particular industries or localities that are now experiencing economic difficulty. Much the same would be true of a monetary policy that permitted rapid growth of money and credit. There is no justification for such fateful steps at this time....

COURT ON CLASS ACTION SUITS
May 28, 1974

Dealing a severe blow to the average citizen's use of class action suits to remedy improper practices of business or government, the Supreme Court May 28 ruled that persons initiating a federal class action suit must notify, at their expense, all other persons in that class. The cost of such notice was expected to deter many individuals from bringing such suits. Class actions, in which individuals with relatively small and similar claims can join to seek relief through the courts, had been used increasingly by consumer and environmental groups since the late 1960s. The rules for federal class action suits were revised and approved by Congress in 1966.

Upset by the fact that each time he purchased an odd lot of stock—fewer than, or not a multiple of, 100 shares—he had to pay an extra surcharge on top of the usual commission, Morton Eisen filed a class action suit in May 1966. On his behalf and on that of all other odd-lot purchasers from 1962 to 1966, he sued the brokerage firms which handled 99 per cent of the New York Stock Exchange's odd-lot business, charging them with violating the antitrust and securities laws, and seeking damages. His own stake in the damage award was about $70.

Justice Lewis F. Powell Jr., writing the Court's opinion in the case, pointed out Eisen's need to maintain this case as a class action: "No competent attorney would undertake his complex antitrust action to recover so inconsequential an amount. Economic reality dictates that petitioner's suit proceed as a class action or not at all." All the litigation over the ensuing eight years had focused on whether or not Eisen's case could stand as a class action. In 1968, the federal district court reversed an earlier decision *and found that the case did satisfy the requirements for a class action. Construing liberally the requirement that Eisen notify each identifiable member of that class, the lower court held that this would be satisfied by notifying a limited number of members—at a cost of about $22,000—compared to $225,000 for mailing notice to each of the more than two million identifiable members.*

Because even $22,000 was a large price for Eisen to pay in his suit for $70, the court held a preliminary hearing, decided Eisen had a good chance of winning the case, and ordered the brokerage firms to pay 90 per cent of the cost of notifying the class members. The notification requirement was designed to allow members of a class to withdraw from the class, if they desired, or to enable them to share in the award which resulted. The U.S. Court of Appeals, second circuit, rejected the lower court's findings and ordered that the suit be dismissed as an unmanageable class action—"a Frankenstein monster posing as a class action." Eisen appealed to the Supreme Court.

Supreme Court Opinion

The Supreme Court was virtually unanimous on the key point of the case: Eisen did have to notify all identifiable members of the class at his own expense. The language of the rules was unmistakable in its meaning, Powell wrote. Despite Eisen's argument that the high cost of such notice would end his class action and frustrate his challenge to the policies concerning 'odd-lot' purchases, this notice requirement was "not a discretionary consideration to be waived in a particular case." Therefore, Powell said it must stand as a prerequisite to his class action case. Furthermore, Powell held for the Court, the person bringing the suit must bear the entire notification cost; the lower court had exceeded its authority in ordering the brokerage firms to bear part of that cost.

Justices William O. Douglas, William J. Brennan Jr. and Thurgood Marshall dissented in part. They argued that the case should be sent back to the lower courts where the class which Eisen represented might be subdivided into a smaller subclass which he could afford to notify. "The class action is one of the few legal remedies the small claimant has against those who command the status quo," wrote Douglas. "I would strengthen his hand with the view of creating a system of law that dispenses justice to the lowly as well as to those liberally endowed with power and wealth."

In an earlier class action ruling in December 1973, the Court had held that where no federal law or question is involved, a class action for damages may only come into the federal courts if each person in the class has a claim of $10,000 or more.

Excerpts from the Supreme Court's May 28 opinion follow on the next page:

No. 73-203

Morton Eisen, Etc., Petitioner, *v.* Carlisle & Jacquelin et al.	On Writ of Certiorari to the United States Court of Appeals for the Second Circuit.

[May 28, 1974]

MR. JUSTICE POWELL delivered the opinion of the Court.

On May 2, 1966, petitioner filed a class action on behalf of himself and all other odd-lot traders on the New York Stock Exchange (the Exchange). The complaint charged respondents with violations of the antitrust and securities laws and demanded damages for petitioner and his class. Eight years have elapsed, but there has been no trial on the merits of these claims. Both the parties and the courts are still wrestling with the complex questions surrounding petitioner's attempt to maintain his suit as a class action under Rule 23 of the Federal Rules of Civil Procedure. We granted certiorari to resolve some of these difficulties....

I

Petitioner brought this class action in the United States District Court for the Southern District of New York. Originally, he sued on behalf of all buyers and sellers of odd-lots on the Exchange, but subsequently the class was limited to those who traded in odd-lots during the period from May 1, 1962, through June 30, 1966.... Throughout this period odd-lot trading was not part of the Exchange's regular auction market but was handled exclusively by special odd-lot dealers, who bought and sold for their own accounts as principals. Respondent brokerage firms Carlisle & Jacquelin and DeCoppet & Doremus together handled 99% of the Exchange's odd-lot business.... They were compensated by the odd-lot differential, a surcharge imposed on the odd-lot investor in addition to the standard brokerage commission applicable to round-lot transactions. For the period in question the differential was 1/8 of a point (12½ cents) per share on stocks trading below $40 per share and 1/4 of a point (25 cents) per share on stocks trading at or above $40 per share.

Petitioner charged that respondent brokerage firms had monopolized odd-lot trading and set the differential at an excessive level in violation of § 1 and 2 of the Sherman Act...and he demanded treble damages for the amount of the overcharge. Petitioner also demanded unspecified money damages from the Exchange for its alleged failure to regulate the differential for the protection of investors in violation of § 6 and 19 of the Securities Exchange Act of 1934.... Finally, he requested attorneys' fees and injunctive prohibition of future excessive charges.

A critical fact in this litigation is that petitioner's individual stake in the damage award he seeks is only $70. No competent attorney would undertake his complex antitrust action to recover so inconsequential an amount. Economic reality dictates that petitioner's suit proceed as a class action or not at all. Opposing counsel have therefore engaged in prolonged combat over the various requirements of Rule 23. The result has been an exceedingly complicated series of decisions by both the District Court and the Court of Appeals for the Second Circuit. To understand the labyrinthian history of this litigation, a preliminary overview of the decisions may prove useful.

In the beginning, the District Court determined that petitioner's suit was not maintainable as a class action. On appeal, the Court of Appeals issued two decisions known popularly as *Eisen I* and *Eisen II*. The first held that the District Court's decision was a final order and thus appealable. In the second the Court of Appeals intimated that petitioner's suit could satisfy the requirements of Rule 23, but it remanded the case to permit the District Court to consider the matter further. After conducting several evidentiary hearings on remand, the District Court decided that the suit could be maintained as a class action and entered orders intended to fulfill the notice requirements of Rule 23. Once again, the case was appealed. The Court of Appeals then issued its decision in *Eisen III* and ended the trilogy by denying class action status to petitioner's suit....

II

At the outset we must decide whether the Court of Appeals in *Eisen III* had jurisdiction to review the District Court's orders permitting the suit to proceed as a class action and allocating the cost of notice. Petitioner contends that it did not. Respondents counter by asserting two independent bases for appellate jurisdiction: first, that the orders in question constituted a "final" decision...and were therefore appealable as of right...and second, that the Court of Appeals in *Eisen II* expressly retained jurisdiction pending further development of a factual record on remand and that consequently no new jurisdictional basis was required for the decision in *Eisen III*. Because we agree with the first ground asserted by respondents, we have no occasion to consider the second....

III

Turning to the merits of the case, we find that the District Court's resolution of the notice problem was erroneous in two respects. First, it failed to comply with the notice requirements of Rule 23..., and second, it imposed part of the cost of notice on respondents,

A

Rule 23 (c)(2) provides that, in any class action maintained under subdivision (b)(3), each class member shall be advised that he has the right to exclude himself from the action on request or to enter an appearance through counsel, and further that the judgment, whether favorable or not, will bind all class members not requesting exclusion. To this end, the court is required to direct to class members "the best notice practicable under the circumstances, *including individual notice to all members who can be identified through reasonable effort.*" We think the import of this language is unmistakable. Individual notice must be sent to all class members whose names and addresses may be ascertained through reasonable effort....

[In] *Mullane v. Central Hanover Bank and Trust Co....*the Court... observed that notice and an opportunity to be heard were fundamental requisites of the constitutional guarantee of procedural due process. It further stated that notice must be "reasonably calculated, under all the circumstances, to apprise interested parties of the pendency of the action and afford them an opportunity to present their objections...."

The Court then held that publication notice could not satisfy due process where the names and addresses of the beneficiaries were known. In such cases, "the reasons disappear for resort to means less likely than the mails to apprise them of [an action's] pendency"....

Petitioner contends, however, that we should dispense with the requirement of individual notice in this case, and he advances two reasons for doing so. First, the prohibitively high cost of providing individual notice to 2,250,000 class members would end this suit as a class action and effectively frustrate petitioner's attempt to vindicate the policies underlying the antitrust and securities laws. Second, petitioner contends that individual notice is unnecessary in this case, because no prospective class member has a large enough stake in the matter to justify separate litigation of his individual claim. Hence class members lack any incentive to opt out of the class action even if notified.

The short answer to these arguments is that individual notice to identifiable class members is not a discretionary consideration to be waived in a particular case. It is, rather, an unambiguous requirement of Rule 23. As the Advisory Committee's Note explained, the Rule was intended to insure that the judgment whether favorable or not, would bind all class members who did not request exclusion from the suit.... Accordingly, each class member who can be identified through reasonable effort must be notified that he may request exclusion from the action and thereby preserve his opportunity to press his claim separately or that he may remain in the class and perhaps participate in the management of the action. There is nothing in Rule 23 to suggest that the notice requirements can be tailored to fit the pocketbooks of particular plaintiffs.

Petitioner further contends that adequate representation, rather than notice, is the touchstone of due process in a class action and therefore satisfies Rule 23. We think this view has little to commend it.... We therefore conclude that Rule 23 (c)(2) requires that individual notice be sent to all class members who can be identified with reasonable effort.

B

We also agree with the Court of Appeals that petitioner must bear the cost of notice to the members of his class. The District Court reached the contrary conclusion and imposed 90% of the notice cost on respondents. This decision was predicated on the court's finding, made after a preliminary hearing on the merits of the case, that petitioner was "more than likely" to prevail on his claims. Apparently, the court interpreted Rule 23 to authorize such a hearing as part of the determination whether a suit may be maintained as a class action. We disagree.

We find nothing in either the language or history of Rule 23 that gives a court any authority to conduct a preliminary inquiry into the merits of a suit in order to determine whether it may be maintained as a class action....

In the absence of any support under Rule 23, petitioner's effort to impose the cost of notice on respondents must fail. The usual rule is that a plaintiff must initially bear the cost of notice to the class. The exceptions cited by the District Court related to situations where a fiduciary duty pre-existed between the plaintiff and defendant, as in a shareholder derivative suit. Where, as here, the relationship between the parties is truly adversarial, the plaintiff must pay for the cost of notice as part of the ordinary burden of financing his own suit.

Petitioner has consistently maintained, however, that he will not bear the cost of notice under subdivision (c) (2) to members of the class as defined in his original complaint.... We therefore remand the cause with instructions to dismiss the class action as so defined.

The judgment of the Court of Appeals is vacated and the cause remanded for proceedings consistent with this opinion.

MR. JUSTICE DOUGLAS, with whom MR. JUSTICE BRENNAN and MR. JUSTICE MARSHALL concur, dissenting in part.

While I am in general agreement with the phases of this case touched on by the Court, I add a few words because its opinion does not fully explore the issues which will be dispositive of this case on remand to the District Court.

Rule 23 (c)(4) provides, "When appropriate (A) an action may be brought or maintained as a class action with respect to particular issues, or (B) a class may be divided into subclasses and each subclass treated as a class, and the provisions of this rule shall then be construed and applied accordingly."...

The power to create a subclass is clear and unambiguous. Who should be included and how large it should be are questions that only the District Court should resolve. Notice to each member of the subclass would be essential under Rule 23 (c) (2); and under Rule 23 (c) (2) (A) any notified member may opt out. There would remain the question whether the subclass suit is manageable. But since the subclass could be chosen in light of the nonmanageability of the size of the class whose claims are presently before us, there is no apparent difficulty in that sense....

The purpose of Rule 23 is to provide flexibility in the management of class actions, with the trial court taking an active role in the conduct of the litigation.... Lower federal courts have recognized their discretion to define those subclasses proper to prosecute an action without being bound by the plaintiff's complaint.... And, as Rule 23 (c)(1) clearly indicates, the courts retain both the power and the duty to realign classes during the conduct of an action when appropriate....

I agree...that a class action serves not only the convenience of the parties but also prompt, efficient judicial administration. I think in our society that is growing in complexity there are bound to be innumerable people in common disasters, calamities, or ventures who would go begging for justice without the class action but who could with all regard to due process be protected. Some of these are consumers whose claims may seem *de minimis* but who alone have no practical recourse for either remuneration or injunctive relief. Some may be environmentalists, who have no photographic development plant about to be ruined because of air pollution by radiation but who suffer perceptibly by smoke, noxious gases, or radiation. Or the unnamed individual may be only a ratepayer being excessively charged by a utility or a homeowner whose assessment is slowly rising beyond his ability to pay.

The class action is one of the few legal remedies the small claimant has against those who command the status quo. I would strengthen his hand with the view of creating a system of law that dispenses justice to the lowly as well as to those liberally endowed with power and wealth.

SYRIAN-ISRAELI DISENGAGEMENT
May 31, 1974

Syria and Israel signed an agreement in Geneva May 31 providing for a cease-fire and separation of their forces in the Golan Heights, thus clearing the way for further negotiations toward settlement of the October 1973 war in the Middle East. Left unmentioned in the text were many controversial points, including the status of the Palestinians and policing of the disengagement, which were dealt with separately in unpublished understandings between the United States and Syrian President Hafez Assad and Israeli Prime Minister Golda Meir. Following month-long negotiations during which U.S. Secretary of State Henry A. Kissinger shuttled back and forth between Damascus and Jerusalem, the Israeli Knesset (Parliament) and Syria's ruling Baath Party approved the accord May 30.

Under the agreement Syria regained 300 square miles held by Israel since the October 1973 war, plus a strip of the Golan Heights, including the town of Quneitra, which had been in Israeli hands since the 1967 war. Israel agreed to withdraw about 350 yards from the outskirts of Quneitra but kept three hills overlooking the town, thereby protecting Israeli settlements. The pact established a 1/4 mile-wide buffer zone, including Quenitra, to be patrolled by a 1,250-man United Nations Disengagement Observer Force.

Long the champions of the Palestinian militants, the Syrians were unwilling to agree formally to stop Syrian-based commando raids into Israel, a major Israeli demand. But Assad was reported to have privately assured Kissinger that Syria would try to prevent such attacks. Assad's statement, it was understood, represented a major breakthrough in reaching the final

435

pact. Added to Assad's assurances were private U.S. statements to Israel promising American support of Israeli actions taken against guerrillas in self-defense. Without going into details, Mrs. Meir told the Knesset about that promise and also indicated that the United States had entered into understandings with Israel providing for aerial reconnaissance of the disengagement area and further economic and military aid for Israel. In deference to Syrian demands for return of all Israeli-held territory, Kissinger informed Assad privately that the United States did not regard the disengagement line as a permanent boundary. Kissinger was also reported to have promised to work for Palestinian representation at the Geneva peace talks.

Triumph for Kissinger

The accord, which marked the first formal agreement between Syria and Israel since the armistice ending the 1948 Israeli war of independence, was signed at U.N. headquarters in Geneva by Israeli Maj. Gen. Herzl Shafir and Syrian Gen. Adnan Wajih Tayara. It was widely interpreted as a personal triumph for Kissinger. Said Assad, "It could not have been done without him."

Within half an hour after the disengagement agreement was signed in Geneva, the fighting on the Golan Heights stopped—after 81 days of conflict. Withdrawal of forces began June 5 when Syrian and Israeli negotiators at Geneva set the precise lines of troop and weapons disengagement and established the buffer zone. The first U.N. troops arrived the same day. Sporadic clashes between Israelis and Palestinian guerrillas nevertheless continued, according to reports by both sides.

The prospect of American aid was believed to have strengthened Kissinger's hand during the disengagement talks. Appearing June 4 before the U.S. House of Representatives Foreign Affairs Committee, Kissinger stressed that no commitments on aid to Syria had been made during the negotiations. However, he acknowledged that a $100-million "Special Requirements Fund" in the administration's foreign aid request might be earmarked for Syria, and he indicated that the United States would "look favorably on a request for economic reconstruction" in the evacuated territories.

Israeli reaction to the disengagement emphasized its provisional nature. Outgoing Israeli Defense Minister Moshe Dayan said, "This is the end of the first stage of the war. But what will come next?" Israeli restraint contrasted with Syrian elation over what was regarded as a major Arab victory. In a statement issued June 5, the Syrian government declared that the United States understood Syrian attitudes and that its friendship would be cultivated as a means of weakening Israel. The pact effectively ended the isolation of Egyptian President Anwar Sadat, who had been severely attacked by Arab militants for agreeing to the Egyptian-Israeli disengagement of Jan. 18. (See p. 29-32.) As a Sadat aide said, the accord "vindicated" Sadat "in front of all the Arabs."

By joining with Egypt in moving toward a negotiated settlement of the Middle East problem, Syrians further eroded radical Palestinian hopes of replacing Israel with a secular state. Meeting in Cairo June 1-9, the Palestinian National Council, a parliament of the Palestine Liberation Organization (PLO), agreed to seek admission to forthcoming Geneva peace talks but specified that "the national rights of the Palestinian people" must be a topic of discussion there. (PLO at the U.N., see p. 919.) The term "national rights" was variously interpreted by participants in the conference to mean either acceptance of a Palestinian state on the west bank of the Jordan River or in the Gaza Strip, or dismantlement of Israel itself. The council authorized the PLO, which represents various guerrilla groups, to increase its military operations "inside occupied lands," that is, in Israel and Israeli-held territories.

Text of the accord signed May 31 by Syria and Israel providing for separation of their forces on the Golan Heights.

THE AGREEMENT
[A]

Israel and Syria will scrupulously observe the ceasefire on land, sea and air and will refrain from all military action against each other from the time of the signing of this document, in implementation of the United Nations Security Council Resolution 338 dated Oct. 22, 1973.

[B]

The military forces of Israel and Syria will be separated in accordance with the following principles:

1. All Israeli military forces will be west of the line designated as Line A on the map attached hereto except in the Quneitra area where they will be west of Line A-1.

2. All territory east of Line A will be under Syrian administration and Syrian civilians will return to this territory.

3. The area between Line A and the line designated as Line B on the attached map will be an area of separation. In this area will be stationed the United Nations Disengagement Observer Force established in accordance with the accompanying protocol.

4. All Syrian military forces will be east of the line designated as Line B on the attached map.

5. There will be two equal areas of limitation in armament and forces, one west of Line A and one east of Line B as agreed upon.

Air Forces of the two sides will be permitted to operate up to their respective lines witout interference from the other side.

[C]

In the area between Line A and Line A-1 on the attached map there shall be no military forces.

[D]

This agreement and the attached map will be signed by the military representatives of Israel and Syria in Geneva not later than May 31, 1974, in the Egyptian-Israeli military working group of the Geneva peace conference under the aegis of the United Nations, after that group has been joined by a Syrian military representative and with the participation of representatives of the United States and the Soviet Union.

The precise delineation of a detailed map and a plan for the implementation of the disengagement of forces will be worked out by a military working group who will agree on the stages of this process.

The military working group described above will start their work for this purpose under the aegis of the United Nations within 24 hours after the signing of this agreement. They will complete this task within five days.

Disengagement will begin within 24 hours after the completion of the task of the military working group. The process of disengagement will be completed not later than 20 days after it begins.

[E]

The provision of paragraphs A, B and C shall be inspected by personnel of the United Nations comprising the U.N. Disengagement Observer Force under this agreement.

[F]

Within 24 hours after the signing of this agreement in Geneva all wounded prisoners of war which each side holds of the other as certified by the I.C.R.C.—International Committee of the Red Cross—will be repatriated. The morning after the completion of the task of the military working group, all remaining prisoners of war will be repatriated.

[G]

The bodies of all dead soldiers held by either side will be returned for burial in their respective countries within 10 days after the signing of this agreement.

[H]

This agreement is not a peace agreement. It is a step toward a just and durable peace on the basis of Security Council Resolution 338 dated Oct. 22, 1973.

THE PROTOCOL

Israel and Syria agreed that: The function of the United Nations Disengagement Observer Force under the agreement will be to use its best efforts to maintain the cease-fire and to see that it is scrupulously observed. It will supervise the agreement and protocol thereto with regard to the areas of separation and limitations.

In carrying out its mission, it will comply with generally applicable Syrian laws and regulations and will not hamper the functioning of local civil administrators.

It will enjoy freedom of movement and communication and other facilities that are necessary for its mission. It will be mobile and provided with personal weapons of a defensive character and shall use such weapons only in self-defense.

The number of the U.N.D.O.F. shall be about 1,250, who will be selected by the Secretary General of the United Nations in consultation with the parties from members of the United Nations who are not permanent members of the Security Council.

The U.N.D.O.F. will be under the command of the United Nations vested in the Secretary General under the authority of the Security Council. The U.N.D.O.F. shall carry out inspections under the agreement and report thereon to the parties on a regular basis not less often than once every 15 days and in addition when requested by either party.

It shall mark on the ground the respective lines shown on the map attached to the agreement. Israel and Syria will support a resolution of the U.N. Security Council which will provide for the U.N.D.O.F. contemplated by the agreement. The initial authorization will be for six months subject to renewal by further resolution of the Security Council.

▼▼▼

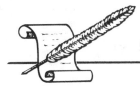

June

COLSON'S GUILTY PLEA
June 3, 1974

Charles W. Colson, former special counsel to President Richard M. Nixon, pleaded guilty June 3 in a federal court in the District of Columbia to a charge of obstructing justice by his activities against Pentagon Papers defendant Daniel Ellsberg. By agreeing to plead guilty, Colson obtained from Watergate special prosecutor Leon Jaworski the dismissal of all other charges against him involving the Ellsberg and Watergate coverup cases. Colson also agreed to testify in ongoing government investigations or trials arising from the Watergate scandal, an offer which was reported by the Washington Post *to have created considerable consternation among his former White House associates. Colson was the first member of the President's inner circle to agree to cooperate with the special prosecutor. For that reason, and the substantiality of the charges the special prosecutor had agreed to drop, it was generally assumed that he had significant knowledge to share in relation to still unresolved questions raised by the Watergate cases. Colson's vow to "tell everything I know about the Watergate" fed speculation that his testimony might implicate President Nixon in the coverup or in matters pertaining to the ITT controversy and to political contributions from the dairy industry.*

In two separate indictments handed down on March 1 and March 7, respectively, Colson had been charged with conspiring to impede the investigation into the Watergate break-in and with conspiring to violate the civil rights of Dr. Lewis J. Fielding, at one time Daniel Ellsberg's psychiatrist, by breaking into his office in Los Angeles. Colson had pleaded not guilty on all counts, and he continued to maintain his innocence of the charges concerning Fielding and obstruction of the Watergate investigation

*even as he unexpectedly pleaded guilty for actions against Ellsberg. What
Colson admitted to was masterminding a plan to defame and degrade the
credibility and public image of Ellsberg, who had been indicted in June
1971 on charges of leaking the then-classified Pentagon Papers to the
media. The charges against Colson were stated in a one-count criminal information which said that Colson's intent had been to "influence, obstruct
and impede the conduct and outcome" of Ellsberg's 1973 trial* (see Historic
Documents 1973, p. 537). *A criminal information is an indictment prepared
by a prosecutor rather than by a grand jury.*

*Colson's guilty plea came after a week of plea-bargaining with the
Watergate prosecutors and an intense prayer meeting held the night
before his court appearance. In December 1973, Colson reportedly had undergone a religious conversion which had been greeted with skepticism
because of his previous self-cultivated image as the White House "tough
guy." The best-known statement about Colson had been one he made
himself in a celebrated memorandum to other White House aides, seeking
to fire them up for the 1972 election by demonstrating his own zeal. Wrote
Colson, "I would walk over my grandmother if necessary." Colson had
joined the White House staff in 1969 as special counsel, concentrating on
defining and cultivating political interest groups.*

Colson's Career as Hatchetman

*Colson's career as the political hatchetman of the Nixon administration
began with the 1970 congressional elections, during which he was reported
to have planned political advertisements associating Democratic candidates with extremist causes. The dissemination of damaging stories
about then Democratic Senator Joseph D. Tydings, campaigning for re-
election in Maryland, was also attributed to Colson. Thereafter a string of
"dirty tricks" was laid on Colson's doorstep—including schemes for
firebombing and burglarizing the Brookings Institution, and forging a
State Department cable purporting to link the assassination of South Vietnamese president Ngo Dinh Diem in 1963 with the late President Kennedy.
The two latter charges, made by former presidential counsel John W. Dean
III, were denied by Colson.*

*However, his reputation for hardnosed action caused apprehension even
at the White House. "That is your fatal flaw in Chuck," former chief of
staff H. R. Haldeman once told Nixon. "He is an operator in expediency,
and he will pay at the time and where he is to accomplish whatever there is
to do." Against this background, Colson's plea bargain initially raised
questions of credibility. Despite "some evidence that he is cooperating
fully," one government source was reported to be "very skeptical after all
that has happened...the nearly two years in which he protested his innocence so vehemently." Senator Harold E. Hughes (D Iowa), who had
been instrumental in Colson's conversion, vouched for his sincerity: "The
guilty plea is a result of his conversion," said Hughes. "(Colson) said he was*

not guilty of what he was charged with and he went in search of what he had done that was criminal.... I'm convinced he intends to tell all he knows to the appropriate authority."

In a statement issued after he entered his guilty plea, Colson said his decision had been influenced by remarks of U.S. District Court Judge Gerhard A. Gesell, who had said during pre-trial arguments on May 21 that the government of the United States was one of laws and not of men. The statement had come as a "profound" revelation, Colson said.

On June 21, Colson was sentenced to serve one to three years and to pay a $5,000 fine. Colson's disbarment from the practice of law, automatic as a result of his guilty plea to a felony charge, followed on June 25 by order of the U.S. District Court for the District of Columbia. Colson had left the White House staff in March 1973 to return to private law practice, but he had continued to advise President Nixon until early 1974.

The White House response to Colson's surprise move was an effort to minimize speculation about the possibly damaging effects of his testimony. On June 4, Special White House Counsel James D. St. Clair said that he felt Colson's testimony in the impeachment inquiry "would be highly supportive of the President." But transcripts of Nixon's Watergate conversations indicated a deep concern on the President's part over what Colson might reveal about the inner workings of the senior White House team if he were ever to speak publicly or privately with the Watergate prosecutors.

Text of the criminal information filed by the special prosecutor's office June 3 against former White House special counsel Charles W. Colson, and excerpts from a statement released by Colson after entering a plea June 3:

INFORMATION

The United States of America by its attorney, the special prosecutor, Watergate special prosecution force, charges:

1. At all times material herein, up to on or about March 10, 1973, Charles W. Colson, the defendant, was acting in the capacity of an officer and employee of the United States government, as special counsel to the President of the United States, Richard M. Nixon.

2. On or about June 28, 1971, and for a period of time thereafter, in the District of Columbia and elsewhere, Charles W. Colson, the defendant, unlawfully, willfully and knowingly did corruptly endeavor to influence, obstruct and impede the due administration of justice in connection with the criminal trial of Daniel Ellsberg under indictment in the case of United States v. Russo, Criminal Case No. 9373, United States District Court, Central District of California, by devising and implementing a scheme to defame and destroy the public image and credibility of Daniel Ellsberg and those engaged in the legal defense of Daniel Ellsberg, with the intent to in-

fluence, obstruct, and impede the conduct and outcome of the criminal prosecution then being conducted in the United States District Court for the Central District of California.

3. The aforesaid scheme by which Charles W. Colson, the defendant, unlawfully, willfully and knowingly did corruptly endeavor to influence, obstruct and impede the due administration of justice in connection with the criminal prosecution of Daniel Ellsberg consisted of the following acts:

(1) In July and August 1971, the defendant, and others unnamed herein, endeavored to and did release defamatory and derogatory allegations concerning one of the attorneys engaged in the legal defense of Daniel Ellsberg for the purpose of publicly disseminating said allegations, the known and probable consequences of which would be to influence, obstruct, and impede the conduct and outcome of the criminal prosecution of Daniel Ellsberg.

(2) In July and August, 1971, the defendant, and others unnamed herein, endeavored to obtain, receive and release confidential and derogatory information concerning Daniel Ellsberg, including information from the psychiatric files of Daniel Ellsberg, for the purpose of publicly disseminating said information, the known and probable consequences of which would be to influence, obstruct, and impede the conduct and outcome of the criminal prosecution of Daniel Ellsberg.

(In violation of Title 18, United States Code Section 1503)

Respectfully submitted,
s/LEON JAWORSKI
Special Prosecutor
Watergate Special Prosecution Force

1425 K Street, N.W.
Washington, D.C. 20005
Attorney for the United States
Dated: June 3, 1974

Excerpts from Colson's statement:

I have pleaded guilty today to the information filed by the special prosecutor in the District Court. The charges in the information are not those contained in the two indictments previously returned against me—that is the Watergate cover-up and the Ellsberg break-in.

I pleaded not guilty to those charges; I can in complete conscience, however, plead guilty to the particular charges of this information.

I have taken this action for reasons which are very important to me.

1. To have fought the two indictments might well have resulted in my eventual exoneration. As a defendant, I would have been necessarily concerned with protecting my position in the trials. That would have limited

my ability to tell everything I know about the Watergate and Watergate related matters.

I have told the truth from the beginning but I have not been able to testify fully; for example, because of a threatened indictment I could not appear at the Ervin committee.

I have watched with a heavy heart the country I love being torn apart these past months by one of the most divisive and bitter controversies in our history. The prompt and just resolution of other proceedings, far more important than my trial, is vital to our democratic process. I want to be free to contribute to the resolution no matter who it may help or hurt—me or others. That, at least is the way I see my duty; that is the dictate of my conscience.

2. During the pre-trial motions, I listened very intently to many of the arguments related to the national security justification of the Ellsberg break-in. Judge Gesell's words from the bench—to the effect that if this is to be a government of laws and not of men, then those men entrusted with enforcing the law must be held to account for the natural consequences of their own actions—had a profound effect on me. Whether at the time certain actions seemed totally justified and indeed essential to the national interest is not the issue. If the overriding national interest requires extraordinary action, then every possible legal sanction must be observed, every right to individual due process respected. We cannot accept the principle that men in high government office can act in disregard of the rights of even one individual citizen.

My plea acknowledges that I endeavored to disseminate derogatory information about Dr. Ellsberg and his attorney at a time when he was under indictment by the same government of which I was an officer. Judge Gesell's words had particular impact upon me because I have either been under indictment or been the target of serious accusations for the past two years. I know what it feels like—what it must have felt like to Dr. Ellsberg—to have the government which is prosecuting me also to try me in the public press. I know how it feels to be subjected to repeated and in some cases deliberate leaks from various congressional committees. In fact, there are records showing that the CIA deliberately planted stories with several major news organizations accusing me of involvement in criminal activities.

I regret what I attempted to do to Dr. Ellsberg. It is wrong whether it is done to him, to me or to others. Not only is it morally right therefore that I plead to this charge but I fervently hope that this case will serve to prevent similar abuses in the future. Government officials must know that under our system of government, every individual—whether a potential or actual criminal defendant—is entitled to a fair trial and that anyone who attempts to interfere with that right must suffer the consequences....

NIXON'S MIDDLE EAST TRIP
June 10-19, 1974

The diplomatic efforts of the Nixon administration were demonstrated clearly in June 1974 as President Nixon made two major trips abroad to underscore his administration's achievements in promoting world peace. The President received a hero's welcome when he toured five Middle East nations June 12-19 symbolizing the dramatic turnabout in U.S.-Arab relations brought about during the nine months of negotiations following the October Arab-Israeli war. It was the first time an American President had visited Egypt, Saudi Arabia, Syria, Israel and Jordan. In the Middle East, Nixon pledged to provide Egypt with a nuclear reactor with guarantees that it be used only for peaceful purposes, announced the resumption of diplomatic relations between the United States and Syria and promised continued American military and economic support for Israel.

President Nixon stopped over in Salzburg, Austria, June 10-11 for talks with Austrian Chancellor Bruno Kreisky on Middle East and East-West relations. Moreover, scarcely a week after returning to this country from the Middle East, he flew June 25 to Brussels, Belgium, for a meeting with NATO leaders (see p. 529) and on to Moscow June 27 for the third annual summit meeting with Soviet leaders (see p. 535). With the conclusion of the Middle East and Soviet trips, Nixon had logged a presidential travel record of 137,000 miles. Only Secretary of State Henry A. Kissinger's emotional threat to resign, made in Salzburg June 11, over alleged involvement in the wiretapping of his aides (see p. 487) and reports that outspoken Soviet Jewish dissidents had been detained for the length of Nixon's Soviet visit, marred the otherwise triumphant tours. The drama of the trips in fact was underscored June 24 when it was reported that President Nixon was suffer-

*ing from a potentially dangerous attack of phlebitis in his left leg and had
made the Middle East trip over the objections of his doctors.*

*But the drama of the Middle East trip—the first by an American Presi-
dent except for Roosevelt's meetings with war allies in Egypt in 1943—
could not overshadow the President's domestic problems with the economy
and Watergate. Back in Washington, the President's critics charged
that the trips were calculated political attempts to supplant the ever-
breaking Watergate headlines with stories of Nixon's indispensability to
world peace efforts. The Supreme Court, in his absence, agreed to decide
whether the special prosecutor could have access to 64 presidential
tapes and whether the grand jury had been within its authority when it
named Nixon an unindicted coconspirator in the plan to cover up the
Watergate scandal. (See p. 225, 621.) Kissinger incisively related
the foreign trips to the domestic problems: "If we did not go," he
said, "we would be saying we are not a functioning government." But,
the administration's foreign affairs accomplishments, dramatized by
the trips, were vital to Nixon's public image. The President had seemingly linked his presidency to his ability to promote the importance of
these accomplishments and thereby drown out Watergate allegations.*

Middle East Accomplishments

*Ceremonial receptions played centerstage throughout the Middle East
trip. On his arrival at Cairo, the first stop of the Middle East tour, Nixon
was greeted by throngs of cheering Egyptians, waving palm fronds and
throwing rose petals in his path. Saudi princes accorded him a stately
welcome in Jidda, Saudi Arabia. A more restrained military welcome took
place in Damascus, Syria. In all, official White House estimates placed the
crowd turnout at seven million.*

*By far the most controversial of Nixon's actions while in the Mideast was
his announcement that the United States would provide Egypt and Israel
with nuclear technology for peaceful purposes. Details were to be worked
out. Before Nixon's return, a number of members of Congress had expressed doubts about providing nuclear fuel and reactors to the volatile
Middle East and promised a close look at the terms of the agreements
when negotiations on them were completed. Some members expressed
concern because Congress had not been consulted in advance of the trip
about the nuclear offers. The agreements were to be scrutinized by the
Joint Committee on Atomic Energy, the Senate Foreign Relations Committee and the House Foreign Affairs Committee.*

*Nixon and Egyptian President Anwar Sadat announced in a joint
statement June 14 that the United States would sell nuclear reactors and
fuel to Egypt for generating electricity. The agreement on the sales was to
include appropriate safeguards against the use of the equipment and byproducts for other than peaceful uses. In the joint statement, Nixon also
pledged economic cooperation, with aid to the extent authorized by
Congress for reconstruction and restoring trade. He also pledged assistance*

in encouraging private American investment, increasing agricultural production and in scientific developments.

In Saudi Arabia, discussions with King Faisal were on the implementation of the pact signed June 8 between the two nations on military and economic cooperation and assistance. In Syria, Nixon and President Hafez Assad announced on June 16 the resumption of diplomatic relations between the two countries, broken during the 1967 Arab-Israeli War. While no mention was made of foreign aid to Syria, Kissinger had indicated the possibility of economic assistance for rebuilding war-damaged areas after the signing of the Syrian-Israeli military disengagement pact in May. (See p. 435-439.)

In Israel, Nixon announced continued and expanded military and economic aid and a nuclear technology package similar to Egypt's. The joint statement with Israeli Prime Minister Yitzhak Rabin called for the working out of long-term military aid agreements, rather than annual ones, as well as continued cooperation in a number of areas, including energy production, tourism and industry. The two leaders discussed Israel's long-term military needs. In Jordan, the final stop in the Mideast, Nixon and King Hussein discussed increased U.S. aid to Jordan for maintaining its military and economic strength. The President proposed $207.5-million for Jordan in his fiscal 1975 foreign aid program.

Reaction

During the President's absence, some members of Congress criticized the plans for U.S. sales of nuclear reactors and fuel to Egypt and Israel and promised a close look at the agreements in public hearings. Sen. Henry M. Jackson (D Wash.), a member of the Joint Atomic Energy Committee, said it was a "terrible shock that the government would bring nuclear power plants where terrorists operate with impunity." Sen. Jacob K. Javits (R N.Y.), a member of the Foreign Relations Committee, also expressed concern about greater nuclear technology in "the Middle East tinderbox."

Joint Atomic Energy Committee Chairman Rep. Melvin Price (D Ill.) said in a floor statement June 18 that the committee would give members ample opportunity to comment on the agreements in public hearings. He advised against any legislative action on the proposed agreements until they had been completed and submitted to the Joint Committee. He said the committee planned to report its recommendations on the sales agreements to the House and Senate after the hearings. Nixon assured congressional leaders at a briefing June 20 that tight safeguards would be included in the agreements.

On his return to the White House June 19, Nixon told the waiting greeters that his Middle East trip "could well be remembered centuries from now as one of those great turning points which affect mankind for the better."

*The following documents relating to President Nixon's trip
to the Middle East are included below: (1) remarks by
President Nixon and Egyptian President Anwar Sadat at
the signing of a U.S.-Egyptian agreement for cooperation;
(2) text of the U.S.-Egyptian agreement; (3) remarks by
President Nixon and Saudi Arabian King Faisal at the conclusion of the President's visit to Saudi Arabia;
(4) remarks by President Nixon and Syrian President
Hafez Assad following the leaders' agreement to resume
diplomatic relations between their two countries; (5) joint
U.S.-Israeli statement issued at the end of Nixon's visit in
Israel; (6) joint U.S.-Jordanian statement issued at the end
of Nixon's visit in Jordan; and (7) remarks by Vice President Gerald R. Ford and President Nixon at the welcoming
ceremony at the White House on the return of President
Nixon from his Middle East trip:*

*Remarks of President Nixon and President Sadat upon
signing the "Principles of Relations and Cooperation
Between Egypt and the United States," June 14, 1974:*

President Sadat: *Great guest of Egypt, the President, Richard Nixon,
distinguished guests, ladies and gentlemen:*

I am indeed happy to be able to speak to you once again at the end of this
visit which we all share the view that it is a visit which is both historic and
of paramount importance because of the significance it bears in steering
American-Egyptian relations once again towards the path of friendship
and cooperation and because of the drastic steps which it is taking now in
order to try and bring a settlement to a painful situation that has existed
for over a quarter of a century in the Middle East.

Your visit, Mr. President, has actually come in the wake of concentrated
efforts that have been exerted and which were crowned by the disengagement agreements that were signed on both the Egyptian and Syrian fronts.

And you personally, Mr. President, have had great efforts which we are
indeed thankful for. And at the same time, your Secretary of State, Mr.
Kissinger, who knows no rest and no respite in his efforts, he also has a role
that will always remain known and recognized.

And once again, I find that I have to formulate the situation as we conceive it before you. And this position, we feel, has three main factors: We
find that the disengagement agreement, although it has contributed immensely in breeding the right climate, we believe that it still remains to be
a military issue that had only to do with the implementation of the Security Council resolutions dealing with the cease-fire.

We find that the disengagement agreements have actually opened the
door before an issue that needs a lot of efforts, and we believe that we cannot possibly belittle the dimensions of these great efforts.

And this, in fact, is the only alternative against the painful recurrence of
war.

The second factor is that we have to admit that the crux of the whole problem in the Middle East are the legitimate rights of the Palestine people; and unless this is implemented, we feel that the prospects of peace in the Middle East will be dwindling.

The third factor is that from the bottom of our hearts, we do welcome the change that has occurred in the American position, and we actually welcome and feel satisfied with this new spirit and this positive policy.

We all, and I personally, have been very frank from the very beginning, and I have actually submitted and expressed initiatives to our victorious troops on the front and to the whole world and with full determination to pursue that policy.

But I feel that these efforts cannot possibly implement everything on their own, but I feel that in order to implement this drive of ours, all the parties have to admit that the 6th of October has brought a change, and it has dissipated forever the fantasy that there could be anything that can be achieved by the force of arms or to try and impose a certain will.

And it is upon such conviction by all the parties of such principles that peace can possibly be established. And it is indeed with satisfaction that I have to say that all the bilateral talks that have taken place between President Nixon and myself, or whether President Nixon and United States Secretary Dr. Kissinger and myself, and Minister Ismail Fahmy, that is on the official plane, or whether the meetings that have taken place unofficially during that visit, I believe that this all enhances our feeling that a great deal is being done for the establishment of peace.

We shall do our very best actually to puruse this line of conduct so that the cooperation between our two countries should be based on mutual respect and for a broader sphere of cooperation. Allow me that personally I will say that this visit has been an excellent opportunity for me and for Mrs. Sadat to get to welcome a great statesman and the head of a very great state, President Nixon and Mrs. Nixon, and a tribute to a great lady that stands by her husband in the assumption of a great role.

In the name of the people of Egypt, I would like to express once again our happiness that we have been able to welcome President Nixon and Mrs. Nixon and were to welcome him on that visit, a visit which we feel has been of paramount importance and most fruitful, and we do hope that the practical effect of that visit would appear in the very near future. Thank you.

Nixon's Remarks

President Nixon. *Mr. President and ladies and gentlemen:*

Mr. President, I first want to endorse very enthusiastically your very generous compliment to our Secretary of State for the role he has played, along with members of the U.S. team, in working out the various problems to which you have referred.

And on my part, may I pay my respects to Foreign Secretary Fahmy for the role that he has played, and members of your team, in working out many of the details and also many of the hard, substantive issues that have confronted us.

We are both fortunate, I believe, in the support that we have had, and the talks that have gone forward have been ones that have laid the foundation for not only a continuation of a direct contact between you, President Sadat, and me, through channels that we have established but also direct contacts at the Foreign Minister level and at all levels of government to put meaning and also substance into the papers that we sign, the speeches that we may make, the declarations that may be forthcoming.

Sadat to Come to America

Also, on this occasion, before leaving Cairo, could I express again our grateful appreciation on behalf of not only Mrs. Nixon and myself but all of ours who are in the American party, for the overwhelming hospitality that you have extended to us on this visit. We are most grateful, grateful for that hospitality, and we shall always remember it, and we look forward to the opportunity later this year to have Mrs. Sadat, who stands so strongly and loyally and effectively by your side, as well as you, Mr. President, visit the United States again and get to know our country and our people better, not only at the official level but, as I have had the opportunity, across the Nation among all people from all walks of life.

We have today signed a statement which has as its title, "Principles of Relations and Cooperation Between Egypt and the United States."

I think, Mr. President, as I sign this statement, as you must think, of the many statements and treaties and executive agreements and others that I have signed since I have been in this office. Some have meant a great deal more than others, but there is one important rule which governs statements or agreements or treaties or whatever documents are signed by heads of government, and that is this: that the statement, the treaty, the agreement, is only as good as the will and determination of the parties concerned to keep that agreement.

Now, what we have established in this visit, brief though it is: first, that that will and determination to keep the agreement and not to be satisfied just with it, but to build on it. We have certainly established that that will and determination exists between the two heads of state and heads of government, President Sadat and myself. We have established that it also exists at official levels in other areas of government.

But I think, also, we have something else which is worthy of note. As we saw in the 3 days that we have been in your country, these "Principles of Relations and Cooperation Between Egypt and the United States" have the support of the Egyptian people. We sensed that as we saw your people in such great numbers, and I can assure you, Mr. President, they also have the support of the American people.

And so not only officially, not only at the head of state and head of government level but also among our people there is support for this document that we have signed, and support not only for the specific agreements, declarations that are contained therein but support for the spirit which we have discussed; in which we will go on from this agreement to others in the future that will build on them.   For example, in our discussions we have explored ways and means that in the future we could build on the understandings set forth in this agreement. It is also very significant to note that the relations and principles described herein are relations and cooperation, which are dedicated to the works of peace, and we believe that this is again something which has the support of your people and of the American people, based on what he have seen in our visit here.

You have referred, Mr. President, to the fact that while we have made very significant progress by reason of the negotiations that have taken place today in removing roadblocks which have existed toward a final equitable, permanent peace agreement, that there is still a long road to travel. We recognize that, as you recognize it, and we look forward to attempting to work with you, with other governments involved in attempting to find solutions to these problems, because we believe that in the final analysis it is the permanent peace settlement which is in the interest of every government in the area and every nation in the area. And it is not our intention, as you have indicated it is not your intention, that what we have done to date is final. It is a beginning, a very good beginning, and it has been followed up very substantially by this bilateral understanding which we have signed today. But there is more to be done on both fronts, and we look forward to working with you in accomplishing those goals.

"Egypt Now Is At the Beginning"

And finally, Mr. President, I would not want this moment to pass without reflecting on those few minutes that we had, through your courtesy, standing by the Pyramids, thinking back over the thousands of years of history which your people have known, and history which is the common heritage of the civilization of our world today.

We think of the great things that your people have done in the past, but as we stood there, I thought also of the even greater things that you, your government—now that we move into an era of peace, now that we will have cooperation with the U.S. and with other governments as well, I am sure, in accomplishing peaceful goals, we think that Egypt is not at the beginning—it is almost trite to say it—not only of a new era but the beginning of what can be the greatest progress this nation has known for many generations and even centuries.

That is your goal. You have spoken feelingly to me about that goal as we have seen your people—so many of them—the farmers, the workers, the teachers, the professional people, and the others, whether in the countryside, in Cairo, or in Alexandria.

It is a great goal, and you can be sure, Mr. President, that we in America share that goal with you. And as far as the principles stated in the papers that we have just signed are concerned, you can be sure we do not consider this just another piece of paper. It has the backing of our Government officially, it has my personal backing, and it also has the heartfelt support, I am sure, of the American people.

*Text of the "Principles of Relations and Cooperation
Between Egypt and the United States," June 14, 1974:*

The President of the Arab Republic of Egypt, Muhammed Anwar el-
Sadat, and the President of the United States of America, Richard Nixon,
—Having held wide-ranging discussions on matters of mutual interest to
their two countries,
—Being acutely aware of the continuing need to build a structure of
peace in the world and to that end and to promote a just and durable peace
in the Middle East, and,
—Being guided by a desire to seize the historic opportunity before them
to strengthen relations between their countries on the broadest basis in
ways that will contribute to the well-being of the area as a whole and will
not be directed against any of its states or peoples or against any other
state.
Have agreed that the following principles should govern relations
between Egypt and the United States.

I. General Principles of Bilateral Relations

Relations between nations, whatever their economic or political systems,
should be based on the purposes and principles of the United Nations
Charter, including the right of each state to existence, independence and
sovereignty; the right of each state freely to choose and develop its political,
social, economic and cultural systems; non-intervention in each other's internal affairs; and respect for territorial integrity and political independence.
Nations should approach each other in the spirit of equality respecting
their national life and the pursuit of happiness.
The United States and Egypt consider that their relationship reflects
these convictions.
Peace and progress in the Middle East are essential if global peace is to
be assured. A just and durable peace based on full implementation of U.N.
Security Council Resolution 242 of November 22, 1967, should take into due
account the legitimate interest of all the peoples in the Mid East, including
the Palestinian people, and the right to existence of all states in the area.
Peace can be achieved only through a process of continuing negotiation as
called for by United Nations Security Council Resolution 338, of October 22,
1973, within the framework of the Geneva Middle East Peace Conference.
In recognition of these principles, the Governments of the Arab Republic
of Egypt and the United States of America set themselves to these tasks:
They will intensify consultations at all levels, including further consultations between their Presidents, and they will strengthen their
bilateral cooperation whenever a common or parallel effort will enhance
the cause of peace in the world.
They will continue their active cooperation and their energetic pursuit of
peace in the Middle East.

They will encourage increased contacts between members of all branches of their two governments—executive, legislative and judicial—for the purpose of promoting better mutual understanding of each other's institutions, purposes and objectives.

They are determined to develop their bilateral relations in a spirit of esteem, respect and mutual advantage. In the past year, they have moved from estrangement to a constructive working relationship. This year, from that base, they are moving to a relationship of friendship and broad cooperation.

They view economic development and commercial relations as an essential element in the strengthening of their bilateral relations and will actively promote them. To this end, they will facilitate cooperative and joint ventures among appropriate governmental and private institutions and will encourage increased trade between the two countries.

They consider encouragement of exchanges and joint research in the scientific and technical field as an important mutual aim and will take appropriate concrete steps for this purpose.

They will deepen cultural ties through exchanges of scholars, students, and other representatives of the cultures of both countries.

They will make special efforts to increase tourism in both directions and to amplify person-to-person contact among their citizens.

They will take measures to improve air and maritime communications between them.

They will seek to establish a broad range of working relationships and will look particularly to their respective Foreign Ministers and Ambassadors and to the Joint Commission on Cooperation, as well as to other officials and organizations, and private individuals and groups as appropriate, to implement the various aspects of the above principles.

II. Joint Cooperation Commission

The two governments have agreed that the intensive review of the areas of economic cooperation held by President el-Sadat and President Nixon on June 12 constituted the first meeting of the Joint Cooperation Commission, announced May 31, 1974. This Commission will be headed by the Secretary of State of the United States and the Minister of Foreign Affairs of Egypt. To this end, they have decided to move ahead rapidly on consultations and coordination to identify and implement programs agreed to be mutually beneficial in the economic, scientific and cultural fields.

The United States has agreed to help strengthen the financial structure of Egypt. To initiate this process United States Secretary of the Treasury William Simon will visit Egypt in the near future for high level discussions.

III. Nuclear Energy

Since the atomic age began, nuclear energy has been viewed by all nations as a double-edged sword—offering opportunities for peaceful applications, but raising the risk of nuclear destruction. In its international programs of cooperation, the United States Government has made its nuclear technology available to other nations under safeguard conditions. In this context, the two governments will begin negotiation of an Agreement for Cooperation in the fields of nuclear energy under agreed safeguards. Upon conclusion of such an agreement, the United States is prepared to sell nuclear reactors and fuel to Egypt, which will make it possible for Egypt by the early 1980s to generate substantial additional quantities of electric power to support its rapidly growing development needs. Pending conclusion of this Agreement, the United States Atomic Energy Commission and the Egyptian Ministry of Electricity will this month conclude a provisional agreement for the sale of nuclear fuel to Egypt.

IV. Working Groups

The two governments have agreed to set up Joint Working Groups to meet in the near future to prepare concrete projects and proposals for review by the Joint Commission at a meeting to be held later this year in Washington, D.C. These Joint Working Groups will be composed of governmental representatives from each country and will include the following:

(1) A Joint Working Group on Suez Canal Reconstruction and Development to consider and review plans for reopening the Suez Canal and reconstruction of the cities along the Canal; and the United States role in this endeavor.

(2) A Joint Working Group to investigate and recommend measures designed to open the way for United States private investment in joint ventures in Egypt and to promote trade between the two countries. Investment opportunities would be guided by Egypt's needs for financial, technical, and material support to increase Egypt's economic growth. The United States regards with favor and supports the ventures of American enterprises in Egypt. It is noted that such ventures, currently being negotiated, are in the field of petrochemicals, transportation, food and agricultural machinery, land development, power, tourism, banking, and a host of other economic sectors. The estimated value of projects under serious consideration exceeds two billion dollars. American technology and capital combined with Egypt's absorptive capacity, skilled manpower and productive investment opportunities can contribute effectively to the strengthening and development of the Egyptian economy. The United States and Egypt will therefore negotiate immediately a new Investment Guarantee Agreement between them.

(3) A Joint Working Group on Agriculture to study and recommend actions designed to increase Egypt's agricultural production through the use of the latest agricultural technology.

(4) A Joint Working Group on Technology, Research and Development in scientific fields, including space, with special emphasis on exchanges of scientists.

(5) A Joint Working Group on Medical Cooperation to assist the Government of Egypt to develop and strengthen its medical research, treatment and training facilities. These efforts will supplement cooperation in certain forms of medical research already conducted through the Naval Medical Research Unit (NAMRU), whose mutually beneficial work will continue.

(6) A Joint Working Group on Cultural Exchanges to encourage and facilitate exhibitions, visits, and other cultural endeavors to encourage a better understanding of both cultures on the part of the peoples of the United States and Egypt.

The two governments have agreed to encourage the formation of a Joint Economic Council to include representatives from the private economic sector of both countries to coordinate and promote mutually beneficial cooperative economic arrangements.

In support of their economic cooperation, the United States will make the maximum feasible contribution, in accordance with Congressional authorization, to Egypt's economic development, including clearing the Suez Canal, reconstruction projects, and restoring Egyptian trade. In addition, the United States is prepared to give special priority attention to Egypt's needs for agricultural commodities.

Consistent with the spirit of cultural cooperation, the United States Government has agreed to consider how it might assist the Egyptian Government in the reconstruction of Cairo's Opera House. The Egyptian Government for its part intends to place the "Treasures of Tutankhamen" on exhibit in the United States.

Both governments, in conclusion reiterate their intention to do everything possible to broaden the ties of friendship and cooperation consistent with their mutual interests in peace and security and with the principles set forth in this statement.

In thanking President El-Sadat for the hospitality shown to him and the members of his party, President Nixon extended an invitation to President El-Sadat, which President El-Sadat has accepted, to visit the United States during 1974.

MUHAMMED ANWAR EL-SADAT   RICHARD NIXON

Cairo, Egypt,
June 14, 1974

Remarks of the President and King Faisal at Riasa Palace in Jidda, Saudi Arabia, June 15, 1974

The President. *Your Majesty, Your Royal Highnesses, Your Excellencies, ladies and gentlemen:*

Once again, it has been my great privilege and pleasure to meet with Your Majesty, as well as with Crown Prince Khalid and other members of the Saudi Arabian Government.

Our talks have been constructive and far-reaching, covering problems on the whole world. We have particularly directed our attention to, and have reviewed in detail, the momentous changes that are occurring in this area of the world, the Middle East.

While we both recognize that important steps have already been taken on the long road to permanent peace in this area, there is much that remains to be done in reaching our goal.

And the United States intends to persevere in its active efforts to achieve this difficult but great goal of a permanent and equitable and just peace in this area, and essential elements in the search for peace for the fundamental developments that we are witnessing in American relations with Saudi Arabia and with other nations in the Arab world.

The American and Arab nations are rapidly moving into an era of close cooperation and interdependence, an era unprecedented in the long history of our relationships. It is entirely fitting that one of the first manifestations of this new era should come in the relationships between Saudi Arabia and the United States, the two nations that have been closely bound by ties of friendship for more than three decades.

Saudi-American Cooperation

In exploring avenues of cooperation, His Majesty and I have focused in particular on the work of the joint commissions which were agreed to a week ago during the visit of His Royal Highness Prince Fahd and other senior Saudi Ministers to Washington. These commissions and the goals they represent hold rich promise for the future of Saudi Arabia and for the future of the entire Mideast.

And, Your Majesty, the United States intends to be Saudi Arabia's active and constructive partner in insuring the success of these goals.

His Majesty and I have also reviewed the efforts by the United States to assist Saudi Arabia in maintaining its defense forces. Our two nations are totally dedicated to peace. But to achieve that goal in this area, Saudi Arabia must have a level of security that is consistent with its role as a leader in this part of the world. If Saudi Arabia is strong and secure as it will be, we will enhance the prospects for peace and stability throughout the Middle East and in turn throughout the world.

Ties: "Never Stronger"

As we conclude these talks after having met on several occasions before, I would say that today American ties with Saudi Arabia have never been stronger and have never more solidly been based than they are now. We have long been good friends, and our friendship which now develops into an active partnership will be further strengthened through active cooperation between us in the areas that I have described.

And, Your Majesty, on behalf of all the Americans traveling with me, I would like to express our grateful appreciation to you for the very generous hospitality you have extended to us and also to express appreciation to you for the gestures of hospitality and the counsel you have provided for Secretary Kissinger during his visit to your nation.

And personally, I look forward to meeting you again when you next can plan a trip to the United States. I can assure you of a warm and friendly reception.

King Faisal. *Mr. President, Excellencies, distinguished guests:*

It is a source of great appreciation to meet with you again, Mr. President, only this time in our country, and to receive you so warmly as you may have seen, so genuinely, on the part of the people and the Government of Saudi Arabia.

We greatly appreciate, Mr. President, your genuine expressions of friendship and solidarity and cooperation between our two countries. We have no doubt whatsoever that everybody who is genuine and who knows us well, both sides of us, is absolutely assured of our agreeing with you fully about the strengthening and deepening of our relations.

Improvement of U.S.-Arab Relations

And as I have mentioned to you, Mr. President, I have the conviction that all our Arab brethren are desirous of and are seriously looking forward to improve the relations that bind them to the United States of America in ties of friendship and respect.

It is our sincere hope that all the problems and the blemishes that seem to mar the relationship between the United States of America and some Arab countries will be removed so that the clear waters will go back to their natural course.

We are fully confident in the efficacy of Your Excellency's endeavors to remove all these problems and blemishes so that we can once again, the Arab world and the United States of America, be very close and deep friends.

Americans Should Rally Behind Nixon

But what is very important is that our friends in the United States of America be themselves wise enough to stand behind you, to rally around you, Mr. President, in your noble efforts, almost unprecedented in the history of mankind, the efforts aiming at securing peace and justice in the world.

It goes without saying that in addition to our professions, genuine professions of friendship between us, and our desires to strengthen the ties, there is no doubt that our ultimate objectives, both you and us, are in the same direction, namely aiming at securing peace, justice, stability, and prosperity to the whole world.

And anybody who stands against you, Mr. President, in the United States of America or outside the United States of America, or stands against us, your friends in this part of the world, obviously has one aim in mind, namely that of causing the splintering of the world, the wrong polarization of the world, the bringing about of mischief, which would not be conducive to tranquility and peace in the world.

Therefore, we beseech Almighty God to lend his help to us and to you so that we both can go hand in hand, shoulder to shoulder in pursuance of the noble aims that we both share, namely those of peace, justice, and prosperity in the world.

And we sincerely hope that God will grant us success to our joint efforts in reaching those noble aims for all peoples of the world.

I would like to assure you, Mr. President, that for our part, we will pursue, realize, and carry out every item that we have agreed upon, both sides, between Dr. Kissinger and his Royal Highness Prince Fahd, between the American side and the Saudi side in the fields of cooperation.

And I would like to reiterate my thanks and gratification at your having taken the trouble to grace us with this very kind and most welcome visit and certainly beseech Almighty God to grant you continued success in your noble endeavors.

Thank you.

Remarks of President Nixon and President Asad following agreement to resume diplomatic relations, June 16, 1974:

President Asad. It was a good opportunity to receive in Damascus Mr. Richard Nixon, the President of the United States of America, since his visit afforded us the opportunity to exchange views on matters concerning our bilateral relations and the Middle East issue. Many values of civilization and humanity link the American people and the Syrian-Arab people. It is natural that the American citizens of Syrian descent form one of the bridges of understanding that would pave the way for a new phase in relations between our two peoples, relations based on the mutual interests and the respect of each side for the independence and sovereignty of the other side.

We welcome the participation of the United States of America in the Damascus International Fair this year. We declare our readiness for conducting a dialog to consolidate friendship between the peoples of both countries and to establish ties of cooperation in the educational and economic fields so as to serve the interests of both sides.

The Syrian Arab Republic extends thanks to President Nixon for the constructive efforts which the United States of America exerted for reaching an agreement on the disengagement of forces on the Golan Heights. The Syrian Arab Republic declares its readiness to pursue its sincere and constructive cooperation with the Government of the United States of America for laying down the firm basis for a just and lasting peace in the Middle East region.

Disengagement: Step Toward Just Settlement

The agreement of the disengagement forces and our understanding constitutes a first step towards and an integral part of the comprehensive just settlement of the issue. Such a settlement cannot be reached without Israel's withdrawal from all the occupied Arab territories and the securing of the national rights of the Palestinian people in conformity with our understanding of Security Council Resolution Number 388 of October 22, 1973, this understanding which we communicated to the United Nations in due time.

We are dedicating our utmost efforts for achieving a just and lasting peace in our region. We consider this peace an essential condition for the stability of international peace and security. We believe that peace in any region cannot be consolidated if the people of that region is robbed of his basic rights that are recognized under the Charter of the United Nations and its resolutions.

President Nixon and I have agreed to consolidate dialog and cooperation between our two countries for achieving a just and lasting peace in our region and in the world.

We also agreed to enhance the relations between our countries in all fields.

Finally, we have agreed that diplomatic relations between our two countries be restored as of today at the Ambassadorial level.

Thank you.

President Nixon. President Asad, distinguished guests:

I join President Asad in expressing my pleasure that our two Governments are today reestablishing diplomatic relations. The American and the Syrian peoples have a long history of friendly relations, and we in America are proud to count on many persons of Syrian descent among our citizens.

We look forward now to an expansion in contacts and cooperation between the United States and Syria. President Asad and I have agreed that Ambassabors will be named within 2 weeks.

In the many contacts which have taken place in recent weeks between the United States and Syrian Governments, in the course of the negotiations on disengagement, each side has made clear its respect for the independence and for the sovereignty of the other. I want to reaffirm that relations between our two countries shall be based on this principle of international law. I also want to take this opportunity to express my admiration for the efforts of President Asad and his colleagues, the efforts they have undertaken in the interest of peace. The United States will work closely with Syria for the achievement of a just and lasting peace in implementation of United Nations Security Council Resolution 338—a peace which will bring a new era of growth and prosperity, and progress in the Middle East.

Renewed U.S.-Syrian Contacts

The renewed contacts between our Governments, and especially the intensive discussions leading to the agreement on the disengagement of the Israeli and Syrian military forces, having contributed markedly to a deeper understanding and improvement in the overall relationship between the

United States and Syria and between our two peoples. President Asad and I consider this agreement a first step toward a just and lasting peace in this area.

President Asad and I have agreed our Governments will review and develop further concrete ways in which the United States and Syria can work more closely together for their mutual benefit. A senior Syrian official will visit Washington in the near future to discuss specific plans to achieve this goal. In the general context of strengthening our bilateral relations, I have affirmed that the United States is prepared to resume educational and cultural exchanges. President Asad extended an invitation to the United States to participate in the Damascus International Trade Fair next month, and I have accepted this invitation with great pleasure on behalf of the United States.

I have extended an invitation to President Asad to visit the United States at a time to be agreed, and I am delighted to announce that he has accepted this invitation.

Text of the Joint United States-Israeli statement issued at the conclusion of the President's visit, June 17, 1974:

The President of the United States, Richard Nixon, visited Israel June 16-17, 1974. This is the first visit ever to have been paid by an American President to the State of Israel. It symbolizes the unique relationship, the common heritage and the close and historic ties that have long existed between the United States and Israel.

President Nixon and Prime Minister Rabin held extensive and cordial talks on matters of mutual interest to the United States and Israel and reviewed the excellent relations between their two countries. They discussed in a spirit of mutual understanding the efforts of both countries to achieve a just and lasting peace which will provide security for all States in the area and the need to build a structure of peace in the world. United States Secretary of State Henry Kissinger and members of the Israeli Cabinet participated in these talks.

Prime Minister Rabin expressed Israel's appreciation for the outstanding and effective role of the United States in the quest for peace under leadership of President Nixon assisted by the tireless efforts of Secretary Kissinger and indicated Israel's intention to participate in further negotiations with a view to achieving peace treaties with its neighbors which will permit each State to pursue its legitimate rights in dignity and security.

President Nixon and Prime Minister Rabin agreed that peace and progress in the Middle East are essential if global peace is to be assured. Peace will be achieved through a process of continuing negotiations between the parties concerned as called for by U.N. Security Council Resolution 338 of October 22, 1973.

Basis for Peace

The President and the Prime Minister agreed on the necessity to work energetically to promote peace between Israel and the Arab States. They agreed that States living in peace should conduct their relationship in accordance with the purposes and principles of the United Nations Charter, and the U.N. Declaration on Principles of International Law concerning Friendly Relations and Co-operation among States which provides that every State has the duty to refrain from organizing or encouraging the organization of irregular forces or armed bands including mercenaries for incursion into the territory of another State. They condemned acts of violence and terror causing loss of innocent human lives.

The President and the Prime Minister expressed their great pleasure in the intimate cooperation which characterizes the warm relationship between their two countries and peoples. They agreed to do everything possible to broaden and deepen still further that relationship in order to serve the interests of both countries and to further the cause of peace.

President Nixon reiterated the commitment of the United States to the long-term security of Israel and to the principle that each state has the right to exist within secure borders and to pursue its own legitimate interests in peace.

Prime Minister Rabin expressed his appreciation for the U.S. military supplies to Israel during the October War and thereafter. The President affirmed the continuing and long-term nature of the military supply relationship between the two countries, and reiterated his view that the strengthening of Israel's ability to defend itself is essential in order to prevent further hostilities and to maintain conditions conducive to progress towards peace. An Israeli Defense Ministry delegation will soon come to Washington in order to work out the concrete details relating to long-term military supplies.

Continued U.S. Support of Israel

President Nixon affirmed the strong continuing support of the United States for Israel's economic development. Prime Minister Rabin expressed the gratitude of Israel for the substantial help which the United States has provided, particularly in recent years. The President and Prime Minister agreed that future economic assistance from the United States would continue and would be the subject of long-range planning between their governments. The President affirmed that the United States, in accordance with Congressional authorization, will continue to provide substantial economic assistance for Israel at levels needed to assist Israel to offset the heavy additional costs inherent in assuring Israel's military capability for the maintenance of peace.

In the economic field, the President and the Prime Minister noted with satisfaction the effective working relationship between their governments at all levels and the depth of the relationship between the economies of the two nations. They agreed to strengthen and develop the framework of their bilateral relations. The primary goal will be to establish a firmer and more clearly defined structure of consultation and cooperation. Where appropriate, they will set up special bi-national committees. Both sides recognize the importance of investments in Israel by American companies, the transmission of general know-how and marketing assistance, and cooperation of American companies with Israeli counterparts on research and development. The United States Government will encourage ventures by American enterprises and private investment in Israel designed to increase Israel's economic growth, including in the fields of industry, power, and tourism. They agreed to begin immediately negotiations for concrete arrangements to implement such policy including in the area of avoidance of double taxation.

Nuclear Energy Agreement

The President and the Prime Minister announce that their two governments will negotiate an agreement on cooperation in the field of nuclear energy, technology and the supply of fuel from the United States under agreed safeguards. This agreement will in particular take account of the intention of the Government of Israel to purchase power-reactors from the United States. These will secure additional and alternative sources of electricity for the rapidly developing Israel economy. As an immediate step, Israel and the United States will in the current month reach provisional agreement on the further sale of nuclear fuel to Israel.

Prime Minister Rabin particularly expressed the view that the supply of oil and other essential raw materials to Israel must be assured on a continuous basis. President Nixon proposed that United States and Israeli representatives meet soon in order to devise ways to meeting this problem.

The President and the Prime Minister stressed as an important mutual aim the further encouragement of the fruitful links already existing between the two countries in the scientific and technical field, including space research. Special emphasis will be put on exchanges of scientists and the sponsorship of joint projects. With this end in view they will explore means to widen the scope and substance of existing agreements and activities including those pertaining to the Bi-National Science Foundation.

In the area of water desalination the countries will expand their joint projects.

Future Exchanges and Cultural Ties

The President and the Prime Minister agreed to develop further the cultural ties between the two countries through exchange of scholars, students, artists, exhibitions, mutual visits and musical and other cultural events. In the near future, Israel will send to the United States an archeological exhibition depicting the Land of the Bible. The Israel Philharmonic Orchestra will visit the United States on the occasion of the American bicentennial celebrations.

The President and the Prime Minister noted with gratification the large number of tourists from their respective countries visiting both the United States and Israel and affirmed that they would continue their efforts to foster this movement. To this end, the two governments will resume negotiations on an agreement granting landing rights to the Israel national carrier in additional major cities in the continental Unites States.

The President and the Prime Minister discussed the plight of Jewish minorities in various countries in the spirit of the Universal Declaration of Human Rights. The Prime Minister thanked the President for his efforts in support of the right of free emigration for all peoples without harassment, including members of Jewish monorities. The President affirmed that the United States would continue to give active support to these principles in all feasible ways.

Meeting Between Nixon and Meir

The President was particularly pleased at the opportunity to meet with former Prime Minister Golda Meir, whose courage, statesmanship, patience and wisdom he greatly admires. The President expressed his satisfaction at the constructive cooperation between Israel and the United States under Prime Minister Meir's leadership which had led to the conclusion of the agreements between Egypt and Israel and Syria respectively on the disengagement of their military forces.

In departing, President and Mrs. Nixon expressed their deep appreciation of the warm reception accorded them in Israel and their admiration for the achievements of the Israeli people. They were deeply impressed by the manner in which the overwhelming problems of integrating many hundreds of thousands of immigrants of many various backgrounds and cultures were being successfully overcome. Convinced of the determination of this valiant people to live in peace, the President gave them renewed assurance of the support of the people of the United States.

The Prime Minister and the President agreed that the cordiality of Israel's reception of the President reflected the long friendship between Israel and the United States and pledged their continued energies to nurture and strengthen that friendship. To this end, the President invited Prime Minister Rabin to pay an early visit to Washington.

Text of the joint United States-Jordanian statement issued at the conclusion of the President's visit, June 18, 1974:

On the invitation of His Majesty King Hussein, President Richard Nixon paid the first visit of a President of the United States of America to the Hashemite Kingdom of Jordan on June 17 and 18, 1974.

During this visit President Nixon and His Majesty King Hussein discussed the full range of common interests which have long bound Jordan and the United States in continued close friendship and cooperation.

The United States reaffirmed its continued active support for the strength and progress of Jordan. The President explained to His Majesty in detail the proposal he has submitted to the Congress of the United States for a substantial increase in American military and economic assistance for Jordan in the coming 12 months. The President expressed his gratification over the efforts which Jordan is making under its development plan to expand the Jordanian economy, to give significant new impetus to the development of Jordan's mineral and other resources, and production, and to raise the standard of living for all its people.

The President expressed admiration for His Majesty's wise leadership and stated his view that effective and steady development would make a substantial contribution to peace and stability in the Middle East. The President promised a special effort by the United States Government to provide support in a variety of ways for Jordan's development efforts and in this regard welcomed the recent visit to Washington of His Royal Highness Crown Prince Hassan.

Importance of Jordanian Strength

His Majesty emphasized the importance of maintaining Jordan's military strength if economic progress and development are to be assured.

His majesty expressed the view that resources invested in maintaining the security and stability of the Kingdom are related to its economic growth, for without order and peace it is unrealistic to expect to marshal the energies and investment needed for economic progress. The President agreed with His Majesty and promised, in cooperation with the Congress, to play a strong role in maintaining Jordan's military strength.

His Majesty and the President agreed that they will continue to give U.S.-Jordanian relations their personal attention. In this context, it was agreed that a joint Jordanian-U.S. Commission will be established at a high level to oversee and review on a regular basis the various areas of cooperation between Jordan and the United States in the fields of economic development, trade and investment, military assistance and supply, and scientific, social and cultural affairs.

His Majesty and the President have long agreed on the importance of moving toward peace in the Middle East. The President discussed the steps which have been taken in this regard since His Majesty's visit to Washington in March of this year. His Majesty expressed Jordan's support for the very significant diplomatic efforts which the United States has made to help bring peace to the Middle East. His Majesty and the President discussed the strategy of future efforts to achieve peace and the President promised the active support of the United States for agreement between Jordan and Israel on concrete steps toward the just and durable peace called for in the United Nations Security Council Resolution 338 of October 22, 1973.

The President has invited His Majesty to pay a visit to Washington at an early date. The purpose of the visit will be to hold further talks on the strategy of future efforts to achieve peace in accord with the objectives of the United Nations Security Council Resolution 338. Further discussions of the details of the establishment of the joint commission will also be held. His Majesty has accepted the invitation and the date of the visit will be announced shortly.

The President expressed his gratitude and that of Mrs. Nixon for the warm hospitality extended by His Majesty, by Her Majesty Queen Alia and by the Jordanian people.

Remarks of the President and the Vice President at a welcoming ceremony at the White House following the President's trip to the Middle East, June 19, 1974:

The Vice President. Mr. President, Mrs. Nixon:

It is a great privilege and honor for me to have the opportunity of welcoming both of you back on a very successful peace mission, which you have accomplished with great dignity and distinction.

When you left a few days ago, there was come apprehension in some quarters that this vitally important mission might not achieve the objectives that we all hope for, but I think, as we have followed your journeys in five countries, we have seen that the actions taken by you have cemented the great accomplishments of the Secretary of State during his negotiations.

The welcome given to you and Mrs. Nixon in five countries is a tribute to you, Mr. President, to Mrs. Nixon and I think to the American people.

Over the years it has been my privilege, Mr. President, to welcome you back on a number of peace missions that you undertook. I was in the group that welcomed you when you came back from the Soviet Union in 1972, when you came back from that historic mission to the People's Republic of China.

In each and every case, there have been solid achievements leading us and the world down the road of peace. Of course, it has been wonderful to see, as we did, Mrs. Nixon, not only on this trip but other trips, where she actually charmed and captivated the people of all countries.

Mrs. Nixon: First Lady of the World

Mr. President, I think it is fair to say that Mrs. Nixon could now be called the First Lady of the World.

Mr. President, about 10 days ago, I was here with many others to wish you Godspeed. Our prayers were with you at that time, and I think it might be appropriate now to quote from that Biblical injunction, "Blessed is the peacemaker."

Mr. President, the American people know that the road to peace is long and very, very difficult, but the American people historically have stood tall and strong as they met the conflicts on the battlefield. I am just as confident, Mr. President, that the American people will stand tall and strong as they now move forward in the efforts to achieve the peace that you have worked so strenuously to lay the groundwork for, not only in the Middle East but in Europe and in Southeast Asia.

The American people will be united. They will be tall, and they will back you as they have in the past, in seeking the peace that is sought by all.

There is an Arabic saying that goes something like this, and I hope I can quote it correctly: "May Allah make the end better than the beginning."

It seems to me that this welcome here is indicative of the attitude that the American people have in all 50 States. They appreciate your accomplishments, they appreciate what you have done for America, and they are grateful for the foundation that you have laid for a lasting peace in the world as a whole.

We welcome you back, and are glad you are here.

The President. Thank you.

Mr. Vice President, members of the Cabinet, and all of you who have been so very kind to come out and welcome us back after our trip to the Mideast:

It is hard to realize that over the past 9 days that we have had the opportunity to meet with the leaders of five countries of the Mideast, as well as the President of Portugal and the Prime Minister of Austria.

'A Journey Toward a Lasting Peace'

As I have said, this trip now comes to an end, but it is only the beginning of a much longer journey, a journey that will be difficult, a journey that has many pitfalls, potentially, in it, but one that is worth taking, a journey on which we are embarked and on which we will continue, a journey toward lasting peace, not only in the Mideast but all over the world.

Let me say, too, that with regard to the trip itself, at this point in our relations with the nations in that area, some observations I think can be made.

I have, over the past 21 years, visited that area on several occasions, and I would say that a profound and, I believe, lasting change has taken place in these respects:

First, where there was no hope for peace, there is now hope.

Second, where there was hostility for America in many parts of the world, there is now friendship.

Third, while we did have the opportunity to meet new friends in Egypt and in Syria, we were able to reassure old friends in Israel and in Saudi Arabia and in Jordan.

What this all adds up to, of course, is not that we have instant peace as a result of one series of negotiations or just one very long trip, but what it does mean is that we are on the way, and it does mean, too, that we must dedicate ourselves to stay on the course, as the Vice President has indicated, to stand tall until we reach our goal.

Also, I would like to say a word with regard to those television clips, I am sure many of you saw, of literally millions of people in Cairo and Alexandria, and Damascus, and in Jidda, in Jerusalem, and in Amman—millions of people welcoming the President of the United States and his wife.

U.S. Aim of Peace and Progress

What did this mean? What it really meant was not a welcome in a personal sense, but it meant something far more significant. It meant very simply that millions of people in that part of the world who have known nothing but poverty and war for the last 30 years desperately want peace, and they want progress. They believe that America wants peace and progress not only for ourselves but for them, too. They believe that we will help in achieving peace and progress not only for ourselves but for them, too. They believe that we will help in achieving peace and progress without exacting the price of domination over them.

In other words, what those people were saying to us and that we convey to you, our fellow Americans all over this great Nation, is that for millions and millions of people in that part of the world, there is trust for America, there is respect for America, and really some very strong affection for America.

I would say, as we conclude this part of this very long journey, we must not let these people down. We must help, because America must play and will play the crucial role in continuing the progress toward peace and continuing also to build on the foundations of these new relationships with other nations where those relationships have been broken in times past.

Waging peace is, in fact, more difficult than waging war because it is more complex. The goal sometimes one loses sight of as he becomes involved in the tactics that are necessary to achieve that goal.

But while waging peace is more difficult than waging war, I think, as all of us realize, the rewards are infinitely greater. And I think on this day that every American can be proud that in his country, in that part of the world and I would say in most of the world, is trusted as a nation which first has the responsibility to lead toward achieving the great goal of progress and peace for all peoples but also we can be proud of the fact that we are not backing away from that responsibility.

Let us be worthy of the hopes, of the trust of millions of people that most of us will never meet. This is a great goal.

Thank you.

LIMITS TO MIRANDA RULING
June 10, 1974

Reflecting a conservative approach to criminal law and to the invitation to overturn earlier established rulings, the Supreme Court June 10 limited slightly—but refused to discard—the controversial Miranda *decision concerning the rights of criminal suspects. That decision, announced in June 1966, was probably the most controversial of all the Warren Court's rulings on criminal law. The Court barred the use of any evidence obtained by police from a person in custody but not warned fully of his constitutional rights to remain silent and to have legal counsel, appointed for him at public expenses if necessary. The ruling was based on the Fifth Amendment privilege that no one can be compelled to incriminate himself.*

Thomas W. Tucker was arrested and charged with rape in Pontiac, Mich., in April 1966—two months before the Miranda *ruling was announced. Before questioning him, police advised him of his right to remain silent and to have counsel, but not of his right to have counsel appointed for him, if necessary. The record showed that police asked Tucker if he wanted an attorney; his answer was "no." During subsequent questioning, Tucker said that at the time of the rape, he had been with a friend, Robert Henderson. But when police located and questioned Henderson, his testimony incriminated Tucker.*

Before the trial began, the Miranda *ruling was announced. Tucker's attorney moved to exclude Henderson's testimony from the trial, as obtained through use of Tucker's statements when he had not been fully advised of his constitutional rights. The judge denied this motion, although all of Tucker's own statements under interrogation were excluded from use at* the trial. Henderson testified and Tucker was convicted. His conviction was affirmed by the state courts.

Attacking his conviction then in the federal courts, Tucker won a ruling from the federal district court that Henderson's testimony should not have been admitted since police had used Tucker's statements—which were not admissible—as their lead to look for Henderson. The court of appeals, sixth circuit, affirmed that finding. The prosecutors appealed, inviting the Supreme Court to throw out the strict Miranda guidelines.

Opinion

"Just as the law does not require that a defendant receive a perfect trial, only a fair one, it cannot realistically require that policemen investigating serious crimes make no errors whatsoever," Justice William H. Rehnquist wrote for the eight-man majority, reversing the decisions of the two lower courts. Only Justice William O. Douglas dissented. (Michigan v. Tucker) To ensure that persons interrogated by police were not deprived of their privilege against compulsory self-incrimination, the Court in the Miranda ruling set up procedural safeguards, outlining certain rights of which a person must be advised and barring use of his statements if he was not fully warned of his constitutional privileges, wrote Rehnquist. "These procedural safeguards were not themselves rights protected by the Constitution, but were instead measures to ensure that the right against compulsory self-incrimination was protected."

Tucker's right not to be compelled to incriminate himself was not violated, the Court held. He was not coerced to name Henderson, and, furthermore, his own statements were excluded from use at the trial. The police were acting in keeping with pre-Miranda standards and in good faith, a factor which weakens the need for excluding all products of that interrogation in order to deter future police misconduct. Furthermore, Henderson testified at the trial and so "the reliability of his testimony was subject to the normal testing process of an adversary trial."

Douglas Dissent

In dissent, Douglas argued that the interrogation of Tucker, without his knowing he could have appointed counsel, did violate his Fifth Amendment right against self-incrimination. As a result, he said, Miranda should apply to exclude all evidence resulting from that interrogation, including Henderson's testimony. The fact that the interrogation occurred before the Miranda ruling should not bar its application: "People who are in jail because of a state's use of unconstitutionally derived evidence are entitled to a new trial, with the safeguards the Constitution provides, without regard to when the constitutional violation occurred, when the trial occurred, or when the conviction became 'final,' " he wrote.

Excerpts from the Supreme Court's decision June 10 on the exclusion of evidence under the Miranda *ruling, excerpts from concurring opinions, and excerpts from Justice William O. Douglas's dissenting opinion:*

No. 73-482

State of Michigan,
    Petitioner,
        v.
Thomas W. Tucker

On Writ of Certiorari to
the United States Court
of Appeals for the Sixth Circuit.

[June 10, 1974]

MR. JUSTICE REHNQUIST delivered the opinion of the Court.

This case presents the question whether the testimony of a witness in respondent's state court trial for rape must be excluded simply because police had learned the identity of the witness by questioning respondent at a time when he was in custody as a suspect, but had not been advised that counsel would be appointed for him if he was indigent. The questioning took place before this Court's decision in *Miranda* v. *Arizona*, 384 U.S. 436 (1966), but respondent's trial, at which he was convicted, took place afterwards. Under the holding of *Johnson* v. *New Jersey*, 384 U.S. 719 (1966), therefore, *Miranda* is applicable to this case. The United States District Court for the Eastern District of Michigan reviewed petitioner's claim on a petition for habeas corpus and held that the testimony must be excluded. The Court of Appeals affirmed.

I

On the morning of April 19, 1966, a 43-year-old woman in Pontiac, Michigan, was found in her home by a friend and coworker, Luther White, in serious condition. At the time she was found the woman was tied, gagged, and partially disrobed, and had been both raped and severely beaten. She was unable to tell White anything about her assault at that time and still remains unable to recollect what happened.

While White was attempting to get medical help for the victim and to call for the police, he observed a dog inside the house. This apparently attracted White's attention for he knew that the woman did not own a dog herself. Later, when talking with police officers, White observed the dog a second time, and police followed the dog to respondent's house. Neighbors further connected the dog with respondent.

The police then arrested respondent and brought him to the police station for questioning. Prior to the actual interrogation the police asked respondent whether he knew for what crime he had been arrested, whether he wanted an attorney, and whether he understood his constitutional rights. Respondent replied that he did understand the crime for which he was arrested, that he did not want an attorney, and that he understood his rights. The police further advised him that any statements he might make could be used against him at a later date in court. The police, however, did not advise respondent that he would be furnished counsel free of charge if he could not pay for such services himself.

The police then questioned respondent about his activities on the night of the rape and assault. Respondent replied that during the general time period at issue he had first been with one Robert Henderson and then later at home, alone, asleep. The police sought to confirm this story by contacting Henderson, but Henderson's story served to discredit rather than to bolster respondent's account. Henderson acknowledged that respondent had been with him on the night of the crime but said that he had left at a relatively early time. Furthermore, Henderson told police that he saw respondent the following day and asked him at that time about scratches on his face—"asked him if he got hold of a wild one or something." Respondent answered, "[S]omething like that." Then, Henderson said, he asked respondent "[W]ho it was," and respondent said: "[S]ome woman lived the next block over," adding "She is a widow woman" or words to that effect.

These events all occurred prior to the date on which this Court handed down its decision in *Miranda* v. *Arizona* 384 U.S. 436 (1966), but respondent's trial occurred afterwards. Prior to trial respondent's appointed counsel made a motion to exclude Henderson's expected testimony because respondent had revealed Henderson's identity without having received full *Miranda* warnings. Although respondent's own statements taken during interrogation were excluded, the trial judge denied the motion to exclude Henderson's testimony. Henderson therefore testified at trial, and respondent was convicted of rape and sentenced to 20 to 40 years' imprisonment. His conviction was affirmed by both the Michigan Court of Appeals and by the Michigan Supreme Court.

Respondent then sought habeas corpus relief in federal district court. That court, noting that respondent had not received the full *Miranda* warnings and that the police had stipulated Henderson's identity was learned only through respondent's answers, "reluctantly" concluded that Henderson's testimony could not be admitted. Application of such an exclusionary rule was necessary, the court reasoned, to protect respondent's Fifth Amendment right against compulsory self-incrimination. The court therefore granted respondent's petition for a writ of habeas corpus unless petitioner retried respondent within 90 days. The Court of Appeals for the Sixth Circuit affirmed. We granted certiorari...and now reverse.

II

Although respondent's sole complaint is that the police failed to advise him that he would be given free counsel if unable to afford counsel himself, he did not, and does not now, base his arguments for relief on a right to counsel under the Sixth and Fourteenth Amendments. Nor was the right to counsel, as such, considered to be persuasive by either federal court below....

Respondent's argument, and the opinions of the District Court and Court of Appeals, instead rely upon the Fifth Amendment right against compulsory self-incrimination and the safeguards designed in *Miranda* to secure that right. In brief, the position urged upon this Court is that proper regard for the privilege against compulsory self-incrimination requires, with limited exceptions not applicable here, that all evidence derived solely from statements made without full *Miranda* warnings be excluded at a subsequent criminal trial. For purposes of analysis in this case we believe that the question thus presented is best examined in two separate parts. We will therefore first consider whether the police conduct complained of directly infringed upon respondent's right against compulsory self-incrimination or whether it instead violated only the prophylactic rules developed to protect that right. We will then consider whether the evidence derived from this interrogation must be excluded.

III

The history of the Fifth Amendment right against compulsory self-incrimination, and the evils against which it was directed, have received considerable attention in the opinions of this Court.... At this point in our history virtually every schoolboy is familiar with the concept, if not the language, of the provision that reads: "No person...shall be compelled in any criminal case to be a witness against himself...."

The importance of a right does not, by itself, determine its scope, and therefore we must continue to hark back to the historical origins of the privilege, particularly the evils at which it was to strike. The privilege against compulsory self-incrimination was developed by painful opposition to a course of ecclesiastical inquisitions and Star Chamber proceedings occurring several centuries ago....

Where there has been genuine compulsion of testimony, the right has been given broad scope. Although the constitutional language in which the privilege is cast might be construed to apply only to situations in which the prosecution seeks to call a defendant to testify against himself at his criminal trial, its application has not been so limited. The right has been held applicable to proceedings before a grand jury,...to civil proceedings, ...to congressional investigations,...to juvenile proceedings,...and to other statutory inquiries.... The privilege has also been applied against the States by virtue of the Fourteenth Amendment....

The natural concern which underlies many of these decisions is that an inability to protect the right at one stage of a proceeding may make its invocation useless at a later stage. For example, a defendant's right not to be compelled to testify against himself at his own trial might be practically nullified if the prosecution could previously have required him to give evidence against himself before a grand jury....

In more recent years this concern—that compelled disclosures might be used against a person at a later criminal trial—has been extended to cases involving police interrogation. Before *Miranda* the principal issue in these cases was not whether a defendant had waived his privilege against compulsory self-incrimination but simply whether his statement was "voluntary." In state cases the Court applied the Due Process Clause of the Fourteenth Amendment, examining the circumstances of interrogation to determine whether the processes were so unfair or unreasonable as to render a subsequent confession involuntary.... Where the State's actions offended the standards of fundamental fairness under the Due Process Clause, the State was then deprived of the right to use the resulting confessions in court.

Although federal cases concerning voluntary confessions often contained references to the privilege against compulsory self-incrimination, references which were strongly criticized by some commentators,...it was not until this Court's decision in *Miranda* that the privilege against compulsory self-incrimination was seen as the principal protection for a person facing police interrogation. This privilege had been made applicable to the States in *Malloy* v. *Hogan*,...and was thought to offer a more comprehensive and less subjective protection than the doctrine of previous cases. In *Miranda* the Court examined the facts of four separate cases and stated:

> "In these cases, we might not find the defendants' statements to have been involuntary in traditional terms. Our concern for adequate safeguards to protect precious Fifth Amendment rights is, of course, not lessened in the slightest.... To be sure, the records do not evince overt physical coercion or patent psychological ploys. The fact remains that in none of these cases did the officers undertake to afford appropriate safeguards at the outset of the interrogation to insure that the statements were truly the product of free choice."...

Thus the Court in *Miranda*, for the first time, expressly declared that the Self-Incrimination Clause was applicable to state interrogations at a police station, and that a defendant's statements might be excluded at trial despite their voluntary character under traditional principles.

To supplement this new doctrine, and to help police officers conduct interrogations without facing a continued risk that valuable evidence would be lost, the Court in *Miranda* established a set of specific protective guidelines, now commonly known as the *Miranda* rules. The Court declared that "the prosecution may not use statements, whether exculpatory or inculpatory, stemming from custodial interrogation of the defendant unless it demonstrates the use of procedural safeguards effective to secure the privilege against self-incrimination."... A series of recommended "procedural safeguards" then followed. The Court in particular stated:

> "Prior to any questioning, the person must be warned that he has a right to remain silent, that any statement he does make may be used as evidence against him, and that he has a right to the presence of an attorney, either retained or appointed."...

The Court said that the defendant, of course, could waive these rights, but that any waiver must have been made "voluntarily, knowingly and intelligently."...

The Court recognized that these procedural safeguards were not themselves rights protected by the Constitution but were instead measures to insure that the right against compulsory self-incrimination was protected.... The suggested safeguards were not intended to "create a constitutional straightjacket,"...but rather to provide practical reinforcement for the right against compulsory self-incrimination.

A comparison of the facts in this case with the historical circumstances underlying the privilege against compulsory self-incrimination strongly indicates that the police conduct here did not deprive respondent of his privilege against compulsory self-incrimination as such, but rather failed to make available to him the full measure of procedural safeguards associated with that right since *Miranda*. Certainly no one could contend that the interrogation faced by respondent bore any resemblance to the historical practices at which the right against compulsory self-incrimination was aimed. The District Court in this case noted that the police had "warned [respondent] that he had the right to remain silent,"...and the record in this case clearly shows that respondent was informed that any evidence taken could be used against him. The record is also clear that respondent was asked whether he wanted an attorney and that he replied that he did not. Thus, his statements could hardly be termed involuntary as that term has been defined in the decisions of this Court. Additionally, there were no legal sanctions, such as the threat of contempt, which could have been applied to respondent had he chosen to remain silent. He was simply not exposed to "the cruel trilemma of self-accusation, perjury, or contempt."...

Our determination that the interrogation in this case involved no compulsion sufficient to breach the right against compulsory self-incrimination does not mean there was not a disregard, albeit an inadvertent disregard, of the procedural rules later established in *Miranda*. The question for decision is how sweeping the judicially imposed consequences of this disregard shall be. This Court said in *Miranda* that statements taken in violation of the *Miranda* principles must not be used to prove the prosecution's case at trial. That requirement was fully complied with by the state court here: respondent's statements, claiming that he was with Henderson and then asleep during the time period of the crime were not admitted against him at trial. This Court has also said, in *Wong Sun* v. *United States*...that the "fruits" of police conduct which actually infringed a defendant's Fourth Amendment rights must be suppressed. But we have already concluded that the police conduct at issue here did not abridge respondent's constitutional privilege against compulsory self-incrimination, but departed only from the prophylactic standards later laid down by this Court in *Miranda* to safeguard that privilege. Thus, in deciding whether Henderson's testimony must be excluded, there is no controlling precedent of this Court to guide us. We must therefore examine the matter as a question of principle.

IV

Just as the law does not require that a defendant receive a perfect trial, only a fair one, it cannot realistically require that policemen investigating serious crimes make no errors whatsoever. The pressures of law enforcement and the vagaries of human nature would make such an expectation unrealistic. Before we penalize police error, therefore, we must consider whether the sanction serves a valid and useful purpose.

We have recently said, in a search and seizure context, that the exclusionary rule's "prime purpose is to deter future unlawful police conduct and thereby to effectuate the guarantee of the Fourth Amendment against unreasonable searches and seizures."...In a proper case this rationale would seem applicable to the Fifth Amendment context as well.

The deterrent purpose of the exclusionary rule necessarily assumes that the police have engaged in willful, or at the very least, negligent conduct which has deprived the defendant of some right. By refusing to admit evidence gained as a result of such conduct, the courts hope to instill in those particular investigating officers, or in their future counterparts, a greater degree of care towards the right of an accused. Where the official action was pursued in complete good faith, however, the deterrence rationale loses much of its force.

We consider it significant to our decision in this case that the officers' failure to advise respondent of his right to appointed counsel occurred prior to the decision in *Miranda*. Although we have been urged to resolve the broad question of whether evidence derived from statements taken in violation of the *Miranda* rules must be excluded regardless of when the interrogation took place, we instead place our holding on a narrower ground. For at the time respondent was questioned these police officers were guided, quite rightly, by the principles established in *Escobedo*,...particularly focusing on the subject's opportunity to have retained counsel with him during the interrogation if he chose to do so. Thus, the police asked respondent if he wanted counsel, and he answered that he did not. The statements actually made by respondent to the police, as we have observed, were exluded at trial in accordance with *Johnson* v. *New Jersey, supra*. Whatever deterrent effect on future police conduct the exclusion of those statements may have had, we do not believe it would be significantly augmented by excluding the testimony of the witness Henderson as well.

When involuntary statements or the right against compulsory self-incrimination are involved, a second justification for the exclusionary rule also has been asserted: protection of the courts from reliance on untrustworthy evidence. Cases which involve the Self-Incrimination Clause must, by definition, involve an element of coercion, since the clause provides only that a person shall not be *compelled* to give evidence against himself. And cases involving statements often depict severe pressures which may override a particular suspect's insistence on innocence....

But those situations are a far cry from that presented here. The pressures on respondent to accuse himself were hardly comparable even with the least prejudicial of those pressures which have been dealt with in our cases. More important, the respondent did *not* accuse himself. The evidence which the prosecution successfully sought to introduce was not a confession of guilt by respondent, or indeed even an exculpatory statement by respondent, but rather the testimony of a third party who was subjected to no custodial pressures. There is plainly no reason to believe that Henderson's testimony is untrustworthy simply because *respondent* was not advised of *his* right to appointed counsel. Henderson was both available at trial and subject to cross-examination by respondent's counsel, and counsel fully used this opportunity, suggesting in the course of his cross-examination that Henderson's character was less than exemplary and that he had been offered incentives by the police to testify against respondent. Thus the reliability of his testimony was subject to the normal testing process of an adversary trial.

Respondent contends that an additional reason for excluding Henderson's testimony is the notion that the adversarial system requires "the government in its contest with the individual to shoulder the entire load.".... To the extent that this suggested basis for the exclusionary rule in Fifth Amendment cases may exist independently of the deterrence and trustworthiness rationales, we think it of no avail to respondent here. Subject to applicable constitutional limitations, the Government is not forbidden all resort to the defendant to make out its case. It may require the defendant to give physical evidence against himself,...and it may use statements which are voluntarily given by the defendant after he receives full disclosure of the rights offered by *Miranda*. Here we deal not with the offer of defendant's own statements in evidence, but only with the testimony of a witness whom the police discovered as a result of defendant's statements. This recourse to respondent's voluntary statements does no violence to such elements of the adversarial system as may be embodied in the Fifth, Sixth, and Fourteenth Amendments.

In summary, we do not think that any single reason supporting exclusion of this witness' testimony, nor all of them together, are very persuasive. By contrast, we find the arguments in favor of admitting the testimony quite strong. For, when balancing the interests involved, we must weigh the strong interest under any system of justice of making available to the trier of fact all concededly relevant and trustworthy evidence which either party seeks to adduce. In this particular case we also "must consider society's interest in the effective prosecution of criminals in light of the protection our pre-*Miranda* standards afford criminal defendants.".... These interests may be outweighed by the need to provide an effective sanction to a constitutional right,...but they must in any event be valued. Here respondent's own statement, which might have helped the prosecution show respondent's guilty conscience at trial, had already been excised from the prosecution's case.... To extend the excision further under the circumstances of this case and exclude relevant testimony of a third-party witness would require far more persuasive arguments than those advanced by respondent.

This Court has already recognized that a failure to give interrogated suspects full *Miranda* warnings does not entitle the suspect to insist that statements made by him be excluded in every conceivable context. In *Harris* v. *New York*,...(1971), the Court was faced with the question of whether the statements of the defendant himself, taken without informing him of his right of access to appointed counsel, could be used to impeach defendant's direct testimony at trial. The Court concluded that they could, saying:

> "Some comments in the *Miranda* opinion can indeed be read as indicating a bar to use of an uncounseled statement for any purpose, but discussion of that issue was not at all necessary to the Court's holding and cannot be regarded as controlling. *Miranda* barred the prosecution from making its case with statements of an accused made while in custody prior to having or effectively waiving counsel. It does not follow from *Miranda* that evidence inadmissible against an accused in the prosecution's case in chief is barred for all purposes, provided of course that the trustworthiness of the evidence satisfies legal standards."...

We believe that this reasoning is equally applicable here. Although *Johnson* enabled respondent to block admission of his own statements, we do not believe that it requires the prosecution to refrain from all use of those statements, and we disagree with the courts below that Henderson's testimony should have been excluded in this case.

Reversed.

MR. JUSTICE BRENNAN, with whom MR. JUSTICE MARSHALL joins, concurring.

...The Court, in answering this question, proceeds from the premise that *Johnson* v. *New Jersey*,...makes *Miranda* applicable to all cases in which a criminal trial was commenced after the date of our decision in *Miranda*, and that, since respondent's trial was post-*Miranda*, the effect of *Miranda* on this case must be resolved. I would not read *Johnson* as making *Miranda* applicable to this case....

In *Johnson* v. *New Jersey*,...the Court was called upon to determine whether the newly announced procedures in *Miranda* v. *Arizona* should be retroactively applied to upset final convictions based in part upon confessions obtained without the prior warnings required by *Miranda*. Aware that *Miranda* provided new safeguards against the possible use at trial of unreliable statements of the accused, we nonetheless concluded that the decision should not be retroactively applied. The probability that the truth-determining process was distorted by, and individuals were convicted on the basis of, coerced confessions was minimized, we found, by the availability of strict pre-*Miranda* standards to test the voluntariness of confessions. In addition, we recognized that law enforcement agencies had justifiably relied on our prior rulings and that retroactive application would necessitate the wholesale release and subsequent retrial of vast numbers of prisoners....

The conclusion that the *Miranda* rules should be applied to post-*Miranda* trials made good sense, where criminal defendants were seeking to exclude *direct statements* made without prior warning of their rights. Exclusion of possibly unreliable pre-*Miranda* statements made in the inherently coercive atmosphere of in-custody interrogation...could be obtained at a relatively low cost. For, although the police might have relied in good faith on our prior rulings in interrogating defendants without first advising them of their rights, *Miranda* put the police on notice that pre-*Miranda* confessions obtained without prior warnings would be inadmissible at defendants' trials. Since defendants who had made pre-*Miranda* confessions had not yet gone to trial, and the police investigations into those cases were still fresh, *Johnson* envisioned "no undue burden being imposed upon prosecuting authorities by requiring them to find evidentiary substitutes for statements obtained in violation of the constitutional protections afforded by *Miranda*....

Application of the *Miranda* standards to the present case, however, presents entirely different problems. Unlike the situation contemplated in *Johnson*, the burden imposed upon law enforcement officials to obtain evidentiary substitutes for inadmissible "fruits" will likely be substantial. The lower courts, confronted with the question of the application of *Miranda* to fruits, have provided differing answers on the admissibility issue. The police, therefore, could not reasonably have been expected to know that substitute evidence would be necessary. As a result, in a case such as the present one, in which law enforcement officials have relied on trial and appellate court determinations that fruits are admissible, a contrary ruling by this Court, coming years after the commission of the crime, would severely handicap any attempt to retry the defendant....

Since excluding the fruits of respondent's statements would not further the integrity of the factfinding process and would severely handicap law enforcement officials in obtaining evidentiary substitutes, I would confine the reach of *Johnson* v. *New Jersey* to those cases in which the *direct statements* of an accused made during a pre-*Miranda* interrogation were introduced at his post-*Miranda* trial. If *Miranda* is applicable at all to the fruits of statements made without proper warnings, I would limit its effect to those cases in which the fruits were obtained as a result of post-*Miranda* interrogations....

Since I agree that the judgment of the Court of Appeals must be reversed, I concur in the judgment of the Court.

MR. JUSTICE WHITE, concurring.

For the reasons stated in my dissent in that case, I continue to think that *Miranda* v. *Arizona*,...was ill-conceived and without warrant in the Constitution. However that may be, the *Miranda* opinion did not deal with the admissibility of evidence derived from in-custody admissions obtained without the specified warnings, and the matter has not been settled by subsequent cases....

Miranda having been applied in this Court only to the exclusion of the defendant's own statements, I would not extend its prophylactic scope to bar the testimony of third persons even though they have been identified by means of admissions that are themselves inadmissible under *Miranda*. The arguable benefit from excluding such testimony by way of possibly deterring police conduct that might compel admissions are, in my view, far outweighed by the advantages of having relevant and probative testimony, not obtained by actual coercion, available at criminal trials to aid in the pursuit of truth. The same results would not necessarily obtain with respect to the fruits of involuntary confessions. I therefore concur in the judgment.

MR. JUSTICE DOUGLAS, dissenting.

In this case the respondent, incarcerated as a result of a conviction in a state court, was granted a writ of habeas corpus by the District Court.... The District Court concluded that "the introduction by the prosecution in its case in chief of testimony of a third person which is admittedly the fruit of an illegally obtained statement by the [accused violates the accused's] Fifth Amendment rights."...

I

I cannot agree when the Court says that the interrogation here "did not abridge respondent's constitutional privilege against self-incrimination, but departed only from the prophylactic standards later laid down by this Court in *Miranda* to safeguard that privilege."... The Court is not free to prescribe preferred modes of interrogation absent a constitutional basis. We held the "requirement of warnings and waiver of rights [to be] fundamental with respect to the Fifth Amendment privilege,"...and without so holding we would have been powerless to reverse Miranda's conviction. While *Miranda* recognized that police need not mouth the precise words contained in the Court's opinion, such warnings were held necessary "unless other fully effective means are adopted to notify the person" of his rights. There is no contention here that other means were adopted. The respondent's statements were thus obtained "under circumstances that did not meet *constitutional* standards for the protection of the privilege [against self-incrimination]."

II

With the premise that respondent was subjected to an unconstitutional interrogation, there remains the question whether not only the testimony elicited in the interrogation but also the fruits thereof must be suppressed.... The petitioner has stipulated that the identity and the whereabouts of the witness and his connection with the case were learned about only through the unconstitutional interrogation of the respondent. His testimony must be excluded to comply with *Miranda's* mandate that "*no* evidence obtained as a result of interrogation [not preceded by adequate warnings] can be used against" an accused.

III

In *Johnson* v. *New Jersey*, 384 U.S. 719 (1966), the Court held that statements obtained in violation of *Miranda* standards must be excluded from all trials occurring after the date of the *Miranda* decision.... I disagree, as I disagreed in *Johnson*, that any defendant can be deprived of the full protection of the Fifth Amendment, as the Court has construed it in *Miranda*, based upon an arbitrary reference to the date of his interrogation or his trial....

People who are in jail because of a State's use of unconstitutionally derived evidence are entitled to a new trial, with the safeguards the Constitution provides, without regard to when the constitutional violation occurred, when the trial occurred or when the conviction became "final."...

I would affirm the judgment below.

KISSINGER'S THREAT TO RESIGN
June 11, 1974

Stung by press allegations that he had concealed his role in initiating federal wiretaps, Secretary of State Henry A. Kissinger threatened at a June 11 news conference to resign unless cleared of all charges. Kissinger complained that the attacks on his character and credibility made it impossible for him to conduct United States foreign policy. Speaking to the press in Salzburg, Austria, a stopover preparatory to President Nixon's Middle East tour, (see p. 449.) Kissinger asserted that his involvement in a federal wiretapping effort from 1969 to 1971 had been limited to alerting Nixon to leaks and supplying names of individuals with access to sensitive information to the Federal Bureau of Investigation (FBI). He strongly denied that the wiretaps had been improper or that he had misrepresented his role in them. Kissinger's statements at Salzburg reaffirmed his testimony on wiretaps to the Senate Foreign Relations Committee during his confirmation hearings in September 1973.

After Kissinger's confirmation by the Senate Sept. 21, 1973, news stories based on sources in the FBI and House Judiciary Committee—which was investigating Watergate and related cases as part of its presidential impeachment inquiry—had cast doubts on his version of his role in the wiretaps. Those doubts increased after a June 6 closed session of the committee heard evidence on the Nixon administration's secret domestic surveillance activities. Leaked materials from the House committee were widely interpreted as showing that Kissinger had misled the Senate Foreign Relations Committee about the extent of his involvement in the wiretaps.

Specifically, Kissinger was charged with having initiated the 1969-71 wiretaps which were undertaken by the FBI against 13 federal officials and four newsmen. The order to end the "national security" wiretaps was reported to have come from Kissinger's office; and it was also alleged that then National Security Council (NSC) aide Gen. Alexander M. Haig Jr., presumably acting for Kissinger, had vetoed at least two and possibly three FBI proposals in mid-1969 to terminate one tap, at the home of former NSC staffer Morton I. Halperin, because it was unproductive. Kissinger also was reported to have had prior knowledge of the formation of a White House investigative unit known as the "plumbers" in 1971, knowledge which he had denied to the Foreign Relations Committee in 1973 and at the Salzburg press conference. The "plumbers" were involved in the break-in at the office of Dr. Lewis Fielding, the psychiatrist who had treated Pentagon Papers defendant Daniel Ellsberg. (See p. 33-40, 205-214, 411-417, 661-669; Historic Documents 1973, p. 537-548.)

Reporters had previously confronted Kissinger with the charges at a Washington news conference June 6, the same day the Judiciary Committee met in closed session. Having just returned from a month of shuttling between Damascus and Jerusalem in a diplomatic effort which achieved the Syrian-Israeli troop disengagement (see p. 435), Kissinger later said he had been unprepared to answer questions on the wiretaps. Initially he referred reporters to his 1973 Senate testimony, but when asked if he had "retained counsel in preparation for a defense against a possible perjury indictment," he snapped, "I have not retained counsel, and I am not conducting my office as if it were a conspiracy."

Kissinger Details His Role

At Salzburg, Kissinger acknowledged that the June 6 news conference on the wiretaps and his alleged knowledge of the "plumbers" had "irritated, angered, flustered [and] discombobulated" him because "after five weeks in the Middle East, I was not thinking about the various investigations going on in the United States." Kissinger reaffirmed his original statements to the Senate Foreign Relations Committee and announced that he had, by letter, asked the committee to conduct a new review of the wiretapping charges. The wiretaps in question had been "legal" and in accord with "established procedures," Kissinger said. In submitting the names, Kissinger acknowledged, "we knew that an investigation was certain and that a wiretap was probable."

Support for the beleaguered Kissinger materialized quickly after his conference in Salzburg. On the same day, White House Press Secretary Ronald L. Ziegler released a statement saying that the President would be very reluctant to accept Kissinger's resignation, although he understood "the Secretary's strong feeling that he be able to carry out his responsibilities unencumbered by...anonymous attack." Also on June 11, the Senate Foreign Relations Committee unanimously agreed to review Kissinger's previous testimony. Late the following day, June 12, a resolution supporting Kissinger's integrity was introduced in the Senate. By June 13, 52 senators had signed the resolution including Majority Leader Mike

Mansfield (D Mont.) and Minority Leader Hugh Scott (R Pa.). Vice President Gerald R. Ford June 12 claimed that the leaks of derogatory information about Kissinger had come from House Judiciary Committee members favoring the impeachment of President Nixon.

Nevertheless, reports of Kissinger's wiretapping role continued to appear. Along with accounts of Kissinger's Salzburg news conference, three major newspapers on June 12 carried excerpts from FBI documents on the domestic surveillance program. The Washington Post, The New York Times *and the* Boston Globe *published FBI documents dated May 12 and May 13, 1973, respectively. The May 12 document said specific requests for the wiretaps had come from either Kissinger, then national security adviser, or his aide, Gen. Haig. The document dated May 13, 1973, said "it appears that the project of placing electronic surveillance at the request of the White House had its beginning in a telephone call to Mr. J. Edgar Hoover [then FBI director] on May 9, 1969, from Dr. Henry A. Kissinger."*

In a report issued August 6, the Senate Foreign Relations Committee, unanimously reaffirmed its decision that Kissinger's role in the wiretaps of subordinates "did not constitute grounds to bar his confirmation as Secretary of State." The committee had held six closed hearings during which it received testimony, reviewed all Justice Department files on the matter (unavailable during the original confirmation hearings) and received written answers to questions from President Nixon, former Attorney General John Mitchell and former FBI official William C. Sullivan. "The committee was unable to settle to its satisfaction some questions about the initiation and termination of certain wiretaps," the report said. "But it did establish to its satisfaction that Secretary Kissinger's role in the program was essentially as he described it in testimony last year."

Following release of the report, State Department spokesman Robert Anderson said Kissinger was "gratified" by the report and "no longer sees any reason for resignation."

Excerpts from statements by Secretary of State Henry A. Kissinger during a press conference at Salzburg, Austria, on June 11, 1974:

Last Thursday [at a Washington press conference, June 6] a number of you commented on the fact that I seemed irritated, angered, flustered, discombobulated. All these words are correct. After five weeks in the Middle East I was not thinking about the various investigations going on in the United States. I did not prepare myself for the press conference by reading the records of investigations that I believed had been completed....

Since that press conference there have been many articles and several editorials. I was prevented by the short time interval between the press conference and the President's departure from holding a press conference in the United States before we left.

However, I got in touch with Senator [J.W.] Fulbright, Chairman of the Senate Foreign Relations Committee on Sunday, and I sent him the following letter yesterday morning which I will now read to you.

"Dear Mr. Chairman:

"You have no doubt seen the news reports and editorial comments relating to my testimony before the Senate Foreign Relations Committee at the time of my confirmation hearing. They involve fundamental issues concerning the truthfulness and completeness of my testimony; hence they raise issues of public confidence and directly affect the conduct of our foreign policy.

"You will remember that my testimony concerning the national security wiretaps ordered by the President and carried out by the FBI under the authority of the Attorney General was in three parts: public testimony, an extensive executive session, and a session with Senators [John] Sparkman and [Clifford P.] Case in which we went over relevant FBI files.

"The meeting with Senators Sparkman and Case was conducted in the presence of then Attorney General [Elliot L.] Richardson and the then Deputy Attorney General [William D.] Ruckelshaus. I emphasize this because no new material has appeared since my testimony except a brief excerpt from a Presidential tape, a large part of which is described as unintelligible.

"The documents now being leaked were available to me before my testimony. They were given to Senators Sparkman and Case prior to my meeting with them. In a few cases my recollection differed in emphasis from the documents. In those cases I pointed out apparent discrepancies and explained them at the time.

"The innunendoes which now imply that new evidence contradicting my testimony has come to light are without foundation. All the available evidence is to the best of my knowledge contained in the public and closed hearings which preceded my confirmation....

"Nevertheless, at this sensitive period, I feel it important that the committee which first examined the evidence and which has a special concern with the conduct of foreign affairs should have an opportunity to review it once again.

"I should add that if the committee decides on a review, I would not object should it wish to examine relevant security files and reports on wiretaps sent to my office. I, of course, stand ready to appear at any time."

Since sending this letter, there have been many more articles and more are undoubtedly in the process of preparation. In these circumstances, it is not appropriate for me, as Secretary of State, to go with the President to the Middle East without having a full discussion of the facts as I know them, keeping in mind only that I do not have all my records here with me.

I shall now discuss these facts with you. I shall afterwards stay for as long as there are any questions. There will be no ending of the question period as long as there are any questions left to be asked.

Charges Against Kissinger

First, what is it we are talking about? The impression has been created that I was involved in some illegal or shady activity that I am trying to obscure with misleading testimony. The fact of the matter is that the wiretaps in question were legal, they followed established procedures. When they were established, the then Attorney General and the then Director of the Federal Bureau of Investigation assured me that they were reinstituting procedures that were carried out in previous administrations.

Before public reputations are attacked or destroyed, elementary fairness requires that this particular statement be looked into and that it be made clear whether the national security wiretaps were in fact carried out in previous administrations. The history of these wiretaps derived from a series of leaks that occurred in the spring of 1969. As Assistant to the President for National Security Affairs, I had the duty to call the attention of the President to what seemed to me violations of national security.

These violations cannot be assessed only by analyzing the intrinsic merit of individual documents, but they must be also analyzed in terms of the confidence other governments can have in a government that seems totally incapable of protecting its secrets. After a series of egregious violations, the President ordered, on the advice of the Attorney General and the Director of the Federal Bureau of Investigation, the institution of a system of national security wiretaps.

I repeat, I was informed when I was told about this system, that it was reinstituted, a system that had existed in previous administrations, even though it may have been administered from different offices. I was asked to have my office supply names in three categories: individuals who had adverse information in their security files, individuals who had access to information that had leaked, and individuals whose names had appeared as a result of the investigation that submission of the previous two lists might entail.

My office, for which I bear full responsibility, submitted those names in carrying out this program. I would be prepared to let any appropriate investigative body examine the list to make certain that no name was submitted through my office that did not fit into one of these categories.

"A Wiretap Was Probable"

In submitting these names, we knew that an investigation was certain and that a wiretap was probable and I so testified in the Executive Session of the Senate Foreign Relations Committee, no matter how sentences are now taken out of context.

I testified both to Senator Case and to Senator [Edmund S.] Muskie that in submitting the names, we knew, of course, that a wiretap was a probable outcome. The basic issue is whether through my office or with my knowledge any names were submitted for any purpose other than the protection of national security and whether the information was used for any purpose other than the protection of national security.

When a wiretap was installed, the FBI would send a report to my office only when, in the judgment of the FBI, the conversation involved violations of national security. It is totally incorrect and outrageous to say that these tapes that were submitted to my office involved a description of extramarital affairs or pornographic descriptions....

One of the leaks that I have read recently speaks of 54 logs that were allegedly sent to my office. The word "logs" of course, is a lie. What was sent to my office was a page and a half summary....

After May, 1970, it was decided that my office was not equipped to deal with internal security matters. And after May, 1970, no reports from the FBI were sent to my office for the remainder of the period that the national security wiretaps remained in force.

During this period, General [Alexander M.] Haig maintained, at my direction, contact with Director [William C.] Sullivan of the FBI. The reports from that time on were sent to Mr. [H.R.] Haldeman's office. [Haldeman was then White House chief of staff.] If a report of sufficient gravity had been sent to Mr. Haldeman's office, Mr. Sullivan might inform General Haig and if in the judgment of General Haig the report was sufficiently serious, I would be informed of the content, but I would not see the report....

Of course, in the sense that we submitted the names of individuals who belonged in the categories which we were ordered to produce, we initiated submitting names. The point I am making is my office did not initiate any requests for wiretaps that were not triggered either by a security violation or by fulfilling the criteria of adverse information in the security files and that last criterion was met only once at the beginning of the program.

These are the facts of the national security wiretap program as I remember. I do not apologize for it. It is not a shady affair, as has been alleged. It followed legal proceedings. I fully testified to it and I stand ready to testify again before any appropriate committee.

The "Plumbers" and David Young

Now let me turn to another matter that is also constantly being invoked: the issue of the plumbers and David Young. [Young had worked for Kissinger at the National Security Council but left in 1971 to join the special White House investigative unit known as the "plumbers."] I testified before the Senate Foreign Relations Committee and I said in a press conference that I did not know about the existence of the plumbers by that or any other name. I did not know that David Young was working for the plumbers.

I said this under oath and I repeat it today. I hope none of you are ever in a position that you have to prove the negative of a knowledge....

The question which I answered before the Senate Foreign Relations Committee was as follows: "Did you, when he, namely David Young, left your employment and was transferred to Mr. [John D.] Ehrlichman, have any idea at that time or any subsequent time that he was to be requested to engage in illegal activities, burglary, conspiracy to burglary or whatever they might be?" [Ehrlichman was White House domestic affairs advisor.]

This, ladies and gentlemen, is the question I was answering before the Senate Foreign Relations Commission, not the question whether I ever heard anything of David Young....

I joined this Administration five years ago when this country was deeply divided. I felt that with my particular background I had a special obligation to understand the dangers of national division and to do my best to overcome them....

But it seems to me that our national debate has now reached a point where it is possible for documents that have already been submitted to one committee to be selectively leaked by another committee without the benefit of any explanation, where public officials are required to submit their most secret documents to public scrutiny, but unnamed sources can attack the credibility and the honor of senior officials of the Government without even being asked to identify themselves....

I have believed that I should do what I could to heal division in this country. I believed that I should do what I could to maintain the dignity of American values and to give Americans some pride in the conduct of their affairs.

I can do this only if my honor is not at issue and if the public deserves to have confidence. If that cannot be maintained, I cannot perform the duties that I have exercised, and in that case, I shall turn them over immediately to individuals less subject to public attack....

Question-and-answer session:

Q: How can there be a public accounting of those as you suggested at the end of your remarks?

KISSINGER: I believe that if public officials must give an accounting of their activities, those who print the accusations should state where these accusations come from so that a judgment can be made about the motive of the individuals making them. I have submitted all the documents that I have voluntarily, to the Senate Foreign Relations Committee last year and I explained every document of which I had personal knowledge to the Senate, first in the session with Senator Sparkman and Senator Case and then in the meeting of the full committee....

Q: Do you expect that campaign [of leaks]—if you can characterize it that way—will continue?

KISSINGER: I do not want to make any estimate of whether this will continue, nor do I even want to question the good faith of those who are leaking the documents. I know the documents that are being leaked. I submitted them to the Senate Foreign Relations Committee. Individuals reading them without an explanation of their context can easily come to some of the conclusions that have been made. I understand this....

Q: Mr. Secretary, you seem to imply here that if this campaign is not stopped, you are going to resign. Is that a fair assumption from what you said?

KISSINGER: I am not concerned with the campaign. I am concerned with the truth. I do not believe that it is possible to conduct the foreign policy of the United States under these circumstances when the character and credibility of the Secretary of State is at issue. And if it is not cleared up, I will resign....

Q: Dr. Kissinger, are you suggesting that it is the responsibility of reporters who have written stories of those leaks and/or editors who have printed those stories that they should come forward and identify their sources?

KISSINGER: I am suggesting that when the credibility of senior officials is put in question on the basis of unnamed sources for the selective leaking of documents and when this attack affects not only the individual concerned, which may be a personal injustice, but affects the standing of the United States in the world, then I believe an obligation exists in one way or another to do this, yes....

Q: If the Senate Foreign Relations Committee resumed its hearings and went through the whole matter again and gave you a clean bill of health, would you then withdraw your threat to resign?

KISSINGER: Yes.

Q: Is that the method that you prefer?

KISSINGER: I will not propose a method.

Q: Do you think these leaks are designed to force you to resign, sir?

KISSINGER: I don't believe that, and I do not believe that I am surrounded by a conspiracy. I have not had unfortunate experiences with the press. I think if this can happen to someone whose relationship with the press has been as good as I believe mine has been, then we are facing a national problem, not a personal problem. I do not believe there is the slightest animosity against me about this.

Q: Dr. Kissinger, I am still not quite clear in my own mind what you feel your role was in initiating the wiretapping program. Now you said the decision, if I understand you correctly, was actually made at a meeting between the President, the Attorney General, then Mr. Mitchell, and the head of the FBI, then Mr. Hoover. Now, do you feel that you played a major role in getting that program started or do you feel you were kind of an innocent bystander who, in effect, played a minor role? What is your own concept of your role?

KISSINGER: My concept of my role to which I testified before the Senate Foreign Relations Committee, and which Elliot Richardson also supported, I may say, from the record—not on the basis of conversations with me as has been alleged in a newspaper article—my concept of my role was that on a number of occasions I called to the attention of the President, it would seem to me, very significant security leaks. This, then, led the President, I believe on the recommendation of the Attorney General and the Director of the FBI, to institute a program of wiretapping. I did not, myself, propose this program. I was new in the Government and, therefore, I was unaware of the fact that such a program, according to the Director of the FBI, had also been carried out in every previous administration since Franklin Roosevelt. So, in retrospect, I would have to say I undoubtedly contributed, by my description of the security problem, and being new in Government, it is possible that in one or two cases I may have taken an exaggerated view of them. I did not recommend the program as such, though this does not mean that I disagreed with it. I find wiretapping distasteful. I find leaks distasteful, and therefore, a choice had to be made....

Q: Dr. Kissinger, did you at the time when these decisions were made have any doubt about the ethicality—save the legal aspects—did you at that time have a question in your own mind whether it was ethical or not and now with the benefit of hindsight do you have any doubt at all in your mind that it was ethical.

KISSINGER: At the time I found it an extremely painful process. It involved threats to individuals, who if they had been found to be security leaks, would have reflected badly on my own judgment. So I did not find it a task that was particularly pleasant. But I could not quarrel with the judgment and I did not quarrel with the judgment of those who found it necessary.... At my confirmation hearings I testified in executive session...that stricter regulations than were then in force or had been in force in previous Administrations would be compatible with the objective of national security....

▼▼▼

WORLD MONETARY REFORM
June 14, 1974

Abandoning a two-year attempt to forge a permanent reform of the international money system, 20 nations instead adopted interim measures, announced in Washington June 14. Further efforts to devise a fixed-rate currency exchange system were postponed indefinitely. Agreement on a package of provisional measures was reached at the sixth and final meeting of the International Monetary Fund's (IMF) Committee of 20. The group had been authorized at the IMF's September 1972 meeting (see Historic Documents, 1972, p. 815) *to negotiate a replacement for the Bretton Woods system. Since then, soaring worldwide inflation and fourfold increases in oil prices had so strained troubled monetary relationships that the committee had been forced to change "objectives, approach and timing," according to IMF officials.*

There was little in the June agreement that had not been previously disclosed in general terms. The major decision, to put off negotiations for a new, permanent monetary system, had been taken at the committee's January meeting in Rome. The June agreement spelled out guidelines for currency "floating," a practice already in operation which featured flexible exchange rates and expressed the values of one currency in terms of another, such as the number of Japanese yen a dollar will buy. The value of IMF's international reserve money, called Special Drawing Rights (SDRs), was changed from a dollar-based figure to one fixed by the combined worth of 16 currencies. The committee also issued an outline of general goals for a future, permanent monetary system. The interim measures stressed attention to the problems of developing nations, many of which were staggering under huge oil import bills. Unanimous adoption of the measures came only after the United States had agreed to review its opposition to linking aid for less-developed countries to future issuance of SDRs.

Monetary Crisis

Since August 1971, when President Richard M. Nixon declared that the United States would no longer convert dollars to gold upon demand, the dollar had undergone two devaluations, forcing its abandonment as the standard for measuring the value of other currencies. Termination of dollar convertibility precipitated the collapse of the Bretton Woods monetary system, based on a stable dollar, which had operated since its adoption in July 1944 by 44 nations. Even before Nixon's action, the Bretton Woods system had been seriously compromised by a buildup of trade imbalances, an accelerated rate of currency revaluations, and inflation.

The need for a new system to curb broad fluctuations in international payments and currency exchange had, since 1971, prompted temporary and limited measures. These generally were efforts to manage floating exchange rates in anticipation of a major stabilization of the system. By the IMF's June agreement, those temporary measures were systematized and legitimitized as a first step in the "evolution" of permanent, long-term reform.

Immediate Steps

The IMF communique on "immediate steps" warned the fund's present 126 member nations against competitive devaluation or undervaluation of currencies. Members were asked to refrain voluntarily from using trade restrictions to improve their balance of payments problems. The SDR was given a new value based on the combined worth of 16 currencies, including the dollar, weighted according to their importance in world trade. Freed from its prior dependence on the value of the dollar, the SDR was expected to gain in stability as a result of the new agreement.

Starting June 28, the value of the SDR was to be recalculated each day in terms of all the 16 currencies, a technique known as the "standard basket." Also, the interest rate on SDRs was raised from 1.5 per cent to 5 per cent per annum. The SDR was developed by the IMF as a monetary standard to replace gold or the dollar. A country could use its SDRs when, because of a deficit in its balance of payments, it needed dollars or other foreign currency. It could exchange its SDRs with another country, designated by the IMF, for the needed currency. SDRs had been in use prior to the June agreement; the new consideration was the method by which their value was established.

The key element of the IMF package was the complex "guidelines for floating," essentially a voluntary code of good conduct governing intervention by central banks in daily currency trading to influence exchange rates. Other interim measures included establishment of two new lending operations. A temporary "oil facility" was created to aid nations with unmanageable deficits in their balance of payments, resulting from higher oil prices. A second "extended" lending operation, pegged to the needs of less developed countries, offered larger and longer-term loans than had previously been available from IMF. Two new committees were also set up, one to continue work towards permanent monetary reform, the other to examine the "transfer of real resources to developing countries," with special attention to nations hit hardest by spiraling oil, food and fertilizer prices.

Long-Term Reform

In a separate "outline of reform" the committee described in general terms what form a permanent system should take. The central feature, according to the document, would be a "stable but adjustable" currency exchange rate system; most countries would maintain fixed "par values" and could intervene in currency trading, within limits, to correct balance of payments deficits and surpluses. Major interventions would require IMF approval.

No agreement was reached on how to set the limits for automatic intervention by individual countries. What sanctions or what degree of pressure could be used against uncooperative member nations was also not resolved. Other matters of dispute were the future role of gold and the means which could be used to control the growth of total world currency reserves—"liquidity." The most publicized dispute was whether the SDRs should be distributed to less-developed countries as an indirect form of aid. The United States had consistently blocked this proposal, reportedly on the grounds that it was inflationary and that it would create a new form of foreign aid without congressional approval. Underdeveloped countries had pressed for the measure. In a major concession the United States agreed to reconsider its position on the SDR-aid link. Both the seriousness of the matters under dispute, and the shifting alliances from issue to issue, were credited by observers with having prevented final agreement on long-term reform.

U.S. Secretary of the Treasury William E. Simon hailed the interim measures as "comprehensive" and "resourceful." But commentators questioned how effective an entirely voluntary pact could be. The major areas of disagreement, unresolved after two years of negotiation, signaled the points at which the new system could break down.

> *Excerpts from the communique of the Committee of the Board of Governors on International Monetary Reform and Related Issues (Committee of 20), Jan. 18, 1974; followed by excerpts from the report by the Committee of 20, June 14, 1974:*

The Committee concluded its work on international monetary reform; agreed on a program of immediate action; and reviewed the major problems arising from the current international monetary situation.

The program of immediate action is as follows:

(a) Establishment of an Interim Committee of the Board of Governors of the Fund with an advisory role, pending establishment by an amendment of the Articles of Agreement of a Council with such decision-making powers as are conferred on it.

(b) Strengthening of Fund procedures for close international consultation and surveillance of the adjustment process.

(c) Establishment of guidelines for the management of floating exchange rates.

(d) Establishment of a facility in the Fund to assist members in meeting the initial impact of the increase in oil import costs.

(e) Provision for countries to pledge themselves on a voluntary basis not to introduce or intensify trade or other current account measures for balance of payments purposes without a finding by the Fund that there is balance of payments justification for such measures.

(f) Improvement of procedures in the Fund for management of global liquidity.

(g) Further international study in the Fund of arrangements for gold in the light of the agreed objectives of reform.

(h) Adoption for an interim period of a method of valuation of the SDR based on a basket of [16] currencies and of an initial interest rate on the SDR of 5 per cent.

(i) Early formulation and adoption of an extended Fund facility under which developing countries would receive longer-term balance of payments finance.

(j) Reconsideration by the Interim Committee, simultaneously with the preparation by the Executive Board of draft amendments of the Articles of Agreement, of the possibility and modalities of establishing a link between development assistance and SDR allocation.

(k) Establishment of a joint ministerial Committee of the Fund and World Bank to carry forward the study of the broad question of the transfer of real resources to developing countries and to recommend measures.

(l) Preparation by the Executive Board of draft amendments of the Articles of Agreement for further examination by the Interim Committee and for possible recommendation at an appropriate time to the Board of Governors....

Members of the Committee expressed their serious concern at the acceleration of inflation in many countries. They agreed on the urgent need for stronger action to combat inflation, so as to avoid the grave social, economic and financial problems that would otherwise arise. They recognized that, while international monetary arrangements can help to contain this problem, the main responsibility for avoiding inflation rests with national governments. They affirmed their determination to adopt appropriate fiscal, monetary and other policies to this end....

The Committee noted that, as a result of inflation, the energy situation and other unsettled conditions, many countries are experiencing large current account deficits that need to be financed. The Committee recognized that sustained cooperation would be needed to ensure appropriate financing without endangering the smooth functioning of private financial markets and to avert the danger of adjustment action that merely shifts the problem to other countries. Particular attention was drawn to the pressing difficulties of the most severely affected developing countries. Members of the Committee therefore strongly emphasized their request to all countries with available resources and to development finance institutions to make every effort to increase the flow of financial assistance on concessionary terms to these countries.

Excerpts from the report by the Committee of 20 including excerpts from the Outline of Reform, June 14, 1974:

Since the Nairobi meeting [an interim Committee of 20 meeting, September 1973], the uncertainties affecting the world economic outlook, related to inflation, the energy situation and other unsettled conditions, have increased. Major changes are occurring in the world balance of payments structure, and it is not yet clear to what extent the positions of individual countries will be altered or how adjustment will be achieved.

These conditions of greater uncertainty have led to a change of emphasis in the work of the Committee. It has been recognized that priority should be given to certain aspects of reform which have become all the more urgent. Thus, for example, during the current period of exceptional and widespread payments imbalances, there is a particular need to maintain close international consultation and surveillance of countries' balance of payments policies in the Fund, and to develop orderly means of financing these imbalances, including means of supplying on appropriate terms the increased needs of many developing countries for financial resources. On the other hand, it is recognized that other aspects of reform will need to be developed and implemented at a later date. Thus, for example, it may be some time before there is a return to a system based on stable but adjustable par values or to general convertibility; nor will the full arrangements for management of the adjustment process and of global liquidity necessarily be feasible in the period immediately ahead.

Given, therefore, that there will be an interim period before a reformed system can be finally agreed and fully implemented, the Committee regards it as of the highest importance that immediate steps should be taken to begin an evolutionary process of reform, and that other action taken in this field during the interim period should be consistent with the principles of reform....

The general direction in which the Committee believes that the system could evolve in the future[:] This involves an enlargement of the scope of international surveillance and management in a number of important areas, and a consequently larger role for the Fund. It is envisaged that there should be more effective and symmetrical adjustment procedures which, while leaving the choice of particular policies as far as possible to the country concerned, will nevertheless ensure, through a process of assessment supported by reserve indicators [a measure of reserves on either a stock or a flow basis] and by graduated pressures, that appropriate action is taken where necessary; that the convertibility system should promote the better management of global liquidity and the avoidance of uncontrolled growth of reserve currency balances, and that the SDR should become the principal reserve asset, with the role of gold and of reserve currencies being reduced; and that there should be arrangements to give positive encouragement to economic development and to promote an increasing net flow of real resources to developing countries....

OUTLINE OF REFORM

1. It is agreed that there is need for a reformed world monetary order, based on cooperation and consultation within the framework of a strengthened International Monetary Fund, that will encourage the growth of world trade and employment, promote economic development, and help to avoid both inflation and deflation.

2. The main features of the international monetary reform will include:

(a) an effective and symmetrical adjustment process, including better functioning of the exchange rate mechanism, with the exchange rate regime based on stable but adjustable par values and with floating rates recognized as providing a useful technique in particular situations;

(b) cooperation in dealing with disequilibriating capital flows;

(c) the introduction of an appropriate form of convertibility for the settlement of imbalances, with symmetrical obligations on all countries;

(d) better international management of global liquidity, with the SDR becoming the principal reserve asset and the role of gold and of reserve currencies being reduced;

(e) consistency between arrangements for adjustment, convertibility and global liquidity; and

(f) the promotion of the net flow of real resources to developing countries....

Adjustment

4. There will be a better working of the adjustment process in which adequate methods to assure timely and effective balance of payments adjustment by both surplus and deficit countries will be assisted by improved international consultation in the Fund, including the use of objective indicators. To this end:

(a) Countries will take such prompt and adequate adjustment action, domestic or external, as may be needed to avoid protracted payments imbalances. In choosing among different forms of adjustment action, countries will take into account repercussions on other countries as well as internal considerations.

(b) Countries will aim to keep their official reserves within limits which will be internationally agreed from time to time in the Fund and which will be consistent with the volume of global liquidity. For this purpose reserve indicators will be established on a basis to be agreed in the Fund....

The Exchange Rate Mechanism

11. In the reformed system exchange rates will continue to be a matter for international concern and consultation. Competitive depreciation or undervaluation will be avoided. The exchange rate mechanism will remain based on stable but adjustable par values, and countries should not make inappropriate par value changes. On the other hand, countries should, whether in surplus or deficit, make appropriate par value changes promptly. Changes in par values will continue to be subject to Fund approval. The Fund may establish simplified procedures for approving small par value changes under appropriate safeguards.

12. Countries will undertake obligations to maintain specified maximum exchange rate margins for their currencies, except when authorized to adopt floating rates. The Fund will be empowered to vary the specified maximum margins on a qualified majority. It is agreed that it would be desirable that the system of exchange margins and intervention should be more symmetrical than that which existed in practice under the Bretton Woods system.

13. Countries may adopt floating rates in particular situations, subject to Fund authorization, surveillance and review. Such authorization will relieve a country of its obligations with regard to the maintenance of specified margins. Authorization to float may be withdrawn if the country fails to conform with the guidelines for conduct, or if the Fund decides that continued authorization to float would be inconsistent with the international interest....

Controls

14. There will be a strong presumption against the use of controls on current account transactions or payments for balance of payments purposes....

15. Countries will not use controls over capital transactions for the purpose of maintaining inappropriate exchange rates or, more generally, of avoiding appropriate adjustment action. Insofar as countries use capital controls, they should avoid an excessive degree of administrative restriction which could damage trade and beneficial capital flows and should not retain controls longer than needed....

16. Wherever possible developing countries will be exempted from controls imposed by other countries, particularly from import controls and controls over outward long-term investment. The special circumstances of developing countries will be taken into account by the Fund in assessing controls which these countries feel it necessary to apply. In addition,

developed countries should seek to remove legal, institutional and administrative obstacles to the access of developing countries to their financial markets. For their part, developing countries should seek to avoid policies which would discourage the flow of private capital to them....

Convertibility, Consolidation and the Management of Currency Reserves

18. It is agreed that the basic objectives to be accommodated in the reformed convertibility system should be symmetry of obligations on all countries including those whose currencies are held in official reserves; the better management of global liquidity and the avoidance of uncontrolled growth of reserve currency balances; adequate elasticity; and as much freedom for countries to choose the composition of their reserves as is consistent with the overall objectives of the reform.

19. As part of the better international management of global liquidity, the aggregate volume of official currency holdings will be kept under international surveillance and management in the Fund....

20. All countries maintaining par values will settle in reserve assets those official balances of their currencies which are presented to them for conversion. The Fund will establish appropriate arrangements to ensure sufficient control over the aggregate volume of official currency holdings....

21. Elasticity within the settlement system, particularly to finance disequilibrating capital flows, may be provided by credit facilities, including Fund credit and official bilateral or regional short-term credit. The Fund may establish as necessary new credit facilities to assist countries exposed to disequilibrating capital flows, particularly those without sufficient access to bilateral or regional credit....

Primary Reserve Assets

24. The SDR will become the principal reserve asset and the role of gold and of reserve currencies will be reduced. The SDR will also be the *numeraire* in terms of which par values will be expressed.

25. As part of the better international management of global liquidity, the Fund will allocate and cancel SDRs so as to ensure that the volume of global reserves is adequate and is consistent with the proper functioning of the adjustment and settlement systems. In the assessment of global reserve needs and the decision-making process for SDR allocation and cancellation the Fund will continue to follow the existing principles.... However, it is agreed that the methods of assessing global reserve needs must remain the subject of study, and it has been suggested that they may need to give additional emphasis to a number of economic factors.

26. The effective yield on the SDR will be high enough to make it attractive to acquire and hold, but not so high as to make countries reluctant to use the SDR when in deficit. The value of the SDR in transactions against currencies will be determined in such a way as to protect the capital value of the SDR against depreciation....

27. ...Consideration will be given to other aspects of the SDR, including its name, with a view to promoting public understanding.

28. Appropriate arrangements will be made for gold in the reformed system, in the light of the agreed objectives that the SDR should become the principal reserve asset and that the role of gold should be reduced. At the same time it is also generally recognized that gold reserves are an important component of global liquidity which should be usable to finance balance of payments deficits. It is not yet settled what arrangements for gold would be best in the reformed system, having due regard to the interests of all member countries....

The Link and Credit Facilities in Favor of Developing Countries

29. In the light of the agreed objective to promote economic development, the reformed monetary system will contain arrangements to promote an increasing net flow of real resources to developing countries.... If these arrangements were to include a link between development assistance and SDR allocation, this could take one of [several] forms....

30. It is envisaged that there will be a new facility in the Fund, under which developing countries would receive longer-term balance of payments finance.

The Institutional Structure of the Fund

31. A permanent and representative Council, with one member appointed from each Fund constituency, will be established. The Council will meet regularly, three or four times a year as required, and will have the necessary decision-making powers to supervise the management and adaptation of the monetary system, to oversee the continuing operation of the adjustment process and to deal with sudden disturbances which might threaten the system. The Managing Director will participate in meetings of the Council.

SEX EQUALITY RULES IN SCHOOLS
June 18, 1974

The Department of Health, Education and Welfare (HEW) on June 18 proposed regulations to outlaw sex discrimination in a host of school and college activities. The draft rules would ban discriminatory funding of athletic programs, teacher hiring, admissions, dormitory curfews, and other common practices in schools from pre-elementary to graduate level. But provision was made for numerous exemptions, and one extremely controversial item—sex discrimination in textbooks and other curricular materials—was omitted from the regulations on the ground of possible unconstitutionality. An HEW statement noted that "sex stereotyping" in textbooks was a "serious problem," but said that any attempt to regulate content could pose "grave constitutional questions under the 1st Amendment."

The rules were designed to implement Title IX of the Educational Amendments of 1972, which forbade sex discrimination in schools receiving federal aid. Lawsuits brought under the 1972 act, challenging disparate funding of male and female athletic programs in public schools, were pending in New York and Ohio at the time that HEW proposed the regulations. Charges under Title IX had also been filed with HEW. The rules were issued on a provisional basis, which gave interested parties until Oct. 15 to comment or suggest changes.

Funding for athletics provoked the greatest controversy during the preparation of the rules. Reportedly, earlier drafts circulated among interested parties had stipulated equal facilities, coaching and per-diem and travel expenses for women's and men's teams. However, the final version stopped short of requiring "equal aggregate" expenditures; instead, it proposed "equal opportunity" for men and women. The rules permitted but

507

did not require teams of mixed sexes. If a school chose to establish separate teams, "comparable" types and levels of competition—also equipment and supplies—would have to be provided for women. The regulations left unclear whether offering equal athletic scholarships to college was required, or whether such scholarships had to be offered in the same ratio as the proportion of women and men involved in inter-collegiate athletics.

Military institutions, and church-related institutions whose compliance would violate religious tenets, had been exempted from all coverage by the 1972 law. The major exception in the HEW regulations was in the areas of recruiting and admissions. Private undergraduate colleges, pre-elementary, elementary and secondary schools were not affected by the ban on discriminatory admissions. That ban applied to high school-level vocational schools, coeducational public colleges and all graduate and professional schools. But even those schools and colleges exempt from admissions controls were subject to the remaining rules, which covered financial aid and other benefits, access to courses and extracurricular activities, also recruiting, pay and fringe benefits for teachers.

Implementation of Rules

Once adopted in final form, the rules could be enforced in several ways. HEW could withdraw federal aid through administrative proceedings, or the agency could refer violations to the Justice Department for prosecution. In announcing the proposed regulations, HEW Secretary Casper W. Weinberger said that the government counted on voluntary action by schools and colleges. Some rules purposely avoided "rigid" formulas, said Weinberger, to allow institutions flexibility.

Representatives of women's organizations were criticial of the proposed regulations. Margot Polivy, a Washington lawyer representing the Association of Intercollegiate Athletics for Women, said the rules left many issues "up in the air." Commenting on the provisions for athletics, she said that "without a requirement for equal expenditures, I don't know what standard they are going to use." An HEW official acknowledged that provisions in the rules for "ability grouping" might have the effect of segregating some physical education classes, in spite of requirements for desegregation of noncompetitive sports.

> *Excerpts from the Department of Health, Education and Welfare's official explanation of proposed regulations prohibiting sex discrimination under Title IX of the Education Amendments of 1972, June 18, 1974:*

Coverage

Except for the specific limited exemptions set forth below, the proposed regulation applies to all aspects of all education programs or activities of a school district, institution of higher education, or other entity which receives Federal funds for any of those programs.

With respect to admissions to educational institutions, the proposed regulation applies only to: Vocational, professional and graduate schools, and to institutions of public undergraduate education (except those few public undergraduate schools which have been traditionally and continually single sex).

The proposed regulation does not cover admission to: Recipient preschools, elementary, and secondary schools (except vocational schools), private undergraduate institutions and, as noted above, to those few public undergraduate educational institutions that have been traditionally and continually single sex.

Even institutions whose admissions are exempt from coverage must treat all students nondiscriminatorily once they have admitted members of both sexes.

Military institutions at both the secondary and higher education level are entirely exempt from coverage under Title IX. Practice in schools run by religious organizations also are exempt to the extent compliance would be inconsistent with religious tenets. Thus, for example, if a religious tenet relates only to employment, the institution would still be prohibited from discriminating against students.

Admissions

The proposed regulation covers recruitment as well as all admissions policies and practices of those recipients not exempt as to admissions. It includes specific prohibitions of sex discrimination through separate ranking of applicants, application of sex-based quotas, administration of sex-biased tests or selection criteria, and granting of preference to applicants based on their attendance at particular institutions if the perference results in sex discrimination. The proposed regulation also forbids application in a discriminatory manner of rules concerning marital or parental status, and prohibits discrimination on the basis of pregnancy and related conditions, providing that recipients shall treat disabilities related to pregnancy in the same way as any other temporary disability or physical condition.

Generally, comparable efforts must be made by recipients to recruit members of each sex. Where discrimination previously existed, additional recruitment efforts directed primarily toward members of one sex must be undertaken to remedy the effects of the past discrimination.

EXAMPLES

An institution whose admissions are covered by the regulation may not set quotas on the number of men or women who will be admitted. Thus, a medical school may not set such quotas, although a private undergraduate school may do so.

An institution whose admissions are covered may not set different standards of admission for one sex than for the other. Thus, a graduate school may not require a lower grade point average for men than for women, although a private undergraduate school may do so.

An institution of graduate, professional or vocational education which prior to enactment of Title IX had limited its admissions primarily to members of one sex must undertake special efforts to notify and recruit members of the sex previously barred or restricted in order to overcome the effects of past discrimination.

Treatment

As stated before, although some schools are exempt from Title IX with regard to admissions, all schools must treat their admitted students without discrimination on the basis of sex. With regard to treatment of students, therefore, the proposed regulation applies to recipient preschools, elementary and secondary schools, vocational schools, colleges and universities at the undergraduate, graduate and professional levels, as well as to other agencies, organizations and persons which receive Federal funds for educational programs and activities.

Specifically, the treatment sections of the regulation cover the following areas:

[1]

Access to and participation in course offerings and extracurricular activities, including campus organizations and competitive athletics.

[2]

Eligibility for and receipt or enjoyment of benefits, services, and financial aid.

[3]

Use of facilities, and comparability of, availability of, and rules concerning housing (except that single-sex housing is permissible).

There is no provision in the regulation which would prohibit discrimination in textbooks and other curricular materials. As noted in the preamble to the proposed regulation, the department recognizes that sex stereotyping in curricula is a serious matter, but has concluded that any specific regulatory provision in this area would raise grave constitutional questions under the First Amendment. The department assumes that recipients will deal with this problem in the exercise of their general authority and control over curricula and course content. For its part, the department will increase its efforts, through the Office of Education, to provide research, assistance, and guidance to local educational agencies in eliminating sex bias from curricula and educational material.

Access and Participation Generally

The regulation prohibits discrimination by recipients in granting access to or providing for participation in any course offering or extra-curricular activity, including a campus organization or competitive athletics. No classes, including physical education, may be offered separately on the basis of sex.

Athletics

Where selection is based on competitive skill, athletics may be provided through separate teams for males and females or through a single team open to both sexes. Institutions must determine, at least annually, in what sports students desire to participate. If separate teams are offered, a recipient institution may not discriminate on the basis of sex in provision of necessary equipment or supplies, or in any other way, but equal aggregate expenditures are not required. The goal of the regulation in the area of competitive athletics is to secure equal opportunity for males and females while allowing schools and colleges flexibility in determining how best to provide such opportunity.

Where athletic opportunities for students of one sex have been limited, an institution must make affirmative efforts to inform members of that sex of the availability of equal opportunities and to provide support and training to enable them to participate.

Campus Organizations

Generally, a recipient may not, in connection with its education program or activity, support or assist any organization, agency or person which discriminates on the basis of sex. The proposed regulation does not specify in more detail what organization, agencies, or persons could not, if they operated discriminatorily, be supported by a recipient consistent with its obligations under Title IX. It does, however, set out the major criteria to be applied in determining existence of a violation in this area, which are (1) the substantiality of the relationship between the recipient and the organization (including financial support and housing), and (2) the closeness of the relationship between the organization's functions and the educational program or activity of the recipient.

EXAMPLES

A recipient school district may not require boys to take shop and girls to take home economics, exclude girls from shop and boys from home economics, or operate separate home economics or shop classes for boys and girls.

A recipient school district may not require segregation of boys into one health, physical education, or other class, and segregation of girls into another such class.

A recipient institution which admits male and female students may not provide sports opportunities exclusively or virtually exclusively for male students. However, it is not required to provide women access to men's teams if it furnishes women separate opportunities to participate in competitive athletics of comparable types and at comparable levels of competition (e.g. varsity, junior varsity, etc.).

511

Benefits, Services and Financial Aid

Generally, a recipient subject to the regulation is prohibited from discriminating in making available, in connection with its educational program or activity, any benefits, services, or financial aid. Benefits and services include medical and insurance policies and services for students, counseling, and assistance in obtaining employment. Financial aid includes scholarships, loans, grants-in-aid and workstudy programs.

The general prohibition does not apply to administration by a recipient of a scholarship or similar financial assistance program which is restricted to members of one sex and is established under a foreign will, trust or similar legal instrument or by a foreign government.

Facilities

Generally, all facilities must be available without discrimination on the basis of sex. As provided in the statute, however, the regulation permits separate housing based on sex as well as separate locker rooms, toilets and showers. A recipient may not make available to members of one sex locker rooms, toilets and showers which are not comparable to those provided to members of the other sex. With respect to housing, the regulation requires comparability as to the facilities themselves and nondiscrimination as to their availability and as to the rules under which they are operated, including fees, hours, and requirements for off-campus housing.

EXAMPLES

An institution which has one swimming pool must provide for use by members of both sexes on a non-discriminatory basis.

Administration by a recipient institution of different rules based on sex regarding elegibility for living off-campus, curfews, availability of cleaning and janitorial assistance, etc. would violate the regulation.

Employment

All employes in all institutions are covered, both full- and part-time, except those in military schools, and in religious schools, to the extent compliance would be inconsistent with the controlling of religious tenets. Employment coverage under the proposed regulation generally follows the policies of the Equal Employment Opportunity Commission and the Department of Labor's Office of Federal Contract Compliance.

As to fringe benefits, employers must provide either equal contributions to or equal benefits under pension plans for male and female employes; as to pregnancy, leave and fringe benefits to pregnant employes must be offered in the same manner as are leave and benefits to temporarily disabled employes.

EXAMPLES

A recipient employer may not recruit and hire employes solely from discriminatory sources in connection with its educational program or activity.

A recipient employer must provide equal pay to male and female employes performing the same work in connection with its educational program or activity.

A recipient employer may not discriminate against or exclude from employment any employe or applicant for employment on the basis of pregnancy or related conditions.

COURT ON OBSCENITY
June 24, 1974

The U.S. Supreme Court on June 24 unanimously overturned a ruling by the Supreme Court of Georgia affirming a jury's conviction of the manager of a theater that had shown the motion picture Carnal Knowledge. *In a second decision the same day, the Court upheld the finding of a lower federal court which banned use of the mails for the circulation by a private enterprise of an allegedly obscene brochure promoting the sale of* The Illustrated Presidential Report of the Committee on Obscenity and Pornography. *The report, published in 1970, urged an end to all legal bars on the purchase by adults of sexually explicit books and magazines or on the viewing by adults of sexually explicit films.*

Taken together, the two rulings appeared to narrow the scope of Supreme Court decisions in 1973 which held that questions of obscenity could be judged against local, non-national standards, and which formulated guidelines for the observance of those standards (see Historic Documents, 1973, p. 611). The 1974 opinions appeared to signal a return to case-by-case obscenity decisions by the Court, a course which the justices had tried to avoid by their 1973 rulings.

Carnal Knowledge, an award-winning film which depicted the contrasting sex lives and marriages of two friends from college years to middle age, had been declared obscene by an Albany, Ga., trial jury. The Georgia Supreme Court, applying the high court's 1973 obscenity standards, upheld the Albany jury. But the Supreme Court found that the film did not depict sexual conduct in a patently offensive way under the standards it had established a year earlier. Delivering the opinion of the Court, Justice

William H. Rehnquist stated that "It would be a serious misreading of Miller [one of the 1973 decisions] to conclude that juries have unbridled discretion in determining what is patently offensive." In the 1973 ruling, he pointed out, "we made it plain that…'no one will be subject to prosecution for the sale or exposure of obscene materials unless these materials depict or describe patently offensive "hardcore" sexual conduct'…. It would be wholly at odds with this aspect of Miller to uphold an obscenity conviction based upon a defendant's depiction of a woman with a bare midriff." The 1973 guidelines were established to ban hardcore pornography, not whatever a jury might find disagreeable, Rehnquist said.

Justice William J. Brennan Jr., in a concurring opinion joined by Justices Potter Stewart and Thurgood Marshall, pointed out that the latest ruling confirmed his observation in 1973 that the course then laid out did "not extricate us from the mire of case-by-case determinations of obscenity," nor did it avert the "attendant uncertainty of such a process and its inevitably institutional stress upon the judiciary." Justice William O. Douglas also concurred, "being of the view that any ban on obscenity is prohibited by the First Amendment."

Obscenity Conviction Upheld

The second Court decision upheld by a 5-4 vote the conviction of six Los Angeles parties for sending through the mails a one-page brochure including a collage of photographs from The Illustrated Presidential Report of the Commission on Obscenity and Pornography—which pictured sexual acts and behavior in violation of the 1973 guidelines. The advertisement had depicted "heterosexual and homosexual intercourse, sodomy and a variety of deviate sexual acts," according to the U.S. 9th Circuit Court of Appeals, which had affirmed the jury's decision. The jury had not been able to decide whether the report itself was obscene.

Speaking for the Court, Justice Rehnquist again addressed the question of community standards. By rejecting a nationwide standard, the Court had not required the use of a standard for a smaller particular geographic area, he said. "A juror is entitled to draw on his own knowledge of the view of the average person in the community…from which he comes."

Justice Douglas dissented, holding that "If officials may constitutionally report on obscenity, I see nothing in the First Amendment that allows us to bar the use of a glossary factually to illustrate what the report discusses." Justice Brennan, joined by Justices Stewart and Marshall in another dissenting opinion, said that "whatever the constitutional power of government to regulate the distribution of sexually oriented materials, the First and Fourteenth Amendments…deny the Federal and State Governments power wholly to suppress their distribution."

Excerpts from the opinion of the Court, handed down June 24, in two obscenity cases—one involving the film Carnal

Knowledge *(Jenkins* v. *Georgia) and the other an advertise-ment for* The Illustrated Presidential Report of the Commission on Obscenity and Pornography *(Hamling et al.* v. *United States):*

Billy Jenkins, Appellant, } On Appeal from
          v.   } the Supreme Court
State of Georgia. } of Georgia.

[June 24, 1974]

MR. JUSTICE REHNQUIST delivered the opinion of the Court.

Appellant was convicted in Georgia of the crime of distributing obscene material. His conviction, in March 1972, was for showing the film "Carnal Knowledge" in a movie theater in Albany, Georgia. The jury that found appellant guilty was instructed on obscenity pursuant to the Georgia statute, which defines obscene material in language similar to that of the definition of obscenity set forth in this Court's plurality opinion in *Memoirs* v. *Massachusetts...:*

> "Material is obscene if considered as a whole applying community standards, its predominant appeal is to prurient interest, that is, a shameful or morbid interest in nudity, sex or excretion, and utterly without redeeming social value and if, in addition, it goes substantially beyond customary limits of candor in describing or representing such matters."...

We hold today in *Hamling* v. *United States...*that defendants convicted prior to the announcement of our *Miller* decisions but whose convictions were on direct appeal at that time should receive any benefit available to them from those decisions. We conclude here that the film "Carnal Knowledge" is not obscene under the constitutional standards announced in *Miller* v. *California...*and that the First and Fourteenth Amendments therefore require that the judgment of the Supreme Court of Georgia affirming appellant's conviction be reversed....

We agree with the Supreme Court of Georgia's implicit ruling that the Constitution does not require that juries be instructed in state obscenity cases to apply the standards of a hypothetical statewide community. *Miller* approved the use of such instructions; it did not mandate their use. What *Miller* makes clear is that state juries need not be instructed to apply "national standards." We also agree with the Supreme Court of Georgia's implicit approval of the trial court's instructions directing jurors to apply "community standards" without specifying what "community." *Miller* held that it was constitutionally permissible to permit juries to rely on the understanding of the community from which they came as to contemporary community standards, and the States have considerable latitude in framing statutes under this element of the *Miller* decision. A State may choose to define an obscenity offense in terms of "contemporary community standards" as defined in *Miller* without further specification, as was done here, or it may choose to define the standards in more precise geographic terms, as was done by California in *Miller*....

There is little to be found in the record about the film "Carnal Knowledge" other than the film itself. However, appellant has supplied a variety of information and critical commentary, the authenticity of which appellee does not dispute. The film appeared on many "Ten Best" lists for 1971, the year in which it was released. Many but not all of the reviews were favorable....

Miller states that the questions of what appeals to the "prurient interest" and what is "patently offensive" under the obscenity test which it formulates are "essentially questions of fact."... "When triers of fact are asked to decide whether 'the average person, applying community standards' would consider materials 'prurient' it would be unrealistic to require that the answer be based on some abstract formulation.... To require a State to structure obscenity proceedings around evidence of a *national* 'community standard' would be an exercise in futility."...

But all of this does not lead us to agree with the Supreme Court of Georgia's apparent conclusion that the jury's verdict against appellant virtually precluded all further appellate review of appellant's assertion that his exhibition of the film was protected by the First and Fourteenth Amendments. Even though questions of appeal to the "prurient interest" or of patent offensiveness are "essentially questions of fact," it would be a serious misreading of *Miller* to conclude that juries have unbridled discretion in determining what is "patently offensive." Not only did we there say that "the First Amendment values applicable to the States through the Fourteenth Amendment are adequately protected by the ultimate power of appellate courts to conduct an independent review of constitutional claims when necessary,"...but we made it plain that under that holding "no one will be subject to prosecution for the sale or exposure of obscene materials unless these materials depict or describe patently offensive 'hard core' sexual conduct...."

We also took pains in *Miller* to "give a few plain examples of what a state statute could define for regulation under part (b) of the standard announced," that is, the requirement of patent offensiveness.... These examples included "representations or descriptions of ultimate sexual acts, normal or perverted, actual or simulated," and "representations or descriptions of masturbation, excretory functions, and lewd exhibition of the genitals." While this did not purport to be an exhaustive catalog of what juries might find patently offensive, it was certainly intended to fix substantive constitutional limitations, deriving from the First Amendment, on the type of material subject to such a determination. It would be wholly at odds with this aspect of *Miller* to uphold an obscenity conviction based upon a defendant's depiction of a woman with a bare midriff, even though a properly charged jury unanimously agreed on a verdict of guilty.

Our own view of the film satisfies us that "Carnal Knowledge" could not be found under the *Miller* standards to depict sexual conduct in a patently offensive way. Nothing in the movie falls within either of the two examples given in *Miller* of material which may constitutionally be found to meet the "patently offensive" element of those standards, nor is there anything sufficiently similar to such material to justify similar treatment. While the subject matter of the picture is, in a broader sense, sex, and there are scenes in which sexual conduct including "ultimate sexual acts" is to be understood to be taking place, the camera does not focus on the bodies of the actors at such times. There is no exhibition whatever of the actors' genitals, lewd or otherwise, during these scenes. There are occasional scenes of nudity, but nudity alone is not enough to make material legally obscene under the *Miller* standards.

Appellant's showing of the film "Carnal Knowledge" is simply not the "public portrayal of hard core sexual conduct for its own sake, and for ensuing commercial gain" which we said was punishable in *Miller*. We hold that the film could not, as a matter of constitutional law, be found to depict sexual conduct in a patently offensive way, and that it is therefore not outside the protection of the First and Fourteenth Amendments because it is obscene. No other basis appearing in the record upon which the judgment of conviction can be sustained, we reverse the judgment of the Supreme Court of Georgia.

Reversed.

Mr. Justice Brennan, with whom Mr. Justice Stewart and Mr. Justice Marshall join, concurring in result.

...Today's decision confirms my observation in *Paris Adult Theater I* v. *Slaton*...that the Court's new formulation does not extricate us from the mire of case-by-case determinations of obscenity. I there noted that:

> "Ultimately, the reformulation must fail because it still leaves in this Court the responsibility of determining in each case whether the materials are protected by the First Amendment. The Court concedes that even under its restated formulation, the First Amendment interests at stake require 'appellate courts to conduct an independent review of constitutional claims when necessary,'...

After the Court's decision today, there can be no doubt that *Miller* requires appellate courts—including this Court—to review independently the constitutional fact of obscenity. Moreover, the Court's task is not limited to reviewing a jury finding under part (c) of the *Miller* test that "the work, taken as a whole, lack[ed] serious literary, artistic, political, or scientific value." *Miller* also requires independent review of a jury's determination under part (b) of the *Miller* test that "the work depicts or describes in a patently offensive way, sexual conduct specifically defined by the applicable state law."...

In order to make the review mandated by *Miller*, the Court was required to screen the film Carnal Knowledge and make an independent determination of obscenity *vel non*. Following that review, the Court holds that Carnal Knowledge "could not, as a matter of constitutional law, be found to depict sexual conduct in a patently offensive way, and that therefore it is not outside the protection of the First and Fourteenth Amendments because it is obscene."

Thus, it is clear that as long as the *Miller* test remains in effect "one cannot say with certainty that material is obscene until at least five members of this Court, applying inevitably obscure standards, have pronounced it so." *Paris Adult Theater I* v. *Slaton...* (BRENNAN, J., dissenting). Because of the attendant uncertainty of such a process and its inevitable institutional stress upon the judiciary, I continue to adhere to my view that, "at least in the absence of distribution to juveniles or obtrusive exposure to unconsenting adults, the First and Fourteenth Amendments prohibit the State and Federal Governments from attempting wholly to suppress sexually oriented materials on the basis of their allegedly 'obscene' contents." *Paris Adult Theater I* v. *Slaton....* It is clear that, tested by that constitutional standard, the Georgia obscenity statutes under which appellant Jenkins was convicted are constitutionally over-broad and therefore facially invalid. I therefore concur in the Court's judgment reversing Jenkins' conviction.

MR. JUSTICE DOUGLAS, being of the view that any ban on obscenity is prohibited by the First Amendment, made applicable to the States through the Fourteenth, concurs in the reversal of this conviction.

<table>
<tr><td>William L. Hamling et al.,
Petitioners,
v.
United States</td><td>On Writ of Certiorari
to the United States
Court of Appeals
for the Ninth Circuit.</td></tr>
</table>

[June 24, 1974]

MR. JUSTICE REHNQUIST delivered the opinion of the Court.

On March 5, 1971, a grand jury in the United States District Court for the Southern District of California indicted petitioners William L. Hamling, Earl Kemp, Shirley R. Wright, David L. Thomas, Reed Enterprises, Inc., and Library Service, Inc., on 21 counts of an indictment charging use of the mails to carry an obscene book, The Illustrated Presidential Report of The Commission on Obscenity and Pornography, and an obscene advertisement, which gave information as to where, how, and from whom and by what means the Illustrated Report might be obtained, and of conspiracy to commit the above offenses.... Prior to trial, petitioners moved to dismiss the indictment on the grounds that it failed to inform them of the charges, and that the grand jury had insufficient evidence before it to return an indictment and was improperly instructed on the law. Petitioners also challenged the petit jury panel and moved to strike the venire on ground that there had been an unconstitutional exclusion of all persons under 25 years of age. The District Court denied all of these motions.

Following a jury trial, petitioners were convicted on 12 counts of mailing and conspiring to mail the obscene advertisement. On appeal, the United

States Court of Appeals for the Ninth Circuit affirmed.... The jury was unable to reach a verdict with regard to the counts of the indictment which charged the mailing of the allegedly obscene Illustrated Report....

Miller rejected the view that the First and Fourteenth Amendments require that the proscription of obscenity be based on uniform nationwide standards of what is obscene, describing such standards as "hypothetical and unascertainable."... But in so doing the Court did not require as a constitutional matter the substitution of some smaller geographical area into the same sort of formula; the test was stated in terms of the understanding of "the average person, applying contemporary community standards."... When this approach is coupled with the reaffirmation in *Paris Adult Theater I* v. *Slaton* of the rule that the prosecution need not as a matter of constitutional law produce "expert" witnesses to testify as to the obscenity of the materials, the import of the quoted language from *Miller* becomes clear. A juror is entitled to draw on his own knowledge of the views of the average person in the community or vicinage from which he comes for making the required determination, just as he is entitled to draw on his knowledge of the propensities of a "reasonable" person in other areas of the law.... Our holding in *Miller* that California could constitutionally proscribe obscenity in terms of a "statewide" standard did not mean that any such precise geographic area is required as a matter of constitutional law....

The *Miller* cases, important as they were in enunciating a constitutional test for obscenity to which a majority of the Court subscribed for the first time in a number of years, were intended neither as legislative drafting handbooks or as manuals of jury instructions....

It is plain from the Court of Appeals' description of the brochure involved here that it is a form of hard-core pornography well within the types of permissibly proscribed depictions described in *Miller*.... Whatever complaint the distributor of material which presented a more difficult question of obscenity *vel non* might have as to the lack of a previous limiting construction,...these petitioners have none.

Mr. Justice Douglas, dissenting.

In 1970 the President's Commission on Obscenity and Pornography issued its Report....

What petitioners did was to supply the Report with a glossary—not in dictionary terms but visually. Every item in the glossary depicted explicit sexual material within the meaning of that term as used in the Report. Perhaps we should have no Reports on Obscenity. But imbedded in the First Amendment is the philosophy that the people have the right to know. Sex is more important to some than to others but it is of some importance to all. If officials may constitutionally report on obscenity, I see nothing in the First Amendment that allows us to bar the use of a glossary factually to illustrate what the Report discusses.

MR. JUSTICE BRENNAN, with whom MR. JUSTICE STEWART and MR. JUSTICE MARSHALL join, dissenting.

Whatever the constitutional power of government to *regulate* the distribution of sexually oriented materials, the First and Fourteenth Amendments, in my view, deny the Federal and State Governments power wholly to *suppress* their distribution. For I remain of the view that, "at least in the absence of distribution to juveniles or obtrusive exposure to unconsenting adults, the First and Fourteenth Amendments prohibit the State and Federal Governments from attempting wholly to suppress sexually oriented materials on the basis of their allegedly 'obscene' contents."... (BRENNAN, J., dissenting). Since amended 18 U.S.C. § 1461, as construed by the Court, aims at total *suppression* of distribution by mail of sexually oriented materials, it is, in my view, unconstitutionally overbroad and therefore invalid on its face. On that ground alone, I would reverse the judgment of the Court of Appeals and direct the dismissal of the indictment. Several other reasons, however, also compel the conclusion that petitioners' convictions should be set aside....Under today's "local" standards construction...the guilt or innocence of distributors of identical materials mailed from the same locale can now turn on the dicey course of transit or place of delivery of the materials.... National distributors choosing to send their products in interstate travels will be forced to cope with the community standards of every hamlet into which their goods may wander. Because these variegated standards are impossible to discern, national distributors, fearful of risking the expense and difficulty of defending against prosecution in any of several remote communities, must inevitably be led to retreat to debilitating self-censorship that abridges the First Amendment rights of the people. For it "would tend to restrict the public's access to forms [of sexually oriented materials] which the [United States] could not constitutionally suppress directly...a censorship...hardly less virulent for being privately administered...[for]...[t]hrough it, the distribution of all [sexually oriented materials], both obscene and not obscene, would be impeded." Thus, the people of many communities will be "protected" far beyond government's constitutional power to deny them access to sexually oriented materials. A construction that has such consequences necessarily renders the constituionality of amended § 1461 facially suspect under the First Amendment.

COURT ON "RIGHT TO REPLY"
June 25, 1974

In a case which had stirred widespread concern in the communications industry, the Supreme Court June 25 struck down a Florida "right to reply" law requiring a newspaper to print a rebuttal of a political candidate attacked in its columns. The unanimous decision came after more than two years of stepped-up demands for "media access" from government officials including President Nixon and former Vice President Agnew, from minority groups and legal scholars. Critics charged that monopolistic control of the news media gave unwarranted importance to the biases of a few powerful owners, whose opinions determined both what was reported and how issues were interpreted to the public.

Without a competitive news industry open to a broad range of views, critics argued, minority groups, unpopular candidates and average citizens were denied opportunities to influence public opinion and government processes. It was also charged that recent court decisions made it difficult for citizens to protect themselves from libel. In a March 8 message to Congress Nixon asserted that the Court's 1968 Sullivan decision gave the press "virtually a license to lie," and he said he had asked the Justice Department to "explore the possibility" of right to reply legislation. (In New York Times v. Sullivan, the Court had established the "actual malice" standard governing libel suits by public officials against their detractors.)

The Florida case arose when Pat L. Tornillo Jr., a teachers' union official, invoked a little-used 1913 law to demand that the Miami Herald print his replies to two critical editorials that appeared in September 1972, while he was running for a seat in the state House of Representatives. After his election defeat, Tornillo took the Herald to court. The Dade County Circuit

Court agreed with the newspaper's contention that the Florida statute un-constitutionally abridged the freedom of the press and dismissed the case. On appeal, the Florida Supreme Court, by a vote of six to one, reversed the lower court ruling, and upheld the statute on the grounds that it expanded rather than limited free speech and encouraged the flow of public information.

Opinion of the Court

Recognizing the legitimate concern of many who felt that the increasing concentration of the media was imperiling the public's right to know, the U.S. Supreme Court in its June 25 ruling nevertheless declined to approve a law requiring newspapers to print certain material. Writing for the Court, Chief Justice Warren E. Burger stated that previous court rulings clearly implied that statutory requirements for publication of particular material would constitute unconstitutional government interference with the press. The compulsory publication of replies could subject a newspaper to extra expenses or force it to omit news or commentary, a possibility that might tempt editors to avoid controversy at the expense of vigorous political coverage, Burger held. Even if it were possible to eliminate these "penalties," Burger said, the Florida law trespassed upon the editorial function.

Justices William J. Brennan Jr. and William H. Rehnquist concurred, adding a brief statement that the Court's opinion did not imply any view as to the constitutionality of laws which required newspapers to print retractions of statements proved to be false as well as defamatory. In another concurring opinion Justice Byron R. White said the Florida statute "runs afoul of the elementary First Amendment proposition that government may not force a newspaper to print copy which, in its journalistic discretion, it chooses to leave on the newsroom floor."

Among major news organizations the Florida case had been considered a serious threat to editorial freedom. Only one other state, Mississippi, had a "right to reply" law on the books, but leaders in all branches of the communications business feared that a Supreme Court ruling upholding the Florida law would encourage passage of similar statutes by other state legislatures. Friend-of-the-court briefs on behalf of the Herald *were filed by the American Newspaper Publishers Association, the National Newspaper Association, the American Society of Newspaper Editors, the National Association of Broadcasters and individual papers.*

The decision was hailed by the Herald's *publisher, Lee Hills, as "a victory for the American people." William Hornby, chairman of the Freedom of Information Press-Bar Committee of the American Society of Newspaper Editors said: "The unanimous character of the Court decision should put to rest this particular doctrine of publication—that editors must print material by government order."*

*Excerpts from Supreme Court opinion, June 25, 1974,
invalidating Florida's "right to reply" law:*

No. 73-797

The Miami Herald Publishing
Company, A Division of
Knight Newspapers,
Inc., Appellant,
 v.
Pat. L. Tornillo, Jr.

On Appeal from the Su-
preme Court of Florida

[June 25, 1974]

Mr. Chief Justice Burger delivered the opinion of the Court.

The issue in this case is whether a state statute granting a political candidate a right to equal space to reply to criticism and attacks on his record
by a newspaper, violates the guarantees of a free press....

The challenged statute creates a right to reply to press criticism of a candidate for nomination or election. The statute was enacted in 1913 and this
is only the second recorded case decided under its provisions.

Appellant contends the statute is void on its face because it purports to
regulate the content of a newspaper in violation of the First Amendment.
Alternatively it is urged that the statute is void for vagueness since no
editor could know exactly what words would call the statute into operation.
It is also contended that the statute fails to distinguish between critical
comment which is and is not defamatory.

The appellee and supporting advocates of an enforceable right of access
to the press vigorously argue that Government has an obligation to ensure
that a wide variety of views reach the public. The contentions of access
proponents will be set out in some detail. It is urged that at the time the
First Amendment to the Constitution was enacted in 1791 as part of our
Bill of Rights the press was broadly representative of the people it was serving. While many of the newspapers were intensely partisan and narrow in
their views, the press collectively presented a broad range of opinions to
readers. Entry into publishing was inexpensive; pamphlets and books
provided meaningful alternatives to the organized press for the expression
of unpopular ideas and often treated events and expressed views not
covered by conventional newspapers. A true marketplace of ideas existed in
which there was relatively easy access to the channels of communication.

Access advocates submit that although newspapers of the present are
superficially similar to those of 1791 the press of today is in reality very
different from that known in the early years of our national existence....Chains of newspapers, national newspapers, national wire and
news services, and one-newspaper towns, are the dominant features of a
press that has become noncompetitive and enormously powerful and influential in its capacity to manipulate popular opinion and change events....

The elimination of competing newspapers in most of our large cities, and
the concentration of control of media that results from the only newspaper

being owned by the same interests which own a television station and a radio station, are important components of this trend toward concentration of control of outlets to inform the public.

The result of these vast changes has been to place in a few hands the power to inform the American people and shape public opinion....In effect, it is claimed, the public has lost any ability to respond or to contribute in a meaningful way to the debate on issues. The monopoly of the means of communication allows for little or no critical analysis of the media except in professional journals of very limited readership....

The obvious solution, which was available to dissidents at an earlier time when entry into publishing was relatively inexpensive, today would be to have additional newspapers. But the same economic factors which have caused the disappearance of vast numbers of metropolitan newspapers have made entry into the marketplace of ideas served by the print media almost impossible. It is urged that the claim of newspapers to be "surrogates for the public" carries with it a concomitant fiduciary obligation to account for that stewardship. From this premise it is reasoned that the only effective way to insure fairness and accuracy and to provide for some accountability is for government to take affirmative action. The First Amendment interest of the public in being informed is said to be in peril because the "marketplace of ideas" is today a monopoly controlled by the owners of the market.

Proponents of enforced access to the press take comfort from language in several of this Court's decisions which suggests that the First Amendment acts as a sword as well as a shield, that it imposes obligations on the owners of the press in addition to protecting the press from government regulation....

However much validity may be found in these arguments, at each point the implementation of a remedy such as enforceable right of access necessarily calls for some mechanism, either governmental or consensual. If it is governmental coercion, this at once brings about a confrontation with the express provisions of the First Amendment and the judicial gloss on that amendment developed over the years....

We see that beginning with *Associated Press* v. *United States* [1945] the Court has expressed sensitivity as to whether a restriction or requirement constituted the compulsion exerted by government on a newspaper to print that which it would not otherwise print. The clear implication has been that any such compulsion to publish that which " 'reason' tells them should not be published" is unconstitutional. A responsible press is an undoubtedly desirable goal, but press responsibility is not mandated by the Constitution and like many other virtues it cannot be legislated.

Appellee's argument that the Florida statute does not amount to a restriction of appellant's right to speak because "the statute in question here has not prevented the *Miami Herald* from saying anything it wished" begs the core question. Compelling editors or publishers to publish that which " 'reason' tells them should not be published" is what is at issue in this case. The Florida statute operates as a command in the same sense as a statute or regulation forbidding appellant from publishing specified matter. Governmental restraint on publishing need not fall into familiar or traditional patterns to be subject to constitutional limitations on governmental powers....The Florida statute exacts a penalty on the basis of the content of a newspaper. The first phase of the penalty resulting from the compelled printing of a reply is exacted in terms of the cost in printing and composing time and materials and in taking up space that could be devoted to other material the newspaper may have preferred to print. It is correct, as appellee contends, that a newspaper is not subject to the finite technological limitations of time that confront a broadcaster but it is not correct to say that, as an economic reality, a newspaper can proceed to infinite expansion of its column space to accommodate the replies that a government agency determines or a statute commands the readers should have available.

Faced with the penalties that would accrue to any newspaper that published news or commentary arguably within reach of the right of access statute, editors might well conclude that the safe course is to avoid controversy and that, under the operation of the Florida statute, political and electoral coverage would be blunted or reduced. Government enforced right of access inescapably "dampens the vigor and limits the variety of public debate."

Even if a newspaper would face no additional costs to comply with a compulsory access law and would not be forced to forego publication of news or opinion by the inclusion of a reply, the Florida statute fails to clear the barriers of the First Amendment because of its intrusion into the function of editors. A newspaper is more than a passive receptacle or conduit for news, comment, and advertising. The choice of material to go into a newspaper, and the decisions made as to limitations on the size of the paper, and content, and treatment of public issues and public officials—whether fair or unfair—constitutes the exercise of editorial control and judgment. It has yet to be demonstrated how governmental regulation of this crucial process can be exercised consistent with First Amendment guarantees of a free press as they have evolved to this time. Accordingly, the judgement of the Supreme Court of Florida is reversed.

It is so ordered.

MR. JUSTICE BRENNAN, with whom MR. JUSTICE REHNQUIST joins, concurring.

I join the Court's opinion which, as I understand it, addresses only "right of reply" statutes and implies no view upon the constitutionality of "retraction" statutes affording plaintiffs able to prove defamatory falsehoods a statutory action to require publication of a retraction.

MR. JUSTICE WHITE, concurring.

...A newspaper or magazine is not a public utility subject to "reasonable" governmental regulation in matters affecting the exercise of journalistic judgment as to what shall be printed....We have learned, and continue to learn, from what we view as the unhappy experiences of other nations where government has been allowed to meddle in the internal editorial affairs of newspapers. Regardless of how beneficent-sounding the purposes of controlling the press might be, we prefer "the power of reason as applied through public discussion" and remain intensely skeptical about those measures that would allow government to insinuate itself into the editorial rooms of this Nation's press....

NATO DECLARATION
June 26, 1974

President Nixon joined 14 other heads of state in signing a Declaration on Atlantic Relations at a meeting of member states of the North Atlantic Treaty Organization (NATO) in Brussels, Belgium, June 26. The President had stopped in Brussels en route to the Soviet summit (see p. 535) *to put his signature on the agreement approved June 18 in Ottawa, Canada, by Secretary of State Henry A. Kissinger and foreign ministers of other NATO member states. The 14-point declaration, which affirmed the "common destiny" of the allies, was seen as a step toward mending relations that had been strained by economic, military and political disagreements. The document grew out of a proposal for a "new Atlantic Charter," put forward by Kissinger on April 23, 1973,* (see Historic Documents 1973, p. 487-498), *in support of a reinvigorated policy of "shared ideals and common purposes with our friends." Kissinger had sought to include Japan as well as the North Atlantic nations in that agreement. But the European allies, preferring a narrower approach, insisted on a separate agreement between the United States and the other NATO countries.*

The key provision of the document signed June 26 called on the member nations of NATO "to keep each other fully informed and to strengthen the practice of frank and timely consultations by all means that may be apappropriate on matters relating to their common interests." At the drafting session in Ottawa, a U.S. move—to make consultations between NATO members a legally binding obligation—had run aground when France, in particular, opposed such language. Said French Foreign Minister Jean Sauvagnargues: "We are in perfect harmony.... We don't need a legal brief to consult with each other." As recently as March, a dis-

pute over prior consultations between European countries and the United States had been triggered by a European Economic Community (EEC) offer of special aid to Arab states. (See p. 185.) The proposal, widely interpreted as a unilateral attempt by the European countries to secure oil supplies, was set forth to the Arab oil producers without prior discussion of the plan with the United States. Evidencing the anger engendered in Washington by that move, Kissinger was quoted March 11 as saying, "the biggest problem American foreign policy confronts is...how to bring our friends to a realization that there are greater common interests than simple self-assertiveness."

European-American relations were bruised all the more because less than a month earlier, in February, the EEC countries had joined the United States, Canada and Japan in endorsing a joint effort to guarantee continued production and equitable distribution of oil supplies. (See p. 123.) Against this background, questions were raised as to whether European countries would abide by the new declaration's pledge of consultations. Two weeks before the Declaration on Atlantic Relations was signed in Brussels, foreign ministers of EEC countries had agreed in Bonn, West Germany, to pursue the proposal of aid to Arab states. Under that agreement, consultations between the EEC and the United States would be allowed, but only after the unanimous approval of the members was obtained.

Other Key Passages

Among other key provisions of the Declaration on Atlantic Relations was a reiteration of the tenet set forth in the 1949 treaty establishing NATO that equated an attack against one member of the alliance with an attack against all members. In a June 19 statement, Kissinger underscored the significance of the language when he said NATO members "hold the view that events in troubled areas in many parts of the world can influence alliance security." The Middle East was one of those areas, he added.

In the field of East-West relations, the declaration struck a pessimistic note, asserting that despite the laudable progress made toward detente, "essential elements in the situation which gave rise to the [1949 NATO] treaty have not changed." Stressing the need to maintain military defenses, the declaration also noted the role Great Britain and France could play—by means of their nuclear capability—in deterring aggressive action.

In other areas, the new agreement called for NATO allies to "work to remove sources of conflict between their economic policies and to encourage economic cooperation with one another." On June 19, NATO officials called the passage on the economy "the strongest statement ever included in a NATO document." On the issue of the level of American troops stationed in Europe, a topic simultaneously under discussion in Vienna at the 19-nation European Security Conference, the document said that the United States had agreed "to maintain forces in Europe at the level required to sustain the credibility of the strategy of deterrence and to maintain the capacity to defend the North Atlantic area should deterrence fail."

*Text of the Declaration on Atlantic Relations, signed in
Brussels, Belgium, June 26 by President Nixon and the
heads of other North Atlantic Treaty Organization (NATO)
countries:*

Declaration on Atlantic Relations

Text of the Declaration Signed at the Meeting of the North Atlantic Council in Brussels. June 26, 1974

1. The members of the North Atlantic Alliance declare that the Treaty signed 25 years ago to protect their freedom and independence has confirmed their common destiny. Under the shield of the Treaty, the Allies have maintained their security, permitting them to preserve the values which are the heritage of their civilization and enabling Western Europe to rebuild from its ruins and lay the foundations of its unity.

2. The members of the Alliance reaffirm their conviction that the North Atlantic Treaty provides the indispensable basis for their security, thus making possible the pursuit of detente. They welcome the progress that has been achieved on the road towards detente and harmony among nations, and the fact that a Conference of 35 countries of Europe and North America is now seeking to lay down guidelines designed to increase security and co-operation in Europe. They believe that until circumstances permit the introduction of general, complete and controlled disarmament, which alone could provide genuine security for all, the ties uniting them must be maintained. The Allies share a common desire to reduce the burden of arms expenditure on their peoples. But States that wish to preserve peace have never achieved this aim by neglecting their own security.

3. The members of the Alliance reaffirm that their common defense is one and indivisible. An attack on one or more of them in the area of application of the Treaty shall be considered an attack against them all. The common aim is to prevent any attempt by a foreign power to threaten the independence or integrity of a member of the Alliance. Such an attempt would not only put in jeopardy the security of all members of the Alliance but also threaten the foundations of world peace.

4. At the same time they realize that the circumstances affecting their common defense have profoundly changed in the last ten years: the strategic relationship between the United States and the Soviet Union has reached a point of near equilibrium. Consequently, although all the countries of the Alliance remain vulnerable to attack, the nature of the danger to which they are exposed has changed. The Alliance's problems in the defense of Europe have thus assumed a different and more distinct character.

5. However, the essential elements in the situation which gave rise to the Treaty have not changed. While the commitment of all the Allies to the common defense reduces the risk of external aggression, the contribution to the security of the entire Alliance provided by the nuclear forces of the United States based in the United States as well as in Europe and by the presence of North American forces in Europe remains indispensable.

6. Nevertheless, the Alliance must pay careful attention to the dangers to which it is exposed in the European region, and must adopt all measures necessary to avert them. The European members who provide three quarters of the conventional strength of the Alliance in Europe, and two of whom possess nuclear forces capable of playing a deterrent role of their own contributing to the overall strengthening of the deterrence of the Alliance, undertake to make the necessary contribution to maintain the common defense at a level capable of deterring and if necessary repelling all actions directed against the independence and territorial integrity of the members of the Alliance.

7. The United States, for its part, reaffirms its determination not to accept any situation which would expose its Allies to external political or military pressure likely to deprive them of their freedom, and states its resolve, together with its Allies, to maintain forces in Europe at the level required to sustain the credibility of the strategy of deterrence and to maintain the capacity to defend the North Atlantic area should deterrence fail.

8. In this connection the member states of the Alliance affirm that as the ultimate purpose of any defense policy is to deny to a potential adversary the objectives he seeks to attain through an armed conflict, all necessary forces would be used for this purpose. Therefore, while reaffirming that a major aim of their policies is to seek agreements that will reduce the risk of war, they also state that such agreements will not limit their freedom to use all forces at their disposal for the common defense in case of attack. Indeed, they are convinced that their determination to do so continues to be the best assurance that war in all its forms will be prevented.

9. All members of the Alliance agree that the continued presence of Canadian and substantial US forces in Europe plays an irreplaceable role in the defense of North America as well as of Europe. Similarly the substantial forces of the European Allies serve to defend Europe and North America as well. It is also recognized that the further progress towards unity, which the member states of the European Community are determined to make, should in due course have a beneficial effect on the contribution to the common defense of the Alliance of those of them who belong to it. Moreover, the contributions made by members of the Alliance to the preservation of international security and world peace are recognized to be of great importance.

10. The members of the Alliance consider that the will to combine their efforts to ensure their common defense obliges them to maintain and improve the efficiency of their forces and that each should undertake, according to the role that it has assumed in the structure of the Alliance, its proper share of the burden of maintaining the security of all. Conversely, they take the view that in the course of current or future negotiations nothing must be accepted which could diminish this security.

11. The Allies are convinced that the fulfilment of their common aims requires the maintenance of close consultation, co-operation and mutual trust, thus fostering the conditions necessary for defense and favourable for detente, which are complementary. In the spirit of the friendship, equality and solidarity which characterize their relationship, they are firmly resolved to keep each other fully informed and to strengthen the practice of frank and timely consultations by all means which may be appropriate on matters relating to their common interests as members of the Alliance, bearing in mind that these interests can be affected by events in other areas of the world. They wish also to ensure that their essential security relationship is supported by harmonious political and economic relations. In particular they will work to remove sources of conflict between their economic policies and to encourage economic co-operation with one another.

12. They recall that they have proclaimed their dedication to the principles of democracy, respect for human rights, justice and social progress, which are the fruits of their shared spiritual heritage and they declare their intention to develop and deepen the application of these principles in their countries. Since these principles, by their very nature, forbid any recourse to methods incompatible with the promotion of world peace, they reaffirm that the efforts which they make to preserve their independence, to maintain their security and to improve the living standards of their peoples exclude all forms of aggression against anyone, are not directed against any other country, and are designed to bring about the general improvement of international relations. In Europe, their objective continues to be the pursuit of understanding and co-operation with every European country. In the world at large, each Allied country recognizes the duty to help the developing countries. It is in the interest of all that every country benefit from technical and economic progress in an open and equitable world system.

13. They recognize that the cohesion of the Alliance has found expression not only in co-operation among their governments, but also in the free exchange of views among the elected representatives of the peoples of the Alliance. Accordingly, they declare their support for the strengthening of links among Parliamentarians.

14. The members of the Alliance rededicate themselves to the aims and ideals of the North Atlantic Treaty during this year of the twenty-fifth Anniversary of its signature. The member nations look to the future, confident that the vitality and creativity of their peoples are commensurate with the challenges which confront them. They declare their conviction that the North Atlantic Alliance continues to serve as an essential element in the lasting structure of peace they are determined to build.

SOVIET-AMERICAN SUMMIT
June 27-July 3, 1974

Pursuing hopes for a breakthrough on a permanent agreement to limit offensive nuclear weapons, President Nixon made his second summit visit to the Soviet Union June 27-July 3. (First Soviet Summit, see Historic Documents 1972, p. 431-463.) During the week-long meetings, Nixon and Soviet Communist Party General Secretary Leonid I. Brezhnev signed agreements to place further limits on Soviet and American underground nuclear tests and on the number of anti-ballistic missile sites each country could maintain. The leaders also signed accords in the fields of energy, medicine and housing. But the sought-after broadening and extension of the five-year 1972 strategic arms limitation (SALT) treaty was not achieved. Nonetheless, the personal rapport between Nixon and Brezhnev that had marked the 1973 summit meetings in the United States (see Historic Documents 1973, p. 587-609), continued to characterize the 1974 visit. Brezhnev disclosed early in the conversations that he had accepted President Nixon's invitation to visit the United States in 1975.

The Soviet trip, following hard on the heels of the President's journey to five Middle East countries (see p. 449), dramatized the diplomatic clout of the Nixon administration. But foreign affairs successes could not muffle the continuing controversy in the United States over the Watergate scandal nor stifle concern over the inflation-ridden U.S. economy. (See p. 287 and p. 419.) As members of Congress continued to call on President Nixon to resign, the House Judiciary Committee moved closer toward voting on various articles of impeachment directed against Nixon. (See p. 655.) Meanwhile, inflation continued to drive up prices as the country appeared headed for the deepest recession since the end of World War II.

And Nixon's critics charged that the President's trips to the Soviet Union and the Middle East had been calculated attempts to shift public attention away from domestic worries and focus it on the administration's foreign policy achievements.

Indications that Soviet leaders were aware of President Nixon's domestic worries turned up early in the summit meetings. Detente had been possible, Nixon suggested June 27, offering a toast to his Soviet hosts, "because of a personal relationship that was established between the General Secretary and the President of the United States." The Russian translation of those remarks June 28 by the Soviet press agency TASS gave rise to a minor controversy that suggested a different Soviet view. The TASS translation deleted the word "personal" when it reported that Nixon had credited detente to "the relations that have developed between us." Although the director of TASS denied that any particular significance could be attached to the rewording, the translation heightened suspicions that the Soviet Union, aware that Nixon might be removed from office, was seeking to base detente on ground firmer than the man Richard Nixon. Brezhnev was already known to be attempting to establish ties with various Democrats.

Accomplishments

Two nuclear accords and four agreements in the areas of housing, energy, medicine and trade were signed by the two leaders during the summit talks. But the agreement that they failed to reach—on the limitation of strategic arms—took prominence. Secretary of State Henry A. Kissinger had sought before the summit to discourage optimism that a firm agreement could be reached at the talks. But a joint communique that was released July 3 by Brezhnev and Nixon gave surprisingly strong indication that the two sides were further apart in efforts to curb the arms race than had been believed. Although Nixon and Brezhnev had pledged at the 1973 summit to attempt to work out in 1974 a permanent agreement limiting strategic offensive arms, no such agreement was reached at the 1974 summit. The two leaders also failed to reach a hoped-for limited agreement curbing multiple warheads—multiple independently targeted re-entry vehicles (MIRVs). (Tentative accord reached in November, between President Ford and Brezhnev, see p. 955-972.)

Instead of permanent agreements, they pledged to seek a new interim accord which would cover the period until 1985 and would include both quantitative and qualitative limitations. The two agreed that the new accord should be concluded as soon as possible—prior to the 1977 expiration date of the interim agreement limiting offensive missile launchers reached at the 1972 summit. Negotiators for both sides were scheduled to return to the Geneva bargaining table to begin work on the new agreement. The two leaders were reported to have failed to agree on a mandate on arms limitation for their negotiators at the strategic arms limitation talks (SALT). Kissinger said that both sides would formulate new instructions for their delegations "from certain basic principles" agreed on at the Moscow summit.

Agreement on a formula balancing the Soviet missile advantage and the U.S. warhead advantage had proved to be the key stumbling block at the summit. "It did not prove possible to find a balance between overall numbers and the numbers of missiles with multiple warheads," Kissinger stated in Brussels July 4. The secretary said that the Soviets could not accept the number of missiles the United States had proposed as the upper limit. The Soviet Union had received a numerical advantage in missile launchers under the 1972 accord. In addition, Soviet deployment of heavier missiles gave them an advantage in throw weight—the amount of destructive force that can be delivered by a missile to a target. The U.S. advantage included a decided edge in numbers of multiple warheads, which were not covered by the 1972 agreement. The United States had deployed MIRVs, while the Soviet MIRV was still in the testing stage. Once the Soviets acquired a MIRV capability, the greater throw weight of their missiles would permit deployment of a larger number of MIRVs than the United States, American officials contended.

The issue was further complicated by reports of disagreement between Kissinger and the Pentagon over how to approach the arms limitation problem. Kissinger was said to have been willing to conclude a more limited accord on MIRVs, while the Pentagon reportedly wanted a broader agreement covering other strategic weapons. During a Moscow press conference July 3, Kissinger stated: "Both [Washington and Moscow] have to convince their military establishments of the benefits of restraint, and that does not come easily to either side." Defense Secretary James R. Schlesinger July 3 denied that the military had blocked any agreement. "We have firm civilian control in this country," he asserted.

Underground Test Agreement

At photographed ceremonies July 3, Nixon and Brezhnev signed a partial test ban treaty on underground nuclear explosions. Because seismic detectors could monitor blasts above the magnitude set by the accord, the agreement could be easily policed. The Soviets continued to oppose policing procedures that required on-site inspections within the country. At the same time, the leaders signed a protocol agreeing to forego the option of establishing a second anti-ballistic missile system site as provided for in the treaty signed May 26, 1972. The 1972 ABM accord had allowed each country to defend its national capital and maintain one other intercontinental ballistic missile site. But each country had deployed only one system of ABM interceptors by mid-1974: the Americans at Grand Forks, N.D., and the Soviets around Moscow. By the 1974 accord, both countries agreed to limit to one the number of ABM sites within their territory.

Four agreements were signed June 28 and 29 concerning housing, energy, medicine and trade. They provided for joint projects in housing and con-

struction, particularly residential buildings in earthquake areas; joint research and development programs in non-nuclear forms of energy; cooperation in research and development of artificial hearts, and exchanges of information on economic undertakings and possible cooperation between American companies and Soviet organizations. Other agreements reached involved cooperative environmental research and cultural exchanges.

Reaction

The non-controversial agreements signed at the 1974 summit drew little congressional reaction. One State Department official conceded June 29 that most of the accords could have been concluded at lower diplomatic levels. Opposition to the administration's nuclear policy, however, came June 25 from 37 senators, including Senate Majority Leader Mike Mansfield (D Mont.). In a letter to the President, the senators expressed "serious reservations" over a limited test ban that did not ban all tests. Moreover, Nixon's pledge to the Soviets to promote passage of trade reform legislation in Congress that would grant concessions to the Soviet Union came under fire from Sen. Henry M. Jackson (D Wash.), who had offered an amendment to the trade reform bill to require freer Soviet emigration policies as a prerequisite to the granting of most-favored-nation trade status to the Soviet Union. Jackson, Sen. Jacob K. Javits (D N.Y.) and Sen. Abraham Ribicoff (D Conn.) had told Kissinger before the summit that they would oppose granting the trade concessions until the Soviets topped their pledge to permit 45,000 Jews to emigrate each year.

Texts of agreements signed at Moscow summit conference June 27-July 3, 1974; of President Nixon's address to the people of the Soviet Union, July 2; and of Joint U.S.-Soviet communique issued at conclusion of the conference:

Energy

Agreement Between the United States of America and the Union of Soviet Socialist Republics on Cooperation in the Field of Energy. June 28, 1974

The United States of America and the Union of Soviet Socialist Republics;

Attaching great importance to meeting the energy needs of the two countries, with proper regard to the protection of the environment;

Recognizing that the development of cooperation in the field of energy can benefit the peoples of both countries and all mankind;

Desiring to expand and to deepen the cooperation now existing between the two countries in the field of energy research and development;

Recognizing the need to create better mutual understanding of each country's national energy programs and outlook;

Convinced that cooperation in the field of energy will contribute to the overall improvement of relations between the two countries;

In accordance with and in development of the Agreement between the Government of the United States of America and the Government of the Union of Soviet Socialist Republics on Cooperation in the Fields of Science and Technology of May 24, 1972, and the agreement on Cooperation in the Field of Environmental Protection between the United States of America and the Union of Soviet Socialist Republics of May 23, 1972, as well as in accordance with the Agreement between the United States of America and the Union of Soviet Socialist Republics on Scientific and Technical Cooperation in the Field of Peaceful Uses of Atomic Energy of June 21, 1973, and the General Agreement between the United States of America and the Union of Soviet Socialist Republics on Contacts, Exchanges and Cooperation of June 19, 1973;

Have agreed as follows:

Article I

The Parties will expand and strengthen their cooperation in the field of energy on the basis of mutual benefit, equality and reciprocity.

Article II

The main objectives of such cooperation under this Agreement are:

a. to use the scientific and technical potential of both countries to accelerate by cooperative efforts research and development in the areas of existing and alternative sources of energy as well as to increase effectiveness in the use of energy and its conservation, and

b. to achieve a better mutual understanding of each country's national energy programs and outlook.

Article III

1. Cooperation will be implemented in the following areas:

a. technologies concerning the exploration, extraction, processing and use of fossil fuels, including but not limited to oil, shale, natural gas and coal, and, in particular, new methods of drilling and of increasing the rate of extraction and degree of recovery of oil and natural gas from strata, and of mining, extracting and processing coal and shale;

b. the exchange of relevant information, views and methods of forecasting concerning the natural energy programs and outlooks of the respective countries, including all questions of mutual interest related to production, demand and consumption of the major forms of fuels and energy;

c. technology for developing non-conventional sources of energy, such as solar and geothermal energy and synthetic fuels;

d. energy-related environmental technology; and

e. measures to increase the efficiency of energy use and to restrain demand.

2. Other areas of cooperation may be added by mutual agreement.

Article IV

1. Cooperation between the Parties may take the following forms:

a. exchange of scientists and specialists;

b. exchange of scientific and technical information, documentation and results of research;

c. establishment of groups of experts for the planning and execution of joint research and development programs;

d. joint work by theoretical and experimental scientists in appropriate research centers of the two countries; and

e. holding joint consultations, seminars and panels.

2. Other forms of cooperation may be added by mutual agreement.

3. Cooperation under this Agreement will be carried out in accordance with the laws and regulations of the respective countries.

Article V

1. In furtherance of this Agreement, the Parties will, as appropriate, encourage, facilitate and monitor the development of contacts and cooperation between organizations, institutions and firms of the respective countries, including the conclusion, as appropriate, of implementing agreements for carrying out cooperative activities under this Agreement.

2. To assure fruitful development of cooperation, the Parties will render every assistance for the travel of scientists and specialists to areas of the respective countries appropriate for the conduct of activities under this Agreement.

Article VI

1. For implementation of this Agreement, there shall be established a US-USSR Joint Committee on Cooperation in the Field of Energy. Meetings of the Joint Committee will be convened once a year in the United States and the Soviet Union alternately, unless otherwise mutually agreed.

2. The Joint Committee shall take such action as is necessary for effective implementation of this Agreement including, but not limited to, consultations on the energy situation and outlook of the respective countries; approval of specific projects and programs of cooperation; designation of appropriate participating organizations and institutions responsible for carrying out cooperative activities; and making recommendations, as appropriate, to the two Governments. The Joint Committee shall establish the necessary working groups to carry out the programs, projects and exchange of information contemplated by this Agreement.

3. Each Party shall designate its Executive Agent which will be responsible for carrying out this Agreement. During the period between meetings of the Joint Committee, the Executive Agents shall maintain contact with each other, keep each other informed of activities and progress in implementing this Agreement, and coordinate and supervise the development and implementation of cooperative activities conducted under this Agreement.

Article VII

Nothing in this Agreement shall be interpreted to prejudice or modify any existing agreements between the Parties, except that energy projects within the Agreement between the Government of the United States of America and the Government of the Union of Soviet Socialist Republics on Cooperation in the Fields of Science and Technology of May 24, 1972 and the Agreement between the United States of America and the Union of Soviet Socialist Republics on Cooperation in the Field of Environmental Protection of May 23, 1972 which clearly fall under this Agreement henceforward will be implemented pursuant to this Agreement.

Article VIII

Unless an implementing agreement contains other provisions, each Party or participating institution, organization or firm, shall bear the costs of its participation and that of its personnel in cooperative activities engaged in pursuant to this Agreement.

Article IX

1. This Agreement shall enter into force upon signature and remain in force for five years. It will be automatically extended for successive five-year periods unless either Party notifies the other of its intent to terminate this Agreement not later than six months prior to the expiration of this Agreement.

2. This Agreement may be modified at any time by mutual agreement of the Parties.

3. The termination of this Agreement will not affect the validity of implementing agreements concluded under this Agreement between institutions, organizations and firms of the respective countries.

Done at Moscow on June 28, 1974, in duplicate, in the English and Russian languages, both texts being equally authentic.

For the United States of America:
        Richard Nixon
                President of the United States

For the Union of Soviet Socialist Republics:
        N.V. Podgorny
        Chairman, Presidium, USSR Supreme Soviet

Housing Construction

**Agreement Between the United States of America
and the Union of Soviet Socialist Republics on
Cooperation in the Field of Housing and
Other Construction.
June 28, 1974**

The United States of America and the Union of Soviet Socialist
Republics;

Desiring to develop cooperation in the field of housing and other construction;

Realizing that a more effective application of new and traditional building materials and techniques can contribute to more rational utilization
of the resources available to both countries;

Desiring to exchange information and techniques in the field of housing
and other construction;

Believing that cooperation in the field of housing and other construction
offers benefits for both the United States of America and the Union of
Soviet Socialist Republics;

Convinced that such cooperation will serve to contribute to the improvement of relations between the two countries;

Noting cooperation already being implemented in these areas under existing agreements, and in accordance with the General Agreement between
the United States of America and the Union of Soviet Socialist Republics
on Contacts, Exchanges, and Cooperation, signed June 19, 1973;

Have agreed as follows:

Article I

The Parties will develop and carry out cooperation in the field of housing
and other construction on the basis of mutual benefit, equality and
reciprocity.

Article II

This cooperation will be directed to the investigation and solution of
specific problems of mutual interest in the field of housing and other construction.

Initially, cooperation will be implemented in the following areas:

a. innovative techniques for the improvement of life safety, reliability,
quality, and economy of buildings and building materials including:
organization and management of construction, new methods and
materials, and the improved use of traditional methods and materials;

b. performance criteria for housing and other construction in seismic
areas with special consideration of the impact of geophysical conditions;

c. improvement of construction methods in areas of extreme climatic
conditions, such as cold and arid regions, including techniques for erection
and finishing of buildings under sustained freezing, and foundation construction under unusual soil conditions;

d. Services to housing and other buildings, including water supply, waste disposal, heating, lighting, and ventilation, with special reference to combined utility functions; and

e. Planning, design, and construction of new towns. Other areas of cooperation may be added by mutual agreement.

Article III

Cooperation pursuant to this Agreement may be implemented by the following means:

a. exchange of experts, advanced students and delegations;

b. exchange of scientific and technical information and documentation;

c. conducting joint conferences, meetings and seminars;

d. joint development and implementation of research programs and projects; and

e. other forms of cooperation which may be mutually agreed upon.

Such cooperation shall be conducted in accordance with the constitution and applicable laws and regulations of the respective countries.

Article IV

In furtherance of the aims of this Agreement, the Parties will, as appropriate, encourage, facilitate and monitor the development of cooperation and direct contacts between agencies, organizations and firms of the two countries, including the conclusion, as appropriate, of implementing agreements for carrying out specific projects and programs under this Agreement.

Article V

1. For the implementation of this Agreement, there shall be established a US-USSR Joint Committee on Cooperation in Housing and Other Construction. This Committee shall meet, as a rule, once a year alternately in the United States and the Soviet Union, unless otherwise mutually agreed.

2. The Joint Committee shall take such action as is necessary for the effective implementation of this Agreement, including, but not limited to, approval of specific projects and programs of cooperation, designation of appropriate agencies, organizations, and joint working groups to be responsible for carrying out cooperative activities, and making recommendations, as appropriate, to the Parties.

3. Each Party shall designate its Executive Agent which will be responsible for coordinating and carrying out this Agreement, and, as appropriate, in their respective countries, shall assure the cooperation of other participating institutions and organizations. During the period between meetings of the Joint Committee, the Executive Agents will maintain contact with each other and will coordinate and supervise the development and implementation of cooperative activities conducted under this Agreement.

543

4. Unless an implementing agreement contains other provisions, each Party or participating institution, organization or firm shall bear the costs of its participation and that of its personnel in cooperative activities engaged in under this Agreement.

Article VI

Nothing in this Agreement shall be interpreted to prejudice other agreements between the Parties or their respective rights and obligations under such other agreements.

Article VII

1. This Agreement shall enter into force upon signature and remains in force for five years. It will be automatically extended for successive five year periods unless either party notifies the other of its intent to terminate this Agreement not later than six months prior to the expiration of this Agreement.

2. This Agreement may be modified at any time by mutual agreement of the Parties.

3. The termination of this Agreement shall not affect the validity of implementing agreements concluded under this Agreement between interested agencies, organizations and firms of the two countries.

Done at Moscow on June 28, 1974, in duplicate in the English and Russian languages, both texts being equally authentic.

For the United States of America:

> Richard Nixon
> President of the United States

For the Union of Soviet Socialist Republics:

> A.N. Kosygin
> Chairman of the Council of Ministers
> of the USSR

Heart Research

Agreement Between the Government of the United States of America and the Government of the Union of Soviet Socialist Republics on Cooperation in Artificial Heart Research and Development.
June 28, 1974

The Government of the United States of America and the Government of the Union of Soviet Socialist Republics;

Reaffirming the importance that medical science has for mankind today;

Realizing the advisability of further uniting the efforts of both countries in resolving the pressing problems of medical science;

Recognizing the great importance of scientific research and the study of heart disease, which is one of the leading causes of mortality in both their countries as well as throughout the world;

Desiring to expand and strengthen common efforts to promote the development of an artificial heart;

Realizing that the development of an effective artificial heart could eventually lead to a reduction in mortality;   In pursuance and further development of the Agreement between the Government of the United States of America and the Government of the Union of Soviet Socialist Republics on Cooperation in the Field of Medical Science and Public Health, signed May 23, 1972;

In accordance with the General Agreement between the United States of America and the Union of Soviet Socialist Republics on Contacts, Exchanges and Cooperation, signed June 19, 1973;

Have agreed as follows:

Article I

Both parties undertake to develop and extend scientific and technical cooperation in artificial heart research and development on the basis of equality, reciprocity and mutual benefit.

Article II

The cooperation will be concentrated in the areas of research on, and joint development and testing of devices, materials, instruments and control mechanisms which will provide cardiovascular support including total heart replacement.

Article III

The cooperation provided for in the preceding Articles may be implemented principally in the following ways:

a. exchange of scientific and technical information;

b. organization of joint conferences, workshops and meetings of experts;

c. exchanges of specialists and delegations;

d. preparation of joint publications and technical manuals; and

e. familiarization with and exchange of technical aids and equipment.

In the course of implementing this Agreement, other forms of cooperation may also be determined by mutual agreement.

Article IV

The parties will delegate practical implementation of this Agreement to the US-USSR Joint Committee for Health Cooperation. The Committee shall approve the programs of cooperation, designate the participating organizations responsible for the realization of these programs, and periodically review the progress of the cooperation.

Article V

Cooperation shall be financed on the basis of reciprocal agreements worked out by the Joint Committee, using the resources of the Department of Health, Education, and Welfare of the United States of America and the Ministry of Health of the Union of Soviet Socialist Republics, as well as the resources of those organizations and institutions taking part in the cooperation.

Article VI

Such cooperation will be carried out in accordance with the laws and regulations of the respective countries.

Nothing in this Agreement shall be construed to prejudice or modify other agreements concluded between the two parties.

Article VII

This Agreement shall enter into force upon signature and shall remain in force for three years after which it will be extended for successive five year periods unless one party notifies the other of its intent to terminate this agreement not less than six months prior to its expiration.

This Agreement may be modified by mutual agreement of the parties.

Done at Moscow on June 28, 1974, in duplicate, in the English and Russian languages, both texts being equally authentic.

For the United States of America:

> Henry A. Kissinger
> The Secretary of State

For the Union of Soviet Socialist Republics:

> N. V. Podgorny
> Chairman, Presidium, USSR Supreme
> Soviet

Economic, Industrial, and Technical Cooperation

Long Term Agreement Between the United States of America and the Union of Soviet Socialist Republics To Facilitate Economic, Industrial, and Technical Cooperation.
June 29, 1974

The United States of America and the Union of Soviet Socialist Republics,

Desiring to promote continuing orderly expansion of economic, industrial, and technical cooperation and the exchange of relevant information to facilitate such cooperation between the two countries and their competent organizations, enterprises, and firms on a long term and mutually beneficial basis,

Guided by the Basic Principles of Relations between the United States of America and the Union of Soviet Socialist Republics of May 29, 1972, the Joint American-Soviet Communique of June 24, 1973, and the principles set forth in the Agreement between the Government of the United States of America and the Government of the Union of Soviet Socialist Republics Regarding Trade dated October 18, 1972,

Have agreed as follows:

Article I

The Parties shall use their good offices to facilitate economic, industrial, and technical cooperation in keeping with established practices and applicable laws and regulations in the respective countries.

Article II

Cooperation which shall be facilitated as contemplated in Article I shall include:

a. purchases and sales of machinery and equipment for the construction of new enterprises and for the expansion and modernization of existing enterprises in the fields of raw materials, agriculture, machinery and equipment, finished products, consumer goods, and services;

b. purchases and sales of raw materials, agricultural products, finished products, consumer goods, and services;

c. purchases, sales and licensing of patent rights and proprietary industrial know-how, designs, and processes;

d. training of technicians and exchange of specialists; and

e. joint efforts, where appropriate, in the construction of industrial and other facilities in third countries, particularly through supply of machinery and equipment.

Article III

In order to assist relevant organizations, enterprises, and firms of both countries in determining the fields of cooperation most likely to provide a basis for mutually beneficial contracts, a working group of experts convened by the Commission mentioned in Article V shall meet not less frequently than once a year to exchange information and forecasts of basic economic, industrial, and commercial trends.

Article IV

To promote the cooperation foreseen in this Agreement the Parties undertake to facilitate, as appropriate, the acquisition or lease of suitable business and residential premises by organizations, enterprises, and firms of the other party and their employees; the importation of essential office equipment and supplies; the hiring of staffs; the issuance of visas, including multiple entry visas, to qualified officials and representatives of such organizations, enterprises, and firms and to members of their immediate families; and travel by such persons for business purposes in the territory of the receiving country.

Article V

The US-USSR Commercial Commission established pursuant to the Communique of May 26, 1972, is authorized and directed to monitor the practical implementation of this Agreement, when necessary jointly with other American-Soviet bodies created by agreement between the Governments of the two countries, with a view to facilitating the cooperation contemplated in this Agreement.

Article VI

This Agreement shall enter into force on the date of its signature, and shall remain in force for 10 years.

The Parties shall agree not later than six months prior to the expiration of the above period upon measures which may be necessary to facilitate further development of economic, industrial, and technical cooperation.

Done at Moscow on June 29, 1974, in duplicate, in the English and Russian languages, both texts being equally authentic.

For the United States of America:

> Richard Nixon
> President of the United States of
> America

For the Union of Soviet Socialist Republics:

> L. I. Brezhnev
> General Secretary of the Central
> Committee of the CPSU

Address to the People of the Soviet Union

The President's Radio and Television Address. July 2, 1974

Dobryy vecher [Good evening]:

Two years ago, at the first of these summit meetings, your Government gave me the opportunity to speak directly with you, the people of the Soviet Union. Last year, at our second meeting, General Secretary Brezhnev spoke on radio and television to the people of the United States. And now, tonight, I appreciate this opportunity to continue what has become a tradition, a part of our annual meetings.

In these past 2 years, there has been a dramatic change in the nature of the relationship between our two countries. After a long period of confrontation, we moved to an era of negotiation, and now we are learning cooperation. We are learning to cooperate not only in lessening the danger of war, but in advancing the work of peace.

We are thereby helping to create not only a safer but also a better life for the people of both of our countries. By reflecting on how far we have advanced, we can better appreciate how strong a foundation we have laid for even greater progress in the future.

At our first summit meeting 2 years ago, we signed the first agreement ever negotiated for the limitation of strategic nuclear arms. This was an historic milestone on the road to a lasting peace—and to mankind's control over the forces of his own destruction.

We have many difficulties yet to be overcome in achieving full control over strategic nuclear arms. But each step carries us closer and builds confidence in the process of negotiation itself.

Our progress in the limitation of arms has been vitally important. But it has not been the only product of our work at the summit. We have also been steadily building a new relationship that over time will reduce the causes of conflict.

In the basic principles for our mutual relations, agreed to in Moscow in 1972, and in the agreement on prevention of nuclear war, signed last year in Washington, we have established standards to guide our actions toward each other in international affairs generally so that the danger of war will be reduced and the possibility of dangerous confrontations will be lessened.

"New Avenues of Cooperation"

What is particularly significant is that our negotiations have been far wider than the reduction of arms and the prevention of wars and crises. The pattern of agreements reached between us has opened new avenues of cooperation across the whole range of peaceful relations.

For example, we are working together in programs which will bring better health, better housing, a better environment, as well as in many other fields. Trade between our two countries totaled a record $1.4 billion in 1973. That is more than twice the level of the previous year. This means more goods and a greater choice available for the people of both of our countries.

It was exactly 15 years ago next month when I was here in Moscow as Vice President that I first spoke to the people of the Soviet Union on radio and television. In that speech I said, "Let our aim be not victory over other peoples, but the victory of all mankind over hunger, want, misery and disease, wherever it exists in the world."

The agreements we have reached at these summit meetings—on health, for example, including this year's agreement on artificial heart research—will help us toward that great victory. At the same time, they will give the people of both of our countries a positive stake in peace.

This is crucially important. Traditionally, when peace has been maintained, it has been maintained primarily because of the fear of war. Negotiators have been spurred in their efforts either by the desire to end a war or by the fear that their failure would begin a war.

The peace we seek now to build is a permanent peace. And nothing permanent can be built on fear alone. By giving both of our nations a positive stake in peace—by giving both of our peoples hope, something to look forward to as the results of peace—we create a more solid framework on which a lasting structure of peace can be built and on which it then can stand strong through the years.

"Peace: A Richer and Fuller Life"

The peace we seek to build is one that is far more than simply the absence of war. We seek a peace in which each man, woman, and child can look forward to a richer and a fuller life. This is what the people of the Soviet Union want. This is what the people of America want. And this is what the people of all nations want.

Our two nations are great nations. They are strong nations, the two strongest nations in the world.

Too often in the past, the greatness of a nation has been measured primarily in terms of its success in war. The time has come to set a new standard for the measure of greatness of a nation. Let our measure of greatness be not by the way we use our strength for war and destruction, but how we work together for peace and for progress for ourselves and for all mankind.

Let us recognize that to be great, a strong nation need not impose its will on weaker nations. A great nation will establish its place in history by the example it sets, by the purposes for which its power is used, by the respect that it shows for the rights of others, by the contribution it makes toward building a new world in which the weak will be as safe as the strong.

In these meetings, we have been seeking to ensure that the power of both of our nations will be used not for war and destruction, but rather for peace and for progress.

Our two nations will continue to have differences. We have different systems. And, in many respects, we have different values. Inevitably our interests will not always be in accord.

But the important thing is that we are learning to negotiate where we have differences, to narrow them where possible, and to move ahead together in an expanding field of mutual interests.

One of the most important aspects of our developing new relationship might be stated this way: Just as a cloth is stronger than the threads from which it is made, so the network of agreements we have been weaving is greater than the sum of its parts. With these agreements, we have been creating a pattern of interrelationships, of habits of cooperation and arrangements for consultation—all of which interact with one another to strengthen the fabric of the new relationship. Thus each new agreement is important not only for itself but also for the added strength and stability it brings to our relations overall.

"Practical About Peace"

We have been weaving this fabric of cooperation not just because we are idealistic about peace—and we are—but because we are practical about peace. The words of the agreements we sign are important; even more important is how we carry them out in practice—how we translate the ideal of peaceful cooperation into the practice of peaceful cooperation. In this growing network of agreements, of exchanges, of patterns of cooperation, we are demonstrating not just the ideal of peace but the practice of peace.

In the course of many years, I have visited memorials to the dead of many wars, in many countries. Yesterday, I laid a wreath at one of the most moving memorials I have ever seen—the Khatyn Memorial, outside Minsk. A huge bronze statue of Joseph Kaminsky, the village blacksmith, carrying his 15-year-old dead son in his arms, stands today above the graves of what was the village of Khatyn.

Chimneys stand where the houses were, with a memorial bell in each chimney tolling for the dead, not only for Khatyn but also for the hundreds of other villages that were destroyed and the millions of others who died—a stark reminder to all nations, and for all time, of the terrible cost of war.

As I laid the wreath, I thought of the people of Khatyn, and I thought especially of the children of Khatyn. I reflected on the fact that our efforts now must be directed not against any one nation or group of nations, but against the evil of war itself.

And I also thought of the living memorial that we today must build—the living memorial of a lasting peace, so that the children of those who sacrificed in war, and their children's children, can be spared the tragedy of Khatyn, and can know instead the security of a human brotherhood that reaches across the boundaries of all nations.

When we first met at the summit 2 years ago, both sides were venturing into the untried waters of something new. And we were, perhaps, a bit uncertain, even apprehensive, about where it would lead.

But now, we and the leaders of the Soviet Union have come to know one another. Each of us has a much fuller understanding of the policies of the other country, even where those policies differ.

Thus, we have been able to meet this year, as we will meet again next year in the United States, not in an atmosphere of crisis, but rather in an atmosphere of confidence—confidence that the work we have embarked on is going forward.

In fact, it might be said that the most remarkable thing about this summit meeting is that it is taking place so routinely, so familiarly—as a part of a continuing pattern that would have seemed inconceivable just a few years ago.

Peace is not only a condition; if it is to last, it must also be a continuing process. And these meetings are an example of that process in action.

As allies in World War II, we fought side by side in the most terrible war in all human history. And together with our allies we won the victory. In winning that victory, the people of the Soviet Union and the people of the United States shared a common hope that we also had won a lasting peace. That hope was frustrated, but now we have a new opportunity.

Winning victory in war is difficult. It requires extraordinary courage, stamina, and dedication from every individual citizen in the nation. But in some ways, the building of a lasting peace is even more difficult than waging war because it is more complex. We must bring to the task of building that peace the same kind of courage, of stamina, of dedication that inspired us in our struggle for victory in war.

And the fact that our task of building peace is more complex does not mean that we cannot succeed.

Soviet-American Space Mission

Let me give a striking example which demonstrates that point. In the whole field of modern technology, no mission is more complex than the mission of sending men into space. The joint Soviet-American space mission planned for next year—the joint Soyuz-Apollo mission—is in many ways symbolic of the new relationship we are building between our two nations.

It is symbolic for several reasons—reasons which carry important lessons about that new relationship.

For one thing, the rocket technology developed for war is being used for peace.

And for another, Soviet and American spacemen, starting from their separate countries, will find their way toward one another and join with one another—just as we are doing and must continue to do across the whole range of our relationship.

By standardizing their docking techniques, they will make international rescue missions possible in case future space missions encounter trouble in space; thus they will make space safer for the astronauts and the cosmonauts of both of our countries—just as our new relationship can make life on earth safer for the people of both of our countries.

Finally, and perhaps more important, this joint mission—for which our astronauts are now here in the Soviet Union training alongside your cosmonauts—is being made possible by careful planning, by precise engineering, by a process of working and building together, step by step, to reach a goal that we share, and this is the way that together we can build a peace, a peace that will last.

One of the greatest of your writers, Leo Tolstoy, once told this story. A very old man was planting apple trees. He was asked: "What are you planting apple trees for? It will be a long time before they bear fruit, and you will not live to eat a single apple."

The old man replied, "I will never eat them, but others will, and they will thank me."

Our two nations bear a shared responsibility toward the entire world. And we, too, must plant now so that future generations will reap a harvest of peace—a peace in which our children can live together as brothers and sisters, joining hands across the ocean in friendship, and ushering in a new era in which war is behind us, and in which together, in peace, we can work toward a better life for our people and for all people.

Spasibo, y do svidaniye. [Thank you and goodby.]

Limitation of Anti-Ballistic Missile Systems

Protocol to the Treaty Between the United States of America and the Union of Soviet Socialist Republics on the Limitation of Anti-Ballistic Missile Systems.
July 3, 1974

The United States of America and the Union of Soviet Socialist Republics, hereinafter referred to as the Parties,

Proceeding from the Basic Principles of Relations between the United States of America and the Union of Soviet Socialist Republics signed on May 29, 1972,

Desiring to further the objectives of the Treaty between the United States of America and the Union of Soviet Socialist Republics on the Limitation of Anti-Ballistic Missile Systems signed on May 26, 1972, hereinafter referred to as the Treaty,

Reaffirming their conviction that the adoption of further measures for the limitation of strategic arms would contribute to strengthening international peace and security.

Proceeding from the premise that further limitation of anti-ballistic missile systems will create more favorable conditions for the completion of work on a permanent agreement on more complete measures for the limitation of strategic offensive arms,

Have agreed as follows:

Article I

1. Each Party shall be limited at any one time to a single area out of the two provided in Article III of the Treaty for deployment of anti-ballistic missile (ABM) systems or their components and accordingly shall not exercise its right to deploy an ABM system or its components in the second of the two ABM system deployment areas permitted by Article III of the Treaty, except as an exchange of one permitted area for the other in accordance with Article II of this Protocol.

2. Accordingly, except as permitted by Article II of this Protocol: the United States of America shall not deploy an ABM system or its components in the area centered on its capital, as permitted by Article III(a) of the Treaty, and the Soviet Union shall not deploy an ABM system or its components in the deployment area of intercontinental ballistic missile (ICBM) silo launchers permitted by Article III(b) of the Treaty.

Article II

1. Each Party shall have the right to dismantle or destroy its ABM system and the components thereof in the area where they are presently deployed and to deploy an ABM system or its components in the alternative area permitted by Article III of the Treaty, provided that prior to initiation

553

of construction, notification is given in accord with the procedure agreed to by the Standing Consultative Commission, during the year beginning October 3, 1977, and ending October 2, 1978, or during any year which commences at five year intervals thereafter, those being the years for periodic review of the Treaty, as provided in Article XIV of the Treaty. This right may be exercised only once.

2. Accordingly, in the event of such notice, the United States would have the right to dismantle or destroy the ABM system and its components in the deployment area of ICBM silo launchers and to deploy an ABM system or its components in an area centered on its capital, as permitted by Article III(a) of the Treaty, and the Soviet Union would have the right to dismantle or destroy the ABM system and its components in the area centered on its capital and to deploy an ABM system or its components in an area containing ICBM silo launchers, as permitted by Article III(b) of the Treaty.

3. Dismantling or destruction and deployment of ABM systems or their components and the notification thereof shall be carried out in accordance with Article VIII of the ABM Treaty and procedures agreed to in the Standing Consultative Commission.

Article III

The rights and obligations established by the Treaty remain in force and shall be complied with by the Parties except to the extent modified by this Protocol. In particular, the deployment of an ABM system or its components within the area selected shall remain limited by the levels and other requirements established by the Treaty.

Article IV

This Protocol shall be subject to ratification in accordance with the constitutional procedures of each Party. It shall enter into force on the day of the exchange of instruments of ratification and shall thereafter be considered an integral part of the Treaty.

Done at Moscow on July 3, 1974, in duplicate, in the English and Russian languages, both texts being equally authentic.

For the United States of America:

> Richard Nixon
> President of the United States of America

For the Union of Soviet Socialist Republics:

> L. I. Brezhnev
> General Secretary of the Central Committee of the CPSU

Limitation of Underground Nuclear Weapons Tests

Treaty Between the United States of America and the Union of Soviet Socialist Republics on the Limitation of Underground Nuclear Weapons Tests.
July 3, 1974

The United States of America and the Union of Soviet Socialist Republics, hereinafter referred to as the Parties,

Declaring their intention to achieve at the earliest possible date the cessation of the nuclear arms race and to take effective measures toward reductions in strategic arms, nuclear disarmament, and general and complete disarmament under strict and effective international control,

Recalling the determination expressed by the Parties to the 1963 Treaty Banning Nuclear Weapon Tests in the Atmosphere, in Outer Space and Under Water in its Preamble to seek to achieve the discontinuance of all test explosions of nuclear weapons for all time, and to continue negotiations to this end,

Noting that the adoption of measures for the further limitation of underground nuclear weapon tests would contribute to the achievement of these objectives and would meet the interests of strengthening peace and the further relaxation of international tension,

Reaffirming their adherence to the objectives and principles of the Treaty Banning Nuclear Weapon Tests in the Atmosphere, in Outer Space and Under Water and of the Treaty on the Non-Proliferation of Nuclear Weapons,

Have agreed as follows:

Article I

1. Each Party undertakes to prohibit, to prevent, and not to carry out any underground nuclear weapon test having a yield exceeding 150 kilotons at any place under its jurisdiction or control, beginning March 31, 1976.

2. Each Party shall limit the number of its underground nuclear weapon tests to a minimum.

3. The Parties shall continue their negotiations with a view toward achieving a solution to the problem of the cessation of all underground nuclear weapon tests.

Article II

1. For the purpose of providing assurance of compliance with the provisions of this Treaty, each Party shall use national technical means of verification at its disposal in a manner consistent with the generally recognized principles of international law.

2. Each Party undertakes not to interfere with the national technical means of verification of the other Party operating in accordance with paragraph 1 of this Article.

3. To promote the objectives and implementation of the provisions of this Treaty the Parties shall, as necessary, consult with each other, make inquiries and furnish information in response to such inquiries.

Article III

The provisions of this Treaty do not extend to underground nuclear explosions carried out by the Parties for peaceful purposes. Underground nuclear explosions for peaceful purposes shall be governed by an agreement which is to be negotiated and concluded by the Parties at the earliest possible time.

Article IV

This Treaty shall be subject to ratification in accordance with the constitutional procedures of each Party. This Treaty shall enter into force on the day of the exchange of instruments of ratification.

Article V

1. This Treaty shall remain in force for a period of five years. Unless replaced earlier by an agreement in implementation of the objectives specified in paragraph 3 of Article I of this Treaty, it shall be extended for successive five-year periods unless either Party notifies the other of its termination no later than six months prior to the expiration of the Treaty. Before the expiration of this period the Parties may, as necessary, hold consultations to consider the situation relevant to the substance of this Treaty and to introduce possible amendments to the text of the Treaty.

2. Each Party shall, in exercising its national sovereignty, have the right to withdraw from this Treaty if it decides that extraordinary events related to the subject matter of this Treaty have jeopardized its supreme interests. It shall give notice of its decision to the other Party six months prior to withdrawal from this Treaty. Such notice shall include a statement of the extraordinary events the notifying Party regards as having jeopardized its supreme interests.

3. This Treaty shall be registered pursuant to Article 102 of the Charter of the United Nations.

Done at Moscow on July 3, 1974, in duplicate, in the English and Russian languages, both texts being equally authentic.

For the United States of America:

Richard Nixon
The President of the United States
of America

For the Union of Soviet Socialist Republics:

L. I. Brezhnev
General Secretary of the Central
Committee of the CPSU

Protocol

TO THE TREATY BETWEEN THE UNITED STATES OF AMERICA AND THE UNION OF SOVIET SOCIALIST REPUBLICS ON THE LIMITATION OF UNDERGROUND NUCLEAR WEAPON TESTS

The United States of America and the Union of Soviet Socialist Republics, hereinafter referred to as the Parties,

Having agreed to limit underground nuclear weapon tests,

Have agreed as follows:

1. For the Purpose of ensuring verification of compliance with the obligations of the Parties under the Treaty by national technical means, the Parties shall on the basis of reciprocity, exchange the following data:

a. The geographic coordinates of the boundaries of each test site and of the boundaries of the geophysically distinct testing areas therein.

b. Information on the geology of the testing areas of the sites (the rock characteristics of geological formations and the basic physical properties of the rock, i.e., density, seismic velocity, water saturation, porosity and depth of water table).

c. The geographic coordinates of underground nuclear weapon tests, after they have been conducted.

d. Yield, date, time, depth and coordinates for two nuclear weapon tests for calibration purposes from each geophysically distinct testing area where underground nuclear weapon tests have been and are to be conducted. In this connection the yield of such explosions for calibration purposes should be as near as possible to the limit defined in Article I of the Treaty and not less than one-tenth of that limit. In the case of testing areas where data are not available on two tests for calibration purposes, the data pertaining to one such test shall be exchanged, if available, and the data pertaining to the second test shall be exchanged as soon as possible after a second test having a yield in the above-mentioned range. The provisions of this Protocol shall not require the Parties to conduct tests solely for calibration purposes.

2. The Parties agree that the exchange of data pursuant to subparagraphs a, b, and d of paragraph 1 shall be carried out simultaneously with the exchange of instruments of ratification of the Treaty, as provided in Article IV of the Treaty, having in mind that the Parties shall, on the basis of reciprocity, afford each other the opportunity to familiarize themselves with these data before the exchange of instruments of ratification.

3. Should a Party specify a new test site or testing area after the entry into force of the Treaty, the data called for by subparagraphs a and b of paragraph 1 shall be transmitted to the other Party in advance of use of that site or area. The data called for by subparagraph d of paragraph 1 shall also be transmitted in advance of use of that site or area if they are

available; if they are not available, they shall be transmitted as soon as possible after they have been obtained by the transmitting Party.

4. The Parties agree that the test sites of each Party shall be located at places under its jurisdiction or control and that all nuclear weapon tests shall be conducted solely within the testing areas specified in accordance with paragraph 1.

5. For the purposes of the Treaty, all underground nuclear explosions at the specified test sites shall be considered nuclear weapon tests and shall be subject to all the provisions of the Treaty relating to nuclear weapon tests. The provisions of Article III of the Treaty apply to all underground nuclear explosions conducted outside of the specified test sites, and only to such explosions.

This Protocol shall be considered an integral part of the Treaty.

Done at Moscow on July 3, 1974.

For the United States of America:

> Richard Nixon
> The President of the United States of
> America

For the Union of Soviet Socialist Republics:

> L. I. Brezhnev
> General Secretary of the Central
> Committee of the CPSU

Dangers of Environmental Warfare

U.S.-U.S.S.R. Joint Statement Concerning Future
Discussions on the Dangers of Environmental
Warfare.
July 3, 1974

The United States of America and the Union of Soviet Socialist Republics:

Desiring to limit the potential danger to mankind from possible new means of warfare;

Taking into consideration that scientific and technical advances in environmental fields, including climate modification, may open possibilities for using environmental modification techniques for military purposes;

Recognizing that such use could have widespread, long-lasting, and severe effects harmful to human welfare;

Recognizing also that proper utilization of scientific and technical advances could improve the inter-relationship of man and nature;

1. Advocate the most effective measures possible to overcome the dangers of the use of environmental modification techniques for military purposes.

2. Have decided to hold a meeting of United States and Soviet representatives this year for the purpose of exploring this problem.

3. Have decided to discuss also what steps might be taken to bring about the measures referred to in paragraph 1.

Moscow, July 3, 1974

For the United States of America:

Richard Nixon
The President of the United States of
America

For the Union of Soviet Socialist Republics:

L. I. Brezhnev
General Secretary of the Central
Committee of the CPSU

JOINT COMMUNIQUE

Text of the Joint United States-Soviet Communique Issued at the Conclusion of the President's Visit.
July 3, 1974

In accordance with the agreement to hold regular US-Soviet meetings at the highest level and at the invitation, extended during the visit of General Secretary of the Central Committee of the Communist Party of the Soviet Union L. I. Brezhnev to the USA in June 1973, the President of the United States of America and Mrs. Richard Nixon paid an official visit to the Soviet Union from June 27 to July 3, 1974.

During his stay President Nixon visited, in addition to Moscow, Minsk and the Southern Coast of the Crimea.

The President of the United States and the Soviet leaders held a thorough and useful exchange of views on major aspects of relations between the USA and USSR and on the present international situation.

On the Soviet side the talks were conducted by L. I. Brezhnev, General Secretary of the Central Committee of the Communist Party of the Soviet Union; N. V. Podgorny, Chairman of the Presidium of the USSR Supreme Soviet; A. N. Kosygin, Chairman of the USSR Council of Ministers; and A. A. Gromyko, Minister of Foreign Affairs of the USSR.

Accompanying the President of the USA and participating in the talks was Dr. Henry A. Kissinger, US Secretary of State and Assistant to the President for National Security Affairs....

The talks were held in a most businesslike and constructive atmosphere and were marked by a mutual desire of both Sides to continue to strengthen understanding, confidence and peaceful cooperation between them and to contribute to the strengthening of international security and world peace.

I. Progress in Improving US-Soviet Relations

Having considered in detail the development of relations between the USA and the USSR since the US-Soviet summit meeting in May 1972, both

Sides noted with satisfaction that through their vigorous joint efforts they have brought about over this short period a fundamental turn toward peaceful relations and broad, mutually beneficial cooperation in the interests of the peoples of both countries and of all mankind.

They emphasized the special importance for the favorable development of relations between the USA and the USSR of meetings of their leaders at the highest level, which are becoming established practice. These meetings provide opportunities for effective and responsible discussion, for the solution of fundamental and important bilateral questions, and for mutual contributions to the settlement of international problems affecting the interests of both countries.

Both Sides welcome the establishment of official contacts between the Congress of the US and the Supreme Soviet of the USSR. They will encourage a further development of such contacts, believing that they can play an important role.

Both Sides confirmed their mutual determination to continue actively to reshape US-Soviet relations on the basis of peaceful coexistence and equal security, in strict conformity with the spirit and the letter of the agreements achieved between the two countries and their obligations under those agreements. In this connection they noted once again the fundamental importance of the joint documents adopted as a result of the summit meetings in 1972 and 1973, especially of the Basic Principles of Relations Between the USA and the USSR, the Agreement on the Prevention of Nuclear War, the Treaty on the Limitation of Anti-Ballistic Missile Systems, and the Interim Agreement on Certain Measures with Respect to the Limitation of Strategic Offensive Arms.

Both Sides are deeply convinced of the imperative necessity of making the process of improving US-Soviet relations irreversible. They believe that, as a result of their efforts, a real possibility has been created to achieve this goal. This will open new vistas for broad mutually beneficial cooperation, and for strengthening friendship between the American and Soviet peoples, and will thus contribute to the solution of many urgent problems facing the world.

Guided by these worthy goals, both Sides decided to continue steadfastly to apply their joint efforts—in cooperation with other countries concerned, as appropriate—first of all in such important fields as:

—removing the danger of war, including particularly war involving nuclear and other mass-destruction weapons;

—limiting and eventually ending the arms race especially in strategic weapons, having in mind as the ultimate objective the achievement of general and complete disarmament under appropriate international control;

—contributing to the elimination of sources of international tension and military conflict;

—strengthening and extending the process of relaxation of tensions throughout the world;

—developing broad, mutually beneficial cooperation in commercial and economic, scientific-technical and cultural fields on the basis of the principles of sovereignty, equality and noninterference in internal affairs with a view to promoting increased understanding and confidence between the peoples of both countries.

Accordingly, in the course of this summit meeting both Sides considered it possible to take new constructive steps which, they believe, will not only advance further the development of US-Soviet relations but will also make a substantial contribution to strengthening world peace and expanding international cooperation.

II. Further Limitation of Strategic Arms and Other Disarmament Issues

Both sides again carefully analyzed the entire range of their mutual relations connected with the prevention of nuclear war and limitation of strategic armaments. They arrived at the common view that the fundamental agreements concluded between them in this sphere continue to be effective instruments of the general improvement of US-Soviet relations and the international situation as a whole. The USA and the USSR will continue strictly to fulfill the obligations undertaken in those agreements.

In the course of the talks, the two Sides had a thorough review of all aspects of the problem of limitation of strategic arms. They concluded that the Interim Agreement on offensive strategic weapons should be followed by a new agreement between the Soviet Union and the United States on the limitation of strategic arms. They agreed that such an agreement should cover the period until 1985 and deal with both quantitative and qualitative limitations. They agreed that such an agreement should be completed at the earliest possible date, before the expiration of the Interim Agreement.

They hold the common view that such a new agreement would serve not only the interests of the Soviet Union and the United States but also those of a further relaxation of international tensions and of world peace.

Their delegations will reconvene in Geneva in the immediate future on the basis of instructions growing out of the summit.

Taking into consideration the interrelationship between the development of offensive and defensive types of strategic arms and noting the successful implementation of the Treaty on the Limitation of Anti-Ballistic Missile Systems concluded between them in May 1972, both Sides considered it desirable to adopt additional limitations on the deployment of such systems. To that end they concluded a Protocol providing for the limitation of each Side to a single deployment area for ABM systems instead of two such areas as permitted to each Side by the Treaty.

At the same time, two protocols were signed entitled "Procedures Governing Replacement, Dismantling or Destruction, and Notification Thereof, for Strategic Offensive Arms" and "Procedures Governing Replacement, Dismantling or Destruction, and Notification Thereof for ABM Systems and their Components." These protocols were worked out by the

Standing Consultative Commission which was established to promote the objectives and implementation of the provisions of the Treaty and the Interim Agreement signed on May 26, 1972.

The two Sides emphasized the serious importance which the US and USSR also attach to the realization of other possible measures—both on a bilateral and on a multilateral basis—in the field of arms limitation and disarmament.

Comprehensive Test Ban

Having noted the historic significance of the Treaty Banning Nuclear Weapon Tests in the Atmosphere, in Outer Space and Under Water, concluded in Moscow in 1963, to which the United States and the Soviet Union are parties, both Sides expressed themselves in favor of making the cessation of nuclear weapon tests comprehensive. Desiring to contribute to the achievement of this goal the USA and the USSR concluded, as an important step in this direction, the Treaty on the Limitation of Underground Nuclear Weapon Tests providing for the complete cessation, starting from March 31, 1976, of the tests of such weapons above an appropriate yield threshold, and for confining other underground tests to a minimum.

The Parties emphasized the fundamental importance of the Treaty on the Non-Proliferation of Nuclear Weapons. Having reaffirmed their mutual intention to observe the obligations assumed by them under that Treaty, including Article VI thereof, they expressed themselves in favor of increasing its effectiveness.

A joint statement was also signed in which the US and USSR advocate the most effective measures possible to overcome the dangers of the use of environmental modification techniques for military purposes.

Both Sides reaffirmed their interest in an effective international agreement which would exclude from the arsenals of states such dangerous instruments of mass destruction as chemical weapons. Desiring to contribute to early progress in this direction, the USA and the USSR agreed to consider a joint initiative in the Conference of the Committee on Disarmament with respect to the conclusion, as a first step, of an international Convention dealing with the most dangerous, lethal means of chemical warfare.

Both Sides are convinced that the new important steps which they have taken and intend to take in the field of arms limitation as well as further efforts toward disarmament will facilitate the relaxation of international tensions and constitute a tangible contribution to the fulfillment of the historic task of excluding war from the life of human society and thereby of ensuring world peace. The US and the USSR reaffirmed that a world disarmament conference at an appropriate time can play a positive role in this process.

III. Progress in the Settlement of International Problems

In the course of the meeting detailed discussions were held on major international problems.

Both Sides expressed satisfaction that relaxation of tensions, consolidation of peace, and development of mutually beneficial cooperation are becoming increasingly distinct characteristics of the development of the international situation. They proceed from the assumption that progress in improving the international situation does not occur spontaneously but requires active and purposeful efforts to overcome obstacles and resolve difficulties that remain from the past.

The paramount objectives of all states and peoples should be to ensure, individually and collectively, lasting security in all parts of the world, the early and complete removal of existing international conflicts and sources of tension and the prevention of new ones from arising.

The United States and the Soviet Union are in favor of the broad and fruitful economic cooperation among all states, large and small, on the basis of full equality and mutual benefit.

The United States and the Soviet Union reaffirm their determination to contribute separately and jointly to the achievement of all these tasks.

Europe

Having discussed the development of the situation in Europe since the last American-Soviet summit meeting, both Sides noted with profound satisfaction the further appreciable advances toward establishing dependable relations of peace, good neighborliness and cooperation on the European continent.

Both Sides welcome the major contribution which the Conference on Security and Cooperation in Europe is making to this beneficial process. They consider that substantial progress has already been achieved at the Conference on many significant questions. They believe that this progress indicates that the present stage of the Conference will produce agreed documents of great international significance expressing the determination of the participating states to build their mutual relations on a solid jointly elaborated basis. The US and USSR will make every effort, in cooperation with the other participants, to find solutions acceptable to all for the remaining problems.

Both Sides expressed their conviction that successful completion of the Conference on Security and Cooperation in Europe would be an outstanding event in the interests of establishing a lasting peace. Proceeding from this assumption the USA and the USSR expressed themselves in favor of the final stage of the Conference taking place at an early date. Both Sides also proceed from the assumption that the results of the negotiations will permit the Conference to be concluded at the highest level, which would correspond to the historic significance of the Conference for the future of Europe and lend greater authority to the importance of the Conference's decisions.

Both Sides reaffirmed the lasting significance for a favorable development of the situation in Europe of the treaties and agreements concluded in recent years between European states with different social systems.

They expressed satisfaction with the admission to the United Nations of the Federal Republic of Germany and the German Democratic Republic.

Both Sides also stressed that the Quadripartite Agreement of September 3, 1971, must continue to play a key role in ensuring stability and detente in Europe. The US and USSR consider that the strict and consistent implementation of this Agreement by all parties concerned is an essential condition for the maintenance and strengthening of mutual confidence and stability in the center of Europe.

The USA and the USSR believe that, in order to strengthen stability and security in Europe, the relaxation of political tension on this continent should be accompanied by measures to reduce military tensions.

They therefore attach importance to the current negotiations on the mutual reduction of forces and armaments and associated measures in Central Europe, in which they are participating. The two Sides expressed the hope that these negotiations will result in concrete decisions ensuring the undiminished security of any of the parties and preventing unilateral military advantage.

Middle East

Both Sides believe that the removal of the danger of war and tension in the Middle East is a task of paramount importance and urgency, and therefore, the only alternative is the achievement, on the basis of UN Security Council Resolution 338, of a just and lasting peace settlement in which should be taken into account the legitimate interests of all peoples in the Middle East, including the Palestinian people, and the right to existence of all states in the area.

As Co-Chairmen of the Geneva Peace Conference on the Middle East, the USA and the USSR consider it important that the Conference resume its work as soon as possible, with the question of other participants from the Middle East area to be discussed at the Conference. Both Sides see the main purpose of the Geneva Peace Conference, the achievement of which they will promote in every way, as the establishment of just and stable peace in the Middle East.

They agreed that the USA and the USSR will continue to remain in close touch with a view to coordinating the efforts of both countries toward a peaceful settlement in the Middle East.

Indochina

Both Sides noted certain further improvements in the situation in Indochina. In the course of the exchange of views on the situation in Vietnam both Sides emphasized that peace and stability in the region can be preserved and strengthened only on the basis of strict observance by all parties concerned of the provisions of the Paris Agreement of January 27, 1973, and the Act of the International Conference on Vietnam of March 2, 1973.

As regards Laos, they noted progress in the normalization of the situation as a result of the formation there of coalition governmental bodies. Both Sides also pronounced themselves in favor of strict fulfillment of the pertinent agreements.

Both Sides also stressed the need for an early and just settlement of the problem of Cambodia based on respect for the sovereign rights of the Cambodian people to a free and independent development without any outside interference.

Strengthening the Role of the United Nations

The United States of America and the Soviet Union attach great importance to the United Nations as an instrument for maintaining peace and security and the expansion of international cooperation. They reiterate their intention to continue their efforts toward increasing the effectiveness of the United Nations in every possible way, including in regard to peace-keeping, on the basis of strict observance of the United Nations Charter.

IV. Commercial and Economic Relations

In the course of the meeting great attention was devoted to a review of the status of and prospects for relations between the USA and the USSR in the commercial and economic field.

Both Sides reaffirmed that they regard the broadening and deepening of mutually advantageous ties in this field on the basis of equality and non-discrimination as an important part of the foundation on which the entire structure of US-Soviet relations is built. An increase in the scale of commercial and economic ties corresponding to the potentials of both countries will cement this foundation and benefit the American and Soviet peoples.

The two Sides noted with satisfaction that since the previous summit meeting US-Soviet commercial and economic relations have on the whole shown an upward trend. This was expressed, in particular, in a substantial growth of the exchange of goods between the two countries which approximated $1.5 billion in 1973. It was noted that prospects were favorable for surpassing the goal announced in the joint US-USSR communique of June 24, 1973, of achieving a total bilateral trade turnover of $2.3 billion during the three-year period 1973-1975. The Joint US-USSR Commercial Commission continues to provide an effective mechanism to promote the broad-scale growth of economic relations.

The two Sides noted certain progress in the development of long-term cooperation between American firms and Soviet organizations in carrying out large-scale projects including those on a compensation basis. They are convinced that such cooperation is an important element in the development of commercial and economic ties between the two countries. The two Sides agreed to encourage the conclusion and implementation of appropriate agreements between American and Soviet organizations and firms. Taking into account the progress made in a number of specific projects, such as those concerning truck manufacture, the trade center, and chemical fertilizers, the Sides noted the possibility of concluding appropriate contracts in other areas of mutual interest, such as pulp and paper, timber, ferrous and non-ferrous metallurgy, natural gas, the engineering industry, and the extraction and processing of high energy-consuming minerals.

Both Sides noted further development of productive contacts and ties between business circles of the two countries in which a positive role was played by the decisions taken during the previous summit meeting on the opening of a United States commercial office in Moscow and a USSR trade representation in Washington as well as the establishment of a US-Soviet Commercial and Economic Council. They expressed their desire to continue to bring about favorable conditions for the successful development of commercial and economic relations between the USA and the USSR.

Both Sides confirmed their interest in bringing into force at the earliest possible time the US-Soviet trade agreement of October 1972.

Desirous of promoting the further expansion of economic relations between the two countries, the two Sides signed a Long-Term Agreement to Facilitate Economic, Industrial and Technical Cooperation between the USA and the USSR. They believe that a consistent implementation of the cooperation embodied in the Agreement over the ten-year period will be an important factor in strengthening bilateral relations in general and will benefit the peoples of both countries.

Having reviewed the progress in carrying out the Agreement Regarding Certain Maritime Matters concluded in October 1972 for a period of three years, and based on the experience accumulated thus far, the two Sides expressed themselves in favor of concluding before its expiration a new agreement in this field. Negotiations concerning such an agreement will commence this year.

V. Progress in Other Fields of Bilateral Relations

Having reviewed the progress in the implementation of the cooperative agreements concluded in 1972-1973, both Sides noted the useful work done by joint American-Soviet committees and working groups established under those agreements in developing regular contacts and cooperation between scientific and technical organizations, scientists, specialists and cultural personnel of both countries.

The two Sides note with satisfaction that joint efforts by the USA and USSR in such fields of cooperation as medical science and public health, protection and improvement of man's environment, science and technology, exploration of outer space and the world ocean, peaceful uses of atomic energy, agriculture and transportation create conditions for an accelerated solution of some urgent and complicated problems facing mankind.

Such cooperation makes a substantial contribution to the development of the structure of American-Soviet relations, giving it a more concrete positive content.

Both Sides will strive to broaden and deepen their cooperation in science and technology as well as cultural exchanges on the basis of agreements concluded between them.

On the basis of positive experience accumulated in their scientific and technological cooperation and guided by the desire to ensure further progress in this important sphere of their mutual relations, the two Sides decided to extend such cooperation to the following new areas.

Energy

Taking into consideration the growing energy needs of industry, transportation and other branches of the economies of both countries and the consequent need to intensify scientific and technical cooperation in the development of optimal methods of utilizing traditional and new sources of energy, and to improve the understanding of the energy programs and problems of both countries, the two Sides concluded an agreement on cooperation in the field of energy. Responsibility for the implementation of the Agreement is entrusted to a US-USSR Joint Committee on Cooperation in Energy, which will be established for that purpose.

Housing and Other Construction

The two Sides signed an agreement on cooperation in the field of housing and other construction. The aim of this Agreement is to promote the solution by joint effort of problems related to modern techniques of housing and other construction along such lines as the improvement of the reliability and quality of buildings and building materials, the planning and construction of new towns, construction in seismic areas and areas of extreme climatic conditions. For the implementation of this Agreement there will be established a Joint US-USSR Committee on Cooperation in Housing and Other Construction which will determine specific working programs.

For the purpose of enhancing the safety of their peoples living in earthquake-prone areas, the two Sides agreed to undertake on a priority basis a joint research project to increase the safety of buildings and other structures in these areas and, in particular, to study the behavior of prefabricated residential structures during earthquakes.

Artificial Heart Research

In the course of the implementation of joint programs in the field of medical science and public health, scientists and specialists of both countries concluded that there is a need to concentrate their efforts on the solution of one of the most important and humane problems of modern medical science, development of an artificial heart. In view of the great theoretical and technical complexity of the work involved, the two Sides concluded a special agreement on the subject. The US-USSR Joint Committee for Health Cooperation will assume responsibility for this project.

Cooperation in Space

The two Sides expressed their satisfaction with the successful preparations for the first joint manned flight of the American and Soviet spacecraft, Apollo and Soyuz, which is scheduled for 1975 and envisages their docking and mutual visits of the astronauts in each other's spacecraft. In accordance with existing agreements fruitful cooperation is being carried out in a number of other fields related to the exploration of outer space.

Attaching great importance to further American-Soviet cooperation in the exploration and use of outer space for peaceful purposes, including the development of safety systems for manned flights in space, and considering the desirability of consolidating experience in this field, the two Sides agreed to continue to explore possibilities for further joint space projects following the US-USSR space flight now scheduled for July 1975.

Transport of the Future

Aware of the importance of developing advanced modes of transportation, both Sides agreed that high-speed ground systems of the future, including a magnetically levitated train, which can provide economical, efficient, and reliable forms of transportation, would be a desirable and innovative area for joint activity. A working group to develop a joint research cooperation program in this area under the 1973 Agreement on Cooperation in the Field of Transportation will be established at the Fall meeting of the Joint US-USSR Transportation Committee.

Environmental Protection

Desiring to expand cooperation in the field of environmental protection, which is being successfully carried out under the US-USSR Agreement signed on May 23, 1972, and to contribute to the implementation of the "Man and the Biosphere" international program conducted on the initiative of the United Nations Educational, Scientific and Cultural Organization (UNESCO), both Sides agreed to designate in the territories of their respective countries certain natural areas as biosphere reserves for protecting valuable plant and animal genetic strains and ecosystems, and for conducting scientific research needed for more effective actions concerned with global environmental protection. Appropriate work for the implementation of this undertaking will be conducted in conformity with the goals of the UNESCO program and under the auspices of the previously established US-USSR Joint Committee on Cooperation in the Field of Environmental Protection.

Cultural Exchanges

The two Parties, aware of the importance of cultural exchanges as a means of promoting mutual understanding, express satisfaction with the agreement between the Metropolitan Museum of Art of New York City and the Ministry of Culture of the USSR leading to a major exchange of works of art. Such an exchange would be in accordance with the General Agreement on Contacts, Exchanges and Cooperation signed July 19, 1973, under which the parties agreed to render assistance for exchange of exhibitions between the museums of the two countries.

Establishment of New Consulates

Taking into consideration the intensive development of ties between the US and the USSR and the importance of further expanding consular relations on the basis of the US-USSR Consular Convention, and desiring to promote trade, tourism and cooperation between them in various areas, both Sides agreed to open additional Consulates General in two or three cities of each country.

As a first step they agreed in principle to the simultaneous establishment of a United States Consulate General in Kiev and a USSR Consulate General in New York. Negotiations for implementation of this agreement will take place at an early date.

Both Sides highly appreciate the frank and constructive atmosphere and fruitful results of the talks held between them in the course of the present meeting. They are convinced that the results represent a new and important milestone along the road of improving relations between the USA and the USSR to the benefit of the peoples of both countries, and a significant contribution to their efforts aimed at strengthening world peace and security.

Having again noted in this connection the exceptional importance and great practical usefulness of US-Soviet summit meetings, both Sides reaffirmed their agreement to hold such meetings regularly and when considered necessary for the discussion and solution of urgent questions. Both Sides also expressed their readiness to continue their active and close contacts and consultations.

The President extended an invitation to General Secretary of the Central Committee of the CPSU, L.I. Brezhnev, to pay an official visit to the United States in 1975. This invitation was accepted with pleasure.

Richard Nixon
    President of the United States of America

L.I. Brezhnev
    General Secretary of the Central Committee CPSU

▼▼▼

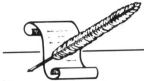

July

BUDGET REFORM LEGISLATION
July 12, 1974

President Nixon signed into law July 12 legislation setting up a framework for tightening congressional control over government spending. The budget reform procedures, when fully implemented in 1976, were intended to force Congress into tying spending decisions and fiscal policy objectives into an over-all budget package. President Nixon characterized the legislation as "the most significant reform of budget procedures since the Congress and this country began." He pledged "the full support of the executive branch in helping fulfill the great promise of this bill."

Enactment of the budget reform legislation, some members of Congress apparently believed, would bring to an end the years of presidential domination of federal budget decisions. But as one retired federal budget official pointed out, "the only question is, will it work?" The extent of congressional concern for ending inflation and the willingness of members to sacrifice political and jurisdictional interests for the sake of more reasoned budget policy were seen as the main determinants of whether or not the new reform procedures would be effective. "To make it work," observed Samuel M. Cohn, a former assistant director of the Office of Management and Budget, "Congress and its individual members will have to act a lot differently than they do now." On Aug. 22, 1974, Sen. Walter F. Mondale (D Minn.) warned his colleagues on the newly formed Senate Budget Committee: "We have a task that might be impossible, but if we don't try, we'll all be condemned."

On paper at least, the budget reform measure established an institutional and procedural structure aimed at enabling Congress to give more orderly and informed scrutiny to the annual federal budget. "The idea is a great idea," said Cohn. "For the first time, if it works, we'll be able to see that Congress has to reconcile its action on the totals with its action on the pieces." Under previously existing procedures, Congress had rarely looked at budget totals—of expenditures on the one hand and of revenues on the other—contenting itself instead with piece-by-piece action on the President's requests for authority to spend the government's money. As a remedy, the budget reform measure created new House and Senate committees—aided by a staff of budget experts—to focus congressional attention on the totals, and on how action on the pieces would affect the budget.

When fully implemented, the new law would require Congress to examine the total, setting target figures in a budget resolution, before acting on the pieces through authorization and appropriation bills. Once the customary appropriations process is completed, moreover, Congress would have to review both the target totals and the pieces, reconciling any discrepancies. Other provisions promised major changes in the way Congress conducts its business. One would give the House and Senate a chance to review new backdoor spending programs (legislation that bypasses the regular appropriations process, such as veterans' benefits) that create obligations that Congress must later meet by making the required appropriations. Another major innovation would spell out procedures by which the President could impound funds merely to defer their expenditure, but be required to ask Congress to rescind its earlier appropriations if he intended not to spend the money at all. To fit the expanded budget-making procedures into the annual sessions of Congress, the measure shifted the start of the fiscal year back to Oct. 1 from July 1—starting with fiscal 1977 on Oct. 1, 1976—and it set a detailed timetable for completing congressional action on the necessary legislation before that date.

Signing of the bill capped years of efforts to draw Congress more effectively into the over-all budget-making process. Given its constitutional "power of the purse," Congress had found it a source of frustration that its ability to control federal expenditures was rather severely limited during the period following World War II. A number of procedural reforms were attempted—namely a plan for congressional overview of the budget ceiling and another measure aimed at achieving one appropriations bill rather than several smaller ones.

The Legislative Reorganization Act of 1946 established a Joint Committee on the Legislative Budget to review the President's budget and recommend ceilings on expenditures and appropriations. The committee did so in 1947, but the Senate and House failed to reach agreement on its recommendations. In 1948, both chambers agreed that expenditures should be cut by $2.5-billion; but, in fact, fiscal 1949 outlays were $2.4-billion higher than estimated. The Democratic-controlled 81st Congress dropped the Legislative Budget in 1949.

In 1950, for the first time since the early days of the Republic, Congress lumped all regular appropriations into one bill, action which was supported *by the belief that it was a more effective way to limit spending than the discarded Legislative Budget. But the omnibus measure was completely outmoded before its enactment by the outbreak of war in Korea, and another $37-billion in supplemental funds was required before the end of 1950. In 1951, Congress returned to the practice of acting on a dozen or so regular appropriation acts, and the omnibus approach was not tried again.*

Controversies over the ever increasing presidential domination of the budget-making process was fueled during the Nixon years by executive-congressional clashes over federal spending ceilings and the unprecedented impoundment by Nixon of $40-billion of congressional appropriations. A significant move to reassert a congressional role in budget-making procedures resulted from the creation by law in 1972 of the Joint Study Committee on Budget Control. That body recommended that a committee be created in the House and another in the Senate to report out concurrent resolutions governing appropriations and spending. Bills incorporating that recommendation were introduced in the House and Senate on April 18, 1973. The House passed the bill Dec. 5, 1973, and the Senate followed suit on March 22, 1974.

Excerpts from provisions of the law enacted July 12 to reform procedures followed by the House and Senate in handling the federal budget:

DECLARATION OF PURPOSES

The Congress declares that it is essential—

(1) to assure effective congressional control over the budgetary process;

(2) to provide for the congressional determination each year of the appropriate level of Federal revenues and expenditures;

(3) to provide a system of impoundment control;

(4) to establish national budget priorities; and

(5) to provide for the furnishing of information by the executive branch in a manner that will assist the Congress in discharging its duties.

DEFINITIONS

IN GENERAL.—For purposes of this Act—

(1) The terms "budget outlays" and "outlays" mean, with respect to any fiscal year, expenditures and net lending of funds under budget authority during such year.

(2) The term "budget authority" means authority provided by law to enter into obligations which will result in immediate or future outlays involving Government funds, except that such term does not include authority to insure or guarantee the repayment of indebtedness incurred by another person or government.

(3) The term "tax expenditures" means those revenue losses attributable to provisions of the Federal tax laws which allow a special exclusion, exemption, or deduction from gross income or which provide a special credit,

575

a preferential rate of tax, or a deferral of tax liability; and the term "tax expenditures budget" means an enumeration of such tax expenditures.

(4) The term "concurrent resolution on the budget" means—

(A) a concurrent resolution setting forth the congressional budget for the United States Government for a fiscal year as provided in section 301;

(B) a concurrent resolution reaffirming or revising the congressional budget for the United States Government for a fiscal year as provided in section 310; and

(C) any other concurrent resolution revising the congressional budget for the United States Government for a fiscal year as described in section 304.

(5) The term "appropriation Act" means an Act referred to in section 105 of title 1, United States Code....

TITLE I—ESTABLISHMENT OF HOUSE AND SENATE BUDGET COMMITTEES

BUDGET COMMITTEE OF THE HOUSE OF REPRESENTATIVES

Sec. 101. ... (a) Committee on the Budget, [will] consist of twenty-three Members as follows:

"(1) five Members who are members of the Committee on Appropriations;

"(2) five Members who are members of the Committee on Ways and Means;

"(3) eleven Members who are members of other standing committees;

"(4) one Member from the leadership of the majority party; and

"(5) one Member from the leadership of the minority party. No Member shall serve as a member of the Committee on the Budget during more than two Congresses in any period of five successive Congresses beginning after 1974 (disregarding for this purpose any service performed as a member of such committee for less than a full session in any Congress). All selections of Members to serve on the committee shall be made without regard to seniority."

(b) ...the Committee on the Budget or any subcommittee thereof is authorized to sit and act at such times and places within the United States, whether the House is in session, has recessed, or has adjourned, to hold such hearings, to require the attendance of such witnesses and the production of such books or papers or documents or vouchers by subpoena or otherwise, and to take such testimony and records, as it deems necessary. Subpoena may be issued over the signature of the chairman of the committee or of any member of the committee designated by him; and may be served by any person designated by such chairman or member. The chairman of the committee, or any member thereof, may administer oaths to witnesses."...

(c) ...All concurrent resolutions on the budget...and other matters required to be referred to the committee.... The committee shall have the duty—

"(1) to report the matters required to be reported by it under titles III and IV of the Congressional Budget Act of 1974;

"(2) to make continuing studies of the effect on budget outlays of relevant existing and proposed legislation and to report the results of such studies to the House on a recurring basis;

"(3) to request and evaluate continuing studies of tax expenditures, to devise methods of coordinating tax expenditures, policies, and programs with direct budget outlays, and to report the results of such studies to the House on a recurring basis; and

"(4) to review, on a continuing basis, the conduct by the Congressional Budget Office of its functions and duties."

BUDGET COMMITTEE OF THE SENATE

Sec. 102. (a) ...Committee on the Budget,...

"(2) Such committee shall have the duty—

"(A) to report the matters required to be reported by it under titles III and IV of the Congressional Budget Act of 1974;

"(B) to make continuing studies of the effect on budget outlays of relevant existing and proposed legislation and to report the results of such studies to the Senate on a recurring basis;

"(C) to request and evaluate continuing studies of tax expenditures, to devise methods of coordinating tax expenditures, policies, and programs with direct budget outlays, and to report the results of such studies to the Senate on a recurring basis; and

"(D) to review, on a continuing basis, the conduct by the Congressional Budget Office of its functions and duties."...

(d) Each meeting of the Committee on the Budget of the Senate, or any subcommittee thereof, including meetings to conduct hearings, shall be open to the public, except that a portion or portions of any such meeting may be closed to the public if the committee or subcommittee, as the case may be, determines by record vote of a majority of the members of the committee or subcommittee present that the matters to be discussed or the testimony to be taken at such portion or portions—

(1) will disclose matters necessary to be kept secret in the interests of national defense or the confidential conduct of the foreign relations of the United States;

(2) will relate solely to matters of committee staff personnel or internal staff management or procedure;

(3) will tend to charge an individual with crime or misconduct, to disgrace or injure the professional standing of an individual, or otherwise to expose an individual to public contempt or obloquy, or will represent a clearly unwarranted invasion of the privacy of an individual;

(4) will disclose the identity of any informer or law enforcement agent or will disclose any information relating to the investigation or prosecution

of a criminal offense that is required to be kept secret in the interests of effective law enforcement; or

(5) will disclose information relating to the trade secrets or financial or commercial information pertaining specifically to a given person if—

(A) an Act of Congress requires the information to be kept confidential by Government officers and employees; or

(B) the information has been obtained by the Government on a confidential basis, other than through an application by such person for a specific Government financial or other benefit, and is required to be kept secret in order to prevent undue injury to the competitive position of such person....

TITLE II—CONGRESSIONAL BUDGET OFFICE
ESTABLISHMENT OF OFFICE

Sec. 201. (a) In General.—

(1) There is established an office of the Congress to be known as the Congressional Budget Office (hereinafter in this title referred to as the "Office"). The Office shall be headed by a Director; and there shall be a Deputy Director who shall perform such duties as may be assigned to him by the Director and, during the absence or incapacity of the Director or during a vacancy in that office, shall act as Director.

(2) The Director shall be appointed by the Speaker of the House of Representatives and the President pro tempore of the Senate after considering recommendations received from the Committees on the Budget of the House and the Senate, without regard to political affiliation and solely on the basis of his fitness to perform his duties. The Deputy Director shall be appointed by the Director.

(3) The term of office of the Director first appointed shall expire at noon on January 3, 1979, and the terms of office of Directors subsequently appointed shall expire at noon on January 3 of each fourth year thereafter. Any individual appointed as Director to fill a vacancy prior to the expiration of a term shall serve only for the unexpired portion of that term. An individual serving as Director at the expiration of a term may continue to serve until his successor is appointed. Any Deputy Director shall serve until the expiration of the term of office of the Director who appointed him (and until his successor is appointed), unless sooner removed by the Director.

(4) The Director may be removed by either House by resolution.

(5) The Director shall receive compensation at a per annum gross rate equal to the rate of basic pay, as in effect from time to time, for level III of the Executive Schedule in section 5314 of title 5, United States Code. The Deputy Director shall receive compensation at a per annum gross rate equal to the rate of basic pay, as so in effect, for level IV of the Executive Schedule in section 5315 of such title.

(b) PERSONNEL.—The Director shall appoint and fix the compensation of such personnel as may be necessary to carry out the duties and functions of the Office. All personnel of the Office shall be appointed without regard to political affiliation and solely on the basis of their fitness to perform their duties. The Director may prescribe the duties and responsibilities of the personnel of the Office, and delegate to them authority to perform any of the duties, powers, and functions imposed on the Office or on the Director. For purposes of pay (other than pay of the Director and Deputy Director) and employment benefits, rights, and privileges, all personnel of the Office shall be treated as if they were employees of the House of Representatives.

(c) EXPERTS AND CONSULTANTS.—In carrying out the duties and functions of the Office, the Director may procure the temporary (not to exceed one year) or intermittent services of experts or consultants or organizations thereof by contract as independent contractors, or, in the case of individual experts or consultants, by employment at rates of pay not in excess of the daily equivalent of the highest rate of basic pay payable under the General Schedule of section 5332 of title 5, United States Code.

(d) RELATIONSHIP TO EXECUTIVE BRANCH.—The Director is authorized to secure information, data, estimates, and statistics directly from the various departments, agencies, and establishments of the executive branch of Government and the regulatory agencies and commissions of the Government. All such departments, agencies, establishments, and regulatory agencies and commissions shall furnish the Director any available material which he determines to be necessary in the performance of his duties and functions (other than material the disclosure of which would be a violation of law). The Director is also authorized, upon agreement with the head of any such department, agency, establishment, or regulatory agency or commission, to utilize its services, facilities, and personnel with or without reimbursement; and the head of each such department, agency, establishment, or regulatory agency or commission is authorized to provide the Office such services, facilities, and personnel.

(e) RELATIONSHIP TO OTHER AGENCIES OF CONGRESS.—In carrying out the duties and functions of the Office, and for the purpose of coordinating the operations of the Office with those of other congressional agencies with a view to utilizing most effectively the information, services, and capabilities of all such agencies in carrying out the various responsibilities assigned to each, the Director is authorized to obtain information, data, estimates, and statistics developed by the General Accounting Office, the Library of Congress, and the Office of Technology Assessment, and (upon agreement with them) to utilize their services, facilities, and personnel with or without reimbursement. The Comptroller General, the Librarian of Congress, and the Technology Assessment Board are authorized to provide the Office with the information, data, estimates, and statistics, and the services, facilities, and personnel, referred to in the preceding sentence.

(f) APPROPRIATIONS.—There are authorized to be appropriated to the Office for each fiscal year such sums as may be necessary to enable it to carry out its duties and functions. Until sums are first appropriated pursuant to the preceding sentence, but for a period not exceeding 12 months following the effective date of this subsection, the expenses of the Office shall be paid from the contingent fund of the Senate....

DUTIES AND FUNCTIONS

Sec. 202. (a) ASSISTANCE TO BUDGET COMMITTEES.—It shall be the duty and function of the Office to provide to the Committees on the Budget of both Houses information which will assist such committees in the discharge of all matters within their jurisdictions, including (1) information with respect to the budget, appropriation bills, and other bills authorizing or providing budget authority or tax expenditures, (2) information with respect to revenues, receipts, estimated future revenues and receipts, and changing revenue conditons, and (3) such related information as such Committees may request.

(b) ASSISTANCE TO COMMITTEES ON APPROPRIATIONS, WAYS AND MEANS, AND FINANCE.—At the request of the Committee on Appropriations of either House, the Committee on Ways and Means of the House of Representatives, or the Committee on Finance of the Senate, the Office shall provide to such Committee any information which will assist it in the discharge of matters within its jurisdiction, including information described in clauses (1) and (2) of subsection (a) and such related information as the Committee may request.

(c) ASSISTANCE TO OTHER COMMITTEES AND MEMBERS.—

(1) At the request of any other committee of the House of Representatives or the Senate or any joint committee of the Congress, the Office shall provide to such committee or joint committee any information compiled in carrying out clauses (1) and (2) of subsection (a), and, to the extent practicable, such additional information related to the foregoing as may be requested.

(2) At the request of any Member of the House or Senate, the Office shall provide to such Member any information compiled in carrying out clauses (1) and (2) of subsection (a), and, to the extent available, such additional information related to the foreging as may be requested.

(d) ASSIGNMENT OF OFFICE PERSONNEL TO COMMITTEES AND JOINT COMMITTEES.—At the request of the Committee on the Budget of either House, personnel of the Office shall be assigned, on a temporary basis, to assist such committee. At the request of any other committee of either House or any joint committee of the Congress, personnel of the Office may be assigned, on a temporary basis, to assist such committee or joint committee with respect to matters directly related to the applicable provisions of subsection (b) or (c).

(e) TRANSFER OF FUNCTIONS OF JOINT COMMITTEE ON REDUCTION OF FEDERAL EXPENDITURES.—

(1) The duties, functions, and personnel of the Joint Committee on Reduction of Federal Expenditures are transferred to the Office, and the Joint Committee is abolished....

(f) REPORTS TO BUDGET COMMITTEES.—

(1) On or before April 1 of each year, the Director shall submit to the Committees on the Budget of the House of Representatives and the Senate a report, for the fiscal year commencing on October 1 of that year, with respect to fiscal policy, including (A) alternative levels of total revenues, total new budget authority, and total outlays (including related surpluses and deficits), and (B) the levels of tax expenditures under existing law, taking into account projected economic factors and any changes in such levels based on proposals in the budget submitted by the President for such fiscal year. Such report shall also include a discussion of national budget priorities, including alternative ways of allocating budget authority and budget outlays for such fiscal year among major programs or functional categories, taking into account how such alternative allocations will meet major national needs and affect balanced growth and development of the United States.

(2) The Director shall from time to time submit to the Committees on the Budget of the House of Representatives and the Senate such further reports (including reports revising the report required by paragraph (1)) as may be necessary or appropriate to provide such Committees with information, data, and analyses for the performance of their duties and functions.

(g) USE OF COMPUTERS AND OTHER TECHNIQUES.—The Director may equip the Office with up-to-date computer capability (upon approval of the Committee on House Administration of the House of Represenatives and the Committee on Rules and Administration of the Senate), obtain the services of experts and consultants in computer technology, and develop techniques for the evaluation of budgetary requirements.

PUBLIC ACCESS TO BUDGET DATA

Sec. 203. (a) RIGHT TO COPY.—Except as provided in subsections (c) and (d), the Director shall make all information, data, estimates, and statistics obtained under sections 201(d) and 201(e) available for public copying during normal business hours, subject to reasonable rules and regulations, and shall to the extent practicable, at the request of any person, furnish a copy of any such information, data, estimates, or statistics upon payment by such person of the cost of making and furnishing such copy.

(b) INDEX.—The Director shall develop and maintain filing, coding and indexing systems that identify the information, data, estimates, and statistics to which subsection (a) applies and shall make such systems available for public use during normal business hours.

(c) EXCEPTIONS.—Subsection (a) shall not apply to information, data, estimates, and statistics—

(1) which are specifically exempted from disclosure by law; or

(2) which the Director determines will disclose—

(A) matters necessary to be kept secret in the interests of national defense or the confidential conduct of...foreign relations....

(B) information relating to trade secrets or financial or commercial information pertaining specifically to a given person if the information has been obtained by the Government on a confidential basis, other than through an application by such person for a specific financial or other benefit, and is required to be kept secret in order to prevent undue injury to the competitive position of such person; or

(C) personnel or medical data or similar data the disclosure of which would constitute a clearly unwarranted invasion of personal privacy, unless the portions containing such matters, information, or data have been excised.

(d) INFORMATION OBTAINED FOR COMMITTEES AND MEMBERS.—Subsection (a) shall apply to any information, data, estimates, and statistics obtained at the request of any committee, joint committee, or Member unless such committee, joint committee, or Member has instructed the Director not to make such information, data, estimates, or statistics available for public copying.

TITLE III—CONGRESSIONAL BUDGET PROCESS
TIMETABLE

Sec. 300. The timetable with respect to the congressional budget process for any fiscal year is as follows:

On or before:	Action to be completed:
November 10	President submits current services budget
15th day after Congress meets	President submits his budget.
March 15	Committees and joint committees submit reports to Budget Committees.
April 1	Congressional Budget Office submits report to Budget Committees.
April 15	Budget Committees report first concurrent resolution on the budget to their Houses.
May 15	Committees report bills and resolutions authorizing new budget authority.
May 15	Congress completes action on first concurrent resolution on the budget.
7th day after Labor Day	Congress completes action on bills and resolutions providing new budget authority and new spending authority.
September 15	Congress completes action on second required concurrent resolution on the budget.
September 25	Congress completes action on reconciliation bill or resolution, or both, implementing second required concurrent resolution.
October 1	Fiscal year begins ...

TITLE IV—ADDITIONAL PROVISIONS TO IMPROVE FISCAL PROCEDURES

BILLS PROVIDING NEW SPENDING AUTHORITY

Sec. 401. (a) LEGISLATION PROVIDING CONTRACT OR BORROWING AUTHORITY.—It shall not be in order in either the House of Representatives or the Senate to consider any bill or resolution which provides new spending authority described in subsection (c) (2) (A) or (B) (or any amendment which provides such new spending authority), unless that bill, resolution, or amendment also provides that such new spending authority is to be effective for any fiscal year only to such extent or in such amounts as are provided in appropriation Acts.

(b) LEGISLATION PROVIDING ENTITLEMENT AUTHORITY.—

(1) It shall not be in order in either the House of Representatives or the Senate to consider any bill or resolution which provides new spending authority described in subsection (c) (2) (C) (or any amendment which provides such new spending authority) which is to become effective before the first day of the fiscal year which begins during the calendar year in which such bill or resolution is reported.

(2) If any committee of the House of Representatives or the Senate reports any bill or resolution which provides new spending authority described in subsection (c) (2) (C) which is to become effective during a fiscal year and the amount of new budget authority which will be required for such fiscal year if such bill or resolution is enacted as so reported exceeds the appropriate allocation of new budget authority reported under section 302 (b) in connection with the most recently agreed to concurrent resolution on the budget for such fiscal year, such bill or resolution shall then be referred to the Committee on Appropriations of that House with instructions to report it, with the committee's recommendations, within 15 calendar days (not counting any day on which that House is not in session) beginning with the day following the day on which it is so referred. If the Committee on Appropriations of either House fails to report a bill or resolution referred to it under this paragraph within such 15-day period, the committee shall automatically be discharged from further consideration of such bill or resolution and such bill or resolution shall be placed on the appropriate calendar.

(3) The Committee on Appropriations of each House shall have jurisdiction to report any bill or resolution referred to it under paragraph (2) with an amendment which limits the total amount of new spending authority provided in such bill or resolution.

(c) DEFINITIONS.—

(1) For purposes of this section, the term "new spending authority" means spending authority not provided by law on the effective date of this section, including any increase in or addition to spending authority provided by law on such date.

583

(2) For purposes of paragraph (1), the term "spending authority" means authority (whether temporary or permanent)—

(A) to enter into contracts under which the United States is obligated to make outlays, the budget authority for which is not provided in advance by appropriation Acts;

(B) to incur indebtedness (other than indebtedness incurred under the Second Liberty Bond Act) for the repayment of which the United States is liable, the budget authority for which is not provided in advance by appropriation Acts; and

(C) to make payments (including loans and grants), the budget authority for which is not provided for in advance by appropriation Acts, to any person or government if, under the provisions of the law containing such authority, the United States is obligated to make such payments to persons or governments who meet the requirements established by such law.

Such terms does not include authority to insure or guarantee the repayment of indebtedness incurred by another person or government.

(d) EXCEPTIONS.—

(1) Subsections (a) and (b) shall not apply to new spending authority if the budget authority for outlays which will result from such new spending authority is derived—

(A) from a trust fund established by the Social Security Act (as in effect on the date of the enactment of this Act); or

(B) from any other trust fund, 90 percent or more of the receipts of which consist or will consist of amounts (transferred from the general fund of the Treasury) equivalent to amounts of taxes (related to the purposes for which such outlays are or will be made) received in the Treasury under specified provisions of the Internal Revenue Code of 1954.

(2) Subsections (a) and (b) shall not apply to new spending authority which is an amendment to or extension of the State and Local Fiscal Assistance Act of 1972, or a continuation of the program of fiscal assistance to State and local governments provided by that Act, to the extent so provided in the bill or resolution providing such authority.

(3) Subsections (a) and (b) shall not apply to new spending authority to the extent that—

(A) the outlays resulting therefrom are made by an organization which is (i) a mixed-ownership Government corporation (as defined in section 201 of the Government Corporation Control Act), or (ii) a wholly owned Government corporation (as defined in section 101 of such Act) which is specifically exempted by law from compliance with any or all of the provisions of that Act; or

(B) the outlays resulting therefrom consist exclusively of the proceeds of gifts or bequests made to the United States for a specific purpose. . . .

TITLE V—CHANGE OF FISCAL YEAR

FISCAL YEAR TO BEGIN OCTOBER 1

Sec. 501. Section 237 of the Revised Statutes (31 U.S.C. 1020) is amended to read as follows:

"Sec. 237. (a) The fiscal year of the Treasury of the United States, in all matters of accounts, receipts, expenditures, estimates, and appropriations—

"(1) shall, through June 30, 1976, commence on July 1 of each year and end on June 30 of the following year; and

"(2) shall, beginning on October 1, 1976, commence on October 1 of each year and end on September 30 of the following year. "(b) All accounts of receipts and expenditures required by law to be published annually shall be prepared and published for each fiscal year as established by subsection (a)."

TRANSITION TO NEW FISCAL YEAR

Sec. 502. (a) As soon as practicable, the President shall prepare and submit to the Congress—

(1) after consultation with the committees on Appropriations of the House of Representatives and the Senate, budget estimates for the United States Government for the period commencing July 1, 1976, and ending on September 30, 1976, in such form and detail as he may determine; and

(2) proposed legislation he considers appropriate with respect to changes in law necessary to provide authorizations of appropriations for that period.

(b) The Director of the Office of Management and Budget shall provide by regulation, order, or otherwise for the orderly transition by all departments, agencies, and instrumentalities of the United States Government and the government of the District of Columbia from the use of the fiscal year in effect on the date of enactment of this Act to the use of the new fiscal year prescribed by section 237 (a) (2) of the Revised Statutes. The Director shall prepare and submit to the Congress such additional proposed legislation as he considers necessary to accomplish this objective.

(c) The Director of the Office of Management and Budget and the Director of the Congressional Budget Office jointly shall conduct a study of the feasibility and advisability of submitting the Budget or portions thereof, and enacting new budget authority or portions thereof, for a fiscal year during the regular session of the Congress which begins in the year preceding the year in which such fiscal year begins. The Director of the Office of Management and Budget and the Director of the Congressional Budget Office each shall submit a report of the results of the study conducted by them, together with his own conclusions and recommendations, to the Congress not later than 2 years after the effective date of this subsection....

TITLE VI—AMENDMENTS TO BUDGET AND ACCOUNTING ACT, 1921

MATTERS TO BE INCLUDED IN PRESIDENT'S BUDGET

Sec. 601. Section 201 of the Budget and Accounting Act, 1921 (31 U.S.C. 11), is amended by adding at the end thereof the following new subsections:

"(d) The Budget transmitted pursuant to subsection (a) for each fiscal year shall set forth separately the items enumerated in section 301(a) (1)—(5) of the Congressional Budget Act of 1974.

"(e) The Budget transmitted pursuant to subsection (a) for each fiscal year shall set forth the levels of tax expenditures under existing law for such fiscal year (the tax expenditure budget), taking into account projected economic factors, and any changes in such existing levels based on proposals contained in such Budget. For purposes of this subsection, the terms 'tax expenditures' and 'tax expenditures budget' have the meanings given to them by section 3(a) (3) of the Congressional Budget Act of 1974.

"(f) The Budget transmitted pursuant to subsection (a) for each fiscal year shall contain—

"(1) a comparison, for the last completed fiscal year, of the total amount of outlays estimated in the Budget transmitted pursuant to subsection (a) for each major program involving uncontrollable or relatively uncontrollable outlays and the total amount of outlays made under each such major program during such fiscal year;

"(2) a comparison, for the last completed fiscal year, of the total amount of revenues estimated in the Budget transmitted pursuant to subsection (a) and the total amount of revenues received during such year, and with respect to each major revenue source, the amount of revenues estimated in the Budget transmitted pursuant to subsection (a) and the amount of revenues received during such year; and

"(3) an analysis and explanation of the difference between each amount set forth pursuant to paragraphs (1) and (2) as the amount of outlays or revenues estimated in the Budget submitted under subsection (a) for such fiscal year and the corresponding amount set forth as the amount of outlays made or revenues received during such fiscal year.

"(g) The President shall transmit to the Congress, on or before April 10 and July 15 of each year, a statement of all amendments to or revisions in the budget authority requested, the estimated outlays, and the estimated receipts for the ensuing fiscal year set forth in the Budget transmitted pursuant to subsection (a) (including any previous amendments or revisions proposed on behalf of the executive branch) that he deems necessary and appropriate based on the most current information available. Such statement shall contain the effect of such amendments and revisions on the summary data submitted under subsection (a) and shall include such supporting detail as is practicable. The statement transmitted on or before July 15 of any year may be included in the supplemental summary required to be transmitted under subsection (b) during such year. The Budget transmitted to the Congress pursuant to subsection (a) for any fiscal year, or the supporting detail transmitted in connection therewith, shall include a statement of all such amendments and revisions with respect to the fiscal year in progress made before the date of transmission of such Budget.

"(h) The Budget transmitted pursuant to subsection (a) for each fiscal year shall include information with respect to estimates of appropriations for the next succeeding fiscal year for grants, contracts, or other payments under any program for which there is an authorization of appropriations for such succeeding fiscal year and such appropriations are authorized to be included in an appropriation Act for the fiscal year preceding the fiscal year in which the appropriation is to be available for obligation.

"(i) The Budget transmitted pursuant to subsection (a) for each fiscal year, beginning with the fiscal year ending September 30, 1979, shall contain a presentation of budget authority, proposed budget authority, outlays, proposed outlays, and descriptive information in terms of—

"(1) a detailed structure of national needs which shall be used to reference all agency missions and programs;

"(2) agency missions; and

"(3) basic programs.

To the extent practicable, each agency shall furnish information in support of its budget requests in accordance with its assigned missions in terms of Federal functions and subfunctions, including mission responsibilities of component organizations, and shall relate its programs to agency missions"....

YEAR-AHEAD REQUESTS FOR AUTHORIZATION OF NEW BUDGET AUTHORITY

Sec. 607. Notwithstanding any other provision of law, any request for the enactment of legislation authorizing the enactment of new budget authority to continue a program or activity for a fiscal year (beginning with the fiscal year commencing October 1, 1976) shall be submitted to the Congress not later than May 15 of the year preceding the year in which such fiscal year begins. In the case of a request for the enactment of legislation authorizing the enactment of new budget authority for a new program or activity which is to continue for more than one fiscal year, such request shall be submitted for at least the first 2 fiscal years.

TITLE VII—PROGRAM REVIEW AND EVALUATION

REVIEW AND EVALUATION BY THE COMPTROLLER GENERAL

...Sec. 702. (a) Section 204 of the Legislative Reorganization Act of 1970 (31 U.S.C. 1154) is amended to read as follows:

"REVIEW AND EVALUATION

"Sec. 204. (a) The Comptroller General shall review and evaluate the results of Government programs and activities carried on under existing law when ordered by either House of Congress, or upon his own initiative, or when requested by any committee of the House of Representatives or the Senate, or any joint committee of the two Houses, having jurisdiction over such programs and activities.

"(b) The Comptroller General, upon request of any committee of either House or any joint committee of the two Houses, shall—

"(1) assist such committee or joint committee in developing a statement of legislative objectives and goals and methods for assessing and reporting actual program performance in relation to such legislative objectives and goals. Such statements shall include, but are not limited to, recommendations as to methods of assessment, information to be reported, responsibility for reporting, frequency of reports, and feasibility of pilot testing; and

"(2) assist such committee or joint committee in analyzing and assessing program reviews or evaluation studies prepared by and for any Federal agency.

Upon request of any Member of either House, the Comptroller General shall furnish to such Member a copy of any statement or other material compiled in carrying out paragraphs (1) and (2) which has been released by the committee or joint committee for which it was compiled.

"(c) The Comptroller General shall develop and recommend to the Congress methods for review and evaluation of Government programs and activities carried on under existing law.

"(d) In carrying out his responsibilities under this section, the Comptroller General is authorized to establish an Office of Program Review and Evaluation within the General Accounting Office. The Comptroller General is authorized to employ not to exceed ten experts on a permanent, temporary, or intermittent basis and to obtain services as authorized by section 3109 of title 5, United States Code, but in either case at a rate (or the daily equivalent) for individuals not to exceed that prescribed, from time to time, for level V of the Executive Schedule under section 5316 of title 5, United States Code.

"(e) The Comptroller General shall include in his annual report to the Congress a review of his activities under this section....

TITLE VIII—FISCAL AND BUDGETARY
INFORMATION AND CONTROLS
AMENDMENT TO LEGISLATIVE REORGANIZATION ACT
OF 1970

Sec. 801. (a) So much of title II of the Legislative Reorganization Act of 1970 (31 U.S.C. chapter 22) as precedes section 204 thereof is amended to read as follows:

"Part 1 ... "Sec. 201. The Secretary of the Treasury and the Director of the Office of Management and Budget, in cooperation with the Comptroller General of the United States, shall develop, establish, and maintain, for use by all Federal agencies, standardized data processing and information systems for fiscal, budgetary, and program-related data and information. The development, establishment, and maintenance of such systems shall be carried out so as to meet the needs of the various branches of the Federal Government and, insofar as practicable, of governments at the State and local level.

"STANDARDIZATION OF TERMINOLOGY, DEFINITIONS, CLASSIFICATIONS, AND CODES FOR FISCAL BUDGETARY, AND PROGRAM-RELATED DATA AND INFORMATION

"Sec. 202. (a) (1) The Comptroller General of the United States, in cooperation with the Secretary of the Treasury, the Director of the Office of Management and Budget, and the Director of the Congressional Budget Office, shall develop, establish, maintain, and publish standard terminology, definitions, classifications, and codes for Federal fiscal, budgetary, and program-related data and information. The authority contained in this section shall include, but not be limited to, data and information pertaining to federal fiscal policy, revenues, receipts, expenditures, functions, programs, projects, and activities. Such standard terms, definitions, classifications, and codes shall be used by all Federal agencies in supplying to the Congress fiscal, budgetary, and program-related data and information.

"(2) The Comptroller General shall submit to the Congress, on or before June 30, 1975, a report containing the initial standard terminology, definitions, classifications, and codes referred to in paragraph (1), and shall recommend any legislation necessary to implement them. After June 30, 1975, the Comptroller General shall submit to the Congress additional reports as he may think advisable, including any recommendations for any legislation he may deem necessary to further the development, establishment, and maintenance, modification, and executive implementation of such standard terminology, definitions, classifications, and codes.

"(b) In carrying out this responsibility, the Comptroller General of the United States shall give particular consideration to the needs of the Committees on the Budget of the House and Senate, the Committees on Appropriations of the House and Senate, the Committee on Ways and Means of the House, the Committee on Finance of the Senate, and the Congressional Budget Office.

"(c) The Comptroller General of the United States shall conduct a continuing program to identify and specify the needs of the committees and Members of the Congress for fiscal, budgetary, and program-related information to support the objectives of this part.

"(d) The Comptroller General shall assist committees in developing their information needs, including such needs expressed in legislative requirements, and shall monitor the various recurring reporting requirements of the Congress and committees and make recommendations to the Congress and committees for changes and improvements in their reporting requirements to meet congressional information needs ascertained by the Comptroller General, to enhance their usefulness to the congressional users and to eliminate duplicative or unneeded reporting.

"(e) On or before September 1, 1974, and each year thereafter, the Comptroller General shall report to the Congress on needs identified and specified under subsection (c); the relationship of these needs to the existing reporting requirements; the extent to which the executive branch reporting presently meets the identified needs; the specification of changes to standard classifications needed to meet congressional needs; the activities, progress and results of his activities under subsection (d); and the progress that the executive branch has made during the past year.

"(f) On or before March 1, 1975, and each year thereafter, the Director of the Office of Management and Budget and the Secretary of the Treasury shall report to the Congress on their plans for addressing the needs identified and specified under subsection (c), including plans for implementing changes to classifications and codes to meet the information needs of the Congress as well as the status of prior year system and classification implementations....

TITLE IX—MISCELLANEOUS PROVISIONS;

EFFECTIVE DATES

Sec. 905. (a) Except as provided in this section, the provisions of this Act shall take effect on the date of its enactment.

(b) Title II (except section 201(a)), section 403, and section 502(c) shall take effect on the day on which the first Director of the Congressional Budget Office is appointed under section 201(a).

(c) Except as provided in section 906, title III and section 402 shall apply with respect to the fiscal year beginning on October 1, 1976, and succeeding fiscal years, and section 401 shall take effect on the first day of the second regular session of the Ninety-fourth Congress.

(d) The amendments to the Budget and Accounting Act, 1921, made by sections 601, 603, and 604 shall apply with respect to the fiscal year beginning on July 1, 1975, and succeeding fiscal years, except that section 201(g) of such Act (as added by section 601) shall apply with respect to the fiscal year beginning on October 1, 1975, and succeeding fiscal years and section 201(i) of such Act (as added by section 601) shall apply with respect to the fiscal year beginning on October 1, 1978, and succeeding fiscal years. The amendment to such Act made by section 602 shall apply with respect to the fiscal year beginning on October 1, 1976, and succeeding fiscal years.

APPLICATION OF CONGRESSIONAL BUDGET PROCESS TO FISCAL YEAR 1976

Sec. 906. If the Committees on the Budget of the House of Representatives and the Senate both agree that it is feasible to report and act on a concurrent resolution on the budget referred to in section 301(a), or to apply any provision of title III or section 401 or 402, for the fiscal year beginning on July 1, 1975, and submit reports of such agreement to their respective Houses, then to the extent and in the manner specified in such reports, the provisions so specified and section 202(f) shall apply with respect to such fiscal year. If any provision so specified contains a date, such reports shall also specify a substitute date.

TITLE X—IMPOUNDMENT CONTROL

PART A—General Provisions

DISCLAIMER

Sec. 1001. Nothing contained in this Act, or in any amendments made by this Act, shall be construed as—

(1) asserting or conceding the constitutional powers or limitations of either the Congress or the President;

(2) ratifying or approving any impoundment heretofore or hereafter executed or approved by the President or any other Federal officer or employee, except insofar as pursuant to statutory authorization then in effect;

(3) affecting in any way the claims or defenses of any party to litigation concerning any impoundment; or

(4) superseding any provision of law which requires the obligation of budget authority or the making of outlays thereunder.

AMENDMENT TO ANTIDEFICIENCY ACT

Sec. 1002. Section 3679(c) (2) of the Revised Statutes, as amended (31 U.S.C. 665), is amended to read as follows:

"(2) In apportioning any appropriation, reserves may be established solely to provide for contingencies, or to effect savings whenever savings are made possible by or through changes in requirements or greater efficiency of operations. Whenever it is determined by an officer designated in subsection (d) of this section to make apportionments and reapportionments that any amount so reserved will not be required to carry out the full objectives and scope of the appropriation concerned, he shall recommend the recission of such amount in the manner provided in the Budget and Accounting Act, 1921, for estimates of appropriations. Except as specifically provided by particular appropriations Acts or other laws, no reserves shall be established other than as authorized by this subsection. Reserves established pursuant to this subsection shall be reported to the Congress in accordance with the Impoundment Control Act of 1974"....

RECISSION OF BUDGET AUTHORITY

Sec. 1012. (a) TRANSMITTAL OF SPECIAL MESSAGE.—Whenever the President determines that all or part of any budget authority will not be required to carry out the full objectives or scope of programs for which it is provided or that such budget authority should be rescinded for fiscal policy or other reasons (including the termination of authorized projects or activities for which budget authority has been provided), or whenever all or part of budget authority provided for only one fiscal year is to be reserved from obligation for such fiscal year, the President shall transmit to both Houses of Congress a special message specifying—

(1) the amount of budget authority which he proposes to be rescinded or which is to be so reserved;

(2) any account, department or establishment of the Government to which such budget authority is available for obligation, and the specific project or governmental functions involved;

(3) the reasons why the budget authority should be rescinded or is to be so reserved;

(4) to the maximum extent practicable, the estimated fiscal, economic, and budgetary effect of the proposed recission or of the reservation; and

(5) all facts, circumstances, and considerations relating to or bearing upon the proposed recission or the reservation and the decision to effect the proposed recission or the reservation, and to the maximum extent practicable, the estimated effect of the proposed recission or the reservation upon the objects, purposes, and programs for which the budget authority is provided.

(b) REQUIREMENT TO MAKE AVAILABLE FOR OBLIGATION.—Any amount of budget authority proposed to be rescinded or that is to be reserved as set forth in such special message shall be made available for obligation unless within the prescribed 45-day period, the Congress has completed action on a recission bill rescinding all or part of the amount proposed to be rescinded or that is to be reserved.

DISAPPROVAL OF PROPOSED DEFERRALS OF BUDGET AUTHORITY

Sec. 1013. (a) TRANSMITTAL OF SPECIAL MESSAGE.—Whenever the President, the Director of the Office of Management and Budget, the head of any department or agency of the United States, or any officer or employee of the United States proposes to defer any budget authority provided for a specific purpose or project, the President shall transmit to the House of Representatives and the Senate a special message specifying—

(1) the amount of the budget authority proposed to be deferred;

(2) any account, department, or establishment of the Government to which such budget authority is available for obligation, and the specific projects or governmental functions involved;

(3) the period of time during which the budget authority is proposed to be deferred;

(4) the reasons for the proposed deferral, including any legal authority invoked by him to justify the proposed deferral;

(5) to the maximum extent practicable, the estimated fiscal, economic, and budgetary effect of the proposed deferral; and

(6) all facts, circumstances, and considerations relating to or bearing upon the proposed deferral and the decision to effect the proposed deferral, including an analysis of such facts, circumstances, and considerations in terms of their application to any legal authority and specific elements of legal authority invoked by him to justify such proposed deferral, and to the maximum extent practicable, the estimated effect of the proposed deferral upon the objects, purposes, and programs for which the budget authority is provided.

A special message may include one or more proposed deferrals of budget authority. A deferral may not be proposed for any period of time extending beyond the end of the fiscal year in which the special message proposing the deferral is transmitted to the House and the Senate.

(b) Requirement to Make Available for Obligation.—Any amount of budget authority proposed to be deferred, as set forth in a special message transmitted under subsection (a), shall be made available for obligation if either House of Congress passes an impoundment resolution disapproving such proposed deferral.

(c) Exception.—The provisions of this section do not apply to any budget authority proposed to be rescinded or that is to be reserved as set forth in a special message required to be transmitted under section 1012....

REPORTS BY COMPTROLLER GENERAL

Sec. 1015. (a) Failure to Transmit Special Message.—If the Comptroller General finds that the President, the Director of the Office of Management and Budget, the head of any department or agency of the United States, or any other officer or employee of the United States—

(1) is to establish a reserve or proposes to defer budget authority with respect to which the President is required to transmit a special message under section 1012 or 1013; or

(2) has ordered, permitted, or approved the establishment of such a reserve or a deferral of budget authority; and that the President has failed to transmit a special message with respect to such reserve or deferral, the Comptroller General shall make a report on such reserve or deferral and any available information concerning it to both Houses of Congress. The provisions of this part shall apply with respect to such reserve or deferral in the same manner and with the same effect as if such report of the Comptroller General were a special message transmitted by the President under section 1012 or 1013, and, for purposes of this part, such report shall be considered a special message transmitted under section 1012 or 1013.

(b) INCORRECT CLASSIFICATION OF SPECIAL MESSAGE.—If the President has transmitted a special message to both Houses of Congress in accordance with section 1012 or 1013, and the Comptroller General believes that the President so transmitted the special message in accordance with one of those sections when the special message should have been transmitted in accordance with the other of those sections, the Comptroller General shall make a report to both Houses of the Congress setting forth his reasons.

SUITS BY COMPTROLLER GENERAL

Sec. 1016. If, under section 1012(b) or 1013(b), budget authority is required to be made available for obligation and such budget authority is not made available for obligation, the Comptroller General is hereby expressly empowered, through attorneys of his own selection, to bring a civil action in the United States District Court for the District of Columbia to require such budget authority to be made available for obligation, and such court is hereby expressly empowered to enter in such civil action, against any department, agency, officer, or employee of the United States, any decree, judgment, or order which may be necessary or appropriate to make such budget authority available for obligation. The courts shall give precedence to civil actions brought under this section, and to appeals and writs from decisions in such actions, over all other civil actions, appeals, and writs. No civil action shall be brought by the Comptroller General under this section until the expiration of 25 calendar days of continuous session of the Congress following the date on which an explanatory statement by the Comptroller General of the circumstances giving rise to the action contemplated has been filed with the Speaker of the House of Representatives and the President of the Senate.

PROCEDURE IN HOUSE AND SENATE

Sec. 1017. (a) REFERRAL.—Any recission bill introduced with respect to a special message or impoundment resolution introduced with respect to a proposed deferral of budget authority shall be referred to the appropriate committee of the House of Representatives or the Senate, as the case may be.

(b) DISCHARGE OF COMMITTEE.—

(1) If the committee to which a recission bill or impoundment resolution has been referred has not reported it at the end of 25 calendar days of continuous session of the Congress after its introduction, it is in order to move either to discharge the committee from further consideration of the bill or resolution or to discharge the committee from further consideration of any other recission bill with respect to the same special message or impoundment resolution with respect to the same proposed deferral, as the case may be, which has been referred to the committee.

(2) A motion to discharge may be made only by an individual favoring the bill or resolution, may be made only if supported by one-fifth of the

Members of the House involved (a quorum being present), and is highly privileged in the House and privileged in the Senate (except that it may not be made after the committee has reported a bill or resolution with respect to the same special message or the same proposed deferral, as the case may be); and debate thereon shall be limited to not more than 1 hour, the time to be divided in the House equally between those favoring and those opposing the bill or resolution, and to be divided in the Senate equally between, and controlled by, the majority leader and the minority leader or their designees. An amendment to the motion is not in order, and it is not in order to move to reconsider the vote by which the motion is agreed to or disagreed to.

(c) FLOOR CONSIDERATION IN THE HOUSE.—

(1) When the committee of the House of Representatives has reported, or has been discharged from further consideration of, a recission bill or impoundment resolution, it shall at any time thereafter be in order (even though a previous motion to the same effect has been disagreed to) to move to proceed to the consideration of the bill or resolution. The motion shall be highly privileged and not debatable. An amendment to the motion shall not be in order nor shall it be in order to move to reconsider the vote by which the motion is agreed to or disagreed to.

(2) Debate on a recission bill or impoundment resolution shall be limited to not more than 2 hours, which shall be divided equally between those favoring and those opposing the bill or resolution. A motion further to limit debate shall not be debatable. In the case of an impoundment resolution, no amendment to, or motion to recommit, the resolution shall be in order. It shall not be in order to move to reconsider the vote by which a recission bill or impoundment resolution is agreed to or disagreed to.

(3) Motions to postpone, made with respect to the consideration of a recission bill or impoundment resolution, and motions to proceed to the consideration of other business, shall be decided without debate.

(4) All appeals from the decisions of the Chair relating to the application of the Rules of the House of Representatives to the procedure relating to any recission bill or impoundment resolution shall be decided without debate.

(5) Except to the extent specifically provided in the preceding provisions of this subsection, consideration of any recission bill or impoundment resolution and amendments thereto (or any conference report thereon) shall be governed by the Rules of the House of Representatives applicable to other bills and resolutions, amendments, and conference reports in similar circumstances.

(d) FLOOR CONSIDERATION IN THE SENATE.—

(1) Debate in the Senate on any recission bill or impoundment resolution, and all amendments thereto (in the case of a recission bill) and debatable motions and appeals in connection therewith, shall be limited to not more than 10 hours. The time shall be equally divided between, and controlled by, the majority leader and the minority leader or their designees.

(2) Debate in the Senate on any amendment to a recission bill shall be limited to 2 hours, to be equally divided between, and controlled by, the mover and the manager of the bill. Debate on any amendment to an amendment, to such a bill, and debate on any debatable motion or appeal in connection with such a bill or an impoundment resolution shall be limited to 1 hour, to be equally divided between, and controlled by, the mover and the manager of the bill or resolution, except that in the event the manager of the bill or resolution is in favor of any such amendment, motion, or appeal, the time in opposition thereto, shall be controlled by the minority leader or his designee. No amendment that is not germane to the provisions of a recission bill shall be received. Such leaders, or either of them, may, from the time under their control on the passage of a recission bill or impoundment resolution, allot additional time to any Senator during the consideration of any amendment debatable motion, or appeal.

(3) A motion to further limit debate is not debatable. In the case of a recission bill, a motion to recommit (except a motion to recommit with instructions to report back within a specified number of days, not to exceed 3, not counting any day on which the Senate is not in session) is not in order. Debate on any such motion to recommit shall be limited to one hour, to be equally divided between, and controlled by, the mover and the manager of the concurrent resolution. In the case of an impoundment resolution, no amendment or motion to recommit is in order.

(4) The conference report on any recission bill shall be in order in the Senate at any time after the third day (excluding Saturdays, Sundays, and legal holidays) following the day on which such a conference report is reported and is available to Members of the Senate. A motion to proceed to the consideration of the conference report may be made even though a previous motion to the same effect has been disagreed to.

(5) During the consideration in the Senate of the conference report on any recission bill, debate shall be limited to 2 hours, to be equally divided between, and controlled by, the majority leader and minority leader or their designees. Debate on any debatable motion or appeal related to the conference report shall be limited to 30 minutes, to be equally divided between, and controlled by, the mover and the manager of the conference report.

(6) Should the conference report be defeated, debate on any request for a new conference and the appointment of conferees shall be limited to one hour, to be equally divided between, and controlled by, the manager of the conference report and the minority leader or his designee, and should any motion be made to instruct the conferees before the conferees are named, debate on such motion shall be limited to 30 minutes, to be equally divided between, and controlled by, the mover and the manager of the conference report. Debate on any amendment to any such instructions shall be limited to 20 minutes, to be equally divided between, and controlled by, the mover and the manager of the conference report. In all cases when the manager of the conference report is in favor of any motion, appeal, or

amendment, the time in opposition shall be under the control of the minority leader or his designee.

(7) In any case in which there are amendments in disagreement, time on each amendment shall be limited to 30 minutes, to be equally divided between, and controlled by, the manager of the conference report and the minority leader or his designee. No amendment that is not germane to the provisions of such amendments shall be received.

And the Senate agree to the same.

That the House recede from its disagreement to the amendment of the Senate to the title of the bill and agree to the same with an amendment as follows:

In lieu of the amendment of the Senate, amend the title to read as follows: "An Act to establish a new congressional budget process; to establish Committees on the Budget in each House; to establish a Congressional Budget Office; to establish a procedure providing congressional control over the impoundment of funds by the executive branch; and for other purposes."

And the Senate agree to the same.

Sam J. Ervin, Jr.,
Edmund S. Muskie,
Abraham Ribicoff,
Lee Metcalf,
Howard W. Cannon,
Claiborne Pell,
Robert C. Byrd,
James B. Allen
C.H. Percy,
W.V. Roth, Jr.,
Bill Brock,
M.W. Cook,
Hugh Scott,
Robert P. Griffin,
Managers on the Part of the Senate.

Richard Bolling,
Bernie Sisk,
John Young,
Gillis W. Long,
Dave Martin,
Delbert Latta,
Del Clawson,
Managers on the Part of the House

SENATE WATERGATE REPORT

July 12, 1974

Eighteen months after it began the most intensive investigation into presidential campaign corruption in American history, the Senate Select Committee on Presidential Campaign Activities issued its final report. The scene in the Senate caucus room July 12 when the 2,217-page document was handed out was almost anticlimactic, because most of the committee's preliminary findings had been leaked to the press over the preceding months. Yet the impact of the three volumes was significant. The report laid out all together, for the first time, the details of the comprehensive scandals lumped under the umbrella of Watergate. (See also House Judiciary Committee Report, p. 713-763.) *It started with the background of the Watergate break-in—Tom Charles Huston's intelligence plan, the "enemies" list and the White House "plumbers" unit—and moved on to the coverup, the campaign practices of the Committee for the Reelection of the President, the Nixon administration's "responsiveness program," the financing of the 1972 presidential campaign and the Hughes-Rebozo investigation. The report concluded with recommendations by the committee designed to forestall future abuses of power and campaign financing.* (Excerpts below, p. 606.)

The findings, adopted unanimously by the seven members of the select committee, were couched in laconic prose, devoid of almost any indignation or emotion, and they scrupulously avoided assessing whether President Nixon was implicated in the Watergate coverup. The committee said it purposely refrained from making any judgments because of the House Judiciary Committee's impeachment inquiry and the Watergate-related trials either scheduled or already in progress. The report, however, in-

cluded "general observations based on the evidence." "The Watergate affair," it said, "reflects an alarming indifference displayed by some in high places to concepts of morality and public responsibility and trust. Indeed, the conduct of many Watergate participants seems grounded on the belief that the ends justified the means, that the laws could be flouted to maintain the present administration in office." The report exonerated the chairmen of the Republican and Democratic National Committees in 1972—Republican Sen. Robert Dole (Kan.) and Democrat Lawrence F. O'Brien—of any involvement in the scandal. But Sen. Sam J. Ervin Jr. (D N.C.), the committee chairman, left little doubt about the committee's underlying conclusions. During a press conference at which the report was released, Ervin was asked if the deletion of analysis had weakened the report. "There are two ways to indicate a horse," Ervin replied. "One is to draw a picture that is a great likeness. And the other is to draw a picture that is a great likeness and write under it, 'This is a horse.' We just drew the picture."

The committee was created by the Senate by a vote of 77-0 on Feb. 7, 1973. (See Historic Documents 1973, p. 549-556.) The resolution establishing the committee gave it full investigative powers and wide latitude to examine the 1972 presidential election, the Watergate break-in and coverup and any other matters found to be relevant to those subjects. The committee's high point came in the spring and summer of 1973, when it heard testimony from 62 witnesses in three months of public sessions. Those sessions, televised nationally, provided the first detailed public account of how the Watergate break-in and subsequent coverup were conceived and conducted. (See Historic Documents 1973, p. 659-679; 697-701.)

Break-In and Coverup

The report recounted the familiar story of the break-in at the Democratic national headquarters in the Watergate office building on June 17, 1972, presenting the break-in as an outgrowth of White House domestic intelligence activities that had started two years earlier. "The Watergate break-in cannot be understood unless viewed in the context of similar White House activities," the report said. "The evidence presented...shows that, from the early days of the present administration, the power of the President was viewed by some in the White House as almost without limit. Especially when national or internal security was invoked, even criminal laws were considered subordinate to presidential decision or strategy."

The Senate committee considered the Committee for the Re-election of the President (CRP) to be the creature of the White House, especially of Nixon's closest aides. "The evidence accumulated by the Select Committee demonstrates that CRP was a White House product, answerable to top White House leadership. It appears that H. R. Haldeman, the President's Chief of Staff, was principally responsible for organizing CRP, and John Mitchell (the former attorney general) has stated that Haldeman was the moving force," the report said.

The story of the "Gemstone" bugging plan was brought out at the committee's hearings in 1973, as were the beginning and the unraveling of the coverup of the Watergate burglary. Acknowledging the committee's role in breaking the silence, the report noted, "On May 17 the committee opened its public hearings into the Watergate burglary and its aftermath. By August 7, 1973, when the first phase of hearings ended, the Gemstone plan, the break-in, the details of the coverup and much more had been revealed." The report conceded that the committee's hearings had failed to establish conclusively who had approved the electronic surveillance of the Democratic National Committee's headquarters. But it noted that the initial hearings provided the first public forum for accusations that former Attorney General John N. Mitchell, while director of Nixon's re-election committee, had "reluctantly" approved the operation, possibly with the knowledge of higher-ups in the Nixon administration.

Campaign Practices

Political intelligence-gathering played an important part in the Nixon re-election drive, along with the use of federal agencies to harass Nixon's opponents, the select committee found. The report focused on those activities, which, it said, began almost 3½ years before the 1972 presidential election. "The campaign to re-elect President Nixon in 1972 was expensive, intense and long," the report said. "It began in late March 1969, soon after the President's inauguration, when John Ehrlichman, Counsel to the President, hired Jack Caulfield to gather political intelligence and derogatory information on individuals considered to be unfriendly to the new administration." The investigations were carried out by Anthony T. Ulasewicz, a former New York City policeman who had been hired by Caulfield and Ehrlichman. Ulasewicz was paid secretly by Herbert W. Kalmbach, Nixon's personal attorney, from an unused reserve of 1968 Nixon campaign funds.

The committee said the White House political activities raised serious questions about campaign practices in a free society. "The 1972 presidential campaign was replete with abuses of positions, power, and prerogatives, particularly by White House personnel....A corollary to the abuse of presidential incumbency for political gain is the considerable extent to which objectionable campaign practices were conceived, encouraged, and controlled by high-level presidential aides. "Another important theme," the report added, "is the misuse of large amounts of money, especially difficult-to-trace cash that was held in secret places in the White House and elsewhere."

As part of the administration's "attack strategy" aimed at putting Democrats on the defensive, White House officials, according to the report, used the Internal Revenue Service (IRS), the FBI and the Secret Service to obtain sensitive or derogatory information about their opponents.

The report called the IRS "a preferred target of the White House staff in its attempts to politicize independent agencies.... The Political Enemies project, White House efforts to have the IRS focus on left wing organizations, White House efforts to get IRS information for political purposes, and the White House concern with tax exemptions given to liberal foundations all attest to the serious efforts made by the White House to use an independent agency for political purposes." The FBI was used by administration aides such as former White House Counsel John W. Dean III as a source of information that they could "leak" to the press to smear political opponents, the committee found. It was also used by the White House, according to the report, to investigate alleged administration critics such as CBS news correspondent Daniel Schorr.

While the report did not find anything "improper in itself" in the White House strategy of trying to undercut Sen. Edmund S. Muskie (Maine) in the Democratic presidential primaries and to divide the Democratic Party, it charged that that strategy ultimately led to the dirty tricks carried on by the Committee for the Re-election of the President. "The absence of primary opponents for the President allowed his political strategists to target their efforts on the Democrats," it said. The abundance of money in the CRP allowed the political operatives to set up a concerted effort to infiltrate and interfere with the Democratic primaries. "The result," the committee found, "was a campaign to re-elect President Nixon that was filled with illegal, improper, and unethical activity...."

Donald H. Segretti conducted dirty-tricks operations in the Florida presidential primary, and the re-election committee was behind vote-siphoning operations in the Democratic primaries in Illinois and New Hampshire. The Senate committee uncovered improper campaign activities directed against the Nixon re-election drive. But the report said that "except for a few isolated examples..., there is presently no evidence indicating that these improper activities were directly or indirectly related to the campaign of any Democratic candidate."

'Incumbency-Responsiveness Program'

Beginning in the spring of 1971, top White House officials began drawing up plans to use federal agencies to bolster the President's re-election campaign, the report charged. "Documents obtained by the committee indicate that this effort—which had as its main vehicle a White House devised plan known as the Responsiveness Program—was an organized endeavor 'to politicize' the executive branch to ensure that the administration remained in power." The program, the report said, included "plans to redirect federal monies to specific administration supporters and to target groups and geographic areas to benefit the campaign. It entailed instructions to shape legal and regulatory action to enhance campaign goals. It comprised plans to utilize government employment procedures for election benefits." The committee was especially critical of the use of federal funds for Spanish-

speaking groups and the Federation of Experienced Americans, a pro-Nixon organization of elderly persons, calling the grants "flagrant abuses of proper governmental procedures."

"In fact," the report continued, "a question exists whether the planning and implementation of the Responsiveness plan rises to the level of a conspiracy to interfere with the lawful functioning of government, conduct prosecutable under 18 U.S.C. section 371 as a conspiracy to defraud the United States, as that term has been interpreted by the Supreme Court." The report noted the argument that the administration's responsiveness program was nothing more than politics as usual, as practiced by earlier administrations. But the committee dismissed that argument, saying that "to some degree, the contention that other administrations have done the same thing misses the point. For...certain of the activities...not only appear to contravene the notion that our nation's citizens are entitled to equal treatment under the law, but also raise questions as to the applicability of specific federal civil and criminal statutes. "It is also relevant," the report added, "that the major documents promulgating Responsiveness plans were classified 'Confidential,' 'Extremely Confidential' and/or 'Eyes Only' and noted that secrecy in the implementation of the proposal was of paramount necessity in order to avoid adverse publicity."

Campaign Financing

The Senate committee devoted one 838-page volume to the financing of the 1972 presidential campaign. The report focused primarily on the Nixon re-election drive. It also examined contributions to former New York Mayor John V. Lindsay's short-lived campaign for the Democratic nomination and the campaigns of Sen. Hubert H. Humphrey (D Minn.) and Rep. Wilbur D. Mills (D Ark.), and on Democratic nominee George McGovern's settling of campaign bills after his defeat. Investigators found evidence that McGovern was settling bills with creditors at 50 per cent face value—while making substantial transfers to his 1974 senatorial campaign. The investigators learned that Lindsay had accepted a $10,000 cash contribution from a group of contractors who later won a $1.7-million New York City asphalt contract. And the investigators charged that the primary election campaigns of Humphrey and Mills had received thousands of dollars in illegal corporate contributions.

The Nixon presidential campaign, according to the report, received illegal contributions from at least 13 corporations. The contributions totaled $780,000 in corporate funds, the report stated. "While there is no evidence that any fund-raiser for President Nixon directly solicited a corporate contribution," the committee said, "there is evidence that a number of them either were indifferent to the source of the money or, at the very least, made no effort whatsoever to see to it that the source of the funds was private rather than corporate. In any event, there is no evidence that any *fund-raiser who was involved in these contributions sought or obtained assurances that the contribution was legal at the time it was made."*

The committee's investigators explored the sources of money for the corporate contributions. The largest source was foreign subsidiaries, but corporate expense accounts and corporate bonuses to reimburse executives for their contributions were also used, they found. Most of the contributions were given in untraceable cash to the Finance Committee to Re-elect the President, headed by former Commerce Secretary Maurice H. Stans. The corporate contributions were not disclosed until July 6, 1973, "—or 15 months after almost all of them were made," the report stated. The disclosure was forced by a lawsuit by Common Cause, the so-called citizens' lobby, to compel disclosure of contributions to the Finance Committee to Re-elect the President made before April 7, 1972 (the date the 1971 Federal Election Campaign Act became effective, requiring disclosure of contributions).

The report was a primer of questionable contribution practices. It detailed how $1.8-million was collected in contributions from ambassadors appointed by Nixon, and the apparent relationship between campaign contributions and ambassadorial appointments. It also examined the role of Herbert W. Kalmbach, the President's personal attorney, as a chief Nixon fund-raiser. Kalmbach began raising money for the 1972 campaign in late 1970, and investigators gave an insight into some of his techniques. "Kalmbach sought out friends in an effort to obtain what amounted to commitments for campaign contributions," the committee reported. "Kalmbach states that he never asked for a commitment in so many words, but rather approached people, suggested an amount to them and asked if they would accept a 'goal figure.'... Kalmbach acknowledged that he told contributors that there were different classes of contributors, and he had different 'cut-off points,' for example at $25,000, $50,000 and $100,000. Kalmbach said that on occasion he referred to a '100 Club'—meaning contributors who gave $100,000. He indicated that he told contributors that there were a lot of people in the $25,000 class, and if one wanted to be known as a major contributor, he should give more."

One of the major areas of the committee's investigation was the $2-million pledge to the Nixon re-election campaign in 1971 from the Associated Milk Producers Inc., a dairy cooperative, at the time it was seeking an increase in milk price supports. (White House Paper on Milk Supports, see p. 3-21.) White House aides and dairy industry representatives denied there was a quid pro quo of dairy contributions in exchange for the milk price increase, and the report noted that "much of what the President says is supported by surrounding events: the dairy lobby had successfully gathered the support of about a quarter of each House in support of bills to raise the support level and at least some dairy leaders had considered boycotting further Republican fundraising efforts because of the administration's position on price supports." But investigators found strong *links between Nixon's decision on milk price supports and dairy industry political influence. "The crux of the committee's investigation was...not whether it was the correct decision but whether the President made the decision for the 'wrong' reason," the report said.*

After reviewing the dealings between Nixon aides and dairy industry officials on the eve of the price support decision, the report concluded, "Whatever the legal circumstances of the 1971 price support increase and these and other matters, the fact is that the dual role played by many Nixon officials of both policymaker and fundraiser gave, at the very least, the appearance of impropriety and provided circumstances that were ripe for abuse. Whether or not these two roles were directly tied, they appeared to be linked, and this had a significant impact on the approach taken by the dairymen."

Investigators also broke new ground in their examination of a $100,000 campaign contribution by billionaire Howard R. Hughes to Charles G. Rebozo, Nixon's close friend, and Rebozo's expenditures of Hughes' money for improvements to Nixon's property in Key Biscayne, Florida.

Personal Views of Senators

Six of the seven committee members presented their personal views on the Watergate investigation at the end of the report. Only Sen. Herman E. Talmadge (D Ga.) did not. In a statement replete with biblical and classical references, Chairman Ervin called Watergate "a conglomerate of various illegal and unethical activities in which various officers and employees of the Nixon re-election committees and various White House aides of President Nixon participated...." He accused them of trying to "destroy insofar as the presidential election of 1972 was concerned the integrity of the process by which the President of the United States is nominated and elected" and to "hide...the identities and wrongdoing" of Nixon campaign and White House officials. Trying to explain why Watergate occurred, Ervin attributed it to "a lust for political power." The President's men "apparently believed that the President is above the Constitution, and has the autocratic power to suspend its provisions if he decides in his own unreviewable judgment that his action in so doing promotes his own political interests or the welfare of the nation. They resorted to evil means to promote what they conceived to be a good end."

Sen. Howard H. Baker Jr. (R Tenn.), committee vice chairman, had issued his report July 2 detailing the role of the Central Intelligence Agency in the Watergate scandal. That was not included in the Watergate committee's final report. In his own Watergate statement, Sen. Lowell P. Weicker Jr. (R Conn.) charged that "every major substantive part of the Constitution was violated, abused or undermined during the Watergate period." The only committee member to deal directly with what the investigation found about Nixon's role in the scandal was Sen. Edward J.

Gurney (R Fla.), the President's staunchest defender on the committee. "In my opinion," he wrote, "there has been no proof gathered by the committee to indicate that the President of the United States participated in or approved of the planning or had advance knowledge of the break-in. The testimony and documents presented to the committee also clearly show that there was a conspiracy to cover-up the Watergate break-in and that certain persons at the White House were involved in that conspiracy. In my opinion, the evidence gathered...does not indicate that the President had knowledge of the coverup until March 1973." Senators Daniel K. Inouye (D Hawaii) and Joseph M. Montoya (D N.M.) called for the public financing of federal elections in their joint statement.

Excerpts from the recommendations of the Senate Watergate Committee's report, July 12, 1974:

Recommendations

Watergate Break-In and Cover-Up

I

The Committee recommends that Congress enact legislation to establish a permanent office of public attorney which would have jurisdiction to prosecute criminal cases in which there is a real or apparent conflict of interest within the executive branch. The public attorney would also have jurisdiction to inquire into (with power to gain access to executive records) the status and progress of complaints and criminal charges concerning matters pending in or involving the conduct of federal departments and regulatory agencies. The public attorney would be appointed for a fixed term (e.g., five years), be subject to Senate confirmation and be chosen by members of the judicial branch to ensure his independence from executive control or influence.

In each of the nation's two major scandals during the past half century, Teapot Dome and Watergate, the appointment of a special prosecutor was essential to preserve the integrity of the criminal justice system and public confidence in the rule of law. In both situations, the office was created after serious abuses had occurred....

It is thus essential that an independent public attorney's office be created to investigate and prosecute where conflicts of interest in the executive branch exist. This office should be given power to inquire fully into corruption in the executive branch and have access to all records relating to such corruption. The operations of the current special prosecution force demonstrate the effective role such an entity can play.

The preventative role this office could fulfill must be emphasized. Permanent status for this office could help ensure responsible action by executive branch officials who have primary responsibility to administer and enforce the law. Indeed, it is reasonable to speculate that the existence of a public attorney's office might have served as a deterrent against some of the wrongful acts that comprise the Watergate scandal. Because of this preventive role, it is unwise to wait until another national crisis to re-institute the office of special prosecutor. It is far better to create a permanent institution now than to consider its wisdom at some future time when emotions may be high and unknown political factors at play.

The public attorney we recommended would not be only a "special prosecutor" but an ombudsman having power to inquire into the administration of justice in the executive branch. With the power of access to executive records, he could appropriately respond to complaints from the public, the Congress, the Courts and other public and private institutions. If he became aware of misconduct in the executive branch, he could assume the role of special prosecutor. The public attorney should also be required to make periodic reports to Congress on the affairs of his office and the need for new legislation within his jurisdiction, a function that should be of great assistance to the relevant Congressional oversight committees.

The Attorney General should find such an office advantageous in cases involving charges against Administration officials or persons otherwise close to high executive officers, particularly where a proper exercise of discretion not to prosecute would give rise to public suspicion of cover-up. Such cases could be referred by the Attorney General to the public attorney. The public attorney would also have jurisdiction to prosecute all criminal cases referred to it by the Federal Elections Commission, which is elsewhere recommended in this report.

It is not anticipated that there would be substantial jurisdictional disputes between the Justice Department and the public attorney. The statute establishing the public attorney should grant him discretionary jurisdiction in any situation where there is a reasonable basis to conclude that a conflict of interest exists. He should have exclusive jurisdiction over criminal cases referred to him by the Federal Elections Commission. As to cases where a jurisdictional dispute cannot be resolved, provision should be made for special judicial determination on an expedited basis. Deciding such jurisdictional disputes is well within the competence of the courts for the question would primarily be one of statutory interpretation....

The present immunity statute would have to be amended to allow the independent prosecutor to grant use immunity without the consent of the Attorney General. The procedure by which the public attorney obtains immunity should be made similar to that applicable to Congressional requests for immunity. The Attorney General would be informed of an immunity request, but he could only delay the immunity, not prevent it. Similarly, the Attorney General would inform the public attorney of his immunity decisions; the public attorney would have the power to delay, not prevent, immunity.

To guarantee true independence from the executive branch, the public attorney should be appointed for a fixed term.... He should be removable only by the appointing authority...for gross improprieties. Because it is highly important that the special prosecutor act solely in the interest of justice and not for personal benefit, he should be ineligible for appointment or election to federal office for a period of two years after his term expires or he resigns or is removed.

Crucial to the independence of the public attorney is the appointing authority. If the appointing authority is vested in the President or the Attorney General (who is responsible to the President), the appearance of political influence would remain even if the public attorney has such tenure. The argument in favor of Presidential appointment is that criminal prosecution is an executive function and there is a presumption of regularity respecting the exercise of Presidential power that should not be discarded because of the unique abuses of Watergate. But Watergate at least teaches that the abuse of power must be anticipated....

...the Congress should vest the appointment power as follows: the Chief Justice should be given the power and duty to select three retired circuit court judges who, in turn, would appoint the public attorney. After the Chief Justice makes the initial appointment of the three circuit court judges, the Chief Justice's responsibilities would be ended; the three retired circuit court judges—who would not sit on any cases either at trial or in an appellate capacity in which the public attorney's office was involved—would make the actual appointment, which would be subject to confirmation by the Senate.... At the end of the five-year period, the Chief Justice would appoint (or reappoint) three retired circuit judges and they, in turn, would choose a new public attorney, or reappoint the outgoing public attorney for one additional term only....

II

The Committee recommends that, in connection with its revision of the federal criminal code, Congress should treat as a separate federal offense, with separate penalties, any felony defined in the code (except those felonies that specifically relate to federal elections) that is committed with the purpose of interfering with or affecting the outcome of a federal election or nominating process.

The purpose of this proposal is primarily to establish as a separate federal crime the commission of certain traditional common law offenses such as burglary and larceny where these crimes are committed with the intent of interfering with or affecting a federal election or nominating process....

Adoption of the above proposal would not add redundancy to the criminal law. Rather, it would allow the prosecution of crimes in which there is a federal interest in the federal courts....

III

The Committee recommends that Congress enact legislation making it unlawful for any employee in the Executive Office of the President, or assigned to the White House, directly or indirectly to authorize or engage in any investigative or intelligence gathering activity concerning national or domestic security not authorized by Congress.

The evidence received concerning the establishment, by direction of the President, of a special investigative unit in the White House (the Plumbers) and the operations of the Plumbers illustrates the danger to individual rights presented by such a secret investigative activity....

IV

The committee recommends that the appropriate Congressional oversight committees should more closely supervise the operations and internal regulations of the intelligence and law enforcement "community." In particular, these committees should continually examine the relations between federal law enforcement and intelligence agencies and the White House, and promptly determine if any revision of law is necessary relating to the jurisdiction or activities of these agencies.

From its beginning, the Central Intelligence Agency has been prohibited from performing police and internal security functions within the United States....

Notwithstanding this clear and long-standing prohibition, the select committee found that the White House sought and achieved CIA aid for the Plumbers and unsuccessfully sought to involve the CIA in the Watergate cover-up....

As for law enforcement agencies, testimony of the former acting director of the Federal Bureau of Investigation, Patrick Gray, as well as evidence received by the Committee of efforts by the White House to interfere with the IRS, indicate that similar oversight functions should be strengthened with regard to the FBI, and IRS and similar agencies.

V

The Committee recommends that Congress amend:

(1) The false declaration prohibition of 18 U.S.C. 1623 to make it equally applicable to Congressional proceedings under oath.

(2) Section 1621 of Title 18 to provide that, once the oath has been properly administered by a Congressman in a public or private Congressional hearing, it is not a defense to a perjury charge that subsequently a quorum was absent or no Congressman was present when the alleged perjurious statement was made....

VI

The Committee recommends that the Congress refrain from adopting proposed revisions of Title 18 which would unjustifiably broaden the present defenses to criminal charges of official mistake of law and execution of public duty. The Committee supports the predominant rule of law adopted in the American Law Institute's model penal code, that any reliance on a mistake of law or superior orders must be objectively reasonable to constitute a valid defense....

VII

The Committee recommends that the appropriate committees of Congress study and reconsider Title III of the Omnibus Crime and Safe Streets Act of 1968 for the purpose of determining whether the electronic surveillance provisions contained in that act require revision or amendment.

The Committee's investigation has revealed incidents of unlawful violations of privacy through electronic surveillance, some...directly or indirectly under federal branch auspices in whose trust Congress placed the protection of privacy under the provisions of Title III of the Safe Streets Act of 1968. The restrictions contained in that act have proved to be inadequate to protect individuals against unjustified invasions of privacy.

Campaign Practices

I

The Committee recommends that Congress enact criminal legislation to prohibit anyone from obtaining employment, voluntary or paid, in a campaign of an individual seeking nomination or election to any federal office by false pretenses, misrepresentations or other fraudulent means for the purpose of interfering with, spying on, or obstructing any campaign activities of such candidate. Furthermore, such legislation should make it unlawful for anyone to direct, instruct, or pay anyone to join any such campaign by such means or for such purposes as are outlined above.

New legislation is needed to prevent the infiltration of Presidential and federal campaigns. The activities of Donald Segretti, Robert Benz, Michael McMinoway, Elmer Wyatt, Tom Gregory and others are abundant documentation of the numerous infiltration efforts in the 1972 campaign.

Dangers of this infiltration range from the confusion and suspicion resulting from leaked information to the opponents or newspapers to more systematic disruption and sabotage of the opposition campaign....

II

The Committee recommends that Congress enact legislation to make it unlawful to request or knowingly disburse or make available campaign funds for the purpose of promoting or financing violations of federal election laws.

This recommendation is an effort to deter individuals with control over campaign funds from blindly and automatically providing money for campaign activities whenever they are so instructed. For example, Herb Kalmbach, the custodian of left-over 1968 campaign funds, funded Tony Ulasewicz's activities for nearly three years as well as the travels and illegal activities of Donald Segretti.

III

The Committee recommends that Congress enact new legislation which prohibits the theft, unauthorized copying, or the taking by false pretenses of campaign materials, documents, or papers not available for public dissemination belonging to or in the custody of a candidate for federal office or his aides.

IV

The Committee recommends that Congress should make it unlawful for any individual to fraudulently misrepresent by telephone or in person that he is representing a candidate for federal office for the purpose of interfering with the election.

Responsiveness Program

I

Prosecution for violations of the existing criminal statutes [relating to impairment of government agency functions], insofar as they relate to federal elections, and the criminal statutory enactments recommended below should be entrusted to the public attorney....

II

The Federal Elections Commission...should be given authority to investigate and restrain violations of federal civil and criminal statutes insofar as those violations relate to federal elections. The commission should also be empowered to refer evidence of such violations to the public attorney....

III

The Committee recommends that Congress enact legislation making it a felony to obstruct, impair or pervert a government function, or attempt to obstruct, impair or pervert a government function, by defrauding the government in any manner....

...there is currently in the federal code a statute (18 U.S.C. 371) making it unlawful to conspire to defraud the United States. The Supreme Court has ruled that a conspiracy to interfere with the lawful functioning of government is prosecutable under this provision. The Committee's recommendation...would make illegal *individual* conduct that fraudulently interferes with lawful government function....

IV

The Committee recommends that Congress preserve as part of the United States Code 18 U.S.C. 595, which makes it illegal for a government official connected with the awarding of federal grants and loans to use his official authority to affect a federal election, but recommends that this offense be upgraded to a felony. The committee recommends that 18 U.S.C. 600, which makes illegal the promise of government benefit for political support, be upgraded to a felony.

The Committee also recommends that the scope of Section 595 be expanded to include misuse of official authority in connection with the dispensing of other federal funds such as government contracts payments and federal subsidies....

V

The Committee recommends that Congress preserve in the United States Code 18 U.S.C. 611, which proscribes political contributions by or solicitations to government contractors, and 18 U.S.C. 602, which makes illegal political solicitations by persons receiving federal compensation for services rendered to other such persons—but appropriately amend these provisions to make illegal contributions by or knowing solicitations to (a) any person receiving, during the calendar year a contribution or solicitation is made, other federal monies (e.g. grants, loans, subsidies) in excess of $5,000, and (b) the principals or dominant shareholders of corporations receiving, during the calendar year a contribution or solicitation is made,...federal funding designed to benefit disadvantaged and minority groups....

The evidence before the Committee indicates that, respecting minority groups, plans were laid to solicit recipients of grants or loans. Also, there appear to have been particular pressures to contribute on minority businessmen whose corporations were quite dependent on government business....

The current major bills to revise the criminal code before Congress...generally weaken the proscriptions in Sections 602 and 611 and lessen the penalties for their violation. In view of the abuses discovered, a weakening of the law in this area seems unwise.

VI

The Committee recommends that Congress amend the Hatch Act to place all Justice Department officials—including the Attorney General—under its purview.

The evidence the Select Committee has gathered indicated that various federal officials took an active part in the President's 1972 re-election campaign. Some of the officials apparently involved were covered by the Hatch Act, which prohibits certain federal employees from engaging in political campaigns and political management, but some were not. Some of the federal officials involved in political activities were employed at the Department of Justice....

VII

The Committee recommends that the appropriate committees of both houses of Congress, in accordance with their constitutional responsibilities, maintain a vigilant oversight of the operations of the executive branch in order to prevent abuses of governmental processes to promote success in a federal election....

Campaign Financing

In making its legislative recommendations the Select Committee has made a number of proposals that it believes will reduce the likelihood of future abuses. In so doing, it wishes to emphasize two points. First, full disclosure of contributions and expenditures as well as of governmental action affecting contributors is the critical minimum of campaign financing reform. But for even this minimum to be an effective tool, the data must be accessible and reviewed by those with an interest in the government process, including candidates and the press. Second, the temptation to over-regulate must be viewed in terms that such action would have on the willingness of citizens to participate voluntarily in the electoral process....

I

The Committee recommends that the Congress enact legislation to establish an independent, nonpartisan Federal Elections Commission which would replace the present tripartite administration of the clerk of the House, secretary of the Senate, and GAO Office of Federal Elections and would have certain enforcement powers. With...exceptions...the Committee adopts sections 308 and 309 of S 3044 which would create a Federal Elections Commission and vest in it certain enumerated powers.

Under the Senate bill, the commission would be composed of seven members appointed by the President with the advice and consent of the Senate who would serve seven-year terms. Not more than four of the commissioners would be members of the same political party....

II

The Committee recommends enactment of a statute prohibiting cash contributions and expenditures in excess of $100 in connection with an election for nomination and election for federal office.

III

The Committee recommends enactment of a statute requiring each candidate for the office of President or Vice President to designate one political committee as his central campaign committee with one or more banks as his campaign depositories....

Laundering of funds is often accomplished by contributing and transferring funds from committee to committee so as to obscure the original source and make it impossible to trace the money to the intended beneficiary or use. The Select Committee believes that the requirements of a central campaign committee and a designated depository increase the traceability of campaign funds by putting the responsibility for collecting and reporting campaign financial information in a centralized place.

IV

The Committee recommends enactment of a statutory limitation on over-all campaign expenditures of Presidential candidates. The committee proposes a limit of expenditures of 12 cents times the voting age population during a general election....

The Select Committee further recommends a limitation on expenditures of Presidential candidates in primary elections...provided for in Section 504(a)(2)(a) of S 2044. This section provides for an expenditure limit of "two times the amount which a candidate for nomination for election to the office of Senator from that State may expend in that State in connection with his primary election campaign."...

V

The Committee recommends enactment of a statutory limitation of $3,-000 on political contributions by any individuals to the campaign of each Presidential candidate during the prenomination period and a separate $3,-000 limitation during the post-nomination period. A contribution to a Vice-Presidential candidate of a party would be considered, for purposes of the limitation, a contribution to that party's Presidential candidate.

A necessary corollary to a limit on contributions to Presidential candidates is a limitation on independent expenditures on behalf of a candidate without his authorization. Such expenditures, if unrestricted, could be used to avoid and thereby undermine any limitation on contributions.... On the other hand, there are serious constitutional arguments against an outright prohibition on independent campaign expenditures in view of the right of expression guaranteed by the First Amendment. A reasonable solution seems to be the adoption of a rule to the effect that if an individual acted on his own, and not at the suggestion or request of the candidate, he could expend a separate $1,000 on behalf of one or more candidates during the prenomination and general election periods and would have the responsibility for reporting expenditures aggregating over $100 on behalf of any candidate. Such independent expenditures on behalf of a candidate would not count toward the over-all expenditure limit of the candidate.

VI

The Committee recommends that the Internal Revenue Code be amended to provide a credit in a substantial amount of individual and joint federal income tax returns for any contribution made in a calendar year to a political party or any candidate seeking election to any public office, federal, state, or local.

The incentive which the committee suggests is a 100 per cent tax credit for contributions up to a certain level, for example, $25 for an individual return and $50 for a joint return.

VII

The Committee recommends against the adoption of any form of public financing in which tax monies are collected and allocated to political candidates by the federal government.... While recognizing the basis of support for the concept of public financing and the potential difficulty in adequately funding campaigns in the midst of strict limitations on the form and amount of contributions, the committee takes issue with the contention that public financing affords either an effective or appropriate solution. Thomas Jefferson believed "to compel a man to furnish contributions of money for the propagation of opinions which he disbelieves and abhors, is sinful and tyrannical."

The Committee's opposition is based like Jefferson's upon the fundamental need to protect the voluntary right of individual citizens to express themselves politically as guaranteed by the First Amendment. Furthermore, we find inherent dangers in authorizing the federal bureaucracy to fund and excessively regulate political campaigns....

VIII

The Committee recommends enactment of a statute prohibiting the solicitation or receipt of campaign contributions from foreign nationals.

Under present law...it is a felony to solicit, accept or receive a political contribution from a foreign principal or an agent of a foreign principal.... Since the term "principal" connotes the existence of an agency relationship, it is the [Justice] Department's view that a foreign national is a foreign principal...only if the principal has an agent within the United States....

Thus the present statute permits political contributions from individuals who neither reside in the United States nor have the right to vote in elections within the United States....

In addition to direct contributions by foreign nationals during 1972, hundreds of thousands of dollars were laundered through foreign banks and foreign companies....

The proposed statute would prohibit political contributions by foreign nationals whether or not they have agents within the United States....

IX

The Committee recommends that no government official whose appointment required confirmation by the Senate or who was on the payroll of the Executive Office of the President be permitted to participate in the solicitation or receipt of campaign contributions during his or her period of service and for a period of one year thereafter.

During the 1972 campaign there was a widespread transfer of key Administration officials from the White House and from departments and agencies to high positions in the campaign effort. In certain cases, these officials or their assistants went to the very persons over whom they previously wielded regulatory or other power to solicit campaign contributions. Particularly in view of the likelihood that many of these officials would return to the government, solicitation by them may well have had undesirable coercive aspects. While the entire practice of carving the campaign force out of the Administration on a temporary basis seems highly questionable, the committee recommends as a minimum step that high Administration officials who leave to enter the campaign be barred from engaging in fund-raising activities for a period of one year.

X

The Committee recommends that stringent limitations be imposed on the right of organizations to contribute to Presidential campaigns.

One of the major abuses investigated by the Select Committee was the apparent attempt on the part of several large dairy cooperatives to utilize their contribution potential of millions of dollars to influence Administration decisions. The power of associations and organizations...individuals, corporations or unions—to band together and pool their contributions has given rise to enormous contributions.... In the context of a Presidential race it appears that a limit of $6,000—the figure contained in S 3044—would tend to avoid the problem of undue influence by organizations while providing them an opportunity to participate in the political process....

XI

The Committee recommends that violations of the major provisions of the campaign financing law, such as participating in a corporate or union contribution in excess of the limit, and making a foreign contribution shall constitute a felony.

Rebozo-Hughes Investigation and Related Matters

I

Communications between the White House and the Internal Revenue Service should be more strictly regulated, specifically:

1. Any requests, direct or indirect, for information or action made to the IRS by anyone in the Executive Office of the President, up to and including the President, should be recorded by the persons making the request and by the IRS. Requests and responses by the IRS (i.e. whether information was provided), should be disclosed at least once a year to appropriate Congressional oversight committees.

2. On "sensitive case reports," which cover special cases, the IRS should be permitted to disclose to persons in the Executive Office of the President, up to and including the President, only the name of the person or group in the report and the general nature of the investigation.

3. All persons in the Executive Office of the President, up to and including the President, should be prohibited from receiving indirectly or directly any income tax return.

4. All requests for information or action and all IRS responses should be disclosed periodically to the appropriate Congressional oversight committees.

There were numerous efforts by the White House to use the IRS for political purposes between 1969 and 1972. Particularly striking examples, such as attempts to use the IRS to harass persons perceived as "enemies," have already been exposed and discussed at great length by the Select Committee and other groups. In addition, there was misuse of the IRS by the White House regarding the IRS investigations of Rebozo, the President's brothers, and people connected with the Hughes operation. Because of the close relationship of several of the parties to the President, questions of improper White House influence in this case are particularly acute....

II

Congress should enact legislation requiring full financial disclosure by the President and Vice President of the United States to the Government Accounting Office each year of all income, gifts and things of value that they or their spouses have received during the year or expenditures made for their personal benefit or the benefit of their spouses by other individuals.

Presently, legislation requires that Congressmen and Senators file statements of financial disclosure each year. Certainly, the head of the executive branch of the government should be held to no less a standard than the members of the legislature, and perhaps even held to a higher standard of disclosure because of the significance of his position....

Examples of items which should be disclosed include the following:

(a) Copies of tax returns, declarations, statements, or other documents which were made individually or jointly for the preceding year in compliance with the provisions of the Internal Revenue Code;

(b) The identity of each interest in real or personal property having a value of $10,000 or more which the President or Vice President or spouses owned at any time during the preceding year;

(c) The identity of each trust or other fiduciary relation in which the President or Vice President or spouses held a beneficial interest having a value of $10,000 or more, and the identity, if known, of each interest of the trust or other fiduciary relation in real or personal property in which he or she held a beneficial interest having a value of $10,000 or more at any time during the preceding year;

(d) The identity of each liability of $5,000 or more owned by the President or Vice President or by them jointly with their spouses, at any time during the preceding year; and

(e) The source and value of all gifts received by the President, Vice President, or spouses in the aggregate amount or value of $50 or more from any single source received during the preceding year.

III

Suggestion: State and local bar associations should conduct a study of the attorney-client privilege in light of the abuses of the privilege uncovered during the Select Committee's investigations....

In at least four instances...the lawyer-client privilege has been pleaded as part of an attempt to cover up illegal or questionable activities that had nothing to do with the rendering of legal advice:

(1) Mardian and Liddy in the Watergate cover-up;

(2) Dean and Segretti in the Watergate dirty-tricks cover-up;

(3) Kalmbach and Rebozo in the Hughes-Rebozo cover-up;

(4) Wakefield-Rebozo, also in the Hughes-Rebozo area....

The Courts

I

The Committee recommends that Congress enact legislation giving the United States District Court for the District of Columbia jurisdiction over suits to enforce Congressional subpoenas issued to members of the executive branch, including the President. This statute, which would apply to all subpoenas issued by Congressional bodies, would replace the special statute passed for and limited to the Select Committee that is now codified as 28 U.S.C. 1364. The statute should provide that a Congressional body has standing to sue in its own name and in the name of the United States and may employ counsel of its own choice in such a suit. The statute should provide that suits brought to enforce Congressional subpoenas must be handled on an expedited basis by the courts.

II

The Select Committee recommends that Congress give careful consideration to the bill now before the Senate (S 2567) that would establish a

Congressional Legal Service and thus give Congress a litigation arm that would allow it to protect its interest in court by its own counsel.

III

The Select Committee recommends that Congress amend 2 U.S.C. 190a-1(b) to allow a senatorial committee or its staff to take testimony and evidence in private session upon an express determination by the committee that the requirements of efficient and productive investigation so require and that the investigation would be materially harmed if a regimen of confidentiality were not imposed. The amended statute, however, should provide that testimony or evidence taken in confidence for these reasons should be released to the public as soon as the requirements of efficient investigation no longer demand confidentiality.

SUPREME COURT ON NIXON'S TAPES

July 24, 1974

It was a central irony of the Watergate scandal that the Supreme Court—to which President Nixon had carefully appointed four justices sympathetic to his own viewpoints—resoundingly rejected Nixon's claim of absolute privilege to withhold evidence from the Watergate prosecutor. The President's general need to preserve the confidentiality of his conversations was not strong enough to justify Nixon's withholding of evidence relevant to a criminal trial, the unanimous Court held July 24. Were he to do so, it "would cut deeply into the guarantee of due process of law and gravely impair the basic function of the courts.... Without access to specific facts, a criminal prosecution may be totally frustrated." With no dissent but without the participation of Justice William H. Rehnquist, one of Nixon's appointees, the Court affirmed the order of Federal Judge John J. Sirica directing Nixon to turn over to him the tapes of 64 White House conversations subpoenaed by Special Watergate Prosecutor Leon Jaworski for use as evidence in the Watergate coverup trial. (Watergate Coverup Indictments, see p. 157.) Sirica would listen to the tapes privately, excise the portions that were not useful as evidence and turn over to Jaworski those that were potentially relevant and admissible as evidence. (Released tapes, see p. 301-387, p. 673-682 and p. 991-1002.)

Since July 1973, when it came to light that presidential conversations had been secretly recorded (see Historic Documents 1973, p. 697-701), the White House tapes had become a focal point in the Watergate controversy. Debate over whether the conversations should have been recorded at all—especially without the knowledge of most of the participants—gave way to debate over whether the tapes could answer the ultimate question of the Watergate scandal: did President Nixon have foreknowledge of the Watergate break-in and did he participate in the Watergate coverup?

Nixon claimed immediately that the principle of executive privilege barred disclosure of the tapes. A subpoena for nine of the recordings, filed by Special Watergate Prosecutor Archibald Cox on July 23, 1973, resulted in three surprising actions: (1) a presidential order to Cox not to seek additional White House documents through the judicial system, (2) the firing of Cox, preceded by the resignation of two top Justice Department officials who refused to carry out Nixon's order to dismiss Cox, and eventually (3) the release of the nine tapes to the Watergate grand jury. (See Historic Documents 1973, p. 839-857; 859-880.)

Early in 1974, when the House Judiciary Committee launched its impeachment inquiry (see p. 137), various tapes were subpoenaed for evidence in that probe. Instead of the subpoenaed tape recordings, President Nixon submitted White House-edited transcripts of the tapes to the committee on April 30 and again claimed that executive privilege barred release of the tapes themselves. (See p. 287.) The House Judiciary Committee then informed Nixon in writing that the transcripts did not constitute compliance with its subpoena. But it was Special Watergate Prosecutor Jaworski's insistence on access to the tapes for use in the Watergate coverup trial that led to the Supreme Court's decision July 24.

Summary of Court's Opinion

Dealing first with several threshold questions, the court found that it could review the Sirica order even though Nixon had not officially refused to comply and had not been held in contempt. "Here...the traditional contempt avenue to immediate appeal is peculiarly inappropriate due to the unique setting in which the question arises. To require a President of the United States to place himself in the posture of disobeying an order of the court merely to trigger the procedural mechanism for review of the ruling would be unseemly and present an unnecessary occasion for constitutional confrontation between two branches of the government." Rejecting presidential counsel James D. St. Clair's contention that this was a dispute between two parts of the executive branch and therefore was not a matter for the courts to decide, the Court held that the special prosecutor had been delegated "unique authority and tenure" including the "explicit power to contest the invocation of executive privilege in the process of seeking evidence deemed relevant to the performance of his specially delegated duties."

Reaffirming its 1803 decision, Marbury v. Madison, establishing the power of the courts to review the actions of the other two branches, Chief Justice Burger wrote for the Court that "notwithstanding the deference each branch must accord to the others, the 'judicial power of the United States' vested in the federal courts by Article III, Section 1 of the Constitution can no more be shared with the Executive Branch than the Chief Executive, for example, can share with the Judiciary the veto power, or the Congress share with the Judiciary the power to override a presidential veto.

Any other conclusion would be contrary to the basic concept of separation of powers and the checks and balances....We therefore reaffirm that it is 'emphatically the province and the duty' of this Court 'to say what the law is' with respect to the claim of privilege presented in this case." No mention was made of the pending impeachment inquiry or St. Clair's argument that the Court's decision would interfere in that process.

"Neither the doctrine of separation of powers, nor the need for confidentiality of high-level communications, without more, can sustain an absolute, unqualified, presidential privilege of immunity from judicial process under all circumstances. The President's need for complete candor and objectivity from advisers calls for great deference from the courts. However when the privilege depends solely on the broad undifferentiated claim of public interest in the confidentiality of such conversations, a confrontation with other values arises. Absent a claim of need to protect military, diplomatic or sensitive national security secrets, we find it difficult to accept the argument that even the very important interest in confidentiality...is significantly diminished by production of such material for in camera inspection...

"To read the Article II powers of the President as providing an absolute privilege as against a subpoena essential to enforcement of criminal statutes on no more than a generalized claim of the public interest in confidentiality of nonmilitary and nondiplomatic discussions would upset the constitutional balance of 'a workable government' and gravely impair the role of the courts under Article III [of the Constitution]." There is a limited executive privilege with a constitutional base, wrote Burger: "A President and those who assist him must be free to explore alternatives in the process of shaping policies and making decisions and to do so in a way many would be unwilling to express except privately. These are the considerations justifying a presumptive privilege for presidential communications...fundamental to the operation of government and inextricably rooted in the separation of powers." To the extent that confidentiality relates to the President's ability to discharge his presidential powers effectively, that privilege has a constitutional basis, he wrote.

Rule Of Law Must Take Priority

"But," Burger continued, "this presumptive privilege must be considered in light of our historic commitment to the rule of law." The rights to a fair trial and to due process are guaranteed by the Constitution, he pointed out, and "it is the manifest duty of the Court to vindicate those guarantees and, to accomplish that, it is essential that all relevant and admissible evidence be produced. We cannot conclude that advisers will be moved to temper the candor of their remarks by the infrequent occasions of disclosure because of the possibility that such conversations will be called for in the context of a criminal prosecution," the Court held...."The President's broad interest in confidentiality of communications will not be

*vitiated by disclosure of a limited number of conversations preliminarily
shown to have some bearing on the pending criminal cases. We conclude
that when the ground for asserting privilege as to subpoenaed materials
sought for use in a criminal trial is based only on the generalized interest
in confidentiality, it cannot prevail over the fundamental demands of due
process of law in the fair administration of criminal justice. The
generalized assertion of privilege must yield to the demonstrated specific
need for evidence in a pending criminal trial."*

> *Full text of the Supreme Court's decision July 24, 1974, re-
> quiring President Nixon to produce certain tapes and
> documents relating to precisely identified conversations
> and meetings between the President and others (footnotes,
> pagination references, and citations not part of the text
> proper have been omitted); and the statement released by
> President Nixon, through his counsel James D. St. Clair,
> announcing his intended compliance:*

Nos. 73-1766 and 73-1834

United States, Petitioner,
73-1766 Richard M. Nixon, President
of the United States,
et al.

Richard M. Nixon, President
of the United States,
Petitioner,
73-1834 v.
United States.

*On Writs of Certiorari to
the United States Court
of Appeals for the Dis-
trict of Columbia Circuit
before judgment.*

[July 24, 1974]

MR. CHIEF JUSTICE BURGER delivered the opinion of the court.

These cases present for review the denial of a motion, filed on behalf of
the President of the United States, in the case of *United States v. Mitchell
et al.* to quash a third-party subpoena *duces tecum* issued by the United
States District Court for the District of Columbia, pursuant to Fed. Rule
Crim. Proc. 17 (c). The subpoena directed the President to produce certain
tape recordings and documents relating to his conversations with aides and
advisers. The court rejected the President's claims of absolute executive
privilege, of lack of jurisdiction, and of failure to satisfy the requirements
of Rule 17 (c). The President appealed to the Court of Appeals. We granted
the United States' petition for certiorari before judgment, and also the
President's responsive cross-petition for certiorari before judgment,
because of the public importance of the issues presented and the need for
their prompt resolution.

On March 1, 1974, a grand jury of the United States District Court for the
District of Columbia returned an indictment charging seven named in-
dividuals with various offenses, including conspiracy to defraud the United
States and to obstruct justice. Although he was not designated as such in

the indictment, the grand jury named the President, among others, as an unindicted coconspirator. On April 18, 1974, upon motion of the Special Prosecutor, a subpoena *duces tecum* was issued pursuant to Rule 17 (c) to the President by the United States District Court and made returnable on May 2, 1974. This subpoena required the production, in advance of the September 9 trial date, of certain tapes, memoranda, papers, transcripts, or other writings relating to certain precisely identified meetings between the President and others. The Special Prosecutor was able to fix the time, place and persons present at these discussions because the White House daily logs and appointment records had been delivered to him. On April 30, the President publicly released edited transcripts of 43 conversations; portions of 20 conversations subject to subpoena in the present case were included. On May 1, 1974, the President's counsel, filed a "special appearance" and a motion to quash the subpoena, under Rule 17 (c). This motion was accompanied by a formal claim of privilege. At a subsequent hearing, further motions to expunge the grand jury's action naming the President as an unindicted coconspirator and for protective orders against the disclosure of that information were filed or raised orally by counsel for the President.

On May 20, 1974, the District Court denied the motion to quash and the motions to expunge and for protective orders. It further ordered "the President or any subordinate officer, official or employee with custody or control of the documents or objects subpoenaed," to deliver to the District Court, on or before May 31, 1974, the originals of all subpoenaed items, as well as an index and analysis of those items, together with tape copies of those portions of the subpoenaed recordings for which transcripts had been released to the public by the President on April 30. The District Court rejected jurisdictional challenges based on a contention that the dispute was nonjusticiable because it was between the special prosecutor and the Chief Executive and hence "intra-executive" in character; it also rejected the contention that the judiciary was without authority to review an assertion of executive privilege by the President. The court's rejection of the first challenge was based on the authority and powers vested in the Special Prosecutor by the regulation promulgated by the Attorney General; the court concluded that a justiciable controversy was presented. The second challenge was held to be foreclosed by the decision in *Nixon* v. *Sirica*, (1973).

The District Court held that the judiciary, not the President, was the final arbiter of a claim of executive privilege. The court concluded that, under the circumstances of this case, the presumptive privilege was overcome by the Special Prosecutor's prima facie "demonstration of need sufficiently compelling to warrant judicial examination in chambers...." The court held, finally, that the Special Prosecutor had satisfied the requirements of Rule 17 (c). The District Court stayed its order pending appellate review on condition that review was sought before 4 p.m., May 24. The court further provided that matters filed under seal remain under seal when transmitted as part of the record.

On May 24, 1974, the President filed a timely notice of appeal from the District Court order, and the certified record from the District Court was docketed in the United States Court of Appeals for the District of Columbia Circuit. On the same day, the President also filed a petition for writ of mandamus in the Court of Appeals seeking review of the District Court order.

Later on May 24, the Special Prosecutor also filed, in this Court, a petition for a writ of certiorari before judgment. On May 31, the petition was granted with an expedited briefing schedule. On June 6, the President filed, under seal, a cross-petition for writ of certiorari before judgment. This cross-petition was granted June 15, 1974, and the case was set for argument on July 8, 1974.

I
JURISDICTION

The threshold question presented is whether the May 20, 1974, order of the District Court was an appealable order and whether this case was properly "in," 28 U.S.C. § 1254, the United States Court of Appeals when the petition for certiorari was filed in this court. Court of Appeals jurisdiction under 28 U.S.C. § 1291 encompasses only "final decisions of the district courts." Since the appeal was timely filed and all other procedural requirements were met, the petition is properly before this Court for consideration if the District Court order was final.

The finality requirement of 28 U.S.C. § 1291 embodies a strong congressional policy against piecemeal reviews, and against obstructing or impeding an ongoing judicial proceeding by interlocutory appeals. See, e.g., *Cobbledick* v. *United States*, (1940). This requirement ordinarily promotes judicial efficiency and hastens the ultimate termination of litigation. In applying this principle to an order denying a motion to quash and requiring the production of evidence pursuant to a subpoena duces tecum, it has been repeatedly held that the order is not final and hence not applicable. This court has

> "consistently held that the necessity for expedition in the administration of the criminal law justifies putting one who seeks to resist the production of desired information to a choice between compliance with a trial court's order to produce prior to any review of that order, and resistance to that order with the concomitant possibility of an adjudication of contempt if his claims are rejected on appeal."

The requirement of submitting to contempt, however, is not without exception and in some instances the purposes underlying the finality rule require a different result. For example, in *Perlman* v. *United States*, (1918), a subpoena had been directed to a third party requesting certain exhibits; the appellant, who owned the exhibits, sought to raise a claim of privilege. The Court held an order compelling production was appealable because it was unlikely that the third party would risk a contempt citation in order to allow immediate review of the appellant's claim of privilege. That case fell within the "limited class of cases where denial of immediate review would render impossible any review whatsoever of an individual's claims," *United States* v. *Ryan*.

Here too the traditional contempt avenue to immediate appeal is peculiarly inappropriate due to the unique setting in which the question arises. To require a President of the United States to place himself in the posture of disobeying an order of the court merely to trigger the procedural mechanism for review of the ruling would be unseemly, and present an unnecessary occasion for constitutional confrontation between two branches of the Government. Similarly, a federal judge should not be placed in the posture of issuing a citation to a President simply in order to invoke a review. The issue whether a President can be cited for contempt could itself engender protracted litigation, and would further delay both review on the merits of his claim of privilege and the ultimate termination of the underlying criminal action for which his evidence is sought. These considerations lead us to conclude that the order of the District Court was an appealable order. The appeal from that order was therefore properly "in" the Court of Appeals, and the case is now properly before this Court on the writ of certiorari before judgment.

II
JUSTICIABILITY

In the District Court, the President's counsel argued that the court lacked jurisdiction to issue the subpoena because the matter was an intrabranch dispute between a subordinate and superior officer of the Executive Branch and hence not subject to judicial resolution. That argument has been renewed in this Court with emphasis on the contention that the dispute does not present a "case" or "controversy" which can be adjudicated in the federal courts. The President's counsel argues that the federal courts should not intrude into areas committed to the other branches of Government. He views the present dispute as essentially a "jurisdictional" dispute within the Executive Branch which he analogizes to a dispute between two congressional committees. Since the Executive Branch has exclusive authority and absolute discretion to decide whether to prosecute a case, *Confiscation Cases*, (1869), *United States* v. *Cox*, (1965), it is contended that a President's decision is final in determining what evidence is to be used in a given criminal case. Although his counsel concedes the President has delegated certain specific powers to the Special Prosecutor, he has not "waived nor delegated to the Special Prosecutor the President's duty to claim privilege as to all materials...which fall within the President's inherent authority to refuse to disclose to any executive officer." Brief for the President 47. The Special Prosecutor's demand for the items therefore presents, in the view of the President's counsel, a political question under *Baker* v. *Carr*, (1962), since it involves a "textually demonstrable" grant of power under Art. II.

The mere assertion of a claim of an "intra-branch dispute," without more, has never operated to defeat federal jurisdiction; justiciability does not depend on such surface inquiry. In *United States* v. *ICC*, (1949), the Court observed, "courts must look behind names that symbolize the parties to determine whether a justiciable case or controversy is presented."

Our starting point is the nature of the proceeding for which the evidence is sought—here a pending criminal prosecution. It is a judicial proceeding in a federal court alleging violation of federal laws and is brought in the name of the United States as sovereign. *Berger* v. *United States* (1935). Under the authority of Art. II § 2, Congress has vested in the Attorney General the power to conduct the criminal litigation of the United States Government. It has also vested in him the power to appoint subordinate officers to assist him in the discharge of his duties. Acting pursuant to those statutes, the Attorney General has delegated the authority to represent the United States in these particular matters to a Special Prosecutor with unique authority and tenure. The regulation gives the Special Prosecutor explicit power to contest the invocation of executive privilege in the process of seeking evidence deemed relevant to the performance of these specially delegated duties.

So long as this regulation is extant it has the force of law. In *Accardi* v. *Shaughnessy*, (1953), regulations of the Attorney General delegated certain of his discretionary powers to the Board of Immigration Appeals and required that Board to exercise its own discretion on appeals in deportation cases. The Court held that so long as the Attorney General's regulations remained operative, he denied himself the authority to exercise the discretion delegated to the Board even though the original authority was his and he could reassert it by amending the regulations. *Service* v. *Dulles*, (1957), and *Vitarelli* v. *Seaton*, (1959), reaffirmed the basic holding of *Accardi*.

Here, as in *Accardi*, it is theoretically possible for the Attorney General to amend or revoke the regulation defining the Special Prosecutor's authority. But he has not done so. So long as this regulation remains in force the Executive Branch is bound by it, and indeed the United States as the sovereign composed of the three branches is bound to respect and to enforce it. Moreover, the delegation of authority to the Special Prosecutor in this case is not an ordinary delegation by the Attorney General to a subordinate officer: with the authorization of the President, the Acting Attorney General provided in the regulation that the Special Prosecutor was not to be removed without the "consensus" of eight designated leaders of Congress.

The demands of and the resistance to the subpoena present an obvious controversy in the ordinary sense, but that alone is not sufficient to meet constitutional standards. In the constitutional sense, controversy means more than disagreement and conflict; rather it means the kind of controversy courts traditionally resolve. Here at issue is the production or nonproduction of specified evidence deemed by the Special Prosecutor to be relevant and admissible in a pending criminal case. It is sought by one official of the Government within the scope of his express authority; it is resisted by the Chief Executive on the ground of his duty to preserve the confidentiality of the communications of the President. Whatever the correct answer on the merits, these issues are "of a type which are traditionally justiciable." *United States* v. *ICC*. The independent Special Prosecutor with his asserted need for the subpoenaed material in the underlying criminal prosecution is opposed by the President with his stead-fast assertion of privilege against disclosure of the material. This setting assures there is "that concrete adverseness which sharpens the presenta-tion of issues upon which the court so largely depends for illumination of difficult constitutional questions." *Baker* v. *Carr*. Moreover, since the matter is one arising in the regular course of a federal criminal prosecution, it is within the traditional scope of Art. III power.

In the light of the uniqueness of the setting in which the conflict arises, the fact that both parties are officers of the Executive Branch cannot be viewed as a barrier to justiciability. It would be inconsistent with the applicable law and regulation, and the unique facts of this case to conclude other than that the Special Prosecutor has standing to bring this action and that a justiciable controversy is presented for decision.

III
RULE 17 (c)

The subpoena *duces tecum* is challenged on the ground that the Special Prosecutor failed to satisfy the requirements of Fed. Rule Crim. Proc. 17(c), which governs the issuance of subpoenas *duces tecum* in federal criminal proceedings. If we sustained this challenge, there would be no occasion to reach the claim of privilege asserted with respect to the subpoenaed material. Thus we turn to the question whether the requirements of Rule 17 (c) have been satisfied. See *Arkansas-Louisiana Gas Co. v. Dept. of Public Utilities* (1938); *Ashwander* v. *Tennessee Valley Authority*, (1936). (Brandeis, J., concurring.)

Rule 17 (c) provides:

> "A subpoena may also command the person to whom it is directed to produce the books, papers, documents or other objects designated therein. The court on motion made promptly may quash or modify the subpoena if compliance would be unreasonable or oppressive. The court may direct that books, papers, documents or objects designated in the subpoena be produced before the court at a time prior to the trial or prior to the time when they are to be offered in evidence and may upon their production permit the books, papers, documents or objects or portions thereof to be inspected by the parties and their attorneys."

A subpoena for documents may be quashed if their production would be "unreasonable or oppressive," but not otherwise. The leading case in this Court interpreting this standard is *Bowman Dairy Co. v. United States*, (1950). This case recognized certain fundamental characteristics of the sub-poena *duces tecum* in criminal cases: (1) it was not intended to provide a means of discovery for criminal cases. (2) its chief innovation was to ex-pedite the trial by providing a time and place *before* trial for the inspection of subpoenaed materials. As both parties agree, cases decided in the wake of *Bowman* have generally followed Judge Weinfeld's formulation in *United States* v. *Iozia*, (SDNY 1952), as to the required showing. Under this test, in order to require production prior to trial, the moving party must show: (1) that the documents are evidentiary and relevant; (2) that they are not otherwise procurable reasonably in advance of trial by exercise of due diligence; (3) that the party cannot properly prepare for trial without such production and inspection in advance of trial and that the failure to obtain such inspection may tend unreasonably to delay the trial; (4) that the application is made in good faith and is not intended as a general "fishing expedition."

Against this background, the Special Prosecutor, in order to carry his burden, must clear three hurdles: (1) relevancy; (2) admissibility; (3) specificity. Our own review of the record necessarily affords a less comprehensive view of the total situation than was available to the trial judge and we are unwilling to conclude that the District Court erred in the evaluation of the Special Prosecutor's showing under Rule 17 (c). Our conclusion is based on the record before us, much of which is under seal. Of course, the contents of the subpoenaed tapes could not at that stage be described fully by the Special Prosecutor, but there was a sufficient likelihood that each of the tapes contains conversations relevant to the offenses charged in the indictment. *United States* v. *Gross*, (SDNY 1959). With respect to many of the tapes, the Special Prosecutor offered the sworn testimony or statements of one or more of the participants in the conversations as to what was said at the time. As for the remainder of the tapes, the identity of the participants and the time and place of the conversations, taken in their total context, permit a rational inference that at least part of the conversations relate to the offenses charged in the indictment.

We also conclude there was a sufficient preliminary showing that each of the subpoenaed tapes contains evidence admissible with respect to the offenses charged in the indictment. The most cogent objection to the admissibility of the taped conversations here at issue is that they are a collection of out-of-court statements by declarants who will not be subject to cross-examination and that the statements are therefore inadmissible hearsay. Here, however, most of the tapes apparently contain conversations to which one or more of the defendants named in the indictment were party. The hearsay rule does not automatically bar all out-of-court statements by a defendant in a criminal case. Declarations by one defendant may also be admissible against other defendants upon a sufficient showing, by independent evidence, of a conspiracy among one or more other defendants and the declarant and if the declarations at issue were in furtherance of that conspiracy. The same is true of declarations of coconspirators who are not defendants in the case on trial. *Dutton* v. *Evans*, (1970). Recorded conversations may also be admissible for the limited purpose of impeaching the credibility of any defendant who testifies or any other coconspirator who testifies. Generally, the need for evidence to impeach witnesses is insufficient to require its production in advance of trial. See, *e.g. United States* v. *Carter*, (D. D. C. 1954). Here, however, there are other valid potential evidentiary uses for the same material and the analysis and possible transcription of the tapes may take a significant period of time. Accordingly, we cannot say that the District Court erred in authorizing the issuance of the subpoena *duces tecum*.

Enforcement of a pretrial subpoena *duces tecum* must necessarily be committed to the sound discretion of the trial court since the necessity for the subpoena most often turns upon a determination of arbitrariness or that the trial court finding was without record support, an appellate court will not ordinarily disturb a finding that the applicant for a subpoena complied with Rule 17 (c). See, *e.g. Sue* v. *Chicago Transit Authority,* (CA7 1960); *Shotkin* v. *Nelson* (CA10 1944).

In a case such as this, however, where a subpoena is directed to a President of the United States, appellate review, in deference to a coordinate branch of government, should be particularly meticulous to ensure that the standards of Rule 17 (c) have been correctly applied. *United States* v. *Burr,* (1807). From our examination of the materials submitted by the Special Prosecutor to the District Court in support of his motion for the subpoena, we are persuaded that the District Court's denial of the President's motion to quash the subpoena was consistent with Rule 17 (c). We also conclude that the Special Prosecutor has made a sufficient showing to justify a subpoena for production *before* trial. The subpoenaed materials are not available from any other source, and their examination and processing should not await trial in the circumstances shown.

IV
THE CLAIM OF PRIVILEGE
A

Having determined that the requirements of Rule 17 (c) were satisfied, we turn to the claim that the subpoena should be quashed because it demands "confidential conversations between a President and his close advisors that it would be inconsistent with the public interest to produce." App. 48a. The first contention is a broad claim that the separation of powers doctrine precludes judicial review of a President's claim of privilege. The second contention is that if he does not prevail on the claim of absolute privilege, the court should hold as a matter of constitutional law that privilege prevails over the subpoena *duces tecum*.

In the performance of assigned constitutional duties each branch of the Government must initially interpret the Constitution, and the interpretation of its powers by any branch is due great respect from the others. The President's counsel, as we have noted, reads the Constitution as providing the absolute privilege of confidentiality for all presidential communications. Many decisions of this court, however, have unequivocally reaffirmed the holding of *Marbury* v. *Madison,* (1803), that "it is emphatically the province and duty of the judicial department to say what the law is."

No holding of the Court has defined the scope of judicial power specifically relating to the enforcement of a subpoena for confidential presidential communications for use in a criminal prosecution, but other exercises of powers by the Executive Branch and the Legislative Branch have been found invalid as in conflict with the Constitution. *Powell* v. *McCormack, Youngstown.* In a series of cases, the Court interpreted the explicit immunity conferred by express provisions of the Constitution on Members of the House and Senate by the Speech or Debate Clause, U.S. Const. Art. I, § 6. *Doe* v. *McMillan* (1973); *Gravel* v. *United States*, (1973); *United States* v. *Brewster*, *(1972)*; *United States* v. *Johnson*, (1966). Since this Court has consistently exercised the power to construe and delineate claims arising under express powers, it must follow that the Court has authority to interpret claims with respect to powers alleged to derive from enumerated powers.

Our system of government "requires that federal courts on occasion interpret the Constitution in a manner at variance with the construction given the document by another branch." *Powell* v. *McCormack*. And in *Baker* v. *Carr*, 369 U.S., at 211, the Court stated:

> "[d]eciding whether a matter has in any measure been committed by the Constitution to another branch of government, or whether the action of that branch exceeds whatever authority has been committed, is itself a delicate exercise in constitutional interpretation, and is a responsibility of this Court as ultimate interpreter of the Constitution.

Notwithstanding the deference each branch must accord the others, the "judicial power of the United States" vested in the federal courts by Art. III, § 1 of the Constitution can no more be shared with the Executive Branch than the Chief Executive, for example, can share with the Judiciary the veto power, or the Congress share with the Judiciary the power to override a presidential veto. Any other conclusion would be contrary to the basic concept of separation of powers and the checks and balances that flow from the scheme of a tripartite government. The Federalist, No. 47. We therefore reaffirm that it is "emphatically the province and the duty" of this Court "to say what the law is " with respect to the claim of privilege presented in this case. *Marbury* v. *Madison*.

B

In support of his claim of absolute privilege, the President's counsel urges two grounds one of which is common to all governments and one of which is peculiar to our system of separation of powers. The first ground is the valid need for protection of communications between high government officials and those who advise and assist them in the performance of their manifold duties; the importance of this confidentiality is too plain to require further discussion. Human experience teaches that those who expect public dissemination of their remarks may well temper candor with a concern for appearances and for their own interests to the detriment of the decisionmaking process. Whatever the nature of the privilege of confidentiality of presidential communications in the exercise of Art. II powers the privilege can be said to derive from the supremacy of each branch within its own assigned area of constitutional duties. Certain powers and privileges flow from the nature of enumerated powers; the protection of the confidentiality of presidential communications has similar constitutional underpinnings.

The second ground asserted by the President's counsel in support of the claim of absolute privilege rests on the doctrine of separation of powers.

Here it is argued that the independence of the Executive Branch within its own sphere, *Humphrey's Executor* v. *United States, Kilbourn* v. *Thompson*, (1880), insulates a president from a judicial subpoena in an ongoing criminal prosecution, and thereby protects confidential presidential communications.

However, neither the doctrine of separation of powers, nor the need for confidentiality of high level communications, without more, can sustain an absolute, unqualified presidential privilege of immunity from judicial process under all circumstances. The President's need for complete candor and objectivity from advisers calls for great deference from the courts. However, when the privilege depends solely on the broad undifferentiated claim of public interest in the confidentiality of such conversations, a confrontation with other values arises. Absent a claim of need to protect military, diplomatic or sensitive national security secrets, we find it difficult to accept the argument that even the very important interest in confidentiality of presidential communications is significantly diminished by production of such material for *in camera* inspection with all the protection that a district court will be obliged to provide.

The impediment that an absolute, unqualified privilege would place in the way of the primary constitutional duty of the Judicial Branch to do justice in criminal prosecutions would plainly conflict with the function of the courts under Art. III. In designing the structure of our Government and dividing and allocating the sovereign power among three coequal branches, the Framers of the Constitution sought to provide a comprehensive system, but the separate powers were not intended to operate with absolute independence.

> "While the Constitution diffuses power the better to secure liberty, it also contemplates that practice will integrate the dispersed powers into a workable government. It enjoins upon its branches separateness but interdependence, autonomy but reciprocity." *Youngstown Sheet & Tube Co.* v. *Sawyer*, (1952) (Jackson, J., concurring).

To read Art. II powers of the President as providing an absolute privilege as against a subpoena essential to enforcement of criminal statutes on no more than a generalized claim of the public interest in confidentiality of nonmilitary and nondiplomatic discussions would upset the constitutional balance of "a workable government" and gravely impair the role of the courts under Art. III.

C

Since we conclude that the legitimate needs of the judicial process may outweigh presidential privilege, it is necessary to resolve those competing interests in a manner that preserves the essential functions of each branch. The right and indeed the duty to resolve that question does not free the judiciary from according high respect to the representations made on behalf of the President. *United States* v. *Burr*, (1807).

The expectation of a President to the confidentiality of his conversations and correspondence, like the claim of confidentiality of judicial deliberations, for example, has all the values to which we accord deference for the privacy of all citizens and added to those values the necessity for protection of the public interest in candid, objective, and even blunt or harsh opinions in presidential decisionmaking. A President and those who assist him must be free to explore alternatives in the process of shaping policies and making decisions and to do so in a way many would be unwilling to express except privately. These are the considerations justifying a presumptive privilege for presidential communications. The privilege is fundamental to the operation of government and inextricably rooted in the separation of powers under the Constitution. In *Nixon* v. *Sirica*, (1973), the Court of Appeals held that such presidential communications are "presumptively privileged," and this position is accepted by both parties in the present litigation. We agree with Mr. Chief Justice Marshall's observation, therefore, that "in no case of this kind would a court be required to proceed against the President as against an ordinary individual." *United States* v. Burr, (CCD Va. 1807).

But this presumptive privilege must be considered in light of our historic commitment to the rule of law. This is nowhere more profoundly manifest than in our view that "the twofold aim [of criminal justice] is that guilt shall not escape or innocence suffer." *Berger* v. *United States*, (1935). We have elected to employ an adversary system of criminal justice in which the parties contest all issues before a court of law. The need to develop all relevant facts in the adversary system is both fundamental and comprehensive. The ends of criminal justice would be defeated if judgments were to be founded on a partial or speculative presentation of the facts. The very integrity of the judicial system and public confidence in the system depend on full disclosure of all the facts, within the framework of the rules of evidence. To ensure that justice is done, it is imperative to the function of courts that compulsory process be available for the production of evidence needed either by the prosecution or by the defense.

Only recently the Court restated the ancient proposition of law, albeit in the context of a grand jury inquiry rather than a trial,

> " 'that the public...has a right to every man's evidence' except for those persons protected by a constitutional, common law, or statutory privilege, *United States* v. *Bryan*, (1949); *Blackmer* v. *United States*, *Branzburg* v. *United States*, (1973).

The privileges referred to by the Court are designed to protect weighty and legitimate competing interests. Thus, the Fifth Amendment to the Constitution provides that no man "shall be compelled in any criminal case to be a witness against himself." And, generally, an attorney or a priest may not be required to disclose what has been revealed in professional confidence. These and other interests are recognized in law by privileges against forced disclosure, established in the Constitution, by statute, or at common law. Whatever their origins, these exceptions to the demand for every man's evidence are not lightly created or expansively construed, for they are in derogation of the search for truth.

In this case the President challenges a subpoena served on him as a third party requiring the production of materials for use in a criminal prosecution on the claim that he has a privilege against disclosure of confidential communications. He does not place his claim of privilege on the ground they are military or diplomatic secrets. As to these areas of Art. II duties the courts have traditionally shown the utmost deference to presidential responsibilities. In *C. & S. Air Lines* v. *Waterman Steamship Corp.*, (1948), dealing with presidential authority involving foreign policy considerations, the Court said:

> "The President, both as Commander-in-Chief and as the Nation's organ for foreign affairs, has available intelligence services whose reports are not and ought not to be published to the world. It would be intolerable that courts, without the relevant information, should review and perhaps nullify actions of the Executive taken on information properly held secret."

In *United States v. Reynolds*, (1952), dealing with a claimant's demand for evidence in a damage case against the Government the Court said:

> "It may be possible to satisfy the court, from all the circumstances of the case, that there is a reasonable danger that compulsion of the evidence will expose military matters which, in the interest of national security, should not be divulged. When this is the case, the occasion for the privilege is appropriate, and the court should not jeopardize the security which the privilege is meant to protect by insisting upon an examination of the evidence, even by the judge alone, in chambers."

No case of the Court, however, has extended this high degree of deference to a President's generalized interest in confidentiality. Nowhere in the Constitution, as we have noted earlier, is there any explicit reference to a privilege of confidentiality, yet to the extent this interest relates to the effective discharge of a President's powers, it is constitutionally based.

The right to the production of all evidence at a criminal trial similarly has constitutional dimensions. The Sixth Amendment explicitly confers upon every defendant in a criminal trial the right "to be confronted with the witnesses against him" and "to have compulsory process for obtaining witnesses in his favor." Moreover, the Fifth Amendment also guarantees that no person shall be deprived of liberty without due process of law. It is the manifest duty of the courts to vindicate those guarantees and to accomplish that it is essential that all relevant and admissible evidence be produced.

In this case we must weigh the importance of the general privilege of confidentiality of presidential communications in performance of his responsibilities against the inroads of such a privilege on the fair administration of criminal justice. The interest in preserving confidentiality is weighty indeed and entitled to great respect. However we cannot conclude that advisers will be moved to temper the candor of their remarks by the infrequent occasions of disclosure because of the possibility that such conversations will be called for in the context of a criminal prosecution.

On the other hand, the allowance of the privilege to withhold evidence that is demonstrably relevant in a criminal trial would cut deeply into the guarantee of due process of law and gravely impair the basic function of the courts. A President's acknowledged need for confidentiality in the communications of his office is general in nature, whereas the constitutional need for production of relevant evidence in a criminal proceeding is specific and central to the fair adjudication of a particular criminal case in the administration of justice. Without access to specific facts a criminal prosecution may be totally frustrated. The President's broad interest in confidentiality of communications will not be vitiated by disclosure of a limited number of conversations preliminarily shown to have some bearing on the pending criminal cases.

We conclude that when the ground for asserting privilege as to subpoenaed materials sought for use in a criminal trial is based only on the generalized interest in confidentiality, it cannot prevail over the fundamental demands of due process of law in the fair administration of criminal justice. The generalized assertion of privilege must yield to the demonstrated, specific need for evidence in a pending criminal trial.

D

We have earlier determined that the District Court did not err in authorizing the issuance of the subpoena. If a president concludes that compliance with a subpoena would be injurious to the public interest he may properly, as was done here, invoke a claim of privilege on the return of the subpoena. Upon receiving a claim of privilege from the Chief Executive, it became the further duty of the District Court to treat the subpoenaed material as presumptively privileged and to require the Special Prosecutor to demonstrate that the presidential material was "essential to the justice of the [pending criminal] case." *United States* v. *Burr.* Here the District Court treated the material as presumptively privileged, proceeded to find that the Special Prosecutor had made a sufficient showing to rebut the presumption and ordered an *in camera* examination of the subpoenaed material. On the basis of our examination of the record we are unable to conclude that the District Court erred in ordering the inspection. Accordingly we affirm the order of the District Court that subpoenaed materials be transmitted to that court. We now turn to the important question of the District Court's responsibilities in conducting the *in camera* examination of presidential materials or communications delivered under the compulsion of the subpoena *duces tecum.*

E

Enforcement of the subpoena *duces tecum* was stayed pending this Court's resolution of the issues raised by the petitions for certiorari. Those issues now having been disposed of, the matter of implementation will rest with the District Court. "[T]he guard, furnished to [President] to protect him from being harassed by vexatious and unnecessary subpoenas, is to be looked for in the conduct of the [district] court after the subpoenas have issued; not in any circumstances which is to precede their being issued." *United States* v. *Burr.* Statements that meet the test of admissibility and relevance must be isolated; all other material must be excised. At this stage the District Court is not limited to representations of the Special Prosecutor as to the evidence sought by the subpoena; the material will be available to the District Court. It is elementary that *in camera* inspection of evidence is always a procedure calling for scrupulous protection against any release or publication of material not found by the court, at that stage, probably admissible in evidence and relevant to the issues of the trial for which it is sought. That being true of an ordinary situation, it is obvious that the District Court has a very heavy responsibility to see to it that presidential conversations, which are either not relevant or not admissible, are accorded that high degree of respect due the President of the United States. Mr. Chief Justice Marshall sitting as a trial judge in the *Burr* case, was extraordinarily careful to point out that:

"[I]n no case of this kind would a Court be required to proceed against the President as against an ordinary individual." *United States* v. *Burr*, (No. 14,694).

Marshall's statement cannot be read to mean in any sense that a President is above the law, but relates to the singularly unique role under Art. II of a President's communications and activities, related to the performance of duties under that Article. Moreover, a President's communications and activities encompass a vastly wider range of sensitive material than would be true of any "ordinary individual". It is therefore necessary in the public interest to afford presidential confidentiality the greatest protection consistent with the fair administration of justice. The need for confidentiality even as to idle conversations with associates in which casual reference might be made concerning political leaders within the country or foreign statesmen is too obvious to call for further treatment. We have no doubt that the District Judge will at all times accord to presidential records that high degree of deference suggested in *United States* v. *Burr*, and will discharge his responsibility to see to it that until released to the Special Prosecutor no *in camera* material is revealed to anyone. This burden applies with even greater force to excised material; once the decision is made to excise, the material is restored to its privileged status and should be returned under seal to its lawful custodian.

Since this matter came before the Court during the pendency of a criminal prosecution, and on representations that time is of the essence, the mandate shall issue forthwith.

Affirmed

MR. JUSTICE REHNQUIST took no part in the consideration or decision of these cases.

President Nixon's reaction to the Supreme Court tapes decision. Nixon's statement was made through his counsel, James D. St. Clair, July 24 at San Clemente, Calif.:

I have reviewed the decision of the Supreme Court with the President. He's given me this statement, which he's asked me to read to you. And this is the President's statement as he gave it to me:

"My challenge in the courts to the subpoena of the special prosecutor was based on the belief that it was unconstitutionally issued, and on my strong desire to protect the principle of presidential confidentiality in a system of separation of powers.

"While I am, of course, disappointed in the result, I respect and accept the Court's decision, and I have instructed Mr. St. Clair to take whatever measures are necessary to comply with that decision in all respects. For the future it will be essential that the special circumstances of this case not be permitted to cloud the right of Presidents to maintain the basic confidentiality without which this office cannot function. I was gratified, therefore, to note that the Court reaffirmed both the validity and the importance of the principle of executive privilege, the principle I had sought to maintain. By complying fully with the Court's ruling in this case, I hope and trust that I will contribute to strengthening rather than weakening this principle for the future, so that this will prove to be not the precedent that destroyed the principle but the action that preserved it."

That concludes the President's statement. As we all know, the President has always been a firm believer in the rule of law, and he intends his decision to comply fully with the Court's ruling as an action in furtherance of that belief. Therefore, in accordance with his instructions, the time-consuming process of reviewing the tapes subject to the subpoena, and the preparation of the index and analysis required by Judge Sirica's order, will begin forthwith.

Thank you all very much.

COURT ON CROSS-DISTRICT BUSING

July 25, 1974

Declaring that boundary lines could be ignored only where each school district had been found to practice racial discrimination or where the boundaries had been deliberately drawn to promote racial segregation, the Supreme Court July 25, in a 5-4 decision, reversed a lower court ruling ordering cross-county busing between Detroit, Mich., and 53 surrounding communities. "Boundary lines may be bridged where there has been a constitutional violation calling for inter-district relief, but the notion that school district lines may be casually ignored or treated as a mere administrative convenience is contrary to the history of public education in our country," Chief Justice Warren E. Burger wrote for the majority. The long-awaited decision was expected to have a major impact on attempts to desegregate northern metropolitan areas where a majority of black students were concentrated in inner cities and a majority of white students were clustered in surrounding suburbs. The court remanded the case requiring the lower court to come up with a desegregation plan for the Detroit school system alone. Burger was joined in his opinion by Justices Stewart, Blackmun, Powell and Rehnquist. Justices Douglas, Brennan, White and Marshall dissented.

"Today's holding, I fear, is more a reflection of a perceived public mood that we have gone far enough in enforcing the Constitution's guarantee of equal justice than it is the product of neutral principles of law," Marshall wrote. The decision came in the midst of a heated congressional debate over legislation that would severely limit the authority of a court to order transportation of students to overcome racial discrimination.

Accepting the lower court findings that the Detroit system was racially discriminatory, Burger noted that no one had claimed that any of the suburban communities had failed to provide equal opportunity and protection to any of its students. "An inter-district remedy might be in order where the racially discriminatory acts of one or more school districts caused racial segregation in an adjacent district or where district lines have been deliberately drawn on the basis of race," Burger said. But "without an inter-district violation and inter-district effect, there is no constitutional wrong calling for an inter-district remedy." In a dissenting opinion, Douglas rejected that thesis: "Metropolitan treatment of metropolitan problems is commonplace. If this were a sewage problem or a water problem or an energy problem, there can be no doubt that Michigan would stay well within...constitutional bounds if she sought a metropolitan remedy."

State Segregation Action

Burger rejected the contention made by the original plaintiffs that state and local personnel had engaged in official actions that led to the segregation of black children in Detroit and that the state and its agencies should thus be responsible for correcting the wrong. "The Michigan education structure...in common with most states, provides for a large measure of local control," Burger said. "It is obvious from the scope of the inter-district remedy itself that absent a complete restructuring of the laws of Michigan...the district court will become first a de facto 'legislative authority' to resolve these complex questions, and then the 'school superintendent' for the entire area." But Marshall insisted that state actions causing segregation must be considered. "The essential foundation of inter-district relief in this case was not to correct conditions within outlying districts who themselves engaged in purposeful segregation. Instead, inter-district relief was seen as a necessary part of any meaningful effort by the state of Michigan to remedy the state-caused segregation within the city of Detroit.

Marshall also questioned whether a plan limited solely to Detroit could effectively end discrimination. Claiming that the growing majority of black students in the city would continue to drive whites out of the city and into the surrounding suburbs, Marshall said a plan involving only Detroit "does not promise to achieve actual desegregation."

> Excerpts from the Court's majority opinion barring busing of students across school district lines without first proving that deliberate actions by surrounding school districts have encouraged segregation. Chief Justice Burger wrote the majority opinion. Excerpts also from concurring opinion by Justice Stewart and from dissenting opinions by Justices Douglas, White and Marshall:

Nos. 73-434, 73-435, and 73-436

William G. Milliken, Governor of Michigan et al.,
Petitioners,
73-434   v.
Ronald Bradley and Richard
Bradley, by Their Mother
and Next Friend, Verda
Bradley, et al.

Allen Park Public Schools
et al., Petitioners,
73-435   v.
Ronald Bradley and Richard
Bradley, by Their Mother
and Next Friend, Verda
Bradley, et al.

The Grosse Point Public
School System,
Petitioner,
73-436   v.
Ronald Bradley and Richard
Bradley, by Their Mother
and Next Friend, Verda
Bradley, et al.

On Writs of Certiorari to
the United States Court
of Appeals for the Sixth
Circuit.

[July 25, 1974]

MR. CHIEF JUSTICE BURGER delivered the opinion of the Court.

We granted certiorari in these consolidated cases to determine whether a federal court may impose a multi-district, areawide remedy to a single district *de jure* segregation problem absent any finding that the other included school districts have failed to operate unitary school systems within their districts, absent any claim or finding that the boundary lines of any affected school district were established with the purpose of fostering racial segregation in public schools, absent any finding that the included districts committed acts which effected segregation within other districts, and absent a meaningful opportunity for the included neighboring school districts to present evidence or be heard on the propriety of a multidistrict remedy or on the question of constitutional violations by those neighboring districts.

I

The action was commenced in August of 1970 by the respondents, the Detroit Branch of the National Association for the Advancement of Colored People and individual parents and students, on behalf of a class later defined by order of the United States District Court, ED Michigan, dated February 16, 1971, to include "all school children of the City of Detroit and all Detroit resident parents who have children of school age." The named defendents in the District Court included the Governor of Michigan, the

Attorney General, the State Board of Education, the State Superintendent of Public Instruction, and the Board of Education of the city of Detroit, its members and its former superintendent of schools. The State of Michigan as such is not a party to this litigation and references to the State must be read as references to the public officials, State and local, through whom the State is alleged to have acted. In their complaint respondents attacked the constitutionality of a statute of the State of Michigan known as Act 48 of the 1970 Legislature on the ground that it put the State of Michigan in the position of unconstitutionally interfering with the execution and operation of a voluntary plan of partial high school desegregation....The complaint also alleged that the Detroit Public School System was and is segregated on the basis of race as a result of the official policies and actions of the defendants and their predecessors in office, and called for the implementation of a plan that would eliminate "the racial identity of every school in the [Detroit] system and...maintain now and hereafter a unitary non-racial school system...."

...On September 27, 1971, the District Court issued its findings and conclusions on the issue of segregation finding that "Government actions and inaction at all levels, federal, state and local, have combined, with those of private organizations, such as loaning institutions and real estate associations and brokerage firms, to establish and to maintain the pattern of residential segregation throughout the Detroit metropolitan area."...

The District Court found that the Detroit Board of Education created and maintained optional attendance zones within Detroit neighborhoods underdoing racial transition and between high school attendance areas of opposite predominant racial compositions. These zones, the court found, had the "natural, probable, forseeable and actual effect" of allowing White pupils to escape identifiably Negro schools....Similarly, the District Court found that Detroit school attendance zones had been drawn along north-south boundary lines despite the Detroit Board's awareness that drawing boundary lines in an east-west direction would result in significantly greater desegregation. Again, the District Court concluded, the natural and actual effect of these acts was the creation and perpetuation of school segregation within Detroit....

With respect to the Detroit Board of Education's practices in school construction, the District Court found that Detroit school construction generally tended to have segregative effect with the great majority of schools being built in either overwhelmingly all Negro or all White neighborhoods so that the new schools opened as predominantly one race schools. Thus, of the 14 schools which opened for use in 1970-1971, 11 opened over 90% Negro and one opened less than 10% Negro....

The District Court found that the State, through Act 48, acted to "impede, delay and minimize racial integration in Detroit schools...."

The District Court also held that the acts of the Detroit Board of Education, as a subordinate entity of the State, were attributable to the State of Michigan thus creating a vicarious liability on the part of the State....

Accordingly, the District Court proceeded to order the Detroit Board of Education to submit desegregation plans limited to the segregation problems found to be existing within the city of Detroit. At the same time, however, the state defendants were directed to submit desegregation plans encompassing the three-county metropolitan area despite the fact that the school districts of these three counties were not parties to the action and despite the fact that there had been no claim that these outlying counties, encompassing some 85 separate school districts, had committed constitutional violations. An effort to appeal these orders to the Court of Appeals was dismissed on the ground that the orders were not appealable....

[F]ollowing the completion of hearings on the Detroit-only desegregation plans, the District Court issued the four rulings that were the principal issues in the Court of Appeals.

(a) On March 24, 1972,...the District Court...rejected the state defendants' arguments that no state action caused the segregation of the Detroit schools, and the intervening suburban districts' contention that interdistrict relief was inappropriate unless the suburban districts had themselves committed violations....

(b) On March 28, 1972, the District Court issued its findings and conclusions on the three "Detroit-only" plans submitted by the city Board and the respondents. It found that the best of the three plans "would make the Detroit system more identifiably Black...thereby increasing flights of Whites from the city and the system."...From this the court concluded that the plan "would not accomplish desegregation within the corporate geographical limits of the city."...Accordingly, the District Court held that "it must look beyond the limits of the Detroit school district for a solution to the problem," and that "[s]chool district lines are simply matters of political convenience and may not be used to deny constitutional rights."...

(c) During the period from March 28, 1972 to April 14, 1972, the District Court conducted hearings on a metropolitan plan....Thereafter, on June 14, 1972, the District Court issued its ruling on the "desegregation area" and related findings and conclusions. The court acknowledged at the outset that it had "taken no proofs with respect to the establishment of boundaries of the 86 public school districts in the counties [in the Detroit area], nor on the issue of whether, with the exclusion of the city of Detroit school district, such school districts have committed acts of *de jure* segregation." Nevertheless, the court designated 53 of the 85 suburban school districts plus Detroit as the "desegregation area" and appointed a panel to prepare and submit "an effective desegregation plan" for the Detroit schools that would encompass the entire desegregation area....

(d) ...On June 12, 1973, a divided Court of Appeals, sitting en banc, affirmed in part, vacated in part and remanded for further proceedings....The Court of Appeals held, first, that the record supported the District Court's findings and conclusions on the constitutional violations committed by the Detroit Board,...and by the state defendants....It stated that the acts of racial discrimination shown in the record are "casually related to the substantial amount of segregation found in the Detroit school system,"...and that "the District Court was, therefore, authorized and required to take effective measures to desegregate the Detroit Public School System."...

The Court of Appeals also agreed with the District Court that "any less comprehensive a solution than a metropolitan area plan would result in an all black school system immediately surrounded by practically all white suburban school systems, with an overwhelming white majority population in the total metropolitan area."...

Accordingly, the Court of Appeals concluded that "the only feasible desegregation plan involves the crossing of the boundary lines between the Detroit School District and adjacent or nearby school districts for the limited purpose of providing an effective desegregation plan."...It reasoned that such a plan would be appropriate because of the State's authority to control local school districts. Without further elaboration, and without any discussion of the claims that no constitutional violation by the outlying districts had shown and that no evidence on that point had been allowed, the Court of Appeals held:

> "[T]he State has committed *de jure* acts of segregation and...the State controls the instrumentalities whose action is necessary to remedy the harmful effects of the State acts."...

An inter-district remedy was thus held to be "within the equity powers of the District Court."

II

...The target of the *Brown* v. *Board of Education*, 347 U.S. 483 (1954), holding was clear and forthright: the elimination of state mandated or deliberately maintained dual school systems with certain schools for Negro pupils and others for White pupils. This duality and racial segregation was held to violate the Constitution in the cases subsequent to 1974.... In *Brown* v. *Board of Education*, 349 U.S. 294 (1955) *(Brown II)*, the Court's first encounter with the problem of remedies in school desegregation cases, the Court noted that:

> "In fashioning and effectuating the decrees the courts will be guided by equitable principles. Traditionally, equity has been characterized by a practical flexibility in shaping its remedies and by a facility for adjusting and reconciling public and private needs."...

Proceeding from these basic principles, we first note that in the District Court the complainants sought a remedy aimed at the *condition* alleged to offend the Constitution—the segregation within the Detroit City school district. The court acted on this theory of the case....

Thereafter...the District Court abruptly rejected the proposed Detroit-only plans on the ground that "while it would provide a racial mix more in keeping with the Black-White proportions of the student population, [it] would accentuate the racial identifiability of the [Detroit] district as a Black school system and would not accomplish desegregation."..."[T]he racial composition of the student body is such," said the court, "that the plan's implementation would clearly make the entire Detroit public school system racially identifiable."...Consequently, the court reasoned, it was imperative to "look beyond the limits of the Detroit school district for a solution to the problem of segregation in the Detroit schools..." since "school district lines are simply matters of political convenience and may not be used to deny constitutional rights."

While specifically acknowledging that the District Court's findings of a condition of segregation were limited to Detroit, the Court of Appeals approved the use of a metropolitan remedy largely on the grounds that it is:

"impossible to declare 'clearly erroneous' the District Judge's conclusion that any Detroit only segregation plan will lead directly to a single segregated Detroit school district overwhelmingly black in all of its schools, surrounded by a ring of suburbs and suburban school districts overwhelmingly white in composition in a state in which the racial composition is 87 per cent white and 13 per cent black.

Viewing the record as a whole, it seems clear that the District Court and the Court of Appeals shifted the primary focus from a Detroit remedy to the metropolitan area only because of their conclusion that total desegregation of Detroit would not produce racial balance which they perceived as desirable. Both courts proceeded on an assumption that the Detroit schools could not be truly desegregated—in their view of what constituted desegregation—unless the racial composition of the student body of each school substantially reflected the racial composition of the population of the metropolitan area as a whole....

The clear importance of...*Swann* [v. *Charlotte-Mecklenburg Board of Education*, 402 U.S. 1 (1971)] is that desegregation, in the sense of dismantling a dual school system, does not require any particular racial balance in each "school, grade or classroom." See *Spencer* v. *Kugler*....

Here the District Court's approach to what constituted "actual desegregation" raises the fundamental question,...as to the circumstances in which a federal court may order desegregation relief that embraces more than a single school district. The court's analytical starting point was its conclusion that school district lines are no more than arbitrary lines on a map "drawn for political convenience." ...but, the notion that school district lines may be casually ignored or treated as a mere administrative convenience is contrary to the history of public education in our country. No single tradition in public education is more deeply rooted than local control over the operation of schools; local autonomy has long been thought essential both to the maintenance of community concern and support for public schools and to quality of the educational process....

[A] review of the scope and character of these local powers indicates the extent to which the inter-district remedy approved by the two courts would disrupt and alter the structure of public education in Michigan. The metropolitan remedy would require, in effect, consolidation of 54 independent school districts historically administered as separate units into a vast new super school district....Entirely apart from the logistical and other serious problems attending large-scale transportation of students, the consolidation would give rise to an array of other problems in financing and operating this new school system....

It may be suggested that all of these vital operational problems are yet to be resolved by the District Court, and that this is the purpose of the Court of Appeals' proposed remand. But it is obvious from the scope of the inter-district remedy itself that absent a complete restructuring of the laws of Michigan relating to school districts the District Court will become first, a *de facto* "legislative authority" to resolve these complex questions, and then the "school superintendent" for the entire area. This is a task which few, if any, judges are qualified to perform and one which would deprive the people of control of schools through their elected representatives.

Of course, no state law is above the Constitution. School district lines and the present laws with respect to local control, are not sacrosanct and if they conflict with the Fourteenth Amendment federal courts have a duty to prescribe appropriate remedies....We therefore turn to address, for the first time, the validity of a remedy mandating cross-district or inter-district consolidation to remedy...segregation found to exist in only one district....

The controlling principle consistently expounded in our holdings is that the scope of the remedy is determined by the nature and the extent of the constitutional violation....Before the boundaries of separate and autonomous school districts may be set aside by consolidating the separate units for remedial purposes or by imposing a cross-district remedy, it must first be shown that there has been a constitutional violation within one district that produces a significant segregative effect in another district. Specifically it must be shown that racially discriminatory acts of the state or local school districts, or of a single school district have been a substantial cause of inter-district segregation. Thus an inter-district remedy might be in order where the racially discriminatory acts of one or more school districts caused racial segregation in an adjacent district, or where district lines have been deliberately drawn on the basis of race. In such circumstances an inter-district remedy would be appropriate to eliminate the inter-district segregation directly caused by the constitutional violation. Conversely, without an inter-district violation and an inter-district effect, there is no constitutional wrong calling for an inter-district remedy.

The record before us, voluminous as it is, contains evidence of *de jure* segregated conditions only in the Detroit schools; indeed, that was the theory on which the litigation was initially based and on which the District Court took evidence....Disparate treatment of White and Negro students occurred within the Detroit school system, and not elsewhere, and on this record the remedy must be limited to that system....

The constitutional right of the Negro respondents residing in Detroit is to attend a unitary school system in that district....The view of the dissenters, that the existence of a dual system *in Detroit* can be made the basis for a decree requiring cross-district transportation of pupils cannot be supported on the grounds that it represents merely the devising of a suitably flexible remedy for the violation of rights already established by our prior decisions. It can be supported only by drastic expansion of the constitutional right itself, an expansion without any support in either constitutional principle or precedent.

III

...The Court of Appeals, for example, relied on five factors which, it held, amounted to unconstitutional state action with respect to violations found in the Detroit system:

(1) It held the State derivatively responsible for the Detroit Board's violations on the theory that actions of Detroit as a political subdivision of the State were attributable to the State...With a single exception, discussed later, there has been no showing that either the State or any of the 85 outlying districts engaged in activity that had a cross-district effect....Where the schools of only one district have been affected, there is no constitutional power in the courts to decree relief balancing the racial composition of that district's schools with those of the surrounding districts.

(2) There was evidence introduced at trial that, during the late 1950's Carver School District, a predominantly Negro suburban district, contracted to have Negro high school students sent to a predominantly Negro school in Detroit....[T]his isolated instance affecting two of the school districts would not justify the broad metropolitan-wide remedy contemplated by the District Court and approved by the Court of Appeals....

(3) The Court of Appeals cited the enactment of state legislation (Act 48) which had the effect of rescinding Detroit's voluntary desegregation plan (the April 7 plan). That plan, however, affected only 12 of 21 Detroit high schools and had no causal connection with the distribution of pupils by race between Detroit and the other school districts within the tri-county area.

(4) The court relied on the State's authority to supervise school site selection and to approve building construction as a basis for holding the State responsible for the segregative results of the school construction program in Detroit....This brief comment, however, is not supported by the evidence taken at trial....

(5) The Court of Appeals also relied upon the District Court's finding that:

> "This and other financial limitations, such as those on bonding and the working of the state aid formula whereby suburban districts were able to make far larger per pupil expenditures despite less tax effect, have created and perpetuated systematic educational inequalities."...

This again, underscores the crucial fact that the theory upon which the case proceeded related solely to the establishment of Detroit city violations as a basis for desegregating Detroit schools and that, at the time of trial, neither the parties nor the trial judge were concerned with a foundation for inter-district relief.

IV

...It is clear that the District Court, with the approval of the Court of Appeals, has provided an inter-district remedy in the face of a record which shows no constitutional violations that would call for equitable relief except within the city of Detroit. In these circumstances there was no occasion for the parties to address, or for the District Court to consider whether there were racially discriminatory acts for which any of the 53 outlying districts were responsible and which had direct and significant segregative effect on schools of more than one district.

We conclude that the relief ordered by the District Court and affirmed by the Court of Appeals was based upon an erroneous standard and was unsupported by record evidence that acts of the outlying districts affected the discrimination found to exist in the schools of Detroit. Accordingly, the judgment of the Court of appeals is vacated and the case is remanded for further proceedings consistent with this opinion leading to prompt formulation of a decree directed to eliminating the segregation found to exist in Detroit city schools, a remedy which has been delayed since 1970.

Reversed and remanded.

MR. JUSTICE STEWART, concurring.

In joining the opinion of the Court, I think it is appropriate, in view of some of the extravagant language of the dissenting opinions, to state briefly my understanding of what it is that the Court decides today....

In the present posture of the case...the Court does not deal with questions of substantive constitutional law. The basic issue now before the Court concerns...the appropriate exercise of federal equity jurisdiction....

The [lower] courts were in error for the simple reason that the remedy they thought necessary was not commensurate with the constitutional violation found. Within a single school district whose officials have been shown to have engaged in unconstitutional racial segregation, a remedial decree that affects every individual school may be dictated by "common sense,"...and indeed may provide the only effective means to eliminate segregation "root and branch,"...and to "effectuate a transition to a racially nondiscriminatory school system".... But in this case the Court of Appeals approved the concept of a remedial decree that would go beyond the boundaries of the district where the constitutional violation was found, and include schools and school children in many other school districts that have presumptively been administered in complete accord with the Constitution....

This is not to say, however, that an inter-district remedy of the sort approved by the Court of Appeals would not be proper, or even necessary, in other factual situations....

In this case, however, no...inter-district violation was shown. Indeed, no evidence at all concerning the administration of schools outside the city of Detroit was presented other than the fact that these schools contained a higher proportion of white pupils than did the schools within the city. Since the mere fact of different racial compositions in contiguous districts does not itself imply or constitute a violation of the Equal Protection Clause in the absence of a showing that such disparity was imposed, fostered, or encouraged by the State or its political subdivisions, it follows that no inter-district violation was shown in this case. The formulation of an inter-district remedy was thus simply not responsive to the factual record before the District Court and was an abuse of that court's equitable powers.

In reversing the decision of the Court of Appeals this Court is in no way turning its back on the proscription of state-imposed segregation first voiced in *Brown* v. *Board of Education*,...or on the delineation of remedial powers and duties most recently expressed in *Swann* v. *Charlotte-Mecklenburg Board of Education*....

By approving a remedy that would reach beyond the limits of the city of Detroit to correct a constitutional violation found to have occurred solely within that city the Court of Appeals thus went beyond the governing equitable principles established in this Court's decisions.

Mr. Justice Douglas dissenting.

...Metropolitan treatment of metropolitan problems is commonplace. If this were a sewage problem or a water problem, or an energy problem, there can be no doubt that Michigan would stay well within federal constitutional bounds if she sought a metropolitan remedy....Education in Michigan is a state project with very little completely local control, except that the schools are financed locally, not on a statewide basis....

The issue is not whether there should be racial balance but whether the State's use of various devices that end up with black schools and white schools brought the Equal Protection Clause into effect. Given the State's control over the educational system in Michigan, the fact that the black schools are in one district and the white schools are in another is not controlling—either constitutionally or equitably....It is conceivable that ghettos develop on their own without any hint of state action. But since Michigan by one device or another has over the years created black school districts and white school districts, the task of equity is to provide a unitary system for the affected area where, as here, the State washes its hands of its own creations.

Mr. Justice White, with whom Mr. Justice Douglas, Mr. Justice Brennan and Mr. Justice Marshall join, dissenting.

...Regretfully, and for several reasons, I can join neither the Court's judgment nor its opinion. The core of my disagreement is that deliberate acts of segregation and their consequences will go unremedied, not because a remedy would be infeasible or unreasonable in terms of the usual criteria governing school desegregation cases, but because an effective remedy would cause what the Court considers to be undue administrative inconvenience to the State. The result is that the State of Michigan, the entity at which the Fourteenth Amendment is directed, has successfully insulated itself from its duty to provide effective desegregation remedies by vesting sufficient power over its public schools in its local school districts. If this is the case in Michigan, it will be the case in most states.

There are undoubted practical as well as legal limits to the remedial powers of federal courts in school desegregation cases. The Court has made it clear that the achievement of any particular degree of racial balance in the school system in not required by the Constitution; nor may it be the primary focus of a court devising an acceptable remedy for *de jure* segregation. A variety of procedures and techniques are available to a district court engrossed in fashioning remedies in a case such as this; but the courts must keep in mind that they are dealing with the process of *educating* the young, including the very young. The task is not to devise a system of pains and penalties to punish constitutional violations brought to light. Rather, it is to desegregate an *educational* system in which the races have been kept apart, without, at the same time losing sight of the central *educational* function of the schools....

I am even more mystified how the Court can ignore the legal reality that the constitutional violations, even if occurring locally, were committed by governmental entities for which the State is responsible and that it is the State that must respond to the command of the Fourteenth Amendment. An interdistrict remedy for the infringements that occurred in this case is well within the confines and powers of the State, which is the governmental entity ultimately responsible for desegregating its schools....

The unwavering decisions of this Court over the past 20 years support the assumption of the Court of Appeals that the District Court's remedial power does not cease at the school district line....

Until today, the permissible contours of the equitable authority of the district courts to remedy unlawful establishment of a dual school system have been extensive, adaptable, and fully responsive to the ultimate goal of achieving "the greatest possible degree of actual desegregation." There are indeed limitations on the equity powers of the federal judiciary, but until now the Court has not accepted the proposition that effective enforcement of the Fourteenth Amendment could be limited by political or administrative boundary lines demarcated by the very State responsible for the constitutional violation and for the disestablishment of the dual system. Until now the Court has instead looked to practical considerations in effectuating a desegregation decree, such as excessive distance, transportation time and hazards to the safety of the school children involved in a proposed plan. That these broad principles have developed in the context of dual school systems compelled or authorized by state statute at the time of *Brown* v. *Board of Education*, (1954) *(Brown I)*, does not lessen their current applicability to dual systems found to exist in other contexts, like that in Detroit, where intentional school segregation does not stem from the compulsion of state law, but from deliberate individual actions of local and state school authorities directed at a particular school system....

The result reached by the Court certainly cannot be supported by the theory that the configuration of local governmental units is immune from alteration when necessary to redress constitutional violations....

Nor does the Court's conclusion follow from the talismanic invocation of the desirability of local control over education. Local autonomy over school affairs, in the sense of the community's participation in the decisions affecting the education of its children, is, of course, an important interest. But presently constituted school district lines do not delimit fixed and unchangeable areas of a local educational community....The majority's suggestion that judges should not attempt to grapple with the administrative problems attendant on a reorganization of school attendance patterns is wholly without foundation. It is precisely this sort of task which which the district courts have been properly exercising to vindicate the constitutional rights of Negro students since *Brown I* and which the Court has never suggested they lack the capacity to perform.

Finally, I remain wholly unpersuaded by the Court's assertion that "the remedy is necessarily designed, as all remedies are, to restore the victims of discriminatory conduct to the position they would have occupied in the absence of such conduct."...In the first place...there would have been no, or at least not as many, recognizable Negro schools and no, or at least not as many, white schools, but "just schools," and neither Negroes nor whites would have suffered from the effects of segregated education, with all its shortcomings....Moreover,...it is unrealistic to suppose that the children who were victims of the State's unconstitutional conduct could now be provided the benefits of which they were wrongfully deprived. Nor can the benefits which accrue to school systems in which school children have not been officially segregated, and to the communities supporting such school systems, be fully and immediately restored after a substantial period of unlawful segregation. The education of children of different races in a desegregated environment has unhappily been lost, along with the social, economic, and political advantages which accompany a desegregated school system as compared with an unconstitutionally segregated system....

I am therefore constrained to record my disagreement and dissent.

MR. JUSTICE MARSHALL, with whom Mr. Justice Douglas, Mr. Justice Brennan, and Mr. Justice White join, dissenting.

...After 20 years of small, often difficult steps toward that great end, the Court today takes a giant step backwards....Ironically purporting to base its result on the principle that the scope of the remedy in a desegregation case should be determined by the nature and the extent of the constitutional violation, the Court's answer is to provide no remedy at all for the violation proved in this case, thereby guaranteeing that Negro children in Detroit will receive the same separate and inherently unequal education in the future as they have been unconstitutionally afforded in the past.

I cannot subscribe to this emasculation of our constitutional guarantee of equal protection of the laws and must respectfully dissent. Our precedents, in my view, firmly establish that where, as here, state-imposed segregation has been demonstrated, it becomes the duty of the State to eliminate root and branch all vestiges of racial discrimination and to achieve the greatest possible degree of actual desegregation. I agree with both the District Court and the Court of Appeals that, under the facts of this case, this duty cannot be fulfilled unless the State of Michigan involves outlying metropolitan area school districts in its desegregation remedy. Furthermore, I perceive no basis either in law or in the practicalities of the situation justifying the State's interpretation of school district boundaries as being absolute, barriers to the implementation of an effective desegregation remedy. Under established and frequently used Michigan procedures, school district lines are both flexible and permeable for a wide variety of purposes, and there is no reason why they must stand in the way of meaningful desegregation relief.

The rights at issue in this case are too fundamental to be abridged on grounds as superficial as those relied on by the majority today. We deal here with the right of all of our children, whatever their race to an equal start in life and to an equal opportunity to reach their full potential as citizens. Those children who have been denied that right in the past deserve better than to see fences thrown up to deny them that right in the future. Our Nation, I fear, will be ill-served by the Court's refusal to remedy separate and unequal education, for unless our children begin to learn together, there is little hope that our people will ever learn to live together....

We recognized only last Term in *Keyes [v. School District No. 1]* that it was the State itself which was ultimately responsible for *de jure* acts of segregation committed by a local school board. A deliberate policy of segregation by the local board, we held, amounted to "state-imposed segregation."...Wherever a dual school system exists, whether compelled by state statute or created by a local board's systematic program of segregation, "the *State* automatically assumes an affirmative duty 'to effectuate a transition to a racially nondiscriminatory school system' [and] to eliminate from the public schools within their school system 'all vestiges of state-imposed segregation.' "...

[S]everal factors in this case coalesce to support the District Court's ruling that it was the State of Michigan itself, not simply the Detroit Board of Education, which bore the obligation of curing the condition of segregation within the Detroit city schools. The actions of the State itself directly contributed to Detroit's segregation. Under the Fourteenth Amendment, the State is ultimately responsible for the actions of its local agencies. And finally, given the structure of Michigan's educational system, Detroit's segregation cannot be viewed as the problem of an independent and separate entity. Michigan operates a single statewide system of education, a substantial part of which was shown to be segregated in this case.

II

B

What action, then, could the District Court require the State to take in order to cure Detroit's condition of segregation?...

Under our decisions, it was clearly proper for the District Court to take into account the so-called "white flight" from the city schools which would be forthcoming from any Detroit-only decree....

[S]urely...school authorities must, to the extent possible, take all practicable steps to ensure that Negro and white children in fact go to school together. This is, in the final analysis, what desegregation of the public schools is all about.

Because of the already high and rapidly increasing percentage of Negro students in the Detroit system, as well as the prospect of white flight, a Detroit-only plan simply has no hope of achieving actual desegregation....

Racially identifiable schools are one of the primary vestiges of state-imposed segregation which an effective desegregation decree must attempt to eliminate....

Under a Detroit-only decree, Detroit's schools will clearly remain racially identifiable in comparison with neighboring schools in the metropolitan community. Schools with 65% and more Negro students will stand in sharp and obvious contrast to schools in neighboring districts with less than 2% Negro enrollment. Negro students will continue to perceive their schools as segregated educational facilities and this perception will only be increased when whites react to a Detroit-only decree by fleeing to the suburbs to avoid integration....

The rippling effects on residential patterns caused by purposeful acts of segregation do not automatically subside at the school district border. With rare exceptions, these effects naturally spread through all the residential neighborhoods within a metropolitan area....The state must also bear part of the blame for the white flight to the suburbs which would be forthcoming from a Detroit-only decree and would render such a remedy ineffective. Having created a system where whites and Negroes were intentionally kept apart so that they could not become accustomed to learning together, the State is responsible for the fact that many whites will react to the dismantling of that segregated system by attempting to flee to the suburbs. Indeed, by limiting the District Court to a Detroit-only remedy and allowing that flight to the suburbs to succeed, the Court today allows the State to profit from its own wrong and to perpetuate for years to come the separation of the races it achieved in the past by purposeful state action....

III

...First of all, the metropolitan plan would not involve the busing of substantially more students than already ride buses....

With respect to distance and amount of time traveled, 17 of the outlying school districts involved in the plan are contiguous to the Detroit district. The rest are all within 8 miles of the Detroit city limits....

As far as economies are concerned, a metropolitan remedy would actually be more sensible than a Detroit-only remedy. Because of prior transportation aid restrictions,...Detroit largely relied on public transportation, at student expense, for those students who lived too far away to walk to school. Since no inventory of school buses existed, a Detroit-only plan was estimated to require the purchase of 900 buses to effectuate the necessary transportation. The tri-county area, in contrast, already has an inventory of 1,800 buses, many of which are now underutilized....

Desegregation is not and was never expected to be an easy task. Racial attitudes ingrained in our Nation's childhood and adolescence are not quickly thrown aside in its middle years. But just as the inconvenience of some cannot be allowed to stand in the way of the rights of others, so public opposition, no matter how strident, cannot be permitted to divert this Court from the enforcement of the constitutional principles at issue in this case. Today's holding, I fear, is more a reflection of a perceived public mood that we have gone far enough in enforcing the Constitution's guarantee of equal justice than it is the product of neutral principles of law. In the short run, it may seem to be the easier course to allow our great metropolitan areas to be divided up each into two cities—one white, the other black— but it is a course, I predict, our people will ultimately regret. I dissent.

IMPEACHMENT ARTICLES
July 27-30, 1974

A committee of the House of Representatives, acting in a capacity only once before paralleled in American history, voted July 27-30 to recommend the impeachment of President Richard M. Nixon on the grounds of obstruction of justice, abuse of power and contempt of Congress. The historic votes adopting the articles capped six months of deliberate—and often partisan—consideration by the House Judiciary Committee. That committee had launched an impeachment probe in February in response to charges that the Watergate scandal traced a path to the President's Oval Office. (See p. 137-143.) The committee began televised committee deliberation of impeachment articles on July 24, adjourning July 30 after approving three articles and rejecting two others.

On July 27, a majority of the committee soundly indicated their approval of removing Nixon from office and approved an article of impeachment. Article I, approved by a 27-11 vote, charged President Nixon with obstruction of justice for his participation in a scheme to cover up White House involvement in the Watergate affair and to block the investigation of that affair. The committee approved Article II by a 28-10 vote July 29, charging Nixon with abusing the powers of his office by subverting the activities of the Central Intelligence Agency and the Internal Revenue Service. Article III, charging Nixon with contempt of Congress for his refusal to honor the committee's subpoenas, was approved July 30 by a 21-17 vote. The committee July 30 rejected two other proposed articles, both on a vote of 12-26. The first charged the President with authorizing and ratifying the concealment from Congress of the facts concerning the bombing in Cambodia in 1972 in derogation of Congress' constitutional power to declare war. The sec-

ond accused Nixon of knowingly and fraudulently evading portions of his federal income taxes from 1969 through 1972 and violating his oath of office by receiving unconstitutional emoluments.

Following the House Judiciary Committee's decisive votes July 27-30, the mood on Capitol Hill clearly indicated that legislators had accepted impeachment of Nixon as highly likely and were already looking ahead to the Senate trial scheduled to begin in September. Senators had been informed by the leadership that 6-day work weeks could be expected during the trial of Nixon, an effort aimed at concluding the proceedings before the November 1974 elections.

On the question of Nixon's resignation, legislators—for the moment—subdued their predictions that President Nixon would resign and instead were taking at face value Nixon's reiterated vows not to "walk away from the job that the people of the United States elected me to do for the people of the United States." The White House announced that Nixon's impeachment by the House was expected but predicted that the Senate would fail to convict him.

What could not be seen as the month of July ended was the effect that would be felt as a result of the Supreme Court's unanimous decision July 24 ordering Nixon to surrender White House tapes as evidence for upcoming Watergate trials. (Supreme Court decision, see p. 621-638.) *As a result of that decision, Nixon Aug. 5 released transcripts of three conversations held June 23, 1972, six days after the Watergate break-in, that clearly linked him directly with the Watergate coverup as an original participant in the scheme.* (June 23, 1972, transcripts, see p. 673-682.)

As public outrage mounted as a result of the Nixon admission, resignation emerged as an imminent possibility. Crowds surrounded the White House awaiting the historic moment. On the evening of Aug. 8, President Nixon went on national television to inform the country that he would submit his resignation effective at noon, Aug. 9. (President Nixon's resignation, see p. 683-693.)

> *Following are complete texts of the three articles of impeachment voted by the House Judiciary Committee and two articles rejected by the committee:*

Texts of Articles

Article I

In his conduct of the office of President of the United States, Richard M. Nixon, in violation of his constitutional oath faithfully to execute the office of President of the United States and, to the best of his ability, preserve, protect, and defend the Constitution of the United States, and in violation of his constitutional duty to take care that the laws be faithfully executed, has prevented, obstructed, and impeded the administration of justice, in that:

On June 17, 1972, and prior thereto, agents of the Committee for the Re-election of the President committed unlawful entry of the headquarters of the Democratic National Committee in Washington, District of Columbia, for the purpose of securing political intelligence. Subsequent thereto, Richard M. Nixon, using the powers of his high office, engaged personally and through his close subordinates and agents, in a course of conduct or plan designed to delay, impede, and obstruct the investigation of such unlawful entry; to cover up, conceal and protect those responsible; and to conceal the existence and scope of other unlawful covert activities.

The means used to implement this course of conduct or plan included one or more of the following:

(1) making false or misleading statements to lawfully authorized investigative officers and employees of the United States;

(2) withholding relevant and material evidence or information from lawfully authorized investigative officers and employees of the United States;

(3) approving, condoning, acquiescing in, and counseling witnesses with respect to the giving of false or misleading statements to lawfully authorized investigative officers and employees of the United States and false or misleading testimony in duly instituted judicial and congressional proceedings;

(4) interfering or endeavoring to interfere with the conduct of investigations by the Department of Justice of the United States, the Federal Bureau of Investigation, the Office of Watergate Special Prosecution Force, and Congressional Committees;

(5) approving, condoning, and acquiescing in, the surreptitious payment of substantial sums of money for the purpose of obtaining the silence or influencing the testimony of witnesses, potential witnesses or individuals who participated in such unlawful entry and other illegal activities;

(6) endeavoring to misuse the Central Intelligence Agency, an agency of the United States;

(7) disseminating information received from officers of the Department of Justice of the United States to subjects of investigations conducted by lawfully authorized investigative officers and employees of the United States, for the purpose of aiding and assisting such subjects in their attempts to avoid criminal liability;

(8) making or causing to be made false or misleading public statements for the purpose of deceiving the people of the United States into believing that a thorough and complete investigation had been conducted with respect to allegations of misconduct on the part of personnel of the executive branch of the United States and personnel of the Committee for the Re-election of the President, and that there was no involvement of such personnel in such misconduct; or

(9) endeavoring to cause prospective defendants, and individuals duly tried and convicted, to expect favored treatment and consideration in

return for their silence or false testimony, or rewarding individuals for their silence or false testimony.

In all of this, Richard M. Nixon has acted in a manner contrary to his trust as President and subversive of constitutional government, to the great prejudice of the cause of law and justice and to the manifest injury of the people of the United States.

Wherefore Richard M. Nixon, by such conduct, warrants impeachment and trial, and removal from office.

—Adopted July 27 by a 27-11 vote

Article II

Using the powers of the office of President of the United States, Richard M. Nixon, in violation of his constitutional oath faithfully to execute the office of President of the United States and, to the best of his ability, preserve, protect, and defend the Constitution of the United States, and in disregard of his constitutional duty to take care that the laws be faithfully executed, has repeatedly engaged in conduct violating the constitutional rights of citizens, impairing the due and proper administration of justice and the conduct of lawful inquiries, or contravening the laws governing agencies of the executive branch and the purposes of these agencies.

This conduct has included one or more of the following:

(1) He has, acting personally and through his subordinates and agents, endeavored to obtain from the Internal Revenue Service, in violation of the constitutional rights of citizens, confidential information contained in income tax returns for purposes not authorized by law, and to cause, in violation of the constitutional rights of citizens, income tax audits or other income tax investigations to be initiated or conducted in a discriminatory manner.

(2) He misused the Federal Bureau of Investigation, the Secret Service, and other executive personnel, in violation or disregard of the constitutional rights of citizens, by directing or authorizing such agencies or personnel to conduct or continue electronic surveillance or other investigations for purposes unrelated to national security, the enforcement of laws, or any other lawful function of his office; he did direct, authorize, or permit the use of information obtained thereby for purposes unrelated to national security, the enforcement of laws, or any other lawful function of his office; and he did direct the concealment of certain records made by the Federal Bureau of Investigation of electronic surveillance.

(3) He has, acting personally and through his subordinates and agents, in violation or disregard of the constitutional rights of citizens, authorized and permitted to be maintained a secret investigative unit within the office of the President, financed in part with money derived from campaign contributions, which unlawfully utilized the resources of the Central Intelligence Agency, engaged in covert and unlawful activities, and attempted to prejudice the constitutional right of an accused to a fair trial.

(4) He has failed to take care that the laws were faithfully executed by failing to act when he knew or had reason to know that his close subordinates endeavored to impede and frustrate lawful inquiries by duly constituted executive, judicial, and legislative entities concerning the unlawful entry into the headquarters of the Democratic National Committee, and the cover up thereof, and concerning other unlawful activities including those relating to the confirmation of Richard Kleindienst as Attorney General of the United States, the electronic surveillance of private citizens, the break-in into the offices of Dr. Lewis Fielding and the campaign financing practices of the Committee to Re-elect the President.

(5) In disregard of the rule of law, he knowingly misused the executive branch, including the Federal Bureau of Investigation, the Criminal Division, and the Office of Watergate Special Prosecution Force, of the Department of Justice, and the Central Intelligence Agency, in violation of his duty to take care that the laws be faithfully executed.

In all of this, Richard M. Nixon has acted in a manner contrary to his trust as President and subversive of constitutional government, to the great prejudice of the cause of law and justice and to the manifest injury of the people of the United States.

Wherefore Richard M. Nixon, by such conduct, warrants impeachment and trial, and removal from office.

—Adopted July 29 by a 28-10 vote

Article III

In his conduct of the office of President of the United States, Richard M. Nixon, contrary to his oath faithfully to execute the office of President of the United States and, to the best of his ability, preserve, protect, and defend the Constitution of the United States, and in violation of his constitutional duty to take care that the laws be faithfully executed, has failed without lawful cause of excuse to produce papers and things as directed by duly authorized subpoenas issued by the Committee on the Judiciary of the House of Representatives on April 11, 1974, May 15, 1974, May 30, 1974, and June 24, 1974, and willfully disobeyed such subpoenas. The subpoenaed papers and things were deemed necessary by the Committee in order to resolve by direct evidence fundamental, factual questions relating to Presidential direction, knowledge, or approval of actions demonstrated by other evidence to be substantial grounds for impeachment of the President. In refusing to produce these papers and things Richard M. Nixon, substituting his judgment as to what materials were necessary for the inquiry, interposed the powers of the Presidency against the lawful subpoenas of the House of Representatives, thereby assuming to himself functions and judgments necessary to the exercise of the sole power of impeachment vested by the Constitution in the House of Representatives.

In all of this, Richard M. Nixon has acted in a manner contrary to his trust as President and subversive of constitutional government, to the great prejudice of the cause of law and justice, and to the manifest injury of the people of the United States.

Wherefore, Richard M. Nixon by such conduct, warrants impeachment and trial, and removal from office.

—Adopted July 30 by a 21-17 vote

Articles Not Approved

Income Taxes

In his conduct of the office of President of the United States, Richard M. Nixon, in violation of his constitutional oath faithfully to execute the office of the President of the United States, and, to the best of his ability, preserve, protect and defend the Constitution of the United States and in violation of his constitutional duty to take care that the laws be faithfully executed, did receive emoluments from the United States in excess of the compensation provided by law pursuant to Article II, Section 1, Clause 7 of the Constitution, and did willfully attempt to evade the payment of a portion of Federal income taxes due and owing by him for the years 1969, 1970, 1971, and 1972, in that:

(1) He, during the period for which he has been elected President, unlawfully received compensation in the form of government expenditures at and on his privately-owned properties located in or near San Clemente, California, and Key Biscayne, Florida.

(2) He knowingly and fraudulently failed to report certain income and claimed deductions in the year 1969, 1970, 1971, and 1972 on his Federal income tax returns which were not authorized by law, including deductions for a gift of papers to the United States valued at approximately $576,000.

In all of this, Richard M. Nixon has acted in a manner contrary to his trust as President and subversive of constitutional government, to the great prejudice of the cause of law and justice and to the manifest injury of the people of the United States.

Wherefore Richard M. Nixon, by such conduct, warrants impeachment and trial, and removal from office.

Cambodia Bombing

In his conduct of the office of President of the United States, Richard M. Nixon, in violation of his constitutional oath faithfully to execute the office of President of the United States and, to the best of his ability, preserve, protect, and defend the Constitution of the United States, and in disregard of his constitutional duty to take care that the laws be faithfully executed, on and subsequent to March 17, 1969, authorized, ordered, and ratified the concealment from the Congress of the facts and the submission to the Congress of false and misleading statements concerning the existence, scope and nature of American bombing operations in Cambodia in derogation of the power of the Congress to declare war, to make appropriations and to raise and support armies, and by such conduct warrants impeachment and trial and removal from office.

SENTENCING OF THE "PLUMBERS"
July 31, 1974

John D. Ehrlichman, for four years one of President Nixon's two closest advisers, and the man in overall charge of the White House Special Investigations Unit known as the "plumbers," was sentenced July 31 to serve at least 20 months in prison. Ehrlichman had been convicted July 12 along with G. Gordon Liddy, Bernard L. Barker and Eugenio R. Martinez (three of the Watergate burglars, see Historic Documents 1973, p. 413-425; 499-512; 537-548; 549-556; 563-574; 659-679) on charges of conspiring to violate the civil rights of Dr. Lewis J. Fielding, a Los Angeles psychiatrist who had been consulted by Daniel Ellsberg. The four men were convicted of violating Fielding's rights by burglarizing his office in September 1971, purportedly in an effort to uncover damaging information about Ellsberg who at the time stood accused of leaking classified documents to national newspapers. (Pentagon Papers case, see Historic Documents 1973, p. 537-548.) Ehrlichman was also convicted on three counts of perjury arising from the attempt to coverup the activities of the "plumbers." One of the three charges was dismissed by U.S. District Judge Gerhard A. Gesell as too vague. The men had been indicted by a federal grand jury in Washington, D.C., on March 7 (see p. 205-214 and p. 411-417.)

At sentencing July 31, Ehrlichman, told by Gesell that he must bear "major responsibility for this shameful episode in the history of our country," was ordered to serve three concurrent sentences of 20 months to five years. The maximum sentence which could have been imposed on each count was 20 years in prison and a $30,000 fine. Ehrlichman, after the conviction, continued to assert his innocence and his faith that on appeal he would be exonerated. Gesell sentenced Liddy to prison for one

661

to three years, a sentence which was to run concurrently with the six to 20 years that he was serving for the Watergate break-in. The two other men convicted in the Fielding break-in, Barker and Martinez, were placed on three years' probation. Both already had served sentences for their role in the Watergate case. Gesell told them they had been "duped" by high government officials and had been punished sufficiently.

Key Point of the Trial

What is meant by the term "covert operation"? Does it mean only a secret mission or does it mean an illegal act such as a break-in? The fate of Ehrlichman had rested on how the jurors in U.S. District Court in Washington, D.C., answered that question. The definition of those words had been the central issue when the trial opened July 1.

As the prosecution got underway, the government brought forward its two key witnesses, David R. Young Jr. and Egil Krogh Jr., former codirectors of the "plumbers," to prove that "covert operations" were synonymous with "break-in" and that Young, Krogh and Ehrlichman knew that. Young testified July 2 that he believed Ehrlichman had specifically authorized the "examination" of Daniel Ellsberg's psychiatric records in Fielding's office without the knowledge or consent of the psychiatrist. "It was presumed that someone would have to enter those offices" without consent, Young said. "That was understood in the light of Dr. Fielding's refusal to speak with the FBI." Krogh said he told Ehrlichman on Aug. 5, 1971, that if the unit was to be successful in obtaining information for the profile, "we would have to conduct an operation on our own." Krogh said he did not recall the specific terminology used, but that he thought he said, "covert operation...clandestine...something to that effect." At that meeting, Krogh related, Ehrlichman asked for his assurance that the operation would not be traceable to the White House.

Krogh said approval came in an Aug. 11 memorandum in which Ehrlichman initialed his acquiescence to a "covert operation to examine psychiatric files" held by Fielding, to which Ehrlichman added, "If it is not traceable." After receipt of that memo, Krogh said, "It was clear to me that an entry operation would have to be undertaken to examine those files." He said the Aug. 11 memo referred specifically to the Aug. 5 meeting with Ehrlichman.

Charles W. Colson, the former special counsel to the President who had pleaded guilty to a charge of smearing Ellsberg, recalled in his testimony on July 3 how, at Ehrlichman's request, he had obtained $5,000 to finance the break-in. But Colson said he was not aware in advance that a burglary was being planned. He said he spoke to Ehrlichman after the unsuccessful break-in, and Ehrlichman told him words to the effect that "the boys tried to get Dr. Ellsberg's psychiatric records, but they failed...." The only other thing Ehrlichman said at that meeting, Colson said, was that "the matter was not to be discussed outside that office, with anyone else."

In summation remarks wrapping up the prosecution's case, Assistant Special Watergate Prosecutor William H. Merrill said July 11 that to find former White House assistant John D. Ehrlichman guilty, all the jurors needed to conclude was that he knew of a "covert operation to examine the files" of Dr. Lewis J. Fielding. Merrill contended that the evidence that Ehrlichman knew of the break-in in September 1971 was overwhelming. His closing statement lasted an hour and 20 minutes. "Everyone else knew that someone was going to go into Dr. Fielding's office to examine his files without his consent, and they might not have known there was going to be a break-in, but that's not what the indictment charges," Merrill continued. The indictment charged Ehrlichman with approving the unauthorized examination of Fielding's files, and the evidence showed him guilty of that charge, Merrill said. But, with the eight days of testimony behind him, William S. Frates, Ehrlichman's chief defense lawyer, replied that the government had failed to prove its case against the former presidential adviser. Frates suggested that prosecutors had tried to trick Ehrlichman into committing perjury and he attacked the credibility of the former codirector of the White House "plumbers" unit, David R. Young Jr., one of the prosecution's chief witnesses.

Ehrlichman Testimony

The high point of the trial came when Ehrlichman took the witness stand for two days to deny steadfastly that he had done anything illegal. In seven hours of testimony July 8 and 9, Ehrlichman said that he did not approve the break-in at Fielding's office, that he did not know about it in advance and that he did not examine files brought to him in March 1973 by Young or remove "sensitive" memoranda from them. The jury's assessment of Ehrlichman's testimony was crucial, for the prosecution had hammered away the week before at his alleged involvement with the break-in plans and his subsequent lying to FBI agents and a federal grand jury about his involvement. Prosecutors had introduced several memoranda from August 1971 that dealt with the break-in plans. In one memo, dated Aug. 11, 1971, Ehrlichman specifically approved a covert operation to examine Fielding's files. Ehrlichman said July 8 that when he approved the operation, he thought he was clearing "a legal, conventional investigation." The means to be employed in the investigation "didn't enter my thought process," the former White House official said.

Ehrlichman had rested his defense, in part, on his contention that he did not know that a covert operation would involve any illegal activities. "Covert to me means a private investigation—where the people don't identify themselves as from the FBI—a conventional investigation like the FBI would conduct," he said. He thought that perhaps the files "could be examined by request" or "by some third party," he continued, adding that he did not even know where the files were and thought that maybe Fielding was an employee of the Rand Corporation, where Ellsberg had worked. The other leg of his defense was his memory—more aptly his poor recollection.

Under stiff cross examination by Merrill, Ehrlichman maintained that he could not recall a great many of the details testified to by Young and Krogh, even though many of them were documented by memoranda. He explained his faulty memory by saying that "a great deal of this was jury grist I was glancing at and setting aside because it wasn't of any great moment." It was, he said, "part of the great mass of stuff I had sort of trained myself not to pack around in my memory." But Merrill pointed out the selectivity of Ehrlichman's memory. Ehrlichman could remember conversations and meetings that helped his defense, but said he had trouble recollecting meetings and conversations that specifically dealt with plans for getting psychiatric information on Ellsberg.

Kissinger and Nixon Statements

The defense succeeded in obtaining Secretary of State Henry A. Kissinger as a witness for Ehrlichman. In 108 seconds of testimony on July 10, Kissinger said that he never requested a psychological profile of Ellsberg. In a written statement made under oath and submitted voluntarily the same day, Nixon reiterated that he did not authorize the Fielding break-in. He also said that he recalled "repeatedly emphasizing to Mr. Ehrlichman that this was a highly classified matter which could be discussed with others only on an absolutely 'need to know' basis."

Before dismissing the jury so that it could reach a verdict, Judge Gesell instructed panel members July 12 that they need not find that Ehrlichman had known in advance that the "covert operation" to obtain Ellsberg's psychiatric files included a forcible break-in. That instruction cut sharply into one of Ehrlichman's defenses to the conspiracy count, that he merely approved a "covert operation" to examine the files and never knew in advance that there would be a break-in. Gesell said, in effect, that any search of private files without permission or a court order would be illegal and would violate the Fourth Amendment to the Constitution, which guarantees against unreasonable searches.

After the jury was dismissed for its deliberations, Ehrlichman's attorneys objected to the judge's instructions because he did not instruct the jury generally about their defense theory. Judge Gesell answered that "there is no coherent statement of his defense...his defense has been one of guarding and dodging around various issues." Several hours later, Ehrlichman, Liddy, Barker and Martinez were found guilty.

> *Excerpts from the proceedings July 31 in U.S. District Judge Gerhard A. Gesell's Washington courtroom. At the sentencing were John D. Ehrlichman and his lawyer William S. Frates; G. Gordon Liddy, Bernard L. Barker and Eugenio R. Martinez and their lawyers Peter Maroulis and Daniel Schultz. The proceedings, which begin on the next page, followed the defendants' convictions on charges of violating the civil rights of Dr. Lewis J. Fielding.*

THE COURT: ...You may come forward, Mr. Ehrlichman, with your counsel.

(Whereupon Defendant Ehrlichman and Mr. Frates approached the lectern.)

THE COURT: Mr. Frates, is there anything you wish to say to the Court before sentence is imposed on Mr. Ehrlichman?

MR. FRATES: No, Your Honor, there is not. Thank you, sir.

THE COURT: Mr. Ehrlichman, is there anything you wish to say to the Court before sentence is imposed?

DEFENDANT EHRLICHMAN: May it please the Court, I believe that I am the only one in this room who really knows whether I am guilty or not guilty of the charges. Your Honor, I am innocent of each and every one of these charges involved in this case.

THE COURT: Mr. Ehrlichman, the Court, of course, accepts the verdict of the jury.

You are a lawyer and among the Defendants you held the highest position of public trust in our Government and the major responsibility for this shameful episode in the history of our country.

The Constitution was ignored; the rights of citizens abused; the important Ellsberg Federal prosecution was tainted and had to be dismissed by Judge Byrne; falsehoods and concealment were employed to thwart the lawful inquiry into this abuse; and the jury has found that all of this occurred with your approval and your affirmative participation.

The Court has put out of the Court's mind all accusations concerning you in Watergate matters and all other pending indictments; and after giving heavy weight to the many affirmative aspects of your life, without which the Court would impose a far more severe sentence, you are sentenced to twenty months to five years on each count, the counts to run concurrently.

That is the sentence of the Court.

Mr. Liddy, if you will come forward with your attorney.

(Whereupon Defendant Liddy and Mr. Maroulis approached the lectern.)

THE COURT: Is there anything you wish to say, Mr. Maroulis, before sentence is imposed on Mr. Liddy?

MR. MAROULIS: May it please the Court, I should like to insure that the Court is accurately informed concerning Mr. Liddy's present situation. I say that because there have been repeated reports in the media which are misleading to the effect that Mr. Liddy is currently under sentence of six years and eight months.

I would like to hand to the Court a copy of the official sentence computation of the Federal Bureau of Prisons. It reflects accurately that Mr. Liddy is currently under sentence of twenty years and a $40,000 fine.

THE COURT: That is the Court's understanding.

MR. MAROULIS: Yes, sir.

(Whereupon the document was submitted to the Court.)

MR. MAROULIS: The document reflects—and I direct the Court's attention to the bottom of the page—that the sentence is inoperative until October 3 of this year. The net effect of that is to adjust the dates listed by the addition of one and a half years, which happens to be exactly the time Mr. Liddy has served in prison, as he stands here.

Mr. Liddy will not be eligible for parole, much less receive it, until April 1, 1981, at which time he will have served eight years and two months in prison.

Thank you, sir.

THE COURT: Is there anything you wish to say to me, Mr. Liddy, before sentence is imposed?

DEFENDANT LIDDY: Nothing at all, Your Honor.

THE COURT: Mr. Liddy, as the Court views the evidence, a middle level degree of responsibility in this case was yours. Your involvement, of course, remains unexplained.

The Court is well aware that you are an experienced trial lawyer. The evidence demonstrates your violation was deliberate and your offense is clear.

You are now serving a civil commitment imposed by Judge Sirica. The Court is going to impose a sentence of one-to-three years, to run concurrently with your sentence in the earlier criminal matter tried before Judge Sirica; and your sentence is to commence on October 3 of this year or such earlier date, in the event that civil commitment is in any manner modified or set aside.

The Court is very concerned that you are in the D.C. Jail, which I don't think is a fit place for you or anyone else to be. I cannot affect the civil commitment order of Judge Sirica; but I strongly recommend that as soon as you start serving this sentence, concurrently or otherwise with Judge Sirica's sentence, depending on how that comes out on appeal, that you be committed to the Lewisburg Federal Penitentiary.

That is the sentence of the Court.

Now I think Mr. Barker and Mr. Martinez can come up together with you, Mr. Schultz.

MR. SCHULTZ: Yes, sir.

(Whereupon Defendant Barker and Defendant Martinez and Mr. Schultz approached the lectern.)

THE COURT: Is there anything, Mr. Schultz, you wish to say before sentence is imposed on each of these men?

MR. SCHULTZ: Just briefly, Your Honor.

In January of this year Mr. Barker was released from jail after spending twelve and a half months incarcerated in connection with his eighteen-month-to-five-year sentence imposed in the original Watergate case. If we lose the appeal that is pending now, he will return to jail for another five and a half months before he would become eligible for parole.

In January of this year, Mr. Martinez also had the ability to be released by the Court of Appeals on his personal recognizance pending the appeal. At the same time the Parole Board had set his parole date, as he had become eligible after a sentence of one-to-four years and had served his year.

I had lengthy discussions with Mr. Martinez, because there were two months to go before the parole date; and the conclusion of those discussions was that Mr. Martinez continued to want to remain in jail for that additional two months, because he did not want to have to come out and worry about going back in. He thought it would be better for him to finish out his time than to have to worry about having his life disrupted in returning to jail.

He came out on March 7 of 1974 and on the same day he was indicted again in connection with this case.

I have represented Mr. Barker and Mr. Martinez for eighteen months. I deeply believe that they have been punished enough. The reasons why I believe that I have stated during the course of this trial. The facts on which I base that by and large have come out during the course of this trial.

Thank you, Your Honor.

THE COURT: Mr. Barker, is there anything you want to say to me before sentence is imposed?

DEFENDANT BARKER: No, Your Honor.

THE COURT: Mr. Martinez?

DEFENDANT MARTINEZ: Yes, Your Honor.

Really, this is not the place in which I had decided to be when I became an American citizen. It was never in my mind to do any wrongdoing.

I believe if I had been in front of this Court, what we did in this case, which happened prior, for which I was convicted after, the same people who brought us to this charge took us, after nine months, to the other place. They were not apprehended or they came back in the same condition. They do not represent to us any other change in attitude or purpose or motivation.

If I have committed an offense, that it looks like I did according to the conviction of the thing, I feel sorry; but my motivation was not to become a criminal or an offender.

My guilt, I tried to find out in my conscience, with my family, is to have trust or to have faith in those people who were running this country. The same ones who have had the trust of the people of this country.

I never thought that to carry out orders, as you have found out in Court, that came out from the White House could lead me into becoming a criminal, Your Honor. My motivations have never been to be a criminal.

It is nothing new: We went to the Bay of Pigs. Cubans have died in the Congo. They have been called mercenaries. They are not. They have died in

Vietnam. And now we are facing in Washington a similar case, Your Honor.

If I have done something wrong, I hope that in your mind at least, if I did it not according with the law, you do not think that my motivation or my intention are criminal.

I have become an American citizen about two years, a year prior to my conviction. Never was it my intention to become a criminal or a felon, Your Honor.

That is all.

THE COURT: I want to say something to each of you to give you the view of the Court.

Without giving the matter adequate thought, it appears to the Court that you contributed to illegal activity by our Government which in many ways was typical of the very regime you so strenuously and courageously opposed in Cuba.

As you both should well know, it is impossible to preserve freedom anywhere when zealots take over and the rule of law is ignored.

You have never sought to conceal your minor, non-policy roles. You were duped by high Government officials. Your good names have been tarnished by your impulsive, misguided conduct. You have each already served time for similar conduct in a related matter.

The Court feels that you have been adequately punished. The Court will suspend sentence and place each of you on probation for a period of three years.

Now, I want to say on the matter of bond, while you are both before me, that you, of course, have your right to appeal. If you choose to serve your probation during the pendency of the appeal—which is what the Court would recommend to you, though it is your choice and your choice alone to make—it would be the Court's purpose to transfer the question of probation supervision to the Miami probation office, where you both live, and where you can proceed pending the appeal.

DEFENDANT MARTINEZ: Thank you, Your Honor.

DEFENDANT BARKER: Thank you.

THE COURT: If you decide not to do so, Mr. Schultz can so advise the probation office later today or tomorrow. The thought I would then have is that you would remain on your personal recognizance under the present arrangements we have with respect to your bond. If you choose not to go forward and serve your probation pending the appeal.

DEFENDANT MARTINEZ: Thank you, Your Honor.

MR. SCHULTZ: Thank you very much, Your Honor.

DEFENDANT BARKER: Thank you.

THE COURT: Now, Mr. Frates, as far as Mr. Ehrlichman's bond is concerned, I am sure there is no objection from the United States. Mr.

Ehrlichman will be continued on the same bond he has been on, pending appeal, with the understanding, of course, that he will report to you or directly to the Bail Agency here any change in address if he moves from the address we now have as to his residence.

MR. FRATES: Thank you, sir. We appreciate that.

THE COURT: Return of Court.
(Whereupon at 9:50 a.m., the proceedings were concluded.)

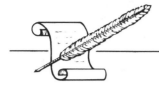

August

SELF-INCRIMINATING NIXON TAPES

August 5, 1974

A brief packet of information released by the White House Aug. 5 inflicted the final blow on the beleaguered Nixon administration. In a statement issued along with the White House transcripts of three taped conversations, President Nixon admitted that six days after the Watergate break-in of June 17, 1972, he ordered a halt to the investigation of that affair for political as well as national security reasons. He also admitted in the statement that he kept evidence of his action from his staff and lawyers and, later, from those members of the House Judiciary Committee who opposed reporting an impeachment resolution. (See p. 655.) The President said he deeply regretted "this...serious act of omission," but he fully acknowledged that he had withheld the contents of the tapes despite the fact that they contradicted his previous declarations of non-involvement and lack of knowledge of the Watergate coverup. (Previous statements, see Historic Documents 1973, p. 499-512, 563-574, 737-751, 859-880, 897-909 and 947-963.)

Nixon's statement accompanied the transcripts of conversations with former White House Chief of Staff H.R. Haldeman on June 23, 1972. The tapes of those conversations were turned over to U.S. District Judge John J. Sirica Aug. 2 in accordance with a unanimous Supreme Court decision July 24 ordering the President to make the tapes available as evidence in various upcoming Watergate trials. (See p. 621.) In the statement accompanying release of the transcripts Aug. 5, Nixon made it plain that neither his staff nor his Watergate lawyer, James D. St. Clair, had known of the contents of the conversations.

On Capitol Hill, reactions to the Nixon disclosure were swift and highly negative. The House Judiciary Committee had concluded its inquiry into

673

grounds for impeachment of the President and had voted three articles of impeachment that were scheduled for full House debate Aug. 19. (Final House Judiciary Committee report, p. 713.) Members of the House Judiciary Committee who had voted against the articles were moved by the latest turn of events to reconsider their position. Every one of the 10 Republicans who had opposed impeachment—for lack of direct, specific and hard evidence—switched to the other side. Rep. Charles E. Wiggins (R Calif.), Nixon's most eloquent defender on the committee, announced shortly after release of the transcripts that he would support impeachment. "The facts...known to me have now changed," said Wiggins. "I am now possessed of information which establishes beyond a reasonable doubt that on June 23, 1972, the President personally agreed to certain actions, the purpose and intent of which were to interfere with the FBI investigation of the Watergate break-in.... After considerable reflection, I have reached the painful conclusion that the President of the United States should resign." If the President did not resign, Wiggins added, "I am prepared to conclude that the magnificent career of public service of Richard Nixon must be terminated involuntarily and shall support those portions of Article I [of the impeachment resolution] which are sustained by the evidence."

Wiggins' view was voiced more strongly by other legislators. "The most devastating thing that can be said of it," said Speaker Carl Albert (D Okla.), "is that it speaks for itself." Nixon should resign, said Robert McClory (R Ill.), the most senior Republican on the House Judiciary Committee to support impeachment. Any delay was now "only a question of his personal stubbornness, personal stonewalling," he said. Majority Leader Thomas P. O'Neill Jr. (D Mass.) said he felt no more than 75 members would oppose impeachment. The evening of Aug. 5, Vice President Gerald R. Ford announced that he would cease repeating his still-held belief in the President's innocence. He had not been informed of the contents of the President's statement in advance.

As statements from members of Congress in favor of Nixon's departure from office—by resignation or impeachment—flooded Capitol Hill Aug. 6, Nixon called a sudden Cabinet meeting. Queried afterwards, Cabinet members insisted that Nixon said he would not resign but would "fight on" to stay in office. Treasury Secretary William E. Simon said, "The President sincerely believes he has not committed an impeachable offense."

In mid-afternoon Aug. 6, House Minority Leader John J. Rhodes (R Ariz.) made his announcement: he would vote for impeachment based on Article I, obstruction of justice, and perhaps—based on the new evidence—for Article II, abuse of powers. Representatives Barber B. Conable Jr. (R N.Y.) and John B. Anderson (R Ill.), the third and fourth ranking members of the House, also expressed their support for impeachment. All three expressed doubts about the suggestion that the President be granted immunity, by Congress, from prosecution after he left office. And Sen. Robert Dole (R Kan.), who was national party chairman during the 1972 campaign, said Aug. 6 that if the President had 40 votes the previous week in the Senate against conviction, he had no more than 20 left, far short of the 34 needed to survive a trial in that body. But Sen. Carl T. Curtis (R Neb.) continued to defend the President, warning against panic. The United States would become like a "banana republic," he said, if it ousted Nixon, placing Ford and Ford's choice for vice president—neither of whom had been elected to their offices—in the nation's highest posts.

Nixon's Aug. 5 statement, conceding he had withheld crucial evidence from the Watergate prosecutors and the public, stirred an outcry against the President that soon brought an end to the five and one-half year administration. On Aug. 8, President Nixon told the nation via national television that he would resign, effective at noon the next day. (See p. 683.) On Aug. 9, Gerald R. Ford became the thirty-eighth President of the United States. (See p. 695-705.)

> *Following are excerpts from White House tape transcripts made public by President Nixon Aug. 5. The excerpts are from three conversations on June 23, 1972, with H. R. Haldeman, then his chief of staff. In these excerpts, the President approves a plan suggested by Haldeman to have top officials of the Central Intelligence Agency (CIA) tell the FBI to stay out of certain investigations of the Watergate break-in which could lead to employees of the Nixon re-election committee. On June 23, about two hours after getting the President's approval, Haldeman met with CIA Director Richard C. Helms and Gen. Vernon A. Walters, the deputy director. Walters later testified that he was "ordered" by Haldeman to inform L. Patrick Gray III, then acting FBI director, that unspecified CIA activities in Mexico might be uncovered if the bureau pursued its investigation there:*

Meeting: The President and Haldeman, Oval Office, June 23, 1972, (10:04—11:39 a.m.):

H. Now, on the investigation, you know the Democratic break-in thing, we're back in the problem area because the FBI is not under control, because Gray doesn't exactly know how to control it and they have—their investigation is now leading into some productive areas—because they've been able to trace the money—not through the money itself—but through the bank sources—the banker. And, and it goes in some directions we don't want it to go. Ah, also there have been some things—like an informant came in off the street to the FBI in Miami who was a photographer or has a friend who is a photographer who developed some films through this guy Barker and the films had pictures of Democratic National Committee letterhead documents and things. So it's things like that that are filtering in. Mitchell came up with yesterday, and John Dean analyzed very carefully last night and concludes, concurs now

675

with Mitchell's recommendation that the only way to solve this, and we're set up beautifully to do it, ah, in that and that—the only network that paid any attention to it last night was NBC—they did a massive story on the Cuban thing.

P. That's right.

H. That the way to handle this now is for us to have Walters call Pat Gray and just say, "Stay to hell out of this—this is ah, business here we don't want you to go any further on it." That's not an unusual development, and ah, that would take care of it.

P. What about Pat Gray—you mean Pat Gray doesn't want to?

H. Pat does want to. He doesn't know how to, and he doesn't have, he doesn't have any basis for doing it. Given this, he will then have the basis. He'll call Mark Felt in [W. Mark Felt, FBI deputy associate director in 1972], and the two of them—and Mark Felt wants to cooperate because he's ambitious—

P. Yeah.

H. He'll call him in and say, "We've got the signal from across the river to put the hold on this." And that will fit rather well because the FBI agents who are working the case, at this point, feel that's what it is.

P. This is CIA? They've traced the money? Who'd they trace it to?

H. Well they've traced it to a name, but they haven't gotten to the guy yet.

P. Would it be somebody here?

H. Ken Dahlberg.

P. Who the hell is Ken Dahlberg?

H. He gave $25,000 in Minnesota and, ah, the check went directly to this guy Barker.

P. It isn't from the Committee, though, from Stans?

H. Yeah. It is. It's directly traceable and there's some more through some Texas people that went to the Mexican bank which can also be traced to the Mexican bank—they'll get their names today.

H. —And (pause)

P. Well, I mean, there's no way—I'm just thinking if they don't cooperate, what do they say? That they were approached by the Cubans. That's what Dahlberg has to say, the Texans too, that they—

H. Well, if they will. But then we're relying on more and more people all the time. That's the problem and they'll stop if we could take this other route.

P. All right.

H. And you seem to think the thing to do is get them to stop?

P. Right, fine.

H. They say the only way to do that is from White House instructions. And it's got to be to Helms and to—ah, what's his name....? Walters.

P. Walters.

H. And the proposal would be that Ehrlichman and I call them in, and say, ah—

P. All right, fine. How do you call him in—I mean you just—well, we protected Helms from one hell of a lot of things.

H. That's what Ehrlichman says.

P. Of course, this Hunt, that will uncover a lot of things. You open that scab there's a hell of a lot of things and we just feel that it would be very detrimental to have this thing go any further. This involves these Cubans, Hunt, and a lot of hanky-panky that we have nothing to do with ourselves. Well what the hell, did Mitchell know about this?

H. I think so. I don't think he knew the details, but I think he knew.

P. He didn't know how it was going to be handled though—with Dahlberg and the Texans and so forth? Well who was the asshole that did? Is it Liddy? Is that the fellow? He must be a little nuts!

H. He is.

P. I mean he just isn't well screwed on is he? Is that the problem?

H. No, but he was under pressure, apparently, to get more information, and as he got more pressure, he pushed the people harder to move harder—

P. Pressure from Mitchell?

H. Apparently.

P. Oh, Mitchell. Mitchell was at the point (unintelligible).

H. Yeah.

P. All right, fine, I understand it all. We won't second-guess Mitchell and the rest. Thank God it wasn't Colson.

H. The FBI interviewed Colson yesterday. They determined that would be a good thing to do. To have him take an interrogation, which he did, and that—the FBI guys working the case concluded that there were one or two possibilities—one, that this was a White House—they don't think that there is anything at the Election Committee—they think it was either a White House operation and they had some obscure reasons for it—non-political, or it was a—Cuban and the CIA. And after their interrogation of Colson yesterday, they concluded it was not the White House, but are now convinced it is a CIA thing, so the CIA turnoff would—

P. Well, not sure of their analysis, I'm not going to get that involved. I'm (unintelligible).

H. No, sir, we don't want you to.

P. You call them in.

H. Good deal.

P. Play it tough. That's the way they play it and that's the way we are going to play it.

H. O.K.

P. When I saw that news summary, I questioned whether it's a bunch of crap, but I thought, er, well it's good to have them off us awhile, because when they start bugging us, which they have, our little boys will not know how to handle it. I hope they will though.

H. You never know.

P. Good.

(Other matters are discussed. Then the conversation returns to the break-in coverup strategy.)

Return to Strategy

P. When you get in—when you get in (unintelligible) people, say, "Look the problem is that this will open the whole, the whole Bay of Pigs thing, and the President just feels that ah, without going into the details—don't, don't lie to them to the extent to say there is no involvement, but just say this is a comedy of errors, without getting into it, the President believes that it is going to open the whole Bay of Pigs thing up again. And, ah, because these people are plugging for (unintelligible) and that they should call the FBI in and (unintelligible) don't go any further into this case period!

P. (Inaudible) our cause—

H. Get more done for our cause by the opposition than by us.

P. Well, can you get it done?

H. I think so.

Second Meeting

Meeting: The President and Haldeman, Oval Office, June 23, 1972 (1:04—1:13 p.m.)

P. O.K., just postpone (scratching noises) (unintelligible) Just say (unintelligible) very bad to have this fellow Hunt, ah, he knows too damned much, if he was involved—you happen to know that? If it gets out that this is all involved, the Cuba thing it would be a fiasco. It would make the CIA look bad, it's going to make Hunt look bad, and it is likely to blow the whole Bay of Pigs thing which we think would be very unfortunate—both for CIA, and for the country, at this time, and for American foreign policy. Just tell him to lay off. Don't you?

H. Yep. That's the basis to do it on. Just leave it at that.

P. I don't know if he'll get any ideas for doing it because our concern political (unintelligible). Helms is not one to (unintelligible)—I would just say, lookit, because of the Hunt involvement, whole cover basically this.

H. Yep. Good move.

P. Well, they've got some pretty good ideas on this Meany thing. Shultz did a good paper. I read it all (voices fade).

Third Meeting

Meeting: The President and Haldeman, Executive Office Building, June 23, 1972 (2:20—2:45 p.m.)

H. No problem

P. (Unintelligible)

H. Well, it was kind of interesting. Walters made the point and I didn't mention Hunt, I just said that the thing was leading into directions that were going to create potential problems because they were exploring leads that led back into areas that would be harmful to the CIA and harmful to the government (unintelligible) didn't have anything to do (unintelligible).

(Telephone)

P. Chuck? I wonder if you would give John Connally a call he's on his trip—I don't want him to read it in the paper before Monday about this quota thing and say—look, we're going to do this, but that I checked, I asked you about the situation (unintelligible) had an understanding it was only temporary and ah (unintelligible) O.K.? I just don't want him to read it in the papers. Good. Fine.

H. (unintelligible) I think Helms did to (unintelligible) said, I've had no—

P. God (unintelligible).

H. Gray called and said, yesterday, and said that he thought—

P. Who did? Gray?

H. Gray called Helms and said I think we've run right into the middle of a CIA covert operation.

P. Gray said that?

H. Yeah. And (unintelligible) said nothing we've done at this point and ah (unintelligible) says well it sure looks to me like it is (unintelligible) and ah, that was the end of that conversation (unintelligible) the problem is it tracks back to the Bay of Pigs and it tracks back to some other the leads run out to people who had no involvement in this, except by contacts and connection, but it gets to areas that are liable to be raised? The whole problem (unintelligible) Hunt. So at that point he kind of got the picture. He said, he said we'll be very happy to be helpful (unintelligible) handle anything you want. I would like to know the reason for being helpful, and I made it clear to him he wasn't going to get explicit (unintelligible) generality, and he said fine. And Walters (unintelligible). Walters is going to make a call to Gray. That's the way we put it and that's the way it was left.

Money

P. How does that work though, how, they've got to (unintelligible) somebody from the Miami bank.

H. (unintelligible). The point John makes—the Bureau is going on on this because they don't know what they are uncovering (unintelligible) continue to pursue it. They don't need to because they already have their case as far as the charges against these men (unintelligible) and ah, as they pursue it (unintelligible) exactly, but we didn't in any way say we (unintelligible). One thing Helms did raise. He said, Gray—he asked Gray why they thought they had run into a CIA thing and Gray said because of the characters involved and the amount of money involved, a lot of dough. (unintelligible) and ah, (unintelligible)

P. (Unintelligible)

H. Well, I think they will.

P. If it runs (unintelligible) what the hell who knows (unintelligible) contributed CIA.

H. Yeah, it's money CIA gets money (unintelligible) I mean their money moves in a lot of different ways, too.

P. Yeah. How are (unintelligible)—a lot of good—

H. (Unintelligible)

P. Well you remember what the SOB did on my book? When I brought out the fact, you know—

H. Yeah.

P. that he knew all about Dulles? (Expletive Deleted) Dulles knew. Dulles told me. I know, I mean (unintelligible) had the telephone call. Remember, I had a call put in—Dulles just blandly said and knew why.

H. Yeah.

P. Now, what the hell! Who told him to do it? The President? (Unintelligible)

H. Dulles was no more Kennedy's man than (unintelligible) was your man (unintelligible)

P. (unintelligible) covert operation—do anything else (unintelligible)

Following is the text of President Nixon's Aug. 5 statement issued with the release of the transcripts of three June 23, 1972, White House tape recordings:

I have today instructed my attorneys to make available to the House Judiciary Committee, and I am making public, the transcripts of three conversations with H. R. Haldeman on June 23, 1972. I have also turned over the tapes of these conversations to Judge Sirica, as part of the process of my compliance with the Supreme Court ruling.

On April 29, in announcing my decision to make public the original set of White House transcripts, I stated that "as far as what the President personally knew and did with regard to Watergate and the cover-up is concerned, these materials—together with those already made available—will tell it all."

Shortly after that, in May, I made a preliminary review of some of the 64 taped conversations subpoenaed by the Special Prosecutor.

Among the conversations I listened to at that time were two of those of June 23. Although I recognized that these presented potential problems, I did not inform my staff or my Counsel of it, or those arguing my case, nor did I amend my submission to the Judiciary Committee in order to include and reflect it. At the time, I did not realize the extent of the implications which these conversations might now appear to have. As a result, those arguing my case, as well as those passing judgment on the case, did so with information that was incomplete and in some respects erroneous. This was a serious act of omission for which I take full responsibility and which I deeply regret.

Since the Supreme Court's decision twelve days ago, I have ordered my Counsel to analyze the 64 tapes, and I have listened to a number of them myself. This process has made it clear that portions of the tapes of these June 23 conversations are at variance with certain of my previous statements. Therefore, I have ordered the transcripts made available immediately to the Judiciary Committee so that they can be reflected in the Committee's report, and included in the record to be considered by the House and Senate.

In a formal written statement on May 22 of last year, I said that shortly after the Watergate break-in I became concerned about the possibility that the FBI investigation might lead to the exposure either of unrelated covert activities of the CIA, or of sensitive national security matters that the so-called "plumbers" unit at the White House had been working on, because of the CIA and plumbers connections of some of those involved. I said that I therefore gave instructions that the FBI should be alerted to coordinate with the CIA, and to ensure that the investigation not expose these sensitive national security matters.

That statement was based on my recollection at the time—some eleven months later—plus documentary materials and relevant public testimony of those involved.

The June 23 tapes clearly show, however, that at the time I gave those instructions I also discussed the political aspects of the situation, and that I was aware of the advantages this course of action would have with respect to limiting possible public exposure of involvement by persons connected with the re-election committee.

My review of the additional tapes has, so far, shown no other major inconsistencies with what I have previously submitted. While I have no way at this stage of being certain that there will not be others, I have no reason to believe that there will be. In any case, the tapes in their entirety are now in the process of being furnished to Judge Sirica. He has begun what may be a rather lengthy process of reviewing the tapes, passing on specific claims of executive privilege on portions of them, and forwarding to the Special Prosecutor those tapes or those portions that are relevant to the Watergate investigation.

It is highly unlikely that this review will be completed in time for the House debate. It appears at this stage, however that a House vote of impeachment is, as a practical matter, virtually a foregone conclusion, and that the issue will therefore go to trial in the Senate. In order to ensure that no other significant relevant materials are withheld, I shall voluntarily furnish to the Senate everything from these tapes that Judge Sirica rules should go to the Special Prosecutor.

I recognize that this additional material I am now furnishing may further damage my case, especially because attention will be drawn separately to it rather than to the evidence in its entirety. In considering its implications, therefore, I urge that two points be borne in mind.

The first of these points is to remember what actually happened as a result of the instructions I gave on June 23. Acting Director Gray of the FBI did coordinate with Director Helms and Deputy Director Walters of the CIA. The CIA did undertake an extensive check to see whether any of its covert activities would be compromised by a full FBI investigation of Watergate. Deputy Director Walters then reported back to Mr. Gray that they would not be compromised. On July 6, when I called Mr. Gray, and when he expressed concern about improper attempts to limit his investigation, as the record shows, I told him to press ahead vigorously with his investigation—which he did.

The second point I would urge is that the evidence be looked at in its entirety, and the events be looked at in perspective. Whatever mistakes I made in the handling of Watergate, the basic truth remains that when all the facts were brought to my attention I insisted on a full investigation and prosecution of those guilty. I am firmly convinced that the record, in its entirety, does not justify the extreme step of impeachment and removal of a President. I trust that as the Constitutional process goes forward, this perspective will prevail.

▼▼▼

PRESIDENT NIXON'S RESIGNATION
August 8-9, 1974

President Richard M. Nixon, under fire for nearly two years because of the Watergate scandal and facing imminent impeachment by the House of Representatives, resigned from the presidency at noon Aug. 9. Nixon, the first man ever to resign from the nation's highest office, had announced his resignation in a nationwide television address Aug. 8 in which he said that he no longer had sufficient support in Congress to justify continuing the effort to complete his term. Nixon's resignation was precipitated by his own release Aug. 5 of transcripts of three conversations with former White House chief of staff H.R. Haldeman. The conversations, held June 23, 1972, six days after the June 17 Watergate break-in, demonstrated that Nixon had participated in the coverup from its initial stages. In his talks with Haldeman, Nixon approved a plan to use the Central Intelligence Agency to obstruct any Federal Bureau of Investigation efforts to trace funds used to finance the break-in. (June 23, 1972, transcripts, see p. 673-682.)

Release of the June 23, 1972, transcripts was followed by an abrupt change of position by the eleven members of the House Judiciary Committee who had voted against an article of impeachment charging Nixon with obstruction of justice. All eleven announced that they would support impeachment on the floor of the House. (Articles of impeachment, see p. 655-660.) *Following the defection of Nixon's supporters in the Judiciary Committee, members of Congress with few exceptions were left with no choice but to call for his departure from office—by resignation or by impeachment. On Aug. 7, House Minority Leader John J. Rhodes (R Ariz.) and others of Nixon's own party leaders told the President that he could muster no more than 10 to 15 votes in each chamber against impeachment.*

Nixon's decision to resign, made Wednesday evening Aug. 7, was an agonizing one. The emotion which he controlled while giving his resignation speech was evident as he met with 50 of his closest congressional supporters an hour before the historic speech. At the meeting, Nixon was described by those present as a man struggling against breaking down.

Nixon's Resignation Speech

In the speech, estimated to have been delivered to the largest television audience in history, Nixon said he believed it was his duty to "persevere" and "complete the term of office to which you elected me," so long as he retained congressional support. But, he continued, because his political base in Congress was no longer strong enough "to justify continuing that effort," he believed "that the constitutional purpose has been served and there is no longer a need for the process to be prolonged." As a result, even though he had never been a "quitter," Nixon said he would resign to spare the nation the ordeal of his trying to vindicate himself, at a time when world peace and domestic inflation required the full attention of the government. Discussing his role in the Watergate affair, Nixon said: "I would only say that if some of my judgments were wrong—and some were wrong—they were made in what I believed at the time to be the best interest of the nation." Thanking those persons who had supported him, Nixon said he likewise held "no bitterness" against those who had not. "More than anything," he said in concluding, he hoped his efforts to achieve world peace would be "my legacy to you, to our country, as I leave the presidency."

Farewell and Relief

On Aug. 9, his last morning in office, Nixon gave an emotional farewell to his cabinet members and the White House staff and then left the White House for San Clemente, no longer the Western White House. His letter of resignation reached Secretary of State Henry A. Kissinger shortly after 11:30 a.m. There was no effective time specified in the letter, making it effective upon receipt. Vice President Gerald R. Ford automatically became the nation's 38th President at that time, minutes before he was sworn in by Chief Justice Warren E. Burger. (See p. 695-705.)

Reaction in Congress to the resignation and Ford's move to the Oval Office was one of overwhelming relief. Rhodes called it "an act of supreme statesmanship." Congressional leaders hailed Ford, noting that he was "one of ours"—a man who had served in Congress for years with many of them.

Congressional reaction was largely representative of the public reaction. With some exceptions, the news of Nixon's decision to leave office brought public relief. Vice President Ford was viewed as a refreshingly simple and forthright man, and many Americans hoped that his ascension to the presidency would bring a quick end to the political turmoil that had weakened the country.

Following are the texts of Richard M. Nixon's televised address to the nation Aug. 8 announcing his intention to resign the office of the President effective at noon, Aug. 9, 1974; Vice President Gerald R. Ford's remarks outside his home Aug. 8 following the telecast of Nixon's address; Nixon's farewell remarks to his cabinet and the White House staff Aug. 9; and President Nixon's letter of resignation:

ADDRESS TO THE AMERICAN PEOPLE

The President's Address Announcing His Intention To Resign. August 8, 1974

Good evening.

This is the 37th time I have spoken to you from this office, where so many decisions have been made that shaped the history of this Nation. Each time I have done so to discuss with you some matter that I believe affected the national interest.

In all the decisions I have made in my public life, I have always tried to do what was best for the Nation. Throughout the long and difficult period of Watergate, I have felt it was my duty to persevere, to make every possible effort to complete the term of office to which you elected me.

In the past few days, however, it has become evident to me that I no longer have a strong enough political base in the Congress to justify continuing that effort. As long as there was such a base, I felt strongly that it was necessary to see the constitutional process through to its conclusion, that to do otherwise would be unfaithful to the spirit of that deliberately difficult process and a dangerously destabilizing precedent for the future.

But with the disappearance of that base, I now believe that the constitutional purpose has been served, and there is no longer a need for the process to be prolonged.

I would have preferred to carry through to the finish whatever the personal agony it would have involved, and my family unanimously urged me to do so. But the interest of the Nation must always come before any personal considerations.

From the discussions I have had with Congressional and other leaders, I have concluded that because of the Watergate matter I might not have the support of the Congress that I would consider necessary to back the very difficult decisions and carry out the duties of this office in the way the interests of the Nation would require.

I have never been a quitter. To leave office before my term is completed is abhorrent to every instinct in my body. But as President, I must put the interest of America first. America needs a full-time President and a full-time Congress, particularly at this time with problems we face at home and abroad.

To continue to fight through the months ahead for my personal vindication would almost totally absorb the time and attention of both the President and the Congress in a period when our entire focus should be on the great issues of peace abroad and prosperity without inflation at home.

Announcement of Resignation

Therefore, I shall resign the Presidency effective at noon tomorrow. Vice President Ford will be sworn in as President at that hour in this office.

As I recall the high hopes for America with which we began this second term, I feel a great sadness that I will not be here in this office working on your behalf to achieve those hopes in the next 2½ years. But in turning over direction of the Government to Vice President Ford, I know, as I told the Nation when I nominated him for that office 10 months ago, that the leadership of America will be in good hands.

In passing this office to the Vice President, I also do so with the profound sense of the weight of responsibility that will fall on his shoulders tomorrow and, therefore, of the understanding, the patience, the cooperation he will need from all Americans.

As he assumes that responsibility, he will deserve the help and the support of all of us. As we look to the future, the first essential is to begin healing the wounds of this Nation, to put the bitterness and divisions of the recent past behind us, and to rediscover those shared ideals that lie at the heart of our strength and unity as a great and as a free people.

By taking this action, I hope that I will have hastened the start of that process of healing which is so desperately needed in America.

I regret deeply any injuries that may have been done in the course of the events that led to this decision. I would say only that if some of my judgments were wrong, and some were wrong, they were made in what I believed at the time to be the best interest of the Nation.

To those who have stood with me during these past difficult months, to my family, my friends, to many others who joined in supporting my cause because they believed it was right, I will be eternally grateful for your support.

And to those who have not felt able to give me your support, let me say I leave with no bitterness toward those who have opposed me, because all of us, in the final analysis, have been concerned with the good of the country, however our judgments might differ.

So, let us all now join together in affirming that common commitment and in helping our new President succeed for the benefit of all Americans.

I shall leave this office with regret at not completing my term, but with gratitude for the privilege of serving as your President for the past 5½ years. These years have been a momentous time in the history of our Nation and the world. They have been a time of achievement in which we can all be proud, achievements that represent the shared efforts of the Administration, the Congress, and the people.

But the challenges ahead are equally great, and they, too, will require the support and the efforts of the Congress and the people working in cooperation with the new Administration.

Accomplishments During Nixon Years

We have ended America's longest war, but in the work of securing a lasting peace in the world, the goals ahead are even more far-reaching and more difficult. We must complete a structure of peace so that it will be said of this generation, our generation of Americans, by the people of all nations, not only that we ended one war but that we prevented future wars.

We have unlocked the doors that for a quarter of a century stood between the United States and the People's Republic of China.

We must now ensure that the one quarter of the world's people who live in the People's Republic of China will be and remain not our enemies but our friends.

In the Middle East, 100 million people in the Arab countries, many of whom have considered us their enemy for nearly 20 years, now look on us as their friends. We must continue to build on that friendship so that peace can settle at last over the Middle East and so that the cradle of civilization will not become its grave.

Together with the Soviet Union we have made the crucial breakthroughs that have begun the process of limiting nuclear arms. But we must set as our goal not just limiting but reducing and finally destroying these terrible weapons so that they cannot destroy civilization and so that the threat of nuclear war will no longer hang over the world and the people.

We have opened the new relation with the Soviet Union. We must continue to develop and expand that new relationship so that the two strongest nations of the world will live together in cooperation rather than confrontation.

Around the world, in Asia, in Africa, in Latin America, in the Middle East, there are millions of people who live in terrible poverty, even starvation. We must keep as our goal turning away from production for war and expanding production for peace so that people everywhere on this earth can at last look forward in their children's time, if not in our own time, to having the necessities for a decent life.

Here in America, we are fortunate that most of our people have not only the blessings of liberty but also the means to live full and good and, by the world's standards, even abundant lives. We must press on, however, toward a goal of not only more and better jobs but of full opportunity for every American and of what we are striving so hard right now to achieve, prosperity without inflation.

"I Have Tried to the Best of My Ability"

For more than a quarter of a century in public life I have shared in the turbulent history of this era. I have fought for what I believed in. I have tried to the best of my ability to discharge those duties and meet those responsibilities that were entrusted to me.

Sometimes I have succeeded and sometimes I have failed, but always I have taken heart from what Theodore Roosevelt once said about the man in the arena, "whose face is marred by dust and sweat and blood, who strives valiantly, who errs and comes short again and again because there is not effort without error and shortcoming, but who does actually strive to do the deed, who knows the great enthusiasms, the great devotions, who spends himself in a worthy cause, who at the best knows in the end the triumphs of high achievements and who at the worst, if he fails, at least fails while daring greatly."

I pledge to you tonight that as long as I have a breath of life in my body, I shall continue in that spirit. I shall continue to work for the great causes to which I have been dedicated throughout my years as a Congressman, a Senator, a Vice President, and President, the cause of peace not just for America but among all nations, prosperity, justice, and opportunity for all of our people.

There is one cause above all to which I have been devoted and to which I shall always be devoted for as long as I live.

When I first took the oath of office as President 5½ years ago, I made this sacred commitment, to "consecrate my office, my energies, and all the wisdom I can summon to the cause of peace among nations."

I have done my very best in all the days since to be true to that pledge. As a result of these efforts, I am confident that the world is a safer place today, not only for the people of America but for the people of all nations, and that all of our children have a better chance than before of living in peace rather than dying in war.

This, more than anything, is what I hoped to achieve when I sought the Presidency. This, more than anything, is what I hope will be my legacy to you, to our country, as I leave the Presidency.

To have served in this office is to have felt a very personal sense of kinship with each and every American. In leaving it, I do so with this prayer: May God's grace be with you in all the days ahead.

The Vice President's Remarks to Reporters

Remarks of Vice President Ford Following the President's Address to the Nation.   August 8, 1974

I think that this is one of the most difficult and very saddest periods and one of the very saddest incidents that I have ever witnessed.

Let me say that I think the President of the United States has made one of the greatest personal sacrifices for the country and one of the finest personal decisions on behalf of all of us as Americans by his decision to resign as President of the United States.

It has been my opportunity to watch over a period of nearly 25 years a foreign policy in the last 5 years that has been most successful in the achievement of peace for all of us here, and hopefully the rest of the world. It has been a policy that I think can continue—peace in the months and years ahead.

Let me say without any hesitation or reservation that the policy that has achieved peace and built the blocks for future peace will be continued, as far as I am concerned, as President of the United States.

We have been fortunate in the last 5 years to have a very great man in Henry Kissinger who has helped to build the blocks of peace under President Nixon.

I think those policies should be continued, and those policies of peace will be continued. I have asked Henry Kissinger, as Secretary of State, to stay on and to be the Secretary of State under the new Administration.

I have known Henry Kissinger for a great many years. I knew him before he came with the Nixon Administration. I want him to be my Secretary of State, and I am glad to announce that he will be the Secretary of State, which means that he and I will be working together in the pursuit of peace in the future as we have achieved it in the past.

We have many other problems. We have problems at home which must be resolved. They can be resolved and will be resolved by the cooperation of the Congress with the President and those who work with him.

I have been very fortunate in my lifetime in public office to have a good many adversaries in the political arena, in the Congress, but I don't think I have a single enemy in the Congress, and the net result is that I think tomorrow I can start out working with Democrats and with Republicans in the House as well as in the Senate to work on the problems, serious ones which we have at home, in the spirit of cooperation which I believe will be exhibited with the Congress and the new President, and the problems overseas and the problems at home will be beneficial not only to 211 million fine Americans but to the world as a whole.

I pledge to you tonight, as I will pledge tomorrow and in the future, my best efforts and cooperation, leadership, and dedication that is good for America and good for the world.

Thank you very much.

Remarks to Members of the Cabinet and the White House Staff

The President's Remarks Prior to His Departure From the White House. August 9, 1974

Members of the Cabinet, Members of the White House Staff, all of our friends here:

I think the record should show that this is one of those spontaneous things that we always arrange whenever the President comes in to speak, and it will be so reported in the press, and we don't mind because they have to call it as they see it.

But on our part, believe me, it is spontaneous.

You are here to say goodby to us, and we don't have a good word for it in English. The best is *au revoir*. We will see you again.

I just met with the members of the White House staff, you know, those who serve here in the White House day in and day out, and I asked them to do what I ask all of you to do to the extent that you can and, of course, are requested to do so: to serve our next President as you have served me and previous Presidents—because many of you have been here for many years—with devotion and dedication, because this office, great as it is, can only be as great as the men and women who work for and with the President.

This house, for example, I was thinking of it as we walked down this hall, and I was comparing it to some of the great houses of the world that I have been in. This isn't the biggest house. Many, and most, in even smaller countries are much bigger. This isn't the finest house. Many in Europe, particularly, and in China, Asia, have paintings of great, great value, things that we just don't have here, and probably will never have until we are 1,-000 years old or older.

White House Is "Best House"

But this is the best house. It is the best house because it has something far more important than numbers of people who serve, far more important than numbers of rooms or how big it is, far more important than numbers of magnificent pieces of art.

This house has a great heart, and that heart comes from those who serve. I was rather sorry they didn't come-down. We said goodby to them upstairs. But they are really great. And I recall after so many times I have made speeches, and some of them pretty tough, yet, I always come back, or after a hard day—and my days usually have run rather long—I would always get a lift from them because I might be a little down, but they always smiled.

And so it is with you. I look around here, and I see so many on this staff that, you know, I should have been by your offices and shaken hands, and I would love to have talked to you and found out how to run the world—everybody wants to tell the President what to do, and boy he needs to be told many times—but I just haven't had the time. But I want you to know that each and every one of you, I know, is indispensable to this Government.

I am proud of this Cabinet. I am proud of all the members who have served in our Cabinet. I am proud of our sub-Cabinet. I am proud of our White House Staff. As I pointed out last night, sure we have done some things wrong in this Administration, and the top man always takes the responsibility, and I have never ducked it. But I want to say one thing: We can be proud of it—5½ years. No man or no woman came into this Administration and left it with more of this world's goods than when he came in. No man or no woman ever profited at the public expense or the public till. That tells something about you.

Nixon Years: Mistakes But No Personal Gain

Mistakes, yes. But for personal gain, never. You did what you believed in. Sometimes right, sometimes wrong. And I only wish that I were a wealthy man—at the present time I have got to find a way to pay my taxes—[laughter]—and if I were, I would like to recompense you for the sacrifices that all of you have made to serve in Government.

But you are getting something in Government—and I want you to tell this to your children, and I hope the Nation's children will hear it, too—something in Government service that is far more important than money. It is a cause bigger than yourself. It is the cause of making this the greatest nation in the world, the leader of the world, because without our leadership the world will know nothing but war, possibly starvation, or worse, in the years ahead. With our leadership it will know peace, it will know plenty.

We have been generous, and we will be more generous in the future as we are able to. But most important, we must be strong here, strong in our hearts, strong in our souls, strong in our belief, and strong in our willingness to sacrifice, as you have been willing to sacrifice, in a pecuniary way, to serve in Government.

There is something else I would like for you to tell your young people. You know, people often come in and say, "What will I tell my kids?" They look at government and say it is sort of a rugged life, and they see the mistakes that are made. They get the impression that everybody is here for the purpose of feathering his nest. That is why I made this earlier point—not in this Administration, not one single man or woman.

And I say to them, "There are many fine careers. This country needs good farmers, good businessmen, good plumbers, good carpenters."

I remembered my old man. I think that they would have called him sort of a little man, common man. He didn't consider himself that way. You know what he was? He was a streetcar motorman first, and then he was a farmer, and then he had a lemon ranch. It was the poorest lemon ranch in California, I can assure you. He sold it before they found oil on it. [*Laughter*].

And then he was a grocer. But he was a great man because he did his job, and every job counts up to the hilt, regardless of what happens.

Nixon's Mother

Nobody will ever write a book, probably, about my mother. Well, I guess all of you would say this about your mother—my mother was a saint. And I think of her, two boys dying of tuberculosis, nursing four others in order that she could take care of my older brother for 3 years in Arizona, and seeing each of them die, and when they died, it was like one of her own.

Yes, she will have no books written about her. But she was a saint.

Now, however, we look to the future. I had a little quote in the speech last night from T.R. As you know, I kind of like to read books. I am not educated, but I do read books—[*laughter*]—and the T.R. quote was a pretty good one.

Here is another one I found as I was reading, my last night in the White House, and this quote is about a young man. He was a young lawyer in New York. He had married a beautiful girl, and they had a lovely daughter, and then suddenly she died, and this is what he wrote. This was in his diary.

He said: "She was beautiful in face and form and lovelier still in spirit. As a flower she grew and as a fair young flower she died. Her life had been

691

always in the sunshine. There had never come to her a single great sorrow. None ever knew her who did not love and revere her for her bright and sunny temper and her saintly unselfishness. Fair, pure and joyous as a maiden, loving, tender and happy as a young wife. When she had just become a mother, when her life seemed to be just begun and when the years seemed so bright before her, then by a strange and terrible fate death came to her. And when my heart's dearest died, the light went from my life forever."

That was T.R. in his twenties. He thought the light had gone from his life forever—but he went on. And he not only became President but, as an ex-President, he served his country always in the arena, tempestuous, strong, sometimes wrong, sometimes right, but he was a man.

Never An End, Always A Beginning

And as I leave, let me say, that is an example I think all of us should remember. We think sometimes when things happen that don't go the right way; we think that when you don't pass the bar exam the first time—I happened to, but I was just lucky; I mean my writing was so poor the bar examiner said, "We have just got to let the guy through." [*Laughter*] We think that when someone dear to us dies, we think that when we lose an election, we think that when we suffer a defeat, that all is ended. We think, as T.R. said, that the light had left his life forever.

Not true. It is only a beginning always. The young must know it; the old must know it. It must always sustain us because the greatness comes not when things go always good for you, but the greatness comes when you are really tested, when you take some knocks, some disappointments, when sadness comes, because only if you have been in the deepest valley can you ever know how magnificent it is to be on the highest mountain.

And so I say to you on this occasion, as we leave, we leave proud of the people who have stood by us and worked for us and served this country.

We want you to be proud of what you have done. We want you to continue to serve in Government, if that is your wish. Always give your best, never get discouraged, never be petty; always remember others may hate you, but those who hate you don't win unless you hate them, and then you destroy yourself.

And so, we leave with high hopes, in good spirit and with deep humility, and with very much gratefulness in our hearts. I can only say to each and every one of you, we come from many faiths, we pray perhaps to different gods, but really the same God in a sense, but I want to say for each and every one of you, not only will we always remember you, not only will we always be grateful to you but always you will be in our hearts and you will be in our prayers.

Thank you very much.

Resignation of President Nixon

The President's Letter to the Secretary of State.   August 9, 1974

Dear Mr. Secretary:

I hereby resign the Office of President of the United States.

Sincerely,

 Richard Nixon

[The Honorable Henry A. Kissinger, The Secretary of State, Washington, D.C. 20520]

GERALD R. FORD: 38TH PRESIDENT
August 9, 1974

"Our long national nightmare is over. Our Constitution works. Our great republic is a government of laws and not of men." With these words, Gerald R. Ford attempted to put the Watergate scandal to rest when he took office at noon Aug. 9 as the 38th President of the United States. To those gathered at the inaugural ceremony in the East Room of the White House and to a national audience via television and radio, Ford said: "I assume the Presidency under extraordinary circumstances, never before experienced by Americans. This is an hour of history that troubles our minds and hurts our hearts." He therefore felt it was his first duty "to make an unprecedented compact with my countrymen," and he would do so by means of "just a little straight talk among friends." He pledged to be "the President of all the people" (a reference to earlier criticism that he had an anti-minority voting record), (See Historic Documents 1973, p. 969-973), to embark on "an uninterrupted and sincere search for peace", and to "follow my instincts of openness and candor with full confidence that honesty is always the best policy in the end." For President Nixon, who had left the White House only hours before, Ford asked the prayers of Americans and added: "May our former President, who brought peace to millions, find it for himself."

The new President said he would delay until the following Monday, Aug. 12, a presentation of his views on "the priority business of the nation." He asked the Speaker of the House and the President pro tempore of the Senate to allow him to address a joint session of Congress that day. (Text of speech, below.) Immediately following his inaugural remarks, Ford met with congressional leaders of both parties. Later in the day, he met with economic advisers and told them that control of inflation was his "high and first priority." He had announced Aug. 8 that Secretary of State Henry A. Kissinger would stay on in the Ford administration. That statement was made during a television interview outside Ford's Alexandria, Va., residence following Nixon's speech that evening announcing his resignation. (See p. 683-693.)

Ford's swift and unprecedented ascent from House Minority Leader to President was made possible by two of the greatest scandals in American history. He was chosen by President Nixon as vice president after Spiro T. Agnew resigned that post in October 1973, pleading "no contest" to tax evasion charges based on his acceptance of bribes. Ford was sworn in as Vice President Dec. 6, 1973. Nine months later Ford became President upon Nixon's resignation—a resignation which came the day after Republican congressional leaders informed him that his only alternative was certain impeachment in the House and likely conviction in the Senate.

For many Republicans, the succession of Gerald R. Ford to the presidency brought with it the promise of an end to despair within the party—a despair which grew as the Watergate scandal unfolded and deepened into panic as the 1974 congressional elections approached. It was agreed that Ford himself would have a honeymoon period during which his popularity would depend more on his presence than on any of his specific programs. But would that honeymoon help Republican candidates avert the disaster that was predicted for them in November? No one could be sure. What was certain was that things had rarely looked worse for the Republican Party than they did at the close of Richard Nixon's presidency. Many Republicans were joining in predictions that Democrats would gain enough seats in November to impose congressional government upon the nation. The year's primaries indicated that Republican voters were using a simple method to express their dissatisfaction with President Nixon. They were not voting. Confirming Republican fears, Democrats did make significant gains in Congress as a result of the November elections.

Ford's Message to Congress

Ford made it clear in his televised message to Congress Aug. 12 that he wanted to work with Congress in meeting the nation's problems. He said, "As President within the limits of basic principles, my motto towards the Congress is communication, compromise and cooperation." He told the legislators: "I do not want a honeymoon with you. I want a good marriage." Senators and Representatives reacted warmly. Many members said they believed Ford's speech opened an "era of good feelings" between the executive and legislative branches after five years of coolness during the Nixon period. Capitol Hill had learned from the Watergate tapes that the Nixon White House men regarded Congress as a group of "clowns."

Ford delighted members of the Senate by accepting a proposal for a "domestic summit meeting" to explore ways of dealing with some of the national problems that had gone so long unattended during the past year of Watergate. Calling inflation "our domestic public enemy number one," Ford said the meeting should take place "in full view of the American public" at an "early date" and he promised to preside over it personally. (Economic summit, see p. 861-880.)

> *Included in this entry are the following: (1) the text of the oath of office taken by Gerald R. Ford when he was sworn in as President of the United States Aug. 9, (2) the text of his remarks following the inaugural ceremonies, and (3) the text of Ford's televised message to Congress Aug. 12 setting forth his views on the nation's priorities:*

SWEARING IN OF THE PRESIDENT

Oath of Office Taken by the President at a Ceremony in the East Room at the White House. August 9, 1974

I, Gerald R. Ford, do solemnly swear that I will faithfully execute the Office of President of the United States, and will to the best of my ability, preserve, protect and defend the Constitution of the United States, so help me God.

The President's Remarks Following His Swearing In as the 38th President of the United States. August 9, 1974

Mr. Chief Justice, my dear friends, my fellow Americans:

The oath that I have taken is the same oath that was taken by George Washington and by every President under the Constitution. But I assume the Presidency under extraordinary circumstances, never before experienced by Americans. This is an hour of history that troubles our minds and hurts our hearts.

Therefore, I feel it is my first duty to make an unprecedented compact with my countrymen. Not an inaugural address, not a fireside chat, not a campaign speech—just a little straight talk among friends. And I intend it to be the first of many.

I am acutely aware that you have not elected me as your President by your ballots, and so I ask you to confirm me as your President with your prayers. And I hope that such prayers will be the first of many.

If you have not chosen me by secret ballot, neither have I gained office by any secret promises. I have not campaigned either for the Presidency or the Vice Presidency. I have not subscribed to any partisan platform. I am indebted to no man, and only to one woman—my dear wife—as I begin this very difficult job.

I have not sought this enormous responsibility, but I will not shirk it. Those who nominated and confirmed me as Vice President were my friends and are my friends. They were of both parties, elected by all the people and

697

acting under the Constitution in their name. It is only fitting then that I should pledge to them and to you that I will be the President of all the people.

Thomas Jefferson said the people are the only sure reliance for the preservation of our liberty. And down the years, Abraham Lincoln renewed this American article of faith asking, "Is there any better way or equal hope in the world?"

I intend, on Monday next, to request of the Speaker of the House of Representatives and the President pro tempore of the Senate the privilege of appearing before the Congress to share with my former colleagues and with you, the American people, my views on the priority business of the Nation and to solicit your views and their views. And may I say to the Speaker and the others, if I could meet with you right after these remarks, I would appreciate it.

Even though this is late in an election year, there is no way we can go forward except together and no way anybody can win except by serving the people's urgent needs. We cannot stand still or slip backwards. We must go forward now together.

To the peoples and the governments of all friendly nations, and I hope that could encompass the whole world, I pledge an uninterrupted and sincere search for peace. America will remain strong and united, but its strength will remain dedicated to the safety and sanity of the entire family of man, as well as to our own precious freedom.

I believe that truth is the glue that holds government together, not only our Government, but civilization itself. That bond, though strained, is unbroken at home and abroad.

In all my public and private acts as your President, I expect to follow my instincts of openness and candor with full confidence that honesty is always the best policy in the end.

My fellow Americans, our long national nightmare is over. Our Constitution works; our great Republic is a Government of laws and not of men. Here the people rule. But there is a higher power, by whatever name we honor Him, who ordains not only righteousness but love, not only justice but mercy.

As we bind up the internal wounds of Watergate, more painful and more poisonous than those of foreign wars, let us restore the golden rule to our political process, and let brotherly love purge our hearts of suspicion and of hate.

In the beginning, I asked you to pray for me. Before closing, I ask again your prayers, for Richard Nixon and for his family. May our former President, who brought peace to millions, find it for himself. May God bless and comfort his wonderful wife and daughters, whose love and loyalty will forever be a shining legacy to all who bear the lonely burdens of the White House.

I can only guess at those burdens, although I have witnessed at close hand the tragedies that befell three Presidents and the lesser trials of others.

With all the strength and all the good sense I have gained from life, with all the confidence my family, my friends, and my dedicated staff impart to me, and with the good will of countless Americans I have encountered in recent visits to 40 states, I now solemnly reaffirm my promise I made to you last December 6: to uphold the Constitution, to do what is right as God gives me to see the right, and to do the very best I can for America.

God helping me, I will not let you down.

Thank you.

ADDRESS TO CONGRESS

The President's Address Delivered Before a Joint Session of the Congress. August 12, 1974

Mr. Speaker, Mr. President, distinguished guests and my very dear friends:

My fellow Americans, we have a lot of work to do. My former colleagues, you and I have a lot of work to do. Let's get on with it.

Needless to say, I am deeply grateful for the wonderfully warm welcome. I can never express my gratitude adequately.

I am not here to make an inaugural address. The Nation needs action, not words. Nor will this be a formal report of the State of the Union. God willing, I will have at least three more chances to do that.

It is good to be back in the People's House. But this cannot be a real homecoming. Under the Constitution, I now belong to the executive branch. The Supreme Court has even ruled that I am the executive branch, head, heart, and hand.

With all due respect to the learned Justices—and I greatly respect the judiciary—part of my heart will always be here on Capitol Hill. I know well the co-equal role of Congress in our constitutional process. I love the House of Representatives. I revere the traditions of the Senate despite my too-short internship in that great body. As President, within the limits of basic principles, my motto toward the Congress is communication, conciliation, compromise, and cooperation.

This Congress, unless it has changed, I am confident, will be my working partner as well as my most constructive critic. I am not asking for conformity. I am dedicated to the two-party system, and you know which party I belong to.

I do not want a honeymoon with you. I want a good marriage.

I want progress, and I want problem-solving which requires my best efforts and also your best efforts.

I have no need to learn how Congress speaks for the people. As President, I intend to listen.

But I also intend to listen to the people themselves—all the people—as I promised last Friday. I want to be sure that we are all tuned in to the real voice of America.

Seeking Unity in Diversity

My Administration starts off by seeking unity in diversity. My office door has always been open, and that is how it is going to be at the White House. Yes, Congressmen will be welcomed—if you don't overdo it. *[Laughter]*

The first seven words of the Constitution and the most important are these: We, the people of the United States. We, the people, ordained and established the Constitution and reserved to themselves all powers not granted to Federal and State government. I respect and will always be conscious to that fundamental right of freedom.

Only 8 months ago, when I last stood here, I told you I was a Ford, not a Lincoln. Tonight I say I am still a Ford, but I am not a Model T.

I do have some old-fashioned ideas, however. I believe in the very basic decency and fairness of America. I believe in the integrity and patriotism of the Congress. And while I am aware of the House rule that no one ever speaks to the galleries, I believe in the first amendment and the absolute necessity of a free press.

But I also believe that over two centuries since the First Continental Congress was convened, the direction of our Nation's movement has been forward. I am here to confess that in my first campaign for President—of my senior class in South High School in Grand Rapids, Michigan—I headed the Progressive Party ticket, and lost. Maybe that is why I became a Republican. *[Laughter]*

Now I ask you to join with me in getting this country revved up and moving.

My instinctive judgment is that the state of the Union is excellent. But the state of our economy is not so good. Everywhere I have been as Vice President, some 118,000 miles in 40 States some 55 press conferences, the unanimous concern of Americans is inflation.

For once all the polls seem to agree. They also suggest that the people blame Government far more than either management or labor for the high cost of everything they have to buy.

You who come from 50 States, three territories, and the District of Columbia, know this better than I do. That is why you have created, since I left, your new Budget Reform Committee. I welcome it, and I will work with its members to bring the Federal budget into balance in fiscal year 1976.

The fact is that for the past 25 years that I had the honor of serving in this body, the Federal budget has been balanced in only six.

Mr. Speaker, I am a little late in getting around to it, but confession is good for the soul. I have sometimes voted to spend more taxpayers' money for worthy Federal projects in Grand Rapids, Michigan, while I vigorously opposed wasteful spending boondoggles in Oklahoma. *[Laughter]*

Necessity for Keeping Down Federal Spending

Be that as it may, Mr. Speaker, you and I have always stood together against unwarranted cuts in national defense. This is no time to change that nonpartisan policy.

Just as escalating Federal spending has been a prime cause of higher prices over many years, it may take some time to stop inflation. But we must begin right now.

For a start, before your Labor Day recess, Congress should reactivate the Cost of Living Council through passage of a clean bill, without reimposing controls, that will let us monitor wages and prices to expose abuses.

Whether we like it or not, the American wage earner and the American housewife are a lot better economists than most economists care to admit. They know that a government big enough to give you everything you want is a government big enough to take from you everything you have.

If we want to restore confidence in ourselves as working politicians, the first thing we all have to do is to learn to say, "No."

The first specific request by the Ford Administration is not to Congress but to the voters in the upcoming November elections. It is this, very simple: Support your candidates, Congressmen and Senators, Democrats or Republicans, conservatives or liberals, who consistently vote for tough decisions to cut the cost of government, restrain Federal spending, and bring inflation under control.

I applaud the initiatives Congress has already taken. The only fault I find with the Joint Economic Committee's study on inflation, authorized last week, is that we need its expert findings in 6 weeks instead of 6 months.

A month ago, the distinguished majority leader of the United States Senate asked the White House to convene an economic conference of the best economic brains from labor, industry, and agriculture.

Later, this was perfected by resolution to assemble a domestic summit meeting to devise a bipartisan action for stability and growth in the American economy. Neither I nor my staff have time right now for letterwriting. So, I will respond. I accept the suggestion, and I will personally preside.

Furthermore, I propose that this summit meeting be held at an early date, in full view of the American public. They are as anxious as we are to get the right answers.

My first priority is to work with you to bring inflation under control. Inflation is domestic enemy number one. To restore economic confidence, the Government in Washington must provide some leadership. It does no good to blame the public for spending too much when the Government is spending too much.

I began to put my Administration's own economic house in order starting last Friday.

I instructed my Cabinet officers and Counsellors and my White House Staff to make fiscal restraint their first order of business, and to save every taxpayer's dollar the safety and genuine welfare of our great Nation will permit. Some economic activities will be affected more by monetary and fiscal restraint than other activities. Good government clearly requires that we tend to the economic problems facing our country in a spirit of equity to all of our citizens in all segments of our society.

Tonight, obviously, it no time to threaten you with vetoes. But I do have the last recourse, and I am a veteran of many a veto fight right here in this great chamber. Can't we do a better job by reasonable compromise? I hope we can.

Minutes after I took the Presidential oath, the joint leadership of Congress told me at the White House they would go more than half way to meet me. This was confirmed in your unanimous concurrent resolution of cooperation, for which I am deeply grateful. If, for my part, I go more than half way to meet the Congress, maybe we can find a much larger area of national agreement.

Outline Of "What We Must Do"

I bring no legislative shopping list here this evening. I will deal with specifics in future messages and talks with you, but here are a few examples of how seriously I feel about what we must do together.

Last week, the Congress passed the elementary and secondary education bill, and I found it on my desk. Any reservations I might have about some of its provisions—and I do have—fade in comparison to the urgent needs of America for quality education. I will sign it in a few days.

I must be frank. In implementing its provisions, I will oppose excessive funding during this inflationary crisis.

As Vice President, I studied various proposals for better health care financing. I saw them coming closer together and urged my friends in the Congress and in the Administration to sit down and sweat out a sound compromise. The Comprehensive Health Insurance Program goes a long way toward providing early relief to people who are sick.

Why don't we write—and I ask this with the greatest spirit of cooperation—why don't we write a good health bill on the statute books in 1974, before this Congress adjourns.

The economy of our country is critically dependent on how we interact with the economies of other countries. It is little comfort that our inflation is only a part of a worldwide problem or that American families need less of their paychecks for groceries than most of our foreign friends.

As one of the building blocks of peace, we have taken the lead in working toward a more open and a more equitable world economic system. A new round of international trade negotiations started last September among 105 nations in Tokyo. The others are waiting for the United States Congress to grant the necessary authority to the executive branch to proceed.

With modifications, the trade reform bill passed by the House last year would do a good job. I understand good progress has been made in the Senate Committee on Finance. But I am optimistic, as always, that the Senate will pass an acceptable bill quickly as a key part of our joint prosperity campaign.

I am determined to expedite other international economic plans. We will be working together with other nations to find better ways to prevent shortages of food and fuel. We must not let last winter's energy crisis happen again. I will push Project Independence for our own good and the good of others. In that, too, I will need your help.

Successful foreign policy is an extension of the hopes of the whole American people for a world peace and orderly reform and orderly freedom. So, I would say a few words to our distinguished guests from the governments of other nations where, as at home, it is my determination to deal openly with allies and adversaries.

Continuance of Nixon Foreign Policy

Over the past 5½ years in Congress and as Vice President, I have fully supported the outstanding foreign policy of President Nixon. This policy I intend to continue.

Throughout my public service, starting with wartime naval duty under the command of President Franklin D. Roosevelt, I have upheld all our Presidents when they spoke for my country to the world. I believe the Constitution commands this. I know that in this crucial area of international policy I can count on your firm support.

Now, let there be no doubt or any misunderstanding anywhere, and I emphasize anywhere: There are no opportunities to exploit, should anyone so desire. There will be no change of course, no relaxation of vigilance, no abandonment of the helm of our Ship of State as the watch changes.

We stand by our commitments and we will live up to our responsibilities in our formal alliances, in our friendships, and in our improving relations with potential adversaries.

On this, Americans are united and strong. Under my term of leadership, I hope we will become more united. I am certain America will remain strong.

A strong defense is the surest way to peace. Strength makes detente attainable. Weakness invites war as my generation—my generation—knows from four very bitter experiences.

Just as America's will for peace is second to none, so will America's strength be second to none.

We cannot rely on the forbearance of others to protect this Nation. The power and diversity of the Armed Forces, active guard, and reserve, the resolve of our fellow citizens, the flexibility in our command to navigate international waters that remain troubled are all essential to our security.

I shall continue to insist on civilian control of our superb military establishment. The Constitution plainly requires the President to be Commander in Chief, and I will be.

Our job will not be easy. In promising continuity, I cannot promise simplicity. The problems and challenges of the world remain complex and difficult. But we have set out on a path of reason, of fairness, and we will continue on it.

As guideposts on that path, I offer the following:

—To our allies of a generation in the Atlantic community and Japan, I pledge continuity in the loyal collaboration on our many mutual endeavors.

—To our friends and allies in this hemisphere, I pledge continuity in the deepening dialog to define renewed relationships of equality and justice.

—To our allies and friends in Asia, I pledge a continuity in our support for their security, independence, and economic development. In Indochina, we are determined to see the observance of the Paris agreement on Vietnam and the cease-fire and negotiated settlement in Laos. We hope to see an early compromise settlement in Cambodia.

—To the Soviet Union, I pledge continuity in our commitment to the course of the past 3 years. To our two peoples, and to all mankind, we owe a continued effort to live, and where possible, to work together in peace; for in a thermonuclear age there can be no alternative to a positive and peaceful relationship between our nations.

—To the People's Republic of China, whose legendary hospitality I enjoyed, I pledge continuity in our commitment to the principles of the Shanghai communique. The new relationship built on those principles has demonstrated that it serves serious and objective mutual interests and has become an enduring feature of the world scene.

—To the nations in the Middle East, I pledge continuity in our vigorous efforts to advance the progress which has brought hopes of peace to that region after 25 years as a hotbed of war. We shall carry out our promise to promote continuing negotiations among all parties for a complete, just, and lasting settlement.

—To all nations, I pledge continuity in seeking a common global goal: a stable international structure of trade and finance which reflects the interdependence of all peoples.

—To the entire international community—to the United Nations, to the world's nonaligned nations, and to all others—I pledge continuity in our dedication to the humane goals which throughout our history have been so much of America's contribution to mankind.

So long as the peoples of the world have confidence in our purposes and faith in our good word, the age-old vision of peace on earth will grow brighter.

I pledge myself unreservedly to that goal. I say to you in words that cannot be improved upon: Let us never negotiate out of fear, but let us never fear to negotiate.

On the Ethics of Government

As Vice President, at the request of the President, I addressed myself to the individual rights of Americans in the area of privacy. There will be no illegal tappings (tapings), eavesdropping, buggings, or break-ins by my Administration. There will be hot pursuit of tough laws to prevent illegal invasion of privacy in both government and private activities.

On the higher plane of public morality, there is no need for me to preach tonight. We have thousands of far better preachers and millions of sacred scriptures to guide us on the path of personal right-living and exemplary official conduct. If we can make effective and earlier use of moral and ethical wisdom of the centuries in today's complex society, we will prevent more crime and more corruption than all the policemen and prosecutors governments can ever deter. If I might say so, this is a job that must begin at home, not in Washington.

I once told you that I am not a saint, and I hope never to see the day that I cannot admit having made a mistake. So I will close with another confession.

Frequently, along the tortuous road of recent months from this chamber to the President's House, I protested that I was my own man. Now I realize that I was wrong.

I am your man, for it was your carefully weighed confirmation that changed my occupation.

The truth is I am the people's man, for\you acted in their name, and I accepted and began my new and solemn trust with a promise to serve all the people and do the best that I can for America.

When I say all the people, I mean exactly that.

To the limits of my strength and ability, I will be the President of black, brown, red, and white Americans, of old and young, of women's liberationists and male chauvinists—*[laughter]*—and all the rest of us in between, of the poor and the rich, of native sons and new refugees, of those who work at lathes or at desks or in mines or in fields, of Christians, Jews, Moslems, Buddhists, and atheists if there really are any atheists after what we have all been through.

Fellow Americans, one final word:

I want to be a good President.

I need your help.

We all need God's sure guidance.

With it, nothing can stop the United States of America.

Thank you very much.

ROCKEFELLER NOMINATION
August 20, 1974

Nelson A. Rockefeller, the 66-year-old former Republican governor of New York, was nominated Aug. 20 by President Ford to be the 41st Vice President of the United States. Once confirmed by the House Judiciary Committee and the Senate Rules Committee (confirmation hearings, p. 987), Rockefeller was to fill the vacancy created when Ford succeeded Richard M. Nixon as President on Aug. 9. (See p. 695-705.) Ford was praised by many who felt he had shown true statesmanship in selecting a man who, in some respects, might be considered to overshadow the President himself. The Vice President-designate was recognized as a man of many sides. Despite his great wealth, he had championed the interests of the common man. He exuded an image of glamor and charisma and collected Picassos. At the same time, he moved freely among small-town Americans and spoke the no-nonsense language of labor union hard-hats. An heir to the Rockefeller millions, he nonetheless had chosen to pursue a career in politics, following in the footsteps of his maternal grandfather and namesake, Nelson W. Aldrich, who had served 30 years as a U.S. Senator from Rhode Island. During his 15-year career as governor of New York, Rockefeller had been a constant friend of business interests. During most of that time he had been a conservative in fiscal matters. But he also initiated liberal policies in transportation, education, housing, the environment, health and welfare.

Before his nomination by Ford Aug. 20, political observers agreed that Rockefeller might make a last stab at the presidency in 1976. But these observers were almost unanimous in agreeing that he would have had serious opposition. Conservatives in the party never had forgiven him com-

pletely for not supporting the candidacy of Arizona Sen. Barry Goldwater in 1964. And many Republicans west of the Mississippi and in the South disliked him as a symbol of the wealthy eastern establishment. The fall of Richard Nixon and the rise of Gerald Ford evidently put an end to Rockefeller's presidential hopes. Ford obviously was the front-runner for the 1976 nomination, and by 1980 Rockefeller would be too old—72. In accepting Ford's nomination Rockefeller agreed to take a post that he once had dismissed as "standby equipment."

Rockefeller's image as a liberal dated from his early days as a director of the Creole Petroleum Company, which operated in Venezuela. He once declared at an annual board meeting that "the only justification for ownership is that it serves the broad interest of the people. We must recognize the social responsibilities of corporations, and the corporations must use their ownership of assets to reflect the best interests of the people." That was in 1937, when Rockefeller was 29 years old.

Later, as governor, civil rights became a priority in Rockefeller's legislative proposals. In 1960, he advanced a plan to combat discrimination in private multiple dwellings. In 1961 it became the first statewide law in the nation prohibiting discrimination in private housing. In 1963, Rockefeller pushed legislation to extend the coverage of the antidiscrimination law to all private housing with the exception of apartments in two-family homes and rented rooms in one-family homes. Passage of this bill placed 95 per cent of the housing in New York under the coverage of anti-discrimination laws. These and other civil rights measures were largely responsible for Rockefeller's reputation as a liberal.

Under Rockefeller's leadership, New York also inaugurated a dramatic increase of state services. Among other things, the governor:

●Stressed the coordination of transportation policy as a factor in "creating a more favorable economic climate";

●Pushed increases in state aid to local elementary and secondary schools and forcefully advocated better higher education. One of the achievements he said he was especially proud of was the establishment of a powerful New York state university system;

● Worked to inject private capital in the construction of low- and middle-income housing;

●Pioneered in establishing statewide air and water pollution control measures;

●Supported moves to extend state health and welfare programs.

Rockefeller for many years ran New York on a balanced-budget, "pay-as-you-go" basis, forcing one tax increase after another through the legislature. But by the beginning of his fourth term he had capitulated to deficit spending, creating agencies to sell bonds to fund state projects such as his higher education program. At the same time, however, Rockefeller was noticeably swinging toward the right in other areas. Beginning in 1968 he increasingly criticized welfare chiselers and pushed through stiffer drug abuse laws. Critics said these changes in direction were intended to pacify conservative Republicans, whose support Rockefeller would need for the 1976 nomination. If so, time and events overtook the former governor.

Prospects for Rockefeller Confirmation

From the outset, the vast Rockefeller wealth was earmarked as the major target of inquiry for the House Judiciary Committee and the Senate Rules Committee, which would hold hearings on Rockefeller's nomination. Congressional leaders were careful to point out that the object of their investigation into Rockefeller's finances was not to titillate the public. "The important consideration is to make sure there is no conflict of interest," said Sen. Robert C. Byrd (D W. Va.), majority whip and a member of the Rules Committee. Rockefeller, whose net worth was estimated at between $100-million and $600-million, had always been secretive about his finances. After President Ford announced his nomination, the former New York governor promised to comply with "whatever the law says" regarding his wealth. He also pledged to cooperate with Congress during the confirmation process.

The Rockefeller holdings had been called the greatest family fortune in the world. It started with John D. Rockefeller Sr., who founded the Standard Oil Company in 1870. The family has been sensitive about financial disclosures ever since the first "John D." was called a "robber baron" by those who questioned his business ethics. Historian Allan Nevins estimated the elder Rockefeller to have been worth more than $1-billion. In 1968, Fortune *magazine placed the net worth of Nelson, his four brothers and one sister, all grandchildren of John D. Sr., at more than $200-million each with annual income of about $5-million each. In his 1964 book,* The Rich and the Super-Rich, *author Ferdinand Lundberg placed Rockefeller's personal fortune at $500-million, including his extensive art collection. In all, the family fortune is divided between three major areas: real estate, such as the Rockefeller Center in New York City; family trusts, many administered by Rockefeller Brothers Inc.; and "venture capital," such as the International Basic Economy Corp. (IBEC), designed to provide impoverished nations, especially in Latin America, with inexpensive food and housing while still turning a profit.*

Following are the texts of President Ford's announcement of his nomination of Nelson A. Rockefeller as Vice President and of Rockefeller's acceptance of the nomination:

Ford's Statement:

Mr. Speaker, Members of the leadership of the House and Senate, members of the Cabinet:

After a great deal of soul searching, after considering the advice of Members of the Congress, Republicans as well as the Democratic leadership, after consulting with many, many people within the Republican Party, and without, I have made a decision which I would now like to announce to the American people.

This is a difficult decision, but the man that I am selecting as nominee for Vice President is a person whose long record of accomplishment in the Government and outside is well-known. He comes from a family that has long been associated with the building of a better America. It is a family that has contributed significantly to many accomplishments, both at home and abroad, for the American people.

His achievements in Government are well, well-known. He served in the Department of State under former President Franklin Delano Roosevelt. He served under the Presidency of Harry Truman. He served in the Department of HEW under President Eisenhower.

He has served as Governor of the great Empire State, the State of New York, for 15 years, the longest period of time in the history of the State of New York. He is known across the land as a person dedicated to the free enterprise system, a person who is recognized abroad for his talents, for his dedication to making this a peaceful world.

It was a tough call for a tough job. The number of people who were considered by me in the process were all men and women of great quality. They came from those suggested to me who serve in the Congress, the Senate and the House of Representatives.

The names included individuals who had served their respective states with great credit. The names included individuals who were in Government, but not in Washington. The names included individuals who were not connected with Government.

But after a long and very thoughtful process, I have made the choice and that choice is Nelson Rockefeller of New York State. It is my honor and privilege to introduce to you a good partner for me and I think a good partner for our country and the world.

So I announce officially that I will send the name of Nelson Rockefeller to the Congress of the United States for confirmation.

Rockefeller's acceptance statement:

Mr. President, Mr. Speaker and leaders of the Congress, Mr. Secretary of State and Members of the Cabinet, and friends:

Mr. President, your nomination of me to be Vice President of the United States under the 25th Amendment of the Constitution makes me very humble. If I am confirmed, it will be my great honor to serve you and through you to serve all the people of this great country.

As you pointed out in your moving message to the Congress, these are very serious times. They are times, as you pointed out, that require the closest cooperation between the Congress of the United States and the Executive Branch of Government. They also require the dedication of every American to our common national interest.

You, Mr. President, through your dedication and your openness have already reawakened faith and hope, and under your leadership we, as a people, and we as a nation have the will, the determination and the capability to overcome the hard realities of our times. I am optimistic about the long-term future.

Thank you, Sir.

FINAL IMPEACHMENT REPORT
August 20, 1974

Ending the impeachment inquiry which it authorized Feb. 6 (see p. 137), the House of Representatives Aug. 20 accepted the report of the House Judiciary Committee, officially noted the committee's recommendations on impeachment and commended the committee for its "conscientious and capable efforts" in carrying out its obligations. The committee, chaired by Rep. Peter W. Rodino Jr. (D N.J.), had submitted its report for the record even though Nixon's resignation had rendered moot the question of whether the President should be removed from office. (See p. 683-693.)

The House voted 412-3 on a resolution which formally recorded its recognition of the committee's recommendations and of former President Nixon's resignation, and officially accepted the committee report and authorized its printing. By adoption of the resolution proposed by Majority Leader Thomas P. O'Neill Jr. (D Mass.), the House put its stamp of approval on the committee's seven month inquiry without impeaching the former president. The parliamentary move ended a search begun with Nixon's resignation, for a way in which the House could take official notice of the committee's recommendations without adopting articles of impeachment and setting a Senate trial in motion.

The resolution stated that the House took notice that:

● It had authorized the House Judiciary Committee to investigate possible grounds of impeachment of President Nixon. (See p. 137.)

● The committee had on July 27, 29 and 30 recommended articles of impeachment against Nixon. (See p. 655.)

●Nixon had Aug. 9 resigned the office of president.

The resolution went on to state that the House "accepts the report submitted by the Committee on the Judiciary pursuant to House Resolution 803 and authorizes...that the said report, together with supplemental, additional, separate, dissenting, minority, individual and concurring views be printed in full in the Congressional Record *and as a House Document."*

Limited Meaning

The precise and limited meaning of the House action adopting the resolution and "accepting" the report was pointed out by Charles E. Wiggins (R Calif.), a member of the committee: "There must be no misunderstanding concerning the purpose or intent of this resolution....The language...can only mean that the report of the committee has been formally received by the House.... I am satisfied that its author and the House as a whole reject any implication that this resolution 'approves' the committee report.... It must also be remembered that an approval of the resolution would be tantamount to adoption of the articles of impeachment by the House. No such intent should be imparted to the majority leader...."

Explanation of Impeachment Action

The 528-page Judiciary Committee Report—written for the historical record—explained the basis for the committee's decision recommending impeachment. Aware that they were writing for history, the members of the committee made clear the reason for Nixon's resignation. As Charles B. Rangel (D N.Y.) expressed it in his separate views: "[E]ven on the day of his resignation, President Nixon attempted to convey to the American people the impression that his resignation was caused by erosion of his political base as a result of some poor judgments he made during his term of office. The record, as set forth in the committee report, makes it abundantly clear that Richard M. Nixon violated his oath of office as President...that he committed impeachable crimes, and that on the available evidence he would have been impeached by the House of Representatives."

The majority views of the committee, covering 223 pages, were chiefly a statement of the committee's findings and the evidence supporting them. The second half of the report consisted of individual, additional, supplemental and minority views. The minority views were those of the 10 Republicans who had opposed impeachment—until Nixon Aug. 5 released the last, fatal transcripts. (See p. 673-682.)

Many committee members added separate statements, but those who had played the most crucial roles in the committee's work—Charles E. Wiggins (R Calif.) and Walter Flowers (D Ala.) and most of the Republicans who supported impeachment—did not.

> *Following are excerpts from the final report of the House Judiciary Committee, accepted by the full House of Representatives Aug. 20 and excerpts from the Supplemen-*

tal, Additional, Separate, Dissenting, Minority, Individual
and Concurring Views:

ARTICLE I

INTRODUCTION

Before entering on the execution of his office as President of the United
States, Richard M. Nixon has twice taken, as required in Article II, Section
1, Clause 7 of the Constitution, the following oath:

> I do solemnly swear that I will faithfully execute the Office of the President of
> the United States, and will to the best of my ability, preserve, protect and defend
> the Constitution of the United States.

Under the Constitution, the Executive power is vested in the President.
In Article II, Section 3, the Constitution requires that the President "shall
take care that the laws be faithfully executed."

On June 17, 1972, and prior thereto, agents of the Committee for the Re-
Election of the President committed unlawful entry into the headquarters
of the Democratic National Committee in Washington, D.C. for the purpose
of securing political intelligence.

For more than two years, Richard M. Nixon continuously denied any personal or White House responsibility for the burglaries; he continuously
denied any direction of or participation in a plan to cover up and conceal the
identities of those who authorized the burglaries and the existence and
scope of other unlawful and covert activities committed in the President's
interest and on his behalf.

In the course of his public statements, from June 22, 1972, until August
5, 1974, the President repeated these denials.... [See p. 41-42, 52-53, 145-154,
189-203, 287-299, 301-387, 673-682; Historic Documents 1973, p. 337-342,
499-512, 563-574, 737-751, 897-909, 947-963.]

On July 27, 1974, the Committee on the Judiciary decided that since June
17, 1972, Richard M. Nixon, using the power of his high office, engaged, personally and through his subordinates and agents, in a course of conduct or
plan designed to delay, impede and obstruct the investigation of the unlawful entry into the headquarters of the Democratic National Committee;
cover-up; conceal; and protect those responsible and to conceal the existence and scope of the unlawful and covert activities.

This report is based on the evidence available to the Committee at the
time of its decision. It contains clear and convincing evidence that the
President caused action—not only by his own subordinates but by agencies
of the United States, including the Department of Justice, the Federal
Bureau of Investigation, and the Central Intelligence Agency—to cover up
the Watergate break-in. This concealment required perjury, destruction of

evidence, obstruction of justice—all of which are crimes. It included false and misleading public statements as part of a deliberate, contrived, continued deception of the American people.

On August 5, 1974, the President submitted to the Committee on the Judiciary three additional edited White House transcripts of Presidential conversations, which only confirms the clear and convincing evidence, that from the beginning, the President, knowingly directed the cover-up of the Watergate burglary.

The evidence on which the Committee based its decision on Article I is summarized in the following sections....

CONCLUSION

After the Committee on the Judiciary had debated whether or not it should recommend Article I to the House of Representatives, 27 of the 38 Members of the Committee found that the evidence before it could only lead to one conclusion: that Richard M. Nixon, using the powers of his high office, engaged, personally and through his subordinates and agents, in a course of conduct or plan designed to delay, impede, and obstruct the investigation of the unlawful entry, on June 17, 1972, into the headquarters of the Democratic National Committee; to cover up, conceal and protect those responsible; and to conceal the existence and scope of other unlawful covert activities.

This finding is the only one that can explain the President's involvement in a pattern of undisputed acts that occurred after the break-in and that cannot otherwise be rationally explained.

1. The President's decision on June 20, 1972, not to meet with his Attorney General, his chief of staff, his counsel, his campaign director, and his assistant John Ehrlichman, whom he had put in charge of the investigation—when the subject of their meeting was the Watergate matter.

2. The erasure of that portion of the recording of the President's conversation with Haldeman, on June 20, 1972, which dealt with Watergate—when the President stated that the tapes had been under his "sole and personal control."

3. The President's public denial on June 22, 1972, of the involvement of members of the Committee for the Re-election of the President or of the White House staff in the Watergate burglary, in spite of having discussed Watergate, on or before June 22, 1972, with Haldeman, Colson, and Mitchell—all persons aware of that involvement.

4. The President's directive to Haldeman on June 23, 1972, to have the CIA request the FBI to curtail its Watergate investigation.

5. The President's refusal, on July 6, 1972, to inquire and inform himself what Patrick Gray, Acting Director of the FBI, meant by his warning that some of the President's aides were "trying to mortally wound" him.

6. The President's discussion with Ehrlichman on July 8, 1972, of clemency for the Watergate burglars, more than two months before the return of any indictments.

7. The President's public statement on August 29, 1972, a statement later shown to be untrue, that an investigation by John Dean "indicates that no one in the White House staff, no one in the Administration, presently employed, was involved in this very bizarre incident."

8. The President's statement to Dean on September 15, 1972, the day that the Watergate indictments were returned without naming high CRP and White House officials, that Dean had handled his work skillfully, "putting your fingers in the dike every time that leaks have sprung here and sprung there," and that "you just try to button it up as well as you can and hope for the best."

9. The President's discussion with Colson in January, 1973 of clemency for Hunt.

10. The President's discussion with Dean on February 28, 1973, of Kalmbach's upcoming testimony before the Senate Select Committee, in which the President said that it would be hard for Kalmbach because "it'll get out about Hunt," and the deletion of that phrase from the edited White House transcript.

11. The President's appointment in March, 1973, of Jeb Stuart Magruder to a high government position when Magruder had previously perjured himself before the Watergate Grand Jury in order to conceal CRP involvement.

12. The President's inaction in response to Dean's report of March 13, 1973, that Mitchell and Haldeman knew about Liddy's operation at CRP, that Sloan has a compulsion to "cleanse his soul by confession," that Stans and Kalmbach were trying to get him to "settle down," and that Strachan had lied about his prior knowledge of Watergate out of personal loyalty; and the President's reply to Dean that Strachan was the problem "in Bob's case."

13. The President's discussion on March 13, 1973, of a plan to limit future Watergate investigations by making Colson a White House "consultant without doing any consulting," in order to bring him under the doctrine of executive privilege.

14. The omission of the discussion related to Watergate from the edited White House transcript, submitted to the Committee on the Judiciary, of the President's March 17, 1973, conversation with Dean, especially in light of the fact that the President had listened to the conversation on June 4, 1973.

15. The President's instruction to Dean on the evening of March 20, 1973, to make his report on Watergate "very incomplete," and his subsequent public statements misrepresenting the nature of the instruction.

16. The President's instruction to Haldeman on the morning of March 21, 1973, that Hunt's price was pretty high, but that they should buy the time on it.

17. The President's March 21st statement to Dean that he had "handled it just right," and "contained it;" and the deletion of the above comments from the edited White House transcripts.

18. The President's instruction to Dean on March 21, 1973, to state false-ly that payments to the Watergate defendants had been made through a Cuban Committee.

19. The President's refusal to inform officials of the Department of Justice that on March 21, 1973, Dean had confessed to obstruction of justice and had said that Haldeman, Ehrlichman, and Mitchell were also involved in that crime.

20. The President's approval on March 22, 1973, of a shift in his position on executive privilege "in order to get on with the cover-up plan," and the discrepancy, in that phrase, in the edited White House transcript.

21. The President's instruction to Ronald Ziegler on March 26, 1973, to state publicly that the President had "absolute and total confidence" in Dean.

22. The President's action, in April, 1973, in conveying to Haldeman, Ehrlichman, Colson and Kalmbach information furnished to the President by Assistant Attorney General Petersen after the President had assured Petersen that he would not do so.

23. The President's discussions, in April, 1973, of the manner in which witnesses should give false and misleading statements.

24. The President's directions, in April, 1973, with respect to offering assurances of clemency to Mitchell, Magruder and Dean.

25. The President's lack of full disclosure and misleading statements to Assistant Attorney General Henry Petersen between April 15 and April 27, 1973, when Petersen reported directly to the President about the Watergate investigation.

26. The President's instruction to Ehrlichman on April 17, 1973, to give false testimony concerning Kalmbach's knowledge of the purpose of the payments to the Watergate defendants.

27. The President's decision to give Haldeman on April 25 and 26, 1973, access to tape recordings of Presidential conversations, after Assistant Attorney General Petersen had repeatedly warned the President that Haldeman was a suspect in the Watergate investigation.

28. The President's refusal to disclose the existence of the White House taping system.

29. The President's statement to Richardson on May 25, 1973, that his waiver of executive privilege, announced publicly on May 22, 1973, did not extend to documents.

30. The refusal of the President to cooperate with Special Prosecutor Cox; the President's instruction to Special Prosecutor Cox not to seek additional evidence in the courts and his firing of Cox when Cox refused to comply with that directive.

31. The submission by the President to the Committee on April 30, 1974, and the simultaneous release to the public of transcripts of 43 Presidential conversations and statements, which are characterized by omissions of words and passages, misattributions of statements, additions, paraphrases, distortions, non-sequiturs, deletions of sections as "Material Unrelated to Presidential Action," and other signs of editorial intervention;

the President's authorization of his counsel to characterize these transcripts as "accurate"; and the President's public statement that the transcripts contained "the whole story" of the Watergate matter.

32. The President's refusal in April, May, and June 1974, to comply with the subpoenas of the Committee issued in connection with its impeachment inquiry.

In addition to this evidence, there was before the Committee the following evidence:

1. Beginning immediately after June 17, 1972, the involvement of each of the President's top aides and political associates, Haldeman, Mitchell, Ehrlichman, Colson, Dean, LaRue, Mardian, Magruder, in the Watergate coverup.

2. The clandestine payment by Kalmbach and LaRue of more than $400,000 to the Watergate defendants.

3. The attempts by Ehrlichman and Dean to interfere with the FBI investigation.

4. The perjury of Magruder, Porter, Mitchell, Krogh, Strachan, Haldeman and Ehrlichman.

Finally, there was before the Committee a record of public statements by the President between June 22, 1972, and June 9, 1974, deliberately contrived to deceive the courts, the Department of Justice, the Congress and the American people.

President Nixon's course of conduct following the Watergate break-in, as described in Article I, caused action not only by his subordinates but by the agencies of the United States, including the Department of Justice, the FBI, and the CIA. It required perjury, destruction of evidence, obstruction of justice, all crimes. But, most important, it required deliberate, contrived, and continuing deception of the American people.

President Nixon's actions resulted in manifest injury to the confidence of the nation and great prejudice to the cause of law and justice, and was subversive of constitutional government. His actions were contrary to his trust as President and unmindful of the solemn duties of his high office. It was this serious violation of Richard M. Nixon's constitutional obligations as President, and not the fact that violations of Federal criminal statutes occurred, that lies at the heart of Article I.

The Committee finds, based upon clear and convincing evidence, that this conduct, detailed in the foregoing pages of this report, constitutes "high crimes and misdemeanors" as that term is used in Article II, Section 4 of the Constitution. Therefore, the Committee recommends that the House of Representatives exercise its constitutional power to impeach Richard M. Nixon.

On August 5, 1974, nine days after the Committee had voted on Article I, President Nixon released to the public and submitted to the Committee on the Judiciary three additional edited White House transcripts of Presidential conversations that took place on June 23, 1972, six days following the DNC break-in. Judge Sirica had that day released to the Special Prosecutor transcripts of those conversations pursuant to the mandate of the United States Supreme Court. The Committee had subpoenaed the tape recordings of those conversations, but the President had refused to honor the subpoena.

These transcripts conclusively confirm the finding that the Committee had already made, on the basis of clear and convincing evidence, that from shortly after the break-in on June 17, 1972, Richard M. Nixon, acting personally and through his subordinates and agents, made it his plan to and did direct his subordinates to engage in a course of conduct designed to delay, impede and obstruct investigation of the unlawful entry of the headquarters of the Democratic National Committee; to cover up, conceal and protect those responsible; and to conceal the existence and scope of other unlawful covert activities.

ARTICLE II

INTRODUCTION

On July 29 the Committee adopted Article II, as amended, by a vote of 28 to 10. The Article provides:

Using the powers of the office of President of the United States, Richard M. Nixon, in violation of his constitutional oath faithfully to execute the office of President of the United States, and to the best of his ability, preserve, protect, and defend the Constitution of the United States, and in disregard of his constitutional duty to take care that the laws be faithfully executed, has repeatedly engaged in conduct violating the constitutional rights of citizens, impairing the due and proper administration of justice and the conduct of lawful inquiries, or contravening the laws governing agencies of the executive branch and the purposes of these agencies.

Article II charges that Richard M. Nixon, in violation of his constitutional duty to take care that the laws be faithfully executed and his oath of office as President, seriously abused powers that only a President possesses. He engaged in conduct that violated the constitutional rights of citizens, that interfered with investigations by federal authorities and congressional committees, and that contravened the laws governing agencies of the executive branch of the federal government. This conduct, undertaken for his own personal political advantage and not in furtherance of any valid national policy objective, is seriously incompatible with our system of constitutional government.

Five instances of abuse of the powers of the office of President are specifically listed in Article II. Each involves repeated misuse of the powers of the office, and each focuses on improprieties by the President that served no valid national policy objective. Each of them individually and all of them together support the ground of impeachment charged in Article II—that Richard M. Nixon, using the power of his office, repeatedly engaged in conduct violating the constitutional rights of citizens, impairing the due and proper administration of justice and the conduct of lawful inquiries, or contravening the laws governing agencies of the executive branch and the purposes of these agencies.

Richard M. Nixon violated the constitutional rights of citizens by directing or authorizing his subordinates to interfere with the impartial and nonpolitical administration of the internal revenue laws. He violated the constitutional rights of citizens by directing or authorizing unlawful electronic surveillance and investigations of citizens and the use of information obtained from the surveillance for his own political advantage. He violated the constitutional rights of citizens by permitting a secret investigative unit within the office of the President to engage in unlawful and covert activities for his political purposes. Once these and other unlawful and improper activities on his behalf were suspected, and after he knew or had reason to know that his close subordinates were interfering with lawful investigations into them, he failed to perform his duty to see that the criminal laws were enforced against these subordinates. And he used his executive power to interfere with the lawful operations of agencies of the executive branch, including the Department of Justice and the Central Intelligence Agency, in order to assist in these activities, as well as to conceal the truth about his misconduct and that of his subordinates and agents....

CONCLUSION

In recommending Article II to the House, the Committee finds clear and convincing evidence that Richard M. Nixon, contrary to his trust as President and unmindful of the solemn duties of his high office, has repeatedly used his power as President to violate the Constitution and the law of the land.

In so doing, he has failed in the obligation that every citizen has to live under the law. But he has done more, for it is the duty of the President not merely to live by the law but to see that law faithfully applied. Richard M. Nixon has repeatedly and willfully failed to perform that duty. He has failed to perform it by authorizing and directing actions that violated or disregarded the rights of citizens and that corrupted and attempted to corrupt the lawful functioning of executive agencies. He has failed to perform it by condoning and ratifying, rather than acting to stop, actions by his subordinates that interfered with lawful investigations and impeded the enforcement of the laws.

Article II, section 3 of the Constitution requires that the President "shall take Care that the Laws be faithfully executed." Justice Felix Frankfurter described this provision as "the embracing function of the President";

President Benjamin Harrison called it "the central idea of the office." "[I]n a republic," Harrison wrote, "the thing to be executed is the law, not the will of the ruler as in despotic governments. The President cannot go beyond the law, and he cannot stop short of it."

The conduct of Richard M. Nixon has constituted a repeated and continuing abuse of the powers of the Presidency in disregard of the fundamental principle of the rule of law in our system of government. This abuse of the powers of the President was carried out by Richard M. Nixon, acting personally and through his subordinates, for his own political advantage, not for any legitimate governmental purpose and without due consideration for the national good.

The rule of law needs no defense by the Committee. Reverence for the laws, said Abraham Lincoln, should "become the political religion of the nation." Said Theodore Roosevelt, "No man is above the law and no man is below it; nor do we ask any man's permission when we require him to obey it."

It is a basic principle of our government that "we submit ourselves to rulers only if [they are] under rules." *[Youngstown Sheet and Tube Co. v. Sawyer (1952), Justice Jackson concurring]* "Decency, security, and liberty alike demand that government officials shall be subjected to the same rules of conduct that are commands to the citizen," wrote Justice Louis Brandeis....

In asserting the supremacy of the rule of law among the principles of our government, the Committee is enunciating no new standard of Presidential conduct. The possibility that Presidents have violated this standard in the past does not diminish its current—and future—applicability. Repeated abuse of power by one who holds the highest public office requires prompt and decisive remedial action, for it is in the nature of abuses of power that if they go unchecked they will become overbearing, depriving the people and their representatives of the strength of will or the wherewithal to resist.

Our Constitution provides for a responsible Chief Executive, accountable for his acts. The framers hoped, in the words of Elbridge Gerry, that "the maxim would never be adopted here that the chief Magistrate could do no wrong." They provided for a single executive because, as Alexander Hamilton wrote, "the executive power is more easily confined when it is one" and "there should be a single object for the...watchfulness of the people."

The President, said James Wilson, one of the principal authors of the Constitution, "is the dignified, but accountable magistrate of a free and great people." Wilson said, "The executive power is better to be trusted when it has no screen.... [W]e have a responsibility in the person of our President: ...he cannot roll upon any other person the weight of his criminality...." As both Wilson and Hamilton pointed out, the President should not be able to hide behind his counsellors; he must ultimately be accountable for their acts on his behalf. James Iredell of North Carolina, a leading proponent of the proposed Constitution and later a Supreme Court

Justice, said that the President "is of a very different nature from a monarch. He is to be...personally responsible for any abuse of the great trust reposed in him."

In considering this Article the Committee has relied on evidence of acts directly attributable to Richard M. Nixon himself. He has repeatedly attempted to conceal his accountability for these acts and attempted to deceive and mislead the American people about his own responsibility. He governed behind closed doors, directing the operation of the executive branch through close subordinates, and sought to conceal his knowledge of what they did illegally on his behalf. Although the Committee finds it unnecessary in this case to take any position on whether the President should be held accountable, through exercise of the power of impeachment, for the actions of his immediate subordinates, undertaken on his behalf, when his personal authorization and knowledge of them cannot be proved, it is appropriate to call attention to the dangers inherent in the performance of the highest public office in the land in an air of secrecy and concealment.

The abuse of a President's powers poses a serious threat to the lawful and proper functioning of the government and the people's confidence in it. For just such Presidential misconduct the impeachment power was included in the Constitution. The impeachment provision, wrote Justice Joseph Story in 1833, "holds out a deep and immediate responsibility, as a check upon arbitrary power; and compels the chief magistrate, as well as the humblest citizen, to bend to the majesty of the law." And Chancellor James Kent wrote in 1826:

> If...neither the sense of duty, the force of public opinion, nor the transitory nature of the seat, are sufficient to secure a faithful exercise of the executive trust, but the President will use the authority of his station to violate the Constitution or law of the land, the House of Representatives can arrest him in his career, by resorting to the power of impeachment.

The Committee has concluded that, to perform its constitutional duty, it must approve this Article of Impeachment and recommend it to the House. If we had been unwilling to carry out the principle that all those who govern, including ourselves, are accountable to the law and the Constitution, we would have failed in our responsibility as representatives of the people, elected under the Constitution. If we had not been prepared to apply the principle of Presidential accountability embodied in the impeachment clause of the Constitution, but had instead condoned the conduct of Richard M. Nixon, then another President, perhaps with a different political philosophy, might have used this illegitimate power for further encroachments on the rights of citizens and further usurpations of the power of other branches of our government. By adopting this Article, the Committee seeks to prevent the recurrence of any such abuse of Presidential power.

The Committee finds that, in the performance of his duties as President, Richard M. Nixon on many occasions has acted to the detriment of justice, right, and the public good, in violation of his constitutional duty to see to the faithful execution of the laws. This conduct has demonstrated a contempt for the rule of law; it has posed a threat to our democratic republic. The Committee finds that this conduct constitutes "high crimes and misdemeanors" within the meaning of the Constitution, that it warrants his impeachment by the House, and that it requires that he be put to trial in the Senate.

In recommending Article II to the House, the Committee finds clear and convincing evidence that Richard M. Nixon has not faithfully executed the executive trust, but has repeatedly used his authority as President to violate the Constitution and the law of the land. In so doing, he violated the obligation that every citizen has to live under the law. But he did more, for it is the duty of the President not merely to live by the law but to see that law faithfully applied. Richard M. Nixon repeatedly and willfully failed to perform that duty. He failed to perform it by authorizing and directing actions that violated the rights of citizens and that interfered with the functioning of executive agencies. And he failed to perform it by condoning and ratifying, rather than acting to stop, actions by his subordinates interfering with the enforcement of the laws.

ARTICLE III

INTRODUCTION

On February 6, 1974, the House of Representatives adopted H. Res. 803, authorizing and directing the Committee on the Judiciary to investigate whether sufficient grounds exist to impeach President Richard M. Nixon. This resolution authorized the Committee "to require...by subpoena or otherwise... production of such things...as deemed necessary to such investigation."

On February 25, 1974, Special Counsel to the Committee wrote to the President's counsel requesting tape recordings of designated presidential conversations and related documents. Some of these items had previously been provided by the President to the Special Prosecutor; others had not. In response to this request, the President agreed to produce only those materials he had previously given to the Special Prosecutor.

By subsequent letters and, ultimately, by service of eight subpoenas upon the President, the Committee sought:

(1) tape recordings, notes and other writings relating to 147 specified conversations;

(2) a list of the President's meetings and telephone conversations known as "daily diaries," for five special periods in 1971, 1972 and 1973;

(3) papers and memoranda relating to the Watergate break-in and its aftermath and to the activities of the White House special investigative

unit (the Plumbers), prepared by, sent to, received by or at any time contained in the files of seven named former members of the President's staff; and

(4) copies of the President's daily news summaries, for a 3½ month period in 1972, that contain his handwritten notes pertaining to the hearings before the Senate Judiciary Committee on Richard Kleindienst's nomination to be Attorney General and matters involving ITT antitrust litigation.

The President was informed that the materials demanded by these eight subpoenas were necessary for the Committee's inquiry into the Watergate matter, domestic surveillance, the relationship between a governmental milk price support decision and campaign contributions by certain dairy cooperatives, the conduct of ITT antitrust litigation and alleged perjured testimony by administration officials during the Kleindienst confirmation hearings, and the alleged misuse of the Internal Revenue Service.

In response to these subpoenas the President produced:

(1) edited transcripts of all or part of 33 subpoenaed conversations and 6 conversations that had not been subpoenaed, all but one of which related to the Watergate matter;

(2) edited copies of notes made by John Ehrlichman during meetings with the President, which had been previously furnished to Ehrlichman and the Special Prosecutor in connection with the trial *United States v. Ehrlichman*, and

(3) copies of certain White House news summaries, containing no handwritten notes by the President.

The Committee did not receive a single tape recording of any of the 117 subpoenaed conversations. Nor, apart from the edited notes of Ehrlichman and the copies of news summaries, did the Committee receive any of the other papers or things sought by its subpoenas.

Shortly after the President's response, the Committee informed the President that his refusal to comply might be regarded as a ground for impeachment.

At the conclusion of its inquiry, the Committee approved by a vote of 21-17 the following Article of Impeachment:

Article III

...In refusing to produce these papers and things, Richard M. Nixon substituted his judgment as to what materials were necessary for the inquiry, interposed the powers of the presidency against the lawful subpoenas of the House of Representatives, thereby assuming to himself functions and judgments necessary to the exercise of the sole power of impeachment vested by the Constitution in the House of Representatives.

In all of this, Richard M. Nixon has acted in a manner contrary to his trust as President and subversive of constitutional government, to the great prejudice of the cause of law and justice, and to the manifest injury of the people of the United States.

Wherefore, Richard M. Nixon by such conduct, warrants impeachment and trial, and removal from office.

The refusal of the President to comply with the subpoenas was an interference by him with the efforts of the Committee and the House of Representatives to fulfill their constitutional responsibilities. It was, as Article III states, an effort to interpose "the powers of the presidency against the lawful subpoenas of the House of Representatives, thereby assuming to himself functions and judgments necessary to this exercise of the sole power of impeachment vested by the Constitution in the House of Representatives."

Evidence of the President's refusal to comply with the Committee's subpoenas seeking evidence with respect to the Watergate matter could be introduced as proof of the allegations in Article I—which charges interference with investigations by Congressional Committees as one of the means used to obstruct justice in the Watergate matter. But the refusal by the President to comply with subpoenas issued after the Committee was satisfied there was other evidence pointing to the existence of impeachable offenses, is a grave interference with the efforts of the Committee and the House to fulfill their constitutional responsibilities, regardless of whether it is part of a course of conduct or plan to obstruct justice. Only Article III is concerned with enforcing general standards requiring Presidential compliance with subpoenas in impeachment inquiries.

The Committee has been able to conduct an investigation and determine that grounds for impeachment exist—even in the face of the President's refusal to comply. But this does not mean that the refusal was without practical import. The Committee had enough evidence to recommend the adoption of two other articles, but it does not and did not have at the time it deliberated and voted—despite the President's contentions to the contrary—the "full story." Had it received the evidence sought by the subpoenas, the Committee might have recommended articles structured differently or possibly ones covering other matters. Article III states, the evidence sought was "deemed necessary by the Committee in order to resolve by direct evidence fundamental, factual questions relating to presidential direction, knowledge or approval of actions demonstrated by other evidence to be substantial grounds for impeachment of the President." It is the defiance of the Committee's subpoenas under these circumstances that gave rise to the impeachable offense charged by Article III.

The President's statement on August 5, 1974, that he would transmit to the Senate certain material subpoenaed by the Committee, did not lessen the need for Article III. The President said on August 5 that he would supply to the Senate, for an impeachment trial, those portions of recordings of 64 conversations that Judge Sirica decides should be produced for the Special Prosecutor for use in the Watergate criminal trial. This assurance did not remove the interference with the exercise of their responsibilities by the Committee and the House charged in Article III.

Article III charges the President with interfering with the discharge of the Committee's responsibility to investigate fully and completely whether sufficient grounds exist to impeach him. The Committee's duty is different from the duty of a prosecutor, a grand jury, or a trial jury, whose task it is to determine whether specific criminal statutes have been violated. What may be relevant or necessary for the Watergate criminal trial would not necessarily coincide with what is relevant and necessary for this inquiry. And, in any event, it is for the Committee—not a trial judge in a criminal case—to determine what is relevant and necessary to the Committee's inquiry. Thus, even if the President had, on August 5, 1974, consented to deliver to the House the portions of the 64 recordings that Judge Sirica eventually found relevant and necessary to the Watergate criminal trial, the President's refusal to comply with the Committee's subpoenas would nonetheless constitute an interference with the duty of this Committee.

Similarly, the President's willingness to furnish to the Senate some material that was sought by the Committee's subpoenas does not remove the obstruction of the constitutional process. In the first place, the President's assurance related only to a portion of the material sought by the Committee. But more fundamentally, providing material to the Senate did not eliminate the interference with this Committee's responsibilities because the duty of the Committee differs also from that of the Senate. The responsibility of the Senate is to determine whether the evidence is sufficient to remove the President on the basis of specific articles of impeachment previously transmitted to it by the House. The duty of the Committee is to investigate first and then to recommend to the House whether there is sufficient evidence to transmit articles of impeachment to the Senate. In order for this Committee and the House to be able to perform their responsibilities, it is not sufficient for the President to meet the demands of other bodies seeking evidence for other purposes; the demands of the Committee and House must also be met.

Rather than removing the need for Article III, the events of August 5 underscore its importance. On that day, the President not only made the statement concerning transmittal of materials to the Senate, but also released edited transcripts of three conversations that took place on June 23, 1972 between himself and Haldeman. These conversations were requested by the Committee by letter dated April 19, 1974 and subpoenaed on May 15, 1974. The President, by letter dated May 22, 1974, refused to comply with the subpoena stating that "the Committee has the full story of Watergate, insofar as it relates to Presidential knowledge and Presidential actions."

There is no question that the three June 23, 1972 conversations bear significantly upon presidential knowledge and presidential actions. There is also no question that, prior to sending his May 22, 1974 letter defying the Committee's subpoena, the President listened to recordings of two of these conversations. Both of these facts were admitted in his August 5 statement. Yet the President did not make the June 23 conversations available until after the Committee had completed its deliberations, and then only as a consequence of the Supreme Court decision in *United States v. Nixon* directing that the conversations be produced for the Watergate criminal trial. The President's defiance of the Committee forced it to deliberate and make judgments on a record that the President now acknowledges was "incomplete." His actions demonstrate the need to ensure that a standard be established barring such conduct in impeachment inquiries. That is the function of Article III....

CONCLUSION

The undisputed facts, historic precedent, and applicable legal principles support the Committee's recommendation of Article III. There can be no question that in refusing to comply with limited, narrowly drawn subpoenas—issued only after the Committee was satisfied that there was other evidence pointing to the existence of impeachable offenses—the President interfered with the exercise of the House's function as the "Grand Inquest of the Nation." Unless the defiance of the Committee's subpoenas under these circumstances is considered grounds for impeachment, it is difficult to conceive of any President acknowledging that he is obligated to supply the relevant evidence necessary for Congress to exercise its constitutional responsibility in an impeachment proceeding. If this were to occur, the impeachment power would be drained of its vitality. Article III, therefore, seeks to preserve the integrity of the impeachment process itself and the ability of Congress to act as the ultimate safeguard against improper presidential conduct.

PROPOSED ARTICLE ON CONCEALMENT OF INFORMATION ABOUT BOMBING OPERATIONS IN CAMBODIA

On July 30, 1974, the Committee considered a proposed Article of Impeachment dealing with the unauthorized bombing of Cambodia and the concealment from the Congress of that bombing *[Text, see p. 655-660]...*

The Committee, by a vote of 26-12, decided not to report the proposed Article to the House.

The Article charged that the President had concealed the bombing in Cambodia from the Congress and that he had submitted, personally and through his aides, false and misleading statements to the Congress concerning that bombing. The investigation of those allegations centered upon the initial decision to bomb Cambodia; the type, scope, extent and nature of the bombing missions; the reporting and recording system used internally within the military and the Administration; and the statements made by Administration officials to Congress and to the public both during the military operation and after it had ceased.

On February 11, 1969, the President received the initial request to institute the bombing from his military advisors. On March 17, 1969, after a series of National Security Council meetings, the President approved the request and directed that the operation be undertaken under tight security.

On March 18, 1969, the bombing of Cambodia commenced with B-52 strikes under the code name MENU OPERATION. These strikes continued until May 26, 1970, almost one month after the American incursion into Cambodia. The operational reports prepared after each mission stated that these strikes had taken place in South Vietnam rather than in Cambodia.

Between April 24 and May 24, 1970, American planes conducted tactical air strikes in Cambodia under the code name "regular" PATIO. No operational reports were made with respect to these strikes. Similarly, prior to June 30, 1970, an unspecified number of tactical air strikes occurred in various parts of Cambodia. Again no regular reports were prepared.

On May 14, 1970, a one day series of "special" PATIO sorties were conducted, operational reports stated that the strikes had occurred in Laos rather than Cambodia. The tactical air sorties with the code name "regular" FREEDOM DEAL were accurately reported as having occurred in Cambodia. A series of tactical air bombing missions in Cambodia called "special" FREEDOM DEAL occurred outside the boundaries designated for FREEDOM DEAL bombing, although the operational reports indicated otherwise.

On July 1, 1973, Congress enacted P.L. 93-50 and P.L. 93-52 providing for the cessation of all bombing in Cambodia by August 15, 1973. At that time the bombing had not been formally acknowledged by the President or his representatives.

Later, during the Senate Armed Services Committee hearings on the Cambodian bombing, military and Administration officials explained that the bombing was not publicized because of the delicate diplomatic and military situation in Southeast Asia prior to the American incursion into Cambodia. They stated that it was their understanding that Cambodia's ruler, Prince Sihanouk, had privately agreed to the bombing of Cambodia prior to his overthrow. It was further stated that certain Members of Congress had been informed of the military action and that this constituted sufficient notice to Congress of the President's military decision. Finally, the submission of false data to Congress was said to have resulted from the highly classified nature of the accurate bombing statistics.

The Committee considered the views of the supporters of this proposed Article of Impeachment that the President's conduct constituted ground for impeachment because the Constitution vests the power to make war in Congress and implicitly prohibits the Executive from waging an undeclared war. Stating that impeachment is a process for redefining the powers of the President, the supporters argued that the President, by issuing false and misleading statements, failed to provide Congress with complete and accurate information and thereby prevented Congress from responsibly exercising its powers to declare war, to raise and support armies, and to make appropriations. They stated that informing a few selected members of the Congress about the Cambodian bombing did not constitute the constitutionally required notice, particularly inasmuch as the President's contemporaneous public statements were contrary to the facts and the selected Members were committed to a course of action involving war that did not represent the views of a substantial portion of American citizens. The supporters also stated that Congress had not ratified the President's conduct through inaction or by its 1973 limitation on bombing because Congress did not know of the bombing until after it voted the authorization. Finally, they asserted that the technicalities or merits of the war in Southeast Asia, the acquiescence or protests of Prince Sihanouk, and the arguably similar conduct of past Presidents were irrelevant to the question of President Nixon's constitutional accountability in usurping Congress' war-making and appropriations powers.

The Committee did not agree to the article for a variety of reasons. The two principal arguments in opposition to it were that President Nixon was performing his constitutional duty in ordering the bombing and that Congress had been given sufficient notice of the bombing. Several Members stated that the President as Commander-in-Chief was acting to protect American troops and that other Presidents had engaged in similar military activities without prior Congressional consent. Examining the bombing of Cambodia from the perspective of Congressional responsibility, the opponents of the Article concluded that, even if President Nixon usurped Congressional power, Congress shared the blame through acquiescence or ratification of his actions. They stated that the President had provided sufficient notice of the military actions to Congress by informing key Members. Finally, they said that the passage of the War Powers Resolution in 1973 mooted the question raised by the Article....

PROPOSED ARTICLE ON EMOLUMENTS
AND TAX EVASION

On July 30, 1974, the Committee considered the following [Article on Emoluments and Tax Evasion].... *[Text of Article, see p. 655-660.]*

After debate, by a vote of 26 to 12, the Committee decided not to report the Article to the House.

This Article was based upon allegations in two areas. The expenditure of federal funds on the President's privately-owned properties at San Clemente, California, and Key Biscayne, Florida, was alleged to constitute a violation of Article II, Section 1, Clause 7, of the Constitution. That clause reads, "The President shall, at stated Times, receive for his Services, a Compensation, which shall neither be increased nor diminished during the Period for which he shall have been elected, and he shall not receive within that Period any other Emolument from the United States, or any of them." The second allegation is that the President knowingly and fraudulently failed to report certain income and claimed certain improper deductions on his federal income tax returns.

A. Expenditure of Federal Funds on the President's Properties

Several investigations have been undertaken with regard to the amount and propriety of Federal expenditures at or near the President's properties in San Clemente, California, and Key Biscayne, Florida. The House Committee on Government Operations found that a total of $17 million had been spent by the Federal Government in connection with the President's properties, including personnel costs, communication costs, and amounts expended on adjacent Federal facilities.... The staff of the Joint Committee on Internal Revenue Taxation found that the President realized more than $92,000 in personal income from government expenditures on his properties in the years 1969 through 1972.... The Internal Revenue Service concluded that the President realized more than $67,000 in personal income from government expenditures on his properties in those years....

The federal expenditures at San Clemente which were found to be primarily for the President's personal benefit included payments for such items as a sewer system, a heating system, a fireplace exhaust fan, enlargement of den windows, refurbishing or construction of outbuildings, paving, and boundary and structural surveys.... Expenditures brought into question at Key Biscayne included expenditures for such items as the reconstruction of a shuffleboard court and the building of a fence and hedge system.... The Government also made significant expenditures for landscape construction and maintenance on both properties....

The proponents of this section of the Article argued that the President, personally and through his agents, supervised the planning and execution of non-protective government expenditures at his private homes for his personal enrichment. The opponents maintained that a majority of the questionable expenditures were made pursuant to a Secret Service request, that there was no direct evidence of the President's awareness at the time of the expenditures that payments for these items were made out of public rather than personal funds, and that this section of the Article did not rise to the level of an impeachable offense.

B. Internal Revenue Code Violations

In examining the President's income tax returns for the years 1969 through 1972, the Internal Revenue Service found that his reported income should have been increased by more than $230,000 and that deductions claimed in excess of $565,000 should be disallowed, for a total error in reported taxable income of more than $796,000.... The staff of the Joint Committee on Internal Revenue Taxation determined that the President's improper deductions and unreported income for that period totaled more than $960,000.... Central to the tax section of the proposed Article was the charitable deduction claimed by the President for the years 1969-1972 for a gift of his private papers claimed to have been made to the Government in 1969 which was allegedly worth $576,000....

Both the IRS and the Joint Committee staff disallowed this deduction as not having been made on or before July 25, 1969, the last day on which a gift of such papers could entitle the donor to a tax deduction.... While the papers allegedly donated were physically delivered to the National Archives on March 27, 1969, they were part of a larger mass of papers, and the selection of the papers given was not completed until March 27, 1970.... The President's attorneys argued that in February 1969, the President told an aide that he wanted to make a gift..., but no contemporary record of this instruction was produced. A deed of gift, signed not by President Nixon but by a White House attorney who had no written authority to sign on behalf of the President..., was not delivered to the Archives until April 1970, although on its face it appears to have been executed on April 21, 1969.... The IRS and Joint Committee staff investigations established that the deed was actually executed on April 10, 1970, and backdated to the 1969 date (before the deduction cut-off date of July 25, 1969).... It was found that through the end of 1969, the National Archives, the donee, thought that no gift had been made.... Finally, even though the deed contained restrictions limiting access to the papers, the President's 1969 tax return stated that the gift was made without restrictions....

The IRS assessed a five percent negligence penalty against the President.... An internal IRS memorandum recommending against the assertion of a fraud penalty stated that as of late March 1974 there was not sufficient evidence available to assert such a penalty.... On April 2, 1974, IRS Commissioner Alexander wrote to Special Prosecutor Jaworski recommending a grand jury investigation into possible violations of law arising out of the preparation of the President's 1969 income tax return. Commissioner Alexander stated that the IRS was unable to complete its processing of the matter because of the lack of cooperation of some of the witnesses and because of many inconsistencies in the testimony of in-individuals to the IRS.... The Joint Committee staff report did not address the question of fraud...

The Joint Committee staff did submit questions to the President concerning the gift-of-papers deduction and other tax matters.... The President did not answer the questions.

The proponents of this Article argued that the President knew that no gift of papers had been made by July 25, 1969, and that the deduction was improper. They noted that it was contrary to rational tax planning for such a large gift to be made so early in the year. They pointed to the President's personal involvement in a similar gift in 1968, and memoranda and incidents in 1969 which showed his interest in his personal financial affairs in general and the gift-of-papers deduction in particular. They referred to the opinion of an expert on criminal tax fraud matters that if this were the case of an ordinary taxpayer, the case would be referred to a grand jury for prosecution. It was argued that the President took advantage of his office in claiming this unlawful deduction, knowing that the tax return of a President would receive only cursory examination by the IRS.

The opponents of the tax fraud section stated that the President had not knowingly underpaid his taxes, but relied on attorneys and agents; that the IRS failure to assess a fraud penalty was dispositive; and that even if fraud were shown, the offense of tax evasion did not rise to the level of an impeachable offense. Some who voted against the Article were of the opinion that the evidence before the Committee did not satisfy the standard of "clear and convincing proof" which some Members thought applicable.

Some of the Members who opposed the proposed Article argued that there was no clear and convincing evidence that the President had committed tax fraud and stated that the President had not knowingly underpaid his taxes, but rather relied on attorneys and agents. Opponents of the proposed Article also asserted that an impeachment inquiry in the House and trial in the Senate are inappropriate forums to determine the President's culpability for tax fraud, and that this kind of offense can be properly redressed through the ordinary processes of the criminal law. Finally they argued that even if tax fraud were proved, it was not the type of abuse of power at which the remedy of impeachment is directed.

SUPPLEMENTAL, ADDITIONAL, SEPARATE, DISSENTING, MINORITY, INDIVIDUAL, AND CONCURRING VIEWS

CONCURRING VIEWS OF MESSRS. RAILSBACK, FISH, HOGAN, BUTLER, COHEN AND FROEHLICH

For reasons we articulated in debate before the Judiciary Committee, the undersigned voted to recommend Articles I and II to the House. We agree in substance with this Report as it relates to those two articles. However, lest anyone infer that we agree without reservation to every point made, and given the lack of adequate time to prepare a detailed response to such points, suffice it to say that we do not necessarily agree that there is clear and convincing evidence to support every conclusion contained in the Report or that every fact referred to is necessary or relevant to support such articles.

ADDITIONAL VIEWS OF MESSRS. BROOKS, KASTENMEIER, EDWARDS, CONYERS, EILBERG, SEIBERLING, DANIELSON, RANGEL, MS. JORDAN, MS. HOLTZMAN, AND MR. MEZVINSKY

....[T]he House Judiciary Committee has recommended three articles of impeachment against Richard M. Nixon. These articles are fully supported by the evidence presented to the Committee. They do not, however, include all of the offenses committed by Richard Nixon for which he might be impeached, tried and removed from office.

There is ample evidence that Richard Nixon has violated the Constitution and the laws of the United States in an effort to enrich himself at the cost of the American taxpayer.

Shortly after his election in 1968, Mr. Nixon purchased three private homes. He then prevailed upon agencies of the Federal government to spend thousands of dollars of public funds at those properties. Intensive investigations by the House Government Operations Committee, the General Accounting Office, the Joint Committee on Internal Revenue Taxation, and the U.S. Internal Revenue Service have concluded that many of these expenditures were for Mr. Nixon's personal benefit and served no proper government function.

To preclude the possibility that a President might, because of personal financial considerations, either misuse the office for his own benefit or be held hostage to a hostile Congress, the drafters of our Constitution provided:

> The President shall, at stated times, receive for his services, a compensation, which shall neither be increased nor diminished during the period for which he shall have been elected, and he shall not receive within that period any other emolument from the United States or any of them.

The meaning of this clause is both clear and certain. Alexander Hamilton, writing in the *Federalist Papers No. 73*, succinctly stated its purpose as follows:

> It is impossible to imagine any provision which would have been more eligible than this. The legislature, on the appointment of a President, is once for all to declare what shall be the compensation for his services during the time for which he shall have been elected. This done, they will have no power to alter it, either by increase or diminution, till a new period of service by a new election commences.... Neither the Union, nor any of its members, will be at liberty to give, nor will he be at liberty to receive, any other emolument than that which may have been determined by the first act.

...Clearly, the payment of thousands of dollars by the Federal government for new heating systems, remodeling den windows, a sewer line, boundary surveys, landscape maintenance, sprinkler systems, and a shuffle board court constitutes additional "emoluments."...

In addition to receiving unlawful emoluments while in office, Mr. Nixon has attempted to evade the payment of his lawful taxes. There is substantial evidence that when Mr. Nixon signed his Federal income tax returns for 1969, 1970, 1971 and 1972, he knowingly attested to false information intending to defraud the American people of approximately one-half million dollars....

...[T]he Committee should have adopted an article citing Mr. Nixon for violation of the emoluments provision of the Constitution and violation of the tax laws of the United States.

A number of Members of the Committee agreed that Mr. Nixon had "set a very sorry example," or that he "did knowingly underpay his taxes in the four years in question by taking unauthorized deductions," or that he was "guilty of bad judgment and gross negligence." Those Members, however, for reasons of their own, chose not to view such actions on the level of impeachable offenses. That, of course, is a matter for each Member to determine. For myself, I find that these offenses bring into focus, in a manner every American can understand, the nature and gravity of the abuses that permeate Mr. Nixon's conduct in office.

The integrity of the Office of President cannot be maintained by one who would convert public funds to his own private benefit and who would refuse to abide by the same laws that govern every American taxpayer. All doubt should be removed that any American, even if he be President, can disregard the laws and the Constitution of the United States with impunity.

SUPPLEMENTAL VIEWS OF MR. EDWARDS

I fully and without reservation concur with the majority views of this report. I add supplementary views only to emphasize that there is a profoundly important aspect to the grievous and sustained misconduct of Mr. Nixon that in my opinion constituted a grave threat to the liberties of the American people.

In his attempts to subvert the processes of representative government and the guarantees of the Bill of Rights, Mr. Nixon and his associates used repeatedly the justification he described as "national security."

It was a familiar theme, referred to by James Madison in a letter to Jefferson in 1786. "Perhaps it is a universal truth," wrote the author of the Bill of Rights, "that the loss of liberty at home is to be charged to the provisions against dangers, real or pretended, from abroad."...

I found it immensely disturbing that the talented and distinguished counsel for Mr. Nixon in the impeachment inquiry supported the view that the mere invocation of the catch phrase "national security" justified illegal wiretaps and personal surveillances. Indeed, he told the Judiciary Committee that in his view a President should be impeached for *not* proceeding as Mr. Nixon did.

So, I am writing these supplementary views to emphasize the urgency of Madison's two hundred year old warning. Congress, the press, and indeed all of the American people must be vigilant to the perils of the subversive notion that any public official, the President or a policeman, possesses a kind of inherent power to set aside the Constitution whenever he thinks the public interest, or "national security" warrants it. That notion is the essential postulate of tyranny.

ADDITIONAL VIEWS OF MR. CONYERS

...In my judgment, this course of presidential conduct...specified in Articles I, II, and III, provides irrefutable evidence that Richard Nixon was not fit to enjoy the trust and authority which reposes in the Presidency of the United States.

But of at least equal importance is the uncontroverted evidence that Mr. Nixon authorized an illegal war against the sovereign nation of Cambodia, and sought to protect himself from criticism and possible repudiation by engaging in deliberate policies of concealment, deception, and misrepresentation.

On July 30, 1974, I proposed the...article [charging that]:

Richard M. Nixon, in violation of his constitutional oath...authorized, ordered and ratified the concealment from the Congress of the facts and the submission to the Congress of false and misleading statements concerning the existence, scope and nature of American bombing operations in Cambodia in derogation of the power of the Congress to declare war, to make appropriations, and to raise and support armies, and by such conduct warrants impeachment and trial and removal from office.

Although this article was not recommended by the Committee, it is fully supported by the facts and the Constitution.

...The manner in which the Cambodian bombing was initiated, conducted, and reported clearly exceeded the constitutional powers of the presidency, and presented indisputable evidence of impeachable conduct.

President Nixon unilaterally initiated and authorized a campaign of bombing against the neutral nation of Cambodia. For the next four years, he continually deceived the Congress and the American people as to when the bombing began and how far it extended. In so doing, he exceeded his constitutional power as commander-in-chief. He usurped the power of Congress to declare war, and he expended monies for a purpose not authorized or approved by the Congress. In so doing, he also denied the people of the United States their right to be fully informed about the actions and policies of their elected officials....

...We cannot sanction such a policy of deliberate deception, intended to nullify the constitutional powers of the Congress to legislate for the people we represent.

By the same policies of secrecy and deception, Richard Nixon also violated a principal tenet of democratic government: that the President, like every other elected official, is accountable to the people. For how can the people hold their President to account if he deliberately and consistently lies to them? The people cannot judge if they do not know, and President Nixon did everything within his power to keep them in ignorance. In all good conscience, we must condemn his deception regarding Cambodia with the same fervor and outrage we condemn his deception regarding Watergate.

The difficult question is not whether the secret bombing of Cambodia constitutes impeachable conduct. That is too obvious to require further argument. Instead, the question we must ponder is why the Congress has not called the President to judgment. The painful answer is that condemning the Cambodian bombing would also have required us to indict previous administrations and to admit that the Congress has failed to fully meet its own constitutional obligations.

Whether intentionally or not, the Congress has participated in the degeneration of its power to declare war. Although a War Powers Act was passed recently, over the veto of President Nixon, no legislation is self-executing. Whatever its limitations and faults, this legislation, and the constitutional provisions on which it is based, will only have meaning to the extent that the Congress invests them with meaning. Instead of merely ratifying the decisions and recommendations of the executive branch, the Congress must demonstrate that it is once again prepared to play an active and constructive role in the formulation of foreign policy—in the creation of policies which will direct this nation toward war or peace....

It has frequently been argued during the past weeks that this Committee's inquiry and the President's subsequent resignation demonstrate that "the system works." But such satisfaction or complacency is misguided. We must recognize that we were presented with a seemingly endless series of public revelations and presidential actions which did more to undermine Mr. Nixon's position than any independent investigation undertaken by this Committee or its staff. Our inquiry has been the beneficiary of literally years of work by investigative reporters, the Special Prosecutor's office, and the Senate Select Committee on Presidential Campaign Activities. And most importantly, the President himself documented his words and actions through his secret taping system, without which our inquiry might never have even begun. The President himself did more than anyone or anything to insure his removal from office.

If the system has worked, it has worked by accident and good fortune. It would be gratifying to conclude that this House, charged with the sole power of impeachment, exercised vigilance and acted on its own initiative. However, we would be deluding ourselves if we did not admit that this inquiry was forced on us by an accumulation of disclosures which, finally and after unnecessary delays, could no longer be ignored.

Perhaps ironically, and certainly unintentionally, we have ourselves jeopardized the future of the impeachment process. Before this inquiry, the prospect of impeaching a president was disquieting because it had not been attempted in more than a century. Now with our inquiry as a precedent, future Congresses may recoil from ever again exercising this power. They may read the history of our work and conclude that impeachment can never again succeed unless another President demonstrates the same, almost uncanny ability to impeach himself. If this is our legacy, our future colleagues may well conclude that ours has been a pyrrhic victory, and that impeachment will never again justify the agony we have endured. It is imperative, therefore, that we speak to them clearly; impeachment is difficult and it is painful, but the courage to do what must be done is the price of remaining free.

SEPARATE COMMENTS OF MR. WALDIE

Impeachment of a President should be undertaken not to punish a President but to constitutionally redefine and to constitutionally limit the powers of the Presidency when those powers have been dangerously extended and abused....

...I believe we should have approved an Article of Impeachment dealing with the exercise of the War Power....

...[I]f ever a power of the President desperately needed a Constitutional redefinition and thereby a Constitutional limitation, it is the War Power.

I regret we did not recommend an Article of Impeachment based on the conduct of the President in concealing and deceiving the American People with respect to the exercise of the War Power in the bombing of Cambodia. Failing to do so, we may have unintentionally ratified such conduct for future Presidents. And if we have done that, all the good we might have done in redefining and limiting Presidential power in other fields may be of little avail....

...[T]he certainty that the long run best interests of the Nation will be served only exists if we assure that the lessons of Richard Nixon's "nightmare" are fully understood.

Those lessons would essentially, I believe, distil down to the principle that no man, "be he President or pauper" is above the law.

Mr. Nixon never understood that. The Congress was slow in coming to its comprehension. The people never wavered or doubted in their instinctive belief in that principle.

That all in the future might comprehend that vital lesson, it is necessary that the full extent of Mr. Nixon's abuse of America—that a full record of the "nightmare" he visited upon us, be made.

The process whereby that will occur will include the Congress and the Report of the House Judiciary Committee—now—and additional reports as evidence accumulates. It will also include the Courts of our land. The full extent of Richard Nixon's participation in illegal activities will only unravel as accountability to the institution of justice is accomplished. To deny that process by granting immunity to Mr. Nixon would materially detract from the necessity of a full exposition of the "nightmare."

It would also essentially deny the basic lesson that no man, "be he President or pauper," is above the law. We upheld that principle when we forced the resignation of President Richard Nixon under the certainty of impeachment and conviction. We would shatter that princple, so hard fought and dearly won, if we place Richard Nixon, citizen, above the law; beyond accountability for his conduct....

ADDITIONAL VIEWS OF MESSRS. SARBANES AND SEIBERLING, JOINED BY MESSRS. DONOHUE, EILBERG, MANN, DANIELSON, THORNTON, SMITH AND HOGAN

While in the majority who voted against the proposed Article concerning President Nixon's concealment from Congress of the bombing of Cambodia, we certainly did not intend our vote to indicate approval of such conduct on his part. In fact, as some of us stated during the debate, we consider his action to have been a usurpation of Congress' power to declare war and to make appropriations.

The issue in the proposed article was the wrongful withholding of information from the Congress and the falsification of reports to the Congress....

Despite the grave and deplorable implications of this policy, there are certain reasons why impeachment is not the appropriate remedy in this instance. Although neither the House of Representatives nor the Senate nor any Congressional committee was advised of the bombing prior to May, 1970, when the clandestine air operations had been underway for 14 months, a few key members of the Congress in positions of responsibility had been informally advised of the bombing. Clearly, the informing by the Administration of a few, carefully selected individuals in the Congress is not the same as informing the Congress and cannot be considered proper or adequate notice. Nonetheless, the situation as to executive responsibility is clouded by the fact that certain members of the Congress were made aware of the bombing.

Furthermore, it appears likely that had the President formally consulted the Congress prior to April, 1970, the Congress would have acquiesced in the bombing policy. Although air operations were openly conducted over Cambodian territory from July, 1970 until mid-August, 1973, it should be noted that the Congress took no action, until June, 1973, to stop them. On the contrary, the Congress during this period repeatedly approved major authorizations and appropriations bills which provided authority for the continuation of these bombing operations. These considerations raise doubts about here invoking the impeachment remedy, although they in no sense justify the concealment from Congress of information about the bombing.

...Impeachment of a President should not be foreclosed in situations where Congress was forced by events to support a military venture initiated by a President acting in excess of his authority; indeed, such actions go to the very heart of the Constitutional allocation of powers and would require a serious impeachment inquiry. But where—as here—Congress over a considerable period of time had accepted and condoned Presidential encroachments on its powers, Congress' own inaction makes it questionable whether invoking the impeachment remedy in this instance is appropriate.

Finally, it is not necessary for Congress to take such action in this case in order to establish a proper precedent for the future. By enacting, over a Presidential veto, the War Powers Resolution of 1973 (PL 93-148) Congress has laid down specific guidelines requiring the President to report promptly to Congress whenever United States Armed Forces are introduced into hostilities or into the territory, airspace or waters of a foreign nation. Certainly any President who violated the provisions of that Law would invite Congressional action through the impeachment remedy to protect the Constitutional separation of powers against abuse by the Executive.

ADDITIONAL VIEWS OF MR. DANIELSON

IMPEACHABLE CONDUCT

...I am convinced...that impeachable conduct need not be criminal conduct. It is enough to support impeachment that the conduct complained of be conduct which is grossly incompatible with the office held and which is subversive of that office and of our Constitutional system of government. With respect to a President of the United States it is clear, in my mind, that conduct which constitutes a substantial breach of his oath of office, is impeachable conduct.

ROLE OF PRESIDENT'S COUNSEL IN IMPEACHMENT INQUIRY

In the Nixon inquiry, the President's counsel participated actively and to a degree that is without precedent in our history.... In my opinion, this expanded role of the President's counsel was improvidently permitted, for it gravely threatened to transform the proceeding from its constitutional role of the "Grand Inquest of the Nation" to that of an adversary proceeding similar to a judicial trial. I would urge that in any future impeachment inquiries the role of the counsel of the person subject to the impeachment process not be extended beyond that of an observer and auditor. In the Nixon hearings, the extensive participation was permitted out of an overabundance of caution that the hearings be conducted with fairness and that due process be observed. Those goals were not only achieved, but surpassed, and because of excessive participation by President's counsel, both fairness and due process were threatened.

THE SUFFICIENCY OF PLEADING THE ARTICLES OF IMPEACHMENT

A careful reading of the three articles of impeachment returned by the Committee clearly demonstrates that they are finely drawn and sufficient to meet fully any objections or demands as to whether the person impeached would be adequately informed of the charges against him. Impeachment is neither a civil nor a criminal judicial procedure. It is a parliamentary procedure.... In the Nixon inquiry, much debate centered on whether the articles contained sufficient specificity. That was a false issue. It is submitted that each of the articles returned by the Committee was drawn with sufficient specificity to inform the person accused fully of the charges placed against him, thus enabling him adequately to prepare his defense. In addition, the President was furnished, through his counsel, with a full and complete copy of every item of evidence in the possession of the Committee....

THE CONDUCT CHARGED IN ARTICLE II CONSTITUTES IMPEACHABLE CONDUCT

...Article II, on Monday, July 29, 1974...is the most important article...considered by the committee.

The offenses charged in this Article II are truly high crimes and misdemeanors within the purest meaning of those words as established in Anglo-American parliamentary law over a period of now some 600 years. The offenses charged against the President in this article are uniquely Presidential offenses. No one else can commit them. Anyone, the most lowly citizen, can obstruct justice. Anyone, the most lowly citizen, can violate any of the laws in our criminal code. But only the President can abuse the powers of the Office of the President....

Only the President can harm the Presidency. No one but the President can destroy the Presidency. It is our responsibility, acting under the impeachment clause, to preserve and protect the Presidency as we preserve and protect every other part of our marvelous structure of government, and we do it through this impeachment process....

I ask "Is not the violation of the solemn oath of office an impeachable offense?" It is not found in our criminal code. It is implicit in our Constitution. It is necessarily implicit in the Constitution for otherwise why would there be an oath of office?

EMOLUMENTS RECEIVED BY THE PRESIDENT

...The investigations have all concluded that many of the expenditures on Mr. Nixon's private homes were for his personal benefit. They were paid for by...the United States Government....

There is no way under the U.S. Constitution that Mr. Nixon can receive and retain such emoluments. Therefore, it necessarily follows that he is holding the full money value of those expenditures as a constructive trustee for the United States, and that the matter cannot be resolved until he has paid the full money value thereof to the United States.

SUPPLEMENTAL VIEWS OF MR. DRINAN

Contemporary commentators and future historians will have reason, it seems to me, to raise the most serious questions as to why the House Judiciary Committee did not more adequately investigate the deliberate and persistent cover-up by President Nixon of the clandestine bombing which he personally authorized over the neutral nation of Cambodia between March 18, 1969 and May 19, 1970....

CAMBODIAN ISSUE ACCORDED LOW PRIORITY

The fact is that the House Judiciary Committee made its decision against the Cambodian bombing as an impeachable offense upon inadequate evidence. The concurring statement contained in this report by Congresswoman Holtzman, joined in by myself and several other members of the Committee, indicates that "the statistical information regarding [Cambodia] is incomplete because the inquiry staff declined to obtain it." Congresswoman Holtzman continues by stating that "unfortunately, the investigation in general of the secret Cambodian bombing was not pursued as fully by the staff as its seriousness required."...

I am not minimizing the seriousness and the gravity of the three articles of impeachment set forth and justified in this report. I have concurred in the judgment that all of them constitute impeachable offenses. At the same time it seems paradoxical that a bipartisan majority emerged for votes to impeach the President on the basis of strictly domestic offenses whereas a bipartisan majority did not emerge with respect to the presumably bipartisan role which the President fulfilled as Commander-in-Chief. Only history will be able to decide the reasons for this phenomenon. I feel compelled to state at this time, however, that I find it incongruous that a President be impeached for unlawful wiretapping but not for unlawful war making. Similarly, I find it disturbing that the Committee voted to impeach a President for concealing a burglary but not for concealing a massive bombing.

...A careful review of the written record of the debate in the Judiciary Committee on the Cambodian question indicates that many of the members did not have answers to the questions which in their judgment were essential to a decision on the impeachability of the President's conduct in ordering that information concerning bombing in Cambodia be withheld from Congress and the American people.

Members did not have that information because from the beginning of the impeachment inquiry the Cambodian question was given a very low priority. The members of the Judiciary Committee did not establish that low priority. Clearly the inherent seriousness of the matter could not justify the paucity of staff assigned to the Cambodian issue. Only history will be able to decide whether a Congress which funded a war in Indo-China even after it had repealed the Gulf of Tonkin Resolution in December, 1970, was so confused about its own role in the Vietnam War that it was unable or unwilling to delve into presidential conduct more shocking and more unbelievable than the conduct of any president in any war in all of American history....

CONCLUSION

...The Framers of the Constitution devised the remedy of impeachment for those members of the executive branch of government who would bring the ultimate tyranny of war on the people of America without the Congress officially and formally declaring that war.

The manner in which President Nixon unilaterally conducted an air war in Cambodia and the subsequent course of conduct in which he covered up that period of massive bombing in a neutral country cannot be justified by the Constitution, by the relevant laws, or by any traditional relationship between the Congress and the President in a period of war. The fact is that President Nixon, in the concealment and cover-up of the war in Cambodia, violated the most fundamental right of the Congress and usurped the most basic constitutional privileges of the people of America. He committed offenses for which the remedy of impeachment is uniquely suited and for which that extraordinary remedy was placed in the Constitution....

It is exceedingly regrettable that the unconscionable and unconstitutional conduct of Richard Nixon with respect to the neutral nation of Cambodia was not also deemed by the Committee to be an impeachable offense. I can only hope that future generations will not interpret this decision of the Judiciary Committee as implied consent and sanction of such conduct.

SEPARATE AND ADDITIONAL VIEWS OF MR. RANGEL, CONCERNING ARTICLES OF IMPEACH-MENT AGAINST THE PRESIDENT OF THE UNITED STATES, RICHARD M. NIXON

...[H]ad not the President resigned, it is clear that he would have been impeached by the House of Representatives and convicted in the Senate for his criminal activities.

This record needs to be established for the sake of historical accuracy in view of the fact that even on the day of his resignation President Nixon attempted to convey to the American people the impression that his resignation was caused by erosion of his political base as a result of some poor judgments he made during his term of office. The record, as set forth in the Committee report, makes it abundantly clear that Richard M. Nixon violated his oath of office as President of the United States, that he committed impeachable crimes, and that on the available evidence he would have been impeached by the House of Representatives.

For only the second time in the one hundred and ninety-eight years of our Constitutional history the House of Representatives is presented with articles of impeachment against the President of the United States....

What Richard Nixon has done is to substitute power for law, to define and attempt to impose a standard of amorality upon our government that gives full rein to the rich and powerful to prey upon the poor and weak. What Richard Nixon has done is to demean the importance of national security by using it as a handy alibi to protect common burglars. What Richard Nixon has done is attempt to stain the reputation of the agencies of our government by using them to obstruct justice, harass political enemies, illegally spy upon citizens, and cover-up crimes. What Richard Nixon has done is show contempt for the Congress by refusing to provide information necessary for the Constitutionally legitimate conduct of an inquiry into the question of impeachment by the Committee on the Judiciary of the House of Representatives. What Richard Nixon has done is threaten the Constitution by declaring himself and the Office of the Presidency beyond the reach of law, the Congress, and the courts.

To a large extent he has succeeded. We have reached a state in our national life where responsible members of Congress argue that the President does not have to account for his actions to anyone or recognize any higher authority. Thus we stand on the brink of total subversion of our Constitutional government and dictatorship....

DISSENTING VIEWS CONCERNING THE TWO ARTICLES PRESENTED TO, BUT NOT VOTED BY THE COMMITTEE

I do not believe, however, that we will have fulfilled our Constitutional duty if we vote impeachment solely on the basis of the three articles recommended by the Committee. The very nature of the impeachment process, we have recognized in the Judiciary Committee, infuses our decision on the grounds for impeachment with the weight of historical precedent. We are not merely making a judgment on the conduct of the Richard M. Nixon Presidency, we are making judgments that will determine the limits of Presidential, legislative, and judicial power. For this reason I supported the two articles of impeachment which were recommended to the Committee on the Judiciary, but which have not been recommended by the Committee to the House. These two articles, based upon the President's authorization of the secret bombing of Cambodia without the lawful direction of the Congress and the President's use of his office for his self-enrichment in derogation of the Constitutional provision forbidding the taking of emoluments, are as equally indicative of the President's contempt for the law as the three articles recommended by the Committee. The Presidential conduct to which these articles are addressed is as potentially destructive of the Constitution as the President's obstruction of justice, abuse of power and contempt of Congress even though the particular activity involved did not appear to offend as large a number of members of the Judiciary Committee as the activity addressed in the first three articles.

...[I]f we are to prevent future Presidents from committing the lives of American youth to adventurous forays, we have a duty to seriously consider President Nixon's authorization of the secret bombing of Cambodia as an abuse of Presidential power constituting an impeachable offense....

It is clear to me from the evidence that President Nixon directed or knowingly received the benefit of improper expenditures on his San Clemente and Key Biscayne properties in violation of the law and the emoluments clause of the Constitution. It is equally clear that Richard Nixon had knowledge of and bears full responsibility for the willful evasion of his income tax obligation.

Richard M. Nixon did this while preaching economy in government and imposing devastating cuts on vital social programs in his budgets and through the impoundment of Congressionally appropriated funds. He enriched himself at the taxpayers' expense while children were going hungry and uncared for, the poor and elderly were being denied adequate housing, and growing hope was being turned into despair as Federal assistance to help people out of the bondage of poverty was being brutally terminated in the name of economy. Perhaps the greatest indictment against Richard Nixon that can be voted by the House is that by his actions he created a moral vacuum in the Office of the Presidency and turned that great office away from the service of the people toward the service of his own narrow, selfish interests.

CONCLUSION

...Yet at the same time I am heartened, and my faith in the Constitution and in our democracy is strengthened by the now irrefutable proof that the Constitution is not a dead instrument, that truly no man is above the law, and that if a President acts unlawfully he can be impeached and sent to the Senate for a trial to determine whether he should be removed from office. I am encouraged that our Constitution works, for I am especially dependent upon its protection. I am encouraged that the American system permits a black nightwatchman and the son of an Italian immigrant family sitting as a District Court judge, each through applying the law, to be the instruments of uncovering the most extensive and highly placed corruption in our national history and the bringing to justice of the most powerful men in our society. I am encouraged that what the Judiciary Committee has done, and what the full House must now do, in voting Articles of Impeachment against Richard M. Nixon, will begin a process of restoring the faith of the American people in our government.

ADDITIONAL VIEWS OF MS. HOLTZMAN

...First, Richard Nixon's resignation was in response to the certainty of his impeachment, conviction and removal from office. The evidence was overwhelming.

Second, the Watergate break-in—which precipitated his downfall—was not an accident. It was the logical outgrowth of President Nixon's repeated condonation of wiretapping and break-ins for political purposes. That pattern of lawlessness began only four months after President Nixon first took office....

Third, the Watergate break-in was not an isolated abuse of Richard Nixon's re-election campaign; it was but one element in a pervasive pattern of immoral, unethical and criminal conduct....

Nor was President Nixon's abuse of his powers restricted to attacks on the Constitutional freedoms of the American citizens and his political opponents. He also systematically arrogated to himself the powers of Congress; he waged a secret war in the neutral country of Cambodia; he unlawfully impounded funds appropriated by Congress; he attempted to dismantle social programs mandated by law.

The conclusion is inescapable that Richard Nixon engaged personally in wrongful acts, allowed and encouraged his subordinates to do the same, and indeed stretched the Constitution beyond its breaking point, because he felt he would not have to answer for his conduct. Concealment, deception, and cover-up became a way of life in the Oval Office.

This impeachment proceeding—in the thoroughness, fairness and gravity of its approach, as well as the strength of its findings—stands as a warning to all future Presidents that they will be held accountable to their oaths of office. Nonetheless, it will be an empty warning unless the American public and the Congress continue to demand from their Presidents and other public officials respect for the Constitution, acknowledgment of the supremacy of law and commitment to decency and honesty.

DISSENTING VIEWS OF MS. HOLTZMAN, JOINED BY MESSRS. KASTENMEIER, EDWARDS, HUNGATE, CONYERS, WALDIE, DRINAN, RANGEL, OWENS AND MEZVINSKY

PROPOSED ARTICLE IV: SECRET BOMBING OF CAMBODIA

We believe that Richard Nixon committed a high crime and misdemeanor when, as President, he unilaterally ordered the bombing of Cambodia and deliberately concealed this bombing from Congress and the American public, through a series of false and deceptive statements, for more than four years....

It is difficult to imagine Presidential misconduct more dangerously in violation of our constitutional form of government than Mr. Nixon's decision, secretly and unilaterally, to order the use of American military power against another nation, and to deceive and mislead the Congress about this action. By depriving Congress of its constitutional role in the war-making and appropriations processes, the President denied to the American people the most basic right of self-government: the right to participate, through their elected representatives, in the decisions that gravely affect their lives....

The decision to make war has enormous human, economic and ethical implications. It is intolerable in a constitutional democracy to permit that decision to be made in secret by a President and to be hidden through deception from the law-making bodies and the public....

The sole remedy which Congress can employ to bring a President to account for usurpation of the war-making and appropriations powers is impeachment. Only the use of that power is an effective deterrent; and, failure to employ it, when necessary, sets a dangerous precedent....

The Constitution does not permit the President to nullify the war-making and appropriations powers given to the Congress. Secrecy and deception which deny to the Congress its lawful role are destructive of the basic right of the American people to participate in their government's life-

and-death decisions. Adoption of Article IV would give notice to all future Presidents that the American people and the Congress may not be excluded from those decisions.

By failing to recommend the impeachment of President Nixon for the deception of Congress and the American public as to an issue as grave as the systematic bombing of a neutral country, we implicitly accept the argument that any ends—even those a President believes are legitimate—justify unconstitutional means. We cannot permit a President to sidestep constitutional processes simply because he finds them cumbersome....

ADDITIONAL VIEWS OF MR. OWENS

ARTICLE IV: THE CAMBODIAN WAR

...I fully realize that this matter involves the expansion of a war begun by Democratic Presidents, and at times one of those Presidents, Lyndon B. Johnson himself misled the Congress and the public about the course of that war. But past transgressions of this gravity, even if accepted or ratified by a Congress victimized by deceit, do not make a later repetition Constitutionally acceptable.

I believe the Committee should have supported this article of impeachment, in addition to the three voted by the Committee, to set a precedent for the future. In this time of growing nuclear capability around the world, Congress must make clear to future presidents that which we have tried to set forward [in] this Congress with passage over the President's veto of the War Powers Act: No more wars of any nature must be started without the consent of the people's elected representatives, exactly as set forth in the Constitution.

ARTICLE V: THE PRESIDENT'S TAXES

The evidence before the Congress demonstrates that the President engaged in unethical, shabby, and disgraceful conduct by grossly underpaying his income taxes while in office. There is, however, no clear and convincing evidence available to the Committee to show the two elements necessary to make this offense impeachable.

To become an impeachable offense here, in my opinion, there must be clear proof of fraud by the President himself, coupled with clear indications that he used the power of his presidential office to avoid being audited by the IRS.

This test is not met by evidence available to us. Although I do not find that they rise to the level of impeachability, I do join other Americans in condemning these unconscionable acts which indicate serious violations of Richard Nixon's obligation as a taxpayer.

But there are other remedies for these abuses. Prosecution by the IRS for civil or criminal fraud are still available, even if President Nixon were allowed to serve out his full term. The unique power of impeachment is not needed here. The people of the United States have other remedies. The other impeachable offenses voted by the Committee have only one method of correction—the ultimate weapon of impeachment—which should be used only when it is the sole adequate response....

CONCLUSION

...It was the overwhelming cumulative effect of the evidence, viewed in its entirety, which persuaded so many members of the Committee—both liberal and conservative, Republican and Democratic—that Articles of Impeachment were required. Any member of Congress, or any citizen who carefully examines this evidence would, I believe, support the Committee's actions....

By acting so responsibly and by submerging their political allegiances and fortunes for this difficult process, the members of the Committee have strengthened the Congress. By voting to impeach the President for conduct which violated our guarantees of liberty, the Committee has strengthened the Constitution and the Bill of Rights. And by creating clear precedents for future Presidential conduct, it will strengthen the Presidency....

And impeachment is the only tool the Constitution provides to control a President who has refused to obey the laws or his Constitutional obligations.

I believe the significance of what this Committee has done will endure for many years to come. If our standards of impeachment had been too low or insubstantial, we would have seriously weakened the presidency and created a precedent for future use of the impeachment power when charges may be trivial or partisan. We have avoided this mistake. On the other hand, if we had rejected these Articles of Impeachment with this clear and convincing evidence of serious wrongdoing before us, no president would ever have been impeached, and the impeachment power, which the Constitution vested in Congress as the last resort to prevent serious abuses of power by a president, would be rendered impotent.

ADDITIONAL VIEWS OF MR. MEZVINSKY, JOINED BY MESSRS. BROOKS, KASTENMEIER, EDWARDS, CONYERS, EILBERG, DANIELSON, RANGEL AND MS. HOLTZMAN CONCERNING INCOME TAX EVASION BY THE PRESIDENT

...The President...is not an ordinary taxpayer; his willful tax evasion affects the very integrity of our government. Such conduct calls for the constitutional remedy of impeachment....

The facts set forth...show that the Committee had before it evidence of tax evasion by the President which met the most stringent standards of proof. The use of tape recordings and similar documentary evidence to prove the charges set forth in the Articles recommended by the Committee perhaps led some to expect that type of evidence for all of the Articles. Most cases, however, whether criminal or civil, do not turn on the availability of tape recordings. They are decided on an evaluation of all the proven facts and circumstances and the logical inferences to be drawn from those facts and circumstances. Whatever the applicable standard of proof, the evidence presented to the Committee demonstrated that the President of the United States was guilty of willful income tax evasion for the years 1969 through 1972. He should have been impeached for such conduct....

As with any other citizen, the President's evasion of taxes constituted a serious felony—which, even under the "criminality" standards urged on the Committee by the President, constitutes an impeachable offense. But because of his position, the President's acts went beyond criminal wrongdoing; they necessarily involved taking advantage of the power and prestige of the Presidency.

As Chief Executive, President Nixon could expect that his tax returns would not be subject to the same scrutiny as those of other taxpayers. The superficial examination of his 1971 and 1972 returns conducted in May, 1973, which caused the IRS to write the President commending him (instead of sending him a bill for the more than $180,000 by which he had underpaid his taxes for those two years) bears out this expectation of favoritism....

Had his entire Presidency not been subjected to public scrutiny—for the reasons contained in Articles I and II—Mr. Nixon's tax evasion would have succeeded.

A President's noncompliance with the revenue laws does not merely deprive the Treasury of funds from one taxpayer; it affects the very foundation of our voluntary system of tax collection. Allowing such conduct to go unchecked threatens to damage seriously the ability of the government to efficiently raise from all the citizens of the Nation the funds necessary to govern our society. If a President commits willful tax evasion and is not brought to account by the Congress, then not only the tax system, but our entire structure of government risks corrosion. For this most fundamental reason we believe that the willful tax evasion by President Nixon should have been considered an impeachable offense by the Committee, and that the Article charging this offense should have been reported to the House.

ADDITIONAL VIEWS OF MR. McCLORY ON ARTICLE III CONCURRED IN BY MR. DANIELSON AND MR. FISH

The power of impeachment is the Constitution's paramount power of self-preservation. This power is textually committed by the Constitution solely to the House of Representatives. The power to impeach includes within it the power to inquire. Without the corollary power to inquire, the power to impeach would be meaningless—and dangerous....

The principle that is the subject of this discussion is clear and simple: the Constitution does not give to the House of Representatives, exercising its power to impeach, a power to ask while giving to the President—as President—an equal power to refuse. It is respectfully submitted that our Constitution makes more sense than that. The Constitution does not give to the President a privilege to refuse *by virtue of his office* when his use or abuse of that office is at issue.

When the trustee of the highest office in the land is called upon by the representatives of the people to make an accounting of his performance, his assertion that Presidents need not answer is contemptuous of his trust and of the people who have placed their trust in him.

...The President's basic answer to the subpoenas was that Presidents do not have to comply with such subpoenas by virtue of the office and that if the power to impeach included within it the power to inquire, then no President ever again would be safe.

All that I ask of my colleagues is to think through the ramifications of the President's position. For me, I do not wish to have a Presidency that is safe from the power of the people's representatives to demand an accounting. And that is precisely what is at stake in Article III...

It is also suggested that simply because two branches have disagreed over their respective roles, the third branch should be called on to referee. But is this how our government works? If the Congress and the Supreme Court disagree on the constitutionality of a bill, does the President act as a referee, or does the Court's view prevail because of its assigned role under the Constitution?...

Article III is no make-weight article. For posterity, it is the most important article. It preserves for future generations the power to hold their public servants accountable....

It was not our subpoena that brought to light the additional evidence on August 5, 1974. The same sadly can be said of much of the substantial evidence which we possess. Our subpoenas still stand unanswered. It was only by the coincidence of an investigation into the conduct of private citizens who formerly worked at the White House that evidence necessary to our inquiry into Presidential conduct fell into our hands. By experiencing that coincidence, have we acquitted ourselves of our responsibility to preserve for our grandchildren a workable government wherein even the highest remain accountable to the people through their representatives? Shall we protect the people's rights and prevent the crippling of the Constitution's essential check against unconstitutional government?

In recommending Article III to the House the Committee has sought to answer these questions in the affirmative.

[W]e concur in full with the foregoing views on Article III...

CONCURRING VIEWS OF MR. FISH

...Much attention has been given, and properly, to the specific charges against the President; but there are also larger considerations involved. The issue for history is the constitutional standard by which this President, or any future President, shall be held to account for his own acts or omissions and those of his immediate subordinates....

Impeachment is appropriate only where the President's action involves an undermining of the integrity of office, an arrogation of power, a disregard of constitutional duties, or otherwise has a substantial adverse impact on the system of government....

Under the "take Care" clause...the President may not knowingly countenance—let alone authorize or direct—serious unlawful conduct in an official capacity on the part of any agency or executive official within the executive establishment. Furthermore, whatever may be the responsibility of the President for the conduct of those executive officers in the various agencies of government, his responsibility for the conduct of his immediate subordinates in the White House is even more compelling....

Although the clause does not require day-to-day supervisory responsibility for each executive department or agency, neither does the size and complexity of the executive branch excuse the President's failure to take reasonable steps calculated to ensure that his subordinates have faithfully carried out his responsibility of faithful execution of the laws. The President must exercise due diligence in overseeing the acts of his immediate subordinates. He can neither mislead them by offering ambiguous instructions and then fail to police their actions, nor can he with impunity simply ignore available facts bearing on their wrongful official conduct. He must remain always alert for any hint or suggestion of improper official conduct on their part. If a President has knowledge that the laws are being violated or improperly executed, he is under a duty to take appropriate steps to remedy these wrongs....

MINORITY VIEWS OF MESSRS. HUTCHINSON, SMITH, SANDMAN, WIGGINS, DENNIS, MAYNE, LOTT, MOORHEAD, MARAZITI AND LATTA

PRELIMINARY STATEMENT

...[T]he resignation of Richard Nixon from the Presidency...rendered moot, in our view, the sole question to which this Committee's impeachment inquiry was addressed, namely, whether sufficient grounds exist for the House of Representatives to exercise its constitutional power to impeach Mr. Nixon. We see no need for the Members of the House to take any action whatsoever with respect to the filing of this Committee Report, other than to read it and the individual and minority views included herein.

It is perhaps less *urgent*, but it is surely no less *necessary*, that we record our views respecting the more significant questions of law and fact which we perceive to be posed by the record compiled by the Committee in the course of its Impeachment Inquiry.... [W]e have an obligation, both to our contemporaries and to posterity, not to perpetuate, unchallenged, certain theories of the evidence, and of law, which are propounded by the majority but which we believe to be erroneous....

Our gratitude for his having by his resignation spared the Nation additional agony should not obscure for history our judgment that Richard Nixon, as President, committed certain acts for which he should have been impeached and removed from office. Likewise, having effectively admitted guilt of one impeachable offense—obstruction of justice in connection with the Watergate investigation—Richard Nixon is not consequently to be presumed guilty of all other offenses with which he was charged by the majority of the Committee that approved recommending to the full House three Articles of Impeachment against him. Indeed, it remains our view that, for the most part, he was not guilty of those offenses and that history should so record.

Our views respecting the merits of each of the major allegations made by the majority of the Committee against President Nixon are set out more fully in the separate discussions of the three proposed Articles which follow. To summarize:

(1) With respect to proposed Article I, we believe that the charges of conspiracy to obstruct justice, and obstruction of justice, which are contained in the Article in essence, if not in terms, may be taken as substantially con-

fessed by Mr. Nixon on August 5, 1974, and corroborated by ample other evidence in the record....

(2) With respect to proposed Article II, we find sufficient evidence to warrant a belief that isolated instances of unlawful conduct by presidential aides and subordinates did occur during the five-and-one-half years of the Nixon Administration, with varying degrees of direct personal knowledge or involvement of the President in these respective illegal episodes. We roundly condemn such abuses and unreservedly favor the invocation of existing legal sanctions, or the creation of new ones, where needed, to deter such reprehensible official conduct in the future, no matter in whose Administration, or by what brand or partisan, it might be perpetrated.

Nevertheless, we cannot join with those who claim to perceive an invidious, pervasive "pattern" of illegality in the conduct of official government business generally by President Nixon. In some instances, as noted below, we disagree with the majority's interpretation of the evidence regarding either the intrinsic illegality of the conduct studied or the linkage of Mr. Nixon personally to it. Moreover, even as to those acts which we would concur in characterizing as abusive and which the President appeared to direct or countenance, neither singly nor in the aggregate do they impress us as being offenses for which Richard Nixon, or any President, should be impeached or removed from office, when considered, *as they must be*, on their own footing, apart from the obstruction of justice charge under proposed Article I which we believe to be sustained by the evidence.

(3) Likewise, with respect to proposed Article III, we believe that this charge, standing alone, affords insufficient grounds for impeachment. Our concern here...is that the Congressional subpoena power itself not be too easily abused as a means of achieving the impeachment and removal of a President against whom no other substantive impeachable offense has been proved by sufficient evidence derived from sources other than the President himself....

We know that it has been said, and perhaps some will continue to say, that Richard Nixon was "hounded from office" by his political opponents and media critics. We feel constrained to point out, however, that it was Richard Nixon who impeded the FBI's investigation of the Watergate affair by wrongfully attempting to implicate the Central Intelligence Agency; it was Richard Nixon, who created and preserved the evidence of that transgression and who, *knowing that it had been subpoenaed by this Committee and the Special Prosecutor*, concealed its terrible import, even from his own counsel, until he could do so no longer. And it was a unanimous Supreme Court of the United States which, in an opinion authored by the Chief Justice whom he appointed, ordered Richard Nixon to surrender that evidence to the Special Prosecutor, to further the ends of justice.

The tragedy that finally engulfed Richard Nixon had many facets. One was the very self-inflicted nature of the harm. It is striking that such an able, experienced and perceptive man, whose ability to grasp the global implications of events little noticed by others may well have been unsurpassed by many of his predecessors, should fail to comprehend the damage that accrued daily to himself, his Administration, and to the Nation, as day after day, month after month, he imprisoned the truth about his role in the Watergate cover-up so long and so tightly within the solitude of his Oval Office that it could not be unleashed without destroying his Presidency....

Meaning of "Treason, Bribery, or other high Crimes and Misdemeanors"

...We do not believe that a President or any other civil officer of the United States government may constitutionally be impeached and convicted for errors in the administration of his office....

...We have never had a British parliamentary system in this country, and we have never adopted the device of a parliamentary vote of no-confidence in the chief executive. If it is thought desirable to adopt such a system of government, the proper way to do so is by amending our written Constitution—not by removing the President....

The language of the Constitution indicates that impeachment can lie only for serious criminal offenses....

...An impeachment power exercised without extrinsic and objective standards would be tantamount to the use of bills of attainder and *ex post facto* laws, which are expressly forbidden by the Constitution and are contrary to the American spirit of justice.

It is beyond argument that a violation of the President's oath or a violation of his duty to take care that the laws be faithfully executed, must be impeachable conduct or there would be no means of enforcing the Constitution. However, this elementary proposition is inadequate to define the impeachment power. It remains to determine what kind of conduct constitutes a violation of the oath or the duty. Furthermore, reliance on the summary phrase, "violation of the Constitution," would not always be appropriate as a standard, because actions constituting an apparent violation of one provision of the Constitution may be justified or even required by other provisions of the Constitution.

There are types of misconduct by public officials—for example, ineptitude, or unintentional or "technical" violations of rules or statutes, or "maladministration"—which would not be criminal; nor could they be made criminal, consonant with the Constitution, because the element of criminal intent or *mens rea* would be lacking. Without a requirement of criminal acts or at least criminal intent, Congress would be free to impeach these officials. The loss of this freedom should not be mourned; such a use of the impeachment power was never intended by the Framers, is not supported by the language of our Constitution, and, if history is to guide us, would be seriously unwise as well....

The evidence before the Committee on the Judiciary

On August 5, 1974, the President released to the Committee and to the public the transcripts of three conversations between himself and H. R. Haldeman on June 23, 1972. Suffice it to say that these transcripts, together with the circumstances of their belated disclosure, foreclosed further debate with respect to the sufficiency of proof of the charges embodied in proposed Article I and led inevitably to the President's resignation three days later.

In the wake of these sudden and decisive events it may seem academic to discuss the character of the evidence which, prior to August 5, 1974, had been adduced in support of the allegations against the President. We are nevertheless constrained to make some general observations about that evidence, for two reasons. First, the disclosure of the June 23, 1972, transcripts, though dispositive of the case under proposed Article I, did not substantially affect the nature of the evidence in support of proposed Article II. Second, the fact that this disclosure cured the evidentiary defects earlier associated with proposed Article I must not be allowed to obscure the fact that a majority of the Members of the Committee had previously, and in our view wrongly, voted to recommend to the House the adoption of that Article on the basis of information then at their disposal....

Standard of Proof

...Because of the fundamental similarity between an impeachment trial and an ordinary criminal trial, therefore, the standard of proof beyond a reasonable doubt is appropriate in both proceedings. Moreover, the gravity of an impeachment trial and its potentially drastic consequences are additional reasons for requiring a rigorous standard of proof. This is especially true in the case of a presidential impeachment. Unlike a federal judge, an appointed officer who enjoys lifetime tenure during good behavior, the President is elected to office for a fixed term. The proper remedy for many instances of presidential misbehavior is the ballot box. The removal of a President by impeachment in mid-term, however, should not be too easy of accomplishment, for it contravenes the will of the electorate. In providing for a fixed four-year term, not subject to interim votes of No Confidence, the Framers indicated their preference for stability in the executive. That stability should not be jeopardized except on the strongest possible proof of presidential wrongdoing....

On balance, it appears that prosecution is warranted if the prosecutor believes that the guilt of the accused is demonstrated by clear and convincing evidence.

Without unduly overemphasizing the aptness of the analogy to a public prosecutor, we therefore take the position that a vote of impeachment is justified if, and only if, the charges embodied in the articles are proved by clear and convincing evidence....

ARTICLE I

THE PRESIDENT ENTERS THE CONSPIRACY

Given the varied motives of these principal actors to suppress the facts in their own interests, as well as in what they jointly, but mistakenly, perceived to be the best interests of the President, it is wholly plausible that the cover-up conspiracy arose immediately and spontaneously as word of the arrest of McCord *et al.* spread, just as Dean suggested.... Since there is no logical need to hypothesize an all-knowing, all-powerful President at the center of the conspiracy from its beginning, organizing and directing the cover-up activities of each of his aides and subordinates (at least in general outline) in order adequately to explain the events that transpired in the first several days following the discovery of the burglars, we consider it our Constitutional mandate not to do so unless and until specific evidence convinces us that it is *at least* more probable than not that the President had become involved....

Interpreting Events in Light of the June 23, 1972 Transcripts

We do not consider it nit-picking to suggest that, even with the benefit of the additional evidence produced by the President on August 5, 1974, some of the specific allegations made against him in the majority report are not well founded. It is still important—perhaps even more important, now that Mr. Nixon is not able to mount a formal defense to the Committee's accusations in an appropriate forum—for us to caution against the indiscriminate adoption of each and every adverse interpretation that could be placed upon specific presidential actions and statements, merely because the President has been shown to be culpable *to some extent* at an early stage of the cover-up....

ARTICLE II

Legal Considerations

Duplicity

...Article II...is a catch-all repository for...miscellaneous and unrelated presidential offenses which were thought to have sufficient support among Committee Members to warrant inclusion. If this Article has any organizing principle at all, it is not a common factual basis but rather a common legal theory supposedly applicable to each specified offense....

Our opposition to the adoption of Article II should not be misunderstood as condonation of the presidential conduct alleged therein. On the contrary, we deplore in strongest terms the aspects of presidential wrongdoing to which the Article is addressed. However, we could not in conscience recommend that the House impeach and the Senate try the President on the basis of Article II in its form as proposed, because in our view the Article is duplicitous in both the ordinary and the legal senses of the word. In common usage, duplicity means belying one's true intentions by deceptive words; as a legal term of art, duplicity denotes the technical fault of uniting two or more offenses in the same count of an indictment. We submit that the implications of a vote for or against Article II are ambiguous and that the Committee debate did not resolve the ambiguities so as to enable the Members to vote intelligently. Indeed, this defect is symptomatic of a generic problem inherent in the process of drafting Articles of impeachment, and its significance for posterity may be far greater than the substantive merits of the particular charges embodied in Article II....

One must therefore look for an organizing principle in the three legal theories advanced in Article II. Parenthetically, it may be observed that if the Article had been restricted to the first three specifications (discriminatory use of the IRS; warrantless wiretapping; the Plumbers), a specific and possibly useful legal theory could have been established as a framework for analysis. These three alleged offenses all potentially involve violations of individual rights guaranteed under the First Amendment, the Fourth Amendment, or both. The fourth and fifth specifications, however, do not fit within that framework. Consequently the legal theories applicable to the charges had to be so broadened that they are not useful as an organizing principle. For example, it is hard to understand why the fourth specification (failure to prevent subordinates from impeding inquiries) is included in this Article at all, since it seems much more germane to Article I....

...Article II represents an unwieldy agglomeration of alleged abuses of power by President Nixon: efforts to procure discriminatory income tax audits, warrantless wiretapping, covert activities of the "Plumbers," etc. In order to evaluate the gravity of these allegations, it is instructive to compare them with certain historical incidents illustrative of the alarming growth of executive power during the past forty years....

ARTICLE III

We believe that adoption of Article III would have unnecessarily introduced an element of brittleness at the heart of our system of Constitutional checks and balances, and for this reason would have been unwise. Furthermore, there may appear to be an element of unfairness, or even circularity, in removing a President from office for failure to cooperate in his own impeachment—for failure to furnish information to his accusers, as it were—particularly where other grounds for impeachment are thought to exist....

The adoption of proposed Article III by the full House would have set an unwise and potentially mischievous precedent. No President should be impeached for failing to comply with subpoenas issued by an impeachment inquiry Committee for materials which were subject to a colorable claim of Executive or other privilege, unless his noncompliance amounted to contempt of the House, adjudicated in the customary manner, after notice and opportunity for him to appear personally or by counsel before the House and show cause why his failure to comply was not contemptuous.

To those Members who may believe that in this case the claim of Executive privilege was asserted by the President in bad faith, at least as to some materials, we would reiterate our view that this alone should not have deprived the President of an opportunity to make his defense before the full House, like any putative contemnor. Even so, the House would not have been without recourse, inasmuch as a willful refusal to furnish relevant subpoenaed material based on a bad faith claim of privilege, if proved or admitted, would have been relevant to the obstruction of justice charge contained in Article I. It is in that context that we believe the President's response to the Committee's subpoenas should have been examined.

We, the undersigned Members of the Committee on the Judiciary, hereby subscribe to the "Minority Views" respecting Articles I, II and III of the proposed Bill of Impeachment ordered reported to the House on July 30, 1974, which views, together with a "Preliminary Statement," are to be filed with the Committee Report on said Bill of Impeachment:

> EDWARD HUTCHINSON.
> HENRY P. SMITH, III.
> CHARLES W. SANDMAN, JR.
> CHARLES E. WIGGINS.
> DAVID W. DENNIS.
> WILEY MAYNE.
> TRENT LOTT.
> CARLOS J. MOORHEAD.
> JOSEPH MARAZITI.
> DELBERT L. LATTA.

I concur in the views of the minority with respect to Articles I and III but not Article II.

> WILEY MAYNE.

We, the undersigned Members of the Committee on the Judiciary, hereby subscribe to the "Minority Views" respecting Article III of the proposed Bill of Impeachment ordered reported to the House on July 30, 1974, which views are to be filed with the Committee Report on said Bill of Impeachment:

> TOM RAILSBACK.
> WALTER FLOWERS.
> M. CALDWELL BUTLER.
> HAROLD V. FROEHLICH.

INDIVIDUAL VIEWS OF MR. HUTCHINSON

...Impeachment of a President is a drastic remedy and should be resorted to only in cases where the offenses committed by him are so grave as to make his continuance in office intolerable. Unlike criminal jurisprudence, where the sentencing judge has large discretion as to the punishment to be inflicted, the conviction of an impeached President removes him from office, nothing less. The charges against him should be so serious as to fit removal. The three articles of impeachment, when measured against this standard, fall short in all but a single count in my opinion.

I reject the proposition that the impeachment function of the House is nothing more than the indictment function of a grand jury, and that a Member who votes to impeach is merely sending the case to the Senate for trial.... This is a much greater burden than that of a grand jury which represents only that there is probable cause to believe a particular offense was committed and that the indicted person committed it. The grand jury has no burden to maintain its cause before any court.

In my judgment, a Member who votes to impeach is recommending to the Senate the removal of the President from office, nothing less. In order to warrant such drastic action, the offenses charged should be serious and grievous violations by the President of his Constitutional duties.... In a divided government, with the Congress in control by one political party and the President of another, impeachment becomes a threatening political tool, if one group of politicians can decide over another what is an abuse of power.

In weighing this evidence, if an inference or conclusion favorable to the President can be drawn as well as an inference or conclusion unfavorable to him, I believe the President should be given the benefit of the doubt.

In my judgment, not any of the three articles of impeachment are drawn with the particularity which is required to give the House information of the precise offenses charged and the overt acts claimed to be supportive of them; nor to give the President the notice which constitutional process accorded him, had he chosen to defend against those charges in the Senate.

ARTICLE I

...Until the August 5th release of conversations held between the President and Mr. Haldeman on June 23, 1972, there was no direct evidence of complicity by the President in the cover-up. The President said he knew nothing about any cover-up until his conversations with John Dean in mid-March 1973; there was no direct evidence to the contrary and he was entitled to the benefit of the doubt.

It is now evident that the President knew as early as June 23, 1972, six days following the Watergate break-in, of a plan to obstruct the FBI investigation into that event, and that he authorized the plan....

But without the evidence of the June 23, 1972, conversation I was prepared to defend the President against the charge of obstructing justice on the basis that he had no knowledge of it until March 1973....

ARTICLE II

...In my opinion, Article II is as weak a basis for removing a President from the office as is Article III.

Article II is a catch-all. Culling from tens of thousands of transactions between the White House and the agencies of the Executive branch a few isolated instances of conceived pressure described as abuses of power, and with no evidence of the President's personal involvement, the proponents allege repeated engagement, that is time after time, by the White House in such a course of action....

ARTICLE III

The idea that a President should be removed from office because he does not comply with a subpoena of a committee of the House, even if the precedent be limited to impeachment cases, is frightening....

I opposed issuance of subpoenas by the Committee to the President because such subpoenas would be unenforceable; and because I do not believe the House can order presidential action any more than the President can order the House. The President and the House are co-equal in our system. Neither is above or below the other.

I think Article III does not state an impeachable offense.

CONCLUSION

History will deal more kindly with Richard Nixon than did his contemporaries. As the Watergate affair moves into the past it may be seen for what a little thing a President was forced to resign from office when compared with the accomplishments of his administration. A legal case of obstruction of justice was made against him. But instructions by other Presidents have undoubtedly altered the course of other investigations without controversy. The abuses of power charged against the President were probably no greater than have occurred in some other administrations. What to one man seems an abuse of power appears to another to be strong executive discretion. The President should not have been impeached under Article II. And I believe the House would have rejected Article III....

ADDITIONAL VIEWS OF MR. RAILSBACK, JOINED BY MESSRS. SMITH, SANDMAN, DENNIS, MAYNE, BUTLER, FROEHLICH, MOORHEAD, MARAZITI AND LATTA, IN OPPOSITION TO ARTICLE III

Refusal to fully comply with a Congressional subpoena in and of itself without further action on the part of the Congress is not a ground upon which an impeachment can be based. The House has neither exhausted available remedies on this issue nor can the House in this instance be the ultimate judge of the scope of its own power....

ADDITIONAL AND SEPARATE VIEWS OF MR. MAYNE

ARTICLE II

I file views separate from those of my minority colleagues for the following reasons:

1. I would vote in the House to impeach under Article II because I believe a case for impeachment has now been made under Paragraphs 1, 4 and 5 of that Article.

2. The minority views do not give sufficient treatment to the evidence in support of the grave allegations of Paragraph 1, Article II that the President tried to obtain income tax audits or other income tax investigations to be initiated or conducted in a discriminatory manner, i.e. to harass political opponents....

In weighing whether a sufficient case had been made against the President under Article II, I had to consider the fact that Paragraph 1 alleging abuse of the Internal Revenue Service had unfortunately been lumped together with 4 other Paragraphs, which had little if any connection with each other and were supported by less proof than Paragraph 1. Paragraph 3 relative to a special investigative unit set up in the White House to identify and plug national security leaks struck me as especially weak. I could not accept the argument based on inferences alone that a President who had been advised by his closest foreign policy and national defense advisers that it was necessary to take decisive action to stop leaks which were threatening the security of the United States, could be subject to impeachment for taking such action, even though he did not implement it in the best way and it would have been much wiser to rely on the FBI which is the established agency responsible for National Security investigations....

Faced with the choice of voting for a 5 paragraph Article in which there did not seem to me to be clear and convincing evidence sufficient to impeach on 4 of the 5 Paragraphs, I voted against Article II on July 29....

When the presidential admissions of August 5, 1974, are viewed against the background of the evidence already considered by the Committee with reference to Paragraph 5, I must conclude that the President did in fact misuse his executive power in the manner in which he interfered with the Federal Bureau of Investigation, the Criminal Division of the Department of Justice and the Central Ingelligence Agency.

His admissions of August 5 also further strengthen the evidence that he violated the constitutional rights of citizens as alleged in Paragraph 1 relating to abuse of the Internal Revenue Service.

Three of the 5 Paragraphs of Article II having now been proved by clear and convincing evidence I would vote to impeach on this Article in the full House....

PRESIDENT FORD'S
FIRST NEWS CONFERENCE
August 28, 1974

No major surprises marked President Ford's Aug. 28 news conference, his first since he became President Aug. 9. (See p. 695-705.) The televised question-and-answer session was more notable for the ways it contrasted with Richard Nixon's meetings with the press. Appearing relaxed and confident, Ford fielded 29 questions during the 28-minute conference. Nine dealt with the economy, seven with the legal problems Nixon could face resulting from Watergate, two each with the effects of Watergate, Ford's political plans and his national defense and foreign policies. This presidential news conference was the first to be held since the last Nixon conference March 6. Ford, who had held 55 scheduled press conferences during his eight-month tenure as Vice President, earlier had promised to hold such meetings regularly. Nixon held 37 conferences in 5½ years.

Unlike Nixon, Ford wore no makeup during his appearance. He spoke from a taller, slimmer podium under a new layout in the East Room of the White House. Instead of standing before a blue velvet backdrop, Ford stood in front of an open door with a long red-carpeted corridor visible in the background. Aides said the change was designed to eliminate the atmosphere of a television studio. The mood of the meeting also contrasted with Nixon's press conferences, particularly those he held during the Watergate scandal. Both the new President and the reporters were less tense.

On the subject of the inflation-ridden economy, Ford flatly ruled out returning to government controls to halt inflation. "Wage and price controls are out, period," he said, adding that reduced federal spending would be the key to the administration's war against inflation. Ford said the *government would spend less than $300-billion in the current fiscal year. He urged wage-earners to follow the administration's example and "watch every penny." The President also referred to the planned domestic summit conference on the economy, saying the administration was gathering advice from "a wide variety of the segments of our population to see if they have any better ideas for us to win the battle against inflation."*

Fate of Former President Nixon

Ford said he was deferring a decision on how he would deal with former President Nixon's legal troubles until the matter went into litigation. "In this situation, I am the final authority," he said. "There have been no charges made, there has been no action by the courts, there has been no action by any jury, and until any legal process has been undertaken, I think it is unwise and untimely for me to make any commitment." However, the President hinted strongly that he would be inclined to intercede in Nixon's behalf at some point. At his swearing-in, Ford recalled, he had said he hoped Nixon would find "peace." He said that he now agreed with Vice President-designate Nelson A. Rockefeller's statement Aug. 23 that Nixon already had been "hung" and should not also be "drawn and quartered." Ford stressed that he was not ruling out the option of pardoning Nixon. "Of course, I make the final decision," he said. "Until it gets to me, I make no commitment one way or the other. But I do have the right as President of the United States to make that decision." In response to another question, Ford also declined to rule out the option of granting a pardon before any trial took place. However, at still another point, he indicated that he would not seek to limit the activities of Special Prosecutor Leon Jaworski with respect to other Watergate defendants. Jaworski "has an obligation to take whatever action he sees fit in conformity with his oath of office, and that should include any and all individuals," Ford declared. On Sept. 8, a Sunday morning, Ford granted Nixon a "full, free and absolute pardon... for all offenses against the United States which he...has committed or may have committed during his years as president. (See p. 811-817.)

Other Statements

In response to other questions at the Aug. 28 news conference, Ford:

• *Reiterated that he "probably" will be a candidate for the Republican presidential nomination in 1976. "I think Gov. Rockefeller and myself are a good team, but, of course, the final judgment in this matter will be that of the delegates to the national convention."*

• *Indicated that Rockefeller "can be extremely important in the new administration as my teammate in doing effective work in the area of the Domestic Council" and in helping prepare legislative proposals for the 94th Congress when it convenes in January 1975. Other duties Ford has in mind for Rockefeller, he said, include taking over the President's responsibilities in heading the Domestic Council's subcommittee on privacy, contributing to foreign policy decision-making and helping "in the political arena under certain guidelines and some restrictions."*

- *Stressed the need to "accelerate every aspect of Project Independence," the Nixon administration's program for becoming self-sufficient in the field of energy by 1980.*

- *Urged cutting "any fat in the defense budget," while maintaining that a strong defense program is needed.*

- *Indicated that the United States would abide by any decision by the Organization of American States to relax economic and political sanctions against Cuba.*

- *Said the sole surviving component of the Johnson administration's Office of Economic Opportunity, the Community Action Program, might be phased out under the housing and urban development act he had signed into law Aug. 22.*

- *Declared that his administration would be "open" and that he would be "as candid and forthright as I possibly can." There will be no code of ethics for the executive branch, he added. "The code of ethics that will be followed will be the example that I set."*

Following is the text of President Ford's nationally televised Aug. 28 news conference, his first since taking office as President:

NEWS CONFERENCE TEXT

THE PRESIDENT: Please sit down. Good afternoon.

At the outset, I have a very important and a very serious announcement. There was a little confusion about the date of this press conference. My wife, Betty, had scheduled her first press conference for the same day. Obviously, I had scheduled my first press conference for this occasion. So, Betty's was postponed.

We worked this out between us in a calm and orderly way. She will postpone her press conference until next week, and until then, I will be making my own breakfast, my own lunch and my own dinner. (Laughter)

Helen?

Q: Mr. President, aside from the Special Prosecutor's role, do you agree with the Bar Association that.the laws apply equally to all men, or do you agree with Governor Rockefeller that former President Nixon should have immunity from prosecution, and specifically, would you use your pardon authority, if necessary?

P: Well, let me say at the outset that I made a statement in this room in the few minutes after the swearing-in, and on that occasion I said the following. That I had hoped that our former President, who brought peace to millions, would find it for himself.

Now, the expression made by Governor Rockefeller, I think, coincides with the general view and the point of view of the American people. I subscribe to that point of view, but let me add in the last ten days or two weeks I have asked for prayers for guidance on this very important point.

In this situation, I am the final authority. There have been no charges made, there has been no action by the courts, there has been no action by any jury, and until any legal process has been undertaken, I think it is unwise and untimely for me to make any commitment.

Political Movement

Q: Mr. President, you have been in office 19 days now, and already some of your naturally conservative allies are grumbling that you are moving too far to the left. Does this trouble you?

P: I don't think I have deviated from my basic philosophy nor have I deviated from what I think is the right action. I have selected an outstanding person to be the Vice President. I have made a decision concerning amnesty, which I think is right and proper—no amnesty, no revenge—and that individuals who have violated either the draft laws or have evaded Selective Service or deserted can earn their way, or work their way, back. I don't think these are views that fall in the political spectrum right or left.

I intend to make the same kind of judgments in other matters because I think they are right and I think they are for the good of the country.

Q: Mr. President, may I follow that with one more example, possibly, that is there is a report the Administration is considering a $4 billion public works program in case the inflation [unemployment] rate gets higher than it is, say six percent. Is that under consideration?

P: I think most of you do know that we have a public service employment program on the statute books which is funded right today, not for any major program, but to take care of those areas in our country where there are limited areas of unemployment caused by the energy crisis or any other reason.

There is a recommendation from some of my advisers saying that if the economy gets any more serious, that this ought to be a program, a broader, more expensive public service program. We will approach this problem with compassion and action where there is a need for it.

Running in 1976

Q: Mr. President, there are two political questions: Do you definitely plan to run for President in 1976, and if so, would you choose Governor Rockefeller as your running mate, or would you leave that choice up to the Convention's free choice?

P: I will repeat what has been said on my behalf, that I will probably be a candidate in 1976, I think Governor Rockefeller and myself are a good team, but of course, the final judgment in this matter will be that of the delegates to the national Convention.

Q: May I just follow up on Helen's question: You are saying, sir, that the option of a pardon for former President Nixon is still an option that you will consider, depending on what the courts will do.

P: Of course, I make the final decision. Until it gets to me, I make no commitment one way or the other. But I do have the right as President of the United States to make that decision.

Q: And you are not ruling it out?

P: I am not ruling it out. It is an option and a proper option for any President.

Q: Do you feel the Special Prosecutor can in good conscience pursue cases against former top Nixon aides as long as there is the possibility that the former President may not also be pursued in the courts?

P: I think the Special Prosecutor, Mr. Jaworski, has an obligation to take whatever action he sees fit in conformity with his oath of office, and that should include any and all individuals.

Open Administration

Q: What do you plan to do as President to see to it that we have no further Watergates?

P: Well, I indicated that, one, we would have an open Administration. I will be as candid and as forthright as I possibly can. I will expect any individuals in my Administration to be exactly the same. There will be no tightly controlled operation of the White House staff. I have a policy of seeking advice from a number of top members of my staff. There will be no one person, nor any limited number of individuals, who make decisions. I will make the decisions and take the blame for them or whatever benefit might be the case.

I said in one of my speeches after the swearing in, there would be no illegal wiretaps or there would be none of the other things that to a degree helped to precipitate the Watergate crisis.

Q: Do you plan to have a code of ethics for the Executive Branch?

P: The code of ethics that will be followed will be the example that I set.

Fighting Inflation

Q: Mr. President, do you have any plans now for immediate steps to control and curtail inflation, even before your summit conference on the economy?

P: We have announced that as far as fiscal control is concerned, we will spend less in the Federal Government in the current fiscal year than $300 billion. That is a reduction of $5 billion 500 million at a minimum.

This, I think, will have two effects: Number one, it will be substantively beneficial, it will make our borrowing from the money market less, freeing more money for housing, for the utilities to borrow, and in addition, I think it will convince people who might have some doubts that we mean business.

But in the meantime, we are collecting other ideas from labor, from management, from agriculture, from a wide variety of the segments of our population to see if they have any better ideas for us to win the battle against inflation.

Q: Mr. President, as you know, a number of people have questioned your opposition to a return to wage and price controls. Gardner Ackley, a University of Michigan economist that you have listened to in the past, recently testified before Congress that if we are really frightened about inflation, we ought to think about returning to wage and price controls.

Can you foresee any circumstances under which you would be willing to do that and make them work?

P: I foresee no circumstances under which I can see the reimposition of wage and price controls. The situation is precisely this: This past week I had a meeting with the Democratic and Republican leadership, plus my own advisers in the field of our national economy.

There was an agreement, number one, that I would not ask for any wage and price control legislation. There was agreement by the leadership on both sides of the aisle that there was no possibility whatsoever that this Congress in 1974 would approve any such legislation. Number three, labor and management almost unanimously agree that wage and price controls at the present time or under any foreseeable circumstances were unwise.

Under all those circumstances, it means that wage and price controls are out, period.

The Vice President

Q: Can you give us your present thinking on how best you might use Mr. Rockefeller as Vice President once he is confirmed?

P: I have a lot of ideas. Until Congress confirms Mr. Rockefeller, we are sort of in a honeymoon period. I really shouldn't make any commitments until we actually get married.

But to be serious, if I might, I think Governor Rockefeller can be extremely important in the new Administration as my teammate in doing effective work in the area of the Domestic Council. We have to prepare legislative proposals that will go to the Congress when the new Congress comes back in January.

I believe that Governor Rockefeller will take over my responsibilities heading the subcommittee of the Domestic Council on privacy. Governor Rockefeller, with his vast experience in foreign policy, can make a significant contribution to some of our decision-making in the area of foreign policy. Obviously, in addition, he can be helpful, I think, in the political arena under certain guidelines and some restrictions.

Q: Mr. President, you just ruled out wage and price controls, but I just would like to ask you why Mr. Nixon, when he was President, felt he was compelled to go back to them because the situation was getting out of hand? Can you just reinforce what you told Mr. Brokaw, why you think the situation is [not] that much out of hand yet?

P: I can only refer you to the circumstances and the decision of President Nixon in August of 1971. That was a decision he made under quite different circumstances. We are in totally different circumstances today. We have gone through a 3-year period, more or less. I think we have learned a few economic lessons that wage and price controls in the current circumstances didn't work, probably created more dislocations and inequities. I see no justification today, regardless of the rightness or wrongness of the decision in 1971, to reimpose wage and price controls today.

Q: Mr. President, you are still working with the same team of economic advisers who advised your predecessor. As a matter of putting your own stamp on your own Administration, and inspiring confidence, do you plan to change the cast of characters?

P: There is one significant change. Just within the last 48 hours, Herb Stein, who did a superb job for President Nixon, is going back to the University of Virginia, and Alan Greenspan is taking over and he has been on board, I think two days.

That is a distinct change. I think Mr. Greenspan will do an excellent job. We are soliciting, through the economic summit, the views of a great many people from the total spectrum of the American society. Their ideas will be vitally important in any new, innovative approaches that we take. So, I think, between now and the 28th of September, when I think the second day of the summit ends, we will have the benefit of a great many wise, experienced individuals in labor, management, agriculture, et cetera, and this will give us, I hope, any new approaches that are wise and beneficial.

Oil Prices

Q: Some oil governments and some commercial cartels, notably Aramco in Saudi Arabia are restricting oil production in order to keep oil prices artifically high. Now the U.S. can't do anything about Venezuela, but it can conceivably vis a vis cartels like Aramco. What steps and actions do you plan to take in this regard?

P: I think this points up very vividly the need for us to accelerate every aspect of Project Independence, I think it highlights the need and necessity for us to proceed with more oil and gas drilling a greater supply domestically. I believe it points up the requirements that we expedite the licensing processes for new nuclear reactors. I think it points up very dramatically the need that we expand our geothermal, our solar research and development in the field of energy.

In the meantime, it seems to me that the efforts that we made several months ago to put together a group of consumer-industrial nations requires that this group meet frequently and about as much as possible in concert, because if we have any economic repercussions because of high oil prices and poor investment policies, it could create serious economic problems throughout the industrial world. So it does require, I believe, the short-term action by consumer nations and the long-term actions under Project Independence.

Q: Mr. President, to pursue Helen's inquiry, has there been any communication between the Special Prosecutor's office and anyone on your staff regarding President Nixon?

P: Not to my knowledge.

Q: Mr. President, the beneficial effects of the present accounting on inflation will take some time to dribble down to the wage earner. What advice would you give the wage earner today that is having trouble stretching his dollar over his plate?

P: I think every wage earner has to realize we are going through a serious economic problem with inflation in double digits, not as bad as people in many Western European countries, but it will require him or her to follow the example of their Federal Government which is going to tighten its belt and likewise for an interim period of time watch every penny.

Q: Mr. President, you said last March in an interview, I think in Seapower magazine, that you came down quite strongly in favor of establishing a U.S.-Indian Ocean fleet with the necessary bases to support it. Do you still favor that and do you favor the development of Diego Garcia?

P: I favor the limited expansion of our base at Diego Garcia. I don't view this as any challenge to the Soviet Union. The Soviet Union already has three major naval operating bases in the Indian Ocean. This particular proposed construction, I think, is a wise policy and it ought not to ignite any escalation of problems in the Middle East.

Yes, Sarah.

Veterans Benefits

Q: I want to ask about this new veterans benefits bill which Congress passed in the last hours. I understand this is a bill that you favored and maybe spurred the Congress to pass. It saves $200 million.

My question is: Is that a real savings when it gives the disabled man less money than an able man and disrupts completely the veterans going to college in September?

P: I had no part in just how that House action was taken. I did discuss, coming back from the VFW meeting in Chicago, with a number of Members of the House and Senate, the problem that I faced with the bill that came out of conference, which would have added $780-some million over and above the budget for this year and a substantial increase for a number of succeeding years.

But that particular compromise was put together and brought to the Floor of the House without any participation by me. I think there are some good provisions in that particular House action. It does tend to equalize the benefits for Vietnam veterans with the benefits that were given to World War II and to Korean veterans.

There are some, I think, inequities, and you probably pointed out one. I hope when the Congress reconvenes within a week or so that they will go back to conference, take a good look and hopefully eliminate any inequities and keep the price down because it is inflationary the way it was and it may be the way it was proposed by the House.

Q: Mr. President, concerning the Federal budget, will domestic social programs have to bear the whole brunt of the anti-inflationary fight or can some money come out of the defense budget, and if so, how much?

P: No budget for any department is sacrosanct, and that includes the defense budget. I insist, however, that such money be made available to the Army, the Navy and the Air Force so that we are strong militarily for the purpose of deterring war or meeting any challenge by any adversary. But if there is any fat in the defense budget, it ought to be cut out by Congress or eliminated by the Secretary of Defense.

In the meantime, all other departments must be scrutinized carefully so that they don't have any fat and marginal programs are eliminated.

Mrs. Tufty?

Other Priorities

Q: Mr. President, you had given top priority to inflation. Do you have a list of priorities and if so, what is number two?

P: Well, of course, public enemy number one, and that is the one we have to lick, is inflation. If we take care of inflation and get our economy back on the road to a healthy future, I think most of our other domestic programs or problems will be solved.

We won't have high unemployment. We will have ample job opportunities. We will, I believe, give greater opportunities to minorities to have jobs. If we can lick inflation, and we are going to try, and I think we are going to have a good program, most of our other domestic programs will be solved.

Q: Do you have any plans to revive the Office of Economic Opportunity, and if so, in what areas?

P: As I am sure you know, the old poverty program has been significantly changed over the last several years. The Headstart program has been taken out of OEO and turned over to the Department of HEW. The health aspect of the old poverty programs are also over in HEW.

The Congress just approved, and Mr. Nixon approved, a Legal Services Corporation, which was another part of the old poverty program. So, we ended up really with just CAP, the Community Action Program.

I think most people who have objectively looked at the Community Action Program and the model cities program and maybe some of the other similar programs, there is duplication, there is overlapping.

And under the new housing and urban development bill, local communities are given substantial sums to take a look at the model cities programs and related programs, and they may be able to take up the slack of the ending of the Community Action Programs.

Q: Mr. President, my question applies to a 1972 statement in which you said that an impediment to a regional peace settlement is an impediment to preserve the fiction that Jerusalem is not the capital of Israel. My question, sir, is would you, now that you set foreign policy, request that the Embassy be shifted from Tel Aviv to Jerusalem along with other national Embassies?

P: Under the current circumstance and the importance of getting a just and lasting peace in the Middle East, I think that particular proposal ought

773

to stand aside. We must come up with some answers between Israel and the Arab nations in order to achieve a peace that is both fair and durable.

Q: Mr. President, do you contemplate any changes in our policy with Cuba?

P: The policy that we have toward Cuba today is determined by the sanctions voted by the Organization of American States and we abide by those actions that were taken by the members of that organization.

Now if Cuba changes its policy toward us and toward its Latin neighbors, we, of course, would exercise the option depending on what the changes were to change our policy. But before we made any change, we would certainly act in concert with the other members of the Organization of American States.

Question of Pardon

Q: Mr. President, you have emphasized here your option of granting a pardon to the former President.

P: I intend to.

Q: You intend to have that option. If an indictment is brought, would you grant a pardon before any trial took place?

P: I said at the outset that until the matter reaches me, I am not going to make any comment during the process of whatever charges are made.

Q: Mr. President, two questions related, how long will the transition last in your opinion, and, secondly, how soon would it be proper and fair for Democrats on the campaign trail this fall to hold you accountable for the economic policy and the economic problems this country faces?

P: I can't judge what the Democrats are going to say about my policies. They have been very friendly so far and very cooperative. I think it is a fair statement that our problems domestically, our economic problems, are the joint responsibility of Government. As a matter of fact, I think the last poll indicated that most Americans felt that our difficulties were caused by Government action and that, of course, includes the President and the Democratic Congress. So we are all in this boat together with labor and management and everybody else. I don't think making partisan politics out of a serious domestic problem is good politics.

Q: Mr. President, in your fight against inflation, what, if anything, do you intend to do about the next Federal pay raise?

P: I have made no judgment on that yet, the recommendation has not come to my desk.

Q: Mr. President, when do you expect the SALT talks to resume? Is there disagreement over our position in the Pentagon and the State Department and other agencies?

P: At the present time, there is an effort being made to bridge the Department of Defense, the State Department and any others together for a resolution of our, the United States position regarding SALT 2. This decision will be made in the relatively near future. I don't think there is any basic difficulty that cannot be resolved internally within our Government. I believe that Secretary Kissinger is going to be meeting with representatives from the Soviet Union in the near future, I think in October, if my memory is correct, and we, of course, will then proceed on a timetable to try and negotiate SALT 2. I think a properly negotiated effective strategic arms limitation agreement is in the best interests of ourselves, the Soviet Union and a stable international situation.

THE PRESS: Thank you, Mr. President.

U.N. WORLD
POPULATION AGREEMENT
August 30, 1974

Agreement on concerted global action to bring population levels into balance with available food supplies remained beyond the reach of delegates at the U.N. World Population Conference that concluded its 10-day meeting in Bucharest, Rumania, on Aug. 30. Instead, the representatives from 130 nations signed a vaguely worded agreement calling for voluntary compliance in slowing world population growth. A global consensus on strict measures to meet head-on the population growth problem had been precluded by serious disagreements on approaches between industrialized nations and the less developed nations. The former favored strict population control in order to stem hunger, poverty, environmental deterioration and raw material shortages, while the developing nations supported a population expansion program aimed at bolstering economic development and a redistribution of the world's wealth. In the end, the pact stopped short of setting national and international population goals or of dealing directly with the problem of overpopulation. Instead, it ranked economic and social development ahead of direct population control as methods for curbing spiraling population rates. The agreement thus appeared more closely aligned with the views of Communist and Latin American countries which had led efforts to shape the final pact, stressing the need to redistribute the world's resources. While the document was acclaimed overwhelmingly by the delegates, world food experts generally expressed disappointment that it did not emphasize the urgency of dealing with the population situation and the related problems such as food shortages. Said one French agricultural expert, Rene Dumont: "It will be said that the conference was convened on the eve of the greatest famine and the conference failed to recognize it."

The U.N. World Population Conference followed the 1972 U.N. General Assembly approval of the resolution which called for a world parley. The aim of the conference was to gain a global consensus on the population problem and on possible means of meeting it. World population experts were specifically concerned with the annual two per cent population growth rate, which added 70-million people to the world in 1974. If this growth rate continued, the 1974 estimated world population of 4-billion people would double in 35 years. Tied in with this problem were the shortages of food and other raw materials, shortages which experts believed would be aggravated by continuing population growth.

Rationale for Population Expansion

Rumanian President Nicolae Ceausescu took a different view when he spoke before the delegates gathered in his country. He declared that the population problem could be alleviated by a redistribution of the world's wealth and cited "the imperialist, colonialist and neo-colonialist exploitation and oppression of many peoples" as the major cause for the disproportionate distribution of wealth. He said that Rumania would continue to attempt to expand its population from 20-million to 25-million by 1980 and affirmed the "sovereign right" of other nations to make such decisions as they deem "most suitable, consonant with...national interests." Ceausescu echoed the views of many developing nations which believed that only through population expansion and economic and social development could they better their position in the world community.

Provisions of the Agreement

In dealing with population control, countries with high birthrates deemed "detrimental to their national purpose" were "invited" by the agreement to take steps to set quantitative goals and to undertake policies aimed at attaining these goals by 1985. However, the pact stressed that "nothing herein should interfere with the sovereignty of any government to adopt such goals." The agreement also affirmed the basic right of couples to decide the number and spacing of any offspring, and recognized their right to be furnished the information and specific means to carry out those decisions. Without setting a date for compliance, the agreement asked nations to furnish their citizens with the necessary information, education and means to plan families.

In reference to the interrelationship between population growth and natural resources shortages, the agreement took note of the disproportionate use by industrialized nations of the world's resources. It urged the industrialized nations "to adopt appropriate policies in population, consumption and investment, bearing in mind the need for fundamental improvement in international equity."

Apparently as a result of extensive lobbying efforts by a group of internationally known women, including U.S. anthropologist Margaret Mead, U.S. feminist author Betty Friedan and Australian writer Germaine Greer, the agreement included a section emphasizing the right of women to participate on an equal basis with men in all spheres of activity. It emphasized the role women could play in the economic sphere. The section noted that participation by women without discrimination would also have an impact on lowering birthrates.

'Culprits' for World Population Problem

Political rivalries emerged throughout the 10-day conference as delegates alternately sought to place the blame for the population problem on their ideological antagonists. China blamed the Soviet Union and the United States, calling them the "chief culprits" of poverty in the less developed nations. The chief Chinese delegate, Huang Shu-tse, called "utterly groundless" the concern over a population explosion and instead accused the "superpowers" of attempting to shift blame for the world's problems to the Third World. Huang said China stood opposed to any outside interference with domestic population growth.

Renewing an earlier Soviet theme (Historic Documents 1973, p. 809-824), U.S.S.R. deputy health minister Lev Volodsky called on all nations to cut their military budgets by 10 per cent in order to divert some of those funds into aid programs for underdeveloped nations. Volodsky cited "imperialists and colonialists" as the group responsible for the problems of the Third World. By contrast, the U.S. position focused on population expansion as the reasons for widespread hunger and poverty. The U.S. view called for a reduction of family size to a level of parents and two children.

A highlight of the conference was an appearance Aug. 26 by John D. Rockefeller III, chairman of the Rockefeller Foundation, who had supported a policy of family planning for 40 years. In a dramatic reversal, Rockefeller said: "I have changed my mind, the evidence has been mounting, particularly in the past decade, that family planning alone is not adequate." He said he now favored an approach which "recognizes that rapid population growth is only one among many problems facing most countries, that it is a multiplier and intensifier of other problems rather than the cause of them. And it recognizes that motivation for family planning is best stimulated by hope that living conditions and opportunities in general will improve." He advocated a birth control policy, but in conjunction with general economic and social development.

Following is the text of Chapter III and of Chapter IV of the World Population Plan of Action, "Recommendations for Action," approved by the delegates to the U.N. World Population Conference in Bucharest, Rumania, on Aug. 30:

CHAPTER III. RECOMMENDATIONS FOR ACTION

A. Population goals and policies

1. Population growth

16. According to the United Nations medium population projections, little change is expected to occur in average rates of population growth either in the more developed or in the less developed regions by 1985. According to the United Nations low variant projections, it is estimated that as a result of social and economic development and population policies as reported by countries in the Second United Nations Inquiry on Population and Development, population growth rates in the developing countries as a whole may decline from the present level of 2.4 per cent per annum to about 2 per cent by 1985; and below 0.7 per cent per annum in the developed countries. In this case the worldwide rate of population growth would decline from 2 per cent to about 1.7 per cent.

17. Countries which consider that their present or expected rates of population growth hamper their goals of promoting human welfare are invited, if they have not yet done so, to consider adopting population policies, within the framework of socio-economic development, which are consistent with basic human rights and national goals and values.

18. Countries which aim at achieving moderate or low population growth should try to achieve it through a low level of birth and death rates. Countries wishing to increase their rate of population growth should, when mortality is high, concentrate efforts on the reduction of mortality, and where appropriate, encourage an increase in fertility and encourage immigration.

19. Recognizing that *per capita* use of world resources is much higher in the more developed than in the developing countries, the developed countries are urged to adopt appropriate policies in population, consumption and investment, bearing in mind the need for fundamental improvement in international equity.

2. Morbidity and mortality

20. The reduction of morbidity and mortality to the maximum feasible extent is a major goal of every human society and should be achieved in conjunction with massive social and economic development. Where death and morbidity rates are very high, concentrated national and international efforts should be applied to reduce them as a matter of highest priority in the context of societal change.

21. The short-term effect of mortality reduction on population growth rates is symptomatic of the early development process and must be viewed as beneficial. Sustained reductions in fertility have generally been preceded by reductions in mortality. Although this relationship is complex, mortality reduction may be a prerequisite to a decline in fertility.

22. It is a goal of this Plan of Action to reduce, to the maximum extent possible, the mortality level, particularly among children, as well as maternal mortality, in all regions of the world, and to reduce national and subnational differentials in mortality levels. The attainment of an average expectation of life of 62 years by 1985 and 74 years by the year 2000 for the world as a whole would require by the end of the century an increase of 11 years for Latin America, 17 years for Asia and 28 years for Africa.

23. Countries with the highest mortality levels should aim by 1985 to have an expectation of life at birth of at least 50 years and an infant mortality rate of less than 120 per thousand live births.

24. It is recommended that national and international efforts to reduce general morbidity and mortality levels be accompanied by particularly vigorous efforts to achieve the following goals:

(a) Reduction of foetal, infant and early childhood mortality and related maternal morbidity and mortality;

(b) Reduction of involuntary sterility, subfecundity, defective births and illegal abortions;

(c) Reduction, or if possible elimination, of differential morbidity and mortality within countries, particularly with regard to differentials between regions, urban and rural areas, social and ethnic groups, and sexes;

(d) Eradication, wherever possible, or control of infectious and parasitic diseases, undernutrition and malnutrition; and the provision of a sufficient supply of potable water and adequate sanitation;

(e) Improvement of poor health and nutritional conditions which adversely affect working age populations and their productivity and thus undermine development efforts;

(f) Adoption of special measures for reducing mortality from social and environmental factors and elimination of aggression as a cause of death and poor health.

25. It is recommended that health and nutrition programmes designed to reduce morbidity and mortality be integrated within a comprehensive development strategy and supplemented by a wide range of mutually supporting social policy measures; special attention should be given to improving the management of existing health, nutritional and related social services and to the formulation of policies to widen their coverage so as to reach, in particular, rural, remote and underprivileged groups.

26. Each country has its own merits and experience in preventing and treating diseases. Promotion of interchange of experience in this regard will help to reduce morbidity and mortality.

3. Reproduction, family formation and the status of women

27. This Plan of Action recognizes the variety of national goals with regard to fertility and does not recommend any world family-size norm.

28. This Plan of Action recognizes the necessity of ensuring that all couples are able to achieve their desired number and spacing of children and the necessity of preparing the social and economic conditions to achieve this desire.

29. Consistent with the Proclamation of the International Conference on Human Rights, the Declaration on Social Progress and Development, the relevant targets of the Second United Nations Development Decade and the other international instruments on the subject, it is recommended that all countries:

(a) Respect and ensure, regardless of their overall demographic goals, the right of persons to determine, in a free, informed and responsible manner, the number and spacing of their children;

(b) Encourage appropriate education concerning responsible parenthood and make available to persons who so desire advice and means of achieving it;

(c) Ensure that family planning, medical and related social services aim not only at the prevention of unwanted pregnancies but also at elimination of involuntary sterility and sub-fecundity in order that all couples may be permitted to achieve their desired number of children; and adoption should be facilitated;

(d) Seek to ensure the continued possibility of variations in family size when a low fertility level has been established or is a policy objective;

(e) Make use, wherever needed and appropriate, of adequately trained professional and auxiliary health personnel, rural extension, home economics and social workers, and non-government channels, to help provide family planning services and to advise users of contraceptives;

(f) Increase their health manpower and health facilities to the level of effectiveness, redistribute functions among the different levels of professionals and auxiliaries in order to overcome the shortage of qualified personnel and establish an effective system of supervision in their health and family planning services;

(g) Ensure that information about, and education in, family planning and other matters which affect fertility, are based on valid and proven scientific knowledge, and include a full account of any risk that may be involved in the use or non-use of contraceptives.

30. Governments which have family planning programmes are invited to consider integrating and coordinating these services with health and other services designed to raise the quality of family life, including family allowances and maternity benefits, and to consider including family planning services in their official health and social insurance systems. As concerns couples themselves, family planning policy should also be directed towards promotion of the psycho-social harmony and mental and physical well-being of couples.

31. It is recommended that countries wishing to affect fertility levels give priority to implementing development programmes and educational and health strategies which, while contributing to economic growth and higher standards of living, have a decisive impact upon demographic trends, including fertility. International co-operation is called for to give priority to assisting such national efforts in order that these programmes and strategies be carried into effect.

32. While recognizing the diversity of social, cultural, political and economic conditions among countries and regions, it is nevertheless agreed that the following development goals generally have an effect on the socio-economic content of reproductive decisions that tends to moderate fertility levels:

(a) The reduction of infant and child mortality, particularly by means of improved nutrition, sanitation, maternal and child health care, and maternal education;

(b) The full integration of women into the development process, particularly by means of their greater participation in educational, social, economic and political opportunities, and especially by means of the removal of obstacles to their employment in the non-agricultural sector wherever possible. In this context, national laws and policies, as well as relevant international recommendations, should be reviewed in order to eliminate discrimination in, and remove obstacles to, the education, training, employment and career advancement opportunities for women;

(c) The promotion of social justice, social mobility, and social development particularly by means of a wide participation of the population in development and a more equitable distribution of income, land, social services and amenities;

(d) The promotion of wide educational opportunities for the young of both sexes, and the extension of public forms of pre-school education for the rising generation;

(e) The elimination of child labour and child abuse and the establishment of social security and old age benefits;

(f) The establishment of an appropriate lower limit for age at marriage.

33. It is recommended that governments consider making provision, in both their formal and nonformal educational programmes, for informing their people of the consequences of existing or alternative fertility behaviour for the well-being of the family, the educational and psychological development of children and the general welfare of society, so that an informed and responsible attitude to marriage and reproduction will be promoted.

34. Family size may also be affected by incentive and disincentive schemes. However, if such schemes are adopted or modified they should not violate human rights.

35. Some social welfare programmes, such as family allowances and maternity benefits, may have a positive effect on fertility and may hence be strengthened when such an effect is desired. However, such programmes should not, in principle, be curtailed if the opposite effect on fertility is desired.

36. The projections in paragraph 16 of future declines in rates of population growth, and those in paragraph 22 concerning increased expectation of life, are consistent with declines in the birth rate of the developing countries as a whole from the present level of 38 per thousand to 30 per thousand by 1985; in these projections, birth rates in the developed countries remain in the region of 15 per thousand. To achieve by 1985 these

levels of fertility would require substantial national efforts, by those countries concerned, in the field of socio-economic development and population policies, supported, upon request, by adequate international assistance. Such efforts would also be required to achieve the increase in expectation of life.

37. In the light of the principles of this Plan of Action, countries which consider their birth rates detrimental to their national purposes are invited to consider setting quantitative goals and implementing policies that may lead to the attainment of such goals by 1985. Nothing herein should interfere with the sovereignty of any government to adopt or not to adopt such quantitative goals.

38. Countries which desire to reduce their birth rates are invited to give particular consideration to the reduction of fertility at the extremes of female reproductive ages because of the salutary effects this may have on infant and maternal welfare.

39. The family is recognized as the basic unit of society. Governments should assist families as far as possible to enable them to fulfill their role in society. It is therefore recommended that:

(a) The family be protected by appropriate legislation and policy without discrimination as to other members of society;

(b) Family ties be strengthened by giving recognition to the importance of love and mutual respect within the family unit;

(c) National legislation having direct bearing on the welfare of the family and its members, including laws concerning age at marriage, inheritance, property rights, divorce, education, employment and the rights of the child, be periodically reviewed, as feasible, and adapted to the changing social and economic conditions and with regard to the cultural setting;

(d) Marriages be entered into only with the free and full consent of the intending spouses;

(e) Measures be taken to protect the social and legal rights of spouses and children in the case of dissolution or termination of marriage by death or other reason.

40. (a) Governments should equalize the legal and social status of children born in and out of wedlock as well as children adopted;

(b) The legal responsibilities of each parent toward the care and support of all their children should be established.

41. Governments should ensure full participation of women in the educational, social, economic, and political life of their countries on an equal basis with men. It is recommended that:

(a) Education for girls as well as boys should be extended and diversified to enable them to contribute more effectively in rural and urban sectors, as well as in the management of food and other household functions;

(b) Women should be actively involved both as individuals and through political and non-governmental organizations, at every stage and every level in the planning and implementation of development programmes, including population policies;

(c) The economic contribution of women in households and farming should be recognized in national economies;

(d) Governments should make a sustained effort to ensure that legislation regarding the status of women complies with the principles spelled out in the Declaration on the Elimination of Discrimination Against Women and other United Nations Declarations, Conventions, and international instruments to reduce the gap between law and practice through effective implementation, and to inform women at all socio-economic levels of their legal rights and responsibilities.

42. Equal status of men and women in the family and in society improves the over-all quality of life. This principle of equality should be fully realized in family planning where both spouses should consider the welfare of other members of the family.

43. Improvement of the status of women in the family and in society can contribute, where desired, to smaller family size, and the opportunity for women to plan births also improves their individual status.

4. Population distribution and internal migration

44. Urbanization in most countries is characterized by a number of adverse factors—drain from rural areas through migration of individuals who cannot be absorbed by productive employment in urban areas, serious disequilibrium in the growth of urban centres, contamination of the environment, inadequate services and housing and social and psychological stress. In many developing countries, adverse consequences are due in large part to the economic structures resulting from the dependent situation of these countries in the international economic system and the correction of these shortcomings requires as a matter of priority the establishment of equitable economic relations among peoples.

45. Policies aimed at influencing population flows into urban areas should be co-ordinated with policies relating to the absorptive capacity of urban centres, as well as policies aimed at eliminating the undesirable consequences of excessive migration. In so far as possible, these policies should be integrated in plans and programmes dealing with over-all social and economic development.

46. In formulating and implementing internal migration policies, governments are urged to consider the following guidelines, without prejudice to their own socio-economic policies:

(a) Measures which infringe the right of freedom of movement and residence within the borders of each State that is enunciated in the Universal Declaration of Human Rights and other international instruments should be avoided;

(b) A major approach to a more rational distribution of the population is in planned and more equitable regional development, particularly in the advancement of regions which are less favoured or developed by comparison with the rest of the country;

(c) In planning development, and particularly in planning the location of industry and business and the distribution of social services and amenities, governments should take into account not only short-term economic

returns of alternative patterns, but also the social and environmental costs and benefits involved as well as equity and social justice in the distribution of the benefits of development among all groups and regions;

(d) Population distribution patterns should not be restricted to a choice between metropolitan and rural life; efforts should be made to establish and strengthen networks of small and medium-size cities to relieve the pressure on the large towns, while still offering an alternative to rural living;

(e) Intensive programmes of economic and social improvement should be carried out in the rural areas through balanced agricultural development which will provide increased income to the agricultural population, permit an effective expansion of social services and include measures to protect the environment and conserve and increase agricultural resources;

(f) Programmes should be promoted to make accessible to scattered populations the basic social services and the support necessary for increased productivity, e.g. by consolidating them in rural centres.

47. Internal migration policies should include the provision of information to the rural population of the economic and social conditions in the urban areas, including information on availability of employment opportunities.

48. In rural areas and areas accessible to rural populations, new employment opportunities including industries and public works programmes should be created, systems of land tenure should be improved and social services and amenities provided. It is not sufficient to consider how to bring the people to existing economic and social activities; it is also important to bring those activities to the people.

49. Considerable experience is now being gained by some countries which have implemented programmes aimed at relieving urban pressure, revitalizing the countryside, inhabiting sparsely populated areas or settling newly reclaimed agricultural land. Countries having such experience are invited to share it with other countries. It is recommended that international organizations make available upon request co-ordinated technical and financial assistance to facilitate the settlement of people.

50. The problems of urban environment are a consequence not only of the concentration of inhabitants, but also of their way of life which can produce harmful effects, such as wasteful and excessive consumption and activities which produce pollution. In order to avoid such effects in those countries experiencing this problem a development pattern favouring balanced and rational consumption is recommended.

5. International migration

51. It is recommended that governments and international organizations generally facilitate voluntary international movement. However, such movements should not be based on racial considerations which are to the detriment of indigenous populations. The significance of international migration varies widely among countries, depending upon their area, population size and growth rate, social and economic structure and environmental conditions.

52. Governments which consider international migration as important to their countries, either in the short or the long run, are urged to conduct, when appropriate, bilateral or multilateral consultations, taking into account the principles of the Charter of the United Nations, the Universal Declaration of Human Rights and other international instruments, with a view to harmonizing their policies which affect these movements. It is recommended that international organizations make available upon request co-ordinated technical and financial assistance to facilitate the settlement of people in countries of immigration.

53. Problems of refugees and displaced persons arising from forced migration, including their right of return to homes and properties, should also be settled in accordance with the relevant Principles of the Charter of the United Nations, the Universal Declaration of Human Rights and other international instruments.

54. Countries that are concerned with the outflow of migrant workers and wish to encourage and assist their remaining or returning should make particular efforts to create favourable employment opportunities at the national level. More developed countries should co-operate, bilaterally or through regional organizations and the international community, with less developed countries, to achieve these goals through the increased availability of capital, technical assistance, export markets and more favourable terms of trade and choice of production technology.

55. Countries receiving migrant workers should provide proper treatment and adequate social welfare services for them and their families, and should ensure their physical safety and security, in conformity with the provisions of relevant ILO conventions and recommendations and other international instruments.

56. Specifically, in the treatment of migrant workers Governments should work to prevent discrimination in the labour market and in society through lower salaries or other unequal conditions, to preserve their human rights, to combat prejudice against them and to eliminate obstacles to the reunion of their families. Governments should enable permanent immigrants to preserve their cultural heritage *inter alia* through the use of their mother tongue. Laws to limit illegal immigration should not only relate to the illegal migrants themselves but also to those inducing or facilitating their illegal action and should be promulgated in conformity with international law and basic human rights. Governments should bear in mind humanitarian considerations in the treatment of aliens who remain in a country illegally.

57. Since the outflow of qualified personnel from developing to developed countries seriously hampers the development of the former, there is an urgent need to formulate national and international policies to avoid the "brain drain" and obviate its adverse effects, including the possibility of devising programmes for large-scale communication of appropriate technological knowledge mainly from developed countries to the extent it can be properly adjusted and appropriately absorbed.

58. Developing countries suffering from heavy emigration of skilled workers and professionals should undertake extensive educational, manpower planning, investment in scientific and technical programmes, and other programmes and measures, to better match skills with employment opportunities, to increase the motivation of such personnel to contribute to the progress of their own country, and also undertake measures to encourage the return of their scientists and skilled personnel to specific job situations where needed.

59. Foreign investors should employ and train local personnel and use local research facilities to the greatest possible extent in conformity with the policies of the host country. Subject to their consent, the location of research facilities in host countries may aid them to a certain extent in retaining the services of highly skilled and professional research workers. Such investment should, of course, in no circumstances inhibit national economic development. International co-operation is needed to improve programmes to induce skilled personnel to return to, or remain in, their own countries.

60. Where immigration has proved to be of a long-term nature, countries are invited to explore the possibilities of extending national civil rights to immigrants.

61. The flow of skilled workers, technicians and professionals from more developed to less developed countries may be considered a form of international co-operation. Countries in a position to do so should continue and increase this flow with full respect for the sovereignty and equality of recipient countries.

62. Countries affected by significant numbers of migrant workers are urged, if they have not yet done so, to conclude bilateral or multilateral agreements which would regulate migration, protect and assist migrant workers, and protect the interests of the countries concerned. The International Labour Organisation should promote concerted action in the field of protection of migrant workers, and the United Nations Human Rights Commission should help, as appropriate, to ensure that the fundamental rights of migrants are safeguarded.

6. Population structure

63. All governments are urged, when formulating their development policies and programmes, to take fully into account the implications of changing numbers and proportions of youth, working age groups and the aged, particularly where such changes are rapid. Countries should study their population structure to determine their most desirable balance between age groups.

64. Specifically, developing countries are urged to consider the implications which the combination of their characteristically young age structure and moderate to high fertility have on their development. The fact of increasingly young population structures in many developing countries requires appropriate development strategies, priorities being required for their subsistence, health, education, training and incorporation

in the labour force through full employment as well as their active participation in political, cultural, social and economic life.

65. Developing countries are invited to consider the possible economic, social and demographic effects of population shifts from agriculture to non-agricultural industries. In addition to fuller utilization of labour and improvements in productivity and the levels of living, promotion of non-agricultural employment should aim at such change in the socio-economic structure of manpower and population that would affect demographically relevant behaviour of individuals. All countries are invited to fully consider the appropriate support and assistance to the World Employment Programme and related national employment promotion schemes.

66. Similarly, the other countries are urged to consider the contrary implications of the combination of their aging structure with moderate to low or very low fertility. All countries should carry out as part of their development programmes, comprehensive, humanitarian and just programmes of social security for the elderly.

67. In undertaking settlement and resettlement schemes and urban planning, governments are urged to give adequate attention to questions of age and sex balances and, particularly, to the welfare of the family.

B. Socio-economic policies

68. This Plan of Action recognizes that economic and social development is a central factor in the solution of population problems. National efforts of developing countries to accelerate economic growth should be assisted by the entire international community. The implementation of the International Development Strategy of the Second United Nations Development Decade, the Declaration and the Programme of Action on the new international economic order as adopted at the sixth Special Session of the United Nations General Assembly should lead to a reduction in the widening gap in levels of living between developed and developing countries and would be conducive to a reduction in population growth rates particularly in countries where such rates are high.

69. In planning measures to harmonize population trends and socio-economic change, human beings must be regarded not only as consumers but also as producers. The investment by nations in the health and education of their citizens contributes substantially to productivity. Consequently, plans for economic and social development and for international assistance for this purpose should emphasize the health and education sectors. Likewise, patterns of production and technology should be adapted to each country's endowment in human resources. Decisions on the introduction of technologies affording significant savings in employment of manpower should take into account the relative abundance of human resources. To this end it is recommended that efforts should be intensified to determine for each country the technologies and production methods best suited to its working population situation and to study the relationship between population factors and employment.

70. It is imperative that all countries, and within them all social sectors, should adapt themselves to more rational utilization of natural resources, without excess, so that some are not deprived of what others waste. In order to increase the production and distribution of food for the growing world population it is recommended that governments give high priority to improving methods of food production, the investigation and development of new sources of food and more effective utilization of existing sources. International co-operation is recommended with the aim of ensuring the provision of fertilizers and energy and a timely supply of foodstuffs to all countries.

C. Promotion of knowledge and policies

71. In order to achieve the population objectives of this Plan of Action and to put its policy recommendations adequately into effect, measures need to be undertaken to promote knowledge of the relationships and problems involved, to assist in the development of population policies and to elicit the cooperation and participation of all concerned in the formulation and implementation of these policies.

1. Data collection and analysis

72. Statistical data on the population collected by means of censuses, surveys or vital statistics registers, are essential for the planning of investigations and to provide a basis for the formulation, evaluation and application of population and development policies. Countries that have not yet done so are urged to tabulate and analyse their census and other data in order to fulfill these objectives.

73. It is up to each country to take a population census in accordance with its own needs and capabilities. However, it is recommended that a population census be taken by each country between 1975 and 1985. It is also recommended that these censuses give particular attention to data relevant to development planning and the formulation of population policies; in order to be of greatest value, it is recommended that these data be tabulated and made available as quickly as possible, with an evaluation both of the quality of information as well as the degree of coverage of the census.

74. All countries that have not yet done so should be encouraged to establish a continuing capability for taking multi-subject household sample surveys and a long-term plan for securing statistics on various demographic and interrelated socio-economic variables on a regular basis. This is recommended particularly with regard to topics relating to the improvement of levels of living and the well-being and level of education of individuals, in view of the close relationship between these variables and the problems affecting population. All countries are invited to co-operate with the World Fertility Survey.

75. In line with the objectives of the World Programme for the Improvement of Vital Statistics, countries are encouraged to establish and improve their vital registration system, as a long-term objective, and to enact laws

relevant to the improvement of vital registration. Until this improvement is completed, the use of alternative methods is recommended, such as sample surveys, which provide up-to-date information on vital events.

76. Less developed countries should be provided with technical co-operation, equipment and financial support to develop or improve the population and related statistical programmes mentioned above. Provision for data gathering assistance should cover fully the need for evaluating, analysing and presenting the data in a form most appropriate to the needs of users.

77. Governments that have not yet done so are urged to establish appropriate services for the collection, analysis and dissemination of demographic and related statistical information.

2. Research

78. This Plan of Action gives high priority to research activities in population problems (including unemployment, starvation and poverty) and to related fields, particularly to research activities that are important for the formulation, evaluation and implementation of the population policies consistent with full respect for human rights and fundamental freedom as recognized in international instruments of the United Nations. Although research for filling gaps in knowledge is very urgent and important, high priority should be given to research oriented to the specific problems of countries and regions, including methodological studies. Such research is best carried out in the countries and regions themselves and by competent persons especially acquainted with national and regional conditions. The following research areas are considered to be of particular importance for filling existing gaps in knowledge:

(a) The social, cultural and economic determinants of population variables in different developmental and political situations, particularly at the family and micro levels;

(b) The demographic and social processes occurring within the family cycle through time and, particularly, through alternative modes of development;

(c) The development of effective means for the improvement of health, and especially for the reduction of maternal, foetal, infant and early childhood mortality;

(d) The study of experiences of countries which have major programmes of internal migration with a view to developing guidelines that are helpful to policy-makers of these countries and of countries that are interested in undertaking similar programmes;

(e) Projections of demographic and related variables including the development of empirical and hypothetical models for monitoring the future;

(f) The formulation, implementation and evaluation of population policies, including methods for integrating population inputs and goals in development plans and programmes; the means for understanding and improving the motivations of people to participate in the formulation and implementation of population programmes; the study of education and communication aspects of population policy; the analysis of population policies in their relationship with other socio-economic development policies, laws and institutions, including the possible influences of the economic system on the social, cultural and economic aspects of population policies; the translation into action programmes of policies dealing with the socio-economic determinants of fertility, mortality, internal migration and distribution, and international migration;

(g) The collection, analysis and dissemination of information concerning human rights in relation to population matters and the preparation of studies aimed at the clarification, systematization and more effective implementation of these human rights;

(h) The review and analysis of national and international laws which bear directly or indirectly on population factors;

(i) Basic biological and applied research on the assessment and improvement of existing and new methods of fertility regulation; the evaluation of the impact of different methods of fertility regulation on ethical and cultural values and on mental and physical health, both in short-term and long-term effects; and the assessment and study of policies for creating social and economic conditions so that couples can freely decide on the size of their families;

(j) The evaluation of the impact of different methods of family planning on the health conditions of women and members of their families;

(k) The interrelationships among patterns of family formation, nutrition and health, reproductive biology, and the incidence, causes and treatment of sterility;

(l) Methods for improving the management, delivery and utilization of all social services associated with population, including family welfare and, when appropriate, family planning;

(m) Methods for the development of systems of social, demographic and related economic statistics in which various sets of data are interlinked, with a view to improving insight into the interrelationships of variables in these fields;

(n) The interrelations of population trends and conditions and other social and economic variables, in particular the availability of human resources, food and natural resources, the quality of the environment, the need for health, education, employment, welfare, housing and other social services and amenities, promotion of human rights, the enhancement of the status of women, the need for social security, political stability, discrimination, and political freedom;

(o) The impact of a shift from one family size pattern to another on biological and demographic characteristics of the population;

(p) Research should be undertaken on the changing structure, functions, and dynamics of the family as an institution, including the changing roles of men and women, attitudes toward and opportunities for women's educa-

tion and employment; the implications of current and future population trends for the status of women; biomedical research on male and female fertility, and the economic, social and demographic benefits to be derived from the integration of women in the development process;

(q) Research dealing with social indicators, to reflect the quality of life as well as the interrelations between socio-economic and demographic phenomena, should be encouraged. Emphasis should also be given to the development of socio-economic and demographic models.

79. Their national research requirements and needs must be determined by governments and national institutions. However, high priority should be given, wherever possible, to research that has wide relevance and international applicability.

80. National and regional research institutions dealing with population and related questions should be assisted and expanded as appropriate. Special efforts should be made to co-ordinate the research of these institutions by facilitating the exchange of their research findings and the exchange of information on their planned and ongoing research projects.

3. Management, training, education and information

81. There is a need for the development of management in all fields related to population, with national and international attention and appropriate support given to programmes dealing with its promotion.

82. A dual approach to training is recommended: an international programme for training in population matters concomitant with national and regional training programmes adapted and made particularly relevant to conditions in the countries and regions of the trainees. While recognizing the complementarity of these two approaches, national and regional training should be given the higher priority.

83. Training in population dynamics and policies, whether national, regional or international, should, in so far as possible, be interdisciplinary in nature. The training of population specialists should always be accompanied by relevant career development for the trainees in their fields of specialization.

84. Training in the various aspects of population activities, including the management of population programmes, should not be restricted to the higher levels of specialization but should also be extended to personnel at other levels, and, where needed, to medical, paramedical, traditional health personnel, and population programme administrators.

85. Training in population matters should be extended to labour, community and other social leaders, to senior government officials, with a view to enabling them better to identify the population problems of their countries and communities and to help in the formulation of policies relating to them. Such training should impart an adequate knowledge of human rights in accordance with international standards and awareness of the human rights aspect of population problems.

86. Owing to the role of education in individuals' and society's progress and its impact on demographic behaviour all countries are urged to further develop their formal and informal educational programmes; efforts should be made to eradicate illiteracy, to promote education among the youth and abolish factors discriminating against women.

87. Educational institutions in all countries should be encouraged to expand their curricula to include a study of population dynamics and policies, including, where appropriate, family life, responsible parenthood and the relation of population dynamics to socio-economic development and to international relations. Governments are urged to co-operate in developing a world-wide system of international, regional and national institutions to meet the need for trained manpower. Assistance to the less developed countries should include, as appropriate, the improvement of the educational infrastructure such as library facilities and computer services.

88. Governments are invited to use all available means for disseminating population information.

89. Governments are invited to consider the distribution of population information to enlighten both rural and urban populations, through the assistance of governmental agencies.

90. Voluntary organizations should be encouraged, within the framework of national laws, policies and regulations, to play an important role in disseminating population information and ensuring wider participation in population programmes, and to share experiences regarding the implementation of population measures and programmes.

91. International organizations, both governmental and non-governmental, should strengthen their efforts to distribute information on population and related matters, particularly through periodic publications on the world population situation, prospects and policies, the utilization of audio-visual and other aids to communication, the publication of non-technical digests and reports, and the production and wide distribution of newsletters on population activities. Consideration should also be given to strengthening the publication of international professional journals and reviews in the field of population.

92. In order to achieve the widest possible dissemination of research results, translation activities should be encouraged at both the national and international levels. In this respect, the revision of the United Nations Multilingual Demographic Dictionary and its publication in additional languages is strongly recommended.

93. The information and experience resulting from the World Population Conference and the World Population Year relating to the scientific study of population and the elaboration of population policies should be synthesized and disseminated by the United Nations.

4. Development and evaluation of population policies

94. Where population policies or programmes have been adopted, systematic and periodic evaluations of their effectiveness should be made with a view to their improvement.

95. Population measures and programmes should be integrated into comprehensive social and economic plans and programmes and this integration should be reflected in the goals, instrumentalities and organizations for planning within the countries. In general, it is suggested that a unit dealing with population aspects be created and placed at a high level of the national administrative structure and that such a unit be staffed with qualified persons from the relevant disciplines.

CHAPTER IV. RECOMMENDATIONS FOR IMPLEMENTATION

A. Role of national Governments

96. The success of this Plan of Action will largely depend on the actions undertaken by national Governments and Governments are urged to utilize fully the support of intergovernmental and non-governmental organizations.

97. This Plan of Action recognizes the responsibility of each Government to decide on its own policies and devise its own programmes of action dealing with the problems of population and economic and social progress. The recommendations made in this Plan of Action, in so far as they relate to national Governments, are made with due regard to the need for variety and flexibility in the hope that they may be responsive to major needs in the population field as perceived and interpreted by national Governments. However, it is strongly recommended that national policies be formulated and implemented without violating, and with due promotion of, universally accepted standards of human rights.

98. An important role of Governments with regard to this Plan of Action is to determine and assess the population problems and needs of their countries in the light of their political, social, cultural, religious and economic conditions; such an undertaking should be carried out systematically and periodically so as to promote informed, rational and dynamic decision-making in matters of population and development.

99. The effect of national action or inaction in the fields of population may, in certain circumstances, extend beyond national boundaries; such international implications are particularly evident with regard to aspects of morbidity, population concentration and international migration, but may also apply to other aspects of population concern.

B. Role of international co-operation

100. International co-operation, based on the peaceful co-existence of States having different social systems, should play a supportive role in achieving the goals of the Plan of Action. This supportive role could take the form of direct assistance, technical or financial, in response to na-

tional and regional requests and be additional to economic development assistance, or the form of other activities, such as monitoring progress, undertaking comparative research in the area of population, resources and consumption, and furthering the exchange among countries of information and policy experiences in the field of population and consumption. Assistance should be provided, as far as possible, with the assurance of support consistent with the national plans of recipient countries. Assistance should be provided on the basis of respect for sovereignty of the recipient country and its national policy.

101. The General Assembly of the United Nations, the Economic and Social Council, the Governing Council of UNDP/UNFPA [U.N. Development Program/U.N. Fund for Population Activities] and other competent legislative and policy-making bodies of the specialized agencies and the various intergovernmental organizations are urged to give careful conconsideration to this Plan of Action and to ensure an appropriate response to it.

102. Countries sharing similar population conditions and problems are invited to consider jointly this Plan of Action, exchange experience in relevant fields and elaborate those aspects of the Plan that are of particular relevance to them. The United Nations regional economic commissions and other regional bodies of the United Nations system should play an important role toward this end.

103. There is a special need for training in the field of population. The United Nations system, governments and, as appropriate, non-governmental organizations are urged to give recognition to this need and priority to the measures necessary to meet it, including information, education and services for family planning.

104. More developed countries, and other countries able to assist, are urged to increase their assistance to less developed countries in accordance with the goals of the Second United Nations Development Decade and, together with international organizations, to make this assistance available in accordance with the national priorities of receiving countries. In this respect, it is recognized, in view of the magnitude of the problems and the consequent national requirements for funds, that considerable expansion of international assistance in the population field is required for the proper implementation of this Plan of Action.

105. It is suggested that the expanding, but still insufficient, international assistance in population and development matters requires increased co-operation; UNFPA is urged, in co-operation with all organizations responsible for international population assistance, to produce a guide for international assistance in population matters which would be made available to recipient countries and institutions and be revised periodically.

106. International non-governmental organizations are urged to respond to the goals and policies of this Plan of Action by co-ordinating their activities with those of other non-governmental organizations, and with those of relevant bilateral and multilateral organizations, by expanding their

support for national institutions and organizations dealing with population questions, and by co-operating in the promotion of widespread knowledge of the goals and policies of the Plan of Action, and, when requested, by supporting national and private institutions and organizations dealing with population questions.

C. Monitoring, review and appraisal

107. It is recommended that monitoring of population trends and policies discussed in this Plan of Action should be undertaken continuously as a specialized activity of the United Nations and reviewed biennially by the appropriate bodies of the United Nations system, beginning in 1977. Because of the shortness of the intervals, such monitoring would necessarily have to be selective with regard to its informational content and should focus mainly on new and emerging population trends and policies.

108. A comprehensive and thorough review and appraisal of progress made towards achieving the goals and recommendations of this Plan of Action should be undertaken every five years by the United Nations system. For this purpose the Secretary-General is invited to make appropriate arrangements taking account of the existing structure and resources of the United Nations system, and in cooperation with Governments. It is suggested that the first such review be made in 1979 and be repeated each five years thereafter. The findings of such systematic evaluations should be considered by the Economic and Social Council with the object of making, whenever necessary, appropriate modifications of the goals and recommendations of this Plan.

109. It is urged that both the monitoring and the review and appraisal activities of this Plan of Action be closely co-ordinated with those of the International Development Strategy for the Second United Nations Development Decade and any new international development strategy that might be formulated.

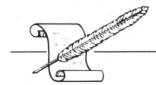

September

U.S.-EAST GERMAN RELATIONS
September 4, 1974

The United States and the German Democratic Republic ended 25 years of diplomatic silence Sept. 4 when their representatives signed an agreement establishing formal diplomatic relations between the two governments. The way had been paved for the opening of ties by the four-power Berlin Treaty, signed by the victorious nations of World War II, France, the Soviet Union, the United Kingdom, and the United States, on June 3, 1972, which set standards for access to West Berlin and called for the recognition of two separate German states. (See Historic Documents 1972, p. 467-470.) *Following the signing of that treaty, the North Atlantic Treaty Organization (NATO) had authorized the establishment of diplomatic relations between its members and East Germany. But the key breakthrough to the establishment of relations between the United States and the Communist bloc country was a policy shift by the East German government. Abandoning a long-standing position, that government agreed for the first time to hold discussions on the possible compensation of Jews who had been victims of the World War II Nazi government. Previously, the East Germans had refused to recognize the legal right of the United States to act as a representative of the victimized Jews or to consider its own government a successor to the Nazi Third Reich and therefore responsible for its outstanding obligations.*

In a joint statement issued after the signing of the agreement to establish relations, the United States and East Germany took note of the scheduled talks on outstanding Jewish claims. Mention was made also of upcoming negotiations of "other financial matters outstanding," apparently a reference to confiscated property that had belonged to Americans un-

der the Nazi regime and to Americans' inheritances that had been withheld following the removal of the Third Reich government. It was also learned that discussions on trade, cultural and consular relations were scheduled to begin before the end of 1975. Following the establishment of diplomatic relations, both countries quickly named ambassadors to head their delegations abroad. Embassies were scheduled to open in the foreign capitals at a later date once adequate facilities could be found.

The formal agreement was signed by Arthur A. Hartman, U.S. assistant secretary of state for European Affairs and Herbert Suss, an East German Foreign Ministry official who had negotiated the final accord for his government. Suss told reporters after the signing that East Germany's desire for "long-term economic cooperation" with the United States had been a factor in the reversal of position regarding the talks on Jewish compensation. Pursuant to that policy shift, the East German government had set up a non-governmental body, the Committee of Anti-Fascist Resistance Fighters, to hold talks on the private claims of Jews. That committee was scheduled to meet first with the U.S. Federal Trade Commission and then with the Conference on Jewish Material Claims Against Germany, a private international organization based in New York City. The West German government had signed an agreement with the organization in 1952.

Traffic Dispute Delayed Diplomatic Recognition

Establishment of U.S.-East German ties had been postponed for a month in July, following difficulties with traffic entering West Berlin. The East German government had allegedly harassed traffic entering the city following the establishment of a West German government environmental office in the divided city. That West German move was interpreted by the East Germans as signaling a transfer of major West German government offices to West Berlin, action seen as threatening to the sovereignty of the East German regime. The United States had suspended the talks on diplomatic relations with East Germany on July 26, following reports of East German police stopping officials bound for the West German environmental office in West Berlin. And on July 31, East German representatives negotiating the new agreement in Washington, D.C., were asked by the State Department to leave the country. The delegates returned Sept. 2 following a resolution of the traffic dispute and signed the final accord Sept. 4. With the opening of U.S.-East German diplomatic relations, Canada became the only NATO country not to have established relations with the German Democratic Republic.

Following is the text of an announcement read to news correspondents on Aug. 30, by Robert Anderson, special assistant to the Secretary of State for press relations, and the text of the joint U.S.-German Democratic Republic communique, issued in Washington, D.C., on Sept. 4 follow-

ing the signing of the agreement between the two countries to establish diplomatic relations. The text of the actual agreement was not made available to the public:

DEPARTMENT ANNOUNCEMENT, AUGUST 30

A delegation from the German Democratic Republic will arrive in Washington on September 2 for meetings with representatives of the Department of State on matters relative to the establishment of diplomatic relations.

The visiting delegation will be headed by Ambassador Herbert Suss, member of the Directorate of the Foreign Ministry of the German Democratic Republic. Assistant Secretary of State for European Affairs Arthur A. Hartman will head the American delegation.

Negotiations between the United States and the German Democratic Republic on the establishment of relations commenced in Washington July 15 and were concluded on July 26.

A team of U.S. adminstrative experts visited Berlin in mid-August to continue to work on arrangements for a U.S. Embassy there. G.D.R. experts have been in Washington since the end of July working on similar arrangements for a G.D.R. Embassy.

TEXT OF JOINT COMMUNIQUE, SEPTEMBER 4

The Governments of the United States of America and the German Democratic Republic, having conducted negotiations in a cordial atmosphere in Washington July 15-26, 1974, have agreed to establish diplomatic relations as of today in accordance with the Vienna Convention on Diplomatic Relations of April 18, 1961 and to base the conduct of these relations on the Charter of the United Nations. The two Governments will exchange diplomatic representatives with the rank of Ambassador Extraordinary and Plenipotentiary.

The two delegations also exchanged views on the future development of relations between the two States. It was agreed that, pending the entry into force of a comprehensive consular agreement, their consular relations will be based in general on customary international law on consular relations. They also agreed to negotiate in the near future the settlement of claims and other financial matters outstanding between them.

Agreement was also reached on a number of practical questions concerning the establishment and future operation of their respective Embassies.

C.I.A. INVOLVEMENT IN CHILE
September 8, 1974

A controversy over U.S. political involvement in the domestic affairs of foreign governments was touched off Sept. 8 by reports that the director of the Central Intelligence Agency (CIA) had testified before a congressional committee that his organization had been authorized to spend more than $8-million in Chile in 1970-1973 to create conditions making it impossible for Marxist President Allende to govern. Allende had died in the military coup which toppled his government on Sept. 11, 1973. According to reports of the April 22, 1974, testimony of CIA Director William E. Colby before a secret session of the House Armed Services Subcommittee on Intelligence, the funds were authorized for covert support of political candidates and news media opposing Allende. The testimony came to light in a letter from Rep. Michael J. Harrington (D Mass.) to Rep. Thomas E. Morgan (D Pa.), chairman of the House Foreign Affairs Committee. The letter, dated July 18, was leaked to the press on Sept. 8.

President Ford acknowledged the CIA activities—a rare presidential admission—at a news conference Sept. 16. Ford said the funds had been used to strengthen opposition parties and newspapers which Allende had been trying to destroy. The President defended these covert activities as "in the best interests of the people of Chile and certainly in our best interests." Ford backed up previous statements of Secretary of State Henry A. Kissinger by insisting that the United States had "no involvement in any way whatsoever" in the coup overthrowing Allende. Kissinger told senators at a Senate Foreign Relations Committee hearing Sept. 19 that the CIA action had not been aimed at subverting the government of Chile, but rather at keeping opposition political parties and opposition media alive. Colby similarly denied Sept. 13 that the CIA had played any direct role in the coup, and he defended that agency's activities. "I think it would be mistaken to deprive our nation of the possibility of some moderate covert action response to a foreign problem and leave us with nothing between a diplomatic protest and sending in Marines," he said. Colby would not discuss any details of CIA activities in Chile, however.

Public Outcry Against CIA Activity

While President Ford, Kissinger and Colby sought to subdue the criticism of the CIA activity, legislators, editorial writers and foreign heads of state expressed their outrage. Rep. Harrington, whose letter had brought the controversy to light, said in his letter that the CIA involvement in Chile was "viewed [by the Nixon administration] as a prototype, or laboratory experiment, to test the techniques of heavy financial investment in efforts to discredit and bring down a government." A New York Times *editorial Sept. 8 said that Colby's testimony indicated that the White House and the State Department had "repeatedly and deliberately misled the public and the Congress about the extent of U.S. involvement in the internal affairs of Chile." Sen. Edward M. Kennedy (D Mass.) charged Sept. 9 that the CIA action represented "not only a flagrant violation of our alleged policy of non-intervention in Chilean affairs but also an appalling lack of forthrightness with the Congress." Sen. Frank Church (D Idaho) declared Sept. 11 that he had been "incensed" by Colby's testimony. Abroad, Cuban Premier Fidel Castro denounced Ford's defense of the CIA intervention, saying that the United States "openly proclaims the right to intervene by any means, no matter how illicit, dirty or criminal, in the internal processes of the nations of the hemisphere."*

More Details On CIA Actions

Following its editorial on CIA funding of opposition parties in Chile, the New York Times *reported Sept. 20 that CIA funds had been used specifically to subsidize strikes by Chilean middle class workers in 1972 and 1973, strikes that had been seen as a key element in the downfall of Allende's government. On Sept. 24, the* Times *reported that the CIA subsidizing of strikers was part of a "get rougher" policy advanced by the Nixon administration following Allende's announcement that nationalized U.S. copper firms would not be compensated and U.S. intelligence reports that Cuban munitions were being smuggled to Chilean leftists.*

Following are excerpts from the letter sent by Rep. Michael J. Harrington (D Mass.) July 18, 1974, to House Foreign Affairs Committee Chairman Thomas Morgan (D Pa.) expressing concern over CIA activity in Chile:

Dear Mr. Chairman:

As you know, for sometime I have been actively interested in the development of United States foreign policy toward Chile, and particularly since the overthrow of the Allende government on September 11, 1973 and my visit to that country shortly thereafter. It is my purpose in writing to discuss some of the fruits of my endeavors in that direction, which I feel pose serious questions about the manner in which our current relations with Chile evolved, how our policies there were implemented, and how Congress has exercised its oversight function. I request that you bear with me on the length of this letter, since I feel that the importance of its subject matter requires a detailed and comprehensive presentation of the evolution of my present concern.

No doubt you are familiar with numerous reports, dating from the time of Salvador Allende's election as President in 1970, alleging that the United States government played an active role in trying to influence Chilean politics. Immediately after the military coup last October, further reports appeared which indicated that the United States was involved, either directly or indirectly. At that time, I made a very brief trip to Chile which enabled me to gain a sense of the prevailing attitude there and helped add some substance to my earlier impression that the United States had engaged in political and economic destabilization efforts that eventually led to President Allende's downfall.

Since that time, I have repeatedly tried to focus attention in Congress on the origins of American policy toward the Allende government to determine its possible influence in the eventual course of events in Chile. In particular, I was concerned with the activities of the Treasury Department and the Central Intelligence Agency, the latter of which is the subject of quite limited Congressional review that is perfunctory and comes after the fact....[M]y efforts have not been productive of any substantial inquiries into our policies toward the Allende government. Instead, the few hearings that have been held focused largely on the internal situation in Chile and allegations of denials of civil and judicial rights....

Following the September 25, 1973 hearing, Chairman Fascell issued a statement which read: "...the [Inter-American Affairs] Subcommittee will hold additional hearings on Chile in the near future. We intend to conduct a full scale investigation of United States policy toward Chile." The committed language of that statement has not been pursued, despite a series of conversations between my office and the Subcommittee both at the staff level and between Chairman Fascell and myself. Finally, a request made in writing by me on March 7, 1974 to Chairman Fascell that he hold hearings on U.S. activities in Chile resulted in an inconclusive exchange of letters over three months, with the end result that the Subcommittee has promised two days of hearings, possibly sometime this summer, with non-government witnesses.

The one possible opportunity that was afforded to probe United States policies toward Chile occurred during the Subcommittee executive session testimony in October, 1973 of CIA director William Colby, who unfortunately refused to respond fully to questions of CIA activities in Chile, citing the jurisdiction of the Armed Services Committee. With little expectation that tangible results would follow because of its past deference to the CIA in such matters, I turned to the Special Subcommittee on Intelligence of the House Armed Services Committee. In my letter of April 2, 1974 to Chairman Nedzi, a copy of which is also attached, I recounted the reluctance of CIA Director William Colby to fully testify before the Foreign Affairs Committee and requested that Chairman Nedzi's Subcommittee hold hearings to question Mr. Colby directly as to covert CIA operations in Chile.

Mr. Colby testified on April 22, 1974 and after some delay, largely due to Chairman Nedzi's desire to obtain clearance from Chairman Hebert, I was notified on or about June 1, 1974 that I would be given access to the transcript. I read the hearing transcript once on June 5 and again on June 12, and the information contained in the Colby testimony convinced me that it is of critical importance for the Congress and the American people to learn the full truth of American activities in Chile. I wish to share this information with you, in the hope that you will feel the same sense of conviction that I experienced upon learning the full details of significant U.S. activities in the affairs of another country without any prior consultation of even the committee charged with overseeing such operations. In fact, actual formal notification of that committee came seemingly as an afterthought, and only after my request was made, many months after the operations had been conducted.

While my memory must serve here as the only source for the substance of the testimony, I submit the following summary of its contents as an indication of what transpired in Chile.

The testimony was given on April 22, 1974 by Mr. Colby, who was accompanied by a Mr. Phillips, who was apparently the Latin American specialist of the CIA. Also in attendance were Chairman Nedzi and Frank Slatinshek, Chief Counsel of the House Armed Services Committee. Approximately one-third of the 48 pages of testimony is devoted to exposition by Mr. Colby of a continuous Central Intelligence Agency involvement in the internal politics of Chile from 1962 through 1973. Most of the remainder of the testimony provides a description of the methods employed by the CIA in conducting such operations, focusing on the details of how activities in Chile were accomplished.

Over the 1962 to 1973 period, the Forty Committee (an inter-departmental body that reviews and authorizes all covert CIA activities and is chaired by the President's Advisor on National Security Affairs) authorized the expenditure of approximately $11 million to help prevent the election of Allende and, in Mr. Colby's words, "destabilize" the Allende government so as to precipitate its downfall. The agency activities in Chile were viewed as a prototype, or laboratory experiment, to test the techniques of heavy financial investment in efforts to discredit and bring down a government.

Funding was provided to individuals, political parties, and media outlets in Chile, through channels in other countries in both Latin America and Europe. Mr. Colby's description of these operations was direct, though not to the point of identifying actual contacts and conduits.

A total of $3 million was sent in 1964 to the Christian Democratic Party in Chile that was opposing Allende in the national elections. Also in 1964, unidentified American corporations suggested that the CIA serve as a conduit for corporate funds that would finance anti-Allende activities, but that idea was rejected as unworkable. Approximately $500,000 was authorized in 1969 to fund individuals who could be nurtured to keep the anti-Allende forces active and intact.

During the 1970 election, in which Allende eventually was elected President, $500,000 was given to opposition party personnel. An expenditure of $350,000 was authorized to bribe the Chilean Congress, which at that time was faced with deciding a run-off election between Allende and the opposition candidate. The bribe would have been part of a scheme to overturn the results of the election in which Allende had gained a plurality, but that plan, although originally approved by the Forty Committee, was later evaluated as unworkable.

The testimony indicates that the Agency role in 1970 was viewed as that of the "spoiler," involving general attempts to politically destabilize the country and discredit Allende to improve the likelihood that an opposition candidate would win.

Following the election of Allende, $5 million was authorized by the Forty Committee for more destabilization efforts during the period from 1971 to 1973. An additional $1.5 million was spent for the 1973 municipal elections. Some of these funds were used to support an unnamed but influential anti-Allende newspaper.

Although a specific request in the summer of 1973 for $50,000 to assist the trucker's strike was turned down, the Forty Committee did authorize in August, 1973 an expenditure of $1 million for further political destabilization activities. This final authorization came without any apparent deterrent being posed by the recently completed hearings into ITT involvement in Chile and the Senate Watergate Committee's disclosure of CIA activities related to Watergate.

The full plan authorized in August was called off when the military coup occurred less than one month later. In the aftermath of the coup, however, funds that had been committed were spent. These included $25,000 to one individual to purchase a radio station and $9,000 to finance a trip to other Latin American capitals to reassure them about the new military leaders.

Since learning this information, I have attempted once again to induce some Members to pursue the facts of our involvement in the Chilean situation to determine how those policies evolved and how they can be justified as being in the national interest. I have had a reasonably extended conversation with Congressman Fraser, and briefer ones with Congressmen Fascell and Hamilton, in which I described what I learned from the Colby testimony. While they were indeed distressed at the details of CIA operations, nothing was forthcoming as a result of those conversations that leads me to believe that there would be further investigations or hearings into the broader policy questions that such activities pose.

I turn to you as a last resort, having despaired of the likelihood of anything productive occurring as a result of the avenues I have already pursued. It is indicative of my frustrations to note that in the five meetings this year of the Subcommittee on Inter-American Affairs, which focused on human rights in Chile, only one government witness with knowledge of U.S. activities in Chile appeared. At that hearing, Congressman Fraser and I questioned Deputy Assistant Secretary of State Harry Shlaudeman on possible CIA involvement in Chile while he was stationed there as Deputy Chief of Mission from 1969 through mid-1973. His answers, a transcript of which is attached, indicated to me some knowledge on his part of CIA activities that he was unwilling to discuss before a duly-constituted Committee of the House. The inherent limitations facing Members of Congress in uncovering the facts of covert activities such as those in Chile requires, I believe, a commitment by those in a position to act beyond the existing, illusory oversight machinery.

At his confirmation hearings on July 2, 1973, Director Colby said:

> "We are not going to run the kind of Intelligence service that other countries run. We are going to run one in the American society and the American constitutional structure, and I can see that there may be a requirement to expose to the American people a great deal more than might be convenient from the narrow intelligence point of view."

I feel it is time to hold Mr. Colby to his commitment, as the Congress and the American people have a right to learn what was done in our name in Chile. Much as I would prefer to see this accomplishment within the channels of the Congressional process, its importance convinces me that our very system of government requires that knowledge of American activities in Chile not remain solely with a handful of officials and Members of Congress. Therefore, I urge you to promptly turn this matter to the attention of the Foreign Affairs Committee for a complete, public investigation of United States relations with Chile. I trust that you will agree that the importance of this matter and its implications for future foreign policies of the United States demands no less.

Yours sincerely,
S/Michael J. Harrington

THE NIXON PARDON
September 8, 1974

In an act of mercy which raised more questions than it resolved, President Ford, on Sunday morning, Sept. 8, granted former President Richard M. Nixon a "full, free and absolute pardon...for all offenses against the United States which he...has committed or may have committed" during his years as president. In a statement from his California home, Nixon accepted the pardon, saying that he would for the rest of his life bear the burden "that the way I tried to deal with Watergate was the wrong way." (Impeachment Articles, p. 655-660, House Judiciary Report, p. 713, Senate Watergate Report, p. 599-619.) *Later, White House Counsel Philip W. Buchen, who oversaw the negotiations with Nixon leading up to the pardon announcement, said that the granting of a pardon "can imply guilt—there is no other reason for granting a pardon." He said that he had so advised President Ford. A spokesman for Watergate Special Prosecutor Leon Jaworski said that the special prosecutor, who did not take part in the decision, accepted it as a constitutional exercise of the President's constitutional power "to grant reprieves and pardons for offenses against the United States, except in cases of impeachment." With that exercise of his power, Ford ended the month-long honeymoon he had enjoyed with Congress and the American people, reopening the questions of Watergate for the upcoming elections and setting off a barrage of criticism of the new President.*

Ford's credibility, one of his strong points, was called into question by his pardon of the former President. Earlier—during his confirmation hearings in 1973 and in response to a question Aug. 28—he had indicated his intention to await the working of the judicial process before considering the exercise of the pardon power. But, he said, in his Sept. 8 statement, cer-

tain difficult decisions "do not look at all the same as the hypothetical questions that I have answered freely and perhaps too fast on previous occasions." Stating his desire to end the "American tragedy" of Nixon and Watergate, Ford said he would follow his conscience, not the public opinion polls. Newsweek magazine reported Sept. 8 that 58 per cent of the American people polled opposed giving Nixon any immunity from prosecution.

"Serious allegations and accusations hang like a sword over our former President's head and threaten his health as he tries to reshape his life, a great part of which was spent in the service of this country," Ford said, referring obliquely to continuing reports of Nixon's unstable mental and physical health in the weeks since his resignation. Through the week, reports mounted of Nixon's depression and ill health, the latter reportedly related to a recurrence of the phlebitis which had affected him earlier in the summer. A month and a half after the pardon, Nixon underwent surgery due to his phlebitis.

In light of the intense publicity of Watergate and impeachment, it would be months or years before Nixon could get a fair jury trial, said Ford. "[A] former President of the United States, instead of enjoying equal treatment with any other citizens accused of violating the law, would be cruelly and excessively penalized either in preserving the presumption of his innocence or in obtaining a speedy determination of his guilt." For the nation's good and because Nixon and his family had suffered enough, Ford therefore signed the statement granting Nixon his pardon.

Criticism of Ford's Pardon of Nixon

Reaction to Ford's pardon of the former President was immediate and largely negative, with the exception of some congressional Republicans who said Ford had tempered justice with mercy. Sen. Edward W. Brooke (R Mass.), the first Republican senator to call publicly for Nixon's resignation, issued a statement Sept. 8, labeling Ford's "blanket pardon without Mr. Nixon's full confession of his involvement in the Watergate scandal, a serious mistake." Democrats questioned the fairness of the pardon to other Watergate figures who had been convicted or faced trial. They said it created a double standard of justice and made it impossible for the nation ever to learn the full story of the Watergate affair. Senate Majority Whip Robert C. Byrd (D W.Va.) said the pardon "demonstrates that someone is above the law" and revives "the lack of faith in government." Sen. Sam J. Ervin Jr. (D N.C.), who had presided over the Senate Watergate hearings during the summer of 1973 (see p. 599-619, Historic Documents 1973, p. 549-556, 659-679, 697-701), called the pardon "expedient, incompatible with good government and bad precedent for the future."

Even within Republican ranks, there were differences of opinion on the pardon. House Republican Leader John J. Rhodes (Ariz.) remarked: "No *man is above the law. But the law is purposely flexible so as to accommodate varying degrees of reality and circumstance." Sen. Robert Taft Jr. (R Ohio) said that by granting the pardon President Ford "had taken another step in putting Watergate behind us." But Rep. Wiley Mayne (R Iowa), a member of the House Judiciary Committee said that his "first impression is that [the pardon] is premature and might well have been deferred" until Special Prosecutor Jaworski indicated what action he would take against the former President. Sen. Howard H. Baker Jr. (R Tenn.), who had served as vice-chairman of the Senate Watergate Committee, expressed the "possibility that this may reopen a caustic and divisive debate in the country." And Sen. Robert W. Packwood (R Ore.) declared: "I don't think Ford should have done it. No man is literally above the law."*

Critics were further outraged by the White House announcement, soon after the pardon, that the expected decision by Ford on some form of amnesty for draft evaders and deserters from the Vietnam war—set to come Sept. 10—would be postponed because of Ford's involvement in the negotiations leading up to Nixon's pardon. The White House later said that some decision on this matter would be reached by the end of September. (Amnesty proposal, see p. 819-831.) And the criticism mounted even higher Sept. 10 when acting White House Press Secretary John W. Hushen said that he was authorized to say that pardons for all the Watergate defendants were under consideration by Ford. The White House retreated the next day, saying Ford was not considering a blanket pardon but would consider individual requests for pardons on their merits, after the individuals involved were tried. A few hours after the White House announcement the Senate, by a vote of 55-24 Sept. 11, adopted a resolution expressing the sense of the Senate that no future pardons should be granted to Watergate defendants until after they were tried, found guilty and had exhausted all appeals.

A Question of Timing

Little question was raised of Ford's power to pardon Nixon, even before any indictment was filed. The questions—and the criticism— were aimed instead at his timing and the wisdom of his short-circuiting the judicial processes already at work. It was later revealed that before announcing the pardon, Ford had asked for and received from Jaworski's office a list of the matters under investigation other than the Watergate coverup possibly involving the former President. They included the question of his tax deductions for the disallowed gift of pre-presidential papers, obstruction of justice in the Pentagon Papers trial, the concealing of FBI wiretap records at the White House, certain wiretaps of White House aides, misuse of the Internal Revenue Service, the dairy industry campaign contribution pledge and the increase in milk price supports, the challenge to The Washington Post ownership of two television stations, false testimony to the Senate about the settlement of the International Telephone and Telegraph Corp. antitrust case and the handling of certain campaign contributions.

*Concerning all the items but the coverup, Deputy Special Prosecutor Henry
S. Ruth Jr. had stated to Jaworski in a memo that "none of these matters at
the moment rises to the level of our ability to prove even a probable
criminal violation by Mr. Nixon."*

Additional Fall-Out: Two Resignations

*Two resignations quickly followed Ford's announcement. The first was
that of his press secretary and long-time friend, Jerald F. terHorst. The
second, Sept. 9, was that of Philip A. Lacovara, counsel to Jaworski and a
lifetime Republican. During the week Jaworski denied rumors that his own
resignation was imminent. By foreclosing the strong possibility—implied
in Ford's Sept. 8 statement—that Nixon would have been indicted had he
not been pardoned, the pardon created considerable consternation within
the office of the special prosecutor and within the ranks of the grand jury
which had earlier named Nixon an unindicted co-conspirator in the
Watergate coverup. (See p. 225-232.) Lacovara, who had assisted Jaworski
in arguing the historic tapes case before the Supreme Court in July and
who had come to that post from the office of the solicitor general in the
Justice Department, said that he resigned as a result of Ford's decision to
pardon Nixon. Jaworski announced Oct. 12 that he would resign as special
Watergate prosecutor effective Oct. 25. Saying that "the bulk of the work"
was "discharged," he denied his action was connected with Ford's pardon of
Nixon.*

*Following are the texts of President Ford's Sept. 8 state-
ment pardoning former President Nixon, the proclamation
by which Ford pardoned Nixon, and former President
Nixon's Sept. 8 statement issued following Ford's pardon:*

President Ford's Pardon of Nixon

Ladies and gentlemen, I have come to a decision which I felt I should tell
you, and all of my fellow American citizens, as soon as I was certain in my
own mind and in my own conscience that it was the right thing to do.

I have learned already in this office that the difficult decisions always
come to this desk. I must admit that many of them do not look at all the
same as the hypothetical questions that I have answered freely and
perhaps too fast on previous occasions. My customary policy is to try and
get all the facts and to consider the opinions of my countrymen and to take
counsel with my most valued friends. But these seldom agree, and in the
end the decision is mine.

To procrastinate, to agonize and to wait for a more favorable turn of
events that may never come, or more compelling external pressures that
may as well be wrong as right, is itself a decision of sorts and a weak course
for a President to follow.

I have promised to uphold the Constitution, to do what is right as God
gives me to see the right, and to do the very best that I can for America. I

have asked your help and your prayers not only when I became President, but many times since.

The Constitution is the supreme law of our land and it governs our actions as citizens. Only the laws of God, which govern our consciences, are superior to it. As we are a nation under God, so I am sworn to uphold our laws with the help of God. And I have sought such guidance and searched my own conscience with special diligence to determine the right thing for me to do with respect to my predecessor in this place, Richard Nixon, and his loyal wife and family.

Theirs is an American tragedy in which we all have played a part. It could go on and on and on, or someone must write "The End" to it.

I have concluded that only I can do that. And if I can, I must.

There are no historic or legal precedents to which I can turn in this matter, none that precisely fit the circumstances of a private citizen who has resigned the presidency of the United States. But it is common knowledge that serious allegations and accusations hang like a sword over our former President's head, threatening his health, as he tries to reshape his life, a great part of which was spent in the service of this country and by the mandate of its people.

After years of bitter controversy and divisive national debate, I have been advised and I am compelled to conclude that many months and perhaps more years will have to pass before Richard Nixon could obtain a fair trial by jury in any jurisdiction of the United States under governing decisions of the Supreme Court.

I deeply believe in equal justice for all Americans, whatever their station or former station. The law, whether human or divine, is no respecter of persons but the law is a respecter of reality. The facts as I see them are that a former President of the United States, instead of enjoying equal treatment with any other citizen accused of violating the law, would be cruelly and excessively penalized either in preserving the presumption of his innocence or in obtaining a speedy determination of his guilt in order to repay a legal debt to society.

During this long period of delay and potential litigation, ugly passions would again be aroused, and our people would again be polarized in their opinions, and the credibility of our free institutions of government would again be challenged at home and abroad. In the end, the courts might well hold that Richard Nixon had been denied due process and the verdict of history would even more be inconclusive with respect to those charges arising out of the period of his presidency of which I am presently aware.

But it is not the ultimate fate of Richard Nixon that most concerns me—though surely it deeply troubles every decent and every compassionate person. My concern is the immediate future of this great country. In this I dare not depend upon my personal sympathy as a longtime friend of the former President nor my professional judgment as a lawyer. And I do not.

As President, my primary concern must always be the greatest good of all the people of the United States, whose servant I am.

As a man, my first consideration is to be true to my own convictions and my own conscience.

My conscience tells me clearly and certainly that I cannot prolong the bad dreams that continue to reopen a chapter that is closed. My conscience tells me that only I, as President, have the constitutional power to firmly shut and seal this book. My conscience says it is my duty, not merely to proclaim domestic tranquility, but to use every means that I have to ensure it.

I do believe that the buck stops here, that I cannot rely upon public opinion polls to tell me what is right. I do believe that right makes might, and that if I am wrong 10 angels swearing I was right would make no difference. I do believe with all my heart and mind and spirit that I, not as President, but as a humble servant of God, will receive justice without mercy if I fail to show mercy.

Finally, I feel that Richard Nixon and his loved ones have suffered enough, and will continue to suffer no matter what I do, no matter what we as a great and good nation can do together to make his goal of peace come true.

Now, therefore, I, Gerald R. Ford, President of the United States, pursuant to the pardon power conferred upon me by Article II, Section 2, of the Constitution, have granted and by these presents do grant a full, free, and absolute pardon unto Richard Nixon for all offenses against the United States which he, Richard Nixon, has committed or may have committed or taken part in during the period from January 20, 1969, through August 9, 1974.

In witness whereof, I have hereunto set my hand this 8th day of September in the year of our Lord Nineteen Hundred Seventy Four, and of the independence of the United States of America the 199th.

Pardon Proclamation

Richard Nixon became the thirty-seventh President of the United States on January 20, 1969, and was re-elected in 1972 for a second term by the electors of forty-nine of the fifty states. His term in office continued until his resignation on August 9, 1974.

Pursuant to resolutions of the House of Representatives, its Committee on the Judiciary conducted an inquiry and investigation on the impeachment of the President extending over more than eight months. The hearings of the committee and its deliberations, which received wide national publicity over television, radio, and in printed media, resulted in votes adverse to Richard Nixon on recommended articles of impeachment.

As a result of certain acts or omissions occurring before his resignation from the office of President, Richard Nixon has become liable to possible indictment and trial for offenses against the United States. Whether or not he shall be so prosecuted depends on findings of the appropriate grand jury and on the discretion of the authorized prosecutor. Should an indictment ensue, the accused shall then be entitled to a fair trial by an impartial jury, as guaranteed to every individual by the Constitution.

It is believed that a trial of Richard Nixon, if it became necessary, could not fairly begin until a year or more has elapsed. In the meantime, the tranquility to which this nation has been restored by the events of recent weeks could be irreparably lost by the prospects of bringing to trial a former President of the United States. The prospects of such trial will cause prolonged and divisive debate over the propriety of exposing to further punishment and degradation a man who has already paid the unprecedented penalty of relinquishing the highest elective office in the United States.

Now, therefore, I, Gerald R. Ford, President of the United States, pursuant to the pardon power conferred upon me by Article II, Section 2, of the Constitution, have granted and by these presents do grant a full, free, and absolute pardon unto Richard Nixon for all offenses against the United States which he, Richard Nixon, has committed or may have committed or taken part in during the period from January 20, 1969, through August 9, 1974.

In witness whereof, I have hereunto set my hand this 8th day of September in the year of Our Lord Nineteen Hundred Seventy-Four, and of the independence of the United States of America the 199th.

Text of Nixon's Statement

I have been informed that President Ford has granted me a full and absolute pardon for any charges which might be brought against me for actions taken during the time I was President of the United States.

In accepting this pardon, I hope that his compassionate act will contribute to lifting the burden of Watergate from our country.

Here in California, my perspective on Watergate is quite different than it was while I was embattled in the midst of the controversy, and while I was still subject to the unrelenting daily demands of the presidency itself.

Looking back on what is still in my mind a complex and confusing maze of events, decisions, pressures and personalities, one thing I can see clearly now is that I was wrong in not acting more decisively and more forthrightly in dealing with Watergate, particularly when it reached the stage of judicial proceedings and grew from a political scandal into a national tragedy.

No words can describe the depths of my regret and pain at the anguish my mistakes over Watergate have caused the nation and the presidency—a nation I so deeply love and an institution I so greatly respect.

I know many fair-minded people believe that my motivations and action in the Watergate affair were intentionally self-serving and illegal. I now understand how my own mistakes and misjudgments have contributed to that belief and seemed to support it. This burden is the heaviest one of all to bear.

That the way I tried to deal with Watergate was the wrong way is a burden I shall bear for every day of the life that is left to me.

FORD'S VIETNAM AMNESTY PLAN
September 16, 1974

Seeking to "bind the nation's wounds," President Ford proclaimed a plan
Sept. 16 whereby Vietnam war draft evaders and military deserters could
wipe their records clean by swearing allegiance to the United States and
performing up to 24 months of low-paid alternate service. The primary purpose of the "earned re-entry" clemency offer was, said Ford, "the reconciliation of all our people and the restoration of the essential unity of
Americans within which honest differences of opinion do not descend to
angry discord, and mutual problems are not polarized by excessive
passion." The President said the reconciliation would not require that the
"serious offense" of desertion or evasion be condoned, but that it would call
for "an act of mercy to...heal the scars of divisiveness." But while Ford
sought to reunite the country through the reconciliation plan, he instead
generated largely critical comment about the program.

Ford had touched off the controversy Aug. 19 when he disclosed to a
hostile audience, the Veterans of Foreign Wars, his intention to institute a
conditional amnesty program. The debate intensified after the Sept. 16 announcement of the plan as amnesty advocates and opponents alike united
in condemning Ford's clemency offer. Advocates of amnesty voiced objections that Ford's approach to military evaders and deserters was fraught
with conditions and regulations while the President's pardon of former
President Richard M. Nixon had been full and absolute. (Ford's pardon of
Nixon, see p. 811-817.) Opponents of amnesty countered that men who had
either fled the country rather than meet their military obligation or
deserted the military once enlisted should be dealt with more seriously
than would be done under Ford's program. Many such opponents of amnes-

ty advocated military court-martials or prison terms for those who had refused to serve.

Reconciliation Plan

Using the words "reconciliation" and "clemency" to describe the plan rather than "amnesty," which meant a pardon, the White House gave Vietnam war draft evaders and military deserters, convicted and unconvicted, until Jan. 31, 1975, to report to the Justice Department or to military authorities to request clemency. The plan offered three choices to returning men. By the first, evaders and deserters could swear allegiance to the United States and present their cases to a newly named clemency board which would review them and decide whether to recommend a complete pardon or prescribe alternate service in hospitals, prisons or other needy areas. President Ford would make the final decisions on pardons. Under the second, described by the Defense Department as a "loophole," a returning deserter could accept an undesirable discharge which would automatically place him outside the Uniform Code of Military Justice and thus relieve him of any obligation to work for clemency. By contrast, draft evaders would remain subject to prosecution under civilian laws if they reneged on their commitment to perform alternate service. The third option under the plan was inaction: draft resisters or military deserters could remain in jail or stay abroad or in hiding, mindful that they were liable for prosecution if they were ever apprehended in the United States.

Men Subject to Clemency

The number of persons subject to clemency was open to question. The White House said approximately 15,500 draft evaders were "potentially eligible," including 8,700 already convicted. About 4,350 were under indictment, including 4,060 listed as fugitives. Some 3,000 were estimated to be living in Canada. Another 2,250 individuals were under investigation for draft law violations. Of the 141 convicted evaders currently under sentence, 46 were free on appeals. Estimates varied even more widely as to the number of deserters. The White House said that there were 500,000 "incidents of desertion," absence without leave of 30 days or more, during the Vietnam era. At House amnesty hearings in March, the American Civil Liberties Union estimated there were 30,000 to 50,000 deserters or evaders living in exile. Other estimates ranged as high as 100,000.

Reaction

Advocates of blanket amnesty protested that deserters and draft resisters who acted out of conscience should not have to be contrite or required to earn amnesty for protesting an immoral war. In the first week after clemency was offered, few of those men who fled the country to avoid service had signaled an intention to return under Ford's conditions. Many draft resisters maintained that Ford's offer of conditional amnesty reduced the chances of unconditional amnesty some time in the future.

Veterans' organizations, retired military officials and some members of Congress stood fast in their insistence that deserters and evaders broke the law and should be punished. They also criticized Ford's choice of former Sen. Charles E. Goodell (R N.Y., 1968-71) as chairman of a Presidential Clemency Board to review cases of men already convicted by military or civilian courts. As a senator, Goodell had been so opposed to the Vietnam war that the Nixon administration helped to engineer his defeat. One of the strongest criticisms came from Sen. Barry Goldwater (R Ariz.), who deplored Ford's action as a "step that is like throwing mud in the faces of the millions of men who have served this country."

Following are the texts of President Ford's speech Sept. 16 announcing the conditional amnesty program, the official proclamation of the program, the executive order establishing the clemency board, and fact sheets issued by the White House explaining the reconciliation plan:

Program for the Return of Vietnam Era Draft Evaders and Military Deserters

The President's Remarks announcing the Program. September 16, 1974

Good morning:

In my first week as President, I asked the Attorney General and the Secretary of Defense to report to me, after consultation with other Governmental officials and private citizens concerned, on the status of those young Americans who have been convicted, charged, investigated, or are still being sought as draft evaders or military deserters.

On August 19, at the national convention of Veterans of Foreign Wars in the city of Chicago, I announced my intention to give these young people a chance to earn their return to the mainstream of American society so that they can, if they choose, contribute, even though belatedly, to the building and the betterment of our country and the world.

I did this for the simple reason that for American fighting men, the long and divisive war in Vietnam has been over for more than a year, and I was determined then, as now, to do everything in my power to bind up the Nation's wounds.

I promised to throw the weight of my Presidency into the scales of justice on the side of leniency and mercy, but I promised also to work within the existing system of military and civilian law and the precedents set by my predecessors who faced similar postwar situations, among them Presidents Abraham Lincoln and Harry S Truman.

My objective of making future penalties fit the seriousness of each individual's offense and of mitigating punishment already meted out in a spirit of equity has proved an immensely hard and very complicated matter, even more difficult than I knew it would be.

But the agencies of Government concerned and my own staff have worked with me literally night and day in order to develop fair and orderly procedures and completed their work for my final approval over this last weekend.

I do not want to delay another day in resolving the dilemmas of the past, so that we may all get going on the pressing problems of the present. Therefore, I am today signing the necessary Presidential proclamation and Executive orders that will put this plan into effect.

The program provides for administrative disposition of cases involving draft evaders and military deserters not yet convicted or punished. In such cases, 2 months of alternate service will be required which may be reduced for mitigating circumstances.

The program also deals with cases of those already convicted by a civilian or military court. For the latter purpose, I am establishing a Clemency Review Board of nine distinguished Americans whose duty it will be to assist me in assuring that the Government's forgiveness is extended to applicable cases of prior conviction as equitably and as impartially as is humanly possible.

The primary purpose of this program is the reconciliation of all our people and the restoration of the essential unity of Americans within which honest differences of opinion do not descend to angry discord and mutual problems are not polarized by excessive passion.

My sincere hope is that this is a constructive step toward a calmer and cooler appreciation of our individual rights and responsibilities and our common purpose as a nation whose future is always more important than its past.

At this point, I will sign the proclamation that I mentioned in my statement, followed by an Executive order for the establishment of the Clemency Board, followed by the signing of an Executive order for the Director of Selective Service, who will have a prime responsibility in the handling of the matters involving alternate service.

Thank you very much.

Program for the Return of Vietnam Era Draft Evaders and Military Deserters

Proclamation 4313. September 16, 1974

By the President of the United States of America a Proclamation

The United States withdrew the last of its forces from the Republic of Vietnam on March 28, 1973.

In the period of its involvement in armed hostilities in Southeast Asia, the United States suffered great losses. Millions served their country, thousands died in combat, thousands more were wounded, others are still listed as missing in action.

Over a year after the last American combatant had left Vietnam, the status of thousands of our countrymen—convicted, charged, investigated or still sought for violations of the Military Selective Service Act or of the Uniform Code of Military Justice—remains unresolved.

In furtherance of our national commitment to justice and mercy these young Americans should have the chance to contribute a share to the rebuilding of peace among ourselves and with all nations. They should be allowed the opportunity to earn return to their country, their communities, and their families, upon their agreement to a period of alternate service in the national interest, together with an acknowledgement of their allegiance to the country and its Constitution.

Desertion in time of war is a major, serious offense; failure to respond to the country's call for duty is also a serious offense. Reconciliation among our people does not require that these acts be condoned. Yet, reconciliation calls for an act of mercy to bind the Nation's wounds and to heal the scars of divisiveness.

NOW, THEREFORE, I, GERALD R. FORD, President of the United States, pursuant to my powers under Article II, Sections 1, 2 and 3 of the Constitution, do hereby proclaim a program to commence immediately to afford reconciliation to Vietnam era draft evaders and military deserters upon the following terms and conditions:

1. *Draft Evaders*—An individual who allegedly unlawfully failed under the Military Selective Service Act or any rule or regulation promulgated thereunder, to register or register on time, to keep the local board informed of his current address, to report for or submit to preinduction or induction examination, to report for or submit to induction itself, or to report for or submit to, or complete service under Section 6(j) of such Act during the period from August 4, 1964 to March 28, 1973, inclusive, and who has not been adjudged guilty in a trial for such offense, will be relieved of prosecution and punishment for such offense if he:

(i) presents himself to a United States Attorney before January 31, 1975,

(ii) executes an agreement acknowledging his allegiance to the United States and pledging to fulfill a period of alternate service under the auspices of the Director of Selective Service, and

(iii) satisfactorily completes such service.

The alternate service shall promote the national health, safety, or interest. No draft evader will be given the privilege of completing a period of alternate service by service in the Armed Forces.

However, this program will not apply to an individual who is precluded from re-entering the United States under 8 U.S.C. 1182(a) (22) or other law. Additionally, if individuals eligible for this program have other criminal charges outstanding, their participation in the program may be conditioned upon, or postponed until after, final disposition of the other charges has been reached in accordance with law.

The period of service shall be twenty-four months, which may be reduced by the Attorney General because of mitigating circumstances.

2. *Military Deserters*—A member of the armed forces who has been administratively classified as a deserter by reason of unauthorized absence and whose absence commenced during the period from August 4, 1964 to March 28, 1973, inclusive, will be relieved of prosecution and punishment under Articles 85, 86 and 87 of the Uniform Code of Military Justice for such absence and for offenses directly related thereto if before January 31, 1975 he takes an oath of allegiance to the United States and executes an agreement with the Secretary of the Military Department from which he absented himself or for members of the Coast Guard, with the Secretary of Transportation, pledging to fulfill a period of alternate service under the auspices of the Director of Selective Service. The alternate service shall promote the national health, safety, or interest.

The period of service shall be twenty-four months, which may be reduced by the Secretary of the appropriate Military Department, or Secretary of Transportation for members of the Coast Guard, because of mitigating circumstances.

However, if a member of the armed forces has additional outstanding charges pending against him under the Uniform Code of Military Justice, his eligibility to participate in this program may be conditioned upon, or postponed until after, final disposition of the additional charges has been reached in accordance with the law.

Each member of the armed forces who elects to seek relief through this program will receive an undesirable discharge. Thereafter, upon satisfactory completion of a period of alternate service prescribed by the Military Department or Department of Transportation, such individual will be entitled to receive, in lieu of his undesirable discharge, a clemency discharge in recognition of his fulfillment of the requirements of the program. Such clemency discharge shall not bestow entitlement to benefits administered by the Veterans Administration.

Procedures of the Military Departments implementing this Proclamation will be in accordance with guidelines established by the Secretary of Defense, present Military Department regulations notwithstanding.

3. *Presidential Clemency Board*—By Executive Order I have this date established a Presidential Clemency Board which will review the records of individuals within the following categories: (i) those who have been convicted of draft evasion offenses as described above, (ii) those who have received a punitive or undesirable discharge from service in the armed forces for having violated Article 85, 86, or 87 of the Uniform Code of Military Justice between August 4, 1964 and March 28, 1973, or are serving sentences of confinement for such violations. Where appropriate, the Board may recommend that clemency be conditioned upon completion of a period of alternate service. However, if any clemency discharge is recommended,

such discharge shall not bestow entitlement to benefits administered by the Veterans Administration.

4. *Alternate Service*—In prescribing the length of alternate service in individual cases, the Attorney General, the Secretary of the appropriate Department, or the Clemency Board shall take into account such honorable service as an individual may have rendered prior to his absence, penalties already paid under law, and such other mitigating factors as may be appropriate to seek equity among those who participate in this program.

IN WITNESS WHEREOF, I have herunto set my hand this sixteenth day of September in the year of our Lord nineteen hundred seventy-four, and of the Independence of the United States of America the one hundred and ninety-ninth.

GERALD R. FORD

Presidential Clemency Board

Executive Order 11803. September 16, 1974

ESTABLISHING A CLEMENCY BOARD TO REVIEW CERTAIN CONVICTIONS OF PERSONS UNDER SECTION 12 OR 6(j) OF THE MILITARY SELECTIVE SERVICE ACT AND CERTAIN DISCHARGES ISSUED BECAUSE OF, AND CERTAIN CONVICTIONS FOR, VIOLATIONS OF ARTICLE 85, 86 OR 87 OF THE UNIFORM CODE OF MILITARY JUSTICE AND TO MAKE RECOMMENDATIONS FOR EXECUTIVE CLEMENCY WITH RESPECT THERETO

By virtue of the authority vested in me as President of the United States by Section 2 of Article II of the Constitution of the United States, and in the interest of the internal management of the Government, it is ordered as follows:

SECTION 1. There is hereby established in the Executive Office of the President a board of 9 members, which shall be known as the Presidential Clemency Board. The members of the Board shall be appointed by the President, who shall also designate its Chairman.

SECTION 2. The Board, under such regulations as it may prescribe, shall examine the cases of persons who apply for Executive clemency prior to January 31, 1975, and who (i) have been convicted of violating Section 12 or 6(j) of the Military Selective Service Act (50 App. U.S.C. § 462), or of any rule or regulation promulgated pursuant to that section, for acts committed between August 4, 1964 and March 28, 1973, inclusive, or (ii) have received punitive or undesirable discharges as a consequence of violations of Article 85, 86 or 87 of the Uniform Code of Military Justice (10 U.S.C. §§ 885, 886, 887) that occurred between August 4, 1964 and March 28, 1973, inclusive, or are serving sentences of confinement for such violations. The Board will only consider the cases of Military Selective Service Act violators who were convicted of unlawfully failing (i) to register or register on time, (ii) to keep the local board informed of their current address, (iii) to report for or submit to preinduction or induction examination, (iv) to report for or submit to induction itself, or (v) to report for or submit to, or complete service under Section 6(j) of such Act. However, the Board will not consider the cases of individuals who are precluded from re-entering the United States under 8 U.S.C. 1182 (a) (22) or other law.

SECTION 3. The Board shall report to the President its findings and recommendations as to whether Executive clemency should be granted or denied in any case. If clemency is recommended, the Board shall also recommend the form that such clemency should take, including clemency conditioned upon a period of alternative service in the national interest. In the case of an individual discharged from the armed forces with a punitive or undesirable discharge, the Board may recommend to the President that a clemency discharge be substituted for a punitive or undesirable discharge. Determination of any period of alternate service shall be in accord with the Proclamation announcing a program for the return of Vietnam era draft evaders and military deserters.

SECTION 4. The Board shall give priority consideration to those applicants who are presently confined and have been convicted only of an offense set forth in section 2 of this order, and who have no outstanding criminal charges.

SECTION 5. Each member of the Board, except any member who then receives other compensation from the United States, may receive compensation for each day he or she is engaged upon the work of the Board at not to exceed the daily rate now or hereafter prescribed by law for persons and positions in GS-18, as authorized by law (5 U.S.C. 3109), and may also receive travel expenses, including per diem in lieu of subsistence, as authorized by law (5 U.S.C. 5703) for persons in the government service employed intermittently.

SECTION 6. Necessary expenses of the Board may be paid from the Unanticipated Personnel Needs Fund of the President or from such other funds as may be available.

SECTION 7. Necessary administrative services and support may be provided the Board by the General Services Administration on a reimbursable basis.

SECTION 8. All departments and agencies in the Executive branch are authorized and directed to cooperate with the Board in its work, and to furnish the Board all appropriate information and assistance, to the extent permitted by law.

SECTION 9. The Board shall submit its final recommendations to the President not later than December 31, 1976, at which time it shall cease to exist.

GERALD R. FORD

The White House,
  September 16, 1974.

Program for the Return of Vietnam Era
Draft Evaders and Military Deserters

Fact Sheets Concerning the Program.
September 16, 1974

The President has today issued a proclamation and Executive orders establishing a program of clemency for draft evaders and military deserters to commence immediately. This program has been formulated to permit these individuals to return to American society without risking criminal prosecution or incarceration for qualifying offenses if they acknowledge their allegiance to the United States and satisfactorily serve a period of alternate civilian service.

The program is designed to conciliate divergent elements of American society which were polarized by the protracted period of conscription necessary to sustain United States activities in Vietnam. Thus, only those who were delinquent with respect to required military service between the date of the Tonkin Gulf Resolution (August 4, 1964) and the date of withdrawal of United States forces from Vietnam (March 28, 1973) will be eligible. Further, only the offenses of draft evasion and prolonged unauthorized absence from military service (referred to hereinafter as desertion) are covered by the program.

Essential features of the program are outlined below.

1. *Number of Draft Evaders.* There are approximately 15,500 draft evaders potentially eligible. Of these some 8,700 have been convicted of draft evasion. Approximately 4,350 are under indictment at the present time, of whom some 4,060 are listed as fugitives. An estimated 3,000 of these are in Canada. A further 2,250 individuals are under investigation with no pending indictments. It is estimated that approximately 130 persons are still serving prison sentences for draft evasion.

2. *Number of Military Deserters.* Desertion, for the purposes of this program, refers to the status of those members of the Armed Forces who absented themselves from military service without authorization for 30 days or more. During the Vietnam era it is estimated that there were some 500,000 incidents of desertion as so defined. Of this 500,000 a number were charged with offenses other than desertion at the time they absented themselves. These other offenses are not within the purview of the clemency program for deserters. Approximately 12,500 of the deserters are still at large of whom about 1,500 are in Canada. Some 660 deserters are at present serving sentences to confinement or are awaiting trial under the Uniform Code of Military Justice.

3. *Unconvicted Evaders.* Draft evaders will report to the U.S. attorney for the district in which they allegedly committed their offense.

Draft evaders participating in this program will acknowledge their allegiance to the United States by agreeing with the United States attorney to perform alternate service under the auspices of the Director of Selective Service.

The duration of alternate service will be 24 months, but may be reduced for mitigating factors as determined by the Attorney General.

The Director of Selective Service will have the responsibility to find alternate service jobs for those who report. Upon satisfactory completion of the alternate service, the Director will issue a certificate of satisfactory completion to the individual and U.S. attorney, who will either move to dismiss the indictment if one is outstanding, or agree not to press possible charges in cases where an indictment has not been returned.

If the draft evader fails to perform the agreed term of alternate service, the U.S. attorney will be free to, and in normal circumstances will, resume prosecution of the case as provided in the terms of the agreement.

Aliens who fled the country to evade the draft will be ineligible to participate in the program.

4. *Unconvicted Military Absentees.* Military absentees who have no other pending charges may elect to participate in the program. Military deserters may seek instruction by writing to:

(a). Army—U.S. Army Deserter Information Point, Fort Benjamin Harrison, Ind. 46216

(b). Navy—Chief of Naval Personnel, (Pers 83), Department of the Navy, Washington, D.C. 20370

(c). Air Force—U.S. Air Force Deserter Information Point, (AFMDC/DPMAK) Randolph Air Force Base, Tex. 78148

(d). Marine Corps—Headquarters, U.S. Marine Corps, (MC) Washington, D.C. 20380

Those who make such an election will be required to execute a reaffirmation of allegiance and pledge to perform a period of alternate civilian service. Those against whom other charges under the Uniform Code of Military Justice are pending will not be eligible to participate in the program until these other charges are disposed of in accordance with the law. Participants in the program will be separated with an undesirable discharge. Although these discharges will not be coded on their face in any manner, the Veterans Administration will be advised that the recipients were discharged for willful and persistent unauthorized absence. They will thus not be eligible for any benefits provided by the Veterans Administration.

The length of required alternate civilian service will be determined by the parent Services for each individual on a case-by-case basis. The length of service will be 24 months but may be reduced for military service already completed or for other mitigating factors as determined by the parent Service. After being discharged each individual will be referred to the Director of Selective Service for assignment to prescribed work. Upon certification that this work has been satisfactorily completed, the individual may submit the certification to his former Service. The Service will then issue a special new type of discharge—a clemency discharge—which will be substituted for the previously awarded undesirable discharge. However, the clemency discharge shall not bestow entitlement to benefits administered by the Veterans Administration.

5. **Alternate Civilian Service.** Determining factors in selecting suitable alternate service jobs will be:

(a) *National health, safety or interest.*

(b) *Noninterference with the competitive labor market.* The applicant cannot be assigned to a job for which there are more numerous qualified applicants than jobs available.

(c) *Compensation.* The compensation will provide a standard of living to the applicant reasonably comparable to the standard of living the same man would enjoy if he were entering the military service.

(d) *Skill and talent utilization.* Where possible, an applicant may utilize his special skills.

In prescribing the length of alternate service in individual cases, the Attorney General, the military department, or the Clemency Board shall take into account such honorable service as an individual may have rendered prior to his absence, penalties already paid under the law, and such other mitigating factors as may be appropriate to seek equity among participants in the program.

6. *No Grace Period.* There will *not* be a grace period for those outside the country to return and negotiate for clemency with the option of again fleeing the jurisdiction. All those eligible for the program and who have no additional criminal charges outstanding who re-enter the United States will have 15 days to report to the appropriate authority from the date of their re-entry. However, this 15-day period shall not extend the final date of reporting of January 21, 1975, as set forth in the proclamation.

7. *Inquiries.* Telephone inquiries may be made to the following authorities:

Evaders:
Department of Justice: (202) 739-4281

Military Absentees:
U.S. Navy:	(202) 694-2007
	(202) 694-1936
U.S. Marine Corps:	(202) 694-8526
U.S. Army:	(317) 542-3417
U.S. Air Force:	(512) 652-4104
U.S. Coast Guard:	(202) 426-1830

Procedures To Be Followed
Unconvicted Draft Evader and
Military Absentee

Draft Evader

Report to United States attorney where offense was committed

Acknowledge allegiance to the United States by agreeing with the United States attorney to perform 24 months alternate service or less based on mitigating circumstances

Perform alternate service under the auspices of the Director of Selective Service

Director of Selective Service issues certificate of satisfactory completion of alternate service

Receipt by United States attorney of a certificate of satisfactory completion of alternate service

Dismissal of indictment or dropping of charges

Apply to Clemency Board

Clemency Board may recommend clemency to the President

Clemency Board may condition recommendation of clemency on period of alternate service

President may grant clemency

Military Absentee

(including Coast Guard)

Report as prescribed by the military department concerned or for members of the Coast Guard report to the Secretary of Transportation

Oath of allegiance to United States

Agree with the concerned military department to perform 24 months alternate service or less based upon mitigating circumstances

Upon request, military department forgoes prosecution and issues undesirable discharge

Perform alternate service under the auspices of the Director of Selective Service

Director of Selective Service issues certificate of satisfactory completion of alternate service

Receipt of a certificate of satisfactory completion of alternate service by the concerned military department

Clemency discharge substituted for undesirable discharge

Apply to Clemency Board

Clemency Board may recommend clemency to the President, including substitution of a clemency discharge for a punitive or undesirable discharge

Clemency Board may condition recommendation of clemency on period of alternate service

President may grant clemency, including substitution of a clemency discharge for a punitive or undesirable discharge

U.N. GENERAL ASSEMBLY OPENING
September 17-24, 1974

The 29th United Nations General Assembly session which convened at U.N. headquarters in New York City Sept. 17 proved a forum for debate on a broad spectrum of global problems, ranging from rapidly rising world inflation and population levels to a growing shortage of food supplies. (See also U.N. World Population Agreement, p. 777-797, U.N. World Food Conference, p. 939-953.) Leading off, General Assembly President, Algerian Foreign Minister Abdel-aziz Bouteflika, surprised delegates with an unusually strident speech avowing the effectiveness of force in liberating oppressed peoples. President Ford addressed the assembly the second day of the session, pledging increased American aid to reduce food shortages and calling upon the Arab states to cease employing their oil resources as a political and economic weapon. Secretary of State Henry A. Kissinger, speaking to the delegates Sept. 23, warned oil producing nations that artificially high oil prices threatened to "engulf us all in a general depression." Soviet Foreign Minister Andrei Gromyko presented his nation's views in an unusually moderate address Sept. 24, focusing particularly on the triumphs of detente and on the continuing conflict in the Middle East.

Bouteflika, who had been elected unanimously by the delegates to serve as president at the 13-week session, opened the 29th meeting of the General Assembly Sept. 17. In a sharp departure from the tradition of previous Assembly presidents, Bouteflika acclaimed the strides toward progress achieved by force. Saying he accepted his post as a manifestation of deference to the "generations of freedom fighters who contributed to making a better world with weapons in their hands," the Algerian official said these fighters had shown that "revolutionary violence is the only way for people to liberate themselves." He condemned "modern capitalist exploitation" and asserted that detente had created merely a fragile international order susceptible to shattering. With regard to the Middle East peace negotiations, Bouteflika warned that only a return of territories captured in earlier wars could lead to peace in that area. He also defended the right of Palestinians "to freely exercise their right of self-determination," an apparent reference to the guerrilla group, the Palestinian Liberation Organization, which claimed it was the sole voice of the Palestinians and whose leader—after controversial approval—addressed the U.N. body two months later. (See p. 919-937.)

Ford's U.N. Address

On Sept. 18, following in the tradition of all American presidents since Harry S Truman, President Ford addressed the General Assembly. He pledged increased American food assistance to countries beset with food shortages and outlined the first glimpses of a new and tougher U.S. position on Arab oil prices, a position Kissinger elaborated upon a week later. Warning that "failure to cooperate on oil and food and inflation could spell disaster for every nation represented in this room," Ford called on all countries to cooperate in a "global strategy for food and energy." Noting that it had not been the U.S. policy to "use food as a political weapon despite the oil embargo and recent oil price and production decisions," Ford told the delegates that the United States was aware of its "special responsibilities" because it was a major source of the world's food supply. But he challenged the oil exporting countries to "define their policies to meet growing needs...[without] imposing unacceptable burdens on the international monetary and trade systems." He warned that oil producers would eventually become "victims of their own actions" if they persisted in "confronting consumers with production restrictions, artificial pricing and the prospect of ultimate bankruptcy."

Zeroing in specifically on the issue of world-wide food shortages, Ford pledged that the United States would increase levels of food shipments to peoples in need during the end of 1974 and into 1975. He also promised increased agricultural production assistance to needy nations and offered U.S. cooperation in establishing an international food reserve system. At the same time, he called on all producers of food and energy to increase their output, mindful that the predicted doubling of the world population by 2000 would necessitate these increases.

A week later, Kissinger followed Ford to the U.N. podium. The secretary of state pursued Ford's theme regarding oil producers, cautioning that largely because of artificially inflated petroleum prices, "the early warning signs of a major economic crisis are evident." Stressing the necessity of world cooperation in meeting the economic dilemma, Kissinger chided delegates because their nations "continue to deal with economic issues on a national, regional or bloc basis at the precise moment that our interdependence is multiplying." He also noted the U.S. departure from that rule, particularly in newly launched programs with such oil producing nations as Saudi Arabia and Iran where the United States had offered assistance in helping to diversify their economies. In a veiled threat, Kissinger said that if such U.S. efforts failed, "what has gone up by political decision can be reduced by political decision." Kissinger's remarks were interpreted by The Washington Post Sept. 25 as an attempt to pressure oil consuming nations into joining together in concerted action against the oil exporters and to persuade underdeveloped nations that they were the victims of petroleum prices that had been raised sharply.

In an unusually mild speech Sept. 24, Soviet Foreign Minister Andrei Gromyko praised the strides he believed had been accomplished by detente between his country and the United States and offered the establishment of relations between the Soviet Union and Israel once conditions in the Middle East had been resolved. On detente, he lauded the improvement in U.S.-U.S.S.R. relations and emphasized what he saw as the fruits of that new relationship. "For the first time international detente has gone further than good wishes and verbal assurances," he asserted. "Not long ago, there was bitter fighting in Indochina, in the Middle East and in South East Asia, and those were not the only areas where events took a dangerous turn. Now several international conflicts have been channeled to a certain extent toward a political settlement. Prospects for a safer peaceful future in Europe have been opened up."

Offering to seek to open diplomatic ties with Israel when genuine progress was made toward peace in the Middle East, Gromyko nonetheless warned Israel against trying to "freeze" the current situation by continuing to hold Arab territory. He similarly cautioned that "militant intoxication" could bring about another outbreak of war in the area. He urged a resumption of the Middle East peace talks in Geneva and said the Palestinians should be allowed to take their "rightful place" at the conference table. Gromyko said the Soviet Union stood "in favor of Israel existing and developing as an independent sovereign state," although he emphasized that his country supported "the legitimate demands of the Arabs" and opposed Israeli retention of occupied Arab lands.

> Following are excerpts from the texts of speeches to the United Nations General Assembly by Algerian Foreign Minister Abdel-aziz Bouteflika, president of the Assembly, Sept. 17; President Ford, Sept. 18; Soviet Foreign Minister Andrei Gromyko, Sept. 24; and Secretary of State Henry A. Kissinger, Sept. 23:
>
> Excerpts from remarks by Abdel-aziz Bouteflika, U.N. General Assembly president, Sept. 17, begin on next page:

...I should like to regard your ruling [electing me General Assembly president] as a recognition of Africa, which is in its full efflorescence. Moreover, certain as I am of your full agreement, I should like to regard it, above all, as a manifestation of your deference to all those generations of freedom fighters, who, like those in my country, have themselves shouldered the historic responsibility for making a decisive contribution to the advent of a better world, if necessary, with weapons in their hands.

If great empires have arisen from oppressive violence, what greater empire could there be than the realm of justice, which itself makes revolutionary violence legitimate—revolutionary violence, which is the only way for peoples to liberate themselves....

...[T]his is the United Nations;...The three principles of justice, freedom and peace which it has in vain tried to rely upon in seeking that universality which was so difficult to bring about have made the existence of this Organization even more indispensable by that very token. The fact that it had to exist could not obviously confer perfection upon it; but it is quite obvious that it can still be improved. Furthermore, it is already in the process of progressively reforming itself, without crisis and without disruption.

Furthermore, throughout the dangerous storms of contemporary history could we for one instant even dare to imagine that the international community could survive its own contradictions without the timely and indeed salutary intervention of the great institutions which watched over its own destiny? But in the world as it is no one would be so bold as to claim that these institutions, however indispensable they may be, can be placed above and act equally towards all the Powers, great and small. It has even occurred that they have become so used to the problems of some that finally they overlook the vital concerns of the majority. Undoubtedly, in the solemn atmosphere of this forum all States are equal. But it would seem that outside it some are more equal than others. A fine tradition perhaps, but not one that speaks very eloquently in favour of the Charter....

[I]s not the prime virtue precisely that of objectivity, scrupulous respect for the real, and the patient search for truth?... In adjusting its conduct faithfully to this ideal our Organization would be simply keeping its promise of peace and universality.

The concept of universality is also a moral necessity.... Our era is in fact characterized by a constant move towards universality, which, in an initial phase, took the form of the gradual recognition of the equality of races, of nations, of States, and in a second phase that of an ever-growing trend towards translating this equality into facts by striving to reduce disparities created by the wealth of some and the poverty of the majority....

Moral Considerations

However decisive the distribution of power may be, moral considerations also have their weight, and this weight can be decisive. In recent years there has been a certain weakening in decolonization but there has just been a giant step forward in the recognition of the right to independence of the remaining territories under foreign domination.... But it is not enough to win a place in this Organization to be proof against hunger and insecurity. We do not wish to be deluded by the fragile appearance of freshly-acquired sovereignty. We are people who have made a religion of struggle....

This gives us greater freedom to underscore international responsibilities regarding development problems.... At the present time the problems of development are spreading beyond national and continental limits. These are world-wide problems, in the same way as imperialist hegemony is a world-wide problem. It is not by chance that I have mentioned these two phenomena in the same breath, because it is modern capitalist exploitation which has brought about the divorce between the wealthy and the poor.

The awareness which has now crystallized around these problems is not simply the expression of a philanthropic impulse; it proceeds from the growing belief that in an organically cohesive world no one's destiny is isolated. In this connection it is obvious that development can not be simply viewed through the cold calculations of utilitarianism but rather as the function of fundamental needs for justice and equity.

For the first time this year these crucial matters have been set down as the subjects of specific debate....

The United Nations, after almost 30 years of its existence, has now entered a decisive phase in its existence.... But its solidity, its ability to become rooted in the awareness of this era, undoubtedly increase its responsibilities and militate in favor of even greater effectiveness in the way it carries out its mission. This means that a greater democratization of its structures and their rigorous adaptation to the realities in which we live today not only would be consonant with an imperative need but would open before the Organization new and undoubtedly heartening prospects....

The Middle East Conflict

...[T]he destiny of the Middle East affects that of all of Europe. And the fate of Europe has world-wide repercussions. Less than ever can the Mediterranean now be regarded as a lake of peace, because the Middle East has become the stake for major rivalries. The repercussions of events in that region which is a nerve center will undoubtedly be felt even beyond adjacent continents. Already, the attention which is being paid by Africa, Asia and Europe to the development of the struggle of Arab peoples is a harbinger of developments of which it is difficult today to measure the full impact. It is my earnest belief that the problems involved here require from us solutions which may well run counter to the traditions which are most strongly anchored in our institutions. No one could ask us to be optimistic, as long as the conquered territories have not been restored, and since the Palestinian homeland has been given up in the circumstances we are aware of, no one expects the international community to bargain with its solidarity with the Palestinian people, until, in accordance with the principles of the Charter and the pertinent resolutions of the United Nations, it has had, like other peoples, the opportunity to exercise freely its right to self-determination....

Impact of Detente

The slackening of East-West tensions has made the chances of dialogue more promising....

We should not wish to minimize the importance of such changes which, if they develop normally, might effectively spell the creation of a new era, one where cooperation would replace confrontation, one in which each member of the international community would bear his measure of responsibility in international affairs. But what is happening in the world today and the legitimate concern for it demonstrates the present fragile balance and the dangers which may grow from upsetting it.

The crisis that has occurred in different continents, one whose development led to the very threshold of a general conflagration, attests to the flaws and the dangers of an international order which rests exclusively on the will of a few powerful nations and is the offshoot of the nature of their relations. That order, however, is the one that has prevailed since the end of the Second World War and for 25 years has shown its virtues but also proved its limitations and its inadequacies.

Emergence of Third World

The movement of the non-aligned nations was born of the awakening awareness of the flaws in the international system, controlled as it was by the great Powers. Its primary objective was precisely to guarantee to small countries safety against the abuses of such a regime....

The development of the movement of the non-aligned in the course of the last few years must be considered as a phenomenon whose importance and ramifications yield in no way to those of the detente that has taken place in the relations between the super-Powers. The new dimensions it has acquired and the dynamism which is constantly shown by it make it a weighty participant in world affairs.

The appearance of this new piece on the world chessboard was not welcomed with joy at all, particularly by those who were troubled by this intrusion of the small nations into a system that thus far had been managed by the great. Others expressed a certain doubt regarding the solidity and effectiveness of such a movement, because of the number and vulnerability of the countries it brought together.

But the movement of non-aligned nations does not wish to rival the great Powers and certainly not to quarrel with them. Its acts are based upon the solidarity of the countries of the Third World and thus are intended above all to bring into relations among nations this new factor of justice and humanity which the prodigious development of the power of some had obscured. What is non-alignment but the expression of the attachment of our peoples to their own independence, but also an expression of their dedication and total devotion to the cause of peace in the world.

In allowing the smaller nations to assume their part of the responsibilities in the management of world affairs, non-alignment appears as an undeniable component of international balance. In so doing it also plays the role of promoter of detente, not only breaking up a confrontation between the super-Powers, often a dangerous one, but more particularly by participating actively in improving relations among States. In losing and setting aside the static and defensive attitude it adopted in the first few years, today it shows a vitality through which it proves that it has achieved maturity and the clarity of its objectives which now allows it to introduce a better harmony into the world. The voice which the non-aligned nations raise may at times still be too feeble, and not always persuasive. But it cannot purely and simply be discarded or disregarded when we propose to free the world of the dangers that threaten it.... Everything is happening as though recent history had once and for all endorsed the vocation and aptitude of the Third World for partnership in the determination of the elements of international balance. This is an undeniable qualitative change....

The United Nations offers the non-aligned nations the right arena wherein to affirm their principles and contribute best to the tasks of safeguarding and strengthening security in the world.

The emergence of the movement of non-aligned nations and its affirmation as the authentic spokesman for the Third World have had considerable influence on the activity of the United Nations, on its orientation and its effectiveness....

I know that it is not customary for a President to address the General Assembly with the directness and frankness to which I have resorted today. From the bottom of my heart I thank you for having allowed me this exceptional privilege, which again I consider to be proof of your friendship and admiration for the Algerian people....

Excerpts from President Ford's address to the 29th session of the General Assembly, September 18, 1974:

Mr. President, Mr. Secretary General, your Excellencies:

In 1946, President Harry Truman welcomed representatives of 55 nations to the first General Assembly of the United Nations. Since then, every American President has had the great honor of addressing this Assembly.

Today, with pleasure and humility, I take my turn in welcoming you, the distinguished representatives of 138 nations....

Since the United Nations was founded, the world has experienced conflicts and threats to peace, but we have avoided the greatest danger—another world war. Today, we have the opportunity to make the remainder of this century an era of peace and cooperation and economic well-being.

The harsh hostilities which once held great powers in their rigid grasp have now begun to moderate. Many of the crises which dominated past General Assemblies are fortunately behind us. And technological progress holds out the hope that one day all men can achieve a decent life.

Nations too often have had no choice but to be either hammer or anvil, to strike or to be struck. Now we have a new opportunity—to forge, in concert with others, a framework of international cooperation. That is the course the United States has chosen for itself.

American Pledges to the World

On behalf of the American people, I renew these basic pledges to you today.

—We are committed to a pursuit of a more peaceful, stable, and cooperative world. While we are determined never to be bested in a test of strength, we will devote our strength to what is best. And in the nuclear era, there is no rational alternative to accords of mutual restraint between the United States and the Soviet Union, two nations which have the power to destroy mankind.

—We will bolster our partnerships with traditional friends in Europe, Asia, and Latin America to meet new challenges in a rapidly changing world. The maintenance of such relationships underpins rather than undercuts the search for peace.

—We will seek out, we will expand our relations with old adversaries. For example, our new rapport with the People's Republic of China best serves the purposes of each nation and the interests of the entire world.

—We will strive to heal old wounds, reopened in recent conflicts in Cyprus, the Middle East, and in Indochina. Peace cannot be imposed from without, but we will do whatever is within our capacity to help achieve it.

—We rededicate ourselves to the search for justice, equality, and freedom. Recent developments in Africa signal the welcome end of colonialism. Behavior appropriate to an era of dependence must give way to the new responsibilities of an era of interdependence.

No single nation, no single group of nations, no single organization can meet all of the challenges before the community of nations. We must act in concert. Progress toward a better world must come through cooperative efforts across the whole range of bilateral and multilateral relations....

In my 25 years as a Member of the Congress of the United States, I learned two basic practical lessons:

First, men of differing political persuasions can find common ground for cooperation. We need not agree on all issues in order to agree on most. Differences of principle, of purpose, of perspective will not disappear. But neither will our mutual problems disappear unless we are determined to find mutually helpful solutions.

Second, a majority must take into account the proper interest of a minority if the decisions of the majority are to be accepted. We who believe in and live by majority rule must always be alert to the danger of the "tyranny of the majority." Majority rule thrives on the habits of accommodation, moderation, and consideration of the interests of others.

A very stark reality has tempered America's actions for decades and must now temper the actions of all nations. Prevention of full-scale warfare in the nuclear age has become everybody's responsibility. Today's regional conflict must not become tomorrow's world disaster. We must assure by every means at our disposal that local crises are quickly contained and resolved.

The challenge before the United States [Nations] is very clear. This organization can place the weight of the world community on the side of world peace. And this organization can provide impartial forces to maintain the peace....

Let the quality of our response measure up to the magnitude of the challenge that we face. I pledge to you that America will continue to be constructive, innovative, and responsive to the work of this great body.

The nations in this hall are united by a deep concern for peace. We are united as well by our desire to ensure a better life for all people.

Today, the economy of the world is under unprecedented stress. We need new approaches to international cooperation to respond effectively to the problems that we face. Developing and developed countries, market and nonmarket countries—we are all a part of one interdependent economic system.

The food and oil crises demonstrate the extent of our interdependence. Many developing nations need the food surplus of a few developed nations. And many industrialized nations need the oil production of a few developing nations.

Energy is required to produce food and food to produce energy—and both to provide a decent life for everyone. The problems of food and energy can be resolved on the basis of cooperation, or can, I should say, [be] made unmanageable on the basis of confrontation. Runaway inflation, propelled by food and oil price increases, is an early warning signal to all of us.

Let us not delude ourselves. Failure to cooperate on oil and food and inflation could spell disaster for every nation represented in this room. The United Nations must not and need not allow this to occur. A global strategy for food and energy is urgently required.

Four Guidelines for A Global Approach

The United States believes four principles should guide a global approach:

First, all nations must substantially increase production. Just to maintain the present standards of living the world must almost double its output of food and energy to match the expected increase in the world's population by the end of this century. To meet aspirations for a better life, production will have to expand at a significantly faster rate than population growth.

Second, all nations must seek to achieve a level of prices which not only provides an incentive to producers but which consumers can afford. It should now be clear that the developed nations are not the only countries which demand and receive an adequate return for their goods. But it should also be clear that by confronting consumers with production restrictions, artificial pricing, and the prospect of ultimate bankruptcy, producers will eventually become the victims of their own actions.

Third, all nations must avoid the abuse of man's fundamental needs for the sake of narrow national or bloc advantage. The attempt by any nation to use one commodity for political purposes will inevitably tempt other countries to use their commodities for their own purposes.

Fourth, the nations of the world must assure that the poorest among us are not overwhelmed by rising prices of the imports necessary for their survival. The traditional aid donors and the increasingly wealthy oil producers must join in this effort.

The United States recognizes the special responsibility we bear as the world's largest producer of food. That is why Secretary of State Kissinger proposed from this very podium last year a world food conference to define a global food policy. And that is one reason why we have removed domestic restrictions on food production in the United States.

It has not been our policy to use food as a political weapon, despite the oil embargo and recent oil prices and production decisions.

It would be tempting for the United States—beset by inflation and soaring energy prices—to turn a deaf ear to external appeals for food assistance, or to respond with internal appeals for export controls. But however difficult our own economic situation, we recognize that the plight of others is worse.

Americans have always responded to human emergencies in the past, and we respond again here today. In response to Secretary General Waldheim's appeal and to help meet the long-term challenge in food, I reiterate: To help developing nations realize their aspirations to grow more of their own food, the United States will substantially increase its assistance to agricultural production programs in other countries.

Next, to ensure that the survival of millions of our fellow men does not depend upon the vagaries of weather, the United States is prepared to join in a worldwide effort to negotiate, establish, and maintain an international system of food reserves. This system will work best if each nation is made responsible for managing the reserves that it will have available.

Finally, to make certain that the more immediate needs for food are met this year, the United States will not only maintain the amount it spends for food shipments to nations in need but it will increase this amount this year.

Thus, the United States is striving to help define and help contribute to a cooperative global policy to meet man's immediate and long-term need for food. We will set forth our comprehensive proposals at the World Food Conference in November.

Now is the time for oil producers to define their conception of a global policy on energy to meet the growing need and to do this without imposing unacceptable burdens on the international monetary and trade system.

Cooperation to Overcome Common Problems

A world of economic confrontation cannot be a world of political cooperation. If we fail to satisfy man's fundamental needs for energy and food, we face a threat not just to our aspirations for a better life for all our peoples but to our hopes for a more stable and a more peaceful world. By working together to overcome our common problems, mankind can turn from fear towards hope.

From the time of the founding of the United Nations, America volunteered to help nations in need, frequently as the main benefactor. We were able to do it. We were glad to do it. But as new economic forces alter and reshape today's complex world, no nation can be expected to feed all the world's hungry peoples.

Fortunately, however, many nations are increasingly able to help. And I call on them to join with us as truly united nations in the struggle to produce, to provide more food at lower prices for the hungry and, in general, a better life for the needy of this world.

America will continue to do more than its share. But there are realistic limits to our capacities. There is no limit, however, to our determination to act in concert with other nations to fulfill the vision of the United Nations Charter, to save succeeding generations from the scourge of war, and to promote social progress and better standards, better standards of life in a large freedom.

Thank you very, very much.

Excerpts from remarks by Andrei A. Gromyko, Minister of Foreign Affairs of the USSR, delivered before the General Assembly, September 24, 1974:

Mr. President, distinguished delegates, each session of the General Assembly is not the same as the previous one—nor is the world situation in which they convene the same.... What remains unchanged, however, is the criterion that the United Nations and every one of its members should be guided by at all times and in all things, namely, concern for the maintenance of international peace and security.... Those who are earnestly seeking for ways to establish and consolidate peaceful relations and to settle disputed problems at the negotiating table can definitely count on the reliable cooperation of the Soviet Union....

Achievements of Detente

The general state of world affairs is taking shape under the impact of a great number of factors—from political and military to national or even psychological ones. It hardly lends itself to a onefold appraisal. But the main trend of international development arouses no doubts: detente and a desire for it are today predominant.

For the first time international detente has gone further than good wishes and verbal assurances....

Through joint efforts by many States it has become possible to reduce the risk of an armed conflict between the two social systems. But of special significance are the well-known agreements of 1972-1974 between the

Soviet Union and the United States of America. This applies above all to the Agreement on the Prevention of Nuclear War....

Not long ago there was bitter fighting in Indochina, in the Middle East, and in South Asia. And those were not the only areas where events took a dangerous turn. Now several international conflicts have been channelled to a certain extent toward a political settlement....

Adjoining this is another major asset of detente—the development of bilateral relations between States with different social systems....

Finally, it was detente that put on the agenda the restructuring of economic relations in the world. The task is to eliminate inequality and discrimination, and to ensure in practice the sovereign right of States to dispose of their natural resources....

On the whole, one can confidently say that the course of international events has now been turned closer to peace.

One should, however, also clearly see another thing: the movement towards peace does not always follow a straight line. Difficulties on this road will not necessarily decrease with each passing year....

In the final account the solution of the accumulated problems is hampered by the deliberate opposition of those forces whose interests are associated with policies contrary to the policy of detente....

The Soviet Union counters them with its own motto, which is not to slacken efforts to ensure that the sound processes which have now begun are consolidated and become irreversible....

Middle East Conflict

For almost thirty years now the Middle East has been in a state of fever. Over this period wars have broken out there time and again, the last one only a year ago. This is enough to convince anyone that the Middle East problem must be solved, and solved justly, with the interests of all the peoples of the region being taken into account.

What does that imply? First of all, the withdrawal of Israeli forces from all the Arab lands seized by them in 1967 and the assurance of the legitimate national rights of the Arab people of Palestine. Otherwise, there can be no stable peace in the Middle East. It takes no prophet to foresee a new flare-up of hostilities if the Middle East settlement should be reduced to half measures, no matter how well advertised.

There are increasing signs that Israel regards the disengagement of forces on the Sinai and at the Golan Heights not as the first step towards a general settlement—the way it should be—but as a maneuver intended to freeze the situation. Plain unwillingness to leave the occupied Arab territories and, moreover, a desire to consolidate Israel's hold on them are quite evident. What other explanation can there be for the militarist intoxication which has again overcome Israel and for the attempts to exert military pressure on the Arab states? Unless this stops, the disengagement of forces may prove to be a mere regrouping of forces prior to a new clash.

The Soviet Union believes there must be no delay in implementing measures leading to a political settlement in the Middle East. What this means is a prompt resumption of the Geneva Peace Conference, the most appropriate forum for considering the Middle East problem in all its complex totality and for finding solutions satisfactory for the parties involved in the conflict. Naturally, this fully applies also to the Arab people of Palestine whose representatives must take their rightful place at the Conference.

We believe the time has surely come to address ourselves in earnest to the problem of Palestine. A wider approach is required here which would open the way to assure, not in words, but in deeds, the legitimate national rights of the Arab people of Palestine. That is why we are in favor of including the question of Palestine in the agenda of this session of the General Assembly as a separate item.

There are some who try to present the Soviet Union's position as one-sided and only serving the interests of the Arab States. Yes, we do support, and we will support the legitimate demands of the Arabs. But it would be wrong to see only this particular aspect in our position. When we insist that territories acquired by force should not become a prize for the aggressor, the purport of our demand goes beyond the limits of the Middle East. It reflects intolerance of aggression in general. What this involves, therefore, is a major international principle, and the question of consistency in policy.

Furthermore, the Soviet Union stands in favor of Israel existing and developing as an independent sovereign State. We have said so many times and we reaffirm it once again. Real, not illusory, progress towards a Middle East settlement will create prerequisites for the development of relations between the Soviet Union and all the States of the Middle East, including Israel....

Excerpts from the speech by Secretary of State Henry A. Kissinger Sept. 23 before the U.N. General Assembly:

...Our deepest problem—going far beyond the items on our agenda—is whether our vision can keep pace with our challenges. Will history recall the 20th century as a time of mounting global conflict or as the beginning of a global conception? Will our age of interdependence spur joint progress or common disaster?

The answer is not yet clear....

The world has dealt with local conflicts as if they were perpetually manageable. We have permitted too many of the underlying causes to fester unattended until the parties believed that their only recourse was war. And because each crisis ultimately has been contained we have remained complacent. But tolerance of local conflict tempts world holocaust. We have no guarantee that some local crisis—perhaps the next—will not explode beyond control.

The world has dealt with nuclear weapons as if restraint were automatic. Their very awesomeness has chained these weapons for almost three decades; their sophistication and expense have helped to keep constant for a

845

decade the number of states who possess them. Now, as was quite foreseeable, political inhibitions are in danger of crumbling. Nuclear catastrophe looms more plausible—whether through design or miscalculation; accident, theft, or blackmail.

The world has dealt with the economy as if its constant advance were inexorable. While postwar growth has been uneven and some parts of the world have lagged, our attention was focused on how to increase participation in a general advance. We continue to deal with economic issues on a national, regional, or bloc basis at the precise moment that our interdependence is multiplying. Strains on the fabric and institutions of the world economy threaten to engulf us all in a general depression.

The delicate structure of international cooperation so laboriously constructed over the last quarter century can hardly survive—and certainly cannot be strengthened—if it is continually subjected to the shocks of political conflict, war, and economic crisis.

The time has come, then, for the nations assembled here to act together on the recognition that continued reliance on old slogans and traditional rivalries will lead us toward:

—A world ever more torn between rich and poor, East and West, producer and consumer.

—A world where local crises threaten global confrontation and where the spreading atom threatens global peril.

—A world of rising costs and dwindling supplies, of growing populations and declining production.

There is another course. Last week before this Assembly, President Ford dedicated our country to a cooperative, open approach to build a more secure and more prosperous world. The United States will assume the obligations that our values and strength impose upon us.

But the building of a cooperative world is beyond the grasp of any one nation. An interdependent world requires not merely the resources but the vision and creativity of us all. Nations cannot simultaneously confront and cooperate with one another....

But we must at least begin to remedy problems, not just manage them; to shape events, rather than endure them; to confront our challenges instead of one another.

The Political Dimension

The urgent political responsibility of our era is to resolve conflicts without war.... Together let us face its realities:

—First, a certain momentum toward peace has been created—in East-West relations and in certain regional conflicts. It must be maintained. But we are only at the beginning of the process. If we do not continue to advance, we will slip back.

—Second, progress in negotiation of difficult issues comes only through patience, perseverance, and recognition of the tolerable limits of the other side. Peace is a process, not a condition. It can only be reached in steps.

—Third, failure to recognize and grasp the attainable will prevent the achievement of the ideal. Attempts to resolve all issues at one time are a certain prescription for stagnation. Progress toward peace can be thwarted by asking too much as surely as by asking too little.

—Fourth, the world community can help resolve chronic conflicts, but exaggerated expectations will prevent essential accommodation among the parties. This Assembly can help or hinder the negotiating process. It can seek a scapegoat or a solution. It can offer the parties an excuse to escape reality or sturdy support in search of a compromise. It can decide on propaganda or contribute to realistic approaches that are responsive to man's yearning for peace....

Let us be realistic about what must be done. The art of negotiation is to set goals that can be achieved at a given time and to reach them with determination. Each step forward modifies old perceptions and brings about a new situation that improves the chances of a comprehensive settlement....

The Nuclear Dimension

The second new dimension on our agenda concerns the problem of nuclear proliferation.

The world has grown so accustomed to the existence of nuclear weapons that it assumes they will never be used. But today, technology is rapidly expanding the number of nuclear weapons in the hands of major powers and threatens to put nuclear-explosive technology at the disposal of an increasing number of other countries.

In a world where many nations possess nuclear weapons, dangers would be vastly compounded. It would be infinitely more difficult, if not impossible, to maintain stability among a large number of nuclear powers. Local wars would take on a new dimension. Nuclear weapons would be introduced into regions where political conflict remains intense and the parties consider their vital interests overwhelmingly involved. There would, as well, be a vastly heightened risk of direct involvement of the major nuclear powers.

This problem does not concern one country, one region, or one bloc alone. No nation can be indifferent to the spread of nuclear technology; every nation's security is directly affected.

The challenge before the world is to realize the peaceful benefits of nuclear technology without contributing to the growth of nuclear weapons or to the number of states possessing them.

As a major nuclear power, the United States recognizes its special responsibility. We realize that we cannot expect others to show restraint if we do not ourselves practice restraint....

Beyond the relations of the nuclear powers to each other lies the need to curb the spread of nuclear explosives. We must take into account that plutonium is an essential ingredient of nuclear explosives and that in the immediate future the amount of plutonium generated by peaceful nuclear reactors will be multiplied many times. Heretofore the United States and a number of other countries have widely supplied nuclear fuels and other nuclear materials in order to promote the use of nuclear energy for peaceful purposes. This policy cannot continue if it leads to the proliferation of nuclear explosives. Sales of these materials can no longer be treated by anyone as a purely commercial competitive enterprise.

The world community therefore must work urgently toward a system of effective international safeguards against the diversion of plutonium or its byproducts. The United States is prepared to join with others in a comprehensive effort.

Let us together agree on the practical steps which must be taken to assure the benefits of nuclear energy free of its terrors:

—The United States will shortly offer specific proposals to strengthen safeguards to the other principal supplier countries.

—We shall intensify our efforts to gain the broadest possible acceptance of International Atomic Energy Agency (IAEA) safeguards, to establish practical controls on the transfer of nuclear materials, and to insure the effectiveness of these procedures.

—The United States will urge the IAEA to draft an international convention for enhancing physical security against theft or diversion of nuclear material. Such a convention should set forth specific standards and techniques for protecting materials while in use, storage, and transfer.

—The Treaty on the Non-Proliferation of Nuclear Weapons, which this Assembly has endorsed, warrants continuing support. The treaty contains not only a broad commitment to limit the spread of nuclear explosives but specific obligations to accept and implement IAEA safeguards and to control the transfer of nuclear materials.

Mr. President, whatever advantages seem to acrue from the acquisition of nuclear-explosive technology will prove to be ephemeral. When Pandora's box has been opened, no country will be the beneficiary and all mankind will have lost. This is not inevitable. If we act decisively now, we can still control the future.

The Economic Dimension

...The economic history of the postwar period has been one of sustained growth, for developing as well as developed nations. The universal expectation of our peoples, the foundation of our political institutions, and the assumption underlying the evolving structure of peace are all based on the belief that this growth will continue.

But will it? The increasingly open and cooperative global economic system that we have come to take for granted is now under unprecedented attack. The world is poised on the brink of a return to the unrestrained economic nationalism which accompanied the collapse of economic order in the thirties. And should that occur, all would suffer—poor as well as rich, producer as well as consumer....

The early warning signs of a major economic crisis are evident. Rates of inflation unprecedented in the past quarter century are sweeping developing and developed nations alike. The world's financial institutions are staggering under the most massive and rapid movements of reserves in history. And profound questions have arisen about meeting man's most fundamental needs for energy and food.

While the present situation threatens every individual and nation, it is the poor who suffer the most. While the wealthier adjust their living standards, the poor see the hopes of a lifetime collapse around them. While others tighten their belts, the poor starve. While others can hope for a better future, the poor see only despair ahead.

It can be in the interest of no country or group of countries to base policies on a test of strength; for a policy of confrontation would end in disaster for all. Meeting man's basic needs for energy and food and assuring economic growth while mastering inflation require international cooperation to an unprecedented degree.

Let us apply these principles first to the energy situation:

—Oil producers seek a better life for their peoples and a just return for their diminishing resources.

—The developing nations less well-endowed by nature face the disintegration of the results of decades of striving for development as the result of a price policy over which they have no control.

—The developed nations find the industrial civilization built over centuries in jeopardy.

Both producers and consumers have legitimate claims. The problem is to reconcile them for the common good.

The United States is working closely with several oil producers to help diversify their economies. We have established commissions to facilitate the transfer of technology and to assist with industrialization. We are prepared to accept substantial investments in the United States, and we welcome a greater role for the oil producers in the management of international economic institutions.

The investment of surplus oil revenues presents a great challenge. The countries which most need these revenues are generally the least likely to receive them. The world's financial institutions have coped thus far, but ways must be found to assure assistance for those countries in need of it. And the full brunt of the surplus revenues is yet to come.

Despite our best efforts to meet the oil producers' legitimate needs and to channel their resources into constructive uses, the world cannot sustain even the present level of prices, much less continuing increases. The prices of other commodities will inevitably rise in a never-ending inflationary spiral. Nobody will benefit. The oil producers will be forced to spend more for their own imports. Many nations will not be able to withstand the pace, and the poorer could be overwhelmed. The complex, fragile structure of global economic cooperation required to sustain national economic growth stands in danger of being shattered....

But the long-range solution requires a new understanding between consumers and producers. Unlike food prices, the high cost of oil is not the result of economic factors—of an actual shortage of capacity or of the free play of supply and demand. Rather it is caused by deliberate decisions to restrict production and maintain an artificial price level. We recognize that the producers should have a fair share; the fact remains that the present price level even threatens the economic well-being of producers. Ultimately they depend upon the vitality of the world economy for the security of their markets and their investments. And it cannot be in the interest of any nation to magnify the despair of the least developed, who are uniquely vulnerable to exorbitant prices and who have no recourse but to pay.

What has gone up by political decision can be reduced by political decision....

At a time of universal concern for justice and in an age of advanced technology, it is intolerable that millions are starving and hundreds of millions remain undernourished. The magnitude of the long-term problem is clear. At present rates of population growth, world food production must double by the end of this century to maintain even the present inadequate dietary level. And an adequate diet for all would require that we triple world production. If we are true to our principles, we have an obligation to strive for an adequate supply of food to every man, woman, and child in the world. This is a technical possibility, a political necessity, and a moral imperative.

The United States is prepared to join with all nations at the World Food Conference in Rome to launch the truly massive effort which is required. We will present a number of specific proposals:

—To help developing nations. They have the lowest yields and the largest amounts of unused land and water; their potential in food production must be made to match their growing need.

—To increase substantially global fertilizer production. We must end once and for all the world's chronic fertilizer shortage.

—To expand international, regional, and national research programs. Scientific and technical resources must be mobilized now to meet the demands of the year 2000 and beyond.

—To rebuild the world's food reserves. Our capacity for dealing with famine must be freed from the vagaries of weather.

—To provide a substantial level of concessionary food aid. The United States will in the coming year increase the value of our own food aid shipments to countries in need. We make this commitment, despite great pressures on our economy and at a time when we are seeking to cut our own government budget, because we realize the dimensions of the tragedy with which we are faced. All of us here have a common obligation to prevent the poorest nations from being overwhelmed and enable them to build the social, economic, and political base for self-sufficiency.

The hopes of every nation for a life of peace and plenty rest on an effective international resolution of the crises of inflation, fuel, and food. We must act now, and we must act together.

The Human Dimension

Mr. President, let us never forget that all of our political endeavors are ultimately judged by one standard—to translate our actions into human concerns.

The United States will never be satisfied with a world where man's fears overshadow his hopes....

Mr. President, we have long lived in a world where the consequences of our failures were manageable—a world where local conflicts were contained, nuclear weapons threatened primarily those nations which possessed them, and the cycle of economic growth and decline seemed principally a national concern.

But this is no longer the case. It is no longer possible to imagine that conflicts, weapons, and recession will not spread.

We must now decide. The problems we face will be with us the greater part of the century. But will they be with us as challenges to be overcome or as adversaries that have vanquished us?...

KENNEDY'S REJECTION
OF 1976 PRESIDENTIAL RACE
September 23, 1974

Sen. Edward M. Kennedy of Massachusetts took himself firmly and finally out of contention for the Democratic presidential or vice presidential nomination in 1976 at a news conference in Boston Sept. 23. "This decision is firm, final and unconditional," said the 42-year old heir to the Kennedy family's political legacy. "There is absolutely no circumstance or event that will alter the decision. I will not accept the nomination. I will not accept a draft. I will oppose any effort to place my name in nomination in any state or at the national convention, and I will oppose any effort to promote my candidacy in any other way."

Kennedy's explanation for his withdrawal from the contest for the 1976 nomination of his party was, according to his prepared statement, based solely on family obligations. A rare form of bone cancer forced the amputation of one leg of his 12-year-old son, Edward Jr., in 1973 and regular treatments were required to prevent the spread of the disease. Kennedy's wife, Joan, had suffered nervous disorders requiring repeated hospitalization for psychiatric treatment. Kennedy was also a surrogate father for the children of his two assassinated brothers, former President John F. Kennedy and former New York Sen. Robert F. Kennedy. "My primary responsibilities are at home," he said in his statement. "It has become quite apparent to me that I would be unable to make a full commitment to a campaign for the presidency. I simply cannot do that to my wife and children and the other members of my family."

Kennedy had been the consistent first choice for the nomination among Democrats surveyed in national public opinion polls. It had been widely assumed that the nomination would have been his for the asking, probably on the first ballot at the national convention, had he decided to seek it. He had said at first that he would announce his plans in mid-1975. Later he had stepped up his timetable to the first of the year. "I have chosen to announce the decision now in order to ease the apprehensions within my family about the possibility of my candidacy, as well as to clarify the situation within my party," he said Sept. 23. He said he would be a candidate for re-election to the Senate in 1976.

The announcement by Kennedy immediately reshaped the Democratic presidential picture for 1976. It opened up fresh speculation about the possible candidacy, either as a Democrat or as a third-party challenger, of Gov. George C. Wallace (D Ala.). It almost certainly cleared the way for a flock of other candidates, a series of free-swinging state presidential primaries and a more uncertain national convention in 1976. Kennedy ducked repeated questions from reporters about his choice of candidates. The decision should be left to the voters, he said.

> *Text of the statement by Sen. Edward M. Kennedy (D Mass.), released Sept. 23, announcing his intention to remove his name from consideration for the 1976 Democratic presidential nomination:*

I appreciate your coming this morning. As I said in my brief statement yesterday, I have requested this conference to announce my future political plans, and I very much wanted to make the announcement here in Massachusetts.

From the campaigns of my brothers before me, I know that seeking the nation's highest office demands a candidate's undivided attention and his deepest personal commitment. If any candidate is unable to make that commitment, he does a disservice to his country and to his party by undertaking the effort.

My primary responsibilities are at home. It has become quite apparent to me that I would be unable to make a full commitment to a campaign for the presidency. I simply cannot do that to my wife and children and the other members of my family.

Therefore, in 1976, I will not be a candidate for President or Vice President of the United States.

This decision is firm, final and unconditional. There is absolutely no circumstance or event that will alter the decision. I will not accept the nomination. I will not accept a draft. I will oppose any effort to place my name in nomination in any state or at the national convention, and I will oppose any effort to promote my candidacy in any other way.

I reached this decision after discussion with my wife and the other members of my family. I have chosen to announce the decision now in order to ease the apprehensions within my family about the possibility of my candidacy, as well as to clarify the situation within my party.

I shall do all I can in the two years ahead to insure the success of my party and its nominees. I appreciate the confidence of those who have expressed their faith in me and who have indicated their support for me as a presidential candidate.

For the past 12 years, I have served the people of Massachusetts in the United States Senate. In 1976, I expect to be a candidate for re-election. I take pride in my service to the people of this commonwealth. In their service, much can be done to influence the direction of the nation, and it is in their service that I have found the greatest satisfaction of my public life.

REVERSAL OF CALLEY CONVICTION
September 25, 1974

Lt. William L. Calley Jr., the only person ever convicted in connection with the 1968 killing of hundreds of civilians in the South Vietnamese hamlet of Mylai, was ordered released from Ft. Leavenworth Sept. 25 when a federal judge overturned Calley's conviction. U.S. District Court Judge J. Robert Elliott in Columbus, Ga., reversed Calley's conviction citing "massive adverse pretrial publicity." The judge also based his decision on the Army's denial of Calley's requests for certain witnesses, on the House of Representatives' denial of access to testimony given before that body, and on the illegality of charges originally pressed against Calley. Although the Army announced plans to appeal Elliott's decision, Calley was set free on Nov. 19 after serving a little less than a third of his original 10-year prison term.

Coming down hard on the Army for failing to control the massive publicity against Calley, the judge devoted 85 pages of his 132-page decision to the role of media coverage in the Mylai case. Said Elliott: "Never in the history of the military justice system, and perhaps in the history of American courts, has any accused ever encountered such intense and continuous prejudicial publicity." The judge said he was referring specifically to phrases such as "atrocity," "slaughter of noncombatants" and "barbaric act" that had appeared in news stories about the 1968 event. Elliott was especially critical of eyewitness accounts of the incident which he believed had exploited and sensationalized the slayings.

The Army's refusal of Calley's request for certain witnesses was the second major factor in the judge's decision to reverse the conviction. Elliott cited the Army's denial of Calley's request to subpoena former

Secretary of Defense Melvin R. Laird and Gen. William C. Westmoreland, commander of American forces in Vietnam during 1968. "The petitioner's [Calley's] superiors could well have been worried about their own possible criminal responsibility as a result of the Mylai incident," wrote Elliott. The judge also ruled illegal the House of Representatives' action refusing Calley access to testimony presented before House committees on the Mylai affair. Moreover, Elliott found that the charges preferred against Calley were inadequate in that they failed to specify the names or descriptions of persons allegedly killed or ordered killed by Calley and to cite the locations of the slayings. During 1969, the total number of slain Mylai civilians was variously reported as ranging from 109 to 567. Elliott noted that Calley could have been convicted several times for the killing of one person.

> *Following are various excerpts from U.S. District Court Judge J. Robert Elliott's decision Sept. 25 overturning the conviction of Lt. William L. Calley Jr., for his alleged role in the killing of civilians in the South Vietnamese village of Mylai:*
>
> *(1) Excerpts from Judge Elliott's opinion dealing with a fair trial. Elliott found that Calley had not received a fair trial due to the inability of the military judicial system to control the extensive pretrial publicity, damaging public remarks by high-ranking military officers and notable civilians, and the refusal of the Justice Department to enforce a military judge's order limiting the comments of persons involved in the case:*

...Never in the history of the military justice system, and perhaps in the history of American courts, has any accused ever encountered such intense and continuous prejudicial publicity as did the Petitioner herein. Virtually every newspaper, periodical, magazine, television station, radio station, and every other news medium carried continuous and extensive interviews, reports, pictures, articles, statements, quotes, and editorial comments concerning the Petitioner's role in the so-called My Lai incident...

In the military justice system there is no continuously sitting judicial officer who may act to protect the rights of the individual accused...

> *(2) Excerpts from Judge Elliott's opinion dealing with the extent of prejudicial pretrial publicity. Elliott noted the extensive reporting by newspapers and networks. He cited publicized comments by members of Congress, the Secretary of the Army, President Nixon, General Westmoreland and Calley's commanding officer at the time of the incident, Capt. Medina, all of whom gave the impression, Elliott wrote, that the government sought to convict "someone" for the slayings and that the "someone" was Calley:*

...In a number of cases in recent years the federal courts have moved away from the earlier doctrine that a denial by a juror on voir dire that he has been affected by damaging publications must be accepted as true, these later cases establishing the principle that adverse and inflammatory publicity has an inherently prejudicial impact on jurors and that it is not necessary that the prejudice be "isolated" and "demonstrated" as a prerequisite to reversal....

[T]he Supreme Court has established...the doctrine of inherent prejudice in regard to the accused's right to a fair trial, the doctrine coming into play when, because of the circumstances, there is such a high probability that prejudice will result until the procedure is deemed inherently lacking in due process. In such cases no showing of identifiable prejudice is necessary....

In the Court's opinion the case before us represents a situation where it is not necessary for the Petitioner to show "isolatable," "identifiable" prejudice as a prerequisite to reversal. However, isolatable prejudice has been shown....

This opinion of the Court should not be construed as holding that if an individual who is charged with offenses achieves sufficient notoriety as a result of his alleged acts the charges should be dismissed. The guidelines enunciated by the Supreme Court in Sheppard v. Maxwell, 384 U.S. 333 (1966) contain the remedies for pretrial publicity problems created by the great majority of cases. Unfortunately, the court-martial system could not and cannot effectively invoke some of these guidelines....

In balancing the right of the press to disseminate news and the right of the accused to have his trial conducted in an atmosphere free from the prejudicial effect of such news coverage, we deal with two separate guarantees of the Constitution which are in direct conflict. Neither guarantee is predominant over the other. Rather, these guarantees must be viewed separately and they both must be observed. Where the guarantees conflict, neither may give way....

> *(3) Excerpts from Elliott's ruling dealing with denials of subpoenas requested by Calley's defense team and of evidence taken before a session of the House of Representatives. In one section, not included, Elliott cited as improper the Army's denial of subpoenas for Laird and Westmoreland, noting that pressures apparently were applied to limit testimony from superior officers due to concern that the officers could be held accountable for not prohibiting Calley's alleged actions. Below are Elliott's remarks dealing with a claim by the House of Representatives that a generalized legislative privilege precluded submission of testimony presented to House committees.*

...Whatever its source, the question here presented is whether the privilege claimed by the House of Representatives or, in this case, by one of its subcommittee chairmen, is an absolute privilege or is limited by application of the Bill of Rights. The answer to this question is made obvious and easy by the recent "definitive" decision of the Supreme Court in the case of U.S. v. Nixon....

If we substitute the word "legislative" for the words "Presidential" or "executive" [in the "Nixon" opinion], we see that the Supreme Court in deciding the "Nixon case" also decided the "Calley case."

The privilege claimed by the President was the generalized privilege of executive confidentiality. The privilege claimed by [the subcommittee] was the generalized privilege of legislative confidentiality.

The President sought to stand behind the doctrine of separation of powers. The Chairman of the House Subcommittee seeks to stand behind the doctrine of separation of powers.

The Supreme Court held that the executive branch was not entitled to invoke the privilege of confidentiality at the expense of the individual accused's right to evidence at his criminal trial. Here we hold that the legislative branch was not entitled to invoke the privilege of confidentiality at the expense of the individual accused's right to evidence at his criminal trial....

> *(4) Excerpts from Elliott's opinion finding that charges preferred against Calley were inadequate in that they did not specify the names or descriptions of any of the 70 or more persons allegedly killed by him or ordered killed by him nor the locations of any of the slayings.*

...Neither the research of the parties nor that of this Court reveals any military or federal cases, other than this case, allowing an offense to be alleged covering multiple unnamed victims in a single specification. Those cases cited by the Petitioner and by the government dealing with multiple victims within an indictment, deal with individuals who were specifically recognizable....

In this case the testimony indicated that there were several various and separate acts allegedly committed by the Petitioner and by others over a period of some few hours. Not all of the people identified by any one individual who testified with regard to the charged multiple killings were alleged to have been killed by the Petitioner alone.... There was, similarly, no specific time frame given by the prosecution as to when the killings took place, and as a result the Petitioner could have been convicted of the crimes charged without there being an agreement on the part of the jurors as to time, identity, location or even number. This raises a problem of unique character, at least as far as American jurisprudence is concerned—the problem of possible double jeopardy within the same criminal proceeding....

In this case there was indeed a risk (even a probability) that the Petitioner was twice convicted for the same individual killing within the same trial....

The constitutionally mandated notice was not present in this case to enable the Petitioner to know what he had to defend against and to protect him from double jeopardy....

▼▼▼

SUMMIT ON THE U.S. ECONOMY
September 27-28, 1974

The long-awaited economic summit conference proposed by President Ford Aug. 12 in response to a Senate request, (see p. 696), concluded on Sept. 28 and Ford and his advisers began putting together the economic policy recommendations he had promised to send to Congress within 10 days. (Ford's Anti-recession and tax proposal, see p. 975-980.) *Although the two-day summit discussions produced no new proposals and little consensus on what should be done, Ford's conference-closing remarks hinted that the administration would call for some form of public service jobs and tax-relief programs for the individuals and industries hurt most by inflation and by flagging economic activity. "Inflation strikes society unevenly," Ford told more than 1,500 participants in the conference on inflation, "and government must concern itself with those on whom this burden falls excessively."*

Summing up the summit findings from the Democratic congressional viewpoint, Sen. Hubert H. Humphrey (D Minn.) told the conference that "any policy that brings higher unemployment and lower real incomes for our people, in the name of controlling inflation, is simply unacceptable. It will not wash." That Democrats would disassociate themselves from any continuation of the policies Ford inherited from the Nixon administration became clear in opening statements delivered Sept. 27 by House Speaker Carl Albert (D Okla.) and Senate Majority Leader Mike Mansfield (D Mont.). Taking pains to point out that the inflation summit had been managed by the White House, Albert termed it "no secret that there is a divergence of views, generally and specifically, between the Republican administration and the Democratic majority in Congress with regard to economic policy." Calling both inflation and recession "social dynamite," Mansfield argued that federal budget restraint was "only a fragment of the answer to our difficulties" and offered his own nine-point program, including such stern steps as mandatory wage, price, rent and profit controls.

Proposals to Curb Inflation

Mansfield was one of only a few participants to endorse a return to wage and price controls. Proposals that won widespread acceptance included:

• *Continued federal budget restraint, although many participants opposed spending cuts that would harm their interests and some questioned whether the resulting reduction in inflation was worth the risk of worsening unemployment.*

• *Some loosening of the Federal Reserve Board's tight restraints on monetary growth to relieve pinched credit markets, although Federal Reserve Chairman Arthur F. Burns and others insisted that monetary restraint still must be applied to retard inflation.*

• *Some kind of action to combat the effects of petroleum price increases forced upon the world by the oil-producing nations.*

• *Re-examination of federal government regulatory policies that discourage price competition.*

Outside of those areas of general consensus, representatives from separate economic sectors presented the divergent views which they had expressed during preparatory pre-summit meetings around the nation.

Organized labor leaders stressed the threat of unemployment and called for public service jobs, lower interest rates, credit allocation for housing and tax relief paid for by tax reforms. They were especially critical of the President's advisers, including Federal Reserve Chairman Burns, and opposed wage controls.

Business and manufacturing interests, while giving surprising support for tax relief at lower income levels, urged measures that would help business expand capacity. Those included tax incentives for capital investment and the lifting of federal regulations that required business to devote resources to nonproductive investments such as pollution control and job safety. Representatives from the banking and finance sector supported budget restraint and easing of monetary policy. They supported lower-income tax relief and tax incentives for investment, including an exemption or credit for savings account interest. To make up lost revenues, they supported tax increases at higher income levels or excise taxes on luxuries.

Views of Housing, Energy and Transportation Sectors

Representatives from agriculture and the housing, oil, gas and transportation industries put forth views on measures that could ease their par-

ticular problems. With their industry gripped by a severe slump, housing leaders called for tax incentives for savings, expansion of federal housing assistance, loosening of credit and a separate construction panel within the Council on Wage and Price Stability. Agriculture representatives urged incentives to greater productivity, including higher subsidy-triggering prices and credit allocations to farmers. Oil and gas industry spokesmen urged a full-scale energy conservation program to reduce dependence on high-priced foreign oil. Decontrol of oil and gas prices was supported as an incentive to domestic production. In addition, transportation industry representatives called for revision of federal regulatory policies, including quicker freight-rate increases, relaxation of environmental protection requirements, tax breaks, termination of unprofitable rail service and relaxation of Interstate Commerce Commission regulations. They also urged reduction of oil prices.

Representing groups who feared that federal programs benefiting them would be cut, participants from the Department of Health, Education and Welfare argued against spending reductions that would harm those who suffered most from inflation. They called for increased spending in public service jobs, national health insurance, more frequent adjustment of Social Security benefits and tax increases at higher income levels. Consumer groups, complaining that they were inadequately represented in the various discussion areas, called for improved economic efficiency that would reduce prices. They urged elimination of federal restrictions on market competition, stepped-up antitrust law enforcement and action to roll back petroleum prices.

At the White House economic summit conference on the economy Sept. 27-28, House Speaker Albert and Senate Majority Leader Mansfield presented the views of the Democratic leadership in Congress Sept. 27. Rep. Barber B. Conable Jr. and Sen. Humphrey summed up the positions of the Republican and Democratic parties, respectively, as the conference closed Sept. 28. President Ford made the closing remarks Sept. 28. Texts of their addresses follow:

Speaker Albert

...I agree with the President that the occasion which brings us together today is an important one.

I wish to thank the President on behalf of the Democratic Members of the House of Representatives for convening this economic summit and for inviting Members of the Congress to participate.

This effort to call upon the best thinking of business, labor, government and the democratic community underscores the extraordinary nature of our current economic problems.

The American people are facing their most severe economic difficulties in a generation.

Our economy is besieged by rapid inflation, growing recession and unemployment.

Inflation in the price of consumer goods is running at a rate of 12 percent annually.

Almost five million workers are already without jobs, and unemployment continues to spread across our land.

In the face of these urgent problems, we have come together to endeavor to work out mutually agreeable and effective solutions.

The Congress has willingly participated in this conference but I think it should be made clear that the conference—and I do not say this critically—has been managed by the Executive Branch, and that Congressional input in its organization has been limited.

I have appointed outstanding Members of Congress to participate in the various economic summit meetings, and I have been informed by them that elements of conference planning, which strongly influenced conclusions, for example, the selection of pre-summit meeting participants, the writing of agendas and the naming of spokesmen for the various panels appearing today have been done entirely by the Executive Branch.

As we begin our work today, it is no secret that there is a divergence of views, generally and specifically between the Republican Administration and the Democratic Majority in Congress with regard to economic policy.

The pre-summit meetings have made this abundantly clear.

The Administration in effect has spoken of the old-time religion, of tight money and fiscal stringency, coupled with tax incentives for business and cutbacks in social programs.

We believe that if this conference gives its entire attention to only those economic factors, we will surely not accomplish what we hoped to achieve today and we will fall short of what our Nation needs.

For example, we must recognize from the outset that several major factors in our current price inflation lie beyond our immediate control, and that some other factors we can readily control, such as federal spending, have had little role in causing price increases.

Among elements to some extent beyond our control—food and oil have been two of the major contributors to rapid price increases in our economy.

While in the past policy errors have led to food price increases, much of our present food price inflation results from bad weather in the Middle West and elsewhere in the world, which has, unfortunately, limited harvests.

There is no recovering these crop losses in the short term.

Similarly, great increases in the price of oil have resulted from a factor beyond our control, particularly the decision of the oil-producing countries to curtail production. This has caused world as well as domestic problems of a magnitude which can hardly be overestimated, and I commend the President for bringing this matter to the attention of the United Nations a few days ago.

The Democratic Party, and particularly the House Democratic Caucus, have searched for broad policies to counteract the many and varied elements which are causing our current price inflation.

Democrats' Proposals

We are on record as supporting expanded public employment programs. We stand for an adequate program of public service employment with the goal of a job for all able and willing to work.

I believe that the prompt creation of 100,000 such jobs is vitally necessary.

Public service employment helps those worst hurt by inflation without unleasing inflationary forces in the economy and, additionally, local governments benefit by obtaining the manpower needed to improve their services.

We Democrats in Congress also favor bringing down interest rates through chanelling credit toward activities that can help people most, such as housing, small business, utilities, food production and other productive capital investment; assisting labor and industry in achieving an equitable wage structure for the worker is also an important goal.

This can be achieved, we believe, through a balanced tax reform package including measures to offset the harm done by inflation to the purchasing power of lower and middle-income families.

We hope for tax reform that includes social security or tax relief to low and middle-income persons balanced by eliminating unjustified tax subsidies wherever found.

We have been very pleased by recent indications that the President intends to cooperate in achieving this urgently needed tax reform.

We would expect the business sector to show equivalent restraint in price behavior. In particular, we want an end to administrative price increases, those introduced by concentrated industries solely as an exercise of their economic might upon a captive consumer market.

This may be achievable through skillful and imaginative use of the Council on Wage and Price Stability—at least we hope so.

Finally, we have proposed a thorough review of the government's own economic policies and machinery and cutting out of waste and unnecessary expenditures. Of course, in all candor, we must admit there are differences in opinion among well-intentioned people and good Americans as to what in any case constitutes waste.

Thus, as we go into today's discussion, it is clear that there have been differences in the views held by the various party participants.

Willingness to Cooperate

But we come here today in the spirit of compromise and conciliation, in the knowledge that the problems we face are too serious to allow partisan wrangling or preconceived ideas about fiscal and monetary policy to delay their solution.

We are truly hopeful that we will find in our sessions today and tomorrow the flexibility of mind and unity of purpose, which will allow us to move and to move quickly to combat our growing economic ills.

We in Congress, I believe, have already shown our spirit of cooperation by quickly passing more than a month ago the legislation authorizing establishment of the Council on Wage and Price Stability.

Let me note parenthetically we hope the Executive Branch will soon name the Members of this Council and that it will begin its important work.

Other actions of the Congress have also shown our willingness to cooperate to solve our Nation's economic problems. The Congress' Joint Economic Committee, for example, has reported unanimously with every Democratic and Republican Member participating in an action program to reduce inflation and restore economic growth.

This program represents a sound initiative and I would hope these recommendations can be considered carefully here today and I believe they have been overlooked at the pre-summit meeting sessions.

Extremely important, for example, is the Committee's conclusion that massive reductions in federal spending would do little to forestall inflation while such reductions might in fact trigger a major inflation.

This conclusion in my view may very well be a breakthrough in economic thinking, second only to Congressional acceptance in the 1964 Revenue Act of the deliberate creation of a budget deficit for the purpose of getting the Nation moving again.

Finally, the Joint Democratic Leadership stands ready to bring the Congress back in session after the elections to receive and to act on proposals from the Executive Branch to address our problem of unemployment, recession and inflation.

In short, we will do all that we can to restore the economic health of our nation without sacrificing longstanding principles of social and economic justice for all Americans.

We hope that the Administration will continue throughout these sessions to demonstrate the spirit shown in the President's decision to follow up on Senator Mansfield's suggestion to hold these economic summit meetings, for only through cooperation and compromise, which I hope we can achieve at this Conference, will we be able to formulate an economic recovery program which will offer relief to the great majority of our people, distribute the burden of inflation more equitably and get this Nation moving again.

After we have achieved these goals, we can turn to the really important business of building America, of guaranteeing every American's right to a job and to economic security as we set out to do under the Full Employment Act, guaranteeing every American's right to a good education, to decent housing, and health care, and to all the other goals which represent the best part of the programs of America.

Senator Mansfield

Mr. President, Mr. Speaker, Senator Scott, Senator Tower, Ladies and Gentlemen: As the President has said, we are all soldiers in the fight against inflation.

As he also said, it applies—inflation—to Democrats, Republicans and independents alike—in other words to all of us.

There have been mini-meetings of this Conference in Washington and across the land. These meetings have been educational and instructive. They have brought to light many views on the state of the economy. But what thing of value to the people of the nation will come out of these meetings?

This is the critical question. As one who was among the first to welcome the President's call for this Summit Conference, I must state in all candor that I am not too optimistic about the results.

This Conference has had the participation of the foremost economists in the country—in and out of government. They have told us what the inflation and recession are all about—in a hundred versions. The talk has been of micro-economics, macro-economics, econometrics and what not.

Of these things, of importance to economists, the public knows nothing. Of inflation, the public knows a great deal. Of recession, the public is learning more and more each day. The public knows too that little has been done to stem the inflation or to halt the march of recession, anywhere by anyone.

Everyone recognizes that petroleum is one of the main sources of the problems which confront us. Yet, today, we are importing 40 percent of our petroleum needs as compared to 35 percent a year ago. The price of crude has sky-rocketed and the end is not in sight. In 1972, $4.7 billion was spent on imports; $8.2 billion in 1973; $27 billion plus in 1974. The trend is up, up, up.

For America and for many other countries, a major source of inflation lies in these figures, in the manipulated spigot of international petroleum flow. As far as the United States is concerned, the other factor is Viet Nam. Viet Nam is water under the bridge only in the sense that we cannot undo what has already been done. Its terrible cost will extend far into the first half of the next century. It will be paid by the sacrifices of several generations.

Inflation has turned the world of the past two decades upside down. Things that are going up should be coming down and they are not. Retail prices are up by 47 percent annually. Unemployment is up. Interest rates are up. Medical costs are up by 36 percent.

Things that are coming down should be going up and they are not. The stock market is down—$500 billion in values have been lost and 31 million people are affected. Real income is down. Our international trade balances have hit a record low. Auto sales are down 22 percent from a year ago. Unemployment in Michigan stands at 9.3 percent, compared to 5½ overall in the country. Housing is down 45 percent and yet in some places, construction wages have been increased by 20 percent. How can more houses be built and sold when prices are higher, interest rates are higher and construction wages are higher?

Need for Action

I am not an economist and make no pretenses. What is clear to me, however, is that the time for words—micro, macro or whatever is at an end. Words will no longer satisfy the nation. Inflation is social dynamite; walk through any food market in any suburb and take note of the comments. Recession is social dynamite; walk through areas of high unemployment in any city and ask what lies ahead. The divisions among people, among societies, among nations are on the rise. They will not wait for the "self-adjusting mechanisms" of the economy to self-adjust.

What is the answer? Mostly, we hear talk about the need for a tight Federal budget and tight money. Of course, we need to keep rein on government expenditures, in good times and bad, and especially on the extravagant and the irrelevant. At best, however, the Federal budget is only a fragment of the answer to our difficulties.

It is said, too, the fault lies with the American consumer. Tell that to the grocery-shopper who feeds a family on inflation-eroded wages or a fixed income. Tell it to the home-owner who uses oil to keep out the cold and the worker who uses gasoline to get to work. The fact is that the laissez faire application of the laws of demand and supply no longer correct the economic ills of a society already bound in by a massive complex of intervention built up over decades. The clock cannot be turned back to Adam Smith's Eighteenth Century England.

The nation is in an economic emergency. The people expect government to confront that emergency and to act on it in the general interests of the people. We have not done so and even now seem to lack the capacity to do so.

Take the problem of energy-supply as an example. A year ago, we talked of crash programs to increase our own production and to develop substitutes to reduce the dependency on imported oil.

Congress has appropriated vast funds and stands ready to appropriate more for this purpose. But what have we really achieved with this year of grace? What have we really done? We have allowed the self-adjusting mechanisms of the economy to operate quite freely in petroleum.

We have let prices find their own level. In a society grown universally dependent on petroleum, that is the cruelest form of rationing. The burden falls heaviest on those with the least income.

The need for new action—equitable action—by this Administration in cooperation with the Congress: It exists not only with regard to petroleum but in many other matters. As the President has already been informed, the Senate majority believes that integrated action in seven fields is needed to curb inflation and to halt the recession.

Multiple Approach

These fields are (1) budget reductions, (2) wage, prices and profit control, (3) selective monetary credit easement, (4) tax adjustments, (5) positive action to deal with shortages and supplies, (6) development of new employment, and (7) readjustment of international policies.

Credit curbs alone are not enough. Budget cutting alone is not enough. Indeed, the budget has already been cut by Congress and will be cut further. But how much inflation can really be squeezed out of the economy by this method and at what price? How much will it cost in lost jobs, lost output, lost public services and business failures?

As for the international economic situation, particularly as it involves petroleum, the Senate and all Americans welcome the call for increased cooperation among consuming nations; and, indeed, there is no reason not to extend the call to the producing nations.

We welcome joint policies designed to assure international distribution of essential commodities. The answer will not be found in confrontation with other nations but in cooperation by our own people with others.

Some countries like Italy and the United Kingdom face bankruptcy. A whole corridor of humanity spanning the African Continent is starving. Along with petroleum these and countless other specific situations are all parts of a world-wide whole. International petroleum problems must be dealt with in that context.

There are many areas that must be addressed in regard to our economic predicament. We must address them candidly and act on their dictates within the framework of this nation's basic tenets.

Nine-Point Plan

At this time, I offer on my own behalf for the consideration of this Conference, a nine-point program of Federal action. I do not think we are going to come to grips with the mounting problems of the economy unless we begin to move in the direction of:

1. Establishing, as needed, mandatory wage, price, rent and profit controls.

2. Reviving the Reconstruction Finance Corporation to deal with the credit needs of ailing businesses such as Penn Central, Lockheed and Grumman, Pan American, TWA and many more headed in the same direction; Congress is not the proper forum for specific decisions involving government bail-outs.

3. Restoring Regulation W to require larger downpayments on credit purchases and shorter periods for repayment and allocating credit on a priority basis in the light of the nation's critical needs.

4. Beginning an equitable rationing system for energy and other scarce materials to the end that dependency on foreign sources of petroleum can be reduced and beginning, too, a stringent conservation system including measures to enforce the speed limit and to bring about a reduction of wastage in the utility and other industrial fields.

5. Developing a broader system of indexing to the end that the real incomes of wage earners can be tied to real living costs.

6. Without delay, to establish a commission on supplies and shortages, legislation for which has already passed the Congress.

7. Curbing excessive profits and controlling the flow of investments abroad through the taxing power while conversely cutting taxes on Americans hardest hit by inflation, those in low and moderate income categories and those on moderate fixed incomes.

8. Creating without delay, a jobs program which puts people to work in public services and elsewhere as necessary to keep down the level of un-employment.

9. Working with all nations prepared to work with us to deal with cartel-created shortages in petroleum or other commodities, and there are other commodities, recognizing that petroleum is only one aspect of the larger question of the interrelationship of the economic well-being of all nations and the stability of the world.

Sacrifices are needed across the board if we are going to restore the nation's economy. In my judgment, the people of this nation are prepared to make those sacrifices. They will do whatever must be done, so long as the burdens are equitable. This is the job of the President and the Congress—to ensure that the sacrifices are fairly distributed.

It is time to put aside the evasions and circumlocutions. The bell is tolling. There is no need to send to find out for whom. It is tolling for all of us.

Senator Humphrey

...The most important finding, as I see it, of this conference is that we have not one, but two public enemies—inflation and recession.

It has been called by Dr. Samuelson "stagflation." May I say out home all they know is that prices are too high, the number of unemployed is too high, and the production too low. That is what we are dealing with.

Any policy that brings higher unemployment and lower real incomes for our people, in the name of controlling inflation, is simply unacceptable. It will not wash and you have to understand it.

The Employment Act of 1946 has scarcely been mentioned here and yet it is law and it established the basic economic contract between the American people and their government. It declares that it is the policy and the responsibility of the Federal Government to promote "maximum employment, production and purchasing power."

Now, this is the law of the land just as surely as the Internal Revenue Code is the law, but that contract has been violated or it has been ignored and often trampled upon and by government.

Some Questions

I ask some questions:

Do really high interest rates promote "maximum employment, production and purchasing power?"

They do not.

Does excessively tight money promote "maximum employment, production and purchasing power?"

It does not.

Does failure to enforce the anti-trust laws promote "maximum employment, production and purchasing power?"

It does not.

Do our incredibly unfair tax laws, jerry-built over the years, that encourage mergers and destroy competition, that extend special tax favors to some promote "maximum employment, production and purchasing power?"

They do not.

We are guilty of violating federal law here in the government of the United States.

Any policy to deal with our economic problems must live up to the promise of the Employment Act of 1946 to the American people unless you want to repeal the law.

Regrettably, we have had no consistent economic policy in recent years.

The freezes, the phases, the variety of economic game plans have resulted for the business community, for everyone, in uncertainty and doubt which in themselves have contributed to inflation and recession.

The proposals and actions resulting from this economic summit, therefore, must result in a reliable, consistent economic policy, faithful to the goals of the Employment Act or this conference will have failed.

Now, it is said that inflation is a thief in the night robbing every American equally. I think we have dispelled that idea because this is wrong. Inflation, as has been brought out here time after time, discriminates against the poor, the disabled, and the minorities, and if you happen to have all of those at one time, you are literally destroyed.

It does hit crippling blows to small business, to housing, to families, to farmers and to the vast majority of wage earners.

The 12 percent inflation that we talked about in the past year is really not factual at all. We are kidding ourselves. It is much higher for low and middle income families who are required to spend about 80 percent or more of their income on food, fuel, housing, transportation, clothing and health care, and it is the price rises on these essentials that must above all be stopped and reduced unless you want unbelievable political and social trouble in this country.

Some have called here for a big budget cut in the federal budget but with little or no regard for the effect on State and local government where government and people meet head-on.

We have summarized here today that there are no quick and easy answers to long-term complex problems, but that does not relieve us from certain steps that can and must be taken now to bring down prices or at least stabilize them, to reduce interest rates, to conserve fuel, and we will see whether we really mean conservation in the next few weeks or whether we have talked it, to create jobs and to get this economy moving again.

Some people can talk about our enduring a recession when you have a job, but talk to the people who don't have one and see how they like it or try it for size when you are out of one. We are living in an economy that is not

871

just economics. We are living in a political society of free people, and they are going to have something to say about their future.

From this conference, therefore, should come an agenda of economic action and this should take the form of a legislative program that the President will present to us, and then there are a number of administrative actions under existing law that can be taken.

Some Agenda Items

As I see it, the agenda for economic action should include, among other things, immediate and some long-term considerations.

There can be, there are and will be budget reductions, but a $5 billion or even a $10 billion budget cut will not put food on the table and it will not put another paycheck in somebody's pocket.

I want to compliment Dr. Heller on his paper in the *Wall Street Journal* of September 27th on the nine myths on budget cutting and inflation.

The watchword as I see it in this summation for all of us is can we be fair? Fairness and justice is what the Constitution calls for—fairness in all segments of the economy.

The other watchword is discipline which the American people really don't like to have—discipline in eliminating waste, discipline in working habits, in private industry and government, and discipline as mentioned here in the administration of governmental programs. Fiscal discipline, yes but wholesale cuts in people programs that save the lives of people which is promoting the general welfare under the Constitution, no.

We must remember that while inflation erodes income, recession and unemployment destroy income.

Now, there has been some talk here about the old-time religion and some people say that is our trouble. I don't happen to think that is all of it. I think the trouble is the revival of old-time sin. Some of that old-time sin is pretty clear here today. The policies of excessively tight money, and I know you must have management of money supply and of high interest that just goes at its own pace, appropriation impoundments and half-way controls administered by people who don't believe in them have not cured our economic ills and won't. In fact, the patient's fever is rising and his paralysis is spreading. The doctors—and most of them are here today—had better change the prescription or we may lose the patient.

And might I say more personally the American family may decide to change the doctors at the executive and legislative levels.

Need for Energy Policy

I will start with a national energy policy which has been emphasized here. We don't have a national energy policy. We have a lot of scattered shots but a national energy policy emphasizing the kind of conservation we have heard of and expanded research that is really something on the Manhattan style and leadership that was pointed out by the United States among the oil importing countries in dealing with the OPEC countries.

We also need a program of immediate tax relief to low- and middle-income Americans and it has to be offset by closing some of the most glaring tax loopholes and increasing revenues from the upper end of the income scale.

We need a national food policy and my fellow Americans we don't have a national food policy and we don't have a secretary that wants one and we ought to understand it.

A national food policy that not only expands production, but provides an assurance of fair and stable incomes to farmers and assures adequate supplies of food at reasonable prices to the American consumer. This may very well include an export licensing system for agricultural commodities determined to be in critically short supply.

You can't have the American people going short of food simply in the name of commerical exports. It won't work.

You have to have a food reserve program in this country for national security purposes. If Mr. Schlesinger can ask for reserves of munitions for the security of our country, I ask for reserves of food to protect the American security and the American consumer and farmer alike.

We need a credit allocation program. We have one now. It is to the highest bidder. That is what you have got and that is not going to work.

A credit allocation program to assure the availability of reasonably priced credit for priority uses such as local government, housing and small business; interest rates can be and must be brought down.

We need a tough new anti-trust enforcement program and it ought to be done.

We need a national health insurance program.

We need a balanced national growth and development policy, some economic planning.

We are the only industrialized country in the world with no economic plans. This is unforgivable.

We need a full employment program with the jobs being primarily in the public sector, but we need public service jobs and we need a national domestic development bank.

If we can lend under the Export-Import Bank at a low rate of interest, why can't we lend it to our own people at the same rate of interest?

We need a stronger role for the Wage-Price Council and get some teeth in it as was said here today and we need a federal action office to break up the bottlenecks of raw materials, fertilizers—

We need a productivity council of labor and business.

I want to say that I want to compliment our President. I will tell you why.

This is open government. This is what he said—a national town meeting of the air. This is more public education on economics than this country has had since the last great depression.

I think we can avoid it and I want to say this is democracy in action, of debate, dialogue, discussion and dissent and we are now going to have decision and the time to act is now. Action delayed is a remedy denied.

Thank you.

Representative Conable

...We are at the end of a very interesting and encouraging experiment in representative government.

As a member of the Steering Committee for this conference, I have been to six of these meetings, and I can attest that a wide range of interests and aspirations have been represented in the pre-summits as in this room. It should be apparent that the process has not been rigged because so many people have been permitted to charge it was.

Here the American people have been able to watch representatives engage in open dialogue with the President and members of Congress about the gravity of a problem that concerns us all.

I hope others are as proud as I am that such a process is possible. Such openness will help renew our confidence.

The President's patience and unfailing good nature in presiding here so long yesterday and his returning under the circumstances of today to close this conference show the high priority he gives to the battle against inflation.

We know difficult decisions lie ahead, and the inspiration of such leadership is essential if we are to accept those decisions and carry the resulting programs to a successful conclusion.

The Members of Congress present are grateful that the President understands the relevance of Congress to this battle and that he will offer and expect more than politics as usual in our mutual relations no matter how imminent the political season.

Here and at the pre-summits, what we have been seeking is understanding and consensus. As a Republican in Congress, I have none of the pleasure in minority status that Professor Galbraith seems to enjoy. My purpose is to summarize here the majority views of these meetings as I see them. The limitations of time and participation yesterday and today may have made the outline sketchy, but the total record of all the meetings will show, I believe, widespread agreement about the following seven points.

Points of Agreement

• First, fiscal discipline is needed even though the immediate trade-off between spending cuts and the short-term rate of inflation is not all that impressive.

Our current calamity results in substantial part from the cumulative impact of careless though well-intentioned over-stimulus from spending more than we taxed.

Further, undisciplined behavior at this time by the Government will rob us of our right to lead America out of the economic swamps because the people understand instinctively what the Government has apparently been a long time learning.

• Second, monetary discipline is also needed although many believe we have reached the point where serious dislocation will occur if pressure is not taken off interest rates.

● Third, to maintain public support for a substantial monetary and fiscal discipline, we in Government must be wisely sensitive to the special problems our troubled economy inflicts on the poor, the potentially unemployed, the elderly, the small businessman and farmer, the housing industry, and the consumer. It is going to require judgment, flexibility, and real leadership to find the right balance between toughness and human concern.

● Fourth, there is virtually no support in industry, labor or among rank-and-file Congressmen for wage and price controls. Talk about their inevitability, which many of us think is cynically based upon the expectation of short public memories, should be discouraged. Things were bad in August of 1971 but they are worse now after three years of controls.

● Fifth, many believe that too many industries have the power to raise prices beyond what a healthier competition would permit. Many also believe that labor should be given incentives rather than coercion to moderate its wage demands even where real wages have been eroded by inflation. Perhaps such incentives should be built into any tax adjustment given to lower-income people.

● Sixth, great emphasis should be put on conservation of resources and the reduction of waste particularly in the energy field.

● Seventh, the world depends upon American prosperity and economic stability.

One of the frightening things to learn as a Congressman is that so often we legislate not just for 210 million people but for the whole world.

The leadership needed from the United States now is not military or political but economic. Cartel-type price-fixing in oil and basic materials can probably be dealt with only if America encourages and leads a collective response from the consuming developed and less-developed nations.

Trade bill completion by the Congress will help as a first step in needed negotiating authority.

Now, the President may see the elements of consensus differently than I do. Since he speaks with one voice while we in Congress speak with many, the advantage in finding consensus and in initiating programs lies with the presidency. In dealing with this problem, complexity is our enemy but strong and decisive leadership can give us faith that the underlying realities are being dealt with. Whether or not we agree about the details, if the program is fair, all Americans will be willing to accept necessary sacrifice even though we as a nation have become quite self-indulgent compared to our grandparents.

But we urge the President, the Government as a whole, the Congress not to lose the momentum of these meetings as a preliminary to action. We understand it is not going to be easy or quick. It cannot be done with mirrors.

An element of consensus that I have not mentioned before is that the problem is urgent and we all want to get at it—everyone who has attended these meetings. We don't just want action for the sake of action. Our economic and political freedoms are at stake. Some of the nostrums which have been proposed will require wise leadership in this voluntary nation of ours to keep our sense of urgency alive and effective as long as it must be kept alive, but those of us in the Congress who know the President so well think both branches of Government now have what it takes.

Thank you.

President Ford

...I thank each and every one of you for your contributions to this summit. For most summits, there is no way to go except down. From this summit, we are going to start going up.

This is not the end, but it is the beginning of a battle against inflation and waste which will not end until it is won.

I have vowed and asked all of you to resolve here that we will celebrate our Nation's 200th birthday with our economy healthy and strong, with prosperity as well as peace that brings the solid realities of a great Republic.

Thousands and thousands of dedicated men and women have come together in this series of inflation conferences to map the strategies and the tactics of our all-out war against America's domestic enemy number one.

All of you will be the Founding Fathers, if we succeed. If we fail, then certainly we will all hang separately.

General George Washington's words at the start of our Nation are equally appropriate at this time, and I quote: "Let us raise the standard to which the wise and honest can repair, the rest is in the hands of God."

And God helps those who help themselves. On this principle, Americans in two centuries have astonished the world and time and time again have confounded the pessimists and the cynics who said it couldn't be done.

You have discussed many ideas. You have spoken candidly, and as a result, I, along with other Americans, have gained a far better understanding of our economic problems. Perhaps we have caught glimpses of the political problems, and we understand those, but even in our controversies, we have all developed a super sense of direction.

His Turn

You have done your homework well; now it is my turn.

In the days immediately ahead, I will offer to the American people and to the Congress a program of action which will help bring balance and vitality to our economy. This program could not be formulated without your participation and without the support of millions of other Americans who have given us their ideas.

I think all agree on one point: Inflation must be stopped. But this Administration will respond not with words but with action and with programs. As your President, the only special interest I have, the only special interest I represent is the American people—housewives struggling with rising grocery prices, workers whose real purchasing power has eroded because of inflation, businessmen trying to control rising costs, families needing new homes, but unable to find mortgage money to buy them, those thousands of unemployed who want work, the elderly locked into pension programs earned years ago, indeed all 213 million Americans.

I pledge to you that I will not shrink from the hard decisions needed to meet the problems facing each and every one of us. This is a critical hour in America's history. It requires that Americans once again rise above our society. The very future of our political and economic institutions, indeed our whole way of life, is literally at stake.

A fundamental fact of human history is precisely this: Nations which cannot impose upon themselves a disciplined management of their fiscal and monetary affairs are doomed to economic disorder and widespread inflation.

Such discipline is imperative. It is urgent if we are to achieve a stable and expanding economy. The American people have repeatedly demonstrated their ability to submerge personal and group interests to the general welfare. When they know the chips are down, they are really down—and they have done it in the past and they will do it again—they will respond as they always have.

As part of the demanded discipline, I will send to the Congress a plan of action to keep Federal outlays for fiscal year 1975 at or under $300 billion. Every dollar the Federal Treasury must borrow is a dollar not available to the home buyer or the businessman trying to expand or other citizens who may be borrowers for good and sufficient reasons.

A coherent national policy on energy is essential for economic stability. It must encourage prudent use of available energy. There must be an assured future energy supply to enable consumers and businessmen to plan in a confident and orderly way.

I will soon propose a national energy program aimed at assuring adequate internal supplies while reducing dependence on external sources.

At this very minute, Secretaries Kissinger and Simon are exploring with their counterparts from four major industrial nations a coordinated plan to cope with a world energy crisis and world economic dislocations.

Today, I can announce three actions I have just taken:

Economic Policy Board

First, I have directed the consolidation by Executive Order of all the Federal Government economic efforts, domestic and international, under a new Economic Policy Board. The Secretary of the Treasury, Bill Simon, will serve as chairman of this board and as my principal spokesman on matters of economic policy.

I have appointed Bill Seidman, who has done so well with this conference, to serve as my assistant for the coordination and the implementation of economic affairs and also as Executive Director of the new Economic Policy Board.

In addition to Secretary Simon and Bill Seidman, I have appointed eight Cabinet officers as members of this board. They include Henry Kissinger, Rogers Morton, Earl Butz, Fred Dent, Pete Brennan, Caspar Weinberger, Jim Lynn and Claude Brinegar.

In addition, membership includes the Director of the Office of Management and Budget, Roy Ash; the Chairman of the Council of Economic Advisers, Alan Greenspan, and the Executive Director of the Council on International Economic Policy, William Eberle.

Dr. Arthur Burns, Chairman of the Board of Governors of the Federal Reserve System, will attend meetings of this board, which will start work immediately.

Labor-Management Committee

Second, I have established by Executive Order a White House Labor-Management Committee whose counsel and recommendations will not only be sought by me but given to me man-to-man and face-to-face.

Eight distinguished labor leaders and eight distinguished business executives comprise its membership. The objective of this committee is not only to serve as advisers to me on major economic policies, but to help assure effective collective bargaining, promote sound wage and price policies, develop higher standards of living, boost productivity and establish more effective manpower policies.

Dr. John T. Dunlop, a dedicated public servant and professor of economics at Harvard University, has agreed, and we are very thankful, to serve as coordinator of this committee.

Representing labor on this committee will be President George Meany of the AFL-CIO, Secretary-Treasurer Lane Kirkland of the AFL-CIO, President I. W. Abel of the United Steel Workers of America, President Murray H. Finley of the Amalgamated Clothing Workers of America, President Paul Hall of the Seafarers International Union of North America, President Frank Fitzsimmons of the Teamsters International Union, and President Leonard Woodcock of the United Auto Workers and President Arnold Miller of the United Mine Workers.

Representing management on the committee will be John Harper of the Aluminum Company of America, Reginald H. Jones of General Electric, Steve Bechtel of the Bechtel group, Richard Gerstenberg of General Motors, Rawleigh Warner of the Mobil Oil Company, Walter Wriston of the First National City Bank, Arthur Wood of Sears, Roebuck and Company, and R. Heath Larry of U.S. Steel.

I am proud to announce this group of 16 distinguished, outstanding Americans.

A third announcement: The Council on Wage and Price Stability recently established by Congress at my request and with my deep appreciation is another arm I will use in the fight on inflation. I have asked Dr. Albert Rees, a distinguished economist and professor of economics at Princeton, to direct the Council's work.

We are fortunate to have Dr. Rees with us.

And may I express to all the people, those that I have mentioned and others that will help, their willingness to step in and help the country and 213 million people. But nobody knows better than I that councils and committees cannot win this war.

The most important weapon in the fight against inflation is the spirit of the American people. This spirit is no secret weapon. It is renowned all over the world, and I call on each of you in this room, but more urgently, on each of you at home watching on television, and all the other Americans across this vast land who either hear or read my words, I urge them as I know they will, to join with all of us in a great effort to become inflation fighters and energy savers.

I know all across our country the question everyone asks me is, "What can I do to help?"

I will tell you how we can start. Right now, make a list of some ten ways you can save energy and you can fight inflation. Little things that become habits—they do become habits. They don't really affect in some instances your health and happiness. They are habits that you can abandon if we are all faced with this emergency.

I suggest that each person exchange your family's list with your neighbors and I urge you and ask you to send me a copy.

Some of the best ideas come from your home rather than from the White House. The success or failure of our fight against inflation rests with every individual American. Our country is above all a union. And you and I can make it a more perfect union as our fathers did.

One of our delegates yesterday, Sylvia Porter, the well-known newspaper columnist on economics, has kindly consented to help me to get this voluntary citizens' program organized and underway, and I thank you very, very much, Sylvia.

It was dramatically pointed out here yesterday that inflation strikes our society very unevenly. Government must concern itself with those on whom the burden falls excessively.

For instance, we must provide productive work for those without jobs. We must adjust our tax system to encourage savings, stimulate productivity, discourage excessive debt, and to correct inflation-caused inequities.

And I can assure the American people that the Executive Branch and the Congress working together will effectuate and implement such a program.

May I add a very special word to our distinguished foreign guests. What you heard here yesterday and today may remind each of you of the current problems of your own country's economy. The problems of people are not very different in these days wherever they live and work.

The whole world suffers from inflation.

I assure you the United States is seeking honest solutions that will help, not hinder, other nations' efforts to advance or restore their economic health.

I will have extensive consultations with leaders of other governments aimed at strengthening international institutions and to assure that we never again experience worldwide and interacting inflations and deflations.

Plan to Congress

There are more difficult decisions ahead for me and for the Congress. From the many alternative policies which we have heard here given in good faith, listened to in good faith, we can and will fashion a coherent and consistent program.

I will present my recommendations to the nation and to the Congress within the next ten days.

Finally, you will understand my two compelling reasons for cancelling all but my most essential appointments and travel plans in order to be here in Washington. I will devote every minute that I can to forging the mass of evidence and the evaluations generated by this conference into concrete action, into concrete plans and legislative proposals.

A great leader of this country—of this century, I should say—in whom the unbeatable willpower of his American heritage, combined with English eloquence, rallied his embattled countrymen from almost certain defeat by a blunt promise of blood, toil, tears and sweat.

I trust we can avoid blood and tears and we will.

But I do offer you plenty of toil and plenty of sweat.

I will roll up my sleeves and work every bit as hard as you do, starting this week-end, until every American is enlisted as an inflation fighter and as an energy saver until this job is done.

Thank you and God bless you.

October

U.S.-POLISH RELATIONS
October 8 and 9, 1974

A new era in American-Polish diplomatic relations was opened October 8 and 9 as President Ford met with Polish Communist Party First Secretary Edward Gierek at the White House. During their two days of meetings, the leaders signed nine agreements, comprised of two treaties of "friendship" and "good political relations" and seven economic and technological accords. At the end of the talks, it was announced that President Ford had accepted an invitation to visit Poland in 1975. According to the State Department, the agreements marked the establishment of the United States' most comprehensive ties with any Communist nation other than the Soviet Union. Gierek, the first Polish Communist Party chief to visit the United States since the Communists gained control of Poland at the end of World War II, met with Ford during an eight-day tour of this country that also included a speech by the Polish Communist Party Leader at the United Nations, meetings with members of Congress and a visit in Houston with Lieut. Col. Karol Bobko, an American astronaut of Polish ancestry.

Ford and Gierek issued a joint communique at the end of their talks, discussing the context of U.S.-Polish relations. They also signed a "joint statement on the development of economic, industrial and technological cooperation" Oct. 9 which anticipated a doubling of American-Polish trade volume by 1980. The second joint statement signed that day, affirming "feelings of friendship" and "friendly relations," endorsed the belief that "mutually beneficial economic relations are conducive to good political relations."

*The seven other agreements were largely technical in nature. They in-
cluded a pact to fund jointly a total of $54-million in scientific and
technological projects; an agreement to cooperate in research on methods of
coal extraction and use; an accord removing double taxation on goods and
individuals between the two countries; an agreement to cooperate in the
area of medicine and health care, including 89 joint research projects; a
pact calling for joint efforts aimed at protection of the environment; a joint
statement.on agricultural trade that called for three-year advance projections of crop yields and import needs; and an accord calling for the establishment of a joint economic council by the Chambers of Commerce of
the two nations.*

*Text of a joint U.S.-Polish communique issued at the con-
clusion of talks between President Ford and Polish Communist Party First Secretary Edward Gierek:*

JOINT U.S.-POLISH COMMUNIQUE

At the invitation of the President of the United States of America,
Gerald R. Ford, and Mrs. Ford, the First Secretary of the Central Committee of the Polish United Workers' Party, Edward Gierek, and Mrs.
Gierek, paid an official visit to the United States October 8 through 13,
1974.

The First Secretary was accompanied by: Mieczyslaw Jagielski, Deputy
Chairman of the Council of Ministers, and Mrs. Jagielski; Stefan
Olszowski, Foreign Minister, and Mrs. Olszowski; Ryszard Frelek, Member
of the Secretariat of the Central Committee of the Polish United Workers'
Party; Witold Trampczynski, Polish Ambassador to the United States of
America.

The First Secretary was also accompanied by a group of advisers and experts.

The official party also visited New York, Pittsburgh, and Houston.

During his stay in Washington, First Secretary Gierek held talks with
President Ford on the development of relations between Poland and the
United States as well as on international issues.

He also met with Secretary of State and Assistant to the President for
National Security Affairs Henry A. Kissinger, Secretary of Agriculture
Earl Butz, Secretary of Commerce Frederick Dent, Secretary of Health,
Education and Welfare Caspar Weinberger, and Chairman of the Export-
Import Bank William Casey.

The First Secretary paid a visit to Congress and met with members of the
Senate and the House of Representatives. He also had talks with leading
American businessmen and bankers.

Talks were also held between Foreign Minister Olszowski and Secretary
of State Kissinger.

The talks and meetings were held in a friendly and businesslike atmosphere and were characterized by a mutual desire to expand and strengthen the relations between Poland and the United States.

In the course of the talks, the President and the First Secretary noted with satisfaction the significant progress which has recently been made in Polish-American relations. Both leaders expressed their desire to further develop these relations, which are based on the long-standing traditions of friendship and sympathy existing between the Polish and American peoples.

They agreed that the "Joint Statement on Principles of U.S.-Polish Relations" signed during the visit provides a firm basis for broad cooperation between the two countries and contributes to the process of strengthening world peace, security, and international cooperation.

The President and the First Secretary also attached importance to the "Joint Statement on the Development of Economic, Industrial and Technological Cooperation between the United States of America and the Polish People's Republic," which they signed. They agreed that the main directions and scope of cooperation stipulated in the field of trade, industrial and technological cooperation should contribute to the further advancement of bilateral economic relations.

The President and the First Secretary noted with satisfaction the rapid growth of trade between the United States and Poland in the past two years, accompanied by a substantial intensification of general economic relations between the two countries. They considered a mutual trade turnover of one billion dollars by 1976 and two billion dollars by 1980 to be a realistic and desirable goal.

They also agreed that the provisions contained in the "Joint Statement on the Development of Agricultural Trade between the United States of America and the Polish People's Republic" create possibilities for a further expansion of trade in food and agricultural products as well as for cooperation in various sectors of the agricultural economy.

They noted that the Joint American-Polish Trade Commission plays an important role in the development of trade and economic cooperation.

President Ford and First Secretary Gierek expressed their deep satisfaction at the conclusion during the visit of agreements in the fields of: Coal research; Health; Environmental Protection; Cooperation in Science and Technology; and Avoidance of Double Taxation.

They also welcomed the conclusion of an agreement on the establishment of working relationships between the U.S. and Polish Chambers of Commerce.

Both leaders stressed the significance of the broad development of cultural and scientific cooperation between the United States and Poland and expressed their conviction that this cooperation should be further developed.

The President and the First Secretary emphasized the importance of historical traditions in strengthening the bonds of sympathy and friendship between the United States and Poland. A positive role in this strengthening of mutual relations has been played by American citizens of Polish descent. Both leaders undertook to encourage and support further development of those and other contacts between the American and Polish people.

The President and the First Secretary conducted a broad and useful exchange of views on the most important international issues with special emphasis on European questions. They agreed that there exist a number of spheres in which both countries can contribute to the strengthening of peace and international security.

Both leaders expressed satisfaction with the results of the talks they held and agreed that consultations will continue between the two countries at various levels on matters concerning their mutual relations, including the assessment of the implementation of the agreements that were concluded as well as on important international issues of mutual interest.

The First Secretary and Mrs. Gierek expressed their warm gratitude for the hospitality and friendliness accorded to them in the United States.

The First Secretary extended an invitation to the President of the United States and Mrs. Ford to pay an official visit to the Polish People's Republic at a time convenient to them. The invitation was accepted with pleasure.

FORD'S TESTIMONY ON
NIXON PARDON

October 17, 1974

In a rare presidential appearance at a formal congressional committee hearing, President Gerald R. Ford Oct. 17 went before the House Judiciary Committee to answer questions about his pardon of Richard M. Nixon. (Pardon of Nixon, see p. 811-817.) While there was little ceremony to mark the occasion, Ford's appearance may have been the first time in history a sitting president testified before a congressional committee. The White House cited two precedents for Ford's appearance: The first was the appearance of George Washington before a special House committee investigating an ill-fated military expedition against a small body of Indians; the second came in 1862 when President Abraham Lincoln went before the House Judiciary Committee to explain the leak of his State of the Union message to the New York Herald. However, the authenticity of these two incidents was questioned by a Library of Congress specialist in executive privilege, Harold Relyea, who told Historic Documents *that the first instance probably never occurred and the second was not well documented.*

In a 45-minute prepared statement, Ford stressed that his appearance before the Judiciary Subcommittee on Criminal Justice was voluntary and did not create a precedent. At one point Ford seemed to hint that he might not answer all the questions that were put to him. Though he came "in a spirit of cooperation," Ford said, "even then we may not mutually agree on what information falls within the proper scope of inquiry by the Congress." He said he respected the right of executive privilege "when it protects advice given to a President in the expectation that it will not be disclosed," since otherwise a president could not obtain frank advice. In addition, Ford declared, executive privilege might extend to Nixon. The principle "may be exercised as well by a past president if the information sought pertains to his official functions when he was serving in office."

Ford Denies Any "Deal"

Ford flatly denied that any secret arrangement on the pardon had been made between him and Nixon before Nixon left office. "I want to assure you, members of this subcommittee, members of Congress and the American people, there was no deal, period, under no circumstances," Ford at one point told Rep. Elizabeth Holtzman (D N.Y.), thumping the witness table for emphasis. Instead, he insisted that he pardoned the former president for the good of the nation.

Ford's decision to testify on the pardon had been announced Sept. 30 by the White House, the day the President informed the subcommittee he would appear before it in person to respond to questions about the pardon. Subcommittee Chairman William L. Hungate (D Mo.) had written the President concerning two resolutions introduced in the House Sept. 12 calling on the President to answer questions about the pardon. Ford responded initially with a letter to Hungate referring the chairman to questions Ford answered at a news conference.

Hungate termed Ford's reply "unsatisfactory" and the subcommittee sent the President another letter requesting him to send a representative to testify on the pardon. In reply, the President informed the subcommittee that he would appear before it personally "to respond to the questions."

> *Excerpts from President Ford's testimony Oct. 17 before the Criminal Justice Subcommittee of the House Judiciary Committee on his Sept. 8 pardon of former President Richard M. Nixon:*

We meet here today to review the facts and circumstances that were the basis for my pardon of former President Nixon on September 8, 1974.

I want very much to have those facts and circumstances known. The American people want to know them. And Members of the Congress want to know them. The two Congressional resolutions of inquiry now before this committee serve those purposes. That is why I have volunteered to appear before you this morning, and I welcome and thank you for this opportunity to speak to the questions raised by the resolutions.

My appearance at this hearing of your distinguished subcommittee of the House Committee on the Judiciary has been looked upon as an unusual historic event—one that has no firm precedent in the whole history of Presidential relations with the Congress. Yet, I am here not to make history, but to report on history....

H Res 1367 before this Subcommittee asks for information about certain conversations that may have occurred over a period that includes when I was a Member of Congress or the Vice President. In that entire period, no references or discussions on a possible pardon for then President Nixon occurred until August 1 and 2, 1974.

You will recall that since the beginning of the Watergate investigations, I had consistently made statements and speeches about President Nixon's innocence of either planning the break-in or of participating in the coverup. I sincerely believed he was innocent.

Even in the closing months before the President resigned, I made public statements that in my opinion the adverse revelations so far did not constitute an impeachable offense. I was coming under increasing criticism for such public statements, but I still believed them to be true based on the facts as I knew them.

Meeting With Haig

In the early morning of Thursday, August 1, 1974, I had a meeting in my Vice Presidential office, with Alexander M. Haig, Jr., chief of staff for President Nixon. At this meeting, I was told in a general way about fears arising because of additional tape evidence scheduled for delivery to Judge Sirica on Monday, August 5, 1974. I was told that there could be evidence which, when disclosed to the House of Representatives, would likely tip the vote in favor of impeachment. However, I was given no indication that this development would lead to any change in President Nixon's plans to oppose the impeachment vote.

Then shortly after noon, General Haig requested another appointment as promptly as possible. He came to my office about 3:30 p.m. for a meeting that was to last for approximately three-quarters of an hour. Only then did I learn of the damaging nature of a conversation on June 23, 1972....

I describe this meeting because at one point it did include references to a possible pardon for Mr. Nixon, to which the third and fourth questions in H. Res. 1367 are directed. However, nearly the entire meeting covered other subjects, all dealing with the totally new situation resulting from the critical evidence on the tape of June 23, 1972. General Haig told me he had been told of the new and damaging evidence by lawyers on the White House Staff who had first-hand knowledge of what was on the tape. The substance of his conversation was that the new disclosure would be devastating, even catastrophic, insofar as President Nixon was concerned. Based on what he had learned of the conversation on the tape, he wanted to know whether I was prepared to assume the Presidency within a very short time and whether I would be willing to make recommendations to the President as to what course he should now follow.

I cannot really express adequately in words how shocked and stunned I was by this unbelievable revelation. First, was the sudden awareness I was likely to become President under these most troubled circumstances; and secondly, the realization these new disclosures ran completely counter to the position I had taken for months, in that I believe the President was not guilty of any impeachable offense....

General Haig asked for my assessment of the whole situation. He wanted my thoughts about the timing of a resignation, if that decision were to be made, and about how to do it and accomplish an orderly change of Administration. We discussed what scheduling problems there might be and what the early organizational problems would be.

General Haig outlined for me President Nixon's situation as he saw it and the different views in the White House as to the courses of action that might be available, and which were being advanced by various people around him on the White House Staff. As I recall there were different major courses being considered:

(1) Some suggested "riding it out" by letting the impeachment take its course through the House and the Senate trial, fighting all the way against conviction.

(2) Others were urging resignation sooner or later. I was told some people backed the first course and other people a resignation but not with the same views as to how and when it should take place.

Nixon's Options on Resignation

On the resignation issue, there were put forth a number of options which General Haig reviewed with me. As I recall his conversation, various possible options being considered included:

(1) The President temporarily step aside under the 25th Amendment.

(2) Delaying resignation until further along the impeachment process.

(3) Trying first to settle for a censure vote as a means of avoiding either impeachment or a need to resign.

(4) The question of whether the President could pardon himself.

(5) Pardoning various Watergate defendants, then himself, followed by resignation.

(6) A pardon to the President, should he resign.

The rush of events placed an urgency on what was to be done. It became even more critical in view of a prolonged impeachment trial which was expected to last possibly 4 months or longer.

The impact of the Senate trial on the country, the handling of possible international crises, the economic situation here at home, and the marked slowdown in the decisionmaking process within the Federal Government were all factors to be considered and were discussed.

General Haig wanted my views on the various courses of action as well as my attitude on the options of resignation. However, he indicated he was not advocating any of the options. I inquired as to what was the President's pardon power, and he answered that it was his understanding from a White House lawyer that a President did have the authority to grant a pardon even before any criminal action had been taken against an individual, but, obviously, he was in no position to have any opinion on a matter of law....

I told General Haig I had to have time to think; further, that I wanted to talk to James St. Clair. I also said I wanted to talk to my wife before giving any response. I had consistently and firmly held the view previously that in no way whatsoever could I recommend either publicly or privately any step by the President that might cause a change in my status as Vice President. As the person who would become President if a vacancy occurred for any reason in that office, a Vice President, I believed, should endeavor not to do or say anything which might affect his President's tenure in office. Therefore, I certainly was not ready even under these new circumstances to make any recommendations about resignation without having adequate time to consider further what I should properly do.

Shortly after 8:00 o'clock the next morning James St. Clair came to my office. Although he did not spell out in detail the new evidence, there was no question in my mind that he considered these revelations to be so damaging that impeachment in the House was a certainty and conviction in the Senate a high probability. When I asked Mr. St. Clair if he knew of any other new and damaging evidence besides that on the June 23, 1972, tape, he said "no." When I pointed out to him the various options mentioned to me by General Haig, he told me he had not been the source of any opinion about Presidential pardon power.

After further thought on the matter, I was determined not to make any recommendations to President Nixon on his resignation. I had not given any advice or recommendations in my conversations with his aides, but I also did not want anyone who might talk to the President to suggest that I had some intention to do so.

For that reason I decided I should call General Haig the afternoon of August 2. I did make the call late that afternoon and told him I wanted him to understand that I had no intention of recommending what President Nixon should do about resigning or not resigning, and that nothing we had talked about the previous afternoon should be given any consideration in whatever decision the President might make. General Haig told me he was in full agreement with this position.

My travel schedule called for me to make appearances in Mississippi and Louisiana over Saturday, Sunday, and part of Monday, August 3, 4, and 5. In the previous 8 months, I had repeatedly stated my opinion that the President would not be found guilty of an impeachable offense. Any change from my stated views, or even refusal to comment further, I feared, would lead in the press to conclusions that I now wanted to see the President resign to avoid an impeachment vote in the House and probable conviction vote in the Senate. For that reason I remained firm in my answers to press questions during my trip and repeated my belief in the President's innocence of an impeachable offense. Not until I returned to Washington did I learn that President Nixon was to release the new evidence late on Monday, August 5, 1974.

At about the same time I was notified that the President had called a Cabinet meeting for Tuesday morning, August 6, 1974. At that meeting in the Cabinet Room, I announced that I was making no recommendations to the President as to what he should do in the light of the new evidence. And I made no recommendations to him either at the meeting or at any time after that.

In summary, I assure you that there never was at any time any agreement whatsoever concerning a pardon to Mr. Nixon if he were to resign and I were to become President.

The first question of H. Res. 1367 asks whether I or my representative had "specific knowledge of any formal criminal charges pending against Richard M. Nixon." The answer is: "no."

I had known, of course, that the grand jury investigating the Watergate break-in and coverup had wanted to name President Nixon as an unindicted co-conspirator in the coverup. Also, I knew that an extensive report had been prepared by the Watergate Special Prosecution Force for the grand jury and had been sent to the House Committee on the Judiciary, where, I believe, it served the staff and members of the Committee in the development of its report on the proposed articles of impeachment. Beyond what was disclosed in the publications of the Judiciary Committee on the subject and additional evidence released by President Nixon on August 5, 1974, I saw on or shortly after September 4 a copy of a memorandum prepared for Special Prosecutor Jaworski by the Deputy Special Prosecutor, Henry Ruth. Copy of this memorandum had been furnished by Mr. Jaworski to my Counsel and was later made public during a press briefing at the White House on September 10, 1974.

I have supplied the Subcommittee with a copy of this memorandum. The memorandum lists matters still under investigation which "may prove to have some direct connection to activities in which Mr. Nixon is personally involved." The Watergate coverup is not included in this list, and the alleged coverup is mentioned only as being the subject of a separate memorandum not furnished to me. Of those matters which are listed in the memorandum, it is stated that none of them "at the moment rises to the level of our ability to prove even a probable criminal violation by Mr. Nixon."

This is all the information I had which related even to the possibility of "formal criminal charges" involving the former President while he had been in office.

The second question in the resolution asks whether Alexander Haig referred to or discussed a pardon with Richard M. Nixon or his representatives at any time during the week of August 4, 1974, or any subsequent time. My answer to that question is: not to my knowledge. If any such discussions did occur, they could not have been a factor in my decision to grant the pardon when I did because I was not aware of them.

Questions three and four of H. Res. 1367 deal with the first and all subsequent references to, or discussions of, a pardon for Richard M. Nixon, with him or any of his representatives or aides. I have already described at length what discussions took place on August 1 and 2, 1974, and how these discussions brought no recommendations or commitments whatsoever on my part. These were the only discussions related to questions three and four before I became President, but question four relates also to subsequent discussions.

At no time after I became President on August 9, 1974, was the subject of a pardon for Richard M. Nixon raised by the former President or by anyone representing him. Also, no one on my staff brought up the subject until the day before my first press conference on August 28, 1974. At that time, I was advised that questions on the subject might be raised by media reporters at the press conference.

As the press conference proceeded, the first question asked involved the subject, as did other later questions. In my answers to these questions, I took a position that, while I was the final authority on this matter, I expected to make no commitment one way or the other depending on what the Special Prosecutor and courts would do. However, I also stated that I believed the general view of the American people was to spare the former President from a criminal trial.

A Prolonged Trial Would Have Disrupted The Country

Shortly afterwards I became greatly concerned that if Mr. Nixon's prosecution and trial were prolonged, the passions generated over a long period of time would seriously disrupt the healing of our country from the wounds of the past. I could see that the new Administration could not be effective if it had to operate in the atmosphere of having a former President under prosecution and criminal trial. Each step along the way, I was deeply concerned, would become a public spectacle and the topic of wide public debate and controversy.

As I have before stated publicly, these concerns led me to ask from my own legal counsel what my full right of pardon was under the Constitution in this situation and from the Special Prosecutor what criminal actions, if any, were likely to be brought against the former President, and how long his prosecution and trial would take.

As soon as I had been given this information, I authorized my Counsel, Philip Buchen, to tell Herbert J. Miller, as attorney for Richard M. Nixon, of my pending decision to grant a pardon for the former President. I was advised that the disclosure was made on September 4, 1974, when Mr. Buchen, accompanied by Benton Becker, met with Mr. Miller....

The fourth question in the resolution also asks about "negotiations" with Mr. Nixon or his representatives on the subject of a pardon for the former President. The pardon under consideration was not, so far as I was concerned, a matter of negotiation. I realized that unless Mr. Nixon actually accepted the pardon I was preparing to grant, it probably would not be effective. So I certainly had no intention to proceed without knowing if it would be accepted. Otherwise, I put no conditions on my granting of a pardon which required any negotiations.

Although negotiations had been started earlier and were conducted through September 6 concerning White House records of the prior administration, I did not make any agreement on that subject a condition of the pardon. The circumstances leading to an initial agreement on Presidential records are not covered by the resolutions before this Subcommittee. Therefore, I have mentioned discussions on that subject with Mr. Nixon's attorney only to show they were related in time to the pardon discussions but were not a basis for my decision to grant a pardon to the former President.

The fifth, sixth, and seventh questions of H. Res. 1367 ask whether I consulted with certain persons before making my pardon decision.

I did not consult at all with Attorney General Saxbe on the subject of a pardon for Mr. Nixon. My only conversation on the subject with Vice Presidential nominee Nelson Rockefeller was to report to him on September 6, 1974, that I was planning to grant the pardon.

Special Prosecutor Jaworski was contacted on my instructions by my Counsel, Philip Buchen. One purpose of their discussions was to seek the information I wanted on what possible criminal charges might be brought against Mr. Nixon. The result of that inquiry was a copy of the memorandum I have already referred to and have furnished to this subcommittee. The only other purpose was to find out the opinion of the Special Prosecutor as to how long a delay would follow, in the event of Mr. Nixon's indictment, before a trial could be started and concluded.

At a White House press briefing on September 8, 1974, the principal portions of Mr. Jaworski's opinion were made public. In this opinion, Mr. Jaworski wrote that selection of a jury for the trial of the former President, if he were indicted, would require a delay "of a period from nine months to a year, and perhaps even longer." On the question of how long it would take to conduct such a trial, he noted that the complexities of the jury selection made it difficult to estimate the time. Copy of the full text of his opinion dated September 4, 1974, I have now furnished to this subcommittee.

I did consult with my Counsel, Philip Buchen, with Benton Becker, and with my Counsellor, John Marsh, who is also an attorney. Outside of these men, serving at the time on my immediate staff, I consulted with no other attorneys or professors of law for facts or legal authorities bearing on my decision to grant a pardon to the former President.

Questions eight and nine of H. Res. 1367 deal with the circumstances of any statement requested or received from Mr. Nixon. I asked for no confession or statement of guilt, only a statement in acceptance of the pardon when it was granted. No language was suggested or requested by anyone acting for me to my knowledge. My Counsel advised me that he had told the attorney for Mr. Nixon that he believed the statement should be one expressing contrition, and in this respect, I was told Mr. Miller concurred. Before I announced the pardon, I saw a preliminary draft of a proposed statement from Mr. Nixon, but I did not regard the language of the statement, as subsequently issued, to be subject to approval by me or my representatives.

Nixon's Health

The tenth question covers any report to me on Mr. Nixon's health by a physician or psychiatrist, which led to my pardon decision. I received no such report. Whatever information was generally known to me at the time of my pardon decision was based on my own observations of his condition at the time he resigned as President and observations reported to me after that from others who had later seen or talked with him. No such reports were by people qualified to evaluate medically the condition of Mr. Nixon's health, and so they were not a controlling factor in my decision. However, I believed and still do, that prosecution and trial of the former President would have proved a serious threat to his health, as I stated in my message on September 8, 1974.

H. Res. 1370 is the other resolution of inquiry before this subcommittee. It presents no questions but asks for the full and complete facts upon which was based my decision to grant a pardon to Richard M. Nixon.

I know of no such facts that are not covered by my answers to the questions in H. Res. 1367. Also:

Subparagraphs (1) and (4): There were no representations made by me or for me and none by Mr. Nixon or for him on which my pardon decision was based.

Subparagraph (2): The health issue is dealt with by me in answer to question 10 of the previous resolution.

Subparagraph (3): Information available to me about possible offenses in which Mr. Nixon might have been involved is covered in my answer to the first question of the earlier resolution.

Other Possible Watergate Pardons

In addition, in an unnumbered paragraph at the end, H. Res. 1370 seeks information on possible pardons for Watergate-related offenses which others may have committed. I have decided that all persons requesting consideration of pardon requests should submit them through the Department of Justice.

Only when I receive information on any request duly filed and considered first by the Pardon Attorney at the Department of Justice would I consider the matter. As yet no such information has been received, and if it does I will act or decline to act according to the particular circumstances presented, and not on the basis of the unique circumstances, as I saw them, of former President Nixon.

By these responses to the resolutions of inquiry, I believe I have fully and fairly presented the facts and circumstances preceding my pardon of former President Nixon. In this way, I hope I have contributed to a much better understanding by the American people of the action I took to grant the pardon when I did. For having afforded me this opportunity, I do express my appreciation to you, Mr. Chairman, and to Mr. Smith, the Ranking Minority Member, and to all the other distinguished Members of this subcommittee; also to Chairman Rodino of the Committee on the Judiciary, to Mr. Hutchinson, the Ranking Minority Member of the full committee, and to other distinguished Members of the full committee who are present.

In closing, I would like to reemphasize that I acted solely for the reasons I stated in my proclamation of September 8, 1974, and my accompanying message and that I acted out of my concern to serve the best interests of my country. As I stated then: "My concern is the immediate future of this great country . . . My conscience tells me it is my duty, not merely to proclaim domestic tranquility, but to use every means that I have to insure it." . . .

CONGRESSMAN WILLIAM L. HUNGATE. Mr. President, on behalf of the subcommittee, we express our appreciation for your appearance here bringing facts that will be helpful to the American people and the Congress.

There will be some who will find the answers fully satisfactory and forthright. There will be others who will not. But I would hope that all would appreciate your openness and willingness to come before the American public and the Congress to discuss this important matter.

The gentleman from Wisconsin, Mr. Kastenmeier.

CONGRESSMAN ROBERT W. KASTENMEIER. Thank you, Mr. Chairman....

Mr. President, you indicated that you wanted to spare Mr. Nixon a criminal trial. Did you specifically have any other end in view in terms of protecting Mr. Nixon in terms of a pardon; that is to say, whatever a pardon would spare the President other than a criminal trial, were there any other adversities which a pardon would help Mr. Nixon with, as you saw it?

THE PRESIDENT. As I indicated in the proclamation that I issued, and as I indicated in the statement I made at the time on September 8, my prime reason was for the benefit of the country, not for any benefits that might be for Mr. Nixon.

I exercised my pardon authority under the Constitution, which relates only to those criminal matters during the period from January 20, 1969, until August 9, 1974.

CONGRESSMAN KASTENMEIER. I appreciate that, Mr. President, but it must have been something you foresaw which could happen to Mr. Nixon which justified a pardon, if in fact you were advised, and perhaps you were not, that there was no proceeding going to be commenced against Mr. Nixon, that nothing would happen to him, really a pardon may have been an empty gesture in that event?

THE PRESIDENT. As I indicated, Mr. Kastenmeier, after the press conference on August 28 where three questions were raised about the pardon or the possibility of a pardon, I asked my Counsel to find out from the Special Prosecutor what, if any, charges were being considered by the Special Prosecutor's office.

As I indicated in my prepared statement, I received from Mr. Jaworski certain information indicating that there were possible or potential criminal proceedings against Mr. Nixon....

CONGRESSMAN HUNGATE. The gentleman from New York, Mr. Smith.

CONGRESSMAN HENRY P. SMITH 3d. Mr. President, [I]n regard to your answer of whether you consulted with certain persons and in that connection and in connection with question number six of H.R. 1367, you stated in regard to the Vice Presidential nominee, Nelson Rockefeller, that your only conversation on the subject with him was to report to him on September 6, 1974, that "I was planning to grant the pardon."

Now, the question asks whether he gave you any facts or legal authorities and my question is, did he do so?

THE PRESIDENT. Nelson Rockefeller did not give me any facts or legal authorities. He was in my office to discuss with me the proceedings concerning his nomination, and at the conclusion of a discussion on that matter, I felt that I should inform him of the possible or prospective action that I would be taking, but he gave no facts, he gave me no legal advice concerning the pardon.

CONGRESSMAN SMITH. Mr. President, as you were minority leader of the Congress before you became Vice President of the United States, did you at any time discuss the wisdom or advisability of a possible Presidential pardon for President Nixon with President Nixon or any of his representatives or any member of the White House Staff?

This was in the period before you became Vice President.

THE PRESIDENT. The answer is categorically no. Before I became Vice President, Mr. Smith, I, on several occasions—I can't recall how many—indicated to President Nixon himself that I thought he should not resign.

If my memory is accurate, Mr. Smith, before I became Vice President, there were individuals both in the Congress and otherwise who were advocating that Mr. Nixon resign.

I do recall on one or more occasions telling Mr. Nixon in my judgment he should not, because I thought that would be an admission of guilt, and on the information I had at that time, I did not believe Mr. Nixon was guilty of any impeachable offense....

CONGRESSMAN DON EDWARDS. Mr. President, put yourself in the position of the high school teacher, shall we say, in Watts or the barrios of San Jose or Harlem, and if you were such a teacher, how would you explain to the young people of America the American concept of equal justice under law?

THE PRESIDENT. Mr. Edwards, Mr. Nixon was the 37th President of the United States. He had been preceded by 36 others. He is the only President in the history of this country who has resigned under shame and disgrace.

I think that that in and of itself can be understood, can be explained to students or to others. That was a major, major step, and a matter of, I am sure, grave, grave deliberations by the former President, and it certainly, as I have said several times, constituted shame and disgrace....

CONGRESSMAN JAMES R. MANN. Mr. President, Mr. Kastenmeier asked you about the termination of the investigation by the Special Prosecutor's office. Was it your intention, by the pardon, to terminate the investigation by the Special Prosecutor's office in the 10 areas that you received the report from that office upon?

THE PRESIDENT. I think the net result of the pardon was, in effect, just that; yes, sir.

CONGRESSMAN MANN. And is that part of the reason that you didn't consult with Mr. Jaworski with reference to the tape agreements as to how that might affect his further investigations?

THE PRESIDENT. Well, as I pointed out, the tape agreement was initiated between my legal counsel and Mr. Nixon sometime before the question of a pardon ever arose.

The reason for that, Mr. Mann, is that I came into office and almost immediately there were demands and requests, not only from the Special Prosecutor, as I recall, but from other sources as to those tapes and other documents. And one of the first things I did when these problems came to my desk was to ask the Attorney General for his opinion as to the ownership of those tapes or any other documents.

And once we got that information, then we felt that there ought to be some discussion as to where the tapes and other documents would be held and under what circumstances....

CONGRESSMAN MANN. What response would you have if the Special Prosecutor's Office now requested access to certain of the tapes now in the custody of the Government?

THE PRESIDENT. The material that is still held by the Government, in my understanding of the Supreme Court decision, permits the Special Prosecutor to obtain any of that material for its responsibility, and I, of course not in a personal way, would make certain that that information was made available to the Special Prosecutor's office....

CONGRESSWOMAN ELIZABETH HOLTZMAN. Thank you, Mr. Chairman, and Mr. Ford, I too, wish to applaud your historical appearance here today. At the same time, however, I wish to express my dismay that the format of this hearing will not be able to provide to the American public the full truth and all of the facts respecting your assurance of a pardon to Richard Nixon.

Unfortunately, each member of this committee will have only 5 minutes in which to ask questions about this most serious matter, and unfortunately, despite my urging, the committee declined to provide sufficient time for each committee member to ask the questions that were appropriate.

The committee declined to prepare fully for your coming by calling other witnesses, such as Alexander Haig, Mr. Buchen, Mr. Becker, and has failed to insist also on full production of documents by you respecting the issuance of this pardon.

I must confess my own lack of easiness at participating in a proceeding that has raised such high expectations and unfortunately, will not be able to respond to them.

I would like to point out, Mr. President, that the resolutions of inquiry which have prompted your appearance here today have resulted from very dark suspicions that have been created in the public's mind.

Perhaps these suspicions are totally unfounded, and I sincerely hope that they are. But nonetheless, we must all confront the reality of these suspicions and the suspicions that were created by the circumstances of the pardon which you issued, the secrecy with which it was issued, and the reasons for which it was issued which made people question whether or not, in fact, it was a deal.

THE PRESIDENT. May I comment there? I want to assure you, the members of this subcommittee, the Members of the Congress and the American people, there was no deal, period, under no circumstances.

CONGRESSWOMAN HOLTZMAN. Mr. President, I appreciate that statement, and I am sure many of the American people do, as well. But they also are asking questions about the pardon, and I would like to specify a few of them for you so that perhaps we can have some of these answered.

I think, from the mail I have received from all over the country, as well as my own district, I know that the people want to understand how you can explain having pardoned Richard Nixon without specifying any of the crimes for which he was pardoned. And how can you explain pardoning Richard Nixon without obtaining any acknowledgement of guilt from him? How do you explain the failure to consult the Attorney General of the United States with respect to the issuance of the pardon, even though in your confirmation hearings you had indicated the Attorney General's opinion would be critical in any decision to pardon the former President?

How can this extraordinary haste in which the pardon was decided on and the secrecy with which it was carried out be explained, and how can you explain the pardon of Richard Nixon, accompanied by an agreement with respect to the tapes which, in essence, in the public's mind, hampered the Special Prosecutor's access to these materials, and this was done, also, in the public's mind, in disregard of the public's right to know the full story about Richard Nixon's misconduct in office.

And, in addition, the public, I think, wants an explanation of how Benton Becker was used to represent the interests of the United States in negotiating a tapes agreement when at that very time, he was under investigation by the United States for possible criminal charges?

And how, also, can you explain not having consulted Leon Jaworski, the Special Prosecutor, before approving of the tapes agreement? And I think, Mr. President, that these are only a few of the questions that have existed in the public's mind before and unfortunately still remain not resolved. And since I have very brief time, I would like to ask you, in addition to these questions, one further one, and that is that suspicions have been raised that the reason for the pardon and the simultaneous tapes agreement was to insure that the tape recordings between yourself and Richard Nixon never came out in public. To alleviate this suspicion once and for all, would you be willing to turn over to this subcommittee all tape recordings of conversations between yourself and Richard Nixon?

THE PRESIDENT. Those tapes, under an opinion of the Attorney General which I sought, according to the Attorney General—and, I might add, according to past precedent—belong to President Nixon. Those tapes are in our control. They are under an agreement which protects them, totally, fully, for the Special Prosecutor's office or for any other criminal proceedings.

Those tapes will not be delivered to anybody until a satisfactory agreement is reached with the Special Prosecutor's office. We have held them because his office did request that, and as long as we have them held in our possession for the Special Prosecutor's benefit, I see no way whatsoever that they can be destroyed, that they can be kept from proper utilization in criminal proceedings.

Now, those tapes belong to Mr. Nixon according to the Attorney General, but they are being held for the benefit of the Special Prosecutor, and I think that is the proper place for them to be kept....

AGREEMENT ON
SOVIET JEWISH EMIGRATION
October 18, 1974

A compromise between Soviet desires for preferential U.S. trade benefits and congressional concerns for the unrestricted emigration of Soviet Jews emerged Oct. 18 in an exchange of letters made public by Sen. Henry M. Jackson (D Wash.). The letters between Jackson and Secretary of State Henry A. Kissinger discussed an informal agreement reportedly reached between Kissinger and Soviet leaders. According to Kissinger, the compromise agreement included Soviet assurances aimed at satisfying Congress regarding Soviet policy on emigration in exchange for congressional passage of long-stalled legislation granting the Soviet Union most-favored-nation status. The preferential trade benefits for imported Soviet goods had been a goal set originally by President Nixon and Soviet Communist Party General Secretary Leonid I. Brezhnev at the first U.S.-Soviet summit in 1972 (see Historic Documents 1972, p. 431-463) *and heavily stressed by Brezhnev at the 1973 summit* (see Historic Documents 1973, p. 587-609).

In an apparent effort to mute publicity on the compromise agreement, Jackson made public the exchange of letters, but not Kissinger or the White House. In fact, neither the White House nor the State Department officially commented on the compromise. While the agreement was immediately hailed as a major breakthrough in international civil liberties, Kissinger cautioned members of Congress Dec. 3 that any attempt "to nail down publicly" additional details or commitments was "likely to backfire." However, Kissinger stressed, that fact did not alter his understanding of certain Soviet assurances incorporated in the compromise package.

In the ensuing months, the publicity prompted by the emigration agreement brought strident denials from the Soviet Union that their leaders had ever given the assurances indicated. Nonetheless, Congress Dec. 20 passed and sent to President Ford trade reform legislation that included provisions authorizing the President for 18 months to grant most-favored-nation status to Communist countries, including the Soviet Union. At the end of the 18 months, the most-favored-nation status could be renewed if Congress, satisfied with Soviet emigration policy, adopted a concurrent resolution extending the President's authority for a year.

On Dec. 18, the day House and Senate conferees reached agreement on the trade reform legislation, linking the Soviet trade benefits with Jewish emigration, the Soviet Union issued a statement denying that it had given any specific assurances that emigration policies would be eased in return for American trade concessions. The statement in particular refuted a claim made by Jackson that emigration would increase. The Soviet Union also released the text of an Oct. 26 letter to Kissinger from Soviet Foreign Minister Andrei Gromyko, criticizing the Jackson-Kissinger letters as a "distorted picture of our position as well as of what we told the American side on that matter." President Ford signed the bill into law Jan. 3, 1975. On Jan. 14, the Soviet Union notified the State Department that it could not accept the trade agreement under the conditions imposed by the Jewish emigration amendment. The Soviet action appeared to deliver a political setback to Jackson as well as mark the trade bill for reconsideration during the 94th Congress.

Following are the full texts of letters released Oct. 18 between Secretary of State Henry A. Kissinger and Sen. Henry M. Jackson (D Wash.) on the agreement regarding emigration of Soviet Jews. Also included is Soviet Foreign Minister Andrei Gromyko's Oct. 26 letter to Kissinger:

Secretary Kissinger's Letter

October 18, 1974

Dear Senator Jackson:

I am writing to you, as the sponsor of the Jackson Amendment, in regard to the Trade Bill (H.R. 10710) which is currently before the Senate and in whose early passage the administration is deeply interested. As you know, Title IV of that bill, as it emerged from the House, is not acceptable to the administration. At the same time, the administration respects the objectives with regard to emigration from the U.S.S.R. that are sought by means of the stipulations in Title IV, even if it cannot accept the means employed. It respects in particular your own leadership in this field.

To advance the purposes we share both with regard to passage of the trade bill and to emigration from the U.S.S.R., and on the basis of discussions that have been conducted with Soviet representatives, I should like on behalf of the administration to inform you that we have been assured that the following criteria and practices will henceforth govern emigration from the U.S.S.R.

First, punitive actions against individuals seeking to emigrate from the U.S.S.R. would be violations of Soviet laws and regulations and will therefore not be permitted by the government of the U.S.S.R. In particular, this applies to various kinds of intimidation or reprisal, such as, for example, the firing of a person from his job, his demotion to tasks beneath his professional qualifications, and his subjection to public or other kinds of recrimination.

Second, no unreasonable or unlawful impediments will be placed in the way of persons desiring to make application for emigration, such as interference with travel or communications necessary to complete an application, the withholding of necessary documentation and other obstacles including kinds frequently employed in the past.

Third, applications for emigration will be processed in order of receipt, including those previously filed, and on a nondiscriminatory basis as regards the place of residence, race, religion, national origin and professional status of the applicant. Concerning professional status, we are informed that there are limitations on emigration under Soviet law in the case of individuals holding certain security clearances, but that such individuals who desire to emigrate will be informed of the date on which they may expect to become eligible for emigration.

Fourth, hardship cases will be processed sympathetically and expeditiously; persons imprisoned who, prior to imprisonment, expressed an interest in emigrating, will be given prompt consideration for emigration upon their release; and sympathetic consideration may be given to the early release of such persons.

Fifth, the collection of the so-called emigration tax on emigrants which was suspended last year will remain suspended.

Sixth, with respect to all the foregoing points, we will be in a position to bring to the attention of the Soviet leadership indications that we may have that these criteria and practices are not being applied. Our representations, which would include but not necessarily be limited to the precise matters enumerated in the foregoing points, will receive sympathetic consideration and response.

Finally, it will be our assumption that with the application of the criteria, practices, and procedures set forth in this letter, the rate of emigration from the U.S.S.R. would begin to rise promptly from the 1973 level and would continue to rise to correspond to the number of applicants.

I understand that you and your associates have, in addition, certain understandings incorporated in a letter dated today respecting the foregoing criteria and practices which will henceforth govern emigration from the U.S.S.R. which you wish the President to accept as appropriate guidelines to determine whether the purposes sought through Title IV of the trade bill and further specified in our exchange of correspondence in regard to the emigration practices of non-market economy countries are being fulfilled. You have submitted this letter to me and I wish to advise you on behalf of the President that the understandings in your letter will be among the considerations to be applied by the President in exercising the authority provided for in Sec. 402 of Title IV of the trade bill.

I believe that the contents of this letter represent a good basis, consistent with our shared purposes, for proceeding with an acceptable formulation of Title IV of the trade bill, including procedures for periodic review, so that normal trading relations may go forward for the mutual benefit of the U.S. and the U.S.S.R.

Best regards,

HENRY A. KISSINGER

Jackson's Reply

October 18, 1974

Dear Mr. Secretary:

Thank you for your letter of Oct. 18 which I have now had an opportunity to review. Subject to the further understandings and interpretations outlined in this letter, I agree that we have achieved a suitable basis upon which to modify Title IV by incorporating within it a provision that would enable the President to waive subsections designated (a) and (b) in Sec. 402 of Title IV as passed by the House in circumstances that would substantially promote the objectives of Title IV.

It is our understanding that the punitive actions, intimidation or reprisals that will not be permitted by the government of the U.S.S.R. include the use of punitive conscription against persons seeking to emigrate, or members of their families; and the bringing of criminal actions against persons in circumstances that suggest a relationship between their desire to emigrate and the criminal prosecution against them.

Second, we understand that among the unreasonable impediments that will no longer be placed in the way of persons seeking to emigrate is the requirement that adult applicants receive the permission of their parents or other relatives.

Third, we understand that the special regulations to be applied to persons who have had access to genuinely sensitive classified information will not constitute an unreasonable impediment to emigration. In this connection we would expect such persons to become eligible for emigration within three years of the date on which they last were exposed to sensitive and classified information.

Fourth, we understand that the actual number of emigrants would rise promptly from the 1973 level and would continue to rise to correspond to the number of applicants, and may therefore exceed 60,000 per annum. We would consider a benchmark—a minimum standard of initial compliance—to be the issuance of visas at the rate of 60,000 per annum; and we understand that the President proposes to use the same benchmark as the minimum standard of initial compliance. Until such time as the actual number of emigrants corresponds to the number of applicants the benchmark figure will not include categories of persons whose emigration has been the subject of discussion between Soviet officials and other European governments.

In agreeing to provide discretionary authority to waive the provisions of subsections designated (a) and (b) in Sec. 402 of Title IV as passed by the House, we share your anticipation of good faith in the implementation of the assurances contained in your letter of Oct. 18 and the understandings conveyed by this letter. In particular, with respect to paragraphs three and four of your letter we wish it to be understood that the enumeration of types of punitive action and unreasonable impediments is not and cannot be considered comprehensive or complete, and that nothing in this exchange of correspondence shall be construed as permitting types of punitive action or unreasonable impediments not enumerated therein.

Finally, in order adequately to verify compliance with the standard set forth in these letters, we understand that communication by telephone, telegraph and post will be permitted.

Sincerely yours,

HENRY M. JACKSON

Gromyko's Letter

Dear Mr. Secretary of State:

I believe it necessary to draw your attention to the question concerning the publication in the United States of materials of which you are aware and which touch upon the departure from the Soviet Union of a certain category of Soviet citizens.

I must say straightforwardly that the above-mentioned materials, including the correspondence between you and Senator Jackson, create a distorted picture of our position as well as of what we told the American side on that matter.

When clarifying the actual state of affairs in response to your request, we underlined that the question as such is entirely within the internal competence of our state. We warned at the time that in this matter we had acted and shall act in strict conformity with our present legislation on that score.

But now silence is being kept precisely about this. At the same time, attempts are being made to ascribe to the elucidations that were furnished by us the nature of some assurances and, nearly, obligations on our part regarding the procedure of the departure of Soviet citizens from the U.S.S.R., and even some figures are being quoted as to the supposed number of such citizens, and there is talk about an anticipated increase of that number as compared with previous years.

We resolutely decline such an interpretation. What we said, and you, Mr. Secretary of State, know this well, concerned only and exclusively the real situation in the given question. And when we did mention figures—to inform you of the real situation—the point was quite the contrary, namely about the present tendency toward a decrease in the number of persons wishing to leave the U.S.S.R. and seek permanent residence in other countries.

We believe it important that in this entire matter, considering its principled significance, no ambiguities should remain as regards the position of the Soviet Union.

A. GROMYKO
Minister of Foreign Affairs of the U.S.S.R.

November

REPORT ON
"PROJECT INDEPENDENCE"
November 12, 1974

Various strategies to reduce continued U.S. reliance on imported oil supplies over the next decade were outlined in detail by the Federal Energy Administration (FEA) Nov. 12 in a report on "Project Independence," a plan for American self-sufficiency in energy supplies put forth by President Nixon in November 1973. (See Historic Documents 1973, p. 914-922.) *Although the study offered no formal recommendations on any of the alternatives, which included an accelerated effort to increase domestic oil production, the emphasis was on mandatory energy conservation measures—a policy that conflicted with the Ford administration's actions to date. "There is little we can do to increase energy supplies in the next two to three years," outgoing FEA Administrator John C. Sawhill said Nov. 12 at a news conference accompanying release of the report. He added that "an inescapable conclusion" of the study was the need "to cut back demand to bring it into balance with supplies." The report also appeared to favor energy conservation as a key feature of any long-range energy policy. While the study acknowledged the importance of increasing domestic energy supplies, accelerated production raised crucial social and environmental questions as well as uncertainties over the amounts of untapped petroleum. Furthermore, a significant drop in the world oil price—about $11 a barrel—could make massive domestic exploration and development economically unfeasible. "One way to hedge against" such uncertainties, Sawhill said, is by "adopting a strong conservation program."*

If the United States took no new policy initiatives, FEA predicted that at world oil prices of $7 a barrel the energy demand growth rate would drop to

*3.2 per cent a year, compared to a 4.5 per cent growth rate during the 1960s,
and that petroleum imports would reach 12.3 million barrels a day by 1985
with 6.2 million barrels coming from insecure sources. A one-year embargo, FEA said, could cost the economy $205-billion. By contrast if world
oil prices stayed at the current $11 rate, the growth rate would drop to 2.7
per cent and the need for imports would drop to 3.3 million barrels a day by
1985, of which only 1.2 million barrels would come from insecure sources.
In that event, a year-long embargo would cost the country $40-billion.
Although $11 prices would make self-sufficiency easier to attain, FEA
cautioned that the nation would be better off economically with lower
world oil prices and the implementation of a limited number of energy
policy actions.*

Accelerated Supply

*Any increase in domestic energy production would depend on develop-
ment of the oil fields in Alaska, on the Outer Continental Shelf in the
Atlantic, Pacific and the Alaskan Gulf and the opening of Naval Petroleum
Reserves to commercial development. But, Sawhill said, "until the wells
are drilled we won't really know" if the areas contain oil or how much.
Development would also have significant environmental impact on
previously undisturbed areas. Secondary and tertiary recovery methods
and the development of synthetic fuels such as shale oil would only be
economically feasible if world oil prices remained at $11. Shale oil develop-
ment would increase solid waste disposal problems and create a demand for
water that might not be easily satisfied.*

*Although its production could be expanded without significant additional
expense, coal was not foreseen as playing a major role in an accelerated
development program unless the government undertook a demand
management policy that would switch consumption of oil and gas to consumption of coal and coal-fed power. While FEA predicted that nuclear
power would generate 30 per cent of all electricity by 1985, the demand for
nuclear power would replace the demand for coal and have no real impact
on oil imports. The study predicted that substitute energy forms such as
solar and geothermal energy would play a minor role at best in relieving
the energy crisis before 1985. Accompanying other drawbacks to an
accelerated supply strategy was the potential for serious manpower and
equipment shortages in the initial years.*

Conservation Policy

*Although it would not eliminate the need for imports totally, the study
said "there are innumerable alternative technical possibilities for energy
conservation." Primary on the list were: a 15-cents-a-gallon gasoline tax,
standards requiring automobiles to give 20 miles per gallon of gas, tax
credits to both private individuals and businesses to improve energy conservation in existing office and national standards for heating and cooling
in new homes and commercial buildings. While conservation standards
would have the least impact on the environment, the study said the*

*program "could reduce economic growth, industrial output and our stan-
dard of living" as well as "require additional federal intervention in the
marketplace."*

*Following are excerpts from the text of the summary of the
Project Independence "blueprint" made public Nov. 12 by
the Federal Energy Administration:*

World Oil Assessment

The world oil price will largely determine U.S. energy prices and, in turn,
affect both United States supply possibilities and rate of energy growth.

World oil prices are highly uncertain and could decline to about $7 per
barrel (FOB U.S.) and might fall somewhat lower.

● World supply/demand can be brought into balance at $7, but would re-
quire significant OPEC production cutbacks from the expected doubling of
their capacity by 1985.

● OPEC has already cut back production 10 per cent in four months to
eliminate the estimated 2-3 million barrel per day (MMBD) world surplus.

Major OPEC cutbacks would be required to sustain $11 world oil prices.

● In the short term, prices can be supported by moderate production cutbacks.

● Much of the expected increase over 1973 OPEC production levels must
be foregone by 1985 to support $11 prices.

● Decisions by major oil exporters will be more political than economic
because greater revenues are not needed by the key suppliers to support
their economic growth.

Foreign sources of oil have a significant probability of being insecure in
the 1974-1985 time frame.

The resolution of pressing international financial, economic and political
problems will ultimately determine world oil prices and security of supply.

● The study contrasts differences in the United States' situation based
on a $7 and on an $11 world oil price.

● The study also estimates potential levels of world oil disruptions and
their impact on the U.S.

Domestic Energy Through 1985: The Base Case

If major policy initiatives are not implemented, the U.S. energy picture
will be substantially different from pre-1974 trends, and is described
below.

Energy Demand

At $11 world oil prices, domestic energy demand will grow at substan-
tially lower rates than it has in the past.

● Total demand will grow at a rate of 2.7 per cent per year between 1972
and 1985, compared to 4-5 per cent during 1960-1970.

● 1985 demand will be about 103 quadrillion Btu's (quads) as contrasted
with most other forecasts in the 115-125 quads range,

• Electric demand will also be below its recent high growth rates,

• Petroleum demand will be about constant between 1974 and 1977 and only grow at about 1-2 per cent per year thereafter.

At $7 prices, total energy demand will grow at 3.2 percent through 1985, and petroleum consumption will be about 5 million barrels per day (MMBD) higher than at $11 levels by 1985.

Energy Supply

Petroleum production is severely constrained in the short run and greatly affected by world oil prices in the long run.

• Between 1974 and 1977, there is little that can prevent domestic production from declining or at best remaining constant.

• By 1985, at $7 world oil prices, production will rise to 8.9 MMBD from the current 8.6 MMBD. "Lower 48" production will decline from 8.2 MMBD to 4.2 MMBD, but is offset by Alaskan and Outer Continental Shelf (OCS) production.

• If oil prices remain at $11, production could reach 12.8 million barrels per day by 1985. This further increase comes mainly from the use of more expensive secondary and tertiary recovery in the lower 48 States.

Coal production will increase significantly, but is limited by lack of markets.

• By 1985, coal use will be between 1.0 and 1.1 billion tons per year depending on world oil prices.

• Production could be expanded greatly by 1985, but lower electric growth, increasing nuclear capacity and environmental restrictions limit this increase.

Potential increases in natural gas production are limited, but continued regulation could result in significant declines.

• Continued regulation at today's price will reduce production 15.2 TCF by 1985, or 38 per cent below the deregulated case.

• With deregulation of gas, production will rise from 22.4 trillion cubic feet (TCF) in 1972 to 24.6 TCF by 1985. Alaska production will be 1.6 TCF of this total.

Nuclear power is expected to grow from 4.5 percent to 30 percent of total electric power generation.

• This forecast is lower than many others due to continued schedule deferments, construction delays and operating problems.

Synthetic fuels will not play a major role between now and 1985.

• At $7 they are marginally economic.

• At $11 they are economic, but given first commercial operation in the late 1970's, their contribution by 1985 is small.

• Research and development (R&D) on these technologies is important if they are to replace a growing liquid and gaseous fuels gap which may develop after 1985.

Shale oil could reach 250,000 B/D by 1985 at $11 prices, but would be lower if expectations for $7 prices prevail.

Geothermal, solar and other advanced technologies are large potential sources, but will not contribute to our energy requirements until after 1985.

- R&D is needed so that these important sources, which can have less environmental impact than current sources and are renewable (do not deplete existing reserves), can be useful beyond 1985.

Constraints and Barriers

Even achieving the Base Case will require actions to alleviate potentially serious barriers.

- Rather than stimulating coal use, current Clean Air Act requirements could, by mid-1975, preclude 225 million tons of coal now used in utilities.
- The financial situation of the electric utility industry is particularly critical, and inadequate rates of return will not only reduce their internal funds, but hamper their ability to attract debt or equity financing.
- Current manpower, equipment, and materials shortages are likely to persist in the short-term and inhibit production increases.
- Continued problems with growth in the nuclear industry are possible, unless reliability problems, future shortages of enrichment capacity, and the waste disposal problem are resolved.

Oil Imports and Domestic Vulnerability

Oil imports will remain level or rise in the next few years, no matter what long-term actions we take.

Our domestic vulnerability to future disruptions is dependent on world oil prices.

- At $7 oil and no new domestic policy actions, imports will reach 12.3 MMBD in 1985, of which 6.2 MMBD are susceptible to disruption. A one year embargo could cost the economy $205 billion.
- At $11, imports will decline to 3.3 MMBD by 1985, and only 1.2 MMBD are susceptible to disruption, at a cost of $40 billion for a one year embargo.

Economic and Environmental Assessment

Higher energy prices are likely in any event, but $11 world oil will magnify these price trends and have several major effects.

- $11 oil prices, as opposed to $7, will reduce U.S. economic growth from 3.7 per cent to 3.2 per cent.
- Dollar outflows for petroleum imports will be higher in the near term for $11 than for $7, but by 1980 the situation will be reversed.
- At $11 oil prices, large regional price disparities exist with eastern oil-dependent regions at the high end of the spectrum.
- At $7 prices, these disparities narrow and the Northeast is no longer the highest cost region.
- Because energy costs as a percentage of total consumption are higher for lower income groups, higher energy costs will impact the poor more heavily.

Energy production through 1985 will have mixed environmental impacts.

● Most sources of water pollution should be below 1972 levels, due to the Federal water pollution standards.

● Emission controls will lessen the air pollution impact of increased energy use, but some regions will still be affected significantly.

● Surface mining will continue to increase and problems of secondary economic development in the West and Alaska are likely.

Alternative Energy Strategies

U.S. options to reduce vulnerability fall into three distinct categories. While each has significant impact, a national energy policy will probably combine elements from each.

Accelerating Domestic Supply

Federal policies to lease the Atlantic OCS, reopen the Pacific OCS and tap the Naval Petroleum Reserves can dramatically increase domestic oil production.

● At $7 prices, domestic production by 1985 could rise from 8.9 MMBD to 12.8 MMBD.

● At $11 prices, production could reach as high as 17 MMBD, although less is needed to achieve zero imports.

Shale oil production could reach one MMBD in 1985.

● Prices close to $11 would be needed for economic viability.

● Potential water and environmental constraints would have to be overcome.

Accelerating nuclear power plant construction does not reduce imports much; in general, it replaces new coal-fired power plants.

Accelerating synthetic fuel production would require by-passing key research steps and may not be cost-effective or practical in the 1985 time frame.

Accelerating domestic energy production could be inhibited by several key constraints:

● In the short-term, many shortages of materials, equipment, and labor will persist.

● By 1985, however, most critical shortages will be overcome sufficiently to meet the requirements of the accelerated supply scenario.

● Availability of drilling rigs and fixed and mobile platforms will be a major constraint in reaching the projected oil levels.

● Financial and regulatory problems in the utility and railroad industries could hamper their ability to purchase needed facilities and equipment.

● Water availability will be a problem in selected regions by 1985.

Energy Conservation and Demand Management

Energy conservation actions can reduce demand growth to about 2.0 per cent per year between 1972 and 1985.

- To achieve reductions beyond those induced by price could require new standards on products and buildings, and/or subsidies and incentives.
- Major actions could include standards for more efficient new autos, incentives to reduce miles traveled, incentives for improved thermal efficiency in existing homes and offices and minimum thermal standards for new homes and offices.
- Petroleum demand could be reduced by 2.2 MMBD by 1985.
- Electricity consumption could be reduced from 12.3 quads to about 11.0 quads in 1985, compared with 5.4 in 1972.

Demand management can further reduce dependence on limited oil and gas supplies by actions that involve switching from petroleum and natural gas consumption to coal or coal-fired electric power.

- Switching existing power plants and industrial users, prohibiting new oil or gas-fired power plants and encouraging electric space heating is most important at lower oil prices, and can substitute 400 million tons of coal per year for 2.5 MMBD of petroleum and 2.5 TCF per year of natural gas.
- Implementation may be limited by environmental restrictions and financial inability of the electric utility industry to support a large electrification strategy.
- Electrification to increase coal use in the pre-1985 period must be weighed against the possibility of increasing coal use by liquefication and gasification in the post-1985 period.

Emergency Programs

Standby conservation or curtailment measures can reduce vulnerability.

- Depending on the level of demand in 1985, curtailment measures in response to an embargo can cut consumption by 1-3 MMBD.
- At higher world oil prices curtailment is less effective because there is less "fat" in energy consumption.
- They involve almost no cost when not needed and relatively small administrative costs and some economic impact when implemented.
- They can be instituted in 60-90 days.

Emergency storage is cost-effective in reducing the impact of an embargo.

- Storage to insure against a one MMBD cutoff for one year would cost $6.3 billion over ten years.
- A one MMBD interruption of oil supply for one year during that period could cost the economy $30-40 billion.
- This cost effectiveness holds for any level of insecure imports, and applies if there is a one-in-five chance of one disruption in ten years.

The International Energy Program (IEP) developed in Brussels will foster consumer nation cooperation and reduce the United States' economic impact of a supply disruption during the next several years.

- It can reduce the likelihood of an import disruption.
- It includes a formula for allocating shortages which avoids excessive bidding and divisive scramble for oil by the participants during the most

vulnerable period of the next five years. If, in the 1980's, the United States achieves the low import levels which are possible at high oil prices and by pursuing aggressive strategies of accelerating supply and conservation, the IEP would still act as a deterrent to an interruption, but its utility in protecting the U.S. against the economic impact of supply disruptions would be diminished.

Comparison of Alternative Energy Strategies

Import Vulnerability

Domestic supply and demand actions can greatly reduce U.S. vulnerability to import disruptions by 1985.

● At $7 per barrel oil with all supply and demand actions implemented, 3 MMBD could still be subject to cutoff.

● At $11, either all the demand actions or only a portion of the supply strategy would completely eliminate our vulnerability.

Domestic supply and demand strategies are cheaper in economic terms than imported oil or any other emergency option.

● At either $7 or $11, they have a lower present resource cost than imports, and reduce insecure imports.

After domestic actions, standby demand curtailment is most effective in reducing vulnerability.

Demand curtailment and storage can be designed to buffer against large levels of insecure imports.

Economic and Regional Impacts

Accelerating domestic supply or reducing demand will mean lower energy costs for the Nation and, hence, higher economic growth.

Reduced energy costs will benefit lower income groups.

Increased domestic supply may result in wider regional price disparities than if no action is taken.

The economy can absorb the increased financial costs of reducing vulnerability.

Both supply and demand actions will have economic impacts, regionally and in key sectors of the economy.

Environmental Impacts

The conservation strategy has the lowest environmental impact.

A demand management strategy which substitutes coal for oil and gas will result in the greatest increase in environmental impact over the base case.

The accelerated supply strategy has mixed environmental impacts.

● Air pollution is lower due to more nuclear plants and increased oil and gas production.

● Solid waste is up dramatically due to increased shale oil production.

● Many virgin resource areas will be disturbed for the first time.

Major Uncertainties

The degree to which price will dampen demand:
- If demand is much less sensitive to price than is assumed, we will be much more vulnerable in 1977 and in 1985 at higher world oil prices.
- Mandatory energy conservation measures or diversification and acceleration of supply hedge against this uncertainty.

The ultimate production potential of frontier oil areas:
- Literally all the new oil production forecast comes from frontier areas in Alaska and the Atlantic OCS, or from improved tertiary recovery techniques.

- If the frontier areas do not prove productive:

1) 1985 domestic production could decline to 5 MMBD at $7 oil prices;
2) at $11 and with accelerated supply actions, total production could still not exceed about 11 MMBD.

- Synthetic fuels, switching from petroleum and gas to coal and mandatory conservation may be necessary if frontier areas are not lucrative.

Time required to implement domestic measures:
- While lead times were taken into account, other factors could delay achievement.
- Federal inaction or local opposition.
- Materials and equipment constraints.
- Delays in private investment decisions due to price uncertainty.

Policy Implications

Although $11 world oil prices make achievement of self-sufficiency easier, the United States is still better off economically with lower world oil prices. The implementation of a limited number of major supply or demand actions could make us self-sufficient. By 1985, we could be at zero imports at $11, and down to 5.6 MMBD of imports at $7 prices.

Not all of these actions may be warranted, but they indicate we have significant flexibility when one considers:
- Some projected imports in 1985 are from secure sources.
- Some insecure imports can be insured against.
- Not all of the supply and demand actions must be implemented to achieve the desired result.

While we cannot delay all action, we can pick from those that make the most economic, environmental and regional sense.

Accelerating domestic supply, while economic, has some important drawbacks:
- It will adversely affect environmentally clean areas.
- It requires massive regional development in areas which may not benefit from or need increased supply.
- It is a gamble on as yet unproved reserves of oil and gas.
- It may well be constrained by key materials and equipment shortages.

Implementing a conservation strategy has positive environmental effects and alleviates constraint problems, but:

- It requires intervention and regulation in previously free market areas.
- It results in increased nonmarket costs due to more limited individual choice and changed lifestyles.

While cost effective, there are several important ramifications to a storage program.

- It will take a few years to implement and our vulnerability will be greatest during that period.
- It requires more imports now, which will act to sustain *cartel prices* in the near term.
- We could suffer major capital losses—$4 billion for each one billion barrels stored if the world oil price drops from $11 to $7.

Our actions to increase domestic self-sufficiency could have an appreciable impact on world oil price.

- U.S. reduction in imports can make even $7 hard for OPEC to maintain.
- World oil price reductions could jeopardize domestic energy investments and could require price guarantees or other supports.

Any domestic energy policy must be designed to resolve uncertainties and minimize the risk of not anticipating world oil prices correctly.

- Policy programs should include actions to reduce domestic uncertainty, such as exploring the frontier areas....
- A flexible and dynamic approach must be balanced against the need for a stable long term policy which encourages domestic energy investment.

▼▼▼

ARAFAT'S U.N. SPEECH
November 13, 1974

In an historic departure from U.N. tradition, Yasir Arafat, leader of the Palestine Liberation Organization (PLO), on Nov. 13 addressed the General Assembly of the United Nations, where he was accorded the privileges of a head of state even though he represented no government. Delivering the opening address in an emotion-charged debate on the question of Palestine, Arafat called for dissolution of the state of Israel and its replacement by a new Palestinian state comprised of Moslems, Christians and Jews. The leader of liberation groups which had claimed credit for numerous terrorist activities included in his speech a warning and a plea, saying: "I have come bearing an olive branch and a freedom fighter's gun. Do not let the olive branch fall from my hand." Arafat, wearing traditional Arab dress, stirred controversy when he raised his arms in a victory gesture and revealed a holster slung beneath his draped garb. A U.N. guard said it contained a gun, but a PLO spokesman insisted the holster was empty.

Asserting that the goal of the Palestine Liberation Organization remained the creation of a secular state of Palestine, Arafat said that "When we speak of our common hopes for the Palestine of tomorrow, we include in our perspective all Jews now living in Palestine who choose to live with us there in peace and without discrimination." He urged Jews to join the new state and "turn away from the illusory promises made to them by Zionist ideology and Israeli leadership," promises which offered them only "perpetual bloodshed, endless war and continuous thralldom." The PLO leader said Israel had staged four wars of aggression against the Arabs. To avert the fifth war, which he accused the Israelis of planning, he declared that the "only alternative open before our Arab na-

tions, chiefly Egypt and Syria, was to expend exhaustive efforts in pre-paring forcefully to resist this barbarous invasion, and this in order to liberate Arab lands and to restore the rights of the Palestinian people."

Israel's Response to Speech

Absent from the General Assembly during Arafat's speech, Israeli delegate Tekoah returned to denounce the Palestinian terrorists as "murderers of athletes in the Olympic Games in Munich, the butchers of children in Maalot, [and] the assassins of diplomats in Khartoum." (Olympic games tragedy, see Historic Documents 1972, p. 751-763.) Attacking the U.N. decision of Oct. 14, 1974, inviting Arafat to address the General Assembly, Tekoah characterized the action as a virtual capitulation "to a murder organization which aims at the destruction of a state member of the United Nations."

Turning to the larger issue of the Palestine problem, Tekoah decried those Arab states "in the vanguard of a fanatical assault on the Jewish people." He charged that they had sought to exploit the Palestinian question as "a weapon of Arab belligerency against Israel." He noted Jordanian King Hussein's remark that Arab leaders "have used the Palestine people for selfish political purposes." Tekoah reiterated Israeli pledges not to permit "the establishment of PLO authority in any part of Palestine." He asserted: "The PLO will not be forced on the Palestinian Arabs. It will not be tolerated by the Jews of Israel." No resolution, the Israeli delegate declared, "can establish the authority of an organization which has no authority...which has no foothold in any part of the territories it seeks." He observed that the Palestinians had a country called Jordan. He recalled the Israeli statement of July 21, 1974, which said that Israel "would work toward negotiating a peace agreement with Jordan, and that in the Jordanian-Palestinian Arab state east of Israel, the specific identity of the Jordanians and Palestinians will find expression in peace and good-neighborliness with Israel."

Arafat's speech before the General Assembly appeared to deliver a setback to Secretary of State Henry A. Kissinger's efforts to bring the parties of the Middle East to a settlement on the long-standing disputes over territory. Stirred by the PLO leader's remarks, Palestinians demonstrated in Israel. Several terrorist raids were staged in the ensuing weeks by Palestinian groups, and they led to retaliatory raids by Israel. In late November, rumors circulated of imminent war in the Middle East. But in late December, postponement of a state visit to the Middle East by Soviet Communist Party General Secretary Leonid I. Brezhnev was interpreted as indicating Egyptian willingness to continue pursuit of a settlement with Israel along lines suggested by Kissinger.

Following are excerpts from the text of the speech delivered before the United National General Assembly

Nov. 13 by Yasir Arafat, leader of the Palestine Liberation
Organization:

In the name of the people of Palestine and the leader of its national struggle, the Palestine Liberation Organization, I take this opportunity to extend to you, Mr. President [Abdelaziz Bouteflika of Algeria], my warmest congratulations on your election to the presidency of the twenty-ninth session of the United Nations General Assembly.

We have, of course, long known you to be a sincere and devoted defender of the cause of freedom, justice and peace. We have known you also to be in the vanguard of the freedom fighters in their heroic Algerian war of national liberation. Today Algeria has attained a distinguished position in the world community and has assumed its responsibilities both in the national and in the international fields, thus earning the support and esteem of the entire human family.

I also avail myself of this opportunity to extend my sincerest appreciation to Mr. Kurt Waldheim, the Secretary-General of the United Nations, for the great efforts he has made and is still making to enable us to assume our responsibilities in the smoothest possible way.

In the name of the people of Palestine I take this opportunity to congratulate three States that have recently been admitted to membership in the United Nations after obtaining their national independence: Guinea-Bissau, Bangladesh and Grenada. I extend our best wishes to the leadership of those Member States and wish them progress and success.

Mr. President, I thank you for having invited the Palestinian Liberation Organization to participate in this plenary session of the United Nations General Assembly. I am grateful to all those representatives of States of the United Nations who contributed to the decision to introduce the question of Palestine as a separate item of the agenda of this Assembly. That decision made possible the Assembly's resolution inviting us to address it on the question of Palestine.

U.N. Debate: Victory For Palestinians

This is a very important occasion. The question of Palestine is being re-examined by the United Nations, and we consider that step to be a victory for the world Organization as much as a victory for the cause of our people. It indicates anew that the United Nations of today is not the United Nations of the past, just as today's world is not yesterday's world. Today's United Nations represents 138 nations, a number that more clearly reflects the will of the international community. Thus today's United Nations is more nearly capable of implementing the principles embodied in its Charter and in the Universal Declaration of Human Rights, as well as being more truly empowered to support causes of peace and justice.

Our peoples are now beginning to feel that change. Along with them, the peoples of Asia, Africa and Latin America also feel the change. As a result, the United Nations acquires greater esteem both in our people's view and in the view of other peoples. Our hope is thereby strengthened that the United Nations can contribute actively to the pursuit and triumph of the causes of peace, justice, freedom and independence. Our resolve to build a new world is fortified—a world free of colonialism, imperialism, neocolonialism and racism in each of its instances, including Zionism.

Our world aspires to peace, justice, equality and freedom. It wishes that oppressed nations at present bent under the weight of imperialism might gain their freedom and their right to self-determination. It hopes to place the relations between nations on a basis of equality, peaceful coexistence, mutual respect for each other's internal affairs, secure national sovereignty, independence and territorial unity on the basis of justice and mutual benefit. This world resolves that the economic ties binding it together should be grounded in justice, parity and mutual interest. It aspires finally to direct its human resources against the scourge of poverty, famine, disease and natural calamity, toward the development of productive scientific and technical capabilities to enhance human wealth—all this in the hope of reducing the disparity between the developing and the developed countries. But all such aspirations cannot be realized in a world that is at present ruled over by tension, injustice, oppression, racial discrimination and exploitation, a world also threatened with unending economic disaster, war and crisis.

Justice of Armed Struggles for Liberation

Great numbers of peoples, including those of Zimbabwe, Namibia, South Africa and Palestine, among many others, are still victims of oppression and violence. Their areas of the world are gripped by armed struggles provoked by imperialism and racial discrimination, both merely forms of aggression and terror. Those are instances of oppressed peoples compelled by intolerable circumstances into a confrontation with such oppression. But wherever that confrontation occurs it is legitimate and just.

It is imperative that the international community should support these peoples in their struggles, in the furtherance of their rightful causes, in the attainment of their right to self-determination.

In Indo-China the peoples are still exposed to aggression. They remain subjected to conspiracies preventing them from the enjoyment of peace and the realization of their goals. Although peoples everywhere have welcomed the agreements on peace reached in Laos and South Viet-Nam, no one can say that genuine peace has been achieved, nor that those forces responsible in the first place for aggression have now desisted from their attacks on Viet-Nam. The same can be said of the present military aggression against the people of Cambodia. It is therefore incumbent on the international community to support these oppressed peoples, and also to condemn the oppressors for their designs against peace. Moreover, despite the positive stand taken by the Democratic Republic of Korea with regard to a peaceful, just solution of the Korean question, there is as yet no settlement of that question.

A few months ago the problem of Cyprus erupted violently before us. All peoples everywhere shared in the suffering of the Cypriots. We ask that the United Nations continue its efforts to reach a just solution in Cyprus, thereby sparing the Cypriots further war and ensuring peace and independence for them instead. Undoubtedly, however, consideration of the question of Cyprus belongs within that of Middle Eastern problems as well as of Mediterranean problems.

Toward A New Economic Order

In their efforts to replace an outmoded but still dominant world economic system with a new, more logically rational one, the countries of Asia, Africa, and Latin America must nevertheless face implacable attacks on these efforts. These countries have expressed their views at the special session of the General Assembly on raw materials and development. Thus the plundering, the exploitation, the siphoning off of the wealth of impoverished peoples must be terminated forthwith. There must be no deterring of these people's efforts to develop and control their wealth. Furthermore, there is a grave necessity for arriving at fair prices for raw materials from these countries.

In addition, these countries continue to be hampered in the attainment of their primary objectives formulated at the Conference on the Law of the Sea in Caracas, at the Population Conference and at the Rome Food Conference. The United Nations should therefore bend every effort to achieve a radical alteration of the world economic system, making it possible for developing countries to develop. The United Nations must shoulder the responsibility for fighting inflation, now borne most heavily by the developing countries, especially the oil-producing countries. The United Nations must firmly condemn any threats made against these countries simply because they demand their just rights.

"Armed Violence...More Likely Everywhere"

The world-wide armaments race shows no sign of abating. As a consequence, the entire world is threatened with the dispersion of its wealth and the utter waste of its energies. Armed violence is made more likely everywhere. We expect the United Nations to devote itself single-mindedly to curbing the unlimited acquisition of arms; to preventing even the possibility of nuclear destruction; to reducing the vast sums spent on military technology; to converting expenditure on war projects for development, for increasing production, and for benefiting common humanity.

And still, the highest tension exists in our part of the world. There the Zionist entity clings tenaciously to occupied Arab territory; Zionism persists in its aggressions against us and our territory. New military preparations are feverishly being made. These anticipate another, fifth war of aggression to be launched against us. Such signs bear the closest possible watching, since there is a grave likelihood that this war would forebode nuclear destruction and cataclysmic annihilation.

The world is in need of tremendous efforts if its aspirations to peace, freedom, justice, equality and development are to be realized, if its struggle is to be victorious over colonialism, imperialism, neo-colonialism, and racism in all its forms, including Zionism. Only by such efforts can actual form be given to the aspirations of all peoples, including the aspirations of peoples whose States oppose such efforts. It is this road that leads to the fulfillment of those principles emphasized by the United Nations Charter and the Universal Declaration of Human Rights. Were the *status quo* simply to be maintained, however, the world would instead be exposed to prolonged armed conflict, in addition to economic, human and natural calamity.

Just Causes Will Triumph

Despite abiding world crises, despite even the gloomy powers of backwardness and disastrous wrong, we live in a time of glorious change. An old world order is crumbling before our eyes, as imperialism, colonialism, neo-colonialism and racism, the chief form of which is Zionism, ineluctably perish. We are privileged to be able to witness a great wave of history bearing peoples forward into a new world which they have created. In that world just causes will triumph. Of that we are confident.

The question of Palestine belongs to this perspective of emergence and struggle. Palestine is crucial amongst those just causes fought for unstintingly by masses labouring under imperialism and aggression. It cannot be, and is not, lost on me today, as I stand here before the General Assembly, that if I have been given the opportunity to address the General Assembly, so too must the opportunity be given to all liberation movements fighting against racism and imperialism. In their names, in the name of every human being struggling for freedom and self-determination, I call upon the General Assembly urgently to give their just causes the same full attention the General Assembly has so rightly given to our cause. Such recognitions once made, there will be a secure foundation thereafter for the preservation of universal peace. For only with such peace will a new world order endure in which peoples can live free of oppression, fear, terror and the suppression of their rights. As I said earlier, this is the true perspective in which to set the question of Palestine. I shall now do so for the General Assembly, keeping firmly in mind both the perspective and the goal of a coming world order.

Politics, Diplomacy Enhance Armed Struggle

Even as today we address the General Assembly from what is before all else an international rostrum we are also expressing our faith in political and diplomatic struggle as complements, as enhancements of armed struggle. Furthermore we express our appreciation of the role the United

Nations is capable of playing in settling problems of international scope. But this capability, I said a moment ago, became real only once the United Nations had accommodated itself to the living actuality of aspiring peoples, towards which an Organization of so truly international a dimension owes unique obligations.

In addressing the General Assembly today our people proclaims its faith in the future, unencumbered either by past tragedies or present limitations. If, as we discuss the present, we enlist the past in our service, we do so only to light up our journey into the future alongside other movements of national liberation. If we return now to the historical roots of our cause we do so because present at this very moment in our midst are those, who, while they occupy our homes, as their cattle graze in our pastures, and as their hands pluck the fruit of our trees, claim at the same time that we are disembodied spirits, fictions without presence, without traditions or future. We speak of our roots also because until recently some people have regarded—and continued to regard—our problem as merely a problem of refugees. They have portrayed the Middle East Question as little more than a border dispute between the Arab States and the Zionist entity. They have imagined that our people claim rights not rightfully its own and fights neither with logic nor valid motive, with a simple wish only to disturb the peace and to terrorize wantonly. For there are amongst you—and here I refer to the United States of America and others like it—those who supply our enemy freely with planes and bombs and with every variety of murderous weapon. They take hostile positions against us. deliberately distorting the true essence of the problem. All this is done not only at our expense, but at the expense of the American people, and of the friendship we continue to hope can be cemented between us and this great people, whose history of struggle for the sake of freedom we honour and salute.

Appeal to American People

I cannot now forgo this opportunity to appeal from this rostrum directly to the American people, asking it to give its support to our heroic and fighting people. I ask it whole-heartedly to endorse right and justice, to recall George Washington to mind, heroic Washington whose purpose was his nation's freedom and independence, Abraham Lincoln, champion of the destitute and the wretched, and also Woodrow Wilson whose doctrine of Fourteen Points remains subscribed to and venerated by our people. I ask the American people whether the demonstrations of hostility and enmity taking place outside this great hall reflect the true intent of America's will? What, I ask you plainly, is the crime of the people of Palestine against the American people? Why do you fight us so? Does such unwarranted belligerence really serve your interests? Does it serve the interests of the American masses? No, definitely not. I can only hope that the American people will remember that their friendship with the whole Arab nation is too great, too abiding, and too rewarding for any such demonstrations to harm it.

In any event, as our discussion of the question of Palestine focuses upon historical roots, we do so because we believe that any question now exercising the world's concern must be viewed radically, in the true root sense of that word, if a real solution is ever to be grasped. We propose this radical approach as an antidote to an approach to international issues that obscures historical origins behind ignorance, denial, and a slavish obeisance to the present.

Roots of the Palestinian Question

The roots of the Palestinian question reach back into the closing years of the 19th century, in other words, to that period which we call the era of colonialism and settlement as we know it today. This is precisely the period during which Zionism as a scheme was born; its aim was the conquest of Palestine by European immigrants, just as settlers colonized, and indeed raided, most of Africa. This is the period during which, pouring forth out of the west, colonialism spread into the furthest reaches of Africa, Asia, and Latin America, building colonies, everywhere cruelly exploiting, oppressing, plundering the peoples of those three continents. This period persists into the present. Marked evidence of its totally reprehensible presence can be readily perceived in the racism practised both in South Africa and in Palestine.

Just as colonialism and its demagogues dignified their conquests, their plunder and limitless attacks upon the natives of Africa with appeals to a "civilizing and modernizing" mission, so too did waves of Zionist immigrants disguise their purposes as they conquered Palestine. Just as colonialism as a system and colonialists as its instrument used religion, colour, race and language to justify the African's exploitation and his cruel subjugation by terror and discrimination, so too were these methods employed as Palestine was usurped and its people hounded from their national homeland.

Just as colonialism heedlessly used the wretched, the poor, the exploited as mere inert matter with which to build and to carry out settler colonialism, so too were destitute, oppressed European Jews employed on behalf of world imperialism and of the Zionist leadership. European Jews were transformed into the instruments of aggression; they became the elements of settler colonialism intimately allied to racial discrimination.

"Zionism: Imperialist, Colonialist, Racist"

Zionist theology was utilized against our Palestinian people: the purpose was not only the establishment of Western-style settler colonialism but also the severing of Jews from their various homelands and subsequently their estrangement from their nations. Zionism is an ideology that is imperialist, colonialist, racist; it is profoundly reactionary and discriminatory; it is united with anti-Semitism in its retrograde tenets and is, when all is said and done, another side of the same base coin. For when what is proposed is that adherents of the Jewish faith, regardless of their national residence, should neither owe allegiance to their national residence nor live on equal footing with its other, non-Jewish citizens—when that is proposed we hear anti-Semitism being proposed. When it is proposed that the only solution for the Jewish problem is that Jews must alienate themselves from communities or nations of which they have been a historical part, when it is proposed that Jews solve the Jewish problem by immigrating to and forcibly settling the land of another people—when this occurs, exactly the same position is being advocated as the one urged by anti-Semites against Jews.

Thus, for instance, we can understand the close connection between Rhodes, who promoted settler colonialism in south-east Africa, and Herzl, who had settler colonialist designs upon Palestine. Having received a certificate of good settler colonialist conduct from Rhodes, Herzl then turned around and presented this certificate to the British Government, hoping thus to secure a formal resolution supporting Zionist policy. In exchange, the Zionists promised Britain an imperialist base on Palestinian soil so that imperial interests could be safeguarded at one of their chief strategic points.

So the Zionist movement allied itself directly with world colonialism in a common raid on our land. Allow me now to present a selection of historical truths about this alliance.

Recent History of Jewish Settlement in Palestine

The Jewish invasion of Palestine began in 1881. Before the first large wave of immigrants started arriving, Palestine had a population of half a million; most of the population was either Moslem or Christian, and only 20,000 were Jewish. Every segment of the population enjoyed the religious tolerance characteristic of our civilization.

Palestine was then a verdant land, inhabited mainly by an Arab people in the course of building its life and dynamically enriching its indigenous culture.

The Balfour Declaration

Between 1882 and 1917 the Zionist Movement settled approximately 50,-000 European Jews in our homeland. To do that it resorted to trickery and deceit in order to implement them in our midst. Its success in getting Britain to issue the Balfour Declaration once again demonstrated the alliance between Zionism and imperialism. Furthermore, by promising to the Zionist movement what was not hers to give, Britain showed how oppressive was the rule of imperialism. As it was constituted then, the League of Nations abandoned our Arab people, and Wilson's pledges and promises came to nought. In the guise of a mandate, British imperialism was cruelly and directly imposed upon us. The mandate document issued by the League of Nations was to enable the Zionist invaders to consolidate their gains in our homeland.

In the wake of the Balfour Declaration and over a period of 30 years, the Zionist movement succeeded, in collaboration with its imperialist ally, in settling more European Jews on the land, thus usurping the properties of Palestinian Arabs.

By 1947 the number of Jews had reached 60,000; they owned about 6 per cent of Palestinian arable land. The figure should be compared with the population of Palestine, which at that time was 1,250,000.

U.N. Had No Right to Partition

As a result of the collusion between the mandatory Power and the Zionist movement and with the support of some countries, this General Assembly early in its history approved a recommendation to partition our Palestinian homeland. This took place in an atmosphere poisoned with questionable actions and strong pressure. The General Assembly partitioned what it had no right to divide—an indivisible homeland. When we rejected that decision, our position corresponded to that of the natural mother who refused to permit King Solomon to cut her son in two when the unnatural mother claimed the child for herself and agreed to his dismemberment. Furthermore, even though the partition resolution granted the colonialist settlers 54 per cent of the land of Palestine, their dissatisfaction with the decision prompted them to wage a war of terror against the civilian Arab population. They occupied 81 per cent of the total area of Palestine, uprooting a million Arabs. Thus, they occupied 524 Arab towns and villages, of which they destroyed 385, completely obliterating them in the process. Having done so, they built their own settlements and colonies on the ruins of our farms and our groves. The roots of the Palestine question lie here. Its causes do not stem from any conflict between two religions or two nationalisms. Neither is it a border conflict between neighboring states. It is the cause of people deprived of its homeland, dispersed and uprooted, and living mostly in exile and in refugee camps.

With support from imperialist and colonialist Powers, it managed to get itself accepted as a United Nations Member. It further succeeded in getting the Palestine Question deleted from the agenda of the United Nations and in deceiving world public opinion by presenting our cause as a problem of refugees in need either of charity from do-gooders, or settlement in a land not theirs.

Path of Israeli Aggression

Not satisfied with all this, the racist entity, founded on the imperialist-colonialist concept, turned itself into a base of imperialism and into an arsenal of weapons. This enabled it to assume its role of subjugating the Arab people and of committing aggression against them, in order to satisfy its ambitions for further expansion on Palestinian and other Arab lands. In addition to the many instances of aggression committed by this entity against the Arab States, it has launched two large-scale wars, in 1956 and 1967, thus endangering world peace and security.

As a result of Zionist aggression in June 1967, the enemy occupied Egyptian Sinai as far as the Suez Canal. The enemy occupied Syria's Golan Heights, in addition to all Palestinian land west of the Jordan. All these developments have led to the creation in our area of what has come to be known as the "Middle East problem." The situation has been rendered more serious by the enemy's persistence in maintaining its unlawful occupation and in further consolidating it, thus establishing a beachhead for world imperalism's thrust against our Arab nation. All Security Council decisions and appeals to world public opinion for withdrawal from the lands occupied in June 1967 have been ignored. Despite all the peaceful efforts on the international level, the enemy has not been deterred from its expansionist policy. The only alternative open before our Arab nations, chiefly Egypt and Syria, was to expend exhaustive efforts in preparing forcefully to resist that barbarous armed invasion—and this in order to liberate Arab lands and to restore the rights of the Palestinian people, after all other peaceful means had failed.

The October 1973 War

Under these circumstances, the fourth war broke out in October 1973, bringing home to the Zionist enemy the bankruptcy of its policy of occupation, expansion and its reliance on the concept of military might. Despite all this, the leaders of the Zionist entity are far from having learned any lesson from their experience. They are making preparations for the fifth war, resorting once more to the language of military superiority, aggression, terrorism, subjugation and, finally, always to war in their dealings with the Arabs.

It pains our people greatly to witness the propagation of the myth that its homeland was a desert until it was made to bloom by the toil of foreign settlers, that it was a land without a people, and that the colonialist entity caused no harm to any human being. No: such lies must be exposed from this rostrum, for the world must know that Palestine was the cradle of the most ancient cultures and civilizations. Its Arab people were engaged in farming and building, spreading culture throughout the land for thousands of years, setting an example in the practice of freedom of worship, acting as faithful guardians of the holy places of all religions. As a son of Jerusalem, I treasure for myself and my people beautiful memories and vivid images of the religious brotherhood that was the hallmark of our Holy City before it succumbed to catastrophe. Our people continued to pursue this enlightened policy until the establishment of the State of Israel and their dispersion. This did not deter our people from pursuing their humanitarian role on Palestinian soil. Nor will they permit their land to become a launching pad for aggression or a racist camp predicated on the destruction of civilization, cultures, progress and peace. Our people cannot but maintain the heritage of their ancestors in resisting the invaders, in assuming the privileged task of defending their native land, their Arab nationhood, their culture and civilization, and in safeguarding the cradle of monotheistic religion.

Israel Supports "Imperialists and Racists"

By contrast, we need only mention briefly some Israeli stands: its support of the Secret Army Organization in Algeria, its bolstering of the settler-colonialists in Africa—whether in the Congo, Angola, Mozambique, Zimbabwe, Azania or South Africa—and its backing of South Viet-Nam against the Viet-Namese revolution. In addition, one can mention Israel's continuing support of imperialists and racists everywhere, its obstructionist stand in the Committee of Twenty-Four, its refusal to cast its vote in support of independence for the African States, and its opposition to the demands of many Asian, African and Latin American nations, and several other States in the Conferences on raw materials, population, the Law of the Sea, and food. All these facts offer further proof of the character of the enemy which has usurped our land. They justify the honourable struggle which we are waging against it. As we defend a vision of the future, our enemy upholds the myths of the past.

The enemy we face has a long record of hostility even towards the Jews themselves, for there is within the Zionist entity a built-in racism against Oriental Jews. While we were vociferously condemning the massacres of Jews under Nazi rule, Zionist leadership appeared more interested at that time in exploiting them as best it could in order to realize its goal of immigration into Palestine.

Israelis Did Not Want to Live Peaceably With Us

If the immigration of Jews to Palestine had had as its objective the goal of enabling them to live side by side with us, enjoying the same rights and assuming the same duties, we would have opened our doors to them, as far as our homeland's capacity for absorption permitted. Such was the case with the thousands of Armenians and Circassians who still live among us in equality as brethren and citizens. But that the goal of this immigration should be to usurp our homeland, disperse our people, and turn us into second-class citizens—this is what no one can conceivably demand that we acquiesce in or submit to. Therefore, since its inception, our revolution has not been motivated by racial or religious factors. Its target has never been the Jew, as a person, but racist Zionism and undisguised aggression. In this sense, ours is also a revolution for the Jew, as a human being, as well. We are struggling so that Jews, Christians and Muslims may live in equality, enjoying the same rights and assuming the same duties, free from racial or religious discrimination.

We do distinguish between Judaism and Zionism. While we maintain our opposition to the colonialist Zionist movement, we respect the Jewish faith. Today, almost one century after the rise of the Zionist movement, we wish to warn of its increasing danger to the Jews of the world, to our Arab people and to world peace and security. For Zionism encourages the Jew to emigrate out of his homeland and grants him an artificially created nationality. The Zionists proceed with their terrorist activities even though these have proved ineffective. The phenomenon of constant emigration from Israel, which is bound to grow as the bastions of colonialism and racism in the world fall, is an example of the inevitability of the failure of such activities.

Urge World Stand Against Zionism

We urge the people and governments of the world to stand firm against Zionist attempts at encouraging world Jewry to emigrate from their countries and to usurp our land. We urge them as well firmly to oppose any discrimination against any human being, as to religion, race, or colour.

Why should our Arab Palestinian people pay the price of such discrimination in the world? Why should our people be responsible for the problems of Jewish immigration, if such problems exist in the minds of some people? Why do not the supporters of these problems open their own countries, which can absorb and help these immigrants?

Those who call us terrorists wish to prevent world public opinion from discovering the truth about us and from seeing the justice on our faces. They seek to hide the terrorism and tyranny of their acts, and our own posture of self defense.

The difference between the revolutionary and the terrorist lies in the reason for which each fights. For whoever stands by a just cause and fights for the freedom and liberation of his land from the invaders, the settlers and the colonialists, cannot possibly be called terrorist, otherwise the American people in their struggle for liberation from the British colonialists would have been terrorists; the European resistance against the Nazis would be terrorism, the struggle of the Asian, African and Latin American peoples would also be terrorism, and many of you who are in this Assembly hall were considered terrorists. This is actually a just and proper struggle consecrated by the United Nations Charter and by the Universal Declaration of Human Rights. As to those who fight against the just causes, those who wage war to occupy, colonize and oppress other people, those are the terrorists. Those are the people whose actions should be condemned, who should be called war criminals: for the justice of the cause determines the right to struggle.

Pillage By Zionist Terrorism

Zionist terrorism which was waged against the Palestinian people to evict it from its country and usurp its land is registered in our official documents. Thousands of our people were assassinated in their villages and towns, tens of thousands of others were forced at gunpoint to leave their homes and the lands of their fathers. Time and time again our children, women and aged were evicted and had to wander in the deserts and climb mountains without any food or water. No one who in 1948 witnessed the catastrophe that befell the inhabitants of hundreds of villages and towns—in Jerusalem, Jaffa, Lydda, Ramle and Galilee—no one who has been a witness to that catastrophe will ever forget the experience, even though the mass blackout has succeeded in hiding these horrors as it has hidden the traces of 385 Palestinian villages and towns destroyed at the time and erased from the map. The destruction of 19,000 houses during the past seven years, which is equivalent to the complete destruction of 200 more Palestinian villages, and the great number of maimed as a result of the treatment they were subjected to in Israeli prisons, cannot be hidden by any blackout.

Their terrorism fed on hatred and this hatred was even directed against the olive tree in my country, which has been a proud symbol and which reminded them of the indigenous inhabitants of the land, a living reminder that the land is Palestinian. Thus they sought to destroy it. How can one describe the statement by Golda Meir which expressed her disquiet about "the Palestinian children born every day." They see in the Palestinian child, in the Palestinian tree, an enemy that should be exterminated. For tens of years Zionists have been harassing our people's cultural, political, social and artistic leaders, terrorizing them and assassinating them. They have stolen our cultural heritage, our popular folklore and have claimed it as theirs. Their terrorism even reached our sacred places in our beloved and peaceful Jerusalem. They have endeavored to de-Arabize it and make it lose its Moslem and Christian character by evicting its inhabitants and annexing it.

Destruction of Sacred Moslem Shrine

I must mention the fire of the Aksa Mosque and the disfiguration of many of the monuments, which are both historic and religious in character. Jerusalem, with its religious history and its spiritual values, bears witness to the future. It is proof of our eternal presence, of our civilization, of our human values. It is therefore not surprising that under its skies the three religions were born and that under that sky these three religions shine in order to enlighten mankind so that it might express the tribulations and hopes of humanity, and that it might mark out the road of the future with its hopes.

The small number of Palestinian Arabs who were not uprooted by the Zionists in 1948 are at present refugees in their own homeland. Israeli law treats them as second-class citizens—and even as third-class citizens since Oriental Jews are second-class citizens—and they have been subject to all forms of racial discrimination and terrorism after confiscation of their land and property. They have been victims of bloody massacres such as that of Kfar Kassim, they have been expelled from their villages and denied the right to return, as in the case of the inhabitants of Ikrit and Kfar-Birin. For 26 years, our population has been living under martial law and was denied the freedom of movement without prior permission from the Israeli military governor, this at a time when an Israeli law was promulgated granting citizenship to any Jew anywhere who wanted to emigrate to our homeland. Moreover, another Israeli law stipulated that Palestinians who were not present in their villages or towns at the time of the occupation were not entitled to Israeli citizenship.

Israeli Rulers Bring Terror

The record of Israeli rulers is replete with acts of terror perpetrated on those of our people who remained under occupation in Sinai and the Golan Heights. The criminal bombardment of the Bahr-al-Bakar School and the Abou Zaabal factory are but two such unforgettable acts of terrorism. The total destruction of the Syrian city of Kuneitra is yet another tangible instance of systematic terrorism. If a record of Zionist terrorism in South Lebanon were to be compiled, the enormity of its acts would shock even the most hardened: piracy, bombardments, scorched-earth, destruction of hundreds of homes, eviction of civilians and the kidnapping of Lebanese citizens. This clearly constitutes a violation of Lebanese sovereignty and is in preparation for the diversion of the Litani River waters.

Need one remind this Assembly of the numerous resolutions adopted by it condemning Israeli aggressions committed against Arab countries, Israeli violations of human rights and the articles of the Geneva Conventions, as well as the resolutions pertaining to the annexation of the city of Jerusalem and its restoration to its former status?

The only description for these acts is that they are acts of barbarism and terrorism. And yet, the Zionist racists and colonialists have the temerity to describe the just struggle of our people as terror. Could there be a more flagrant distortion of truth than this? We ask those who usurped our land, who are committing murderous acts of terrorism against our people and are practicing racial discrimination more extensively than the racists of South Africa, we ask them to keep in mind the United Nations General Assembly resolution that called for the one-year suspension of the membership of the Government of South Africa from the United Nations. Such is the inevitable fate of every racist country that adopts the law of the jungle, usurps the homeland of others and persists in oppression.

Britain and Israel Sought to Usurp Land

For the past 30 years, our people have had to struggle against British occupation and Zionist invasion, both of which had one intention, namely the usurpation of our land. Six major revolts and tens of popular uprisings were staged to foil these attempts, so that our homeland might remain ours. Over 30,000 martyrs, the equivalent in comparative terms of 6 million Americans, died in the process.

When the majority of the Palestinian people was uprooted from its homeland in 1948, the Palestinian struggle for self determination continued under the most difficult conditions. We tried every possible means to continue our political struggle to attain our national rights, but to no avail. Meanwhile, we had to struggle for sheer existence. Even in exile we educated our children. This was all a part of trying to survive.

The Palestinian people produced thousands of physicians, lawyers, teachers and scientists who actively participated in the development of the Arab countries bordering on their usurped homeland. They utilized their income to assist the young and aged amongst their people who remained in the refugee camps. They educated their younger sisters and brothers, supported their parents and cared for their children. All along, the Palestinian dreamt of return. Neither the Palestinian's allegiance to Palestine nor his determination to return waned; nothing could persuade him to relinquish his Palestinian identity or to forsake his homeland. The passage of time did not make him forget, as some hoped he would. When our people lost faith in the international community which persisted in ignoring its rights and when it became obvious that the Palestinians would not recuperate one inch of Palestine through exclusively political means, our people had no choice but to resort to armed struggle. Into that struggle it poured its material and human resources. We bravely faced the most vicious acts of Israeli terrorism which were aimed at diverting our struggle and arresting it.

"Our Undisputed Right To Return To Our Homeland"

In the past 10 years of our struggle, thousands of martyrs and twice as many wounded, maimed and imprisoned were offered in sacrifice, all in an effort to resist the imminent threat of liquidation, to regain our right to self determination and our undisputed right to return to our homeland. With the utmost dignity and the most admirable revolutionary spirit, our Palestinian people has not lost its spirit in Israeli prisons and concentration camps or when faced with all forms of harassment and intimidation. It struggles for sheer existence and it continues to strive to preserve the Arab character of its land. Thus it resists oppression, tyranny and terrorism in their ugliest forms.

It is through our popular armed struggle that our political leadership and our national institutions finally crystallized and a national liberation movement, comprising all the Palestinian factions, organizations, and capabilities, materialized in the Palestine Liberation Organization.

Through our militant Palestine national liberation movement, our people's struggle matured and grew enough to accommodate political and social struggle in addition to armed struggle. The Palestinian individual, qualified to shape the future of our Palestine, not merely content with mobilizing the Palestinians for the challenges of the present.

Cultural And Educational Activities Of The PLO

The Palestine Liberation Organization can be proud of having a large number of cultural and educational activities, even while engaged in armed struggle, and at a time when it faced increasingly vicious blows of Zionist terrorism. We established institutes for scientific research, agricultural development and social welfare, as well as centres for the revival of our cultural heritage and the preservation of our folklore. Many Palestinian poets, artists and writers have enriched Arab culture in particular, and world culture generally. Their profoundly humane works have won the admiration of all those familiar with them. In contrast to that, our enemy has been systematically destroying our culture and disseminating racist, imperialist ideologies, in short, everything that impedes progress, justice, democracy and peace.

The Palestine Liberation Organization has earned its legitimacy because of the sacrifice inherent in its pioneering role, and also because of its dedicated leadership of the struggle. It has also been granted this legitimacy by the Palestinian masses, which in harmony with it have chosen it to lead the struggle according to its directives. The Palestine Liberation Organization has also gained its legitimacy by representing every faction, union or group as well as every Palestinian talent, either in the National Council or in people's institutions. This legitimacy was further strengthened by the support of the entire Arab nation, and it was consecrated during the last Arab Summit Conference, which reiterated the right of the Palestine Liberation Organization, in its capacity as the sole representative of the Palestinian people, to establish an independent national State on all liberated Palestinian territory.

Moreover, the Palestine Liberation Organization's legitimacy was intensified as a result of fraternal support given by other liberation movements and by friendly, like-minded nations that stood by our side, encouraging and aiding us in our struggle to secure our national rights.

Here I must also warmly convey the gratitude of our revolutionary fighters and that of our people to the non-aligned countries, the socialist countries, the Islamic countries, the African countries and friendly European countries, as well as all our other friends in Asia, Africa and Latin America.

The Palestine Liberation Organization represents the Palestinian people, legitimately and uniquely. Because of this, the Palestine Liberation Organization expresses the wishes and hopes of its people. Because of this, too, it brings these very wishes and hopes before you, urging you not to shirk a momentous historic responsibility towards our just cause.

For many years now, our people has been exposed to the ravages of war, destruction and dispersion. It has paid in the blood of its sons that which cannot ever be compensated. It has borne the burdens of occupation, dispersion, eviction and terror more uninterruptedly than any other people. And yet all this has made our people neither vindictive nor vengeful. Nor has it caused us to resort to the racism of our enemies. Nor have we lost the true method by which friend and foe are distinguished.

"We Deplore Crimes Against Jews"

For we deplore all those crimes committed against the Jews; we also deplore all the real discrimination suffered by them because of their faith.

I am a rebel and freedom is my cause. I know well that many of you present here today once stood in exactly the same resistance position as I now occupy and from which I must fight. You once had to convert dreams into reality by your struggle. Therefore you must now share my dream. I think this is exactly why I can ask you now to help, as together we bring out our dream into a bright reality, our common dream for a peaceful future in Palestine's sacred land.

As he stood in an Israeli military court, the Jewish revolutionary, Ahud Adif, said: "I am no terrorist; I believe that a democratic State should exist on this land." Adif now languishes in a Zionist prison among his co-believers. To him and his colleagues I send my heartfelt good wishes.

And before those same courts there stands today a brave prince of the church, Bishop Capucci. Lifting his fingers to form the same victory sign used by our freedom-fighters, he said: "What I have done, I have done that all men may live on this land of peace in peace." This princely priest will doubtless share Adif's grim fate. To him we send our salutations and greetings.

Revolution Makes Dreams Real

Why therefore should I not dream and hope? For is not revolution the making real of dreams and hopes? So let us work together that my dream may be fulfilled, that I may return with my people out of exile, there in Palestine to live with this Jewish freedom-fighter and his partners, with this Arab priest and his brothers, in one democratic State where Christian, Jew and Moslem live in justice, equality, fraternity and progress.

Is this not a noble dream worthy of my struggle alongside all lovers of freedom everywhere? For the most admirable dimension of this dream is that it is Palestinian, a dream from out of the land of peace, the land of martyrdom and heroism, and the land of history, too.

Let us remember that the Jews of Europe and the United States have been known to lead the struggles for secularism and the separation of Church and State. They have also been known to fight against discrimination on religious grounds. How can they then refuse this humane paradigm for the Holy Land? How then can they continue to support the most fanatic, discriminatory and closed of nations in its policy?

Our Plan For Palestine

In my formal capacity as Chairman of the Palestine Liberation Organization and leader of the Palestinian revolution I proclaim before you that when we speak of our common hopes for the Palestine of tomorrow we include in our perspective all Jews now living in Palestine who choose to live with us there in peace and without discrimination.

In my formal capacity as Chairman of the Palestine Liberation Organization and leader of the Palestinian revolution I call upon Jews to turn away one by one from the illusory promises made to them by Zionist ideology and Israeli leadership. They are offering Jews perpetual bloodshed, endless war and continuous thralldom.

We invite them to emerge from their moral isolation into a more open realm of free choice, far from their present leadership's efforts to implant in them a Masada complex.

We offer them the most generous solution, that we might live together in a framework of just peace in our democratic Palestine.

In my formal capacity as Chairman of the Palestine Liberation Organization, I announce here that we do not wish one drop of either Arab or Jewish blood to be shed; neither do we delight in the continuation of killing, which would end once a just peace, based on our people's rights, hopes and aspirations had been finally established.

Appeal to Support PLO Struggle

In my formal capacity as Chairman of the Palestine Liberation Organization and leader of the Palestinian revolution I appeal to you to accompany our people in its struggle to attain its right to self-determination. This right is consecrated in the United Nations Charter and has been repeatedly confirmed in resolutions adopted by this august body since the drafting of the Charter. I appeal to you, further, to aid our people's return to its homeland from an involuntary exile imposed upon it by force of arms, by tyranny, by oppression, so that we may regain our property, our land, and thereafter live in our national homeland, free and sovereign, enjoying all the privileges of nationhood. Only then can we pour all our resources into the mainstream of human civilization. Only then can Palestinian creativity be concentrated on the service of humanity. Only then will our Jerusalem resume its historic role as a peaceful shrine for all religions.

I appeal to you to enable our people to establish national independent sovereignty over its own land.

Today I have come bearing an olive branch and a freedom-fighter's gun. Do not let the olive branch fall from my hand. I repeat: do not let the olive branch fall from my hand.

War flares up in Palestine, and yet it is in Palestine that peace will be born.

U.N. WORLD FOOD CONFERENCE
November 16, 1974

Machinery to coordinate world food policies was approved by representatives of 133 nations and six national liberation movements Nov. 16 at the conclusion of a 12-day World Food Conference in Rome sponsored by the U.N. Food and Agriculture Organization. Delegates to the conference approved broad guidelines aimed at halting "the scourge of hunger and malnutrition," but the agreements reached at Rome stopped short of providing immediate relief for the millions among the world's population currently faced with starvation. The agreements, to be sent to the U.N. General Assembly for final approval, included establishment of a new U.N. agency, a World Food Council, to oversee food programs. In addition, a final declaration called on "all governments" able to do so to increase substantially agricultural aid to developing nations in need of food and urged all nations to "reduce to a minimum the waste of food and of agricultural resources."

A compromise between developed and developing nations was reflected in the agreement to establish the World Food Council as a means of reducing the likelihood of recurrent food shortages. When food shortages had begun to reach crisis proportions in 1974, developing nations had appealed to the richer nations to meet their humanitarian obligations by supplying food for the starving. Developed nations responded with warnings that short-term solutions to food shortages were not sufficient. Populations could not continue to grow unrestrained, they said, lest it become impossible for the earth to continue to feed itself. The situation worsened as crop failures increased the extent of starvation and curbed Western willingness to donate food because of food shortages and higher consumer food prices *at home. Any food surpluses had been depleted. It was against this background that the U.N. World Food Conference was held. The disagreement over approaches to the food crisis was resolved in part by the agreement to establish the World Food Council. The council would be under the immediate supervision of the Economic and Social Council of the United Nations (ECOSOC) where industrialized nations had a predominant voice. But the council would report ultimately to the U.N. General Assembly where developing nations had numerical superiority.*

Composition of Food Council

Under the agreement reached by the delegates, the World Food Council was to be established by the United Nations General Assembly and report to that body via ECOSOC. The council would be comprised of officials at ministerial or plenipotentiary levels and meet several times during the year to coordinate existing as well as any new U.N. policies regarding food production, food aid, food security and nutrition. The council would be staffed through the U.N. Food and Agriculture Organization and would maintain its own full-time secretariat in Rome. In addition, delegates recommended that two subcommittees be established under the World Food Council, a world food security council and a food aid committee.

Other committees or councils approved by the delegates in Rome Nov. 16 included an international agricultural development fund to funnel investment funds into the improvement of agricultural facilities in developing nations. A proposal originally set forth by the Arab states, including the oil-producing countries, the plan called for voluntary contributions from traditional donors as well as from the newly rich nations, particularly the oil states. Two other proposals called for an irrigation, drainage and flood control project and a nutrition aid program. In addition, the delegates called for "achievement of a desirable balance between population and the food supply," without setting specific standards or goals.

Earlier in the conference, delegates pledged establishment of an internationally coordinated system of nationally held grain reserves and a 10-million ton-a-year food aid program for poor nations. Finally agreeing to a plan that had initially brought disagreement from the Soviet Union, the delegates also concurred on establishment of an early-warning system of data sharing to distribute information about weather conditions or other factors which might threaten food supplies either by decreasing supply or increasing demand.

Reaction

The conference had stirred various reactions among observers around the world. Many Americans feared that expectations of receiving free U.S. food aid would be unduly raised among developing nations, many of which were making no effort to control skyrocketing population growth. Others warned that hungry people were dangerous people—especially those in countries with nuclear capability. Still others reminded Americans of their traditional humanitarian nature. Deputy chairman of the U.S. delegation Edwin M. Martin Nov. 16 stressed that the purpose of the conference was not "to get food to people tomorrow but to lay out a plan of action to prevent the crisis that we have now from recurring." His comment was an apparent reference to President Ford's decision not to pledge an additional million tons of food aid, as requested by Democratic senators attending the conference, but to leave open the amount of additional aid to be provided. Martin said the United States "will probably be giving" at least a million tons, but, he added, "it would not be useful to announce a figure."

The acceptance by an Egyptian official of the role of secretary general of the World Food Conference had bolstered world hopes that Arab states with greatly increased oil revenues would assume a more important role in world aid programs. Ahmed Marei, the Egyptian secretary general of the conference, said Nov. 17 that he was "absolutely certain" Arab states would donate "millions, no, hundreds of millions of dollars," to the proposed agricultural development fund. Iranian Interior Minister Jamshid Amouzegar said the same day that Iran was "prepared to give—and give more—provided we do not replace the traditional donors' contributions."

Pope Paul's Controversial Remark

Perhaps the most controversial comment generated by the World Food Conference came from Pope Paul VI. Receiving more than 2,000 conference delegates at the Vatican Nov. 9, the Pope urged immediate steps to alleviate the problem of starvation, while discounting population control as one means of helping to solve that problem. Said the Pope: "It is inadmissible that those who have control of the wealth and resources of mankind should try to resolve the problems of hunger by forbidding the poor to be born." The papal remark drew immediate criticism from those concerned lest it seriously handicap efforts to induce poor nations to take population control measures.

Following are excerpts from selected resolutions adopted by delegates to the U.N. World Food Conference in Rome:

RESOLUTIONS ADOPTED BY THE CONFERENCE

RESOLUTION I

Objectives and strategies of food production

The World Food Conference...

1. *Resolves* that all governments should accept the removal of the scourge of hunger and malnutrition, which at present afflicts many millions of human beings, as the objective of the international community as a whole, and accept the goal that within a decade no child will go to bed hungry, that no family will fear for its next day's bread, and that no human being's future and capacities will be stunted by malnutrition.

2. *Calls on* the government of each developing country to:

(i) accord a *high* priority to agricultural and fisheries development;

(ii) formulate food production and food utilization objectives, targets and policies, for the short, medium and long-term, with full participation of producers, their families, and farmers' and fishermens' organizations, taking into account its demographic and general development goals and consistent with good environment practices;

(iii) take measures for agrarian reform and a progressive change in the socio-economic structures and relationships in rural areas; and

(iv) develop adequate supporting services for agricultural and fisheries development, including those for education, research, extension and training, marketing, storage and processing, transport, as well as credit facilities and incentives to enable producers to buy the required inputs;

3. *Calls on all governments* able to furnish external assistance to substantially increase their official development assistance to agriculture in developing countries, especially the least developed and the most seriously affected countries, including capital assistance on soft terms, technical assistance, transfer of appropriate technology and programme loans for imports of essential inputs;

4. *Requests* governments to make arrangements whereby developing countries will have access to inputs such as fertilizer, pesticides, agricultural machinery and equipment in sufficient quantity and at reasonable prices;

5. *Urges* governments to respond to the appeal of the Secretary-General of the United Nations for contributions to the Special Programme, the urgent implementation of which is essential for ensuring progress in resolving the food problem of the developing countries seriously affected by the economic crisis, and to contribute generously to the International Fund for Agricultural Development proposed by the Conference;

6. *Urges* the developed countries concerned to adopt and to implement agricultural policies which encourage the early expansion of food production while taking into account a satisfactory level of income for producers and world food requirements and the need of maintaining reasonable prices for consumers; such policies should not impede or delay the increase in food production by developing countries, both for domestic consumption and for export;

7. *Requests* all countries to reduce to a minimum the waste of food and of agricultural resources, in particular land, water and all forms of energy; and to ensure the rational utilization of fisheries resources;

8. *Calls on* the regional economic commissions to continue their important contribution to the task of stimulating co-ordinated economic development in their respective regions, by co-operating in the efforts in this direction that the countries in those regions are making;

9. *Urges* FAO in consultation with UNDP and other relevant international institutions, with due regard for national sovereignty:
    (a) to formulate economic, social, physical and biological criteria for selecting suitable additional areas for food production,
    (b) to make an inventory, on the basis of these criteria, of the areas most suitable for additional production,
    (c) to make an inventory of resources available for financing additional production, and
    (d) to indicate ways and means for carrying out programmes and projects for additional food production;

10. *Requests* the World Bank, Regional Banks, UNDP, FAO, UNIDO and other international agencies, through modification of their existing policies and criteria as appropriate, to substantially increase their assistance for agriculture anf fisheries in developing countries giving priority to programmes and projects aimed at benefiting the poorest groups of the population and placing equal emphasis on both economic and social benefits; simplify and streamline the procedures for the granting of such assistance; and mobilize the support of the entire international community including non-governmental organizations, for the urgent task of overcoming hunger and malnutrition.

RESOLUTION II

Priorities for agricultural and rural development

The World Conference...

1. *Calls on* governments to bring about appropriate progressive agrarian reforms in accordance with the political objectives and administrative capabilities of each country, adequate means of information and motivation and other institutional improvements in rural areas aimed at employment and income generation, at organizing, activating and assisting the rural population, including nomads, for participation in integrated rural development and at eliminating exploitative patterns of land tenure, credit and marketing systems where they still prevail, calls on them to improve credit marketing and inputs distribution systems and recommends that existing and experienced institutions and organizations in the developed countries should be mobilized as much as possible to take part in

943

agricultural development work, and also to make all efforts to carry out Economic and Social Council Resolution 1707 (LIII) on Agrarian Reform;

2. *Invites* governments to promote the development of cooperative organizations and other associations for the mass of farmers and rural workers for agricultural and rural development and for generating greater self-reliance, self-sufficiency and motivation;

3. *Requests* all governments to intensify their efforts in both formal and non-formal education of rural people with emphasis on what is relevant to their needs, taking into account the special role of women in agriculture and rural life in many societies, and to aim at the elimination of illiteracy within a decade;

4. *Calls on* each country to identify and implement with greater financial and policy support such food production and rural development programmes as are best suited to its specific national and regional characteristics and circumstances and which are required to achieve its national and international food production objectives, bearing in mind the development of appropriate technology, and the establishment of price relationships which will lead to increased incomes;

5. *Calls on* UNDP, IBRD, FAO and other international and bilateral agencies to review their criteria for financial, technical and other assistance for integrated rural development; to give greater importance to social criteria so as to implement broader and longer-range programmes of rural development; and if necessary improve their technical and administrative capacity for implementing these programmes;

6. *Urges* governments, UNDP and the other international and bilateral agencies to co-operate in accelerating the planning and implementation of integrated rural development programmes and to devote greatly expanded resources to these activities;

7. *Calls on* FAO and other United Nations organizations concerned to collect, evaluate and disseminate the results and experience from past and ongoing rural development programmes, to determine the suitability of these programmes in bringing about both expanding agricultural production and social integration.

RESOLUTION V

Policies and programmes to improve nutrition

The World Food Conference...

RECOMMENDS

1. That all governments and the international community as a whole, in pursuance of their determination to eliminate within a decade hunger and

malnutrition, formulate and integrate concerted food and nutritional plans and policies aiming at the improvement of consumption patterns in their socio-economic and agricultural planning, and for that purpose assess the character, extent and degree of malnutrition in all socio-economic groups as well as the preconditions for improving their nutritional status;

2. That FAO, in cooperation with WHO, UNICEF, WFP, IBRD, UNDP and UNESCO, assisted by PAG, prepare a project proposal for assisting governments to develop intersectoral food and nutrition plans; this proposal to be communicated to the FAO Council at its mid-1975 session through its Food and Nutrition Policy Committee, and to the governing bodies of the other interested agencies;

3. That governments, with their own resources, supplemented with food, financial and technical assistance from multilateral or bilateral external sources, and in close cooperation with agricultural production programmes initiate new or strengthen existing good and nutrition intervention programmes, on a scale large enough to cover on a continuing basis a substantial part of the vulnerable groups;

4. That governments include nutrition education in the curricula for educational programmes at all levels and that all concerned in the fields of agriculture, health and general education be appropriately trained to enable them to further the nutrition education of the public within their domains;

5. That governments strengthen basic health, family well-being and planning services and improve environmental conditions, including rural water supplies and the elimination of water-borne diseases; and provide treatment and rehabilitation of those suffering from protein-energy malnutrition;

6. That governments consider the key role of women and take steps to improve their nutrition, their educational levels and their working conditions; and to encourage them and enable them to breast-feed their children;

7. That governments review special feeding programmes within the context of their food and nutrition strategies to determine desirability and the feasibility of undertaking such new programmes, or improving existing ones, particularly amongst the vulnerable groups (children, pregnant and nursing mothers), but also for school children, workers and others; such programmes should promote increased local food production and processing thereby stimulating local initiative and employment and should also include an element of nutrition-education;

8. That the international agencies, non-governmental agencies and countries which are in a position to provide funds and foods for this purpose, should provide assistance to governments who will request such aid in order to introduce in the period 1975-76, emergency programmes for

supplementary feeding of a substantial number of the malnourished children with due attention to basic health and other essential services for the welfare of all children at risk;

9. That governments should explore the desirability and feasibility of meeting nutrient deficiencies, through fortification of staples or other widely-consumed foods, with amino-acids, protein concentrates, vitamins and minerals, and that, with the assistance of WHO in cooperation with other organizations concerned, should establish a world-wide control programme aimed at substantially reducing deficiencies of vitamin A, iodine, iron/folate, vitamin D, riboflavine, and thiamine as quickly as possible;

10. That FAO, in association with other international and non-governmental organizations concerned, undertakes an inventory of vegetable food resources other than cereals, such as roots, tubers and legumes, vegetables and fruits, including also those from unconventional sources, and that it studies the possibility of increasing their production and consumption, particularly in countries where malnutrition prevails;

11. That governments take action to strengthen and modernize consumer education services, food legislation and food control programmes and the relevant aspects of marketing practices, aiming at the protection of the consumer (avoiding false and misleading information from mass-media and commercial fraud), and that they increase their support of the Codex Alimantarius Commission;

12. That the joint FAO/WHO food contamination monitoring programme, in cooperation with UNEP, be further developed in order to provide early information to the national authorities for appropriate action;

13. That a global nutrition surveillance system be established by FAO, WHO and UNICEF to monitor the food and nutrition conditions of the disadvantaged groups of the population at risk, and to provide a method of rapid and permanent assessment of all factors which influence food consumption patterns and nutritional status;

14. That governments consider establishing facilities and funds for applied nutrition research related to economic, cultural, social and medical aspects of production, processing, preservation, storage, distribution and utilization of food and that FAO, WHO and UNICEF arrange for an internationally coordinated programme in applied nutritional research including establishing priorities, identifying appropriate research centres and generating the necessary fundings;

15. That governments should associate, wherever practicable non-governmental organizations whose programmes include nutrition-related activities, with their nutritional efforts, particularly in the areas of food and nutrition programmes, nutrition education and feeding programmes for the most vulnerable groups.

RESOLUTION VII

Scientific water management: irrigation, drainage and flood control

The World Food Conference...

1. *Recommends* urgent action to be taken by governments and international agencies such as FAO and WMO to implement the following:

(a) Undertake, wherever needed, exhaustive climatic, hydrological and irrigation potential, hydro-power potentials and desert creep surveys;

(b) Rapid expansion of irrigation capacities in areas where surface water and/or groundwater reserves are available for rational exploitation, so as to facilitate both the improvement of productivity and intensity of cropping;

(c) Development of techniques for the safe utilization of brackish water for food production in areas where sweet surface/groundwater is not available;

(d) Reclamation of areas affected by waterlogging, salinity and alkalinity and prevention of salinisation of irrigated areas;

(e) Identification of groundwater resources, exploration of the economic feasibility of using non-conventional sources of water and research and development efforts in the most economical use of water with such techniques as drip and sprinkler irrigation in arid areas where shortage of water, rather than land, is the limiting factor in crop production;

(f) Sound exploitation of groundwater resources, water harvesting and conservation in the soil profile and in run-off farm ponds together with techniques for the efficient use of the water thus made available in semi-arid and in drought-prone areas;

(g) Flood protection and flood control measures, including watershed management and soil conservation to mitigate the damage to crops in high rainfall and flood-prone areas; to render where feasible, the flood-free period into a major cropping season through development of lift irrigation and groundwater exploitation;

(h) Establishment of suitable drainage systems and appropriate steps to control salinity in swampy areas as well as in areas exposed to tidal inundation;

(i) Taking all necessary measures and developing techniques to combat desert creep;

2. *Calls on* international institutions and bilateral and multilateral aid agencies to provide substantially increased external assistance to enable the developing countries to undertake rapidly action set out under paragraph 1;

3. *Urges* governments and international agencies to assess and make appropriate arrangements for meeting the energy requirements for irrigation and to encourage intensive research on using solar hydro-electric power, geo-thermal and wind energy in agricultural operation;

4. *Urges* governments and international agencies to strengthen and where necessary to initiate national, regional research and training in all aspects of water technology related to specific farming systems and to improve the administration and management of water delivery systems.

RESOLUTION VIII

Women and food

The World Food Conference...

1. *Calls on* all governments to involve women fully in the decision-making machinery for food production and nutrition policies as part of total development strategy;

2. *Calls on* all governments to provide to women in law and fact the right to full access to all medical and social services particularly special nutritious food for mothers and means to space their children to allow maximum lactation, as well as education and information essential to the nurture and growth of mentally and physically healthy children;

3. *Calls on* all governments to include in their plan provision for education and training for women on equal basis with men in food production and agricultural technology, marketing and distribution techniques, as well as consumer, credit and nutrition information;

4. *Calls on* all governments to promote equal rights and responsibilities for men and women in order that the energy, talent and ability of women can be fully utilized in partnership with men in the battle against world hunger.

RESOLUTION IX

Achievement of a desirable balance between population and food supply

The World Food Conference...

Now calls on all governments and on people everywhere not only to make every possible effort to grow and equitably distribute sufficient food and income so that all human beings may have an adequate diet—a short-range goal which priority and the best techniques might make possible—but also to support, for a longer-term solution, rational population policies ensuring to couples the right to determine the number and spacing of births, freely and responsibly, in accordance with national needs within the context of an overall development strategy.

RESOLUTION XII

Seed industry development

The World Food Conference...

1. *Urges* the governments of developing countries to make short and long-term commitments of manpower, institutional and financial resources for seed industry development in their national agricultural development plans;

2. *Requests* interested countries and parties to introduce policies and measures for the production, processing, quality control, distribution, marketing, legislation, promotion and education of farmers in the utilization of quality seed;

3. *Recommends* that the international assistance of the FAO Seed Industry Development Programme be strengthened, so that national seed production and utilization efforts, both for domestic use and exports, including the training of competent technical and managerial manpower, can be furthered to meet demands.

RESOLUTION XIII

International Fund for Agricultural Development

The World Food Conference...

Resolves that:

1. An International Fund for Agricultural Development should be established immediately to finance agricultural development projects primarily for food production in the developing countries;

2. All developed countries and all those developing countries that are in a position to contribute to this Fund should do so on a voluntary basis;

3. The Fund should be administered by a Governing Board consisting of representatives of contributing developed countries, contributing developing countries, and potential recipient countries, taking into consideration the need for equitable distribution of representation amongst these three categories and ensuring regional balance amongst the potential recipient representations;

949

4. The disbursements from the Fund should be carried out through existing international and/or regional institutions in accordance with the regulations and criteria to be established by the Governing Board;

5. The Secretary-General of the United Nations should be requested to convene urgently a meeting of all interested countries mentioned in paragraph 3 and institutions to work out the details, including the size of, and commitments to, the Fund;

6. The Fund should become operative as soon as the Secretary-General of the United Nations determines, in consultation with representatives of the countries having pledged contributions to the Fund, that it holds promise of generating substantial additional resources for assistance to developing countries and that its operations have a reasonable prospect of continuity.

RESOLUTION XIV

Reduction of military expenditures for increasing food production

The World Food Conference...

Calls on the states participating in the Conference to take the necessary measures for the most rapid implementation of the Resolutions of the General Assembly and other organs of United Nations pertaining to the reduction of military expenditures on behalf of development, and to allocate a growing proportion of the sums so released to the financing of food production in developing countries and the establishment of reserves to deal with emergency cases.

RESOLUTION XVI

Global information and early-warning system on food and agriculture

The World Food Conference...

1. *Resolves that* a Global Information and Early Warning System on Food and Agriculture (hereinafter referred to as the "System") should be established and agrees that FAO is the most appropriate organization to operate and supervise the System;

2. *Requests* FAO, in co-operation with other concerned international organizations, particularly the International Wheat Council, to formulate arrangements necessary for the establishment of the System, and to submit them for final approval by Governments participating in the System;

3. *Requests* all Governments to participate in the System and extend full co-operation, on a voluntary and regular basis, by furnishing as much current information and forecasts as possible, including current information and forecasts obtained from the statistics and regular studies which are published, initially on basic food products, including in particular wheat, rice, coarse grains, soybeans, and livestock products and, to the extent practicable, other important food products and other relevant aspects of their food supply and demand situation affecting world food security, such as prices and production of inputs and equipment required for agricultural production, the food industry and livestock health, taking account of and respecting in full the sovereign rights of Governments in this regard;

4. *Requests* Governments to take steps, where necessary, to amplify and otherwise improve their data collection and dissemination services in these fields; and further requests FAO, WMO, WHO, the Intergovernmental Bureau for Informatics and other multilateral and bilateral sources to urgently assist interested Governments with technical and financial assistance on particular aspects in strengthening existing arrangements for data collection and dissemination in the fields of food production, nutritional levels at various income levels, input supplies, meteorology and crop/weather relationships, on a national or regional level as appropriate, and to co-ordinate this action with that of the World Food Council provided for in Conference resolution XXI on arrangements for follow-up action;

5. *Requests* that the information thus collected be fully analysed and disseminated periodically to all participating Governments, and for their exclusive use; it being understood that, where requested, certain information provided by Governments would be disseminated in aggregate form particularly in order to avoid unfavourable market repercussions;

6. *Requests* the World Meteorological Organization, in co-operation with FAO (a) to provide, as a part of the System, regular assessments of current and recent weather on the basis of the information presently assembled through the World Weather Watch, so as to identify agriculturally significant changes in weather patterns; (b) to expand and establish joint research projects particularly in arid and semi-arid areas, to investigate weather/crop relationships taking account of the effect of soil moisture conditions; (c) to strengthen the present global weather monitoring systems in regard to the adequacy of meteorological observations, and data processing systems, at the national and regional levels, in order to make them directly relevant to agricultural needs; and (d) to encourage investigations on the assessment of the probability of adverse weather conditions occurring in various agricultural areas, and on a better understanding of the causes of climatic variations.

RESOLUTION XVII

International Undertaking on World Food Security

The World Food Conference...

1. *Endorses* the objectives, policies and guidelines as set out in the text of the proposed international Undertaking on World Food Security, *invites* all Governments to express their readiness to adopt them and *urges* all Governments to co-operate in bringing into operation the proposed International Undertaking as soon as possible;

2. *Calls for* the early completion by the FAO bodies of the operational and other practical arrangements required for the implementation of the proposed International Undertaking, including the examination of practical economic and administrative problems involved;

3. *Invites* Governments of all major food, primarily cereals, producing, consuming and trading countries to enter as soon as possible into discussion in appropriate international fora, with a view to accelerating the implementation of the principles contained in the proposed International Undertaking on World Food Security, and also with a view to studying the feasibility of establishing grain reserves to be located at strategic points;

4. *Urges* Governments and the concerned international and regional organizations to provide the necessary technical, financial and food assistance in the form of grants or on specially favourable terms to develop and implement appropriate national food stocks policies in developing countries, including the extension of storage and transport facilities, within the priorities of their national development programme, so that they are in a position to participate effectively in a world food security policy.

RESOLUTION XVIII

An improved policy for food aid

The World Food Conference...

1. *Affirms* the need for continuity of a minimum level of food aid in physical terms, in order to insulate food aid programmes from the effects of excessive fluctuations in production and prices;

2. *Recommends* that all donor countries accept and implement the concept of forward planning of food aid, make all efforts to provide commodities and/or financial assistance that will ensure in physical terms at least 10 million tons of grains as food aid a year, starting from 1975, and also to provide adequate quantities of other food commodities;

3. *Requests* that interest cereals-exporting and -importing countries as well as current and potential financial contributors meet as soon as possible to take cognizance of the needs and to consider ways and means to increase food availability and financing facilities during 1975 and 1976 for the affected developing countries and, in particular, for those most seriously affected by the current food problem;

4. *Urges* all donor countries to (a) channel a more significant proportion of food aid through the World Food Programme, (b) consider increasing progressively the grant component in their bilateral food aid programmes, (c) consider contributing part of any food aid repayments for supplementary nutrition programmes and emergency relief, (d) provide, as appropriate, additional cash resources to food aid programmes for commodity purchases from developing countries to the maximum extent possible;

5. *Recommends* that the Intergovernmental Committee of the World Food Programme, reconstitute as recommended in Conference resolution XXI on arrangements for follow-up action, be entrusted with the task of formulating proposals for more effective co-ordination of multilateral, bilateral and non-governmental food aid programmes and of co-ordinating emergency food aid;

6. *Recommends* that Governments, where possible, earmark stocks or funds for meeting international emergency requirements, as envisaged in the proposed international Undertaking on World Food Security, and *further recommends* that international guidelines for such emergency stocks be developed as a part of the proposed Undertaking to provide for an effective co-ordination of emergency stocks and to ensure that food relief reaches the neediest and most vulnerable groups in developing countries;

7. *Recommends* that a part of the proposed emergency stocks be placed at the disposal of the World Food Programme, on a voluntary basis, in order to increase its capacity to render speedy assistance in emergency situations.

FORD'S ASIAN SUMMITS
November 18-24, 1974

President Ford traveled to three foreign countries Nov. 18-24, and by his first trip abroad as President symbolically sealed the transition to a new administration in Washington. Ford's initial stop on the Asian tour was Japan, which no other American President had visited officially. There he met with Emperor Hirohito, Premier Kakuei Tanaka, and other government officials and pledged cooperation on problems of energy and food supplies. The presidential entourage on Nov. 22 flew on to South Korea, where Ford and Korean President Park Chung Hee reaffirmed a U.S. pledge to maintain troops in that country. The final and most important leg of the journey took the President on Nov. 23 to the Siberian city of Vladivostok for intensive negotiations with Soviet Communist Party General Secretary Leonid I. Brezhnev. That meeting yielded a surprise tentative agreement to limit the numbers of strategic offensive nuclear weapons and delivery vehicles employed by the United States and the Soviet Union through 1985. Ford's Soviet visit was the second during 1974 by an American president. Former President Nixon had visited the country in late June. (See p. 535-569.)

The Asian summits afforded the foreign officials he met an opportunity to size up the new American president. Press reports indicated they were favorably impressed by Ford's natural warmth. In Japan, the President and Premier Tanaka reaffirmed the "friendly and cooperative relations" between their countries. In an 11-point joint communique signed Nov. 20, the leaders set forth in general terms their positions on a variety of questions. They voiced a desire for cooperation "among consuming countries," apparently referring to nations dependent on foreign sources of energy and food. They also committed their countries to pursuit of "harmonious relations with producing nations." Focusing specifically on "the need for a more efficient and rational utilization and distribution of world resources," they placed particular emphasis on food and suggested "an international framework" to insure stable supplies.

At a banquet honoring President Ford Nov. 19, Emperor Hirohito noted the friendly relations established between the United States and Japan in 1854. By way of what seemed a veiled apology for World War II, the Emperor referred to "bad days" between friendly nations and expressed Japanese appreciation "for the goodwill and aid you gave us in the confusing period after the war." Hirohito also accepted an invitation from Ford to visit the United States at some future date.

In a televised speech before the Japanese Press Club Nov. 20, Ford suggested that Japan join the United States in an exemplary alliance to combat global economic problems. He pointed to the "common resolve" of the two countries "to maintain stability in East Asia, to help in the development of other countries that need our help and to work together to encourage diplomatic and political rather than military solutions of the world's problems." Promising a continued flow of American goods, Ford said that "if shortages occur, we will take special account of the needs of our traditional partners."

Korean Visit

The second and most controversial stop on the presidential tour brought together President Ford and South Korean President Park Chung Hee. The latter's increasingly dictatorial policies had aroused fear at home that Ford's visit might appear to endorse the Korean tactics. Ford was greeted with great fanfare by more than a million Koreans lining the 12-mile route from the airport into Seoul. The welcoming crowds waved friendly banners, one of which hailed "Ford: King of Kings."

After two hours of talks Nov. 22, Ford and Park issued a joint communique reaffirming "the strong bonds of friendship and cooperation" between the two countries. Asserting "no intention to withdraw U.S. forces" from South Korea, the communique noted American support of South Korean efforts to conduct negotiations with North Korea looking toward eventual reunification of north and south. Ford also expressed U.S. willingness to aid South Korea in the further development of its defense industry.

Vladivostok Summit

Ford met Soviet Communist Party Chief Brezhnev for the first time in his official capacity as President Nov. 23 at the start of two days of talks that were apparently marked by substantial personal rapport. After exchanges of banter between the leaders, including an offer by Brezhnev to supply Washington, D.C., with snowplows comparable to ones that handled the heavy Russian snows, Ford and Brezhnev settled into a lengthy negotiating session outside of Vladivostok. The unexpectedly long duration of that session forced cancellation of a scheduled formal dinner. But the outcome was an unexpected restoration of momentum to the stalled **Strategic Arms Limitation Talks (SALT)**, *which the leaders announced would resume in Geneva in January 1975. Ford and Brezhnev issued a joint statement Nov. 24 prescribing guidelines to be followed by delegates at the SALT II talks. Secretary of State Henry A. Kissinger, who had laid the groundwork for the nuclear agreement during talks in October with Brezhnev, characterized that agreement as a "breakthrough" which meant that "a cap has been put on the arms race for a period of 10 years." Kissinger assessed as a "very strong possibility" the conclusion of a final accord on nuclear limitation in time for signing during the summer of 1975, when Brezhnev was expected to visit the United States.*

The Vladivostok guidelines called for acceptance of the principle of equivalence in strategic forces, whereas the 1972 SALT accord had set different but counter-balancing quotas. (See Historic Documents 1972, p. **431-463).** **Each country was to be accorded latitude as to whether it would** *choose land-based strategic missiles, submarine-launched missiles or strategic bombers for delivery vehicles. Broad limits were set on the deployment of multiple independently targeted re-entry vehicle (MIRV) warheads, which had not been covered by the 1972 SALT accord. While mentioning restrictions on the total number of MIRV-equipped vehicles, the agreement left open the number of individual MIRV warheads that could be deployed.*

Kissinger told reporters Nov. 24 that the Soviet Union had made one basic concession to the United States at Vladivostok. It had dropped its earlier insistence that the U.S. total of strategic delivery vehicles include the forward-based fighter bomber system deployed in Europe. Kissinger also said the two countries had reached agreement on the specific number of MIRVs and delivery vehicles that would be permitted. But, he said, these figures would not be released.

The tentative agreement limiting strategic nuclear weapons and delivery vehicles came as a surprise. The administration had made no mention of it in preliminary briefings before the visit, which was billed simply as an opportunity for Ford and Brezhnev to become acquainted and to reaffirm the commitment to detente. Kissinger noted Nov. 24 that progress on detente had been hampered during President Nixon's visit to the Soviet Union in June because the Nixon administration had been weakened by the Watergate scandal and by the fact that Nixon was a "lame duck" President. (Nixon Soviet Trip, see p. 535-569.) *A final communique issued Nov. 24 at Vladivostok reaffirmed the determination of the United States and the Soviet Union "to continue, without a loss in momentum, to expand the scale and intensity of their cooperation efforts in all spheres."*

On Nov. 24, President Ford and his accompanying entourage, including newsmen, were invited by Brezhnev to tour the city of Vladivostok, which reportedly had been closed to Soviet tourists as well as to all Westerners for almost three decades, purportedly because it housed a military base. According to published news reports, the city, only 50 miles from the Chinese border, had not been visited by Americans since 1922.

Following are the texts of (1) President Ford's speech Nov. 20 before the Press Club of Japan, (2) the U.S.-Japanese joint communique issued Nov. 20, (3) the U.S.-South Korean joint communique issued Nov. 22, (4) the U.S.-Soviet joint statement issued Nov. 24 on the limitation of strategic offensive arms, and (5) the U.S.-Soviet joint communique issued Nov. 24:

President Ford Before The
Japan Press Club

The President's Televised Remarks at a Press Club Luncheon at the Imperial Hotel, Tokyo, November 20, 1974

Mr. Watanabe, ladies and gentlemen:

As the first American President to visit Japan while in office, I greet you on this unprecedented occasion. I thank the Japanese Press Club for inviting me and the National Television Network of Japan for the opportunity to speak directly to the people of Japan.

I deeply appreciate the excellent coverage of my visit by the exceptional news media of Japan. I have always sought a good working relationship with the American journalists and have the same feeling toward their Japanese colleagues. It has been my objective at all times to treat journalists and all other people in the same manner that I would like to be treated.

I bring the warmest greetings of the American people. Our bipartisan political leadership in the American Congress sends its very best wishes. The distinguished leaders of both of America's national political parties have asked me to tell you of the very high value that all Americans attach to our partnership with Japan.

It is the American custom for the President to make a report every year to the Congress on our state of the Union. In the same spirit, I thought the people of Japan might welcome a report on the state of another union—the unity of American and Japanese mutual aspirations for friendship as Americans see that relationship.

In my hometown of Grand Rapids, Michigan, a Japanese company is now assembling musical instruments. Not only are the instruments harmonious in the melodies they produce, but the labor-management relationship followed by the Japanese created a model of harmony between workers and business.

In a nearby community, Edmore, another Japanese firm is manufacturing small electrical motors. This is yet another Japanese enterprise that has injected new energy, new goodwill in our industrial life. There are similar examples throughout America, and we welcome them.

The time has long passed when Americans speak only of what we contributed to your society. Today, traffic flows in both directions. We are both learning from each other.

To signify the value the United States attaches to partnership with Japan, I chose this to make my first overseas trip. I also met with your Ambassador to the United States on the first day that I assumed office, August 9.

I have long admired the richness and the diversity of Japan's culture, the products of your industry, the ingenuity, creativity, and the energy of your people, your courage as a fountain of resourcefulness in a troubled world.

My only regret is that Mrs. Ford could not join me on this visit in response to your very kind invitation. We both hope that she can come at some later date.

Americans are very proud of the way that we and the Japanese have worked together during the postwar period. We have had some disagreements, but we have remained friends and we have remained partners. Together, we created conditions under which both nations could prosper. Together we expanded our relations in trade and travel.

U.S. Interdependence With Japan

The reality of America's economic, political, and strategic interdependence with Japan is very obvious. America is Japan's greatest customer and supplier. Japan is America's greatest overseas trading partner. Japan is the best foreign customer for America's agricultural products.

The total trade between our two nations has doubled since 1970. It will surpass $20 billion in 1974. American investments in Japan are the largest of any foreign state. Japan's investment in America is growing rapidly and accounts for one-fifth of all Japanese investment abroad.

The flow of Japanese visitors to the United States has grown from some 50,000 in 1966 to over 700,000 in 1974. This is also a two-way street: Over 350,000 Americans visited Japan last year, accounting for nearly one-half of all foreign visitors.

Together we removed the legacies of World War II. The reversion of Okinawa eliminated the last vestige of that war from our agenda. We have made independent but mutually compatible efforts to improve our relations with the Soviet Union and the People's Republic of China. We have devised better channels for open consultation. I particularly want you to know that I understand the dangers of taking each other for granted.

As we talk to each other, we must ask each other what we regard as the central needs of our times.

959

First, of course, is peace. Americans and Japanese know the value of peace. We want to devote our resources and ourselves to building things, not tearing them down. We do not want to send our sons into battle again.

The alliance between Japan and the United States has helped to secure peace and can continue to help secure it. That alliance is not directed against any other country. It does not prevent us from improving our relations with other countries.

Our alliance does not signify that both nations subscribe fully to identical attitudes or identical styles. It does signify, however, that we clearly share a common resolve to maintain stability in East Asia, to help in the development of other countries that need our help, and to work together to encourage diplomatic and political rather than military solutions to world problems.

Our alliance was forged by peoples who saw their national interest in friendship and in cooperation. I am confident that our relations will remain solid and very substantial. I pledge that we shall work to make it so.

Peace, however, cannot be our sole concern. We have learned that there are many international threats and dangers that can affect the lives of our citizens. We face dwindling supplies of raw materials and food. We face international economic problems of great complexity. We must be more stringent in conservation than ever before.

We have worked together to solve the problems of the cold war. We succeeded because we worked together. Now we confront these new and even more complicated problems.

The Japanese reformer, Sakuma Shozan, wrote some lines in 1854 that provide an insight for 1974. Sakuma said, and I quote, "When I was twenty I knew that men were linked together in one province; when I was thirty I knew that they were linked together in one nation; when I was forty I knew that they were linked together in one world of five continents."

Now, 120 years later, the links between nations are closer than ever. Modern technology has made the world one. What each man or each nation does or fails to do affects every other.

Some Americans wondered why I decided to accept your invitation to come to Japan at a time when we have unsolved problems at home. I replied to those Americans that many of the problems we have at home are not just American problems but the problems of the world as a whole. Like others, we suffer from inflation. Like others, we face recession. Like others, we have to deal with rising prices and potential shortages of fuels and raw materials. America cannot solve those problems alone. Nations can only solve those problems by working together. Just as we worked together to maintain peace, we can work together to solve tomorrow's problems.

A Model of International Cooperation

Our two nations provide the world with a model of what can be achieved by international cooperation. We can also provide a model for dealing with the new difficulties. We both have great technological skills and human resources, great energy and great imagination. We both acknowledge the responsibility to developing states. We envisage the orderly and peaceful sharing of essential national resources. We can work together to meet the global economic issues.

We believe that we are not just temporary allies; we are permanent friends. We share the same goals—peace, development, stability and prosperity. These are not only praiseworthy and essential goals, but common goals.

The problems of peace and economic well-being are inextricably linked. We believe peace cannot exist without prosperity, prosperity cannot exist without peace, and neither can exist if the great states of the world do not work together to achieve it. We owe this to ourselves, to each other, and to all of the Japanese and the American people.

America and Japan share the same national pastime—baseball. In the game of baseball, two teams compete. But neither can play without the other, nor without common respect for each other and for the rules of the game.

Views on the American People

I have taken the liberty of giving you my views on the world we live in. Now let me tell you, the Japanese people, a little bit about the American people. The American people have faced some difficult times in our history. They know they will face others in the future. Their burdens are enormous, both at home and abroad. Some observers, including American observers, say that Americans have lost their confidence, their sense of responsibility and their creativity. It is not true.

I have traveled over much of my country during the past year. Each time I return to Washington refreshed. Our people are determined and realistic; our people are vigorous. They are solving their problems in countless towns and cities across the country. They continue to understand that history has placed great responsibilities on American shoulders. Americans are ready and willing to play their part with the same strength and the same will that they have always shown in the past.

Americans also know that no nation, however strong, can hope to dictate the course of history by itself. But the ability to understand the basic issue, to define our national interest, and to make common cause with others to achieve common purposes makes it possible to influence events. And Americans are determined to do that for constructive purposes and in the true spirit of interdependence.

In that spirit, let me make a pledge to you today. As we face the problems of the future, the United States will remain faithful in our commitments and firm in the pursuit of our common goals. We intend not only to remain a trustworthy ally, but a reliable trading partner.

We will continue to be suppliers of goods you need. If shortages occur, we will take special account of the needs of our traditional trading partners.

We will not compete with our friends for their markets or for their resources. We want to work with them.

The basic concepts of our foreign policy remain unchanged. Those concepts have a solid bipartisan and popular support. The American people remain strong, confident, and faithful. We may sometimes falter, but we will not fail.

Applying Enduring Values

Let me, if I might, end on a personal note. It is a privilege to be the first American President to visit Japan while in office. It is also a very great pleasure. I look forward to seeing Kyoto, the ancient capital of Japan.

Japan has preserved her cultural integrity in the face of rapid modernization. I have never believed all change is necessarily good. We must try to apply the enduring values of the past to the challenges and to the pressures of our times. Americans can learn from Japan to respect traditions even as we, like you, plunge ahead in the last quarter of the 20th century.

I also look forward to another deep privilege. Yesterday, during my call upon His Imperial Majesty, the Emperor of Japan, I renewed our invitation for the Emperor to visit the United States. It would be a great pleasure to be the first American President to welcome the Emperor of Japan to Washington and to show His Imperial Majesty our national shrines and treasures, including the graceful Japanese cherry trees whose blossoms provide a setting for the monuments to the great heroes of our own past.

I hope that my visit shall be the first of many by American Presidents. I hope that the leaders of our two countries will follow the example that our peoples have already set, to visit each other frequently and freely as our nations move together to deal with the many common problems and concerns that will affect the lives of all our citizens and all humanity.

I said in my first Presidential address to the Congress that my Administration was based on communication, conciliation, compromise, and cooperation. This concept also guides my view of American policy towards Japan. We both have much work to do. Let us do it together. Let us also continue the quest for peace. I would rather walk a thousand miles for peace than take a single step toward war.

I thank you.

U.S.-JAPANESE JOINT COMMUNIQUE

Text of the Joint Communique Between President Ford and Prime Minister Tanaka Issued at the Conclusion of Their Meetings, November 20, 1974

I

President Ford of the United States of America paid an official visit to Japan between November 18 and 22 at the invitation of the Government of

Japan. President Ford met Their Majesties the Emperor and Empress of Japan at the Imperial Palace on November 19.

II

In discussions held on November 19 and 20, President Ford and Prime Minister Tanaka agreed on the following common purposes underlying future relations between the United States and Japan.

1. The United States and Japan, Pacific nations sharing many political and economic interests, have developed a close and mutually beneficial relationship based on the principle of equality. Their friendship and cooperation are founded upon a common determination to maintain political systems respecting individual freedom and fundamental human rights as well as market economies which enhance the scope for creativity and the prospect of assuring the well-being of their peoples.

2. Dedicated to the maintenance of peace and the evolution of a stable international order reflecting the high purposes and principles of the Charter of the United Nations, the United States and Japan will continue to encourage the development of conditions in the Asia-Pacific area which will facilitate peaceful settlement of outstanding issues by the parties most concerned, reduce international tensions, promote the sustained and orderly growth of developing countries, and encourage constructive relationships among countries in the area. Each country will contribute to this task in the light of its own responsibilities and capabilities. Both countries recognize that cooperative relations between the United States and Japan under the Treaty of Mutual Cooperation and Security constitute an important and durable element in the evolution of the international situation in Asia and will continue to plan an effective and meaningful role in promoting peace and stability in that area.

3. The United States and Japan recognize the need for dedicated efforts by all countries to pursue additional arms limitation and arms reduction measures, in particular controls over nuclear armaments, and to prevent the further spread of nuclear weapons or other nuclear explosive devices while facilitating the expanded use of nuclear energy for peaceful purposes. Both countries underline the high responsibility of all nuclear-weapon states in such efforts, and note the importance of protecting non-nuclear-weapon states against nuclear threats.

4. The United States and Japan recognize the remarkable range of their interdependence and the need for coordinated responses to new problems confronting the international community. They will intensify efforts to promote close cooperation among industrialized democracies while striving steadily to encourage a further relaxation of tensions in the world through dialogue and exchanges with countries of different social systems.

5. In view of the growing interdependence of all countries and present global economic difficulties, it is becoming increasingly important to

963

strengthen international economic cooperation. The United States and Japan recognize the necessity of the constructive use of their human and material resources to bring about solutions to major economic problems. The establishment of an open and harmonious world economic system is indispensable for international peace and prosperity and a primary goal of both nations. The United States and Japan will, to this end, continue to promote close economic and trade relations between the two countries and participate constructively in international efforts to ensure a continuing expansion of world trade through negotiations to reduce tariff and other trade distortions and to create a stable and balanced international monetary order. Both countries will remain committed to their international pledges to avoid actions which adversely affect the economies of other nations.

6. The United States and Japan recognize the need for a more efficient and rational utilization and distribution of world resources. Realizing the importance of stable supplies of energy at reasonable prices they will seek, in a manner suitable to the economies, to expand and diversify energy supplies, develop new energy sources, and conserve on the use of scarce fuels. They both attach great importance to enhancing cooperation among consuming countries and they intend, in concert with other nations, to pursue harmonious relations with producing nations. Both countries agree that further international cooperative efforts are necessary to forestall an economic and financial crisis and to lead to a new era of creativity and common progress. Recognizing the urgency of the world food problem and the need for an international framework to ensure stable food supplies, the United States and Japan will participate constructively in multilateral efforts to seek ways to strengthen assistance to developing countries in the field of agriculture, to improve the supply situation of agricultural products, and to assure an adequate level of food reserves. They recognize the need for cooperation among food producers and consumers to deal with shortage situations.

7. For the well-being of the peoples of the world, a steady improvement in the technological and economic capabilities of developing countries must be a matter of common concern to all nations. In recognition of the importance of assisting developing countries, particularly those without significant natural resources, the United States and Japan will, individually and with the participation and support of other traditional aid donors and those newly able to assist, maintain and expand programs of cooperation through assistance and trade as those nations seek to achieve sound and orderly growth.

8. The United States and Japan face many new challenges common to mankind as they endeavor to preserve the natural enviroment and to open new areas for exploration such as space and the oceans. In broad cooperation with other countries, they will promote research and facilitate the exchange of information in such fields as science, technology and en-

vironmental protection, in an effort to meet the needs of modern society, improve the quality of life and attain more balanced economic growth.

9. The United States and Japan recognize that their durable friendship has been based upon the continued development of mutual understanding and enhanced communication between their peoples, at many levels and in many aspects of their lives. They will seek therefore to expand further cultural and educational interchange which fosters and serves to increase such understanding.

10. In the spirit of friendship and mutual trust, the United States and Japan are determined to keep each other fully informed and to strengthen the practice of frank and timely consultations on potential bilateral issues and pressing global problems of common concern.

11. Friendly and cooperative relations between the United States and Japan have grown and deepened over the years in many diverse fields of human endeavor. Both countries reaffirm that, in their totality, these varied relationships constitute major foundation stones on which the two countries base their respective foreign policies and form an indispensable element supporting stable international political and economic relations.

III

This first visit to Japan by an incumbent President of the United States of America will add a new page to the history of amity between the two countries.

U.S.-SOUTH KOREAN JOINT COMMUNIQUE

Text of the Joint Communique Between President Ford and President Park Issued at the Conclusion of Their Meetings. November 22, 1974

At the invitation of President Park Chung Hee of the Republic of Korea, President Gerald R. Ford of the United States of America visited the Republic of Korea on November 22 and 23, 1974, to exchange views on the current international situation and to discuss matters of mutual interest and concern to the two nations.

During the visit the two Presidents held discussions on two occasions. Present at these meetings were Prime Minister Kim Chong Pil, Secretary of State Henry Kissinger, Foreign Minister Kim Dong Jo, Presidential Secretary General Kim Chung Yum, Ambassador Richard L. Sneider, Ambassador Hahm Pyong Choon and other high officials of both Governments. President Ford also visited American forces stationed in the Republic of Korea.

President Ford laid a wreath at the Memorial of the Unknown Soldiers. He also visited the grave of Madame Park Chung Hee and expressed his deepest personal condolences to President Park on her tragic and untimely death.

The two Presidents reaffirmed the strong bonds of friendship and cooperation between their two countries. They agreed to continue the close cooperation and regular consultation on security matters and other subjects of mutual interest which have characterized the relationship between the Republic of Korea and the United States.

The two Presidents took note of significant political and economic changes in the situation in Asia in recent years. They recognized that the allied countries in the area are growing strong and more prosperous and are making increasing contributions to their security as well as to that of the region. President Ford explained that the United States, as a Pacific power, is vitally interested in Asia and the Pacific and will continue its best effort to ensure the peace and security of the region. President Park expressed his understanding and full support for United States policies directed toward these ends.

Talks With North Korea

President Park described the efforts being made by the Republic of Korea to maintain a dialogue with North Korea, designed to reduce tensions and establish peace on the Korean Peninsula, and to lead eventually to the peaceful unification of Korea. President Park affirmed the intention of the Republic of Korea to continue to pursue the dialogue despite the failure of the North Korean authorities to respond with sincerity thus far. President Ford gave assurance that the United States will continue to support these efforts by the Republic of Korea and expressed the hope that the constructive initiatives by the Republic of Korea would meet with positive responses by all concerned.

The two Presidents discussed the current United Nations General Assembly consideration of the Korean question. They agreed on the importance of favorable General Assembly action on the Draft Resolution introduced by the United States and other member countries. Both expressed the hope that the General Assembly would base its consideration of the Korean question on a recognition of the importance of the security arrangements which have preserved peace on the Korean Peninsula for more than two decades.

President Park explained in detail the situation on the Korean Peninsula, and described the threat to peace and stability of hostile acts by North Korea, exemplified most recently by the construction of an underground tunnel inside the southern sector of the Demilitarized Zone.

The two Presidents agreed that the Republic of Korea forces and American forces stationed in Korea must maintain a high degree of strength and readiness in order to deter aggression. President Ford reaffirmed the determination of the United States to render prompt and effective assistance to repel armed attack against the Republic of Korea in accordance with the Mutual Defense Treaty of 1954 between the Republic of Korea and the United States. In this connection, President Ford assured President Park that the United States has no plan to reduce the present level of United States forces in Korea.

U.S. Support of South Korea Defense

The two Presidents discussed the progress of the Modernization Program for the Republic of Korea armed forces and agreed that implementation of the program is of major importance to the security of the Republic of Korea and peace on the Korean Peninsula. President Ford took note of the increasing share of the defense burden which the Republic of Korea is able and willing to assume and affirmed the readiness of the United States to continue to render appropriate support to the further development of defense industries in the Republic of Korea.

President Ford expressed his admiration for the rapid and sustained economic progress of the Republic of Korea, accomplished in the face of various obstacles, including the lack of sufficient indigenous natural resources and continuing tensions in the area. President Park noted with appreciation the United States contribution to Korea's development in the economic, scientific and technological fields.

The two Presidents examined the impact of recent international economic developments. They agreed that the two countries should continue to foster close economic cooperation for their mutual benefit, and that they should guide their economic policies toward each other in the spirit of closer interdependence among all nations. They shared the view that coordination of their policies on new problems confronting the international community is necessary. Both Presidents expressed mutual satisfaction over the continuing growth of substantial bilateral economic relations which have been beneficial to both countries. They agreed that continued private foreign investment in Korea by the United States and other foreign countries is desirable. It was agreed that international efforts should focus on the reduction of trade distortions, establishment of a framework for ensuring stable food supplies, and realization of stable supplies of energy at reasonable prices.

President Park expressed his high expectations and respect for the efforts being made by President Ford to establish world peace and to restore world economic order.

On behalf of the members of his Party and the American people, President Ford extended his deepest thanks to President Park and all the people of the Republic of Korea for the warmth of their reception and the many courtesies extended to him during the visit.

President Ford cordially invited President Park to visit the United States of America and President Park accepted the invitation with pleasure. The two Presidents agreed that the visit would take place at a time of mutual convenience.

Limitation of Strategic Offensive Arms

Text of Joint United States-Soviet Statement. November 24, 1974

During their working meeting in the area of Vladivostok on November 23-24, 1974, the President of the USA Gerald R. Ford and General

Secretary of the Central Committee of the CPSU L. I. Brezhnev discussed in detail the question of further limitations of strategic offensive arms.

They reaffirmed the great significance that both the United States and the USSR attach to the limitation of strategic offensive arms. They are convinced that a long-term agreement on this question would be a significant contribution to improving relations between the US and the USSR, to reducing the danger of war and to enhancing world peace. Having noted the value of previous agreements on this question, including the Interim Agreement of May 26, 1972, they reaffirm the intention to conclude a new agreement on the limitation of strategic offensive arms, to last through 1985.

As a result of the exchange of views on the substance of such a new agreement the President of the United States of America and the General Secretary of the Central Committee of the CPSU concluded that favorable prospects exist for completing the work on this agreement in 1975.

Agreement was reached that further negotiations will be based on the following provisions.

1. The new agreement will incorporate the relevant provisions of the Interim Agreement of May 26, 1972, which will remain in force until October 1977.

2. The new agreement will cover the period from October 1977 through December 31, 1985.

3. Based on the principle of equality and equal security, the new agreement will include the following limitations:

   a. Both sides will be entitled to have a certain agreed aggregate number of strategic delivery vehicles;

   b. Both sides will be entitled to have a certain agreed aggregate number of ICBMs and SLBMs equipped with multiple independently targetable warheads (MIRVs).

4. The new agreement will include a provision for further negotiations beginning no later than 1980-1981 on the question of further limitations and possible reductions of strategic arms in the period after 1985.

5. Negotiations between the delegations of the U.S. and USSR to work out the new agreement incorporating the foregoing points will resume in Geneva in January 1975.

November 24, 1974

U.S.-SOVIET JOINT COMMUNIQUE

Text of the Joint United States-Soviet Communique Issued at the Conclusion of the President's Visit. November 24, 1974

In accordance with the previously announced agreement, a working meeting between the President of the United States of America Gerald R. Ford and the General Secretary of the Central Committee of the Communist Party of the Soviet Union L. I. Brezhnev took place in the area of Vladivostok on November 23 and 24, 1974. Taking part in the talks were the Secretary of State of the United States of America and Assistant to the President for National Security Affairs, Henry A. Kissinger and Member of the Politburo of the Central Committee of the CPSU, Minister of Foreign Affairs of the USSR, A. A. Gromyko.

They discussed a broad range of questions dealing with American-soviet relations and the current international situation.

Also taking part in the talks were:

On the American side Walter J. Stoessel, Jr., Ambassador of the USA to the USSR; Helmut Sonnenfeldt, Counselor of the Department of State; Arthur A. Hartman, Assistant Secretary of State for European Affairs; Lieutenant General Brent Scowcroft, Deputy Assistant to the President for National Security Affairs; and William Hyland, official of the Department of State.

On the Soviet side A. F. Dobrynin, Ambassador of the USSR to the USA; A. M. Aleksandrov, Assistant to the General Secretary of the Central Committee of the CPSU; and G. M. Korniyenko, Member of the Collegium of the Ministry of Foreign Affairs of the USSR.

I

The United States of America and the Soviet Union reaffirmed their determination to develop further their relations in the direction defined by the fundamental joint decisions and basic treaties and agreements concluded between the two States in recent years.

They are convinced that the course of American-Soviet relations, directed towards strengthening world peace, deepending the relaxation of international tensions and expanding mutually beneficial cooperation of states with different social systems meets the vital interests of the peoples of both States and other peoples.

Both Sides consider that based on the agreements reached between them important results have been achieved in fundamentally reshaping American-Soviet relations on the basis of peaceful coexistence and equal security. These results are a solid foundation for progress in reshaping Soviet-American relations.

Accordingly, they intend to continue, without a loss in momentum, to expand the scale and intensity of their cooperative efforts in all spheres as set forth in the agreements they have signed so that the process of improving relations between the US and the USSR will continue without interruption and will become irreversible.

Mutual determination was expressed to carry out strictly and fully the mutual obligations undertaken by the US and the USSR in accordance with the treaties and agreements concluded between them.

II

Special consideration was given in the course of the talks to a pivotal aspect of Soviet-American relations: measures to eliminate the threat of war and to halt the arms race.

Both sides reaffirm that the Agreements reached between the US and the USSR on the prevention of nuclear war and the limitation of strategic arms are a good beginning in the process of creating guarantees against the outbreak of nuclear conflict and war in general. They expressed their deep belief in the necessity of promoting this process and expressed their hope that other states would contribute to it as well. For their part the US and the USSR will continue to exert vigorous efforts to achieve this historic task.

A joint statement on the question of limiting strategic offensive arms is being released separately.

Both sides stressed once again the importance and necessity of a serious effort aimed at preventing the dangers connected with the spread of nuclear weapons in the world. In this connection they stressed the importance of increasing the effectiveness of the Treaty on the Non-Proliferation of Nuclear Weapons.

It was noted that, in accordance with previous agreements, initial contacts were established between representatives of the US and of the USSR on questions related to underground nuclear explosions for peaceful purposes, to measures to overcome the dangers of the use of environmental modification techniques for military purposes, as well as measures dealing with the most dangerous lethal means of chemical warfare. It was agreed to continue an active search for mutually acceptable solutions of these questions.

III

In the course of the meeting an exchange of views was held on a number of international issues: special attention was given to negotiations already in progress in which the two Sides are participants and which are designed to remove existing sources of tension and to bring about the strengthening of international security and world peace.

Having reviewed the situation at the Conference on Security and Cooperation in Europe, both Sides concluded that there is a possibility for its early successful conclusion. They proceed from the assumption that the results achieved in the course of the Conference will permit its conclusion at the highest level and thus be commensurate with its importance in ensuring the peaceful future of Europe.

The USA and the USSR also attach high importance to the negotiations on mutual reduction of forces and armaments and associated measures in Central Europe. They agree to contribute actively to the search for mutually acceptable solutions on the basis of principle of undiminished security for any of the parties and the prevention of unilateral military advantages.

Having discussed the situation existing in the Eastern Mediterranean, both Sides state their firm support for the independence, sovereignty and territorial integrity of Cyprus and will make every effort in this direction. They consider that a just settlement of the Cyprus question must be based on the strict implementation of the resolutions adopted by the Security Council and the General Assembly of the United Nations regarding Cyprus.

In the course of the exchange of views on the Middle East both Sides expressed their concern with regard to the dangerous situation in that region. They reaffirmed their intention to make every effort to promote a solution of the key issues of a just and lasting peace in that area on the basis of the United Nations resolution 338, taking into account the legitimate interests of all the peoples of the area, including the Palestinian people, and respect for the right to independent existence of all states in the area.

The Sides believe that the Geneva Conference should play an important part in the establishment of a just and lasting peace in the Middle East, and should resume its work as soon as possible.

IV

The state of relations was reviewed in the field of commercial, economic, scientific and technical ties between the USA and the USSR. Both Sides confirmed the great importance which further progress in these fields would have for Soviet-American relations, and expressed their firm intention to continue the broadening and deepening of mutually advantageous cooperation.

The two Sides emphasized the special importance accorded by them to the development on a long term basis of commercial and economic cooperation, including mutually beneficial large-scale projects. They believe that such commercial and economic cooperation will serve the cause of increasing the stability of Soviet-American relations.

Both Sides noted with satisfaction the progress in the implementation of agreements and in the development of ties and cooperation between the US and the USSR in the fields of science, technology and culture. They are convinced that the continued expansion of such cooperation will benefit the peoples of both countries and will be an important contribution to the solution of world-wide scientific and technical problems.

The talks were held in an atmosphere of frankness and mutual understanding, reflecting the constructive desire of both Sides to strengthen and develop further the peaceful cooperative relationship between the USA and the USSR, and to ensure progress in the solution of outstanding international problems in the interest of preserving and strengthening peace.

The results of the talks provided a convincing demonstration of the practical value of Soviet-American summit meetings and their exceptional importance in the shaping of a new relationship between the United States of America and the Soviet Union.

President Ford reaffirmed the invitation to L. I. Brezhnev to pay an official visit to the United States in 1975. The exact date of the visit will be agreed upon later.

FOR THE UNITED STATES OF AMERICA
 GERALD R. FORD
  President of the United States of America

FOR THE UNION OF SOVIET SOCIALIST REPUBLICS
 L. I. BREZHNEV
  General Secretary of the Central Committee of the CPSU

November 24, 1974

December

FORD'S RECESSION-FIGHTING PLAN
December 11, 1974

Conceding that "the economy is in difficult straits," President Ford Dec.
11 pledged to resist pressure for a sharp shift to stimulative economic
policies to fight unemployment. Especially with inflationary pressures
only starting to let up, the President told business leaders gathered at a
Business Council meeting in Washington, D.C., that he would continue to
treat inflation, recession and energy problems "with a balanced program."
While promising to send the new Congress some alternatives to his Oct. 8
economic proposals, whose 5 per cent surtax on moderate and upper in-
comes already appeared outmoded in light of the worsening recession, Ford
insisted that "if there are many among you who want me to take a 180-
degree turn from inflation fighting to recessionary pump priming, they will
be disappointed." But as Ford spoke, pressures for an all-out effort to
counter recession—or at least for sterner measures than his largely voluntary anti-inflationary program—were building among both Democrats and
Republicans in Congress.

Insisting that "our country is not in an economic crisis," Ford in his
address acknowledged that the emergence of recession and some easing of
inflation required adjustments in federal policies. Reporting on a White
House meeting earlier in the day with congressional leaders, Ford said his
advisers were preparing new or alternative economic proposals for consideration by the Congress when it convenes in January. But while "there
are now early signals that price pressures are beginning to ease," Ford
maintained that "only by acting in a responsible manner can we strengthen
confidence and move toward recovery without destroying the accumulated
anti-inflation pressures that are just now beginning to work."

Ford evidently was responding to growing indications on Capitol Hill that the heavily Democratic incoming 94th Congress would overrule his cautious policies in favor of stimulative spending and tax-cut measures. White House Press Secretary Ron Nessen Dec. 11 admitted to newsmen that the administration's proposal for a 5 per cent surcharge on 1975 income taxes had no chance of winning congressional approval.

Following is the text, as made available by the White House, of President Ford's Dec. 11 speech to the Business Council in Washington, D.C.:

...I don't have to tell you I deeply appreciate the opportunity to meet with you tonight, as leaders of commerce and industry, to discuss some very serious economic problems that we all face.

The mutuality of our problems was never more clearly stated than when I was introduced at a business conference quite recently. The moderator said, and I quote, "The greatness of America is that anyone can grow up to be President of an auto company, President of an airline, President of a utility, or President of the United States." Then he took a long, long pause and added, "That's just one of the chances you have to take!"

Four months ago, in my first words as President, I promised my fellow citizens from time to time "a little straight talk among friends."

I hope I am among friends tonight, because we are all in the same business, trying to keep this country politically and economically stable and strong, and to bring about better lives for more and more people through the genius of our American system.

Businessmen are not the only Americans working toward these goals, but it is very certain they cannot be reached—these goals—without you.

Straight Talk

Now for a little straight talk. The economy is in difficult straits. All the statistics, or most of them, prove that quite conclusively. We are in a recession. Production is declining and unemployment, unfortunately, is rising.

We are also faced with continued high rates of inflation greater than can be tolerated over an extended period of time.

There is some good economic news, but I can concede much or most of it is bad. Nevertheless, our country is not in an economic crisis.

A crisis—in the sense of a national crisis—is something that demands immediate and drastic action. A national problem is something that demands widespread understanding and carefully deliberated solutions—cures that are not worse than the disease.

In my 25-plus years in this capital, our economy has gone through at least five recessions—five in 25 years. And the facts are that we have recovered from every one of them, and I predict without any hesitation that we will recover from this one also. The question is not when but how. And your question to me as President is what am I doing about it? What am I doing about it as President?

I cannot and will not promise you a sudden change for the better. There is no prospect that I can discern for instantaneous improvement in the economy. Without enumerating them, you and I know that today's difficulties stem from policies and developments of past years. The effect of policies adopted today would not be felt for months to come.

Nor do I believe that confidence in the American economy can be restored with rhetoric—mine or that of other political players or sideline sitters. I do not believe it can be restored by Federal Government activity alone. I do believe it can be restored by the effective teamwork and enlightened self-interest of all elements of our American free enterprise economy and our representative free political system.

Long-term success is not assured by short-term panaceas. There appears to be a tendency these days to focus only on the immediate needs or effects of any proposed economic remedy and not to examine its long-term effects. Speaking only for myself, I do not buy that.

Not just the President, not just the Congress, not just business, or labor, or consumer, but all of us must act to renew and invigorate our economy, and everybody's faith in that economy.

Hopefully we will do most things right and only a few wrong things —maybe some of you have done that in business or had the same experience. But I can assure you this Government, as far as I am concerned, will do nothing deliberately wrong. But just because doing something—yes, it might perk up political opinion polls, but I think the facts are in some instances that course would be the worst course of all.

Men survive by instinct but make progress by intelligence. Perhaps we could survive by merely following our instincts now—an immediate return to wage and price controls, as some demand; immediate and mandatory gasoline rationing, as others advocate; the enactment of other compulsory programs that treat the symptoms but retard the cure.

I happen to believe that instincts must be overruled by intelligence and politics must yield to principles if we are to make reasonable economic progress that can honestly be sustained in the future, whether it is short-term or long-term; and let me say without any hesitation or qualification that is what I intend to do.

Meeting With Leadership

Today I met with the bipartisan leaders of the House and Senate at the White House in the Cabinet Room. The campaign is over, the voters have spoken, and the present Congress is about to adjourn. At that meeting there was a spirit of concern for the country in that representative roomful of responsible Democrats and responsible Republicans which I wish I had the eloquence to describe. Really, you would not believe how well we all get along when the doors are closed.

So I asked my former colleagues how well we all could get along, and I think most of them sincerely agreed that it would be wise if we could have a sort of an informal moratorium on partisan economics, at least until the next Congress convenes in January. Could not we sort of bite our tongues when tempted to say things that might further weaken confidence in the economy and compound the confusion in many Americans' minds about their future.

I was encouraged by the meeting this morning—I thought it was wholesome, beneficial, and I think it will have an impact. But for a start let me say this: Do not believe I have made any economic decisions unless you hear those decisions from me personally. There can be only one person that makes those decisions, and when I make them I'll announce them.

I intend to keep my experts working over the holidays translating into specifics a number of new or alternative measures to augment and update the economic package that I will place before the Congress within the next two months. We will meet the changing priorities in the future of our present and based on future realities.

I will have new proposals on the desks of the new Members of Congress when they convene in mid-January, if not sooner. In the few days left before this Congressional session, I assured the leaders that I would communicate, conciliate, compromise and cooperate to the outer limits of my fundamental principles in order to assure prompt enactment of the most urgent economic measures.

Among these are long-delayed trade reform legislation as well as legislation to make sure that unemployed workers receive temporary assistance, including public service jobs and extended unemployment compensation to protect their buying power. If these measures reasonably approximate the criteria I set two months ago, I will support adequate dollar amounts now indicated by worsening employment statistics, especially in some industries.

Tomorrow I intend to meet with leaders of the automotive industry—Roy Chapin of American Motors, Lee Iacocca of Ford, Tom Murphy of General Motors, Lynn Townsend of Chrysler, and Leonard Woodcock of the UAW. This will be a face-to-face discussion of the industry's very special problems, but problems that affect our economy on a very broad basis.

My door has been open, and remains open, for the responsible spokesmen of any segment of our economy which has been unduly damaged by our present economic difficulty.

I will continue to press for legislation and regulatory policies providing increased incentives and assistance for industrial modernization, replacement, and expansion to assure a sound industrial base now and for future generations, so that new jobs will be created. Increased productivity lies at the heart of our free enterprise system which made America what it is today, and I have been a firm believer in that very important ingredient all of my adult life, and I will say without any hesitation I am not going to change that conviction as President of the United States.

No Change in Rules

In short, what I am saying is quite precisely this: that insofar as I can prevent it, the fundamental rules of the economic game are not going to be changed every month or every other year in the short or the long haul. But I am also saying that insofar as I can achieve it, the programs and the policies of the Federal Government will be responsive to changed circumstances and our best available economic forecasts.

Some factors—especially fuel and food production—contribute formidably, as you well know, to our current economic problems. And when I fly to meet the President of France this weekend, I will be by no means neglecting our domestic difficulties if I improve the climate of cooperation among the fuel-consuming industrial nations by a common effort to ensure adequate food and fuel supplies at acceptable prices.

Just as all of your businesses depend upon enough energy, they also depend upon enough customers. Customers is a lovely word to you, and consumers sounds like an organized pressure group. The facts are that they are interchangeable. And consumers in America are concerned about the economy as employees and stockholders—in fact, they are one and the same people.

This Administration, I can assure you, is pledged to protect the consumer buying power, or customer purchasing power, as an essential element of sustaining and strengthening the free enterprise system. This is where the voluntary part of my economic program comes in—primarily in each individual's purposeful determination to reduce conspicuous waste and to spend wisely.

The WIN campaign—a volunteer, nonpartisan citizens' effort—is yet an unexploited success. It has my full support and it deserves yours.

I can tell you this: I have received more than 200,000 pieces of mail in support of the WIN program, by far the largest amount of favorable public response to anything that I have done since taking office.

Now personally I don't care whether WIN spells Whip Inflation Now or Work Is Needed. America needs the winning spirit to surmount its present economic difficulties. Whatever the challenge, Americans like to win. If there are any among you who want me to take a 180 degree turn from inflation fighting to recessionary pump priming, they will be disappointed.

Three Problems

The fact of the matter is I am deeply concerned about all three domestic devils—inflation, recession and energy. They are all part of the same economic torment that now afflicts every industrial nation. I will continue to treat this general economic ailment with a balanced program. We have not, should not and will not concentrate exclusively on a single aspect of our complex economy. I think it is wise and I intend to concentrate on the total picture.

Heretofore I have emphasized the distortions of inflation because price increases must be blunted before we can realistically expect to restore employment gains and capital investment. There are now early signals that price pressures are beginning to ease. I expect inflation will move steadily down from the intolerable double-digit level.

The facts are conditions are changing rapidly. Only by acting in a responsible manner can we strengthen confidence and move toward recovery without destroying the accumulated anti-inflation pressures that are just now beginning to work. I know that the Business Council can rise to this challenge and I will tell you why. I remember a little history. You and your predecessors were a very key factor in helping the Government mobilize the economy for World War II, and what an incredible record that you wrote—in top managerial posts, in Government, in industry and in the war itself.

Gentlemen, you have to—and we need you to—mobilize again. This Administration will do its part. I will personally do my part. The country needs your full cooperation and your full support.

What is needed is to unite our entire American leadership in this effort, not to divide ourselves with self-defeating pessimism.

As a most perceptive Washington news columnist recently wrote under the heading "The Calamity Howlers," he said the following, and I quote.

"Now the situation is awkward, and in the automobile towns it is alarming, but the calamity howlers are adding to the depression psychology and making things even worse than they need be.

"For example, many companies now seem to be holding back on essential purchases for fear of what might happen in 1975, and there is upward pressure on both prices and wages in the belief that President Ford will finally be forced to adopt wage and price controls. In short, many people are beginning to act on their fears, which are worse than the facts.

"Washington," he went on to say, "is a little jittery, too. Because everybody who has a pain sooner or later comes here to complain about it, the capital has a tendency to think everybody has a pain....

"So things are a little mixed up," he went on to say, "and everybody is looking for painless solutions and hoping to get back to where we were before, with cheap gas and 96 fancy new models to choose from. But it's not on, folks. That world is gone. We're going to have to make do and mend for a while, but this is a very strong country and it will get along if we don't talk ourselves into a mess."

End quote.

As Mr. Reston rightly concluded, this is a very strong country. It started weak and disunited, but two centuries later our free economic system and our free political system are both the strongest and the most enduring in the world, and as long as I am President I propose to keep them that way.

Thank you very much.

U.S.-FRENCH RELATIONS: FORD AND GISCARD D'ESTAING

December 15-16, 1974

A change for the better in U.S.-French relations marked the talks between President Ford and French President Valery Giscard d'Estaing on the French West Indies island of Martinique Dec. 15-16. Appearing to resolve recent differences in the approach to major world issues, Ford and Giscard d'Estaing were able to reach agreements on energy, gold and other questions, according to a joint communique issued at the conclusion of their talks. In the early months of 1974, French resistance to American efforts to obtain concerted action by the West on the energy crisis, the oil embargo and world monetary reform had led to a deterioration in relations between the two countries. Unidentified Nixon administration officials had predicted in March that the United Stages would re-evaluate its relations with France in view of French actions seemingly aimed at isolating the United States from Europe. (See p. 123-127, 185-188, 497-505, and 529-533.) By the end of 1974, those differences apparently had been resolved. Discussing an agreement on oil cooperation reached during the talks, Secretary of State Henry A. Kissinger said Dec. 16 that "We should stop talking about Franco-American relations in terms of confrontation and start talking in terms of cooperation." Giscard d'Estaing told reporters that he hoped "to make France an active agent for international cooperation." He said he attached great importance to his personal friendship with President Ford.

The joint communique of Dec. 16 said that France had gained U.S. approval of its proposal to hold a conference between oil-producing and oil-consuming nations. The United States, modifying its earlier intent to hold off such a conference until oil consumers could concur on a joint plan, agreed to participate in the conference "at the earliest possible date." A "preparatory" meeting between producers and consumers of oil, to make procedural arrangements for the conference, was slated for March 1975. The French, on their part, agreed to "intensive consultations among consumer countries in order to prepare positions for the conference," a concession to the United States position in favor of a united front among the oil consumers.

Stressing the importance of "solidarity," both leaders agreed that prior to the March preparatory meeting, oil consumers would work toward further cooperation on energy conservation and development. They also agreed on "setting up of a new mechanism of financial solidarity," an apparent reference to Kissinger's plan to establish a $25-billion emergency fund for use by oil-consuming nations especially hard hit by rapidly rising oil prices. Kissinger announced to newsmen Dec. 16 that France would participate in the fund, under new guidelines amending the ones originally proposed by the United States.

Giscard d'Estaing and Ford also concluded an agreement on gold. According to the communique, the two leaders agreed that "it would be appropriate for any government which wished to do so to adopt current market prices as the basis of valuation for its gold holdings." While Kissinger said he did not foresee such action by the United States in the near future, he noted that the procedure would allow countries to align the fixed rate with the much higher market rate. Giscard d'Estaing said his nation would make the adjustment in gold valuation in the near future.

Compensation for U.S. Troop Pull-out

The two leaders reached a financial agreement settling a dispute that arose in 1966 when France ordered American forces assigned to the North Atlantic Treaty Organization (NATO) to leave its territory. Giscard d'Estaing agreed that France would pay the United States $100-million to compensate for the financial losses incurred as a result of the 1966 troop pull-out. In the field of other U.S.-European affairs, the two presidents declared that both the United States and members of the European Economic Community (EEC) should "adopt consistent economic policies" in their separate efforts to fight domestic inflation while avoiding unemployment. Of significance, they agreed on the importance of avoiding protectionist measures, such as tariff increases which would unfavorably affect their allies.

Following is the text of the joint communique issued Dec. 16 by President Ford and French President Valery Giscard d'Estaing at the conclusion of the two-day talks on Martinique in the French West Indies:

982

MEETINGS WITH PRESIDENT
VALERY GISCARD D'ESTAING OF FRANCE

Communique Issued Following Meetings Between President Ford and President Giscard d'Estaing. December 16, 1974

The President of the United States, Gerald R. Ford, and the President of the French Republic, Valery Giscard d'Estaing, met in Martinique December 14-16, 1974, to discuss current issues of mutual concern. They were joined in their discussions by the Secretary of State and Assistant to the President for National Security Affairs Henry A. Kissinger and Minister of Foreign Affairs Jean Sauvagnargues, and by Secretary of the Treasury William Simon and Minister of Finance Jean-Pierre Fourcade. The Ministers also held complementary side talks.

The meeting took place in an atmosphere of cordiality and mutual confidence. President Ford and President Giscard d'Estaing welcomed the opportunity to conduct detailed substantive discussions on the whole range of subjects of mutual concern. As traditional friends and allies, the two nations share common values and goals and the two Presidents expressed their determination to cooperate on this basis in efforts to solve common problems.

They reviewed the international situation in the economic, financial and monetary fields.

The two Presidents agreed that the Governments of the United States and of the European Community, in the name of which the French President spoke on this subject, must adopt consistent economic policies in order to be effective in avoiding unemployment while fighting inflation. In particular, they agreed on the importance of avoiding measures of a protectionist nature. And they decided to take the initiative in calling additional intergovernmental meetings should they prove necessary for achievement of the desired consistency of basic economic policies among industrial nations.

In the light of the rapid pace of change in international financial positions in the world today, the Presidents were in full agreement on the desirability of maintaining the momentum of consideration of closer financial cooperation both within the International Monetary Fund and through supplementary measures. As one specific measure to strengthen the existing financial framework, the Presidents agreed that it would be appropriate for any Government which wished to do so to adopt current market prices as the basis of valuation for its gold holdings.

Cooperation on Energy, Economy, Oil

The two Presidents considered in depth the energy problem and its serious and disturbing effects on the world economy. They recognized the importance for the USA, the EEC and other industrialized nations of implementing policies for the conservation of energy, the development of existing and alternative sources of energy, and the setting up of new mechanisms of financial solidarity. They stressed the importance of solidarity among oil importing nations on these issues.

The two Presidents also exchanged views on the desirability of a dialogue between consumers and producers and in that connection discussed the proposal of the President of the French Republic of October 24 for a conference of oil exporting and importing countries. They agreed that it would be desirable to convene such a meeting at the earliest possible date. They regard it as important that all parties concerned should be better informed of their respective interests and concerns and that harmonious relations should be established among them in order to promote a healthy development of the world economy.

The two Presidents noted that their views on these matters are complementary and, in this context, they agreed that the following inter-related steps should be taken in sequence:

—They agreed that additional steps should be taken, within the framework of existing institutions and agreements to which they are in a party, and in consultation with other interested consumers, to strengthen their cooperation. In particular, such cooperation should include programs of energy conservation, for the development of existing and alternative sources of energy and for financial solidarity

—Based on substantial progress in the foregoing areas, the two Presidents agreed that it will be desirable to propose holding a preparatory meeting between consumers and producers to develop an agenda and procedures for a consumer/producer conference. The target date for such a preparatory meeting should be March 1975.

—The preparatory discussions will be followed by intensive consultations among consumer countries in order to prepare positions for the conference.

The two Presidents agreed that the actions enumerated above will be carried out in the most expeditious manner possible and in full awareness of the common interest in meeting this critical situation shared by the United States and France and all other countries involved.

Review of World Affairs

President Ford and President Giscard d'Estaing reviewed current developments in East-West relations. They discussed their respective meetings with General Secretary Brezhnev, and Secretary Kissinger reported on his discussions with leaders of the People's Republic of China. They exchanged views on developments in East-West negotiations, including the Conference on Security and Cooperation in Europe. They expressed their conviction that progress in casing tensions was being made.

The two Presidents exchanged views on the present situation in the Middle East. They agreed on the importance of early progress toward a just and lasting peace in that area.

President Giscard d'Estaing described current efforts by France and other members of the European Community to further the process of European unity. President Ford reaffirmed the continuing support of the United States for efforts to achieve European unity.

The two Presidents discussed the situation in Indochina. They noted that progress in Laos toward reconciliation and reunification was encouraging.

The two Presidents agreed on the need for all parties to support fully the Paris Peace Agreements on Vietnam. Regarding Cambodia, they expressed the hope that the contending parties would enter into negotiations in the near future rather than continuing the military struggle. They expressed the hope that following Laos, Cambodia and Vietnam might also find their political way towards civil peace.

The two Presidents renewed the pledges of both Governments to continue close relations in the field of defense as members of the Atlantic Alliance. They agreed that the cooperation between France and NATO is a significant factor in the security of Europe.

They noted with satisfaction that the positive steps in negotiations on SALT taken during the Soviet-American meeting at Vladivostok have reduced the threat of a nuclear arms race. The two Presidents explored how, as exporters of nuclear materials and technology, their two countries could coordinate their efforts to assure improved safeguards of nuclear materials.

The President of France indicated that his Government was prepared to reach a financial settlement in connection with the relocation of American forces and bases committed to NATO from France to other countries in 1967. The French offer of $100 million in full settlement was formally accepted by President Ford.

The two Presidents concluded that the personal contact and discussion in this meeting had demonstrated accord on many questions and expressed their determination to maintain close contact for the purpose of broad cooperation in areas of common concern to the two countries.

SWEARING-IN OF
VICE PRESIDENT ROCKEFELLER
December 19, 1974

Nelson A. Rockefeller became the nation's 41st vice president Dec. 19 shortly after the House of Representatives confirmed his nomination by President Ford, 287-128. (Ford's nomination of Rockefeller, see p. 707-711.) *The Senate had given its approval of the nomination Dec. 10, 90-7, in accordance with the 25th Amendment requiring vice presidential vacancies to be filled by majority approval of the President's nominee by each chamber of Congress. Rockefeller was administered the oath of office by Supreme Court Chief Justice Warren E. Burger at 10:12 p.m. during the first proceedings of the Senate ever to be televised. In brief remarks following the ceremony, Rockefeller expressed his appreciation for being able to serve his country as vice president. He drew applause for his statement: "There is nothing wrong with America that Americans cannot right." With Rockefeller's swearing-in, for the first time in history, the nation's two highest offices were held by men who had not faced a national electorate. Not until the presidential elections of 1976 would American voters as a whole express their preference for the nation's top leaders.*

Rockefeller's confirmation ended a chain of events that had begun when Spiro T. Agnew resigned as vice president in October 1973, pleading no contest to a charge of income tax evasion. (See Historic Documents 1973, p. 827-838.) *Congress, in December 1973, approved President Richard Nixon's choice of Rep. Gerald R. Ford (R Mich.), then House Minority Leader, to succeed Agnew.* (See Historic Documents 1973, p. 969-973.) *Ford became President Aug. 9, 1974, when Nixon resigned.* (See p. 683-693 and 695-705.) *Ford nominated Rockefeller to be Vice President on Aug. 20.* (See p. 707-711.)

The House confirmation followed release earlier on Dec. 19 of the House Judiciary Committee's report of its nine days of hearings on the nomination, plus several evening sessions. The committee noted in the conclusion of its report that "not every member of the committee subscribing to this report finds himself in agreement with the totality of Mr. Rockefeller's record or with all aspects of his general philosophy of government. Some members who voted in the affirmative specifically announced certain reservations during debate in the committee." However, the report stated, "Looking at the total record...the committee finds Nelson A. Rockefeller fit and qualified to be vice president and believes his nomination merits confirmation pursuant to the 25th Amendment." The report concluded, "Nothing in the committee's hearing record or in its investigative files was found to disqualify Mr. Rockefeller from service. On the contrary, the evidence warrants an endorsement of his capacity and fitness to serve as vice president."

In supplemental views, Robert McClory (R Ill.) and Henry P. Smith III (R N.Y.) listed some of Rockefeller's qualifications for office, complaining that the majority report "does not adequately review the substantial record of public service and experience" of Rockefeller. Objections to the nomination were detailed in dissenting views filed by Robert W. Kastenmeier (D Wis.), Don Edwards (D Calif.), John Conyers (D Mich.), Joshua Eilberg (D Pa.), Jerome R. Waldie (D Calif.), Paul S. Sarbanes (D Md.), Robert F. Drinan (D Mass.), Elizabeth Holtzman (D N.Y.), Wayne Owens (D Utah) and Edward Mezvinsky (D Iowa).

Opposition and Support for Rockefeller

Initially, Ford's nomination of Rockefeller had been greeted favorably on Capitol Hill. However, the nomination appeared headed for trouble by mid-October after the disclosure of a long list of Rockefeller's gifts and loans to New York state officials and his involvement in the 1970 financing of an unflattering biography of Arthur J. Goldberg, who was then Rockefeller's opponent for governor. Critics contended that the Goldberg biography was reminiscent of the campaign dirty tricks revealed in the Watergate scandal, a charge Rockefeller heatedly denied. The hearings also delved into the vast Rockefeller fortune and into charges that Rockefeller could not possibly avoid conflicts of interest if he became president.

Supporters contended that Rockefeller's 36 years of experience in state and national government and his good motives outweighed the arguments of his critics, who included conservatives unhappy with the former governor's fiscal policies in New York. Kastenmeier summed up the objections to the nomination held by many liberals Dec. 19 during the House debate. He questioned Rockefeller's judgment in making the gifts and loans and in his involvement with the Goldberg book. He also criticized Rockefeller's handling of the 1971 Attica (N.Y.) prison uprising in which 39 hostages and prisoners were killed when authorities recaptured the institution.

(See Historic Documents 1972, p. 783-788.) *Kastenmeier cited the conflict of interest question, Rockefeller's strong support of "almost every manifestation of American military power" and his support of continued CIA and FBI covert operations.*

Kastenmeier also declared that there was a "valid concern that the 25th Amendment has not served the nation well" in this case, since it brought to office an unelected president and vice president. He predicted that the 94th Congress would re-examine the 25th Amendment in light of the Ford and Rockefeller experience. However, House Minority Leader John J. Rhodes (Ariz.) said in a statement that Rockefeller "has been probed, provoked, tried, tested and observed from virtually every conceivable angle and perspective." In spite of this "meticulous scrutiny," Rhodes declared, "not a single shred of evidence was produced to even remotely suggest that Nelson Rockefeller profited financially from his service in the government."

Following is the text of remarks by Vice President Nelson A. Rockefeller following his swearing-in Dec. 19:

Mr. President, Mr. Speaker, President pro tem Eastland, Chief Justice, your excellencies, the members of the diplomatic corps, distinguished guests and fellow Americans.

As I stand before you, I feel a great sense of humility. I feel a great sense of gratitude for the privilege of serving the country I love.

I feel a deep sense of gratitude to President Ford, to the Congress of the United States and to the people of America.

To the President for his trust and confidence and the opportunity he has given me to serve this great nation in working with him, a man for whom I have profound respect, admiration and warmth of affection. A man of integrity, sincerity, openness, dedication. A man bearing the lonely burdens of the Presidency with deep human understanding and total devotion to his country. And my admiration to the First Lady, Betty Ford, and her great warmth and courage.

And if you'll forgive me for a personal note, my love and admiration to my own gallant wife, Happy.

I feel deeply grateful to the committees and the members of the United States Senate and the House of Representatives for their confirmation of my nomination.

Among the many reasons I look forward with pride and keen anticipation to serving the Senate as their presiding officer is the fact that my mother's father, my grandfather, Senator Nelson W. Aldrich, represented the great state of Rhode Island in this very chamber for 31 years after serving for three years in the House of Representatives.

The thoroughness with which the Congress exercised its responsibility on behalf of the American people under the 25th Amendment has been another dramatic evidence of the enduring strength and vitality of our Constitution and our unique American system.

Educational Experience

I've learned a great deal from this experience of the past four months. And I've come out of it with an even greater respect for the Congress of the United States, a more profound appreciation of the collective wisdom of the American people as expressed through the Congress, and a deeper understanding of the breadth of the responsibility of the people of this great free land that falls upon those of us in positions of public trust.

I deeply appreciate the outstanding work of all those in government agencies involved in the investigation and preparation of material for the Congressional committee. I admire and respect the vigilant coverage of the free American press, radio and television, through which the people of America were so well-informed.

I would like to thank all of those citizens who participated directly in the process by expressing themselves to their representatives in the Senate and in the House, and to those who sent words of encouragement to Happy and to me.

And finally, especially to you, Mr. Chief Justice, my thanks for your administration of the oath and symbolizing as you do the rule of law by which this great Republic functions.

In this—or—this is a period in which our country faces tremendous difficulties and unprecedented problems, both at home and abroad. Problems that affect every section of our country and every family in America. But there is nothing wrong with America that Americans cannot right. I pledge myself to the fullest limit of my capacity to work with you, Mr. President, and the Congress in the great task of building the strength of America to meet the grave new problems which we confront as a nation and as a people. I thank you.

END OF WATERGATE COVERUP TRIAL

December 30, 1974-January 1, 1975

As 1974 ended, the trial of the Watergate coverup defendants drew to a close, apparently bringing to an end the final sorry chapter in the tangled tale of Watergate. From Oct. 1, through Jan. 1, 1975, five high-ranking officials in the Nixon administration stood trial in a District of Columbia federal court for their alleged roles in a conspiracy to obstruct the investigation of the June 17, 1972, break-in at the Watergate office building. The five defendants were John N. Mitchell, former attorney general; H.R. Haldeman, former White House chief of staff; John D. Ehrlichman, former White House chief domestic adviser; Robert C. Mardian, former assistant attorney general; and Kenneth W. Parkinson, a lawyer who had been hired by the 1972 Nixon re-election committee after the Watergate break-in. (Indictments of the Watergate coverup defendants, see p. 157-184.)

Not physically present at the trial was its central figure, Richard M. Nixon. The disgraced former President had resigned Aug. 9 (see p. 683-693) and had been pardoned by President Ford Sept. 8 (see p. 811-817.) Although Nixon was subpoenaed by Ehrlichman, Judge John J. Sirica ruled that his testimony was not essential for the trial. During the three-month trial Nixon remained 3,000 miles away at his San Clemente, Calif., estate recuperating from surgery for a blood clot in his leg. Nixon's voice, however, played a crucial role as tapes of incriminating White House conversations among Nixon and his aides discussing Watergate were heard at the trial. An April 25, 1973, tape revealed that Nixon had offered to help pay the legal expenses of both Haldeman and Ehrlichman out of funds remaining from the 1972 election contributions. During other conversations April 25, 1973, with Haldeman, Nixon expressed concern that John W. Dean III, former White House counsel, who had pointed the prime accusatory finger at Nixon during the 1973 Senate Watergate hearings, might have himself recorded the crucial March 21, 1973, conversation in which Nixon discussed payment of "hush money" to the original Watergate defendants. On Nov. 4, another bombshell fell in the courtroom with the disclosure of a memo written Nov. 14, 1972, by E. Howard Hunt, one of the original Watergate defendants. In the memo, Hunt listed commitments from the White House that he said were understood to be in exchange for the silence of himself and the other defendants.

Verdict: Guilty

Judge Sirica charged the jury Dec. 30. In his instructions, Sirica directed the jurors to disregard the pardon of Nixon by President Ford and concentrate instead on determining the truth of the case. As the year ended, the jury had been deliberating for less than two days. From indications gained from the jury's requests for documents, it was proceeding rapidly toward a final verdict. At 4:25 p.m. Jan. 1, 1975, the 3-man, 9-woman panel returned its final finding: Mitchell, Haldeman, Ehrlichman and Mardian: guilty on all counts; Parkinson: not guilty.

The four convicted were expected to appeal. No date was set for sentencing. The defendants were referred to a probation officer for a presentence investigation. In the meantime, they remained free without bond. An aide to former President Nixon said Jan. 2 that Nixon, while "deeply anguished by Watergate," on the advice of his attorney would not comment on the convictions of his former aides.

> *Following are (1) the text of the Hunt memo introduced at the trial Nov. 4 listing commitments allegedly given by the White House to the original Watergate defendants in exchange for their silence, (2) excerpts from the transcript of a tape recording introduced at the trial Nov. 21, indicating the concern of President Nixon that John W. Dean III had himself recorded a March 21, 1973, conversation between Dean and the President and (3) excerpts from the transcripts of various tape recordings introduced at the trial Dec. 4, one of which reveals Nixon offering to help pay the legal expenses of his aides H.R. Haldeman and John D. Ehrlichman:*

> *(1) The Hunt memo:*

Review and Statement of Problem

The seven Watergate defendants, and others not yet indicted, bugged D.N.C. offices initially against their better judgment, knowing that Larry O'Brien was seldom there, and that many items of interest were being moved to Florida. Furthermore, the defendants pressed an alternate plan to bug O'Brien's Fontainebleau convention suite, before occupancy, a low-risk, high-gain operation which was rejected.

The seven defendants again protested further bugging of D.N.C. headquarters on June 16-17, the intercepted conversations by then having shown clearly that O'Brien was not using his office. Again, objections were overridden and the attempt was loyally made even though money for outside guards was struck from the operational budget by Jeb Magruder. In fact the entire history of Gemstone was characterized by diminishing funding coupled with increasing demands by those who conceived and sponsored the activity.

If initial orders to bug D.N.C. headquarters were ill-advised, the defendants' sponsors compounded the fiasco by the following acts:

1. Indecisiveness at the moment of crisis.

2. Failure to quash the investigation while that option was still open.

3. Allowing Hunt's safe to be opened and selected contents handed to the F.B.I.

4. Permitting an F.B.I. investigation whose unprecedented scope and vigor caused humiliation to families, friends and the defendants themselves.

5. Granting immunity to Baldwin.

6. Permitting defendants to fall into the hands of a paranoid judge and three self-admitted liberal Democrat prosecutors.

7. Failure to provide promised support funds on a timely and adequate basis; continued postponements and consequent avoidance of commitments.

8. An apparent wash-hands attitude now that the election has been won, heightening the sense of unease among all defendants who have grown increasingly to feel that they are being offered up as scapegoats ultimately to be abandoned.

Items for Consideration

1. Once the criminal trial ends, the D.N.C. civil suit resumes. In his deposition John Mitchell may well have perjured himself.

2. Pending are three investigations by Congressional committees. The Democratic Congress is not going to simply let the Watergate affair die away.

3. The media are offering huge sums for defendants' stories, for example, an offer to one defendant for his "autobiography" now stands at $745,000.

4. The Watergate bugging is only one of a number of highly illegal conspiracies engaged in by one or more of the defendants at the behest of senior White House officials. These as yet undisclosed crimes can be proved.

5. Immunity from prosecution and/or judicial clemency for cooperating defendants is a standing offer.

6. Congressional elections will take place in less than two years.

Defendants' Position

The defendants have followed all instructions meticulously, keeping their part of the bargain by maintaining silence. They have not, until now, attempted to contact persons still in positions of responsibility in an effort to obtain relief and reassurance, believing pre-election security to be a primary consideration.

The Administration, however, remains deficient in living up to its commitments. These commitments were and are:

1. Financial support.
2. Legal defense fees.
3. Pardons.
4. Rehabilitation.

Having recovered from post-election euphoria, the Administration should now attach high priority to keeping its commitments and taking affirmative action in behalf of the defendants.

To end further misunderstandings the seven defendants have set Nov. 27 at 5 P.M. as the date by which all past and current financial requirements are to be paid, and credible assurances given of continued resolve to honor all commitments. Half-measures will be unacceptable.

Accordingly, the defendants are meeting on Nov. 25 to determine our joint and automatic response to evidence of continued indifference on the part of those in whose behalf we suffered the loss of our employment, our futures and our reputations as honorable men.

The foregoing should not be misinterpreted as a threat. It is among other things a reminder that loyalty has always been a two-way street.

(2) Excerpts from the April 25, 1973, transcript:

April 25, 1973

Telephone Conversation: The President and Haldeman, April 25, 1973 (7:46—7:53 p.m.)

Following is a partial text of a telephone conversation between the President and White House Chief of Staff H.R. Haldeman on April 25, 1973.

The tape showed Nixon still worried about the possibility that White House counsel John W. Dean III had tape recorded their March 21, 1973, meeting. Nixon asked Haldeman if there was any way to find out whether Dean had recorded the session. If he did not, Nixon said, it would only be the President's word against Dean's. Nixon also remarked that while things would get tough, he would survive the scandal.

The tape, transcribed by the prosecution, was introduced at the Watergate coverup trial on Nov. 21, 1974.

P. ...Is there any, uh, way that, uh, even surreptitiously or discreetly or otherwise I mean, that, ah, way you could determine whether uh, this matter of whether Dean might have walked in there with a recorder on him? I don't know.

H. No, I don't think there is any way. I think ya gotta, so remote as to be almost beyond possibility. And uh, and if he did (unintelligible).

P. Well we've gotta I mean, its, it (unintelligible), but the point is that that's ah, that's a real bomb isn't it?

H. Ah, ya.

P. Sure is. That, that's what may be his bomb. In other words he (unintelligible).

H. No...

P. Put that on the desk with Henry Petersen and says, "I gotta recording of the President of the United States and here's what he said."

H. Well, that would be very hard.

P. If he did it, then we'd say, "yes..."

H. (Unintelligible) virtually impossible.

P. (Unintelligible) Not virtually impossible. If he did it we'd say, "Yes, sir, that was a recording and I was investigating..."

H. That's right.

P. On the other hand (laughs) it'd be god damn hard on, I mean, he'd run that in the press that'd be (unintelligible).

H. Yeah

P. Well, no way to, no way to find out is there?

H. No, there isn't any, there isn't any (unintelligible) no way anybody would know—

P. We have no—

H. Except him.

P. record of uh, we don't have any (unintelligible) as to whether he has done—

H. None

P. that before, have we?

H. None. We have no evidence at any time under any circumstances, and I've, you know, been involved in enough, you know, what is going on that I, I just find it impossible to think that, that there would (unintelligible) you know, it could possibly be the case.

P. Ummh. One thing about those things, you think that you know when a fellow walks into me, and I didn't look at him that closely, but you were there, god damn I mean, I, I'd think that it's a little, it's, it's, even the smallest ones are bulky enough that you mean, with a fellow like Dean you'd sort of see that wouldn't ya, where do you carry them, in your hip pocket or your breast pocket?

H. Oh, under your arm, you know, where they carry a pistol holster or somethin.

P. Um hmm, ya. Well...

H. (Unintelligible) I really don't think it's—it's so remote as to be almost beyond the—

P. Ya, ya

H. —realm of possibility.

P. In this matter nothing is beyond the realm of possibility. (laughter)...

H. No, that's true but ah—

P. Ya—

H. And, and—

P. But of course we draw the sword on that if ah, if ah...

H. (clears throat) I think if, if that's the subject he has in mind, that he, he's just going to do it on the basis of his own, you know, his own record afterwards, there's no check.

P. Oh well, on that we'll destroy him.

H. And ah...

P. It's his word against...

H. You know from the big (unintelligible)...

P. His word against...

H. Something like that...

P. His word—what? His word against the President's the ah, the ah, (unintelligible) you were there but particularly the President's on that (unintelligible). The only other thing is of course his conversation with regard to the, I mean, the little slip in your office about the...

H. But that.

P. That was so casual.

H. I don't think you're going to have the, have the problem with that. I mean, other than, other than perhaps an effort to, to base it on his conversation and you know, his memorandum afterwards or had he done something like that, but he didn't usually do that.

P. Didn't he?

H. Ummh ummh.

P. He didn't write conversations memorandum?

H. Not usually.

P. Hm. He probably did on this one. But uh, (unintelligible).

H. As I said it sounds as if he had notes which you, you said he thought he did to speak from you know he might have used that ah...

P. Ya that, but I mean, but he didn't make any notes in any conversation I ever had with him, he always sat there and then probably as a (unintelligible) with a good memory, you can go back and write everything down you can remember.

H. Ya, ya.

P. But ah, he's always had or made a memorandum of the

conversation afterwards and I said this and that, on the other hand, Ziegler had a good point about Dean which he made a few days ago, he said John Dean's credibility is nil because...

H. Right.

P. The Dean report has proved to be false and everything else and...

H. Right.

P. And you have something to say and that's what we gotta have in mind here now without you and John to get too god damned discouraged about this because basically John Dean, ah, his report, uh, that he now claims that he didn't make, his subornation of perjury, his everything else...

H. That's right.

The Scapegoat

P. He's ah, who the hell is to believe what he's going to say now, and he's saying it now for what purpose? He's going to be, of course, saying, "Well I, they're making me the scape goat and all the rest, and therefore I'm going to tell all," and he's going, and as he says, "I'll try this," his attorney says, "This administration right up to the President," he didn't say the President, but you know that's what they said.

H. Yeah, but that's (unintelligible) the purpose—when you get down to trying to do it, they got a very tough time.

P. Purpose of course was to get everybody—which now the Prosecutor Chuck, Bob, is not about to give 'em.

H. Really?

P. No, sir, they're not. Oh, Petersen says that I said, "Now all right, you make your judgment on your own," I said, "not on my behalf." He said "No," he says, "he's just—much involved as a principal. We just can't do it." And frankly I think it's just as well. I think if...

H. He's right.

P. I think if you—I think if you're in a position now, that if you gave him immunity, he would sit there the rest of our lives.

H. That's right.

P. Hanging it over ya, and the point is that ah, now if he's going to have this pissing contest (unintelligible) all right, bring it out and fight it out and it'll be a bloody god damn thing, you know in a strange kind of way that's life, isn't it (unintelligible) probably be understood and be rough as a cob, and we'll survive and some people you'll even find (unintelligible) in Mississippi you'll find a half a dozen people that will be for the President. Who knows?

H. (Laughs) Be a lot more than that.

P. (unintelligible) No. We do still have some support in the country, I hope. But, uh...

H. Yep.

P. But we shall see, do you agree?

H. Absolutely.

P. (Laughs)

H. No question.

P. Ya, ya, that's right...Despite all the polls and all the rest, I think there's still a hell of a lot of people out there, and from what I've seen, they're—you know, they, they want to believe, that's the point, isn't it?

H. Why sure. Want to, and do.

P. All right. By the way, I thought there was just a th— thought that maybe you could check th-that thing...

H. No...

P. But there is no way you can check it.

H. There isn't anything to check.

P. You've never heard that, uh, that he's ever done that before.

H. Never, never.

P. Um hmm. Although as I say, if worse comes to worse, and he has one, well, we've got one. (Laughs).

H. Yup.

P. No. But what I mean is—you've gotta live with it, that's it...

H. We'll know it's there at least, an uh—

P. That's right, that's right, that's right. Tomorrow th-, th-, there's a little left on what the one you had this day, right?

H. Yep.

P. Um hmm. But-but you were there during that discussion.

H. Yep.

P. And I suppose that we probably discussed how the hell we get the 120, right? I don't remember it.

H. No, no. I don't think so, I think it was, you know, just sort of a rehash of the other thing...

P. That's right.

H. and basically going into the impossibility of doing it.

P. And the next day you, I suppose the question is, well, did you get the 120, I may have asked him that, I don't know. I don't think I did but I...(laughs).

H. I'm not even sure there was a second.

P. Well anyway—I—listen to it tomorrow an' lemme know. Will ya?

H. Yep.

(3) Following are excerpts from four partial transcripts of conversations between former President Nixon and his aides that were entered into evidence Dec. 4 by the Watergate special prosecutor at the cover-up trial. Speakers are denoted by "P" for President, "H" for Haldeman and "E" for Ehrlichman:

April 25, 1973, from 11:06 a.m. to 1:55 p.m.

P. Could have discussed there the problem of these, of, of, uh, defendants, and, you know what I mean?

H. Yeah (unintelligible).

P. But the payoff, uh, uh, and whether I said anything which would of led him to believe that he should pay them off...

H. Let's...

P. Don't think so.

H. ...Let's not worry about it. It's either, it's either there or it isn't...

P. That's right.

H. But, let's see what's there...

P. And if it is?...

H. Let's listen to it...

P. If it is? Then we have to play in terms of I was having to find out what its implication was.

E. I think then it becomes very important how you couch your decision on being...

P. That's right... Did we say, "Let's go out and get the money?"

H. Yeah, I don't remember the specifics, I just remember the...

P. Was there any—do you remember my saying, "Look, we've got to get the money, can't you find somebody to get the money?"

H. You didn't—I don't remember your saying, "We've got to get it." I remember you saying, "Can't some—we ought to be able to raise that kind of money, or..."

P. "A million dollars."

H. "...There ought to be that kind of money available."

P. Yeah, a million dollars.

H. (Unintelligible) something like that, yeah.

P. That's right.

E. But you didn't say to do it, or that you would, or anything like that.

P. Well, you've got to find out, got to find out...

Telephone Conversation April 25, 1973, from 6:57 p.m. to 7:14 p.m.

P. Hello.

H. Yes, sir.

P. Oh, Bob, you got home?

H. Yeah.

P. Oh, fine. Ya rushing off?

H. No, no, not at all.

P. No, I'll just take a second. Ah, were you able to hear any of the rest of that?

H. No, I, I didn't, I'm gonna, I'm trying to get a different machine that I can....

P. Right.

H. ...Hear better on. Go back to it...

P. And uh, the uh—now with regard to the piece of paper I gave you on Ehrlichman, they have sent that you know out to the....

P. ...Prosecutor. They had to do that for this reason that, uh, that Dean basically, was—that was basically a little blackmail by him, on them, you see.

H. Yeah.

P. Uh, which they said if we didn't put it out—I mean if they didn't —they'd say why did you withhold it from the Ellsberg case, you see.

H. Yeah.

P. So, uh—but that is likely—it could come out I mean, Byrne may, Byrne may ask for, divulge the source. It will be Dean, and Dean will have to testify if he does, then that, uh, piece of thing, that Watergate buggers involved in the Ellsberg thing—it will not blow the Ellsberg case, in, you know, in, in his opinion, due to the fact that it wasn't used. On the other hand, the fact of it will come out. But I think that that was gonna come out anyway, don't you feel so?

H. Probably, probably. Yeah, and I think we gotta assume any of the stuff is.

P. But the point is...

H. I'm not sure that's bad if it does. Well, it adds confusion to the whole thing.

P. Yeah, the, uh, Watergate buggers, uh, try to knock over Ellsberg's psychiatrist...

P. ...They, they, uh, uh—you see, what, what else could I tell Kleindienst, forget it? Get my point?

H. Yeah.

P. I just couldn't do that.

H. Yeah.

P. And, uh, you know, I could say look, this is national security, and you cannot turn it over to 'em, because Dean, another (unintelligible)....Uh, the other point that it, uh, I went—I leveled with Petersen on the, uh, on all the conversation that we had, and I said now I want you to know this, and I said we'll not be blackmailed on it, we didn't do anything about it but, uh, that's when I started my investigation. And that's, that's our line there, I think. The more I...

H. Yeah.

P. ...The more I think of that, you know I'm—I know that I'm in no illusions on it, and incidentally, I think that should just be between you and me...

P. My own belief at this point is that, ah, for yours and John's information, that we just gotta stand god-damn firm today, tomorrow, Friday, the week-end, you know what I mean?

H. Yeah.

P. And, as the Ellsberg thing blows, I'd, I just as soon, you know, just as...

H. Get it all out now.

P. I wouldn't just as soon, but I think it's gonna come anyway. Whatever John Dean knows is gonna come out, Bob.

H. That's right. That's right.

P. But, ah, incidentally, you know, I always wondered about the taping equipment, but I'm damn glad we have it, aren't you?

H. Yes sir, I think it's, it's just one thing I went through today it was very helpful.

P. Yes, It's helpful because while it has some things in there that, as,...

H. (unintelligible).

P. We prefer we wouldn't have said, but on the other hand, we also have some things in there that we know we've, that I've said that weren't, that were pretty good, I mean.

H. That's right.

P. "This is wrong," and, ah, "blackmail" and "how much is this gonna cost" and so forth and so on. Then, on the other hand, I said well, "Let's, ah, we could get that, but how would you handle it?" But that, of course, those are all leading questions. I don't know how you analyze it, but I don't know...

P ...I was just thinking a little bit more about the impeachment thing, that I don't see the Senate or any Senators starting an impeachment of the President based on the word of John Dean.

H. That's right.

P. But, ah, even there, I mean, here is...

H. Still, his word, unless he's got a tape recording. Still, his word unless he has a tape recording.

P. Mhmm....

April 17, 1973, 5:20 p.m.

P. ....Let me ask you this, uh, (pause), legal fees will be sub-stantial (unintelligible). But there's a way we can get it to you, and, uh—two or three hundred thousand dollars (unin-telligible) huh? No, No, now, let me tell you now. I know the problems with families and all the rest. Just let me handle it. Now, how could we do it?

E. Let's let's wait and see if it is necessary, this—that whole thing, I. I, it may not be nec—.

P. Let me say, it would be investigations, legal, that will lead—you will find that you, you have to do it in cash.

E. Yeah.

P. That you got a civic, you got, you got a Government duty. (Unintelligible) important thing.

H. (Unintelligible).

P. (Unintelligible-stuttering). No strain. Doesn't come outa me. I didn't, I never intended to use the money at all. As a matter of fact, I told B-B-Bebe, uh, basically, be sure that people like, uh—who, who have contributed money over the contributing years are, uh, favored and so forth in general. And he's used it for the purpose of getting things out, paid for in check and all that sort of thing....

April 25, 1973, 11:06 p.m.

P. Let me ask you this, to be quite candid. Is there any way you can use cash?

E. I don't think so.

H. I don't think so.

P. As I said, there're a few, not much I think as 200 there's available in '74 campaign already.

H. That compounds the problem. That really does.

P. That's what I think. O.K. I'd just like you to know that....

CUMULATIVE INDEX, 1972-74

CUMULATIVE INDEX, 1972-74

A

ABM. *See* Anti-Ballistic Missile.
ABORTION
  Population Growth and the American Future, 301, 307-310 *(1972)*
  State Laws on, 102 *(1973)*
  Supreme Court on, 101-114 *(1973)*
ABOUREZK, JAMES (D S.D.)
  Senate Election, 1972, 16 *(1973)*
ABRAMS, CREIGHTON W.
  Secret Bombing of Cambodia, 730 *(1973)*
ACCIDENT PREVENTION
  State of the Union, 93-94 *(1972)*
AFL-CIO
  Committee on Political Education Enemies List, 678 *(1973)*
  Foreign Trade, 380 *(1973)*
  Youth Vote Turnout, 36 *(1973)*
AFRICA
  Arafat U.N. Speech, 919-937 *(1974)*
  Democratic Party Platform, 577 *(1972)*
  Republican Party Platform, 661 *(1972)*
  Third World Solidarity, 256 *(1974)*
AGED
  Democratic Party Platform, 544-545 *(1972)*
  GOP Keeps Winning Team, 719-720 *(1972)*
  Nixon Re-election Campaign, 603 *(1974)*
  Republican Party Platform, 700-702 *(1972)*
  State of the Union, 94-95 *(1972)*; 308, 311 *(1973)*
AGNEW, SPIRO T.
  Ford as Vice President, 969 *(1973)*
  GOP Keeps Winning Team, 711, 713-717 *(1972)*
  Nixon on Charges Against, 737, 746, 747, 750 *(1973)*
  Press Relations, 634 *(1973)*
  Resignation, 827-838, 898, 899 *(1973)*
  Watergate: White House Shake-up, 499 *(1973)*
AGRICULTURE. *See also* Food Supply.
  American Party Platform, 619 *(1972)*

Boumediene on Third World, 261-262 *(1974)*
Democratic Party Platform, 538, 568-572 *(1972)*
Economic Controls, Phase IV, 709, 710 *(1973)*
Ford Economic Summit, 863 *(1974)*
Milk Price Supports, 948, 949, 963 *(1973)*
Nixon Budget, 174 *(1973)*
Phase III, 60-day Price Freeze, 579-582 *(1973)*
Republican Party Platform, 683-685 *(1972)*
Soviet-U.S. Pact, 588-608 *(1973)*
State of the Union, 99-101 *(1972)*; 222 *(1973)*; 44, 45 *(1974)*
U.S.-Soviet Environment Pact, 808 *(1972)*
AID TO FAMILIES WITH DEPENDENT CHILDREN, 304, 310, 311 *(1973)*
AIR FORCE
  Cost Overruns of Contracts, 194, 202 *(1973)*
  POW's Slang, 248-253 *(1973)*
  Secret Bombing of Cambodia, 729-735 *(1973)*
AIR POLLUTION. *See* Environmental Quality.
AIRCRAFT
  Anti-hijacking Pact, 265-268 *(1973)*
  Nixon Energy Speech, 914, 916 *(1973)*
  SST, Environmental Risks of, 235-244 *(1973)*
ALASKA
  Abortion Law, 102 *(1973)*
  National Parks for the Future, 802 *(1972)*
  Pipeline, 271-282 *(1972)*; 472, 473, 805, 914, 919 *(1973)*; 120 *(1974)*
  Project Independence, 912, 914, 917 *(1974)*
  Republican Party Platform, 705-706 *(1972)*
ALBERT, CARL (D Okla.)
  Agnew Resignation, 827, 832-834 *(1973)*
  Congressional War-Making Powers, 4 *(1973)*
  Ford as Vice President, 970 *(1973)*
  Ford Economic Summit, 861, 863-866 *(1974)*

B

BACTERIOLOGICAL WARFARE. *See* Biological and Chemical Warfare.
BAKER, BOBBY, 99 *(1973)*
BAKER, HOWARD H. JR. (R Tenn.)
C.I.A. Role in Watergate, 605 *(1974)*
Courts on White House Tapes, 841 *(1973)*
Dean's Watergate Testimony, 664, 665, 672 *(1973)*
Firing of Watergate Prosecutor, 860, 861, 870 *(1973)*
Nixon on National Security, 954, 956 *(1973)*
Nixon Pardon, 813 *(1974)*
Watergate Hearings, 549-556 *(1973)*
Watergate Transcripts, 316, 386 *(1974)*
White House Tapes, 698, 902 *(1973)*
BALDWIN, ALFRED C. 3d, 424 *(1973)*
BANGLADESH. *See* India-Pakistan War.
BANKS, DENNIS
Wounded Knee, 532 *(1973)*
BARKER, BERNARD L., 414, 415, 419, 423-425, 550 *(1973)*
BAYH, BIRCH (D Ind.)
Kleindienst and the ITT Affair, 396, 404-406 *(1972)*
BAZELON, DAVID L., 842 *(1973)*
BEALL, GEORGE
Agnew Resignation, 828, 830-832 *(1973)*
BEARD, DITA D.
Kleindienst and the ITT Affair, 395-398, 400, 403-404 *(1972)*
BERLIN. *See* Germany.
BEST, JUDAH, 828, 829, 832 *(1973)*
BIBLE. *See also* Prayer in Schools.
Evolution or Creation, 843-844 *(1972)*
BIDEN, JOSEPH R. (D Del.)
Senate Election, 1972, 16 *(1973)*
BIOLOGICAL AND CHEMICAL WARFARE
Biological Disarmament, 323-328 *(1972)*
U.N. Message, 759 *(1973)*
U.N. Report on Napalm, 837-841 *(1972)*
BIRTH CONTROL. *See also* Abortion.
Democratic Platform, 548 *(1972)*
Population Growth and the American Future, 307, 309 *(1972)*
U.N. World Food Conference, 940-941, 948 *(1974)*
U.N. World Population Plan, 782 *(1974)*
BIRTH DEFECTS
Marihuana and Health, 160 *(1972)*
Smoking Report, 63-77 *(1973)*
BLACK PANTHER PARTY
Newsmen's Privilege and the Public Interest, 507, 511-513 *(1972)*
POW's Slang, 248 *(1973)*
BLACKMUN, HARRY A. *See also* Supreme Court.

Abortion Guidelines, 102, 103-109 *(1973)*
Cruel and Unusual Punishment, 504-505 *(1972)*
Watergate and Ethics, 723-727 *(1973)*
BLACKS. *See also* Black Panther Party. Busing. Equal Opportunity.
Conversation of Dan Rather with President Nixon, 11-12 *(1972)*
Court Desegregation Plan for Richmond, 15-21 *(1972)*
Cross-District Busing, 639-654 *(1974)*
Navy Race Relations, 901-906 *(1972)*
State of the Union, 96 *(1972)*; 59 *(1974)*
Virginia Redistricting, 280 *(1973)*
Voter Turnout, '72, 38 *(1973)*
Blumenstein, James F., Tennessee v., 283-290 *(1972)*
BOERMA, A. H.
Action on Third World Poverty, 859-860, 865-866 *(1972)*
BOLIVIA
President Nixon's Policy on Expropriation, 67 *(1972)*
BORK, ROBERT H.
Firing of Watergate Prosecutor, 859, 862, 863, 877, 878 *(1973)*
Nixon's Reasons for Firing Cox, 898, 901 *(1973)*
BOUMEDIENE, HOUARI
U.N. Speech on Raw Materials, 255 *(1974)*
Washington Energy Conference, 124 *(1974)*
BOUTEFLIKA, ABDEL-AZIZ
Arafat U.N. Speech, 921 *(1974)*
U.N. General Assembly Speech, 833, 835-839 *(1974)*
Bradley v. School Board, Richmond, 15-21 *(1972)*
BRANDT, WILLY
Soviet-West German Treaties, 557-562 *(1973)*
BRANZBURG, PAUL M.
Newsmen's Privilege and the Public Interest, 507-519 *(1972)*
BRENNAN, WILLIAM J. JR. *See also* Supreme Court.
Apportionment in State Legislatures, 278, 279, 284 *(1973)*
Cruel and Unusual Punishment, 501 *(1972)*
Miranda Ruling Limits, 482-483 *(1974)*
Obscenity, New Rules, 612-613, 622-628 *(1973)*
Obscenity Scope Narrowed, 516, 519, 522 *(1974)*
Right to Reply Law, 524, 527 *(1974)*
BRETTON WOODS SYSTEM, 387 *(1973)*; 497-498, 503 *(1974)*
BREZHNEV, LEONID I.
Blockade of North Vietnam, 408 *(1972)*
China's Party Congress, 777 *(1973)*

I

K

L

X, Y, Z